Ninth Edition

The Press and America

AN INTERPRETIVE HISTORY OF THE MASS MEDIA

Michael Emery

Late, Professor of Journalism
California State University, Northridge

Edwin Emery

Late, Professor Emeritus of Journalism
and Mass Communication
University of Minnesota

Nancy L. Roberts

Professor of Journalism
and Mass Communication
University of Minnesota

ALLYN and BACON

Boston   London   Toronto   Sydney   Tokyo   Singapore

Vice President, Editor-in-Chief: Paul Smith
Series Editor: Karon Bowers
Series Editorial Assistant: Jennifer Becker
Marketing Manager: Jackie Aaron
Composition and Prepress Buyer: Linda Cox
Manufacturing Buyer: Megan Cochran
Cover Administrator: Linda Knowles
Cover Designer: Susan Paradise
Editorial-Production Service: Omegatype Typography, Inc.
Electronic Composition: Omegatype Typography, Inc.

Internet: www.abacon.com

Between the time Website information is gathered and published, some sites may have
closed. Also, the transcription of URLs can result in typographical errors. The publisher
would appreciate notification where these occur so that they may be corrected in subsequent editions.

Many of the designations used by manufacturers and sellers to distinguish their products
are claimed as trademarks. Where those designations appear in this book, and Allyn and
Bacon was aware of a trademark claim, the designations have been printed in initial or
all caps.

Library of Congress Cataloging-in-Publication Data

Emery, Michael C.
   The press and America : an interpretive history of the mass media
   / Michael Emery, Edwin Emery, Nancy L. Roberts. — 9th ed.
      p.   cm.
   Includes bibliographical references (p.   ) and index.
   ISBN 0-205-29557-6
      1. Press—United States—History.   2. Journalism—United States—
   History.   3. Mass media—United States—History.   4. American
   newspapers—History   I. Emery, Edwin.   II. Roberts, Nancy L.
   III. Title
   PN4855.E6   2000
   071'.3—dc21   99-44295
                                                           CIP

Printed in the United States of America

10 9 8 7 6 5 4 3 2 1   04 03 02 01 00 99

Contents

15   A WORLD AT WAR   339

16   TELEVISION TAKES CENTER STAGE   361

17   CHALLENGES AND DISSENT   393

18 A CRISIS OF CREDIBILITY   433

19 EFFORTS TO IMPROVE THE MEDIA   507

Preface

Journalism history is the story of humanity's long struggle to communicate: to discover and interpret news and to offer intelligent opinion and entertaining thoughts in the marketplace of ideas. Part of the story has as its theme the continuing efforts to break down the barriers that have prevented the flow of information and ideas on which public opinion is so largely dependent. A separate and less appreciated challenge has been the internal battle by some journalists against the bias and self-censorship that has plagued so much of journalism.

Another aspect of the story is concerned with the means, or media, by which essential news, opinion, and other desired information reach the public, from the days of the handwritten "newes letter" to the printed page, radio, television, and more recently, enhanced cable and computer services. Important to this story are the heroes and villains, as well as the bit actors, who created the complex matrix of modern communication. The development of America's journalism is thus inherently and integrally related to the cultural identity of its people.

This ninth edition of *The Press and America* honors the inestimable contributions of Edwin Emery and Michael Emery to the field of journalism history. Until his death in September 1993, Edwin Emery was involved in planning the rewriting, organization, and illustration of text, along with changes in the extensive bibliography that was his province from the book's debut in 1954. This ninth edition also marks the passing of Mary Emery, Edwin's wife and Michael's mother, whose love and support quietly helped shepherd *The Press and America*'s first eight editions to press. And the ninth edition marks the passing of Michael Emery, who began his association with the third edition and assumed responsibility for updating and strengthening the manuscript. Michael Emery died in December 1996, just as the eighth edition, for which my assistance had been procured, was being published.

With little warning, I found myself assuming single-handedly the responsibility for the ninth edition, fulfilling a promise to my coauthor and his family. It has been both challenge and privilege. Edwin Emery was my doctoral advisor and colleague at the University of Minnesota, and his son Michael was my good friend and colleague. I have tried to honor their ideas, contributions, and memory while providing a fresh, critical perspective.

The ninth edition, the first without the Emerys' direct voice, has both familiar features and innovations. The examination of American life and the American media remains the heart of the book. The Bibliography and Notes are again presented chapter by chapter at the back of the text, an organization that facilitates both the listing of rapidly expanding new research and the shifting of extensive data listings to the Notes as reference sources. Mass communication researchers may locate in earlier editions some secondary data and older bibliographical citations necessarily eliminated from these pages in the updating process. For this edition the annotated bibliography has been completely revised to reflect current research and to remain an invaluable research tool for students wishing to undertake further research.

The title, *The Press and America,* was chosen in 1949 when work began on the first edition because the newspaper industry was dominant. There was only a smattering of interest in the history of radio, and television was in its infancy. Since then there have been many changes in media roles and communications technologies. For reasons of tradition and continuity, our title remains the same, reflecting as always the emphasis placed on the correlation of journalism history with political, social, economic, and cultural trends. In this interaction, the media have had their influence on the course taken by the United States. Conversely, the conditions and influences present in each historical era have cumulatively determined the shape and character of the media. Within this framework emerges the special story of the men and women of journalism and of the institutions and traditions they created. This story ranges from newspaper editor James Franklin to Katharine Graham; from opinion-molder Horace Greeley to Edward R. Murrow; from radical publicist Sam Adams to I. F. Stone; from talented writer Tom Paine to Tom Wolfe.

There is extensive examination of all the media: newspapers, press associations, magazines, book publishing, advertising, public relations, photojournalism, motion pictures, radio, television, cable, and the Internet. Thus in the 1920s, the stories of radio's David Sarnoff and *Amos 'n' Andy,* of Hollywood's David Wark Griffith and Charlie Chaplin, of the newspapers' Adolph Ochs and the *New York Daily News,* of the *Reader's Digest* and the *New Yorker,* and of the rise of advertising agencies and public relations counsels become interrelated. With words and pictures the book surveys landmark events in communications history, probing significant issues, personalities, media organizations, and trends, all the while tracing how major events in U.S. history were covered by reporters, editors, and broadcasters and how other writers, advertisers, and advocates influenced American life.

For this edition, the historiography was completely revised to reflect the most up-to-date scholarly interpretations for every period of U.S. history, from the colonial period to the present. The aim is to help students understand and interpret journalism history as well grounded within the context of sound historical scholarship.

The last four chapters, dealing with more contemporary mass media developments, have been extensively updated to reflect current debate as well as a historical perspective on issues such as media technology (the Internet and cyberpublishing), the impact of media mergers, public journalism, media ethics (for example, the paparazzi and privacy), and the First Amendment (for example, implications of the Telecommunications Act of 1996). The previous edition's Chapter 20, The Surviving Newspaper Press, has been eliminated, with the most essential information incorporated elsewhere in the book. This results from one of the major objectives that guided this revision: to present students with the most essential information by adding more interpretation and analysis rather than simply recounting overwhelming factual data (as a sort of "textbook of record").

Other key characteristics of this edition include an examination of the Clinton presidency; a continuing critical look at distressing trends in the journalism world; continued analysis of problems with sex and violence in television programming; data about women and minorities in the media and the gay/lesbian press; updates on the ownership patterns of major media organizations; new public opinion surveys regarding media credibility; revised circulation, audience, and sales data for major media, with the addition of new tables; and profiles of leading television news figures and networks and discussion of the pros and cons of new technology, including privacy and other ethical and legal concerns.

ACKNOWLEDGMENTS

Thanks are due many people who have aided this venture during five decades. For this edition, criticisms and suggestions for change in the sections dealing with contemporary mass media and society were elicited from Professor Jean Ward, emerita, and Marilyn Jackson, adjunct, University of Minnesota, the School of Journalism and Mass Communication. Katherine Meerse and David E. Woodard, Ph.D. graduates in history, University of Minnesota, provided an invaluable critique of the book's historiography.

I have been greatly aided by my graduate research assistant, Genelle Belmas, who took special responsibility for updating the media ethics and law sections as well as writing completely new sections on public journalism, the Internet, and the Telecommunications Act. She also provided outstanding general research assistance as well as great help in securing photo copyright permissions, always with good humor. A Ph.D. candidate at the University of Minnesota, she holds a master's degree in political science from the University of Wisconsin. Her studies at Minnesota have emphasized media law and ethics, journalism history, and graphic design, and her dissertation is a study of Internet law, including the areas of pornography, privacy, and hate speech. She brought a rich intellectual background and perspective to this project, and it is much better because of her contributions, for which I am deeply grateful.

Other University of Minnesota students and colleagues who read parts of the manuscript, offered suggestions, and/or gave considerable moral support were Hazel Dicken-Garcia, Sara Evans, Kathleen Hansen, Nahid Kahn, and Al Tims. Ben Huset contributed information on satellites, and Rodger Streitmatter of American University provided current circulation figures on the gay and lesbian press.

The debts for aid with earlier editions can be acknowledged here only in part. A substantial acknowledgment is due Professor Henry Ladd Smith, then of the University of Wisconsin, co-author with Edwin Emery of the first edition. Of great assistance was research compiled by the late Professor Emeritus Robert W. Desmond of the University of California, as well as research findings organized and compiled for *Journalism History* by its founder, Professor Tom Reilly of California State University, Northridge, and his successors, Professor Susan Henry, also of Northridge, and Professor Barbara Cloud, University of Nevada, Las Vegas. Professor Harold L. Nelson of the University of Wisconsin has given many suggestions for text revisions, particularly in the colonial period, and gave invaluable assistance during work on the first edition. Others who provided aid for previous editions are Professor Victoria Goff, University of Wisconsin–Green Bay, who contributed to material dealing with Spanish-language and frontier journalism for the eighth edition; Dr. Félix Gutiérrez, Freedom Forum; Professor Emeritus Donald M. Gillmor of the University of Minnesota in the legal area; and Professor Irving Fang, also at Minnesota, in sections dealing with broadcasting. Journalism bibliographers on whom we have most depended are Warren C. Price, University of Oregon; Calder M. Pickett, University of Kansas; Eleanor Blum, University of Illinois; and Christopher H. Sterling. Thanks are also due Jan Nyberg, Sevareid Librarian at the University of Minnesota.

Manuscript critics (with university affiliations) have been Professors Ralph D. Casey, Minnesota; Frederick B. Marbut, Pennsylvania State; Kenneth E. Olson and Richard A. Schwarzlose, Northwestern; William H. Taft, Missouri; Bruce Westley, Kentucky; Calder M. Pickett, Kansas; Sam Kuczun, Colorado; Ted C. Smythe, California State, Fullerton; George Everett, Tennessee; Ernest C. Hynds, Georgia; Peter Mayeux, Nebraska-Lincoln; and Peter Mellini, San Francisco State. Mention must be made of past aid by journalism professors (with affiliation): Ralph O. Nafziger and William A. Hachten, Wisconsin; Quintus C. Wilson, Northern Illinois; Roland E. Wolseley, Syracuse; Paul Jess, Kansas; Sharon Murphy, Bradley; Barbara Reed, Rutgers; Corban Goble, Kentucky; Warren Francke, Nebraska-Omaha; Betty Winfield, Missouri; Henry G. La Brie III, Boston; John D. Stevens and Marion Marzolf, Michigan; and Everette E. Dennis, Freedom Forum.

Other critics: David Nord, Indiana; Jeffery Smith, Iowa; William E. Ames and Richard B. Kielbowicz, Washington; Donald L. Shaw, North Carolina; Randall L. Murray, California Polytechnic, San Luis Obispo; Ralph E. Kliesch, Ohio; Joseph P. McKerns and Paul Peterson, Ohio State; Harvey Saalberg, Angelo State; Fenwick Anderson, Southern Connecticut State; Robert V. Hudson, Michigan State; R. Smith Schuneman, Hazel Dicken-Garcia, Raymond B. Nixon, Edwin H. Ford, and J. Edward Gerald, Minnesota; Catherine Cassara, Bowling Green State University; and Rodger Streitmatter, American University. The debt to the many scholars and writers whose contributions to media history are listed in the notes and bibliographies also is acknowledged.

Special thanks is given to our editor at Allyn and Bacon, Karon Bowers, and her assistant Scout Reilly. The indexing work of David E. Woodard was greatly appreciated. Thank you to the many friends who offered help and encouragement, especially John Arnold, who provided much relief dog care. And I deeply appreciate the kindness and support of all members of the Emery family, especially Allison and Laurel (Edwin and Mary Emery's daughters and Michael Emery's sisters) and Lu (Michael Emery's widow).

N. L. R.

About the Authors

The first edition of *The Press and America* won the coveted Sigma Delta Chi national research award, the highest in the field of journalism.

Michael Emery, Ph.D., was Professor of Journalism at California State University, Northridge. He was author of *On the Front Lines: Following America's Foreign Correspondents Across the Twentieth Century,* and co-editor of *Readings in Mass Communication* and of *America's Front Page News, 1690–1970.* He was a contributing editor of *Journalism History* and a consultant to the Freedom Forum's Newseum project. He was a United Press International correspondent and was a freelance foreign correspondent who contributed to the *Village Voice, Los Angeles Times,* and other media while reporting from the Middle East, Yugoslavia, and Central America.

Edwin Emery, Ph.D., was Professor Emeritus of Journalism and Mass Communication at the University of Minnesota, where he was a faculty member from 1945 to 1984. He was president of the Association for Education in Journalism and Mass Communication, editor of its research journal, *Journalism Quarterly,* from 1964 to 1973, and author or co-author of 11 books, including *Introduction to Mass Communications.* He was honored with the Sigma Delta Chi national award for his *History of the American Newspaper Publishers Association,* the AEJ Bleyer and Blum awards, the American Journalism Historians Association's Kobre award, and a Guggenheim Fellowship. He was a former United Press bureau manager and World War II war desk editor.

Nancy L. Roberts, Ph.D., is Professor of Journalism and Mass Communication at the University of Minnesota, where she is also an adjunct faculty member of the Program in American Studies. She has been president of the American Journalism Historians Association, book review editor for its journal, *American Journalism,* and head of the History Division, Association for Education in Journalism and Mass Communication. She is author of *American Peace Writers, Editors, and Periodicals: A Dictionary; Dorothy Day and the "Catholic Worker,"* and numerous articles for magazines and newspapers including *Americana,* the *Christian Science Monitor,* and the *Philadelphia Inquirer.*

Introductory Bibliography

Indispensable references for students of the history of American journalism are Margaret Blanchard, ed., *History of the Mass Media in the United States: An Encyclopedia* (Chicago, London: Fitzroy Dearborn, 1998), whose entries provide excellent overviews and bibliographies relative to the economic, political, technological, and other developments that affected the mass media and/or vice versa; Warren C. Price, *The Literature of Journalism: An Annotated Bibliography* (Minneapolis: University of Minnesota Press, 1959), which has 3147 entries; and Warren C. Price and Calder M. Pickett, *An Annotated Journalism Bibliography, 1958–1968* (Minneapolis: University of Minnesota Press, 1970), which has 2172 entries, including some from pre-1958. Entries are particularly full in the areas of general journalism histories, specialized and individual histories, biographies, and narratives of journalists at work. Other sections cover press appraisals, press law, international communication, magazines, radio and television, public opinion and propaganda, communication theory, techniques of journalism, journalism education, periodicals of the press, bibliographies, and directories. British and Canadian journalism is well covered.

A superb single volume of bibliography for mass communication, and one that updates the Price-Pickett work by two decades, is Eleanor Blum and Frances Wilhoit, *Mass Media Bibliography: An Annotated Guide to Books and Journals for Research and Reference* (Urbana: University of Illinois Press, 1990), continuing Dr. Blum's 1972 and 1980 editions of *Basic Books in the Mass Media.* The compilers selected 1947 entries. Also extremely useful are Eleanor S. Block and James K. Bracken, *Communication and the Mass Media: A Guide to the Reference Literature* (Englewood, CO: Libraries Unlimited, 1991); Christopher H. Sterling, James K. Bracken, and Susan M. Hill, *Mass Communications Research Resources: An Annotated Guide* (Mahwah, NJ: Lawrence Erlbaum Associates, 1998); and Jo A. Cates, *Journalism: A Guide to the Reference Literature,* 2nd ed. (Englewood, CO: Libraries Unlimited, 1997), which presents about 800 sources on print, broadcast, and Internet journalism. Current annotated bibliography is reported in *Communication Booknotes Quarterly,* edited by Christopher H. Sterling and published by Lawrence Erlbaum Associates.

For listings of American newspaper files, Clarence S. Brigham's *History and Bibliography of American Newspapers, 1690–1820* (Worcester, MA: American Antiquarian Society, 1947) is the guide to surviving early newsprint (updated and corrected in the April 1961 *Proceedings* of the Society and a 1962 edition; the Society published chronological tables to accompany Brigham in 1972). Winifred Gregory's *American Newspapers, 1821–1936: A Union List of Files Available in the United States and Canada* (New York: Wilson, 1937) has diminished usefulness since libraries began to discard their more recent bound volumes in favor of microfilm. The Library of Congress publishes *Newspapers on Microfilm,* updating periodically, listing microfilm holdings of libraries newspaper by newspaper.

The largest single newspaper collection for the entire period of American history is at the Library of Congress; the largest for the colonial period, at the American Antiquarian Society. Ranking high in overall strength are the libraries of the Wisconsin State Historical Society and Harvard University; the Bancroft Library of the University of California is famous for its western U.S. collections as well. Strong in importance for their regions are the New York Historical Society, New York Public Library, Chicago Historical Society, University of Chicago, Pennsylvania Historical Society, Boston Public Library, Connecticut Historical Society, and the Kansas State Historical Society. Noteworthy for general collections are the University of Missouri, University of Minnesota, Yale University, University of Washington, UCLA, University of Illinois, University of Texas, Duke University, and the Western Reserve Historical Society. The motion picture, broadcast, and recorded sound division of the Library of Congress houses 100,000 motion picture films, 80,000 television programs, a half-million radio broadcasts, and more than 1.5 million sound recordings.

The major U.S. museum exhibit is the Newseum, opened in 1996 by Freedom Forum at its Arlington, Virginia headquarters. The Smithsonian Institution in Washington offers an artifacts exhibit, "Information Age: People, Information & Technology." New York City is home to the extensive Museum of Television and Radio, the American Museum of the Moving Image, and the Museum of Modern Art's research center for film study. Another film museum is California's Hollywood Studio Museum. The International Center of Photography has New York showings. Portland houses the substantial American Advertising Museum, and the Smithsonian has established a Center for Advertising History. Broadcast collections are found at the Vanderbilt University Television News Archive, the Library of Congress, the National Archives, the Museum of Broadcast Communications, Chicago (especially early radio), and at UCLA. Cartoon museums are housed in Boca Raton and Orlando, Florida, and in San Francisco.

Among bibliographies for specific subjects are Joseph P. McKerns, *News Media and Public Policy: An Annotated Bibliography* (New York: Garland, 1985); Wm. David Sloan, *American Journalism History: An Annotated Bibliography* (Westport, CT: Greenwood Press, 1989); Roland E. and Isabel Wolseley, *The Journalist's Bookshelf: An Annotated and Selected Bibliography of United States Print Journalism* (Indianapolis, IN: R. J. Berg, 1986); Richard A. Schwarzlose, *Newspapers: A Reference Guide* (Westport, CT: Greenwood Press, 1987); Jon Vanden Heuvel, *Untapped Sources: America's Newspaper Archives and Histories* (New York: Gannett Foundation Media Center, Columbia University, 1991); Ellen Mazur Thomson, compiler, *American Graphic Design: A Guide to the Literature* (Westport, CT: Greenwood, 1992); Robert Armour, *Film: A Reference Guide* (Westport, CT: Greenwood Press, 1980), a selective list, particularly for U.S. films; Fred and Nancy Paine, *Magazines: A Bibliography for Their Analysis with Annotations and Study Guide* (Metuchen, NJ: Scarecrow Press, 1987); Arthur F. Wertheim, *American Popular Culture: A Historical Bibliography* (New York: ABC-Clio Information Services, 1984); and J. William Snorgrass and Gloria T. Woody, *Blacks and Media: A Selected, Annotated Bibliography, 1962–1982* (Tallahassee: Florida A&M University Press, 1985). James P. Danky was editor and Maureen E. Hady compiler of two major listings: *Native*

American Periodicals and Newspapers, 1828–1982: Bibliography, Publishing Record and Holdings (Westport, CT: Greenwood Press, 1984), and *Women's Periodicals and Newspapers from the 18th Century to 1981* (Boston: G. K. Hall, 1982). For broadcasting, see Diane Foxhill Carothers, *Radio Broadcasting from 1920 to 1990: An Annotated Bibliography* (New York: Garland, 1991), an indispensable guide, and Michael Murray, "Research in Broadcasting: An Overview of Major Resource Centers," *American Journalism,* I:2 (1984), 77.

Two encyclopedias are a chronological history: *Mass Media* (New York: Garland Publishing, 1987), by Robert V. Hudson, and *The Encyclopedia of American Journalism* (New York: Facts on File, 1983), edited by Donald Paneth. Two valuable reference-research guides are *The Aspen Handbook on the Media,* edited by William L. Rivers, Wallace Thompson, and Michael J. Nyhan (New York: Praeger, 1977), and *Electronic Media: A Guide to Trends in Broadcasting and Newer Technologies, 1920–1983,* edited by Christopher H. Sterling (New York: Praeger, 1984). Three biographical dictionaries are Joseph P. McKerns, *The Biographical Dictionary of American Journalism* (Westport, CT: Greenwood Press, 1989), detailing some 500 newspeople in a variety of media positions; *Encyclopedia of Twentieth-Century Journalists* (New York: Garland, 1986), edited by William H. Taft; and *American Newspaper Journalists,* edited by Perry J. Ashley in four volumes of the *Dictionary of Literary Biography* (Chicago: Gale Research, 1983 ff.), followed by four volumes, *American Magazine Journalists,* edited by Sam G. Riley. Also quite useful are these Dictionary of Literary Biography volumes: *American Literary Journalists, 1945–1995,* edited by Arthur J. Kaul (Detroit: Gale Research, 1997); *American Book and Magazine Illustrators to 1920,* edited by Stephen E. Smith et al. (Detroit: Gale Research, 1998); and *American Newspaper Publishers, 1950–1990* (Detroit, Gale Research, 1993).

The earliest annual directory of U.S. periodicals was *George P. Rowell & Co.'s American Newspaper Directory* (1869), superseded by *N. W. Ayer & Son's American Newspaper Annual* (1880), later titled the *Directory of Newspapers & Periodicals* and after 1990 the *Gale Directory of Publications and Broadcast Media.* A standard U.S. source is the *Editor & Publisher International Yearbook* (1921), which also includes international listings. From London, *Benn's Press Directory* (1846) has separate *United Kingdom* and *International* volumes annually. The *Willings Press Guide* (1874) is international in scope, focusing on Britain.

Two major bibliographies for the study of American history are *A Guide to the Study of the United States of America* (Washington, DC: Library of Congress, 1960), and the *Harvard Guide to American History* (Cambridge, MA: Harvard University Press, 1974). The former, although less voluminous, carries extensive annotations lacking in the latter. The United States Information Agency (USIA) in 1989 published a *Handbook for the Study of the United States,* edited by William Bate and Perry Frank, with basic bibliographies in American studies, including journalism and the media, film, popular culture, history, law, and politics. Two source books are *The American History Sourcebook* (Englewood Cliffs, NJ: Prentice Hall, 1988), edited by Joel Makower, and John A. Garraty's *1001 Things Everyone Should Know about American History* (New York: Doubleday, 1989).

HISTORIOGRAPHY

Discussions of historical method are found in Michael Kammen, ed., *The Past Before Us: Contemporary Historical Writing in the United States* (Ithaca, NY: Cornell University

Press, 1980), a book of 20 essays planned by the American Historical Association; John Higham and Paul K. Conkin, *New Directions in American Intellectual History* (Baltimore: Johns Hopkins University Press, 1979); John Clive, *Not by Fact Alone* (New York: Knopf, 1989), essays on the writing and reading of history; David W. Noble, *The End of American History* (Minneapolis: University of Minnesota Press, 1985), a revisionist's denial of America's uniqueness; and Barbara Tuchman, *Practicing History* (New York: Knopf, 1981), which discusses her views on the writing of history and the role of history in society. Richard E. Beringer, *Historical Analysis* (New York: Wiley, 1978), explores 19 approaches to historical study; James West Davidson and Mark Hamilton Lytle examine historical method in terms of debatable episodes in *After the Fact: The Art of Historical Detection* (New York: Knopf, 1986); and quantification techniques are discussed in Robert P. Swierenga, *Quantification in American History* (New York: Atheneum, 1970), and Roderick Floud, *An Introduction to Quantitative Method for Historians* (Princeton, NJ: Princeton University Press, 1973).

For well-balanced discussions of trends in American historiography, see *The New American History,* rev. and exp. ed. edited by Eric Foner (Philadelphia: Temple University Press, 1997), a book of 13 essays planned by the American Historical Association that examine recent trends in U.S. history; and Gerald N. Grob and George A. Bilias, *Interpretations of American History: Patterns and Perspectives,* Vol. 1, *To 1877,* 6th ed. (New York: Free Press, 1992), and Vol 2, *Since 1877,* 6th ed. (New York: Free Press, 1992). Also useful may be Richard Hofstadter, *The Progressive Historians: Turner, Beard, Parrington* (New York: Knopf, 1968), by a one-time consensus advocate; John Higham, *Writing American History* (Bloomington: Indiana University Press, 1970), by a critic of the newer schools; and C. Vann Woodward, ed., *The Comparative Approach in American History* (New York: Basic Books, 1968). Bibliographies in this volume identify leading exponents of these various approaches to American history.

For historiography in journalism and mass communication, the best single volume is John D. Stevens and Hazel Dicken-Garcia, *Communication History* (Beverly Hills: Sage, 1980). Others include James D. Startt and Wm. David Sloan, *Historical Methods in Mass Communication* (Hillsdale, NJ: Erlbaum, 1989); Lucy Shelton Caswell, ed., *Guide to Sources in American Journalism History* (Westport, CT: Greenwood Press, 1989); Jo A. Cates, *Journalism: A Guide to the Reference Literature,* 2nd ed. (Englewood, CO: Libraries Unlimited, 1997); and M. Gilbert Dunn and Douglas W. Cooper, "A Guide to Mass Communication Sources," *Journalism Monographs,* LXXIV (November 1981). Two chapters on historiography by David Paul Nord and MaryAnn Yodelis Smith are found in Guido H. Stempel, III, and Bruce H. Westley, eds., *Research Methods in Mass Communication,* 2nd ed. (Englewood Cliffs, NJ: Prentice Hall, 1989). Also consult Hanno Hardt, *Critical Communication Studies: Communication, History, and Theory in America* (London, New York: Routledge, 1992). The Freedom Forum Media Studies Center at Columbia University in 1991 published for the American Society of Newspaper Editors' Newspaper History Task Force a book containing a lengthy bibliographical essay on books about journalists and a detailed inventory of major U.S. newspaper archives. Titled *Untapped Sources: America's Newspaper Archives and Histories,* it was written by Jon Vanden Heuvel.

Among journal articles, an overview of journalism and mass communication historiography is found in Michael Emery, "The Writing of American Journalism History," *Journalism History,* 10:3–4 (Autumn–Winter 1983), 38–93. Also see the special media history section of *Journalism and Mass Communication Quarterly,* 74:3 (Autumn 1997), which includes articles by Michael Schudson, "Toward a Troubleshooting Manual for Journalism History" (463–476); Carolyn Kitch, "Changing Theoretical Perspectives on

Women's Media Images: The Emergence of Patterns in a New Area of Historical Scholarship" (477–489); and others. Additional articles include 22 in an issue entitled, "Defining Moments in Journalism," *Media Studies Journal,* 11:2 (Spring 1997), 1–177; Wm. David Sloan, "Historians and the American Press, 1900–1945," *American Journalism,* 3:3 (1986), 154–166; "A Conversation with Edwin Emery," *Journalism History,* 7:1 (Spring 1980), 20–23; ". . . A Conversation with James W. Carey," *Journalism History,* 12:2 (Summer 1985), 38–50; and a symposium, "Seeking New Paths in Research," with essays by Garth S. Jowett, Richard A. Schwarzlose, John E. Erickson, Marion Marzolf, and David H. Weaver, in *Journalism History,* 2:2 (Summer 1975), 33–47.

Notes for the 20 chapters begin on page 576. In some cases, chapter notes will include supplementary reference material (names of individuals, lists of newspapers, other valuable research resource data). Annotated bibliographies listing books, monographs, and periodical articles in mass communication—as well as representative background histories—appear chapter by chapter beginning on page 607. The index begins on page 681.

1

The Heritage of the American Press

Give me but the liberty of the press and I will give to the minister a venal House of Peers . . . and servile House of Commons . . . I will give him all the power that place can confer upon him to purchase up submission and overawe resistance—And yet, armed with liberty of the press . . . I will attack the mighty fabric he has reared and bury it amidst the ruins of the abuses it was meant to shelter.

—*Richard Brinsley Sheridan*

The modern press system is the gift of no one nation. It is only the current stage in the evolution of communications efforts, spanning all continents and at least 10,000 years. A series of developments in printing and writing, beginning in the Middle East and Asia, slowly spreading to Europe and finally to America, led to today's marvelous linkage of reporting talent, computers, high-speed color presses, and satellites. Each historic breakthrough was motivated by the need to keep track of trading records, communicate to far-flung empires, spread religious ideas, or leave behind artistic records of accomplishments. The story of American journalism would not be complete without tracing a number of these notable achievements.

THE DEVELOPMENT OF PRINTING

The first systematic attempt to collect and distribute information was *Acta Diurna,* the hand-lettered "daily gazette" posted regularly in the Roman Forum between 59 B.C. and A.D. 222. Prepared by *actuarii,* the earliest known news writers, the reports told of both senate votes and popular events. These were in turn copied by scribes and carried throughout the empire. This enlightened program, enjoyed by Romans who learned of government decrees, legal notices, and even the latest gladiatorial results, had been preceded by many attempts to make the storage and distribution of information convenient. Around 3500 B.C. the Sumerians of the Middle East devised a system of preserving records by inscribing

The Daily Courant.

Wednesday, March 11. 1702.

From the Harlem Courant, Dated March 18. N. S.

Naples, Feb. 22.

ON Wednesday last, our New Viceroy, the Duke of Escalona, arriv'd here with a Squadron of the Galleys of Sicily. He made his Entrance dreſt in a French habit ; and to give us the greater Hopes of the King's coming hither, went to Lodge in one of the little Palaces, leaving the Royal one for his Majeſty. The Marquis of Grigni is also arriv'd here with a Regiment of French.

Rome, Feb. 25. In a Military Congregation of State that was held here, it was Resolv'd to draw a Line from Aſcoli to the Borders of the Eccleſiaſtical State, thereby to hinder the Incurſions of the Tranſalpine Troops. Orders are ſent to Civita Vecchia to fit out the Galleys, and to ſtrengthen the Garriſon of that Place. Signior Caſali is made Governor of Perugia. The Marquis del Vaſto, and the Prince de Caſerta continue ſtill in the Imperial Embaſſador's Palace ; where his Excellency has a Guard of 50 Men every Night in Arms. The King of Portugal has deſir'd the Arch-Biſhoprick of Lisbon, vacant by the Death of Cardinal Souſa, for the Infante his ſecond Son, who is about 11 Years old.

Vienna, Mar. 4. Orders are ſent to the 4 Regiments of Foot, the 2 of Cuiraſſiers, and to that of Dragoons, which are broke up from Hungary, and are on their way to Italy, and which conſiſt of about 14 or 15000 Men, to haſten their March thither with all Expedition. The 6 new Regiments of Huſſars that are now raiſing, are in ſo great a forwardneſs, that they will be compleat, and in a Condition to march by the middle of May. Prince Lewis of Baden has written to Court, to excuſe himſelf from coming thither, his Preſence being ſo very neceſſary, and ſo much deſir'd on the Upper-Rhine.

Francfort, Mar. 12. The Marquiſs d' Uxelles is come to Straſburg, and is to draw together a Body of ſome Regiments of Horſe and Foot from the Gariſons of Alſace ; but will not leſſen thoſe of Straſburg and Landau, which are already very weak. On the other hand, the Troops of His Imperial Majeſty, and his Allies, are going to form a Body near Germeſhein in the Palatinate, of which Place, as well as of the Lines at Spires, Prince Lewis of Baden is expected to take a View, in three or four days. The Engliſh and Dutch Miniſters, the Count of Friſe, and the Baron Vander Meer ; and likewiſe the Imperial Envoy Count Lowenſtein, are gone to Nordlingen, and it is hop'd that in a ſhort time we ſhall hear from thence of ſome favourable Reſolutions for the Security of the Empire.

Liege, Mar. 14. The French have taken the Cannon de Longie, who was Secretary to the Dean de Mean, out of our Caſtle, where he has been for ſome time a Priſoner, and have deliver'd him to the Provoſt of Maubeuge, who has carry'd him from hence, but we do not know whither.

Paris, Mar. 13. Our Letters from Italy ſay, That moſt of our Reinforcements were Landed there ; that the Imperial and Eccleſiaſtical Troops ſeem to live very peaceably with one another in the Country of Parma, and that the Duke of Vendome, as he was viſiting ſeveral Poſts, was within 100 Paces of falling into the Hands of the Germans. The Duke of Chartres, the Prince of Conti, and ſeveral other Princes of the Blood, are to make the Campaign in Flanders under the Duke of Burgundy ; and the Duke of Maine is to Command upon the Rhine.

From the Amſterdam Courant, Dated Mar. 18.

Rome, Feb. 25. We are taking here all poſſible Precautions for the Security of the Eccleſiaſtical State in this preſent Conjuncture, and have deſir'd to raiſe 3000 Men in the Cantons of Switzerland. The Pope has appointed the Duke of Berwick to be his Lieutenant-General, and he is to Command 6000 Men on the Frontiers of Naples : He has alſo ſettled upon him a Penſion of 6000 Crowns a year during Life.

From the Paris Gazette, Dated Mar. 18. 1702.

Naples, Febr. 17. 600 French Soldiers are arrived here, and are expected to be follow'd by 3400 more. A Courier that came hither on the 14th. has brought Letters by which we are aſſur'd that the King of Spain deſigns to be here towards the end of March ; and accordingly Orders are given to make the neceſſary Preparations againſt his Arrival. The two Troops of Horſe that were Commanded to the Abruzzo are poſted at Peſcara with a Body of Spaniſh Foot, and others in the Fort of Montorio.

Paris, March. 18. We have Advice from Toulon of the 5th inſtant, that the Wind having long ſtood favourable, 22000 Men were already ſail'd for Italy, that 3500 more were Embarking, and that by the 15th it was hoped they might all get thither. The Count d' Eſtrees arriv'd there on the Third inſtant, and ſet all hands at work to fit out the Squadron of 9 Men of War and ſome Fregats, that are appointed to carry the King of Spain to Naples. His Catholick Majeſty will go on Board the *Thunderer*, of 110 Guns.

We have Advice by an Expreſs from Rome of the 18th of February, That notwithſtanding the preſſing Inſtances of the Imperial Embaſſadour, the Pope had Condemn'd the Marquis del Vaſto to loſe his Head and his Eſtate to be confiſcated, for not appearing to Anſwer the Charge againſt him of Publickly Scandalizing Cardinal Janſon.

ADVERTISEMENT.

IT will be found from the Foreign Prints, which from time to time, as Occaſion offers, will be mention'd in this Paper, that the Author has taken Care to be duly furniſh'd with all that comes from Abroad in any Language. And for an Aſſurance that He will not, under Pretence of having Private Intelligence, impoſe any Additions of feign'd Circumſtances to an Action, but give his Extracts fairly and Impartially ; at the beginning of each Article he will quote the Foreign Paper from whence 'tis taken, that the Publick, ſeeing from what Country a piece of News comes with the Allowance of that Government, may be better able to Judge of the Credibility and Fairneſs of the Relation : Nor will he take upon him to give any Comments or Conjectures of his own, but will relate only Matter of Fact ; ſuppoſing thoſe People to have Senſe enough to make Reflections for themſelves.

This Courant (as the Title ſhews) will be Publiſh'd Daily ; being deſign'd to give all the Material News as ſoon as every Poſt arrives : and is confin'd to half the Compaſs, to ſave the Publick at leaſt half the Impertinences, of ordinary News-Papers.

LONDON. Sold by E. Mallet, next Door to the King's-Arms Tavern at Fleet-Bridge.

Facsimile of the first daily newspaper in the English language

signs and symbols in wet clay tablets using cylinder seals and then baking them in the sun, They also devised a cuneiform system of writing, using bones to mark signs in wet clay. Stamp seals, engraved objects used to denote ownership, had been common 1000 years earlier. Pictographs or ideographs—drawings of animals, commonly recognized objects, and humans—were popular in the Mediterranean area, China, India, what is now Mexico, and Egypt, where they became known as hieroglyphs. There is evidence that a system of movable type was devised in Asia Minor prior to 1700 B.C., the date of a flat clay disk found in Crete. The disk contained 45 different signs that had been carved on individual pieces of type and then pressed onto the clay.

Elaborate carvings in stone and wood became common in the eastern Mediterranean around 1500 B.C., roughly the same time that the Phoenicians, successful traders and bankers for 1000 years, introduced symbols for sounds and created an alphabet. Colored fluids were used to outline the "letters" of the alphabet and to produce the pictographs. Around 500 B.C. the Egyptians used reeds found along the Nile River to make papyrus. Scribes using brushes or quills could then "write" their hieroglyphics, and sheets of papyrus could be joined to make a scroll. For several hundred years, the scroll collections were housed at the centers of learning. Whereas the clay and stone tablets were heavy and difficult to store or carry any distance, the papyrus sheets and scrolls allowed information to be shared easily.

Vellum was used as another writing surface beginning about A.D. 100. The parchment, made from animal skins, was used in the Greek and Roman empires for special manuscripts or scrolls. At this same time the Chinese invented a smooth, white paper from wood pulp and fibers and also discovered a way to transfer an ideograph from stone to paper after inking the surface. These "rubbings" were joined together to produce beautifully colored scrolls.

Wang Chieh published what is considered the world's oldest preserved book from wood blocks in A.D. 868. Large blocks could be carved so that one sheet of paper, printed on both sides, could be folded into thirty-two pages of booksize. Feng Tao printed the Confucian classics between 932 and 953, and in about 1045 the artisan Pi Sheng was inspired to devise a set of movable clay carvings—a sort of earthenware "type"—that could be reused. The process was also used in Persia and Egypt. Wood-block printing was introduced to Europe when Marco Polo returned from China in 1295 and became popular in Europe during the fourteenth and fifteenth centuries. Its most striking use came in the production of illustrated books. Meanwhile, in Asia, the innovations continued; movable type cast in copper or bronze was used in Korea in 1241.

Johann Gutenberg of Mainz and Strasbourg is credited with introducing printing from movable type in Europe. Beginning about 1450, with the help of his partner Johann Fust, Gutenberg used a mixture of lead and other metals to cast individual letters in reverse and high relief. Apparently he was unaware this was being done in China. After printing several books using an adapted wine press, he began to reproduce the Bible in 1456. However, unable to pay his loans to Fust, Gutenberg lost his shop the following year, and Fust finished the printing of the Bible in 1460. William Caxton imported the first printing press into England in 1476, and by 1490 at least one printing press was operating in every major European city.

THE PRINTING PRESS AS AN AGENT OF CHANGE

The effect of the advent of the printing press upon life in Western Europe was tremendous. Dr. Elizabeth Eisenstein, in her probing study,[1] assembled evidence to support her thesis that the spread of printing in the late fifteenth and sixteenth centuries ripped apart the social and structural fabric of life in Western Europe and reconnected it in new ways that gave shape to modern patterns. The availability of printed materials made possible societal, cultural, familial, and industrial changes facilitating the Renaissance, the Reformation, and the scientific revolution.

How could movable type make such a change in thinking and habits accepted for centuries? First, it made it possible to produce literature and printed materials cheaply enough to reach the masses. Each copy of a hand-produced book or newsletter cost as much to make as the last, and took as long. The printing press reduced the unit cost and produced copies in bulk. This meant that knowledge was no longer the exclusive property of the privileged classes. Availability of cheap printed reading matter encouraged the growth of literacy. Learning to read is likely to make a man or woman curious, simply because matters are brought into focus that have never been imagined. As the Middle Ages ended, various tendencies broke the crust of fixed custom and ushered in an age of discussion.

The so-called cradle books of the fifteenth century were much like their handwritten predecessors. But soon the printing press spewed forth simpler books, pamphlets, and single sheets. Book production spread from universities and monasteries to smaller towns and villages. Martin Luther and his supporters spread the word of Protestantism throughout the German countryside after 1520 on printed sheets that were widely copied and argued about. Since many in the audience lacked the requisite literacy background and experience for reasoning, appeals were often made through the emotions. When people react to emotion rather than to rational thinking, they sometimes forsake the orderliness of the status quo and the safety of docility, hallmarks of medieval society's ruling nobility and the Catholic church. The traditional elite groups had good cause to fear the social consequences of custom-breaking appeals to emotions through the printing press. Thus Henry VIII, noting Luther's success in Germany with a Protestant-based Reformation rooted in reading, would quickly move to limit printing in England.

The newspaper was the most novel product of the printing press. As it began to develop its role of providing news and entertainment, it became the primary catalyst of the printing press for influencing social and political change. Telling the story of those newspapers and their printers and writers is a major theme of this book. Later the story of the print media merges with those of the visual and electronic media, equally important today as agents of change. Central to their influence is their transmission of information and news.

EARLY WRITINGS: PRESERVING HISTORY

The longest continuing information program on record was in China, where, beginning about A.D. 750, the imperial court published semiannual reports on the condition of the people, in addition to monthly bulletins and calendars. Known as *Tching-pao,* these bulletins were printed weekly beginning around 1360; by 1830 they had become daily publications. Known later as the *Peking Gazette,* the reports lasted until the end of the empire in 1911. Another publication for provincial governors appeared in about 950 and also lasted until 1911.

The preservation of history was a goal of writers from the earliest of times. In the opening pages of his monumental four-volume history of world news reporting, the press historian Dr. Robert W. Desmond suggests that the first writers were performing functions "akin to those performed later by literary men and by journalists of the printed media. They were writing of their own times and people; they were gathering and recording information."[2] Desmond included here the Greek epic poet Homer and his *Iliad* and *Odyssey,* the "father of history" Herodotus, who traveled throughout the Middle East, and Demosthenes of Athens, who often wrote speeches for others and was something of a public relations expert. Confucius dealt with his times and contemporaries in China, Thucydides wrote eight volumes on the history of the war between Athens and Sparta, Julius Caesar reported the Roman wars in his *Commentaries,* and Plutarch turned out numerous "profiles" of prominent leaders. The reports on the life of Jesus Christ, known as the New Testament, and the letters of the traveling Paul have influenced untold millions, as has the *Qur'an,* Islam's sacred scriptures. Copies of the *Acta Diurna* were kept for the public in a special building, just as scrolls were preserved in many lands.

Marco Polo's detailed, handwritten accounts of his two trips to China, totaling 33 years, were recopied and distributed for more than 250 years. Finally *The Travels of Marco Polo* was one of the first books to appear in Europe, in 1559. A history of the entire world was written by Mongol historian Rashid al-Din in the early fourteenth century. At least three volumes appeared in Arabic, dealing with the conquests of Genghis Khan, the prophet Muhammad, the history of China, the history of India including the life of Buddha, Old Testament history, and reflections on other peoples whom Mongols encountered during their thirteenth-century invasions. A lavishly illustrated partial manuscript of the second volume was sold in London for $2 million in 1980, after having been lost for nearly 500 years.[3]

THE SPANISH INFLUENCE IN AMERICAN JOURNALISM

The oldest known preserved report of a current event describes a 1541 storm and earthquake in Guatemala. Written by a notary public named Juan Rodríquez, the eight-page booklet was printed in Mexico City by Juan Pablos, an Italian who was the representative in New Spain of Juan Cromberger, the owner of a well-known Seville printing house. Entering the world of the highly developed Aztecs, Incas, and Mayans, the Spanish brought the first printing press to the Americas in 1536. Bishop Juan de Zumárraga delivered the press to Mexico City, and Esteban Martín was said to have done the first printing. But surviving examples are of Pablos's work, dating from 1539 when he, pressman Gil Barbero, and an unnamed black slave turned out their first pages.[4] A translation of the "headline" on the cover sheet of the storm report of 1541 reads:

> Report of the Terrifying Earthquake Which Has Reoccurred In the Indies in a City Called Guatemala.
> It is an event of great astonishment and great example so that we all repent from our sins and so that we will be ready when God calls us.
> Summary of what happened in Guatemala:

A second center for printing in the Americas was Lima, where a press was established in 1583. The first printer there was Antonio Ricardo, who printed a catechism in Indian languages the following year. Much of the early work was the bilingual printing of religious materials, many of them colorfully decorated. By 1600 at least 174 books, possibly more, had been published. Primitive news sheets called *hojas volantes* (flying pages or bulletins), *noticias, relaciones, sucesos,* or *relatos* also appeared in Spain. Some were printed in the Americas in the late sixteenth century; one, printed by Ricardo in Lima in 1594, was preserved. It gave an account of the capture of the English pirate "John of Aquines," son of John Hawkins, off the coast of Peru. The *hojas,* which predated the

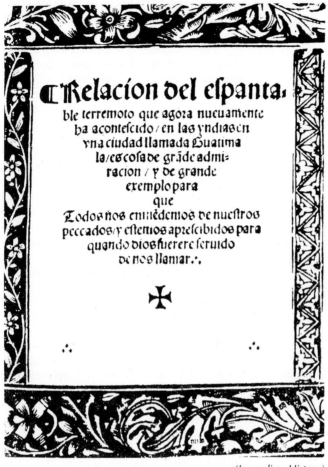

Oldest known preserved news report, printed in 1541 in Mexico City

C Relacion del espanta,
ble terremoto que agora nueuamente
ha acontefcido / en las yndias en
yna ciudad llamada Guatima
la/es cofa de grãde admi=
racion / y de grande
exemplo para
que
Todos nos emmédemos de nueftros
peccados/y eftemos aprefcibidos para
quando dios fuerere feruido
de nos llamar.

✠

(Journalism History)

better-known English news sheets called *corantos,* remained popular into the eighteenth century. Parallel to the technological achievements, there is evidence that the widows of printers carried on their husbands' work in a manner similar to that of the "printers' widows" in U.S. colonial history.[5]

Although the development of a regular periodical press was delayed in the Americas by Spanish censorship and the high cost of printing news for a small group of literate persons, publications of approximately monthly frequency began to appear in Lima in 1618. These *noticias* reflected the excitement over European news, and some of them were copies of European news sheets. Scholars have not determined that any real periodicals came into being during the seventeenth century, although a *Gaceta de Mexico* was published irregularly in 1667, and four volumes of *Mercurio Volante* were published by Carlos de Siguenzay Gongora in 1693, detailing the military campaigns in Mexico. It appears that the first regular periodical was Mexico's *Gaceta de Mexico,* which began carrying both local and foreign news in 1722. It was published monthly by a church official, Juan Ignacio Castorena Ursua y Goyeneche, who included items from California, Manila, Havana,

Guatemala, Acapulco, and other cities of New Spain. In his first issue Castorena asked governors and church officials in other cities to send him items "worthy of the public light and for good example."[6] Castorena's paper lasted only six months because he was transferred, but it was revived in 1728 and continued until about 1739. The second periodical appeared in Guatemala in 1729, *Gazeta de Goatemala,* and the third in Lima, *Gaceta de Lima,* in 1744. Although all three publications were short-lived, they provided the foundation for the strong Spanish-language press of the future.

EUROPEAN NEWS REPORTING

The oldest known and preserved copies of a titled, regularly published news sheet were produced in Germany in 1609, but the existing copies do not indicate the city of publication, the printer, or the publisher. From an analysis of paper, type, printing technique, political content, and religious coloring, experts deduced that the site of this earliest known newspaper had to be in northern Germany. According to Dr. Ralph O. Nafziger, who made a lengthy study of the evidence produced by German researchers, the 1609 *Aviso* appeared in Wolfenbüttel rather than in nearby Bremen as was thought earlier. This was a weekly publication, as were the *Relation* of Strasbourg and the *Avisa Relation oder Zeitung* of Augsburg. Both of these publications also date from 1609.[7]

Between 1610 and 1661, titled news sheets appeared in Switzerland, England, Spain, Austria, Belgium, Holland, Sweden, Italy, Poland, and elsewhere. Amsterdam printers issued untitled *corantos* for readers in both Holland and England as early as 1603. From around 1620 to 1631 a French version was sent to Paris. This ended when the first titled-weekly appeared in Paris in that year. Desmond's research indicates that European printers produced untitled, small "flysheets" from wood blocks as early as 1415. These sheets, printed on one side only, were sold to the public in the Germanic states and Central Europe. Reportedly an account of the Battle of Agincourt in 1415 and a letter from Christopher Columbus in 1493 were published.[8] Newsletters were also common, the most famous being the Fugger newsletters from the Fugger banking house in Augsburg. Between 1568 and 1604 a general readership learned of such historic events as the execution of Mary Queen of Scots, the defeat of the Spanish Armada, and early voyages of Sir Francis Drake. A court newspaper begun in Stockholm in 1645 still appears and is the world's oldest known continuously published newspaper.[9] A German newspaper begun in 1616, the *Frankfurter Oberpostamtzeitung* (renamed the *Postzeitung*), later became the first daily newspaper in the world.[10] It continued until 1866, when it merged with the famed *Frankfurter Zeitung.* Minute-by-minute reports of the English Parliament were published daily for four consecutive weeks in 1660 by Oliver Williams in his *Perfect Diurnal,* a small booklet.

THE PRESS DEVELOPS IN ENGLAND

The point to all this is that England has no special claim as the home of the modern press, even though it advanced beyond all other countries journalistically. In England, as in other lands, news was exchanged long before there was even the most primitive form of newspaper. One of the great attractions at the country fairs of the Middle Ages was the opportunity to exchange gossip and information. Country folk and gentry traveled annually to Bartholomew, Donnybrook, or Stourbridge as much to swap news as to buy yearly supplies of staples. Newspapers did not create news; news created newspapers.

Under twentieth-century standards a true newspaper must meet the following qualifications: it must be published regularly, on a daily or weekly basis; it must appeal to a general-interest audience rather than a specialized one; and it must offer timely news. When these standards are applied to the seventeenth century, "true newspapers" are slow to appear. The criterion most often noted here is continuity of publication using as much timely general interest material as feasible.

To produce a publication of this type, there had to be some incentive for gathering and processing information of interest to the general public—news. News thereupon became a commodity, like food or merchandise, produced for profit to meet a demand. Up to about 1500, the word *Tydings* usually described reports of current events. The word *newes* was coined to differentiate between the casual dissemination of information and the deliberate attempt to gather and process the latest intelligence.

It is significant that the newspaper first flourished in areas where central authority was weak, as in Germany, which at that time was divided into a patchwork of small principalities, or where rulers were more tolerant, as in the Low Countries. This explains why the development of the press lagged in England. True, William Caxton set up the first press in England in 1476, but nearly two centuries elapsed before the country had a genuine newspaper.

Caxton had learned about printing on the continent, where it had been a craft since the middle of the fifteenth century. He had been governor of a chartered association of "adventurers," or merchants interested in foreign enterprise. Caxton was a learned man, the author and translator of several volumes, and a collector of fine books. He believed that it was his mission to bring the culture of the continent to his compatriots. His king, Edward IV, encouraged these ideas. Edward had just come to power, following a long civil war that had split the country. Not until 1471 was he safely in control of his government.[11] At once he began to repair the ravages of the internal conflict. Edward was responsible for progress in law, industry, and culture. It was under such circumstances that Caxton set up his tiny press "at the Sign of the Red Pale" in the almonry of the abbey at Westminster in London in 1476.[12]

THE TUDOR REIGN: PRIOR RESTRAINT THROUGH LICENSING

The Battle of Bosworth Field in 1485 brought a new English dynasty into being. Henry Tudor, the victor, ended the long feud between the royal houses of York and Lancaster, thereby bringing the country back to the stability it so desperately needed. A Lancastrian by blood and a Yorkist by marriage, Henry emerged from the Wars of the Roses, as the civil strife was called, with powers that were eventually to make the Tudors as nearly absolute in power as English monarchs could be. The nobility, which had previously restrained the powers of the English kings, was decimated by the long years of fighting. The Tudor monarchs took full advantage of the situation. Most of them were brilliant and able administrators. Under Tudor leadership England experienced a golden age. It was not, however, conducive to the progress of the press.

Caxton enjoyed relative freedom from royal interference, mostly because he never tried to test his status. Printing was not a social force for about 50 years after its establishment in England. Under the Tudors, however, the press became a matter of kingly concern, for that strong dynasty was noted for its attempts to grasp all possible power. Henry VIII started the government control of the press in 1529 with a list of prohibited books. His purpose was to set up a bulwark against the rising tide of Protestantism. The first licensing system under government control was established a year later, and by a proclamation on Christmas Day 1534, Henry VIII required printers to have royal permission before setting up shop. Thus the concept of "prior restraint" became law.

During this period the powers of the Privy Council were also increased, at the expense of Parliament and the older courts but to the advantage of the Crown. The Council supervised the administration of laws, regulated trade, kept an eye on the courts, and controlled the press. Beginning in 1542 the records of the Council show a continuous report of proceedings against individuals for "unfitting worddes," seditious utterances, and the like. As early as 1540 the Council made arrests for the printing of street ballads about political matters.[13]

Despite these repressive measures, a kind of literary black market supplied the forbidden information and entertainment. We know, for example, that Henry VIII was angered in the thirty-sixth year of his reign by accounts of a battle in Scotland. The news was peddled by London "broadsheet" vendors (a broadsheet was a paper printed specifically to describe a certain event). The king's complaint was not so much that the reports were false but that the news had been printed without his permission.

One way to control an industry is to make it a monopoly and then to hold its directors responsible for abuses. The Tudors did that with the printing industry in 1557 when Queen Mary established the Stationers Company. This organization had existed since 1357 as a society of court and text writers, to which the "limners," or illustrators, were admitted after 1404. By 1500 the printers had also been admitted, but by Mary's time the word "stationer" was applied to the publishers and dealers in books, as distinct from the printers.[14] The Stationers Company was a kind of printing trust, which made it easier for authorities to run down rebel printers who were not members of the elite group. In 1576, for example, the Stationers adopted an order for weekly searches of London printing houses (where almost all printing was concentrated). Pairs of searchers reported on work in progress, number of orders on hand, identity of customers, number of employees, and wages paid. This constituted an effective check on extensive bootleg printing.

The infamous Star Chamber court, originally set up to protect the public but later the symbol of repression, was another barrier to free expression during the long period preceding the appearance of the English newspaper. By edicts of the Privy Council in 1566 and the Star Chamber in 1586, the pattern of restrictions for the next hundred years was outlined. Severe penalties were prescribed for printers foolish enough to defy the authorities. Strange as it may seem, there were printers willing to run that risk. One was William Carter, who was hanged for printing pamphlets favorable to the Catholic cause. Arrested and tortured in 1580, Carter was executed in 1584.[15] Puritan rebels against the Established Church included Hugh Singleton, Robert Waldegrave, John Stroud, and John Hodgkins. The attack on the monopoly control was led by John Wolfe, Roger Ward, William Holmes, and John Charlewood. Waldegrave was the printer of the first "Martin Marprelate" tracts, the Puritan arguments published surreptitiously against the Established Church. Hodgkins carried on when Waldegrave was hounded from the country.

The Tudor control of the press was said to be in the interest of public safety. From Henry VIII to Elizabeth I, the Crown acted on the principle that peace demanded the suppression of unwarranted dissent. On the whole the Tudors were able rulers who "had the feel" of the country. Not so with their successors, the Stuarts, who came to power in 1603. James I (who was James VI of Scotland) was sincere and well meaning, but he was never in tune with the times or with his subjects. He was the son of the unfortunate Mary Queen of Scots, whose life had been marked by scandal and violence. As the son of Mary, James was early suspected of "Papist" sympathies in a day when that was religious jargon for treason. Under the Stuarts, beginning with James, the opposing factions formed battle lines. That the press thrives in such a climate, if restraints break down, perhaps partially explains the rapid development of journalism during the seventeenth century.

During the early part of that century news became of great importance to the English people. The religious disputes, the rise of England as a maritime power, the struggles between king and Parliament, and the changing social conditions made the public more interested in events beyond its local sphere. The balladeers and broadsheet vendors could not meet the demand. Prose pamphlets were much more effective, as evidenced by the success of the Marprelate tracts, but such publications were not enough. The newsletter writers, or "intelligencers," as the publishers of handwritten sheets were called, were capable journalists, but the average person could not afford their products.[16] The time was ripe for a new type of publication.

FIRST ENGLISH *CORANTOS*

In the summer of 1621, nearly a century and a half after Caxton had introduced printing to England, rudimentary prototypes of the modern newspaper appeared on the streets of London. These primitive news sheets were called *corantos.* They lacked the regularity that is necessary for a true newspaper, and they were too specialized in content, but they did fulfill a need.

In 1620 the English were interested in continental developments. The popular Princess Elizabeth had married Frederick, Elector of the Palatinate, in 1613. He was a Protestant, highly favored by nonconformists both on the continent and in England. When he decided to accept the crown of Bohemia against the wishes of the Holy Roman Emperor, he precipitated the Thirty Years' War.

Printers in the Netherlands were quick to capitalize on this interest. At least 25 English-language *corantos* reporting war news were produced, nearly all in Amsterdam, by George Veseler and Broer Jonson. These single sheets, now in the British Museum, were dated December 2, 1620, to September 18, 1621. Nathaniel Butter, a bookseller, was the English distributor. Sales were so brisk that in the summer of 1621 Butter decided to do the publishing himself, pirating his news from Dutch news sheets. Thomas Archer, a printer, was probably his partner. Copies of their first sheets, printed in the summer of 1621, have not survived. Six smaller *corantos,*[17] dated September 24 to October 22, have. But by that time printer Archer had run afoul of the law.

When Frederick, the newly elected king of Bohemia, led his forces to defeat in revolt against the Hapsburgs at a battle near Prague, English sentiment favored intercession by James I for his son-in-law. James could not make up his mind, however. The *corantos* were critical of his foreign policy, and in retaliation the king cracked down on the editors, using the old rules of the Tudors. In December 1620 and again in July 1621, the king issued proclamations against "the great liberty of discourse concerning matters of state." He followed this with an order suppressing *corantos,* but apparently some of the printers flouted his orders, for there is a report of the Stationers Company calling Archer for a hearing in August. He was imprisoned.

Then Nicholas Bourne entered the picture. He was a respected printer, and it is possible that Butter teamed up with him because of his prestige. Their first *coranto* was authorized in September 1621, and undoubtedly bore the legend "Published With Authority" at the top of the page, as did later issues. The earliest surviving *coranto* of this press is dated May 23, 1622. Archer, now out of prison, was the printer. Butter was probably the editor and Bourne was the publisher, or responsible promoter. The paper was printed on one side only, and the sheet was somewhat smaller than a page of modern typewriter paper.

It was not until 1624 that the *corantos* began to be identified by name, thus supplying something of the continuity required of a true newspaper. The earliest known *coranto* published by title was *The Continuation of Our Weekly Newes,* from the office of Bourne and Butter. Because this title appeared on at least 23 consecutive issues, the offering marks another step in the development of the newspaper.

The earliest *corantos* printed nothing but foreign news. The first domestic reports can be traced back to the publication by the Westminster clerks of Parliamentary proceedings dated about 1628. Out of these accounts developed the *diurnals,* or daily reports of local

Numbr 45

A
PERFECT
DIVRNALL
OF THE
PASSAGES
IN
PARLIAMENT.

From Munday the 17. of Aprill till Munday the 24. *Aprill.*

Collected by the same hand that formerly drew up the Copy for William Cooke *in Furnivals Inne. And now Printed by J. Okes and F. Leach and are to be sold by Francis Coles in the Old Baily.*

Munday the 17. of Aprill 1643.

THe Lords and Commons taking into considerati-on a late Proclamation dated at Oxford the first of this instant Aprill, for the holding and continuing of the Court of Chanchery and all proceedings herein the Receipt of his Majesties Exchequer, and of the first fruits and tenthes, the Court of the Dutchies of Lancaster, Court of wards, an Live-ies, and Covrts of Requests, at the City of Ox-ford for the whole Terme of Easter then next en-suing. and for the adjourning the Courts of Kings Bench, Common Pleas, and Exchequer from *Quindena Pasche,* untill the returne of *Quinque Septianas Pasche,* next doe finde that it will much end to the prejudice of the Common-wealth to have the said Courts and Receipts held and continued at Oxford where great part of an
Army

Note that here is al-so a true and pun-&uall re-lation of the whole proceed-ings of the siedge at Reading for all the last weeke unto this present.

events. The diurnals flourished during the struggle between king and Parliament, when it was safe to comment on local news because neither side was strong enough to take punitive measures and when both factions were seeking public support. Many of the restrictions on the press were modified by the Long Parliament, and after 1640 diurnals appeared by the score. The oldest known paper of this type is John Thomas's *Diurnall Occurrences,* which first appeared November 29, 1641.

CIVIL WAR: MILTON'S *AREOPAGITICA*

From 1642 to 1649 England was engulfed in a civil war that pitted the Puritans led by Oliver Cromwell against the supporters of the Stuarts and James's successor, Charles I. The conflict stimulated a duel between the two groups for public support, which meant a period of relaxation for the press. The Long Parliament abolished the dreaded Star Chamber in 1641. Voices began to be raised in favor of a greater freedom of expression. On November 24, 1644, the poet John Milton published his famous *Areopagitica,* probably the best known of the great pleas for a free press.[18] Milton spoke eloquently for the right of discussion and declared that

> though all the winds of doctrine were let loose to play upon the earth, so truth be in the field, we do injuriously by licensing and prohibiting to misdoubt her strength. Let her [truth] and falsehood grapple; who ever knew truth put to the worse, in a free and open encounter?[19]

Milton gave the most perfect expression to the idea of a free press, but just as courageous and articulate were such journalistic heroes as William Walwyn, who argued for liberty of the press following his studies on religious toleration; Henry Robinson, who based his theory of a free press on economic principles and free enterprise; Richard Overton, the Tom Paine of his day, who expanded his Separatist views on religion into principles of democracy; and John Lilburne, who did more than any of his compatriots to make them conscious of their right of discussion.[20] As a matter of fact, Milton had very little effect in bringing about any improvement. His words were not widely disseminated at the time. The ideas expressed in the *Areopagitica* were picked up nearly 100 years later by people all over the world, notably in America, struggling to obtain even greater freedom than they already enjoyed.

 With the execution of Charles I in 1649 and the rise of the Commonwealth under Oliver Cromwell, the press again fell upon evil days. Cromwell's "Roundheads" had taken over the royal prerogatives, which had at times so restricted Puritan writers and publishers, but the new regime was no more tolerant of the press than the Crown had been. Cromwell permitted only administration organs to be published, such as *Mercurius Politicus,* censored by the great Milton; *A Perfect Diurnall,* also controlled for a time through Milton; and later the *Publick Intelligencer* (1655). All unauthorized publications were treated roughly. Marchamont Nedham was Cromwell's leading editor.

 The mercury and intelligencer followed the *coranto* and diurnal as publications in the progression of English news reporting. Carrying a wide range of information, their pages were numbered consecutively, week by week, for the life of the publication. There were similar innovations on the continent. In England most printers had broken away from the booklet form by the 1660s.

 The restoration of Charles II in 1660 resulted in the establishment of an exclusive patent, or monopoly, system under Henry Muddiman and Roger L'Estrange. For a time the ancient, handwritten newsletters were the only means of disseminating information with any degree of freedom. Printed newspapers could be liquidated by confiscating the presses, whereas newsletters could be produced as long as scribes could find a hideaway or were willing to defy authorities. During this period ultimate control was divided between the Crown and Parliament. Regulations and restrictions were fewer, but they were clearly stated, and enforcement was effective under the Surveyor of the Press.

Under Charles, a new era of journalism was ushered in with the publication of the *Oxford Gazette* in 1665. Edited by Muddiman while the royal court was fleeing from the London plague, it was, strictly speaking, the first periodical to meet all the qualifications of a true newspaper. It was printed twice a week, by royal authority. After 23 issues, the publication became the *London Gazette,* when the court moved back to the capital. It continued to be published into the twentieth century as the official court organ.

LICENSING ENDS

The old licensing powers appeared to be crumbling as the Restoration period drew to a close. This was not through choice of the authorities but was more likely a result of the growing tendency for class and political alignments. In 1679 Parliament allowed the Licensing Act of 1662 to lapse. It was revived from time to time, but with the increasing tension between the Crown and Parliament, each side sought to protect its own spokespeople. The so-called Regulation of Printing, or Licensing, Act expired in 1694, not because authorities were convinced of the injustice of licensing, but because licensing was politically unsound. From 1694 to the passage of the first Stamp Act of 1712, the only controls were the laws of treason and seditious libel and regulations against reporting proceedings of Parliament. Prior restraint had ended.

One last victim under Charles was Benjamin Harris, a brash and somewhat reckless journalist. Harris was convicted of violating the king's laws. He was fined and pilloried. Unable to pay the fine, he spent two years in prison. When his office was again raided in 1686, Harris fled to Bristol with his family and took passage for America. He appears again soon in these pages as the publisher of one of the first newspapers in America.

After the Revolution of 1688, which brought a change in the monarchical institution, journalists were accorded considerable freedom. William and Mary were rulers by right of public opinion, and they had the common sense not to antagonize printers and publishers, who were factors in the development of public opinion. There are no serious persecutions in their reign. By 1694 the old Licensing Act died of senility and neglect. With the rise of the two-party system during the reign of William and Mary, it was difficult to maintain licensing. Without the decisive action of the old monarchs, it was impossible to continue such an archaic system. The attack on the Act in Commons centered around the commercial unfairness of the monopoly system, the restrictions on the printing industry, the tendency of suspected violators to use bribery, and the inadequacy of censorship. But as Macaulay declared in his *History of England,* "on the great question of principle, on the question whether the liberty of unlicensed printing be, on the whole, a blessing or a curse to society, not a word is said."[21]

RISE OF A MIDDLE CLASS

Journalistic progress was speeded up by the development of the English party system of government. It is significant that parties emerged at the very time that the newspaper began to be a force in the political and social affairs of a people interested more and more in government. The *corantos* were printed during the death throes of an outworn social system. England was moving steadily from feudalism, whose economic manifestation was production for use, to capitalism, translated economically into production for profit. The change brought social strains as power was grasped by one class at the expense of another.

A new type of citizen began to emerge, the commercial person—the trader, the merchant, and (later) the manufacturer. A great middle class was arising. Standing between the producer and the consumer, it profited from the processing and distributing of goods. In so doing, it helped to raise living standards to the highest level. And the wealth accumulated during this process was inevitably translated into power. The emerging middle class could win recognition and influence only by acquiring some of the feudal privileges and powers of the traditional classes.

Three groups struggled for power. One was largely Anglican in religion, Tory in politics, and aristocratic as a class. The second was likely to be Presbyterian, Whig, and middle class. The third was made up of religious dissenters, radicals, and people of more lowly station. All three classes produced newspapers and journalists; perhaps inevitably the Whig middle class would provide the capital and the printing equipment for writers and editors emerging from the working class, dissenters or radicals though they might be.

EIGHTEENTH-CENTURY JOURNALISM

The popularity of the newspaper was so great that publishers were encouraged to print daily issues. On March 11, 1702, the *Daily Courant* appeared on the streets of London. It was the first daily newspaper printed in the English language. It was produced and "sold by E. Mallet," and authorities differ on the sex of the founder—Elizabeth or Edward? Whichever, the initial venture lasted only a few days.

The real hero of the *Daily Courant* was Samuel Buckley, who revived the daily and made it into a remarkable newspaper. Buckley insisted on a standard of journalism quite unheard of at the time.[22] It was a *news* paper, not a rumor mill. Buckley insisted upon reporting factual news, rather than opinion. He was impartial in his publication of these facts. He was careful to dateline the articles, "that the Publick, seeing from what Country a piece of News comes with the Allowance of that Government, may be better able to Judge of the Credibility and Fairness of the Relation."[23] He practiced what he preached. Although Buckley was a Whig, he did not manipulate news of that party to its favor, even when the Whigs were engaged in a desperate struggle for power. Printing on a single sheet of paper, with the reverse largely devoted to profitable advertising (except on exceptional news days), he had little opportunity for experimentation in makeup. Occasionally, however, Buckley used maps and tabulated figures to clarify his reports. Much of the advertising was spurious by modern standards, but Buckley made money from it. Undoubtedly this revenue made possible his excellent coverage of foreign news.

The high literary quality of eighteenth-century journalism is indicated by the "essay papers," read by students on both sides of the Atlantic even today. The *Tatler* (1709 to 1711) and the *Spectator* (1711 to 1712, 1714) were the products of first Richard Steele and then Steele and Joseph Addison. Printed on one side of a sheet and selling for a penny, this type of paper was enormously popular. The *Spectator* was issued daily and at one time reached 60,000 readers, its promoters boasted. Moreover, its literary form was widely imitated, in America by Benjamin Franklin.

The greatest English journalist of the period was Daniel Defoe, who edited *Mist's Journal* from 1717 through 1720. Steele probably got the idea for his *Tatler* series from reading Defoe's brilliant offerings in earlier papers. Some authorities go so far as to hold that Defoe was the founder of the modern editorial. He discussed all manner of topics in a most charming and persuasive style. He, too, was widely copied by American journalists. But Defoe, like all other editors, was always in danger of arrest for seditious libel, especially for reporting news of Parliament. Newsletter writers like John Dyer, the Tory adherent, smuggled handwritten reports to select readers.

CATO'S LETTERS

In the great controversy between the Tories and the Whigs, Dean Swift wrote some of his greatest satire while he was editing the *Examiner* (1710). The conflict brought out other great writers whose ideas were conveyed to the masses mostly through the newspapers. Influential both in England and America were the so-called Cato Letters, written by John Trenchard and Thomas Gordon over the pen name "Cato." The series appeared between 1720 and 1723 in the *London Journal,* later called the *British Journal.*[24] In convincing, readable form they discussed theories of liberty, representative government, and freedom of expression. In 1724 this series was collected and published in four volumes. Copies were in great demand in the colonies, where the first stirrings of revolution were beginning to be felt. Through American newspapers and pamphlets, the influence of "Cato" can be seen right up to the signing of the Declaration of Independence.

Such progress came at great cost, however. Although party conflict raised the voices of free expression, a reactionary government was able to force new restrictions. In 1712 the Tories succeeded in imposing a tax on newspapers and advertisements. These "taxes on knowledge" tended to curb the press by economic sanction. Even worse, they kept the price of papers high, so that the masses did not have ready access to such publications— which was certainly one of the intentions of the authorities. Advertisement taxes and the stamp tax on news sheets were not fully removed for another 140 years. The British newspaper, as a result, was low in circulation and small in size until the 1850s. Thanks to the satire of Dr. Samuel Johnson and the courage of newspaper publisher John Wilkes, whose jailing for sedition in the 1760s aroused widespread public reaction, the ban on reporting proceedings of the Commons was dropped in 1771. But the threat of trial for seditious libel still hung over those who defied authority.

It is clear from a study of this period that modern journalists can learn much from the experiences of the past. The story of press freedom shows that the press belongs to those who rule. If power is concentrated in the hands of a monarch or an elite group, there is no need for the public to receive information and ideas pertaining to political or social matters. Indeed, providing the public with intelligence (news) may actually constitute a threat to national security and stability, and hence the press must be confined strictly to entertainment or innocuous comment under such a system. On the other hand, if the public participates in government, it must have access to information in direct ratio to its place in the political scheme.

Another lesson to be learned from this period is that the more secure a government is, the less it fears undermining, and the more freedom it accords its press. This is true right up to the present moment. During and after wars, when political leaders and their followers are apprehensive about national safety, liberty of speech and press are in danger of restrictions. Henry VIII's insecurity after his establishment of the English church resulted in strict enforcement of press regulations. Elizabeth cracked down on the press when her claim to the throne was in some doubt. On the other hand, the stability of the English government from the end of the seventeenth century was accompanied by press freedom such as the world had never seen. As Dr. Fredrick Siebert says, "It is axiomatic that government does not exert itself in its own protection unless it is attacked, or believes itself to be seriously threatened."[25]

In the next chapter we shall see the process carried over to America, where the concept of a free press was eventually to prevail as it had in no other country. The philosophy providing the stimulus for this progress developed from the English, however, and the American debt to English press traditions is incalculable.

2

The
Colonial Years

They that can give up essential liberty to obtain a little temporary safety deserve neither liberty nor safety.

—Benjamin Franklin

The time-honored view of the colonial period holds above all that it was heroic:

> Bold men and women, often fired by a sense of divine mission or by a quest for a fuller and juster life than Europe could offer, braved the severities of an Atlantic crossing, attacked the 'howling wilderness,' erected their tiny settlements, established large and thriving families, and somehow still found time to create the free institutions that remain even today the basis for our democratic society.[1]

However, contemporary U.S. historians note on balance that when European colonists arrived in the Americas they encountered a native population that exceeded 70 million. Ultimately, European exploration, conquest, and settlement meant the loss of at least 40 million and perhaps even as many as 60 million lives, many of them Amerindians whose immune systems were ravaged by European diseases. Wars between European settlers and Native Americans also took a heavy toll. Meanwhile, until the 1808 Anglo-American abolition of the slave trade, more than eight million African slaves were brought against their will to the Americas. So the history of colonial America is much more than the history of European settlers (particularly in New England, as the older accounts emphasize). It is the story of three peoples: Native Americans, settlers, and slaves, whose complex experiences have forged both tragedy and innovation.[2]

Against this backdrop, New England was the birthplace of the American newspaper, but it was not until 1704, or 84 years after the establishment of the first successful colony

The first effort at a North American colonial newspaper, and the order banning it

in that area, that a publication meeting all the qualifications of a true newspaper appeared. Printers were available from the very beginning. William Brewster and Edward Winslow, two of the "elders," or leaders, of the Pilgrims who came to Plymouth in December 1620, were printers. They had published religious tracts for the Separatists, the more radical off-shoot of English Protestantism, and they had lived for a time near George Veseler, who was printing the first English *coranto* in the Netherlands while the Pilgrims were on the way to America on the *Mayflower.* Despite this background, the Plymouth colony existed for nearly a century before it enjoyed a newspaper or popular periodical.

Ten years after the arrival of the Pilgrims, another group settled around Boston, a day's sail to the north of Plymouth. This Massachusetts Bay Colony, as it was known, was to be the cradle of American journalism. Many of its members were prosperous. The educational level was high, and some of the settlers were respected scholars. Unlike the Plymouth settlement, which grew slowly, the Massachusetts Bay Colony increased rapidly in population and area of influence. From the beginning it had a high degree of self-government. The charter of the organization had been brought to America, where it served as a kind of constitution beyond the tampering of jealous officials in the home government. In effect the colony had a form of autonomy, or at least a participating home rule, that was to be of great significance in the political development of New England.

THE NEW ENGLAND ENVIRONMENT

Massachusetts Bay colonists were concerned about the education of their children. Having enjoyed educational advantages themselves, they wished to pass on the heritage to succeeding generations. In 1636, six years after the founding of the settlement, they established Harvard College. The larger towns had "grammar schools," which prepared boys for Harvard. As part of this educational process, the authorities established the first press in the English colonies in Cambridge in 1638. Its function was to produce the religious texts needed in school and college; its first book was the *Bay Psalm Book* of 1640.[3] A second press was set up not long after. Later, these presses printed cultural material, including the first history of the colony and some poetry. A word on literacy: the historian Sara Evans notes that although some girls were taught "the rudiments of reading," it was their brothers who "were far more likely to be literate."[4] Also, because reading and writing were viewed as distinct skills and taught separately, far fewer colonial women could write than could read.[5]

It was the colonists' interest in education and cultural dissemination that made Boston famous as the intellectual capital. Here were all the ingredients for the development of a newspaper—high literacy, interest in community matters, self-government, prosperity, and cultural leadership—yet no successful newspaper appeared until the fourth generation.

There was good reason for the lag. At first, the wilderness absorbed the energies of the colonists. Any demand for news was satisfied well enough by the English papers, which arrived on every ship from home. The colonists had few ties with other communities in the New World. Years after they arrived, the settlers were still oriented toward the homeland, not toward their neighbors.

New England colonists established small farms on the rocky soil. Because they lived near each other in the narrow valleys, town life, with the meeting hall and town government, became important to them. In the authoritarian society the settlers established, theological disagreements were seen as threats to the political and social order. Dissenters such as Roger Williams were driven into exile, as was Anne Hutchinson, who joined a small settlement in Rhode Island after being excommunicated by the Massachusetts Bay Puritans.[6]

Life in New England was closely shaped by peoples' beliefs. The theology behind the Puritans was Calvinism. John Calvin, the sixteenth-century reformer in Geneva, Switzerland, formed his theology around predestination, the belief that God has a chosen elect that he will call to himself to be saved. The famed Puritan work ethic—work hard and then you will have success—springs from the popular belief that prosperity is a sign of God's election.

These New England settlers thus had great appreciation for property, especially in the form of land. Land had been the symbol of prestige and standing in England. The decline of feudalism and the emergence of the capitalist class brought many dispossessed English farmers to America as their manor lords substituted wool raising for subsistence farming. In America they could not only work the land they loved, but they could acquire property, the mark of a superior person.[7]

The New England woman was another significant factor in the development of the region. Women joined men as original settlers, working to create homes and businesses. They also reared large families, enabling their society to keep its identity. This was also true in other North American colonies of the British, Germans, Swedes, and Dutch, but not of the Spanish in Latin America and to some extent of the French in Canada. The New England pioneer preserved the traditions of an old race and the characteristics of a great culture.

COMMERCE: FORERUNNER OF THE PRESS

The commercial stimulation that encourages the development of a popular press was brought to New England in a curious way. Because farming paid such a small return on the energy invested in it, the New England Yankee turned to fishing as an easier way of earning a living. Surrounding waters teemed with fish. Soon Yankees were the main suppliers of fish to the Mediterranean basin, where a combination of religions and diet provided a ready market.

Fishing made New Englanders into great seafarers. Soon they were building their own vessels, designed for special purposes and superior to anything under sail up to then. The forests provided the raw materials for a thriving shipbuilding industry. The region abounded in excellent harbors. Shipbuilding and ocean commerce stimulated the growth of lumbering, wood manufacture, and other small industries, for which there was abundant water power. As a result, a class of shrewd, tough, independent businesspeople began to win renown for New England. Many of them became wealthy and were ready to help support a publication that could advertise wares and spread pertinent information.

For a time the coffeehouses had sufficed as a news medium, in the same way that the marketplaces and fairs had served Europe in previous centuries. Here people of congenial interests met to exchange gossip and useful information. Buyers, as well as retailers, were interested in the arrival and departure of ships. Businesspeople were curious about conditions in areas largely ignored by the English papers. Commerce along the North American coast was slowly increasing, for example, and there was a thriving trade with the West Indies. What was being done to disperse local pirates? Was it true that a new postal system was about to be established by His Majesty's Government? Finally, as rivalry spurred trade in the growing communities, merchants discovered that they could move their goods to the local customers faster if they printed notices, or advertisements, in publications read by their customers. The emphasis on this aspect of journalism is indicated by the number of early newspapers with the word "Advertiser" in the name plate. The development of commerce, then, had an important bearing on the establishment of the first newspaper in New England, and all the early publications appeared in commercial centers.

THE SOUTHERN AND MIDDLE COLONIES

In the South the topography favored the growth of large plantations. The general viewpoint remained agrarian rather than commercial, and towns grew slowly. While the "Puritan emphasis on the ability to read the Bible and to understand theology made New England the most literate society in the world during the seventeenth century," the situation in the Southern and middle colonies was quite different.[8] Education was less emphasized, and also since few slaves were taught to read, the overall literacy rate was much lower than in the northern free colonies.[9] Communications develop slowly in such a society. Although Virginia, the "Old Dominion," was settled 13 years before the Pilgrims landed at Plymouth, it lagged far behind in press progress. But the South contributed great ideas and spokespeople, essential to the development of democracy, with which the press was to be so closely integrated. And indeed, Virginia contributed the first reportorial writing in English from the colonies, by Captain John Smith, leader of the 1607 settlement at Jamestown. His *Newes from Virginia* was published as "a true relation" of 40 pages in London in 1608, and has been judged more journalistic than five earlier published news pamphlets about America,[10] among the pre-newspaper newsletters and *corantos* described in Chapter 1.

The Middle Atlantic, or "bread," colonies helped to fuse the regional characteristics of the colonies. Philadelphia and New York were the great commercial centers. In this respect the middle colonies resembled the New England of Boston, Salem, and Providence in this first century of North American colonial history. But the middle colonies attracted settlers of various national and religious backgrounds. Along the Delaware River the Swedes had established communities dating from the early seventeenth century. In 1621 the Dutch West India Company established New Netherland colony. Parts of Pennsylvania became almost as Germanic as the cities in the Palatinate whence the "Pennsylvania Dutch" (Deutsch) had come. The region also absorbed religious expatriates, such as Catholics, Lutherans, Quakers, and Dutch Reformers.

By the end of the seventeenth century there were about 250,000 inhabitants of European descent in the North American colonies. Massachusetts had grown from about 100 in 1620 to 45,000 in 1700. Virginia had a white population of about 50,000. Maryland was next, with 20,000. The others were much smaller but were growing fast. A few families had accumulated respectable fortunes by this time, but the general income level was relatively low.

POLITICAL UNREST

The colonies reflected the religious and political troubles of Europe. Many Americans had emigrated because of differences in beliefs, and they brought their problems with them. The restoration of Charles II after the revolution of the 1640s was a period of political reaction. Once again the king exerted his old powers—or tried to. James II, who succeeded Charles, should have learned that it was dangerous to flout the good will of his subjects, but James was even more unpopular than his predecessors. Under James, revolt seethed. The unrest was reflected in the colonies.

In 1664 the British vanquished the Dutch and took as one of the spoils of war the New Netherland colony, renaming it New York. In the next few years the king tried to strengthen his power in England. It is not surprising that the same process was apparent in the colonies. The General Court of Massachusetts, for example, passed the first formal act restricting the press in 1662. The only printing plant in the colony at the time was the one at Harvard, consisting of two presses, but the authorities were taking no chances with possible subversive literature, and the law provided for rigorous censorship.

One of the governors sent out to the colonies about this time was Sir Edmund Andros. He first took over the seat of government in New York in 1674. It was Andros's understanding that his commission gave him jurisdiction over the area between the Delaware and Connecticut rivers. This was interpreted by colonial leaders as proof that the Crown wished to establish a more effective control of this area by means of centralization of authority. The charters of the New England colonies were declared invalid, and Andros believed he had a mandate to take over this region, too. By 1686 he was in control of most of the populated and prosperous colonies.

Two years later (1688) Parliament deposed James II in the "Glorious Revolution." The Crown was then offered jointly to his eldest daughter, Mary, and her husband, William of Orange. William and Mary were wise rulers. Aware of the circumstances under which they had been offered the crowns, they tended to be conciliatory. The counterpart of these events in America was the revolt against royal authority in the guise of Andros. He was sent back to England in 1689 for trial.[11]

BENJAMIN HARRIS, PRINTER

It was at this time that an ex-London bookseller and publisher decided to offer a periodical that the ordinary colonist could afford and could understand. Boston then had a population of nearly 7000 and was the largest city in America. It offered sufficient sales potential for the type of publication the promoter had in mind. Cultural and literacy levels were sufficient to warrant the financial risk. There was a demand by the commercial interests for such an organ, and they could offer the essential support. The situation was made-to-order for a newspaper, and the man of the hour was at hand.

The hero of this episode was the exiled printer, Benjamin Harris, who was last seen fleeing from the law. Harris arrived in Boston in 1686. Already he had had considerable experience in the London publishing business. Unfortunately, Harris was a troublemaker, and shortly after he had started his London newspaper in 1679, he was arrested for having seditious literature in his possession. He was pilloried and spent two years in prison. When his shop was again raided in 1686, Harris fled with his family to Boston, where he opened a combined coffee and book shop at the corner of State and Washington streets.

The shop was a favorite meeting place for some of Boston's most interesting citizens. Judge Sewall, chronicler of his times and a former publisher, was a regular customer. Most of the local wits and writers made the shop their headquarters. The progressive views of the proprietor are indicated by the fact that his was the only coffee shop in the city where respectable women were welcome.

Harris was a shrewd businessperson. He succeeded against formidable opposition. There were seven booksellers in the neighborhood when Harris set up shop. He sat down and wrote a spelling book that was a best seller in the country for many years. He published books for a distinguished clientele and thus acquired a respect and prestige that some of his rivals lacked. He was not a printer at this time, but rather the promoter of literary works. The downfall of Andros gave Harris the opportunity to go back to his first love, the publication of a newspaper.

PUBLICK OCCURRENCES, 1690

On September 25, 1690, the printing shop of R. Pierce issued a four-page newspaper. It was printed on only three sides. The fourth page was blank so the reader could add his or her own news items before passing it on. The pages measured only 6 by 10¼ inches. There was very little attempt at makeup. This was Harris's *Publick Occurrences, Both Forreign and Domestick,* called by some authorities the first American newspaper. It might very well have been, except that it was banned after the first issue, and one of the qualifications of a newspaper is periodicity, or continuity. If continuity is ignored, there are even earlier examples of broadsheets and reprints of big news events. The characteristic that set *Publick Occurrences* apart was that, unlike the others, it looked like a newspaper, it read like a newspaper, and it was intended as a permanent news organ.[12] Harris was a good reporter for his time. His style was concise—"punchy," the modern editor would call it. The paper included both foreign and local news—another distinction from earlier news publications. Indeed, his "occurrences" covered a multitude of interests. Thus, we find at the bottom of the outside column on page one:

> The *Small-pox* which has been raging in *Boston,* after a manner very Extraordinary is now very much abated. It is thought that far more have been sick of it than were visited with it, when it raged so much twelve years ago, nevertheless it has not been so Mortal. The number of them that have dyed in *Boston* by this last Visitation is about three hundred and twenty, which is not perhaps half so many as fell by the former.[13]

Harris got into trouble with the local authorities, not because he printed libels, but because he printed the truth as he saw it. He had also violated licensing restrictions first imposed in 1662. One of Harris's items reported that Indian allies of the "English Colonies & Provinces of the West" had forced an army under General Winthrop to postpone an attack on the French. The Indians, Harris wrote, had failed to provide "canoo's" for the transportation of the forces into enemy territory. War chiefs had explained that their warriors were too weakened from smallpox to fulfill their commitments, and that was probably true. They were not too weak to make individual raids, however. From one of these raids, Harris reported, they "brought home several *Prisoners,* whom they used in a manner too barbarous for any English to approve." The journalist referred to these Indian allies as "miserable savages, in whom we have too much confided."

All these remarks could be taken as criticism of colonial policy, which at that moment was concerned with winning, not alienating, Native American neighbors. Harris was also accused of bad taste. He had spiced up his paper by reporting that the French king had been taking immoral liberties with the prince's wife, for which reason the prince had revolted. Judge Sewall wrote in his diary that the Puritan clergy were scandalized by this account in a publication reaching the Boston public.

It was the Massachusetts licensing act that ended Harris's career as an American newspaper publisher, however. How he expected to get around that restriction is not at all clear. Harris eventually returned to England, where he faded out of the scene as the penurious vendor of quack medicines.

Not for another 14 years was there a newspaper in the North American colonies. All of the successful Boston publishers in the next 30 years were careful to notify their publics that they printed "by authority." More important, they had the protection of an important office, for the journalists who followed immediately after Harris were all postmasters.

In Europe there had been a long tradition of affiliation between the postal service and journalism. Many of the early continental newspapers had been published by postmasters. There was good reason for this. Postmasters were especially interested in disseminating information. That was their principal business. They had access to most of the intelligence available to the community. They broke the seals of official pouches and delivered important dispatches. Postmasters then, as today, heard much of the local gossip. They were "in the know." Until 1692 there had been no official postal service in the colonies. In that year the British government authorized an intercolonial mail system—an indication that the respective colonies were beginning to take note of each other.

JOHN CAMPBELL'S *NEWS-LETTER,* 1704

One of the postmasters appointed by the Crown for the new intercolonial service was John Campbell, who took over the Boston post office in 1700. From the very beginning Campbell made use of the postal service to supply information to special correspondents in other colonies. He issued this intelligence in the form of a newsletter—the primitive, handwritten report that had been the common medium of communication in Europe before the invention of printing. Most of the information sent out by Campbell was concerned with commercial and governmental matters. Boston was the most important city in the colonies then, and the postmasters' information was therefore highly pertinent all along the Atlantic seaboard. Meetings, proclamations, complaints, legal notices, actions in court, available cargo space, and the arrivals of important persons provided the grist for Campbell's news mill. There was such a demand for his newsletter that Campbell sought the help of Bartholomew Green, one of the few printers in the area.

On the morning of April 24, 1704, Green's shop on Newbury Street printed the first continuous American newspaper. It was called the *Boston News-Letter,* an appropriate title since it was merely a continuation of the publication Campbell has been producing since 1700. The *News-Letter* was printed on both sides of a sheet just a little larger than the dimensions of Harris's paper—that is, slightly larger than a sheet of typewriter paper.

The news in the first issue was not very startling. The publisher-editor-postmaster had simply clipped the incoming London newspapers, already weeks old, and inserted the items as foreign exchanges. Since he did not have space for all the European dispatches, he put aside excess information for future use. As a result, some of his news was months old before it reached the readers. On the other hand, the local news was fairly timely. It was terse, but surprisingly informative. For example:

> Boston, April 18. Arrived Capt. Sill from Jamaica, about four Weeks Passage, says, they continue there very sickly.
>
> Mr. Nathaniel Oliver, a principal Merchant of this place dyed April 15 & was decently inter'd. April 18, Aetatis 53. . . .
>
> The 20 the R'd Mr. Pemberton Preached an Excellent Sermon on 1 Thes. 4:11. "And do your own business"; Exhorting all Ranks & Degrees of Persons to do their own work, in order to a REFORMATION; which His Excellency has ordered to be printed.
>
> The 21 His Excellency Dissolved the Gen. Assembly.[14]

But it was savorless journalism, after Harris's reports on bloodthirsty savages and lustful kings. Campbell cleared all the copy with the governor, or with his secretary. That made his paper libel-proof, censor-proof, and well-nigh reader-proof. Campbell never had enough subscribers to make his venture profitable. His circulation seldom exceeded 300.

Campbell's choice of stories and writing style reflect the religious roots of New England journalism. Research shows that the doctrine of divine providence shaped a teleological order oriented to current events, with conventional and patterned subject matter.[15] Thus, of a suicide of a poor woman, Campbell wrote that "he hoped the Inserting of such an awful Providence here may not be offensive, but rather a Warning to all others to watch against the Wiles of our Grand Adversary." He obviously regretted having to print the account of a prisoner's whipping, but the culprit had cheated the public by selling tar mixed with dirt. The news, Campbell explained sadly, "is here only Inserted to be a caveat to others, of doing the like, least a worse thing befal them." These were typical of the journalism of this period.

Unimpressive as it was, the *Boston News-Letter* was like the biblical mustard seed. From it stemmed the mighty American Fourth Estate, a force no one could ignore.

COMPETITION: THE *BOSTON GAZETTE,* 1719

Colonial readers had a choice of newspapers for the first time after December 21, 1719, when Campbell fell from political favor. William Brooker won the appointment as Boston's postmaster. He was encouraged by his sponsors to continue publication of a semi-official newspaper. Campbell refused to relinquish the *News-Letter,* however, so Brooker had to start a new publication. Thus, after 15 years of monopoly, the pioneer North American newspaper faced "opposition." The new rival was the *Boston Gazette.*

Competition did not noticeably improve either the semiofficial *Gazette* or the free-enterprise *News-Letter.* The *Gazette* started out as an imitator, and a stodgy one at that. Except for a market page, it offered nothing that Campbell had not given his readers. Brooker had one great advantage, however: as postmaster, he could distribute his publication at lower cost.

Five successive postmasters continued the *Gazette* until 1741, when it was merged with another rival that had appeared in the meantime: the *New England Weekly Journal.* The merger was only noteworthy as the first such transaction in the history of American journalism, since these early newspapers were all rather dull. Campbell, Brooker, and their successors, as minor bureaucrats, were careful not to offend the officials upon whom they were dependent for privileges and subsidies. Every issue of the papers was approved by a government representative before publication, even though formal licensing laws had lapsed before 1700 in England. The line "published by authority" also provided an aura of credibility to the contents at a time when it was difficult for the printer to indicate the sources of his news and verify the reliability of specific items.

THE *NEW ENGLAND COURANT,* 1721

This safe policy was brought to an abrupt end in 1721 with the establishment of the *New England Courant.* This vigorous little sheet was published by James Franklin, elder brother of the more famous Benjamin, but a notable American in his own right. James had been printer of the *Gazette* when Brooker was postmaster. When the publisher lost his appointment and the *Gazette* passed on to the succeeding postmaster, the paper was printed in another shop. Franklin was irked by this turn of events, and when a group of leading citizens opposed to the governing group encouraged him to start another paper, he agreed to the proposal.

The spirit of rebellion was manifest in the *Courant* from the start. Although it lasted only five years, it exerted a great influence upon the American press. It was a fresh breeze in the stale journalistic atmosphere of Boston. The *Courant* was the first North American newspaper to supply readers with what they liked and needed, rather than with information controlled by self-interested officials. Its style was bold and its literary quality high. James Franklin had one of the best libraries in the city. He was also familiar with the best of the London literary publications. Here was a publisher who knew how to interest

THE
New-England Courant.

From MONDAY September 3. to MONDAY September 10. 1722.

Quod eſt in corde ſobrii, eſt in ore ebrii.

To the Author of the New-England Courant.

SIR,

[No XII.

T is no unprofitable tho' unpleaſant Purſuit, diligently to inſpect and conſider the Manners & Converſation of Men, who, inſenſible of the greateſt Enjoyments of humane Life, abandon themſelves to Vice from a falſe Notion of *Pleaſure* and *good Fellowſhip.* A true and natural Repreſentation of any Enormity, is often the beſt Argument againſt it and Means of removing it, when the moſt ſevere Reprehenſions alone, are found ineffectual.

I WOULD in this Letter improve the little Obſervation I have made on the Vice of *Drunkenneſs,* the better to reclaim the *good Fellows* who uſually pay the Devotions of the Evening to *Bacchus.*

I DOUBT not but *moderate Drinking* has been improv'd for the Diffuſion of Knowledge among the ingenious Part of Mankind, who want the Talent of a ready Utterance, in order to diſcover the Conceptions of their Minds in an entertaining and intelligible Manner. 'Tis true, drinking does not *improve* our Faculties, but it enables us to *uſe* them ; and therefore I conclude, that much Study and Experience, and a little Liquor, are of abſolute Neceſſity for ſome Tempers, in order to make them accompliſh'd Orators. *Dic. Ponder* diſcovers an excellent Judgment when he is inſpir'd with a Glaſs or two of *Claret,* but he paſſes for a Fool among thoſe of ſmall Obſervation, who never ſaw him the better for Drink. And here it will not be improper to obſerve, That the moderate Uſe of Liquor, and a well plac'd and well regulated Anger, often produce this ſame Effect ; and ſome who cannot ordinarily talk but in broken Sentences and falſe Grammar, do in the Heat of Paſſion expreſs themſelves with as much Eloquence as Warmth. Hence it is that my own Sex are generally the moſt eloquent, becauſe the moſt paſſionate. " It has been ſaid in the Praiſe of ſome Men, " (ſays an ingenious Author,) that they could talk " whole Hours together upon any thing ; but it " muſt be owned to the Honour of the other Sex, " that there are many among them who can talk " whole Hours together upon Nothing. I have " known a Woman branch out into a long extempo- " re Diſſertation on the Edging of a Petticoat, and " chide her Servant for breaking a China Cup, in all " the Figures of Rhetorick."

BUT after all it muſt be conſider'd, that no Pleaſure can give Satisfaction or prove advantageous to a *reaſonable Mind,* which is not attended with the *Reſtraints of Reaſon.* Enjoyment is not to be found by Exceſs in any ſenſual Gratification ; but on the contrary, the immoderate Cravings of the Voluptuary, are always ſucceeded with Loathing and a pal-led Appetite. What Pleaſure can the Drunkard have in the Reflection, that, while in his Cups, he retain'd only the Shape of a Man, and acted the Part of a Beaſt ; or that from reaſonable Diſcourſe a few Minutes before, he deſcended to Impertinence and Nonſenſe ?

I CANNOT pretend to account for the different Effects of Liquor on Perſons of different Diſpoſitions, who are guilty of Exceſs in the Uſe of it. 'Tis ſtrange to ſee Men of a regular Converſation become rakiſh and profane when intoxicated with Drink, and yet more ſurprizing to obſerve, that ſome who appear to be the moſt profligate Wretches when ſober, become mighty religious in their Cups, and will then, and at no other Time addreſs their Maker, but when they are deſtitute of Reaſon, and actually affronting him. Some ſhrink in the Wetting, and others ſwell to ſuch an unuſual Bulk in their Imaginations, that they can in an Inſtant underſtand all Arts and Sciences, by the liberal Education of a little vivifying *Punch,* or a ſufficient Quantity of other exhilerating Liquor.

AND as the Effects of Liquor are various, ſo are the Characters given to its Devourers. It argues ſome Shame in the Drunkards themſelves, in that they have invented numberleſs Words and Phraſes to cover their Folly, whoſe proper Sgnifications are harmleſs, or have no Signification at all. They are ſeldom known to be *drunk,* tho they are very often *boozey, cogey, tipſey, fox'd, merry, mellow, fuddl'd, groatable, Confoundedly cut, See two Moons, Among the Philiſtines, In a very good Humour, See the Sun,* or, *The Sun has ſhone upon them* ; they *Clip the King's Engliſh,* are *Almoſt froze, Feavouriſh, In their Altitudes, Pretty well enter'd,* &c. In ſhort, every Day produces ſome new Word or Phraſe which might be added to the Vocabulary of the *Tiplers :* But I have choſe to mention theſe few, becauſe if at any Time a Man of Sobriety and Temperance happens to *cut himſelf confoundedly,* or is *almoſt froze,* or *feavouriſh,* or accidentally *ſees the Sun,* &c. he may eſcape the Imputation of being *drunk,* when his Misfortune comes to be related.

I am SIR,
Your Humble Servant,

SILENCE DOGOOD.

FOREIGN AFFAIRS.

Berlin, May 8. Twelve Pruſſian Batallions are ſent to Mecklenburg, but for what Reaſon is not known. 'Tis ſaid, the Emperor, ſuſpecting the Deſigns of the Czar, will ſecure all the Domains of the Duke of Mecklenburg. His Pruſſian Majeſty, to promote the intended Union of the Reformed and Lutherans in his Dominions, has charged the Miniſters of thoſe two Communions, not to make the leaſt mention in the Pulpits of the religious Differences about ſome abſtruſer Points, particularly the Doctrine of Predeſtination, and to forbear all contumelious Expreſſions againſt one another.

Hamburg, May 8. The Imperial Court has order'd the Circles of Lower Saxony, to keep in Rea-

Ben Franklin's "Silence Dogood" essay on drunkenness

readers. He lightened his pages by poking fun at rivals. His personality sketches appealed to local interests.

James Franklin was also the first to use a device that was almost an essential of the newspaper at a much later date. This was the "crusade" type of journalism, involving an editorial campaign planned to produce results by presenting news in dramatic form. A crusading editor is not content with the mere reporting of events but knows how to generate stories of interest to the public. Franklin was an expert in the use of this device.

James Franklin was much more than just a tough and independent newspaper owner. The *Courant* also filled a great literary vacuum. Literature of a high standard for popular consumption was rare in colonial North America in the first quarter of the eighteenth century. Now and then a peddler sold a copy of some such classic as Hakluyt's *Voyages,* but most of the available reading of that day was heavily laced with moral lessons and religious doctrines. James Franklin was a cultured man, for his day and society, and while learning the printing trade in England he had enjoyed the essay papers that were then so popular.

Franklin, and many editors who followed him, offered a starved reading public something new in literary fare. Most of the *Spectator* and *Guardian* essays were reprinted in colonial newspapers. Addison and Steele were introduced to hundreds of Americans through such papers as the *Courant.* Such writers were imitated in the colonies, and some of this local material was very good. The young Benjamin Franklin, apprenticed to his brother James at an early age, secretly authored such essays for publication in his brother's newspaper. Indeed, Ben Franklin's "Silence Dogood" essays rank as about the best of the American imitations, even though he was just 16 when he wrote them.

The literature in the *Courant* was witty, pertinent, and even brilliant at times. But after its appearance the colonial press also offered more solid cultural contributions. Daniel Defoe's great book, *Robinson Crusoe,* was printed serially in many colonial papers as fast as installments could be pirated from abroad. Not every reader could discern the significance of Defoe's work, which expressed in the novel form his criticism of the existing social structure. But those who missed the social message could still enjoy the excellent narrative, and indeed it is still read for this purpose alone. In thus broadcasting the new literature, the American newspaper made another contribution to the culture of a new society.

JAMES FRANKLIN, REBEL

But the most important contribution of James Franklin was his unshackling of the American press from the licenser. All previous publishers had bowed to official pressures to print "by authority" despite the end of actual licensing. Franklin printed his paper not "by authority" but in spite of it. He thus helped establish the tradition of editorial independence.

The restrictive authorities were both spiritual and temporal. Censorship was supervised by government officials, of course, but the influence of the church leaders was nearly as great, if less direct. Puritan thought dominated the region, and the hierarchy was directed by two brilliant and strong-willed clergymen, Increase Mather and his son, Cotton. Many citizens secretly detested their stern discipline.

A man of James Franklin's intellectual independence was certain to be irked by the type of restraint imposed by the Mathers. Franklin began his attack at once. One wishes that he might have selected some other issue to contest with the Mathers, however, because in this case he actually obstructed medical progress.

The issue was a smallpox inoculation. The disease took an enormous toll of life in those days; an epidemic that began in Boston in May 1721 had claimed 844 lives by the following March. Cotton Mather was aware of experiments in which blood from recovered smallpox patients had been injected into the bodies of other persons. He encouraged Boston's doctors to try this, and in June Dr. Zabdiel Boylston inoculated his own young son and two slaves. There was a popular outcry, supported by the *News-Letter.* The *Gazette* published the letters of the proinoculation forces, including the Mather camp.

Thus the issue of inoculation had become political and social as well as medical. Coming into the arena in August 1721 with his *Courant,* for a time James Franklin used the inoculation quarrel as a means of attacking the Mathers. What he did in his first issue was to launch a front-page attack on Boylston and the Puritan ministers who were supporting inoculation. The *Courant* was both witty and vindictive in its crusade-like news and comments. The rebels against Increase and Cotton Mather gathered around Franklin, contributing articles and spurring public attention for the new paper. The insufferable Mathers[16] discovered the tide of public opinion was strong against them. They defended themselves in vain in the *Gazette.* Eventually the tide turned in their favor; inoculation began to prove its worth in both England and Boston. Even Franklin came to report favorable news items about inoculation as the issue waned.[17]

But when the spunky journalist turned around and fired a fusillade at the administration, the authorities believed it was time to swat this gadfly. Franklin accused the government of ineffective defense against pirates in the vicinity. Called before the Council in 1722 on a charge of contempt, Franklin was as outspoken as he had been in the columns of his paper. For such impertinence the editor-publisher was thrown into jail.

BENJAMIN FRANKLIN, APPRENTICE

James showed not the slightest remorse for his rude appraisal of the administration, and jail had no effect upon him in that respect. Once free, he stepped up his criticism of authorities—both religious and political. By the end of the year both factions agreed on one thing, at least: James Franklin was too troublesome to be allowed in the community without restriction. At this point the General Court declared that "James Franklin be strictly forbidden . . . to print or publish the *New-England Courant* or any Pamphlet or paper of the like Nature, Except it be first Supervised, by the Secretary of this Province."[18] This, of course, was a reaffirmation of the old licensing power.

James evaded the order by making his brother, Ben, the official publisher of the paper. No such restriction had been imposed upon the younger Franklin. But in carrying out this evasion, James eventually lost the services of his essential brother. James ostensibly canceled Ben's apprenticeship in order to name the boy publisher. At the same time, he made Ben sign secret articles of reapprenticeship. This was the chance Ben had been waiting for. True, the secret articles were binding, and under the law James could return his brother if Ben tried to run away. But if James did so, he would thereby acknowledge that he had flouted the Court's order. Young Ben was clever enough to size up the situation. The next time we meet him is as a printer in his own right in Philadelphia.

The *Courant* declined in popularity and influence after that. Five and a half years after he had established the paper, James abandoned it. Later he accepted the position of government printer for Rhode Island. At Newport in 1732 he founded the *Rhode Island Gazette,* first newspaper in that colony. It survived only a short time, and James never did achieve his former eminence in journalism.[19] If he did nothing else but establish the principle in North America of printing "without authority," James Franklin would deserve a high place in America's journalistic hall of fame. He had accomplished much more, however. He had shown that when a newspaper is aggressive and readable in serving the public cause, it will elicit support sufficient to protect it from powerful foes.

PHILADELPHIA'S JOURNALISM BEGINS

The second largest city in the English colonies at this time was Philadelphia. Two years after the founding of that city in 1683, William Bradford set up the first printing press in the colony. At first he printed only pamphlets and religious tracts for Quaker patrons, but because he had the only press in the region, he was also useful to the administration. Soon he was devoting much of his time to the printing of government documents. Unfortunately, he quarreled with his Quaker superiors, and in 1693 he moved his printing shop to New York, where many years later, in 1725, he established the first newspaper in that city.

William Bradford's son, Andrew, published the first newspaper in Philadelphia. It was also the first colonial newspaper outside Boston. His *American Weekly Mercury* first appeared on December 22, 1719, the day after Brooker had published the first issue of the *Gazette,* Boston's first rival to the *News-Letter.* The *Mercury* was another postmaster paper, but it was a little more outspoken than the usual safe, semiofficial publications of that type that were to appear in the next two decades. On occasion the *Mercury* criticized the administration. It defended James Franklin when the Boston journalist was jailed by angry authorities. It printed the controversial "Cato Letters," which had first appeared in London as arguments for civil and religious liberties. But Bradford was overshadowed in Philadelphia by the greatest printer-journalist of the period.

BENJAMIN FRANKLIN'S *PENNSYLVANIA GAZETTE*

He was Benjamin Franklin, who arrived almost penniless in the City of Brotherly Love after running away from his apprenticeship to his brother James. Within five years he was a successful and prosperous citizen of the town. Ben Franklin's whole career was one of success, color, and usefulness. There has never been another American quite like him. He was "the complete man," like Leonardo, Michelangelo, or Roger Bacon. First of all a printer and journalist, he was also an inventor, scientist, politician, diplomat, pioneer sociologist, business leader, educator, and world citizen.

Franklin took over the management of the *Pennsylvania Gazette* in October 1729 from its founder, Samuel Keimer. Keimer had employed Franklin when he first arrived in Philadelphia, but Ben outgrew that role after traveling to London to learn printing and engraving from England's best. With a friend, Hugh Meredith, he opened his own shop in the spring of 1728 and planned a paper to rival Andrew Bradford's *Mercury.* Keimer, learning of Franklin's project, issued the *Pennsylvania Gazette* in December 1728. It attracted some readership until a new feature began to appear in the rival *Mercury*—a series of clever essays in the Addison and Steele style that soon brought delighted patrons to Bradford's shop for copies of the *Mercury.* The series came to be known as the "Busy-Body Papers." The anonymous author was actually Benjamin Franklin, and his most frequent target of

THE
Pennſylvania GAZETTE.

Containing the freſheſt Advices Foreign and Domeſtick.

From July 24. to July 31. 1735.

TO BE SOLD,
At the House of the Widow Richardſon in Front-Street, near the North-Eaſt Corner of Market-Street.

A LIKELY Negroe Wench about 16 or 18 Years old. ſingle and double refin'd Loaf-Sugar, Barbadoes white and muſcovado Sugar. Alſo Choice Barbadoes Limes in Barrels at reaſonable Rates.

Juſt Imported from London and Briſtol,
And to be SOLD by JOHN INGLIS, at his Store below the Draw-Bridge, in Front-Street, Philadelphia :

B ROAD-Cloths, Kerſeys and Plains, Ruggs, Blankets, Oznabrigs, Checks, London Shalloons, Tammies, Calimancoes, ſeven eighths and yard wide Garlix, Men and Womens worſted Stockings, Men and Womens Shammy Gloves, Pinns, Baladine Silk, ſilk Laces, faſhionable Fans, Paduaſoy, Ribbons, ſilk Ferrits, Gartering, Caddis, Buttons and Mohair, cotton Romals, linnen Handkerchiefs, Chiloes, Mens worſted Caps, Bunts, fine Bed-Ticks made up in Suits, India Taffities, Damasks and Perſians, ſix quarter Muſlins, Suits of ſuper fine Broad-Cloth, with Lining and Trimmings, London double refin'd Sugar, Bird, Pidgeon, Duck, Gooſe and Swan Shot, Bar Lead, 8, 10 and 20 penny Nails, Window Glaſs, Patterns of Chintz for Beds, ſarſnet Handkerchiefs, Briſtol quart Bottles ; and ſundry other Goods, for ready Money, or the uſual Credit.

W Hereas George Carter, a thick ſhort Man, with light buſhy Hair, about 40 Years old, born in White Pariſh, ſix Miles from New-Sarum, in Wiltſhire, by Trade a Baker, went on board a Ship at Briſtol, bound to Penſilvania, about the Year 1722 : Theſe are to deſire the ſaid George Carter (if living) to return to his native Country, or to give Notice where he lives to John Atkinſon, at the White Lyon Tavern, on Cornhil, London, or to Iſrael Pemberton, jun. of Philadelphia, who can inform him of ſomething conſiderable to his Advantage : If he be deceas'd, Information is deſir'd when and where he died. And if any of his Children be living they may have the ſame Advantage, by applying as aforeſaid.

TO BE SOLD,

B Y James Oſwald in Front-Street, at the Houſe of Mr. Joſeph Turner, and by William Wallace, at the Upper-End of Second-Street, Sugar Bakers, Choice double refin'd LOAF-SUGAR at Eighteen-pence the Pound, ſingle refin'd, Sugar Candy, Mollaſſes, &c. at reaſonable Prices.

R U N away from the Subſcriber, the 4th Day of November laſt, a Servant Woman, aged about 28 Years, fair Hair'd, wants ſome of her Teeth before, a little deafiſh, named Suſannah Wells, born near Biddeford, in England : She had on when ſhe went away, a Callico Gown, with red Flowers, blue Stockings, with Clocks, new Shoes, a quilted Petticoat, Plat Hat. Whoever ſecures ſaid Servant, and delivers her to ſaid Subſcriber at Wilmington, or to Robert Dixon in Philadelphia, ſhall have Twenty-five Shillings Reward, and reaſonable Charges paid by Robert Dixon, or   Thomas Downing.
Philad. December 4. 1740.
N. B. It's believed the ſaid Servant was carried from New-Caſtle in the Ship commanded by Capt. Lawrence Dent, now lying at Philadelphia.

Juſt Publiſhed.

P OOR Richard's ALMANACKS, for the Year 1741.   Alſo, Jerman's Almanacks, and Pocket and Sheet Almanacks.   Printed and Sold by B. Franklin.

A LL Perſons are hereby deſired to take Notice, That the Bills of Credit of the Province of Pennſylvania, bearing Date any time before the Year 1739, are by an Act of Aſſembly of the ſaid Province, made in the Year aforeſaid, declared to be null and void, ſince the tenth Day of the Month called Auguſt laſt paſt : And that the ſame ſhould be no longer the current Bills of the ſaid Province.   Therefore all Perſons who are poſſeſſed of any of the ſaid Bills, are deſired forthwith to bring them in to the General Loan-Office of the ſaid Province at Philadelphia, where Attendance will be given to Exchange them for New-Bills.   J. KINSEY.

R U N away from the Subſcriber the 3d Inſt. a Servant Man named Thomas Wenn, by trade a Barber, appears by his looks to be at leaſt 40 Years old, but pretends he is not 30, middle Stature, well ſet, fore ey'd, and near ſighted : Had on when he went away, a ſmall Hat but good, a ſmall black Wig, but may have taken another of ſome other colour, a kerſey Coat almoſt new of a mixt colour rediſh and white, lin'd through with a red half thick or ſerge, large flat metal Buttons, old white dimity Jacket, a pair of ſtout buck ſkin Breeches almoſt new with braſs Buttons, a pair of new thick mill'd Stockings of a bluiſh colour, Shoes about half worn.   Whoever ſecures the ſaid Servant ſo that he may be had again, ſhall have if twenty Miles off this City Twenty Shillings, if thirty, thirty Shilings, and if forty, forty Shillings Reward, paid by Philad. January 5. 1740.   William Croſthwaite.

TO BE SOLD
By ELIZABETH COMBS, at her Houſe over the Draw-Bridge,

A LL kinds of white and check Linnens, Dimities, Callimancoes, Friſes, Hankerchiefs, Cotton Gowns, ſortable Shot, Sail Cloth, and ſeveral other Goods, for ready Money or ſhort Credit.

For SOUTH-CAROLINA directly,
The Ship Loyal-Judith, LOVELL PAYNTER, Commander,

W ILL Sail when the Weather permits. For Freight or Paſſage agree with the ſaid Maſter on board the ſaid Ship, now lying at Mr. Samuel Auſtin's Wharff ; or with Benjamin Shoemaker, Merchant, in High-Street Philadelphia.

Juſt Imported,

A Parcel of likely Negro Men, Women, and Children : As alſo, choice London double and ſingle refin'd, clay'd and Muſcovado SUGARS, and GINGER ; to be ſold by Joſeph Marks, at the Corner of Walnut and Second-Street, Philadelphia.

Juſt Imported,
And to be Sold very reaſonably by Peter Turner, at his Store over againſt the Poſt-Office in Market-Street, Philadelphia ;

A Large Sortment of Kerſeys, napt and fine Drab Kerſeys, Broad-Cloths, London Shalloons, Embo'd Flannens, Womens Shoes and Cloggs, Hat Lineings, fine Gulic and Kingham Holland, Seven-eights Garlix, Callicoes, Writing Paper, crimſon, blue and green haratoens for Beds, fine half Ell crimſon, blue and green worſted Damasks, 3, 4, 8 penny Nails, London Steel, Scythe, Wool-Cards, Shot and Lead, fine and coarſe Bolting Cloths, Hungary Water, fine Green Tea, fine lackered Sconces, ell wide Perſians, black and coloured Taffitys, with ſundry other Goods.

PHILADELPHIA: Printed by B. FRANKLIN, POST-MASTER, the NEW PRINTING-OFFICE, near the Market. Price 10 s. a Year.

The *Pennsylvania Gazette* advertises sales of Negroes and *Poor Richard's Almanack*.

satire was none other than Samuel Keimer. With his sales down to fewer than 100 copies, Keimer gave up the struggle. On October 2, 1729, Ben Franklin took over as publisher.

Franklin had little difficulty winning public acceptance, and with this acceptance came a volume of profitable advertising. In addition to being a readable paper, his was a bold one. Franklin's experience in Boston, plus his innate common sense, kept him from getting into serious trouble with the authorities. But he took a stand on issues, just the same. People have many opinions, he explained to his readers, and printers publish these opinions as part of their business. "They are educated in the belief," he added, "that when men differ in opinion, both sides ought equally to have the advantage of being heard by the public; and that when truth and error have fair play, the former is always an overmatch for the latter [shades of Milton and his *Areopagitica*]. . . . If all printers were determined not to print anything till they were sure it would offend nobody," said he, "there would be very little printed."[20]

With Keimer out of the way, Andrew Bradford remained Franklin's only serious rival. He had what amounted to a government subsidy through his contract for official printing. Franklin met that challenge by writing up an important legislative address, which he then sent to every member of the Pennsylvania Assembly at his own expense. The same report appeared in the *Mercury,* but the *Gazette* story was so much better that Franklin made a great impression on the lawmakers. He continued this reporting, and within a year had won away the government printing contract.

Franklin now bought out his partner, Meredith, with money loaned to him by influential businesspeople he had cultivated in his short career in Philadelphia. Thus, at the age of 24, he was the sole proprietor of the best newspaper in the American colonies. It soon had the largest circulation, most pages, highest advertising revenue, and most literate columns of any paper in the area.

Franklin excelled as a printer, engraver, and type founder. He is regarded as a patron saint not only of printers but also of the advertising world, in recognition of his own advertising copywriting and business skill. Franklin's shop made 60 percent of its money on the *Gazette* and 40 percent on other printing, including the fabulously successful *Poor Richard's Almanack,* begun in 1732. Franklin also tried to issue a magazine in 1741, as did his rival Bradford, but both failed. It was Franklin, too, who helped establish the first foreign-language paper at Germantown, near Philadelphia. When he retired from the active management of the *Gazette* at 42, he busied himself helping young men set up newspapers in other colonies. He became deputy postmaster general for the colonies and employed postriders to carry newspapers between colonies. His role as diplomat and statesman lay ahead.

But Franklin's greatest contribution to American journalism was that he made it respectable. Franklin showed that a good journalist and businessperson could make money in the publishing field. That was, and is, an effective way of making any business respectable. When intelligent and industrious youths saw the possibilities of journalism, as developed by the grand old man of the press, they began to turn more often to this calling. Getting this improved type of personnel into the craft was the best possible tonic for American journalism.

PAPERS IN OTHER COLONIES

After 1725, newspapers sprouted all over the colonies. In Boston, Samuel Kneeland established the *New England Weekly Journal* on March 20, 1727. It is worth a mention because it was the first newspaper to have correspondents in nearby communities whose duty it was to send in pertinent information about their neighborhoods, a practice still followed by newspaper publishers. Another important Boston paper was the *Weekly Rehearsal,* founded in 1731 by Jeremy Gridley, a lawyer. A year later Gridley turned over the publication to Thomas Fleet, James Franklin's old printer. A few years later Fleet changed the name of the paper to the *Evening Post.* Under Fleet, the *Evening Post* became the best and most popular paper in Boston. It lasted until Revolutionary War times. Gridley went on to become editor of Boston's *American Magazine* (1743 to 1746).

Maryland was the fourth colony to have a newspaper.[21] William Parks, a former English editor, set up the *Maryland Gazette* at Annapolis in 1727. His paper reflected good taste, literary skill, and pride in the craft he had learned so well under the best English masters. Later, in 1736, Parks founded the *Virginia Gazette,* the first newspaper in Virginia, at Williamsburg. That little shop has been restored and is now one of the interesting exhibits at the old colonial capital. Because it tells us what the printing business must have been like in colonial days, it might be worth a moment to look into this building.

THE ENGLISH COMMON PRESS

The printing office in Williamsburg is on the ground floor of a small brick building. In the center stands the English Common Press, which was shipped over in pieces from London, for no presses were to be made in America until Isaac Doolittle of Connecticut began turning them out in 1769. Close at hand are the accessories: the imposing stones, upon which the type is gathered; the "horse" and "bank" tables, from which the paper is fed to the press; the wetting trough, for the preparation of the paper; an ink grinding stand; and the matrix punches, made in England by William Caslon himself, for cutting the beautiful type that bears his name. The press stands seven feet high and weighs about 1500 pounds. It is firmly braced to the floor and ceiling by heavy oak beams to ensure rigidity when heavy pressure is applied to the type forms.

From this clumsy apparatus colonial printers such as the Bradfords, Greens, Sowers, Parks, and Franklins produced letterpress work of the highest quality.[22] There was much

A colonial wooden hand press

bad printing during this period, too, but that was often the fault of poor work quality and worn equipment. There is abundant proof that the colonial printing press was capable of turning out superb work, under the supervision of a skilled printer. The printer had to know his business, however. A single impression, or "token," required 13 distinct operations. Two expert craftspeople and an apprentice might turn out about 200 tokens an hour.

Let us watch the colonial printer working. The bed of the press is rolled out by means of a wheel and pulley arrangement. The type, all set by hand, is locked tight in the form and is placed on the bed. A young apprentice, or "devil," applies the homemade ink to the type, using a doeskin dauber on a stick. The paper is then moistened in a trough so that it will take a better impression. It is placed carefully over the type. The bed is rolled back under the press. The "platen," or upper pressure plate, is then pressed against the type by means of a screw or lever device. The platen is released; the bed is wheeled out; and the sheet is hung on a wire to dry before it is ready for its second "run" for the reverse side.

The usual colonial newspaper consisted of four pages, often about 10 by 15 inches in dimension. The paper was rough foolscap. There were no headlines, as we know them, until after 1750, and even then they were uncommon. The only illustrations were the colophons, or printers' trademarks, on the title page, and an occasional woodcut to embellish an advertisement. The Greens and Sowers made their own paper, but most paper was imported from England. It was made of rags and was of surprising durability, despite its mottled appearance. With this primitive equipment printer-journalists not only produced fine graphic art, but they also had at hand implements that were soon to make the press truly a Fourth Estate.

THE RISE OF THE FOURTH ESTATE

In the second quarter of the eighteenth century the newspaper found its place. True, the infant newspaper mortality rate was high, usually as a result of financial malnutrition. For example, more than half of the 2120 newspapers established between 1690 and 1820 expired before they were two years old.[23] Only 34 lasted a generation. Nevertheless, by 1750 most literate Americans had access to some journal of information. In that year there were 14 weekly newspapers in the six most populous colonies, and soon afterward, there was a rapid increase in such publications, as we shall see in the next chapter.

The product was better, too. Semiweekly and even triweekly newspapers, which had first appeared even earlier, were available after the mid-eighteenth century. Circulation was rising. A few publishers had won fame and fortune in the business. Rapid increase in populations, better transportation and communication facilities, and rising political tensions partly explain the growth of the press. Many colonists had become prosperous and were looking for ways of investing capital. Ports such as New York began to achieve world importance. About a third of the ships in the British merchant fleet were launched by New England shipwrights. There were 360 whalers operating from American ports. There were skillful artisans in the towns. The famous "Pennsylvania Rifle," one of the greatest weapons of the time, was a product of such craftspeople. Despite the restrictions of the home country, manufacture of finished articles continued to furnish employment for many hands. In one year alone during this period New Englanders shipped out 13,000 pairs of shoes.[24]

The press was useful to the ambitious trader and merchant. Advertising was the cheapest way to move goods offered for sale by the rising commercial class. Business intercourse between the colonies increased, and accordingly there was need for information only American journalists could provide quickly and cheaply.

Better roads led to better communications. Early editor-postmasters had a double reason for improving roads. Benjamin Franklin, who reversed the process by being appointed postmaster *after* taking up journalism, was named as deputy postmaster of all the colonies, along with William Hunter of Virginia, another printer-journalist. When Franklin took office in 1753, it required six weeks to bring the posts from Boston to Philadelphia by land, and there was a mail pickup only fortnightly. Franklin, who took over most of the postal responsibility because of Hunter's ill health, cut the travel time in half and established weekly service.

There was also improvement in education, always a factor in developing publics favorable to the newspaper. Many parents could now afford to send their children to school, and seminaries and academies were available in the urban centers. Colleges in many colonies produced not only teachers and ministers, effective foes of illiteracy, but also writers and political leaders.

The great technical advances in printing were far in the future, but better type was available during this period. About 1720 William Caslon began modifying Nicolas Jenson's fifteenth-century type into a more readable form. Caslon type was adopted by American printers soon after, and it is still popular. The best standard press was the invention of Willem Janszon Blaeu, a Dutch craftsman of the seventeenth century. Not until around 1800, when Adam Ramage and the Earl of Stanhope came out with the iron press, was there any great improvement in this essential equipment.

THE FIRST ADVERTISING MESSAGES

The development of commerce led to progress in the advertising field. Advertising and printing had been closely associated almost from the beginning. William Caxton, who set up the first press in England, issued a broadside advertising his service (religious) book, *The Pyes of Salisbury Use,* in 1480. Number 62 of the *London Gazette,* the first complete newspaper in the English language, included an announcement of a special advertising supplement in June 1666. An interesting use of advertising is shown in Number 94 of the same paper. After the great fire of London in the fall of 1666, the paper opened its columns to those seeking word of missing loved ones. There were also advertisements concerning salvaged furniture, addresses of scattered families, and houses offering shelter to the homeless.

Presbrey calls John Houghton the father of modern advertising.[25] Houghton was an apothecary; merchant of coffee, tea, and chocolate; book critic; Fellow of the Royal Society; and publisher. In 1692 he established a newspaper for commercial readers. This prototype of the *Wall Street Journal* was the first newspaper to emphasize the role of advertising. Houghton had an appreciation of advertising ethics in an age when the margin between quackery and professional knowledge was narrower than it is today. He was willing to advertise almost any product, but he would not give his seventeenth-century "seal of approval" to statements he believed to be dangerously dishonest. That advertising was a topic for debate and criticism 200 years ago, as it is today, is implied by a comment of the famous pundit, Dr. Samuel Johnson, in the *Idler* of January 20, 1758:

> Advertisements are now so numerous that they are very negligently perused, and it is therefore become necessary to gain attention by magnificence of promises and by eloquences sometimes sublime and sometimes pathetick. Promise—large promise—is the soul of advertising. . . . The trade of advertising is now so near perfection that it is not easy to propose any improvement.[26]

The advertisers could teach the journalists some important lessons on the subject of reader response. For example, the advertisers quickly discovered that their messages must be simply stated to reach the most people. It took the news writers a long time to learn this lesson. Advertisers also understood the value of attractive presentation. They led the way in experimentation with type, illustrations, makeup, and legibility. The press owes much to these practical psychologists and graphics artists.

RISING POLITICAL TENSION

The greatest stimulus to the development of the American press of this period was the rising political tension that was to culminate in the War of Independence. The press had an essential role in the drama about to unfold. The newspaper thrives on controversy, provided it is able to take part in the discussions with any degree of freedom. The great development of the press during the first half of the eighteenth century was its victory over the forces that would have restricted that liberty. This victory made the press the most powerful weapon of the American revolutionaries. Almost forgotten today are the battles and sacrifices by which this concept won general acceptance.

In 1692, before the first successful newspaper had been born in America, a Philadelphia printer boldly stated one of the cardinal principles of a free press. He was William Bradford, founder of a remarkable printing dynasty. Bradford had to placate both a jealous government and a sensitive Quaker hierarchy when he set up his little shop. Every now and then he was threatened by one or the other because of ideas expressed in pamphlets he turned out at regular intervals. Arrested in 1692 for a minor infraction, Bradford declared he was tired of such interference and notified the authorities he was taking his press to a more congenial community. Officials were alarmed by this threat, for they depended upon Bradford for the dissemination of governmental, religious, and commercial information. The General Assembly therefore quashed the charge and induced Bradford to remain by granting him a yearly retainer of 40 pounds and all the printing he could handle by himself.

Because of the disposition of this case, Bradford's defense was not widely known, but it is worth mentioning here because it brought up an issue that was hotly debated a generation later. The printer had insisted that the jury in such cases was responsible for judging both the *law* and the *fact.* Courts at the time had held that when seditious libel (criticism of government) was charged, it was the duty of the jury only to establish the authorship of the statement. This was a point of *fact.* It was up to the judges to determine whether the statement was punishable. This was a point of *law.* Bradford objected to this. Some 40 years later, the issue that Bradford had successfully pressed in 1692 was to become a principal point in the trial of John Peter Zenger.

THE ZENGER CASE: BACKGROUND

The most celebrated case involving freedom of the press was the Zenger case of 1734–35. It has been much overrated for its effect on legal reform, and it settled nothing because of the dubious circumstances under which it was conducted. Its inspirational impact, however, was tremendous.

At this point we meet again William Bradford, late of Philadelphia. The senior Bradford had moved to New York when he was offered the position of government printer there. As a subsidized businessperson, Bradford printed nothing that would antagonize his patrons. On November 8, 1725, he printed the first newspaper in the colony: the *New York Gazette.* Of course it favored the administration on all issues. Like many an editor who followed, Bradford rebelled when persecuted, as in Philadelphia, but conformed when offered special privileges and inducements by the same group he might have fought under different circumstances.

By 1733, New York was experiencing a mild revolution. A group of wealthy merchants and landowners was insisting upon a greater share of control in the colony's affairs, but it had no way of communicating its ideas. Bradford had the only newspaper, and he was firmly committed to the royal faction. However, Bradford's former apprentice and partner had opened his own print shop. He was John Peter Zenger, an immigrant from the German Palatinate who had been apprenticed at the age of 13. In the fall of 1733, a delegation of the commercial faction asked Zenger if he would be willing to edit a paper that would be a medium for expressing their news and views.

The situation that prompted this request was complex. The colonial governor had died in 1731, and it was 13 months before his replacement, Sir William Cosby, arrived from London. Rip Van Dam, member of the governor's council for 30 years and a colonial Dutch leader, served as acting governor. Cosby demanded half the fees Van Dam had collected for his services; Van Dam refused. Money cases were to be heard in regular courts, but Cosby moved his case to a court of chancery that he controlled. In the ensuing struggle, Chief Justice Lewis Morris sided with Van Dam and was removed by the governor. Van Dam and Morris now sought to have Cosby recalled by London. The antiadministration forces had other grievances close to their pocketbooks: Cosby was accused of demanding one-third of the price of all public lands sold under his jurisdiction; there was suspected illegal acquisition of land around what is now Utica; and Cosby was seeking to juggle the council membership so that it would approve his new chief justice, young James Delancey.[27]

The leaders of the antiadministration forces were articulate and able citizens. They included men like Van Dam; Justice Morris; James Alexander, a member of the council and also surveyor general for the colonies of New York and New Jersey; and William Smith, noted for his *History of the Colony of New York from Its Founding to 1762* and a well-known public figure at the time of the trial. They, and other important citizens, were interested in having Zenger start a newspaper that would express their views.

The first issue of Zenger's *New York Weekly Journal* appeared on November 5, 1733. From the very first day, the *Journal* clashed with the administration. Bradford at the *Gazette* was no match for Zenger and the brains behind his venture. The main voice was that of lawyer Alexander, who with his friends had successfully put up Lewis Morris for an Assembly seat in a by-election. The first *Journal* issue reported Morris's election despite what was called the harassment of voters over their qualifications. On December 3, a story appeared in Zenger's paper attacking Governor Cosby for permitting French warships to spy on lower bay defenses. In the same issue, an irate New Jersey settler (who wrote very much like Alexander) denounced the colonial bureaucracy for incompetence, referring to the Van Dam–Morris controversy.

The public enjoyed this show, and Zenger had to run off extra copies to satisfy customers. The governor was not so enthusiastic about such journalistic enterprise. Charging Zenger with "Scandalous, Virulent and Seditious Reflections upon the Government," Cosby ordered his hand-picked chief justice, Delancey, to obtain an indictment against the brash editor. But the grand jury refused to return a true bill. The Assembly likewise balked at filing any charges. Finally, a selected group of the governor's council agreed to start an action against Zenger. On a Sunday afternoon, November 17, 1734, Zenger was arrested on a charge of "raising sedition."

ZENGER'S TRIAL, 1735

The trial did not begin until August 4, 1735. Richard Bradley, Cosby's attorney general, filed an "information" that held Zenger in jail. The *Journal* continued to appear, with Zenger's wife, Anna, running the shop and Alexander filling the editor's role. When Alexander and Smith disputed the validity of the prosecution, they were disbarred. John Chambers, appointed to the case, asked for a postponement until August. The Zenger defense then prevailed on a frail, 60-year-old Philadelphia lawyer, famed for his courtroom presence, to risk traveling to New York for the trial. He was Andrew Hamilton. With him, the stage was set for a drama.

Chambers made a plea to Justice Delancey, then Hamilton arose, his white hair falling to his shoulders. His first words were a bombshell: "I cannot think it proper to deny the Publication of a Complaint which I think is the right of every free born Subject to make," he declared, "and therefore I'll save Mr. Attorney the trouble of examining his Witness to that point; and I do confess (for my Client) that he both printed and published the two Papers set forth in the Information, I do hope in so doing he has committed no Crime."

Bradley, delighted at this apparent easy victory, said that since publication of the offending articles had been admitted by the defense, there was nothing more for the jury to do but bring in a verdict of guilty. To this Hamilton replied calmly but firmly: "Not so, neither, Mr. Attorney. There are two Sides to that Bargain. I hope it is not our bare printing or publishing a Paper that will make it a Libel. You will have something more to do before you make my client a libeller. For the words themselves must be libelous—that is, *False, Malicious, and Seditious*—or else we are not guilty."

Bradley approached the bench and renewed his arguments. One by one Hamilton demolished them. He went back to the Magna Carta and to the abolishing of the Star Chamber to prove that the concept he was upholding—freedom to express justifiable truth—had long been accepted in the older courts and that colonial New York was behind the times. His arguments were worded in decisive language, but his manner was so courtly, and his voice so mild, that the fascinated crowd listened as though hypnotized. When the spectators began to cheer during a lull, however, the prosecution objected to Hamilton's statements, and when Hamilton insisted that "the *Falsehood* makes the *Scandal,* and both the *Libel,*" and then offered to "prove these very Papers that are called Libel to be *True,*" Justice Delancey remonstrated.

"You cannot be admitted, Mr. Hamilton," said the judge sternly, "to give the Truth of a Libel in evidence. . . . The Court is of the Opinion you ought not to be permitted to prove the Facts in the Papers," and he cited a long list of supporting authorities.

"These are Star Chamber Cases," answered Hamilton patiently, "and I was in hopes that Practice had been dead with that Court."

Angered by this veiled criticism of his legal knowledge, the youthful Delancey cried out angrily: "The Court have delivered their Opinion, and we expect you will use us with good Manners. You are not permitted to argue against this Court."

ANDREW HAMILTON'S GREAT PLEA

Hamilton paused a moment. He looked at the jury, then at the audience, and then at Zenger, like a great actor sensing the mood of his public. Then he turned to the judge and bowed courteously.

"I thank you," he replied without a trace of rancor. Then, turning his back upon the bench, he acknowledged the jury with a courtly flourish. He spoke to the jurors directly, in a voice loud enough to carry to all parts of the room: "Then it is to you, Gentlemen, we must now appeal for Witnesses to the Truth of the Facts we have offered, and are denied the Liberty to prove."

Hamilton was talking as though Delancey were not even in the room. He exhorted the jury to act like free people and to follow their own consciences, without fear of official reprisals, as guaranteed under the English system of law. His emphasis upon truth was in keeping with their strong religious roots. He ended:

> . . . old and weak as I am, I should think it my Duty if required, to go to the utmost Part of the Land, where my Service could be of any Use in assisting to quench the Flame of Prosecutions upon Informations, set on Foot by the Government, to deprive a People of the Right of Remonstrating (and complaining too), of the arbitrary Attempts of Men in Power. *Men who injure and oppress the People under their Administration provoke them to cry out and complain; and then make that very Complaint the Foundation for new Oppressions and Prosecutions.*
>
> . . . But to conclude; the Question before the Court and you Gentlemen of the Jury, is not of small nor private Concern. It is not the Cause of the poor Printer, nor of *New York* alone, which you are now trying; No! It may in its Consequence affect every Freeman that lives under a British Government on the main of *America.* It is the best Cause. It is the Cause of Liberty; and I make no Doubt but your upright Conduct, this Day, will not only entitle you to the Love and Esteem of your Fellow-Citizens; but every Man who prefers Freedom to a Life of slavery will bless and honour You, as Men who have baffled the Attempt of Tyranny; and by an impartial and uncorrupt Verdict, have laid a Noble Foundation for securing to ourselves, our Posterity and our Neighbors, That, to which Nature and the Laws of our Country have given us a Right—the Liberty—both of exposing and opposing arbitrary Power (in these Parts of the World, at least) by speaking and writing—Truth.

On that note, Hamilton won his case. The jury returned a verdict of "not guilty," and Zenger was freed. He has now become a hero of American journalism. Less known, but equally heroic, was Andrew Hamilton, who argued the cause of liberty so ably.

THE ZENGER TRIAL ANALYZED

But there are some negative aspects of the Zenger case. The verdict had no effect on libel law for more than half a century. Pennsylvania was the first state to recognize the principles of truth as a defense and the right of the jury to decide both the law and the fact, by including them in its 1790 constitution. New York accepted them in 1805. It was 1792 in England before Fox's Libel Act gave the jury power of decision, and it was 1843 before Lord Campbell's Act recognized truth as a defense.

It is very possible that expediency, rather than principle, guided the authorities after trial. They admitted no new legal precedent in the Zenger case. It is quite probable that Zenger would have been rearrested for his very next offense, except for circumstances. Governor Cosby was cautious for a time after the trial ended, because Justice Morris was in England arguing for Cosby's dismissal, and the governor had no wish to achieve any further notoriety for himself. Then he fell desperately ill during the winter of 1735–36 and died the following March. Had he lived, he might not have accepted defeat so easily.

Again, all the reports of the trial are one-sided. The only complete account of the trial is in Zenger's own newspaper. The Crown never did issue a report giving its side of the verdict. Since the accused had good reason to paint the picture in black and white,

THE
New-York Weekly JOURNAL.

Containing the freſheſt Advices, Foreign, and Domeſtick.

MUNDAT Auguſt 18th, 1735.

To my Subſcribers and Benefactors.

Gentlemen ;

I Think my ſelf in Duty bound to to make publick Acknowledgment for the many Favours received at your Hands, which I do in this Manner return you my hearty Thanks for. I very ſoon intend to print my Tryal at Length, that the World may ſee how unjuſt my Sufferings have been, ſo will only at this Time give this ſhort Account of it.

On *Munday* the 4th Inſtant my Tryal for Printing Parts of my Journal *No.* 13. and 23. came on, in the Supreme Court of this Province, before the moſt numerous Auditory of People, I may with Juſtice ſay, that ever were ſeen in that Place at once ; my Jury ſworn were,

1 *Harmanus Rutgers,*
2 *Stanley Holms,*
3 *Edward Man,*
4 *John Bell,*
5 *Samuel Weaver,*
6 *Andrew Marſchalk,*
7 *Egbert Van Borſen,*
8 *Thomas Hunt,*
9 *Benjamin Hildrith,*
10 *Abraham Kiteltaſs,*
11 *John Goelet,*
12 *Hercules Wendover,*

John Chambers, Eſq; had been appointed the Term before by the Court as my Council, in the Place of *James Alexander* and *William Smith,* who were then ſilenced on my Account, and to Mr. *Chambers*'s Aſſiſtance came *Andrew Hamilton,* Eſq; of *Philadelphia* Barreſter at Law ; when Mr Attorney offered the Information and the Proofs, Mr. *Hamilton* told him, he would acknowledge my Printing and Publiſhing the Papers in the Information, and ſave him the Trouble of that Proof, and offered to prove the Facts of thoſe Papers true, and had Witneſſes ready to prove every Fact ; he long inſiſted on the Liberty of Making Proof thereof, but was over-ruled therein. Mr. Attorney offered no Proofs of my Papers being *falſe, malicious* and *ſeditious,* as they were charged to be, but inſiſted that they were Lybels tho' true. There were many Arguments and Authorities on this point, and the Court were of Opinion with Mr. Attorney on that Head : But the Jury having taken the Information out with them, they returned in about Ten Minutes, and found me *Not Guilty* ; upon which there were immediately three Hurra's of many Hundreds of People in the preſence of the Court, before the Verdict was returned. The next Morning my Diſcharge was moved for and granted, and ſufficient was ſub-

(Library of Congress)

Zenger announces his vindication and lists the jury.

the Crown arguments and principles have been largely ignored. O'Callaghan's *Documents Relative to the Colonial History of New York* (Albany, 1849, V) include statements of Governor Cosby to the Lords of Trade, and they are the nearest thing to a presentation of the other side of the argument.[28]

Justice Delancey, who has always been portrayed as an arrogant judge, showed great restraint in refusing to set aside the verdict and in not overruling Hamilton. He might even have had the old lawyer arrested for contempt of the bench. The British government in this case, as in many others, including the Stamp Act of 1765, did not use its powers to curb opinion, but backed down in the face of overwhelming public dissatisfaction.

This is an important point. The courts as much as the press guard the freedom so jealously maintained by a democratic people. To flout the law for the sake of expediency in a press case is a dangerous precedent. When defendants are acquitted because of political feelings, rather than because of a calm appraisal of the known law, that is a threat to a system that is every bit as important to our freedom as the liberty of the press.

Justice Delancey appears somewhat ridiculous today in his opinion that truth could not be offered as a defense in this type of libel action. The fact is, he had considerable precedent to support him, because the principle recognized by the courts of that day was "the greater the truth, the greater the libel." The logic behind this doctrine was this: Public accusations, or criticisms of those in authority, might upset the entire community and cause a serious breach of the public peace. In Zenger's case, popular opinion was behind him, but this did not sway colonial writers on the subject of seditious libel. Almost all of them agreed that government could be libeled and that to do so was properly to be considered a crime. However, research by Professor Jeffery Smith shows that these viewpoints ran counter to the libertarian press theories held by many journalists, who rejected the theory of seditious libel. But for them the threat of punishment for criticizing officials remained alive until the close of the eighteenth century, when the struggle over the Sedition Act of 1798 brought the issue to a climax.[29]

These negative aspects of the case are counteracted by the inspirational contributions of Zenger and Hamilton and the psychological effects of the trial. For the trial did enunciate a principle—even if it did not establish legal precedent—and this principle is vital to our libertarian philosophy today in matters of free speech and press. The right to criticize officials is one of the main pillars of press freedom.[30] Psychologically, the Zenger trial advanced this goal, for after 1735 no other colonial court trial of a printer for seditious libel has come to light. A few printers were found to be in contempt by their own colonial legislatures or governors' councils, but none was tried by the Crown.[31] Popular opinion had proved its power. The Zenger case thus merits its place in history as a forerunner of what was to follow.

3

The Press and the Revolution

The United Voice of all His Majesty's free and loyal Subjects in America—Liberty and Property, and no Stamps.

—*Motto of various colonial newspapers*

Many believe today that the American Revolution was strictly a struggle by freedom-loving people for independence from a tyrannical British king. Actually, the reasons for the Revolution were much more complex. The clash of debtor and creditor was a factor. The weakness of British policy, inept leadership, and overemphasis of the mercantile system (by which Europeans exploited colonies) were all involved in the dispute. Colonists resented restraints on American development of commerce and industry. They complained that their frontier was being denied to them after their hard-won victory over the French, which they had expected would open up vast new areas to expansion. Refusal of the British to grant home rule was another point of dispute.

But no one of these was sufficient *reason* for the war. Rather, the movement toward revolution was gradually shaped by the influence upon American colonial thinking of the writings of the English opponents of the Stuart kings and their monarchial powers that had survived the Glorious Revolution. Most important of these writings were the "Cato Letters" written by John Trenchard and Thomas Gordon. Viscount Bolingbroke and James Burgh were others who helped shape the ideological prism through which colonials viewed political activity. Historian Bernard Bailyn identified the English-originated themes that appeared in colonial pamphlets, writings, and arguments: a fear of standing armies; an insistence on a government with checks and balances; a yearning for an agrarian society; a stern view of corruption, luxury, and vice; and an obsession with fear that wicked and designing men would deprive the people of their liberties.[1]

Thurſday, October 31, 1765.

THE
PENNSYLVANIA JOURNAL;
AND
WEEKLY ADVERTISER.

NUMB. 1195.

EXPIRING: In Hopes of a Reſurrection to LIFE again.

Adieu, Adieu to the LIBERTY of the PRESS

Facsimile of the famed "Tombstone Edition" protesting the 1765 Stamp Act

A key concept in understanding the political culture of the revolutionary period is republicanism. As the historian Linda Kerber explains, republicanism is complex, and it emphasizes civic virtue as "the cement that held the republic together." Among civic virtue's assumptions are "that the citizen was male, that he was made independent by his control of property, and that he undertook to restrain his passions and selfishness" for the higher good of the republic. Essentially, republicanism is conservative in its emphasis upon citizens who control property; at the same time, republican theory taught the colonists that "politics could be a force for change."[2]

STEPS TOWARD REVOLUTION

As specific changes of policy and abrasive incidents occurred affecting relations between England and the colonies, political spokespersons found support for their views in this ideological background. John Dickinson found backing for his cry of no taxation without representation; Sam Adams could arouse fears of a standing English army occupying and subjugating Boston. Different groups of colonists found reason to resist new policies and laws.

It is significant that the Stamp Act of 1765 alienated two very influential groups: the lawyers and the journalists. The new law placed a heavy duty on the paper used in publishing newspapers and a heavy tax on all legal documents. Thus, the lawyer, who swayed people by the spoken word, and the journalist, who had even wider influence through the written word, were both turned against those who favored the unpopular act. However, from the start the Stamp Act also aroused considerable crowd action. Historians have made a convincing case for popular support of the Revolution.[3]

Yet one can scarcely blame the British for proposing some such law as the Stamp Act. After the Seven Years' War, which saw the British triumphant over the French in North America and India, Great Britain emerged as a great empire—one of the greatest of all time. On the other hand, victory found the British nearly bankrupt. Some way had to be found to pay the cost of defending the wide frontiers. Since the Americans had gained so much from the victory over the French, they should be willing to pay a small share of the defense costs, the politicians in London insisted.

The colonists were indeed willing to offer help—in their own fashion. Colonial legislatures were ready to raise levies, but they did not raise enough, and they did not exert themselves enough to turn over such funds when needed. Since the legislatures controlled the colonial purse strings, not much could be done when levies were in arrears. Empire leaders believed the solution was the imposition of special taxes that could be collected more effectively for this purpose. The Stamp Act was one such attempt. The British themselves paid such a tax. George Grenville, sponsor of the hated measure, pointed out that even Massachusetts had imposed a similar tax in 1755. A little later New York did the same.

The colonists replied that the local stamp acts were imposed by the people paying the tax. As Sam Adams brought out in his resolutions of 1765, the colonies had no direct representation in Parliament. He recognized that this would be impracticable, considering the distance apart of the two areas. That was why he insisted that the colonies be given home rule under a common king.[4] But that was no solution to the immediate problem.

The opposition of the editors took many forms. Some suspended publication. Some publications appeared without title or masthead, which technically took them out of the newspaper classification. A few appeared without the required stamp but with the notice that none could be procured, which may have been true since mobs prevented the sale of stamps in every colony. Several publications satirized the event. On the day before the tax was to be enforced, the *Pennsylvania Journal and Weekly Advertiser* appeared with heavy black column margins, or "turned rules," the traditional symbol of journalistic mourning now represented in the shape of a tombstone.

The Stamp Act agitation was actually only an episode in a long conflict between Great Britain and its colonies. The British were leading exponents of the "mercantile system." Under this program, colonies were to be developed as sources for raw materials and again as markets for finished products. Essential to the system was a favorable balance of trade for Great Britain, meaning that the value of exports must exceed that of imports. This policy was fostered by whatever party gained control. That was why the British government had imposed restrictions on trade, industry, and finances in the colonies beginning in 1651. Scarcity of money in the colonies became a serious matter, for example, but the refusal of British creditors to ease the debt burden embittered many a colonial.[5]

The colonists did not make violent objection, however, until after the victory over the French. Smuggling went on openly, engaged in by respected citizens as a legitimate way around measures believed to be unsound by local consensus. But after 1763, the British began to enforce old laws and to impose new ones. The reaction to this is seen in the colonial attempts to present their grievances peaceably at first and then by more direct action when this policy failed. The Stamp Act Congress, which succeeded in bringing about the repeal of the hated law, showed the colonies what could be accomplished by united, decisive action. Granted all this, one must still conclude that economics were only one factor in the coming revolution. For ideas were stirring people, too. Indeed, it can be said that the revolution was completed by 1775, if ideas are the criteria, in which case the war was only the means of defending the new thoughts against those who could not subscribe to them.

The conflicting ideas that developed as the Revolution progressed can be followed conveniently by studying the products of three journalists who represented their respective classes or groups. They were James Rivington, the Tory spokesperson; John Dickinson, "the Penman of the Revolution," representing the Whig philosophy; and Samuel Adams, the evangelist of democracy and leader of the "agitators," or Radicals.

JAMES RIVINGTON, VOICE OF THE TORIES

Americans are likely to think of the Tories as traitors because of their refusal to bear arms against the British in the War of Independence. Actually, it was the Tories who remained loyal to their country when others rebelled. Only defeat in war made the Tories traitors. Readers of Kenneth Roberts's historical novel, *Oliver Wiswell,* can understand that there were many sincere and honest Americans who believed in the Tory cause in the middle of the eighteenth century. About 20 to 30 percent were Tories in 1776.

The goal of the Tories, apparently, was to retain the basic structure of colonial society. They wished to continue governing by right of property, heredity, position, and tradition—which would appear to be the attributes of a nobility. This seems a strange and distasteful desideratum by democratic standards, but it had its persuasive proponents. Such a one was James Rivington.

"Jemmy" Rivington came to the colonies in 1762, after he had lost his fortune at the race track—not the last newspaperperson to suffer in this way, it might be added. Despite this preoccupation with the sport of kings, Rivington was a credit to journalism and to his class. One can hardly blame him for his Tory views. For generations his family had been official publishers of religious books for the Church of England—the Established Church,

THURSDAY MAY 25 1775.   **[Nº 110.]**

RIVINGTON's
NEW-YORK GAZETTEER

Connecticut, Hudson's River,   New-Jersey and Quebec

WEEKLY ADVERTISER

PRINTED at his OPEN and UNINFLUENCED PRESS fronting HANOVER SQUARE.

Affize of Bread.—*Flour at 16s. per cwt.*	High Water at New-York, this Week.	Wheat, per Bushel,	PRICE CURRENT, in New-York.	
A wheaten Loaf of the finest Flour, to weigh 2 lb. 13 oz. for 4 coppers.	Thursday 57 min. after 6	Monday 50 min. after 9	Flour,	Muscovado Sugar, 50 to 60s.	Fine Salt 3s. 6d. Coarse 2s. 3d.
	Friday 45 min. after 7	Tuesday 27 min. after 10	Brown Bread,	Single refined do. 12s. 6d.	Indian Corn, per Bushel, 3s.
	Saturday 10 min. after 8	Wednesday 50 min. after 10	West India Rum,	Molasses, 2s. od.	Bills of Exchange,
Published the 3d of April, 1775.	Sunday 10 min. after 9		New-England do.	Beef, per Barrel,	Do. at Philadelphia,
				Pork,	Do. at Boston,

PHILADELPHIA, MAY 13.

AFFIDAVITS and depositions relative to the commencement of the late hostilities in the province of Massachusetts-Bay; continued from our last:

Lexington, April 25, 1775.
JOHN PARKER, of lawful age, and commander of the militia in Lexington, do testify and declare, that on the 19th instant, in the morning, about one of the clock, being informed that there was a number of regular officers riding up and down the road, stopping and insulting people as they passed the road; and also was informed that a number of regular troops were on their march from Boston, in order to take the province stores at Concord; ordered our militia to meet on the common in said Lexington, to consult what to do, and concluded not to be discovered, nor meddle or make with said regular troops (if they should approach) unless they should insult or molest us, and upon their sudden approach I immediately ordered our militia to disperse and not to fire; immediately said troops made their appearance and rushed furiously, fired upon and killed eight of our party, without receiving any provocation therefor from us.   JOHN PARKER.

We, Nathaniel Clarkhurst, Jonas Parker, John Munroe, junr., John Winship, Solomon Pierce, John Muzzy, Abner Meeds, John Bridge, junr., Ebenezer Bowman, William Munroe, 3d, Micah Hager, Samuel Sanderson, Samuel Hastings, and John Brown, of Lexington, in the county of Middlesex, and colony of Massachusetts-Bay, in New England; and all of lawful age, do testify and say, that on the morning of the nineteenth of April inst. about one or two o'clock, being informed that a number of regular officers had been riding up and down the road the evening and night preceding, and that some of the inhabitants as they were passing had been insulted by the officers, and stopped by them; and being also informed that the regular troops were on their march from Boston, in order (as it was said) to take the colony stores there deposited at Concord! We met on the parade of our company in this town; after the company had collected, we were ordered by Captain John Parker (who commanded us) to disperse for the present, and be ready to attend the beat of the drum; and accordingly the company went into houses near the place of parade. We further testify and say, that about five o'clock in the morning we attended the beat of our drum and were formed on the parade—we were faced towards the regulars then marching up to us, and some of our company were coming to the parade with their backs towards the troops; and others on the parade began to disperse when the regulars fired on the company, before a gun was fired by any of our company on them; they killed eight of our company, and wounded several, and continued the fire until we had all made our escape.

Signed by each of the above Deposers.

NEW-JERSEY, MAY 16.—

SPEECH of his Excellency WILLIAM FRANKLIN, Esq., Captain General, Governor and Commander in Chief, in and over the Province of NEW-JERSEY, and Territories thereon depending in America, Chancellor and Vice Admiral of the same, &c.

To the GENERAL ASSEMBLY of the said Province, Convened at Burlington.

Gentlemen of the Council, and
Gentlemen of the General Assembly.

THE sole occasion of my calling you together at this time is to lay before you a resolution of the House of Commons wisely and humanely calculated to open a door to the restoration of that harmony between Great-Britain and her American colonies on which their mutual welfare and happiness so greatly depend.

This resolution, having already appeared in the public papers, and a great variety of interpretations put upon it, mostly according to the different views and dispositions by which men are actuated and scarcely any having seen it in its proper light, I think I cannot at this juncture better answer the gracious purposes of his Majesty, nor do my country more essential service than to lay before you as full an explanation of the occasion, purport and intent of it as is in my power. By this means you, and the good people you represent, will be enabled to judge for yourselves how far you ought or ought not to acquiesce with the plan it contains, and what steps it will be prudent for you to take on this very important occasion.

You will see in the King's answer to the joint address of both Houses of Parliament on the 7th of February, how much attention his Majesty was graciously pleased to give to the assurance held out in that address, of the readiness of Parliament to afford every just and reasonable indulgence to the colonies whenever they should make a proper application on the ground of any real grievance they might have to complain of. This address was accordingly soon followed by the resolution of the House of Commons now laid before you. A circumstance which afforded his Majesty great satisfaction, as it gave room to hope for a happy effect, and would, at all events, ever remain an evidence of their justice and moderation and manifest the temper which has accompanied their deliberations upon that question which has been the source of so much disquiet to the King's subjects in America.

His Majesty, ardently wishing to see a reconciliation of the unhappy differences by every means through which it may be obtained without prejudice to the just authority of Parliament, which his Majesty will never suffer to be violated, has approved the resolution of his faithful Commons, and has commanded it to be transmitted to the governors of his colonies, not doubting that this happy disposition to comply with every just and reasonable wish of the King's subjects in America will meet with such a return of duty and affection on their part as will lead to a happy issue of the present dispute, and to a re-establishment of the public tranquility on those grounds of equity, justice and moderation which this resolution holds forth.

What has given the King the greater satisfaction in this resolution, and the greater confidence in the good effects of it, is his having seen that, amidst all the in-

---

James Rivington balances a colonial account of the Battle of Lexington with a speech by Tory William Franklin, Ben's son.

and therefore the one that had the most general appeal to most good Tories. King and bishop represented authority, by which order could be maintained most effectively, the Tory argued. Thus, an attack on the authority of the state was also a threat to the authority of the church, people like Rivington insisted, and the history of revolution has shown that this is indeed the usual consequence. It was the duty of all citizens, therefore, to support the forces of law and order against anarchistic elements.

Rivington was influential in America and could do much for the Tory cause. He was proprietor of the first chain of bookstores in America, with branches in Boston, New York, and Philadelphia. He had been so successful in this venture that he decided to publish a newspaper. In 1773, on the eve of the revolt in the colonies, he founded *Rivington's New-York Gazetteer or the Connecticut, Hudson's River, New-Jersey and Quebec Weekly Advertiser,* a local paper, despite its impressive, regional title. The paper was well edited and skillfully printed. It was also very profitable, as shown by the fact that it averaged about 55 percent advertising.

Rivington merited respect for his venture because he was willing to discuss both sides of political questions—an objectivity that was not the standard in his era. Such objectivity was just what the "Patriot" rivals resented, however. They were not interested in fair and accurate reports. That was no way to fight for a cause, they believed, and so we find Rivington complaining in his issue of April 20, 1775:

> The Printer is bold to affirm that his press has been open to publication from ALL PARTIES. . . . He has considered his press in the light of a public office, to which every man has a right to have recourse. But the moment he ventured to publish sentiments which were opposed to the dangerous views and designs of certain demagogues, he found himself held up as an enemy of his country.

Rivington's complaint was a common one for Tories in the decade preceding outbreak of war. Power was slipping away from the English authorities into the hands of the colonial assemblies. In their eyes, criticism of the Crown was no longer seditious libel. But criticism of the assemblies, or of the Patriot cause, might well be seditious or contemptuous. Freedom of expression meant largely freedom for your side—and the Tory was on the losing side.

The troubles of the Tory printers came largely from public pressures generated by such Radical "agitators" as Sam Adams rather than from official actions. An organized campaign of threats and economic coercion was reinforced at times by mob action against printers who were not all-out for the Radical cause. The Tories, or Loyalists, were nearly all hounded out of business; those who tried to be neutral were either forced into the Radical camp or into suspension.[6]

In Boston, for example, the well-organized Radical group used threats to persuade some reluctant printers to use their propaganda and to mute Tory voices. When John Mein's stoutly Tory *Chronicle* refused to cower but instead attacked the Radical leaders, Mein was hanged in effigy, attacked on the street, and finally mobbed. He had to flee to England, and his paper was suspended in 1770. Thomas Fleet's *Evening Post,* which tried to print both sides of the argument, closed down in 1775, as did the Tory *Post-Boy.* The last Tory voice in Boston, the *News-Letter,* died early in 1776. In Philadelphia, Patriot William Goddard was roughed up for publishing pro-Crown materials in his *Pennsylvania Chronicle.* Rivington thus could complain about the experiences of others, as well as his own, in opposing the Radical-generated tide of public opinion.

After the battles of Lexington and Concord, Rivington ceased to be objective. During the war he was as partisan as his Patriot rivals. His wartime paper, renamed the

Royal Gazette, reeked with unfounded charges against American leaders. He appeared to relish vicious rumors that might harm the rebels—but this was in time of war, whose first casualty is objectivity. And he had little reason to feel charitable toward his political and social enemies. He had been burned in effigy by mobs for expressing his views. Twice his shop had been raided, the type destroyed on one occasion. He had been forced to sign a humiliating public apology for merely voicing his opinions. He had even been driven back to England in 1776, to return as king's printer in 1777. When, in 1781, the news of Yorktown reached the *Royal Gazette,* Rivington became conciliatory. He objectively reported the scene in which General Washington bade farewell to his officers in New York City, after the British had departed. But the Radicals, led by Isaac Sears, were unrelenting; the same mob that had burned him out in 1775 came back on New Year's Eve of 1783 to close him down. Unlike other Tories, Rivington did not leave; he died in New York in 1802.

JOHN DICKINSON, THE WHIG PHILOSOPHER

Advocates for other groups disputed Tory views—some mildly, and some violently. The American Tory was opposed by a rising capitalist faction—it could not as yet be called a party—often referred to as the Colonial Whigs. One articulate Whig was John Dickinson of Pennsylvania, sometimes called "the Penman of the Revolution."

Although not a publisher or printer, Dickinson deserves to be ranked with the great journalists of the period. By newspaper and pamphlet he spread the gospel of his political faith. The gist of his philosophy appeared in a series of articles entitled "Letter from a Farmer

(Magazine of American History)
James Rivington, leading Tory editor

(Pennsylvania Magazine of History and Biography)
John Dickinson, the Colonial Whig

in Pennsylvania." The first such letter was printed in the *Pennsylvania Chronicle* in 1767. Eleven others followed on into 1768. They were widely reprinted up and down the seaboard.

Two 1767 events had alarmed Dickinson: the imposition of the Townshend Acts as direct taxes by Parliament, and the suspension of the New York Assembly for not granting tax money to the governor. The Colonial Whigs, to be safe in their properties, had to control taxes in their own assembly, argued Dickinson. This emphasis upon property was the hallmark of sound government.

Dickinson had no wish to bring on a war for independence, but he, more than any other writer except Sam Adams, prepared public opinion for the Revolution, since he stated basic principles that Colonial Whigs came to feel they must defend. Ironically, this mild Quaker became the author of the *Declaration of Rights of the Stamp Act Congress* and two *Petitions to the King* and coauthor of the Articles of Confederation.

Dickinson was as contemptuous of rabble-rousers as were Rivington and the rest of the Tories, for the Whigs had rather narrow ideas of liberty. The great battle cry of the Whigs, for example, was "no taxation without representation," which is strictly an economic aspect of the struggle. The Whigs had no great interest in the rise of the common person. They had only the vaguest of ideas regarding the "natural rights" philosophy of social reform, for they thought more in terms of property than of human rights. Yet they, too, were fighting for a principle, and in the conflict they brought liberties to others less able to fight on fair terms. The curious twist to all this was that the worst enemies of the American Whigs were their counterparts in England. The British Whigs imposed commercial restrictions that were considered harmful to American business interests. The Americans argued that if British businesspeople in control of the government both at home and abroad could impose taxes arbitrarily without colonial representation, then their American business rivals could be driven into oblivion.

When the Revolution had to be defended by arms, the American Whigs had to choose between loyalty to the Crown, which provided the law and order they so prized, or loyalty to the local government, which held the promise of the unrestricted enterprise they coveted. The dilemma forced the Whigs into becoming either Loyalists or Patriots during the shooting war, for there was by that time no place for compromisers. Dickinson himself had to make this choice. He could not bring himself to stand for outright independence from his beloved homeland, and he refused to sign the Declaration of Independence. But he carried a musket in defense of his home.

Dickinson was influential because he was respected by the propertied class—a group generally regarded as hardheaded, practical, and unemotional. Once convinced, the businesspeople could do more than anyone else in swinging their neighbors in favor of a cause, for their neighbors reasoned that if a "sound" businessperson believed in proposed changes, there must be good reason for this attitude. Dickinson reached this group by articles geared to their interests. His letters were brilliant, convincing, and readable. They were widely printed. All but three of the newspapers of the period carried the complete series by the "Pennsylvania Farmer." Ideas expressed in these contributions were reflected in the press for weeks and even for years.

SAMUEL ADAMS, THE RADICAL PROPAGANDIST

The weakest group at the beginning of the struggle, and the most important at the end of the conflict, was the so-called Radicals, or Patriots—terms not at all synonymous at a later date. The Tory had great interest in hereditary rights, the Whig was preoccupied with eco-

Samuel Adams, the Radical   Isaiah Thomas, Patriot editor

nomic issues, but the Radical carried on into a very different field. The Radicals were the only ones seriously interested in social change. They might have been overcome in America, as they had been in England, however, had it not been for their very effective leadership. Probably the best example of the Radical leader was Samuel Adams, one of the most prolific journalists of his time.

As a propagandist, Adams was without peer. He understood that to win the inevitable conflict, he and his cohorts must achieve five main objectives: they must justify the course they advocated; advertise the advantages of victory; arouse the masses—the real "shock troops"—by instilling hatred of enemies; neutralize any logical and reasonable arguments proposed by the opposition; and finally phrase all the issues in black and white, so that the purposes might be clear even to the common laborer. Adams was able to do all this, and his principal tool was the colonial newspaper. Caution should be taken, however, not to overemphasize Adams's role. Although historians once ascribed tremendous importance to the "machinations of Samuel Adams and other 'pioneers in propaganda'" in building support for the Patriots, more contemporary interpretations point to the pivotal role of "authentic popular feeling, stemming from a deep and widespread distrust of the corruption of British politics."[7]

Adams believed that the American colonies were justified in repudiating the home country because Parliament continued to ignore their basic rights. It was the British who broke the contract, he argued, and hence the obligations of the colonials no longer applied. (The theory of the law of contracts was, and still is, that violation by one party releases all other contractors from obligations.) Adams made it appear as though his class and party fought for the traditional rights that were now being ignored by the British Parliament. Technically, then, it was the British who were in revolt—the colonists were the people maintaining the traditional ways.

Sam Adams was not the only propagandist of the Revolution, but he was the greatest. Not surprisingly, his enemies dubbed him the "Master of the Puppets," and he was perfectly fitted for the role. Adams had turned away from the ministry, from law, and from teaching, although he was familiar with all these professions. As a young Radical, Adams met regularly with the Caucus Club, founded by his father and other aggressive Boston spirits. The club sponsored a newspaper, the *Independent Advertiser,* and in 1748, at the age of 26, Sam Adams became editor of that publication. Later, he was a regular contributor to the *Boston Gazette and Country Journal,* descendant of the second newspaper published in the colonies.

Adams made a strike for liberty in May 1764, when he was appointed one of a committee of five to instruct his town's representative to the legislature. Included was a denial of Parliament's right to impose Grenville's hated Stamp Act. A final paragraph of the document also suggested a union of all the colonies for the most effective expression of grievances.[8] These instructions were printed by the *Gazette,* and since this paper was closely followed as the mouthpiece of the Patriot element, the stirring message was broadcast up and down the seaboard.

EDES AND GILL'S *BOSTON GAZETTE*

At once Adams was recognized as leader of a small but vociferous group. Two of this band were Benjamin Edes and John Gill, boyhood friends and now proprietors of the *Gazette.* By the end of 1764 the newspaper was the nerve center of the Boston Radicals. Many famous Americans wrote for the paper, especially after the passage of the obnoxious Townshend Acts of 1767, which levied new duties on colonial imports, but none was more effective than Sam Adams.

Adams was more than a writer; he was an expert news gatherer. His Committees of Correspondence, organized in 1772, kept him alert to every movement and sentiment throughout the colonies. His agents "covered" every important meeting as ably as modern reporters gather information for the press services today. In a remarkably short time all such news reached Adams's local committee, which then processed it for effective dissemination where such information was needed. This primitive news service was highly efficient, yet no one in the colonies had thought of such a device until Adams came along.

He was just as successful at instilling his enthusiasm for the cause into the hearts of useful helpers. Since a person's greatness can be measured by the caliber of his or her associates, we must assume that Adams was a great man indeed. Cousin John, who later became second president of the United States, sometimes disappointed Sam, as in John's defense of the British soldiers involved in the Boston Massacre, but on the whole the two respected each other, as indicated by the fact that Sam used his influence in John's behalf even while the two argued. They were both honest men. John was useful in enlisting the more dignified members of the community, especially the legal fraternity, who were disdainful of Sam's noisier methods.

Another associate was Josiah Quincy, who understood what some organizers now refer to as "solidarity." Quincy argued that to think justly was not enough; citizens must also think *alike* before there could be a united force of public opinion strong enough to make warriors of the cause invincible. Still another great co-worker was Joseph Warren, the charming and kindly physician, who spoke with great logic for the Patriot cause. Warren insisted upon taking direct action when the shooting began. He lost his life as a high-ranking officer in the first pitched battle of the war at Breed's (Bunker) Hill. James Otis was the spellbinder of the group—one of the great orators of his day. The British feared Otis most of all, because of his persuasive powers.

THE SONS OF LIBERTY

The Boston Radicals who gathered about Sam Adams at the *Gazette* office were the core of the revolutionary movement. But they needed a way to win the support of other colonies for the hard line toward the British they were developing in Massachusetts. This was supplied by the Sons of Liberty, whose chapters sprang into being during the spontaneous popular uprising over the Stamp Act of 1765. Adams, printer Benjamin Edes, and engraver Paul Revere were among the key Boston members from the *Gazette* group. Other printers rated as strong activists in the Sons of Liberty propaganda network were fellow Bostonian Isaiah Thomas of the *Massachusetts Spy;* John Holt of the *New York Journal;* Peter Timothy of Charleston's *South Carolina Gazette;* William Goddard of Philadelphia's *Pennsylvania Chronicle* and Baltimore's *Maryland Journal;* and Solomon Southwick of the *Newport Mercury.* William Bradford III was an officer of the Sons of Liberty in Philadelphia but did not fully commit his *Pennsylvania Journal* to the Radical line.

The Townshend Acts of 1767 permitted the Radicals to develop their Non-Importation Agreements, which bound merchants not to import British goods and citizens not to use them. Dickinson's letters had given support to the Boston group, and James Otis and Joseph Warren made bitter attacks on Governor Francis Bernard in the *Gazette.* Bernard played into their hands by persuading London to send two additional regiments of soldiers to Boston to ensure his control. The Boston press and public greeted these troops with indignation and hostility.

Adams and the Sons of Liberty decided to cash in with an intensive campaign of intercolonial propaganda communications that has been called "the most sustained effort to spread ideas through news items that was made in the entire 20 years (1763–83)."[9] This was the "Journal of Occurrences" of 1768 to 1769, which began with the arrival of the new British troops and ended when Governor Bernard was replaced by Thomas Hutchinson.

The still unidentified authors of the "Journal of Occurrences," working under Adams's direction, compiled a record of alleged events involving the British troops and sent it to John Holt to publish in his *New York Journal.* Other papers from New England to Georgia picked up items. The writers chronicled misdeeds of the British troops garrisoned in Boston, ranging from insults and indignities to assault and attempted rape. Since the events were reported in the Boston papers approximately two months after Holt printed the "Journal of Occurrences" in New York, rather than concurrently, researchers have concluded that Tory complaints of falseness were probably justified. What the "Journal of Occurrences" did was foster the public feeling that the occupying military force was treating people badly and that London was thus punishing Patriots in Boston.

John Holt was the major conduit for this activity of the Sons of Liberty and the most important Radical printer outside Boston. He had worked with Franklin's associate James Parker before launching his *New York Journal* as a Whig paper in late 1766. He became increasingly activist as events occurred that fed the Sons of Liberty movement: the Boston Massacre of 1770; the Tea Act of 1773, which precipitated the Boston Tea Party in

December; and the retaliatory passage of the Intolerable Acts and closing of the port of Boston in 1774. Holt ran stories from the Boston papers, funneling the Radical arguments to Timothy in Charleston, Goddard in Baltimore, and others.

This communication helped keep intercolonial support for the hard line the Boston Radicals were proposing. When tempers flared in Massachusetts in September 1774, Joseph Warren wrote the Suffolk Resolves, which were carried by Paul Revere on horseback to Philadelphia. There the Continental Congress, barely organized, adopted them at the urging of Sam Adams. The action pledged support for the Massachusetts rebels who soon were to be facing British rifles. Not everyone who voted that day realized what Adams had accomplished.

SAM ADAMS'S KEY ROLE

Sam Adams could sense victory in 1774. Behind him lay 20 years of propagandizing, organizing, and using every device to forward his aims. Day after day Adams had pressed his foes through newspaper and through pamphlet. Late at night passersby looked up at the lighted window of the Adams home, and they knew the veteran revolutionary was still at work, writing a piece for the *Gazette,* perhaps, making it hot for the Tories. Adams knew how to find the soft spots in the Tory shell.

The ways of the idol wrecker may not be pretty. Governor Hutchinson was correct when he called Adams an assassin of reputations. The governor knew whereof he spoke, for the last British administrator was a favorite target for the caustic rebel journalist. In the end, Hutchinson, who traced his ancestry back to the independent Anne (the first outstanding woman in American public life), was forced to leave his native land for England.

The "Master of the Puppets" did his work well. On the morning of April 19, 1775, the "shot heard 'round the world" was fired at the battles of Lexington and Concord. From then on, the country was in arms, fighting for the ultimate victory that Adams had helped to engineer.

ISAIAH THOMAS, PATRIOT EDITOR

Printers, publishers, and editors were important influences in preparing the public for Revolution and in maintaining the fighting spirit during the War of Independence. Edes and Gill, proprietors of the Radical *Boston Gazette,* were examples of the patriot-journalist. William Bradford III, grandson of the founder of the famous printing dynasty, wielded both the pen and the sword during the war. His *Pennsylvania Journal* was faithful to the Patriot ideology. But the greatest journalist of the period was Isaiah Thomas, one of the important pioneers of the American Fourth Estate.

Thomas began his career, as an apprentice printer, when he was only six. He had to help support his widowed mother and therefore missed the advantages of formal education. Later, he became a great scholar, owner of one of the finest private libraries in the country, first president of the learned Antiquarian Society, and historian of the colonial press.

Thomas learned to spell by setting type. He broadened his knowledge by studying galley proofs. Zechariah Fowle, Thomas's master, was an inconsiderate employer who turned over much of the actual operation of the shop to his apprentice without appropriate recognition of the young man's worth. The resentful Thomas ran away to Halifax. When he returned to Boston in 1770, Fowle welcomed his runaway apprentice and offered to take

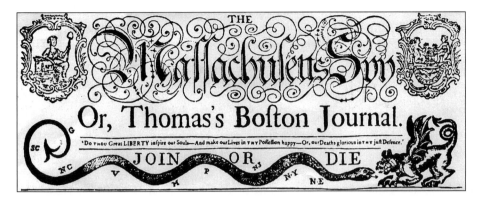

Masthead of Isaiah Thomas's *Massachusetts Spy* with the famed "Join or Die" slogan

him into partnership. Together they founded the *Massachusetts Spy,* a newspaper that lived until 1904.

Thomas soon bought out his shiftless partner. Under his proprietorship the *Spy* became one of the most successful newspapers in the colonies. It was nominally nonpartisan, but it followed the Whig philosophy for the most part. Until hostilities began this was a successful formula, for at 21 the handsome publisher owned a paper exceeded in circulation and bulk only by Rivington's.

Thomas began to shift his Whig doctrine as it became apparent that conciliationists like Dickinson were ineffective. Soon he was the acknowledged spokesperson for the independence group in his area. When British troops arrived in Boston to enforce laws formerly flouted by the colonials, Thomas became the leader of the underground movement. It was they who flashed the signal light from the steeple of Old North Church warning the Minutemen couriers of the impending British raid on Lexington and Concord.[10]

The next day Thomas was an eyewitness to the first battle in the War of Independence. If he did not hear "the shot heard 'round the world," he at least understood its significance. His report of the encounter remains today as the most notable war reporting of that conflict. He would have been the first to deny that his "story" of the fight was objective. By that time he was committed to the use of his press as an instrument of war, and his report is therefore highly colored with propaganda favorable to his compatriots. Even so, his word picture of the event was probably accurate in its main theme, and there are so much color and vigor in his writing that the account deserves mention here. According to Thomas's report:

> About ten o'clock on the night of the 18th of April, the troops in Boston were discovered to be on the move in a very secret manner, and it was found they were embarking in boats (which they privately brought to the place in the evening) at the bottom of the Common; expresses set off immediately to alarm the country, that they might be on their guard. When the expresses got about a mile beyond Lexington, they were stopped by about fourteen officers on horseback, who came out of Boston in the afternoon of that day, and were seen lurking in bye-places in the country till after dark. One of the expresses immediately fled [this was probably Dr. Samuel Prescott], and was pursued two miles by an officer, who, when he got up with him presented a pistol, and told him he was a dead man if he did not stop, but he rode on till he came up to a house, when stopping of a sudden his horse threw him off, having the presence of mind to halloo [the rider, of course, not the horse] to the people in the house.

"Turn out! Turn out! I have got one of them!"

The officer immediately retreated and fled as fast as he had pursued. The other express [Paul Revere], after passing through a strict examination, by some means got clear.

The body of troops in the meantime, under the command of Lieutenant Colonel Smith, had crossed the river and landed at Phipp's Farm. They immediately, to the number of 1000, proceeded to Lexington, six miles below Concord, with great silence. A company of militia, of about eighty men, mustered near the meeting house; the troops came in sight of them just before sunrise. The militia, upon seeing the troops, began to disperse. The troops then set out upon the run, hallooing and hussaing, and coming within a few rods of them, the commanding officer accosted the militia, in words to this effect,

"Disperse, you damn'd rebels—Damn you, disperse."

Upon which the troops again hussaed and immediately one or two officers discharged their pistols, which were instantaneously followed by the firing of four or five of the soldiers and then there seemed to be a general discharge from the whole body. Eight of our men were killed and nine wounded.[11]

The war was hard on Patriot editors and publishers. They had committed themselves to the cause so wholeheartedly that it was impossible to stay in business under British occupation. Both the *Gazette* and the *Spy* printing plants had to be smuggled out of Boston, if these two Patriot organs were to continue beating the drums for the American cause. The *Gazette* was moved at night across the Charles River to Watertown, where it was published until the British were forced out of Boston in 1776. Thomas had his press sent by trusted employees to Worcester on the eve of the Lexington battle, and he made that city his permanent home thereafter.

Once firmly established in Worcester, Thomas again began to thrive as a journalist and publisher. By the time his fellow Patriots had emerged from war triumphant, he was the leading publisher of his day. Seven presses and 150 employees kept his shop in Worcester humming. Under his imprint appeared more than 400 books on law, medicine, agriculture, and science. He was the first American to publish Blackstone's *Commentaries,* a Greek grammar, printed music, and a novel by a native author: William Hill Brown's *Power of Sympathy.* The first American dictionary, by William Perry, was brought out by Thomas and sold 50,000 copies. Later Thomas also published Perry's speller, with sales of various editions totaling 300,000 copies. Among his hundred children's books were the first American versions of *Mother Goose* and *Little Goody Two-Shoes.* Thomas had something for everyone. When he retired from business in 1802, he wrote his two-volume *History of Printing in America* (1810), a classic, and founded the American Antiquarian Society, whose Worcester building today houses the leading collection of colonial printing.

TOM PAINE, THE RADICAL WRITER

Thomas did much to *prepare* the public for the conflict. Another effective journalist of the war was a penniless and somewhat disreputable stranger to the American shores.[12] He was Tom Paine, a Quaker from Thetford, England, who arrived on the eve of the war. He was then 37 years old, and his life up to that point had been anything but inspiring. His mother, whom he disliked, belonged to the Established church. Apparently there was philosophical friction between parents and son from the beginning. After an unsuccessful attempt to work in the corset-making business, young Tom Paine was appointed an exciseman. He was soon accused of incompetency and neglect of duty. Reinstated, he was discharged again for what we would now call "unionization." He had been chosen by the excisemen of his district to represent them in their agitation for higher pay, and it was partly because of his failure as an agitator that he left his homeland.

By a fortunate coincidence, he met Benjamin Franklin, then at the height of his career as the American spokesperson in Europe. Franklin, a shrewd judge of character, saw enough in Paine to write a letter of recommendation. Paine was advised to go to America, where Franklin's son-in-law, Richard Bache, would offer helpful advice. Paine arrived in Philadelphia sick in mind and body. He later said that the very air of America was his tonic. With every breath of freedom he grew stronger. He spoke wonderingly of being able to sit in the same coffeehouses with the "gentry." Paine's first contributions were to Robert Aitken's *Pennsylvania Magazine,* one of several such periodical ventures that flowered and withered during this period. Aitken's magazine was one of the better ones. It did not survive, but Paine wrote for it long enough to establish a reputation as a stimulating commentator. Already he was arguing against the institution of Negro slavery and British arrogance and in favor of universal suffrage and education.

Paine's fame as a writer was achieved by means of a pamphlet copied by many of the colonial newspapers of 1776. This was *Common Sense,* which helped to bring the lukewarm Patriots into the revolutionary movement. *Common Sense* appeared in January 1776, just a little more than a year after the arrival of the uncouth English immigrant. Its popularity was instantaneous and amazing. More than 120,000 copies were sold in the first three months. "I challenge the warmest advocate for reconciliation to show a single advantage that this continent can reap by being connected with Great Britain," he wrote. This challenge was hurled at the Dickinsonian Whigs, who shuddered at the word "independence," and they replied in the local newspapers with condemnation of this upstart. In a matter of weeks, however, Paine's views in *Common Sense* were known to virtually every literate American, and it is significant that only six months later, the Declaration of Independence committed the former colonies to this doctrine.

THE DECLARATION OF INDEPENDENCE

Congress declared the colonies independent of Great Britain on July 2, 1776, approving the motion offered on June 7 by Richard Henry Lee of Virginia and seconded by John Adams of Massachusetts. Benjamin Towne added this one-line insert in his triweekly *Pennsylvania Evening Post* as he went to press that day: "This day the CONTINENTAL CONGRESS declared the UNITED COLONIES FREE and INDEPENDENT STATES."[13] On July 4, Congress asked John Dunlap, the printer of the *Pennsylvania Packet or The General Advertiser,* to print broadsides of the document that had been penned by Thomas Jefferson and edited by Franklin and Adams. In fact, on the fourth, Jefferson and Franklin worked in the printing room with Dunlap, helping him correct typographical errors. Towne carried the full text on July 6, Dunlap on July 8, and by the end of the month at least 29 papers had carried the glorious news.[14]

The next task of Congress was to mobilize world opinion against the British. Despite censorship in many countries, it was impossible to keep the news of this shocking announcement from spreading. The *London Chronicle* and the *Daily Advertiser* in London carried accounts on August 17, and two weeks later King George III made more news by denouncing the "daring and desperate" colonists before the House of Lords. The news was welcomed in oppressed lands such as Ireland and India, but kept secret or ignored in

The *American* CRISIS,
N U M B E R   I.
By the Author of COMMON SENSE.
Will be published in a Hand-Bill this evening.

Advertisement for Tom Paine's first *Crisis* paper in the *Pennsylvania Packet*

authoritarian countries such as Spain, the German states, and Russia. The greatest impact was in France, where the Declaration and various state constitutions were printed as part of a propaganda campaign against the British.

Indeed, from the French Revolution of 1789 to Ho Chi Minh's 1945 revolt in Indochina, the words of the Declaration were copied in recognition of this dramatic, creative challenge to European practices.

PAINE'S *CRISIS* PAPERS

After fighting broke out later in 1776, the rebels found themselves in a difficult situation. The ideology of the conflict was still vague to the tattered troops. Companies were breaking up fast. The British cut the Americans to pieces at Amboy, New Jersey, where Tom Paine fought as a volunteer. Making his way to Washington's headquarters at Fort Lee, Paine saw the defeated Americans licking their wounds, preparing to withdraw to the Delaware River line. His curious status as a foreigner who was neither an officer nor an enlisted man gave him access to both groups, and he talked with all types of Americans as he walked along the wintry roads. Actually the season was unusually mild, but for the ill-clad troops the nightly bivouac brought only misery. At this crucial moment Paine wrote his first *Crisis* paper.

Whether it is true that he wrote it at Washington's direction, by candlelight on a drum head, is inconsequential. There is no doubt, however, that it was written from the heart and under pressure. There was nothing new in what Paine said, but like a poet, he expressed what others could only feel. His work was rough, but that made it all the more appealing to the common people for whom it was written. The foot-slogging militiamen understood that one of their own was speaking.

And who can overestimate the power of words in arousing the will to fight? Down through history hopeless wars and battles have been won when words have doubled the force of arms. So it was with Paine's *Crisis*. His style had a kind of biblical resonance and rhythm. Like Winston Churchill's "We shall fight them on the beaches" speech of World War II, the words rallied weary people by that most potent of spiritual tonics: dedication to a cause. Paine's words have lived through the generations. In the bleak days of World War II, when there were no victories to report, the conquered peoples, despairing of freedom, listened with kindling hope as these words, written December 19, 1776, came through the ether to their secret radio receivers:

> These are the times that try men's souls. The summer soldier and the sunshine patriot will, in this crisis, shrink from the service of his country; but he that stands it NOW, deserves the love and thanks of man and woman. Tyranny, like hell, is not easily conquered; yet we have this consolation with us, that the harder the conflict the more glorious the triumph. What we obtain too cheap, we esteem too lightly—Tis dearness only that gives every thing its value. Heaven knows how to put a proper price upon its goods; and it would be strange indeed if so celestial an article as FREEDOM should not be highly rated.

The first *Crisis* paper exceeded *Common Sense* in popularity. Printed first in John Dunlap's *Pennsylvania Packet* on December 27, the clarion call was echoed in Patriot newspapers throughout the colonies. Washington had the *Crisis* papers read to his numb troops as the words emerged fresh from Paine's pen. It is significant that the week after Paine made his first plea to the dejected, they turned on the foe and won a needed victory at Trenton.

Other *Crisis* papers appeared as the need demanded. More than any other writer of the war, Paine caught the significance of the American Revolution. While others presented political and economic arguments, Paine advocated social revolt as well. But his adopted country rejected him for his radicalism. The author of the *Rights of Man* and the *Age of Reason,* a participant in both the American and French revolutions, Paine died ignored in 1809. His tombstone lists as his most important contribution to democracy his pamphlet *Common Sense.*

THE REVOLUTIONARY PRESS

Only 20 of the 35 newspapers being published at the beginning of the war survived the conflict. Considering the vicissitudes of the times, that was not a bad record. Many would have disappeared had there been no war. And 35 new papers were established during the six years of fighting. Enough of these survived to bring the total number of papers at the end of the war up to the prewar figure. All were weeklies, and most of them were Patriot in sentiment.

Revolutionary newspapers went into about 40,000 homes, but each issue had a larger number of readers per copy than would be true in modern times. Every word was read, even the small "liners" and advertisements. Such enterprise is impressive. On the other hand, any student of the times becomes aware very soon of the primitive communications facilities then available. It took six weeks for the account of Lexington and Concord to reach Savannah. Often the reporting of war events was of the most haphazard type. "The Hartford Post tells us," Hugh Gaine, the turncoat former Patriot editor, wrote in the February 2, 1778, issue of his *New York Gazette and Mercury,* "that he saw a Gentleman in Springfield, who informed him that he (the Gentleman) saw a letter from an Officer in Gen. Howe's Army to another in Gen. Burgoyne's, giving him to understand, war was declared on the sides of France and Spain against the MIGHTY Kingdom of Britain." The news had actually come from a Boston paper already a month old, and the story was not true in any case.[15] Some of the news was high in reporting quality, however. Often it was printed verbatim from participants' accounts, which added to the charm and authenticity. That was how the details of the Battle of Yorktown reached the office of the *Freeman's Journal* in Philadelphia:

> BE IT REMEMBERED
>
> That on the 17th day of October, 1781, Lieut. Gen. Charles Earl Cornwallis, with about 5,000 British troops, surrendered themselves prisoners of war to His Excellency, Gen. George Washington, Commander-in-Chief of the allied forces of France and America. LAUS DEO.[16]

That was all the paper had to tell of the greatest, and final, victory of the war. The account should have been authentic, because the reporter was none other than General Washington. The editor had printed verbatim the dispatch sent out by the general.

If such momentous events were sparsely handled, so was the run of local and colonial news. Close students of colonial newspapers have found only a little local news throughout the eighteenth century. It was largely political, and in times of crisis, military. Pious obituaries, sermons, fires, murders, suicides, epidemics, and the weather were other topics. Considerable attention was paid to local court proceedings, recent research has found, but usually in summary fashion. However, in the 1730s the *Boston News-Letter* ran reports of trials that included descriptions of the reactions of the accused in court.[17] It was another 100 years before detailed crime and court reporting appeared regularly in newspapers; as in England, the colonials had to buy specially produced pamphlets to get such human interest stories. They fared little better in the available selection of foreign items; in the 1760s two-thirds of that space went to governmental and military news, only 15 percent to human interest items (and one-third of that was on crime and justice). Three-fourths of the foreign news came from England. Furthermore, for most items the time lapse between an event and colonial publication was between 6 and 11 weeks.[18]

A serious problem was the shortage of printing supplies. For the most part, paper, ink, and type had come from Europe before the war. Not until 1769 was an American press sold commercially. American paper mills could not begin to supply the demand for stock. Paper at that time was made of linen, and cloth of any kind was scarce, especially in wartime. That was why Washington did not consider it beneath his dignity to issue a plea asking Patriot women to save all available material that might be converted into printing paper, which shows how important the commander in chief considered the press to be. In this connection, it is interesting that he contributed his prestige to encourage the founding, by the Quaker printer Isaac Collins, of the *New Jersey Gazette,* which for a time served as a kind of army newspaper.

An example of journalistic prosperity in wartime was the *Connecticut Courant.* By 1781 it had the then-amazing circulation of 8000 subscribers for each issue. It was full of advertising. Few London papers could boast of such success. The *Courant* printed on paper from its own mill. It was one of the best-printed papers in America. On the other hand, Patriot John Holt had to leave his *New York Journal*'s printing equipment behind in New York when the British came in 1776. He settled down in Kingston, but was routed again by British troops. He finally reestablished the *Journal* in Poughkeepsie, and returned to New York in 1783—only to die the following year a worn-out man.

COLONIAL WOMEN PRINTERS

Research has shown that women played significant roles in early journalism. Many of the 17 colonial women known to have been newspaper printers took up and carried on the trade after the death of their printer husbands, a common practice. Two notable exceptions were Sarah and Mary Katherine Goddard, respectively the mother and sister of printer William Goddard.[19]

The Goddards lived in Providence, Rhode Island, when the widowed Sarah apprenticed William to James Parker in 1755. William came back in 1762, and with his mother and sister founded a print shop and the *Providence Gazette.* William soon disappeared to pursue connections that his work for Parker had given him in New York and Philadelphia, where he founded the *Pennsylvania Chronicle* in 1767. Sarah and Mary Katherine put the nearly defunct *Gazette* back in order and also offered Providence a print shop, bookstore, and post office. Their paper was staunchly Whig. The *Gazette* and *Chronicle* were quick to carry the 12 letters of John Dickinson, for example, and Sarah advised William not to include abusive pieces "against the *Farmer,* who deserves so well of this country."[20] Sarah

(Courtesy of the John Carter Brown Library at Brown University)

Mary Katherine Goddard

(Hartford Courant)

Hannah Bunce Watson became publisher of the *Connecticut Courant* (1778–79) when her husband died of smallpox. She was 28, with five children. She and another widow also owned a paper mill.

possessed a keen sense of political timing, calling the Dickinson letters "the completest pieces ever wrote on the subject in America."[21]

Sarah's and Mary Katherine's success in Providence was interrupted when William called on them for help with his *Pennsylvania Chronicle* in the wake of difficulties caused by his erratic and quarrelsome conduct. Both went to work in the Philadelphia shop in late 1768; Sarah died two years later. Mary Katherine managed the print shop and made it one of the largest in the colonies by 1774. Again, William's wanderlust brought a change. He had founded the *Maryland Journal* in Baltimore in 1773 and needed his sister to manage it while he worked to establish a colonial postal system independent of British control. So Mary Katherine directed the *Maryland Journal* and its print shop for the next ten years. Returning it to William after a quarrel, she ran her bookstore until 1802. She was called "a woman of extraordinary judgment, energy, nerve, and strong, good sense." Isaiah Thomas, the colonial press historian, found she met his exacting standards as an "expert and correct compositor."

So did Elizabeth Timothy of South Carolina, widow of printer Lewis Timothy, and two daughters of James Franklin. Mrs. Timothy was the first colonial woman to publish a newspaper (the *South Carolina Gazette,* 1738–1740), and was the mother of Sons of Liberty hero Peter Timothy. Anne Franklin and her daughters took over her husband James's printshop in Rhode Island in 1735, and Mrs. Franklin ran her son's *Newport Mercury* (1762 to 1763). Margaret Draper, the last printer of the *Boston News-Letter* (1774 to 1776), did battle against the Radicals and left with the British. From Dinah Nuthead, the first colonial woman printer (Maryland, 1696), to the present, women have done their jobs in American printing.[22]

Gazette of the United States.

Number I. | WEDNESDAY, April 15, 1789. | PRICE SIX PENCE.

P L A N
OF THE
GAZETTE of the UNITED STATES.
A NATIONAL PAPER.

To be published at the SEAT *of the* FEDERAL GOVERNMENT, *and to comprise, as fully as possible, the following Objects, viz.*

I. EARLY and authentick Accounts of the PROCEEDINGS of CONGRESS—its LAWS, ACTS, and RESOLUTIONS, communicated so as to form an *HISTORY of the TRANSACTIONS of the FEDERAL LEGISLATURE, under the NEW CONSTITUTION.*

II. Impartial Sketches of the Debates of Congress.

III. ESSAYS upon the great subjects of Government in general, and the *Federal Legislature in particular*; also upon the *national* and *local* Rights of the AMERICAN CITIZENS, as founded upon the Federal or State Constitutions; also upon every other Subject, which may appear suitable for newspaper discussion.

IV. A SERIES of PARAGRAPHS, calculated to catch the "LIVING MANNERS AS THEY RISE," and to point the publick attention to Objects that have an important reference to *domestick, social,* and *publick happiness.*

V. The Interests of the United States as connected with their literary Institutions—religious and moral Objects—Improvements in Science, Arts, EDUCATION and HUMANITY—their foreign Treaties, Alliances, Connections, &c.

VI. Every *species* of INTELLIGENCE, which may affect the *commercial, agricultural, manufacturing,* or *political* INTERESTS of the AMERICAN REPUBLICK.

VII. A CHAIN of DOMESTICK OCCURRENCES, collected through the Medium of an extensive Correspondence with the respective States.

VIII. A SERIES of FOREIGN ARTICLES of INTELLIGENCE, so connected, *as to form a general Idea of publick Affairs in the eastern Hemisphere.*

IX. The STATE of the NATIONAL FUNDS; also of the INDIVIDUAL GOVERNMENTS—Courses of Exchange—Prices Current, &c.

CONDITIONS.

I.
THE Gazette *of the* United States *shall be printed with the same Letter, and on the same Paper as this publication.*

II.
It shall be published every WEDNESDAY *and* SATURDAY, *and delivered, as may be directed, to every Subscriber in the city, on those days.*

III.
The price to Subscribers (exclusive of postage) *will be* THREE DOLLARS *pr. annum.*

IV.
The first semi-annual payment to be made in three months *from the appearance of the first number.*

SUBSCRIPTIONS
are received in all the capital towns upon the Continent; also at the [illegible] *and at* No. 86, William-Street, *until the* 1st *of* May, *from which time at* No. 9, Maiden-Lane, *near the* Oswego-Market, New-York.

N. B. By a new Arrangement made in the Stages, Subscribers at a distance will be duly furnished with papers.

POSTSCRIPT.—*A large impression of every number will be struck off—so that Subscribers may always be accommodated with complete Sets.*

To the PUBLICK.

AT this important Crisis, the ideas that fill the mind, are pregnant with Events of the greatest magnitude—to strengthen and complete the UNION of the States—to extend and protect their COMMERCE, under *equal* Treaties yet to be formed—to explore and arrange the NATIONAL FUNDS—to restore and establish the PUBLICK CREDIT—and *ALL* under the auspices of an untried System of Government, will require the ENERGIES of the Patriots and Sages of our Country—*Hence the propriety of encreasing the Mediums of Knowledge and Information.*

AMERICA, from this period, begins a new Era in her national existence—"THE WORLD IS ALL BEFORE HER"—The wisdom and folly—the misery and prosperity of the EMPIRES, STATES, and KINGDOMS, which have had their day upon the great Theatre of Time, and are now no more, suggest the most important Mementos—These, with the rapid series of Events, in which our own Country has been so deeply interested, have taught the enlightened Citizens of the United States, that FREEDOM and GOVERNMENT—LIBERTY and LAWS, are inseparable.

This Conviction has led to the adoption of the New Constitution; for however VARIOUS the Sentiments, respecting the MERITS of this System, all GOOD MEN are agreed in the necessity that exists, of an EFFICIENT FEDERAL GOVERNMENT.

A paper, therefore, established upon NATIONAL, INDEPENDENT, and IMPARTIAL PRINCIPLES—which shall take up the premised Articles, upon a COMPETENT PLAN, it is presumed, will be highly interesting, and meet with publick approbation and patronage.

The Editor of this Publication is determined to leave no avenue of Information unexplored:—He solicits the assistance of Persons of leisure and abilities—which, united with his own assiduity, he flatters himself will render the Gazette of the United States not unworthy general encouragement—and is, with due respect, the publick's humble servant,

JOHN FENNO.

New-York, April 15, 1789.

EPITOME OF THE PRESENT STATE OF THE UNION.

NEW-HAMPSHIRE,

WHICH is 180 miles in length, and 60 in breadth, contained, according to an enumeration in 1787, 102,000 inhabitants—is attached to the federal Government—engaged in organizing her militia, already the best disciplined of any in the Union—encouraging the domestick arts—and looking forward to the benefits which will result from the operations of the New Constitution. New-Hampshire, from her local adantages, and the hardihood of her sons, may anticipate essential benefits from the operation of equal commercial regulations.

MASSACHUSETTS,

450 miles in length, and 160 in breadth, contained, according to an enumeration in 1787, 360,000 inhabitants—Since the tranquility of the State was restored by the suppression of the late insurrection, the whole body of the people appears solicitous for the blessings of peace and good government. If any conclusion can be drawn from elections for the Federal Legislature, this State has a decided majority in favour of the New Constitution. The great objects of Commerce, Agriculture, Manufactures, and the Fisheries, appear greatly to engage the attention of Massachusetts. Fabrications of Cotton, coarse Woolens, Linens, DUCK, IRON, Wood, &c. are prosecuting with success—and by diminishing her imports, and increasing her exports, she is advancing to that rank and importance in the Union which her extent of territory—her resources—and the genius and enterprise of her citizens entitle her to—and although the collision of parties, at the moment of Election, strikes out a few sparks of animosity, yet the decision once made, the "*Calumet of Peace*" is smoked in love and friendship—"*and like true Republicans they acquiesce in the choice of the Majority.*"

CONNECTICUT,

81 miles in length, and 57 in breadth, contained, agreeably to a Census in 1782, 209,150 inhabitants, enjoying a fertile soil, this truly republican State is pursuing her interest in the promotion of Manufactures, Commerce, Agriculture, and the Sciences—She appears to bid fair, from the peaceable, loyal, and federal Character of the great body of her citizens—from the Enterprise of her men of wealth, and other favourable circumstances, to attain to a great degree of opulence, power, and respectability in the Union.

NEW-YORK,

350 miles in length, and 300 in breadth, contained, agreeably to a Census in 1786, 238,897 inhabitants, This State appears to be convulsed by parties—but the CRISIS is at hand, when it is hoped, that the "*Hatchet*" will be buried. Exertions on one side are making for the re-election of Gov. CLINTON, and on the other for the introduction of the Hon. Judge YATES to the chair—both parties appear sanguine as to their success. It is ardently to be wished, that *temper* and *moderation* may preside at the Elections; and there can be no doubt of it, as that Freedom, for which we fought and triumphed, depends so essentially upon a FREE CHOICE.—It is greatly regretted, that this respectable and important member of the federal Republick, should not be represented in the Most Honourable Senate of the United States. New-York, however, is rising in her federal character, and in manufacturing, agricultural, and commercial consequence: Evidenced in her federal elections—her plans for promoting Manufactures, and the increase of her Exports.

NEW-JERSEY.

160 miles in length, and 52 in breadth, contained, by a Census in 1784, 149,435 inhabitants. This State is at present tranquil, although lately agitated by a very extraordinary contested election—which by a *timely* interference of the Executive, appears to be settled. The inhabitants of this State are warmly attached to the New Constitution—the blessings of peace, an equal trade, and good government, being properly prized by them. The Arts and Sciences are objects of importance in this State, and many of her sons rank high in the Republick of Letters.

PENNSYLVANIA,

288 miles in length, and 156 in breadth—by a Census in 1787, contained 360,000 inhabitants.—This extensive and truly respectable State, is making great proficiency in her Manufactures, Agriculture, Arts and Commerce. Her attachment to the New Constitution is unequivocal, and with a consistency highly honourary to her *national* character, she has lately made an effort, (which, though defeated for a time, will undoubtedly be successful) to conform their State Constitution to that of the Union. The publick buildings in the city of Philadelphia, have been respectfully offered for the accommodation of Congress. Theatrical exhibitions are now permitted by law—and the city has been incorporated: Experience will determine the eligibility of the two latter transactions.

DELAWARE,

92 miles in length, and 16 in breadth; by a Census in 1787, contained 37,000 inhabitants. This State, though circumscribed in its limits, derives great importance from its rank in the Union—attached to the New Constitution, and having the honour to take the lead in its adoption, there is no doubt of its giving efficacy to its righteous administration.

MARYLAND,

134 miles in length, and 110 in breadth, by a Census taken in 1782, contained 253,630 inhabitants. From its favourable situation in the Union, this State bids fair for prosperity, wealth, and eminence. Warmly attached to the New Constitution, and enjoying a central situation, the publications there have teemed with tempting inducements to Congress, to make Baltimore the Seat of the Federal Legislature.

VIRGINIA,

758 miles in length, and 224 in breath—by a census taken in 1782, contains 567,614 inhabitants.

From the natural ardour of her sons in the cause of freedom, is frequently convulsed in her elections, and has been torn by factions.—Possessing an extensive territory and a vast income, her funds are placed on a respectable footing; but as her representation in the federal legislature is decidedly attached to the union and the new constitution—there is now no doubt but that she will see her interest and glory finally connected with a few *temporary* sacrifices upon the principles of mutual concession.

SOUTH-CAROLINA,

200 miles in length, and 125 in breath—and contains, by a census in 1787, 180,000 inhabitants, an important member of the union, has appeared lately to vibrate between opposing sentiments—Her attachment to *national* measures we doubt not will evidentally discover itself when all *tender laws* and *pine barrens* shall be done away. The prohibition of the importation of slaves, and the provision lately made for the reduction of her foreign debt are federal traits—add to these that their electors have given an unanimous vote for his Excellency GENERAL WASHINGTON, as President of the United States—by which the memorable circumstance is authenticated, that the voice of the WHOLE CONTINENT has *once more* called our FABIUS MAXIMUS to rescue our country from impending ruin.

GEORGIA,

600 miles in length, and 250 in breath,—by a Census in 1787, contained 98,000 inhabitants. This state is compleating her federal character by conforming her state constitution to that of the union—and being the youngest branch of the family—and a frontier—she will doubtless experience the supporting and protecting arm of the federal government.

FOREIGN STATES.

RHODE-ISLAND,

Is 68 miles in length, and 40 in breath, and by a Census taken in 1783, contained 51,896 inhabitants. This state has again refused to accede to a union with her sister states, and is now wholly estranged from them; and from appearances, will long continue so, unless the measure of the iniquity of her "KNOW YE" gentry should be speedily filled up—or the delusion which has so long infatuated a majority of her citizens, should be removed.—Anxious of enjoying the protection of the union, the inhabitants of Newport, Providence and other places, are determined to sue for its protection, and to be annexed to Massachusetts or Connecticut. This dismemberment of the State it is to be desired, may be prevented by her being wholly graffed into that stock from whence through blindness she has been broken off.

NORTH-CAROLINA.

Is 758 miles in length, and 110 in breadth, and by a census taken in 1787, contained 270,000 inhabitants. A depreciated paper medium, and a deficiency of political knowledge, are considered as the causes of the anti-national spirit of this State. Her extensive frontier, and being obliged to export the greater part of her productions through Virginia, it is expected will ere long evince the necessity of her acceding to the confederation. This indeed appears already to be the predominant idea of her citizens, by some recent transactions.

NOTE.

Some of the foregoing Observations are transcribed from the Massachusetts Ma[illegible]*; an ingenious periodical publication of I. Thomas and Co. of Boston, now in the fourth month of its progress, as a Candidate for literary eminence, and publick patronage. The Enumeration of the Inhabitants of the several States, is taken from Morse's* AMERICAN GEOGRAPHY—*a new work just published, which from its* [illegible] *and important contents, should be introduced into the families of the United States.*

The first issue of John Fenno's *Federalist* newspaper

4

Founding
the New Nation

**Men who distrust the people and the future may overwhelm us
with their learning, but they do not impress us with their wisdom—thank God.**

—Gerald Johnson

During the Revolution the Tory had disappeared as a political factor in America, but two other groups now struggled for control of the government. One element consisted, for the most part, of citizens engaged in commerce, banking, manufacturing, and property management. Generally, this group—the Federalists—was more interested in preserving and extending its economic advantages than in risking social experiments. The other element was largely made up of the agrarian, small-farmer class, increasingly strengthened by the city wage earners, or "mechanics," as they were called, but with a significant leavening of intellectuals and political philosophers interested in social reform. They came to be known as the Anti-Federalists.

However, these two groups could not be easily separated on the basis of economic class alone; many Federalist and Anti-Federalist leaders actually came from the same social background. It would be inaccurate to portray their struggle over the shape of the Constitution in mainly economic terms. Conflicting ideas—about government, about power—fueled much of their debate. Anti-Federalists were deeply concerned about the power accorded to a distant government; they believed that a republican government had to stay close to the people in order to succeed and so emphasized state and local control. Federalists, on the other hand, felt a strong, centralized federal government was essential.[1]

At the end of the American Revolution, the people of the United States had a choice to make. They might continue to experiment with social change, endorsing the ideas that had been their battle cries. Or they might consolidate strength by making the right of property the fundamental consideration. Or they might work out some arrangements completely satisfactory to neither side but warranting mutual support. Between 1781 and 1788 the states operated under the laws outlined in the Articles of Confederation, the nation's first constitution. While the Confederation underscored the concept of national unity, it was clear from the beginning that Congress' inability to control the often rambunctious states showed the need for a more centralized form of government. The record of the Confederation gave the conservatives hope that public opinion might be swung to their side. The opportunity came with the proposal to draft a new national charter.

State legislatures sent the delegates to the Constitutional Convention at Philadelphia, and state assemblies were dominated by the property group. This was because the big commercial centers were strongholds of the Federalists, where land ownership and voting qualifications disfranchised many "mechanics," or laborers. It was therefore the citizens of means and community standing who brought about the fundamental change in government under the Constitution. They succeeded in placing financial power in the hands of a strong, central government. But they could not have their way entirely. They could not have obtained acceptance of the new charter by the people unless the authors had made concessions. The document they produced is a marvel of balanced forces.

THE BILL OF RIGHTS AND PRESS FREEDOM

One of the concessions made by the Federalists was the Bill of Rights. Offered as the first ten amendments, these articles have since been considered part of the Constitution in the sense that they were the price paid by the authors for the Anti-Federalist consent that made ratification of the document possible. By demanding the Bill of Rights, Linda Kerber writes, "Anti-Federalists forced the Federalists to confront the need for protection of minority rights, giving to the new political order perhaps its most distinctive and important characteristic."[2] However, the Constitution (as well as the Declaration of Independence) had its limits. Slavery was not openly an issue of contention during the Constitutional convention because that would have imperiled ratification by the southern states. Ultimately the Constitution left it up to the states to decide who should vote. State-maintained property qualifications for voting effectively disenfranchised women and slaves.

The first article of the Bill of Rights is of special interest to journalists. It provides that "Congress shall make no law respecting an establishment of religion, or prohibiting the free exercise thereof; or abridging the freedom of speech, or of the press; or the right of the people peaceably to assemble, and to petition the Government for a redress of grievances." This is the cornerstone of our press liberty, but there is evidence that the authors of the Constitution spent little time discussing this issue. James Madison's careful minutes of the convention show only casual and infrequent mention of the press.

But there was long precedent for the protection that finally was provided the press. British common law, as used in the various states, provided great freedom of expression for the times, even though it still recognized seditious libel laws. The same basic principles were stated in the Declaration of Rights written by John Dickinson when the First Continental Congress had convened in 1774. Nine of the 13 states had already provided such constitutional protection by 1787. The Virginia Bill of Rights of 1776 stated: "That freedom of the press is one of the great bulwarks of liberty, and can never be restrained but by despotick governments." Article XVI of the Massachusetts Bill of Rights of 1780 expressed similar sentiments, and other states used variations of this theme to establish the principle.[3]

This probably explains why the authors of the new national charter ignored the press issue. They assumed that full protection was already granted under the states. Charles Pinckney of South Carolina did present a draft of a constitution with a clause similar to the one eventually adopted, but apparently little attention was paid to his suggestion at that time.

It was soon clear, however, that the Constitution could not possibly succeed without concessions to public sentiment. Delegates from Massachusetts reported that it would be impossible to win ratification of the Constitution in that state without a clause concerning freedom of expression. Virginia could not muster enough votes for ratification until Governor Edmund Randolph called upon the framers to add the Bill of Rights. A constitutional committee was appointed to draft such a bill. The resolution was a modification of the Virginia document. Delegates were then told to return to their respective states and to use all influence available in mustering support for ratification of the main document on the promise that the Rights clauses would be included in the charter. It was on this understanding that New York finally approved the Constitution, but even so, it was not an easy victory for the Federalists, as the conservatives came to be known.

Because of promises given, the Bill of Rights was an important issue in the first session of Congress. Madison headed the committee charged with drafting the amendments. When his first draft was read out of committee, it stated: "no state shall violate the equal rights of conscience or of freedom of speech." The select committee to which the report was referred added "or of the press." Modified by House and Senate, the clause became the first amendment, as ratified in 1791.

THE FEDERALIST SERIES

Curiously, the press, which had to be protected as a concession to the public sentiment, was a tool of the Federalists in winning support for the charter they grudgingly admitted was the best document they could obtain in favor of their interests. The best exposition of the Federalist doctrine was a series of articles that first appeared in the semiweekly *New York Independent Journal* from October 1787 to April 1788. Reprinted throughout the country and later published in pamphlet and (with six new essays) in book form, these articles are known collectively as *The Federalist.*

The 85 articles were written for mass consumption, and they were effective enough that they soon gave their name to the party that was actually nationalist in doctrine rather than federalist.[4] Written hastily, much as daily editorials were written later, these are still read not only as revealing political studies but also as good literature. Alexander Hamilton wrote the largest number of Federalist articles over the pen name "Publius." Madison is believed to have written 29, some of which are the best in the series. John Jay, a noted New York state political leader, probably wrote a half dozen. In clear, concise style, *The Federalist* explained the philosophy of the Constitution party. The gist of this doctrine is described in the tenth, supposedly written by Madison. Madison stood somewhere between the two opposing leaders. He disapproved of Hamilton's financial and autocratic ideas, but he veered from his mentor, Thomas Jefferson, in sponsoring a stronger national government. Madison had attended all the meetings of the constitutional committee and had engineered many of the modifications in the document. Said he, in describing the form of government prescribed by the framers of the national charter, "justice must prevail [even] over a majority" to prevent the whims of an unstable public from wrecking the ship of state. This control would be accomplished through a republican form of government, offering protection to the masses, without direct control by them, as under a truly "democratic" system.

ALEXANDER HAMILTON, LEADER OF THE FEDERALISTS

The Federalist firmly established Alexander Hamilton as leader of the party that took the title of the series as its label. He saw himself as the Saint George of the anarchist dragon, fostered, he felt, by the radicalism and disorganization of the liberals. "We should be rescued from democracy," Hamilton insisted, and he looked forward to a restoration of an aristocracy, according to at least one of his biographers.[5] It has been suggested that Hamilton's respect for the aristocracy, and his continual seeking of recognition by those who valued heredity most highly, may have depended on the uncertainty of his paternity. But then why was he a Patriot in the Revolution, instead of a Tory? Born and reared to young manhood in the British West Indies, Hamilton became an American not so much out of hatred for the British social and political structure as out of contempt for British corruption and mismanagement.

That is why he fought for home rule, and there can be no doubt that he had strong feelings on the subject before the cause of revolution was generally endorsed. His war record was excellent. General Washington, who recognized Hamilton's virtues and who understood the youngster's faults (he was 18 at the time of Lexington and Concord), had a hard time keeping the fiery Patriot out of battle and behind the ledgers, where he was much more useful.

This was the man who led the Federalists. One cannot speak of him without indicating bias, one way or the other. In his day he was one of the most respected and reviled men in government. He had little knowledge of social forces. Never having lived the life of toil, he tended to dismiss the problems of the working people. He was quick to see that a government of fine phrases and glittering shibboleths was certain to be ineffective. He believed that the way to make government work was to let those with special interests in it control it, since they had most to lose by inept rule. Let those qualified take command, insisted Hamilton, who always imagined himself as the ideal soldier, ruling by command rather than by consultation.

Hamilton believed it his duty to establish the credit of the country by drastic financial measures, regardless of the luckless victims of an inadequate monetary system. He had no compassion for popular leaders such as Daniel Shays, the Massachusetts war veteran who led a hopeless revolt in 1786 against a taxation and hard money policy that threatened the very livelihood, to say nothing of the freedoms, of the small farmer. Hamilton saw the danger in such uprisings of the common people, and that was one reason he wished to rush through ratification of the Constitution, which he correctly predicted would solve many problems. But he would have taken care of the Shayses by force, rather than by placating the aggrieved. He admired military efficiency. Yet his life was to prove his genius not as a soldier but as a writer and political thinker. As Bowers says:

> He was a natural journalist and pamphleteer—one of the fathers of the American editorial. His perspicacity, penetration, powers of condensation, and clarity of expression were those of a premier editorial writer. These same qualities made him a pamphleteer without peer.[6]

This was the man who led the forces working for the ratification of the Constitution. Curiously, Hamilton did not like the document. It was a "shilly-shally thing of milk and water which could not last and was good only as a step to something better," he once said.[7] In some ways the Constitution was all too liberal for an admirer of aristocracy such as Hamilton. He sponsored it, however, by facing what he believed to be the facts. The document offered a means of drawing together the type of person Hamilton believed should control government. And although he disapproved of its populist concessions, he was shrewd enough to see that such compromise was essential, if any protection of property was to be imposed. When, on a summer day, he drifted slowly down the Hudson River on the New York packet and thereupon decided to subordinate his personal preferences in writing the first of *The Federalist* papers, he reached the height of his greatness. Had he accomplished nothing else in his lifetime, his services as a journalist that day would have justified his niche in the memory of fellow citizens.

THE FEDERALIST EDITORS: FENNO, WEBSTER, COBBETT, AND RUSSELL

The outstanding Federalist newspaper in the lush days of the party was the *Gazette of the United States*. Sponsored and supported by Hamilton, it was edited by John Fenno, who issued the first edition at the national capital, then in New York, April 15, 1789. With Fenno, who had been a schoolteacher, we are already beginning to see the development of the specialized journalist. Most of the previous editors and publishers had come up through the print shop, but Fenno established his reputation as a journalist without benefit of mechanical apprenticeship. Soon his paper was the acknowledged mouthpiece of the Federalist party, and it moved with the government when Philadelphia became the national capital in 1791.

Another powerful Federalist voice was that of Noah Webster, remembered for his dictionary but a man of many talents. Lawyer, pioneer weatherforecaster, translator, historian, economist, and scientific farmer, Webster was recognized in his day as a great editor. He started out as a lawyer and teacher. He was fascinated by words. His avocation resulted in his three-part *Grammatical Institute of the English Language*. The first part, the speller, appeared in 1784 and enjoyed a phenomenal sale—eventually 60 million copies were sold (not all within the author's lifetime, of course). Webster was in New York in 1793 to edit the daily *Minerva* and the semiweekly *Herald* (after 1797 known as the *Commercial Advertiser* and *Spectator,* respectively), as a supporter of Hamilton.

Webster was an articulate and intelligent interpreter of the Federalist program. He defended President Washington against the smear tactics of such editors as Philip Freneau and Benjamin Franklin Bache and stood firm for the party against opposition attacks. Webster was no mere party hack, however. He resented what he called the "betrayal" of President John Adams by Hamilton, the circumstances of which are described later. At any rate, the *Minerva* was an important organ in the Federalist attempt to regain control. Eventually Webster tired of politics, however, and returned to his old love: linguistics. He is remembered now for his dictionary, which appeared in preliminary form in 1803 and as a great contribution to lexicography in 1828.

Another great Federalist editor was William Cobbett, who was never an American at all but who offered severe criticism of the (Jeffersonian) Republicans and defended the Federalists between 1794 and 1800. Cobbett became a refugee in this country after exposing graft and corruption in the British army. He first showed his writing abilities in an attack on Joseph Priestley, whose scientific views were curiously related to his leftist political views. Encouraged by the success of his writing and sponsored by friends in the Federalist party, Cobbett gave up his modest tutoring position in 1797 to edit *Porcupine's Gazette and Daily Advertiser* in Philadelphia. He timed its appearance with the inauguration of John Adams.

In the short span of three years, Cobbett made a name for himself throughout the new country. He made no pretense of objectivity. His purpose was to expose his enemies, and his weapon was his vitriolic pen. Few editors in history have surpassed the British exile in

Benjamin Russell

Philip Freneau

sustained vituperation. His general theme was alliance with Britain, war against France, and perdition for Republicans. Tom Paine was his special target, and his biography of the Revolution's penman was all the more readable because Cobbett never let himself be restrained by the facts. In short, he had a marvelous time lampooning his enemies and their ideas. His pseudonym, "Peter Porcupine," appeared regularly after he "told off" a magazine editor in a pamphlet entitled *A Kick for a Bite.* A reviewer of the piece likened Cobbett to a porcupine, a creature with bristles that stand erect against those who try to manhandle it. That was just the creature Cobbett fancied himself as being, and he gloried in the name.

The oldest Federalist newspaper was Major Benjamin Russell's *Massachusetts* (later *Columbian*) *Centinel,* published in Boston. Russell had fought at Lexington as a lad of 13. He learned the printing trade under Isaiah Thomas and after serving his time as a journeyman founded his own paper in 1784. His first big crusade was his attempt to push his state toward ratification of the Constitution. That put him in the forefront of the forces that eventually rallied under the Federalist banner. Russell was pro-British, anti-French, an advocate of an American nobility, and later a hater of Jefferson. His paper followed the Federalist line 100 percent, but it also had excellent news coverage and enjoyed great prosperity.

THE FRENCH REVOLUTION

With such journalistic big guns trained upon their hapless opponents, the Federalists rapidly consolidated their power. Had it not been for the French Revolution, they might have annihilated the ideas for which many an American had fought. As Colonel Thomas W. Higginson wrote in his voluminous notes of the period, the French Revolution "drew a red hot plow share through the history of America."[8] Whereas America had triggered the

French upheaval after its own fight for freedom, the French were now repaying in kind—and just in time. The French influence stopped the American monarchists in their tracks. It destroyed the last hope of the aristocrats, and it changed the trend toward realliance with the British. It also provided the literature and philosophy needed as ammunition against the skillful journalistic batteries defending the Federalist citadel. All that was needed was a great leader. As usual in such emergencies, a great one emerged.

THOMAS JEFFERSON, ANTI-FEDERALIST

The hero of the Anti-Federalists was Thomas Jefferson, then Secretary of State in Washington's cabinet. Jefferson was the antithesis of his colleague, Hamilton, both in temperament and in ideology. The American yeoman, rather than the commercial person, was Jefferson's ideal of the sovereign citizen. He was convinced that no other people of the world were so well off as the independent, rural landowners of the United States. Having seen the wretchedness of European cities, he was all the more certain that the benefits of the American yeoman must be maintained. It should be pointed out, however, that Jefferson did not stand as tribune for all the groups made up of the common people. He distrusted the proletariat—the workers in the cities. The slum was his measurement of a sick society.

For Jefferson's purposes, a decentralized, states'-rights government was sufficient. Since credit, commerce, and manufacturing were subordinate matters to him, Jefferson would have been content with no more government than was necessary to preserve internal order. Hamilton stood for exactly the opposite. Thus, the Federalist leader insisted upon a *responsible* government—one that could protect property and aid commerce—whereas Jefferson was much more interested in a *responsive* government and was more concerned with the current needs of the people than with security.

PHILIP FRENEAU, JEFFERSON'S EDITOR

Philip Freneau, who helped to start the second, internal revolution, was a lifelong rebel. It is significant that he was of Huguenot extraction; the Huguenots had suffered for generations in the cause of religious freedom. Freneau was graduated from Princeton in 1771, when the college was a hotbed of sedition. Among the students who gathered in the room Freneau shared with James Madison were such "Radicals" as Harry Lee, Aaron Burr, and William Bradford, later a member of Washington's cabinet. Freneau was the most zealous Patriot of the lot. Long before the Revolution he was writing newspaper contributions and fierce poems on liberty. After Lexington and Concord, he took an active part in the conflict—a rather pathetic little man, pitting his feeble efforts uselessly, as it turned out, against the enemy. In disgust, he took to the sea in one of his father's ships.

He was in Bermuda when news arrived of the Declaration of Independence. Here was revolution he could understand. Freneau hurried home to take an active part in the movement. With Letters of Marque (licenses for a civilian to wage war) from the Continental Congress, he put his available resources into a privateer, a vessel he called the *Aurora.* The ship had to strike its colors in the first battle, and Freneau spent weary weeks in the notorious British prison hulks anchored in New York harbor—an experience that left him physically shattered and made him an even more implacable hater of the British. At length he was exchanged. Returning to New York sick and penniless, he turned to his last resource: his pen. Freneau's poem, "The Prison Ship," whipped apathetic Patriots into renewed efforts against the enemy. His account of the exploits of John Paul Jones instilled pride into a dejected nation.

By the end of the war he had given his health, his fortune, and all his soul to the cause of liberty. As he saw it, the sacrifice had been in vain. He charged his old leaders—Washington included—with failure to carry out the promises of 1776. He saw Jeffersonian Republicanism as a movement to carry on the original drives of the Revolution over the opposition of the Federalists.

It was Madison, Freneau's classmate, who brought the little rebel to Jefferson's attention. Madison had told the Anti-Federalist leader that Freneau was just the man to engage in journalistic jousting with such champions as Fenno and Russell. Jefferson was always considerate of the ideas of Madison, who was like a son to the master of Monticello. He offered Freneau a small subsidy as State Department translator if he would found an Anti-Federalist paper. It was not money that lured Freneau to the capital at Philadelphia, however. He saw himself as a journalistic crusader.

FRENEAU VS. FENNO: VITUPERATIVE PARTISANSHIP

And so it was that Freneau became editor of the *National Gazette* in 1791. The early editions were mild enough, but there were hints of what was to come. Fenno, his rival, would never have tolerated a phrase like "public opinion sets the bounds to every government, and is the real sovereign of every free one."[9] The four short columns of comment on page one of the *National Gazette* looked innocuous in those first few months, but while Fenno was ridiculing the right of plain citizens to complain against government officials, Freneau was telling his readers that "perpetual jealousy of the government" was necessary against "the machinations of ambition," and he warned that "where that jealousy does not exist in a reasonable degree, the saddle is soon prepared for the back of the people."[10]

Then one day Freneau discharged both barrels at Hamilton over the injustices of debt funding. He used the pen name "Brutus" that day, and at once the Federalist leader discovered he had a journalistic foe worthy of his steel. Day by day Freneau sent succeeding volleys after the first one, and his brashness encouraged other articulate voices to sound the call to battle stations. Even the less gifted Anti-Federalist editors could arouse readers now by picking up *National Gazette* "exchanges." The alarm of the Federalists was indicated by the torrent of abuse flowing from their editorial pens, but this, too, Freneau could return in double measure.

Freneau was so nettlesome that Hamilton made the mistake of joining in the fray personally, writing an unsigned article for Fenno's paper saying that an employee of the government should not be criticizing its policies. Freneau replied that the small stipend paid him in Jefferson's State Department did not muzzle him. Hamilton's identity as a writer being already revealed, he now accused Jefferson of being the real author of the *National Gazette*'s vilifications. The quarrel between the two cabinet officers had to be refereed by President Washington, but he found the breach beyond repair. Indeed, Washington was dismayed by "that rascal Freneau," as he called him, when he wrote such items as: "The first magistrate of a country . . . seldom knows the real state of the nation, particularly if he be buoyed up by official importance to think it beneath his dignity to mix occasionally with the people." Freneau considered Washington a fair target because, in the editor's opinion, the old general had lent his name as "front man" for Federalism.

In the end, it was neither the opposition nor the government that defeated Freneau. The *National Gazette* simply died of financial malnutrition. There were no "angels" to come to the rescue, as there had been for Fenno under Hamilton's sponsorship. Jefferson could offer some help, but when he left the cabinet in 1793, Freneau had virtually no financial support. When yellow fever drove his workers out of the city, Freneau closed the office. He never reopened it. The paper had lasted only two years, but it is doubtful if any other publication accomplished so much in that time. The end of the paper was just about the end of Freneau as a journalist, too. He tried his hand for a time in New Jersey and New York, but eventually he returned to the sea. Later, he was rediscovered as a poet.

BACHE AND THE *AURORA*

One of the leading journalists who carried the torch of Anti-Federalism dropped by Freneau was Benjamin Franklin Bache, the grandson of Benjamin Franklin. Bache was just 21 in 1790 when he founded the *Philadelphia General Advertiser,* better known as the *Aurora* (the name appeared in small print around the name plate). Bache was a mercurial young man—impetuous, brilliant, and often intemperate in expression. He was influenced by the style of Freneau, and his paper was even more violently partisan than the *National Gazette* had been. Too often he was downright vicious.

Not that the Federalists did not give him cause for his editorial mudslinging. He had seen the statue of his grandfather—one of the great men of the country—desecrated by hoodlums inspired to acts of vandalism by those opposed to the principles so ably enunciated by "Poor Richard" in Franklin's famous *Almanac.* Brought up in France and Switzerland by his doting grandfather, young Bache was sympathetic to the French cause from the beginning of his journalistic career. That put him in opposition to President Washington when the old war hero backed the anti-French party headed by Hamilton and others. Like Freneau, Bache resorted to personal attacks in his campaign to wreck the Federalist party. He even tried to besmirch the character of the "Father of His Country": "If ever a nation was debauched by a man, the American nation has been debauched by Washington," he wrote in the December 23, 1796, issue of the *Aurora.* Federalists wrecked the *Aurora* office and beat the editor in retaliation. Fenno caned Bache in the street, and Cobbett wrote of him in *Porcupine's Gazette:*

> This atrocious wretch (worthy descendant of old Ben) knows that all men of any understanding put him down as an abandoned liar, as a tool and a hireling, . . . He is an ill-looking devil. His eyes never get above your knees. He is of a sallow complexion, hollow-cheeked, dead eyed, and has a *toute ensemble* just like that of a fellow who has been about a week or ten days in a gibbet.[11]

Some historians have called this period the "dark ages of journalism," because of the scurrility of the press. This was a transition period, however, and perhaps violent partisanship, as reflected in the press, was a means of expending some of the venom stored up against the British after the war.[12] Adding to the tension was the war between Great Britain and revolutionary France. It was not easy for Americans to take the advice of Washington, who warned against entangling foreign alliances in the last hours of his administration.[13] The new nation had little to gain by taking sides, but unfortunately, the war was forced on the attentions of Americans by the belligerents.

The French and the British were about equally callous regarding American foreign policy. The "paper" blockades imposed by Napoleon violated international precedent, and American shipping interests were infuriated by the unlawful seizure of their vessels by the

French. But the British were annoying, too. They had fallen back on the "Rule of 1756," which forbade neutrals from trading in wartime with nations not ordinarily regular customers. This made sense to the British, for it was clear to them that otherwise the enemy could supply itself through adjoining neutral countries, despite the blockade. However, the enforcement of this rule threatened the development of American commerce.

THE ISSUE OF FRANCE

But the Federalists saw evil only in France. They were repelled by the excesses of the French Revolution and by the successes of Napoleon. Since the Federalists were in firm control of the government, they could manipulate foreign policy to favor the British. The Anti-Federalists argued that America had the duty of siding with France in the name of Rochambeau, Lafayette, and DeGrasse, who had come from France to help us win our war with Britain. Federalists answered that our promises of assistance to France in time of trouble had been made to a government since overthrown by a regime to which we had no binding ties. The fact is, the Federalists and Anti-Federalists were in conflict over the issue not because of persuasive logic but because of partisan bitterness.

Both sides found ammunition for their cause in the European issue. There was, for example, the case of "Citizen" Edmond Charles Genêt, minister to the United States from the French Republic. Genêt arrived in Charleston in the spring of 1793. Had he arrived in Boston he might have been sent home packing, but the South was Anti-Federalist territory, and on Genêt's month-long trip north, it was roses, roses all the way. By that time he was so certain he had public opinion behind him that when President Washington brushed off suggestions that the French be allowed to use American ports for refitting damaged war vessels, Genêt went right ahead with his plans. Washington was correct in slapping down such a presumptuous guest of the country, and the people, as a whole, approved. The Federalists used the incident to discredit their pro-French opponents.

Even more embarrassing to the Anti-Federalists was the so-called XYZ Affair, in which it appeared that the unscrupulous French foreign minister, Talleyrand, had informed American diplomats that he would receive them as accredited ministers only after they had paid him a bribe. It was very difficult to defend pro-French sentiment in the face of such raw insults to national pride.

On the other hand, the Anti-Federalists were collecting a few rocks to throw at their enemies, too. Genêt's mistake hurt the Anti-Federalist cause in one way, but it did show how many Americans were opposed to Federalist policy. Many a timid Republican was thus encouraged to enlist in Jefferson's party. The treaty signed by John Jay in 1794 was also used against the Federalists. "Jay's Treaty" was an attempt to get the British to meet agreements negotiated during the Treaty of Paris, which ended the War of Independence. It did get the British out of the frontier forts that they had promised to evacuate, but nothing was settled about impressment of American seamen, which irritated many Americans, especially those doomed to the harsh life of the British Navy.

Partisan feeling was running high when John Adams took the oath of office as the second president of the United States, after the election of 1796. With the Federalists in firm control, the administration began to prepare for war with France. Congress dutifully authorized an army of 35,000, which was a larger force than Washington had ever had at his disposal during the Revolution. Two new superfrigates, the *United States* and the *Constitution,* were laid down as part of the war program. To pay for these items Congress levied a tax that fell particularly heavily on the small landowner, who was least interested in foreign wars.

The result was a political and journalistic battle that passed all the bounds of decency. Even during the Revolution, when Tory and Patriot clawed at each other, there had never been such a caterwaul. Bache and Fenno carried their personal feud beyond the pages of their papers by engaging in a street brawl. "Peter Porcupine" (William Cobbett) brought invective to finest flower by attacking well-known Anti-Federalists, living and dead. It should be noted that the bulk of the party press was basically conventional and contributed to the orderly development of the political party system.

THE ALIEN AND SEDITION ACTS OF 1798

This was the situation when the administration tried to throttle such violent opposition in the summer of 1798. In June and July of that year, Congress passed the Alien and Sedition Acts. One was a law aimed at troublesome foreigners living in the country; the other concerned the muzzling of irritating editors.

There were then about 25,000 aliens in the United States. Many of them were refugees from stern authorities in their homelands, and they therefore tended to be on the side of the Jeffersonians, who believed in as little government as possible. Others were poor, or at least had no property, and again such persons were more likely to gravitate into the ranks of the Anti-Federalists. Groups such as the Irish immigrants were by tradition opposed to the British and so could not possibly see any good in the Hamiltonian policy of British appeasement. There were also many intellectuals in this category. Dr. Joseph Priestley, the discoverer of oxygen and seven other gases, was a British expatriate noted for his leftist views. The Du Ponts, at that time aggressive backers of liberalism, brought French ideas into the platform of the Anti-Federalists. And there was Albert Gallatin, destined to be a great secretary of the Treasury under Jefferson, who was already making a name for himself in Pennsylvania, despite his difficulty in adjusting to a country so different from his native Switzerland. Men like these were almost certain to be opposed to the administration. The Alien Act, it was hoped, would reduce the ranks of threatening foreigners. One provision of the law was an extension of the naturalization period from 5 to 14 years. Another clause empowered the president to deport aliens he judged to be subversive (a power Adams did not actually employ).

The Sedition Act was an obvious attempt to control the journalistic spokespeople of the Anti-Federalists. It declared:

> That if any person shall write, print, utter, or publish . . . any false, scandalous, and malicious writing . . . against the government of the United States, or either house of the Congress . . . or the said President . . . or to excite against them the hatred of the good people of the United States . . . or to resist or oppose, or defeat any such law . . . shall be punished by a fine not exceeding two thousand dollars, and by imprisonment not exceeding two years.[14]

The laws were to stand for two years. It should be pointed out that this was a time when the new nation was still sorting out the range and limits of free speech; furthermore, the concept of legitimate opposition in politics was developing only slowly.[15]

One of the cornerstones of press freedom is the right to express criticism of government and its administrators freely. The Alien and Sedition laws reversed a process that had made America the envy of the oppressed. And yet there were important contributions in the laws. Nor have their repressive features been properly appraised in many accounts of the period. The original bill called for a declaration of war with France. The clauses that followed imposed penalties on all who gave any aid or comfort to this enemy. At the last minute, the war declaration was defeated by a narrow margin, but the following clauses concerning aliens and the press were allowed to stand. That was why all pro-French sentiment was so ruthlessly attacked by the administration.

And in some ways the Sedition Act can be called a milestone on the road to freedom of the press. The law did not forbid criticism of the government. It only attempted to curb malicious and false statements published to defame officials. And it provided a pair of safeguards: truth could be offered as a defense, and the jury could determine both the law and the fact. This was the twin argument made by Andrew Hamilton in the John Peter Zenger trial. Now it was enacted into the law of 1798.[16]

At first glance, the Sedition Act may appear to merit support. But experience has shown time and again that the party in power will inevitably abuse such controls in the interest of expediency. It was so in 1798. President Adams, an honest man despite his political ineptitude, did what he could to modify the bill. Unfortunately, extremists had taken over control, and they were intent on revenge for all the indignities heaped upon them by opposition editors. Fearful for their personal safety, Jefferson and his friends gathered at Monticello and planned the Virginia and Kentucky Resolutions, affirming the right of states to nullify federal actions. Missing in 1798 was the far better safety valve of "judicial review," or the right of the United States Supreme Court to declare a legislative act unconstitutional. Not until 1803 did John Marshall establish that court function in *Marbury* v. *Madison.* Having taken the only available course, Jefferson then sat back to await the next step.

SEDITION ACT PROSECUTIONS

The Adams administration played right into his hands. The Federalists abused the new laws so openly that for a time freedom of the press was seriously threatened in America. It was far from being the "reign of terror" charged by the opposition, but the record is not one of which Americans can be proud. Timothy Pickering, the secretary of state, spent half his time reading Anti-Federalist papers so that he could ferret out violators of the law.

One of the victims of the Sedition Act was Matthew Lyon of Vermont. Born in Ireland, Lyon had landed in America as an indentured servant. He had worked his way up to a position of respect and prestige in his community and was the representative to Congress from his state. Lyon was one of the famous "Green Mountain Boys" in the War of Independence. Cashiered from the army for an act that should have earned him a medal, he was later reinstated and promoted to the rank of colonel.

One afternoon in the House of Representatives, Roger Griswold, a leading Federalist from that citadel of Federalism, Connecticut, made insulting remarks about Lyon's war record. The Vermonter ignored Griswold at first, but when his colleague grasped his coat and repeated the insult, Lyon replied in the uncouth but effective manner of the frontier— he spat in Griswold's eye. The next day Griswold walked up to Lyon's desk in the House and began beating him with a cane. Lyon grabbed a handy pair of fire tongs and beat back his adversary. The Federalists tried to expel Lyon from the House but failed to muster the needed two-thirds vote.

The Sedition Act was used to settle scores with such persons. The crime charged against Lyon under the act was the publication of a letter to an editor accusing President Adams of "ridiculous pomp, foolish adulation, and selfish avarice." For such remarks, Lyon was hauled before a Federalist judge, who sentenced the defendant to four months in jail and a fine of $1000. The vindictiveness of the judge was indicated by the fact that although the trial was held in Rutland, Vermont, where there was a passable jail, Lyon was condemned to a filthy cell at Vergennes, some 40 miles distant. Thousands of local citizens signed a petition requesting parole for the prisoner. It was ignored. When editor Anthony Haswell printed an advertisement in his *Vermont Gazette* announcing a lottery to raise money for paying the fine, he, too, was hustled off to jail for abetting a "criminal."

The Federalists should have heeded the warning, for the public reaction to such injustice was positive and immediate. Lyon was jailed in October 1798, convicted by what he called a packed jury of political opponents. In December he was reelected to the House by a two-to-one vote over his closest opponent. Freed in February 1799, after money had flowed in to pay his fine, the Vermonter returned in triumph to the capital at Philadelphia. At one time the procession behind his carriage was 12 miles long.

The persecutions under the Alien and Sedition Acts have sometimes been described as insignificant. In all, there were 14 indictments under the Sedition Act. Eleven trials resulted, with 10 convictions. During the same time span there were at least 5 other convictions for seditious libel under the provisions of British common law in state or federal courts. Eight of the convictions involved newspapers.[17] Whatever the numbers, the uproar over the prosecutions was enough to make it clear that the states had erred during the Revolution in enacting laws perpetuating the concept of seditious libel. What caught a Tory then caught a Republican now. There were a few more seditious libel cases after 1800, but the example of the Sedition Act proved conclusive. People saw that the test of tyranny is not necessarily the number of prosecutions but the number of men and woman restrained from speaking freely because of fear.

THE END OF THE BATTLE

By 1800 the battle was over. Fenno and Bache both died in the terrible yellow fever epidemic that scourged Philadelphia in the summer of 1798, while Bache was still under indictment. Freneau, driven out by the fever, never reestablished his *Gazette.* Cobbett had left the country, following a libel suit that forced him into bankruptcy.

On the whole, the press improved after the leading character assassins were silenced in one way or the other. The widow Bache married her husband's assistant, William Duane, whose wife had died of the fever. The *Aurora* continued to back Jefferson and his party, but it was much more reasonable in tone under Duane. He was as courageous as Freneau, without Freneau's shrillness and bad taste. He was as colorful in his writing as Cobbett, but without Cobbett's recklessness. Duane suffered for the cause, along with other Anti-Federalists: he was beaten by hoodlums. He was also arrested under the Sedition Act.

The party battle in the House over the Sedition Act continued after the close 44–41 passage vote in 1798. Attempts were made to amend or repeal it in 1799 and again in 1800. In February 1801, a Federalist effort to extend it two more years was defeated 53–49, with 6 Federalists from the South deserting the party to join all 47 supporters of the new President Jefferson. The law expired March 3, 1801, under its own terms and was the last federal sedition law until the wartime of 1917. Jefferson promptly pardoned all those in jail and canceled remaining trials.[18]

The removal of the national capital from Philadelphia to Washington ended an epoch and began a new one, for with the move there had been a complete change in party and administration control, too. In the election year of 1800, Federalists were dominant in the House, the Senate, the presidency, the cabinet, the courts, the churches, business, and education. Up to four-fifths of the newspapers opposed Jefferson and his party. Yet Jefferson won.

A close student of the press of the early national period, Professor David Sloan, argues that its newspapers should not be judged by present-day standards of nonpartisanship because their overriding purpose was to serve a partisan cause. They shaped their news and opinion to condition the faithful for political action. Sloan perceives this party press as one that enjoyed widespread approval by both the public and journalists, and one that contributed to the stabilization of the political party system that was vital to the growth of the new country.

But, Sloan continues, the two major parties and their press supporters played starkly contrasting roles. The Federalists generally were supporters of traditional values and defenders of a disappearing political and social style. The Anti-Federalists reflected contemporary or emerging conditions, and advocated chances toward greater political freedom and widespread participation by the "people."[19] The dominant Federalist press chose to defend its status quo position by attacking Jefferson and his press supporters as subversive radicals—a tactic common to conservatives in any age. The effort failed by 1800.

As the historian Arthur M. Schlesinger, Jr., has written: "When a party starts out by deceiving the people, it is likely to finish by deceiving itself."[20] Since there is good evidence that this statement is true, the press, as demonstrated in this chapter, is more essential than ever in its role of disclosing party deceptions, for without such disclosures the vast majority of the public would not remain free long. Unfortunately, men had to suffer before this was generally understood—men like Lyon, Bache, Duane, and Thomas Adams of the *Boston Independent Chronicle*. Adams and his brother, Abijah, refused to be intimidated by their Federalist persecutors in 1798, although prison and worse confronted them. Sick and near death, Thomas Adams answered his detractors in double-space, double-measure Caslon bold type: "The Chronicle is destined to persecution. . . . It will stand or fall with the liberties of America, and nothing shall silence its clarion but the extinction of every principle which leads to the achievement of our independence."[21]

5

Westward Expansion

**I have lent myself willingly as the subject of a great experiment
. . . to demonstrate the falsehood of the pretext that freedom of the
press is incompatible with orderly government.**

—Thomas Jefferson to Seymour

Jefferson's victory in 1800 made his party subject to the same type of attack that had so recently been launched against the Federalists while they were in power. The Jeffersonian "Republicans" had gained control of the administration, but the president estimated that up to three-fifths of the newspaper editors continued to support Federalist policies. In some areas Federalist newspapers outnumbered their political rivals by as much as five to one. The rank-and-file voters were not impressed by this "one-party" press, apparently, for they continued to return to office a long succession of candidates representing the Republican party (as the Anti-Federalists became known before eventually adopting the name Democratic party).

The disparity between public and editorial opinion in the periods of Jefferson and Andrew Jackson, and of Franklin Roosevelt and Harry Truman, has concerned students of the press. They point to the occasions when overwhelming popular mandates coincided with preponderant press opposition to the popular cause, and critics sometimes wonder if the American press is the power the journalists say it is. This history indicates that the power of the press is not in its persuasion by opinion, but in its dissemination of information and its arousal of interest in issues, whether important or superficial.

THE *NEW YORK EVENING POST,* 1801

One of the important Federalist organs was founded by Alexander Hamilton a year after the defeat of this party in 1800. The Federalist leader believed that a reputable party paper

National Intelligencer.

was needed more than ever to stem the tide of Republican popularity. The result was the *New York Evening Post,* destined to become the city's oldest newspaper. Hamilton chose William Coleman as the first editor. That Coleman was a lawyer and former court reporter again indicates the trend of journalism since the days when the printer-editor was the rule. He was an able editor, but while "the General," as Hamilton liked to be called, was around, it was plain to all that Coleman was subordinate in the office.

Coleman was, nonetheless, a writer of some literary pretensions. He could express his convictions in a slashing style that often cut down wavering opposition within and without the party. He had also had great personal charm and courage. Eventually, Coleman broke with Hamilton because of his loyalty to Aaron Burr,[1] but in the founding days of the *Post,* Coleman did not make an editorial move without consulting his sponsor. It is significant that Coleman was a shorthand expert, and that was one reason he had been selected by Hamilton. Late at night Coleman could have been seen in the empty streets hurrying to the home of the Federalists' great leader to take dictation for the next day's editorials. These editorials needed no reworking: they were the work of Hamilton at his journalistic best. Picked up by Federalist editors around the country, they exerted an important party influence. Rival party papers appeared in new western settlements, serving as spokespersons for the Federalists and Republicans and nationalizing the tendency toward two major parties (later to emerge as the Republicans and Democrats).

The victorious party in 1800 needed opposition, as does any party in power. Jefferson had committed himself frequently as a believer in press freedom. His party had fought against the Alien and Sedition Acts in accordance with this doctrine. He had sponsored and encouraged the Virginia and Kentucky Resolutions as attacks on press restrictions by the Federalists. He had helped Freneau and Thomas Ritchie establish newspapers to attempt to stem the tide of Federalist dominance.[2] Now, after his party's victory, he found himself accused of press restrictions by the Federalists. This is a pattern commonly found in the history of American journalism—the reversal of free-expression policies once a group wins power.

JEFFERSON'S VIEW OF THE PRESS

Jefferson appears to have been sincere in his defense of a free press. Even when the press humiliated him, he defended its freedom. Wrote Jefferson to his friend Carrington in 1787:

> I am persuaded that the good sense of the people will always be found to be the best army. They may be led astray for a moment, but will soon correct themselves. The people are the only censors of their governors; and even their errors will tend to keep these to the true principles of their institution. To punish these errors too severely would be to suppress the only safeguard of the public liberty. The way to prevent these irregular interpositions of the people, is to give them full information of their affairs through the channel of the public papers, and to contrive that those papers should penetrate the whole mass of the people. The basis of our government being the opinion of the people, the very first object should be to keep that right; and were it left to me to decide whether we should have a government without newspapers, or newspapers without a government, I should not hesitate a moment to prefer the latter.

This part of Jefferson's letter to Carrington is widely quoted. But the second part of his letter is not so well known, though it is a qualification essential to the preceding statement. The great statesman went on to say:

> But I should mean that every man should receive those papers, and be capable of reading them.

Later, when the Federalist editors had made life miserable for him, he wrote in exasperation to a friend:

> The newspapers of our country by their abandoned spirit of falsehood, have more effectually destroyed the utility of the press than all the shackles devised by Bonaparte.[3]

But that was in 1813, when Jefferson was very tired. His more considered views of the vicious opposition press are better summed up in the following 1802 letter:

> They [Federalists] fill their newspapers with falsehoods, calumnies, and audacities. . . . We are going fairly through the experiment of whether freedom of discussion, unaided by coercion, is not sufficient for the propagation and protection of truth, and for the maintenance of an administration pure and upright in its actions and views. . . . I shall protect them in the right of lying and calumniating.[4]

Although Jefferson's views on the press were well known to his followers, and although he wielded strong control over his party, he could not keep his subordinates from trying to impose restrictions on opposition editors, now that the Jeffersonians were in power.

An example of this vindictiveness was the prosecution of Joseph Dennie for remarks deemed by Republican party leaders to be seditious. Dennie, a grandson of Bartholomew Green, Jr., onetime printer of the *Boston News-Letter,* was one of the ablest editors of his day. His *Farmer's Weekly Museum,* published at Walpole, New Hampshire, was so popular that it achieved national recognition. Later, Dennie took over the editorial direction of the *Port Folio,* an outspoken Federalist magazine published in Philadelphia. Shortly after Jefferson moved into the unfinished White House, Dennie wrote a series of editorials pointing out the weaknesses of popular rule. Although he did not attack the American government specifically, he made it clear that he believed democracy to be futile. These remarks were declared by government officials to be seditious, and the editor was indicted on that charge. After all that Jefferson had written about the press as a rightful censor of its government, the administration action appeared to be highly hypocritical. The jury must have thought so, too, for after a brilliant defense by Joseph Hopkinson, composer of the Patriot song, "Hail Columbia," Dennie was acquitted.

The most celebrated case involving the press during this period was prosecuted under a state law, as recommended by the president. The defendant was Harry Croswell, editor of a Federalist paper at Hudson, New York. Croswell called his little weekly *The Wasp,* and it stung political opponents in every column. One day Croswell reported that Jefferson had paid James Callender, a Richmond editor, to spread the word that George Washington had been a robber, traitor, and perjurer. This was a serious charge against Jefferson and the dignity of his office. Croswell was indicted in 1804. He was found guilty, but appealed the case.

When the trial was called, a titan arose to argue for the defense. He was Alexander Hamilton, Jefferson's arch rival. The four judges listened with obvious respect. The press, Hamilton argued, had "the right to publish with impunity truth, with good motives, for justifiable ends, though reflecting on Government, Magistracy, or individuals." Since the "good motives" and "justifiable ends" would have to be disproved by the complainant, Hamilton was essentially saying that truth, and truth alone, was a defense in a libel action. It so happened that Hamilton lost the case, because the four judges were evenly divided in their opinions. Hamilton also had insisted on the right of a jury to determine both the law and the fact. Both issues had been raised in the Zenger case, but only in Pennsylvania had they been recognized in law (in 1790).

The significance of the Croswell trial can be seen in legislation immediately following Hamilton's plea. Even before the judges had handed down the verdict, a bill was introduced in the New York Legislature providing that truth thereafter was to be admitted in defense. The same bill gave the jury the right to determine both the law and the fact. By 1805, these principles had become law in New York—70 years after Zenger's trial. Soon other states followed suit and the shadow of the British common law of seditious libel was lifted. In 1812 the Supreme Court held that the federal government could not prosecute under the old law.

Hamilton did not live to see his eventual triumph. A remark attributed to Hamilton that appeared in an Albany newspaper while the Croswell case was being tried angered New York's second most imposing political figure—Aaron Burr. He challenged Hamilton to a duel. Hamilton might have declined with no great blackening of his honor, but he accepted the gage. On July 11, 1804, his seconds rowed him across the Hudson River to the grassy bank near Weehawken, where his son had been killed in a duel several months before. Burr was an expert marksman, and in the exchange of shots he wounded Hamilton so critically that the great leader died the next day.

GROWTH OF THE PRESS: FIRST DAILIES

The first daily newspaper in America was established by Benjamin Towne in Philadelphia in 1783. His *Pennsylvania Evening Post* was as characterless as its publisher. Towne was a Patriot in 1776 and was one of the first to print the Declaration of Independence for the public. Later, he became a Tory. After the surrender he confessed his sins and reattained a partial state of grace in his community. However, this little mediocre daily lasted only 17 months.

It was succeeded by a very good daily, the *Pennsylvania Packet and Daily Advertiser,* published by the partnership of John Dunlap and David C. Claypoole. Like Towne's *Evening Post,* the *Packet* was originally a weekly publication that had been founded by Dunlap in 1771. Switching from triweekly to daily status in 1784, the Dunlap and Claypoole venture was successful from the beginning. The first American daily in a foreign language was the *Courrier Français* published in Philadelphia between 1794 and 1798, one of several short-lived French papers that appeared while American loyalties were divided between France and England.

By 1800, most big American ports and commercial centers were supporting daily papers: Philadelphia had six; New York, five; Baltimore, three; and Charleston, two. But for some curious reason Boston, the home of the American newspaper, had no daily paper at this time. Many of these publications had been forced into the daily field to meet the competition of the coffeehouses, where the London papers were available and where news was freely exchanged. The American journalists met the challenge by issuing first semiweekly, then triweekly, and finally daily editions.

Philadelphia even had an all-day newspaper for a time. It was the *New World,* published by Samuel Harrison Smith in morning and evening editions. It was not successful, but it indicated the growing interest in fresh news presentation. Of 512 papers being printed in 1820, 24 were dailies, 66 were semiweeklies or triweeklies, and 422 were weeklies. They were still generally slanted toward the more prosperous citizens, for the price was more than the average person could afford. Circulations were not impressive; one of 1500 was considered adequate in all but the largest centers.

In the hinterlands the press was also booming. The number of newspapers beyond the urban fringe increased sixfold during this period.[5] Advertising helped to support this newspaper boom, because although most families tended to buy their supplies in whole-sale lots for seasonal storage, there was already some development of the retail trade that was to sustain the press in later years. The development of the postal system also accounted for some of this expansion. By the postal acts of 1782 and 1792, educational and informational matter could be mailed at very low rates.

THE PRESS MOVES WESTWARD

The expansion of the press reflected the spirit of the country. It had taken 150 years to settle the seaboard colonies, and on the basis of that record, it should have taken another 200 years to push the frontier to the Mississippi River. But once the Appalachian Mountains were conquered, the lands to the west were rapidly taken up. In 1803 Jefferson, who had always opposed national imperialism, had a chance to purchase the vast Louisiana Territory, and the bargain was too good to turn down on principle. When this domain was added to the United States as a vast territory for exploitation, settlers poured in from the East. The lust for western lands is indicated by the numerous petitions for statehood during this period: between 1790 and 1820, nine new states joined the Union.

The waterways were the highways into these frontier regions. Along the Ohio, Kanawha, and Cumberland rivers, tiny communities began to appear that would some day become teeming cities. By present standards they were mere hamlets, but each served a wide trading area. They were thus far more important as markets and social centers than their populations alone indicate. If they were county seats, with courts, law-enforcing agencies, and land offices, they were even more important. And usually among the first to set up shop in such communities were the frontier printer-editors. They were the enthusi-astic promoters of the villages that they were certain would one day rival London. They were leading businesspeople. But most of all they were the people who, more than any-one else, knit the communities into organizations that could begin to bring civilization to the remote areas.

The first newspaper in this new West was John Scull's venture of 1786, the *Pitts-burgh Gazette,* which is still printing as the *Post-Gazette.* A year later, John Bradford, who bore a name well known in the printing industry although he was only indirectly related to the famous Philadelphia publishing family, set up his shop in Lexington, Kentucky. His *Kentucky Gazette* might have been the first paper in the West, had his equipment not been wrecked in transit the year before the establishment of the Pittsburgh enterprise. By 1800, 21 newspapers had been started west of the mountains. The Ohio River was the most im-portant artery of commerce in this early period, but there were also important settlements, and newspapers, along the Wabash and lesser streams, such as the Muskingum, Scioto, Maumee, and Cuyahoga.

Advertising was rarely adequate to support the news business, but fortunately there needed to be some means of publishing legal information in this new area, and that was often sufficient inducement to start up a paper. Elihu Stout, for example, poled himself up the Wabash with his press to found the *Indiana Gazette* at Vincennes in 1804. He had been in-duced to give up his business in Frankfort, Kentucky, on the promise that he would be awarded the territorial legal printing contract—enough of a stake for him to establish a paper.

The northern route to the frontier was along the Mohawk Valley, straight across New York State from the Hudson River. This was the route of the Erie Canal, which was soon to make New York City the largest metropolis in the land, but even before that, it was an important highway. At the end of the valley, the Great Lakes served as transportation and

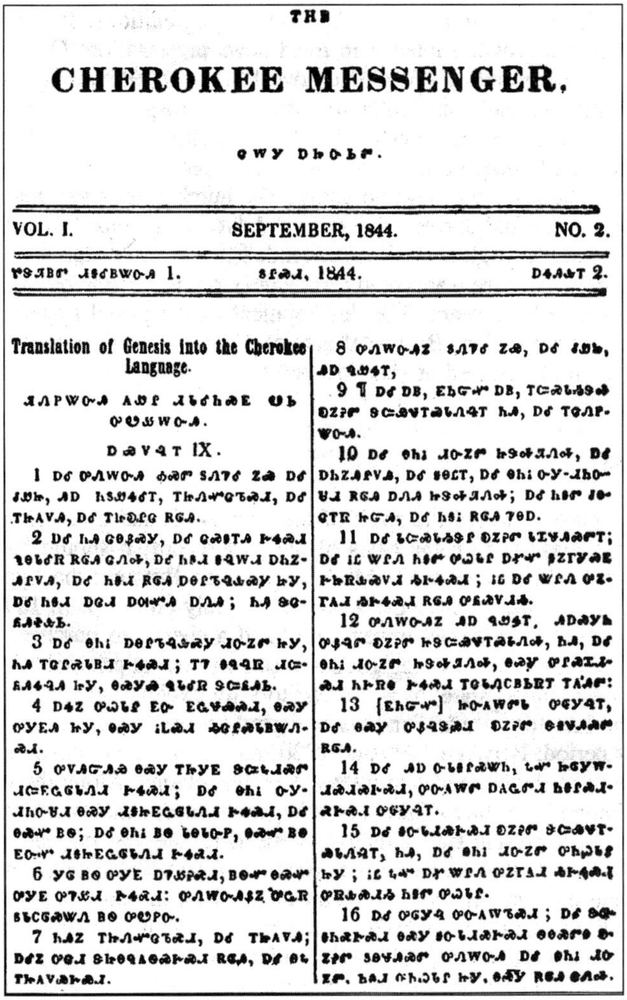
THE

CHEROKEE MESSENGER.

VOL. I. SEPTEMBER, 1844. NO. 2.

Translation of Genesis into the Cherokee Language.

One of the first publications for Native Americans

communication routes between the vast wilderness and the East. Detroit, one of the outer bastions of the frontier then, had a newspaper, the *Gazette,* by 1817. Soon other communities in the area could boast the same. A congressional act of 1814 provided that all federal laws must be printed in two (later, three) newspapers in each state and territory. This was a logical way of letting electors know what their representatives were doing, but it also encouraged the founding of pioneer papers in communities not quite ready to support such ventures.[6]

The first New Orleans paper, begun in 1794, was the *Moniteur de la Louisiane,* a four-page edition for the French population living under Spanish control. It lasted until 1814. The first Spanish-language newspaper in the United States was *El Misisipí,* founded by the English-speaking firm of William H. Johnson in 1808 in New Orleans, the city linking the new nation with Spanish-speaking countries. *El Misisipí* was published for two years in Spanish and English. Texas's first paper, *La Gaceta,* appeared in 1813. Another early Texas paper was *El Mexicano.* These early Spanish-language papers reported the wars between Spain and its colonies and the divisions between groups seeking power.

A few years later, in 1828, the Cherokee Nation had founded the first Native American newspaper, the *Cherokee Phoenix,* in Georgia. Editor Elias Boudinot printed four pages, partly in English and partly in Cherokee, using an 86-character alphabet devised by Sequoyah. Boudinot, a Cherokee schoolteacher, published Cherokee laws, spelling lessons, news, and his own observations, 20 of which were reprinted in *Niles' Weekly Register,* a widely read compilation of speeches and documents. Boudinot resigned in 1832 and the paper finally died in 1834. It was followed by the *Cherokee Advocate,* authorized by the Cherokee National Council in 1843. The bilingual weekly, edited by Princeton-educated William P. Ross, son of Cherokee chief John Ross, was published from 1844 to 1853 in Oklahoma. Baptist missionaries, who had printed the *Shawnee Sun* in Native American dialect in Kansas in 1835, printed 12 issues of the bilingual *Cherokee Messenger* in magazine format in Oklahoma from 1844 to 1846.[7]

THE FRONTIER NEWSPAPER

The flimsy little weeklies of the isolated villages and booming river towns had much to do with the crystallization of public opinion that made the West a new factor in American politics. What were they like, these newspapers that exerted such influence in the West? On the whole, they were small, hand-set, scrubby publications. It is apparent that there was no place on them for large staffs, regular correspondents, or columnists furnishing opinions for readers too busy to form their own. There was plenty of opinion, of course, but most if it was contributed by readers. Usually there was a column or two of local news, sometimes printed as scattered items without benefit of headlines. There might be half a column of exchanges or news gleaned from other newspapers arrived by the last post. The remaining material, exclusive of the notices, or advertisements, was very likely submitted by readers. Every subscriber who could wield a pen sooner or later appeared in the columns. All the aggrieved wrote out their pet complaints for the pages of the local mercury. Even government officials participated in this exchange, not always openly, true, but with sufficient identity to warrant spirited replies. Often this material was strident and in bad taste. "Straight news" tended toward distortion, flamboyance, and vindictiveness. But whatever its faults, it was a robust, colorful press. The great French observer, Alexis de Tocqueville, described the institution at a somewhat later period, but his remarks are pertinent to this decade. He was impressed by the virility of the American press even while repelled by its provincialism. Western crudeness shocked him, but he was amazed at the success of the democratic experiment, and he conceded that the press had been an important implement in this development. Tocqueville found a close relationship between the press and its public, fostered, no doubt, by the active participation of readers in the local journalistic effort. The public appeared to respect the Fourth Estate, he reported, and this was manifest in the great freedom accorded the institution.

By the end of the first decade of the nineteenth century, the western press was lusty and influential. Editors and politicians who understood their constituencies saw that the region had its special problems. They tended to side with the Jeffersonians on the rights of the common people, but their dependence on the federal government to defend their settlements in the Native American territories made them favor strong, centralized administration.

THE INFLUENCE OF THE WEST

The new states also turned to the federal government for the development of transportation, so essential to their growth and prosperity. Again, the great land companies, organized to promote colonization at a profit, were dependent on the national administration rather than on the territorial or parent-state politicians. There was a tendency, then, for the westerners to demand local and statewide autonomy to work out their destinies; they visualized government as a kind of public-service corporation, not as a dispenser of privileges for the wealthy and powerful. Under the Northwest Ordinances, land was set aside to be sold for educational revenue. Suffrage was likely to be broader than in more settled regions; property might be a voting requisite, but it was easy to acquire.

The West certainly influenced the development of the new nation. But the importance of that influence has been disputed since Professor Frederick Jackson Turner suggested in 1893 that the frontier was a political and social laboratory that had produced a distinctive American national character (whose traits include love of independence and democracy, hardiness and self-reliance, and a strong sense of community).[8] Most historians today reject the Turner thesis, noting, for example, that Turner ignored the presence of many people in the West, including women, Native Americans, and nonwhites in general. The attention of contemporary historians focuses more on the conflict and the cultural interplay and exchange that occurred among the West's many different peoples. And ecological historians are paying attention to the West's physical environment (especially its aridity), looking at how it shaped and was shaped by both human and nonhuman inhabitants.[9]

THE WAR OF 1812

The War of 1812 reflects little of merit on either of the belligerents. We do not like to be reminded of General William Hull's abject surrender to an inferior British and Native American force at Detroit or the burning of our national capitol by the British. There were heroic episodes, too, such as Commodore Oliver Hazard Perry's useless naval victory on Lake Erie;[10] the courageous but futile sea battles of American naval vessels and privateersmen against the world's greatest sea power; and General Andrew Jackson's victory at New Orleans on January 8, 1815, two weeks *after* the peace had been signed at Ghent.[11]

An early view attributed great power to Western newspapers in influencing public opinion to support the War of 1812, but voting analysis demonstrates that the vote for the war reflected partisan rather than sectional influence.[12] Most contemporary historians agree that British policies posed both a spiritual and a material challenge to the new country.[13]

GOVERNMENT REPORTING: THE *NATIONAL INTELLIGENCER*

The most important press development at this time was in government reporting. The right to report meetings of interest to the general public is one of the tests of a free press, by the English-American concept. Reporters had access to the national House of Representatives from April 8, 1789, two days after it was established. For a time the Senate was more secretive, since it excluded not only reporters but also members of the House from its debates. By December 9, 1795, the Senate had completed a gallery for reporters, however. When the capital was transferred from New York to Philadelphia, the gallery was too far from the rostrum for the reporters to hear clearly, but on January 2, 1802, the Senate (by then in Washington) voted the reporters access to the floor. There was some squabbling between reporters and the House over arrangements. In Philadelphia, reporters were assigned "four seats on the window sill," and in Washington, after some agitation, they won the right to report the debates.[14]

One of the most effective reports of government was provided by the *National Intelligencer,* an outstanding newspaper of the period. Its founder was Samuel Harrison Smith, who was only 28 when Jefferson had induced him to give up his promising publishing venture in Philadelphia to start a newspaper in the new capital in Washington. Jefferson was head of the learned American Philosophical Society of Philadelphia (founded by Franklin), and Smith had been secretary of the organization. Jefferson was much impressed with the young man. The *National Intelligencer* soon became the semiofficial organ of the administration, but it served papers of all factions outside Washington with its remarkably objective reporting of congressional debates.

Smith retired from the paper in 1810, but his work was carried on ably by the partners who succeeded him, Joseph Gales, Jr., and William W. Seaton, who reported proceedings in the House and the Senate, respectively. Both were experts in a recently perfected shorthand technique, and they were able to offer complete, accurate reports of the debates. Gales and Seaton made the *National Intelligencer* a daily when they assumed control (it had been a triweekly since its founding in 1800).

A patronage system for publishing the acts and journals of the Congress was vital to the development of the *National Intelligencer* and its rivals in the capital. Under this system the House, Senate, and other agencies selected their own printers. John Fenno had held a Senate contract from the Federalists before 1800, and the *National Intelligencer* had the House contract from 1801 to 1805. Then printing firms got the work on low bids until Congress decided to give the business to the hardworking newspaper reporters covering the debates and providing the country's press with the only immediately available accounts. Gales and Seaton held the Senate contract from 1819 to 1826 and the House award from 1819 to 1829. As political fortunes tilted to the Democrats, Duff Green's *United States Telegraph* won the contracts in voting battles on the floor, later sharing them with Francis P. Blair's *Washington Globe.* Congress ended the patronage plan for newspapers in 1846 and established the Government Printing Office in 1860. During 26 years of patronage, the *National Intelligencer* had $1 million in contracts, the *Washington Globe* had $500,000, and the *United States Telegraph* had some $400,000. The system provided financial support for at least two, sometimes three, high-quality capital papers.[15]

Gales and Seaton earned another $650,000 for printing the *Annals of Congress* (1789–1824) and the *American State Papers* series. They began the *Register of Debates* in 1824, which was superseded by the *Congressional Globe* in 1834, which was in turn replaced by the official *Congressional Record* in 1873. The *National Intelligencer* was the voice of the Whig party and briefly became the administration paper when the Whigs elected William Henry Harrison in 1840 and Millard Fillmore became president in 1850. Daniel Webster, a close friend of Gales and Seaton, was secretary of state in both administrations. The Whig party collapse, and the death of Gales in 1860, reduced the once great *National Intelligencer* to a minor role, but it survived until the close of the Civil War.

MAGAZINES GAIN A FOOTHOLD

But the *National Intelligencer* was not typical of the press of the "era of good feeling."[16] Few other newspapers won historical recognition at this time. On the other hand, there was an interesting development in the magazine field during the period. Efforts to publish magazines had been made occasionally since 1741, when Benjamin Franklin was thwarted in his plans by Andrew Bradford, who had published the first periodical three days before Franklin's magazine appeared.

Five magazines were established in the Revolutionary period. By that time there was some indication that the magazine might one day be self-supporting. It was the *Pennsylvania Magazine,* published in Philadelphia by Robert Aitken, which offered the American public its first taste of Tom Paine. This periodical was well edited, and it was full of interesting political information, literary contributions of good quality, and discussions of important issues. Eventually it failed, but it showed that the magazine had possibilities.

An interesting publication started in the period of the party press was the *Farmer's Weekly Museum,* printed at Walpole, on the New Hampshire side of the Connecticut River. Founded by Isaiah Thomas, who retained his interest in it, it gained its greatest fame under the same Joseph Dennie who later got into trouble for his attacks on democracy printed in the *Port Folio* during Jefferson's first administration. Dennie was so witty, critical, and readable that his paper was in demand all over the nation. It was actually a forerunner of the news magazine.

Other magazines that were available at the end of the eighteenth century are now valuable sources of information for the historian. The *Columbian Magazine,* founded in 1786, was elaborately illustrated (with copperplate engravings) and thus pointed the way to the picture magazine. According to Frank Luther Mott, the leading authority on magazine history in this country, Mathew Carey's *American Museum,* founded a year later, was the best-edited periodical of its day. It has been a mine of information on political, social, and economic history for students of the period. Some issues ran to more than 100 pages.

NILES' WEEKLY REGISTER

Mott estimates that several hundred quarterly, monthly, and weekly magazines were printed at one time or another in the first third of the nineteenth century. Most of them have long since been forgotten. One that deserves special mention, however, was *Niles' Weekly Register.* Edited by Hezekiah Niles, a printer with common sense, integrity, and a flare for concise reporting on current trends, the *Register* is known to every historian of the period. Although it was published in Baltimore, it was read in every state in the Union. The *Register* was the early nineteenth-century equivalent of the modern news magazine. At first Niles's publication, started in 1811, contained a minimum of opinion. Most of the material was a weekly roundup of speeches, important documents, and statements of leaders everywhere concerning current problems. Niles was an objective journalist. He was conservative in his views, but he was also honest in his evaluation of events. Thus, both sides of a controversy found space in the *Register,* and the material was indexed for ready reference, much to the delight of later researchers. Its files were so important to historians that the entire publication has been reprinted, issue by issue, for libraries all over the world needing authoritative chronicles of the first half of the nineteenth century (to 1849).

AN EXPANSION OF THE PRINTED WORD

That Niles's enterprise could prosper was evidence of widening political interest spurred by increased participation. All the new states followed the Vermont pattern in providing suffrage for all white males. After 1810, state after state in the East dropped restrictive voting qualifications, though not always peaceably. The enfranchisement of the common man was to bring about many changes, but in the 1820s the so-called common man was not yet fully aware of the new power he had won.

Indeed the press was counted on more and more to supply the information, inspiration, agitation, and education of a society often unable to keep up with its need for schools. Newspapers, books, and magazines increased so fast in this period that presses could not meet the craving for such material. There were 375 printing offices in 1810. By 1825 there were three times as many. Between 1820 and 1830, publication of books alone increased 10 percent and still did not supply the need, for Americans continued to buy 70 percent of their books from European publishers. Despite this literary dependence on Europe, Americans were offering every encouragement to journalist promoters. It is significant that by 1820 more than 50,000 titles, including books, magazines, and newspapers, were listed as American. Sales of such products increased by more than a million dollars in the decade beginning in 1820, when publications grossed about $2.5 million.[17]

True, much of the American material was extremely shallow and provincial. The *Port Folio,* one of the most literate of the magazines, rarely exceeded 2000 subscribers. The authoritative *North American Review* had a normal circulation of about 3000 copies. The biggest New York newspapers printed up to 4000 copies an issue, but printing 1500 to 2500 was much more common. Only in the religious field was circulation impressive. The Methodist *Christian Journal and Advocate,* for example, had about 25,000 subscribers in 1826 by its own estimate. But although circulations were small, popular publications were reaching more and more citizens, and their numbers increased yearly.

Unfortunately, most ordinary citizens could not afford to pay $5 to $10 a year in advance for such publications. The prevailing wage scale gave many workers only about $8 a week, which put virtually all magazines, and most newspapers, out of their reach. Even so, enough circulation reached the common people to give the United States the highest per capita newspaper readership in the world. In 1826, newspaper circulation in America exceeded that of Great Britain by more than three million readers annually. In 1810 there were 376 newspapers in the United States. By 1828, at the time of Jackson's election, there were nearly 900 (mainly weeklies). Nevertheless, what the nation needed was a newspaper press that could reach deeper into the population—first to the middle class, then to the workers.

In many communities, newspapers were the only literature available for the bulk of the citizenry. They served as the main educational device until other cultural institutions could develop. Actually, the United States was beginning to fill this vacuum. In the field of letters the country could offer Washington Irving, James Fenimore Cooper, William Cullen Bryant, Margaret Fuller, Nathaniel Hawthorne, and Ralph Waldo Emerson, all of whom would soon be recognized, even in Europe.

JOHN MARSHALL'S COURT DECISIONS

The trend toward a more enlightened age was noticeable by the end of the 1820s. By that time there were 49 colleges in the United States. The increase in endowed institutions of learning was appreciable after the decision of the Supreme Court in the Dartmouth College case of 1819. Until then, the trend had been toward state control of such educational establishments. The apathy of philanthropists in supporting universities is therefore understandable. In the Dartmouth College case the court held that a state had no right to change contracts, specifically, to make a private institution into a state university. Potential

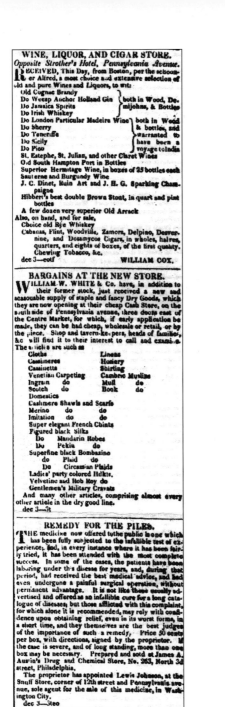
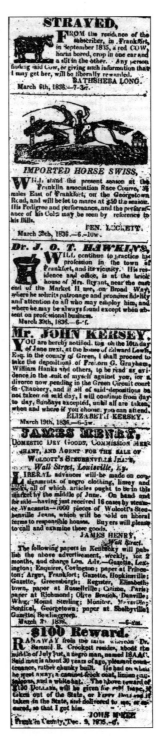

Advertisements from the *National Intelligencer* (1823) and the *Argus of Western America* (1836)

patrons of endowed education had hesitated to make donations to educational institutions threatened by state control.

The Dartmouth College decision was one of a series by which Chief Justice John Marshall guided the Supreme Court in establishing a philosophy of government. Two famous decisions, *McCulloch* v. *Maryland* (1819) and *Gibbons* v. *Ogden* (1824), asserted the supremacy of the national government over the states. Other decisions limited the states from restricting the rights of property holders. Such decisions were indicative of the general attitude regarding the superiority of private controls. This was the heyday of unrestricted enterprise. The attitude on this subject is also reflected in the philosophies of Justice Joseph Story of Massachusetts, author of *Commentaries on the Constitution,* and of James (Chancellor) Kent of New York, who wrote *Commentaries on American Law.* The two eminent and influential jurists interpreted laws so as to make them fit the needs of an increasingly commercial nation. They had no sympathy for an extension of government regulation that might curb the individual businessperson, but they were willing to let the government come to the help of the commercial interests when such aid was convenient.

This was what Senator Thomas Hart Benton of Missouri had in mind when he argued at the end of the decade that the "East," the symbol of business and banking, saw to it that western demands for the homestead laws were obstructed in order to maintain a cheap labor supply for the eastern businesspeople. Another instance of this philosophy in action was the passage of the tariff of 1828—the "tariff of abominations"—which protected the business promoter at the expense of other interests.

THE UNITED STATES OF THE 1820s

But this turn to the right had brought social and political strains. As the businesspeople assumed more dominant places in federal control, and as they began to exert their influence to their own advantages, there was an equal and opposite reaction. It is significant that labor unions and a labor press emerged about this time. The cries of anguish over the "tariff of abominations," especially in the agrarian areas, were a prelude to the battle cries of the Civil War. And yet, curiously, American writers had little to say about the forces shaping the destiny of the country at this time. We can learn more by reading the reports of foreign observers who visited the United States during the first 30 years of the century.

Many, such as Basil Hall and Mrs. Frances Trollope, were devastating in their contempt for American culture and materialism. Others, such as Harriet Martineau, a trained journalist with an understanding heart, saw through the American veneer. In between were reporters, such as Charles Dickens, who were generally severe but reasonably accurate.[18] They were appalled, for the most part, by American provincialism, unmindful that the American was preoccupied with hacking a nation from a wilderness. This complete absorption in the development of native resources had resulted in a strong nationalism obnoxious to the foreign observer. Earlier visitors had confined their observations to the more sophisticated East, but the European reporters of the 1820s to 1830s were more interested in the western regions. They were disgusted by the boastfulness, smugness, superior attitudes, and ill-mannered ignorance of the type of American about to step into control of the government. Most of these observers carried home great disdain for the American concept of popular rule. One who did not was the French observer, Alexis de Tocqueville, whose *Democracy in America* reflects his observations of 1831 to 1832. In 1980 the journalist Richard Reeves retraced de Tocqueville's journey and discovered the same basic values that had made America attractive so many years before. Another early admirer was Sandor Farkas, a Hungarian intellectual who compiled *Journey in North America* following his 1831 visit. In Europe, governments acted and thought for the people; in America, Farkas noted human associations:

> In Europe it is considered something of a magic solution that America so quickly raised the national level of enlightenment. That magic at work in America is the printing of newspapers. For instance, stagecoaches regularly carry newspapers, whose delivery in the wilderness delighted and surprised me. No matter how remote from civilization or poor the settler may be, he reads the newspaper. As the stagecoach approaches a clearing in the wilderness, it sounds a horn and then the driver reaches under the seat box and tosses newspapers by the roadside. The scene repeats itself all day: tossing newspapers at roadside settlements (sometimes only a lonely log cabin).[19]

The full consequence of the Industrial Revolution in America would not be apparent until a later date, but the trend had already started in the 1820s. The opening of the Erie Canal in 1825 was to make New York truly the "Empire State" and its metropolis one of the world's great commercial centers. In 1830, only about 7 percent of Americans lived in cities, but the influence of industry was manifested by the obsession of political leaders with such issues as tariffs and the working man's vote.

On the whole, the new class emerging out of the Industrial Revolution was at first inarticulate. But as early as 1820 there was the beginning of populist revolt in Massachusetts, where workers were insisting upon a greater voice in government. New York experienced the same thing in 1821. In Rhode Island, where the worker was less successful at first, pressure built up into actual violence (Dorr's Rebellion), although the denouement dragged out into a later period. The issue was the rights of property versus the rights of the individual. The mechanics, as the urban workers were called at that time, resented being paid in wildcat banknotes that sometimes depreciated to less than half of their contracted wages. It is significant that in 1829 about 75,000 people were jailed for debt. More than half of these victims owed less than $20. Conditions of labor, especially for women and children, brought out a long line of social reformers who insisted on protective legislation.

Slowly the common man began to realize his power at the polls. In 1824, only six states still chose presidential electors through the legislators, heretofore the frequent tools of the property group. By 1832, only South Carolina maintained this system, and it was in that year that the party convention took at least some of the power away from "King Caucus"—the selection of candidates by a secret conclave of political leaders.

THE MARKET REVOLUTION

The name of Andrew Jackson has often been used as an adjective for the era from 1815 to 1848. This period has also been called the "era of the common man," referring to its democratic reforms.[20] Certainly by 1824 a realignment in American politics was under way.

A financial panic in 1819 had brought distress to speculators and debtors in the South and West, where the Bank of the United States became a great absentee landlord through foreclosures. Those affected saw politics as a way out, if they could get relief laws and new public land and tariff policies and make war on the older money interests of the East, typified by the national bank. But presidential politics were fragmented in 1824, and party lines were blurred. Andrew Jackson, military hero and westerner, led in the small popular vote and had the largest electoral total, but not a majority. John Quincy Adams, typifying the Federalist elitist tradition, ran a strong second. Henry Clay threw his support to Adams in the balloting in the House of Representatives; when Adams named Clay as secretary of state, Jackson labeled it a "deal" and began campaigning as a Democrat for 1828.

In his strongholds in the South and West, Jackson appeared to be one of their kind: a militant nationalist who could "handle" the Native Americans, a natural enemy of the older eastern money power, and a champion of egalitarianism, particularly a symbol of equal access to office. As Richard Hofstadter puts it, "So far as he can be said to have had a popular mandate, it was to be different from what the people imagined Adams had been and to give expression to their unformulated wishes and aspirations."[21] Like all victors in political revolutions, Jackson was bound to disappoint some of the groups who had supported him. The growing support for the Jacksonian Democratic party in the East included many of the workers and immigrants, but it also counted some of the skilled workers and small and large traders and merchants who were more immediate beneficiaries of the democratization of politics. Shifting trends in transportation and manufacturing had also created a democratization of business; the new entrepreneurs and capitalists were sometimes alienated by the older money power and its symbolic political strength in Federalism and Adams. The unfortunate Adams was painted as an intellectual snob, aristocrat, and defender of the old order—images that won votes both West and East for Jackson.

But Jackson clearly began as the candidate of the South and West; only later did the Jacksonian Democrats make a temporary inroad in the East. In 1828 Jackson won 56 percent of the popular vote and defeated Adams 178 to 83 in the electoral college. But Jackson won only Pennsylvania and New York in the East, while Adams won only Maryland and Delaware in the South and West. In 1832 Jackson added Maine, New Hampshire, and New Jersey to his eastern total, while holding onto 54 percent of the popular vote against a weak Whig candidate, Henry Clay, who carried only his home state of Kentucky in the West. Martin Van Buren, Jackson's astute political manager from the East, won all that area except Massachusetts and New Jersey as the 1836 Democratic candidate against three Whig rivals. But when the Whigs united behind a western military hero, William Henry Harrison, in 1840, against a depression-plagued Van Buren, the Jacksonian party coalition was shattered.

Amos Kendall, the West's contribution to the Jacksonian leadership, saw the conflict as a fight between the "producing" classes of farmers, laborers, and skilled workers, and the "nonproducing" capitalists and landlords. Although outnumbered, this nonproducing class remained dominant through control of banks, education, most of the churches, and the bulk of the press. Thus, Kendall pointed out, "those who produce all the wealth are themselves left poor."[22]

Meanwhile, the sanctity of property was explained very comfortably by the ultra-Whig *American Quarterly Review,* published in Philadelphia, which reported just after the end of the decade: "The lowest orders of society ordinarily mean the poorest—and the highest the richest. Sensual excess, want of intelligence, and moral debasement distinguish the former—knowledge, intellectual superiority, and refined, social and domestic affections the latter." As Arthur M. Schlesinger, Jr., the Pulitzer Prize–winning historian of this period remarks: "Property, in [Whig] reflexes, became almost identified with character." Nicholas Biddle, who as head of the powerful Second Bank of the United States believed he was the leader of a class too strong for any attempted restraint by the Jacksonians, smugly summed up the opposition Democrats as a party made up of "men with no property to assess and no character to lose."[23]

The pompous Biddle was utterly astounded when, in the summer of 1832, Jackson vetoed a bill for rechartering the Bank of the United States. "Biddled, diddled, and undone," Charles Gordon Greene of the *Boston Post* wrote of Jackson's veto. In his veto message Jackson paid respects to the farmers, mechanics, and laborers who were seeking protection against governmental injustices, but he also declared that government should provide equal protection for both high and low, rich and poor—something with which the new entrepreneurs could agree. Unfortunately for Jackson and his party, the destruction of Biddle's bank opened the door to poor fiscal policies, wildcat banking, and inflation. By 1837 both rich and poor were victims of a "panic" of major proportions. Van Buren, rather than "Old Hickory," as Jackson was called, caught the blame. But, all told, does Jackson deserve having his name attached to an "era" of political reform, expanded economic opportunity, better schools, a growing literature, and a popular press? Such a designation has long been made, but most historians debate it today. Some argue that the reforms instituted by Jackson were truly democratic; they point, for example, to the replacement of the caucus system with political conventions, which made it easier for ordinary citizens to run for office, and argue that with more citizens able to vote, party leaders couldn't so easily ignore their wishes. But other historians note that race and gender still defined citizenship. And even with more white men voting, they argue, power still was not redistributed in any meaningful way. Political leaders continued to be wealthier and better educated than their constituents. Historians also observe that Jackson's reforms helped certain entrepreneurs and speculators more than they helped the "common man."[24] Furthermore, historians such as Anthony Wallace remind us that removal of Native Americans was fundamental to many of Jackson's reforms. Wallace connects the period's striking market transformations and economic expansion and Jackson's Native American policies, while Sean Wilentz provides an excellent overview of many of these debates.[25] Perhaps the most accurate label for the period is one that emphasizes the economic development and changes—the market revolution—that had such an impact on social relations and virtually every aspect of American life.

FIRST LABOR PAPERS

A direct result of the Industrial Revolution and the growing need for recognition of a new type of citizen was the development of the labor press. A depression during the icy winter of 1828–29 and the rising cost of living fostered the beginning of a long-overdue labor revolt. The appearance of the first labor paper in 1827—the *Journeyman Mechanic's Advocate* of Philadelphia—was a clear signal that laborers intended to fight for their advantages, as property owners had long fought for theirs. The first labor paper lasted only a year. The times were too difficult for workers to provide sufficient support. It was a significant "first," however, for in conjunction with the success of the populists at the polls in 1828, the attempt of labor to express itself was prophetic. Two months before Jackson's election, the first workers' party was organized. It was sponsored by the Mechanic's Union of Trade Associations. In the same year the *Mechanic's Free Press* was established as the first successful labor newspaper. Until the depression of 1837 killed it, the *Free Press* had an average weekly circulation of around 1500—very good for a period when even the biggest New York dailies rarely exceeded 4000.

In many ways, the early labor papers were superior to modern labor organs. Their functions were primarily to counteract prejudices against working people, to supply labor information that the commercial press ignored, and to offer inspiration to the dispirited. The reports were concise, reasonably factual for the time, and well written.

This agitation led to the organization of the first national labor association: the National Trades Union, founded in 1834. A strong supporter of the labor-organization movement was the *Working Man's Advocate,* founded in New York in 1829 by George H. Evans, an English printer. Another important publication supporting labor's cause (along with other social issues) was the *Free Enquirer,* edited in New York by the charming and talented Frances "Fanny" Wright. Fanny Wright, who came to the United States from Scotland in 1818, became a power in the New Harmony utopian experiment conducted by Robert Dale Owen. She had helped put out the *New Harmony Gazette,* published in New York from 1829 as the *Free Enquirer.* Among her many admirers was a young carpenter who was a great believer in democracy, and whose poems in the *Leaves of Grass* were to sing of the people. The poet was Walt Whitman, himself then a journalist and a printer in Brooklyn.

Most of the standard newspapers had scant regard for this labor movement, but one or two helped the cause. William Cullen Bryant, the poet and editor of the *New York Evening Post,* pleaded the case of the working people. The stand of the *Post* indicated how far it had veered since its establishment by the founder of Federalism, Alexander Hamilton. Bryant had been employed in 1825 by William Coleman, the militant Federalist editor of the paper. Four years later Bryant was in full charge of the *Post,* and remained with the paper, except for a few lapses, for half a century. Under Bryant, the *Post* cast off much of its Federalist tradition. On many issues the paper sided with the Jacksonian Democrats. Thus, denouncing what it believed to be an unjust verdict against a "criminal conspiracy" (strike) by the Society of Journeyman Tailors, the *Post* said:

> They were condemned because they were determined not to work for the wages offered them. . . . If this is not SLAVERY, we have forgotten its definition. Strike the right of associating for the sale of labour from the privileges of a freeman, and you may as well at once bind him to a master.[26]

William Leggett, part-owner of the *Post* and interim editor after Bryant went abroad in 1834, was even more prolabor than was Bryant. He was so outspoken, indeed, that the more temperate Bryant had to cool him down on occasion. Later, as we shall see, the cause of the working people was taken up by another famous editor, Horace Greeley. There were magazines, too, fighting for labor during this period. One was the *Democratic Review,* edited by the fiery John L. O'Sullivan. Despite these editorial champions of the underprivileged, however, the press in general took a dim view of the labor movement.

KENDALL AND BLAIR: THE *WASHINGTON GLOBE*

As obnoxious to the Whigs as the labor movement was the "Kitchen Cabinet" of President Jackson. Some of the most influential members of this inner circle were journalists. Duff Green, the editor of the party paper in Washington, was one of the cronies until his endorsement of Calhoun lost him Jackson's support. Isaac Hill, the crippled, rebellious, and vituperative New Hampshire editor, was another intimate of the president. The two important powers behind the party, however, were Amos Kendall and Francis Preston Blair.

Amos Kendall was the most important member of the group. Reared on a New England farm, he was too frail for such rugged work. He had a passion for scholarship, and his family recognized this bent. After he was graduated from Dartmouth College, Kendall headed for the frontier, where opportunities were better for inexperienced lawyers. He hung out his shingle in Kentucky.

As a lawyer, Kendall easily turned his energies to politics. He was a protégé of a regional political chieftain, who insisted that the erudite New Englander take over the editorship of the Democratic party organ. The newspaper was the *Argus of Western America,* published in Frankfort. Kendall made it the party voice of the entire region. An able, honest,

ARGUS OF WESTERN AMERICA.

[Number 39.]   FRANKFORT, KENTUCKY, WEDNESDAY, NOVEMBER 17, 1824.   [Volume XVII.]

This pro-Jackson frontier paper was edited by Amos Kendall and Francis P. Blair.

and articulate journalist, his fame as a party spokesperson eventually came to the attention of General Jackson. Perhaps their physical ills gave them a common bond. The president was old and full of the miseries. Kendall was something of a hypochondriac, but he had always been frail, so perhaps his attitude was justified. At any rate, there was a strong bond between the two men. Jackson was not a polished writer, and he was happy to have Kendall edit his important statements. Time and again Kendall took down the dictation of the wan warrior. Jackson would lie on a faded sofa beneath the portrait of his beloved wife, Rachel, while Kendall skillfully interpreted his chief's rough ideas and put them into presentable form.

When Jackson first moved into the White House, the administration organ in Washington was the *United States Telegraph,* founded in 1826.[27] Duff Green was editor of the paper. He had worked hard to elect Jackson, but his other hero was John C. Calhoun, Jackson's party rival. The split in loyalty cost Green the support of the president. The Jacksonian faction decided to make Francis P. Blair Green's successor. Blair had taken over the editorship of the *Argus* after Kendall went to Washington.

Blair's paper, the *Washington Globe,* appeared at the end of 1830. By that time Jackson and Blair were on the best of terms. "Give it to Bla-ar," the president used to say when he had a particularly trenchant statement requiring journalistic finesse. From Blair's pencil, on scraps of paper held on his knee, came the fighting editorials that helped to knit the party even closer.

But Kendall was the most important of them all. As one of Jackson's rivals put it, Kendall was "the President's *thinking* machine, and his *writing* machine—ay, and his *lying* machine. . . . He was chief overseer, chief reporter, amanuensis, scribe, accountant general, man of all work—nothing was well done without the aid of his diabolical genius."[28] And ex-President Adams, not given to exaggeration, once stated of Van Buren and Jackson, "Both . . . have been for 12 years the tool of Amos Kendall, the ruling mind of their dominion." Kendall became postmaster general in 1835.

INVENTIONS FOR A PEOPLE'S PRESS

The Industrial Revolution, which resulted in less expensive goods, also made it possible to produce less expensive paper. A newspaper publisher could now print more pages and provide more space for advertising these goods and other services in better style than had been available earlier. There was a vast, untapped public tempting the promoter, if only the product could be made attractive. And by 1833, technical progress had reached the point at which this was possible.

In 1822, Peter Smith, connected with R. Hoe & Company, printing-press makers, invented a hand press with a much faster lever action than had existed to that time. Five years later Samuel Rust of New York put out the Washington hand press, which is still seen in some small offices. It had many automatic devices: a platen raised and lowered by springs; an ingenious toggle device for quick impressions; a faster-moving bed; and later, automatic ink rollers.

The next step was to harness power to the press. This came with the age of steam, and at once inventors set themselves to the problem. Daniel Treadwell of Boston had partial success in 1822. A steam book press was developed by Isaac Adams of Boston in 1830 and was popular for many years, but it was a European who perfected the process for speedy power printing. He was Friedrich Koenig of Saxony, who after many delays produced the

An American adaptation of Friedrich Koenig's power press

first of his presses in London in 1811. Koenig's press had a movable bed that carried the type back and forth for inking after each impression. Paper was fed into the top of a cylinder. Three years later Koenig invented a two-cylinder press that printed both sides of the paper—the so-called perfecting press. Late in 1814 the *Times* of London was the first to use this press for newspaper work. The paper proudly stated that it could outstrip all rivals by printing papers at the unbelievable rate of 1100 an hour.

In 1830 David Napier of England perfected the Koenig steam press and tripled the speed of printing. America's R. Hoe & Company, which was to become a byword in newspaper plants, chose the Napier press as the prototype of a new product for American printers. The new Hoe was actually a great improvement over the Napier, and it was able to produce 4000 double impressions an hour. Such technical progress was essential to the production of an inexpensive newspaper that the masses could afford.

By 1833 all the ingredients were available for the establishment of such a venture. It was possible to print a paper that would sell for one cent, in contrast to the six cents then charged by the average commercial dailies. To a worker, six cents was the equivalent of a quarter-pound of bacon or a pint of local whiskey. In England, Henry Hetherington had published two periodicals for the masses. He failed, not because of the price he charged but because he was caught evading the so-called taxes on knowledge, which kept the price of British newspapers out of the reach of the common people, as intended. John Wight, the Bow Street police reporter, had also demonstrated by 1820 the type of news that would make the presses for the mass successful.

In 1829, Seba Smith founded a daily paper at Portland, Maine, that was smaller than a standard newspaper but cheaper by half than the usual daily. It cost $4 a year, payable in advance. A year later, Lynde M. Walter, a Boston Brahmin, bought an existing paper and made it into the daily *Transcript,* also offered for $4. More popular because it offered spicier items, perhaps, was the *Boston Morning Post,* founded as a $4-a-year daily by Charles G. Greene in 1831. Two years later Captain John S. Sleeper founded the *Boston Mercantile Journal,* offered at the same price. All were successful, but they were sold by subscription only.

In Philadelphia, Dr. Christopher Columbus Conwell established a penny paper, *The Cent,* in 1830. Although interesting as a forerunner of the press for the masses, it survived only a short time. A serious and nearly successful attempt to put out a genuine penny paper for the masses, to be sold by the issue as well as by subscription, was made by Horace Greeley in partnership with Dr. H. D. Shepard, a dentist, in January 1833. This was the *New York Morning Post.* A violent snowstorm kept so many citizens indoors the first few days of this paper's appearance that the promoters had to give up the venture.

The time was ripe for a successful penny paper, however. Indeed, the next attempt to produce a penny paper was to bring such a significant change to American journalism as to warrant the description "revolutionary."

6

A Press
for the Masses

But the world does move, and its motive power under God is the
fearless thought and speech of those who dare to be in advance of
their time—who are sneered at and shunned through their days of
struggle as lunatics, dreamers, impracticables, and visionaries;
men of crotchets, vagaries, and isms. They are the masts and sails
of the ship to which conservatism answers as ballast. The ballast is
important—at times indispensable—but it would be of no account
if the ship were not bound to go ahead.

—Horace Greeley

Whenever a mass of people has been neglected too long by the established organs of communication, agencies have eventually been devised to supply that want. Invariably this
press of the masses is greeted with scorn by the sophisticated reader because the content
of such a press is likely to be elemental and emotional. Such scorn is not always deserved.
Just as the child ordinarily starts reading with Mother Goose and fairy stories before grad-
uating to more serious study, so the public first reached by a news agency is likely to prefer what the critics like to call *sensationalism,* which is the emphasis on emotion for its
own sake. This pattern can be seen in the periods when the most noteworthy developments
in popular journalism were apparent. In 1620, 1833, the 1890s, and 1920, this tapping of
a new, much-neglected public started with a wave of sensationalism.

The phenomenon is clearly exhibited in the period of the 1830s and 1840s covered
by this chapter, for it was in 1833 that the first successful penny newspaper tapped a reservoir of readers collectively designated "the common people." The first offerings of this
poor people's newspaper tended to be highly sensational. This was only a developmental
phase, however. Very quickly the penny newspapers began to attract readers from other
social and economic brackets. And the common people, as their literacy skills improved,
also demanded a better product. Within a decade after the appearance of the first penny
paper, the press of the common people included respectable publications that offered significant information and leadership.

Before the appearance of the penny papers, publishers charged from $6 to $10 a year
in advance for a newspaper subscription. That was more than most skilled workers earned

James Gordon Bennett of the *New York Herald*

Horace Greeley of the *New York Tribune*

in a week, and in any case, people of limited means could not pay that much in a lump sum. The standard newspapers were usually edited for people of means, which partially accounted for the preponderance of conservatism in the press. It was also a factor in keeping circulations small, although mechanical limitations certainly had a similar effect. In 1833 the largest dailies in New York were the morning *Courier and Enquirer,* published by the colorful and irascible Colonel James Watson Webb, and the *Journal of Commerce,* founded by Arthur Tappan in 1827 but soon taken over by Gerard Hallock and David Hale.[1] The largest afternoon paper was William Cullen Bryant's *Post.* These and the other eight city papers sold for six cents a copy, and most of them were distributed by subscription, rather than by the street sale that was to characterize the penny press.

DAY'S *NEW YORK SUN,* 1833

Journalism began a new epoch on September 3, 1833, with the appearance of a strange little newspaper, the *New York Sun* ("It Shines for ALL"). Its founder was Benjamin H. Day, who arrived in New York as a lad of 20 after an apprenticeship on Massachusetts's excellent *Springfield Republican.* That was in 1831. For two years, Day operated a printing shop without much success; there were financial disturbances, and in 1832 a plague further cut into the city's prosperity. In desperation, Day decided to publish a paper in an effort to take up some of the slack in his declining job-printing business. He had watched the early attempts to establish penny papers in Boston, Philadelphia, and New York, and it appeared to him that such a publication would be successful if it could be sold and financed on a per-issue basis. He discussed the proposal with two friends, Arunah S. Abell and William M. Swain. They warned him against the undertaking, a bit of advice they had to eat sometime later when they founded their own successful penny papers in Philadelphia and Baltimore. Day went ahead with his plans anyway.

The *Sun* that appeared that September day did not give the impression that it would soon outshine all rivals in circulation.[2] It was printed on four pages, each about two-thirds the size of the modern tabloid page. The front page was three columns wide and devoid of any display devices. Emphasis was on local happenings and news of violence. Most of the material was trivial, flippant—but highly readable. Most important, it was inexpensive. Within six months the *Sun* had a circulation of around 8000, nearly twice that of its nearest rival.

The reporting of George Wisner accounted for some of this success. Remembering the popularity of the Bow Street police-station news in the London forerunners of the penny press, Day hired Wisner to write similarly for the *Sun.* He was an instant success. Wisner received $4 a week for covering the courts, plus a share of the profits of the paper. Within a year he had become co-owner.

"Human-interest" news was a specialty of the *Sun.* Here is a sample of the *Sun* technique taken from a typical issue after the paper was firmly established:

> Some six years ago a young gentleman, the oldest son of a distinguished baronet in England, after completing his course in education, returned home to pay his respects to his parents, and to participate in the pleasures of their social circle.[3]

The account goes on to describe how the handsome youth fell in love with a girl his father had adopted as a ward. Eventually the couple ran off together because such marriages were forbidden, and the scion was disinherited by the angry baron. On the death of the father, however, the son was declared heir to the title. A younger son tried to wrest the estate by charging his elder brother with incest. This part of the story fills all of the *Sun's* first page for that day. No names are used. It could have been complete fabrication, except that the word "recent" is used to give a news flavor to the piece. The fate of the heir is never determined, although the account is embellished:

> And while our hero was unsuspiciously reposing on the soft bosom of his bride, a brother's hand, impelled by a brother's hate, was uplifted with fratricidal fierceness for destruction.

The only concession to the commercial interests of the community in this typical issue was a column of shipping news on the third page. Obviously, the paper was not printed for the property class. And yet anyone could see that it was bringing in plenty of advertising revenue. The back page was solid advertising, and about half the third page was devoted to classified notices, including "want ads." Even page one contained advertising, such as the ad about Robert Hoe & Son, the printing-press maker at 29 Gold Street, who had just installed a new cylinder press for the *Sun* that was the fastest in the city: 1500 complete papers an hour.

A PENNY PRESS FOR THE COMMON PEOPLE

We have suggested that the appearance of the penny press and the rise of the common people in the Jacksonian democracy were integrated. Sociologist Michael Schudson gives support for this, saying the penny press emerged in response to the needs of what he calls a "democratic market society" created by the growth of mass democracy, a marketplace ideology, and an urban society. The new papers "were spokesmen for egalitarianism ideals in politics, economic life, and social life through their organization of sales, their solicitation of advertising, their emphasis on news, their catering to large audiences, and their decreasing concern with the editorial," he sums up—all trends documented in detail in these pages. In his essay Schudson analyzes in depth, but rejects, three theories, each basing the reason for appearance of the penny press on a single primary cause: technological innovation, the spread of literacy (both contributing causes), and a natural evolution of press growth.[4]

Politics for the laboring class, which was beginning to win recognition in the Jacksonian era, had some of the flaws corresponding to the faults of the factory system. Too often majority rule encouraged the spoils system, bossism, and mediocrity in government. And too often the early penny papers lowered standards. The *Sun,* for example, was ready to sacrifice truth if that would bring in more customers. The fact is, the paper nearly trebled in circulation in 1835 when one of its reporters, a descendant of the political philosopher John Locke, wrote a series of articles purporting to describe life on the moon. The so-called moon hoax of Richard Adams Locke may not have increased public confidence in the paper, but readers did not appear to resent the journalistic trick that had been played on them.

And yet there was much that was revealed as good in the sunrise of this new journalism. White male workers had already won the right to vote. The penny papers could reach out to them with something other than the erudite opinions comprising the main fare of the orthodox press. The newly recognized public was more interested in *news* than in *views.* The penny papers concentrated on supplying this type of intelligence in readable form. The *Sun* and its galaxy of imitators proved that news was a valuable commodity, if delivered in a sprightly manner.

Another person began to take a special interest in the newspaper for the masses. This was the advertiser, who was impressed by the amazing circulations of the new medium. Putting an ad in every publication bought by small splinter groups was expensive and ineffective sales promotion. The large circulations of the penny papers now made it feasible to publicize articles for sale that formerly would not have warranted the advertising expense. The first advertising agency man, Volney B. Palmer, who opened shop in 1849 as a liaison between the papers and businesspeople, soon had offices in several cities.

On the other hand, advertising revenue made it possible for editors and publishers to expand and to experiment with new methods of news gathering. Since advertising flowed to the circulation leaders, and since news appeared to be the most popular type of literature, publishers began to invest heavily in various devices for improving news coverage. The full scope of this development is described in the next chapter, but the relation between advertising and the penny press deserves mention at this point. As publishers began to understand the technique of obtaining mass circulations, they had to have better presses. Moses Y. Beach, Ben Day's brother-in-law, who took over the *Sun* in 1837, used part of his profits to buy a new steam-driven Hoe cylinder press capable of producing 4000 papers an hour. It was the most advanced printing equipment of its day.

The penny papers also brought changes in distribution methods. Commercial and standard newspapers had been sold on a subscription basis. Workers not only could not pay large sums in advance, but many also moved around too much to subscribe regularly. There were times when the workers could not read at all because of their jobs or because of their poverty. The penny papers reached such readers by depending primarily on street sales, under the so-called London Plan. Vendors bought the papers from the publisher at a rate of 100 copies for 67 cents, to be sold for 1 cent each. The distribution system also inevitably changed the appearance of the paper, as editors tried to lure readers from rival publications through the use of better makeup and more readable type.

BENNETT'S *NEW YORK HERALD,* 1835

One of the most successful promoters of a newspaper that cut through the partisanship of the times was James Gordon Bennett.[5] Bennett was strictly a reporter and editor, in contrast to the printer-publishers who have figured so prominently in this history. He had gained valuable experience as a Washington correspondent, which was to stand him in good stead when he began to develop national news as a commodity. As editor for Colonel James Watson Webb, he had engineered the 1829 merger of the *Courier* and the *Enquirer,* which made it the largest newspaper in New York. Twice he had tried to found a paper of his own, but without success. The newspaper he produced on the morning of May 6, 1835, changed this picture.

Bennett was 40 years old, disillusioned, and deep in debt when he founded the *New York Morning Herald.* His capital was only $500; he also had some credit from his printers. His office was a cellar in the basement of a building at 20 Wall Street. Equipment consisted of a desk made from a plank spanning two dry-goods boxes, a secondhand chair, and a box for files. His entire staff consisted of himself. On this basis Bennett built one of the most profitable newspaper properties of his time.

There was a month's delay between the first and second issues of the *Herald,* but from June 1835, the paper boomed. The *Herald* was an imitator of the *Sun* in using sensational material, but Bennett added many tricks of his own. When it came to crime reporting the *Herald* knew no equal. The issue of June 4, 1836, a year after regular publication of the paper had begun, showed the typical *Herald* treatment of such news. The whole front page, unrelieved by headlines, was devoted to the Robinson-Jewett case. This involved the murder of a prostitute in a brothel by a notorious man about town, and Bennett gave the sordid murder all the resources of his paper. He stirred up so much interest in the case that the court could not continue hearing testimony when the defendant was up for trial. The tone of *Herald* reporting is indicated by this "precede" to the main story of the trial and the disturbances in the court room:

> The major—the sheriff, all endeavored to restore order—all in vain. A terrible rain storm raged out doors—a mob storm indoors. The Judges and the Officers left the hall. Robinson was carried out of court, and the Public Authorities were trying to clear the hall of the mob, when this extra went to press.
> Why is not the militia called?
> We give the additional testimony up to the latest hour. . . . The mystery of the bloody drama increases—increases—increases.[6]

The "extra" feature of this news coverage (an "extra" is a special edition) was typical of Bennett's aggressive style of journalism. Soon this type of news treatment gave way to an increasing interest in more significant news. Bennett himself had no qualms about using violent news, for he was certain his paper was getting better every day. He got out of the penny-paper category in the summer of 1836 and defended his policy by stating that his readers were getting more for their money—the new price was two cents—than they could get anywhere else.

Year by year the *Herald* branched out into other fields of journalism. The paper appealed to the business class by developing the best financial section of any standard journal. Bennett, a former teacher of economics, wrote what he called the "money page." He had had experience in such reporting, and he took a special interest in this phase of journalism. When administrative duties at last forced him to give up this work, he saw to it that his best staff were assigned to the Wall Street run. In the meantime, he was offering more serious background material than his rivals on the *Sun*. His editorial comment was seldom profound, but it was decisive, reasoned, and informative. The *Herald* led the pack in hounding news from all areas—local, foreign, and national, as we shall see in the next chapter. Bennett built up an interesting "letters" column in which readers could comment on the paper as well as on events. He helped develop the critical review column and society news. Long before other editors recognized the appeal of the subject, Bennett was offering sports news. Thus it was all along. The great contribution of the *Herald* was as an innovator and perfecter.

This aggressive policy paid big dividends. The *Herald* was full of advertising and was on its way to circulation leadership. It had 20,000 readers in 1836 and would be the world's largest daily, at 77,000, by 1860. Such success for a disliked rival brought a movement to boycott the *Herald*. The attack by Bennett's critics was started in May 1840 by Park Benjamin of the *New York Signal*. Colonel James Watson Webb, Bennett's one-time employer, joined in the fray (he had once administered a caning to the editor of the *Herald*), and soon all the opposition papers joined the "moral war" against the upstart journalist. Bennett was accused of blasphemy (he had carried his saucy style into the coverage of religious news), and some of the leading clergy used their influence to make the boycott effective. Advertisers who feared to offend the moral experts withdrew their accounts.

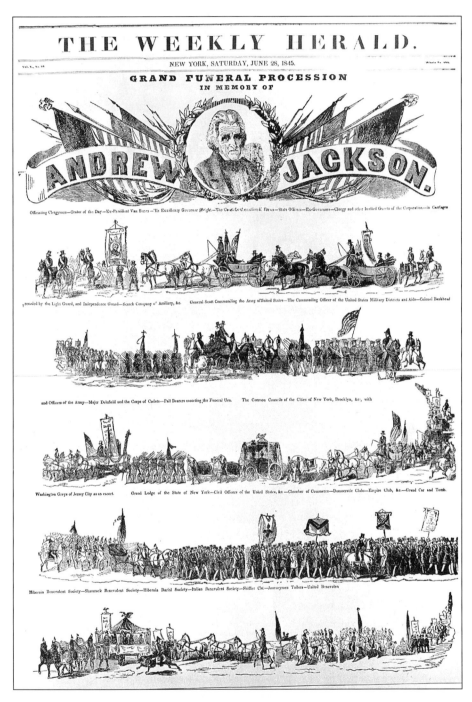

One of Bennett's most famous front pages, using 1845 woodcuts

Bennett solved the problem confronting the *Herald* in characteristic manner. He sent his best reporters out to cover the church beats, including all religious meetings of any consequence. A man of little religious feeling, he had the news sense to understand that here was another neglected public worth cultivating. He also toned down some of the obvious charlatanism that had made the *Herald* the symbol of publicized wickedness. The result was victory for Bennett.

Bennett put some needed ingredients into American journalism. He added spice and enterprise and aggressive news coverage. He proved that a publisher devoted to the continual improvement of the product could expect rich rewards. It cost a large fortune to provide all the machinery and personnel that put the *Herald* ahead of its rivals, but the investment paid huge dividends. Bennett left a valuable property to his son, and he died a rich man. But the *Herald* was remembered not so much for *what* it said as for *how* it said it.

PENNY-PRESS EXPANSION: PHILADELPHIA AND BALTIMORE

Other publishers spread the gospel of penny-press journalism to other cities. Benjamin Day's printer friends, William M. Swain and Arunah S. Abell, saw the *Sun* thrive despite the pessimistic advice they had offered, but they fully admitted their errors when they began the *Philadelphia Public Ledger* in March 1836, with Azariah H. Simmons as partner. Philadelphia had already been introduced to penny-press journalism by Dr. Christopher Columbus Conwell, who had experimented unsuccessfully with a penny paper, *The Cent,* in 1830. In 1835 William L. Drane founded the *Daily Transcript* and was operating successfully when the three partners founded the *Public Ledger.* But the new paper was soon to become one of the great American dailies. It was a cleaned-up version of the *Herald*—full of sensational news but without the extreme bad taste of the New York paper. It was an effective policy. Within two years after its founding, the *Public Ledger* had absorbed its rival, the *Transcript,* and was printing more than 20,000 copies a day. Like the *Herald,* the *Public Ledger* made full use of the most modern technical and news-coverage developments.

Swain was the dominant figure on the *Public Ledger,* and after an interval, Abell decided to strike out for himself. He selected Baltimore as a likely city. It was second only to New York as a trade center and was then third in population. At first, Swain and Simmons were not enthusiastic about the undertaking. Eventually they underwrote the investment, but Abell promoted the Baltimore publication pretty much by himself. The *Baltimore Sun* first rose May 17, 1837. Its appearance coincided with a depression that had already closed the banks. The first issue of the paper played up the story of a city council meeting the day before, at which $100,000 worth of fractional currency ("shinplasters") was authorized to meet the financial crisis. This was scarcely the appropriate time to found a new paper, it would seem, but the *Sun* prospered, like its New York namesake, and appeared to be safely established at the end of the first year, with a circulation of 12,000. Like its Philadelphia affiliate, the *Sun* was always noted for its enterprise and technical progress. It was a pioneer in the development of telegraph news. Both the Baltimore and Philadelphia penny papers worked with the *New York Herald* in exchanging the latest news. The arrangement accounted for numerous scoops, especially during the Mexican War. But the *Baltimore Sun* made a contribution of its own when it developed the Washington bureau of correspondence in its first year of operation. Soon other papers came to value the Baltimore publication for its complete and accurate coverage of national news. Government officials also began to follow the paper closely for trends in political development.

The success of the penny-paper pioneers encouraged other publishers to follow the pattern; 35 penny papers were started in New York in the 1830s. All but the *Sun* and *Herald* succumbed, but in other cities the promoters fared better. By 1840, the four largest American cities had penny papers. Most of them had similar news policies: much local news, great attention to human-interest stories, and a fat budget for entertainment material. But more and more significant news was creeping into the columns, and the penny papers led in aggressive news gathering.

GREELEY'S *NEW YORK TRIBUNE,* 1841

The maturing of the press for the masses was best indicated by the newspaper founded at the very beginning of the fifth decade of the nineteenth century. The paper was the *New York Tribune,* and its founder was Horace Greeley, soon to become one of the most influential editors in the history of American journalism. More books have been written about Greeley than about any other American of the period, except Lincoln.

Horace Greeley was like a character from a Dickens novel—so real that he appeared to be a caricature. He had the angularity of the Vermonter (which he was), a stiff, homespun personality, coupled with the shyness that makes the New England breed so difficult for others to understand. His inconsistencies were legendary. A professed Whig (the party opposed to popular rule), he worked all his life to bring a greater share of material and political benefits to the common people. A leader of the group standing for a continuance of the status quo, he was one of the most "radical" persons of his age. At a time when the democratic process was under great stress, Greeley "put his faith in the unshackled mind."

He saw the ample resources of the United States, and he was certain that every American could enjoy the abundant life, if only simple justice could be made to prevail. He believed in what he called "beneficent capitalism." The practical application of this theory was the American System, sponsored by Henry Clay. Clay was Greeley's great hero. Until death ended the career of the "Great Compromiser," as Clay was known, Greeley devoted a column of his paper to discussions of current issues under the standing headline, "Henry Clay." Greeley, like Clay, honestly believed that if the proceeds of the protective tariff could be used to develop markets for the farmers, all the workers of the country would be prosperous. Because Greeley advocated the high tariff, he was sometimes suspected by the masses of opposing their interests. Because he had scant regard for agrarian dominance in an age of expanding industrialism, he was accused by the farmers of hypocrisy. Because he believed in the organization of unions to prevent exploitation of the workers by the privileged, he was frequently attacked by the property interests.

Actually, his idea was to direct the forces of capitalism so that industry, labor, and agriculture could complement each other in improving the common lot. The day Greeley had in mind was one in which opportunity, work, and education would be available to all. Women would be paid at the same rate as men for similar services and would have equal civil rights. Temperance would prevail in all things. Labor would be well organized for its own protection. Capital would reap the benefits of a prosperous community, but would feel responsible for improving living standards. Slavery and imprisonment for debt would be abolished. John R. Commons, the great authority on the labor movement, called the *Tribune* "the first and only great vehicle this country has known for the ideas and experiments of constructive democracy."[7]

The man who proposed these revolutionary ideas was hardly messianic in appearance. He looked as though he had stepped out of a modern comic strip. He walked with a shambling, uncertain gait, as though he were feeling his way in the dark. His usual garb was a light-gray "duster," or gown, which he had purchased from an immigrant for $3 and wore winter and summer over his ill-fitting, nondescript suits. His guileless, baby-blue eyes were set in a moonlike face fringed with wispy whiskers sprouting out of his collar like reeds around a mossy stone. A high-pitched, whiny voice added nothing to this unimpressive ensemble. Yet this was the man who was to capture the loyalties of newspaper readers as few editors have in the history of American journalism.

Greeley began his career at the age of 15 as an apprentice to a printer whose business soon failed. Greeley traveled around New York State as a tramp printer for five years, reading voraciously all the while. When he arrived in New York City in 1831 he had just $10 to his name. After part-time work as a compositor, he finally landed a permanent position on the *Evening Post*.

Soon he and a partner, Francis Story, set up a shop of their own. They printed a small weekly on contract, but the main revenue was from lottery advertising, a circumstance his later foes and rivals never let him forget. The attempt of the partners to found a penny paper in the winter of 1833 has already been described. In 1834 Greeley founded the *New Yorker,* a stimulating and well-edited publication mainly devoted to literary fare. While publishing this paper he wrote editorials for the *Daily Whig* and had entire charge of a political paper published in Albany by the Whig party leaders. For six months during the presidential campaign of 1840 Greeley edited and published a campaign paper, the *Log Cabin.* He was an experienced journalist, therefore, when he announced in the *Log Cabin* that beginning April 10, 1841, he would publish a daily penny paper, the *New York Tribune.*

His political activities had made Greeley one of the New York Whig triumvirate, which also included state party boss Thurlow Weed, the *Albany Evening Journal* editor, and Governor William H. Seward. Now was the time to found a newspaper that could carry the Whig message to the common people. It is significant that the *Tribune* appeared just a month after President William Henry Harrison's inauguration following the Whig victory of 1840. But the president died a month after his inauguration, and many ambitions were thereby cut short. Not Greeley's, however.[8]

With $1000 of borrowed money and about that much of his own, plus a mortgage on his shop—a total capitalization of not more than $3000—Greeley issued the first *New York Tribune* as a penny paper. It was not much to look at. Its four pages were five columns wide and about the dimensions of a modern tabloid. The printing was good, however, and so was the content, apparently. At least it attracted readers, for Greeley boasted of a circulation in excess of 11,000 after the second month. This was about one-fourth the print order of the *Herald,* the most popular paper in America, but it was enough to establish the *Tribune* firmly.

The *Tribune* always trailed both the *Sun* and the *Herald* in daily circulation, but part of its great reputation was to rest on its weekly edition, which was a phenomenal success. It first appeared September 2, 1841. Offered at $2 a year, or $1 a year when purchased by "clubs" of 20 members (which was very common), the weekly *Tribune* largely established Greeley's reputation as the greatest editor of his day. It was said to have reached a status in the Midwest as being "next to the Bible" as its national circulation reached 200,000.

Admittedly, much of the *Tribune*'s content was rational only in the broad sense. Any offbeat social philosopher could express him- or herself in the paper, if he or she wrote forcefully. The common criticism of Greeley, indeed, was that he was utterly irrational. But some of his "idealism" was founded on sound reasoning. He saw that Jeffersonian ideas, based on an agrarian society, were not applicable to a nation fast becoming an industrial power. He also realized the dangers of unrestricted industrialism. The slums of Europe warned of that.

So Greeley groped for the way out. Lacking formal education, he knew little about social and political philosophers. He preferred to learn by experimentation. That is why he allowed Albert Brisbane the use of his columns. Brisbane was the American prophet of Fourierism, a scheme for curing the ills of capitalism by a form of collective living he called *associationism.* Greeley and Brisbane were both visitors to Brook Farm, an 1840s communitarian experiment in the socialist mold of Charles Fourier. There Greeley met his later staff members Charles A. Dana and George Ripley. In the 1850s the *Tribune* spent many pages explaining socialism, and Greeley himself debated the issue publicly with brilliant opponents, including Henry Raymond of the *New York Times.* For a decade one of the London correspondents Dana hired for the *Tribune* was Karl Marx, cofounder of communism. Greeley also fought steadily for agrarian reforms, including the Homestead Bill, which offered land in the West that immigrants could afford to develop. All this completely violated Whig doctrine, and yet Greeley was one of the leaders of the party. No wonder his critics were confused.

But it should be clear that Greeley did not endorse all the opinions ventilated in the *Tribune.* He was aware that most of the suggestions were impractical. But he was also aware that America was still groping toward a goal and that it would have to continue experimenting if democracy were to be kept dynamic. His readers appeared to understand.

The secret of Greeley's popularity was his consciousness of his responsibility to the reader. His flights into socialistic fancy were erratic and irresponsible, perhaps, but the average reader appeared to understand that the motives were sincere. That was why the farmers, who often disagreed violently with Greeley's views, read the "Try-bune," as they usually called it. How could anyone doubt the sincerity of a man who advocated a fairer distribution of wealth and who lived up to his advice by giving his employees all but a few shares of the gold mine he had made out of the *Tribune?* He took the press of the masses from the vulgar level of sensationalism to a position of promoting culture and stimulating ideas, and made it pay dividends. His protégés also raised the standards of the Fourth Estate. For many years Charles Dana, who appears again in these pages, was Greeley's assistant, and much of the early success of the *Tribune* has been ascribed to Dana. Henry J. Raymond, soon to establish the *New York Times,* started out under Greeley. Margaret Fuller, one of the truly great literary figures of the period, wrote regularly for the *Tribune.* Carl Schurz, John Hay, Whitelaw Reid, Henry James, William Dean Howells, George Ripley, and Richard Hildreth, all of whom made names for themselves in various fields of literature, journalism, and history, served under "Uncle Horace."

The identification of Greeley with his paper is brought out by an anecdote told by Joseph Bishop, the former editor of the *Post.* Bishop was in Vermont a year or so after Greeley's death in 1872 and made some remark about an article that had recently appeared in the *Tribune.* "Does the Try-bune still print?" asked a farmer in the audience. "Why, I thought Greeley was dead."[9]

RAYMOND'S *NEW YORK TIMES,* 1851

A thesis was advanced at the beginning of this chapter that when a new public is first tapped by the mass media, the appeal is invariably on an emotional plane. The result is a "sensational" vehicle of communication. Readers of the *Sun* first bought the paper primarily for its police reports. Many of these readers matured with the years, however, for as time went on, cheap papers competing successfully with the *Sun* offered more nourishing fare. Greeley proved that a publisher could reach the masses without resorting to sensationalism. Even the *Sun* and the *Herald* offered more substantial material over time. They had to in order to keep up with the increasing skills of their readers. Eventually, such papers left the semiliterate public behind, and another wave of sensational papers had to be established (as in the 1890s) to take up the slack. The completion of this cycle is exemplified by Henry J. Raymond of the *New York Times.*

As a college student, Raymond contributed to Greeley's *New Yorker,* which the youth admired greatly. After a visit to the New York editor, Raymond became Greeley's chief assistant in 1841, the year the *Tribune* was founded. George Jones was a colleague in the business office of the *Tribune.* Together they planned to put out the "ideal daily." Neither had sufficient money, however, for already it was impossible to establish a New York paper with $500 and a few packing-box desks, as Bennett had.

Raymond and Greeley were naturally incompatible. The younger man could never appreciate the erratic mental behavior of his employer, and soon Raymond left to work for Colonel James Watson Webb on the *Courier and Enquirer.* During this interim he established a reputation as an orator and budding politician. He was elected to the State Assembly in 1849 and became speaker in 1851. At this point he broke with Webb on the Free Soil Party issue. He took a position as an editor of *Harper's New Monthly Magazine* (established in June 1850), where he remained until 1856 as a part-time editor.

It was in 1851 that Raymond and Jones realized their old ambition of publishing a New York newspaper of their own. The first issue of the *New York Daily Times* appeared September 18, 1851. It sold for one cent, and thus showed its intention of being a paper for the masses, but it eschewed the sensationalism of the *Sun* and *Herald,* and the whimsy of the *Tribune,* as described in the policy expressed in the first issue: ". . . we do not mean to write as if we were in a passion [a slap at Greeley, who was regularly the butt of Raymond's jibes]—unless that shall really be the case; and we shall make it a point to get into a passion as rarely as possible."[10] One of the *Times*'s strong points was the interpreting of foreign news. Raymond sought to excel in reporting European events.

Raymond's contribution was the development of reasonable decency in public reporting. There was a minimum of personal invective in the *Times.* It seldom presented issues in the black-and-white patterns favored by Greeley. It was invariably fair in tone, if not in content, and no rival equaled it in developing the technique of careful reporting. It substituted accuracy for wishful thinking, even when Raymond was deeply involved in politics. Curiously, Raymond, who was addicted to politics, stood for a strangely objective nonpartisanship in his paper. It was as though the man had two completely different personalities.

BOWLES AND THE *SPRINGFIELD REPUBLICAN*

Another outstanding paper at this time was Massachusetts' *Springfield Republican.* Its founder was Samuel Bowles II, although his son, Samuel Bowles III, is more important to this history. The father was reared in Connecticut, where the family had been driven by economic depression. He was apprenticed to a printer at the age of 15. In 1819 he joined with John Francis of Wethersfield as a partner in the *Hartford Times,* a weekly that soon failed under the adverse conditions of the time. He and his wife and family loaded their household possessions and the *Times* press on a flatboat and poled up the Connecticut River to Springfield, Massachusetts. There, a group of Anti-Federalists helped him relocate as a publisher. First copies of the weekly *Springfield Republican* appeared in 1824 for 250 subscribers paying $2 a year. By 1840 Springfield was beginning to boom as a railroad center, and circulation was up to 1200.

Samuel Bowles III made the most of the excellent opportunities presented to him by his father, and it was the son who established the national reputation of the *Republican*. It was he who argued his father into "going daily" in March 1844 (it was an evening paper then but became morning a year later). Bowles made the paper successful by skillful organization of regional correspondence, so that every little community in the upper Connecticut Valley had reason to take the paper.

Partly responsible for the success of the paper were William B. Calhoun, who wrote many of the editorials readers credited to Bowles; Josiah Gilbert Holland, a fluent and articulate writer; and George Ashmun, a friend of Abraham Lincoln and a noted politician. But the main emphasis of the *Republican* was news, and Bowles made that his special department. He took over full control after the death of his father in 1851. Bowles was a sponsor of the new Republican party. By 1860 his weekly edition was a national institution, with a circulation of about 12,000, but with a reputation throughout the country exceeded only by that of the *Tribune*. The daily hovered around 6000, but that, too, was good for a provincial paper.

The reporters and editors of the *Republican* were craftspeople, proud of their product, and absorbed in their work. Young men from all over the United States tried to get on the *Republican* staff. A tour with the Springfield paper was a kind of advanced degree in journalism. A "*Republican* man" was welcome on the biggest papers in the country.

THE RACE FOR NEWS

The pioneers of the penny press probably did not realize what a profound change they were to bring about in American journalism. As the historian-journalist Gerald W. Johnson once pointed out, editors like Day, Bennett, Greeley, and Abell lived in a period of great change—change so profound that by comparison the modifications after the War of Independence were slight.[11] Many institutions were drastically altered after 1830, but none more than the press.

Three factors control the development of a newspaper. They are: (1) the reading public, (2) the system of communications, and (3) improvements in production. In the second quarter of the nineteenth century, all three factors exerted great influence on the press. The public became more discerning as it acquired greater literacy and as more and more publications of various types were offered. The system of communications was developed beyond the wildest dreams of its promoters. The steam press, the beginning of automatic printing, and the perfection of paper making also helped to change the character of the press. The pioneers of the penny press thus found themselves engaged in a game, whose old rules had been canceled and whose new ones were still being formulated. As Johnson says, "To survive, it was necessary to guess what the new rules would be, and to guess correctly most of the time. Conditions demanded alert and supple intelligence, backed by sturdy common sense; for policies whose necessity is as plain as day now were then wrapped in obscurity."[12]

The race for news reflected the American zeal in promoting technological progress. The communications revolution described in this chapter evolved out of this expansionism. Its effect on the press has been measured in a study of news gathering from 1820 to 1860 undertaken at the University of North Carolina. The study's findings showed that the average number of stories of news events published in dailies within a week of occurrence increased from 45 percent to 76 percent during the period. Stories taking more than a month to appear dropped from 28 percent to 8 percent. Increased ability to use telegraphic news would further decrease the lag. Part of this improvement was due to an increased number—from 32 percent to 55 percent—of news items actively gathered by reporters, editors, or correspondents of the sampled papers.[13] This meant a big drop in the use of clipped items, contributions, and other general fare.

NEWS IN THE MAIL

It was Benjamin Franklin who had established the policy of the free exchange of newspapers between editors in 1758 as colonial postmaster general. He also provided regular postal service for publications.

Congress in 1792 and 1794 adapted colonial postal customs to federal control. The generation that drafted the Constitution and the First Amendment adopted below-cost newspaper postage as a means of uniting a fragile nation. Indeed, this represented the first communication policy of the U.S. government, Professor Richard B. Kielbowicz points out. Letter writers underwrote cheap newspaper rates; single-sheet letters paid 25 cents postage beyond 400 miles, while newspapers were carried for a maximum of 1.5 cents regardless of size or weight. Rates for newspapers declined after 1845.

Equally important were special postal services provided to the press. Beginning in 1851, Congress authorized the delivery of newspapers postage-free in the county of publication to offset the advantages enjoyed by the widely circulating metropolitan press. From 1792 to 1873, Congress allowed editors to continue exchanging copies of their papers postage-free, a service that furnished the bulk of newspapers' out-of-town news before the establishment of telegraphic news services. Furthermore, the post office operated expresses intermittently from the 1820s to 1860s that speeded news in advance of the regular mails.[14]

FIRST WASHINGTON REPORTERS

One of the first news sources to be tapped methodically was Congress. The beginning of a Washington press corps can be traced to the establishment by Nathaniel Carter of a capital service for his paper, the *New York Statesman,* in December 1822. Carter's paper used the phrase "Washington Correspondence" from then until 1824. Next on the scene, when Congress convened in December 1827, were three correspondents; James Gordon Bennett of the *New York Enquirer;* Joseph I. Buckingham of the *Boston Courier;* and Samuel L. Knapp of the *Charleston Courier.* These three inaugurated what has been continuous press coverage of Congress ever since. Buckingham left after the session; Knapp stayed into the 1830s. Bennett later become the correspondent of the *Courier and Enquirer* and the most famous member of the early Washington press corps.[15]

Eliab Kingman, who was the first long-term Washington correspondent, ran a stringer service for various clients, including the *Journal of Commerce,* from 1830 to 1861. Matthew L. Davis worked from 1832 to 1840 for the *Times* of London and the *Courier and Enquirer* (who called him "The Spy in Washington"). James and Erastus Brooks, founders of the *New York Express,* reported in the 1830s.

Washington's first important woman journalist was Anne Royall, an unconventional but competent writer and editor who, at age 61 in 1831, founded a four-page paper, *Paul*

Pry. From 1836 to 1854 Royall printed *The Huntress,* which stood for Jacksonian princi-ples, free public education, free speech, and justice for immigrants and Native Americans. Holding the honor of being the first woman to sit in a congressional press gallery was Jane Grey Swisshelm, editor of the antislavery *Saturday Visitor* in Pittsburgh. Swisshelm came to Washington to send her columns to Horace Greeley's *New York Tribune,* at $5 a week. On April 17, 1850, she sat in the Senate press gallery, but then decided not to return. Na-tionally known as a crusader and feminist, she became an editor in Minnesota in 1857, es-caping an unhappy marriage and seeking quiet. But her combative style led a mob to sack her press and throw the type into the river. Undaunted, she made her *St. Cloud Democrat* a voice of the newly founded Republican Party, a fierce opponent of slavery, and a shrill advocate of women's rights.[16] Ranking ahead of these women journalists was Cornelia Walter, who became the first woman editor of a major daily when she ran the family-owned *Boston Transcript* from 1842 to 1847.

Margaret Fuller was in Washington as a *New York Tribune* staff member from 1844 to 1846. She had become editor of *The Dial,* a journal of transcendental philosophy spon-sored by Ralph Waldo Emerson, in 1840 at age 30. Known in Boston for her intellectual leadership, literary skill, and feminist interests, she attracted Greeley, who asked her to write literary reviews and profiles. In 1846 she became the first U.S. woman foreign cor-respondent, and she wrote for the *Tribune* from Britain, France, and Italy. She settled in Rome, adopted socialist thinking, married an Italian revolutionary who fathered her child, and covered the 1848 political upheavals for Greeley. En route home in 1850 to pursue her writing about the role of American women, Fuller died with her husband and child in a shipwreck off the eastern coast.

By 1860 the Senate listed 23 correspondents, the House 51. Lawrence A. Gobright became the Associated Press agent after 1853. Ben: Perley Poore of the *Boston Journal* ar-rived in 1854 for a 33-year career. John Nugent of the *New York Herald* and James W. Si-monton of the *New York Times* both had pre–Civil War brushes with Congress. Noah Brooks of the *Sacramento Union* and Samuel Wilkeson of the *New York Tribune* were among the leaders of the wartime press corps.

Jane Grey Swisshelm (left) and Margaret Fuller, leading women journalists

FOREIGN NEWS

Foreign news, taken from European papers, had always appeared in American newspapers. But not until 1811 was there much concern about offering foreign news reports while they were still fresh. At that time British naval vessels were searching American ships at sea for British deserters. War was imminent, and every message from Europe told of new threats to American commerce. To satisfy the craving of his customers for such information, Samuel Gilbert had provided a reading room in his seven-story Exchange Coffee House, which dominated the Boston waterfront as the tallest building in America. The reading room was typical of coffeehouses in that it supplied foreign newspapers. Gilbert's special contribution was a Marine News Book, which offered much more current and local intelligence for his merchant and shipping office clientele. When the preparation of the news books began to take too much time, Gilbert hired an assistant to carry on this work. On November 20, 1811, he announced in the *Columbian Centinel* that young Samuel Topliff, Jr., would henceforth be in charge of the "Marine and General News Books." Topliff began to meet incoming ships in his rowboat, so that he could return sooner with important news. This was the first systematic attempt in this country to gather foreign news. Later, Topliff hired correspondents in Europe to prepare the dispatches he then received from incoming ship captains.

Other cities perfected similar services. The *Charleston Courier* was first in America with news of the peace with Great Britain in 1814, its ship-news reporter having learned of the event only seven weeks after its occurrence. By 1828 New York had taken the lead in such news gathering. The most enterprising news merchant in the fast-growing city was David Hale, manager of the *Journal of Commerce,* published by Arthur Tappan. The paper was the newest of the ten dailies then being published in New York. Hale soon found that the older publications had established a service for obtaining news from incoming ships. So had Colonel James Watson Webb, owner of the powerful *Courier and Enquirer.* To gain advantage, Hale purchased a fast sloop, which met the European packets as they were trimmed off Sandy Hook for the run up the bay, hours before they would reach Battery Place. Webb met this challenge, as he did others.

Not long after this Hale and his partner, Gerard Hallock, purchased the *Journal of Commerce* and made it into the most aggressive of the six-penny papers. Like the penny-press editors, the partners understood the value of news as a commodity. They sometimes put out extras when there were important stories. They made the front page the show window, as in modern newspaper practice. But above all, they promoted any system that would speed the gathering and dissemination of news. It was Hale and Hallock who inaugurated the pony-express service between Washington and New York. The *Courier and Enquirer* offered stiff competition, but until Bennett came along and outperformed the partners, Hale and Hallock led the New York pack in sniffing out the news.

PONIES, PIGEONS, TRAINS, STEAMBOATS

Bennett was, of course, not content with anything short of the best in news gathering. When Daniel Craig began using carrier pigeons to fly news reports from distant points to eastern cities, Bennett subscribed to the service and even provided his own pigeons. When the steamship, railroad, and magnetic telegraph superseded sailing ships, ponies, and pigeons, Bennett was quick to use the new means of communication, but so were his competitors.

The United States government had a hand in developing the rapid processing of news during this period. Following the lead of the newspaper people, Postmaster General Amos

Kendall established regular pony-express service between Philadelphia and New York, taking over a route from the *Courier and Enquirer* in 1835.[17] By 1836 this express service had been extended across the main routes, cutting the travel time between New York and New Orleans to less than seven days. Express riders did not carry the full newspapers but rather proof sheets of important stories. These "slips," as they were called, preceded the regular papers by as much as a week on such long routes as the New Orleans system. The arrangement enabled newspapers around the country to work out cooperative exchange systems for beating rivals to big news.

In the 1830s and 1840s, railroads gradually began to replace the pony expresses. From 23 miles of track in 1830, up to 9000 miles were completed by 1850. The railroad was a great boon to the newspapers. It not only provided fast distribution but also served as a communications agency. In May 1837, the *Baltimore Sun* rushed President Van Buren's message from Washington in less than two hours by way of the Baltimore & Ohio Railroad. Previously, Abell and his associates would have had to wait until the following morning to obtain such news from the Washington papers.

In 1841, Bennett, Swain (*Philadelphia Public Ledger*), and Abell (*Baltimore Sun*) together hired a special locomotive to carry President Harrison's inaugural address from Washington to Baltimore, Philadelphia, and New York. The *Baltimore Sun* was able to put out an early afternoon extra covering the noonday speech. Proofs of the speech were mailed to the paper's exchanges, which thereby scored a 24-hour scoop over rivals.

The steamship also contributed to the development of fast news gathering. Travel across the Atlantic was reduced from weeks to days. In 1845, when the Oregon question brought a threat of war with England, leading papers cooperated in meeting fast ships at Halifax, the first port of call for the Atlantic steamers. Horses brought the news across the Nova Scotia peninsula to the Bay of Fundy, where a fast steamer relayed the information to Portland, Maine. A railroad train brought the news to Washington less than 50 hours after it had been received in Halifax.

NEWS BY TELEGRAPH

But the biggest boost in speedy transmission of news was given by the telegraph. On May 24, 1844, Samuel F. B. Morse sat at a table in the old Supreme Court chamber in Washington and tapped out a message in code. His assistant in Baltimore decoded the sounds. The message: "What hath God wrought?" Later that afternoon, Morse sent the first telegraphic message published in a newspaper, the *Baltimore Patriot:* "One o'clock—There has just been made a motion in the House to go into committee of the whole on the Oregon question. Rejected—ayes, 79; nays, 86." This was one of the significant reports of the century—not because of the intrinsic news value, but because it portended a whole new system of communication.

Swain, the Philadelphia publisher, was one of the incorporators of the Magnetic Telegraph Company, which promoted Morse's invention. Abell, in Baltimore, used the columns of his paper to demand the help of Congress in subsidizing the inventor's work. He also helped finance the Washington-Baltimore test of the new device. But for conventional reasons, the *Baltimore Sun* gave little space to one of the big stories of the nineteenth century. The Monday paper assigned the first telegraphic news dispatch to the second page, under local news, headed "Magnetic Telegraph." Eleven lines told the story of the experiment that was to do so much for communication throughout the world.

Newspapers were quick to make use of the new invention. In May 1846, President James K. Polk's message to Congress calling for war with Mexico was telegraphed to

Baltimore for the exclusive use of the *Sun*. Bennett became famous for his use of the invention to help him outperform his rivals.

The telegraph also stimulated the growth of small-town dailies. It was high time; unchecked, the metropolitan papers might soon have dominated the field, as they did in Great Britain. In Illinois, where city dailies from St. Louis, Cincinnati, and other big publishing centers had absorbed more and more of the circulation, 30 daily newspapers were founded during the decade following the start of telegraphic news service. The ability of small-town papers to get the same news as their big city rivals was stimulating and pointed to cooperative news. For example, when the telegraph wire from Albany reached Utica early in January 1846, the *Daily Gazette* there received its first telegraphic bulletins. The news was so fresh, and the transmission so novel, that the editor devoted about a column to the dispatches. To share the costs, the publishers at Utica and other upstate papers had organized themselves by March 1846 into what became the New York State Associated Press. Nineteen papers were in that first U.S. news service by August, and news agents were employed in Albany and New York City.[18] The telegraph line linked Albany and Buffalo by July, and Albany and New York City in September. Similar lines were stretching into the interior of the country and to other papers.

THE GENESIS OF THE ASSOCIATED PRESS

The organization of a large-scale news service to reach all these far-flung publications and to meet the needs of the big New York newspapers now seemed a logical step. Many persons had their eyes on the business, including Dr. Alexander Jones, a physician turned reporter; Daniel Craig, the pigeon expert; and various promoters of telegraphic services. But the enterprising New York City dailies proved able to control the situation.

Frederic Hudson, the *Herald*'s managing editor who later wrote a history of journalism, credits Hale of the *Journal of Commerce* with breaking the ice by calling Bennett, whom he despised, and suggesting that the rivals pool their news-gathering resources for the reporting of the Mexican War in 1846.[19] However, nothing resulted on war coverage. But recent exhaustive research has established that the *New York Herald* and the *Tribune* began running identical telegraphic dispatches from Washington on May 7, 1846. These identical routine news stories continued on an almost daily basis.[20] The groundwork was being laid.

Supposedly the publishers of the leading New York papers met in the *Sun* offices in May 1848 and reached an agreement. No record was kept, but later accounts named as those present Bennett and Hudson of the *Herald;* Colonel Webb and his assistant, Henry Raymond, of the *Courier and Enquirer;* Greeley of the *Tribune;* Beach of the *Sun;* Erastus and James Brooks of the *Express;* and Hale and Hallock of the *Journal of Commerce*. They had already chartered the coastal steamer *Buena Vista* to intercept westbound transatlantic steamers and had bought a harbor newsboat.[21] On May 13, 1848, Raymond was writing to the telegraph agent in Boston, telling him that those six papers wished "to procure foreign news by telegraph from Boston in common"—including both news arriving by steamships that docked in Boston before proceeding to New York and news relayed from Halifax. A week later Raymond was agreeing to a contract on behalf of the "Associated Press," providing for a payment of $100 for 3000 words of telegraphic news and stating that the news would also be forwarded to newspapers in Philadelphia and Baltimore.[22]

There is no documentary evidence of a formal organization in 1848, however, and the best precise date for the legal founding of the predecessor organization that grew into the modern Associated Press is January 11, 1849. A copy of the agreement signed that day, forming the Harbor News Association among the six previously named New York dailies, was found in 1967 in the file of the Henry J. Raymond papers in the manuscript division of the New York Public Library by Professor Richard A. Schwarzlose. Its previously unknown details provided that the six partners would operate two boats to gather news from incoming ships in New York harbor, would share the costs, would sell news to papers outside New York City, and would set up membership rules.[23] In 1851, apparently because the selling of news by telegraph was becoming more important, the group signed a new agreement as the Telegraphic and General News Association.

The name "Associated Press" did not come into general use until the 1860s, but the New York City group was the forerunner of that modern-day press association. Dr. Alexander Jones became superintendent of the service and was succeeded in 1851 by Daniel Craig. That year the *Times* became the seventh newspaper member of the combine. In 1856 the group tightened its organization by adopting what was called the "Regulations of the General News Association of the City of New York."[24] Soon called the New York Associated Press, the group established a firm grip on cooperative telegraphic news reporting and sold its service to outsiders. Among its customers were the original New York State Associated Press and AP groups in Boston, Philadelphia, Baltimore, and the South.[25]

THE MEXICAN WAR NEWS

The Mexican War provided the nation's press with an excellent opportunity to demonstrate news enterprise. It became the first foreign war to be covered extensively by American correspondents, and the papers made expensive, elaborate arrangements to have their reports carried back to the United States. By combining the abilities of the pony express, steamers, railroads, and the fledgling telegraph, the press established a 2000-mile communications link that repeatedly beat military couriers and the United States mails with the news from the front lines.

So effective was the express system devised by the press that an exasperated President Polk learned of the American victory at Vera Cruz via a telegram from publisher Abell of the *Baltimore Sun*.[26] Such enterprise boosted newspaper circulations. One Boston writer observed: "If our troops do but make as vigourous a charge upon the enemy as newsboys do upon the public with their extras the victory will be ours without a doubt."[27]

The purpose of the war, however, left a number of editors perplexed. Even though they reported the American victories with a mixture of pride, jingoism, and business sense, some also worried about the moral consequences of the conflict. To Horace Greeley it was a war "in which Heaven must take part against us."[28] James Gordon Bennett, meanwhile, was an adamant supporter of the conflict, arguing, "We are on the verge of vast and unknown changes in the destiny of nations."[29]

The penny-press leaders threw their editorial support behind the war and at the same time established the New York to New Orleans express system to deliver the news from the battle zones. The express system "is a creature of modern times," Bennett explained to his readers, "and is characteristic of the American people."[30] If not characteristic of the people, the system clearly was characteristic of the American press in the 1840s. Led by the New York morning dailies, a number of papers participated, including the *Philadelphia North American* and *Public Ledger,* the energetic *Baltimore Sun,* the *Charleston Courier,* and the *New Orleans Picayune.* During the final six months of the war these papers pooled their efforts to operate the delivery system on a daily basis.

The New Orleans press, closest to the war zones, led the coverage of the conflict.[31] Because newspapers of the day depended heavily on news from their "exchanges"—free copies they received of other newspapers—the reporting by the New Orleans correspondents with the armies was widely reprinted throughout the United States. One of the innovative New Orleans papers was *La Patria,* the nation's first Spanish-language daily. The *Baltimore Sun* and other leading dailies relied on letters from *La Patria*'s correspondents and on translations of Spanish-language papers in Mexico and Latin America.[32] The Spanish-language press in California also paid close attention to battle reports.

The star reporter of the Mexican War was George Wilkins Kendall, editor-publisher of the *New Orleans Picayune.* Kendall covered all the major battles from Monterrey to Chapultepec and gave accurate accounts of the military strategy involved. At least 10 other "special correspondents" followed Kendall into the field, led by Christopher Mason Haile of the *Picayune,* James L. Freaner of the *New Orleans Delta,* and John Peoples for the *Delta, Bee,* and *Crescent.*[33] Haile, a West Point dropout, matched Kendall's reporting ability and added the innovation of providing readers with detailed lists of battle casualties. Freaner and Peoples, former New Orleans printers, became accomplished writers and gained national reputations under their respective pseudonyms of "Mustang" and "Chaparral." Freaner capped his successful career as an army correspondent by personally delivering the peace treaty from Mexico City to Washington in a then-record 17 days.

The reports from the correspondents at the front often supported America's involvement in the war and the principle of Manifest Destiny. They also empathized with the plight of the invading American forces, who were isolated in the interior of Mexico; reflected attitudes of distrust and bias against the Mexicans; and promoted and reinforced the popular war-hero images of generals Zachary Taylor and Winfield Scott. Taylor, benefiting from a wave of favorable newspaper publicity resulting from his battlefield exploits, captured the White House in 1848.

A quixotic chapter in the war was provided by the colorful publisher of the *New York Sun,* Moses Yale Beach. Accompanied by Jane McManus Storms, an editorial writer for his paper, Beach went to Mexico City in 1847 on a secret peace mission for the American government. The effort failed, and Beach, suspected of assisting antiwar forces in Mexico, barely escaped capture by Santa Anna. Storms, a strong advocate of Manifest Destiny, wrote commentaries about the war for the *Sun* and *New York Tribune* from Havana, Vera Cruz, and the Mexican capital under her pseudonym "Montgomery."[34]

The peace treaty of Guadalupe Hidalgo, ratified on May 30, 1848, had long-range effects. Mexicans considered the provisions unfair, causing unhappiness that lasts to this day. They gave up all claims to Texas and lost about 40 percent of their territory—including California. California officially became a state in 1850. Within the United States the victory had strong political and military implications. The issue of slavery in the newly acquired territory became a major story of the 1850s and eventually helped lead the country into civil war.

Of course, differences between the North and the South first emerged early in the nation's history and deepened throughout the antebellum years, as will be discussed in the next chapter. In the midst of those divisions, the acquisition of Mexican land brought the key issue of slavery to the forefront.

PRESSES FOR MASS CIRCULATION

This brings to us the final factor in developing the press. Mass circulation, and all the changes it brought about, could not have been accomplished unless papers could be produced cheaply, quickly, and in general bulk. This problem had to be solved by the technical expert, especially the builder of printing presses.

(R. Hoe & Co., Inc.)

This ingenious Hoe-type revolving press of 1855 printed 20,000 sheets an hour.

The improvement in presses and the need for fast printing are indicated by the experience of the *Philadelphia Public Ledger.* It was founded in 1836 as a penny paper dependent on large circulation for success, but its printing equipment consisted of the usual hand press, seen in a majority of newspaper shops. In six months the paper acquired a circulation of nearly 8000, and it was no longer possible to meet the demands of the public with the cumbersome Clymer press. Swain therefore installed the finest equipment obtainable at the time—a Napier single-cylinder press powered by steam. A year later the publisher had to order another press, this time a double-cylinder machine.

The first cylinder presses merely rolled back and forth over the flat type bed—like some of the proof presses seen in printing shops today. Speed could be doubled by using two cylinders at a time. But even these presses were not fast enough to supply the circulations developed by the penny papers. The problem was solved for the time by Richard Hoe's type-revolving press, first installed in the *Public Ledger* shop in 1846. Hoe substituted horizontal cylinders for the flat beds. Countersunk in these cylinders were curved iron beds, one for each page in the paper. Type matter was locked in these beds by an ingenious system of wedge-shaped rules to keep the type from flying out as the cylinders revolved at high speed. In 1849 the *New York Herald* installed one of these "lightning" presses with six cylinders capable of printing 12,000 impressions an hour. By the outbreak of the Civil War it was possible for an enterprising publisher to print up to 20,000 impressions an hour.

The type-revolving press speeded up the processing of news, but it also imposed limitations on the use of multiple-column makeup. These limitations were overcome by the development of stereotype plates. James Dellagana, a London printer, produced curved, solid plates by making an impression of the type forms in a soft mold, curving this mold to fit the cylinder, and then pouring hot lead onto the mold, or "matrix," to make a type plate. Stereotyping made possible duplicate pages for duplicate presses, bigger headlines, and advertising display devices. Bennett used five duplicate presses during the Civil War.

NEWSPAPERS MOVE WEST

The small-city newspapers changed much less radically than did their big-city rivals, but even in the hinterland the press was experiencing the impact of the communications revolution. The telegraph lines reached Portland, Maine, by 1846, Charleston and St. Louis the next year, and Chicago and Milwaukee in 1848. Pony expresses continued to operate beyond the ends of the lines—notably the overland pony express from St. Joseph, Missouri, to Sacramento, California, which opened in 1860 and continued until the telegraph reached the Pacific in October 1861, with 50,000 miles of wire.

Newspapers in the interior did the best they could. Though local news was a leading commodity, they scrambled to get the Washington and foreign news from proof slips, exchange papers, and meager telegrams. Cincinnati and St. Louis, particularly, were major publishing centers, and both had several daily newspapers by the 1850s. The leaders in Cincinnati were the *Gazette,* founded in 1815 as a weekly and transformed into a daily in 1827, and the *Commercial,* begun in 1843. St. Louis had as its top dailies the *Missouri Republican,* founded as the *Gazette* in 1808, and the *Missouri Democrat,* started in 1852. Secondhand presses, printing equipment, ink, and paper moved out from these centers to smaller towns as the newspaper followed the lines of settlement.

Population was booming in the Great Lakes area, where Chicago and Milwaukee became prominent publishing centers. Chicago's first paper was the *Weekly Democrat,* begun in 1833 and made into a daily in 1840. The *Chicago Tribune* appeared in 1847, and after its purchase by Joseph Medill and his partners in 1855, it became the leading daily. It absorbed the *Weekly Democrat* in 1861. Milwaukee's initial weekly was the *Advertiser,* which was founded in 1836 and lived to become the *Wisconsin News.* The *Milwaukee Sentinel,* started in 1837, became the city's first daily in 1844. The transformation from weekly to daily publication was repeated elsewhere; the *Minnesota Pioneer* of 1849, the state's first paper, became a daily in 1854 and had several competitors in St. Paul.

The establishment of rival papers as mouthpieces for political groups accounted for some of the growth. Some of the western papers were founded as a means of promoting settlement and sale of lands; one such was the *Oregon Spectator,* begun in Oregon City in 1846 as the first Pacific Coast publication. Others were missionary papers, like the first publications in Kansas and the Oklahoma region. Army posts also contributed papers. The weeklies typically carried a good deal of literary material in addition to local news. The dailies, too, attempted to satisfy the hunger for reading matter as well as news. The *Alta California,* which began in San Francisco in 1849 and became the city's first daily in 1850, later achieved fame for publishing the writings of Bret Harte and Samuel Clemens, better known as Mark Twain. Nevada's *Territorial Enterprise,* founded in 1858, boasted Mark Twain as city editor in the early 1860s.

Efforts to publish newspapers for the large Spanish-speaking population in the Southwest and California began in 1834, when *El Crepúsculo de la Libertad* was printed in Santa Fé. But following the Mexican War the journalistic work often appeared first as Spanish-language sections of English-language newspapers. The *Californian* in Monterey (1846), the *Santa Fé Republican* (1847), and the *Los Angeles Star* (1851) were subsidized to print legal notices in Spanish. Later the *Californian* moved to San Francisco and merged with the *California Star* (1846) to form the *California Star and Californian* but dropped its Spanish-language page. Within a few years there were numerous separate Spanish-language papers from Texas to California.[35]

The push into the far West and into the mining country produced other early newspapers: the *Oregonian* in Portland (1850); the *Sacramento Union* (1851); the *San Francisco*

Bulletin (1855) and *San Francisco Call* (1856); the Mormon Church's *Deseret News* in Salt Lake City (1850); and the *Rocky Mountain News* in Denver (1859). Easterners who flocked to the California gold fields and to the Nevada and Colorado mining towns wanted more news than the local papers offered, however. New York papers, particularly the *Herald* and the *Tribune,* issued California editions that were sent by steamer around the Horn or by overland stage. Papers in other eastern cities soon followed suit. For wherever an American went in the expanding nation, he or she wanted the news that an aggressive press corps was providing.

HARPER'S WEEKLY.
A JOURNAL OF CIVILIZATION.

VOL. V.—No. 227.] NEW YORK, SATURDAY, MAY 4, 1861. [SINGLE COPIES SIX CENTS.
$2.50 PER YEAR IN ADVANCE.

Entered according to Act of Congress, in the Year 1861, by Harper & Brothers, in the Clerk's Office of the District Court for the Southern District of New York.

THE HOUSE-TOPS IN CHARLESTON DURING THE BOMBARDMENT OF SUMTER.

A leading picture weekly depicts the start of the Civil War.

7

The Irrepressible Conflict

He who opposes the public liberty overthrows his own.
> —*William Lloyd Garrison*

The Jacksonian era brought out clearly the increasing absorption in America with sectional differences. The beginning of the "irrepressible conflict," as one historian has called the Civil War, can be traced back to colonial times.[1] The petitions to the King long before 1776; the arguments over the Constitution at the Philadelphia convention; the drafting of the Kentucky and Virginia Resolutions after the Alien and Sedition Acts were passed; and the debates over the tariff of 1828 are some of the evidences of the fault line along which the country would one day split. By 1848, people were no longer voting by party but by section. Ultimately, slavery was the *key* cause of the Civil War. One way or another, it was at the root of the sectional divisions that led to war.[2]

There is a tendency to think of the South as turning away from American traditions when it seceded in 1861. But it was the North—meaning the industrial Northeast—not the South, that developed a different way of life after 1820. Generally speaking, the South was about the same in 1861 as it had been in 1761. On the eve of the War between the States, the South retained the impress of the eighteenth century. Slavery was the basis of the Cotton Kingdom's agricultural system. Life centered in the plantation, and so commercial cities did not assume the importance they had in the Northeast. Lacking such centers, the South had only a small middle class and virtually no white proletariat. But it abounded in great orators, great political leaders, and great writers. British cotton and tobacco buyers took the South's main crops, and the southerner bought as well as sold abroad.

From this environment came a governing group with a high sense of honor and morals. Family and land counted for more than money in the South, because money was

121

not as essential to the agrarian as it was to the northern capitalist and wage earner. Money was the sign of success in the North. Land was the criterion in the South. But land values declined in the South some time after 1800, as the staple crops exhausted the soil. Little was known of soil fertilization then, and so immigrants moved to fresh land, thereby reducing the demand for, and consequently the value of, the older lands. Since there was no profit to be made in land speculation, trade, or industry, the capitalist tended to leave the agrarian in full control. The South thus had reason to fear for its future. The industrial North was growing much faster than the South. Population pressure would inevitably give the North political dominance. Already the "tariff of abominations" of 1828 had disclosed what the North would impose upon the South if given free rein.

Both sections turned to the West as an ally when it became clear that the frontier region would determine the outcome of the conflict. The West was agrarian, like the South. It also suffered from high tariffs. Westerners had natural antipathies to the industrial North. They resented the northern sabotage of every legislative attempt to ease the debt of the farmer and to open up free lands. On the other hand, westerners were not as dependent on world markets as were southerners. Westerners were interested in reaching local or regional markets. Their goal was to get their produce to these markets cheaply and easily, and here they found an ally in the northern capitalists. Roads, canals, steamboat subsidies, and railroads were the prices paid by the North for the temporary allegiance of the West against the South.

Westerners also demanded the opening of the frontier to homesteaders. Both the North and South were opposed to this. Southerners feared that the opening of new lands would lead to a preponderance of free states, which would add to the overwhelming weight against the South. Northerners, on the other hand, tended to block westward expansion because it depressed property values in their section, and because free land either kept wages higher than they would otherwise have been or reduced the reservoir of cheap labor in the industrial areas. The point here is that western victory on this issue was a kind of bribe paid by the North for the support of the West. One evidence of this was the Homestead Act, passed on the eve of the war after years of northern objection. Once the West had committed itself, the South had only two choices. It could admit defeat and modify its way of life to suit the North, or it could cast off from an alien system and go its own way—secede.

The Civil War can be viewed as a clash between two contrasting cultures with different social values, much of which stemmed from the institution of slavery. And while other differences were negotiable, there could be no compromise between the two sides on slavery. And so slavery became the issue on which the concept of the American union was tested.

Among the many willing to die for the cause was the abolitionist John Brown, at Harper's Ferry in 1859. To Ralph Waldo Emerson, "Old Ossawatomie" Brown had "made the gallows glorious like the cross." And Walt Whitman, poet and sometime journalist, wrote of Brown's execution:

> I would sing how an old man, with white hair, mounted the scaffold in Virginia, (I was at hand, silent I stood with teeth shut close, I watch'd, I stood very near you old man when cool and indifferent, but trembling with age and your unheal'd wounds, you mounted the scaffold.)[3]

This indicates what the slavery issue meant to people of lofty sentiment. It took some time to sweep the masses into the movement, but eventually the people of the North made slavery a fighting issue, and the press was effective in helping to bring this about. Advocates of the campaigns against slavery were known as "abolitionists." An outstanding abolitionist editor was William Lloyd Garrison, who makes an excellent case study of how the press became such an important factor in the struggle.

GARRISON AND THE *LIBERATOR*

Garrison was born in Newburyport, Massachusetts, of English and Irish stock. His father was a drunkard who abused his family, and Garrison must have been influenced by these circumstances when he took up the temperance issue while still a youth. He was a jack-of-all-trades until he became a printer. That appeared to be his proper niche. Like Benjamin Russell and Isaiah Thomas, Garrison received most of his education at the type case. It was an education that made him literate rather than learned.

He was in his twenties when he met Benjamin Lundy, the gentle Quaker who had started out as a temperance missionary but who had since carried this reforming zeal over into the antislavery movement. It is significant that Quakers had been important in the successful antislavery movement in Great Britain. At any rate, Garrison became one of Lundy's recruits. Soon Garrison had been satisfactorily persecuted—an essential step in the progress of any effective zealot. He emerged from seven months in jail a confirmed abolitionist and with that supreme gift: a cause so absorbing that life itself is not too great a price for it. He moved to Boston, and on January 1, 1831, he issued the first copy of the *Liberator* there.

It was not very impressive, this voice of the abolitionist. Garrison said in 1837 that his publication had never exceeded 3000 subscribers. Much of the time it hovered around 1500, and about one-fourth of that was in black areas, where the readers were either disenfranchised or had little political influence. The editor was always losing entire blocks of readers because of his tactless scorn of men, institutions, and traditions sacred to certain publics. And yet this was part of the medium that was to rouse the North to battle.

Garrison had one weapon, his press, but it was to make him invincible. Through this press he spread his creed far and wide, until the abolitionist movement began to work on the minds of the apathetic. He reached such persons with words like these:

> He who opposes the public liberty overthrows his own. . . . There is no safety where there is no strength; no strength without Union; no Union without justice; no justice where faith and truth are wanting. The right to be free is a truth planted in the hearts of men.[4]

This describes Garrison, a man of courage and determination, imbued with righteousness, narrow and fanatical. What he said was bad for business. Most of the country was prosperous at this time. When people are comfortable, conscience is often half asleep.

Nameplate of Garrison's famed abolitionist paper

Garrison jerked consciences awake—always an unpopular move. Even the religious leaders resented the man, particularly his self-righteousness. One member of the clergy complained that abolitionists like Garrison did not do their work like "Christian gentlemen." To which Garrison replied:

> These are your men of "caution" and "prudence" and "judiciousness." Sir, I have learned to hate those words. Whenever we attempt to imitate our Great Exemplar, and press the truth of God in all its plainness upon the conscience, why, we are imprudent; because, forsooth, a great excitement will ensue. Sir, slavery will not be overthrown without excitement—a most tremendous excitement.[5]

Garrison caused the most violent public reaction since Tom Paine. Amos Kendall, himself a great journalist and a leader of Jacksonian democracy, believed that Garrison should be gagged. As postmaster general, Kendall allowed abolitionist papers to be rifled from the official mail sacks by southern "committees" charged with that task.[6] The state of Massachusetts was ready to forbid the export of the *Liberator,* and in many states, distributors of the paper were intimidated without redress.

ABOLITIONISTS AND "FIRE-EATERS"

James G. Birney, one of the more reasonable abolitionists, was mobbed when he began printing his paper, the *Philanthropist,* in Cincinnati. Note that this was a city in a northern, not a southern, state.

At least one abolitionist died for this cause. He was Elijah Lovejoy, editor of the *St. Louis Observer,* a strident abolitionist weekly founded in 1835. A mass meeting of irate citizens resulted in a resolution informing Lovejoy that free expression as guaranteed in the Bill of Rights did not extend to editors such as Lovejoy who threatened the peace of the community. Lovejoy replied that public resolutions could not fetter an editor.

As an act of good faith, however, Lovejoy moved his press across the river to Alton, Illinois. His office was at once wrecked by a mob. He appealed nationally for support and received enough help to set up another press. This was also demolished. Again he appealed for assistance, and again there was a quick and positive response. The climax came in 1837 while he was setting up his third press in Alton. A group of citizens decided that the Lovejoy nuisance should be abated. They called a mass meeting to devise plans. Lovejoy refused to be intimidated and boldly attended the meeting to present his side. He promised to suspend publication if his readers requested, but he declared he would not be ruled by mob hysteria. He said he would return to his office and would defend his right to publish with his life, if need be. When the mob marched down the street after the meeting, it was motivated not by the desire to destroy a press but to destroy a man who refused his right to think and to express himself. Lovejoy was killed by the mob.

The southern counterpart of the abolitionist was the "fire-eater." Outstanding fire-eaters were William Lowndes Yancey, Edmund Ruffin, and Robert Barnwell Rhett. Yancey was one of the great orators of his era. It was Yancey who led the South from the Democratic convention of 1860. Ruffin was an agricultural writer who had introduced marl as a fertilizer to restore exhausted tobacco land. He was a tireless and indomitable southern patriot. When more timid souls hesitated to fire upon Fort Sumter in 1861, it was Ruffin who snatched the lanyard of the nearest cannon and sent the first ball screaming its message of war. And it was Ruffin who committed suicide rather than take the oath of allegiance after Appomattox. But of all the fire-eaters, Rhett was most effective.

Rhett, sometimes called the "Father of Secession," was editor of the *Charleston Mercury,* which he made into one of the leading papers of the Deep South. By 1832 he was

One-page sheet published by the *Charleston Mercury,* December 20, 1860

declaring openly that the only safety for the South was for it to go its own way. No one paid much attention to Rhett at first. He was treated about as coldly in the South as Garrison had been in the North. But after such magnificent propaganda successes as *Uncle Tom's Cabin,* the South began to depend on its Rhetts, Yanceys, and Ruffins for justification. By 1848, Rhett was once again powerful politically. In 1851 he succeeded to the Senate seat of the great John C. Calhoun.

Ironically, Rhett had no intention of involving his section in a war. He had aroused the South to fighting pitch, but he had assumed all along that the North would not dare fight. On the day Sumter was fired upon, Rhett was still reassuring readers of the *Mercury* that the South would secede peaceably. He should have known better. Lincoln's refusal to evacuate the fort peacefully was proof that this time the North meant business.

BLACK JOURNALISTS SPEAK FOR THEMSELVES

Abolitionists like Garrison and fire-eaters like Rhett attracted both immediate and continuing attention because they represented the extremes of white America's reaction to black slavery, whose emotional clash eventually produced a civil war. Nothing the slaves could do or say for themselves seemed important to a society that viewed them as economic, political, and educational nonequals. In 1850 there were about a half-million free blacks in the American population, half of them in the North and half in the South. But in the South, state laws prohibited blacks from receiving any formal education, and their chances to make decent incomes were few. In the North, state laws restricted black voting rights, and the uneven availability of public schools weighed quickly on children of disfranchised, poor, and illiterate blacks. There was a chance, however, to "get ahead," and some blacks succeeded. A handful of freed blacks won sufficient education to become writers, lawyers, physicians, and business people before the Civil War. To them, and to their friends in the white population, 40 struggling black newspapers were addressed between 1827 and 1865.[7]

These were virtually all dedicated supporters of the antislavery movement. And as such, they rank high in the regard of today's students of the black experience in America. It should not be startling to discover that there were African Americans who spoke out for themselves; what is startling is that they could succeed as well as they did in the face of poverty and illiteracy among most of their audience, and of almost total rejection by a white society that ignored their existence.

Slavery was not abolished everywhere north of the Mason-Dixon Line until 1804, and early leadership among slaves seeking their freedom is found in Massachusetts and Pennsylvania before 1800. By 1830 there were some 50 black antislavery societies, with the most active located in New York, Philadelphia, Boston, and New Haven. Black self-expression had long been centered in the folk songs and spirituals of the slaves. Now a few freed slaves had become adept at oratory, poetry, and autobiographical writing that had produced moving accounts in book form of what it meant to live as a slave. Some freed slaves had seen their articles or letters published in the white press; some had worked with Garrison and his *Liberator* group or for other white abolitionists. Maria W. Stewart (1803–1879), born free in Hartford, Conn., was a passionate antislavery voice in Garrison's *Liberator* from 1831–1833, whose "Ladies' Department" writings, illustrated by a woodcut of a black woman in chains, were reprinted in pamphlets as well. A particularly vicious attack on these black leaders by Mordecai M. Noah, editor of the *New York Enquirer,* is credited with spurring the founding of the first black-published newspaper in the United States.[8]

Freedom's Journal was its name, and in its first issue on March 16, 1827, it printed this simple explanation of the venture: "We wish to plead our own cause. Too long have

FREEDOM'S JOURNAL.

" RIGHTEOUSNESS EXALTETH A NATION."

CORNISH & RUSSWURM, *Editors & Proprietors.*

NEW-YORK, FRIDAY, MARCH 16, 1827.

VOL. I. NO. 1.

TO OUR PATRONS.

IN presenting our first number to our Patrons, we feel all the diffidence of persons entering upon a new and untried line of business. But a moment's reflection upon the noble objects, which we have in view by the publication of this Journal; the expediency of its appearance at this time, when so many schemes are in action concerning our people—encourage us to come boldly before an enlightened publick. For we believe, that a paper devoted to the dissemination of useful knowledge among our brethren, and to their moral and religious improvement, must meet with the cordial approbation of every friend to humanity.

The peculiarities of this Journal, render it important that we should advertise to the world the motives by whic we are actuated, and the objects which we contemplate.

We wish to plead our own cause. Too long have others spoken for us. Too long has the publick been deceived by misrepresentations, in things which concern us dearly, though in the estimation of some mere trifles; for though there are many in society who exercise towards us benevolent feelings; still (with sorrow we confess it) there are others who make it their business to enlarge upon the least trifle, which tends to the discredit of any person of colour; and pronounce anathemas and denounce our whole body for the misconduct of this guilty one. We are aware that there many instances of vice among us, but we avow that it is because no one has taught its subjects to be virtuous: many instances of poverty, because no sufficient efforts accommodated to minds contracted by slavery, and deprived of early education have been made, to teach them how to husband their hard earnings, and to secure to themselves comforts.

Education being an object of the highest importance to the welfare of society, we shall endeavour to present just and adequate views of it, and to urge upon our brethren the necessity and expediency of training their children, while young, to habits of industry, and thus forming them for becoming useful members of society. It is surely time that we should awake from this lethargy of years, and make a concentrated effort for the education of our youth. We form a spoke in the human wheel, and it is necessary that we should understand our pendence on the different parts, and theirs on us, in order to perform our part with propriety.

Though not desirous of dictating, we shall feel it our incumbent duty to dwell occasionally upon the general principles and rules of economy. The world has grown too enlightened, to estimate any man's character by his personal appearance. Though all men acknowledge the excellency of Franklin's maxims, yet comparatively few practise upon them. We may deplore when it is too late, the neglect of these self-evident truths, but it avails little to mourn. Ours will be the task of admonishing our brethren on these points.

The civil rights of a people being of the greatest value, it shall ever be our duty to vindicate our brethren, when oppressed, and to lay the case before the publick. We shall also urge upon our brethren, (who are qualified by the laws of the different states, the expediency of using their elective franchise; and of making an independent use of the same. We wish them not to become the tools of party.

And as much time is frequently lost, and wrong principles instilled, by the perusal of works of trivial importance, we shall consider it a part of our duty to recommend to our young readers, such authors as will not only enlarge their stock of useful knowledge, but such as will also serve to stimulate them to higher attainments in science.

We trust also, that through the columns of the FREEDOM'S JOURNAL, many practical pieces, having for their bases, the improvement of our brethren, will be presented to them, from the pens of many of our respected friends, who have kindly promised their assistance.

It is our earnest wish to make our Journal a medium of intercourse between our brethren in the different states of this great confederacy: that through its columns an expression of our sentiments, on many interesting subjects which concern us, may be offered to the publick: that plans which apparently are beneficial may be candidly discussed and properly weighed; if worthy, receive our cordial approbation; if not, our marked disapprobation.

Useful knowledge of every kind, and every thing that relates to Africa, shall find a ready admission into our columns; and as that vast continent becomes daily more known, we trust that many things will come to light, proving that the natives of it are neither so ignorant nor stupid as they have generally been supposed to be.

And while these important subjects shall occupy the columns of the FREEDOM'S JOURNAL, we would not be unmindful of our brethren who are still in the iron fetters of bondage. They are our kindred by all the ties of nature; and though but little can be effected by us, still let our sympathies be poured forth, and our prayers in their behalf, ascend to Him who is able to succour them.

From the press and the pulpit we have suffered much by being incorrectly represented. Men, whom we equally love and admire have not hesitated to represent us disadvantageously, without becoming personally acquainted with the true state of things, nor discerning between virtue and vice among us. The virtuous part of our people feel themselves sorely aggrieved under the existing state of things—they are not appreciated.

Our vices and our degradation are ever arrayed against us, but our virtues are passed by unnoticed. And what is still more lamentable, our friends, to whom we concede all the principles of humanity and religion, from these very causes seem to have fallen into the current of popular feeling and are imperceptibly floating on the stream—actually living in the practice of prejudice, while they abjure it in theory, and feel it not in their hearts. Is it not very desirable that such should know more of our actual condition, and of our efforts and feelings, that in forming or advocating plans for our amelioration, they may do it more understandingly? In the spirit of candor and humility we intend by a simple representation of facts to lay our case before the publick, with a view to arrest the progress of prejudice, and to shield ourselves against the consequent evils. We wish to conciliate all and to irritate none, yet we must be firm and unwavering in our principles, and persevering in our efforts.

If ignorance, poverty and degradation have hitherto been our unhappy lot; has the Eternal decree gone forth, that our race alone, are to remain in this state, while knowledge and civilization are shedding their enlivening rays over the rest of the human family? The recent travels of Denham and Clapperton in the interior of Africa, and the interesting narrative which they have published; the establishment of the republic of Hayti after years of sanguinary warfare; its subsequent progress in all the arts of civilization; and the advancement of liberal ideas in South America, where despotism has given place to free governments, and where many of our brethren now fill important civil and military stations, prove the contrary.

The interesting fact that there are FIVE HUNDRED THOUSAND free persons of colour, one half of whom might peruse, and the whole be benefitted by the publication of the Journal; that no publication, as yet, has been devoted exclusively to their improvement—that many selections from approved standard authors, which are within the reach of few, may occasionally be made—and more important still, that this large body of our citizens have no public channel—all serve to prove the real necessity, at present, for the appearance of the FREEDOM'S JURNAL.

It shall ever be our desire so to conduct the editorial department of our paper as to give offence to none of our patrons; as nothing is farther from us than to make it the advocate of any partial views, either in politics or religion. What few days we can number, have been devoted to the improvement of our brethren; and it is our earnest wish that the remainder may be spent in the same delightful service.

In conclusion, whatever concerns us as a people, will ever find a ready admission into the FREEDOM'S JOURNAL, interwoven with all the principal news of the day.

And while every thing in our power shall be performed to support the chracter of our Journal, we would respectfully invite our numerous friends to assist by their communications, and our coloured brethren to strengthen our hands by their subscriptions, as our labour is one of common cause, and worthy of their consideration and support. And we do most earnestly solicit the latter, that if at any time we should seem to be zealous, or too pointed in the inculcation of any important lesson, they will remember, that they are equally interested in the cause in which we are engaged, and attribute our zeal to the peculiarities of our situation, and our earnest engagedness in their well-being.

THE EDITORS.

From the Liverpool Mercury.

MEMOIRS OF CAPT. PAUL CUFFEE.

" On the first of the present month of August, 1811, a vessel arrived at Liverpool, with a cargo from Sierra Leone; the owner, master, mate, and whole crew of which are free blacks. The master, who is also owner, is the son of an American slave, and is said to be very well skilled both in trade and navigation, as well as to be of a very pious and moral character. It must have been a strange and an animating spectacle to see this free and enlightened African, entering as an independent trader with his black crew into that port, which was so lately the *nidus* of the slave trade.—*Edinburgh Review for August*, 1811.

We are happy in having an opportunity of confirming the above account, and at the same time of laying before our readers an authentic memoir of Capt. *Paul Cuffee*, the master and owner of the vessel above alluded to, who sailed from this port on the 20th ult. with a licence from the British Government, to prosecute his intended voyage to Sierra Leone.—The father of Paul Cuffee was a native of Africa,—whence he was brought as a slave into Massachusetts. He was there purchased by a person named Slocum, and remained in slavery a very considerable portion of his life. He was named Cuffee, but as it is usual in those parts, took the name of Slocum, as expressing to whom he belonged. Like many of his countrymen he possessed a mind far superior to his condition; although he was diligent in the business of his master, and faithful to his interest, yet by great industry and economy he was enabled to purchase his personal liberty. At the time the remains of several Indian tribes, who originally possessed the right of soil, resided in Massachusetts. Cuffee became acquainted with a woman descended from one of those tribes, named Ruth Moses, and married her. He continued in habits of industry and frugality, and soon afterwards purchased a farm of 100 acres at the point in Massachusetts.

Cuffee and Ruth had a family of ten children. The three eldest sons, David, Jonathan, and John, are farmers in the neighborhood of West Point; filling respectable situations in society, and endowed with good intellectual capacities. They are all married, and have families to whom they are giving good educations. Of six daughters four are respectably married, while two remain single. Paul was born on the Island of Cutterhumpker, one of the Elizabeth Islands, near New-Bedford, in the year 1759—when he was about fourteen years of age, his father died, leaving a considerable property in land, but which being at that time unproductive, afforded but little provision for his numerous family, and thus the care of supporting his mother and sisters devolved upon his brothers and himself. At this time Paul conceived that commerce furnished to industry more ample rewards than agriculture, and he was conscious that he possessed qualities which under proper culture, would enable him to pursue commercial employments with prospects of success—he therefore entered at the age of sixteen, as a common hand on board of a vessel destined to the bay of Mexico, on a whaling voyage. His second voyage was to the West Indies, but on his third he was captured by a British ship during the American war, about the year 1776—after three month detention as a prisoner, at New-York, he was permitted to return home to Westport, where owing to the unfortunate continuance of hostilities he spent about two years in his agricultural pursuits. During this interval Paul and his brother John Cuffee, were called on by the collector of the district, in which they resided, for the payment of a personal tax. It appeared to them, that by the laws and constitution of Massachusetts, taxation and the whole rights of citizenship were united. If the laws demanded of them the payment of the personal taxes, the same laws must necessarily and constitutionally invest them with the right of representing and being represented in the state legislature. But they had never been considered as entitled to the privilege of voting at elections, nor of being elected to places of trust and honor. Under these circumstances they refused payment of the demands. The collector resorted to the force of the laws, and after many delays and detentions, Paul and his brohter deemed it most prudent to silence them by paying the demands; but they resolved, if it were possible to obtain the rights which they believed to be connected with taxation. They presented a respectful petition to the state legislature. From some individuals it met with a warm, and almost indignant opposition. A considerable majority was, however, favorable to their object. They perceived the propriety and justice of the petition, and with an honorable magnanimity, in defiance of the prejudice of the times, they passed a law rendering all free persons of color liable to taxation, according to the established ratio, for white men, and granting them all the privileges, belonging to the other citizens. This was a day equally honorable to the petitioners and the legislature—a day which ought to be gratefully remembered by every person of color, within the boundaries of Massachusetts, and the names of John and Paul Cuffee, should always be united with its recollection.

To be Continued.

COMMON SCHOOLS IN NEW-YORK.—It appears from the report of the Superintendent of Common Schools in the state of New-York, presented last week to the House of Assembly, that of the 723 towns and wards in the State, 721 have made returns according to law: That in these towns there are 8114 school districts, and of course the same number of schools; from 7544 of which returns have been received: That 341 new school dis-

The first issue of the first black-published newspaper in the United States: "Too long have others spoken for us."

others spoken for us." Its editors were John B. Russwurm, the first black to graduate from a college in the United States (Bowdoin in 1826), and Reverend Samuel Cornish, a Presbyterian who edited three weeklies in New York City in this period. A four-page paper, 10 by 15 inches in size, *Freedom's Journal* agitated ruthlessly against the inhumanity of slavery but also ran newsy items, sermons, poetry, and other literary fare. Russwurm left in 1828 to work as an editor and government official in Liberia, and Cornish continued the paper under the name *Rights of All.* The known file ceases in October 1829.[9]

In 1829 David Walker issued his *Appeal* out of Boston, advocating violent measures to eliminate slavery, and George Moses Horton protested in Raleigh through the columns of his *Hope of Liberty.* During the racial turmoil in 1965 Walker's call for militant resistance was republished in paperback form.

Another major effort at a black paper in New York City came in 1837, when Phillip A. Bell founded the *Weekly Advocate,* renamed two months later *The Colored American.* It was published until 1842. Its first editor was Reverend Samuel Cornish, and the publisher was a Canadian, Robert Sears of Toronto. Cornish and Bell retired from the paper in May 1839, and Dr. Charles Bennet Ray became the guiding force of the spirited little paper. He made it not only an antislavery organ but also a "paper devoted primarily to the interests of the colored population, and . . . a first-rate family paper." Circulation reached 2000 in an area from Maine to Michigan.[10]

When the regular dailies in Pittsburgh refused to run contributions by blacks in 1843, Dr. Martin R. Delaney, first of his race to graduate from Harvard, founded *The Mystery.* William Wells Brown, a black writer of the period, described the physician as "decided and energetic in conversation, unadulterated in race, and proud of his complexion."[11] Delaney became involved in a libel suit but managed to keep his paper going until 1848, when it was purchased by the African Methodist Episcopal Church. It was renamed the *Christian Herald,* and then moved to Philadelphia in 1852 as the *Christian Recorder.* By 1970 it had become the oldest of the black religious weeklies.[12]

There were other notable efforts. One was the *Alienated American,* published from 1852 to 1856 in Cleveland by W. H. Day, a graduate of Oberlin College. Another was the *New Orleans Daily Creole,* an 1856 effort that was the first black-owned paper in the South and the first black daily in the United States. Bell, the founder of the *Advocate* in New York, migrated to San Francisco and in 1865 began publishing *The Elevator,* which survived until 1889, unusual longevity for a black paper. But the most famous of the pre–Civil War black papers were edited by the dynamic leader, Frederick Douglass.

FREDERICK DOUGLASS, EDITOR

In the 1970s, Frederick Douglass emerged as a symbol of black achievement and inspiration—his home in Washington had become a national shrine, his autobiographical writings enjoyed fresh printings, his face was on a postage stamp, young black males spelled their names with a double "s" if they were named Douglas. All of which was merited, for this son of a black slave woman and a white man ran away from a Maryland plantation to make himself a leader of those of the black race who needed his skill at writing and oratory to assert their cause.

Born in 1817, he escaped slavery in 1838 and went to New England to work and gain additional education with the encouragement of William Lloyd Garrison, the abolitionist. He began to write for the newspapers and to speak as an eyewitness to the tragedy of the slavery system. In 1845 he went to England, where friends raised enough money to buy

(Bettmann Archive)

Frederick Douglass

his freedom from his Maryland owner. Back in the United States and known for the first of his autobiographical books (*Narrative of the Life of Frederick Douglass*), he was named an editor of *The Ram's Horn*. The paper was started in January 1847 by Willis A. Hodges as a black protest to such practices as those of the *New York Sun,* which had printed a letter from him and then sent him a bill for $15. Hodges's venture failed the next year, but its columns had carried this announcement in late 1847:

> PROSPECTUS for an antislavery paper; to be entitled *North Star.* Frederick Douglass proposes to publish in Rochester a weekly Anti-slavery paper, with the above title. The object of the *North Star* will be to Attack Slavery in all its forms and aspects: Advocate Universal Emancipation; exalt the standard of Public Morality; promote the Moral and Intellectual improvement of the COLORED PEOPLE; and hasten the day of FREEDOM to the Three Millions of our Enslaved Fellow Countrymen.[13]

Publication of *The North Star* began November 1, 1847. It quickly rose to a circulation of some 3000 and was both read in and received contributions from Europe and the West Indies as well as much of the United States. In addition to articles about slavery and blacks, *The North Star* carried a good cross-section of national and world news. The masthead proclaimed: "Right is of no Sex—Truth is of no Color—God is the Father of us all, and we are all Brethren." Not everyone in Rochester thought so; just as the white abolitionists were terrorized, Douglass saw his house burned and his papers destroyed. But the spunky character of the paper and its literary quality were both so high that it survived financial difficulties and racial antagonism. Renamed *Frederick Douglass' Paper* in 1851 after a merger with a weaker sheet, the paper was symbolic of its editor's position as the recognized leader of the black population.

By mid-1860, with the issue of slavery clearly bringing the country to the verge of civil war, Douglass found the financial struggle too great and suspended his weekly. For the next three years he put out *Douglass' Monthly,* an abolitionist magazine aimed at a British audience, to aid the northern war cause. In 1870 he became contributing editor of a Washington weekly, the *New Era,* that sought to aid the now-freed black people. The paper was no more popular than the cause; Douglass invested money in it, renamed it the *New National Era,* and became its fighting editor before admitting defeat (and a $10,000 loss) in 1875.[14] His second autobiographical effort, *My Bondage and My Freedom,* had appeared in 1855; now the final volume, *Life and Times of Frederick Douglass,* appeared in 1878. The remarkable ex-slave, skillful editor, polished orator, and inspirational fellow citizen died in 1895 at the age of 78.

THE NORTHERN PRESS AND THE SLAVERY ISSUE

The important standard papers of the day picked up the slavery issue presented to them by the black editors, the abolitionists, and the fire-eaters. By 1852 Horace Greeley's weekly *New York Tribune* had a circulation of more than 200,000, much of it in the crucial West. It was the acknowledged leader of those opposed to slavery. Greeley felt so strongly on the subject that he was willing to cast off his lifetime allegiances to the Whigs to help organize the new party that brought Abraham Lincoln to the White House in 1860.

In January 1861, Greeley published the first of his "stand firm" editorials—accepted by readers, at least, as Lincoln's own commandments. In February he called for unity against the South by a slogan in large type at the head of the editorial column: "NO COMPROMISE/NO CONCESSIONS TO TRAITORS/THE CONSTITUTION AS IT IS." When the first shot of the war was fired April 12, 1861, Greeley wrote: "Sumter is temporarily lost, but Freedom is saved! It is hard to lose Sumter, but in losing it we have gained a united people. Long live the Republic." He asked for patience when critics, including Henry Raymond of the *New York Times,* offered unreasonable suggestions for breaking the stalemate, but by summer Greeley too was demanding action. On June 26 appeared the memorable editorial: "The Nation's War Cry: 'Forward to Richmond! The Rebel Congress must not be allowed to meet there on July 20. By that date the place must be held by the National Army.' " This was repeated in subsequent issues. After all this pressure, Greeley had a heavy conscience following the rout of the Union army at the first battle of Bull Run. Managing editor Charles A. Dana had been in charge of the paper while Greeley was traveling, and Fitz-Henry Warren, the *Tribune*'s Washington correspondent, had actually written the editorials.

All this time the "reasonableness" of Raymond's *New York Times* had made the paper's editor important journalistically and politically. When Greeley broke with the Whigs Governor Seward and Thurlow Weed, Raymond largely succeeded as the mouthpiece of the old group. When the Whigs foundered on the free soil issue, Raymond threw in his lot with the new Republican party. He wrote its statement of principles at the Pittsburgh convention in 1856. It is noteworthy that he was lukewarm on abolitionism, however, until after Sumter. An early critic of Lincoln (possibly because his rival, Greeley, had helped nominate the Rail-Splitter), Raymond quickly adjusted to circumstance. Once the fighting began, Raymond was a staunch defender of the president.

The *New York Herald,* on the other hand, was mostly opposed to the abolitionist movement. It endorsed the Kansas-Nebraska Act, which the South looked upon as a victory for slavery. Bennett wrote on February 28, 1854: "for twenty odd years, through good and evil report, the *New York Herald* has been the only Northern journal that has unfailingly vindicated the constitutional rights of the South." Naturally, the *Herald* was popular with Southern leaders, who quoted it often. The *Herald* was the most popular American newspaper in Great Britain, and because the British were inclined to favor the South through the close relationship of their textile industry and the cotton growers, it was widely reprinted.

Although Bennett was an annoyance to Lincoln and may have given readers of his editorials a false notion of the North's temper on the eve of the war, the *Herald*'s news columns offered clues to Lincoln's determination to protect federal laws. Virtually every detail about the Lincoln family was reported for the *Herald* and other New York Associated Press members by 25-year-old Henry Villard, the first person to cover a president-elect. Villard met with Lincoln in Springfield almost daily for three months and accompanied him on the long trip to Washington, as Lincoln changed from "a relatively unknown regional politician into a nationally known figure who commanded the public's interest and growing support."[15]

In the West, Joseph Medill's *Chicago Tribune* thundered against slavery. Founded in 1847, the paper made rapid progress after Medill and five partners took it over in 1855. Medill was one of the western leaders of the Republican party and was said to have suggested the name of the new political organization. The *Tribune* was an early supporter of Lincoln. Medill was largely responsible for the Lincoln boom. He enthusiastically followed the future president, reporting the speeches that are now history. Usually Medill followed his reports with a lively editorial on the subject. Lincoln often came to the *Tribune* office for conferences with the West's leading spokesperson. Medill's intimacy with Lincoln is indicated by the crude familiarity with which he conversed with the rising politician. "Dammit, Abe, git your feet off my desk," Medill is said to have told the lanky backwoodsman on one occasion.

When Lincoln assumed office, faced with the virtually impossible task of preserving peace, the newspaper press that watched his every move was highly developed. The typical daily was likely to be drab, by modern standards, but the makeup and readability had improved since the first penny papers. The standard paper was six columns wide. Eight pages usually sufficed, although Raymond's *Times* often ran to ten pages. There were few pictures or graphic illustrations. Many of the penny papers actually sold for twice that by the end of the period, and the *Times* was up to three cents. Headlines were mostly confined by the column rules to one-column labels, and the great development in display headlines was still waiting on the war. Advertising was increasing steadily. Three of the eight pages of the conservative-looking weekly edition of the *Springfield Republican* were usually devoted to classified notices, and this was common throughout the country.

As a whole, the press was strong and prosperous. It was well that the publishing industry was so healthy, for it was about to be tested as it never had been. The test began on the day Edmund Ruffin sent the first shot of the Civil War toward Fort Sumter: April 12, 1861.

WAR AND THE NEW YORK PRESS

By the close of 1861, the *New York Tribune* was engaged in a campaign to free slaves in conquered areas. The president had already discussed the issue with his cabinet, and he had definite plans for accomplishing emancipation. The climax of the *Tribune* crusade was Greeley's famous "Prayer of Twenty Millions" editorial of August 20, 1862, which was a call for action on the slavery issue. Lincoln replied by a personal letter to Greeley, which he also gave to the *National Intelligencer* for publication on August 23. The letter included the paragraph familiar to students of the period:

> My paramount object in this struggle *is* to save the Union, and is *not* either to save or destroy Slavery. If I could save the union without freeing *any* slave, I would do it; and if I could save it by freeing *all* the slaves, I would do it; and if I could do it by freeing some and leaving others alone, I would also do that.

Greeley wrote another open letter to the president urging more concern with the issue. When Lincoln announced his preliminary Emancipation Proclamation a month later, to be effective January 1, 1863, many readers of the *Tribune* assumed that "Uncle Horace" had done it again. "It is the beginning of the new life of the nation," Greeley exulted in his September 23 issue. The president and his cabinet had worked out the details, however, after the battle of Antietam had ended a southern offensive.

By the time of the election of 1864, Lincoln and Greeley appear to have tired of each other. "You complain of me—what have I done, or omitted to do, that has provoked the hostility of the *Tribune*?" asked the president.[16] But eventually Greeley swung around behind his old friend again. Of the 17 New York daily newspapers, only five were solid supporters of the administration: the *Tribune,* the *Times,* the *Evening Post,* the *Sun,* and the *Commercial Advertiser.* Greeley did not hesitate to take unpopular stands when wartime passions made such outspokenness highly dangerous. When Greeley supported the president's draft call of 1863, the *Tribune* was stoned.

War was the golden age for Henry J. Raymond, who had made the *New York Times* one of the outstanding dailies of its time. The paper offered reasonable, penetrating, and thorough reportage. The feeling for objectivity on the part of the *Times* writers is indicated by the four open letters Raymond wrote to Yancey, the southern fire-eater. They were able and dispassionate antisecession arguments that showed an understanding of the southern viewpoint. But on essential issues, the *Times* gave Lincoln strong support.

Raymond was an expert correspondent and writer, and his partner, George Jones, had wisely urged him to confine his energy to journalism rather than politics. The temptation was too great, however. By 1863, he was chairman of the Republican National Committee, one of the key political positions in the nation. He managed the 1864 campaign in which Lincoln and his "union" ticket partner, Andrew Johnson of Tennessee, defeated General George B. McClellan, the Democratic candidate, thanks to solid Union army victories in the fall. Raymond also wrote the party platform and was elected to the House of Representatives.

When Congress convened in 1865, it was assumed that Raymond represented the administration. He proved to be no match, however, for Thaddeus Stevens and other advocates of punishment for the South. Lincoln's assassination removed his party sponsor. He lost his national committee seat and declined to run for Congress again in 1866. He then bolted the party, ending his political career. "Shocking Cruelty to a Fugitive Slave," Greeley headlined the account of the episode in the *Tribune.* Later, Raymond and the *Times* returned to solid ground with the Republicans, but the paper's founder died of a cerebral hemorrhage in 1869 while waging an editorial fight against the infamous Tweed ring of political corruptionists that was looting the city treasury.

Bennett and his *Herald* caused the Lincoln administration considerable annoyance. The paper was politically independent, but it was definitely "soft" toward the South, where it had great influence. Because of its extensive news coverage, particularly of business and commerce, the *Herald* was the most popular American newspaper in Europe. The British government at this time was making friendly overtures to the South, which had provided British mills with cotton in normal times. The attitude of the widely read *Herald* was therefore of concern to Lincoln and his cabinet, for it was important that European neutrals have a fair evaluation of the issues.

After the first battle of Bull Run, Bennett gave his full, but somewhat grudging, support to the Lincoln administration and the war. Even so, it was necessary from time to time for the president to "sweeten up"—as Lincoln put it—the aggressive editor of the *Herald.* "I write this to assure you that the Administration will not discriminate against the *Herald,* especially while it sustains us so generously," Lincoln wrote to Bennett after personally interceding for a *Herald* reporter who had been refused a pass to go down the Potomac river with a military detachment.[17] There were other instances in which *Herald* reporters tangled with authorities. Actually, the aggressiveness of the *Herald* could have caused it much more trouble, if military officials had exerted their authority. At any rate, the editorial tactics paid off, for the *Herald* climbed to a circulation of more than 100,000 soon after the beginning of the war. It was then the most popular newspaper in the United States.[18]

Few presidents suffered more from editorial abuse than Lincoln. Opposition editors and disappointed favor-seekers accused him in print of vicious deeds, which the patient president usually ignored. He was falsely accused of drawing his salary in gold bars, while his soldiers were paid in deflated greenbacks. He was charged with drunkenness while making crucial decisions, with granting pardons to secure votes, and with needlessly butchering armies in his lust for victories. Once he was accused of outright treason. Typical of his press detractors was the *La Crosse Democrat,* a Wisconsin weekly, which said of the draft: "Lincoln has called for 500,000 more victims."

Continuous and unlicensed criticism was voiced by political opponents. Democrats actually polled a larger vote than Republicans in 1860.[19] They were so split by sectional differences, however, that they could not agree on a candidate. The Republicans were aware that they had won by default.

Most northern Democrats were loyal during the war, although they tended to welcome peace overtures short of total victory for Lincoln's aims. There were some who served as a kind of fifth column for the South, however. They were called Copperheads, after the dangerous reptile that gives no warning of its attack. Some formed underground groups engaged in treasonable acts; others were vocal, above-ground Copperheads. In distant California both the English- and Spanish-language press offered extensive coverage. English-speaking readers, many from the South, had mixed loyalties, while the majority of Hispanic readers were pro-North, and their papers supported Lincoln's party.

Clement Laird Vallandigham, an Ohio editor and politician, was a well-known Copperhead. In 1847 he became co-owner of the *Dayton Empire,* an antiabolitionist magazine, and won a seat in Congress in 1858. As secretary of the Democratic National Committee in 1860, he sought to avoid war. By 1863 he was one of the Copperheads arrested by order of General Ambrose E. Burnside. Sentenced to prison, he was banished behind the Confederate lines by Lincoln's order.

MILITARY CENSORSHIP IN THE NORTH

No war had ever been so fully and freely reported. New York newspapers usually devoted at least a third of their space to war news. But sooner or later the press had to work out an understanding with military authorities in the interest of public security. The problem was aggravated by the fact that the American press had become so prosperous, aggressive, and independent before the war that it was sensitive to any form of restriction. The telegraph and the railway posts were other factors to be considered. They made it possible to disseminate news much faster than before. The potential danger of providing information that could be useful to the enemy was therefore all the greater. On the other hand, this was the first of the all-out wars involving civilian populations, and since public morale was now a much more important factor in prosecuting the war, the channels of information had to be kept open.[20]

Civil War military censorship progressed in three stages. In August 1861, after concern within the high command in Washington over the open use of telegraph lines by journalists and civilians for sending military-related information, General George B. McClellan, commanding the Army of the Potomac, formed a voluntary censorship plan with Washington correspondents. This was nullified in October when Secretary of State Seward instructed official censor H. E. Thayer to prohibit telegraphic messages from Washington that related to military *and civil* operations of the government. A frustrated press then reverted to its old system of getting news as best it could.[21]

The second phase began when the censor was taken from the State Department and placed under the direction of the secretary of war, Edwin M. Stanton. By an order of February 25, 1862, field correspondents were to submit copy to provost marshals for approval before transmission. But it was understood that deletions would apply only to military matters. Now reporters knew about how far they could go in reporting.

General William T. Sherman, known for his personal battles with reporters, won his argument that all war correspondents must be *accredited,* or recognized, journalists and that they must be *acceptable* to field commanders. Thus was established a precedent for future military correspondents. From 1864 to the end of the war, censorship entered its third and successful phase. For example, General Sherman marched his army from Atlanta to the sea without once having his plans disclosed by the press. On the whole, journalists were cooperating with the military by the end of the war.

SUSPENSIONS OF NORTHERN NEWSPAPERS

In the main, the northern press enjoyed great freedom throughout the war. The great power of the president after his suspension of habeas corpus was used sparingly. Most of the punitive actions were taken by military commanders. In June 1863, the *Chicago Times* was suspended by order of General Ambrose Burnside. Wilbur F. Storey, publisher of the *Times,* used the most violent language in attacking Lincoln after the Emancipation Proclamation was issued. He repeatedly ignored military warnings to stop fomenting Copperhead dissatisfaction in the area. But the president also had definite ideas about freedom of expression. After three days he rescinded the military order.

Other newspapers ran afoul of the censor. One was the *New York World,* established in 1860 as a penny paper with religious overtones. At first the *World* was a supporter of the Lincoln administration. It lost money and continued to fail even after it absorbed the assets of the famous old *Courier and Enquirer.* Eventually it was taken over by Manton Marble, an able editor who increased circulation by espousing the cause of the "Peace Democrats." After the Emancipation Proclamation, the *World* was openly hostile to the administration. It became the focus of Copperhead activity in an area in which the war was already unpopular. In May 1864, the military authorities had a chance to strike back, when the *World* and the *Journal of Commerce* published a forged presidential proclamation purporting to order another draft of 400,000 men. The document was actually the product of Joseph Howard, Jr., city editor of the *Brooklyn Eagle,* who had hoped to make a profit in the stock market by this hoax. Releasing such a story in the tense metropolis was almost certain to cause bloodshed. When the *World* and the *Journal of Commerce* appeared with the article prominently displayed, General John A. Dix promptly suppressed them. After two days, during which the editors were severely reprimanded, they were allowed to resume publication.

One of the most celebrated suspension cases outside New York was that of Samuel Medary, editor of the *Crisis* and of the *Ohio Statesman* in Columbus. The *Crisis* was a special organ of the Copperheads, and it supported C. L. Vallandigham, the Copperhead candidate for governor. In 1864 Medary was indicted by a federal grand jury as the spokesperson for a group then declared to be subversive. He was released from jail on bond furnished by the editor of the *Cincinnati Enquirer,* who wished to test the wartime freedom of the press. Medary died before the case was tried in court.

THE NORTH REPORTS THE WAR

Indeed, when it came to reporting of military actions, Civil War correspondents, or "specials," as they were called, enjoyed a freedom that would not be tolerated in modern times. Many of the battles were fought in remote areas, and the struggle to publish first-hand accounts was often heroic. Some of the best reporting in American journalism was done by the hundreds of correspondents during this time.

News reporters were everywhere. They roamed the South long after their detection might have resulted in their execution as spies. Some were famous already, including Raymond of the *Times,* who was at Bull Run, and William Howard Russell, the world-renowned British war correspondent fresh from his triumphs in the Crimea.

Some of the best war reporters earned their spurs after the conflict began, however. One of these was B. S. Osbon, a minister's son who had embarked on a life of seafaring and adventure. He was working for the *New York World* at $9 a week on that April morning in 1861 when the curtain went up on one of the great American tragedies. From the deck of a naval cutter, Osbon watched the bombardment of Fort Sumter. The lead of the story he sent back was a prototype of the news style developed during the war:

CHARLESTON, APRIL 12—*The ball is opened. War is inaugurated.*
The batteries of Sullivan's Island, Morris Island, and other points were opened on Fort Sumter at four o'clock this morning. Fort Sumter has returned the fire, and a brisk cannonading has been kept up.[22]

Not long after, Bennett hired Osbon to report for the *Herald* at $25 a week. He was on the quarter deck with Admiral Farragut at the siege of New Orleans; he seemed to be wherever a good story was about to break.

But there were other stars, too. Albert D. Richardson of the *Tribune* sent reports from the Deep South through the line by transmitting his stories in cipher by way of the New York banks. He watched the great battle of Fort Henry from a treetop observation post. He saw Island Number Ten at the Vicksburg approaches reduced to rubble as he stood with Commodore Foote on the hurricane deck of a Union ironclad. He ran the blockade of Vicksburg, was knocked from the deck by the shock of a cannon ball that nearly struck him, and was then picked up from the water and imprisoned by the Confederates. His escape through the lines was one of the exciting journalistic feats of the time.

George W. Smalley, later one of the pioneer foreign correspondents, first gained fame while covering the war for the *Tribune*. At the battle of Antietam, where he served as a dispatch rider for General Hooker, he lost two horses by gunfire. It was Smalley who first got the news of the battle to Washington, where Lincoln was anxiously waiting for some encouraging report before announcing his plans for emancipation.

Many of the correspondents wrote under pen names. There was "Agate," for example, who was actually Whitelaw Reid, the successor to Greeley at the *Tribune* in the early 1870s. He was already famous for his report on the battle of Shiloh when he sent a dispatch from Gettysburg. His story, datelined "Field of Battle, Near Gettysburg, July 2," took up 14 of the 48 columns of the *Cincinnati Gazette*. It remains as a classic of Civil War reporting. Standing on Cemetery Hill, the point most exposed to rebel fire, Reid turned in an eyewitness account of the decisive battle, of which the following is an excerpt:

> Hancock was wounded; Gibbon succeeded to command—approved soldier, and ready for the crisis. As the tempest of fire approached its height, he walked along the line, and renewed his orders to the men to reserve their fire. The rebels—three lines deep—came steadily up. They were in pointblank range.
>
> At last the order came! From thrice six thousand guns there came a sheet of smoky flame, a crash of leaden death. The line literally melted away; but there came a second, resistless still. It had been our supreme effort—on the instant we were not equal to another.
>
> Up to the rifle pits, across them, over the barricades—the momentum of their charge, the mere machine strength of their combined action swept them on. Our thin line could fight, but it had not weight enough to oppose this momentum. It was pushed behind the guns. Right on came the rebels. They were upon the guns, were bayoneting the gunners, were waving their flags over our pieces.
>
> But they had penetrated to the fatal point.[23]

In the Confederate camp near Hagerstown, Maryland, the reporter for the *Richmond Enquirer,* retreating with Lee's army, sent back this eloquent version of the same battle to soften the blow to the bereaved at home:

> Though many a Virginia home will mourn the loss of some noble spirit, yet at the name of Pickett's division and the battle of Gettysburg, how the eye will glisten and the blood course quicker, and the heart beat warm, as among its noble dead is recalled the name of some cherished one. They bore themselves worthy of their lineage and their state. Who would recall them from their bed of glory? Each sleeps in a hero's grave.[24]

The *New York Herald,* true to its tradition, exceeded its rivals in aggressive war coverage. It had more than 40 specials in the field at any given time. One of its foremost reporters was a young Bavarian immigrant, Henry Hilgard, who soon changed his name to Villard after his arrival in 1853. While learning the language, Villard edited the *Volksblatt,* a German paper published in Racine, Wisconsin. Later he covered the Lincoln-Douglas debates for the *Staats-Zeitung* of New York. His account of Lincoln's departure from Springfield for Washington, and of the long train ride under increasing national tension, established Villard as one of the best correspondents of his day. He was only 25 when he began reporting the war for the *Herald.* He is best remembered for two great reporting "scoops." The first was his account of the first battle of Bull Run, the first accurate one to reach New York. The second exclusive account was his report of the battle of Fredericksburg.

THE NEW YORK HERALD.

WHOLE NO. 10,451.　　　　　　NEW YORK, MONDAY, APRIL 10, 1865.　　　　　　PRICE FOUR CENTS.

THE END

SURRENDER

OF

LEE

AND HIS

WHOLE ARMY

TO

GRANT.

TERMS OF SURRENDER.

All Honor to Grant, Meade, Sheridan, Ord, Humphreys, Wright, Griffin, Parke, and their Brave Troops.

Highly Interesting Details of the Fighting Before the Surrender.

Ord Makes a Forced March of Thirty Miles a Day South of Lee's Line of Retreat.

Our Main Columns Follow Closely in the Enemy's Rear.

The Woods Filled with Rebel Stragglers and the Roads Strewn with Cannon, Caissons, Wagons, Ambulances, Muskets, Sabres, Knapsacks and Cartridge Boxes.

Announcement of the Capture of Richmond to the Troops.

INTENSE ENTHUSIASM.

Our Men Clamor to be Led Forward.

&c., &c., &c.

JEFF. DAVIS AT DANVILLE,

&c., &c., &c.

THE SURRENDER.

THE TERMS.

THE PREVIOUS FIGHTING.

THE PURSUIT.

NATIONAL SALUTE.

THANKS TO GRANT AND HIS ARMY.

The New York Herald, *leader in war correspondence, records the South's surrender.*

THE SOUTH REPORTS THE WAR

Not much has been said about the southern press up to this point, although it played an important part in the fortunes of the Confederacy. In many ways editorial reactions were the same in the North and South. Southern editors were highly critical of military strategy, and journalists such as Rhett, for example, attacked the Confederate administration just as violently as Lincoln was being attacked in the North. War aims were not as much an issue as they were in the North, however, nor was there anything quite corresponding to the Copperhead press.

Most of the news of the battles was supplied to southern editors by the Press Association of the Confederate States of America, better known as "PA," which, appropriately enough, was just the reversed logotype of the biggest northern news agency, the AP.[25] When the war began, the South had no system for preparing or transmitting news of public interest to replace the severed connection with the New York AP. Publishers realized that to meet the enormous expense of covering a war, they would have to work together. Following a series of conferences, Joseph Clisby of the *Macon Telegraph* summoned the editor of every daily in the South to attend a meeting in Augusta on February 4, 1862. The Association of the Richmond Press had just been organized, and the plan was to expand the idea by organizing the PA. A board of directors hired a superintendent, J. S. Thrasher, "at a salary not to exceed $3,000," and the organization was ready to function.

The value of the association was at once apparent in the signing of contracts with telegraph agencies and the abolishing of onerous postal regulations. On May 15, 1863, the directors passed a resolution defending Thrasher for his stand against unwarranted military censorship.

On the whole, the PA served its clients well. When General P. G. T. Beauregard began to hold up dispatches, Thrasher called on him personally and told the general that the aim of the press association was to obtain accurate reports for the good of the public, consistent with military security. The general was impressed. He told Thrasher that the PA reporters "should have every facility for early access to intelligence compatible with the public interests," and he wrote letters to high military authorities recommending similar cooperation. Thrasher won the confidence of other leaders. In return, he instructed PA correspondents to send no opinions or comments on events—the procedure that had so irritated northern commanders. They were warned to sift rumors and to offer no information that would aid the enemy. The objectivity of the PA stories has been regarded as constituting a "complete revolution" in journalistic writing.[26]

The development of the PA was a big step in the progress of southern journalism. The 43 daily papers in the South that were still surviving by this point in the war were all members. The editorial weight of this group was impressive. Dispatches were transmitted over the Military Telegraph Lines, the army system, at half rates. Newspapers that seldom had access to regular wire news budgets were now able to keep readers up to date on the war. Reporters with the armies were paid $25 a week, which was good for that time, and the writing was of good quality. On the whole the PA gave a good account of itself until the crumbling Confederacy saw a collapse of restraints and organization.

There were perhaps 800 newspapers being published in the 11 states of the Confederacy in 1861, of which about 10 percent were dailies. Hand presses were in use in most of these newspaper offices, and circulations were small. The *Richmond Dispatch,* with 18,000 subscribers when war broke out, was outranked only by the largest New Orleans dailies, and had more readers than the Richmond *Enquirer, Whig,* and *Democrat* combined. The *Enquirer* was the organ of the Jefferson Davis administration until 1863, when the *Sentinel* was established for that purpose. Richmond also spawned a *Southern Illustrated News* in 1862 to fill the void left by the disappearance of *Harper's Weekly;* it soon had 20,000 readers.[27]

Southern publishers were plagued by a shortage of paper; they were reduced eventually to printing single sheets, to printing extras on galley proof slips, and even to printing on the back of old wallpaper. They also ran out of ink, type, and people to staff their shops. After 1863, when Vicksburg fell, their cities were overrun by federal troops. Only about 20 of the dailies were still printing when Lee surrendered. But they had compiled a journalistic record of the Confederate arms, and had sent more than 100 correspondents to cover the southern armies.

The historian of Civil War correspondents, J. Cutler Andrews, ranks two of these men as head and shoulders above the others.[28] One was Felix Gregory de Fontaine, who signed himself "Personne" in his dispatches to the *Charleston Courier.* The other was Peter W. Alexander, primarily identified with the *Savannah Republican,* but whose "P.W.A." signature was also found in the *Atlanta Confederacy,* the *Columbus Sun,* the *Mobile Advertiser,* the *Richmond Dispatch,* and the *Times* of London. Ranking behind them were such versatile war reporters as Samuel C. Reid, Jr., of the *New Orleans Picayune* and other papers; James B. Sener and William G. Shepardson of the *Richmond Dispatch;* Albert J. Street of the *Mobile Register;* John H. Linebaugh of the *Memphis Appeal;* and an unidentified "Shadow" who covered the battle of Atlanta and who may have been Henry Watterson of future Louisville fame.

De Fontaine and Alexander crossed paths as "regulars" in the major campaigns; both were at Antietam in September 1862, when Lee was repulsed in his invasion of the North but escaped a vastly superior McClellan. De Fontaine wrote a seven-column story of more than 8000 words about the campaign, in what Andrews calls his greatest story of the war. It appeared in the *Charleston Courier* first. At one point the young but war-weary correspondent described the scene in front of the Confederate center along a sunken road called "Bloody Lane":

> From twenty different standpoints great volumes of smoke were every instant leaping from the muzzles of angry guns. The air was filled with the white fantastic shapes that floated away from bursting shells. Men were leaping to and fro, loading, firing and handling the artillery, and now and then a hearty yell would reach the ear, amid the tumult, that spoke of death or disaster from some well aimed ball. Before us were the enemy. A regiment or two had crossed the river, and, running in squads from the woods along its banks, were trying to form a line. Suddenly a shell falls among them, and another and another, until thousands scatter like a swarm of flies, and disappear in the woods. A second time the effort is made, and there is a second failure. Then there is a diversion. The batteries of the Federals open afresh; their infantry try another point, and finally they succeed in effecting a lodgement on this side. Our troops, under D. H. Hill, meet them, and a fierce battle ensues in the centre. Backwards, forwards, surging and swaying like a ship in a storm, the various columns are seen in motion. It is a hot place for us, but is hotter still for the enemy. They are directly under our guns, and we mow them down like grass. The raw levies, sustained by the veterans, come up to the work well, and fight for a short time with an excitement incident to their novel experiences of a battle; but soon a portion of their line gives way in confusion. Their reserves come up, and endeavor to retrieve the fortunes of the day. Our centre, however, stands firm as adamant, and they fall back.[29]

This was at noon; by two o'clock Hill was out of men to defend the center—but McClellan failed to mount a breakthrough and settled for less than an overwhelming victory. More soldiers died in a single day at Antietam than in any other battle in American history—casualties totaled 23,000.

Alexander was also at Antietam and composed his battle account for the *Mobile Advertiser* in the midst of the wounded and dying in an army hospital. "There is a smell of death in the air," he wrote, "and the laboring surgeons are literally covered from head to foot with the blood of the sufferers." It was Alexander who wrote the most penetrating southern account of the battle of Gettysburg, questioning Lee's wisdom in committing himself to full-scale assault the second day and wondering if Lee and his staff had not exhibited too much confidence in the ability of their troops to win against any odds. Most of the southern press reprinted his story.[30]

ARTISTS AND PHOTOGRAPHERS: MATHEW BRADY

A small army of artists covered the war, describing the events in almost photolike drawings that were printed by a laborious process of engraving by hand on a wooden block. Such woodcuts were not new, but they were used in newspapers much more regularly after 1861 to depict battle scenes and the likenesses of leading wartime figures. In another development, some of the metropolitan papers printed large maps to illustrate campaigns, thereby leading the way to new makeup no longer limited by column rules.[31] The *Herald* of September 12, 1863, is a good example of this technique. The paper was a little smaller than a modern standard daily and ran to eight pages, six columns wide. About a quarter of page one of this particular issue was devoted to a map accompanying a story on the Arkansas campaign. On page three a huge map of the Morris Island success in Charleston harbor filled all but two columns of the page from top to bottom.

Illustrations were also the touchstone for success in magazine publishing. Two forerunners of twentieth-century news and picture weeklies were *Frank Leslie's Illustrated Newspaper,* a 16-page, 10-cent weekly founded in 1855, and *Harper's Weekly,* begun in 1857. Their superb artists' drawings for woodcuts brought the war visually to 100,000 or more subscribers. They also covered sports, crime, and disasters. *Harper's Monthly,* an 1850 entry from the same publishing house, achieved a record 200,000 circulation before the war by featuring woodcut illustrations along with its fiction in issues double the usual size. Hand-colored engravings of fashionable clothing for ladies and gentlemen were one of the secrets of *Godey's Lady's Book,* founded in 1830 by Louis Godey and edited from 1836 to 1877 by Sarah J. Hale. The illustrations and copious fiction and poetry brought a 150,000 circulation in the 1850s. Hale's famed contribution was "Mary Had a Little Lamb"; she also wrote or edited 50 books, promoted Thanksgiving as a national holiday, and discussed women's rights in *Godey's.* A rival in fashion illustration was *Peterson's Magazine,* begun in 1842 by Charles J. Peterson with Ann Stephens as associate editor and fiction writer. It exceeded *Godey's* in circulation during the war, indicating the growing recognition of women in the economic picture.

The most notable contribution to pictorial journalism in the 1860s was the photograph. English cameramen Roger Fenton and James Robertson had photographed the British army in the Crimea but did not have the equipment to record battle scenes. During the American Civil War 300 photographers were issued passes by the Army of the Potomac. The best, and truly a pioneer war photographer, was Mathew Brady. True, his photographs could not be used in newspapers of the time, since a practical method of transferring light and shade in the printing process was not perfected for another decade. But artists could copy almost perfect likenesses, and Brady was famous for his war pictures. The photographic record of the conflict taken by him and 20 associates comes down to us as one of the finest examples of reporting.

Brady himself was everywhere during the war. He recorded on his clumsy plates the scene at Fort Sumter. He was at Bull Run, Antietam, and Gettysburg; he photographed Lincoln visiting the Union troops and shot the famous picture of Robert E. Lee after the surrender at Appomattox. His photographic interpretations of famous battles and war leaders could not be matched in mood and accuracy by the printed word. In an era when few persons owned cameras, great men flocked to pose for Brady.[32]

Brady was born in 1832, in upper New York State. As a youth he worked for A. T. Stewart, the pioneer New York department-store owner. Stewart took an interest in the bright lad. When Brady took up the study of photography, the wealthy merchant brought his protégé to the attention of Samuel F. B. Morse, famed as the inventor of the telegraph but equally interested in the science of optics. Morse made Brady his understudy. Together they worked with Professor J. W. Draper of New York University, who was to make the first instantaneous photographic exposure in America.[33] In 1839, Morse took Brady to Europe, where they met Louis Jacques Mandé Daguerre, inventor of the "daguerreotype," a photograph on metal. Other European pioneers included Joseph Nièpce of France and Fox Talbot of Britain.

Brady returned to America and set up a daguerreotype shop at the corner of Broadway and Fulton Street, opposite P. T. Barnum's museum. That was about 1842. Soon he was famous as a photographer of the great and the near-great.[34] Five years in a row he won the American Institute award for his contributions to photography.

But Brady was not satisfied with this success. The daguerreotype was too slow to be adaptable to anything but portrait work, and he sought a faster process. In 1855 he went to Scotland to learn about a new and faster "wet plate" developed by the scientist Scott-Archer. Brady returned with Alexander Gardner, Scott-Archer's associate, and they set up offices in Washington as semiofficial government photographers. When the war loomed, Brady left his lucrative business in the hands of others.

He persuaded his friends President Lincoln and Allan Pinkerton of the Secret Service to let him make an encyclopedic photographic record of the war along with Gardner, Timothy H. O'Sullivan, and other Brady cameramen. They were permitted to go anywhere, protected by the Secret Service. Soon Brady's little black wagon, which was his portable dark room, was a familiar sight on the active fronts. Soldiers dreaded the sight of Brady arriving on the scene, for they knew that soon thereafter the shooting would begin. He was often under sniper fire as he set up his camera at exposed vantage points. By the end of the war he had collected about 3500 photographs, which survive in the National Archives and the Library of Congress (some of the best are by Gardner and O'Sullivan). Brady's postwar publishing projects languished and he died forgotten in 1896—but his pictures live on.[35] Somehow he was able to capture through his lens the hysteria, horror, and occasional glory of war.

WARTIME TECHNICAL ADVANCES

War brought important technical changes to the press. Dependence on the telegraph led to modification in news writing, as correspondents tried to save tolls by striving to be more concise. One way to compress stories was to omit opinion and coloration. By modern standards, Civil War reporting was rambling and colored, but compared with the journalism of an earlier day it was much more readable. Some of the copy, such as that transmitted out of Washington by the New York Associated Press and out of Richmond by the Confederate Press Association, would not be much out of place in a modern newspaper.

The summary lead, which put the main feature of the story in the first paragraph, was developed during the war by reporters in the field who feared that their complete dispatches might not get through. Bennett once said that the cable, rather than the telegraph, was responsible for this, but the cable was not in successful operation until 1866, and the summary lead was fairly common by that time. Here, for example, is the way the *New York Times* started off one of its important front-page articles of April 16, 1865:

> WASHINGTON, Saturday, April 15—12 A.M. Andrew Johnson was sworn into office as President of the United States by Chief Justice Chase today, at eleven o'clock.

Because vital news streamed from the telegraph by the hour, metropolitan papers began to bulletin the highlights, and soon the smallest papers were imitating this procedure. These bulletins led to the modern newspaper headline, which summarizes the story in a few lines.

Most of the newspapers continued to use the eight-page, six-column makeup carried over from before the war. By modern standards they were likely to be drab, with their small type, lack of pictures, and dreadful uniformity of one-column makeup limitations. But the use of huge maps was breaking down the confines of the column rule, and the experimentation of headlines indicated the contrast with the page dress of only a decade earlier.

Presses had to be fast to keep up with other developments in journalism. On the Sunday following the fall of Fort Sumter, the *Herald* printed 135,000 newspapers—a record press run up to that date. In 1863, William Bullock brought out the web perfecting press, which printed both sides of a continuous roll of paper on a rotary press. Although it was not until 1871 that R. Hoe & Company produced such presses as standard equipment, the stimulus of the war is nevertheless apparent.

It was indeed an exciting era that came to a close on the evening of April 14, 1865. Lawrence A. Gobright of the New York Associated Press was working late in his office. He had already sent out dispatches about President Lincoln's theater party, reporting that General Grant had declined an invitation to see the play *Our American Cousin,* in order to go to New Jersey with Mrs. Grant. The door burst open and an excited friend rushed in with news of the tragedy at Ford's Theater. Gobright quickly wrote out a bulletin before going to work on an extended account of the evening's development. No modern reporter could have broken the news more succinctly. The lead said:

> WASHINGTON, FRIDAY, APRIL 14, 1865—The President was shot in a theater tonight, and perhaps mortally wounded.

8

A Revolution
in National Life

The newspaper has a history; but it has, likewise, a natural history. The press, as it exists, is not, as our moralists sometimes seem to assume, the wilful product of any little group of living men. On the contrary, it is the outcome of a historic process.

—Robert E. Park

In many respects American history starts afresh at the close of the Civil War. This is not to deny the obvious fact that two-and-a-half centuries of the American experience had produced fundamental guiding forces that would continue to influence the maturing of the nation's economy and the development of its political and social fabric. But great new forces were at work, and between 1865 and 1900 the United States was to pass through a revolution that affected every phase of the national scene. The forces were those of intensive industrialization, mechanization, and urbanization, which brought with them sweeping social, cultural, and political changes. At some point between the Civil War and the turn of the century, the slow maturing process of virtually every aspect of American life was given the powerful new impetus of redirection.

So it was with the nation's journalism. The great development of communication and of journalistic techniques that had come in the Jacksonian period of American growth continued through the war period. There was a popular press that had appealed to the human interests of its readers, utilized the new communication facilities to develop news enterprise, and sometimes developed editorial force. But the patterns that had emerged and the techniques that had been created were changed. Paralleling this change was the passing from the scene of famous figures of the newspaper movement that had begun in the 1830s. Between 1869 and 1878, five leaders of the era of personal journalism died: Henry J. Raymond, founder of the *New York Times;* James Gordon Bennett, Sr., founder of the *New York Herald;* Horace Greeley, founder of the *New York Tribune;* Samuel Bowles III,

FRANK LESLIE'S ILLUSTRATED NEWSPAPER

Entered according to Act of Congress in the year 1857, by FRANK LESLIE, in the Clerk's Office of the District Court for the Southern District of New York. (Copyrighted May 10, 1858.)

No. 128 — VOL. V.]   NEW YORK, SATURDAY, MAY 15, 1858.   [PRICE 6 CENTS.

OUR EXPOSURE OF THE MILK TRADE OF NEW YORK AND BROOKLYN.

FROM a hundred sources we are receiving, day by day, thanks for our public spirit and fearless exposure of a nefarious and revolting trade, and good wishes and prayers for the ultimate and speedy success of our undertaking.

We feel sincerely gratified and deeply grateful for the outside encouragement we receive; it will move us to new exertions, for we feel that we have obtained the ear of the public; that its sympathies and hopes are with us, and armed with this assurance we feel our power equal to the emergency. That our blows have been dealt strongly and truly we have ample evidence. Our exposure has not only broken up all the milk routes we have published, but one whose name we were fortunately enabled to give, is selling off his swill milk cows. His stable is broken up, his swill trade, gone, and mark the consequence—he has contracted with the country dairies for the milk he requires for his customers. Is not the good work begun? May we not hope for the future?

An early crusade was the 1858 "swill milk" campaign in *Frank Leslie's Illustrated Newspaper.*

most famous of his name to edit the *Springfield Republican;* and William Cullen Bryant, for half a century editor of the *New York Evening Post.*

There was good reason for the development of new approaches to news reporting and editorial expression. The problems the United States faced after the Civil War were heavy ones. The political leadership at hand was not equal to the tasks. There was no really great president between 1865 and the turn of the century, although Grover Cleveland won considerable recognition, primarily for his honesty and courage. But whatever the shortcomings in presidential leadership, the remainder of the political scene was far more depressing. The effort at the political reconstruction of the South degenerated into an ugly battle between a vengeful Congress and an inept president; carpetbaggers and scalawags put in power in the South through arbitrary reconstruction policies gave way, in turn, to southern home rule without participation by the blacks; scandals rocked the Grant administration; corruption permeated city governments; a "consistent rebellion" flared against economic maladjustments, money-supply inequities, and life-squeezing transportation and interest rates assessed against the farmer. In such a setting an independent-thinking editor devoted to presentation of the news was definitely encouraged, as were Charles A. Dana and Edwin Lawrence Godkin.

The journalism of Dana and Godkin was the product of an American society in transition; what was happening to the national life for the first dozen years after the close of the Civil War could be called a transition. But then, the swelling tide of economic and social change brought not transition but revolution.

In journalism, as in all other aspects of American life, the result was an emergence of new concepts and practices more akin to the twentieth century than to the immediate past. New leaders were to revolutionize the newspaper and the magazine by responding to the abruptly changed environment rather than by clinging to the older patterns. The contrast, by the 1890s, between Dana's cranky, change-resisting journalism and that of the dynamic symbol of the new order—Joseph Pulitzer—was glaring indeed. It was no more glaring, however, than the differences that had developed in literature, in science, in political and economic thought, in business and industry, and in the way Americans lived and worked. American journalism, like American history, is marked by what historian Henry Steele Commager calls "the watershed of the nineties," whose topography is as blurred as those of all watersheds, but whose grand outlines emerge clearly.[1]

POLITICAL AND FINANCIAL CRISES

Before we consider what the editors did, we should examine in more detail the society in which they worked. Historians used to view Reconstruction as a unilaterally tragic time when northern carpetbaggers and southern scalawags took advantage of the unpreparedness of black voters for democratic responsibilities and disrupted southern life, until southern home rule was restored in 1877. Current interpretations are much more nuanced. Historians such as Eric Foner view Reconstruction "as part of a prolonged struggle over the new system of labor, racial, and political relations that would replace the South's peculiar institution."[2] During Reconstruction, carpetbaggers, scalawags, African Americans, and federal troops worked together to institute some significant reforms, including improved educational opportunities, greater participation in voting, and employment for blacks. When the federal government withdrew in 1877, southern whites reasserted their power, and blacks returned to second-class citizenship; the next 50 years saw Jim Crow laws, an active Ku Klux Klan, and lynchings of African Americans.[3]

The political landscape of the Reconstruction years was complex. The Republican party, which had elected Abraham Lincoln as its first president in 1860, found it necessary to run a Union ticket in 1864, pairing Lincoln with a Tennessee Democrat, Andrew Johnson. Even then, Lincoln polled only 400,000 more votes than the Democratic candidate, General George B. McClellan, with the South excluded from voting. In light of this, many Republicans viewed the immediate return of the South to full voting privileges with real alarm. They feared the result of accepting Lincoln's theory that since the Union was indissoluble, southern states would automatically return to their former status when fighting ceased. Freed from this policy by Lincoln's death, Representative Thaddeus Stevens of Pennsylvania and Senator Charles Sumner of Massachusetts gave leadership to a group that maintained that the South had committed "state suicide" and should be considered as conquered territory. They and their followers, who came to dominate the postwar Congresses, were named the "radical Republicans."

In Andrew Johnson, the radical Republicans found an opponent who was made vulnerable by personality weaknesses that obscured his other qualities. When southern states readmitted to the Union by Johnson ignored black political rights, the radical Republicans moved to handle the South on their own terms. They passed a civil-rights bill; they submitted the Fourteenth Amendment to the Constitution for ratification; they passed, over Johnson's veto, the reconstruction acts that forced all southern states to again seek reentry into the Union on radical-Republican terms; and they instituted military rule in the South. The contest between the radical Republicans and the president was climaxed by the impeachment of Johnson, who was saved from removal from office by a single vote in the Senate. Thereupon the Republican party turned to General Ulysses S. Grant as its candidate in 1868, and won the election easily.

Political reconstruction was thus a challenge, but financial reconstruction was even more so. Commodity prices in the North had doubled during the five years of war. Running of the printing presses to create legal tender paper money, dubbed "greenbacks," had driven coinage into hiding, intensifying the usual wartime inflationary trend. In 1866 Congress therefore voted to retire the greenbacks gradually over an 11-year period. The argument was advanced that retirement of the greenbacks, which constituted a part of the large federal debt, would deflate prices and increase the value of the dollar. Such action would be to the benefit of creditors and of wage earners whose incomes had not kept pace with prices. But farmers, who generally were debtors, would find money dearer and prices for their products lower. Opposition to retirement of the greenbacks from circulation began to develop in the Middle West agricultural areas and of course in the South, whose economy had been prostrated by the collapse of the Confederate currency and the ravages of war. Opponents of paper money forced final retirement of the greenbacks beginning in 1879, further intensifying the problem of an inadequate money supply for the rapidly expanding American economy. Currency supply was not the only complaint of the agricultural West and South. Farmers found interest rates on their borrowed money excessively high and impossible to pay in years of poor crops or low prices. They found that the railroads, which were extending their tracks across the country, were basing their rates on the axiom "all the traffic will bear."

By the early 1870s a depression was closing in on a country that had fought a costly and devastating war, that was expanding capital investment faster than it was producing wealth, and that was still borrowing large amounts of money from European investors for its expansion. When the financial crash came in 1873, with declining prices for agricultural products, the farmers were certain that their lot was unbearable. A "consistent rebellion" began as the agricultural West and South sought economic redress. Currency reform, banking reform, regulation of railroad and grain-elevator rates, and lowering of interest charges were the major political issues, The Greenback party flourished as a result, to be followed by the rise of the Populists. The Patrons of Husbandry formed their Grange organizations that forced passage of state laws in the Middle West fixing maximum railroad rates, and in a famous decision (*Munn* v. *Illinois,* 1877) the United States Supreme Court upheld the doctrine that the railroads were subject to regulation in the public interest.[4]

GREELEY'S "MUGWUMP" PRESIDENTIAL RACE

In this troubled political and economic setting, the press found much significant news. And as the news principle gained ascendancy, the editorial columns showed definite signs of rebelling against unswerving loyalty to political parties and their beliefs. The way was eased by rebellion within the ranks of the political parties themselves and particularly by the emergence of a "reform Republican" faction opposing the radical Republicans and their president, General Grant. Independence of editorial expression meant primarily the freedom to criticize the leaders and policies of the party the editor might normally support, but for some it also meant freedom to bolt the party and support a rival. Those who bolted were called "mugwumps" by their opponents.

The mugwumps of 1872 were led by a group of editors. The reform Republicans, meeting in convention to find a suitable candidate to oppose Grant, included many editors, the most important of whom were Samuel Bowles of the *Springfield Republican,* Horace White of the *Chicago Tribune,* Murat Halstead of the *Cincinnati Commercial,* and Carl Schurz of the St. Louis *Westliche Post.* The convention ended with the selection of another famous editor, Horace Greeley, as the candidate. Greeley was also nominated by the Democrats, and thus an important segment of the Republican-aligned press found itself allied with pro-Democratic papers. But Greeley's bid for the presidency was ill-starred. Many liberals could not find their way clear to support the aging editor, and others commented cruelly on his eccentricities. Thus such critics of the Grant administration as the *New York Evening Post* and *New York Sun,* and the influential magazines *Harper's Weekly* and the *Nation,* shied away from the Greeley cause. And despite growing discontent with the radical Republicans' reconstruction policies, the administrative shortcomings of the Grant regime, and unsolved economic problems, Grant was reelected handily. Greeley died a few weeks later.

Even though the Greeley campaign had failed, the effect of the mugwump rebellion by such influential editors was a substantial gain in journalistic prestige. It added new proof that editors could shift their political positions and survive, and encouraged those newspapers that felt obliged to attack strong political groups.

SCANDALS IN GOVERNMENT

Scandals in government offer a tempting target for any editor, and the political ineptness and moral laxity that characterized the postwar years further stimulated newspapers and magazines to action. The most notorious example of corruption at the city level was in the operations of the Tweed Ring in New York City. Tammany boss William M. Tweed and his Democratic party cohorts, who milked the city of $200 million, had grown so bold and brazen by 1870 that they had listed a plasterer's pay at $50,000 a day for an

THE TAMMANY TIGER LOOSE —"What are you going to do about it?"

Thomas Nast's famed Tammany Tiger cartoon in *Harper's Weekly* in 1871: "What are you going to do about it?"

entire month while constructing a courthouse. The Tweed Ring controlled some newspapers and frightened others into silence, but it met its masters in the *New York Times* and *Harper's Weekly*. The *Times,* published by George Jones and edited by Louis J. Jennings after the death of Henry J. Raymond in 1869, obtained documentary proof of the Tweed Ring's thefts in 1871 and broke the astounding story. *Harper's Weekly,* ably edited by George William Curtis, provided a gallery for Thomas Nast, the great political cartoonist who used his pen and ink against Tweed in devastating fashion. Jones and Nast were offered bribes to halt the attacks. The answer was the driving of the Tweed Ring from power.[5]

The scandals that left the reputation of the Grant administration blackened were being hinted at before the 1872 presidential election, but it was not until the closing days of the campaign that the *New York Sun* publicized what became known as the Crédit Mobilier affair. When the evidence was developed fully after the election, it proved that promoters of the Union Pacific and Central Pacific railroads had developed a simple system for influencing legislators and others whose support was needed to obtain federal land grants for railroad construction. The railroad builders, operating under the name Crédit Mobilier of America, had sold stock to many public leaders, lending them the money to pay for the stock and then declaring such huge profits that the loans could be repaid in a single year. Exposure of what amounted to gifts from those seeking legislative favor ruined some politicians and cast suspicion on many more, including the prominent Republican leader James G. Blaine of Maine.

Other disclosures of weaknesses in the Grant administration came rapidly: the whiskey tax frauds in the Treasury Department, the bribing of the Secretary of War, and the acceptance of improper gifts by Grant's private secretary. The dazed Grant was himself untouched by the scandals, but his party lost control of the House of Representatives to the Democrats in 1874, and politics became a seesaw affair. The country was entering a period of "dead center" government. For 16 of the next 22 years, control of the two houses of Congress and the presidency was split between the two major parties, so closely was the popular vote divided. Little political progress could be made in such a situation, and eventually the protective tariff became the principal issue of frustrated political aspirants who could not cope with the problems that were generating the "consistent rebellion" of the economically discontented West and South.

DANA AND THE *NEW YORK SUN*

Of the editors who worked in this turbulent postwar period, two stand out as leaders. Their contributions are sharply different. In his years as editor of the *New York Sun,* Charles A. Dana taught the journalism world new lessons in the art of news handling and writing. In his years as editor of the *Nation* and of the *New York Evening Post,* Edwin Lawrence Godkin provided solid editorial-page leadership.

In many respects Dana and his *Sun* represent the bridge between the older press and a "new journalism" that would develop before the end of the century. A New Englander who had been attracted to the Brook Farm socialist experiment in the 1840s along with other intellectuals seeking the answer to the problems created by the Industrial Revolution, Dana had met Horace Greeley there. He joined Greeley's staff and became managing editor of the *Tribune* in 1849—the first American to hold such a position. When the Dana-Greeley association was broken in the early days of the Civil War, Dana entered government service and emerged to struggle for a year as editor of a new Chicago paper, the *Daily Republican* (forerunner of the famous *Inter Ocean*). The newspaper venture was successful, but Dana wearied of Chicago. Returning to New York, he obtained sufficient backing to buy the *Sun,* the original penny newspaper. Its plant and circulation of 43,000 were priced at $175,000 by Moses S. Beach, whose father had taken over Ben Day's paper. A career with Greeley on the *Tribune* already behind him, in 1868 Dana began a 29-year career as editor of the *Sun.*

Dana's audience consisted mainly of average New Yorkers: workers and small merchants. To them he addressed his first editorial in the *Sun,* which expressed his ideas on newspaper making. The *Sun,* he said, would present "a daily photograph of the whole world's doings in the most luminous and lively manner." Its staff would write simply and clearly as it tried to present that photograph of the life of the people of New York as well as of the world's doings. The *Sun* would be low-priced and readable, yet it would use enterprise and money to be the best possible newspaper.

Dana insisted that the journalist must be interested in politics, economics, and government, but first of all in people. The average American, Dana knew, was hard at work, yet loved sentiment and fun and enjoyed stories reflecting a skillful touch of tenderness or wit. As one of the biographers of Dana and the *Sun* put it, Dana had "the indefinable newspaper instinct that knows when a tomcat on the steps of the City Hall is more important than a crisis in the Balkans."[6] By 1876 his circulation had tripled to 130,000.

(Bettmann Archive)

(New York Post)

Charles A. Dana of the *New York Sun*

E. L. Godkin of the *Nation* and *Evening Post*

Brilliant as the *Sun* was, however, it had serious weaknesses. Because Dana insisted on limiting its size to four pages, comprehensive coverage of significant news suffered. And the editorial page that could originate such ringing phrases as "No king, no clown, to rule this town!" to combat Tweed, and "Turn the rascals out!" to harass Grant, could also be so intellectually "smart" as to approach cynicism.

In its discussions of issues, the *Sun* became increasingly conservative. The paper detested labor unions. It poked fun at civil-service reform advocates and others interested in good government, even though the *Sun* itself crusaded against misconduct in office. And it long advocated imperialistic schemes for the annexation of Canada, Cuba, and other neighboring areas.

GODKIN, THE *NATION,* AND THE *POST*

It remained for an English-born journalist to give the United States the vigorous and intelligent editorial leadership it needed in the postwar period. He was Edwin Lawrence Godkin, the founder of the magazine the *Nation* and the successor to William Cullen Bryant as the driving spirit of the *New York Evening Post.*

Of Godkin, historian Allan Nevins has written: "Godkin showed at once a distinctive style, a refreshing penetration, and a skill in ironic analysis never before equalled in American journalism." And because this was so, philosopher William James could write: "To my generation his was certainly the towering influence in all thought concerning public affairs, and indirectly his influence has assuredly been more pervasive than that of any other writer of the generation, for he influenced other writers who never quoted him, and determined the whole current of discussion."[7] President Charles W. Eliot of Harvard University, President Daniel Coit Gilman of Johns Hopkins, James Russell Lowell, James Bryce, Charles Eliot Norton—the intellectual leaders of Godkin's generation—all publicly acknowledged the debt they owed to the pages of the *Nation*. Not, of course, that they always agreed with its editor's viewpoints.

Godkin had been a reporter and editorial writer for English newspapers and had written editorials for Raymond's *New York Times* before deciding that the United States needed a high-grade weekly journal of opinion and literary criticism, similar to those in England. In 1865 he found the financial backing for the *Nation* and announced its aims.

The *Nation*, Godkin said, would discuss the political and economic questions of the day "with greater accuracy and moderation than are now to be found in the daily press." It would advocate "whatever in legislation or in manners seems likely to promote a more equal distribution of the fruits of progress and civilization." It would seek to better the conditions of the blacks. It would fix "public attention upon the political importance of education, and the dangers which a system like ours runs from the neglect of it in any portion of our territory." And it would print sound and impartial criticisms of books and works of art.[8]

Godkin was a mid-Victorian English liberal of the John Stuart Mill school of economic thought. Therefore, he believed that government should not intervene in economic matters. But unlike many of his time, he did believe that government should take action in social spheres. To a twentieth-century world that has used government as a regulatory force in both economic and social situations, Godkin thus appears at times to be reactionary.

But in many areas, Godkin was in the forefront of progressive thought. He urged complete reconciliation with the South during the period of military rule; he was one of the earliest advocates of civil-service reform to end the spoils system; he believed in women's suffrage when it was an unpopular idea; he was a strong supporter of public education and the new land-grant universities; and, as mentioned, he wrote in behalf of the blacks. Above all, the *Nation* ceaselessly badgered politicians who were more interested in personal gain than in progressive improvement of government. Its influence ran far beyond its 10,000 circulation.

In 1881, Godkin moved on to a bigger but actually less influential journalistic stage. That year, Henry Villard, a Civil War correspondent who later made a fortune building railroads, purchased the *New York Evening Post* and hired a trio of outstanding editors for the newspaper. One was Horace White, who had edited the *Chicago Tribune* from 1866 to 1874, taking that newspaper into the liberal Republican camp for a brief period as he advocated tariff reduction, civil-service reform, and currency policies favorable to the farmers. A second was Carl Schurz, the former editor of the St. Louis *Westliche Post* who had become Secretary of the Interior in President Hayes's cabinet and who was a leading American liberal. The third was Godkin, who had sold the *Nation* to Villard but continued to edit it as the weekly edition of the *Evening Post*. Within two years, Schurz and Godkin quarreled over Godkin's antilabor union views, and Schurz resigned, leaving Godkin in control of the *Evening Post* with White as his assistant.

Under Godkin, the *Evening Post* and the *Nation* rose to new fame in the presidential election year of 1884. The contest lay between James G. Blaine, the Republican congressional leader from Maine, and Grover Cleveland, Democratic governor of New York. Godkin, declaring that Blaine was unacceptable because of the post–Civil War scandals, fought his election with all his editorial skill. As the campaign progressed, charges of immoral conduct were made against Cleveland, and emotionalism ran high. Some stalwart Republican newspapers in leading cities found themselves opposing Blaine in company with the usual dissenters: the *Evening Post,* the *New York Times,* the *Springfield Republican, Harper's Weekly,* and the *Nation.* Dana of the *Sun,* who would support neither major-party candidate, fastened on these papers the name "mugwump," indicating desertion of party regularity. The name applied particularly to the *Evening Post,* which had been Republican since the founding of the party in 1856.

The *Evening Post*'s particular contribution was Godkin's famous "deadly parallel" column, in which he matched Blaine's campaign statements and congressional record against his personal associations with railroad builders and financiers. The campaign became exceedingly bitter, and it was evident that the New York State vote would decide the election. When Cleveland carried New York by 23,000 votes and became the first Democrat to win the presidency since the Civil War, many explanations were advanced. A Blaine supporter who had described the Democrats as a party of "rum, Romanism, and rebellion" received heavy blame, as did the antilabor *New York Tribune,* whose advocacy of Blaine was judged to be a handicap in the wooing of working men's votes. But Godkin asserted, with some justice, that the victory was proof of the creation of a group of independent voters who would put public welfare ahead of party loyalty.

Godkin stood in the early 1880s as New York's leading editor primarily because of his great ability, but also because of the shortcomings of his contemporaries. After the death of Raymond, the *Times* was slowly going downhill and exhibited spirit and influence only sporadically. Dana's *Sun* was erratic, and the Bennetts' *Herald* had little editorial force. Greeley's *Tribune,* after the founding editor's death in 1872, switched position and became the voice for the dominant conservative wing of the Republican party. The *Tribune*'s new editor was a famous journalistic figure, Whitelaw Reid, but his editorial stand lacked the qualities of independence shown by an increasing number of editors. While Godkin was urging reconciliation with the South, the *Tribune* was waving the bloody shirt as late as 1880 to preserve Republican supremacy. Godkin was for tariff reform; the *Tribune,* for high tariffs and the protection of the industrial interests of the expanding capitalism. Godkin long supported civil-service reform, which found favor with the Republican leadership only after the assassination of President James A. Garfield in 1881 by a disturbed patronage-seeker. And the *Tribune* more than matched Godkin's opposition to labor unions, fighting a printers' strike against itself for 15 years.[9] Still, the *Tribune*'s standards of news coverage and presentation were such that it was a formidable competitor for the readership of those whom the *Evening Post* called the "gentlemen and scholars."

Unfortunately, Godkin was not a newsperson, despite his editorial genius. He cared little for the news policies of the *Evening Post* beyond his specialized interests. He disliked sentiment and color in the news, and he would have liked to have kept all news of crime and violence out of the paper. Whatever merit there was to his viewpoints, they put the *Evening Post* at a serious disadvantage in the competition for circulation, and the paper never attained the readership its editorial leadership deserved.

Godkin retired as editor of the *Evening Post* and the *Nation* in 1899. He died in 1902. When Henry Villard died in 1900, his son, Oswald Garrison Villard, became publisher and editorial leader of the two publications. They continued to be fighting liberal organs.[10]

WATTERSON'S *COURIER-JOURNAL* AND SCOTT'S *OREGONIAN*

Other strong editorial voices were raised outside New York during the period of Godkin's dominance. The most notable were those of Henry Watterson of the *Louisville Courier-Journal* and Harvey W. Scott of the *Oregonian* in Portland. Both enjoyed long careers that began at the close of the Civil War and continued until World War I, but both belong primarily in this transitional period of journalism history. Arthur Krock, an associate of Watterson on the *Courier-Journal* staff before becoming a *New York Times* fixture, offers one reason for setting Watterson apart from later editors: "he was the last of those editors who wrote with the power of ownership."[11] The same was true of Scott. Other editors, like Godkin, exercised free rein because of their relationships to the owners of their papers, and they have continued to do so since, but admittedly with increasing difficulty as the newspaper became a corporate institution.

Watterson was editor of the *Courier-Journal* for 50 years, and his personality did much to make the newspaper one of the foremost in the country. He was a colorful representative of the era of personal journalism who loved to engage in editorial-page duels with other editors. One of his worst foes was Dana, and he lived to banter with the editors of another journalistic generation in the twentieth century. He himself said that he belonged to the era of "the personal, one-man papers—rather blatant, but independent."[12]

Watterson had varied youthful ambitions: to be a great historian, a great dramatist, a great novelist, a great musician. He came no closer to those dreams than writing a rejected novel and serving as a music critic in New York, but his catholic interests served in time to make him a versatile and engaging writer of editorials. He was an editorial writer in Washington when the Civil War began, and he cast his lot with the South, editing a Tennessee newspaper named the *Rebel.* After stints on newspapers in Cincinnati, Atlanta, and Nashville, at the age of 28 Watterson found his lifetime work in Louisville.

There Walter N. Haldeman, editor of the *Courier,* was in the process of consolidating the *Journal* and the *Democrat* with his newspaper, and the editorship and part-ownership of the new *Courier-Journal* went to Watterson. The year was 1868. Watterson, who despite his work for the southern cause had believed secession to be wrong, raised his voice in behalf of reconciliation of the North and South and gave advice freely to both sections. He told the North that military rule should be relaxed, and he was listened to because he also had sympathy for the blacks. He told the South that Lincoln was a great man and that much of its misery had come about as a result of his assassination. And the South listened, because Watterson was a southerner of good family, not a reforming Yankee. Soon the *Courier-Journal* editorial columns, and particularly its weekly edition, won a position as a leading voice of the new South.

In the Far West, another voice was raised by an editor whose intellectual powers and forceful writing brought him attention as the leading spokesperson of his area. He was Harvey W. Scott, who for 45 years edited the *Oregonian* in Portland. The *Oregonian,* founded in 1850 in a village near the junction of the Willamette and Columbia rivers, grew with the community. Scott gave up a law career to become its editor in 1865, and in 1877 he and Henry L. Pittock became the owners.[13]

Like Godkin, Scott was scholarly and forceful in his expression of opinion, but like Godkin, too, he lacked Watterson's human touch. There was one major reason why Scott's editorials were widely read and quoted: he had the ability to grapple with complex problems that many an editor shied away from and to present new viewpoints originating in his own reasoning and analysis. His range of information seemed unlimited, and he used this resource as he thought an editor should: to guide public opinion in the public interest. The *Oregonian* was Republican by choice, but Scott wrote as an independent editor, taking his stand on the basis of his conception of the public good. An editor with Scott's abilities is rare in any period, and his fame spread from his home city, in which he was a leading figure, as the *Oregonian* won statewide circulation and its editorial voice became nationally recognized.

Dana, Godkin, Watterson, and Scott—particularly the latter two—lived through the enormous changes that were occurring in American life as the Industrial Revolution hit full stride. They were aware of change and accepted it. They and their fellow workers contributed new strengths to American journalism as it approached the "watershed of the nineties."

AN INDUSTRIAL ECONOMY

What was happening? Industrialization was advancing on a major scale, with the mechanization of production processes, the rise of the city, the vast expansion of communication facilities, the coming of the age of steel, the harnessing of electricity for light and power, and a host of inventions and new businesses.

This was the true nationalization of the United States, the achievement of economic and social interdependence.[14] National growth and increased wealth meant cultural progress in literature, science, and the social sciences. But the wealth was not equally distributed, and there was sharp questioning of the theory of individualism that permitted unrestrained exploitation, enormous concentrations of wealth and economic power, and the many injustices of a materialistic-minded age. Political unrest, the rise of labor unions, and demands for economic and social reform thus were added to the scene.

America was a rich continent for the aggressive and the ingenious to master. Between 1865 and 1880 the national wealth doubled, and by 1900 it had doubled again. The population doubled in those 35 years. The nation's iron ore, its oil, its lumber, and its western agricultural lands were sources of yet untapped wealth. Its people, who by and large admired the successful enterprisers, eagerly provided investment and speculative capital. Only when it became clear that the division of the spoils had been in favor of a few to the detriment of the many did the protests take effect. In the meantime, the patterns had been set. The dynamic capitalism of an expanding America, seizing on unparalleled natural resources and utilizing the new machines of the Industrial Revolution, had transformed the national economy.[15]

Familiar symbols of this new economic order are John D. Rockefeller and the oil monopoly, and Andrew Carnegie and the steel combine. But similar concentrations of wealth and business control developed throughout American industry and trade. Cornelius Vanderbilt, Jay Gould, and J. Pierpont Morgan in finance; Leland Stanford, Collis P. Huntington, James J. Hill, and George Pullman in railroading; C. C. Washburn and Charles A. Pillsbury in the milling industry that centered in Minneapolis as the Great Plains opened; Philip D. Armour and Gustavus F. Swift in the meat-packing industry that grew in Chicago and Kansas City as cattle raising became big business; the makers of machine-sewed shoes, ready-made clothes, packaged foods, watches, cameras, farm machinery, and hardware; the timber owners; and the mining kings—all rose to dominate the American scene in the late nineteenth century.

The captains of industry and finance obtained power through a variety of means. Some gained control of large segments of natural resources. A few held patents on basic inventions. Others, of whom Rockefeller was the most noted, won supremacy in part through manipulation of transportation rates and ruthless competitive tactics. Some were lucky in the world of financial speculation. Most important, the Rockefellers and the Carnegies usually were successful because they had, or could hire, the brains necessary to create a new manufacturing or financial empire.

But, as usual, there was a flaw in the new order. As the machine revolutionized the American economy, it brought with it the threat of overproduction and disastrous competition among the new producers. The dislocation of labor that resulted and the bankrupting of weaker businesses also promoted economic instability. The heads of industry cast about for ways of avoiding the industrial and financial panics that threatened the strong as well as the weak.

One effort to overcome these dangers took the form of the pool agreement. Direct competitors sought by voluntary secret agreement to limit industrywide production, to allocate production quotas, and to stabilize prices. The trouble was that in times of distress the rule quickly became "every man for himself."

A more successful form of industry control was the trust, developed by the Standard Oil group around 1880. By this method the shareholders in the original companies assigned their capital stock to a board of trustees and received trust certificates in return. The trustees thus obtained legal control of the individual units. They could decide production quotas, set selling prices, and eliminate competition.

Hosts of other industries followed the lead of the oil companies before 1890. Sugar, salt, whiskey, rope, lead, tin plate, crackers, matches, newsprint, fence wire, and many other products fell under near-monopolistic control. The number of producing companies declined sharply in such fields as woolen goods, iron and steel, leather, and farm machinery. Congress passed the Sherman Anti-Trust Act of 1890 in an attempt to restore open competition, but the result was hardly satisfactory to opponents of monopoly. The sugar trust simply became an incorporated company under the laws of New Jersey, and the Standard Oil group developed the holding-company technique. The amalgamation of many businesses now took the form of a single great corporation, whether in manufacturing, in railroading, or in mining and cattle raising.

Finally, it is important to note that both business and government began looking for foreign outlets for America's surplus of goods during this era, which witnessed the beginning of an active foreign policy and American imperialism.[16]

THE RISE OF THE CITY

The industrial concentration that was maturing between 1880 and 1900 was of vital significance, but it was only a part of the enormous change in American life. Mechanization, industrialization, and urbanization brought swift and extensive social, cultural, and political developments. People were being uprooted physically and mentally by the effects of the economic revolution, and in the new environment no social institution could remain static. Even a brief examination of the character of this new environment will indicate the basic causes of the tremendous changes that developed in the daily newspapers of American cities by the 1880s.

Arthur M. Schlesinger, Sr., chose the phrase "the rise of the city" to characterize the period from 1878 to 1898.[17] Census figures show that the number of American towns and cities of 8000 or more population doubled between 1880 and 1900. The total population of those urban places more than doubled, jumping from some 11 million to 25 million. In 1880 there were 50 million Americans, of whom 22.7 percent were living in towns and cities of more than 8000. By 1900 that figure had risen to 32.9 percent of a total population of 76 million.

The most rapid gain in urbanization occurred during the ten years between 1880 and 1890, which were the years of greatest ferment in the daily newspaper business. The rise of the city was particularly evident in the northeastern industrial states, where urban centers now predominated over declining rural areas, and in the older states of the Middle West. New York City jumped in population from a million to a million and a half during the decade. Chicago, the rail and trade center of inland America, doubled its size, passing the million mark in 1890 to become the nation's second city. Next in line were Philadelphia, at a million; Brooklyn, at 800,000; and Boston, Baltimore, and St. Louis, in the half-million class. Altogether there were 58 cities with more than 50,000 in population in 1890; 80 percent of them were in the East and Middle West, and 50 percent of them were in the five states of New York, Pennsylvania, Massachusetts, New Jersey, and Ohio.

Into these cities was pouring an ever-rising tide of immigration, which brought new blood and new problems for American society. Again the decade of 1880 to 1890 stands out, since in those ten years more than five million immigrants came to America, double the number for any preceding decade. All told, approximately nine million foreign-born were added to the population in the 20 years between 1880 and 1900, as many as had come during the 40 years preceding 1880. As a result, the newspapers of New York City in 1890 were serving a population that was 80 percent foreign-born or of foreign parentage, and as might be expected, the character of some of the newspapers changed. Other American cities had from 25 percent to 40 percent foreign-born residents. To the older Irish, British, and German streams of migration were added great numbers of Scandinavians, Poles, French-Canadians, Italians, Russians, and Hungarians. Of these, particularly the Germans and the Scandinavians migrated to the Middle West, while the other groups tended to remain in the Atlantic states.

The rise of the city meant a quickening of material progress, reflected first in the life of the city dweller and transmitted gradually to the rest of the country. The new American cities hastened the installation of water and sewage systems after the Civil War. They paved their streets with asphalt and bricks, and they bridged their rivers with steel structures patterned after the Roeblings' famed Brooklyn Bridge of 1883. A ten-story Chicago building, constructed around a steel and iron skeleton in 1885, heralded the coming of the skyscraper.

Electricity was becoming a great new servant, both as a source of power for industry and transportation and as a source of light. American cities had barely begun to install arc lights in 1879 when Thomas A. Edison invented a practicable incandescent bulb. When the current flowed out from his Pearl Street generating station in 1882 to light the Stock Exchange and the offices of the *New York Times* and *New York Herald,* a new era in living had begun. By 1898 there were nearly 2800 central electric power stations in the country, as businesses and homes were lighted, electric elevators were installed in the new tall buildings, and electric motors became widely used in industry.

THE COMMUNICATIONS NETWORK

The United States was being tied together by its industrial revolution, and its communications network kept pace with the sense of urgency that was characteristic of the new order. The telephone, invented by Alexander Graham Bell in the 1870s, already had one user for every thousand persons in 1880. By 1900 there was one telephone for each hundred. Intercity lines multiplied during the 1880s, until by 1900 the Bell System covered the country. Western Union quadrupled its telegraph lines between 1880 and 1900. The railroads, with 93,000 miles of track in 1880, reached a near-saturation point of 193,000 miles by 1900. The federal postal service, still the primary means of communication, greatly extended its free carrier service in cities during the two decades and instituted free rural delivery in 1897. Congress, by clearly defining second-class matter in the Postal Act of 1879 and by providing a penny-a-pound rate for newspapers and magazines in 1885, opened the way for low-cost delivery of publications. In business offices the introduction of the typewriter and adding machine speeded the work pace and simplified the handling of increased correspondence and records.

AN EXPANSION OF NEWSPAPERS

The most striking evidence of what was happening to the newspaper is obvious from a bare statistical summary. Between 1870 and 1900, the United States doubled its population and tripled the number of its urban residents. During the same 30 years the number of daily newspapers quadrupled, and the number of copies sold each day increased almost sixfold. Both in numbers and in total circulation the daily newspaper was rising even more rapidly than the city that spawned it. The number of English-language, general-circulation dailies increased from 489 in 1870 to 1967 in 1900.[18] Circulation totals for all daily publications rose from 2.6 million copies in 1870 to 15 million in 1900. A similar advance was being made by weekly newspapers, which served mainly the small towns and rural areas, but also the suburbs and sections of the cities. Between 1870 and 1900, the number of weekly publications tripled, increasing from approximately 4000 to more than 12,000. The weeklies, however, still represented personal journalistic ventures, and the revolution in newspaper methods was taking place at the level of the big-city daily.

There were many less tangible reasons the newspaper was making such tremendous strides as an American social institution. The forces of social and economic interdependence, products of industrialization and urbanization, played a leading part in the creation of the lusty "new journalism." The people of the cities, being molded together as economic and cultural units, increasingly turned to the daily newspapers for the story of their urban life and their common interests. At the same time the country itself was being rapidly unified by the rush toward economic interdependence. Improved communications facilities were a manifestation of this nationalizing influence that pervaded all American life. And again, the daily newspaper was the chronicler of the national scene, the interpreter of the new environment. The city reader, whether seated in new-found comfort on a streetcar or in a better-lighted home, was the eager customer of the publisher who met successfully the new challenge to journalism.

ADVANCES IN EDUCATION

As American social and economic life became more complex and as the national wealth accumulated, many cultural advances were possible that in turn promoted new interest in the newspaper. The cities, with their concentrated populations and earning capacities, naturally led in the expansion of social and intellectual activity. But they also set the pace for a nationalized cultural development. The bookstores, libraries, art galleries, museums, theaters, opera houses, churches, retail stores, schools, and newspapers that brought higher standards in the cities stimulated the interests and the desires of the entire country. Progress in education, the result of this general thirst for knowledge and a better life, was particularly important to the expansion of the mass media: newspapers, magazines, books. The percentage of children attending public schools in the United States rose from 57 percent to 72 percent between 1870 and 1900, and illiteracy declined from 20 percent to 10.7 percent of the population. The number of high schools jumped from approximately 100 in 1860 to 800 by 1880, and then skyrocketed to 6000 by 1900.

At higher educational levels, the growth of state universities and private colleges financed by America's newly wealthy resulted in notable advances in the social sciences, as well as progress in the natural and physical sciences and the humanities. Federal land subsidies provided by the Morrill Act of 1862 encouraged the founding and expansion of state universities, particularly in the Middle West and West, where such state-supported universities as Wisconsin, California, Minnesota, and Illinois began to flourish. The private colleges and universities gained in numbers and influence with the founding of Cornell University in 1865 by Ezra Cornell, whose millions came from the electric telegraph; of Johns Hopkins University in 1876 by a Baltimore merchant; of Leland Stanford University in 1885 by a California railroad and businessperson; of the University of Chicago in 1892 by John D. Rockefeller's benefaction. Johns Hopkins, by emphasizing the role of research in higher education, and Harvard, by giving its students an elective choice of courses, set new patterns for the universities. And university presidents such as Charles W. Eliot of Harvard, Daniel Coit Gilman of Johns Hopkins, and Andrew D. White of Cornell gave effective leadership. No longer was it necessary for Americans interested in scholarly pursuits to go abroad, and the number of graduate students in the United States increased from 400 in 1880 to some 5600 in 1900. Nor were women ignored in the new spread of education. The state universities became coeducational institutions; Smith College for women was founded in 1875, and was soon followed by Bryn Mawr and Radcliffe, fruits of the women's suffrage movement.

NEW SOCIOECONOMIC PHILOSOPHIES

The scholars of the universities and other men and women whose intellectual and cultural achievements were supported by the new wealth of the nation made great advances between 1880 and 1900. Most importantly, they challenged the socioeconomic philosophies that had developed in nineteenth-century society and suggested new concepts better fitted to the revolutionized character of American life. They organized areas of knowledge needed if the country was to understand and cope with its problems, and in doing so they laid the groundwork for the vast growth of research and interpretation in the twentieth century.[19]

A socioeconomic theory of individualism had been well developed by 1880 to bolster the argument that government should not interfere in economic affairs. The individual, this school of thought declared, supplies the enterprise that makes possible industrial progress, wealth, and national power. Therefore government should do nothing that would adversely affect individual economic enterprise. Government's function, ran the argument, is to provide an orderly society in which the individual is protected as he or she fulfills his or her destiny.

Powerful support for the theory of individualism was drawn from the work of the English scientist Charles Darwin, who published his *Origin of Species* in 1859 and *The Descent of Man* in 1871. Darwin's emphasis on the struggle for individual existence in the process of evolution fit nicely into the pattern. Another major influence on American thinking came from the writings of the English philosopher Herbert Spencer. The Spencerian doctrine declared that the ultimate achievement of a perfect society would be the result of a natural process—an inevitable development that people themselves should not attempt to hasten or to alter. In the United States, sociologist William Graham Sumner, historian John Fiske, and political scientist John W. Burgess shaped their teaching and writing to conform with Social Darwinism and Spencer's ideas of individualism. The influence of this socioeconomic doctrine became so strong, particularly in the rendering of Supreme Court decisions nullifying reform legislation, that Justice Oliver Wendell Holmes was led to protest that Spencer's *Social Statics* was not part of the Constitution.[20]

Those who decried the negativism of this theory of individualism were being heard by the 1880s. They contended that individuals did have the ability to control their own destinies, and to shape their economic and political actions as the general welfare of society might require. Unrestricted exercise of individual power by some only brings misery and poverty to others, and the outcome is not national strength but national weakness, said this school of thought. True progress, they stated, depends on cooperation and the use of government's powers in the common good.

A sociologist, Lester Ward, who published the first volume of his *Dynamic Sociology* in 1883, provided logical arguments for the belief that government should be regarded as a positive force and that it should actively seek ways of achieving social improvement. Economist Richard T. Ely attacked the pat theories of the laissez-faire advocates, which he and other economics professors argued were not conforming to the facts of industrial life. Ely's *Socialism, Its Nature, Strength, and Weakness,* published in 1894, made definite proposals for reasonable reform legislation. Economist Thorstein Veblen compared the theories of economic individualists with the actual practices of industrial capitalism and voiced his bitter protest in 1899 with his *Theory of the Leisure Class.* Henry George assailed the unearned increment of wealth through land ownership in his *Progress and Poverty* (1879), and Henry Demarest Lloyd denounced the oil monopoly in *Wealth against Commonwealth* (1894), an effective plea for socioeconomic cooperation.

Newspaper editors Dana, Godkin, and Reid, as we have observed, were supporters of the theory of individualism and opposed government interference in economic spheres. One might expect, in light of what was happening, that other editors would appear who would support the principles of social cooperation and the use of governmental power to regulate economic life. And, indeed, one of the characteristics of the "new journalism" came to be the expression of editorial-page support for the common people. What publishers and editors like Joseph Pulitzer and E. W. Scripps represented in journalism was only an expression of a larger movement in American thought and life.

ADVANCES IN KNOWLEDGE

Those who thus argued directly with the supporters of individualism were aided by those whose contributions to knowledge widened the country's understanding of its history, its government, and human thought and action. The period of the 1880s and 1890s was one of intense activity in study and publication, and in every field there were major achievements that helped Americans to meet the challenge of economic and social change.

Historians broke new ground by studying and writing about social and economic history as well as politics. John Bach McMaster pointed the way by using newspapers as source materials for his significantly titled *History of the People of the United States,* begun in 1883. Henry Adams produced his brilliant history of the Jefferson and Madison administrations in 1889, and James Ford Rhodes began publication of his *History of the United States* in 1892. Frederick Jackson Turner's famous essay on the "Significance of the Frontier in American History" appeared in 1893 and fostered a new school of historical interpretation. Colonial history was being rewritten by people with an understanding of economic and social conditions of the early American period.

The landmark for this period in the field of government and political science was James Bryce's *American Commonwealth* of 1888, in which the talented English writer gave to the United States a description of its new environment. Among many other groundbreaking social science books were John Dewey's *School and Society* (1899) and William James's *Principles of Psychology* (1890).

Literature offered Henry James's *Portrait of a Lady* (1881); Samuel Clemens's *Life on the Mississippi* (1883) and *Huckleberry Finn* (1885); and William Dean Howells's *The Rise of Silas Lapham* (1885), an early example of realism in American literature. In the

1890s, poets Emily Dickinson and Edwin Arlington Robinson and novelists Stephen Crane and Hamlin Garland were making major contributions, while such realistic writers as Theodore Dreiser and Frank Norris were on the verge of fame.

Earlier, women novelists such as Susan B. Warner had discovered a huge audience. Warner's *The Wide, Wide World* paved the way for later best-selling books. *The Curse of Clifton* by Mrs. E.D.E.N. Southworth, *Tempest and Sunshine* by Mary J. Holmes, and *The Lamplighter* by Maria S. Cummins were enormously popular. By the 1880s the domestic novel was in great demand.

Nor was this great cultural stirring and extension of factual information limited to an intellectual class. Millions shared in the new knowledge through the chautauquas and public study courses that became of major importance as means of adult education toward the close of the century. The world fairs and expositions that caught America's fancy in this period were another means of mass education. At the Philadelphia Centennial of 1876 and Chicago's Columbian Exposition of 1893, millions of Americans viewed the material and artistic achievements of their generation. Free public libraries, spreading across the country after 1880, found their great benefactor in Andrew Carnegie. In these libraries were available the literary triumphs and the popular writings of American and British authors.

INFLUENCE OF MAGAZINES

Magazines came to have increasing influence on American life. Earlier ventures like the *North American Review* (1815) and the *Knickerbocker,* a more popular magazine published from 1833 to 1865, had been eclipsed by *Harper's Monthly,* begun in 1850 by the New York book publishing firm. *Harper's* introduced extensive woodcut illustrations, published the writings of leading English and American authors, and ran up a world-record circulation of 200,000 before the Civil War. Two women's magazines, *Godey's Lady's Book* and *Peterson's,* began their careers in 1830 and 1842, respectively, and offered hand-colored engravings of fashions and fiction stories to more than 150,000 readers each by the 1850s.

On the West Coast, San Francisco's *The Golden Era* (1852–1895) reigned as a leading literary magazine, offering cultural and literary content with a Gold Rush slant. Mark Twain was among its contributors.[21] In 1881, the *Century* joined *Harper's* in the highly literary and artistic class of magazines. *Scribner's* made it a trio in 1886. Unillustrated, but of equal literary quality, was the *Atlantic Monthly,* which was begun in 1857 and specialized in publishing the writings of the New England authors. In the weekly field were two illustrated periodicals, *Frank Leslie's Illustrated Newspaper* (1855) and *Harper's Weekly* (1857). The latter exercised strong influence in public affairs, along with E. L. Godkin's weekly, the *Nation* (1865). In addition, the *Independent* (1848), the *North American Review,* and such newcomers as the *Forum* (1886), the *Arena* (1889), and the *Outlook* (1893) all discussed the new political and social environment. The *Literary Digest* began summarizing contemporary editorial opinion in 1890.

Coming into the field were publications that depended on humor, cartoons, and political satire. *Puck* (1877) featured Joseph Keppler's dynamic color cartoons. The others were *Judge* (1881) and *Life* (1883), famed for its publication of the "Gibson girl" drawings of Charles Dana Gibson. In the children's magazine competition, *Youth's Companion* (1827) was joined by *St. Nicholas* (1873).

Helped by the cheap postage rates established by Congress under its 1879 act, some new leaders struck out in the 1880s for the mass readership that still awaited American magazine publishers. One was Cyrus H. K. Curtis, who founded the *Ladies' Home Jour-*

nal in 1883 and, with Edward W. Bok as his editor, soon won a half-million circulation. Curtis bought the *Saturday Evening Post* in 1897 and with editor George Horace Lorimer quickly made it a leader in the low-cost weekly field, which *Collier's* entered in 1888. The older, high-quality monthlies found stiff competition from three low-priced popular magazines: *Munsey's,* begun in 1889 by Frank Munsey; *McClure's,* started in 1893 by S. S. McClure; and the *Cosmopolitan* (1886). It was these magazines, circulating more extensively than any of their predecessors, that were to open the minds of more readers to social and cultural trends.

THE SOCIETY'S SHORTCOMINGS AND DISCONTENTS

It must be noted, however, that the general level of cultural attainment was still low. Even by 1900 the average American had received only five years of schooling. If the public bought encyclopedias galore from the book publishers because it wanted to know more, it also bought dime novels by the millions. If the chautauqua was a booming institution, so were horse racing, prizefighting, and baseball. Cultural and business organizations were expanding in number, but growing even faster were fraternal and social groups. In the newspaper world Adolph Ochs would be able to find enough serious readers in the metropolis of New York to support the reborn *New York Times*, but the great mass of readers was attracted by the devices of a journalism that sought a popular level as it both entertained and informed.

It should be noted briefly, too, that not everybody was successful or contented in this new economic and social environment, despite the general blessings that industrialization had bestowed on the country. Sharp divisions began to appear between those who had gained wealth in the process of national economic upheaval and those who had gained only a crowded room in a city tenement, a poverty-stricken tenant farm in the South, or a precarious existence on the dry plains of the West. Falling farm prices in the 1880s spurred the political activities of the discontented in the South and West. There the Grangers, the Greenbackers, the Farmers' Alliance, and the Populists arose to demand economic equality for agriculture and launched third-party movements that showed real strength. Not until 1896 did one of the major political parties answer the call of the "consistent rebellion"; at that time, the merging of the forces of free silver coinage, paper money, and general political and economic reform under the Democratic banner of William Jennings Bryan provided America with the greatest political excitement of a generation. But despite the bitter experience of the depression of 1893, the advocates of William McKinley and political and economic conservatism won the decision.

In the cities the rise of the labor movement on a nationally organized scale provided a much sharper clash than that between business and agriculture. Some craft unions, such as those of the bricklayers, railroad engineers, and printers, had become established before the Civil War, and a National Labor Union of some stature was organized in 1866, only to disintegrate during the depression of 1873. The Knights of Labor, under the leadership of Terence V. Powderly, reached a peak membership of 700,000 during the two years of industrial turbulence that followed the panic of 1884. Powderly advocated cooperative action by all working people to better their pay and working conditions and the use of the strike weapon when necessary. A radical departure from the traditional practice of organizing unions of only skilled craftworkers, the Knights of Labor "one big union" plan would include both skilled and unskilled workers, men and women, and native-born and immigrants. The ultimate goal was to abolish the wage system and replace it with a cooperative economy of worker-owned industry.[22] Unfortunately for the Knights of Labor, their aggressive action was discredited in 1886 following the Haymarket Square riot in Chicago, where a rally in support of the eight-hour day organized by a small group of agitators, some of them anarchists, was disrupted by police. A bomb exploded, touching off violence that killed 11 persons, including seven police officers. Although the prosecution lacked sufficient evidence, eight anarchists were convicted of the bomb throwing, and four of them were hanged. Even though the trial was unjust, adversaries of the labor movement used the incident to attack the Knights of Labor. In the wake of this criticism the American Federation of Labor, built in 1881 as a national organization of the various craft unions, became the principal voice of the labor movement with Samuel Gompers as its newly elected president. A series of strikes in 1886 led to a reduction of the work day to eight or nine hours for some 200,000 of the 350,000 workers involved.

The reaction in many industries was the formation of employers' associations that raised defense funds to fight the carefully planned demands and strikes of the individual craft unions. Although most of the strikes of the 1880s and 1890s were peaceful, several were extensive and led to great violence. National guard troops were used to quell disturbances at Henry C. Frick's Homestead, Pennsylvania, steel plant in July 1892, and at the Coeur d'Alene, Idaho, mines in that same month, following pitched battles between private guards and workers. A strike at the Chicago railways yards in May 1894, by the American Railway Union against the Pullman Company, led to violence in numerous states, as had happened during the widespread railway strike of 1877. During one of many coal-mine strikes deputies killed 18 miners in Pennsylvania in 1897. A decade of mining wars erupted in Colorado in 1894, and teamsters and waterfront workers were met with resistance when they began organizing in a number of cities.

A NEW JOURNALISM EMERGING

In such a swiftly changing and exciting environment, then, the daily newspaper was coming of age. From 850 English-language, general-circulation dailies in 1880 to 1967 in 1900; from 10 percent of adults as subscribers to 26 percent—these were the statistical evidences of the newspaper's arrival as a major business. The enormous success of Joseph Pulitzer's *New York World,* which between 1883 and 1887 broke every publishing record in the United States, was evidence that a "new journalism" had been created that would change the character and the appearance of the daily newspaper and enormously increase its mass influence.

But before focusing attention on the *New York World*, whose triumphs caught the attention of even the most unobservant in the newspaper business, we should briefly examine the changes that were occurring in other cities. Certainly Henry W. Grady in Atlanta, Edward W. Scripps in Cleveland and Cincinnati, Melville E. Stone and Victor Lawson in Chicago, and William Rockhill Nelson in Kansas City were also engaged in the creation of the "new journalism" in the same years that Joseph Pulitzer was exhibiting his skill, first in St. Louis and then in New York. And in many another city, newspapers were being challenged by bright-faced newcomers that, in some cases, were destined to take their places among America's best. The new papers were low-priced, aggressive, and easily read. They believed that the news function was the primary obligation of the press; they exhibited independence of editorial opinion; they crusaded actively in the community interest; they appealed to the mass audience through improved writing, better makeup, use of headlines and illustrations, and popularization of their contents. These were the general characteristics of the "new journalism"; the individual newspapers, of course, exhibited them in varying degrees.

The rise of evening newspapers was a feature of this growth of the daily. The evening field claimed seven-eighths of the increase in numbers of daily newspapers between 1880 and 1900, and by 1890 two out of three papers were evening editions. The swing toward evening publication was due in part to the changing reading habits of the city populations, and it was strengthened by the discovery that the women readers to whom retail-store advertising was directed favored afternoon-delivered newspapers. Mechanical and news-gathering innovations permitted the evening papers to carry "today's news today," particularly in the Middle West and West, where time differentials aided inclusion of news from the East and from Europe on the same day events occurred. Some morning papers found an answer by publishing afternoon editions under the same name plate, while others established separate evening papers.

JOURNALISM OF THE EAST

New York remained primarily a morning-paper city, with only the *Evening Post* achieving distinction as an afternoon paper before the Pulitzer invasion. Two additions to the field in 1867 were the *Evening Telegram,* begun by James Gordon Bennett as the afternoon edition of the *Herald,* and the *Evening Mail.* The *Mail* was merged with the older *Express* in 1882 to form the *Mail and Express.* The circulation winner of the period was the *Daily News,* a one-cent evening paper dating back to 1855. The *Daily News,* cheap in content as well as in price, circulated in the tenement districts so widely that it challenged the *Sun* and *Herald* throughout the 1870s, and its success suggested to other publishers new ways of reaching the immigrant-crowded tenement sections of the city.

Boston's quiet journalism was upset by the appearance of the *Globe.* Founded in 1872, it had a circulation of only 8000 when General Charles H. Taylor became publisher in 1873. Taylor established an evening edition, cut the price to two cents, ran big headlines, emphasized local news, and gave editorial support to the Democratic party. By 1890 the *Globe,* with combined morning and evening circulation of 150,000, ranked among the top ten papers in the country. The staid *Herald* (1846) and the sensationalized *Journal* (1833) kept pace by establishing evening editions. But the morning *Advertiser* (1813) and *Post* (1831), and evening *Transcript* (1830) and *Traveller* (1825), contented themselves with limited circulations. The *Advertiser* did establish an evening edition—the *Record*—in 1884.

The trend was similar in other eastern cities—Philadelphia, Baltimore, Pittsburgh, Buffalo, Brooklyn, Providence, and Washington.[23]

NEW DAILIES IN THE WEST

To the West, the newspaper that is now the *Dallas News* was established in 1885, and its future publisher, George B. Dealey, appeared in Dallas that year. The *Los Angeles Times,* begun in 1881, saw its future owner, Harrison Gray Otis, join its staff in 1882. In San Francisco, the major event of the period was the sale of the *Examiner* (1865) in 1880 to George Hearst, who turned it over to young William Randolph Hearst in 1887. San Francisco journalism had been lively even before the Hearst entry, with the morning *Chronicle* (1865) leading in civic campaigns and political clean-up movements. Its publisher,

Michel H. de Young, one of two brothers who founded the paper, remained in control of the *Chronicle* for 60 years.

THE SOUTH: HENRY W. GRADY OF ATLANTA

Most brilliant of the southern newspaper makers of the period was Henry W. Grady, who in his brief 39 years demonstrated the qualities of a great reporter and managing editor. Grady's talents were widely exhibited in the dozen years before 1880, when he became managing editor of the *Atlanta Constitution.* Indeed, when Grady became editor and one-third owner of the *Atlanta Herald* in 1872, he nearly put the *Constitution,* founded four years before, out of business. But the *Herald,* for all its journalistic superiority, fell victim to the financial depression of 1873 after a four-year struggle. Grady then became a freelance correspondent for such enterprising newspapers as the *Constitution,* the *New York Herald,* the *Louisville Courier-Journal,* the *Philadelphia Times,* and the *Detroit Free Press,* distinguishing himself for his coverage of politics and for his use of the interview technique in reporting and interpreting the news. He traveled widely, and his grasp of events and his acquaintanceships increased accordingly.

When the *Constitution,* published by Evan P. Howell after 1876, obtained Grady as a part-owner and managing editor, things began to hum. A network of correspondents was built up, and Grady spent lavishly to get all the news coverage possible in every field from politics to baseball. Grady continued to report major news events and political affairs himself. His brilliant story of the Charleston earthquake of 1886 won him national attention as a reporter. The same year his address entitled "The New South," which advocated industrial advancement of the South as a means of reestablishing national solidarity, won him national fame as a spokesperson for his region. As a consequence Grady devoted increased attention to the editorial page of the *Constitution* until his death in 1889, and his influence furthered the paper's sharing of southern leadership with the *Louisville Courier-Journal.*[24]

With Grady's death, Clark Howell, Sr., son of the publisher, became managing editor of the *Constitution.* The other event in Atlanta journalism of the 1880s was the founding, in 1883, of the *Journal,* an evening paper that was destined to outmaneuver the Howells' *Constitution* by the 1950s.[25]

A REVOLUTION IN THE MIDWEST: E. W. SCRIPPS

What has been described thus far would suffice to prove that things were happening to the nation's journalism everywhere. Taylor's *Boston Globe* and Grady's *Atlanta Herald* and *Constitution* exhibited the major characteristics of the "new journalism." The appearance of the Butler family in Buffalo, of the Noyes family in Washington, of Josephus Daniels in Raleigh, of the Howell family in Atlanta, and of Harrison Gray Otis in Los Angeles meant in each case the beginning of the building of a noted American newspaper. But it was in the Midwest of the 1870s and 1880s that the biggest revolution in newspapering was brewing, in Detroit, Cleveland, Cincinnati, Chicago, Kansas City, Milwaukee, and St. Louis.

The name Scripps is written boldly into the story of midwestern newspaper making of the 1870s and early 1880s. James E. Scripps, elder half-brother of the famed Edward Wyllis Scripps, started the family on its journalistic mission when, after working on newspapers in Chicago and Detroit, he founded the *Detroit Evening News* in 1873. By the end of 1880, the Scripps family had fostered newspapers in Cleveland, Cincinnati, St. Louis, and Buffalo. The account of the rise of the Scripps newspaper chain belongs later, but the early successes were a part of the general pattern of the development of the "new journalism." Scripps' newspapers were low-priced evening publications; small in size but well written and tightly edited; hard-hitting in both news and editorial-page coverage of the local scene. Above all, they were distinguished for their devotion to the interests of working people.

When James Scripps needed help to keep his *Detroit News* afloat, he called on his brother George and sister Ellen, and eventually on young Edward, who was the thirteenth child of a thrice-married Englishman who had settled on an Illinois farm. Edward helped to build circulation routes for the *News* and reported for it while the struggle to win advertising support was in progress. Detroit already had well-established papers, such as the morning *Free Press* (1831), but by the 1880s the *News* emerged as a leading evening paper known for its business operation as well as for its qualities as a newspaper.

Scripps money went into four one-cent evening papers: the short-lived *Buffalo Evening Telegraph,* the ill-fated *St. Louis Chronicle,* and the famous *Cleveland Press* and *Cincinnati Post.* These two latter papers became the products of Edward Wyllis Scripps's own publishing genius and the parent papers of his eventual chain.

Cleveland of 1878 had three going newspapers: the *Leader* (1854), the *Herald* (1835), and the *Plain Dealer* (1842). When the *Penny Press* appeared as a four-page, five-column evening paper, it looked no more permanent than the alley shack in which it was published. But the editor, Edward Wyllis Scripps, paid the top salary to his advertising solicitor and put his own tremendous energy into the venture in a fashion that drove the circulation to 10,000 within a few months and foreshadowed the rise of the Scripps publishing empire. Its name became the *Press.*

What happened to Cleveland journalism as a result of the rapid growth of the new *Press* can be told briefly. In 1885 one of the first acts of a new owner, L. E. Holden, was to shift the emphasis of the *Plain Dealer* from the evening to the morning field. Holden bought the plant and morning edition of the *Herald;* the evening editions of the *Leader* and the *Herald* were combined as the *News and Herald.* But the *Press* continued to harass its evening competitors, and in 1905 the other afternoon dailies were combined into a new paper, the *Cleveland News.*

The Scripps opposition in Cincinnati was more formidable. In 1880 the evening *Times* (1840) and *Star* (1872) were merged by Charles P. Taft (half-brother of the later president, William Howard Taft). The *Times-Star* was a two-cent, conservative Republican paper; the Scripps entry that year was one cent and Democratic. But in the morning field were the *Enquirer* (1841), published by John R. McLean as a Democratic paper noted for its adoption of the techniques of sensationalism, and the *Commercial Gazette,* edited by the distinguished liberal Republican, Murat Halstead.[26] The Scripps paper, which became the *Cincinnati Post* after Edward Wyllis Scripps took control in 1883, nevertheless soon gained circulation leadership, as the *Press* was doing in Cleveland.

STONE'S *CHICAGO DAILY NEWS*

Another rising star in the Midwest was the *Chicago Daily News.* Together with another newcomer, the *Herald,*[27] the *Daily News* quickly won equal prominence with older Chicago papers. With Joseph Medill as controlling owner and editor after 1874, the *Tribune* (1847) was continuing its development as a substantially edited, alert newspaper leader. The *Inter Ocean* (successor to the *Republican,* founded in 1865 with Charles A. Dana as first editor) became widely known for its enterprise in news gathering and in adopting new journalistic and printing techniques. But circulation leadership went to a newcomer.

Melville E. Stone, the founder of the *Daily News,* was a product both of Chicago journalism and of the new national newspaper environment. Stone became managing editor of the *Republican* in 1872, as an inexperienced young man of 24, and ended up as city editor when the paper became the *Inter Ocean* later that year. In the fall he went on tour for the paper, studying conditions in the South. He records in his autobiography an association with Henry W. Grady and his *Atlanta Herald* partners: "They spent almost every evening with me talking over the profession of journalism. In these discussions we all learned much."[28] On the same trip, Stone studied New Orleans and St. Louis papers, and in St. Louis he met a talented young reporter, Eugene Field. He then left for Washington to serve as correspondent for his and other papers. In his autobiography, Stone also records another major influence: he was watching the successful one-cent *New York Daily News* and was deciding that he would try the same price formula in Chicago.

In January 1876, the *Daily News* appeared in Chicago as a four-page, five-column sheet with only a few thousand dollars in capital investment. Stone believed that his first responsibility was to print news; his second responsibility was to guide public opinion; and his third, to provide entertainment. The paper did not reject sensational techniques; Stone's personal favorite was the newspaper's detection of criminals. Nor did the *Daily News* fail to entertain. Stone brought Eugene Field to Chicago in 1883 from his earlier St. Louis and Kansas City surroundings; Field conducted the famous "Sharps and Flats" column, in which he commented on politics and people. In the first year a young Chicago financier, Victor F. Lawson, took over the business managership of the paper and two-thirds of the stock. But by 1878 the *Daily News* had bought out the *Post and Mail*, obtaining its Associated Press news rights. A morning edition, eventually named the *Record,* was begun in 1881, and by 1885 the combined circulation had passed the 100,000 mark. When Stone sold his interest to Lawson in 1888 for $350,000, only Pulitzer's *New York World* had a larger circulation among American newspapers than the *Daily News'* 200,000.

The editorial staff Stone had built was a famous one: Eugene Field as a columnist, Slason Thompson as an editorial writer; George Harvey, George Ade, and Finley Peter Dunne (Mr. Dooley) as young reporters; and literary figures, scientists, and professors, such as Chicago's James Laurence Laughlin and Wisconsin's Richard T. Ely, as special contributors. Lawson continued the same type of leadership until his death in 1925; Stone comes into the story again as the general manager and builder of the modern Associated Press.

NELSON'S *KANSAS CITY STAR*

Taking his place with Scripps and Stone as one of the leading figures in this midwestern newspaper revolution was William Rockhill Nelson, founder of the *Kansas City Star.* Nelson had been a lawyer and a building contractor before buying into a Fort Wayne, Indiana, newspaper in 1879. But by the time he appeared in Kansas City in the fall of 1880 he was ready to follow the pattern of the times. He and his editors created a small, two-cent evening newspaper, well written and filled with entertaining material as well as news, and possessed of the crusading urge. Notably, however, the *Star* shunned sensational treatment of the news in its headlines and illustrations.

(Chicago Daily News)

Melville E. Stone

(Kansas City Star)

William Rockhill Nelson

One other difference stands out strongly. Unlike the other great figures of journalism before him, Nelson was not a writer. He believed that the reporter was the heart of the newspaper and had seven on his initial staff. He also sought the best news editors and editorial writers.

Kansas City was a rough, growing town of little beauty when Nelson arrived in 1880. It was the gateway to the plains and the receiving point of western cattle. Half-built, cursed with the usual political corruption and vice of the utilitarian United States of the 1880s, it offered a great chance for a strong editor. Nelson was that: a big man, with massive face and head, stubborn qualities of independence, and an air of dignity that gave him the title of colonel. William Allen White, writing about Nelson the year he died, commented: "Not that he was ever a colonel of anything: he was just coloneliferous."[29]

Nelson gave Kansas City what he thought it needed through his relentless crusades for big and little causes. He fought for low-cost and efficient public transportation, which brought cable cars to the city's hills. He battled against politicians and gamblers. He campaigned for years to establish Kansas City's famous parks and boulevards, and then himself built model homes along the boulevards and saw that those who lived in them planted trees and flowers. The *Star* helped to inaugurate the commission form of government in the city and throughout its circulation area in the Missouri Valley.

Kansas City and the state of Kansas were captured by the *Star* by 1890, and before Nelson's death in 1915 its circulation hit 170,000. The subscription price was ten cents a week even after a Sunday edition had been added and the morning *Times* (1868) had sold out to Nelson in 1901. A weekly edition, selling for 25 cents a year, climbed to 150,000 circulation. The price formula, plus the *Star*'s intensive coverage of its region and its human-interest and literary qualities, made the paper invulnerable to the attacks of competitors who tried to win by using the sensational techniques that Nelson shunned.[30]

OTHER MIDWESTERN CITIES: CLIMAX TO ST. LOUIS

In other midwestern cities, changes in newspaper fortunes were in the air. Milwaukee's several dailies greeted a new competitor in 1882, Lucius W. Nieman and his *Milwaukee Journal,* which at once began to show some of the zeal that would drive all its competitors, except the morning *Sentinel* (1837), for cover in the next 60 years. In Minneapolis another *Journal* began its career as a leading evening newspaper in 1878, and the morning *Tribune* (1867) was given new life in the 1890s by William J. Murphy. St. Paul's *Pioneer Press* (1849), run by the distinguished team of editor Joseph A. Wheelock and manager Frederick Driscoll, found competition in the evening *Dispatch* (1868). Another aggressive evening newspaper was the *Indianapolis News* (1869).

But it was in St. Louis that the climax was reached. The river city had long been a newspaper center. The *Missouri Republican* (1808), which became the *St. Louis Republic* in 1888, the *Missouri Democrat* (1852), and Carl Schurz's German-language *Westliche Post* (1857) were leading papers. The first shock was the arrival of J. B. McCullagh from Chicago and his consolidation of the newly founded *Morning Globe* with the *Missouri Democrat* to start the *Globe-Democrat* on its way in 1875. The great event was the appearance of Joseph Pulitzer, a penniless immigrant who within ten years had built the *St. Louis Post-Dispatch* and then startled the publishing world with his *New York World.* All around him a new daily newspaper was developing in keeping with the changed character of American life, but by his genius Pulitzer became the recognized leader of the "new journalism." His story becomes the story of the emergence of the modern newspaper.

9

The New Journalism

... every issue of the paper presents an opportunity and a duty to say something courageous and true; to rise above the mediocre and conventional; to say something that will command the respect of the intelligent, the educated, the independent part of the community; to rise above fear of partisanship and fear of popular prejudice.

—Joseph Pulitzer

Joseph Pulitzer was one of those many immigrants who helped to build the new United States of the post–Civil War period. In so doing, he both gave and received: the two great newspapers he established won him the honor of being named the leading American editor of modern times,[1] and also built him a fortune appraised at his death at nearly $20 million, one of the largest ever accumulated in the newspaper field.

The story of Joseph Pulitzer's journalistic success climaxes the story of the new national environment. Pulitzer made his own contributions to the creation of the "new journalism," but more importantly, he achieved his leadership by being receptive to the ideas of others. His immense energy and his highly developed journalistic sense enabled him to adapt and to develop in his own way the publishing concepts and techniques of his time and to satisfy his passionate desire to win unquestioned recognition as the builder of the brilliant staff and the complex mechanism of a great modern newspaper. This was a notable achievement, but it alone was not enough to win Pulitzer his reputation as the most useful and worthy American editor in the estimate of his craft. His true greatness lay in his high-minded conception of a newspaper's role, particularly in his exercising of editorial leadership and in the way in which he made that conception live in his newspapers.

Joseph Pulitzer, from the portrait by John S. Sargent

JOSEPH PULITZER'S EARLY CAREER

Pulitzer was born in Hungary in 1847. His father was Magyar-Jewish, his mother Austro-German. At 17, after receiving a good private-school education, he ran away from home to join the army. But he had weak eyesight and an unmilitary look that brought rejections from the Austrian army and the French Foreign Legion. Less particular, however, was an American agent who was seeking Europeans who would volunteer for the Union army in that Civil War year of 1864. The agent enlisted Pulitzer, who became a member of the Lincoln Cavalry.

When the war ended, without having seen any real action, Pulitzer found himself in New York, virtually penniless and handicapped by language difficulties. After a series of short-lived, painful job experiences, which included being a waiter in a St. Louis restaurant, his tremendously inquisitive nature and unbounded energy began to lead him forward. In 1867 he became an American citizen, and a year later he was hired as a reporter for Carl Schurz's leading German-language daily, the *Westliche Post.* Pulitzer soon surpassed others who laughed at his awkward mannerisms by working endless hours, digging into every type of news.

In rapid order he was elected as a Republican to the Missouri State Assembly from a normally Democratic district, became his paper's legislative correspondent, joined with Schurz in stumping the German-speaking areas of Missouri for Horace Greeley in the 1872 campaign, and became part-owner of the *Post.* Planning for his own future, Pulitzer sold his stock in that paper for $30,000 and earned another $20,000 by buying a mediocre St. Louis daily that happened to have a valuable AP membership. He offered this to Joseph B. Mc-Cullagh, a Chicago newspaperman who needed the press-association membership to help force a merger between his *Globe* and the rival *Democrat.* Money in his pocket, Pulitzer left St. Louis newspaper work for a few years. He visited Europe four times, was married, and was admitted to the District of Columbia Bar. In the same period he campaigned for Samuel J. Tilden, the 1876 Democratic presidential candidate, and reported for Dana's *New York Sun* on the electoral commission, which decided that disputed election in favor of Rutherford B. Hayes. By 1878, with a greatly increased knowledge of his adopted country and excellent command of the English language, he returned to St. Louis journalism.

Pulitzer's destiny was now to be fulfilled. The *Dispatch,* founded in 1864, was bankrupt and on the block at a sheriff's sale. Pulitzer won it with a $2500 bid on December 9, 1878, again obtaining as his principal prize an Associated Press membership. Three days later he effected a combination with the *Post,* started by John Dillon in 1875 (Dillon was a partner for only one year but remained a Pulitzer associate).

Thus was born one of the country's greatest newspapers, the *Post-Dispatch.* Within four years it was the leading evening paper in St. Louis, netting $45,000 a year and rivaling the morning papers, the influential *Missouri Republican* and McCullagh's powerful *Globe-Democrat.* Behind this achievement lay the talents of the editor-publisher, now in his early 30s. An ambitious and self-contained man, with the artist's love of good music and skilled writing and the scholar's interest in economic, political, and social trends, Pulitzer was driven by his large intellectual capacity and consuming energy.

Pulitzer's flashing eyes expressed his strong will to succeed. Filled with nervous tension, he was not easily approachable, holding even close associates at a distance. But in his own way he showed his appreciation for the work of those who measured up to his exacting standards for newspaper work. Many capable journalists were to serve under the Pulitzer banner in the years ahead, but the most influential was the right-hand man of these early days, John A. Cockerill, who came to the *Post-Dispatch* as managing editor in 1880. A hardworking and pugnacious man capable of carrying out Pulitzer's commands,

Cockerill brought with him a keen sense of newspaper methods, which was to serve Pulitzer well for the crucial next 12 years.[2]

But it was Pulitzer who imparted to the *Post-Dispatch* its distinctive spirit. His statement of policies contains memorable words:

> The *Post and Dispatch* will serve no party but the people; be no organ of Republicanism, but the organ of truth; will follow no causes but its conclusions; will not support the "Administration," but criticize it; will oppose all frauds and shams wherever and whatever they are; will advocate principles and ideas rather than prejudices and partisanship.[3]

Even more memorable are the words written by a more mature Pulitzer in 1907, near the end of his career, which have become the *Post-Dispatch* platform, printed on the editorial page:

> I know that my retirement will make no difference in its cardinal principles; that it will always fight for progress and reform, never tolerate injustice or corruption, always fight demagogues of all parties, never belong to any party, always oppose privileged classes and public plunderers, never lack sympathy with the poor, always remain devoted to the public welfare, never be satisfied with merely printing news, always be drastically independent, never be afraid to attack wrong, whether by predatory plutocracy or predatory poverty.

Not content with reporting the surface news, Pulitzer pushed his staff to "Never drop a thing until you have gone to the bottom of it. Continuity! Continuity! Continuity until the subject is really finished."[4] This resulted in determined crusading in the public interest with an intensity heightened by Pulitzer's personal involvement and Cockerill's techniques in writing and news display. Favorite targets were crooked politicians, wealthy tax dodgers, a police-protected gambling ring, and a free-wheeling public utility.

There were, however, serious blemishes on the Pulitzer record during the early St. Louis years. Cockerill had brought with him a reputation for exploiting stories of murder, sin, and sex, and for sensationalizing accounts of violence, lynchings, public hangings, and dramatic death. Pulitzer found many of these subjects fitting his "apt to be talked about" definition of news. They delighted in printing bits of gossipy scandal about the "best families" of the St. Louis oligarchy under such headlines as "St. Louis Swells," "An Adulterous Pair," "Loved the Cook," and "Does Rev. Mr. Tudor Tipple?" In these and many other stories could be found exaggeration, half-truth, and humor at the expense of embarrassed citizens.[5] This was also true, of course, of other papers of the times.

Editorially, Pulitzer's early *Post-Dispatch* hit hard at the wealthy families who monopolized control of the nation's fifth-largest city. The crusades it developed, however, were focused not on the problems of the poor and working classes but on those of the middle class and the small businesspeople with whom the publisher associated.[6] Everyone benefited, of course, from attacks on monopoly, from battles for cleaner living conditions, from crusades against vice. But the focus on the plight of the oppressed poor that was to be a Pulitzer trademark in New York was not yet present.

In every field of newspaper publishing, Pulitzer, Cockerill, and their associates on the *Post-Dispatch* were learning the lessons they were soon to apply in New York. There were many mistakes, many stories and editorials falling short of the Pulitzer goals. But there were successes, for as his New York paper commented in 1890, "The foundation of the *New York World* was laid in St. Louis. . . . The battle of new ideas and new theories of journalism was fought there under the banner of the *Post-Dispatch*."[7]

PURCHASE OF THE *NEW YORK WORLD,* 1883

By 1883 Pulitzer was a physical wreck, with his eyesight failing and his nerves badly impaired by incessant work. Matters had not been helped when Cockerill shot and killed a prominent St. Louis attorney whom the *Post-Dispatch* had attacked in its columns. Cockerill was successful in his self-defense plea but a discouraged Pulitzer headed for what he thought would be a long European vacation. Instead, when passing through New York, he heard that the *World,* founded in 1860 as a morning Democratic newspaper, was for sale. Once well edited by Manton Marble, the paper had fallen into the hands of the unscrupulous financier, Jay Gould, who wanted $346,000.

The situation was not promising, but Pulitzer, perhaps inspired by his brother Albert's success in starting the breezy one-cent *Morning Journal* the year before with $25,000 capital, closed the deal on May 9. The first installment was paid with profits from the *Post-Dispatch,* but to Gould's surprise, the balance eventually was paid with profits from the *World.*

Pulitzer started with only a 15,000 circulation for his new two-cent, 8-page paper. Its more powerful Park Row rivals were Bennett's *Herald,* running 12 to 16 pages at three cents; Dana's *Sun,* still publishing but 4 pages at two cents; and Whitelaw Reid's *Tribune* and George Jones's *Times,* both selling 8 pages at four cents.

Quickly revamping the *World*'s staff and wiring to St. Louis for two good *Post-Dispatch* editors, Pulitzer issued his first edition on May 11. The lead story was an account of a storm that caused a million dollars in damage in New Jersey. Other front-page features were an interview with a condemned slayer and stories of a Wall Street plunger, a Pittsburgh hanging, a riot in Haiti, and a wronged servant girl. Ordering a press run of 20,000, Pulitzer was matched only by Bennett in sensational coverage. The next day the *World* was the talk of the town.

Exhibiting another important factor in the Pulitzer success formula—aggressive promotion of the newspaper—Pulitzer used the page-one area around the name plate, the "ears," to plug his paper's circulation and exclusives. His first popular cause was to advocate that the new Brooklyn Bridge, hailed as one of the wonders of the world, be free for the people who would cross it every day on their way to work.

But mixed in with the sensation and promotion were good news coverage and a new editorial policy. A concise 10-point program appeared on the editorial page: tax luxuries; tax inheritances; tax large incomes; tax monopolies; tax the privileged corporations; institute a tariff for revenue; reform the civil service; punish corrupt officeholders; punish vote buying; punish employers who coerce their employees in elections. "There is room in this great and growing city for a journal that is not only cheap but bright, not only bright but large, not only large but truly Democratic—dedicated to the cause of the people,"[8] Pulitzer had said in his first issue.

New Yorkers who resented the flaunted wealth of the moneyed class and believed in economic and social reform found the *World* to be delightful reading; those who worshiped successful dollar-chasers found the editorial pages filled with heresy. Pushing harder for the poor and the helpless than he had in St. Louis, the immigrant Pulitzer found New York's mass audience different. Well-developed crusades on behalf of the immigrants, the poor, and the laboring class appeared in his first two years at the *World.* In particular, the injustices of the garment district's sweatshops for immigrant women, the lack of school opportunities, and the inequity of the tax burden were subjects of Pulitzer's pressing editorials and news stories. In July 1883, a heat wave took a terrible toll in the city's teeming slums; the *World* found that of 716 reported deaths the previous week, 392 had been of children

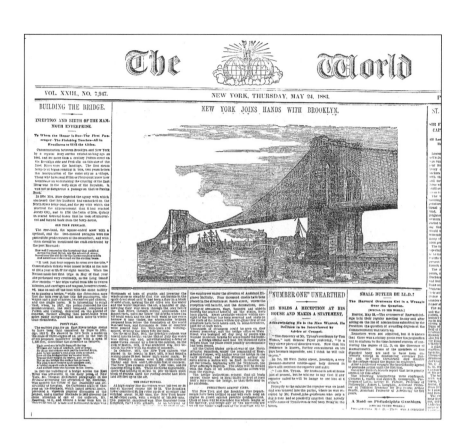

Two examples of crusades from Joseph Pulitzer's *New York World* of the 1880s

under the age of five years. Its reporters went to the scenes of death; its headline writers produced "How Babies Are Baked" and "Line of Little Hearses" in an attempt to shock authorities into concern and action. The *World*'s crusade for tenement-house reform continued in early 1884 when it covered the efforts of Professor Felix Adler to help the poor. Other stories—similar to those that would be found in the *World* for decades—told of meetings of immigrant societies, violence against immigrants, crowded factory conditions, rights of workers to visit museums and other public buildings on Sunday, and prejudice in political organizations.

The *World*'s liberal political and social stands paid circulation dividends in 1884 when Pulitzer supported Grover Cleveland, the Democratic governor of New York, for the presidency against the conservative Republican champion, James G. Blaine. Some of the gains came from the readership of Dana's *Sun,* which followed an erratic course and endorsed the discredited third-party candidate Benjamin Butler. Pulitzer himself was elected to Congress that year but soon abandoned that career.

Meanwhile, Cockerill had arrived from St. Louis to become managing editor. Ever adept in both playing up human-interest news and maintaining a solid display of significant local, national, and international stories, Cockerill also featured women's and sports news, as he had in St. Louis. Typographically the new *World* was using smaller and lighter type faces than its predecessor, but the words spoke for themselves: "Death Rides the Blast," "Screaming for Mercy," "Little Lotta's Lovers," "Baptized in Blood."[9] Alliteration was frequent; so were sex, conflict, and crime.

Daily circulation at the end of its first year was more than 60,000—a fourfold increase that caused other New York papers to cut their prices to meet Pulitzer's threat. The *Herald* even advertised in the *World*'s pages. Four months later the *Sunday World,* effectively using a large number of woodcuts and line drawings,[10] hit the 100,000 mark. Pulitzer's promotion men presented each employee with a tall silk hat and fired 100 cannon shots in City Hall Park by way of celebration. When, in 1887, the 250,000 figure was reached by the *World,* a silver medal was struck in honor of the largest newspaper circulation in the United States. In addition, by 1884 the *World* had passed the *Herald* in the number of advertising columns printed and had jumped in size to 12 or 14 pages daily and 36 to 44 pages on Sunday. However, as expenses mounted and advertising rates were raised, the price to its attentive public remained at two cents.

REASONS FOR THE *WORLD'*S SUCCESS

What had Pulitzer done? First, he had recognized the characteristics of his potential audience. The population of New York City was increasing by 50 percent during the 1880s, and Pulitzer worked to attract the attention of the newcomers to his newspaper. As an immigrant himself, he was alive to the fact that four out of five of the city's residents were either foreign-born or the children of foreign-born parents. And as one who was aware of the social and economic trends of his time, he understood the desire of his readers for both effective, progressive leadership and entertainment. Therefore he had enlivened the *World*'s significant news coverage to satisfy one set of changing conditions and achieved sensationalism both in news content and in newspaper appearance to satisfy another trend.

Pulitzer's answer to critics was that human-interest and sensational stories were needed to win a large circulation and that, having won the circulation, he would create sound public opinion through enticing readers into the editorial columns and news stories about public affairs. He admired the work of the talented Edwin Lawrence Godkin in the

Evening Post, although he disagreed with Godkin's economic theories, but when he was chided about the contrast between the news policies of the *Post* and the *World* he made his famous retort: "I want to talk to a nation, not a select committee."[11]

The following passage from a letter written by Pulitzer to one of his editors in later life reflects his basic highmindedness and the spirit that won for him recognition as a courageous, worthy, and effective editor:

> every issue of the paper presents an opportunity and a duty to say something courageous and true; to rise above the mediocre and conventional; to say something that will command the respect of the intelligent, the educated, the independent part of the community; to rise above fear of partisanship and fear of popular prejudice. I would rather have one article a day of this sort; and these ten or twenty lines might readily represent a whole day's hard work in the way of concentrated, intense thinking and revision, polish of style, weighing of words.[12]

On many days Pulitzer's newspapers fell short of attaining this high goal of journalism, but they approached it often enough to stimulate the efforts of other editors and to win their admiration.[13]

Stunts, as distinguished from useful crusades and promotions, were another specialty of the *World.* Most ambitious was the sending of Nellie Bly around the world in 1889 to see if she could beat the time suggested by Jules Verne in his fictional *Around the World in Eighty Days.* Nellie Bly was a by-line name for Elizabeth Cochrane, a woman reporter who had brightened the pages of the *World* by inviting the attention of mashers and then exposing them and by feigning insanity in order to write about conditions in a New York asylum. As Nellie traveled around the world by ships, trains, horses, and sampans, the *World* ran a guessing contest that drew nearly a million estimates of her elapsed time. Nellie did not fail her newspaper; a special train brought her from San Francisco to New York with banners flying as the country applauded her time of 72 days.[14]

The expanded size of the *World* permitted its editors to enliven its pages with stunts and features and still offer serious and significant news. A large staff of ambitious reporters covered the city in the same manner as Pulitzer had blanketed St. Louis. News editors sought equally hard-to-get national stories and cabled news from abroad. Gradually the coarser sensationalism of the first few years of the *World*'s publication under Pulitzer began to disappear, although there was no letup in the demand for well-written human-interest stories and for reader-pulling illustrations. The editorial page continued to support the Democratic party, and backed Cleveland in 1888 and 1892. Yet at the same time it exhibited its independence by opposing the local Tammany Hall machine. Labor found the *World* a solid champion in 1892, when several strikers were killed by Pinkerton guards during the bitter Homestead steel strike near Pittsburgh.

Pulitzer's publishing empire was expanded in 1887 with the establishment of the *Evening World* on the heels of Dana's decision to publish an evening edition of the *Sun.* The evening paper sold for one cent and soon outdid the morning edition in popular appeal. It never attained the distinctive character of the morning edition, however, and to newspaper people the name *World* still meant the original paper.

A new $2.5 million home for the three *World*s was the next order of business. It was an impressive building, among the tallest of its time, topped with a gilded dome and filled with the newest machines of the printing arts. But before the building was finished, tragedy struck. Pulitzer had become completely blind. His nerves were shattered as well, and he was under the care of European specialists. In October 1890, he announced his retirement from active editorship of his newspapers, and the *Herald,* thinking that it was bidding him goodby, said "We droop our colors to him."

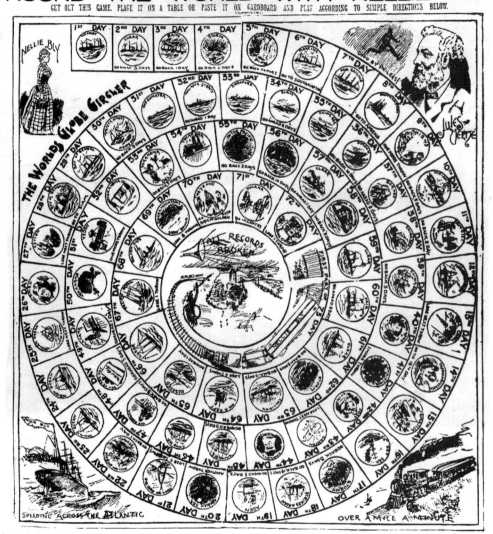

The *World*'s promotion department offers a Nellie Bly game.

But Pulitzer was not gone. He was to live until 1911, and he was to continue to build his personality into the newspapers. His affliction left him incapable of bearing even the slightest noise, and he went to incredible lengths to isolate himself from tormenting sounds. His associates found him infuriatingly difficult, but they also found him keenly aware of the progress of the newspapers. No matter where the blinded and bearded Pulitzer was—aboard his yacht; at Bar Harbor, Maine; or on the Mediterranean coast—he was constantly in touch with the *World* staff. Copies of each issue were read to him by young male secretaries, and streams of his instructions and suggestions came to the offices in the *World*'s gilded dome by cable, mail, and messenger.

There were important editors and managers in the *World* offices. Some of them in the late 1880s and early 1890s included Cockerill, who became editor-in-charge; William H. Merrill, who had come from the *Boston Herald* to be chief editorial writer; Ballard Smith, former managing editor of both the *Louisville Courier-Journal* and the *New York Herald,* who served as managing editor; S. S. Carvalho, ex-*Sun* newsman who was city editor of the *Evening World* and later a Pulitzer executive; Colonel Charles H. Jones, a colorful southerner who served as publisher for Pulitzer in both New York and St. Louis; George Harvey, later to become an important political figure; and Elizabeth Garver Jordan, who began a distinguished literary career with her 1898 *Tales of the City Room,* based on her experiences as a reporter and assistant Sunday editor.

Conflicts between strong-willed rivals for authority and for Pulitzer's favor were inevitable under this policy of assembling many persons of high talent under the *World*'s dome. But no editor or manager became too powerful or long ignored the wishes of the absent owner. Cockerill lost his place in 1891 during one of the upheavals by which Pulitzer enforced his will on the staff. Jones, who was given complete editorial control of the *Post-Dispatch* in 1895, was forced out two years later when he flouted Pulitzer's wishes. By a constant process of seeking loyal and able assistants from among the country's journalists, Pulitzer was able to keep the *World* steadily progressing in the manner he had conceived, as the leading exponent of what was being called the "new journalism."

THE EDITORIAL STAFF EMERGES

The editorial staff of the metropolitan daily newspaper had taken recognizable modern form by 1890 in its numbers and its departmentalized activities. Specialization of duties was necessary as the editing process became more complex and as staffs grew in size. Since the founding of the popular press in the 1830s, the editorial staff had evolved from one person to the scores of newspeople on the staff of the *World.*

Regularly employed reporters were rare even after the penny press had become well established in the 1840s. Newspaper editors ran what local news they encountered or had time to cover, used their telegraph news, clipped their exchanges, and printed the contributions of correspondents, such as the group who covered Congress after the mid-1820s. Some owner-editors added chief assistants, notably Horace Greeley, who employed first Henry J. Raymond and then Charles A. Dana to help him handle the news on the *New York Tribune* in the early 1840s. The chief assistants soon became known as managing editors; two of the earliest to hold that title were Dana of the *Tribune* and Frederic Hudson of the *New York Herald.* In the 1850s chief reporters emerged, as forerunners of the city editors. The *Tribune* of 1854 had 14 reporters and 10 editors, and had introduced editorial writers, literary editors, and other specialists. But these editorial staff advances were found only on leading newspapers.

Intensified reporting of the Civil War by hundreds of correspondents in the field did much to stimulate the rise of news staffs. Some of the Civil War reporters who thus demonstrated their journalistic skills rose to become editors or owners of newspapers: Murat Halstead, Whitelaw Reid, Henry Villard. Others went on to cover wars in Europe or Native American wars on the western American plains. Killed in Custer's Last Stand on the Little Big Horn in 1876 was *Bismarck Tribune* correspondent Mark Kellogg, who earlier had been a Wisconsin reporter and editor of an 1872 Greeley campaign paper in Minnesota.

George W. Smalley was an example of the new type of reporter. A graduate of Yale and of Harvard Law School, he covered the Civil War for the *Tribune,* then reported the Franco-Prussian War and remained in Europe as London correspondent for the paper. Henry M. Stanley of the *New York Herald* covered the Civil War and the Native American wars, went to Asia and Africa as a *Herald* correspondent, and climaxed his career with his expedition to Africa in 1871 to find the missing missionary David Livingstone. Jerome B. Stillson, another *Herald* reporter, obtained an exclusive interview with the Native American chief Sitting Bull in 1877 that filled 14 columns of the paper. John A. Cockerill, Pulitzer's ace reporter and editor, had covered the Russo-Turkish War. Again, these are examples of a limited activity, but they foreshadow the intensified reportorial achievements of the 1890s.

Emphasis increasingly centered on the reporter. Henry Grady, a freelance correspondent before becoming managing editor of the *Atlanta Constitution,* had advanced the art of interviewing as a means of both gathering and interpreting the news. Dana and Pulitzer prized their reporting staffs because they themselves had handled news, as had Henry Raymond of the *Times,* who had covered the Austro-Italian War. Some papers, like the *New York Sun,* Chicago's *Inter Ocean,* Nelson's *Kansas City Star,* and Stone's *Chicago Daily News*—in addition to the large New York dailies—became known as training grounds for young reporters who later moved on to other staffs.

From 1880 to 1900 there was continued development of the notion of "objectivity" in reporting. Offering the appearance of fairness was important to owners and editors trying to gain their share of a growing readership and the resulting advertising revenues. A more organized, less personalized method of news writing, later to be standardized as the "inverted pyramid" style, gained popularity because of the press associations, where high costs and pressure from editors called for clarity and brevity.

The *New York Sun* produced great reporters, among them Julian Ralph, Arthur Brisbane, S. S. Carvalho, Edward W. Townsend, and Richard Harding Davis. Managing editor Amos J. Cummings, an expert in the human-interest story, Chester Lord, managing editor after 1880, and other subeditors molded these careers. Ralph later became a prize Hearst reporter; Brisbane was managing editor of the *Evening Sun* before leaving for a fabulous career with both Pulitzer and Hearst; Carvalho was the *Evening World*'s first city editor before he too joined Hearst and ended up a top executive; Davis left the *Sun* for Hearst's lure but achieved greatest fame with the *Herald.* The *Sun* and the *Tribune* shared the reporting career of Jacob A. Riis, who wrote with discernment about conditions in the New York City slums and the tragedies they bred.

The upsurge of circulations and competition brought increased specialization within the newsrooms. By the 1870s, each leading metropolitan daily had a chief editor, a managing editor or night editor in charge of the news, a city editor to direct the staff of perhaps two dozen reporters, a telegraph editor to handle the increasing volume of wire and cable news, a financial editor, a drama critic, a literary editor, and editorial writers. As the years passed and reporting staffs grew, the city editor's role took on more importance.

However, all was not rosy in the city rooms, where editors often feared for their jobs, and many reporters toiled 14 to 16 hours per day to earn perhaps $20 to $30 per week, instead of a regular salary, under a degrading time and space system. Some top reporters had salaries, and by 1890 they were earning from $50 to $ 100 per week, good pay in 1890 dollars. The managing editor of a large paper might have earned about $125, but many staff members stayed at the same $15 to $25 a week level that had existed for reporters after the

Civil War because there was no effective labor organization in the editorial offices as there was in the mechanical departments. Bennett, Pulitzer, and others kept the pressure on the dozens of lower-ranking reporters by forcing keen competition for space, instituting spy systems, and keeping benefits at a minimum. One effect on the news product was the wide-spread use of combination reporting, in which reporters from competing papers banded together to protect themselves from criticism and to generate enough copy to fill a good deal of valuable space. Another effect was sensationalism, whereby reporters under pressure to come up with exciting stories earned double rates if they reported exclusives. These petty and mean newsroom practices were found even on papers like the *World* that preached different values to the readers. It was years before these practices were minimized.[15]

The newsroom operations became more sophisticated with the use of the telephone, the typewriter, and a rewrite staff. Publishing an increased number of editions caused pressure for the more rapid handling of local news, and the summary lead gained favor as a means of condensing stories. (But the literary stylists and writers of rambling chronological stories were still numerous.) As Sunday papers became common, additional persons were needed to assist the chief editors. Special Sunday staffs were set up, including cartoonists and artists. Along with this attention to regular news, sports news became increasingly important to the mass audience. Pulitzer realized this and arranged the first separate sports department for his *World*. Specialized writers began to appear in each sports field, and several columns of sports news were run in big newspapers by 1890. After the turn of the century regular sports pages began to appear.

CRITICISM OF THE PRESS

There were those who found the "new journalism" "vulgar" and defended the stability of the traditional press. Their voices were to be heard more stridently with the onset of the Spanish-American War and the emergence of the widespread sensationalism dubbed "yellow journalism." The early major critic of the press, Edwin Lawrence Godkin of the *Nation,* was joined by the editors of the *Dial* and in 1911 by Will Irwin in *Collier's.*

Two journalism professors, Marion Marzolf and Hazel Dicken-Garcia, have written books identifying the press critics and analyzing their articles and books. Dicken-Garcia found that the first American book devoted entirely to press criticism was Lambert Wilmer's *Our Press Gang,* appearing in 1860 as a caustic, sweeping indictment covering 14 areas of complaint. The first article of press criticism she located that used the word "ethics" in its title appeared in 1889, the first "code of conduct" in 1890. Press criticism from 1880 to 1950 centered on two issues, Marzolf found: the role of the free press in safe-guarding other freedoms in a democracy and the sociocultural role of the press.[16]

WOMEN IN JOURNALISM

Another development was the rapid influx of women staff members. The industrial boom and expansion of business opportunities had meant jobs for women, and this included the newspaper business. There had been women journalists of note dating back to the Revolutionary War. Before the Civil War Margaret Fuller of the *New York Tribune,* for example, and Jane Grey Swisshelm, a Washington correspondent and Minnesota newspaper editor, gained attention. Victoria Woodhull and her sister, Tennessee Claflin, published their weekly in New York in 1870, championing female emancipation, abortion, and free love. Eliza Jane Poitevant Holbrook was literary editor of the *New Orleans Picayune* in the

1860s, married the publisher, and ran the paper after his death. Ellen Scripps worked with her famous brothers when they started their newspapers in the 1870s and 1880s. Nancy Johnson was the *New York Times'* European travel writer in 1857.

Jennie June Croly—who founded the first American women's press club, the New York Press Club and Sorosis—began the first fashion column and set up a duplicate exchange service, the forerunner to later syndicated services. Her professional career spanned 40 years, beginning with her work for the *New York Herald* in 1855. Kate Field wrote editorials for the *Times* of London before joining the *New York Herald* staff as a reporter and critic. In 1891 she established "Kate Field's Washington," a weekly review of books, music, and art. Writing women's news for some of the first women's pages in the 1890s were Fanny Fern of the *Philadelphia Ledger* and Grace Greenwood of the *New York Times.* Florence Finch Kelly, who worked on several papers and helped establish the Women's Press Club in New York in 1889, joined the *New York Times* in 1906 for a 30-year stint in the book-review section.

Active women writers included Ida M. Tarbell, one of the original muckrakers for *McClure's* beginning in 1893; Winifred Black (Annie Laurie), one of Hearst's early stars; Elizabeth Cochrane (Nellie Bly), the moral crusader for the *World* who had circled the world as a promotional stunt; Nixola Greeley-Smith, the granddaughter of Horace Greeley, who was hired by Pulitzer and spent 20 years as a reporter; and Sally Joy (Penelope Penfeather), fashion writer of the *Boston Herald* and first president of the New England Women's Press Association in the 1880s. Jessie White Mario was the *Nation's* faithful correspondent from Italy from 1866 to 1904, and she provided detailed political news. Helen Campbell wrote slum exposures for the *New York Tribune.*

Women correspondents in Washington multiplied after Jane Swisshelm took her seat in the Senate press gallery in 1850. Among the 166 correspondents listed in the 1879 *Congressional Directory* were 20 women with gallery privileges. However, after each paper was limited to three congressional correspondents, the number of women dropped, since they were not breaking-news reporters. From 1866 to 1880, the foremost women Washington correspondents were Mary Clemmer Ames, whose column appeared in the weekly *New York Independent,* and Emily Edson Briggs, columnist for the *Philadelphia Press.* Sara Clarke Lippincott wrote liberal-oriented columns for the *New York Times* in the 1870s (she also used the pen name Grace Greenwood). Mary Abigail Dodge did conservative articles for the *New York Tribune* in 1877–78.

Carrying on the tradition of many earlier women journalists, Miriam Follin Leslie edited *Frank Leslie's Illustrated Newspaper* after her husband's death. Anna Benjamin covered the Spanish-American War for that publication, and the same year Marie Manning was hired by Hearst as a reporter and ended up as Beatrice Fairfax, lovelorn writer for the *New York Journal.* Later Dorothy Dix (Elizabeth Meriweather Gilmore) wrote a similar column for the Hearst syndicate. One scholar noted that in 1889 the entire issue of the *Journalist,* a professional periodical, was devoted to profiles of 50 women editors and reporters. Ten of them were African Americans, including Mrs. N. F. Mossell, who edited the women's pages of the *New York Freeman,* and popular columnist Lillian Alberta Lewis, whose pen name was Bert Islew. Her work appeared in the *Boston Advocate* and elsewhere.[17]

ADVANCES IN COOPERATIVE NEWS GATHERING

Pressure for speedier and more comprehensive coverage of the news, which stemmed both from increasing competition among the dailies and from the needs of the new social environment, brought changes in cooperative news gathering. Railroads and telegraph lines that had been part of the race for news in the 1840s spurted ahead to cover the country. Between 1880 and 1900 the number of railroad tracks doubled and telegraph lines quadrupled. Bell Telephone lines joined cities in those years; the federal postal service began free rural delivery in 1897 and also improved city carrier service. The Atlantic Cable, which had begun operating in 1866, linked the United States to London, and another cable stretched eastward to India and other parts of Asia.

The opening of the Atlantic Cable had facilitated reciprocal exchanges of news between the Associated Press of New York (founded by the city's morning papers in 1848) and the press agencies of Europe: Reuters in Britain (1851), Havas in France (1835), Wolff in Germany (1849), and Stefani in Italy (1853). An 1870 agreement between Havas, Reuters, and Wolff allowed those agencies to monopolize the distribution of news by designating parts of the world for exclusive reporting and transmission rights for each organization. Some areas were shared by these major contracting parties or with smaller national news organizations. Reuters, with control of more than half of the world's cable lines, dominated the Ring Combination, as the "grand cartel" was called. In 1893 a merger of the New York Associated Press and the Western Associated Press, which formed the Associated Press of Illinois (API), led in turn to an agreement with the Ring Combination whereby the API was allowed to distribute Reuters news in the United States and to share Mexican and Central American news with Reuters and Havas and Canadian and West Indian news with Reuters. The Ring Combination, interrupted by wars and hampered by domestic politics and professional jealousies, lasted until 1934. The Associated Press played a more equal role in the twentieth century.[18]

The AP, controlled by its seven charter-member New York morning newspapers, had formed agreements with Western Union by which preferred treatment and rates could be offered member papers. Regional and local groups that did become members could restrict membership and thus prevent new competitors from obtaining the basic coverage afforded by the AP. To discourage press-service competitors, the New York AP forbade those receiving its service to buy the news of any other agency.

Naturally there were many complaints about this news monopoly. The news service report favored morning newspapers. Rates to clients were arbitrarily assessed, and papers outside of New York felt they were paying too much of the cost and had too little to say about the operations of the service. Despite the fact that in 1880 only half of the morning dailies and a fourth of the evening papers were receiving the service, only the United Press (no relation to the later service of the same name) offered real competition before it was submerged in competition between rival AP factions.[19]

However, some important steps were being taken in cooperative news gathering. A leased wire set up between New York and Washington in 1875 carried up to 20,000 words per day. This improved service reached Chicago in 1884, and by 1900 the AP-leased wires were extended to New Orleans, Denver, and Minneapolis. Smaller dailies were given inexpensive service by the making of thin stereotyped plates that could be set directly into the news columns. The prime distributor of these plates in the 1880s was the American Press Association, which used AP press reports. Feature stories, illustrations, and entertainment material were also available from these syndicates.[20] In addition, some leading papers syndicated proof slips of their exclusive stories by express service, mail, or telegraph. City news services were formally organized in New York and Chicago in the early 1890s. These agencies for the collection of routine city news had taken form during the Civil War.

The new leaders in journalism were willing to spend money for the gathering of news. To supplement their AP coverage they began to send more correspondents to Congress. At the outbreak of the Civil War 45 reporters were in the galleries, but by 1870 this number was 130. The famed Washington Gridiron Club was formed in 1885 by Ben Perley Poore of the *Boston Journal,* dean of the capital press corps. There were major problems that money could not solve, however. The AP, by its cooperative nature, depended heavily on the news collected by member papers and the foreign press services. Often this was unsatisfactory and Western Union operators had to be called on to supply the coverage of spot news events that AP members could not provide. Those papers outside the AP fold were forced to struggle along, waiting for the day when other press associations would provide competition to the AP.

Accompanying changes in the distribution of news was the acceptance of an "objective" method of reporting. This meant that reporters, while continuing to use the terse style dictated by high transmission costs, were expected to keep their personal values out of stories and to stick to verifiable facts. The Associated Press settled into the general use of the "inverted pyramid" lead (the who-what-where-when-why) and thus enhanced its reputation as a reliable agency.

A 1986 study of both local and wire reports from 1865 to 1934 showed the number of "objective" stories rising from about one-third of all stories from 1865 to 1874 to about one-half from 1885 to 1894 to two-thirds from 1905 to 1914 to 80 percent from 1925 to 1934. The researcher Harlan S. Stensaas found a strong relationship between the use of the "inverted pyramid" and authoritative sources. He also stated that there was little difference over the years in the objectivity found in local stories and wire reports, noting there was no demonstrated proof that the press associations had influenced the development of objectivity.[21]

Press historians had long assumed that there was a relationship between the general acceptance of objectivity and the development of tightly written telegraph and wire accounts presented value-free to customers holding obviously different political, social, and economic views. It was to the press associations' economic advantage to avoid alienating those buying the service. This "safe," noninterpretive style was bitterly criticized in the 1960s because it assumed reporters are unemotional and free of subconscious predispositions, and because the supposedly straight reporting of complex events often omits a good deal of the truth. These questions remain unresolved, and more study of the development of objectivity and reporting methods is required.

THE BUSINESS SIDE: ADVERTISING DEVELOPMENTS

The expansion of the editorial staff and its news-gathering activities, which was thus heralding the arrival of modern journalism, was made possible by tremendous developments in the business and mechanical departments of the metropolitan daily newspapers. But these developments in turn brought an overshadowing of the figures of the old-time editors and a relative lessening of their influence in the new era of corporate journalism. This did not mean that editors and news executives were shunted aside, but they could no longer dominate the scene as in the days when an editor-owner stood in command of a less complex enterprise.

Those larger dailies that had become complex business institutions—headed by the *New York World* with its $10 million valuation and its annual $1 million profit in the mid-1890s—were harassed by a host of new problems. It was they who first reflected the corporate nature of the new journalism, although the pressure of the business problems they faced soon came to be felt by an increasing number of middle-sized dailies and to some degree by all newspapers.

The scramble for advertising and circulation supremacy, widespread mechanical innovations and pyramiding capitalization costs, larger payrolls and more difficult labor-relations problems, increasing concern over newsprint supply for skyrocketing circulations—these and other problems brought the rise of a managerial corps in newspaper publishing, just as was happening with managers as a group in American business generally.

Symbolizing the ascendancy of business problems of the daily newspapers was the establishment of the American Newspaper Publishers Association (ANPA) in 1887 to serve as their trade association. The leaders in the association were representatives of aggressive new papers and of older papers that were alive to the problems of the new journalism. Most of the people taking part in association affairs held managerial posts on their newspapers or were publishers primarily interested in business management.

Two of the early presidents were James W. Scott of the *Chicago Herald* and Charles W. Knapp of the *St. Louis Republic,* both news-trained publishers. But men like Colonel Charles H. Jones, S. S. Carvalho, John Norris, and Don C. Seitz—all of whom contended for managerial-side supremacy on Pulitzer's *World* in the 1890s—were more typical leaders of the ANPA. Seitz, who survived as manager of the *World*, and Norris, who became business manager of the *New York Times,* were particularly important leaders of the Publishers Association after the turn of the century. There they spoke for their absent publishers, Pulitzer and Adolph Ochs, respectively.

The ANPA was organized at the call of William H. Brearley, advertising manager of the *Detroit Evening News,* James E. Scripps's successful new paper. There were many state editorial associations—17 had been founded between 1853 and 1880—but most of their members published weeklies and small dailies. The National Editorial Association had been organized among the weeklies and smallest dailies in 1885 by B. B. Herbert of the *Red Wing Daily Republican* of Minnesota.

What Brearley and his associates primarily wanted was a daily newspaper trade association that would help its members with the problems of obtaining national advertising. Although the ANPA soon became deeply involved in issues of labor relations, newsprint supply, government mail rates, and mechanical developments, it centered much of its attention on advertising.

The first advertising agents had appeared in New York and other eastern cities in the 1840s as links between the advertisers and the newspapers. They purchased space for their clients, receiving discounts between 15 percent to 30 percent, and sometimes up to 75 percent, on stated advertising rates. This was their profit. Although larger papers were able to obtain ads on a steady basis and to regulate the agents' commissions, smaller papers were sometimes victimized as agents played one publisher against another.

There were many attempts to regulate advertising practices, and not all agents operated in this manner. The founding of the respected agencies of George P. Rowell, N. W. Ayer & Son, and Lord and Thomas around 1870 helped. Rowell published his *American Newspaper Directory* in 1869 in an effort to locate all of the newly developed newspapers, and Ayer & Son began its continued annual publication in 1880.[22] But true circulations were hard to determine, and it was not until 1914 that the Audit Bureau of Circulations was established, thus solving the problem. Identifying trustworthy ad agencies was another problem, and after years of arguments the ANPA headquarters in New York agreed in 1899 to issue lists of recognized agencies. By common consent the discount figure was set at 15 percent.

The percentage of newspaper revenue coming from advertising, as compared to circulation income, rose from half in 1880 to 64 percent by 1910. Space given to ads in most dailies rose from 25 percent to a 50–50 ratio with editorial material by World War I. While

Two still-famous Chicago department stores advertise in an 1898 *Times-Herald*.

the amount of advertising was rising, the content was changing. Three pioneers in the department-store business, John Wanamaker of Philadelphia, Marshall Field of Chicago, and A. T. Stewart of New York, gave impetus to retail-store advertising. Ivory soap ("It Floats"), Victor phonographs ("His Master's Voice"), and Royal baking powder were

Early copyrighted trademarks and brand advertising

leaders in national advertising in the 1880s, followed in the 1890s by Eastman Kodak, Wrigley's chewing gum, and foods like Kellogg's cereals.

But there was a cloud over the advertising business because the leading clients of newspapers and magazines were the patent medicine makers who pushed Castoria, Scott's Emulsion, and Lydia Pinkham's Female Compound on the unsuspecting public. These misleading, deliberately deceptive, and often outwardly fraudulent advertisements were quickly accepted by most newspaper and magazine representatives because of the great volume of money involved. This practice continued in large scale until Congress began to get involved at the time of World War I. Despite the attempts at governmental regulation, unscrupulous advertisers and dollar-hungry media people continue to the present day to promote useless and sometimes harmful over-the-counter drugs, although television testimonials have replaced the crude newspaper pitches. While consumer advocates protested the overuse of drugs by the American public, the greatest harm came when the cure-alls came to be accepted as proper medical care in remote areas and in crowded tenement districts. Many of the drugs were harmless, as some defenders claimed, but the deception was painful nevertheless, and some did contain deadly poisons.[23]

NEW MAGAZINES: RIVALS FOR ADVERTISING

There were successful new leaders in magazine journalism, just as there were in newspaper making. One was Frank Munsey, a New Englander with a sober and industrious character, who struggled for a decade in New York magazine publishing before achieving success with his *Munsey's,* begun in 1889. Another was S. S. McClure, who, after establishing a feature syndicate service for newspapers, brought out his *McClure's* in 1893. A third was *Cosmopolitan,* founded in 1886 and sold to William Randolph Hearst in 1905.

These well-edited, popularized monthly magazines had found the same key to obtaining mass circulation that the daily newspapers had found in the past. The secret was cutting the price first to 15 cents and then to a dime for magazines that competed with older, 35-cent publications. The low penny-a-pound mail rate, in effect from 1885 until zone rates were established during World War I, helped to make this possible. By the turn of the century *Munsey's* had achieved a 650,000 circulation to lead by a wide margin, and *McClure's* and *Cosmopolitan* were runners-up. The formula for all three was popular fiction, general articles, and illustrations.

Cyrus H. K. Curtis provided new leadership in the women's magazine field with his *Ladies' Home Journal,* founded in 1883. With Edward W. Bok as editor after 1889, the magazine quickly rose to a half-million circulation at a $1 annual subscription price. Among the weekly five-cent magazines the *Saturday Evening Post,* bought by Curtis in 1897, and *Collier's,* founded in 1888, pushed to even higher circulations than those of the monthlies.

These new, popularly circulated magazines made the biggest inroads on available advertising revenue, arising as they did at the moment when national advertising was expanding. But the general illustrated monthly magazines of high literary and artistic quality—*Harper's, Century,* and *Scribner's*—continued to have major influence, even though they were outstripped in circulation. Sharing in the competition for reader attention and revenue were the illustrated weekly periodicals, *Harper's Weekly* and *Leslie's;* the weeklies depending on humor and cartoons, *Puck, Life,* and *Judge*; and the children's magazines, *Youth's Companion* and *St. Nicholas.*

Taking stock of the amount of advertising revenue gained by magazines, newspaper owners formed two business associations, the International Circulation Managers Association in 1898 and the Newspaper Advertising Executives Association in 1900, as well as regional organizations. Beginning in the late 1870s various representatives and associations worked to promote the newspaper as an advertising medium, and in 1913 the American Newspaper Publishers Association was persuaded to sponsor the founding of the Bureau of Advertising. The Bureau, with a paid staff, did an effective job of arguing the case of newspapers. In 1900 magazines were picking up 60 percent or more of national advertising revenue, but by World War I they were sharing the money equally with newspapers. Because newspapers had local advertising as well, they received a total of roughly 70 percent of all advertising revenues in the early years of the twentieth century.

A REVOLUTION IN PRINTING

The growth of the modern newspaper thus far described went hand in hand with the development of better printing techniques, improvements in presenting illustrations and eventually photographs, and changing relationships between management and labor brought by unionization and battles over the price of newsprint.

As part of the Industrial Revolution of the late nineteenth century, achievements in printing included the typesetting machine, faster presses, stereotyping, color printing, dry mats, electrotyping, and photoengraving. Ottmar Mergenthaler's Linotype machine first cast a line of type for newspaper use in 1886 in the *New York Tribune* plant. The time-saving performance of the Linotype helped the large evening dailies, which were under pressure to cover more news close to deadline time. Other slug-casting machines were soon developed, and improvements in the type faces themselves began to help readability. The ugly Gothics began to disappear, and after 1900 the newly designed Cheltenham family, the graceful Bodoni, and other headline types came into favor. The *New York Tribune* won typographical fame for its early use of the Bodoni upper- and lower-case headlines.

The press of deadlines and the rush for big circulations led to the development of bigger and faster presses. The leader here was R. Hoe & Company, which earlier had converted the presses of leading papers from hand to steam power and from flatbed to rotary before the Civil War. Next came the adaptation of the stereotyped plate to the newspaper press to allow the breaking of column rules for illustrations, headlines, and advertising, which had not been practical with type-revolving presses. The use of the curved stereotyped plate permitted an increase in the hourly rate of printing, and extra stereotypes of the same page could be produced for simultaneous use on two or more presses. Other changes allowed the use of a continuous role of newsprint, printing on both sides of the sheet in one operation, automatic folders, and, in the 1890s, color printing.

By 1890 most of the type-revolving presses had been replaced by presses using stereotyped plates and webs. The finest Hoe press could run off 48,000 12-page papers in an hour, and owners of the larger papers were making plans for installing banks of presses to keep up with the skyrocketing circulations. Color inserts printed separately had been used until full-color presses modeled after those in Paris were first built for the *Chicago Inter Ocean* by Walter Scott in 1892. Within a year the *New York World* had color presses, and soon the Sunday comics were a regular feature of the newspaper.

The sweep of all of these mechanical developments included labor specialization and larger working forces that in turn brought new labor-relations problems. The American Federation of Labor had organized printers, pressmen, and engravers, who pushed constantly for shorter working hours and higher pay. The danger of plantwide strikes—suspensions of service that could jeopardize the status of newspapers with their advertisers and the public—was reduced when the International Typographical Union split by specialty into four separate unions.[24] Efforts by labor unions and publishers, led by the American Newspaper Publishers Association, to have local conciliation and arbitration procedures and the right of appeal to a national arbitration board brought comparative peace to the newspaper industry in 1899, during a time of severe labor disturbances in other industries.

The ANPA also took a leadership role in the campaign to bring less expensive newsprint to its members. The Fourdrinier process, introduced from Germany in 1867, which allowed low-cost newsprint to be made from wood pulp to which rag was added, was a basic factor in the growth of the American newspaper. Prior to this, an expensive, limited industry produced paper by hand from rag stock. During the Civil War newspaper costs ran to $440 a ton for paper. By the 1890s a chemically produced wood pulp, called sulphite pulp, replaced rag stock as the toughening element in newsprint. Prices tumbled rapidly, reaching $42 a ton in 1899 and remaining there for years, except for periods of paper shortage.[25]

One problem remained, however. Domestic newsprint manufacturers had obtained a good-sized tariff on imported newsprint and thus had effected a virtual monopolistic control over domestic output and sales prices. The ANPA campaigned for years against the tariff, hoping to free the vast Canadian forest resources for American printing use. Finally, in 1913, Congress carried out the pledge of the Woodrow Wilson administration to lower the tariff, allowing a flood of Canadian newsprint into the country.

PHOTOENGRAVING BRINGS PHOTOGRAPHERS

More than one newspaper owner sensed the need for better illustrations. The *New York Herald* had stood out for its early use of woodcuts, and, beginning about 1870, the *Evening Telegram,* companion paper for the *Herald,* published a daily political cartoon. Of course *Frank Leslie's Illustrated Newspaper, Harper's Weekly,* and later other periodicals did highly artistic work with woodcuts. Women's magazines used engraved-steel fashion plates. But there was a need for a less expensive and faster way of printing illustrations. In the 1870s Zincographs, line cuts produced by etching on zinc plates, began to appear in American papers, and illustrators also found that they could print photos directly onto woodblocks or zinc plates, where they would form a guide for the artist or etcher who completed the cut.

A major breakthrough came when *New York World* editors began to publish line drawings of prominent local citizens, beginning in 1884. Within a short time a number of other leading papers were arranging for the work of the artist Valerian Gribayédoff. In 1891 there were about 1000 artists at work supplying illustrations for 5000 newspapers and magazines.[26] An increasing number of papers began to hire their own artists and to install engraving facilities.

Photoengraving was quickly to curtail this boom for the artists, however. The halftone photoengraving process had been developed in England prior to 1860, but the results were unsatisfactory until Frederic E. Ives went to work on the problems of reproducing photographs in the printing process. Ives was made head of the photographic laboratory at Cornell University in 1876, when he was 20. The next year he produced a photoengraving of a pen-and-ink drawing, which was published in the student paper at Cornell. In

1878 he made his first halftone. Ives saw that the way to break up masses of dark and light was to lay out a series of prominences on a plate that would transfer the ink to paper point by point. If the points were close together, the mass would be dark; and the more widely they were spaced, the lighter the mass would become. Ives moved to Baltimore and then after 1879 to Philadelphia, and produced commercially used halftones. He perfected his process in 1886.

There still remained, however, the problem of how to use the halftones on rotary presses. One of the heroes of the struggle to get pictures into the American newspaper was Stephen H. Horgan. Horgan was the art editor of an illustrated paper called the *New York Daily Graphic,* which began in 1873 and battled bravely until 1889, when it succumbed in the big-city competition. It was Horgan who succeeded in publishing, in 1880, a newspaper halftone of good quality called "Shantytown." And it was Horgan who first had the idea of how to run halftones on rotary presses. He was rebuffed by doubting press operators, however, and it was not until 1897 that he perfected the method for the *New York Tribune.* Within a short time other large papers were running halftone reproductions of photographs.

The artists found the news photographers edging into their field in earnest, now that their photos could be reproduced directly. Both groups covered the Spanish-American War. Syndicates quickly added news and feature photographs to their stock in trade, and big-city papers began to employ local photographers who carried their heavy, awkward equipment and their flashlight powder out on assignments. Pictorial journalism was on its way.

"Shantytown," the first good-quality halftone published in a U.S. newspaper, 1880

> # "KODAK"
>
> ## Stands for all that is best in Photography. *If it isn't an Eastman, it isn't a Kodak.*
>
> **EASTMAN KODAK CO.,**
>
> **Kodaks $5.00 to $35.00.**
>
> **Catalogues at the Dealers or by Mail.**   **Rochester, N. Y.**

Harper's Monthly, 1901

VISUAL MEDIA: DOCUMENTARY AND MOTION PICTURES

Jacob A. Riis, who emigrated from Denmark in 1870, won distinction as a reporter for the *New York Sun* by writing with discernment about the misery and vice of the New York slums where he had lived for seven years. He used a camera and flashlight powder to capture visually the sordid rooms and the faces of the poor. In 1888 the *Sun* published 12 drawings from his photographs with an article headlined "Flashes from the Slums." His famous 1890 book, *How the Other Half Lives,* carried 17 halftones and 19 drawings of his photographs, but the artistic quality was poor. Not until 1947, when enlargements were made from his original glass negatives preserved by the Museum of the City of New York, did Riis become fully recognized as a pioneer in documentary photography.[27] There were other early photojournalists, among them socialite Frances Benjamin Johnston, who at age 23 begged George Eastman to give her one of his first Kodaks. She became a photographer at the White House, documenting life there, and climaxed her exploits by obtaining the last photographs of President William McKinley before his 1901 assassination.[28]

Eastman's marketing of his Kodak camera in 1888 opened a new era. It used a roll of film. Thomas A. Edison's Kinetoscope of 1889 used Eastman film to produce a 50-foot "peep show," and by 1896 his Vitascope was used for the first public showing of a moving picture in a U.S. theater. *The Great Train Robbery,* directed by Edwin S. Porter, made history in 1903 as an eight-minute film telling a unified story. With photography in print and on motion picture film, the era of visual emphasis was launched. New York's dailies would seize upon it.

THE AGE OF YELLOW JOURNALISM

The rapidly expanding American newspaper faced sharp challenges during the 1890s, both as a business institution and as an instrument of society. One challenge was to survive the depression of 1893, a major economic crisis that did not ease until the close of the decade. The other was to respond to the country's growing role in world affairs and to a resulting moral crisis stemming from the ascendancy of a spirit of "Manifest Destiny." The story of how the press responded to these crises is not a happy one; the mixed reactions are traced in this and the following chapter.

The financial stability of the new metropolitan dailies always depended on winning more and more readers in order to attract larger advertising revenues. In depression time, there was even greater pressure to appeal to new readers to replace lost ones. Popularizing a product, though necessary if mass readership were to be achieved, did not need to become mere sensationalizing. Bigger headlines, more readable stories, pictures, and blobs of color could give newspapers new faces, perhaps sometimes even overdoing it, but nevertheless were effective, useful, and desirable devices.

By the same token, these new techniques could also be used to emphasize sensationalism at the expense of news. In the mid-1890s some editors proceeded to do just this, as had been done in earlier periods when new audiences were available. But the difference was that now they had better tools with which to make their sensationalism distinctive and seemingly new. The degrading product of this effort became known as "yellow journalism."

Yellow journalism, at its worst, was the new journalism without a soul. Trumpeting their concern for "the people," yellow journalists at the same time choked up the news channels on which the common people depended with a shrieking, gaudy, sensation-loving, devil-may-care kind of journalism. This turned the high drama of life into a cheap melodrama and led to stories being twisted into the form best suited for sales by the howling newsboy. Worst of all, instead of giving effective leadership, yellow journalism offered a palliative of sin, sex, and violence.

Pulitzer's striking success had demonstrated once again the appeal of the age-old technique of sensation. Other papers, like the *Philadelphia Record* and *Boston Globe,* were playing the same game as the *World*. But it was a mistake to attribute the *World*'s circulation achievements to sensationalism alone, and those who saw the clever promotion and lighter side of the *World* did not see—or disregarded—the solid characteristics of its news coverage and the high qualities of its editorial page. The antics of those who did not make this attempt to balance information and entertainment paid off handsomely in dollars earned. Their competitors were often forced to take on the yellow hue, and although most newspapers eventually recovered from the disease, modern journalism has exhibited some of the effects of this age of yellow journalism ever since.

WILLIAM RANDOLPH HEARST

The man who more than anyone else brought about the era of yellow journalism was watching with sharp interest while Pulitzer was setting New York journalism on its ear in the mid-1880s. He was William Randolph Hearst, who was to become the most controversial figure

Hearst at the peak of his career in the 1930s

(San Francisco Examiner)

in modern journalism before his 64-year publishing career had ended. The youthful Hearst was a calculating witness to Pulitzer's climb to glory, and when he eventually invaded New York to challenge the supremacy of the *World,* he came prepared to dazzle the city with a sensationalized and self-pronounced kind of journalism that would put Pulitzer to shame. The resulting struggle brought repercussions whose effects are still being felt.

Hearst was a Californian, born in 1863, the son of a successful pioneer who struck it rich in the silver mines of the Comstock Lode and who later won more riches in Anaconda copper and western and Mexican ranch lands. The only child of George and Phoebe Hearst, he grew up in San Francisco under the guidance of a busy, ambitious father and a schoolteacher mother, who in later years became a noted philanthropist and the able manager of the family fortune.

Having achieved wealth, George Hearst aspired to political power. In 1880 he acquired the *San Francisco Examiner,* a debt-ridden morning paper that lagged behind the *Chronicle,* and converted it into a Democratic party organ. Young Hearst showed an interest in the paper, but his father took a low view of the newspaperpeople who worked for him and packed his heir off to Harvard in 1883.

Hearst's career at Harvard was sensational, if not successful. He was a free-spending westerner who drank too much beer and listened to too much band music, and who did his best job as business manager of the humor magazine, the *Lampoon.* He was suspended in his sophomore year for celebrating Grover Cleveland's election to the presidency with a noisy fireworks display and was expelled a few months later for perpetrating a practical joke on Harvard's professors. Distinguished faculty members like William James and Josiah Royce could see no humor, it seemed, in finding their likenesses decorating chamber pots.

But the eastern education had not been entirely wasted. Harvard may not have made its impression on Hearst's mind, but the *Boston Globe* and the *New York World* did. Hearst studied the somewhat sensational techniques of General Charles H. Taylor's successful *Globe* and visited its up-to-date mechanical plant. He was more interested in Pulitzer's

World, however, and on one of his vacations he worked as a cub reporter for the newspaper he was to battle later. After bowing out at Harvard, Hearst again spent some time in New York studying the *World*'s techniques and then returned to San Francisco.

HEARST'S *SAN FRANCISCO EXAMINER*

William Randolph Hearst assumed the editorship of the *San Francisco Examiner* in 1887, when George Hearst was named senator from California. He was only 24, but the tall, blue-eyed, shy editor, whose high-pitched voice contrasted with a commanding physical presence, immediately began to staff the paper. Picked as managing editor was Sam S. Chamberlain, who had worked for both Bennett and Pulitzer, edited Bennett's Paris edition of the *Herald,* and in 1884 founded the Paris newspaper *Le Matin.* The brilliant Ambrose Bierce, later famous for his short stories, contributed his "Prattle" column. Star reporters like Edward H. Hamilton signed on, as did Arthur McEwen, an editorial writer who became a key figure in Hearst-style journalism. Homer Davenport began to draw his cartoons, James Swinnerton applied his artist's skill to the new field of comics, and literary flavor was added by Edwin Markham, whose "The Man with the Hoe" first appeared in the paper, and E. L. (Phinney) Thayer, whose contribution was "Casey at the Bat."

Chamberlain's grasp of news techniques made him invaluable. He developed the career of Winifred Black—known as "Annie Laurie" to future generations of Hearst readers—who attracted San Francisco women readers with intense stories. Sent to investigate the city hospital's management, Black conveniently fainted on the street, was carried to the hospital, and turned in a story "with a sob for the unfortunate in every line." The *Examiner* was ever experimenting with crusades, stunts, and devices to present the news in a yet more luring manner. A stalwart Democrat, Hearst attacked the Southern Pacific railroad, the bulwark of the Republican state machine, and attempted to present other types of serious stories. But news that was important but dull took a back seat as the paper strove for what McEwen called the "Gee-Whiz" emotion.[29]

Hearst's experiments on the mechanical side were important and constructive contributions to the new journalism. Trying many new patterns of makeup, arranging headlines in symmetrical patterns, and using attractive type faces, Hearst eventually arrived at a distinctive formula that many another paper imitated. Hearst himself often worked on the page forms, but his mechanical genius was George Pancoast, who joined the *Examiner* staff in 1888 and for the next 50 years perfected the electric drive for presses, improved color printing, and designed 14 printing plants for the Hearst empire.

The *Examiner,* called by the ambitious Hearst "The Monarch of the Dailies," doubled its circulation in the first year, reaching 30,000, and by 1893 had pushed to 72,000. This was more than M. H. de Young's *Chronicle,* the recognized leading daily. Senator Hearst died in 1891 after watching his son turn a losing proposition into a paper averaging a $350,000 to $500,000 yearly profit.[30] And with that success achieved, young Hearst was ready to tackle the challenge he saw in Joseph Pulitzer's city, New York.

HEARST INVADES NEW YORK

The profits from the *Examiner* were now available for an invasion of New York. But Hearst needed more capital, and eventually he persuaded his mother to sell the family holdings in the Anaconda copper mines for $7.5 million and make the cash available for new publishing ventures.[31] Later, when a friend told Mrs. Hearst that she had heard that the *New York Journal* was losing $1 million a year and expressed fear that the family fortune was being thrown away recklessly, Mrs. Hearst replied that, in such an event, her son could hold out for 30 years more.

Somewhat ironically, Hearst entered the New York field by buying the newspaper that Joseph Pulitzer's brother, Albert, had established in 1882. The *Morning Journal* had been a successful one-cent paper appealing to casual newspaper scanners. In 1894 its price was raised to two cents, and circulation fell off. Albert Pulitzer then sold the *Journal* for $1 million to John R. McLean, ambitious publisher of the *Cincinnati Enquirer.* McLean was no stranger to sensational methods of publishing newspapers, but he had been unable to break into the highly competitive New York field. In the fall of 1895, Hearst picked up the paper from the defeated McLean for $180,000.

PULITZER'S *SUNDAY WORLD*

Joseph Pulitzer had been busy during the 10 years since Hearst had left New York to launch his career in San Francisco. Particularly he had expanded the mechanical facilities available to his editors, and he had applied the new techniques to the development of the *Sunday World.*

It was Pulitzer who first demonstrated the full potentialities of the Sunday newspaper as a profitable news and entertainment medium. There had been weeklies issued as Sunday papers since 1796. The daily *Boston Globe* put out a Sunday edition briefly in 1833, but James Gordon Bennett's *Herald* was the first daily to print a Sunday edition steadily, starting in 1841. The demand for news during the Civil War stimulated Sunday publication, but even by the time Pulitzer invaded New York in 1883 only about 100 (out of approximately 900) daily newspapers had Sunday editions. Most were appearing in eastern cities, and a good share were printed in German and other foreign languages. Some carried a four-page supplement filled with entertaining features, fiction, and trivia.

Pulitzer's new *Sunday World* added many more pages of entertainment to the regular news section. Feature material for women, for young readers, and for sports enthusiasts appeared. Humorous drawings and other illustrations were concentrated in the Sunday pages. The offerings of the literary syndicates, such as that developed by S. S. McClure, added to the Sunday paper's appeal. Circulation of the *Sunday World* passed the 250,000 mark in 1887, and by the early 1890s the paper had reached 40 to 48 pages as retail advertisers realized the extent of its readership by families and by women. Other newspapers were quick to follow suit, and in 1890 there were 250 dailies with Sunday editions, crowding the metropolitan areas and driving the independent Sunday weeklies out of the picture.

Heading the *World*'s Sunday staff in the early years was Morrill Goddard, a college graduate who as a young city editor had shown ability to spot the feature angle of news events. But in the Sunday section Goddard jazzed up his page spreads, exaggerating the factual information to the point at which serious news sources, particularly people of science and medicine, shied away. The sensationalism and pseudoscientific stories of this era greatly increased the credibility problem of newspapers, but the issue was ignored.

The installation of color presses in 1893 only gave Goddard another medium to exploit. As many as five colors now could be used in the Sunday color supplement, which included the comic drawings that Goddard knew were most effective in spurring circulation. The *World* had started a regular comic section in 1889 and was the first to use color here (magazines had done so since the 1870s). The most successful of the artists was Richard F. Outcault, whose "Hogan's Alley" depicted life in the tenements. The central figure in each drawing was a toothless, grinning kid attired in a ballooning dress. When the *World*'s printers daubed a blob of yellow on the dress he became the immortal "Yellow Kid."

"YELLOW JOURNALISM" AND THE SPANISH-AMERICAN WAR

When William Randolph Hearst arrived on the New York scene he immediately set out to buy the men who were making the *Sunday World* a success. Using an office the *Examiner* had rented in the *World* building, he hired away Goddard and most of his staff of writers and artists. Hearst's lavish spending habits made Pulitzer's counteroffers hopeless. Soon even the *World*'s publisher, S. S. Carvalho, was working at the *Journal*. The battle on, Pulitzer turned to Arthur Brisbane, socialist Albert Brisbane's brilliant young son, who had broken into newspaper work on the *Sun* before joining Pulitzer's staff. As the new Sunday editor, Brisbane drove the circulation to the 600,000 mark, popularizing the news and pushing hard on Pulitzer's social concerns. Goddard had taken Outcault and the "Yellow Kid" with him, but Brisbane used George B. Luks, later a well-known painter, to continue the cartoon.

Circulation people for both papers used posters featuring the happy-go-lucky, grinning kid with his curiously vacant features. To opposition journalists the "Yellow Kid" seemed symbolic of the kind of sensational journalism that was being practiced, and the public agreed. The phrase "yellow journalism" soon became widely used, and its techniques the object of hard scrutiny. Unfortunately for Pulitzer, Brisbane moved over to the *Evening Journal* as editor in 1897, and Luks also joined Hearst. At this Outcault moaned:

> When I die don't wear yellow crepe, don't let them put a Yellow Kid on my tombstone and don't let the Yellow Kid himself come to my funeral. Make him stay over on the east side, where he belongs.[32]

Besides raiding Pulitzer's staff, Hearst moved in the best of his San Francisco staffers, including Chamberlain, McEwen, Davenport, and Annie Laurie. Dana's *Sun* lost its star reporters Julian Ralph, Richard Harding Davis, and Edward W. Townsend to Hearst's bankroll. Dorothy Dix joined the women's staff, and writers Stephen Crane, Alfred Henry Lewis, and Rudolph Block (Bruno Lessing) were signed, along with a host of other talented reporters, critics, and artists.

Two other events propelled Hearst into the thick of the fight with Pulitzer. In 1896, when the *Journal* reached the 150,000 mark as a one-cent paper, Pulitzer cut his price to a penny, gaining circulation but allowing speculation that he was afraid of his challenger. More importantly, Pulitzer, although in sympathy with many of William Jennings Bryan's ideas, could not support his inflationary monetary policies. But Hearst, as a silver-mine owner, had no problem in arguing against the gold standard. Political partisans were attracted by Hearst's stand for Bryan in the conservative East, where Bryan was looked upon with horror.

Frankly adopting the sins of yellow journalism, the *Journal* continued its surge in circulation figures. One jump of 125,000 came in a single month in the fall of 1896, when the following headlines were typical: "Real American Monsters and Dragons," over a story of the discovery of fossil remains by an archaeological expedition; "A Marvellous New Way of Giving Medicine: Wonderful Results from Merely Holding Tubes of Drugs Near Entranced Patients," a headline that horrified medical researchers; and "Henry James' New Novel of Immorality and Crime; The Surprising Plunge of the Great Novelist in the Field of Sensational Fiction," the *Journal*'s way of announcing publication of *The Other House*.

Other headlines were more routinely sensational: "The Mysterious Murder of Bessie Little," "One Mad Blow Kills Child," "What Made Him a Burglar? A Story of Real Life in New York by Edgar Saltus," "Startling Confession of a Wholesale Murderer Who Begs to Be Hanged." Annie Laurie wrote about "Why Young Girls Kill Themselves" and "Strange Things Women Do for Love."[33]

THE OPEN-AIR SCHOOL IN HOGAN'S ALLEY.

The "Yellow Kid," in his nightshirt, was an 1896 smash hit in the *New York World.*

The *Journal* was crusading, too, but it went beyond other New York newspapers in a manner that enabled it to shout, "While Others Talk the Journal Acts." The paper obtained a court injunction that balked the granting of a city franchise to a gas company, and, pleased by its success, it took similar actions against alleged abuses in government. Hearst then solicited compliments from civic leaders across the country and printed them under such headings as "Journalism That Acts; Men of Action in All Walks of Life Heartily Endorse the Journal's Fight in Behalf of the People" and "First Employed by the Journal, the Novel Concept Seems Likely to Become an Accepted Part of the Function of the Newspapers of This Country."[34]

Before his first year in New York had ended, Hearst had installed large color presses at the *Journal,* added an 8-page colored comic section called *The American Humorist,* and replaced that with a 16-page color supplement, *The Sunday American Magazine* (later, with Brisbane as editor, this was to become the famous *American Weekly*). In late 1896 the *Journal*'s daily circulation was 437,000, and on Sunday it was 380,000. Within a year the Sunday figures had reached the *World*'s 600,000. Circulation figures moved up and down, depending on the street sale appeal of the moment: on the day following the McKinley-Bryan election the *World* and *Journal* each sold approximately 1.5 million copies to break all records.

It was in this atmosphere that the leading papers scrambled for news around the nation and the world. And it was under these conditions that American papers approached the events that led to an international crisis and the Spanish-American War.

THE SPIRIT OF MANIFEST DESTINY

Of all the wars the United States had fought, the Spanish-American War was the most painless. But the results entirely changed the course of American foreign policy. In fewer than four months the Spanish government was forced to request an armistice, at an extraordinarily small cost in American lives, and the American flag floated over an empire stretching from Puerto Rico to the Philippines. Those who have sought to explain the causes of this unwarranted war have often centered the blame on William Randolph Hearst in particular and the newspapers of the country in general. Carefully documented studies made by Marcus M. Wilkerson and Joseph E. Wisan in the early 1930s have ample proof that Hearst's *Journal,* Pulitzer's *World,* the *Chicago Tribune,* the *New York Sun,* and *New York Herald* (and, as is usually ignored, many other American papers) so handled the news of events leading up to the crisis of the sinking of the *Maine* that a war psychosis was developed.[35] It must not be forgotten, however, that the newspapers were cultivating public opinion in a favorable atmosphere.

When viewed in the long perspective, the Spanish-American War was but one in a series of incidents that marked the arrival of the United States as a world and, in particular, a Pacific power. With newly acquired Alaskan territory protecting one flank, Americans moved to gain a foothold in the Samoan Islands. Agitation began in the 1880s for the annexation of Hawaii. Then, with a new modern navy at his disposal, President Grover Cleveland brought his country to the verge of war with Great Britain over a test of the Monroe Doctrine in the Venezuelan crisis of 1895. This was followed by the annexation of Hawaii, the Philippines, Guam, and Puerto Rico, and the building of the Panama Canal. Interest in the Asian mainland brought about John Hay's Open Door Policy in 1899 and President Roosevelt's negotiation of the peace treaty ending the Russo-Japanese War of 1904–5 in a little New Hampshire town. Pan-Americanism became open American intervention in the affairs of Central American countries, and Roosevelt took the United States into European affairs as well by participating in the 1905 Moroccan crisis that had been precipitated by German expansionism.

This desire to be a powerful participant in world affairs was not the only driving force behind the American expansion of interest. There was pride felt by many Americans in the addition of new territories and keen interest in the expansion of trade and foreign investments. But Americans also felt they had a role to play in promoting the idea of peace and justice in the world. There was widespread sympathy for those Cubans, Armenians, and Greeks who were fighting for their freedoms in the 1890s. Both idealism and national pride came into play during the Spanish-American War. However, it must be acknowledged that considerable racism, fueled by Social Darwinism, came into play in the United States's participation in this war, as the historian Richard Dean Burns notes:

> Certain clergymen, historians, political scientists, and political leaders—social Darwinists all—convinced of Anglo-Saxon racial and cultural superiority, sought to extend the beneficent civilization to the less fortunate people by conquest, if necessary. War with Spain, they believed, would lead to acquiring overseas territory where the American mission could be carried out. The political leaders, joined by navalists, were also motivated by nationalism and patriotism, wishing to extend American power in the world and join in the scramble for land and peoples and prestige then in vogue among the European powers.[36]

Newspapers reflected this conflict in goals, reporting both the atrocities committed by Spanish troops against Cuban insurrectionists and the chance for the new American navy to prove itself against Spain. But mainly there was a strong desire to flex the nation's muscles. As the memory of the Civil War faded, many older Americans wondered if their country's military prowess was still secure. Younger citizens were eager to match the exploits of the boys in blue and gray. For them, war, 1898-style, still seemed to be an exciting personal adventure. John D. Hicks, a first-rank American historian who was not unaware of the role of the newspaper as an organ of public opinion, summed up his discussion of the causes of the Spanish-American War by saying:

> Years later, Theodore Roosevelt recaptured the spirit of 1898 when he mourned apologetically, "It wasn't much of a war, but it was the best war we had." America in the spring of 1898 was ripe for any war, and the country's mood was not to be denied.[37]

COVERING CUBAN NEWS, 1895–98

From March 1895, when the Cuban insurrection began, until April 1898, when Spain and the United States went to war, there were fewer than a score of days in which a story about Cuba did not appear in one of the New York newspapers.[38] This was due partly to the aggressive news policies of the big dailies, partly to the manufactured stories by some of the papers (notably the *Journal*), and partly to the increased reader interest in controversial stories. It was also the result of the activities of the Cuban junta that fed information and propaganda to American reporters in New York and at the Florida news bases nearest the island.

A considerable number of Cubans had emigrated to the United States and settled in New York, Philadelphia, Baltimore, Boston, and several Florida cities. The junta had its headquarters in New York, where a Cuban newspaper was published. Through the Cuban residents in the eastern cities, a program of mass meetings was established. Money was raised, and several hundred volunteers were obtained in each city for running arms and taking part in filibustering expeditions. Cuban agents funneled information on the progress of the fighting in Cuba to the American newspapers. The work was well under way in 1895, and as the crisis intensified, the activities of the junta reached greater heights. Ministers, educators, civil leaders, and politicians were reached by the junta.

The Spanish decision in 1896 to use strong repressive measures in Cuba brought Captain-General Valeriano Weyler into the news. All loyal Cubans were ordered to congregate in small areas adjoining Spanish bases, and those who did not were considered enemies. But those huddled in the camps quickly fell victim to epidemics, and many starved to death when food supplies became disrupted. Much of the newspaper copy centered about the effects of famine and pestilence (approximately 110,000 Cubans died in the three years,[39] but newspaper estimates reached 400,000 as part of the exaggeration of these admittedly very serious conditions). Weyler was nicknamed the "Butcher" by American reporters and compared to the "bloodthirsty Cortez and Pizarro" of the days of the conquistadors.

Competition for news became fierce. The Associated Press provided its own coverage and used information from stories printed by member papers.[40] The *Journal* and *World* led the way as papers with correspondents in Cuba sold their stories to other papers. Papers in competing situations fought to sign up as soon as a rival announced it had obtained *World, Journal, Sun, Herald,* or other "big-league" coverage. Striving to keep ahead in every way was Hearst, who persuaded star reporter James Creelman to stop reporting for the *World* and to start working for the *Journal* in 1896, and sent Richard Harding Davis and artist Frederic Remington to join him in Cuba. The impact of pictorial journalism increased in 1897, when New York papers began to use halftone photographs that sometimes were accurate portrayals of Cuban misery and sometimes were fakes. It also was during this time that Remington, according to Creelman's 1901 reminiscences, cabled Hearst that there would be no war and that he was coming home. Whereupon Hearst was supposed to have cabled back: "Remington, Havana. Please remain. You furnish the pictures, and I'll furnish the war. W. R. Hearst."[41] There is no evidence that Hearst actually sent this cable, so often quoted as conclusive evidence against him, but in a sense it reflected the situation. Of all the American papers, Hearst's *Journal* worked the hardest to create public sentiment for war. Episodes like this did much to tag him with "Hearst's war."

In the summer of 1897, after open advocacy of war for about a year and the sensationalizing of several minor incidents, the *Journal* built the story of Evangelina Cisneros into a daily chant for intervention. Miss Cisneros, a niece of the Cuban revolutionary president, had been sentenced to 20 years in prison for her rebellious activity. The *Journal* devoted an incredible number of news columns, 375, to the details of her condition and to her "rescue" by *Journal* reporter Karl Decker. Many notables congratulated the *Journal* on this achievement, and Miss Cisneros was greeted by President McKinley on the White House lawn. Later it was discovered how other New York papers had treated this exciting but out-of-context story: *World,* 12½ columns; *Times,* 10 columns; *Tribune,* 3½ columns; *Sun,* 1 column; *Herald,* 1 column.[42] During the incident, when the *World* published Weyler's account of Miss Cisneros's treatment—which had been exaggerated—the *Journal* accused Pulitzer of unpatriotic motives.

The *Journal*'s most significant "scoop" came on February 9, 1898, when Hearst published a private letter written by Dupuy de Lome, the Spanish ambassador to the United States, to a Spanish newspaper editor visiting in Havana. The letter, stolen in Havana by a Cuban junta member, referred to President McKinley as "weak and catering to the rabble, and besides, a low politician." At the same moment Theodore Roosevelt was commenting that his chief had the backbone of a chocolate eclair, but to have the Spanish ambassador say the same thing, even in a private letter, was a different matter. American opinion of the Spanish government hit a new low, and six days later the *Maine* blew up in Havana harbor. The impact of the two events proved to be the turning point in the diplomatic crisis.

Hearst's *Journal* for February 17, 1898; the *Maine* had sunk on the night of February 15.

THE CORRESPONDENTS GO TO WAR

No one has satisfactorily established the cause of the explosion that sank the *Maine,* with the loss of 266 American lives. But some American newspapers set about making it appear that the Spanish were indirectly responsible for the sinking. The *Journal* offered a $50,000 reward for information leading to the arrest and conviction of the criminals, and three days later the paper's streamer read, "THE WHOLE COUNTRY THRILLS WITH WAR FEVER." Large headlines and striking illustrations became common in big-city papers. Leading the way was Brisbane, who experimented with artist-drawn headlines that virtually filled the front page with two or three words. Later that year Brisbane wrote:

> Before the type size reached its maximum, "War Sure" could be put in one line across a page, and it was put in one line and howled through the streets by patriotic newsboys many and many a time. As war was sure, it did no harm.[43]

Gradually the tide swung toward a declaration of war. Volunteer units such as the Rough Riders were formed, Congress passed a $50 million defense bill for war, and more than once Secretary of State Sherman made statements based on news reports from the *Journal.* In mid-March a leading Republican senator, Proctor of Vermont, made a speech based on his own trip to Cuba. He verified much of what had been published during the previous three years about deaths of Cubans, adding to the pressures on President McKinley to come out for war. The *World* at first urged caution in the handling of the *Maine* matter, but on April 10 Pulitzer published a signed editorial calling for a "short and sharp" war. Most of the nation agreed with this sentiment, and Congress passed a war resolution on April 18.

The *New York Sun,* which under Dana's cynical editorship had been extremely jingoistic, stood with the *Journal* and *World* in demanding intervention. The *New York Herald,* while keeping up in sensational news coverage, opposed intervention in its editorials—an incongruity also true of the *Chicago Times-Herald, Boston Herald, San Francisco Chronicle,* and *Milwaukee Sentinel.* Strongly interventionist were such papers as the *Chicago Tribune, New Orleans Times-Democrat, Atlanta Constitution,* and *Indianapolis Journal.* Keeping calm were such papers as the *New York Tribune, New York Times, Chicago Daily News, Boston Transcript,* and others that reflected the thinking of the business community in their editorial columns. In his study of the newspapers for the period, Wilkerson ranks the *Journal* as the leader in excessive journalism, with the *Chicago Tribune* and the *World* next in order. Joseph Medill's *Chicago Tribune,* strongly nationalistic in its editorial columns, did not originate sensational news stories, as did the *Journal* and *World,* but it ran the cream of those collected by both papers.

It should be pointed out that the *World* was not a jingo newspaper. Pulitzer had opposed the annexation of Hawaii and did not support President Cleveland in the 1895 Venezuelan crisis, when most major papers warned that the United States would fight to uphold Venezuela's boundary claims with British Guiana. During the Cuban crisis the *World* did not stand for the annexation of foreign lands and opposed the taking of the Philippine Islands. The *World* based its call for war on the issue of human liberty and in subsequent actions proved it was not merely jingoistic. Pulitzer later regretted the role the *World* had played in preparing public opinion for killing, and in 1907, when Theodore Roosevelt ordered the American fleet to the Pacific to impress Japan, Pulitzer requested that his editors "show that Spain had granted to Cuba all that we had demanded. . . . Give further details of jingoism causing Cuban War after Spain had virtually granted everything."[44]

But in 1898 only Godkin's *Evening Post,* among the New York dailies, held out to the end against yellow journalism and the decision to force Spain from Cuba. Lashing out against Hearst and Pulitzer, he bitterly attacked with statements like this:

A yellow journal office is probably the nearest approach, in atmosphere, to hell, existing in any Christian state. A better place in which to prepare a young man for eternal damnation than a yellow journal office does not exist.[45]

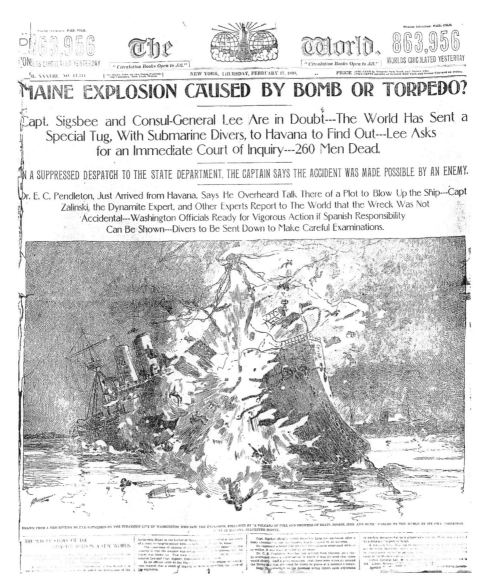

The *World's* February 17, 1898, front page, somewhat more cautious than that of the *Journal*

The newspapers fought the war as determinedly as they had fostered it. Some 500 reporters, artists, and photographers flocked to Florida, where the American army was mobilizing, and to the Cuban and Puerto Rican fronts.[46] Small fleets of press boats accompanied the navy into action. Correspondents sailed with Dewey to Manila and with Schley to Havana. They covered every battle and skirmish in Cuba and more than once took part in the fighting itself. A *Journal* correspondent lost a leg during one fighting charge. Richard Harding Davis, then reporting for the *New York Herald* and the *Times* of London, led another charge and won the praise of Rough Rider Theodore Roosevelt.

Leading the *Journal*'s contingent was the publisher himself, who exuded enthusiasm as he directed his staff of 20 men and women reporters, artists, and photographers, including a motion-picture man. Creelman, who was wounded in one battle, records an image of Hearst—wearing a beribboned straw hat on his head and a revolver at his belt—taking the story from his bleeding reporter and then galloping away on horseback to get to a *Journal* press boat.

American correspondents were learning how to use the boats and cables to speed their messages to the news offices. Stories from Cuba had to be brought to Key West for transmission to New York, with leading papers sending several thousand words a day. All this was expensive, but the race for news was an exciting one. The *World* scored the biggest single beat when Edward W. Harden, one of three correspondents to witness Dewey's amazing victory in Manila Bay, got his story off first by paying the "urgent" priority rate of $9.90 a word. Harden's beat arrived in New York too far into the dawn for the *World* to capitalize on it with a full-blown extra, but the *World*'s news client, the *Chicago Tribune*, had time to revamp its final edition and carry the most dramatic story of the war.

While Hearst said he did not care how much all of this cost (his paper spent $500,000 during the four months and put out as many as 40 extras in one day), Pulitzer began to view the situation with dismay. The *Journal* gleefully asked in its front-page ears, "How do you like the *Journal*'s war?" while Pulitzer began to retreat. In the end, Pulitzer withdrew from the competition in sensationalism at the turn of the century, while Hearst continued to exploit the news in a manner that seriously impeded the effectiveness of his role as a people's champion. By 1900, about one-third of the metropolitan dailies were following the yellow trend, and it was another ten years before the wave of sensationalism subsided and journalists concentrated on the more intelligent use of headlines, pictures, and color printing.

THE TRIUMPH OF MANIFEST DESTINY

The generally enthusiastic public response to the United States's aggressive policy toward Spain in the Caribbean provided the proponents of Manifest Destiny with an excuse for gaining supremacy over as much of Asia as military power could sustain. They included politicians, led by Theodore Roosevelt and Henry Cabot Lodge; historian Brooks Adams; evangelist Josiah Strong; railroad builder James J. Hill; naval strategist Alfred T. Mahan; entrepreneurs like the American-China Development Company; influential newspaper publishers and editors of rural farm journals; and extremely vocal representatives of the powerful farm bloc, such as Senator William V. Allen of Nebraska.

These leaders, agitating on behalf of Americans of all political faiths, generated the ideas and emotions that resulted in the bloody annexation of the Philippine Islands, the capstone of this nation's relentless drive to be a Pacific rather than an Atlantic power. It also was the propellant for future Asian conflicts. Promises made to insurgent leader Emilio

Aguinaldo that American force would guarantee Philippine independence after the overthrow of remaining Spanish troops and that friendly Philippine bases would be used for expanded trade with Japan were not kept. Instead, the United States signaled its determination to become a full-fledged colonial power in East Asia, lured on by the mirage of China as a land of vast and lucrative markets where the surplus crops of America's great midlands could be sold.

This military adventure, which left the United States with an exposed strategic commitment along the axis of Japan's southern expansion, was a colossal blunder that would lead to three more wars in American history. Dewey's victory at Manila had been part of the short but rather exciting 1898 public experience, but the guerrilla war in the Philippines between 1899 and 1902 was, in the words of historian Richard O'Connor, a quickly forgotten "dreary sequel" to the Spanish-American War.[47] At the peak of the fighting approximately 70,000 U.S. troops—fed with notions of racial and religious superiority—were used to crush the insurgency brutally. Horrifying cruelties practiced on Filipino soldiers and massacres of civilians brought the total death count to an estimated 200,000 (American casualties were about 10,000). Fighting against the Moros in the southern Philippines continued until World War I, as the United States strove to subjugate a determined native population. Ironically, as part of this generally confused foreign policy, the United States attempted to atone for what Stanley Karnow called its "naked conquest" by sending thousands of volunteers with missionary zeal to the Philippines to help reconstruct buildings, teach English, and fight disease.[48]

Half a million Americans joined the Anti-Imperialist League that had been founded in Boston. In actions to be repeated years later in protests against the war in Vietnam, they participated in mass meetings, marches, sit-ins, and teach-ins, all the time pressuring their elected representatives against formal annexation of the islands. A bitter Senate debate featured the elderly George H. Hoar of Massachusetts, who tried to awaken his colleagues by telling of concentration camps, burned villages, and the use of the water-cure torture, opposing Albert J. Beveridge of Indiana, a leader of the Senate expansionists.

Carl Schurz, who in an 1893 *Harper's* article had insisted that the United States could obtain economic objectives "without taking those countries into our national household,"[49] was joined in the anti-imperialist movement by Jane Addams, Andrew Carnegie, William James, Samuel Gompers, Samuel Clemens, and other influential citizens. Clemens wrote that a new American flag should be designed with the white stripes painted black, and the stars replaced by a skull and crossbones. But much of the dissent was drowned out by the thunder of editors like "Marse" Henry Watterson of the *Louisville Courier-Journal,* who bluntly spoke for many when he said, "We escape the menace and peril of socialism and agrarianism, as England has escaped them, by a policy of colonialism and conquest . . . we risk Caesarism, certainly, but Caesarism is preferable to anarchism."[50] Those were not the only choices, but many Americans pursued this all-or-nothing approach in an effort to become dominant in new market areas.

The end of the major fighting in the Philippines was followed by the Russo-Japanese War in 1904, and more than 100 correspondents—many of them veterans of the Spanish-American War, the Boer War in South Africa, and the Boxer Rebellion—flocked to Japan. Richard Harding Davis, Frederick Palmer, Jack London, and the photographer Jimmy Hare were among those frustrated by the effective Japanese censorship. The Associated Press coverage from St. Petersburg and Tokyo gave the two versions of the fighting at Port Arthur and in Manchuria. At home, most large newspapers editorialized against the corrupt Russian regime, except a number in California who were so affected by their experience with Asian immigration that they feared a Japanese victory. Finally, in May

1905, the Czar's fleet was destroyed in battle off the coast of Korea, and Japan stood alone in Asia; China had been defeated in 1894. The only possible challengers to Japanese supremacy in the region were the Americans in the Philippines, the new arrivals.

Closer to home and an extension of this hot-blooded American spirit, the Panama Canal had been built in an occupied zone that Colombia complained had been torn from it by an American-backed revolution. This action, and the extension of American military and economic domination in the Central American and Caribbean areas, dissipated hopes for Pan-American understanding. Cuba and Panama virtually became American protectorates under the Platt amendment of 1901. The Dominican Republic, Haiti, and Nicaragua in turn were forced to accept United States intervention in their affairs under the Roosevelt corollary to the Monroe Doctrine, by which the United States undertook to preserve order in those countries and to administer their financial affairs to prevent any possible intervention by European powers. The primary intent was to ensure American security in a vital area, but American trade and financial interests followed the flag—and many persons complained that they sometimes preceded it.

At the same time, however, powerful forces sought to commit America to a quite different role in world affairs. Cultural and religious ties were made with China after the Boxer Rebellion. The Philippines were promised their eventual independence after a period of tutelage. Roosevelt himself acted as a mediator in helping to end the Russo-Japanese War and in smoothing relations among Germany, France, and Britain at the Algeciras conference. The United States accepted the idea of an international court of arbitration, advanced at The Hague Peace Conference of 1899, and negotiated several arbitration treaties. Americans played a leading part in the unsuccessful attempt to create an international court of justice during the second conference at The Hague in 1907. Out of these movements came American leadership in proposing the League of Nations and the World Court at the close of World War I—proposals most of the other nations of the world adopted while the United States slumped back into isolationism.

10

The People's Champions

I have only one principle, and that is represented by an effort to make it harder for the rich to grow richer and easier for the poor to keep from growing poorer.

—*Edward Wyllis Scripps*

The opening of the twentieth century found the United States moving toward a consolidation of its position as an industrial nation. The framework had been completed by 1900: the economic expansion that had begun after the Civil War, the growth in population and the tying together of the country, the rapid development of rich natural resources, the inventive and productive genius, the political and cultural advances—all ensured the future of a new world power.

Vital contests still were in progress, however, that would affect the character of the new United States. These contests assumed critical importance at a moment when the economic, political, and social trends of a new era were being shaped. How would the nation conduct itself in the world community? How democratic would it remain? Would a balance be struck between the advocates of unrestricted economic individualism and the crusaders for social justice? Would the fruits of progress be shared by all the people in the form of better living conditions, educational and cultural opportunities, higher health standards, and personal security? Would government be responsive to the general welfare? What was to be the role of the press in advancing or retarding necessary adjustments?

Men and women had struggled to obtain affirmative answers to these questions ever since the Industrial Revolution had changed the character of American society. The "consistent rebellion" in the agricultural areas against economic inequities represented one phase of the struggle; the rise of the labor unions in the cities another. The growth of strong political movements that sought to place more power in the hands of the people generally; the efforts of the social scientists to impart knowledge on which wise social and

Edward Wyllis Scripps aboard his yacht near the close of his career

political decisions could be based; the appeals of reformers, agitators, political leaders, and writers for an arousing of the country's social conscience—all these had helped to shape the direction in which the country would turn.

But in the first years of the new century there were major divisions of thought and action that indicated the crucial importance of the struggle to shape public opinion and to enforce the popular will. Nationalists and internationalists contended in foreign affairs. Economic individualists and social reformers clashed in the domestic arena. The mass media of the times—newspapers, magazines, books—played a most important role in these national debates.

THE CRISIS OF ECONOMIC POWER

Important as was the contest over foreign policy, it was not the major concern of the American people around the turn of the century. Their attention was instead centered largely on domestic problems created by the Industrial Revolution: the growth of trusts and the centralization of economic power in a few hands; the inadequate incomes of the worker and farmer; corruption and inadequacies in political and business life. To many Americans it seemed that national wealth and strength, while reflecting basic progress for all the people, were actually mainly benefiting a plundering few who were usurping the freedoms of the many.[1]

The concentration of economic power, which had begun to develop rapidly in the 1880s, was greatly accentuated after 1900. A 1904 study listed 318 industrial trusts, three-fourths of which had been incorporated since 1898. These 318 trusts, capitalized at $7 billion, represented the merging of 5300 individual companies. Six big trusts—steel, oil, copper, sugar, tobacco, and shipping—that had been organized in those six years were capitalized at $2.5 billion. Census figures show that in 1914 one-eighth of American businesses employed more than three-fourths of the wage earners and produced four-fifths of the manufactured products.

The newspaper and magazine editors and the reporters and writers who joined in protesting this economic monopoly were even more concerned with the seemingly insatiable appetite of capitalists for power. Those who won domination in one field promptly reached out into other spheres, until the country's financial power fell largely into the hands of two loosely organized groups, the Morgan and the Rockefeller interests and their satellites. The famous Pujo Committee investigation in 1913 reported that four allied financial institutions in New York held 341 directorships in banks, railroads, shipping lines, insurance companies, public utilities, and other businesses with total resources of $22 billion.

The distribution of the wealth being created was heavily one-sided. Two-thirds of the male adult workers failed to earn at least $600 a year in wages, which was the figure set by sociologists as the minimum needed to maintain decent standards at the current cost of living. Many material and social advances were being made: electricity, gas, and plumbing in homes; better schools and parks; the conveniences of city life; telephones, railroads, and highways. But they did not mean much to the millions in the New York tenements whose plight had been reported by Jacob Riis.

Labor-union membership increased between 1900 and 1910, jumping from 3.5 percent of all workers to 7 percent. The gains were being made by skilled workers: the railway workers, building tradespeople, machinists, miners, printing tradespeople, and garment workers. Unskilled workers, women, and immigrants remained victims of the economic order. Immigrants, in particular, faced considerable social problems. The flood of immigrants from 1880 to 1900 was equaled in the single decade 1900 to 1910. The great bulk of the new immigration was from southern and eastern Europe, and a fourth of those arriving were illiterate. By 1910 one-seventh of the United States population was foreign-born, and in the industrial East more than half the population was foreign-born or of foreign-born parentage. These were the "poor and ill-informed" who were to be championed by Progressive newspaper publishers such as Edward Wyllis Scripps. At the same time, Progressivism could be both paternalistic and coercive when its advocates set out to control various racial and ethnic groups.[2]

DEMANDS FOR POLITICAL AND ECONOMIC REFORM

The conditions of the day inevitably demanded reform, and Eugene V. Debs did see his Socialist party win nearly a million votes in the presidential election of 1912, and some 300 cities and towns elected Socialist officeholders. In the labor movement William D. Haywood and his Industrial Workers of the World sought a radical solution to the plight of the unskilled laborer. Also, a vigorous social justice wing of the Progressive movement centered on the establishment of settlement houses for the poor.[3] But political leadership remained in the hands of the two major political parties,[4] and most labor followed the moderate program of Samuel Gompers and his American Federation of Labor.

The instruments for political action on the national level were Theodore Roosevelt's "Square Deal" and Woodrow Wilson's "New Freedom." But the decisions these two administrations won in the fields of monetary reform, government regulation of business, welfare legislation, and tariff revision stemmed from the spirit of the times. This spirit was reflected in various forms by the agitation of the Populists, the great crusade headed by William Jennings Bryan in 1896, the governmental reforms being proposed by Robert La Follette and his individualistic Wisconsin Progressives, the work of the labor-union leaders, the thinking and writing of the intellectuals, and the demands of the women's movement.

In the Roosevelt years a successful antitrust suit against the Northern Securities Company, preventing a monopoly of railroad transportation west of the Mississippi, turned the tide against extreme concentration of economic power. The Hepburn Act brought effective government regulation of transportation rates. And Roosevelt's conservation policies saved a sizable portion of America's natural resources from ruthless exploitation. In the Wilson administration the creation of the Federal Reserve banking system brought a modern currency and credit system to the country for the first time; the Clayton Act struck at the abusive use of court injunctions and contempt citations against striking labor unions; the Federal Trade Commission was given power to regulate unfair business practices; and in other areas government extended its influence to a greater degree than ever before in American history.

But the progress being made, while substantial, was often balked by the supporters of big business. Senators like Nelson Aldrich of Rhode Island were frank spokespeople for the conservative cause, and they had great influence. Congressional representatives like George Norris of Nebraska could clip the wings of House Speaker Joe Cannon, a powerful ally of the big-business forces, but they nevertheless lost many battles to their conservative opposition. William Howard Taft, succeeding Roosevelt as president, was unable to cope with the big-business elements of his Republican party, and an irate Roosevelt launched his third-party Progressive movement in 1912. His Bull Moose crusade failed, but it split the Republican party so thoroughly that Woodrow Wilson entered the White House with a minority of the popular vote to inaugurate a Democratic administration.

Many of the gains were made at state and local levels. Popular election of United States senators, presidential primaries, and adoption of the referendum, initiative, and recall were manifestations of the new trend. State laws protecting working women and children, regulating hours of work, providing for workers' compensation, and advancing social security generally ran the gauntlet of unfavorable court decisions. In the cities, reform movements led by such men as Samuel M. Jones in Toledo, Tom Johnson and Newton D. Baker in Cleveland, Seth Low in New York, and the advocates of commission government in Galveston did yeoman work in restoring government decency. Corruption in municipal councils and in state legislatures was a common mark of the times, and newspaper editors who wished to join with the reformers had almost unbelievable instances of bribe taking and graft to expose.

It should be noted that despite an increasing level of professionalism, many newspapers remained wildly partisan in their election coverage. It would be decades before reporters could claim to be detached observers.

PRESIDENTS AND THE PRESS

Relationships between earlier presidents and the press have been discussed, notably in the cases of Andrew Jackson and Abraham Lincoln. Congress did not provide funds for even a presidential private secretary until 1857; by the time of President William McKinley there was money for six assistants. One of them, George B. Cortelyou, began preparing written statements to distribute to the press. William W. Price of the *Washington Evening Star* had set up a watch outside the White House door in 1895 to interview visitors; Cortelyou moved the press to a table in the corridor near the Executive Offices. In March 1897 McKinley held an East Room reception attended by 120 correspondents. Cortelyou also arranged for a correspondents' railroad car for trips.

Theodore Roosevelt kept Cortelyou on his staff, then nominated him to the cabinet in 1903. William Loeb, Jr., became the press liaison; he shared Roosevelt's distaste for some correspondents. "TR" held informal press sessions, often on Sundays to take advantage of the dull Monday morning news flow. Correspondents who wrote stories the president disputed found themselves inducted into the "Ananias Club." But when Roosevelt built the west wing of the White House in 1904, space was provided for the press adjoining the Executive Offices. The White House Correspondents' Association was formed in 1914.

William Howard Taft was the first president to schedule regular twice-a-week press conferences. But these were soon aborted after an unfortunate session, and Taft relied on giving information to the influential correspondent of his family's *Cincinnati Times-Star.* Woodrow Wilson restored the regular press conferences, but ran them in a manner reminiscent of his professorial days. Under pressure following the sinking of the *Lusitania,* Wilson made his secretary, Joseph P. Tumulty, the news channel for the administration. Presidents Harding, Coolidge, and Hoover maintained the pattern of regular conferences, but Hoover did so only until the oncoming depression soured his press relationships.

THE WOMEN'S EQUALITY MOVEMENT

Coming to a climax in the first two decades of the twentieth century was the women's equality movement, seeking the rights of women in voting, education, and property holding. (Of course, this was just one of a whole group of reforms—including abolition, peace advocacy, and temperance—in which women were involved in the nineteenth and early twentieth centuries.)[5] The growth of women's colleges in the mid-nineteenth century and recognition of the coeducational status of state universities before the close of the century were matched much more slowly on the voting front. The 1848 women's-rights convention, held in Seneca Falls, New York, led to the founding of *The Lily* (1849 to 1859) by the local temperance society. Its editor was Amelia Bloomer (whose loose-fitting trousers worn in protest of the corset bore her name). Women's-rights leader Elizabeth Cady Stanton worked with Bloomer to make *The Lily* a women's-rights monthly with 6000 subscribers. Most famous of the feminist newspapers was Stanton's *The Revolution* (1868 to 1871), which had Susan B. Anthony as its business manager. Advocating a variety of radical causes, it drew only 3000 subscribers. Dismayed by the exclusion of women from the protection of the Fourteenth and Fifteenth amendments, Lucy Stone and other more conservative leaders formed the American Woman Suffrage Association in 1869. Its weekly, the *Woman's Journal,* focused only on the suffrage issue. It was edited by Lucy Stone until 1893, and then by her husband Henry Blackwell and daughter Alice until 1917, by which time it had 6000 readers.

By 1900 the growing number of women in business and professions had resulted in the forming of some 3300 women's clubs and groups; the *National Business Woman* began in 1919 as their federation's voice. But it was hard for the women's movement to get serious, objective coverage from male newspaper editors. The growth of the suffrage campaign led to front-page coverage of mixed support, like this headline in the *New York Press* in May 1912: "20,000 Women in Parade for Vote Cheered by Men," followed by a headline deck, "Crowd of a half million lines Fifth Avenue and shouts approval to rich women who tramp with factory workers and shop girls in pageant led by young society women on horseback, many of them riding astride." By 1917 Emma Bugbee and Eleanor Booth Simmons of the *New York Tribune* and Rheta Childe Dorr of the *New York Mail* were covering women's-movement assemblies.[6] Ratification of the Nineteenth Amendment in 1920 forbade discrimination in voting based on sex, and the movement subsided without resolution of the property-rights issue.

On balance, it should be noted that historians such as Rosalyn Terborg-Penn have come to take a more critical view of the suffrage movement, pointing out that many middle-class, white suffragists exhibited considerable class and race prejudice. Like many Progressives, their story is not straightforwardly heroic.[7]

ALTERNATIVE PRESSES: SOCIALIST

Those who found the country's newspapers too closely conforming in cultural, social, and economic outlooks attempted to publish their own alternative papers, with limited success. The Socialist labor press produced two substantial dailies, the *New York Evening Call* (1908 to 1923) and the *Milwaukee Leader* (1911 to 1942). These founding dates reflect the heyday of the Socialist Party of America in the first two decades of the twentieth century. In 1912, presidential candidate Eugene Debs polled 6 percent of the popular vote, and 79 Socialist mayors were elected in 24 states. Two million copies of 323 Socialist newspapers were circulated in 1913, by far the largest being the weekly *Appeal to Reason* (1901 to 1922), which distributed 760,000 copies by rail all over the country from its shop in Girard, Kansas. On special occasions, it also sent out bundles of papers numbering into the millions. J. A. Weyland, the founder-editor, devoted only about 20 percent of the space to Socialist theory and party activities, concentrating instead on the protest "muckraking" of the era.[8] The Yiddish-language Socialist paper *Vorwärts (Jewish Daily*

Forward), founded in 1897 in New York City, had local daily editions in 11 cities by 1923 and reached a 250,000 circulation under editor Abraham Cahan. The Communist *Daily Worker,* founded in 1924, had a 100,000 circulation in the late 1930s.

"THE PEOPLE'S CHAMPIONS"

The crusading spirit is as old as journalism, but never in American history had there been more opportunities for "the people's champions" than in the first years following 1900. Voices of protest had been raised in colonial days by people like James Franklin and Samuel Adams, in the early years of the republic by Jeffersonian and Jacksonian editors, before the Civil War by the creators of the first mass press, before the close of the century by the leaders of the "new journalism." The struggle between big business and workers and farmers was as old as the struggle between the Hamiltonians and the Jeffersonians for control of the government. The battle for the rights of labor and for a more equitable distribution of wealth was a basic issue of similar standing. And warring on corruption in city governments had been a job for conscientious newspaper people since the rise of urban life. In the ebb and flow of these contests, however, the years following 1900 became critical ones.

Some newspapers were conspicuous in their response to the challenge. So were some of the new popular magazines, which became important vehicles for those whom Teddy Roosevelt eventually termed the "muckrakers." And the school of realistic writers that flowered at the turn of the century added important books to the American literature that dealt with life and problems of the day. Joining hands with politicians and labor leaders, reformers and agitators, professors and ministers, social workers and philanthropists, the men and women of journalism and literature helped to shape the course of the great crusade.

PULITZER'S CRUSADES IN THE *WORLD*

Joseph Pulitzer and his *New York World* became increasingly effective as "people's champions" following the Spanish-American War. In foreign affairs the *World* vigorously opposed the annexation of the Philippines and the imperialism of the Caribbean policy. It continued to support the internationalist movement and the policy of peaceful arbitration of the world's problems, which it had espoused during the Venezuelan crisis. In domestic politics, the *World*'s stand on foreign policy led it to support William Jennings Bryan for president in 1900 on an "anti-imperialism" platform, while ignoring Bryan's radical monetary policies, which Pulitzer disliked.

The independent qualities and the crusading spirit of the *World* reached new heights, both on local and national issues. This was not a sudden manifestation of interest in crusading, as was the case of some other newspapers of the period, but a flowering of the Pulitzer editorial-page philosophy. Pulitzer, while agreeing that the *World* was Democrat in political sympathy, argued that his newspaper was independent of party and supported only those elements in a political party whose objectives coincided with those of the *World.* In looking at the major political parties of his day, Pulitzer put little trust in a Republican party with strong elements representing the big-business interests, although he admired and supported Republican insurgents who fought to break the power of Speaker Cannon or Republican candidates of the caliber of Governor Charles Evans Hughes of New York.

Pulitzer decided that the Democratic party best represented the political philosophy in which he believed and was most likely to act as the defender of individual liberties, grassroots government, and progressive democracy.

Part of the *World*'s new strength in its editorial columns was the result of a revamping of its editorial-page staff. In 1904 the ailing Pulitzer, tortured by the acute nervous disorders that made the last few years of his life a nightmare, found a brilliant young editor who was destined to become the central force of the *World*'s editorial page. His name was Frank I. Cobb.

Cobb was then 35, a veteran of 15 years' newspaper experience, including four years as the chief editorial writer for the *Detroit Free Press.* His somewhat limited formal education had been greatly supplemented by his scholarly interest and wide reading in history, government, and philosophy, and by his experiences as a newspaper reporter and political correspondent. Cobb had demonstrated the maturity of his judgment and his great intellectual capacity early, but he also understood human nature and attracted others to him by his friendliness, his eagerness, and his enthusiasm for living.[9] Within a year he had become recognized as the chief editorial writer and would succeed to the editorship on Pulitzer's death in 1911.

The most famous of all the *World*'s crusades began the same year, 1905. A battle had developed for control of the management of the Equitable Life Assurance Society, one of the life-insurance companies that had built up great financial resources as Americans began to purchase policies and benefits to provide for their personal and family security. Evidence was presented by two *World* reporters, David Ferguson and Louis Seibold, that officials of the company were using funds paid by policyholders for their own private investments and thereby were building huge personal fortunes—gambling with the people's money, the *World* said. Other editors, like Ervin Wardman of the *New York Press,* joined in the battle, and the spotlight was turned on the Mutual Life and New York Life companies as well.

Demand rose for an investigation by a legislative committee, whose counsel was Charles Evans Hughes, a young and forceful attorney who documented the case against the insurance companies. He also substantiated the *World*'s charges that the company had maintained a large fund of money to bribe legislators. The specter of the "money interests" dominating the life-insurance companies so aroused public opinion that strict regulatory legislation was enacted in New York State. Hughes rode into the governorship in 1906.

One other of the *World*'s crusades deserves mention. Late in 1908, Cobb wrote a lengthy editorial demanding a congressional investigation of what he called "the entire Panama Canal scandal." Cobb's ire had been aroused by "a scandalous personal attack" by President Theodore Roosevelt upon the editor of the *Indianapolis News,* who had raised questions about the Canal. Charging that Roosevelt had made "deliberate misstatements of fact," Cobb outlined a story of the needless purchase of the rights of the French company that had originally attempted to construct a canal. Roosevelt retaliated with a special message to Congress attacking Pulitzer by name and saying that the government would prosecute him for criminal libel. When the Justice Department sought indictments, they did so in federal court, claiming that newspaper copies had circulated in the West Point federal reservation. Federal judges ruled that the editors could not be forced into federal court in this manner, since the Sixth Amendment guarantees the accused the right to trial in the state or district where the crime was allegedly committed. The Supreme Court agreed, and Roosevelt dropped the suit rather than proceed in a state court. Cobb called this a sweeping victory for freedom of the press against an oppressive government. His position proved to be essentially correct. Eventually the Congress compensated Colombia for the loss of the Panama area, and in 1979 the United States returned sovereignty of the canal to the Republic of Panama.

Cobb's editorial page represented the realization of Joseph Pulitzer's hopes for the full development of the *New York World.* The editor whom Pulitzer had carefully trained before his own death in 1911 was unexcelled in his forcible expression of logically developed opinions. The *World* commanded deep respect for its intelligent and fair-minded approaches to issues of public importance, for its progressive and hard-hitting crusades that combined the reporting abilities of its news staff and the support of its editorial writers, and for its brilliant, if sometimes erratic, news play. It became one of those favorites of the press world that were called "newspapermen's newspapers."

The *World* helped to "discover" Woodrow Wilson as a presidential candidate, and Cobb and Wilson became close friends. Cobb's often-expressed fear of centralization of authority was in part overcome by his association with Wilson, and the *World* vigorously supported Wilson's far-reaching New Freedom program of economic and social reform that gave the federal government vast new powers. Cobb was one of Wilson's advisers at the Versailles peace conference, which encouraged the hopes for international cooperation that the *World* had long held. His battles in the columns of the *World* for American participation in the League of Nations and the World Court were unavailing, but they further established the paper as the leading voice of the Democratic party.

THE END OF THE *WORLD*

Tragedy struck the *New York World* in 1923, when editor Frank Cobb died at the height of his powers. Just eight years later the *World* itself succumbed, and many a sorrowing newspaper reporter muttered, "If only Cobb had lived. . . ." There probably would have been no difference in the fate of the *World,* but it was true that after Cobb's death the newspaper lacked the genius of leadership it had enjoyed since its purchase by Joseph Pulitzer in 1883.

During the middle 1920s the *World* seemed to be continuing its powerful position. Cobb had left behind a distinguished editorial-page staff, headed now by Walter Lippmann. Among the editorial writers were Maxwell Anderson and Laurence Stallings—more famous for their play, "What Price Glory"—and Charles Merz, later to become editor of the *New York Times.* Appearing on the *World*'s "op. ed." page were Heywood Broun, the liberal-thinking columnist of "It Seems to Me" fame; Franklin P. Adams, conductor of the "Conning Tower"; and Frank Sullivan, who like Anderson and Stallings moved to other creative fields. In this period Rollin Kirby, the cartoonist, won three Pulitzer Prizes for the *World.* (Pulitzer Prizes were made possible with funds from Pulitzer's will, which also provided for journalism education at Columbia University.)

Despite this brilliance and the distinguished record of the paper, Joseph Pulitzer's creation was losing the battle in New York morning journalism. The *World* failed to keep pace with its orthodox rivals in complete coverage of the news, even though it sometimes performed brilliantly, and it saw some of its subway-riding readers succumbing to the lure of the tabloids. Of the Pulitzer heirs, Joseph Pulitzer, Jr., had shown the most ability, but he had assumed control of the *St. Louis Post-Dispatch.* His brothers, Ralph and Herbert, delegated much authority to Herbert Bayard Swope as executive editor, but Swope left the *World* staff in 1928. The newspaper was already running a deficit, and in the depression year of 1930 Pulitzer losses on the morning, evening, and Sunday editions reached nearly $2 million. Then rumors of an impending sale began to be heard, and staff members made a desperate effort to raise enough cash to buy the *World* themselves. They argued, too, that the Pulitzer will forbade the sale of the paper, but in February 1931, a New York court approved its purchase by Roy W. Howard for the Scripps-Howard interests. The evening *World* was merged with the *Telegram.* The morning *World*—symbol of Pulitzer's journalistic genius—was dead, and there was scarcely a newspaperperson who did not feel that something peculiarly precious and irreplaceable had been lost to the craft.

HEARST EXPANDS HIS ROLE

While the *World* was thus rising to greatness, its chief competitor for mass circulation in New York was just as determinedly making a claim to leadership as "the people's champion." William Randolph Hearst, having seen the country start toward annexation of the Philippines and Hawaii, the development of military bases in the Caribbean, and the adoption of other nationalistic policies advocated by the *New York Journal,* turned his attention to domestic affairs. In early 1899 he set forth an editorial platform calling for the public ownership of public franchises, the "destruction of criminal trusts," a graduated income tax, the election of United States senators by popular vote rather than by state legislatures, and national, state, and local improvement of the public school system. Soon Hearst was urging that the coal mines, railroads, and telegraph lines—the symbols of the new industrial era—all be nationalized. And he gave strong encouragement to labor unions.

One example was the *Journal*'s support of striking miners in the anthracite coal fields of Pennsylvania. In September, 1897, a sheriff's posse near Lattimer fired on a parade of immigrant strikers, killing 20 and wounding scores. The sheriff and 66 deputies were charged with murder and tried in February 1898. Desperate working conditions in the mines had been worsened by the importation of Eastern European immigrants, often single, who were regarded by native-born Americans as a threat both to wage levels and cultural standards. Hearst argued that society would be overturned if justice was not given to the workers. Calling the sheriff and his deputies murderers acting for the mine owners, in 24 February issues the *Evening Journal* ran 23 news stories, 8 editorials, and 9 cartoons. Play diminished only after the sinking of the battleship *Maine.* But when the nonimmigrant jury found the defendants innocent, Hearst advised the miners to seek redress without violence. In the bitter anthracite coal-field strikes of 1900 and 1902, the Hearst papers continued their all-out attacks upon the mine owners and their support of the workers.

Not only was this a more radical program than that of the *World* and other liberal newspapers of the day, but the impact of Hearst's editorial technique was also bitter and extreme. In the presidential campaign of 1900, Homer Davenport's cartoons depicting President McKinley as the stooge of a Mark Hanna wearing a suit made of dollar signs were crude but effective. Hanna, a wealthy Ohio politician, had groomed McKinley for public office. When President McKinley was fatally wounded by an anarchist with a copy of the *Journal* in his pocket in September 1901, the Hearst paper's continual assaults on McKinley were recalled. Hearst found it wise to change the name of his morning New York paper to the *American.* But the incident was to haunt him for the rest of his life.

Hearst now sought to advance his political beliefs by seeking office himself. He served two terms in Congress from a Democratic district in New York City from 1903 to 1907, but his eye was on the White House. His high point came in 1904, when 204 delegates cast votes for him in the Democratic national convention (Judge Alton B. Parker, the successful nominee, received 658). The next year Hearst ran as an independent candidate for mayor of New York but lost by some 3500 votes as the result of Tammany's counting him out at the ballot boxes.

This was a notable achievement, and Hearst decided to make the race for the New York governorship in 1906 a stepping-stone to the White House. He won the Democratic nomination in convention but found himself up against Charles Evans Hughes in the November election. Theodore Roosevelt's close associate, Elihu Root, recalled the McKinley assassination episode in a public speech; the *World* and other New York newspapers turned against Hearst, as did Tammany, which he had challenged the year before. Hughes won by 60,000 votes—the only Republican to be elected that year in the statewide balloting—and Hearst's political star had set.

In his political races and in his newspapers, Hearst was making a heavy play for the support of workers, small businessowners, and other ordinary people. His slashing attacks on the "criminal trusts"—the ice trust, the coal trust, the gas trust—and crooked political bosses found favor with those who had grievances against the established order. His forthright support of the labor unions won him the backing of the American Federation of Labor. And the popularized content of his newspapers appealed to the mass of readers. Emphasis on sensational crime and vice stories, human-interest features, pictures and cartoons, and readable typographical display helped draw crowds of new readers to Hearst papers. But despite the following that Hearst had attracted, there was widespread doubting of his journalistic and political motives by the intellectual leaders of the time.[10]

New publishing ventures brought Hearst to the attention of four more large cities in the first few years of the twentieth century. To his *San Francisco Examiner, New York American,* and *New York Evening Journal,* Hearst added eight more papers, which put him in the business of group publishing. In Chicago, the evening *American* was begun in 1900 and the morning *Examiner* in 1902. Boston saw the birth of an evening *American* in 1904, to which Hearst added the century-old *Daily Advertiser* in 1917 and the *Record* in 1920. Hearst also bought Atlanta's *Georgian* in 1912 and the *San Francisco Call* in 1913. Los Angeles was invaded in 1903 with the founding of the morning *Examiner.* The Los Angeles entry was welcomed by local labor unions, which were engaged in a bitter fight with the antilabor *Los Angeles Times.* Hearst rode in a parade between two labor leaders to open the head-on contest with the *Times.*

In the first issue of the *Los Angeles Examiner,* the editors advertised their wares. They listed the Hearst writers: Ella Wheeler Wilcox, "world famous poet and essayist"; Mrs. John A. Logan, wife of a general and writer "on behalf of the American home and American womanhood"; Professor Garrett Serviss, noted astronomer; Dorothy Dix, whose name is the first one recognizable nine decades later; Ambrose Bierce, a truly great writer. The editorial page, the ad said, has "thought-stirring editorials which have done so much to mold public thought in this country." Editorial-page cartoonists listed were Opper, Powers, Davenport, and Howarth; comics included the Katzenjammer Kids and Childe Harold. And, said the editors, "There is nothing in the newspaper world like the magazine section of the Hearst newspapers." Within a month the Examiner claimed 32,500 readers, and it remained a strong paper for half a century.[11]

SCRIPPS AND HIS "PEOPLE'S PAPERS"

Another type of "people's paper" was emerging, meanwhile, under the direction of Edward Wyllis Scripps, the Illinois farm boy who had successfully started the first of his many Scripps newspapers by the time he was 24. Scripps got his start in the Middle West at the moment when Pulitzer was achieving his first success in St. Louis, and when Stone was succeeding in Chicago and Nelson in Kansas City. The *Detroit News,* on which Scripps had served his apprenticeship under his brother James, had been one of the early practitioners of the new journalism. His own first two papers, the *Cleveland Press* and the *Cincinnati Post,* were low-priced afternoon dailies that appealed to the mass of readers (see pages 164–165 for a discussion of Scripps's early career).

But unlike Pulitzer and Hearst, who sought giant circulations in big cities, Scripps set his sights on the working people in the smaller but growing industrial cities of the country. For them he published brightly written, easily read newspapers, small in size but big in heart. Closely edited news, human-interest features, fearless news coverage, local crusades, and hard-fighting independent editorial opinion constituted the Scripps formula.

What made Scripps a distinctive leader as a "people's champion" was his conception of his responsibility to the working people. "The first of my principles," Scripps said, "is that I have constituted myself the advocate of that large majority of people who are not so rich in worldly goods and native intelligence as to make them equal, man for man, in the struggle with individuals of the wealthier and more intellectual class."[12] Scripps viewed his newspapers as the only "schoolroom" the working people had. He believed that nearly all other newspapers were capitalistic and opposed to the working class or else too intellectual in appeal, and he said sadly that the educational system was a failure in its service to his "large majority." So he sought to drive home through his editorial columns the necessity for labor-union organization and collective bargaining as the first prerequisites to a better life for the poor and ill-informed. Scripps was the first to admit that his papers did not always maintain the noble objectives he set for them and that they sometimes made mistakes in "always opposing the rich, always supporting the working man." But Scripps believed that if he kept the focus on such a basic policy he would further the long-range pattern of society that he hoped would emerge.

Above all, the Scripps newspapers reflected a "spirit of protest" that was inherent in the character of their owner-editor. Scripps declared that he protested against everything; his motto was "Whatever is, is wrong." He protested against antiquated governmental systems, against undemocratic political actions, against usurpation of power and prestige by the rich and the intellectuals, against inequality of opportunity, against all sorts of authority in religion and law and politics except that exercised for the benefit of humanity, against corruption, against the power of business interests. He pictured himself as a "damned old crank" who was in rebellion against society. But actually he was seeking to build a progressive democracy, and he was enough of a capitalist to urge the worker to better himself or herself by increasing production and thereby adding to the wealth to be distributed.

Scripps started his newspaper career with an investment of $600 in one share of stock in the *Detroit News.* With the help of his sister Ellen and his brothers James and George, he started the *Cleveland Press* in 1878. In 1883, with an income of $10,000 a year, Scripps turned to Cincinnati and took over management of a struggling penny paper that became the *Post.*

These were the formative years of the Scripps newspaper empire. In Cleveland Scripps found an editor, Robert F. Paine, who for more than 30 years was a leader in editorial policy making. In Cincinnati Scripps found a business manager, Milton A. McRae. In 1889 Scripps and McRae formed the Scripps-McRae League of Newspapers. McRae was to be the speechmaker, the front man, the operations chief. Scripps was to set policy and live as he pleased on a California ranch. And in 1890, at age 36, Scripps did "retire" to a great ranch near San Diego, named Miramar, where he lived a burly life, wearing ranch clothes and cowhide boots, playing poker, drinking whiskey, and smoking innumerable cigars. At Miramar, too, he kept in close touch through correspondence and conferences with his principal editors and managers. There he lived to the age of 71, building himself a fortune of some $50 million.

The Scripps plan for expansion was simple. He and McRae looked for a growing industrial city, usually fairly small and with stodgy newspaper opposition. They put up a few thousand dollars and sent a young, ambitious editor and a business manager off to start a paper. If the young journalists succeeded, they could obtain as much as 49 percent of the stock; if they faltered, new faces replaced them. If the paper failed to make a profit within 10 years, it was abandoned as a failure. As a result of this policy, Scripps papers had a good many employee-stockholders, but they also paid the usual low journalistic salaries of the times to those who were not so blessed. In this respect, Scripps was typically capitalistic in his publishing behavior.

Since the Scripps papers were low-cost afternoon dailies that relied principally on circulation revenue, they had to be edited carefully. Scripps saved newsprint costs by insisting on small headlines and short, concise stories. Saving those extra words so that a Scripps newspaper would be packed with the most news possible became a fine art for Scripps newspeople. Word economy also meant that after the essential news had been told there would be plenty of space for editorial opinion and features.

By 1911 the Scripps-McRae League included 18 papers in Ohio, Indiana, Tennessee, Iowa, Colorado, Oklahoma, and Texas. Meanwhile, Scripps himself was building his own chain of West Coast newspapers. He started by buying the *San Diego Sun* in 1893, and in the next 15 years opened up shop in 10 other West Coast cities. But here, in an only slightly industrialized West, the Scripps record was extremely poor. Only the *San Francisco News* eventually emerged as a strong unit in the Scripps chain. The *Los Angeles Record* and four Pacific Northwest papers seceded from the parent Scripps organization after a quarrel between Scripps and his son James in 1920, and formed the basis for the Scripps League.

Scripps tried another experiment in 1911, when he established in Chicago an adless tabloid named the *Day Book*. Negley D. Cochran was the editor, and the poet Carl Sandburg was the chief reporter. The little paper, which represented Scripps's fondest dream, reached a circulation of 25,000 and was within $500 a month of breaking even when the rising newsprint costs of the first year of World War I, 1917, caused its suspension. A second adless paper, the *Philadelphia News-Post,* started in 1912 but also failed.

Through the years the Scripps papers continued to fight for the right of workers to organize. They crusaded for public ownership and against utility abuses. They attacked political bossism and corruption. They supported Theodore Roosevelt's reforms and his third-party candidacy. And they backed Woodrow Wilson's "New Freedom" and his reelection campaign. In appearance and in content they were closer to being labor papers than any other general circulation newspapers, yet they also won the support of the intellectual liberals whom Scripps sometimes tried to avoid.

WHITE AND THE *EMPORIA GAZETTE*

While publishers like Scripps and Adolph Ochs of the *New York Times* were guiding their newspapers in a relatively impersonal fashion, a small-town Kansas editor was making a highly personal impact on American society. William Allen White was born in Emporia, Kansas, in 1868 and died there in 1944. But between those years he became a citizen of all of the United States and a spokesman for its small towns—of which Emporia became the symbol. The editor of the *Emporia Gazette* was anything but a typical representative of the personal, open approach to journalism. His newspaper editorship was the foundation for his larger activities, first as a conservative, then as a reformer.

White worked as a printer and reporter while he was at the University of Kansas. At 24, he was an editorial writer for William Rockhill Nelson's *Kansas City Star.* He scraped together $3000 by 1895 and bought the *Emporia Gazette,* a rundown Populist party paper with fewer than 600 subscribers. But William Allen White, age 27, was home in Emporia with his wife, Sallie, to stay.

Kansas had been captured during the 1893 depression by the Populists and the Democrats. White was an active Republican editor and politician; he loved politics all his life, and remained a party worker and an intimate of politicians from the time of William McKinley and Theodore Roosevelt to the days of Wendell Willkie and Franklin Roosevelt. On August 15, 1896, White exploded with anger at the Populists in an editorial that shot him into national fame. It was "What's the Matter with Kansas?" which White later referred to as representing "conservatism in its full and perfect flower." The editorial cited evidence that Kansas was declining in population and economic standing, and placed the blame in a fully unrestrained and effective style on the "shabby, wild-eyed, rattle-brained fanatics" of the reform movement.[13] It was reprinted in virtually every Republican newspaper in the country as ammunition against the Democratic candidate for president, William Jennings Bryan. William McKinley's campaign manager, Mark Hanna, adopted the young editor. But Bryan and the Democrats won the election in Kansas.

White now moved to the national stage. He became the friend of political leaders and came to know the young New York Republican Theodore Roosevelt, to whom he

William Allen White

(Emporia Gazette)

became deeply attached and who was his lifelong political hero. More importantly, he met magazine publisher S. S. McClure and became a member of his circle of muckrakers that included Lincoln Steffens, Ray Stannard Baker, John Phillips, and Ida M. Tarbell. White's articles and stories about Kansas and politics appeared in several magazines. White was now in tune with the times, hobnobbing with the muckrakers and becoming, with his wife, a frequent visitor at the Oyster Bay home of the Theodore Roosevelts. The *Emporia Gazette* began to demand reforms: conservation of natural resources, railroad rate control, workers' compensation, direct primaries, the initiative and referendum, the abolition of child labor.

When Roosevelt split with William Howard Taft in 1912 and the Progressive party was formed, White was the Kansas national committee member for the new third party. He was a supporter of the League of Nations—an internationalist in isolationist territory—and when World War II came, he was a leader in the Committee to Defend America by Aiding the Allies. He admired the social gains of the New Deal, but he preferred the leadership of Theodore Roosevelt to that of Franklin Roosevelt.

Another of America's distinctive small-town editors also lived and worked in Kansas. He was Ed Howe, who, at the age of 22 in 1877, founded the daily *Atchison Globe* with $200 capital. Howe was a superlative reporter. He knew people and how to report their little doings. However, he had none of White's expansiveness and sentimentality but rather an amazing ability to make trouble for himself. He told the people of Kansas that religion was all bosh, and he asserted in a time of agitation for women's rights that a woman's place was strictly in the home. His terse, sardonic editorial paragraphs often reflected a keen understanding of human nature, however, and they were widely requoted in the country's newspapers as the work of the "Sage of Potato Hill." His excellent novel, *The Story of a Country Town,* added to his fame.

OTHER NEWSPAPER CRUSADERS

Pulitzer, Hearst, and Scripps were far from being the only champions of the common people among newspaper publishers and editors around the turn of the century. Nor can all those who opposed the business trusts, who fought against one-sided public-utilities franchises, who exposed political inadequacy and corruption, be listed. However, some idea of the contributions made by newspaperpeople can be gained by a look across the country.[14]

One battle against a tightly run political machine was that waged by Charles H. Grasty, editor of the *Baltimore Evening News,* and by the *Baltimore Sun.* Grasty had exposed the policy racket in Baltimore despite a criminal libel charge brought by his political opponents. When in 1895 the *Sun* broke with its Democratic party traditions and attacked Senator Arthur P. Gorman's state Democratic machine, Grasty pitched in to help oust the Gorman group. As a result Maryland elected its first Republican administration since the Civil War, and Gorman lost his Senate seat for one term.

Across the country the spectacular but contradictory career of Fremont Older was unfolding in San Francisco. Older, a typical roving newspaperperson in his early years, settled down as managing editor of the *Bulletin* in 1895. He built the struggling evening sheet into a fairly substantial paper by his sensational methods and then decided to join the solid civic leader, the *San Francisco Chronicle,* in its fights against city machine politics. The target was a Union-Labor party headed by Mayor Eugene E. Schmitz and a political boss, Abram Ruef. Older stepped out of his role as a newspaperperson to become a civic reform leader, and his dominating personality made him the rallying point for the public-spirited of the city. The reform group brought Schmitz and Ruef to court on indictments for accepting payoffs from houses of prostitution and had Ruef sent to prison. Others involved escaped conviction, despite the work of prosecutors Francis J. Heney (who was shot and critically wounded in the courtroom) and Hiram W. Johnson. Older's last great crusade was in behalf of Tom Mooney, who Older eventually decided had been unjustly convicted of the Preparedness Day bombing in San Francisco in 1916. Breaking with the *Bulletin* management on the Mooney issue, Older joined Hearst's *Call* as editor in 1918, saw it become the *Call-Bulletin* in 1929, and died in 1935 before Mooney won his freedom.

Older had been kidnapped and nearly killed during the height of the San Francisco trials. In South Carolina, an editor was assassinated—N. G. Gonzales of the *Columbia State*—in 1903. Gonzales was one of three brothers who battled against political boss Ben Tillman with their newspaper, founded in 1893. The paper continued to exert leadership, however, calling for compulsory public education and opposing child labor and "lynch law."

A less spectacular, but solid, champion of decency was Josephus Daniels of North Carolina, who became editor of the *State Chronicle* in Raleigh in 1885. The paper was a weekly, started by Walter Hines Page two years before. In his first few years in Raleigh, Daniels campaigned against the Southern Railway and its attempt to extend its control over other lines. He advocated a state public-school fund as a means of equalizing educational opportunity, urged financial support of the state university, supported the establishment of teacher-training colleges, and argued for compulsory education as a means of overcoming illiteracy. When the American Tobacco Company was organized by the Duke family in 1890, he began his long campaign against the "tobacco trust."

(*The News & Observer,* Raleigh, NC)

Josephus Daniels

(*Chicago Tribune*)

Joseph Medill

The established daily in Raleigh was the *News and Observer.* Daniels obtained control of it in 1895 and built it into one of the South's leading newspapers. A fervent supporter of the Democratic party, he campaigned for Bryan in his three races for the presidency and backed Woodrow Wilson with full enthusiasm. When Wilson made him Secretary of the Navy in 1913, Daniels's political career was under way.

In Chicago, the *Tribune* that Joseph Medill had built enjoyed a varied record. In the last years of Medill's editorship, before his death in 1899, the *Tribune* was strongly nationalistic in foreign policy and generally conservative in its outlook. It fought the liberal Illinois governor, John P. Altgeld, and bitterly attacked the Eugene Debs–led Chicago labor unions. But the *Tribune* vigorously crusaded against utility and street-railway franchise grabs, and used John T. McCutcheon's front-page cartoons with effectiveness after the artist transferred from the *Record* to the *Tribune* in 1903.

James Keeley, the *Tribune*'s outstanding managing editor, helped develop one of the state's biggest exposés in 1910, when the paper published evidence that William Lorimer had won election to the U.S. Senate by bribing state legislators. Despite the evidence Keeley had obtained, it took two years of campaigning by the *Tribune* and the *Record-Herald* before Lorimer was ousted from the Senate.

THE MAGAZINES: AN ERA OF MUCKRAKING

Highly important as "people's champions" were the magazines that, in the dozen years after 1900, developed a literature of exposure that Theodore Roosevelt dubbed the work of the "muckrakers." Roosevelt used the expression in a derogatory sense, comparing the more sensational writers to the Man with the Muckrake in *Pilgrim's Progress,* who did not look up to see the celestial crown but continued to rake the filth. The reformers, however, came to accept the designation as a badge of honor, and in the history of American magazines the period is known as "the era of the muckrakers."[15]

When in 1893 three new popular magazines—*McClure's, Cosmopolitan,* and *Munsey's*—cut their prices to a dime, their circulation figures started to climb. After the turn of the century these magazines and such others as the *Ladies' Home Journal, Collier's, Everybody's,* and the *Saturday Evening Post* had circulations running into the hundreds of thousands. Most of them joined with great enthusiasm in the crusade against big business and corruption, and for social justice. Their writers, who came largely from newspaper ranks, had national audiences for articles that sometimes were drawn from the stories published by crusading newspapers in various cities. However the articles were obtained, the magazines performed the service of coordinating and interpreting information about social, economic, and political problems for a nationwide audience.

Touching off the muckraking era was S. S. McClure, whose magazine began three significant series of articles in late 1902. McClure, who had founded a newspaper feature syndicate in 1884 and attracted readers and writers to his service, invaded the magazine field in 1893 with a low-priced but unspectacular product filled with interesting and timely articles and literary material. He and his associate editor, John S. Phillips, had selected a staff of talented and responsible writers to handle the nonfiction section of *McClure's.* One was Ida M. Tarbell, whose specialties were biographies and research work. Another was Lincoln Steffens, former reporter for the *Evening Post* and city editor of the *Commercial Advertiser* in New York, who was to become one of the country's most famous crusading liberals. A third was Ray Stannard Baker, who came to *McClure's* from the *Chicago Record* in 1897 and was later to achieve fame as Woodrow Wilson's biographer. Beginning in late 1902 Tarbell exposed the business practices of John D. Rockefeller and the

Standard Oil Company; Steffens opened his attack on corruption in city and state governments; and Baker began discussing the problems of working people. The circulation of *McClure's* mounted past the half-million mark, and the muckraking trend in magazine editing was in full swing.

What McClure was doing was not entirely new to the magazine field. The older magazines of high quality—*Harper's, Scribner's,* the *Century,* and the *Atlantic Monthly*—had paid some attention to current affairs, although they were primarily literary in tone. There were several journals of opinion that had relatively small but influential audiences: Godkin's *Nation,* Albert Shaw's *Review of Reviews,* Lyman Abbott's *Outlook,* the *North American Review,* the *Forum,* and the *Independent.* In the same class but taking an early leadership in crusading for socioeconomic and political reform was Benjamin O. Flower's *Arena.* These magazines and others were giving attention to the rising business trusts, graft, and political machines, but it was *McClure's* that first made a frontal assault of real magnitude.

Tarbell's "History of the Standard Oil Company" ran in *McClure's* until 1904, and her detailed, thoroughly documented account of the unfair business practices used by the company to squeeze out competitors put Rockefeller on the defensive for many years to come. Steffens began his series on "The Shame of the Cities" by recounting the situation in St. Louis that had first been exposed by the *Post-Dispatch,* and followed up with reports on corrupt government in Minneapolis, Pittsburgh, Philadelphia, Chicago, New York, and other cities. George Kibbe Turner, an alumnus of the *Springfield Republican,* continued the city series later in the decade. Baker dealt with labor problems, including child labor and the economic status of the blacks. Other contributors to *McClure's* included Barton J. Hendrick, who wrote about the New York life-insurance companies, and Kansas editor William Allen White. Newspaper reporter Will Irwin served as managing editor and editor in 1906–7.

Cosmopolitan joined the muckrakers when the magazine passed from John Brisben Walker to Hearst by running the series "The Treason of the Senate," which appeared in 1906. The author was David Graham Phillips, one of Pulitzer's editorial writers on the *World* staff who retired from newspaper work to write a series of books examining problems of his time. Phillips denounced a score of conservative senators—both Republican and Democrat—as spokespeople of "the interests." Among other prominent muckrakers, Alfred Henry Lewis attacked the International Harvester Company in *Cosmopolitan* and followed up with a series examining the careers of America's leading millionaires. Charles Edward Russell, who had been managing editor of the *Minneapolis Journal* at 21 and who had worked for several New York and Chicago newspapers, surveyed the weaknesses of state governments in a 1910 series.

Active in the fray, too, was *Everybody's,* founded in 1899 and edited by John O'Hara Cosgrave. When in 1904 it persuaded a colorful Wall Street financier, Thomas W. Lawson, to write "Frenzied Finance," the public appetite for Lawson's inside information drove the magazine's circulation from 200,000 to 735,000 within a year. Less important, but influential, were *Pearson's, Hampton's* (which built a readership of 440,000 in the years 1907 to 1911), and *La Follette's Weekly,* the voice of the Wisconsin Progressives.

Taking the lead from *McClure's* in muckraking after 1905 was *Collier's.* Published by Robert J. Collier and edited by Norman Hapgood, the magazine developed an effective editorial voice in national political affairs. Its articles ranged over many social and economic problems, but it caught popular attention for a series of articles by Samuel Hopkins Adams on the patent-medicine trade. Called "The Great American Fraud," and published in 1905 and 1906, Adams's articles exposed the false claims of many of the popular "cure-alls" and

McClure's Magazine

VOL. XX   *JANUARY, 1903*   NO. 3

THE SHAME OF MINNEAPOLIS

The Rescue and Redemption of a City that was Sold Out

BY LINCOLN STEFFENS

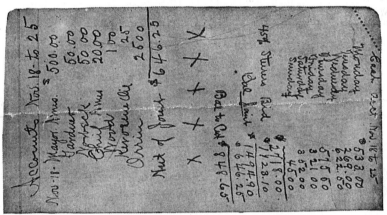

FAC-SIMILE OF THE FIRST PAGE OF "THE BIG MITT LEDGER"

An account kept by a swindler of the dealings of his "Joint" with City Officials, showing first payments made to Mayor Ames, his brother, the Chief of Police and Detectives. This book figured in trials and newspaper reports of the exposure, but was "lost"; and its whereabouts was the mystery of the proceedings. This is the first glimpse that any one, except "Cheerful Charlie" Howard, who kept it, and members of the grand jury, has had of the book

WHENEVER anything extraordinary is done in American municipal politics, whether for good or for evil, you can trace it almost invariably to one man. The people do not do it. Neither do the "gangs," "combines," or political parties. These are but instruments by which bosses (not leaders; we Americans are not led, but driven) rule the people, and commonly sell them out. But there are at least two forms of the autocracy which has supplanted the democracy here as it has everywhere it has been tried. One is that of the organized majority by which, as in Tammany Hall in New York and the Republican machine in Philadelphia, the boss has normal control of more than half the voters. The other is that of the adroitly managed minority. The "good people" are herded into parties and stupefied with convictions and a name, Republican or Democrat; while the "bad people" are so organized or interested by the boss that he can wield their votes to enforce terms with party managers and decide elections. St. Louis is a conspicuous example of this form. Minneapolis is another. Colonel Ed. Butler is the unscrupulous opportunist who handled the non-partisan minority which turned St. Louis into a "boodle town." In Minneapolis "Doc" Ames was the man.

One of the articles that made *McClure's* the leading muckraking magazine demonstrated that some of the patent medicines contained poisonous ingredients. Equally prominent in the attack on the patent-medicine business was Edward W. Bok, editor of the *Ladies' Home Journal.* It was Bok who shocked his women readers by proving that Lydia E. Pinkham, to whom American women were supposed to write for advice, had been dead for 22 years.

The attack on the patent medicines coincided with a drive against adulterated foods and unsanitary practices in packing plants. Under the leadership of Dr. Harvey H. Wiley, chief chemist of the Department of Agriculture, federal and state officials had proved the widespread adulteration of food and the addition of chemicals and artificial dyes by food manufacturers. But the lid was blown off when Upton Sinclair wrote *The Jungle* in 1906, a novel intended to portray the plight of immigrant workers in Chicago's packing houses, but which was terrifying in its charges of unsanitary practices.

Passage of the Pure Food and Drugs Act of 1906 was the outcome. This regulated the activities of manufacturers, but the problem of "truth in advertising" remained. Some newspapers had obtained testimonials from readers, extolling the virtues of the medicines, and had run them in their news columns. This use of "readers," as they were called, had also been extended to cover publicity stories paid for by the column inch. As the campaign for "truth in advertising" grew, newspaperpeople cooperated. State laws making untruthful, deceptive, or misleading advertising statements a misdemeanor were adopted after the trade publication *Printers' Ink* drafted a model statute in 1911, and the federal Newspaper Publicity Law of 1912 required that all matter published for money should be marked "Advertisement."

Other magazines should be noted. One was the *American Magazine,* purchased in 1906 by a group of *McClure's* writers. A disagreement in policy led John S. Phillips, associate editor of *McClure's,* to leave its staff. He took with him Tarbell, Steffens, Baker, William Allen White, and Finley Peter Dunne, "Mr. Dooley." These were the leaders of the muckrakers, and for a few years they constituted a distinguished editorial board for the *American.* The high point of muckraking had been reached in 1906, but liberal insurgency continued, climaxed in 1912 by Theodore Roosevelt's third-party candidacy and Woodrow Wilson's election as president. The *New Republic* began its career in 1914 under editor Herbert Croly, whose *The Promise of American Life* (1909) became a creed for Wilsonian liberals. Croly and staff member Walter Lippmann supported Wilson in wartime. *The Masses,* which was edited by Max Eastman and was a brilliant voice of protest from 1911 to 1917, when its pacifist-socialist line led to wartime persecution and demise, did not. Among its contributors were Lippmann, Carl Sandburg, Sherwood Anderson, and cartoonist Art Young.

THE AGE OF REALISM

Playing a role, too, in the quest for social justice were a group of American writers. William Dean Howells and Henry James had pointed the way toward the realistic novel. Joining them in this movement were novelist Stephen Crane and short-story writers Ambrose Bierce and Hamlin Garland. Of the same school were poets Walt Whitman and Emily Dickinson. From this literary heritage, and from the pressure of the times, came a flowering of realism in literature after 1900.

Californian Frank Norris contributed two volumes of a planned trilogy on the "Epic of Wheat" before his career was cut short by death at 32. His *The Octopus,* which appeared in 1901, told the story of the struggle of California farmers against the power of the Southern Pacific Railroad. His protest against Chicago wheat speculators, *The Pit,* made an equally deep impression. In his stories of adventure and raw, brutal experience another Californian, Jack London, captured a full expression of the rising protest against the capitalistic system. London's *The Iron Heel,* published in 1907, and Upton Sinclair's *The Jungle* were high points in relentless realism. So were Theodore Dreiser's *Sister Carrie* (1900), which was at first suppressed by a frightened publisher, and his later books, *The Financier* (1912) and *The Titan* (1914).

More Americans, it is true, were reading historical novels, adventure stories, and popular favorites like *David Harum* and *Mrs. Wiggs of the Cabbage Patch* than were reading the works of Norris, Sinclair, London, and Dreiser. More Americans, too, were reading fiction in *Munsey's* and the *Saturday Evening Post* than were reading the exposés by Lincoln Steffens, Ida M. Tarbell, and Samuel Hopkins Adams. And among newspaper readers, relatively few were absorbing the editorial arguments of Edward Wyllis Scripps, Joseph Pulitzer, and their contemporaries of equal stature. Still, at a critical moment in American history, when an arousing of public opinion was needed to ensure economic and political progress and a more equitable social pattern, journalism and literature played their part and produced effective leaders.

THE GROWTH OF THE ETHNIC PRESS

Foreign-language publications, which were nearly all in German or French before the Civil War, numbered 300 in 1860, 800 in 1880, and 1200 in 1910. A peak of 1323 ethnic papers was reached in 1917. By the 1970s this had dropped to fewer than 1,000. The German press, beginning in 1732 in Pennsylvania, peaked at 750 publications in 1890, declined to 627 in 1910, and was cut by the impact of war to 258 by 1920. In 1910 the most numerous ethnic papers besides the German ones, by language, were Scandinavian (132), Italian (73), Spanish (58), and Polish (48).

Foreign-language dailies peaked at 160 in 1914; one-third were German (55). Others were French, Italian, and Polish (12 each); Yiddish and Japanese (10 each); Spanish and Bohemian (8 each); and Chinese (5).[16] These dailies circulated a total of 2.6 million copies in 1914, with the German press totaling 823,000 and the Yiddish, 762,000. The largest foreign-language daily was the *New Yorker Staats-Zeitung,* dating from 1845, with a top circulation of 250,000. Its owner, Herman Ridder, was elected a president of the American Newspaper Publishers Association.

The first Jewish publication in the United States, *The Jew,* was founded as a monthly in 1823 by Solomon Henry Jackson, New York's first Jewish printer. Robert Lyon began the first English-language Jewish weekly in New York, the *Asmonean,* in 1849. The Jewish press nurtured immigrants, defended the faith, and defined Jewish identity in its battle with assimilation.[17] The first American newspaper printed in Arabic, *Kawkab America* (Star of America), appeared in 1892 and lasted until 1909. The first Asian newspaper in the United States was San Francisco's *Golden Hills News,* published in 1854 by Methodist missionaries recently returned from China. The Chinese pages of this bilingual paper carried news from China, while an English-language section was used primarily to urge fairness for the Chinese immigrants.

While much of the foreign-language press served immigrants in the bigger cities, the southwestern states developed a distinctive ethnic press serving a native minority population. Close to 150 Spanish-language periodicals were established in that region between 1846 and 1900, with the largest numbers in New Mexico, Texas, and California. The most diverse press was in California, where in the 1870s the editors of Spanish-language papers included *Californios* (native-born Californians of Hispanic descent) as well as journalists from Spain, Mexico, Chile, and Colombia. Spanish-language sections in English papers were maintained throughout the area. Some served as instruments of social control of a minority, while others advocated activism and reflected Hispanic culture.

El Clamor Público (1855 to 1859) was outspoken against mob violence in Los Angeles; *La Crónica* continued the fight in the 1870s. *El Fronterizo* of Tucson urged a boycott of hostile merchants in the 1880s. *El Gato* of Sante Fe urged working-class unity against low pay in 1894, and *El Tiempo* of Las Cruces agitated for New Mexican statehood against anti-Hispanic roadblock tactics.[18] There were 49 Spanish-language publications in the entire country in 1890, 58 in 1910, and 95 in 1920. Together the 8 dailies listed in 1914 had only a 28,000 circulation. But the impact of such ethnic presses was strong among readers, and the general press reflected some of their news and views.

THE BLACK PRESS GROWS

One group of Americans who found little to represent their aspirations and interests in the mass media was the black population. Not until the 1950s did the average American newspaper or magazine exhibit an understanding interest in the black 10 percent of the population, and even then few were sensitive to them as readers. There was a clear need for a black press, but little economic support from a black community with few socio-economic resources. Nevertheless, the black press that had begun in 1827 survived and gained in stature (see pages 126–130 for a discussion of the founding of the black press).

More than 3000 black newspapers—owned and edited by blacks for black readers—have appeared since *Freedom's Journal* made its 1827 bow. The best historical statistics were gathered by Professor Armistead Scott Pride of Lincoln University for his 1951 doctoral dissertation. Pride's figures showed that 1187 black papers were added during the years 1865 to 1900 to the 40 founded before 1865. Another 1500 had been added by 1951, but the survivors numbered only 175. The average life span of a black newspaper, Pride found, was nine years.[19] He gave several reasons for the increase in black papers beginning in the mid-1880s: increased educational opportunities for blacks, support of black papers by religious and welfare groups working in the South, establishment of political sheets for enfranchised blacks, and growth of urban black communities that could support papers.

Just as the standard daily press grew in numbers, circulation, and stature during the era of new journalism between 1880 and World War I, so did the black press. Among today's leaders that have founding dates in that period are the *Philadelphia Tribune* (1884), Baltimore's *Afro-American* (1892), the *Chicago Defender* (1905), New York's *Amsterdam News* (1909), Norfolk's *Journal and Guide* (1909), and the *Pittsburgh Courier* (1910). Historically important from that period are the *New York Age* (1890), *Boston Guardian* (1901), and *The Crisis* (1910).

Ranking in fame with Frederick Douglass and his *North Star* of 1847 are W. E. B. Du Bois and his *The Crisis* of 1910. Other major figures in black publishers' ranks before 1910 included John H. Murphy, Sr., of the *Afro-American* papers, T. Thomas Fortune of the *New York Age,* William Monroe Trotter of the *Boston Guardian,* Robert S. Abbott of the *Chicago Defender,* and Robert L. Vann of the *Pittsburgh Courier.* Their stories, and those of other major black papers, follow.[20]

The semiweekly *Philadelphia Tribune,* which celebrated its centennial in 1984, is the oldest continuously published black newspaper in the United States. Founded by Chris J. Perry, Sr., it became one of the most substantial and best-edited black weeklies. Perry's widow and two daughters continued the *Tribune* after his death in 1921. A son-in-law, E. Washington Rhodes, was publisher and editor until he died in 1970. Criticizing the more affluent blacks for not doing enough to help the poor, the *Tribune* organized charities and scholarship programs as a part of its community responsibility.

The first prominent black woman journalist and editor was Ida B. Wells-Barnett, who during her public career (1887 to 1931) was known as a feminist reformer and race leader, but was essentially a journalist. As co-owner and editor of *Free Speech* in Memphis, she was so determined and aggressive, particularly about the prevalence of lynchings, that the paper was mobbed in 1892. She then worked for the *New York Age* and the weekly *Conservator* in Chicago. She continued to press on racial issues as a journalist and reform leader throughout her career.

John H. Murphy, Sr., is regarded as the founder of the *Afro-American* editions, four regional and one national, centered in Baltimore. Murphy, who did whitewashing for a living and was the superintendent of an African Methodist church Sunday school, began publishing a small paper for the church in his basement. When a Baptist minister, the Reverend William M. Alexander, began another religious paper, the *Afro-American,* in 1892, Murphy gained control of it. The paper gained a national reputation before 1920. Murphy wrote a credo that year calling for the *Afro-American* to keep faith with the common people, to fight to get rid of slums and to provide jobs for all, and to "stay out of politics except to expose corruption and condemn injustice, race prejudice and the cowardice of compromise." The credo still appears in his newspapers, which were continued after his death in 1922 by his son, Dr. Carl J. Murphy.

T. Thomas Fortune was one of the best-known black editors at the turn of the century, and his *New York Age* won national attention. Born to slave parents, Fortune ran errands for a southern newspaper, learned to set type, and entered New York journalism through the back shops. In 1879 a black tabloid named *Rumor* was changed to standard size by George Parker and renamed the *New York Globe;* Fortune and W. Walter Sampson were the printing crew and became Parker's partners. Within a decade Fortune was the principal figure, and the paper had become the *Age.* As its editorial writer, Fortune was quoted by the nation's press and was read by political leaders, including Theodore Roosevelt. Booker T. Washington selected the *Age* as the national voice for the blacks and began to subsidize it. This won the disapproval of W. E. B. Du Bois and other militant black leaders who said that Washington was accepting segregation and subservience to whites. Fortune sold his share of the *Age* in 1907 and in the 1920s supported the back-to-Africa movement of Marcus Garvey, writing for Garvey's widely circulating magazine, *Negro World.* The *Age,* under the editorship of Fred R. Moore, remained a major New York black newspaper until it was sold to the expanding *Defender* group of Chicago in 1952.

William Monroe Trotter, another great black leader at the turn of the century, had a background opposite from Fortune's. His father, a white Union army officer, became interested in racial equality and married a black slave. He then became a merchant in Boston, where his son won election to Phi Beta Kappa at Harvard and earned a master's degree there. In 1901 with George Forbes, an Amherst graduate, Trotter founded the *Boston Guardian.* It was provocative and militant enough to win the praise of Du Bois. When Booker T. Washington spoke in Boston in 1905 the *Guardian* challenged his conservative leadership, particularly on black education and voting. Trotter later led a protest delegation to the national capital to meet with President Woodrow Wilson and plead the cause of blacks. But in the 1920s, his paper languished; Trotter and his wife lost their home, and Trotter died in 1934. His sister continued the *Guardian* until her death in 1957.

Robert S. Abbott's *Chicago Defender,* founded in 1905, fared better in the quest for public support than did Trotter's *Guardian.* By 1915 it reached a circulation of 230,000. The figure declined two-thirds by the depression year of 1935, but rose again to 160,000 in postwar 1947. The Chicago paper, with its national edition, then became the cornerstone of the largest American black newspaper group.

Abbott was born of black parents in Georgia in 1868. When his father died, his mother married John H. H. Sengstacke, the son of a German merchant who had married a slave. Abbott learned printing at Hampton Institute, worked on his stepfather's small paper, studied law, and in 1905 founded the *Defender* among Chicago's 40,000 black population. The paper was run on a shoestring from his landlady's house until Abbott developed a familiar black newspaper formula: muckraking on behalf of his race, sensationalizing through the "race-angling" of headlines and stories, using crime and scandal stories, and mounting resolute challenges to the Ku Klux Klan, racial rioting, lynchings, and other threats to black Americans' security. By the 1930s Abbott had moderated the *Defender's* tone and had added much more personal, social, cultural, and fashion news. When he died in 1940 his successor was John H. Sengstacke, a nephew.

Robert L. Vann's *Pittsburgh Courier,* founded in 1910, became the largest in circulation of all black newspapers, approaching 300,000 in the late 1940s. Vann was a lawyer who took over a church-sponsored publishing venture that he used to fight racial discrimination and the Jim Crow tradition. The *Courier* backed black athletes, which helped Jackie Robinson to break the color barrier in baseball. Vann developed a circulation in the South and used his influence to attract capable black journalists.

P. Bernard Young, another black publisher who developed a national newspaper, took over the *Journal and Guide* in Norfolk in 1910 and ran it as a moderate, nonsensational weekly until his death in 1962. By contrast, the various publishers of New York's *Amsterdam News* have concentrated on local circulation since its founding by James H. Anderson in 1909, and have only gradually won their way to leadership in the competitive Harlem scene.

W. E. B. DU BOIS AND *THE CRISIS*

W. E. B. Du Bois, the militant apostle of protest in the opening decades of the century, became one of the major heroes of the black equality movement of the 1960s. His appeal was strong for the radical left of that movement because late in life he became an advocate of Marxism and went to live in the new African nation of Ghana, where he died in 1963 at 95.

Du Bois was not a newspaperman, although he was a correspondent or columnist for several newspapers. He was primarily a writer and a teacher with a cause to promote—that of rescuing the black race from a crisis that threatened to crush its capability. He is best known for his work between 1910 and 1934 as an executive of the National Association for the Advancement of Colored People and for the founding and editing of its magazine, *The Crisis.* That journal served so well as a combination of a news magazine reporting items of concern to blacks, a journal of editorial opinion, a review of opinion and literature, and a literary magazine that its entire file for the first 50 years has been reproduced as "A Record of the Darker Races."

(Bettmann Archive)

W. E. B. Du Bois

  Born in New England in 1868, Du Bois was raised by his mother in a white society relatively free of discrimination. He himself was of mixed blood. He edited a high-school paper and was correspondent for the *Springfield Republican* and the *New York Age.* At Fisk University he edited the student paper. He studied sociology at Harvard and in Germany, and contributed articles to the *Atlantic* and *World's Work.* After attempting two other black journals, he succeeded with *The Crisis.* In it he set out to challenge the whole concept of white supremacy, then nationally accepted, and its counterpart of black inferiority. He said his object was to "set forth those facts and arguments which show the danger of race prejudice, particularly as manifested today toward colored people. It takes its name from the fact that the editors believe that this is a critical time in the history of the advancement of men."

"Mentally the negro is inferior to the white," said the 1911 *Encyclopedia Britannica.* It was this belief Du Bois set out to destroy. His editorials also attacked immediate ills: wartime discrimination against black soldiers, the widespread race riots and lynchings following World War I, the climax of Ku Klux Klan terrorism, continued white refusal to consider black rights in the fields of voting, education, and housing. Circulation of *The Crisis* passed 100,000 in 1918. But dissension within the NAACP and other factors reduced it to fewer than 10,000 when Du Bois retired as editor in 1934 at age 65. Under editor Roy Wilkins until 1949 and then Henry Lee Moon, circulation revived to well above 100,000.

Du Bois became the head of the sociology department at Atlanta University, founded a scholarly journal on world race problems named *Phylon,* and wrote books and countless articles for major publications. Like Frederick Douglass, his writings were published again in the 1990s as a symbol of achievement by a distinguished member of the black race—and, of course, the human race—who so effectively used the weapon of the journalistic crusade.

11

Bastions of News Enterprise

It will be my earnest aim . . . to give the news impartially, without fear or favor.

—Adolph S. Ochs

The preceding chapters have been concerned with the historical development of patterns of press behavior. A segment of the press was involved successively in important general trends: the rise of the new journalism, the spread of yellow journalism, and service as the "people's champions." But it is difficult to fit all newspapers into such patterns, because each newspaper has an individuality born of its publishing environment. In some cases establishment leaders of this period were more noted for news presentation than for editorial passion. One conspicuous example was the *New York Times,* rescued from near oblivion in 1896 to begin a rise to greatness as a journalistic institution. Others were its New York rivals, the *Herald* and the *Sun; Chicago's Inter Ocean;* and a future western giant, the *Los Angeles Times.* Ensuring the growth of the news-enterprise principle was the rise of the modern press associations, the Associated Press and its new rivals, the United Press and International News Service. Each is delineated in turn.

ADOLPH S. OCHS AND THE *NEW YORK TIMES*

The story of the *New York Times* is the story of the man who rescued it from bankruptcy in 1896 and who guided it until he died in 1935. He was Adolph S. Ochs, a one-time printer's devil from Tennessee, who salvaged the glories of the *Times* of Henry J. Raymond's day and set its course as America's leading newspaper. It was the men and women he selected to staff the *Times* who made it an institution.

"All the News That's Fit to Print."

The New York Times.

THE WEATHER.

Unsettled Tuesday; Wednesday, fair, cooler; moderate southerly winds, becoming variable.

For full weather report see Page 24.

VOL. LXI...NO. 19,535.   NEW YORK, TUESDAY, APRIL 16, 1912.—TWENTY-FOUR PAGES.   ONE CENT   In Greater New York. | Elsewhere, Jersey City, and Newark. TWO CENTS

TITANIC SINKS FOUR HOURS AFTER HITTING ICEBERG;
866 RESCUED BY CARPATHIA, PROBABLY 1250 PERISH;
ISMAY SAFE, MRS. ASTOR MAYBE, NOTED NAMES MISSING

Col. Astor and Bride, Isidor Straus and Wife, and Maj. Butt Aboard.

"RULE OF SEA" FOLLOWED

Women and Children Put Over in Lifeboats and Are Supposed to be Safe on Carpathia.

PICKED UP AFTER 8 HOURS

Vincent Astor Calls at White Star Office for News of His Father and Leaves Weeping.

FRANKLIN HOPEFUL ALL DAY

Manager of the Line Insisted Titanic Was Unsinkable Even After She Had Gone Down.

HEAD OF THE LINE ABOARD

J. Bruce Ismay Making First Trip on Gigantic Ship That Was to Surpass All Others.

Biggest Liner Plunges to the Bottom at 2:20 A. M.

RESCUERS THERE TOO LATE

Except to Pick Up the Few Hundreds Who Took to the Lifeboats.

WOMEN AND CHILDREN FIRST

Cunarder Carpathia Rushing to New York with the Survivors.

SEA SEARCH FOR OTHERS

The Californic Stands By on Chance of Picking Up Other Boats or Rafts.

OLYMPIC SENDS THE NEWS

Only Ship to Flash Wireless Message to Shore After the Disaster.

The Lost Titanic Being Towed Out of Belfast Harbor.

CAPT. E. J. SMITH, Commander of the Titanic.

PARTIAL LIST OF THE SAVED.

Includes Bruce Ismay, Mrs. Widener, Mrs. H. B. Harris, and an Incomplete name, suggesting Mrs. Astor's.

CAPE RACE, N. F., Tuesday, April 16.—Following is a partial list of survivors among the first-class passengers of the Titanic, received by the Marconi wireless station this morning from the Carpathia, via the steamship Olympic:

Ochs, like many another great publisher, struggled up from the ranks to win his place. His parents were German Jews who emigrated to the United States before the Civil War. Adolph, born in 1858 in Cincinnati, was the oldest of six children. The family migrated to Tennessee in a covered wagon, and at 14 Adolph landed an apprenticeship as a printer's devil for the *Knoxville Chronicle*. In 1875 he became assistant composing-room supervisor for the *Louisville Courier-Journal* and did some reporting for Henry Watterson. But he was judged a colorless and awkward writer; his genius lay in his business ability and in his capacity for journalistic leadership.

Back in Knoxville in 1876, Ochs got his chance. The editor of the rival *Tribune,* Colonel John E. MacGowan, wanted to start a newspaper in Chattanooga, a city of 12,000 with no sidewalks, muddy streets, and little interest in newspapers. The city had seen 16 newspapers come and go in 40 years, including the *Dispatch* that Ochs and MacGowan first published. The only survivor was the *Times,* with a circulation of 250. Ochs got control for the same amount of dollars. It was July 1878, and he was not yet 21. But he and his 45-year-old editor promised Chattanooga all the local news, the latest news by telegraph, and a strong business and commercial outlook for a booming city. The *Times* boomed with Chattanooga, and by 1892 it was clearing $25,000 a year. But Ochs owed money on real-estate ventures that were imperiled by the approaching depression of 1893. What he needed, Ochs decided, was another newspaper and its profits. He searched the country, and in March 1896, he learned that there was a chance to buy the *New York Times.*

Ochs was properly impressed by this opportunity. He knew how respected the *Times* had been since its founding by Henry J. Raymond in 1851. After Raymond's death in 1869, the paper had come under the direction of its business manager, George Jones. Jones, editor Louis J. Jennings, and chief assistant John Foord had helped to smash Boss Tweed in the 1870s. John C. Reid had served well as managing editor from 1872 to 1889, and the paper had maintained its place until the death of Jones in 1891. By then the impact of the new journalism was having its effect.

The new guiding spirit on the *Times* became Charles R. Miller, a graduate of Dartmouth and former staff member of the *Springfield Republican,* who assumed the editorship in 1883. In 1893, with associate editor Edward Cary and other staff members, Miller negotiated the purchase of the *Times* from the Jones family heirs for approximately $1 million. But the paper did not prosper. It had the smallest circulation of the city's eight morning dailies, a paltry 9000 paid circulation concealed in a 21,000 press run. This was not far behind the *Tribune*'s 16,000 but was far below the *Sun*'s 70,000 morning circulation, the *Herald*'s 140,000, and the *World*'s 200,000.

OCHS BUYS THE *TIMES,* 1896

Ochs did not have the money to save the *Times,* but he convinced Miller that he had the know-how and the vision needed to put the paper in a sound competitive position. An elaborate refinancing plan was advanced that would give Ochs control of the paper within four years if he succeeded in revitalizing it. Ochs trudged through the Wall Street districts for months persuading financiers, including even J. P. Morgan, to buy bonds in the new enterprise. Finally, in August 1896, an agreement was completed, with Ochs putting up $75,000 of his own money and risking his Chattanooga paper on the outcome. The 38-year-old Tennessean, with 24 years of experience since his printer's devil days, was now competing with Pulitzer, Hearst, Dana, Reid, and Bennett in the New York field.

(New York Times)

Adolph S. Ochs (above) rescued the *New York Times* from bankruptcy in 1896 and made it one of the world's great newspapers before he died in 1935. His longtime managing editor, Carr Van Anda achieved fame as the person most instrumental in developing the Times's superb news coverage. It was Ochs, however, whose leadership made possible the achievements of Van Anda and his staff members.

The plan of attack Ochs had devised to save the *New York Times* was simple. He would not attempt to match the sensationalism of Hearst and Pulitzer, nor would he popularize the paper's offerings in a halfway effort to keep up with the mass-circulation leaders, as some other New York publishers were trying to do. Instead he would publish a paper with solid news coverage and editorial opinion that would be designed for readers who did not like an overemphasis of entertainment and features. Ochs's declaration of principle contained these lines:

> It will be my earnest aim that the *New York Times* give the news, all the news, in concise and attractive form, in language that is parliamentary in good society, and give it as early, if not earlier, than it can be learned through any other reliable medium; to give the news impartially, without fear or favor, regardless of any party, sect or interest involved; to make the columns of the *New York Times* a forum for the consideration of all questions of public importance, and to that end to invite intelligent discussion from all shades of opinion.[1]

Ochs's first steps were unspectacular but effective. The *Times* began to publish a guide listing the out-of-town buyers who were in the city. It reported daily real-estate transactions. And it expanded its market reports, adding to the daily coverage a weekly financial review. The business and financial community began to find these *Times* features increasingly valuable. Lawyers were similarly attracted by another column listing court cases and records. The class of readers to which Ochs was appealing also liked the emphasis placed on government news. It liked Ochs's Sunday magazine, which featured articles of current news significance rather than entertainment. And it liked the *Times* book review section.

Ochs determinedly set his face against the popular features of the new journalism, refusing to run "stunt" stories, banning comics from his columns, and giving pictures short shrift. He sniped at the yellow journalists, advertising the *Times* under the slogan "It Does Not Soil the Breakfast Cloth" before choosing the famous front-page ear, "All the News That's Fit to Print." But circulation in 1898 was still at the 25,000 mark. Ochs decided to make one last gamble, The *Times* was selling for three cents, the *World* and *Journal* for two. Why not cut the price of the *Times* to a penny and thus win the circulation needed to ensure solid advertising support?

Once again the old formula of price adjustment was successful. As a penny paper the *Times* jumped to 75,000 circulation in 1899 and passed the 100,000 mark in 1901. Its advertising linage doubled within two years. The red ink turned to black and Ochs won majority control of the paper's stock under his purchasing agreement. He promptly went into debt again to build the Times Tower on Broadway, in what became Times Square, putting $2.5 million into what in 1904 was one of New York's most spectacular buildings. The strategic location of the *Times* plant in what became the city's nighttime heart and the later development of its moving electric news bulletins helped to establish the paper as one of the city's institutions.

CARR VAN ANDA, MANAGING EDITOR

Far more important to the future of the *Times* was another event of 1904, however. That year Carr V. Van Anda, the foremost managing editor in the United States, began his 25-year-career as the guiding genius of the *Times* news staff. To single out Van Anda as the leading American managing editor perhaps seems extraordinary, for comparisons of the accomplishments of people in different eras and different publishing situations are difficult to make. But it is generally agreed that the chief architect of the superior news department of the *New York Times* was Van Anda, a man who shunned personal publicity so completely that despite his incredible achievements he became almost a legendary figure, even to his own craft.[2]

Alexander Woollcott once remarked that Van Anda "loved the editing of a newspaper more than anything in the world." Apparently he was born with this love, for in 1870, as a boy of six in an Ohio village, he was pasting clippings on sheets of paper and selling them for ten cents a copy. At ten he made a press out of a wooden frame, an ink roller from a cloth-wrapped broom handle, and printed with type salvaged from the village paper. Next he acquired a small press and did job printing, using the profits to finance his study of chemistry and physics. When he entered Ohio University at 16 he had specialized in mathematics and science, and had not the lure of journalism been so strong he would likely have become a scholar of astronomy and physics. As it was, he could always keep step with the keen minds in those fields.

Van Anda left college at 18 to become supervisor for his village paper. Next he set type and reported for the *Cleveland Herald* and other Cleveland papers. When he was 22 he applied for work on the *Baltimore Sun* and was selected for the important post of night editor. Two years later, in 1888, he moved to the *New York Sun,* where after five years he became night editor. When Ochs decided in 1904 that his first managing editor, Henry Loewenthal, should devote full attention to business news, Van Anda's name was suggested as a replacement. The association was to be an ideal one. Ochs was willing to spend money to get the news; Van Anda was more than willing to spend it for him.

Although he was now a managing editor, Van Anda never stopped serving as night editor. For 20 years his routine at the *Times* never varied. He appeared in the newsroom at 1 P.M., went home at 6 P.M. for dinner and a rest, and returned at 10 P.M. to stay until the last person departed at 5 A.M. Usually he was the last person there. Twelve hours a day, seven days a week, Van Anda was riding the news, giving as much attention to the flow of stories as to the major news breaks. He loved to match his speed and wits against a deadline. He loved to exploit an important but undeveloped story and give it painstaking coverage and significant play. But he never lost sight of the importance of the conscientious and intelligent handling of the bulk of the news, and he transmitted this spirit to his staff. He was not a colorful, dynamic leader; rather he was reserved and cold in appearance, and his piercing gaze was called the "Van Anda death ray." But those who worked with him found him a modest, sympathetic chief who backed his workers completely and who never flew into a rage. His secret was in doing his own job so well that the impress was made on both the newspaper and its staff.

There are many stories of Van Anda's almost legendary ability. Soon after he became managing editor of the *Times,* word arrived that the decisive naval battle of the Russo-Japanese War might be at hand. Van Anda recognized the importance of the event and readied himself to handle the story. When the bulletin came, at 4:30 one morning, that the Japanese admiral Togo had smashed the Russian fleet, all of Van Anda's elaborate research and preparation went into play. Within 19 minutes the *Times* had put an extra to press with the bulletin and a half-page of war news on page one, running under headlines written by Van Anda as the page was being remade. Inside was more advance material that Van Anda had long before made ready for this moment. Forty thousand copies were run off, and the managing editor rode about the city with a fleet of horsedrawn wagons at dawn seeing personally that his news beat was prominently displayed on the newsstands.

Van Anda's classic achievement was his handling of the story of the sinking of the liner *Titanic* in 1912. Here, as in other situations, it was Van Anda's personal ability and the functioning of a well-trained staff of high caliber that combined to produce superior news coverage.

It was 1:20 A.M., Monday, April 15, 1912, when the first Associated Press bulletin reached the *Times* newsroom reporting that the luxury liner *Titanic* had struck an iceberg on its maiden voyage from Britain to the United States. An SOS had been picked up by the Marconi wireless station in Newfoundland. The *Titanic* was supposedly unsinkable, but Van Anda's rapid calls to *Times* correspondents in Halifax and Montreal and to the offices of the *Titanic*'s White Star Line told him that the ship's wireless had fallen silent a half-hour after the first call for help and convinced him that the ship must have gone down.

Before 3:30 A.M. Van Anda and his staff had organized the story. Among the more than 2200 aboard were many famous persons. A background story was prepared on the passenger list, and a picture of the *Titanic* was prepared for page one. Two other vessels had reported close scrapes with icebergs in the North Atlantic; this fitted the pattern of the news available about the *Titanic*. In several columns of type the *Times* reported Monday morning that the ship had sunk, while other papers were handling the story in incomplete and inconclusive form.

Tuesday, Wednesday, and Thursday, the story commanded the world's attention, as the liner *Carpathia* sailed toward New York with survivors. On Tuesday Van Anda hired a floor in a hotel a block from the *Carpathia*'s pier and installed four telephone lines directly connected to the *Times'* city room. The entire staff was mobilized under the direction of Arthur Greaves, city editor, to cover the arrival of the rescue ship Thursday night. Van Anda persuaded Guglielmo Marconi, the wireless inventor, to board the ship to interview the wireless operator—and a *Times* reporter slipped through the police lines with the inventor. He got an exclusive story of the last messages from the *Titanic*.

Within three hours after the arrival of the rescue ship the *Times'* first edition appeared, with 15 of its 24 pages devoted to the story of the loss of 1500 lives in the *Titanic* disaster. In coverage and in organization of a great news story, that edition of the *Times* remains a masterpiece.[3]

Van Anda and Ochs both loved speed in the gathering of the news, and this love led the *Times* to leadership in the use of correspondents and communications facilities in such instances as the *Titanic* sinking. Both men had watched the work of Marconi, the Italian scientist who between 1895 and 1900 had devised a practical system of sending telegraphic messages through space by means of electromagnetic waves. Marconi's "wireless" telegraphy was based on the experiments of others, but it was he who obtained the basic patents and formed the first commercial wireless company in London in 1897. Ship-to-shore communication and the use of the wireless by English newspapers and the *New York Herald* to cover sporting events soon followed. In December 1901, Marconi successfully transmitted signals from England to Newfoundland. But it was not until 1907 that a regular trans-Atlantic service opened.[4]

Ranking above all else in bringing the *Times* to greatness was its coverage of the events of World War I. It was in this period that the paper began to publish the texts of documents and speeches, a policy that led to its becoming the leading reference newspaper for librarians, scholars, government officials, and other newspaper editors. The compilation of the *New York Times Index* further ensured the paper this position.

Six full pages in an August 1914 issue of the *Times* presented the British White Paper to American readers. The *Times* had been the first American paper to obtain a copy of the British Foreign Office's correspondence with Germany and Austria, and printed it in full. The next day it published the text of the German version of the events leading up to the war declaration, brought from Berlin by a *Times* correspondent, for another exclusive.

Meanwhile Van Anda was giving his readers minute coverage of the military news, using press-association accounts, the reports of his own correspondents with the various armies, and stories obtained from the *London Chronicle*. War pictures were carried in a rotogravure section, added by Ochs in 1914 after Van Anda had investigated rotogravure printing in Germany. Political and economic reporting from European capitals was given proper emphasis with the military news. When the United States entered the war the *Times* expanded its coverage, spending $750,000 a year on cabled news.

After 25 years of Adolph Ochs's ownership, the *New York Times* of 1921 had achieved major stature. There was one great reason for this success. The paper had taken in some $100 million in those 25 years and had paid out but 4 percent in dividends. Ochs had poured the millions into the *Times* for buildings and equipment, for staff, and for the tremendous news coverage Van Anda had built. Circulation had reached 330,000 daily and more than 500,000 Sunday, while advertising linage had increased tenfold in the 25 years.

Politically the *Times* had been Democratic except during the Bryan campaigns. But it was essentially conservative in tone, particularly in its economic outlook. After going down to defeat on the League of Nations issue with the 1920 Democratic ticket of James M. Cox and Franklin D. Roosevelt, the Times supported Alfred E. Smith in 1928 and Roosevelt in 1932 in the final campaigns before Ochs's death.

The 1920s saw one era of *Times* history ending and another beginning. Editor Miller died in 1922 and was succeeded by Rollo Ogden, longtime *New York Post* editor. Van Anda went into semiretirement in 1925. While still active in management, Ochs groomed his son-in-law Arthur Hays Sulzberger and his nephew Julius Ochs Adler to succeed him. The deaths of Ochs and his business manager, Louis Wiley, in 1935 removed the last of the quartet that had been instrumental in building the *Times*. But the organization they had created continued to carry the paper to new heights in the succeeding years.

THE *NEW YORK HERALD,* A LEADER IN NEWS

The *New York Herald,* under the guidance of founder James Gordon Bennett, had achieved leadership in news enterprise. When James Gordon Bennett, Jr., took control in 1872 the *Herald* ranked first in collecting and presenting the news. Its reporters and correspondents were the best, and its insistence on the use of the fastest means of communication made it a hard-hitting rival for Pulitzer and Hearst when they invaded New York. Its traditions were still those of its adventurous correspondent of the early 1870s, Henry M. Stanley, who spent two years searching in Africa, on an assignment from the younger Bennett, before he found the missing missionary and inquired, "Dr. Livingstone, I presume?" The *Herald* remained a news-enterprise paper in the early twentieth century, contesting vigorously for complete and dramatic coverage of the world's events. It had Joseph L. Stickney accompanying Dewey in Manila; Richard Harding Davis covering the Boer War; Oscar King Davis and W. H. Lewis giving it top coverage of the Russo-Japanese War; Dr. Frederick A. Cook reporting on his trip to the North Pole; and a network of political and war correspondents (supplied in part by the *Paris-Herald*) equaling the work of any such group in World War I. Its use of art and photographs embellished its crack coverage of such events as the sinking of the *General Slocum* and the *Titanic* disaster.[5]

In the struggle for survival in New York, however, the *Herald* was handicapped by the personality and practices of its owner, the younger Bennett. He was intelligent and alert, and his driving force dominated the paper. He established the Paris edition of the *Herald* in 1887, now the famed *International Herald Tribune.* But in his 45 years as a publisher he proved to be a dictator who put his personal whims first. He lived in Paris most of his life, rarely visiting the *Herald* office, and his royal manner of living drained an estimated $30 million from the profits of his papers.[6] No other publisher, save William Randolph Hearst, equaled Bennett in irresponsible personal control of a journalistic enterprise.

George Jean Nathan has described Bennett as he appeared in 1909, at the age of 67.[7] He was tall, slender, full of nervous energy, but bearing himself with a military erectness accented by steel-gray hair and moustache. Though he lived in Paris, his New York editors could neither hire nor fire a reporter without his consent. His editorial committee met at a table with an empty chair at the head—that was Bennett. At his place were set fresh copies of the paper each day, as though he might walk in at any moment.

Bennett's connection with the paper was far from being only a psychological one, however. Cabled instructions arrived from Paris each day. Frequently department heads were called to Paris for conferences. Bennett kept close watch on the work of each employee and practiced a policy of seeing that no individual achieved personal importance. Although he had many good news instincts, he also forced the paper to observe numerous rules of conduct based on his personal idiosyncrasies and promoted his personal beliefs. At Bennett's death in 1918, the *Herald* was sold to Frank Munsey, who could not make the leaderless paper profitable and let it disappear into the *Herald Tribune* in 1924, which would maintain the Bennett news traditions.

THE *NEW YORK SUN* GOES DOWN

The *New York Sun* of the days of editor Charles A. Dana and managing editor Amos J. Cummings had emphasized reporting skill, writing style, and human-interest techniques to a degree worthy of the admiration of the practitioners of the new journalism. It was a city editor of the *Sun,* John B. Bogart, who told a young reporter for the first time: "When a dog bites a man, that is not news; but when a man bites a dog, *that* is news." It was an editorial writer for the *Sun,* Francis P. Church, who in 1897 answered the "Is There a Santa Claus?" inquiry of a little girl named Virginia with an explanation that was reprinted widely for many years. It was a reporter for the *Sun,* Will Irwin, who in 1906 wrote the journalistic masterpiece, "The City That Was," in memory of San Francisco's destruction by earthquake and fire.[8]

Heading the *Sun* news staff from the 1880s to the World War I period were managing editor Chester S. Lord and night city editor Selah M. Clarke, called "Boss" by his associates. They helped to train reporters like Irwin, Arthur Brisbane, Julian Ralph, Samuel Hopkins Adams, Richard Harding Davis, and Jacob Riis. From their night desk, too, Carr Van Anda went to his great career on the *Times.* Succeeding Dana as editor was the highly competent and graceful stylist Edward P. Mitchell. The *Sun* was regarded as a school of journalism for young journalists, and its graduates formed an alumni association. They were dismayed when control of the *Sun* passed in 1916 to Frank A. Munsey, a business-minded purchaser of newspapers who understood little of the journalistic traditions of the craft. The famous morning edition of the *Sun* disappeared in 1920, and the evening *Sun,* bearing little resemblance to the paper of old, trudged on toward eventual oblivion.

CHICAGO'S FAMED *INTER OCEAN*

A newspaper in Chicago's journalism history that for a time attracted a following of reporters was the *Inter Ocean.* It started its career in 1865 as the *Chicago Republican,* edited by Charles A. Dana for the first year. It became the *Inter Ocean* in 1872, a staunchly Republican voice owned by William Penn Nixon. Through its reporting enterprise on the frontier, its religious news, and its agricultural news coverage it built up a midwestern circulation. It also led in introducing mechanical improvements—for example, it installed a color press in 1892, before other American newspapers. During the 1890s the paper lost money and was sold to Charles T. Yerkes, Chicago's traction line boss. Despite its record for conducting crusades in the public interest, the *Inter Ocean* suffered under Yerkes's ownership until he sold it in 1902 to George W. Hinman, who had come from the *New York Sun* to be the *Inter Ocean*'s editor.

Under Hinman the *Inter Ocean* won notice as a training school for newspaperpeople. The paper had been one of those that had catered to the "tramp reporters" of the period and by so doing had obtained the services of many young people with bright journalistic futures. Belonging to the *Inter Ocean* alumni association were the writers Marquis James, William Cuppy, and Ring Lardner; Walter Howey, later a famous Hearst executive; Richard J.

Finnegan, later editor of the *Chicago Times* and *Sun-Times;* and a score of other prominent newspaperpeople. In 1914, however, the *Inter Ocean* fell victim to Chicago's newspaper competition and was added to the list of newspapers that have become reminiscences.[9]

BUILDING THE *LOS ANGELES TIMES*

When local printers in a small town of 12,000 called Los Angeles founded the *Los Angeles Times* in 1881 as a rival to the *Herald* and the *Express,* no one foresaw that both the city and the *Times* would rank in the national forefront a century later. A man who helped build both, Harrison Gray Otis, entered the publishing firm in 1882. He was 45, a Civil War veteran with colonel's rank, and had twice dabbled in newspapering. By 1886 Otis had full control of the 7000-circulation morning daily. A real-estate boom fattened his profits, and by 1900 the *Times,* despite a modest 26,000 circulation, boasted the country's largest advertising linage. Otis began land purchases in California and Mexico that soon totaled a million acres.[10]

Promoted to general when he commanded troops in the Philippines, he became "General Otis"—a hard-fisted capitalist who relished a brawl and used his paper to make vitriolic denunciations of opponents. He castigated some businesspeople as "robber barons" and supported the 1905 Russian Revolution, but otherwise he garnered a widespread reputation for reactionary thought and action. His biggest troubles began in 1890, when he locked out his printers in a dispute with the International Typographical Union (ITU) over the closed shop and rules for resetting advertising mats. In 1894 he formed an employers' group in Los Angeles to oppose the unions. The ITU brought in William Randolph Hearst in 1903 to found a rival morning paper, the *Examiner,* and attempted a boycott of *Times* advertisers. Resistance to Otis and his conservative stance grew, and by 1910 a Socialist candidate won the primaries for mayor of Los Angeles.

Bombings had been used in recent industrial disputes, but the gutting of the *Times* building on October 1, 1910, caused a sensation. Otis and his son-in-law Harry Chandler were absent from the building, thus escaping death, which took 20 of their printers. Detectives traced the bombs to the McNamara brothers, officers of an Indianapolis union. The charges were widely regarded as a frameup engineered by the reactionary Otis, and liberals hired Clarence Darrow to head the defense at the 1911 trial. But one brother confessed, and both pleaded guilty. Darrow withdrew from the case, the Socialist lost the mayoral election, and Otis rebuilt his printing plant in a fortresslike atmosphere with an eagle atop the building. In 1914, three years before his death, he turned the paper over to Harry and Marion Chandler. Their son Norman and grandson Otis would continue the family role.

THE RISE OF THE PRESS ASSOCIATIONS

The rise of the American press associations—organizations dedicated to the rapid, thorough, and impartial collection and dissemination of all the news—was an epochal development in the history of journalism. "The right of the people to know" was greatly advanced by the creation of news agencies that utilized journalistic skills and modern communications techniques to find the news, to report it impartially, and to speed it to every corner of the country and the world. Only a few American dailies ever have attempted to maintain staff correspondents in leading news centers of the world, or even of the country, and the press-association logotypes—AP, UP, INS, UPI—have become the symbols of trustworthy service from outside sources.

The Los Angeles Times

Twenty-fifth Year

PER ANNUM, $9.00 | Per Month, 75 Cents | Per Copy, 5 Cents.

THURSDAY MORNING, APRIL 19, 1906.

On All News Stands, Trains and Streets, 5 CENTS

The stricken city. Panorama of San Francisco before the catastrophe, showing principal buildings that are partially or wholly destroyed.

THE WEATHER.
BRIEF REPORT.

YESTERDAY — Maximum temperature, 73 deg.; minimum, 49 deg. Wind 5 a. m., east; velocity, 1 mile; 5 p. m., west; velocity, 7 miles. At midnight the temperature was 60 deg.; clear.

TODAY—At 5 a. m. the temperature was 52 deg.; clear.

POINTS OF THE NEWS
IN TODAY'S ISSUE OF

INDEX.

SYNOPSIS.

THE CITY, Los Angeles stunned by tidings of sister city's doom, sympathy and money freely offered, nearly 52,000 raised and $100,000 pledged in day; two cities closely connected in business; names of concerns directly affected; panic-stricken crowd besiege telegraph office in vain effort to reach loved ones, and many take trains toward scene of terror; The Times taxes all other papers on hand with the news. Horse Show opens brilliantly, with dainty equines prancing and society a-sparkle... Mayor Powers gets judgment for $10 against man who cut his love with her photograph... Passers of forged checks arrested... City Council places ban on skyscrapers... Maguire defeats Exhibite at billiards... Sanford may take Occidental's coach. Quarantine-breaker Kindgren has inning with Health Office... Fund to send Miss Sutton abroad grows... Leslee L. Smith I...Ex-preacher Wylie and Green woman held on ugly charge.

SOUTHERN CALIFORNIA. See page 1, Part I.

CALIFORNIA'S CALAMITY. At 10 o'clock last night fires following earthquake shocks which practically left all San Francisco in ruins were still burning fiercely in that city and the monetary loss at that hour was estimated at $200,000,000... With loss of more persons killed by falling buildings to ascertain their fears, citizens of the stricken metropolis and surrounding bayside were fleeing to the hills for safety or crowding the ferryboats, on scenes of savage which, more than now became dangerously congested... Gov. Pardee last night telegraphed to the War Department that thousands of persons are homeless and that thousands of tents and such quantities of provisions as can be taken into the city are urgently needed... Federal troops are aiding the police in maintaining order and several looters have been shot... The area covered in San Francisco alone by flames up to 6 o'clock last night was about eight square miles; Insurance companies say they will pay losses in full. "Mayor Schmitz has appointed committee of Safety composed of prominent citizens, on order of questions most needful, answer is have in supply stricken of with water... In the ruin by gunshake and consequent fire, By a merchant's three and four thousand public buildings and commercial structures went down in destruction, and also hundreds of buildings of no interior class, taking hundreds of lives—Often within a radius of many miles of the metropolis were affected by the shocks, and in some of them the blow dealt was terrific, the loss at Salinas alone being $2,500,000—Two dead patients at Agnew's Insane asylum perished when the walls of that institution crumbled—All costumes and scenery of Metropolitan Opera Company destroyed—Sea Marco wharf mains broken, forcing Valley flooded—Oakland, Haven & Co. office store and contents for use of city—It otherwise on San Francisco side of bay were saved in—Twenty persons killed at collapse of Terminal Hotel—Santa Rough not dropped, stand fire well.

HEART IS TORN FROM GREAT CITY.

San Francisco Nearly Destroyed By Earthquakes and Fire—Hundreds of Killed and Injured—Destruction of Other Coast Cities—California's Greatest Horror.

By the Associated Press—P. M.

SAN FRANCISCO, April 19.—It looks now as if the entire city would be burned, following the great quake of yesterday. The government is furnishing tugs to convey news to Oakland, but the confusion is so great that they cannot be relied upon. It will be impossible to send full details for several days.

The latest reports from Leland Sanford University indicate that the magnicent stone buildings of that institution have suffered severe damage Many of the buildings were ruined by cracks, which split them from cornice to foundation. The buildings are practically intact. Only a few structures collapsed in Berkeley, the earthquake shock being slight there.

At 10 o'clock at night, the fire was unabated, and thousands of people are fleeing to the hills and clamoring for places on the ferry boats.

The damage is now believed to have reached $200,000,000 and 50,000 people are thought to be homeless.

Under the fierce heat of the sun today, 29 bodies lay in Washington Square, where they were taken at the order of the Mayor when the morgues and Hall of Justice basement held all that could be cared for.

At 10 p. m. last night the newspapers ceased all effort to collect news, and the Associated Press force is compelled to act independently.

THE PRESIDENT'S MESSAGE:

The President sent the following telegram to Gov. Pardee, Sacramento:

"Sir: Rumors of great disaster from an earthquake in San Francisco, but know nothing of the real facts. Call upon me for any assistance I can render.

(Signed)   THEODORE ROOSEVELT, Washington, April 18."

The President later sent the following additional telegram to Gov. Pardee:

"It was difficult at first to credit the catastrophe that has befallen San Francisco. I feel the greatest concern and sympathy for you and the people, not only of San Francisco, but of California in the terrible disaster. You will let me know if there is anything that the national government can do.

(Signed)   THEODORE ROOSEVELT."

Gov. Pardee sent the following in reply:

"Owing to interruption of telegraphic communication extent of disaster in San Francisco not yet known here, but no doubt calamity is very serious. People of California appreciate your kind inquiry and offer of assistance. State troops doing patrol duty, and if federal assistance is needed will call upon you.   Signed, "GEO. C. PARDEE"

TOSSING SIX HOURS ON SEISMIC WAVES.

SAN FRANCISCO, April 18.—[Special.] During six hours of mortal dread and nameless terror San Francisco was today tossed upon the seismic waves of the most disastrous earthquake known to the history or the traditions of America's west coast. In the mad confusion and helpless horror of this night uncounted bodies of dead men and women are lying in morgues and under unuplifted walls. g through the mists and ferough the mists and fogs that hung in gray warped and creaked, and the rakare lying in morgues and u lieved that nearly 1000 lives have been lost. The noise the wa ers of the placid he waters of the placid bay and over the wait- fell like stacks of cards. The lieved that nearly 1000 lives l not fall far short of that, and it may prove to be much throug t the Golden Gorough the Golden Gate were blowing the ment, the Oakland heights and not fall far short of that, and Fire and f ame have added to the destruction, the winds wit the greeting ofla with the greeting of the sea to the green rocked like forests in the wind. Fire and f ame have added

and despair. The material losses are beyond computation. clad heights and flower-strewn fields that skirted the shores Wounded and hurt inexpressibly the chief city of the West and stretched away into the dim distances beyond. Th lies at this hour humbled to the dust, blackened, battered and sailors still slept in their hammocks in the harbored ships. A charred, her glory of yesterday but a hideous dream, and the few wan-eyed wanderers of the night were stealing through moans from her stricken heart filling the pitying world. the streets, a few early toilers were astir. But that was all.

The first shock came while still the mighty city lay deep Then came the rumble of deep thunder from the mighty in slumber, weary with the revelries and pleasures of the night bowels of the startled earth. The city shook like an aspen leaf, before. In the quiet homes, in the crowded hotels, men had and her gray highways suddenly cracked and split as though not yet awakened to the strifes and endeavors of the new- the batteries of Satan and his America's west coast. In th dawned da . The stars had but waned, and the m orn was against them from underneath ror of this night uncounted

The Los Angeles Times reports a 1906 disaster.

The United States has had three major press associations operating on worldwide scales. One is the Associated Press (AP), which arose out of nineteenth-century efforts in cooperative news gathering. Its twentieth-century competitors were the United Press Associations (UP), founded in 1907 by Edward Wyllis Scripps, and the International News Service (INS), begun in 1909 by William Randolph Hearst. The two merged in 1958 to form the United Press International (UPI). Abroad, major competitors were Reuters of Great Britain, founded in 1851, and Agence France-Presse, which arose after World War II out of the ruins of the old French Havas agency (1835). By 1920 the three American news agencies had expanded their domestic services and had challenged the European agencies—British, French, German—for international news reporting and sales.

THE ASSOCIATED PRESS: GENESIS

The longest history among the American press associations is that of the Associated Press. The modern cooperative news-gathering association with that name took final form in 1900 after a bitter struggle for control of the press-association facilities of the country. The agreement among New York City's leading newspapers in 1849 that brought about the establishment of the Associated Press of New York set the pattern for similar associations. Midwestern dailies formed the Western Associated Press in 1862, which was followed by the New England Associated Press. Other subsidiary regional groups followed. But always the power of the Associated Press of New York was felt (see pages 114 and 182 for more complete accounts of their history).

The New York AP had been well guided by its earliest general agents, Dr. Alexander Jones (1849 to 1851), news-gathering pioneer Daniel H. Craig (1851 to 1866), and former Washington correspondent and San Francisco newspaperperson James W. Simonton (1866 to 1882). Ground was given to restive Western AP members when their agent, William Henry Smith, was named general manager (1882 to 1892), and two of five executive committee seats went to westerners. Despite this, the New York AP faced serious competition from rebels who had tried to form a rival since 1869 and who in 1882 created the United Press (no relation to the later United Press Associations or the present-day UPI). With Walter Polk Phillips as its general manager, the UP had strong modernized dailies as members and good foreign news. William M. Laffan, business manager of the *New York Sun,* was a UP leader.

The actions of the ruling groups within the AP and UP were typical of the times. The two executive committees entered into a secret agreement providing for the two associations to exchange news and thus virtually end competition. There were financial rewards for insiders, but in general AP members were not receiving adequate service. When the deal was uncovered in 1891, a new battle in AP ranks was inevitable.[11] The *New York Sun* and the *Tribune* bolted to the UP in 1892, to be followed the next year by the remaining members of the AP of New York. Taking control of the AP organization was a new corporation, the Associated Press of Illinois, chartered in late 1892.

Melville E. Stone, new AP general manager, obtained exclusive news exchange contracts with Reuters in Britain, Havas in France, and Wolff in Germany. He thus cut the United Press off from the sources of foreign news long enjoyed by its New York members. A four-year struggle finally ended in early 1897 when all the New York dailies except Dana's *Sun* and Hearst's *Journal* were admitted to the AP, and the United Press went into bankruptcy. Hearst had never been an AP member; Laffan of the *Sun* stubbornly organized his own Laffan News Bureau, which operated successfully until 1916.

The Associated Press office on Wall Street at century's turn

Indirectly Laffan was to cause the AP more trouble before the association's course was finally set. The Chicago *Inter Ocean* went to court in 1898 to prevent the AP from discontinuing service to it as punishment for the *Inter Ocean*'s use of Laffan News Bureau copy. An Illinois court decision, handed down in 1900, found that the incorporation papers of the AP were written so broadly as to make the press association a public utility, bound to provide its service to all newspapers wishing it. For the moment the Illinois ruling seemed to put an end to the exclusive membership character of the AP, but its leaders found a way out. The AP of Illinois was dissolved, and a new AP was formed as a nonprofit membership association under New York State law. Stone continued as general manager of the new AP.

THE NEW ASSOCIATED PRESS OF 1900

The most important fact about the new Associated Press of 1900 was that it was a cooperative. Its members were to supply each other with news originating in individual publication areas. They were to share the cost of this exchange of news and of maintaining a press-association staff that would direct the flow of news and augment it with other coverage. The staff, headed by the general manager, was to be responsible only to the membership, through its officers and directors. The AP would thus exist only for the benefit of its member newspapers.

There were some faults, however, in the AP organization. Until 1915 its members could not subscribe to other news services. The original members of 1900 owned bonds that carried additional voting rights, thereby keeping control of the board of directors in the hands of older, larger papers. The smaller dailies were given 3 seats on a board of 18 in 1937. Most serious was the problem of protest rights, by which a member could keep a competitor in its city out of the AP. A four-fifths vote of the entire membership was required to override such a veto and was rarely obtained. The only way to join the AP in larger cities was to buy an existing membership.

Another unhappy situation in which the AP found itself stemmed from the news-exchange contracts it had made in 1893 with European news agencies. This meant that news of the United States that was collected by the AP was distributed abroad by foreign news services. Melville E. Stone, as AP general manager, did his best to open AP news channels in European countries,[12] and the AP established some foreign bureaus before World War I to collect its own news. But lacking the right to sell its foreign news abroad, years would pass before it could build the kind of foreign service it eventually achieved.

There were many notable names in the AP organization during its formative years under Stone's managership. Charles S. Diehl, a veteran of the Illinois AP regime, became an assistant general manager. So did Jackson S. Elliott, news chief during World War I. Frederick Roy Martin, successful editor of the *Providence Journal,* became assistant general manager in 1912 and succeeded Stone as manager in 1921. Among the noted bureau chiefs were Salvatore Cortesi in Rome, Seymour B. Conger in Berlin, and Edwin M. Hood in Washington. World War I correspondents included Charles T. Thompson, Frederick Palmer, and DeWitt Mackenzie, later an AP news analyst.

SCRIPPS AND HEARST CHALLENGE THE AP

Rising alongside the Associated Press as aggressive competing press associations were the United Press Associations of Edward Wyllis Scripps and the International News Service of William Randolph Hearst. The new UP and the INS were not cooperatives, as was the AP. They were regular business enterprises that sold their news services to clients on a contract basis. Both arose in answer to the AP's closed-membership policy. The chain newspaper publishers who started the UP and the INS soon found that the news they collected could be sold both at home and abroad to others who could not obtain, or did not wish to have, AP service. As both the UP and INS soon were serving a variety of clients, their identification with two strong-minded newspaper publishers became only incidental. Their operating staffs were as eager to cover all the news thoroughly and impartially, for the benefit of their readers, as were the AP people or any other newspeople.

Edward Wyllis Scripps once said that he founded the United Press Associations because he was suspicious of his fellow publishers who controlled the AP. He did not take his papers into the AP in 1897, when the old UP folded. "I knew that at least 90 percent of my fellows in American journalism were capitalistic and conservative," he explained. He went on:

> I knew that, at that time at least, unless I came into the field with a new service, it would be impossible for the people of the United States to get correct news through the medium of the Associated Press. . . . I have made it impossible for the men who control the Associated Press to suppress the truth, or successfully to disseminate falsehood.[13]

The rebellious Scripps was undoubtedly too critical of his fellow publishers, but his concept of competing press associations acting as checks on each other proved to be of inestimable value to American journalism.

Scripps had other reasons for establishing his own news service. The AP was most interested in the news report for its big morning-paper members, and Scripps published evening papers. The closed-membership character of the AP meant that Scripps would have trouble obtaining memberships for the new dailies he was establishing. If he ran his own news service, he could fashion its coverage and writing style to better serve the Scripps type of paper. And finally, he expected to make money running a press association.

THE SECOND UNITED PRESS AND ROY HOWARD

After operating two regional news services for his own papers in the Middle West and West for ten years, in 1907 Scripps merged them with the Publishers' Press Association (begun in 1898 by non-AP eastern papers) to form the United Press Associations. A young Scripps newspaperperson named John Vandercook helped create the merger and become head of the United Press, but he died the following year. Succeeding him as general manager was 25-year-old Roy W. Howard, destined to dominate the Scripps publishing empire. Howard had served on the *St. Louis Post-Dispatch* and Scripps papers in Indianapolis and Cincinnati before getting his big chance with the UP. Scripps described the Roy Howard of this period as

> a striking individual, very small of stature, with a large head and speaking countenance, and eyes that appeared to be windows for a rather unusual intellect. His manner was forceful, and the reverse from modest. Gall was written all over his face. It was in every tone and every word he voiced. There was ambition, self-respect and forcefulness oozing out of every pore of his body.[14]

Howard hustled abroad and established bureaus in the major European capitals. He made connections with leading foreign papers and with commercial news agencies not allied with the AP. Howard's biggest break came when the British cut off the cabling of the German news service to belligerents and neutrals during World War I. Two leading Argentine newspapers, *La Prensa* and *La Nación,* rebelled against receiving only the one-sided reports of the French Havas agency and requested Associated Press service. The AP, under its contract agreements, could not enter the South American area, and Howard rapidly rushed in to give the Argentine papers the type of war-news coverage they wanted. Soon the UP was on the way to building an extensive string of clients in South America, where it established its own bureaus.

But Howard and the United Press came a cropper in November 1918, just when the UP was winning attention. Howard was in American naval headquarters at Brest on November 7, when a message arrived from Paris saying the Armistice had been signed at 11 o'clock that morning. Without verifying the message with higher authorities, Howard flashed the news to the New York UP office, and by an incredible stroke of bad luck for his news service, the message passed the censors. The UP bulletin set off wild celebrations in the United States—until several hours later the AP broke the news that the UP had cabled a premature report. The official surrender was signed on November 11. Although Howard argued that he did what any newsperson would have done when he saw the message at naval headquarters (he decided later that the message had originated with a German secret agent in Paris), some telegraph editors never again fully trusted the UP. Even when, in the 1930s, the AP flashed the wrong verdict on the outcome of the trial of Bruno Richard Hauptmann for the kidnapping and murder of the Lindbergh baby, and when, in 1944, the AP flashed the news of the D-Day landing in France prematurely, old-time newspersons still recalled how "Roy Howard ended the First World War four days early."[15]

The United Press survived the false Armistice Day report, however. When Howard left it in 1920 to become a partner in the Scripps newspaper chain, the UP had 780 clients and a fairly good news service. Scripps, who held 51 percent of the controlling common stock, estimated that he received $200,000 in dividends during the first ten years. In the Scripps custom, the remaining 49 percent of the stock went to key United Press people. The intangible "good will" assets were then valued at $2.5 million by Howard.[16]

A common saying among young, low-paid UP reporters was, "They pay you with bylines." Early in its career, the UP began giving enthusiastic young staffers some glory and a chance to develop their own writing styles and news specialties. AP reporters covering World War I were largely anonymous news gatherers. The UP turned loose young correspondents like Webb Miller, Fred S. Ferguson, William Philip Simms, William G. Shepherd, and Westbrook Pegler. Their vividly written and interpretative copy attracted attention and helped to sell the UP service as a second wire for AP member papers. Miller became European news manager and stayed in command until he was killed in a London blackout early in World War II. Pegler became a widely syndicated columnist, as did three UP Washington staffers of the 1920s: Thomas L. Stokes, Paul Mallon, and Raymond Clapper.

THE INTERNATIONAL NEWS SERVICE

The third American press association competitor was the International News Service. Smaller than its rivals and later in establishing itself as a comprehensive news service, the INS nevertheless won prominence for its competitive spirit.

The INS was founded in 1909 as an outgrowth of earlier leased wire facilities of the Hearst newspapers. Richard A. Farrelly was its first manager. By 1918 the INS was serving 400 clients and had a leased wire system approximately half as extensive as those of the AP and UP.

The sparkplug of the INS after 1916 was Barry Faris, editor-in-chief. He established fewer bureaus than the other services, instead concentrating INS resources on the major news centers. His most successful plan was to offer well-known bylines and special coverage of major news events by talented writers. H. R. Knickerbocker, a Pulitzer Prize winner, and Floyd Gibbons were two longtime INS foreign correspondents. James L. Kilgallen began his roving coverage of major national stories in 1921.

THE FEATURE SYNDICATES: ENTERTAINMENT

The impact of the syndicates on newspaper content was heaviest in the nonnews field. The first to relieve newspaper editors of the necessity of clipping column material, fiction, poetry, and other entertainment features from newspaper and magazine exchanges was Ansel N. Kellogg, the Baraboo, Wisconsin, newsperson who founded a ready-print service in Chicago during the Civil War. One side of the newsprint sheets he issued was printed with such items, while the other was left blank for local news and ads. By 1875 stereotyped plates were being supplied to papers by the American Press Association. The giant of the field became the Western Newspaper Union, founded in Des Moines in 1872 and run by George A. Joslyn after 1890. Joslyn eliminated his rivals by 1917 and refined the "patented insides" business, offering editors alternative preprinted materials. The service, which was supplied to nearly 7000 papers at its peak, gradually declined and was abandoned in 1952.

While the Western Newspaper Union was developing in the weekly field, dailies were being offered syndicated literary material for the feature services of Irving Bacheller (1883), S. S. McClure (1884), and Edward W. Bok (1886). McClure and Bok sensed the public demand for entertaining reading, which led to their own more famous careers as magazine publishers. Hearst joined the syndicate movement in 1895, and in 1914 began his King Features Syndicate. George Matthew Adams entered the field in 1907, and John N. Wheeler in 1913.

The early syndicates featured the writings of Robert Louis Stevenson, Rudyard Kipling, Mark Twain, Bret Harte, Henry James, Alfred Henry Lewis, Jack London, and other literary greats. They also could sample the work of a notable group of poetically inclined columnists and humorous writers, which appeared in newspapers throughout the country. Syndication spread the reputation of "M Quad" of the *Detroit Free Press* and *New York Herald;* Bill Nye of Laramie, Wyoming, and the *New York World;* David Ross Locke of the *Toledo Blade,* who created Petroleum V. Nasby; Opie Read of *Arkansaw Traveler* fame; Joel Chandler Harris of the *Atlanta Constitution;* and Finley Peter Dunne, the Chicago newspaperman whose "Mr. Dooley"—a saloon keeper who philosophized on current affairs—became a national institution.

To older newspaperpeople a column was "a little of everything": wit, poetry, sentiment, and comment on personalities and events in the news. One such column conductor was Eugene Field, the St. Louis and Kansas City reporter whom Melville E. Stone brought to the *Chicago Daily News* to write his "Sharps and Flats" before 1900. Another was Bert Leston Taylor, who founded the *Chicago Tribune*'s famed "A Line o' Type or Two" column in 1901. A third was Franklin P. Adams, who wrote for the *Chicago Journal* and *New York Mail* before beginning his "Conning Tower" in the *New York Tribune* in 1914. Don Marquis wrote his "Sun Dial" column, inhabited by "archie," the noncapitalizing cockroach, for the *New York Sun.*

Walter Winchell set the pace for another kind of column. A New Yorker who entered journalism with the racy tabloids of the 1920s, Winchell promoted the "gossip" column as the Broadway reporter of the tabloid *Graphic.* He shifted to the *Mirror* in 1929 and became a star of Hearst's King Features Syndicate. No other columnist ever approached Winchell's sensationalism and intimate coverage of private lives, but such Hollywood columnists as Louella Parsons and Hedda Hopper did their best. Earl Wilson, Leonard Lyons, and Dorothy Kilgallen were other New York scene columnists of the personal type, while O. O. McIntyre and Mark Hellinger wrote about the metropolis in an older literary style.

"All the News That's Fit to Print."

The New York Times.

THE WEATHER
Fair today and Tuesday; diminishing northwest winds.

VOL. LXVIII...NO. 22,206. NEW YORK, MONDAY, NOVEMBER 11, 1918. TWENTY-FOUR PAGES. TWO CENTS

ARMISTICE SIGNED, END OF THE WAR!
BERLIN SEIZED BY REVOLUTIONISTS;
NEW CHANCELLOR BEGS FOR ORDER;
OUSTED KAISER FLEES TO HOLLAND

SON FLEES WITH EX-KAISER

Hindenburg Also Believed to be Among Those in His Party.

ALL ARE HEAVILY ARMED

Automobiles Bristle with Rifles as Fugitives Arrive at Dutch Frontier.

ON THEIR WAY TO DE STEEG

Belgians Yell to Them, "Are You On Your Way to Paris?"

LONDON, Nov. 10.—Both the former German Emperor and his eldest son, Frederick William, crossed then Dutch frontier Sunday morning, according to advices from The Hague. His reported destination is De Steeg, near Utrecht.

The former German Emperor's party, which is believed to include Field Marshal von Hindenburg, arrived at Eysden, [midway between Liège and Maastricht,] on the Dutch frontier, at 7:30 o'clock Sunday morning, according to Daily Mail advices.

The official news that the German General Staff accompanied the former Emperor, and two automobiles carried the party. The automobiles were bristling with rifles, and all the fugitives were armed.

The ex-Kaiser was in uniform. He alighted at the Eysden station and paced the platform, smoking a cigarette.

Many photographs were taken by [of?] the members of the Imperial party. On the whole the people were very quiet, but Belgians among them yelled out "En voyage a Paris." (Are you on your way to Paris?)

Chatting with the members of the staff, the former Emperor, the correspondent says, did not look in the least distressed. A few minutes later an imperial train, including restaurant and sleeping cars, ran into the station. Only servants were aboard.

The engine returned to Vlad, Belgium, and brought back a second train, in which were a large number of staff officers and others, and also stores of food.

The preparations began for the departure at 10 o'clock this morning, but at 10:40 o'clock the train was still at Eysden. The blinds of the train were all drawn.

The Daily Mail remarks that, if the party arrived in Holland armed, all of them must be interned.

While other dispatches confirm...

Kaiser Fought Hindenburg's Call for Abdication; Failed to Get Army's Support in Keeping Throne

By GEORGE RENWICK
Copyright, 1918, by THE NEW YORK TIMES.
Special Cable to THE NEW YORK TIMES.

AMSTERDAM, Nov. 10.—I learn on very good authority that the Kaiser made a determined effort to stave off abdication. He went to headquarters with the deliberate intention of bringing the army around to his side. In this he failed miserably.

His undo-support consisted of a number of officers, nearly all of Prussian regiments, who forced themselves into two regiments and placed themselves at his Majesty's disposal. To anything with such support was seen, of course, to be Gilbertine.

During the night the Kaiser called the Crown Prince, Hindenburg, and General Gröner to him, and the consultation lasted a couple of hours. Both officers strongly pressed the Kaiser to bow to the inevitable, and Hindenburg informed him that any more delay in coming to a decision to abdicate would certainly have the most terrible consequences and lead to serious events in the army. For these consequences Hindenburg said he must refuse responsibility.

The Crown Prince, it is said, was the first to give way. General Gröner fully supported Hindenburg's view, but when the conference broke up the Kaiser remained unconvinced of the advisability of abdication. So it said to have come to the final decision an hour or so later, after several communications had reached him from Berlin and after another short and stormy talk with Hindenburg.

Meanwhile, the son-in-law, the Duke of Brunswick, for himself and his heir, had abdicated. "Brunswick's final Chieftain" was forced without fighting to abdicate. Reports have it that the republican movement in Brunswick, which long before the war was chafing under autocratic conditions, began to be restive even before it was set in motion at Kiel.

Kaiser Shivered as He Signed Abdication

LONDON, Nov. 10.—Emperor William asked his letter of abdication on Saturday morning at the German Grand Headquarters in the presence of Crown Prince Frederick William and Field Marshal Hindenburg, according to a dispatch from Amsterdam to the Exchange Telegraph Company.

The Crown Prince signed his renunciation of the throne shortly afterward.

Before placing his signature to the document, an urgent message from Philipp Scheidemann, who was a Socialist member without portfolio in the Imperial Cabinet, was handed to the Emperor. He read it with a shiver. Then he signed the paper, saying:
"It may be for the good of Germany."

The Emperor was deeply moved. He consented to sign the document only when he got the news of the latest events in the empire.

The ex-Kaiser and former Crown Prince were expected to take leave of their troops on Saturday, but nothing had then been settled regarding their future movements.

GERMAN DYNASTIES BEING WIPED OUT

King of Wuerttemberg Abdicates—Sovereign of Saxony to Follow Suit.

PRINCES MAY BE EXILED

LONDON, Nov. 10.—A Havas dispatch from Basle says:
"Wilhelm II., the reigning King of the monarchy of Württemberg, abdicated on Friday night."

A Wolff Bureau dispatch from Stuttgart, by way of Amsterdam, says that the King has issued a proclamation saying that his person would never serve to hinder the development of the wishes of the people.

According to a report received from Berne, the German Socialists are demanding that every dynasty in Germany be suppressed and all the Princes exiled. It is reported that the Kings of Bavaria and Saxony intend to abdicate soon.

Here is a list of the rulers, well centered days ago, of the various parts of the German Empire. Those who have abdicated and those reported to be so are marked in italic:

ANHALT—Duke Edward, son of the late Duke Friedrich of Anhalt and of Princess Antoinette of Saxe-Altenburg. Succeeded his brother April 18, 1918.
BADEN—Frederick II, succeeded to...

MORE WARSHIPS JOIN THE REDS

Four Dreadnoughts in Kiel Harbor Espouse the Revolutionary Cause.

GUARDSHIPS ALSO GO OVER

Those Protecting Mines in the Great Belt and the Baltic Abandon Their Posts.

LONDON, Nov. 10.—The crews of four German dreadnoughts Posen, Ostfriesland, Nassau, and Oldenburg, in Kiel Harbor, have joined the revolution, says a Copenhagen dispatch. Marines occupied the imperial Government and who was recently released, has issued the following announcement in Berlin in behalf of the Workmen's and Soldiers' Council:

"The Presidency of the police, as well as the Chief Command, is in our hands. Our comrades will be released."

A dispatch from Berne states that the Burgomaster of Berlin has placed himself and his staff at the disposal of the new Government.

Soon German newspapers describe the movement as Bolshevism. The people are shouting "Long live the Republic!" and singing the "Marseillaise."

When revolutionary soldiers attempted to enter a building in Berlin in which they supposed that a number of offi-

BERLIN TROOPS JOIN 'REVOLT

Reds Shell Building in Which Officers Vainly Resist.

THRONGS DEMAND REPUBLIC

Revolutionary Flag on Royal Palace—Crown Prince's Palace Also Seized.

GENERAL STRIKE IS BEGUN

Burgomaster and Police Submit—War Office Now Under Socialist Control.

LONDON, Nov. 10.—The greater part of Berlin is in control of revolutionists, the former Kaiser has fled to Holland, and Friedrich Ebert, the new Socialist Chancellor, has taken command of the situation. The revolt is spreading throughout Germany with great rapidity.

Dispatches received in London today announce these startling developments. The Workmen's and Soldiers' Council is now administering the municipal government of the German capital.

When the cannonade began the people thought the Reichstag bank was being bombarded, and thousands rushed to the square in front of the Crown Prince's palace. It was later determined that other buildings were under fire. Among those killed in the fighting at the "Cockchafer" Barracks was one of the workmen's leaders known as "Comrade" Haberroth.

The Reds, as last reports, were maintaining order.

Berlin was occupied by forces of the Soldiers' and Workmen's Councils on Saturday afternoon, according to a Wolff Bureau report received in Copenhagen. News of Emperor William's abdication was received in the city at that afternoon and general rejoicing, which was immediate. By the fact that it had come too late.

Russians Aid in Outbreak.

How far the example of the Russian Bolsheviki influenced the German upheaval is an interesting question. Red flags figured frequently in the various risings and Chancellor Ebert's motor car floats the international emblem.

The shoulder straps were torn from the uniforms of officers in a number of German cities and even the soldiers' insignia were stripped from them. Delegates of the revolutionary German navy arrived in Berlin on Friday, according to a dispatch from Copenhagen. They conferred for several hours with the Minister of Marine and with members of the Reichstag majority parties.

It is stated that Hugo Haase, a Socialist leader in the Reichstag, has the situation at Hamburg in hand.

It is officially announced from Berlin, according to a Copenhagen dispatch, that the War Ministry has placed itself at the disposal of Chancellor Ebert. This action was taken for the purpose of assuring the provisioning of the army and assisting...

Socialist Chancellor Appeals to All Germans To Help Him Save Fatherland from Anarchy

BERNE, Nov. 10. (Associated Press.)—In an address to the people, the new German Chancellor, Friedrich Ebert, says:

Citizens: The new Government, Prince Max of Baden, in agreement with all the Secretaries of State, has handed over to me the task of liquidating his affairs as Chancellor. I am on the point of forming a new Government in accord with the various parties, and will keep public opinion freely informed of the course of events.

The new Government will be a Government of the people. It must make every effort to secure in the quickest possible time peace for the German people and consolidate the liberty which they have won.

The new Government has taken charge of the administration, to preserve the German people from civil war and famine and to accomplish their legitimate claim to autonomy. The Government can solve this problem only if all the officials in town and country will help.

I know it will be difficult for some to work with the new men who have taken charge of the empire, but I appeal to their love of the people. Lack of organization would in this heavy time mean anarchy in Germany and the surrender of the country to tremendous misery. Therefore, help your native country with honest, indefatigable work for the future, every one at his post.

I demand every one's support in the hard task awaiting us. You know how seriously the war has menaced the provisioning of the people, which is the first condition of the people's existence. The political transformation should not trouble the people. The food supply is the first duty of all, whether in town or country, and they should not endanger, but rather aid, the production of food supplies and their transport to the towns.

Food shortage signifies pillage and robbery, with great misery. The poorest will suffer the most, and the industrial worker will be affected hardest. All who illicitly lay hands on food supplies or other supplies of prime necessity or the means of transport necessary for their distribution will be guilty in the highest degree toward the community.

I ask you immediately to leave the streets and remain quiet and calm.

COPENHAGEN, Nov. 10.—The new Berlin Government, according to a Wolff Bureau dispatch, has issued the following proclamation:

Fellow-Citizens: This day the people's difference has been fulfilled. The Social Democratic Party has undertaken to form a Government. It has invited the Independent Socialist Party to share the Government with equal rights.

In the solution of demobilization problems.

Serious food difficulties are expected in Germany, owing to the stoppage of traffic. The Council of the Regency will take the most drastic steps to re-establish order.

In the new German Government there will be only three representatives of the majority parties, namely, Ebert, Landsberg, and Scheidemann, of the Social Democrats. The other posts will be occupied by Socialists and Independents.

Reds Announce Success.

BERLIN, Nov. 9. (German Wireless to London, Nov. 10.)—(Associated Press.)—The German People's Government has been instituted in the greater part of Berlin. The garrison has gone over to the Government.

The Workmen's and Soldiers' Council has declared a general strike. Troops and machine guns have been placed at the disposal of the Council. Guards which had been stationed at the public offices and other buildings have been withdrawn.

Friedrich Ebert (Vice President of the Social Democratic Party) is carrying on the Chancellorship.

The text of a statement issued by the People's Government reads:

In the course of the forenoon of Saturday the formation of a new German People's Government was initiated. The greater part of the Berlin garrison, and other troops stationed there temporarily, went over to the new Government.

The leaders of the Oppositions of the Social Democratic Party declared that they would not appeal against the people. They will fight on with the masses. The new world, in accordance with the fundamental laws of the empire, restores to them all the legislative power in the State of Germany.

The business of the Imperial Chancellor is being carried on by Friedrich Ebert, and his only aim is the establishment of order.

Scheidemann Exhorts Calm.

Deputy Scheidemann, (leader of the majority Socialists in the Reichstag,) in a speech today said:

"The Kaiser and the Crown Prince have abdicated." The dynasty...

WAR ENDS AT 6 O'CLOCK THIS MORNING

The State Department in Washington Made the Announcement at 2:45 o'Clock

ARMISTICE WAS SIGNED IN FRANCE AT MIDNIGHT

Terms Include Withdrawal from Alsace-Lorraine, Disarming and Demobilization of Army and Navy, and Occupation of Strategic Naval and Military Points.

By The Associated Press.

WASHINGTON, Monday, Nov. 11, 2:48 A. M.—The armistice between Germany, on the one hand, and the allied Governments and the United States, on the other, has been signed.

The State Department announced at 2:45 o'clock this morning that Germany had signed.

The department's announcement simply said: "The armistice has been signed."

The world war will end this morning at 6 o'clock, Washington time, 11 o'clock Paris time.

The armistice was signed by the German representatives at midnight.

This announcement was made by the State Department at 2:50 o'clock this morning.

The announcement was made verbally by an official of the State Department in this form:

"The armistice has been signed. It was signed at 5 o'clock A. M., Paris time, [midnight, New York time,] and hostilities will cease at 11 o'clock this morning, Paris time. [6 o'clock, New York time.]

The terms of the armistice, it was announced, will not be made public until later. Military men have, however, regard it as certain that they include:

Immediate retirement of the German military forces from France, Belgium, and Alsace-Lorraine.

Disarming and demobilization of the German armies.

Occupation by the allied and American forces of such strategic points in Germany as will make impossible a renewal of hostilities.

Delivery of part of the German High Seas Fleet and a certain number of submarines to the allied and American naval forces.

Disarmament of all other German warships...

Continued on Page Two.

Continued on Page Two.

Continued on Page Four.

Continued on Page Four.

Continued on Page Two.

The famous 1918 Armistice Day edition of the *New York Times*

12

War Comes
to the United States

> After the Marne the war grew and spread until it drew in the
> nations of both hemispheres and entangled them in a pattern of
> world conflict no peace treaty could dissolve. . . . The nations were
> caught in a trap, a trap made during the first thirty days out of
> battles that failed to be decisive, a trap from which there was, and
> has been, no exit.
>
> —*Barbara Tuchman, in* The Guns of August

The great war that began in Europe in August 1914 completely altered the pattern of life that a comparatively peaceful nineteenth century had produced. By 1917 it had become a world war, with the United States embarking on a "great crusade" to make the world safe for democracy. But at war's end people found they could neither restore the old order nor build a peaceful new one. Political and social disillusionment, economic depression, and the rise of modern dictatorships brought a second great war, and the designations World War I and II came into the language. After that, war and threat of war seem an unending morass.

In *The Guns of August* Barbara Tuchman agreed with Sir Edward Grey that "the lamps are going out all over Europe; we shall not see them lit again in our lifetime." Tuchman's account began with the pageantry of the funeral procession for King Edward VII in 1910: "the sun of the old world was setting in a dying blaze of splendor never to be seen again." Beside the new king, George V, rode his cousin Wilhelm II, emperor of Germany, mounted on a gray horse and wearing the scarlet uniform of a British field marshal. Behind them, among 9 kings and 50 more royals, were Albert, king of the Belgians, destined for a hero's role; the Archduke Franz Ferdinand, who would be assassinated at Sarajevo; and former President Theodore Roosevelt, who had projected the United States into world pageantry by sending its "Great White Fleet" around the world.

Many of the beplumed, gold-braided riders represented crowns and empires that would disappear in the coming decade: the Hohenzollerns of Germany, the Hapsburgs of

Austria-Hungary, the Romanovs of Russia, the Sultanate of Turkey, the Manchu dynasty of China. But despite the arms rivalries and tensions of the past few years and Kaiser Wilhelm's claim to Germany's "place in the sun," few believed on that 1910 day that so many great dynasties would topple or that the peace of western Europe, unbroken since 1871, would be ruptured. The chancellories of Europe were assuring the world that war was impossible, and their military planners were blueprinting only a short war at most. The failure of the German master battle plan that fateful August 1914 brought the war into the trap from which there was no exit.

AMERICAN REACTION TO EUROPE'S 1914 WAR

No one could foresee in 1914 the ultimate consequences of Germany's transformation of a "Balkan incident" into a general European war. Even though the United States had entered into the world diplomatic arena after its war with Spain, most Americans probably felt secure behind two oceans and were interested only in preserving peace as far as this country was concerned. No doubt the jesting comment of the *Chicago Herald* summarized this attitude: "Peace-loving citizens of this country will now rise up and tender a hearty vote of thanks to Columbus for having discovered America."[1]

Yet underneath this denial of concern by Americans for what was happening in Europe lay the first instinctive reactions to the shattering of peace. As Americans read the vivid account by Richard Harding Davis of the entry of the German army into Brussels—"one unbroken steel-gray column . . . 24 hours later is still coming . . . not men marching, but a force of nature like a tidal wave, an avalanche"—and as they looked almost unbelievingly at pictures of the sacked city of Louvain, they became increasingly uncomfortable.

It is important to record these first American reactions, since in the depths of later disillusionment, when it was evident that our participation in the war had failed to bring a lasting peace, a literature appeared that told a different story.[2] British propagandists, American munitions makers, and cynical politicians had led gullible Americans to an unnecessary slaughter, the theme ran, carrying with it the implication that American newspapers had been duped by foreign propagandists and by war-mongering capitalists, and thereby had misled their readers. A quite convincing case was built on partial evidence for such a thesis, ignoring or overriding such important factors as the impact on American public opinion of crises, such as the sinking of the *Lusitania,* which were predominantly unfavorable to the German side; the effects of Allied censorship and control of overseas communications in shaping the available news (as distinct from overt propaganda efforts); the effects of socially important pressure groups in shaping American thought; the natural ties between English-speaking peoples and the distaste of Americans for German "Kultur"; the legitimate pro-Allied decisions of American officials and diplomats based on German-caused events; the feeling that a strong British navy was less hazardous to American interests than a strong German navy; and, most importantly, the United States objection to one-nation domination of Europe—an objection that led to two wars with German militarism in defense of the American national interest.[3] America opposed one-nation domination of Europe mainly for economic reasons. Perhaps for the first time, the United States realized it had a stake in the world economic system and that its prosperity depended on the widest possible flourishing of liberal capitalism.[4]

News of military actions was delayed by both sides, and official communiqués often attempted to conceal news of reversals.[5] Some correspondents managed to obtain beats on news of important battles, but largely as a matter of luck. Reporters on the front more often won recognition for their feature stories than for their straight factual accounts, while military analysts in the various European capitals provided the continuing story of the fighting along the sprawling western and eastern fronts. This news, after clearing the military censors, still had to funnel through the London communications center, since the British had cut the German Atlantic cable on August 5, 1914. Stories written in Berlin, Vienna, and neutral capitals thereafter had to travel through London to reach the United States.[6]

THE UNITED STATES MOVES TOWARD WAR

The course of events was rapidly bolstering pro-Allied sentiment in the United States. The *New York Times* printed "white papers" giving each belligerent power's version of the events leading up to the war, but Germany's obvious preparation for war and smashing early victories were added reasons to believe the Allied versions, imperfectly as they were presented. The natural ties of many Americans to the English traditions, which were particularly strong among social and intellectual leaders, made it fashionable to be pro-British. Yet large segments of the population opposed American entry into the war up to the last, for various reasons. For one matter, the early twentieth century had seen unprecedented growth in the peace reform movement. Forty-five new peace organizations appeared between 1901 and 1914, including the Carnegie Endowment for International Peace (1910) and the Church Peace Union (1914). In 1915, new peace associations included the Woman's Peace Party and the Fellowship of Reconciliation; the American Union Against Militarism was founded the following year.[7] Now, as U.S. involvement in war loomed, the Middle West was more isolationist than the seaboard sections and was suspicious of the pro-Allied easterners. The Irish, a strong minority, were naturally anti-British because of the Irish civil war, although this did not necessarily make them pro-German. The large groups of German-Americans who were, on the whole, loyal to the United States, were at the same time naturally sympathetic with the aims of their homeland. They regarded Germany's ambitions as no more dangerous or imperialistic than those of Britain, France, and Russia.

One decisive event was the torpedoing of the English Cunard line's *Lusitania,* then the queen of the Atlantic run. When the *Lusitania* went down off the Irish coast on May 7, 1915, with the loss of 1198 of the 1924 persons aboard—including 114 of the 188 American passengers—Germany celebrated the accomplishment of her U-boat captain. But resentment ran high in the United States, particularly when it was remembered that an Imperial Germany Embassy advertisement warning travelers on Allied ships that they did so "at their own risk" had appeared in New York newspapers the morning the *Lusitania* left port. Later it was discovered that the ship had carried munitions.

Even though Germany relaxed its submarine warfare after months of diplomatic note-writing by President Wilson, the summer of 1916 was dominated by pro-Allied arguments and by talk of preparedness. Wilson, whose most effective 1916 campaign slogan had been "He kept us out of war," saw his hopes of the United States serving as a neutral arbiter dashed by two final German actions.

One was the resumption of unrestricted submarine warfare by the Germans in February 1917. This brought a break in diplomatic relations. Clinching the American decision was the Allied interception of German Foreign Minister Zimmermann's note to the Mexican government, offering Mexico the return of Texas, New Mexico, and Arizona after an American defeat, if Mexico would ally itself with Germany. The text of the note, given to the Associated Press unofficially, created a sensation. The sinking in March of three American ships by U-boats brought Wilson's war call on April 2—"The world must be made safe for democracy"—and the declaration of war on April 6. Wilson's masterful phrases played no small part in determining the issue. His denunciation of a group of 11 senators, led by Robert La Follette of Wisconsin, as a "little group of willful men" for filibustering against the arming of American merchant ships in early March did much to discredit the opponents of war.

Some periodicals had been pro-Allies almost from the start. Among the most outspoken were the old *Life* magazine, the *New York Herald,* and Henry Watterson's *Louisville Courier-Journal,* whose editor adopted, in October 1914, the simple but effective battle-cry, "To hell with the Hohenzollerns and the Hapsburgs!" The *New York Times* was solidly pro-Allies, along with the *World* and most other New York newspapers. After the sinking of the *Lusitania,* the number of anti-interventionist newspapers dwindled. William Randolph Hearst's chain of papers stood out as bitterly anti-British and was tarred as pro-German because Hearst made special efforts to obtain German-originated news to balance Allied-originated stories. Other holdouts against the war were the *New York Evening Mail* (which had been bought secretly by German agents), *Chicago Tribune, Cincinnati Enquirer, Cleveland Plain Dealer, Washington Post, Milwaukee Sentinel, Los Angeles Times, San Francisco Chronicle,* and *San Francisco Call.*[8] All, of course, supported the war once it was declared. William Jennings Bryan's *Commoner, La Follette's Weekly,* and Oswald G. Villard's *Nation* and *New York Evening Post* were pacifist.

GEORGE CREEL'S COMMITTEE ON PUBLIC INFORMATION

Only a week after the declaration of war, Wilson appointed a Committee on Public Information (CPI). Its job was primarily one of disseminating facts about the war. It was also to coordinate government propaganda efforts and to serve as the government's liaison with newspapers. It drew up a voluntary censorship code under which editors would agree to refrain from printing material that might aid the enemy. Before it was through, the committee found itself "mobilizing the mind of the world," and Mark Sullivan characterized it as an American contribution to the science of war. George Creel, the newspaper editor who was named by Wilson to direct the committee's work, explained that "it was a plain publicity proposition, a vast enterprise in salesmanship, the world's greatest adventure in advertising."[9]

The opportunity Wilson gave to Creel was a greater one than any other person had enjoyed in the propaganda arena.[10] Creel was a liberal-minded and vigorously competent product of New York, Kansas City, and Denver journalism. He was intensely eager to achieve every possible task his committee might embrace, and he eventually mobilized 150,000 Americans to carry out its varied and far-flung missions.

Creel first opened up government news channels to the Washington correspondents and insisted that only news of troop movements, ship sailings, and other events of strictly military character should be withheld. He issued a brief explanatory code calling on the newspapers to censor such news themselves, voluntarily. Throughout the war, newspaper editors generally went beyond Creel's minimum requests in their desire to aid the war effort. In May 1917, the CPI began publishing an *Official Bulletin* in which releases were reprinted in newspaper form. Before the war was over this publication reached a daily circulation of 118,000. A weekly newspaper editor prepared a digest of the news for rural papers. Still photographs, plates, and mats also were utilized.

A historian who studied the accuracy of CPI news releases years later came to this conclusion: "One of the most remarkable things about the charges against the CPI is that,

James Montgomery Flagg's famous poster for the CPI

of the more than 6,000 news stories it issued, so few were called into question at all. It may be doubted that the CPI's record for honesty will ever be equalled in the official war news of a major power."[11] The historian, however, was referring to sins of commission; the sins of omission—concealment of news by the CPI and the military—were more extensive than considerations of national security required, but less so than those of the Allies.

Creel asked major advertisers and the publications themselves to donate space for various government campaigns, the Red Cross, and other war-related activities. The advertising agencies were organized, and their copy writers and artists were used to create newspaper and magazine advertising, streetcar placards, and outdoor posters. The artists in the CPI's division of pictorial publicity, headed by Charles Dana Gibson, contributed stirring posters. The infant motion-picture industry produced films of a patriotic and instructive nature. Its stars, including Douglas Fairbanks and Mary Pickford, sparked Liberty bond sales. College professors served in a division of pamphleteering that produced a *War Cyclopedia* and 75 million pieces of printed matter. Historian Guy Stanton Ford of the University of Minnesota headed the division, which included such noted historians as Carl Becker of Cornell University, Evarts B. Greene of the University of Illinois, and Frederic L. Paxson of the University of Wisconsin.[12]

Viewed from today's perspective, these endeavors also have a disturbing side. Historians now connect the intolerance of the war and postwar years with the government's propaganda efforts during the war, noting that "the division between patriotism and intolerance proved impossible to maintain."[13]

CENSORSHIP OF GERMAN AND SOCIALIST PAPERS

The Espionage Act of June 15, 1917, provided the opening wedge for the suppression of those who were considered to be disloyal to the American and Allied war cause. Among the crimes that were punishable by heavy fines and imprisonment were willfully made false reports or false statements intended to interfere with the successful operation of the military or naval forces, and willful attempts to promote disloyalty in the armed forces or to obstruct recruitments. A section on use of the mails empowered Postmaster General Albert S. Burleson to declare unmailable all letters, circulars, newspapers, pamphlets, books, and other materials violating provisions of the act.

The restrictions fell most heavily on Socialist organs and German-language newspapers; a few other pacifist or anti-Allies publications also lost their mail privileges. The *American Socialist* was banned from the mails immediately and was soon followed by *Solidarity,* the journal of the left-wing Industrial Workers of the World—the much-feared anticapitalistic IWW. A vociferous advocate of the Irish independence movement, Jeremiah A. O'Leary, lost mailing privileges for his publication, *Bull,* for opposing wartime cooperation with the British. The magazine *The Masses,* brilliantly edited by Max Eastman, felt the ban in August 1917 for publishing an issue containing four antiwar cartoons and a poem defending radical leaders Emma Goldman and Alexander Berkman. An indictment against the editors under the Espionage Act was dismissed in 1919.

Altogether some 44 papers lost their mailing privileges during the first year of the Espionage Act and another 30 retained them only by agreeing to print nothing more concerning the war. The best known were two Socialist dailies, the *New York Call* and Victor Berger's *Milwaukee Leader.* The Austrian-born Berger, in 1910 the first Socialist elected to Congress, was convicted on charges of conspiracy to violate the Espionage Act and was sentenced to 20 years imprisonment. The United States Supreme Court later overturned the decision due to the prejudicial actions of the presiding judge. Twice the House of Representatives denied him the seat to which he had been reelected. For a time during and after the war, all incoming mail was prevented from reaching the *Leader.* The Supreme Court upheld the post office ban on the *Leader* in a 1921 decision, and it was not until June 1921, when Postmaster General Will Hays restored their second-class mailing privileges, that the *Leader* and the *Call* were once again able to reach their numerous out-of-town subscribers. The German-language press likewise was hard hit by mail bans and prosecutions, and declined one-half in numbers and in circulation during the war.

Other papers felt the weight of public opinion against those who did not wholeheartedly support the war. The Hearst newspapers, which had bitterly opposed American entry into the war and continued to be clearly anti-Allies even though they supported the American war effort itself, were widely attacked. Hearst was hanged in effigy, his papers were boycotted in some places, and he himself was denounced as disloyal. His newspapers had vigorously denounced the bringing of charges against Socialist and German-language papers—in contrast to editorial approval of these moves by the *New York Times* and widespread media disinterest in their First Amendment implications. Oswald Garrison Villard's pacifist views and defenses of civil liberties brought such a decline in the fortunes of the *New York Evening Post* that he was forced to sell it in 1918, and one issue of the *Nation* was held up in the New York post office because it carried an editorial titled "Civil Liberty Dead."

THE SEDITION ACT OF 1918

The powers of the government to control the expression of opinion were strengthened by the passage of two other laws. The Trading-with-the-Enemy Act of October 1917 authorized censorship of all communications moving in or out of the United States, and provided that translations of newspaper or magazine articles published in foreign languages could be demanded by the post office—a move to keep the German-language papers in line. The Sedition Act of May 1918 amended and broadened the Espionage Act by making it a crime to write or publish "any disloyal, profane, scurrilous or abusive language about the form of government of the United States or the Constitution, military or naval forces, flag, or the uniform," or to use language intended to bring these ideas and institutions "into contempt, scorn, contumely, or disrepute." The Post Office's application of these broad provisions to ban publications from the mails gave the postmaster general immense powers he hesitated to use. The memory of the blundering Sedition Act of 1798 kept him from using his authority to harass orthodox Republican opponents of the administration, and the brunt of persecution continued to fall on the unpopular radical and pro-German minorities.

Former President Theodore Roosevelt was asking heatedly why the Hearst newspapers had not been denied mail privileges (some Republicans said Hearst escaped because he was a Democrat). Roosevelt also was writing editorials for the *Kansas City Star* criticizing the administration, and he was speaking strongly against what he called its incompetence and softness in dealing with the enemy. Senator Robert La Follette of Wisconsin, who was politically crucified by an error the Associated Press made in reporting one of his speeches,[14] likewise was a possible candidate for prosecution.

The Department of Justice, however, moved against lesser-known persons like the IWW leaders, who were arrested and imprisoned, and Mrs. Rose Pastor Stokes, who got a ten-year sentence for writing a letter to the *Kansas City Star* saying, "No government which is for profiteers can also be for the people, and I am for the people, while the government is for the profiteers." The verdict against Mrs. Stokes was reversed in 1920. But not so fortunate was the four-time Socialist party presidential candidate, Eugene V. Debs. When he told a Socialist convention in June 1918 that the allies were "out for plunder" and then defended the Bolshevists in Russia, he was jailed. Debs's conviction for violation of the Espionage and Sedition Acts was upheld unanimously by the Supreme Court. He received the record Socialist party presidential vote of 920,000 while campaigning in 1920 from federal prison, however, and was pardoned by President Harding in December 1921.

The wartime atmosphere was favorable to the restriction of civil liberties. Generally adopted state laws contained antipacifist, anticommunist, and criminal syndicalism clauses designed to protect business and industry against radical-inspired strikes and violence. Mobs and citizens' committees took care of unpopular persons, including Americans of German ancestry. Many Americans were persuaded by community pressure to buy more Liberty bonds than they wanted. Prosecutors, juries, and judges went beyond the words of the Espionage and Sedition Acts, often because of public pressure. Zechariah Chafee, Jr., the distinguished Harvard law professor, documented the damage done to the spirit of the constitutional guarantee of free speech in his 1920 work, *Freedom of Speech.*[15]

Censorship of foreign communications sent by cable, telephone, or telegraph, as provided in the Trading-with-the-Enemy Act, was carried out by a Censorship Board, which Wilson established in October 1917 to coordinate control of communications facilities. The board was mainly concerned with outgoing messages and news dispatches. There were few complaints against the board, and it received a "job well done" commendation.[16]

LEADING WAR CORRESPONDENTS

Notable among the early war reporters were Richard Harding Davis, whose story of the entry of the German army into Brussels was written for the *New York Tribune* and its syndicate, and Will Irwin, whose beats on the battle of Ypres and the first German use of poison gas were also printed in the *Tribune.* Irwin was one of several correspondents who represented American magazines in Europe; he first wrote for *Collier's* and then for the *Saturday Evening Post.* However, the brunt of the news-coverage responsibility fell on the reporters in the European capital bureaus. Some of the leaders were Karl H. von Wiegand of the United Press and Sigrid Schultz of the *Chicago Tribune* in Berlin; Paul Scott Mowrer of the *Chicago Daily News* and Wythe Williams of the *New York Times* in Paris; and Edward Price Bell of the *Chicago Daily News* in London.

American war correspondents in France found themselves freer to observe the military actions of the American Expeditionary Force (AEF) than those of the other Allied armies. In General Pershing's area correspondents could go into the front lines without military escorts, they could follow the fighting advances, and they could roam the rear areas, living where they chose. This had not been the case for correspondents with the British, French, and German forces in the early years of the war. But everything the correspondents wrote went through the censorship of the press section of the Military Intelligence Service, headed by Major Frederick Palmer, formerly of the Associated Press. News of general engagements, casualties suffered, and troop identifications was released only if it had been mentioned in official communiqués. Press officers were also attached to the training camps and cantonments at home.

There were some 500 American correspondents for newspapers, magazines, press associations, and syndicates in Europe by 1915, and the number was augmented when

American troops joined the fighting. About 40 actually covered the actions of the AEF. Among the best-known byliners was Fred S. Ferguson of the United Press, who beat his competitors in reporting the battle of Saint-Mihiel by writing an advance story, based on the American battle plan, and having it filed section by section as the battle proceeded. Webb Miller of the UP and Henry Wales of the INS also won prominence, along with Edwin L. James of the *New York Times,* Martin Green of the *New York World,* and Junius Wood of the *Chicago Daily News.* Floyd Gibbons of the *Chicago Tribune* was hit by German machine-gun fire and lost an eye.

A soldiers' journalism also sprouted during wartime, the best-known example being the *Stars and Stripes.* The eight-page paper was established in Paris in February 1918. Harold Ross, later editor of the *New Yorker,* became the chief editor, assisted by such well-known writers as Grantland Rice and Alexander Woollcott. Other overseas units had their publications, as did all of the camps in the United States.

DEFEAT OF THE TREATY AND THE LEAGUE

President Wilson had given the world a blueprint for the postwar settlement in his Fourteen Points speech of January 1918 and later addresses before Congress, which called for the establishment of an association of nations (named the League of Nations), international political and economic cooperation, and self-determination in realigning Europe's boundaries. With the defeat of Germany imminent, Wilson made the first of a series of blunders that gave his political opponents a chance to defeat his program.

Wilson erred in asking voters to return Democrats to Congress in the November 1918 election so that he might "be your unembarrassed spokesman at home and abroad." The voters' answer was the election of a Republican majority in both houses. Insensitive to this public reminder that no leader is indispensable, Wilson failed to include any Republican, or any senator, in the American delegation to the Versailles peace conference, even though the treaty would need a two-thirds vote of the Republican-controlled Senate for ratification. He erred finally in making himself the chief negotiator on a daily basis, thereby losing his flexibility and his earlier role as agenda setter for general policy.[17]

By the time the Versailles treaty was signed in June 1919, Wilson's agenda was in disarray. The British, French, and Italian leaders had compromised some of the Fourteen Points; nationalistic rivalries had endangered idealistic territorial adjustments; and a group of 37 senators had announced that they would not vote for a treaty containing a League of Nations, thereby leaving it short of the necessary two-thirds approval. Wilson's answer was to undertake a September cross-country train tour, during which he gave 18 talks in 22 days. He drew large crowds and friendly audiences, and had a good press for his arguments reaffirming basic principles. But right behind him came such relentless Senate opponents as Hiram W. Johnson of California and William E. Borah of Idaho, who picked holes in particular articles of the treaty and made rebuttals in the press. On the final day of his tour, Wilson suffered a physical breakdown and retired into the White House, where he remained partially paralyzed, for the rest of his term.

Wilson's illness left the internationalists leaderless. The Republican Senate leader, Henry Cabot Lodge of Massachusetts, offered a number of conditions affecting American participation in the League as the price for ratification. Moderate Democrats wished to accept, but Wilson denounced the plan as a betrayal and prevented its passage. Thus the United States Senate failed to ratify the treaty, thereby backing out of the international association Wilson had sponsored. In the press, the League had enjoyed reasonably good support from newspapers and magazines, right to the end. Republican politics and Wilson's mistakes killed it. Wilson's supporters sought to make the 1920 presidential election a "solemn referendum," but the Republican slogan of a "return to normalcy" swept the ticket of Warren G. Harding and Calvin Coolidge into office.

THE GREAT "RED SCARE"

The other major postwar reaction was the continuation of a gigantic "Red Scare," stimulated in part by the Russian Revolution and also by reaction to the radical IWW labor movement and Socialist party successes. The persecutions and prosecutions made during wartime under the Espionage and Sedition Acts continued unabated; indeed, the "Red Scare" intensified in 1919. Approximately 2000 persons were prosecuted under the two laws, and nearly half were convicted.

The year 1919 was marked by large-scale strikes. These were called by workers whose often meager salaries had been eroded by wartime inflation and the high cost of living (called "HCL" in the headlines). In Boston police officers whose annual salaries were as low as $1100 joined the American Federation of Labor and finally struck. Governor Calvin Coolidge's laconic "There is no right to strike against the public safety by anyone, anytime, anywhere," doomed the now locked-out police and propelled Coolidge into the vice-presidential nomination and eventually into the White House.

The Industrial Workers of the World (IWW), formed in 1905, had won 100,000 members among unorganized timber workers, longshoremen, miners, migratory workers, and immigrant textile workers. Called the "Wobblies" by their opponents, they aroused public fears with revolutionary rhetoric and loose talk of violence. Their antiwar stand of 1917–18 brought federal raids on their headquarters, arrests, and deportations of alien members. When Legionnaires raided their Centralia, Washington, headquarters in December 1919, and gunfire caused several deaths, the "Red Scare" took over. The IWW movement fell apart, leaving unskilled workers leaderless until the emergence of the CIO in the 1930s. The great steel strike of 1919, in which the AFL sought to unionize the iron and steel industry, succeeded in calling out 340,000 workers in Eastern states. But the strike leader, William Z. Foster, was pilloried as a former Wobblie and a believer in revolutionary programs. His vulnerability aided Elbert H. Gary, president of the U.S. Steel Corporation, in breaking the strike and in preventing unionization of the industry until the 1930s. Foster emerged as a national militant Communist leader.

The "Red Scare" approached a public panic. The display of red flags was forbidden in New York and other states; Attorney General Mitchell Palmer hustled groups of "Reds" to Ellis Island for deportation; the offices of the Socialist daily, the *New York Call,* were raided and wrecked; Socialists were ousted from the New York State Legislature and the Congress; several universities and colleges dismissed tenured professors who were pacifists, Socialists, and of German ancestry; local school boards prescribed loyalty oaths for teachers; many states passed "anti-Red" and criminal syndicalism laws; bombings and a dynamite explosion on Wall Street reinforced the fear of violence. The evangelist Billy Sunday summed up the widespread feeling:

> If I had my way with these ornery wild-eyed Socialists and IWW's, I would stand them up before a firing squad and save space on our ships.[18]

Fortunately it was Palmer who was in charge in December 1919, when a ship dubbed the "Soviet Ark" left New York with 249 Russian aliens aboard, including anarchist leaders

Headings of some of the newspapers which have been the most ardent advocates of "direct action," which when analyzed usually means revolution. Some of their plants have been raided by the Department of Justice and many of their editors and writers are now under arrest.
(C. Pathe Films.)

Types of revolutionists who have been gathered in by the Department of Justice, which has now over 6,000 such in its toils. The foreign aspect of most of the faces is evident. The majority of those arrested are aliens.
(©) N. Y. H. Service.)

Group of radicals, many of whom face deportation, at dinner on Ellis Island. The Island at present is unusually crowded, owing to the unprecedented activity recently shown in rounding up revolutionaries, but the food furnished is good and abundant.
(©) Pathe Films.)

"Reds" snapshotted at Ellis Island while at meals. A riot took place when the arrested men realized that they were being photographed. A rush was made for the cameras, and some of them were smashed, while the mob tried to "manhandle" the operators.
(©) Pathe Films.)

Mid-Week Pictorial, published by the *New York Times,* portrays "revolutionists" with "foreign faces" during the 1919–20 Red Scare.

Emma Goldman and Alexander Berkman, but mostly ordinary workers who had joined the wrong union.

The "Red Scare" also marked the beginning of the career of J. Edgar Hoover in the Justice Department. He was named head in 1919 of the newly created General Intelligence Division, which became the Federal Bureau of Investigation. Hoover directed the FBI until his death in 1972, perceived by the public as a legendary victor over gangsters and a relentless foe of communism. Hoover's 1919 orders were to concentrate on a study of subversive activities; his office provided a list of 60,000 "radicals" within 100 days and a catalogue of 450,000 names in 18 months, including those of 625 "radical" newspapers.[19] Hoover thus began his long career of attacking liberals, blacks, or anyone who in his mind posed a danger to "national security."

The climax of the "Red Scare" came with the Sacco-Vanzetti case. In 1920 a Massachusetts factory payroll manager and guard were shot and killed. Sacco, a shoemaker, and Vanzetti, a fish peddler, were arrested and convicted for the shooting. Defenders said they were framed due to their Italian origins, radical anarchist ideas, and pacifism that had led them to escape military service. Others confessed to the killings, but the "law and order establishment" set its face against a protest by liberals and radicals that reached international proportions. Finally, in 1927, the pair were executed. Upton Sinclair, Maxwell Anderson, John Dos Passos, and James T. Farrell created a literature of protest that made "Sacco-Vanzetti" a symbol of national prejudice and class hatred.

In general, the newspapers failed dismally to defend the civil liberties of those being questionably attacked. The epithet "Reds" was applied to all those caught up in the hunt for disloyal or radical persons. One of the worst offenders on this score was the *New York Times,* whose publisher Adolph Ochs exhibited solid capitalistic preferences and an unreasonable fear of any form of radicalism that might endanger the society in which he had prospered. Walter Lippmann and Charles Merz of the *New York World* editorial-page staff published a documented study, "A Test for the News," as a supplement to the August 4, 1920, issue of the *New Republic,* illustrating the inaccuracy with which the Associated Press and the *New York Times* had reported Russian events from 1917 to 1920 (Merz later became editor of the *Times*). Civil liberties were best defended by the liberal magazines, led by the *Nation* and *New Republic,* and by a handful of newspapers, notably the *St. Louis Post-Dispatch* and the *World* and *Globe* in New York City.

LEGAL CASES: "CLEAR AND PRESENT DANGER"

Out of the prosecutions for political expression arose four landmark cases in the establishment of the First Amendment rights of freedom of speech and freedom of the press. In them Justice Oliver Wendell Holmes advanced what became known as the "clear-and-present-danger" theory.

The first case involved Charles T. Schenck, Elizabeth Baer, and other members of the Philadelphia Socialist party who printed and distributed antiwar leaflets urging young draft inductees to join the Socialist party and work for the repeal of the draft law. It also denounced the war as a ruthless adventure serving the interests of Wall Street. In the Supreme Court's 1919 decision upholding the convictions (*Schenck* v. *U.S.*),[20] Holmes wrote:

> But the character of every act depends upon the circumstances in which it is done. . . . The question in every case is whether the words used, are used in such circumstances and are of

such a nature as to create a clear and present danger that they will bring about the substantive evils that Congress has a right to prevent. It is a question of proximity and degree.

Holmes and the Court found that there had been such a clear and present danger in the Schenck case. In two other Espionage Act cases decided in 1919, the Supreme Court used the same standard to affirm the convictions of Jacob Frohwerk, a German-language newspaper editor, and Eugene Debs, the leader of the American Socialist party.

The second landmark case, the first Supreme Court test of the Sedition Act, was *Abrams* v. *U.S.*[21] Abrams and four other New York radicals had been sentenced to 20 years imprisonment for distributing pamphlets condemning American troop intervention in Russia (they also denounced German militarism). The pamphlets urged a general strike to prevent the production of munitions; for this, Justice John Clarke wrote for the majority, the clear-and-present-danger rule applied to mandate conviction. Holmes and Louis Brandeis dissented, arguing that the best test of truth was by "free trade in ideas" and the "power of the thought to get itself accepted in the competition of the market." Now Holmes wrote:

> Only the emergency that makes it immediately dangerous to leave the correction of evil counsels to time warrants making any exception to the sweeping command, "Congress shall make no law . . . abridging the freedom of speech."

In the 1925 case of Benjamin Gitlow,[22] who was convicted under a New York State criminal anarchy law of issuing Socialist manifestoes, the majority advanced the theory of balancing by the courts of the competing private and public interests represented in First Amendment cases. Holmes and Brandeis dissented, ridiculing the pamphlet, the *Left Wing Manifesto,* as a dreadfully dull political tract. Once more the defendants had lost, but *Gitlow* contained a vitally important statement by the conservative majority that would buttress later defenses of First Amendment rights of speech and press. This statement said it was proper for the Court to apply the protection of the First Amendment to the states under the Fourteenth Amendment. Positive application of this landmark theory came six years later in *Near* v. *Minnesota* (see Chapter 14), when the defendant won.

In 1927, while concurring in the conviction of Anita Whitney under a California law outlawing the Communist party, Brandeis brilliantly restated the clear-and-present-danger theory[23]—cold comfort, perhaps, to the convicted that progressive legal theory was being advanced. In the 1951 case of Eugene Dennis,[24] who was convicted of conspiracy under the sweeping provisions of the anti-communist Smith Act of 1940, the majority once again used the clear-and-present-danger argument to convict Communist party members, citing the world tensions of 1948. Whatever the outcomes, such post-publication trials were preferable to prior restraint mandates, for Schenck and his successors had at least had their say.

LONG-RANGE EFFECTS OF THE "RED SCARE"

The "Red Scare" and the fears the Russian Revolution had generated among most Americans succeeded in fragmenting the American Socialist party and in ostracizing any political movement farther to its left. Socialism and Marxism became tarred with the brush of Communism and a growing image of an evil regime in the Kremlin that sought world dominance and the destruction of all human values.

Historian David Nord, who studied the Socialist party newspaper, *Appeal to Reason,*[25] points out that the consensus view became that Socialism never had any wide appeal because it stood outside the American liberal tradition. The party's successes at the polls in the 1910s were explained because the Socialists had been perceived as social reformers operating within the standard political system. In the 1960s "New Left" historians argued that there had been a genuine anticapitalist mass movement in America, which failed because the radicals fell to fighting among themselves and because the government instituted repression in the "Red Scare" years. In 1981 Warren Beatty made the motion picture *Reds,* again bringing to life John Reed, Emma Goldman, and others of the radical movements that were confounded by the impact of events in Russia and the spread of the "Red Scare." Reed, the brilliant young Harvard graduate who wrote *Ten Days That Shook the World* after joining the Revolution in Moscow, mingled, along with his lover and wife, Louise Bryant, with editor Max Eastman of *The Masses,* writers Upton Sinclair and Eugene O'Neill, and other Greenwich Village figures. Goldman, a Lithuanian-born anarchist editor, lecturer, and literary critic, came to the United States in 1885, only to be deported in 1919 to a Russia she did not admire.

The American Socialist party split into "patriot" and "pacifist" factions when the United States entered into the war. The pacifists were left in control of the party. The Russian Bolshevist Revolution divided the weakened Socialists into a left wing, which wished to affiliate with Moscow and establish a "dictatorship of the proletariat," and a more conservative group that remained loyal to the program of social evolution in a democracy. The left wing split into as many as 16 factional organizations espousing Communism in the names of Marx, Lenin, and the opposition leader Trotsky. William Z. Foster, hero of the 1919 steel strike, organized many of these groups into the Workers' party, which ran national tickets in 1924 and 1928. The orthodox Socialists supported the Progressive party candidacy of Robert La Follette in 1924 before finding an eminently respectable pacifist leader in Norman Thomas by 1928. The party's newspapers disintegrated; the *New York Call* succumbed in 1923, despite the efforts of the garment workers to save it and the installation of Thomas as editor.[26] The *New Masses* replaced the *Masses,* and among the Socialist dailies only the *Milwaukee Leader* survived into the 1930s, before fading away in 1937.

There were no diplomatic relations with the Soviet Union until Franklin Roosevelt's election, and Russian history books recorded in detail the "American invasion" at the close of World War I. In the United States, there was a consolidation of industrial power generated during the war. The Socialists had a chance to temper the drive of the capitalist-industrialist society and to offer the country a socialized democracy. This disappeared during the "Red Scare," and the 1920s saw only hard-fought battles for such innocuous aims as public ownership of utilities. It would take the enormous economic disaster of the Great Depression to bring even such basic social reforms as the right to collective bargaining and a system of social security.

13

The Twenties:
Radio, Movies,
and Jazz Journalism

> **Radio broadcasting is an essential part of the modern press. It shares the same functions and encounters the same problems as the older agencies of mass communication. On the other hand, radio exhibits significant differences. Its ability to draw millions of citizens into close and simultaneous contact with leaders and with events of the moment gives it a reach and an influence of peculiar importance in the management of public affairs.**
>
> *—Commission on Freedom of the Press*

The first American radio stations to seek a regular public audience made their bows in 1920. A half-century later, there were four to five times as many radio and television stations as there were daily newspapers in the United States. In the interval the scratchy-sounding crystal sets of radio's headphone days had been transformed into FM and stereophonic reception. Network radio and big-screen television offered home audiences on-the-spot journalistic coverage of history in the making as well as entertainment.

If the arrival of radio were not enough competition for the print media, in the 1920s going to the movies also became a major activity. During that decade some 20,000 motion-picture theaters opened their doors, and cinema attendance reached its all-time high by 1930—90 million customers weekly.

The atmosphere of the 1920s was conducive to entertainment in the newspaper as well. The sensationalized tabloid gave the period "jazz journalism," but all the press emphasized human-interest stories, pictures, comic strips, and other enticing fare. The great crusade of 1917 was over, and Woodrow Wilson's hopes for American leadership in world affairs had dissolved into a "Red Scare" at home and a nationalist-isolationist outlook toward events abroad. The country's cry was "back to normalcy" insofar as politics were concerned. This did not mean that the United States wanted to stand still; rather it wanted to forget the troubles of the war years and concentrate on "living."

Political conservatism and laissez-faire policies thus prevailed over rebellious but outvoted progressivism. At the same time, Progressivism did not die out. Scholars such as Robert Himmelberg, Louis Galambos, and Ellis Hawley argue that the trade association

Charlie Chaplin and Jackie
Coogan in *The Kid,* 1921;
Graham McNamee broadcast-
ing a Polo Grounds baseball
game in 1926 for WEAF,
New York

movement of the 1920s, as well as the economic mobilization during World War I that created partnerships between government and business, provide strong evidence of the Progressive movement's survival.[1]

Also characteristic of the 1920s was cultural and economic conflict. Examples include immigration restriction and coercive "Americanization" campaigns, Prohibition, the rebirth of the Ku Klux Klan, and the conflict between fundamentalism and Darwinism exemplified by the Scopes trial.[2]

Occupying the White House were three Republicans: the sincere but scandal-plagued Marion, Ohio, newspaper publisher, Warren G. Harding; the close-mouthed Yankee believer in the status quo, Calvin Coolidge; and the efficient but depression-plagued Quaker, Herbert Hoover. America was a relatively complacent land, and business prosperity and the doings of Wall Street outweighed interest in political and social reform or concern for a depressed farm economy.

The press, preoccupied in many instances with sex, crime, and entertainment, reflected the spirit of the times. The majority of newspapers went with the tide, rather than attempting to give the country leadership either by determined display of significant news or through interpretation. There was good copy in the evidences of political laxity that emerge in all postwar periods, however, and even the tabloids played up the Teapot Dome oil-lease scandal and others that issued from the unhappy Harding administration. Dapper Mayor Jimmy Walker's casual handling of New York City affairs was both entertaining and productive of graft exposés. The hue and cry against corruption were valuable, but sober examination of the country's own economic trend and of the world situation went begging in many papers. So did concerns about the racism, sexism, and the generally reactionary attitudes that dominated public and private life.

And, after all, the atmosphere of the 1920s made this inevitable. The national experiment called Prohibition brought rumrunners, speakeasy operators, and gangsters into the spotlight, and they were interesting people. Al Capone, Dutch Schultz, Waxey Gordon, Legs Diamond, and their rivals were sensational copy. Socialites caught in a speakeasy raid made good picture subjects.

Tabloid editors feasted, too, on stories about glamorous and sexy Hollywood and its stars: Rudolph Valentino, Fatty Arbuckle, Clara Bow. They gloried in the love affairs of the great and not-so-great: Daddy Browning and his Peaches, Kip Rhinelander, the Prince of Wales. They built sordid murder cases into national sensations: Judd Gray, Ruth Snyder. They glorified celebrities: Charles A. Lindbergh, Queen Marie of Rumania, Channel swimmer Gertrude Ederle. They promoted the country's sports stars: prizefighter Jack Dempsey, golfer Bobby Jones, tennis champion Bill Tilden, football coach Knute Rockne, home-run hitter Babe Ruth.

Americans also had an eye for business. Advertising expanded enormously as agency copywriters produced legendary slogans for the marketing of automobiles, cigarettes, and other symbols of the "good life." "Blow some my way," said the emancipated woman to her carefully groomed escort in one daring cigarette ad. And if the 1920s saw the emergence of the public-relations concept in the business world, it was also a decade for slapdash press agentry.

EARLY BROADCASTING EXPERIMENTS

When the first commercial American radio station came on the air in 1920, the experimenters found that they had an audience of some size: amateur enthusiasts who had built their own receivers and transmitters to become wireless "hams" and crystal set owners who could pick up broadcasts on their headphones. The magic of radio had been made possible by a number of scientific breakthroughs during the previous half-century, notably Alexander Graham Bell's invention of the telephone in 1876 and Guglielmo Marconi's experiments with the wireless beginning in the 1890s.

Bell's demonstration of the telephone at the Philadelphia Centennial Exposition made it apparent that the instrument could be used to transmit music or information to an audience. During the next few years there were experiments in the United States and Europe whereby music was played by several persons over the telephone; the sound was made more powerful through the intervention of the carbon transmitter. In 1877 music transmitted over the phone from New York City to Sarasota Springs, New York, was accidentally heard in Boston and Providence. This had occurred because electricity had leaked to other trunk lines and because the waves were inducted through the air.[3] This principle was explained later by the German investigator Heinrich Hertz, who in 1888 proved that sound waves could be set in motion and that they could also be detected or received.

A variety of experiments preceded those of Marconi. In the early 1880s Amos Dolbear of Tufts College used a wireless telephone to send messages about a mile. A few years earlier, Thomas Edison had detected the generating of electric sparks from a distance. John Stone developed the concept of modulating a high-frequency wave with the human voice, and beginning in 1892 he conducted experiments designed to lead to voice transmission. But perhaps the most exciting of the early attempts to produce sounds from coils of wire, batteries, and telephones was the work of Nathan B. Stubblefield. In 1892 this Kentucky melon farmer was credited with talking to a friend some distance away, on his farm, using a wireless telephone. During the next ten years Stubblefield conducted several other documented experiments, including one near Washington, D.C., in which he sent a voice message from a boat to shore. Following this Stubblefield told reporters that his invention eventually "will be used for the general transmission of news of every description."[4]

A telephone system in Budapest, Hungary, allowed listeners to receive up to 12 hours of news and music in 1893. The Chicago Telephone Company delivered local and state election results to an estimated 15,000 persons in 1894. But the highly publicized experiments of Marconi gained the most attention. Using the ideas of the German physicist Heinrich Hertz, Marconi successfully transmitted dots and dashes across his family's fields in Italy. In February 1896, the Marconi family traveled to London where Marconi patented his invention, transmitted a signal up to nine miles, and the following year formed the Wireless Telegraph and Signal Company, Ltd., later to be called Marconi's Wireless Telegraph Company, Ltd. His minute-by-minute wireless account of the Kingstown Regatta for the *Dublin Daily Express* in 1898 brought him world acclaim and an invitation from the *New York Herald* to repeat the experiment at the 1899 America's Cup Race. In 1901 he sent a signal from England to Newfoundland, and finally in 1907 he linked Europe and the United States. The headline in the *New York Times* read: "Wireless Joins Two Worlds. Marconi Trans-Atlantic Service Opened With a Dispatch to the *New York Times*."[5]

FESSENDEN, DE FOREST, AND HERROLD

Without the pioneering work of three other men, however, radio history would have been different. Reginald A. Fessenden is credited with being the first to use continuous waves—instead of the series of bursts used by Marconi—to carry a voice or music. His 1902 patent was the first in the United States for a radio-telegraph system using Hertzian waves. Then, on Christmas Eve 1906, Fessenden made what is considered the first broadcast. Ship operators for the United Fruit Company were told to listen for messages coming from Brant Rock, Massachusetts. First came the static and the Morse code. Then operators listening to their headphones heard Fessenden reading from St. Luke's Gospel, playing the violin and a phonograph recording of Handel's "Largo," and wishing them a Merry Christmas. The broadcast was repeated on New Year's Eve and was picked up as far away as the West Indies.[6]

This same month Lee De Forest—called by some "The Father of Radio"—invented the forerunner to the vacuum tube and was able to transmit voice in his laboratory room. This step, adding an element that allowed easier reception and more amplification of sound, was the discovery that would push the growth of radio. De Forest's device was called the Audion.

De Forest began a series of experiments in 1907 that would make him a world celebrity. Using records supplied by the Columbia Phonograph Company, he broadcast concerts that were enjoyed by ship operators and other wireless enthusiasts. The next year he and his wife broadcast music from the top of the Eiffel Tower over a distance of 500 miles. Then, in 1910, he broadcast the voice of Enrico Caruso from the stage of the Metropolitan Opera House to a scattered audience in the New York City area.

Meanwhile, in San Jose, California, Charles David "Doc" Herrold was making broadcasting history. Herrold opened a broadcasting school in 1909 and built an antenna on the roof of the Garden City Bank Building that was so large that the wires spread from the seven-story bank building to the tops of several adjoining buildings. Using a primitive microphone, Herrold began a regularly scheduled, weekly half-hour news and music program, which changed to a daily in 1910. Herrold's wife Sybil may have been the first woman to broadcast her own show, a musical program for young people. A downtown store

Lee De Forest, "The Father of Radio"

(Bettmann Archive)

placed two receiving sets in a "listening room" and hooked up several dozen telephone receivers so customers could sit in comfortable chairs and hear the music. Sybil Herrold even accepted listeners' requests for songs.

Herrold claimed to have been the first "broadcaster" because he aimed his programs at the widest possible audience and because he offered the first regular programming.[7] His 15-watt station, with the call letters FN and then SJN, became KQW in 1921 and finally KCBS in San Francisco in 1949. An interruption in service during and immediately after World War I deprived KCBS of the distinction of being the nation's oldest station, however. Among Herrold's many achievements was a two-way voice-communication system that he set up with another radio station on the roof of the Fairmont Hotel in San Francisco in 1912. At the 1915 Panama-Pacific Exposition in San Francisco, Herrold's demonstrations overshadowed those of De Forest.

But the name De Forest ended up having the same relationship to the history of broadcasting as that of Marconi to wireless telegraphy. Installing a transmitter at the Columbia Phonograph Company, De Forest began daily music broadcasts in 1916. Moving his transmitter to the High Bridge in the Bronx, he broadcast the election returns on November 7, 1916, ending with the statement that Charles Evans Hughes had defeated Woodrow Wilson. This was in error, of course, but the spectacle of broadcasting such important news was impressive.

All nongovernmental radio operations were shut down following the United States entry in World War I, but the government continued making enormous strides in broadcast technology. As early as 1904 the Navy had operated 20 wireless stations, closely following the work of Marconi. To preclude the possibility of interference with Navy signals, Congress passed a law in 1912 whereby the Department of Commerce would issue licenses to private broadcasters and assign them wavelengths that did not conflict with government wavelengths. Then in 1915 the American Telephone & Telegraph Company used a Navy station in Arlington, Virginia, to send signals across the Atlantic, which were also picked up as far away as Honolulu. This kind of experimentation continued throughout the war. Finally, after much debate and planning, the private operation of broadcasting facilities was fully restored on March 1, 1920.

Thus radio became a passive middle-class entertainment medium. According to the historian Susan L. Douglas, its development was shaped in part by press coverage of the early experiments, but also by radio's growing interest to corporations and the military and by its popularity with a generation of amateur hobbyists.[8]

THE FIRST RADIO STATIONS

Dr. Frank Conrad, a Westinghouse engineer who had operated experimental station 8XK in Pittsburgh since 1916, got a jump on postwar broadcasting because of his connection with the Navy, for whom he had designed equipment. On October 17, 1919, Conrad began broadcasting phonograph records, and he received so many requests for music that he began broadcasting for two hours on Wednesday and Sunday evenings. A local department store began advertising the sale of Westinghouse crystal sets to hear "Dr. Frank Conrad's popular broadcasts." Westinghouse decided that a new sales market was waiting and applied for the first full commercial license for standard broadcasting.[9] Its station, KDKA, began operating on November 2, 1920, with a broadcast of returns from the Harding-Cox presidential election. The *Pittsburgh Post* supplied the election bulletins by telephone, and a few thousand persons heard the 18-hour program.

THE FOUR "R'S"—READING, 'RITING, 'RITHMETIC AND RADIO
Miss Sara Muller, teacher at the South Haven school, L. I., one of the smallest schoolhouses in America, instructing her class in calisthenics with the aid of the radio set on the step.
(Fotograms.)

Some of the Manifold Uses of Radio, Wonder Science of the Century

GOVERNOR DONAHEY OF OHIO
in the studio of The Cleveland Plain Dealer listening to the rest of an evening's program to which he had earlier contributed a speech.
(Times Wide World Photos.)

PRESIDENT'S FATHER LISTENING IN ON "CAL"
Colonel John C. Coolidge at the home of a neighbor at Plymouth, Vt., hearing over the radio the address delivered by President Coolidge a. the Associated Press luncheon in New York.
(International.)

DR. MARX, CHANCELLOR OF GERMANY
and head of the German Democratic Party, using the radio to expound his political principles during the recent electoral campaign.
(Times Wide World Photos.)

AN AMBITIOUS PROGRAM
Reginald Gouraud of Paris perfecting a radio telephone transmission set which, he claims, will be strong enough to permit President Coolidge and President Millerand of France to converse with each other.
(Times Wide World Photos.)

SWAYING HIS HIDEOUS HEAD IN HARMONY WITH DULCET STRAINS
The king cobra at the Bronx Zoo, most deadly reptile in the world, charmed by the "concord of sweet sounds" that emanates from the loud speaker of a radio receiving set.
(Times Wide World Photos.)

FASTER THAN ANY PLAYS THEY EVER MADE ON THE DIAMOND
is this radio music transmitted at the rate of 186,000 miles a second to the ears of the Yankee baseball players, Urban, Roettger and Johnson, when rain caused a postponement of the game.
(Times Wide World Photos.)

Page Twenty-four

Mid-Week Pictorial (1924)

KDKA was not the first station to broadcast news regularly, despite its claims. The Herrold contributions in San Jose have been noted. In addition, a Detroit experimental station, 8MK, began daily operation from the *Detroit News* building on August 20, 1920, under the newspaper's sponsorship. A De Forest sales organization—the Radio News and Music Company—had obtained a license for the station, and on August 31 it broadcast the results of a Michigan election. From that time it carried music, talks, and news for a part of each day. The *News* obtained its full commercial license for what became station WWJ in October 1921.

Another pioneer was experimental station 9XM, operated by Professors Earle Terry, Edward Bennett, and others at the University of Wisconsin beginning in 1917. The station was allowed to continue broadcasting throughout World War I, and it aimed its signals to Navy stations in the Great Lakes area. It became WHA in 1922. Although it is certainly the oldest educational station, its claim to be the oldest overall has been muddled by arguments over when it began its daily weather and market reports, whether it had a regular audience, and whether some of its early transmissions were only in Morse code.

Among other active stations in 1921 were KQV in Pittsburgh; WRUC at Union College; 6ADZ in Hollywood, which became KNX; and 4XD in Charlotte, North Carolina.

Radio broadcasting thus began as a means of promoting other enterprises: a department store selling crystal sets, a company wishing to make radios, or a newspaper expanding its domain. Other newspapers followed the *Detroit News* in establishing stations, among them the *Kansas City Star, Milwaukee Journal, Chicago Tribune, Los Angeles Times, Louisville Courier-Journal, Atlanta Journal, Dallas News,* and *Chicago Daily News.*

AT&T, WESTINGHOUSE, AND GE

But the most important elements in the growth of national radio broadcasting were the big companies of the communications and electric manufacturing industries—American Telephone & Telegraph (AT&T), Westinghouse, and General Electric (GE). Radio's growth would mean the expansion of outlets for their products and services.

The pioneer Westinghouse station, KDKA, scored many radio firsts as it pointed the way toward achieving public interest in buying radio sets. During 1921 it broadcast a series of public speeches by national figures, an on-the-spot report of a prizefight, and major league baseball games. Westinghouse also opened stations in New York, Chicago, Philadelphia, and Boston. General Electric built WGY, its powerful Schenectady, New York, station, and American Telephone & Telegraph built WEAF (now WNBC) in New York City.

THE RADIO CORPORATION OF AMERICA

More importantly, the three companies had come together in 1919 to form the Radio Corporation of America (RCA). At government urging, stimulated by United States Navy officers interested in the new medium, the companies had bought up British-owned Marconi patents on radio equipment, which they pooled with their own patent rights in the new RCA. They thus brought into being the future giant of the radio industry, although at first RCA devoted itself to wireless message service.[10]

In 1922 the big companies began a competitive struggle for the control of radio. AT&T held two trump cards. Under its patent-pooling agreements with its competitors, AT&T held considerable power over many stations' rights to charge fees for broadcasting.

And the telephone company observed that KDKA had been successful in using telephone lines to bring religious and theater programs into the studio for broadcasting.

So when WEAF went on the air in August 1922, AT&T announced that it would be an advertising-supported station. Within seven months it had some two dozen sponsors using air time, and the era of commercialization of radio had dawned.[11] At the same time WEAF was experimenting with the use of telephone lines to air intercity broadcasts—telephone lines that AT&T now withheld from its competitors.

SARNOFF, RCA, AND NBC

But despite AT&T's advantage its rivals were not discouraged. Coming to power in RCA was David Sarnoff, the son of a Russian immigrant family, who had begun as a Marconi wireless operator. Sarnoff had been an advocate of mass radio broadcasting since 1915, when he predicted that radio could become a major industry.

And indeed it was clear that radio could become a paying proposition for many. The number of stations in the country had increased from 30 in January 1922 to 556 in March 1923. The number of receiving sets jumped from some 50,000 in 1921 to more than 600,000 in 1922. Newspapers found the story of radio's growth one of continuing interest. In June 1922, the *New York Times* was averaging 40 column inches of radio information daily.[12] The public was demonstrating avid interest in radio's newly developing stars: announcers Graham McNamee and Milton Cross, the vocal duet of Billy Jones and Ernie Hare, and the performers on the *Eveready Hour,* sponsored by a radio battery company. There were objections to radio's introduction of direct advertising to pay the costs of programming, but they were to prove unavailing in the onward rush of the new medium.

The problem faced by Sarnoff and other entrepreneurs was to break the hold AT&T had won on big-time radio. One example of this power was AT&T's role in early World Series baseball reporting. The 1921 Giants-Yankees series, the first for Babe Ruth in New York, was reported for Newark station WJZ by Sandy Hunt, sports editor of the New York *Sunday Call.* Hunt telephoned play-by-play accounts to announcer Tommy Cowan

David Sarnoff, RCA's head

William S. Paley of CBS

in Newark, while KDKA received the information by wire. The following year WJZ joined with WGY in Schenectady and WBZ in Springfield, Massachusetts, and carried the descriptions of Grantland Rice, the legendary sportswriter for the *New York Herald Tribune.* The Giants and Yankees played again and an extensive sales campaign was waged. WJZ was owned by RCA, and newspaper readers were offered "Radiola Score Sheets" for following the games on the $25 receiver sets being advertised. But in stepped AT&T, which refused to allow the WJZ network to lease the telephone lines. Inferior telegraph lines not designed for voice transmission had to be used, which caused distortion. By 1923 AT&T had assumed control of baseball coverage. The third Giant-Yankees series was distributed to a network of stations through WEAF, which hired W. O. McGeehan, baseball expert for the *Herald Tribune,* and Graham McNamee, as announcers, McNamee became an instant celebrity and reported World Series games, in addition to numerous other events, on WEAF until 1935.[13]

The outlook appeared grim as long as RCA was hampered in accepting advertising fees or in using telephone lines for intercity programming. In early 1924 the *Eveready Hour* bought time over a dozen stations—the first use of national radio advertising. A year later the chain headed by WEAF had 26 outlets, reaching as far west as Kansas City. RCA was stuck with its inferior network headed by WJZ and WGY. At the moment Sarnoff was planning to create an RCA subsidiary that could accept unrestricted advertising, the telephone company, secure with the prospect of mounting revenues from leasing its lines, offered to withdraw from the broadcasting business. This occurred in 1926 after a lengthy court battle. WEAF was sold to RCA in 1926, and immediately RCA, GE, and Westinghouse incorporated the National Broadcasting Company (NBC) as an RCA subsidiary, with Merlin H. Aylesworth as president.

NBC made its debut on November 15, 1926, with a spectacular 4½-hour show from the ballroom of the Waldorf-Astoria Hotel in New York and other points around the nation, including Chicago, where Mary Garden sang "Annie Laurie," and Independence, Kansas, where Will Rogers mimicked President Coolidge.[14] It was clear that in the future sponsors would pay for shows featuring big-name bands and singers. By January NBC operated two networks, the Red network with WEAF as the flagship station, and the Blue network headed by WJZ.

On January 1, 1927, the two networks joined to produce the first coast-to-coast broadcast of the Rose Bowl football game with McNamee as announcer. For a year NBC had a third network, the Pacific Coast Network, but this was eliminated in late 1928, when regular coast-to-coast broadcasts linking 58 stations were initiated. In 1930 a federal antitrust action forced GE and Westinghouse to dispose of their holdings in RCA, and the management headed by Sarnoff became supreme. RCA had acquired the Victor phonograph interests and established the RCA-Victor manufacturing unit to produce phonographs, radio sets, and tubes. RCA Communications, Inc., operated a worldwide diotelegraph system. Eventually the Federal Communications Commission forced NBC to sell its Blue network. It was purchased in 1943 by Edward J. Noble, who renamed it the American Broadcasting Company in 1945.

CBS AND PALEY

NBC's first competition came in 1927, when a group of broadcasters trying to syndicate program talent formed the United Independent Broadcasters and allied themselves with a sales company of the Columbia Phonograph Record Company called the Columbia Phonograph Broadcasting System, Inc. United acquired the phonograph company's stock in 1927 and renamed the sales company the Columbia Broadcasting System, Inc. The first network show was on September 18, 1927, when listeners were treated to a variety of music and quite a bit of advertising that one reviewer thought was "aggravating."[15] A year later William S. Paley and his family bought control of United, and in 1929 the firm dissolved the sales company and gave the network its name, CBS. Young Paley, who initially had to prove to his father radio's ability to increase the sales of the family cigar company, used his vigor and enterprise to push CBS into a competitive position with NBC in the battle to gain affiliated stations. By 1934 CBS had 94 affiliates, compared to the 127 owned by the two NBC networks. Paley was to dominate CBS affairs for 50 years, and was recalled from retirement to take an active role in the network's corporate life in a 1986 crisis.

FEDERAL REGULATION: THE FCC

None of this development of radio would have been possible, however, had not the federal government's power been used to avert chaos on the airwaves. Secretary of Commerce Herbert Hoover had endeavored to regulate the growing number of stations, but he lacked sufficient authority under the 1912 law to prevent one station from interfering with the broadcasts of another. By early 1927, when the number of stations had increased to 733, listeners found stations jumping about on the broadcast band to avoid interference, which in metropolitan areas particularly had reached the point of curtailing the sales of radio sets.

National radio conferences held in Washington each year after 1922 urged additional federal regulation of the use of the limited number of available broadcast channels, which by common consent were recognized as being in the public domain. Radio manufacturers wanted the government to unscramble the situation. So did the National Association of Broadcasters, which had been formed in 1923. So did the listening public. The American Newspaper Publishers Association (ANPA), a substantial number of whose members owned stations, also wanted the government to resolve the problem. Walter A. Strong of the *Chicago Daily News* served as chairperson of a coordinating committee that sought passage of a new federal radio act. The bill was approved by Congress in February 1927.

The Radio Act of 1927 established a five-member Federal Radio Commission empowered to regulate all forms of radio communications. The federal government maintained control over all channels, and the commission granted licenses for the use of specific channels for three-year periods. Licenses were to be granted "in the public interest, convenience, or necessity" to provide "fair, efficient and equitable service" throughout the country.

Under this authority the Federal Radio Commission set about eliminating confusion on the broadcast band. The number of stations fell by approximately 150, and the total remained just above the 600 mark for the next ten years. The commission established a group of "clear channels" on which only one station could operate at night. Of the 57 clear channel stations in 1947, designed to give rural areas unimpeded reception of a powerful metropolitan station's programs, 55 were owned or affiliated with the networks. They were the lucrative prizes of radio.[16]

Federal authority was broadened by passage of the Communications Act of 1934, which established the seven-member Federal Communications Commission (FCC). This commission took over not only authority to regulate radio broadcasting but also jurisdiction over all telecommunications. The responsibility of the license holders to operate their radio stations in the public interest was more clearly spelled out, and the commission had the power to refuse renewal of a license in cases of flagrant disregard of broadcasting responsibility. The law forbade, however, any attempt at censorship by the commission; no station could be directed to put a particular program on or off the air. The FCC rarely used its power to cancel the licenses of broadcasters; rather it resorted only to indirect pressure in carrying out its supervision of station operations. However, that pressure was to become substantial in later years.

THE CLASH OVER RADIO NEWS

With the development of widespread broadcasting and the unscrambling of the airwaves by the exercise of federal authority, radio had come of age. But radio's development ran head-on into the interests of other media, particularly incurring the wrath of the newspaper publishers. The major conflict involved radio's growing income, which was taken from the nation's advertising budget. A second involved radio's broadcasting of the news.

Newspaper reaction to radio in the early days of broadcasting was mixed. Newspapers carried the radio log as a reader service, and publicized radio's progress and stars. A report by the American Newspaper Publishers Association's radio committee in 1927 showed that 48 newspapers owned stations, that 69 sponsored programs on unowned stations, and that 97 gave news programs over the air. More than half of the high-grade stations had some newspaper affiliation. The ANPA's radio committee took the position that radio reporting of news events stimulated newspaper sales—a belief borne out fully by later experience.[17] Some of the most exciting broadcasts covered were of the 1924 political conventions; the 1925 Scopes "monkey" trial in Dayton, Tennessee, when listeners of the *Chicago Tribune* station WGN heard the arguments of Clarence Darrow and William Jennings Bryan; Charles Lindbergh's arrival in Washington following his 1927 epic flight to Paris; and the 1927 Jack Dempsey–Gene Tunney prize fight, which was carried over 69 stations, the largest network to that point.

There were some holdouts. The AP, for example, tried to restrict its 1924 presidential election returns for newspaper publication only and fined the Portland *Oregonian* $100 for broadcasting them. There was a great amount of criticism of advertising messages. But there was no stopping radio's ability to cover major events. Some ten million Americans listened in on three million receiving sets to hear of Calvin Coolidge's victory. Four years later, in 1928, the NBC and CBS networks could reach eight million sets. In that bitter campaign both Republican Herbert Hoover and Democrat Alfred E. Smith took to the air, spending $1 million on campaign talks. That year the press associations—the AP, UP, and INS—supplied complete election returns to radio stations, and Ted Husing, the popular sports announcer who doubled as a news announcer during major events, delivered a memorable election broadcast.

Stimulated by public interest in radio's coverage of the election, a few stations began to expand their news operations. In December 1928, KFAB in Lincoln, Nebraska, employed the city editor of the *Lincoln Star* to run its newscasts. Stations followed suit in other cities. The most elaborate early news effort was made by KMPC in Beverly Hills, California, which put ten reporters onto Los Angeles news runs in 1930.[18] Some newspaper publishers complained, justifiably, that radio was using public interest in newscasts as one selling point in attracting advertising.

POPULAR RADIO ENTERTAINMENT

Music was the most popular fare on radio in the late 1920s, most of it classical or semi-classical on shows like the *Palmolive Hour* and the *Maxwell House Hour.* But dance music was catching the public's fancy, and soon the band leaders Guy Lombardo, Paul Whiteman, and others were known nationwide. Many a New Year's Eve ended with millions of listeners dancing to "Auld Lang Syne" as played by Lombardo and his Royal Canadians. Singers became celebrities too, with Vaughn de Leath, Elsie Janis, Bing Crosby, and Kate Smith breaking onto the airwaves. A study of 1927 broadcasts from New York showed that three-fourths of the shows carried music, nearly another 15 percent were religious or educational, and only a few dealt with drama, sports, or information.[19]

The demand for drama began to increase, though, with NBC featuring the *Eveready Hour* and *Real Folks,* and CBS promoting shows like *Great Moments in History, Biblical Dramas, Main Street Sketches,* and *True Story.* In August 1929, one of the most popular comedy shows in broadcasting history made its debut on the NBC network, when Freeman Gosden and Charles Correll starred as *Amos 'n' Andy.* Bringing their blackface vaudeville act to radio, they had first created *Sam 'n' Henry* for WGN in Chicago. Switching to WMAQ, they changed the name to *Amos 'n' Andy.* By 1928 a syndication handled by the *Chicago Daily News* had lined up 30 stations. The five weekly episodes demonstrated how syndication could be used widely in the future: listeners were enticed by the continuing story and waited eagerly for the next dilemma with the "fresh-air taxi." They enjoyed the story line and did not identify it as a form of racial stereotyping—it was just fun to hear.

NBC paid Gosden and Correll $100,000 to join the network. The resulting excitement confirmed what some critics said of radio programming—that its main purpose was

(Bettmann Archive)

Amos 'n' Andy—Freeman Gosden and Charles Correll

to sell radio sets. Sales of radios and supplies increased from $650 million to $842 million between 1928 and 1929.[20] The nation shifted its schedules to fit in the *Amos 'n' Andy* show. Factories closed early, and cab drivers refused to pick up passengers between 7:00 and 7:15 P.M. Eastern Time. Radio was in full force, and the concept of national advertising had been accepted. The 1930s would see spectacular expansion, particularly in news and commentary.

THE RISE OF MOTION PICTURES

Going to the movies became a major preoccupation for Americans in the 1920s. The illusion of movement created by the motion-picture projector and the sense of reality felt by a viewer of the film made the new medium a fascinating one. After Peter Mark Roget (of *Thesaurus* fame) advanced his theory of "persistence of vision" in 1824, inventors worked on the motion-picture concept. The human eye, Roget contended, retains an image for a fraction of a second longer than it actually appears. Thus a series of still pictures printed on a ribbon of celluloid film, and projected at 16 or 24 frames per second, will create for a viewer the illusion of continuous motion.

By 1840 Joseph Niepce and Louis Daguerre in France had developed a photographic process that Mathew Brady used in the American Civil War. In 1877, utilizing 24 cameras, Eadweard Muybridge and John D. Isaacs conducted a famous demonstration of the gait of a galloping horse. "Magic lantern" shows became popular on lecture circuits. In 1888 George Eastman's marketing of his Kodak camera, which used a roll of film, marked another step. Finishing his invention of the phonograph the same year, Thomas A. Edison set his assistant to work on what became the Kinetoscope. William Kennedy Laurie Dickson adapted the Eastman film to the camera by devising a sprocket system and offered a 50-foot "peep show" in the 4-foot Kinetoscope box in 1889. Louis and Auguste Lumière and Charles Pathé in France and Robert W. Paul and William Friese-Greene in England were

(Bettmann Archive)

D. W. Griffith directs one of his films.

simultaneously creating moving pictures. The first public showing in a theater in the United States occurred in 1896, using Edison's improved Vitascope.

Just to see Niagara Falls flowing or a train rushing onward was exciting to the first audiences. But artistry and skill were needed if the nickelodeons were to survive. George Méliès of France, a magician, made 1000 brief films offering ideas for others to use. But it was Edwin S. Porter's eight-minute 1903 film called *The Great Train Robbery* that first told a unified story, utilizing camera-angle shifting, film editing, and parallel development of themes. Porter also set the pace for untold numbers of Westerns to follow.

Three men, working variously as producer-directors and actors, made major imprints on film history in the second decade of the twentieth century. One was David Wark Griffith, first an actor and then a director at Biograph, which had joined Pathé and Vitagraph as a leading picture-making company in New York. In 1915 Griffith completed a 12-reel picture that ran nearly three hours—the first of the "epics" of American film. It was *The Birth of a Nation,* the story of a victimized southern family told in a setting of Civil War battles, Sherman's march to the sea, renegade blacks, and Ku Klux Klansmen. Griffith, the son of a Confederate war veteran, produced a picture sympathetic to that cause with inflammatory racist stereotypes that sometimes triggered antiblack rioting. Its excellence as film-making artistry and its emotional impact, however, give the film a permanent place in movie history.

In 1912 Mack Sennett, also a graduate of the Biograph studio, established the Keystone Film Company in Los Angeles. A master of slapstick, he created the Keystone Kops as a long-running institution. Among those playing in Sennett's films were Mabel Normand, first of the cinematic female comedians, frozen-faced Buster Keaton, and a young English actor named Charlie Chaplin. Gaining fame with *The Tramp* (1915) and *Shoulder Arms* (1918), Chaplin won a $1 million contract to make his own films. Telling largely in pantomime the story of "the little fellow" who never fit in, Chaplin captivated his audiences with his tramp's costume and orchestrated mannerisms for *The Kid* (1921), *The Gold Rush* (1925), and *City Lights* (1931). In *Modern Times* (1936) he rebelled against the assembly line and industrial system; in 1940 he stepped out of character to oppose totalitarianism in *The Great Dictator.* But it was the wistful little tramp who set a dinner table for guests who never came or who shuffled off into the night that won Chaplin his fame.

In 1919, Griffith, Chaplin, the swashbuckling actor Douglas Fairbanks, and "America's sweetheart," Mary Pickford, formed the United Artists Corporation so they could control their own careers and earnings. By then Hollywood was producing three-quarters of the world's films. Most of the major film companies were in place by the early 1920s: Fox, Metro-Goldwyn-Mayer, Paramount, Warner Brothers, Universal, Columbia. Each had producers like Sam Goldwyn, Thomas Ince, Louis B. Mayer, Jesse Lasky, or William Fox. Each had its "stars," such as horseman William S. Hart, comedian Harold Lloyd, actresses Lillian Gish and Gloria Swanson, and Rudolph Valentino, "The Sheik," whose sudden death in 1926 brought about hysterical mourning. Moviegoers lined up at cinema palaces to see such spectaculars as the 1923 pair *The Covered Wagon* and Cecil B. De Mille's *The Ten Commandments.* More sophisticated was *Flesh and the Devil,* starring Greta Garbo and John Gilbert in 1927.

Greta Garbo was part of a foreign influence that enhanced Hollywood in the 1920s. Ernst Lubitsch brought his comedy-making skill from Germany and teamed with singer-actor Maurice Chevalier. Josef von Sternberg directed compatriot Marlene Dietrich. Director Erich von Stroheim made his classic *Greed* in 1924, based on Frank Norris's novel *McTeague,* and then portrayed the futility of war in his 1926 film *What Price Glory?* This was followed by Lewis Milestone's filming of Erich Remarque's German novel *All Quiet on the Western Front* in 1930. Sergei Eisenstein captured the sweep and drama of Russian history in films such as *Potemkin,* his 1925 triumph commemorating the 1905 mutiny aboard that Russian battleship against Czarist misrule.

GOING TO THE MOVIES: THE "TALKIES"

More than 20,000 movie houses were scattered across the country by the mid-1920s. Weekly attendance averaged 46 million people in 1925 and vaulted to an all-time high of 90 million in 1930. Part of the reason for the expanding attendance was the addition of a sound track to movies in 1927. The "talkies" were at first a novelty, then quickly became the standard. Sound scores had been run with movies, and Fox Movietone News had shown Charles A. Lindbergh's Paris and New York receptions in sound after his 1927 flight. But when Al Jolson sang "Mammy" in a Broadway premiere of *The Jazz Singer* in October 1927, the "talking picture" excitement swept the studios. Chaplin could still do *City Lights* in silence in 1931, but other stars whose voices were not congenial retired into the wings.

Going to the movies was a low-priced amusement of the Great Depression years. The movie houses offered double bills, even triple bills, for as little as a quarter, and they were warm places to sit for the underpaid and unemployed. In 1940 weekly attendance still averaged 80 million. Humor was an antidote for the depression; two stars with unique comic elán were Mae West and W. C. Fields. The Marx Brothers solidified their place in film lore with *Duck Soup* (1933). Comedy with a sophisticated touch and elegant setting was offered by comedian Carole Lombard, by William Powell and Myrna Loy in the *Thin Man* series, and by director Frank Capra in the 1934 smash, *It Happened One Night,* starring Clark Gable and Claudette Colbert. There were lavish musicals like *Top Hat* (1935), which featured the flying feet of Fred Astaire and Ginger Rogers. Prohibition and gangsters provided themes for actors Jimmy Cagney, Edward G. Robinson, and Paul Muni.

The art of animation was revolutionized by Walt Disney, who organized teams of artists in his studio to take full advantage of movement, color, sound, musical synchronization, and vocal effects. Mickey Mouse made his debut in 1928, and by 1931 he and Minnie had appeared in 90 short subjects. "Who's afraid of the big bad wolf?" sang Disney's Three Little Pigs in 1933. His full-length features *Snow White and the Seven Dwarfs* (1937) and *Fantasia* (1940) foreshadowed later Disney enterprises on television and theme parks. The 1930s were also the decade of the child stars, led by Jackie Coogan and Shirley Temple. Coogan had been Chaplin's *Kid* of 1921. Temple danced in *Stand up and Cheer* in 1934 and then in a succession of heart-warming films. Mickey Rooney and Judy Garland were the greatest child team before Garland reached stardom in the 1939 version of *The Wizard of Oz.*

The 1930s closed with an epic, *Gone with the Wind,* starring Clark Gable as Rhett Butler and English actress Vivien Leigh as Scarlett O'Hara. The novel had been a best seller, and its story of the Civil War became an all-time fixture on the list of box-office successes in the United States. The 1939 film led that list until 1965, and has been reproduced periodically on film and on television for succeeding generations. A 1986 reprinting of the 1936 book made the best-seller list as total sales exceeded 25 million copies.

Hollywood became a symbol of high living, sex, and sin in the early 1920s, as pitiless publicity and fan worship took effect. A sordid rape case ended "Fatty" Arbuckle's career; the unsolved murder of a leading director brought testimony damaging to stars Mabel Normand and Mary Miles Minter; Wallace Reid was revealed to be a drug addict. In 1922 the alarmed studios selected Postmaster General Will H. Hays to be their czar as head of the Motion Picture Producers and Exhibitors of America. The "Hays Office" exercised informal censorship, made more stringent by its own 1930 production code, city and state censors, and the 1934 Legion of Decency.

JAZZ JOURNALISM: THE TABLOID

A new cycle of sensationalism in journalism began with the close of World War I. Just as in 1833, when the penny press appeared, and in 1897, when the Pulitzer-Hearst duel climaxed the introduction of the new journalism, the times were right for a sensationalized appeal to the people. And there was an untapped audience awaiting such an appeal, just as there had been in 1833 and 1897. In the seven years between 1919 and 1926 three new papers in New York City found more than a million-and-a-half readers without unduly disturbing the circulation balance of the existing dailies. Their sensationalism was accompanied by the use of two techniques that identify the period: the tabloid-style format and the extensive use of photography. As in earlier periods, the wave of sensationalism had its effect on all of the press before it subsided, and, as before, a more substantial journalism followed the era of sensationalized appeal. The 1920s are known as the decade of "jazz journalism,"[21] and the years that followed were marked by a rapid rise in emphasis on the techniques of interpretative reporting, not only in the newspaper field but also in magazine publishing and broadcasting.

The tabloid format introduced so successfully in New York after 1919 was not a stranger to journalism. Before newsprint had become relatively plentiful in the middle of the nineteenth century, small-sized pages were common. The *Daily Graphic,* published in New York between 1873 and 1889 and carrying Stephen H. Horgan's early experimental halftone engravings, had a tabloid format. So did Frank A. Munsey's ill-fated *Daily Continent* of 1891, which like the *Daily Graphic* was heavily illustrated but no more sensationalized than other newspapers. It was not these American efforts that stimulated the tabloid era of the 1920s, however. For better or for worse, the United States owes its tabloids to the cradle of English-language journalism, Great Britain.

Even though English journalistic preoccupation with crime news and court stories played its part in suggesting the advantages of sensationalism to the first American penny-press publishers in 1833, newspapers for the masses lagged in Great Britain because of stamp-tax regulations that did not disappear until 1855. The *Daily Telegraph* then became the first penny paper in England, but its appeal was to the middle classes. Not until after the introduction of compulsory education in England in 1870 was there a market for a truly popularized newspaper. Into that market stepped a discerning young man named Alfred C. Harmsworth, who as Lord Northcliffe was to become one of Britain's giants of the press. His first project, in 1883, was a human-interest weekly magazine named *Answers,* which was modeled after George Newnes's *Tidbits* of 1881. Both publications used the contest to entice working-class readers, and Harmsworth had 250,000 of them within ten years.

Meanwhile Harmsworth was watching the progress of Joseph Pulitzer's *New York World* and of James Gordon Bennett, Jr.'s *Paris Herald,* with its short-lived London edition. He first adapted the new American techniques to the *London Evening News,* which he bought in 1894, and then to his far more famous *Daily Mail,* founded in 1896. Soon Pulitzer was taking lessons from Harmsworth, whom the *World*'s publisher admired so greatly that he permitted Harmsworth, as guest publisher, to turn the January 1, 1901, issue of the *World* into a tabloid representing "the newspaper of the twentieth century." New York was unimpressed, however, and it remained for Harmsworth to do the job in England.

The first widely circulated tabloid was the *Daily Mirror,* which Harmsworth began in London in 1903 as a newspaper for women but soon converted into a "half-penny illustrated," small, sensational, and amusing. By 1909, its circulation had reached a million copies, and the *Daily Sketch* and *Daily Graphic* jumped into the tabloid field. Harmsworth had become Lord Northcliffe and a leading figure in English Journalism by the time of World War I. He still felt that someone should be publishing a tabloid like his *Daily Mirror* in New York, and when he met an American army officer who was overseas from his newspaper desk, Northcliffe told him how lucrative the tabloid could be.

THE FOUNDING OF THE *NEW YORK DAILY NEWS*

The army officer was Captain Joseph Medill Patterson, a partner with his cousin Colonel Robert R. McCormick in the *Chicago Tribune* since 1914. These two grandsons of Joseph Medill met later in France and agreed to start a New York tabloid to be called the *Daily News.* The cousins had other reasons than the arguments Northcliffe had advanced for undertaking the New York venture. Colonel McCormick, as is shown in detail in a later chapter, was a king-sized chip off the conservative Medill block. Captain Patterson, however, was unconventional enough to have written two novels (*A Little Brother of the Rich* and *Rebellion*) that protested social injustice and economic oppression, and was considered socialistic in his thinking by others of his wealthy class. His plan to start a tabloid in New York would thus give him an opportunity to reach the many immigrants and least-literate native-born, as he wished to do, and at the same time would rid Colonel McCormick of an embarrassing copublisher arrangement in Chicago.

So the *Illustrated Daily News,* as the paper was called for its first few months, made its bow in New York on June 26, 1919. Its half-size front page was covered with a picture of the Prince of Wales (later King Edward VIII and then the Duke of Windsor), whose forthcoming visit to America had already stirred feminine hearts. Its promotion gimmick was the sponsoring of its own beauty contest, which was announced to startled readers of the *New York Times* in a full-page ad that read: "SEE NEW YORK'S MOST BEAUTIFUL GIRLS EVERY MORNING IN THE ILLUSTRATED DAILY NEWS." New York newspeople of 1919, like those of 1833 who had sniffed at Benjamin Day's newly founded *Sun,* dismissed the tabloid venture without much concern. But one of them, at least, foresaw the effect its sensationalism, its entertainment emphasis, and its reliance on photography would have. He was Carr Van Anda, the astute managing editor of the *Times,* who realized that the *Daily News* would satisfy a widespread postwar public craving and reach a new reading audience. "This paper," he said, "should reach a circulation of 2,000,000."[22] Patterson and his editors did not disappoint Van Anda. In 1924 the *Daily News* circulation of 750,000 was the largest in the country. By 1929 the figure was 1.32 million—it had increased while the combined circulation of the other New York morning papers stood still. And before World War II it had hit the 2 million mark.

The *Daily News* did badly at first. Its initial circulation of 200,000 dropped to 26,000 the second month, and two of its four reporters were fired. But Captain Patterson was discovering that his circulation potential was not among readers of the *Times* but among the immigrant and poorly educated American-born population of New York. The *News* was put on stands where only foreign-language papers had sold before, and its pictures sold the papers. By 1921 it was second in circulation to Hearst's *Evening Journal.* Hearst's morning *American* tried to capture some of the readership going to the *News* by filling its columns with pictures and features, but the tabloid won the competition. A sharp battle between

Hearst and McCormick circulation people in Chicago was transferred to New York, with lotteries, coupon prizes, and other inducements for readers. Patterson was the victor again with a limerick contest keyed to the popular taste.

THE *MIRROR* AND THE *GRAPHIC*

Direct competition arrived for the *News* in 1924, the year it became America's most widely circulated newspaper. Hearst had experimented unsuccessfully with the tabloid format in Boston—always a poor town for journalistic innovations—but in despair of the *American*'s ever whipping the *News,* he began the tabloid the *Daily Mirror.* Close behind him was Bernarr Macfadden, publisher of the *Physical Culture* and *True Story* magazines and a millionaire with a yen to influence the public and hold high office. But as in his successful *True Story* venture, his newspaper aims were unconventional. He wanted a paper, he said, that "will shatter precedent to smithereens."[23] Macfadden selected Emile Gauvreau, up to that time the managing editor of the respectable *Hartford Courant,* as his chief editor, and the two brought out the *Daily Graphic.* The *Mirror* began to challenge the *News* on more or less straight journalistic terms, but the *Graphic* set out to see just how sensational and lurid it could be. The result was the battle of what Oswald Garrison Villard called "gutter journalism."

The *Graphic* quickly became the most notorious of the tabloids. Indeed, Macfadden had no intention of running a newspaper. He did not bother with subscribing to a press-association service and played only the "gigantic" general news. He was trying to build a million-reader audience on newsstand sales of a daily that was to be the *True Confessions* of the newspaper world. Reporters wrote first-person stories to be signed by persons in the news, and editors headlined them "I Know Who Killed My Brother," "He Beat Me—I Love Him," and "For 36 Hours I Lived Another Woman's Love Life." Gauvreau's retort to criticism was that the public wanted "hot news,"[24] and the evidence seemed to be on his side, as newsstand sales of the *Graphic* mounted.

The climax year of the war of the tabloids was 1926. First the Broadway producer, Earl Carroll, gave a party at which a nude dancing girl sat in a bathtub full of champagne. Before the furor had died down, the tabloids discovered a wealthy real-estate man, Edward Browning, and his 15-year-old shopgirl bride. This was "hot" romance indeed, and the pair became "Daddy" and "Peaches" to all of the country. The *Graphic* portrayed them frolicking on a bed with Daddy saying, "Woof! Woof! I'm a Goof!" Gauvreau decided to thrill his shopgirl audience with the details of Peaches's intimate diary, but at that point the law stepped in.

A sensational murder trial was drummed up in the spring of 1927. A corset salesperson named Judd Gray and his sweetheart, Mrs. Ruth Snyder, had collaborated in disposing of the unwanted Mr. Snyder. When it came time for Mrs. Snyder's execution in the electric chair at Sing Sing, the *Graphic* blared to its readers:

> Don't fail to read tomorrow's *Graphic.* An installment that thrills and stuns! A story that fairly pierces the heart and reveals Ruth Snyder's last thoughts on earth; that pulses the blood as it discloses her final letters. Think of it! A woman's final thoughts just before she is clutched in the deadly snare that sears and burns and FRIES AND KILLS! Her very last words! Exclusively in tomorrow's *Graphic.*[25]

It was the photography-minded *News* that had the last word, however. The *Graphic* might have its "confession," but the *News* proposed to take its readers inside the execution

This 1928 front page represented the extreme in New York tabloid sensationalism.

chamber. Pictures were forbidden, but a photographer, Tom Howard, strapped a tiny camera to his ankle and took his picture just after the current was turned on. The *News* put a touched-up shot on its front page, sold 250,000 extra papers, and later had to run off 750,000 additional copies of the front page.

PATTERSON'S NEWS VALUES CHANGE

Patterson's news and photo enterprise went beyond shocking people. When the steamer *Vestris* sank off the Atlantic coast, with the loss of several hundred lives, Patterson sent all his staffers to interview the survivors on the chance that one of them had taken a picture. One had, and for $1200 the *News* bought one of the greatest action news pictures ever taken, showing the tilted ship's deck and recording the expressions of the victims as they prepared to jump into the water or go down with the ship. Patterson put $750,000 into Associated Press Wirephoto in the early 1930s, when other publishers were balking at using the new photo transmission system, and for a while had exclusive New York use of Wirephoto. The *News* developed its own staff of crack photographers and in addition welcomed shots taken by freelancers in the vast New York area. The payoff was consistent.

With 1929 came the Wall Street crash, the depression, and deepening years of unemployment. Patterson, with his finger on the pulse of the people, told his editors and reporters that the depression and its effects on the lives of all Americans was now the big story. Not that the *News* and other papers stopped playing crime and sex news and features. But they also gave great space to the serious news of a people in trouble. Patterson's *Daily*

(Bettmann Archive)

Readers expected to see the faces of personalities. Senator Gerald P. Nye and John D. Rockefeller are here surrounded by photographers in 1923.

News became a firm supporter of Roosevelt's New Deal through the 1930s, to the disgust of a fiercely anti–New Deal Colonel McCormick in the *Chicago Tribune* tower.

The *Daily News* still wisecracked in its editorial columns and still produced its headlines with a twist that caught any reader's eye. But after 1939 it had no more greetings for the man in the White House. It broke with Roosevelt over involvement in World War II and became bitterly isolationist. Patterson's distrust of the president's foreign policy led him to fight the administration all down the line. After his death in 1946, the *News* was under the control of Colonel McCormick, although its operations were directed by Patterson's former executives. Despite this political break with the Democratic party the *News* remained a "people's paper," climbing to peak circulations of 2.4 million daily and 4.5 million Sunday in 1947, before it felt the effects of a general slackening of metropolitan newspaper circulations and a steep drop in the sales of entertainment-centered papers, which were vulnerable to television's inroads. Yet it still remained a paper sharp enough to produce this 1976 headline on a story on the president's response to the bankrupt city's plea for aid: "FORD TO CITY: DROP DEAD."[26]

THE END OF THE TABLOID ERA

Things did not go so well with the *Mirror* and *Graphic*. Hearst sold the *Mirror* in 1928, had to take it back in 1930, and then bolstered it by stealing columnist Walter Winchell from the *Graphic* and sending Arthur Brisbane in as editor. But the *Mirror* never became a profitable Hearst property and was closed in 1963. The *Graphic* never won any advertising support and died unmourned in 1932, after losing millions of dollars for Macfadden.

Two points should be made clear: very few of the other newspapers that adopted the tabloid format were of the racy character of the New York tabs, and the quest for sensational news did not die with the passing of the *Graphic* and the semitransformation of the *Daily News*. One hopeful tabloid publisher was Cornelius Vanderbilt, Jr., who started crusading, nonsalacious picture papers in Los Angeles, San Francisco, and Miami in the early 1920s. Vanderbilt won good-sized circulations for his papers, but failed to build up advertiser support, and the chain soon withered. The *Los Angeles Daily News* passed to liberal-minded Manchester Boddy, who built it into a pro–New Deal paper much like the orthodox dailies except for its freewheeling style of writing. The *Chicago Times,* founded in 1929, was likewise a liberal, tersely written paper. When Marshall Field combined his *Chicago Sun* with the *Times* in 1947 he kept the tabloid format. The *Daily News* and *Post* in New York and *Newsday* on Long Island were other tabloid leaders.

Although the newspapers of the 1930s devoted far more space to stories about political and economic events and foreign affairs than those of the 1920s, they did not lose the "big story" complex that had characterized postwar Journalism. The trial of Bruno Hauptmann in 1934 for the kidnapping and murder of the Lindbergh baby drew more than 300 reporters, who wired more than 11 million words in 28 days. The publicity-seeking judge turned the trial into a news reporter's paradise, and there was much criticism of "trial by newspaper."

THE *DENVER POST'S* "BUCKET OF BLOOD" DAYS

No account of American journalism history is complete without a mention of the *Denver Post* of the days of Harry H. Tammen and Fred G. Bonfils. With its giant banner lines printed in red ink, its startling and helter-skelter makeup, and its highly sensationalized news play, the *Post* won fame as a dynamic but irresponsible paper. Its owners won fame, too, as ruthless operators of a journalistic gold mine. Tammen, a one-time bartender, and Bonfils, who had come West to make money in real estate and the lottery business, joined forces in 1895 to buy the *Post*. Their yellow-journalism tactics succeeded in the rough-and-tumble newspaper warfare of Denver, and at the height of their fortunes in the 1920s the paper was making more than $1 million a year.

The *Post* was filled with features and sensational stories, but it also engaged in stunts and crusades that spread its fame in the Rocky Mountain area, where it advertised itself as "Your Big Brother." The partners operated from an office with red-painted walls, which Denver promptly called the "Bucket of Blood." Victims of the *Post*'s crusades and exposés filed libel suits against Tammen and Bonfils, and accusations of blackmailing were leveled against the owners. No such charges were ever proved in court, however, and the *Post* continued in its proclaimed role as "the people's champion."

After Tammen's death in 1924, the *Post*'s luck began to change. The conduct of the paper in withholding news of illegal oil leases at Teapot Dome, until Bonfils was in a position to force the lessees to make a contract by which the *Post* would profit by half a million dollars, led the ethics committee of the American Society of Newspaper Editors to recommend that Bonfils be expelled from membership. Instead, however, he was allowed to resign. His reputation was further darkened just before his death in 1933, when he sued the rival *Rocky Mountain News* for libel and then lost interest when the *News* undertook to document many of the stories about the partners.

Still the *Post* roared on, while the stories about life on Denver newspapers multiplied. The entry of the Scripps Howard chain into intensified competition with the *Post* in 1926, through its purchase of the morning *Rocky Mountain News* and the evening *Times* for merger with the Scripps-owned *Express,* brought about one of the country's greatest competitive struggles. No holds were barred by city desks and circulation departments for the next two years, and Denver gorged itself on sensational news and free premium offers. In 1928 a truce was arranged by which the *Times* was killed, leaving the *Post* alone in the evening field and the *News* in the morning. The journalistic habits of the days when anything went continued to haunt Denver, however, for another two decades, until changes in management brought new policies that pushed memories of the Tammen–Bonfils era into the background.

THE WORLD OF COMICS

Highly lucrative for the Sunday papers was their distribution of the drawings of the comic-strip artists. The battle between Pulitzer and Hearst for possession of Richard F. Outcault's "Yellow Kid" in 1896 set off fierce competition in Sunday color comic sections. Early favorites tickled newspaper readers with portrayals of humorous episodes centering about the same characters. Charles E. Schultz's "Foxy Grandpa," who played tricks on boys, and Winsor McKay's childish wonderland of "Little Nemo" appeared in the *New York Herald* at the turn of the century. Hearst offered Rudolph Dirks's "Katzenjammer Kids," longest-lived of all American comics. Dirks began drawing Hans, Fritz, Mama, and the Captain in an 1897 color comic. Also memorable on Hearst pages were James Swinnerton's "Little Jimmy," Frederick Burr Opper's "Happy Hooligan," and George Herriman's "Krazy Kat."

The doings of the "Toonerville Folks" were first portrayed by Fontaine Fox in the *Chicago Post* of 1908. H. C. (Bud) Fisher's "Mutt and Jeff" was the first regular daily cartoon strip, appearing in the *San Francisco Chronicle* in 1907. But most comics came from the Hearst-owned King Features Syndicate or the *Chicago Tribune–New York Daily News* combine, masterminded by Colonel Robert R. McCormick and Captain Joseph M. Patterson.

George McManus began drawing Maggie and Jiggs for Hearst in 1912. Some of the other Hearst comic characters whose names became part of the American vocabulary were Billy De Beck's "Barney Google," owner of Sparkplug the horse; spinach-eating Popeye and Olive Oyl in Elzie C. Segar's "Thimble Theatre"; and Dagwood and Blondie Bumstead in the most popular of all comics, begun in 1930 by Chic Young. Working women of the 1920s were portrayed in "Tillie the Toiler" and "Winnie Winkle."

People still called the comic strips "the funny papers" in this period, but new developments were under way. One was the continuing story strip originated by the McCormick-Patterson group with Sidney Smith's "Andy Gump" in 1917. It is part of comic-strip lore how baby Skeezix was abandoned on Uncle Walt's doorstep in Frank King's "Gasoline Alley" of 1921 to begin a chronicle of family life now in a fourth generation. Less satisfying was Harold Gray's continuity for "Little Orphan Annie," whose waif was lost from Daddy Warbucks every little while and never finished school. King died in 1969 and Gray in 1968, but Skeezix and Annie lived on.

The other development was the action story, which entered the comic pages with United Features' "Tarzan" in 1929. The greatest detective of the comic-strip world operated in Chester Gould's "Dick Tracy" strip beginning in 1931 and starred in a major 1990 motion picture. Swashbuckling adventure was most cleverly portrayed by Milton Caniff in "Terry and the Pirates," a 1934 gold mine, and his 1947 "Steve Canyon." Buck Rogers was the first superhuman, in 1929; Superman caught on in 1939.

Children's humor survived in Edwina Dumm's "Cap Stubbs and Tippie," Carl Anderson's "Henry," Marjorie Buell's "Little Lulu," and Jimmy Hatlo's "Little Iodine." But the best humor has been that of the panel artists. The master performer was H. T. Webster of the *New York World* and *Herald Tribune,* who invented Casper Milquetoast for "The Timid Soul" and who drew "The Thrill That Comes Once in a Lifetime," "Life's Darkest Moment," and "How to Torture Your Wife." Webster also poked fun at bridge addicts and effectively criticized radio and television in "The Unseen Audience."

NEWSPAPER CONSOLIDATIONS, 1910 TO 1930

The years 1910 to 1914 mark the high point in numbers of newspapers published in the United States. The census of 1910 reported 2600 daily publications of all types, of which 2200 were English-language newspapers of general circulation. General-circulation weekly newspapers numbered approximately 14,000. The totals hovered at these peaks until the economic pressures of World War I were felt by American newspapers.

Wartime pressures, while of marked effect on publishing, only accented trends that were developing as early as 1890. These trends were toward suspension of some competing newspapers, merger of others with their rivals, concentration of newspaper ownership in many cities and towns, and creation of newspaper chains or groups. Before 1930, each of these trends had been clearly developed and set the pattern for twentieth-century American journalism.

Statistics can often be confusing, and this is true of those concerned with the number of American newspapers published over the years. For example, it might be assumed that if there were 2200 English-language daily newspapers of general circulation in 1910 and but 1942 in 1930, then 258 newspapers had died in those two decades. Actually, 1391 daily newspapers suspended publication or shifted to weekly status in those 20 years, and another 362 were merged with rival papers. In the same two decades, 1495 dailies were being born,[27] of which only one-quarter enjoyed lengthy lives.

Between 1910 and 1930 the population of the United States increased by 30 million, from 92 to 122 million persons. The number of towns and cities of 8000 or more persons jumped from 768 to 1208. Daily newspaper circulation increased at a faster pace, from 22.4 million copies a day in 1910 to 39.6 million copies in 1930. Sunday newspaper circulation more than doubled in the two decades, moving from 13 million to 27 million copies. Total newspaper advertising revenue tripled in the years 1915 to 1929, increasing from an estimated $275 million to $800 million.[28]

Yet despite this great growth in advertising revenue, in numbers of readers, and in numbers of urban centers that could support a daily newspaper, there was a net loss of 258 daily newspapers in the 20 years. Table 13-1 illustrates daily newspaper publishing trends from 1880 to 1930.

Many reasons can be listed for the decline in numbers of newspapers published, for the curtailment of competition in most communities, and for the increasing concentration of ownership. They fall under seven general headings: (1) economic pressures stemming from technological changes in the publishing pattern; (2) pressures resulting from competition for circulation and advertising revenues; (3) standardization of the product, resulting in loss of individuality and reader appeal; (4) lack of economic or social need for some newspapers; (5) managerial faults; (6) effects of wartime inflation and general business depressions; and (7) planned consolidation of newspapers for various reasons.

METROPOLITAN DAILIES, 1890 TO 1930: MUNSEY, CURTIS, AND KOHLSAAT

New York City boasted 15 general-circulation, English-language daily newspapers in 1890. Eight were morning papers, and seven were afternoon papers. Twelve owners were represented. By 1932 only three morning papers, four evening papers, and two tabloids remained, representing seven ownerships.

The name of Frank A. Munsey plays a large part in that story. Munsey was a successful New Englander whose career had a Horatio Alger ring. He broke into the New York publishing business with a juvenile magazine, the *Golden Argosy,* and then turned to the general magazine field with his *Munsey's.* As a ten-cent monthly, *Munsey's* hit

TABLE 13–1   Growth of One-Daily Cities, 1880–1930[29]

	1880	*1900*	*1910*	*1920*	*1930*
Number of English-language general-circulation dailies	850	1967	2200	2042	1942
Number of cities with dailies	389	915	1207	1295	1402
Number of one-daily cities	149	353	509	716	1002
Number of one-combination cities	1	3	9	27	112
Number of cities with competing dailies	239	559	689	552	288
Percentage of daily cities with competing dailies	61.4	61.1	57.1	42.6	20.6
Total daily circulation (millions)	3.1	15.1	22.4	27.8	39.6

650,000 circulation by 1900 to lead its competitors by a wide margin. The publisher had an income of $1 million a year by 1905. But he dreamt of a great national chain of newspapers, directed from a central headquarters by the most brilliant of American editors and business managers. To Munsey, the successful businessperson, the newspaper business was a disorderly, if not chaotic, enterprise. He proposed to bring efficiency to the newspaper world and thereby improve the product.

In 1901 Munsey bought the old *New York Daily News* and the *Washington Times* to be the nucleus of his chain. In 1902 the *Boston Journal* was added; in 1908 he invaded two more eastern cities, buying the *Baltimore Evening News* and founding the *Philadelphia Evening Times.* Munsey set about to improve the papers, installing color presses, featuring Sunday editions, and seeking increased readership. But the public failed to respond, and by 1917 all the papers were killed or sold to others . . . exactly what a wave of cost-cutting publishers would do in the 1970s and 1980s.

Munsey still owned one newspaper, the *New York Press,* which he had bought in 1912. The *Press,* under the editorship of Ervin Wardman, had a comfortable circulation. But Munsey eyed the New York field for a newspaper that could be combined with it, and his choice was the *Sun.* The *Sun* was still a proud newspaper, edited after the death of Charles A. Dana in 1897 by Edward P. Mitchell. Munsey paid $2.5 million for the *Sun* and the *Evening Sun* in 1916, and merged the *Press* into the morning edition, making Wardman publisher, Mitchell editor, and the *Press*'s renowned Keats Speed managing editor. But wartime publishing difficulties cost Munsey the profit he had hoped to make, and in 1920 he looked about for another prospect for consolidation.

Munsey's first move was to buy the *New York Herald,* the *Telegram,* and the Paris edition of the *Herald* for $4 million. The younger Bennett had spent lavishly during his long lifetime, and when he died in 1918 his newspapers were in neither a financial nor competitive position to continue. Munsey merged the morning *Sun* into the *Herald* and gave the historical name *Sun* to the evening edition.

The next victim was the *Globe.* Started in 1904, it was considered a healthy, liberal newspaper when Munsey killed it in 1923 for its AP evening membership. The next year he bought the conservative *Mail,* which had survived since 1867, merging it with the *Telegram.*

Munsey's morning paper, the *Herald,* was not faring well. He turned his eyes toward the *Tribune,* lowest in circulation of the morning dailies. But the *Tribune*'s owners, Ogden Mills Reid and his able wife, Helen Rogers Reid, refused to sell. Munsey, true to his belief that further consolidation was necessary, thereupon sold the *Herald* and its Paris edition to the Reids for $5 million. Happily, the new *Herald Tribune* successfully added the bulk of the old *Herald's* subscribers to its list and saw its advertising volume expand under the business direction of Mrs. Reid. Of all Munsey's newspaper maneuvering, his part in the creation of the *Herald Tribune* was the happiest, even though it meant the merger of the historic Bennett and Greeley papers.

Death claimed Munsey in 1925. Newspaperpeople generally were bitterly resentful of his cold and businesslike approach toward both them and their profession. William Allen White best expressed the rebels' sentiments in his famed terse obituary published in the *Emporia Gazette:*

> Frank A. Munsey contributed to the Journalism of his day the talent of a meatpacker, the morals of a money-changer and the manners of an undertaker. He and his kind have about succeeded in transforming a once-noble profession into an eight per cent security. May he rest in trust!

Another magazine publisher played a major role in the consolidation of Philadelphia's newspapers. He was Cyrus H. K. Curtis, who entered the Philadelphia newspaper picture by buying the historic *Public Ledger,* founded by William M. Swain in 1836 in the first wave of penny papers. Ably edited by George W. Childs from 1864 until his death in 1894, the *Public Ledger* had been sold in 1902 to Adolph S. Ochs, who put his brother George in charge. By 1913 Ochs was ready to sell to Curtis at a loss.

Curtis, like Munsey, moved in on the competition. The *Evening Telegraph,* dating back to 1864, was bought for its AP membership in 1918 and killed. The *Press,* founded in 1857, was purchased in 1920 for its newsprint contracts, Newspaperpeople mourned again in 1925, when the *North American,* on the scene since 1839 and with a reputation as a crusading force under editor E. A. Van Valkenberg, was killed. Curtis poured money into his newspapers, building them a $15 million plant and developing a famous foreign-news service that was widely syndicated.

But when Curtis died in 1933 the *Public Ledger* was merged into the *Inquirer.* Its evening edition lived until 1942, competing with the *Bulletin* and a tabloid *Daily News* begun in 1925. J. David Stern made the *Record* a liberal morning paper after 1928.

Herman Kohlsaat was the chief figure in Chicago's newspaper consolidations. Enriched by a chain of bakeries and lunch counters and enamored of the newspaper business, Kohlsaat bought into the *Inter Ocean* in 1891. Dissatisfied, he sold out and bought the *Evening Post* and a successful morning Democratic paper, the *Times-Herald.* Kohlsaat was a Republican, and the paper had to compete with the conservative *Tribune.* By 1901 he had to sell out, and the *Times-Herald* disappeared into the *Record,* the morning edition of Victor Lawson's *Daily News.*

Chicago in 1902 thus had four morning papers: the *Tribune, Inter Ocean, Record-Herald,* and William Randolph Hearst's newly established *Examiner.* In the evening field were the *Daily News, Post, Journal,* and Hearst's *American.* T   highly successful *Tribune* and *Daily News,* and the well-financed Hearst papers, were t   e out their competitors in the next 30 years.

One victim was the well-edited *Record-Herald,* whi   en Lawson brought Frank B. Noyes from the *Washington Star* to run it from 1902 t   ranked as one of the country's best. But by 1914 Kohlsaat, back in the picture, v   ging the *Record-Herald* and the *Inter Ocean* as the *Herald,* with James Keeley as e   failed, and in 1918 the Hearst interests established the *Herald & Examiner* as the *T*   s only competitor. Victor Lawson's *Daily News* developed a distinguished forei   ce before passing it to Colonel Frank Knox in 1931. Its only evening rival were *I*   *American* and the liberal tabloid *Times,* founded in 1929.

The sharp reduction in the number of mor   ilies in New York, Philadelphia, and Chicago was part of a nationwide trend. Re?   advertiser preference for afternoon papers, and the time advantage these had in   ing European war news, helped to cut the number of morning papers from 500 in   388 by 1930. By 1933 the journalistic historian Willard G. Bleyer could list 40   more than 100,000 population that had only one morning daily.[30] Mergers had   curred in Detroit, New Orleans, St. Louis, and Kansas City.[31]

HEARST AND SCRIPPS HOWARD CONSOLIDATIONS IN THE 1920s

Activities of the country's two biggest group ownerships—Hearst and Scripps Howard— and of lesser chain aspirants caused newspaper consolidations in still other cities. The Hearst organization, in a buying splurge concentrated in 1918 to 1928, put 16 newspapers to death as consolidations were carried out to bulwark the positions of Hearst-owned dailies. The Scripps Howard group was responsible for the closing of 15 newspapers between 1923 and 1934.

Washington was one of the few large cities to add newspapers during this period, but Hearst promptly consolidated the ownership of two newcomers. The morning *Post* and the Noyes family's evening *Star* were challenged by the founding of the *Times* in 1894 and the *Herald* in 1906. Munsey bought the *Times* in 1901 and killed its morning edition. When he retired from the Washington field in 1917, the *Times* passed to Arthur Brisbane, who sold it to Hearst two years later. The *Herald* was added to the Hearst group in 1922. Scripps Howard gave Washington a fourth ownership when it established the tabloid *Daily News* in 1921.

On the West Coast, Hearst created a strong evening companion for his *San Francisco Examiner* by combining three papers. He bought the *Call* (1855) in 1913 and combined the *Evening Post* with it to obtain an Associated Press membership. In 1929 the *Bulletin* (1856) was absorbed by Hearst to form the *Call-Bulletin.* The mergers left San Francisco with Hearst morning and evening papers, the locally owned morning *Chronicle,* and the Scripps Howard evening *News.* Across the bay in Oakland the *Post-Enquirer* was formed in a 1922 Hearst double purchase and merger as competition for the Knowland family's *Tribune.*

In Los Angeles, Hearst's morning *Examiner* was augmented in 1922 by the purchase of the evening *Herald.* The *Express,* founded in 1871, was swallowed up by Hearst in 1931 to form the *Herald & Express.* In 1947 it became the first major metropolitan paper to hire a woman city editor, Agness Underwood. The *Record,* established by Scripps in 1895, died in the 1920s but was replaced by the *Daily News,* a tabloid that Manchester Boddy developed into a pro–New Deal newspaper. Hearst's solid morning competition in Los Angeles was still Harry Chandler's conservative *Times.*[32]

ADVERTISING: AGENCIES AND COPYWRITERS

Advertising enjoyed a fabulous decade in the 1920s. The advertising agencies expanded and produced legendary managers and copywriters. They in turn created such memorable slogans as "I'd walk a mile for a Camel," "The skin you love to touch" (Palmolive), "Reach for a Lucky instead of a sweet," and "The priceless ingredient" (Squibb). Listeners to Jack Benny's radio comedy hour could chant his sponsor's musical "J-E-L-L-O." And advertising developed research methods to measure radio listenership and the effectiveness of printed messages. The agencies also had art directors who favored the Art Deco style.

The men and women of the 1920s and 1930s were building upon a considerable heritage. George P. Rowell's pioneer agency began in 1869, as did N. W. Ayer & Son, still a 1920s leader. So were J. Walter Thompson, founded in 1878, and Lord & Thomas, opened in 1880. Among the first copywriters had been John E. Powers of department-store copy fame, Earnest Elmo Calkins of the agencies, and inspirational writer Bruce Barton, who made the five-foot shelf of books and correspondence schools vital to intellectual progress. Such phrases as Ivory's "It floats," Victor's "His master's voice," and Kodak's "You press the button, we do the rest," had been written.

A truly legendary ad writer appeared at Lord & Thomas in 1898. He was young Albert Lasker, who was to rise to the agency's presidency and dominate it until 1952. Lord & Thomas boasted copywriters John C. Kennedy and Claude C. Hopkins, who cut a swath through the available advertising accounts. By 1928 the agency attracted the attention of the swashbuckling head of the American Tobacco Company, George Washington Hill, who had contributed "It's toasted" to the Lucky Strike slogans in 1917. According to advertising lore, it was Hill who noticed one woman on a corner eating a candy bar while another more dramatic-looking woman was holding a cigarette. "Reach for a Lucky instead of a sweet" was the message that flashed from Hill to Lasker and his copywriters, and that initiated the relentless campaign that doubled American Tobacco's profits between 1925 and 1931. More intriguing were N. W. Ayer's "The Camels are coming" teaser ads of 1914, the beginning of the first major cigarette ad campaign, which ended with "Camel cigarettes are here." Scarcely believable is the legend that a man walked up to a Camels advertising poster painter and said, "I'd walk a mile for a Camel." Supposedly the painter relayed the now-famous phrase to the sign company, which then relayed it to the agency. Legend notwithstanding, advertising made Camels, Luckies, and Chesterfields ("Blow some my way," said the woman in their daring 1926 ad) into the "big three" selling cigarettes; between them they comprised 80 percent of the United States cigarette market that year.

Young & Rubicam, destined to lead all American agencies in client billings during the early 1980s, was founded in 1923 by two N. W. Ayer & Son employees, account executive John Orr Young and copywriter Raymond Rubicam. It was Rubicam who gave the agency its tone; he had already created the slogans "The instrument of the immortals" for Steinway pianos and "The priceless ingredient" for Squibb pharmaceuticals. J. Walter Thompson had retired from his agency in 1916, turning over control to Stanley Resor and his wife, Helen Lansdowne, products of agency copywriting disciplines. Both the Thompson agency and Young & Rubicam developed research interests. Daniel Starch & Staff began magazine copy testing in 1923; Young & Rubicam first employed the random-sampling techniques of pollster George Gallup in 1932; and Elmo Roper entered the field in 1933. Market research, circulation studies including split-run techniques, and the employment of consumer panels to test products were emerging areas.

The rapidly expanding automobile industry was crowded with dozens of car makers with such still well-known names as Cadillac, Buick, and Ford, and such once-proud appellations as Pierce-Arrow, Hupmobile, and the Apperson Jackrabbit 8. Theodore F. MacManus wrote a Cadillac ad in 1915 that stands as one of the craft's greatest: a full page of copy under the heading, "The penalty of leadership." Henry Ford, the maverick of American business, wrote his own copy introducing the Model T in 1908, and in 1928, the Model A. And it was Ned Jordan, a Lord & Thomas copywriter who had turned to car manufacturing, who in 1923 wrote and published, in the *Saturday Evening Post,* one of the most intriguing advertisements of the century, "Somewhere West of Laramie." Jordan's ad stimulated the sales of the Jordan Playboy car and drew the admiration of generations of creative advertising men and women.

Among the women copywriters of the era whose work was selected for compilations of "the 100 greatest advertisements" were Lillian Eichler of Ruthrauff & Ryan, Miriam Dewey of Young & Rubicam, and Dorothy Dignam and Frances Gerety of N. W. Ayer. And among their slogans were Ivory's "99 and 44/100 pure," Coca-Cola's "The pause that refreshes," Listerine's "Often a bridesmaid but never a bride," and the U.S. School of Music's "They laughed when I sat down at the piano but when I began to play!—"

Historian Roland Marchand, in his book *Advertising the American Dream,* took a cultural approach to the formative years of advertising (1920–40). He saw advertising as both promoting technological modernity and offering relief from self-image anxiety. Its personalized messages and its promise of individuality and equality through consumption cushioned the growing impact of society's impersonality. Its vantage point for all this was that of a white Anglo-Saxon male; men outnumbered women ten to one in the agencies, and non-Nordic types were seldom seen.[33]

The first major cigarette advertising campaign and two famous slogans

Somewhere West of Laramie

SOMEWHERE west of Laramie there's a broncho-busting, steer-roping girl who knows what I'm talking about. She can tell what a sassy pony, that's a cross between greased lightning and the place where it hits, can do with eleven hundred pounds of steel and action when he's going high, wide and handsome.

The truth is—the Playboy was built for her.

Built for the lass whose face is brown with the sun when the day is done of revel and romp and race.

She loves the cross of the wild and the tame.

There's a savor of links about that car—of laughter and lilt and light—a hint of old loves—and saddle and quirt. It's a brawny thing—yet a graceful thing for the sweep o' the Avenue.

Step into the Playboy when the hour grows dull with things gone dead and stale.

Then start for the land of real living with the spirit of the lass who rides, lean and rangy, into the red horizon of a Wyoming twilight.

JORDAN MOTOR CAR COMPANY, Inc., Cleveland, Ohio

A legendary feat of copywriting (1923)

All but two of the top ten advertising agencies of the early 1980s were operating by the 1930s. In addition to Young & Rubicam, J. Walter Thompson, and Lord & Thomas (renamed Foote, Cone & Belding in 1943), two major agencies were created by 1930 mergers of earlier groups, McCann-Erickson and Batten Barton Durstine & Osborn. Also appearing in the 1930s were the Ted Bates, Leo Burnett, and Compton agencies. Other important firms included D'Arcy, 1906; Campbell-Ewald, 1911; Erwin, Wasey, 1912; Grey Advertising, 1917; Dancer-Fitzgerald-Sample, 1923; and three 1929 entries, Benton & Bowles, Kenyon & Eckhardt, and Needham, Louis & Brorby.

Total expenditures for advertising in the United States were $1.5 billion during 1918; the figure jumped to $3 billion by 1920 and to $3.4 billion in 1929. Radio's advertising revenue increased from $4 million in 1927 to $40 million in 1929, with the advent of national networks. By 1933 the depression's impact had cut advertising expenditures to $1.3 billion. As the 1930s progressed, advertising began to be the target of consumer groups and social critics. Regulatory efforts had been encouraged by the formation of Better Business Bureaus after 1913, the establishment of the Audit Bureau of Circulations in 1914 to police print-media circulation claims, the founding of the American Association of Advertising Agencies in 1917, and the creation of the Federal Trade Commission (FTC) in 1914. The Wheeler-Lea Act of 1938 gave the FTC added teeth in dealing with advertisements that deceived consumers.

THE ROOTS OF PUBLIC RELATIONS

The roots of the twentieth-century field of public relations are found in three nineteenth-century developments: the rise of press agentry, the intensification of political campaigning, and the employment by businesses of publicity writers. By the 1920s the image of public relations as an operating concept of management, implemented by a specialized staff function, was beginning to emerge.

Most celebrated of the press agents was Phineas Taylor Barnum, whose skill built his circus into an American institution in post–Civil War years. He and his own press agent, Richard F. (Tody) Hamilton, utilized exaggeration, outright fakery, and staged events to obtain reams of stories in the newspapers. They made household names of Tom Thumb, the midget, and Jenny Lind, "the Swedish Nightingale," who made a dazzling American tour. William F. Cody became "Buffalo Bill" through the skills of a half-dozen press agents. And as Will Irwin noted, the successes of theatrical press agents led to the appearance of thousands of publicists in business, politics, and other areas.

American politics had used pamphlets, posters, emblems, and press releases since the Jacksonian era. The focus on the use of the newspaper became sharper during the 1896 presidential campaign between William Jennings Bryan and William McKinley. Pioneer business publicists like George F. Parker and Ivy Lee cut their teeth in political campaigns. Scott M. Cutlip, a leading public-relations scholar, traces the third strand—business identification with public relations—to pre-1900 events. In 1883 Theodore N. Vail, founding force of AT&T, was mailing sheaves of letters asking for opinions about his American Bell Telephone Company. George Westinghouse hired a personal press representative in 1889. And the Association of American Railroads used the term "public relations" in an 1897 company listing.[34]

The rise of the era of muckraking journalism after 1900, spurred by the political movements led by Presidents Theodore Roosevelt and Woodrow Wilson, brought a new urgency to developments in the publicity field. Roosevelt and Wilson methodically used the press conference and the news release to shape the public image of White House policies. More immediately threatening to business were the muckraking magazines, led by *McClure's,* which published Ida M. Tarbell's 1903 series, "History of the Standard Oil Company." What the methodical Tarbell did in exposing the Rockefeller oil monopoly was matched by the emotion-arousing attack made on the meat packers by Upton Sinclair in 1906 in his book *The Jungle.* Businesspeople now sought defensive publicity and were in some cases more responsive to the managerial concept of public relations.

George F. Parker and Ivy Lee opened a New York City publicity office in 1904. Parker remained primarily a publicist, but Lee moved into the role of advising companies and industries that were in trouble. One was the anthracite coal industry, embroiled in a 1906 strike; in its behalf Lee issued a declaration to the press that his agency would operate only in the open, using prompt and accurate information. He told the Pennsylvania Railroad it should help reporters cover a train wreck, not hide it. It was harder for Lee to maintain his personal image when he became an adviser to John D. Rockefeller, Jr., in 1914, in the wake of vicious strike-breaking activities at the family's Colorado Fuel and Iron Company. Upton Sinclair dubbed Lee "Poison Ivy." Lee's later association with the Guggenheim family brought him more criticism centered on their Chilean mining interests. Nevertheless Lee became identified as a founder of public relations; he formed a public-relations firm with T. J. Ross in 1919.

James D. Ellsworth, later an AT&T staff member, formed a Boston publicity bureau in 1906. Pendleton Dudley, another pioneer, opened his New York office in 1909. Henry Ford, who cannily used the press to publicize his Model-T car, founded his own internal

(Jamie Cope)

Edward L. Bernays

(Wanda Brown)

Doris E. Fleischman

magazine, *The Ford Times,* in 1908. Theodore Vail, becoming AT&T president in 1907, rapidly expanded the Bell company's programs for both customer and press relations. The American Red Cross and National Tuberculosis Association public-relations programs date from 1908. An association of college and university publicists was formed in 1917, and the National Lutheran Council and the Knights of Columbus opened press offices in 1918. Some companies used their advertising agencies, notably N. W. Ayer, for publicity services.

Techniques of publicity, promotion, and propaganda were greatly developed during World War I. President Wilson established the Committee on Public Information (CPI), under the direction of George Creel, to coordinate wartime programs, disseminate information, and stimulate public support of war objectives. Ivy Lee was then working for the Red Cross, but two new figures in the public-relations area joined the CPI. One, the associate chairperson, was Carl Byoir, later founder of one of the largest counseling firms. The other was Edward L. Bernays, who soon proved to be the most articulate advocate of the public-relations concept. The CPI afforded them an opportunity to undertake programs influencing the public mind and to prove the value of publicity campaigns. The lessons were soon used in behalf of products, the corporate image, political candidates, fund-raising drives, and social-work agencies.

Two books of the early 1920s gave direction to the development of the fields of public opinion and public relations. One was Walter Lippmann's 1922 pioneering analysis, *Public Opinion.* Lippmann likened each individual's opinions to "the pictures in our heads" and said that those pictures acted upon by groups of people as "Public Opinion in capital letters." His book examined how opinions are crystallized into a social purpose or a national will. The next year Bernays published *Crystallizing Public Opinion,* in collaboration with his wife and partner, Doris E. Fleischman, who had been a reporter and editor of the *New York Tribune* before their marriage. The first sentence read: "In writing this book I have tried to set down the broad principles that govern the new profession of public relations counsel."[35] Bernays continued as a leading public-relations counsel, teacher, and writer into the 1990s. He died in 1995 at the age of 103. His longtime collaborator, Fleischman, died in 1980.

John W. Hill began a public-relations firm in Cleveland in 1927, and later joined with Don Knowlton to form a major counseling firm. Bernays served as counsel to General Electric and Westinghouse during the 1920s. Arthur W. Page became the first public-relations director of AT&T. Corporate public-relations programs utilizing advertising campaigns were begun by Illinois Central, Metropolitan Life, and General Motors between 1920 and 1923. In the prosperous years of the decade the field expanded steadily. General Motors, facing belt-tightening in 1931, named Paul Garrett as the company's first public-relations director. He set a pattern for corporate public relations and continued in the position for 25 years.

14

Depression
and Reform

Partisanship, in editorial comment which knowingly departs from
the truth, does violence to the best spirit of American journalism;
in the news columns it is subversive of a fundamental principle of
the profession.

—ASNE Canons of Journalism

Criticism of the performance of America's mass media became particularly pointed during
the liberal resurgence of the 1930s known as the New Deal. Driven by the impact of
the Great Depression, the nation established new patterns of social justice and economic
security under the leadership of Franklin D. Roosevelt. In doing so, it vastly expanded governmental participation in socioeconomic affairs. That there was criticism of newspapers
during such years of swift change was nothing new; press critics had been having their say
since the dawn of newspaper publishing. But whereas much of the earlier criticism had
dealt with the cultural and social values of the press, the emphasis in the 1930s was on its
political power. Supporters of Franklin Roosevelt and the New Deal charged that much of
the press was opposed to socioeconomic reforms, sometimes in ways viewed as bitterly
partisan. To the liberals who won sweeping ballot-box victories, it seemed that too often
the press was unresponsive to change and democratic decisions. Their wrath particularly
centered on a group of publishers dubbed the "press lords."

The prologue for this drama came in 1928. There was a great surge of stock prices
on the New York Stock Exchange that carried Radio Corporation of America, for example,
from less than $100 a share to $400. "Two chickens in every pot, two cars in every garage,"
was the slogan of the Republican party, which promised permanent prosperity with the
election of Herbert Hoover as president. A "get-rich-quick" mania brought hundreds of
thousands of small investors into the market in 1929; many of them put their life savings

Radio came of age during the Roosevelt years.

up as margin for speculative accounts. But permanent prosperity was not to be had. The market wavered in September, plummeted in late October, and on "Black Thursday" crashed an average of 40 points. Shoe clerks and stockbrokers were ruined alike, and the boom was over. *Variety* put it simply: "WALL ST. LAYS AN EGG."

The business downturn that ended in the Great Depression was worldwide in character. In the United States, industries had overexpanded, boosting productivity by some 40 percent during the 1920s, but consumers did not have the money to buy the goods thus produced. Too much wealth had fallen into too few hands. Workers' wages had fallen far behind inflation, and farmers were bankrupted by chronically low crop prices. The stock-market collapse added to the momentum. Furthermore, consumer debt rose by 250 percent during the 1920s. A decentralized banking system had allowed banks to divert more funds into speculative investments. Still other factors in the Depression were an unregulated and shaky corporate structure as well as a high tariff.[1]

With unsalable inventories mounting, manufacturers closed plants and laid off workers. In turn, retail stores and businesses failed. More than 1300 banks closed their doors in 1930, and another 3700 in the next two years. There was, for the victims of the spreading chaos, no bank-deposit insurance, no unemployment insurance, no help in warding off foreclosures on farms and homes.

By mid-1932, stocks on Wall Street were worth only 11 percent of their 1929 values. Business failures totaled 86,000; unemployment reached 15 million. Those still working earned an average of $16 a week, or $842 a year. A fourth of the population had no income at all. President Hoover, the advocate of rugged individualism, offered constructive financial aid to big businesses, but none to plain people. He ordered General Douglas MacArthur to drive the ragged "Bonus Army" of war veterans from Washington with gunfire and clubs, a disgraceful episode that was generally condoned by the press.

Hoover won only six states in the 1932 election, against an opponent offering a "New Deal." The new president, Franklin D. Roosevelt, was equally capitalistic in outlook, but compassionate and flexible in seeking new solutions to the problems of a country with one-third of its people "ill-housed, ill-clad, and ill-nourished." Before he took office on March 4, 1933, most of the country's banks had closed, and the economy was at a halt. "The only thing we have to fear is fear itself," Roosevelt said in a reassuring inaugural address. During the "hundred days" that followed, Congress rewrote American political history. "I want to talk a few minutes with the people of the United States about banking," Roosevelt said in his first radio network "fireside chat." A complete reorganization of banking and the financial markets followed. A roll call of 1933 to 1935 legislation includes the establishment of the Federal Deposit Insurance Corporation to insure bank deposits; the Works Progress Administration (WPA) to aid the one-sixth of the population on relief; the National Recovery Administration (NRA) to stimulate industrial production; the Agricultural Adjustment Administration (AAA) to stabilize farm prices; and the Securities Exchange Commission to regulate financial markets. The Social Security Act of 1935 and the Wagner Labor Relations Act of 1935 were cornerstones of personal and job security.

There was heavy criticism of the New Deal among conservatives, businesspeople, financiers, and others whose loyalties lay with the Republican party. Roosevelt had the editorial support of only about one-third of the country's dailies in the 1932 and 1936 elections, including few of the influential ones. He was pilloried by some he called the "press lords." The papers were full of complaints as the economy bettered: the Socialist left denounced Roosevelt for propping up capitalism; the Liberty League, founded in 1936 by 2000 of the wealthiest Americans, berated him for imitating Communist Russia. A conservative Supreme Court declared the NRA and AAA unconstitutional. A *Literary*

Digest poll based on telephone listings and automobile registrations predicted a 1936 Republican victory (an error that hastened the *Digest*'s demise and sale to *Time*).

Accepting his renomination, Roosevelt said confidently: "There is a mysterious cycle in human events. To some generations much is given. Of other generations much is expected. This generation has a rendezvous with destiny." The tumultuous applause that greeted his campaign speeches forecast the solid vote of those without telephones and cars. "FDR" won all but two states from the hapless Alf Landon as five million Republican votes turned Democratic. Flush with victory, Roosevelt took aim at the Supreme Court. But early in 1937 the Court upheld the Wagner Act and Social Security, taking the steam out of his "Court-packing" plan. The New Deal was coming to a halt, but victory came at last on the labor front. Sitdown strikes in the auto plants were unpopular, but they brought unionization of all except Ford. And John L. Lewis's Congress of Industrial Organization (CIO) won contracts with the steel industry after a bloody massacre of workers by police outside a Chicago plant. Thus the efforts of the IWW, Eugene Debs, and earlier labor leaders were bearing fruit.

Historians continue to debate just how far the New Deal went. Writing in the 1950s, Carl N. Degler called it "the third American revolution."[2] William Leuchtenburg also emphasized the changes in U.S. life wrought by the New Deal.[3] On the other hand, New Left historians judged the New Deal as more conservative, arguing that its reforms did not go far enough.[4] Recent scholarship has focused on the ideological, social, economic, and political constraints of the New Deal, as well as the ways in which its programs worked to reinforce gender norms and racial stereotypes, Roosevelt's "Black Cabinet" and his appointment of women to important administrative positions notwithstanding.[5]

A darkening storm of military adventurism brought about by economic and political crises throughout the world periodically interrupted the United States' preoccupation with domestic affairs. Soberly the American people read about the aggressive forces in their newspapers and in newly founded news and picture magazines, listened to radio broadcasts, and watched marching armies in their newsreels, beginning with the Japanese invasion of Manchuria in 1931. Working outside the crumbling League of Nations, the American government attempted to rally world opinion against the Japanese, Italian, and German militarists, but there was no unity of action. Ethiopia fell to Mussolini, the new *Life* magazine pictured a crying Chinese baby in a bomb-destroyed Shanghai railway station, and disturbing headlines recorded Hitler's reoccupation of the Rhineland and *anschluss* with Austria. The disillusionment that had produced the antiwar literature in the 1930s and had set the stage for neutrality legislation was slowly passing. Isolationism died hard, however. In 1935 a Senate committee headed by Gerald P. Nye of North Dakota had advanced the thesis that American munitions makers and bankers were almost solely responsible for the country's entrance into World War I. The neutrality legislation that followed was designed to prevent American loans or sale of war materials to belligerents, on the theory that such a ban would prevent American involvement in "foreign" wars. Even after Americans heard intensive radio coverage of the Munich crisis of September 1938 and Hitler's occupation of the remainder of unhappy Czechoslovakia in March 1939, the isolationists held the upper hand.

THE PRESIDENT AND THE PRESS: FDR

No president had more effective relationships with the press than did Franklin D. Roosevelt. He met the White House correspondents informally, often in his office. He was at ease, communicative, gay, or serious as the news might dictate. Like all presidents he came to be irritated by his critics in the press, once assigning a dunce cap to Robert Post of the conservative *New York Herald Tribune* and another time awarding an iron cross to John O'Donnell of the isolationist *New York Daily News.* But he met the press 998 times during his 12 years in office, for an average of 83 times a year. He was known for his fireside chats, but in his first term he gave only eight; the same four years he communicated with the American people and won 46 states in the next election by holding 340 press conferences, most of which made solid news. He had one of the most capable press secretaries, Stephen T. Early, and built a tradition that would be hard to follow. To look ahead, President Truman dropped the number of press conferences held yearly from 83 to 42; the averages later were Eisenhower, 24; Kennedy, 22; Johnson, 25; Nixon, 7; Ford, 16; Carter, 26; and Reagan, 6. Bush and Clinton had low averages.

As governor of New York Roosevelt had used radio to make direct appeals to the public. In 1932 he flew to Chicago to personally accept his nomination by the Democratic convention on radio—three unprecedented actions. He pointed out that he was breaking tradition and pledged his party to the task of destroying foolish ones. As a radio president, FDR was able to communicate a sense of comfort and reassurance with his personable voice that conveyed sincerity. His fireside chats were truly that.[6]

FDR's warm personality fit the informal "lodge" atmosphere of the press meetings. He was solicitous of the regulars and was sure to ask if they had comfortable places to stay at Hyde Park or Warm Springs. The president would give out a story, and he would provide the correspondents with several laughs as well as a couple of top-head dispatches in a time-saving 20-minute visit. In fact, the Roosevelt press conferences became the greatest regular show in Washington, and FDR knew it. Once, he remarked, "Most of the people in the back row are here for curiosity, isn't that right?"[7]

Roosevelt had conference rules involving direct quotes (only when stipulated), indirect quotes, and "off the record" material. As many as 30 different background questions might be answered in a longer conference; here FDR could employ his full range of news-management techniques. The conferences were useful to him; he could capture the headlines and the lead stories, whether the publishers wanted him to or not.

CRITICISM OF THE "PRESS LORDS"

Political tension, and accompanying criticism of the newspaper's role in elections, made for extensive public acceptance of a literature of criticism of the press. Upton Sinclair's bitter book *The Brass Check* (1919) painted a picture of a false, cowardly press dominated by its business offices and advertisers. Although there were actual newspaper situations that fit these patterns, particularly in crowded metropolitan competitive situations where the loss of an account could endanger a fourth- or fifth-ranking paper, the issue of advertiser influence was not the most pressing one. It was also one that tended to decline later in the century. The issue that had the most immediate impact was that of the political influence of the press, and particularly the misuse of both news and editorial columns by the owners who were called the "press lords" by veteran foreign correspondent and antifascist writer George Seldes. Seldes did not give up his crusade until 1988, when at age 97 he published his twentieth book.

Caustic surveys of the "press lords" began in earnest with Oswald Garrison Villard's *Some Newspapers and Newspaper-Men* (1923). They flourished in the 1930s, which saw the publication of such books as Seldes's *Lords of the Press* (1938) and Harold L. Ickes's *America's House of Lords* (1939), and individual studies such as Ferdinand Lundberg's

Imperial Hearst (1936). These works were valuable as exposés. Adding to these discussions were Casper S. Yost's *Principles of Journalism* (1924), Villard's brief *The Press Today* (1930), Herbert Brucker's *The Changing American Newspaper* (1937), Silas Bent's *Newspaper Crusaders* (1939), and such products of the growing journalism schools as Leon N. Flint's *The Conscience of the Newspaper* (1925), Willard G. Bleyer's *Main Currents in the History of American Journalism* (1927), and *Interpretations of Journalism* (1937), edited by Frank L. Mott and Ralph D. Casey.

In any event, the dynamic and intriguing personalities of some of the "press lords" provided more interesting fare for the American reading public than any other material about newspaperpeople and newspaper problems. To understand, therefore, the bitterness and the extent of the criticisms of the press since the 1930s, it is necessary to examine the roles played by the most-often discussed newspaper publishers of the times.

WILLIAM RANDOLPH HEARST

William Randolph Hearst, as has been suggested in previous chapters, is one of the most difficult men of journalism to study and to evaluate, considering the complex nature of his personality, the variegated social and political impact of his many ventures, and the length and extent of his career. Those who wrote about Hearst were never permitted access to the publisher's private papers or the records of the Hearst empire. As a result, the official Hearst biography released by International News Service when the publisher's 64-year newspaper career closed in 1951 noted in its second paragraph: "And as he fashioned his vast enterprises, there grew progressively in the public mind a picture of the builder himself. It was a strange portrait, obscured by myth and legend, confused by controversy and distortion."

When Hearst had lived out his 88 years, the question became: Did he deserve the criticism that had been heaped upon him more vehemently than on any other publisher? The points most often made in support of a thesis that Hearst made positive contributions to American journalism are these:

1. Hearst built the world's biggest publishing empire in terms of newspapers and their combined circulations. At the peak, in 1935, Hearst printed 26 dailies and 17 Sunday editions in 19 cities. The papers had 13.6 percent of the total daily circulation and 24.2 percent of Sunday circulation in the country. In addition, he controlled the King Features Syndicate, largest of its kind; the money-coining *American Weekly;* the International News Service, Universal Service, and International News Photos; and 13 magazines, 8 radio stations, and 2 motion-picture companies. This, it is argued, spells a success that must be recognized.

2. Hearst's methods and innovations in news writing and news handling—particularly in makeup and headline and picture display—and his utilization of new mechanical processes were very important. Hearst newspapers were edited to appeal to the mass of readers and encouraged millions to increase their reading habits. Because of this and because of Hearst's editorial policies and his own political activities, his newspapers exercised a powerful influence in American life that must be recognized.

3. Hearst was in many ways a constructive force: a stalwart in his Americanism; a believer in popular education and in the extension of the power of the people; and, during different phases of his long career, an advocate of many progressive solutions to national problems. These included his early advocacy of the popular election of senators, the initiative and referendum, a graduated income tax, widespread public ownership of utilities, breaking up of monopolies and trusts, and the rights of labor unions.

These points, the argument runs, are in the record for all to see. Hearst's critics, and the public record, also provided counterarguments:

1. The Hearst empire, for all its one-time size, was not the roaring success a recital of figures would indicate. Its finances were shaky in the 1920s. The crash came for Hearst in 1937, when he was forced to abdicate temporarily and watch a group of trustees liquidate a portion of his empire. Nine dailies and five Sunday editions were dropped by 1940; Universal Service was consolidated with the INS; movie companies, radio stations, and some magazines were sold. The trustees began liquidating $40 million worth of New York City real estate. Many of the $40 million in art treasures that were Hearst's pride and joy were auctioned off at Gimbel's and Macy's. Eventually even many of the 275,000 acres at his San Simeon estate were sold to reclaim some of the $36 million spent there.

   Through it all, however, Hearst continued to live in regal style. The man who had bought a castle in Wales, Egyptian mummies, Tibetan yaks, and a Spanish abbey (which was dismantled stone by stone and shipped to a New York warehouse, after which Hearst never saw it again) had a truly precapitalistic attitude toward money as such. His guests at San Simeon, who were legion, continued to dive into an indoor pool from a sixteenth-century Italian marble balcony, to pick flowers in a mile-long pergola stretching along Hearst's private mountain range, and to eat from kingly silver plates. Before World War II had ended, the trimming down of his empire and wartime publishing profits had accomplished the desired miracle, and the Hearst once thought to be broke was back in full command again.

   When death had claimed its founder in 1951, the Hearst organization had 16 dailies and 13 Sunday editions appearing in a dozen cities. They had 9.1 percent of the country's total daily circulation and 16.1 percent of the Sunday total, a substantial decline in Hearst influence from the 1935 figures of 13.6 percent daily and 24.2 percent Sunday. The Hearst estate was valued at some $56 million, based on estimated stock values, but the profit margins of the Hearst enterprises were below those of other newspapers of their size for which financial reports are available, forecasting further contraction.

2. Undoubtedly, Hearst drew many new newspaper readers to his fold and held more than five million daily and eight million Sunday to the day of his death. But what was the end result? Pulitzer defended the use of sensationalism in his *World* by arguing that it attracted readers who would then be exposed to the columns of his carefully planned, high-quality editorial page. The same could never be said of a Hearst newspaper. Nor did Hearst ever exercise the powerful influence in American life that his great circulations might indicate. Among the men whom he wanted to see become president of the United States were William Jennings Bryan, Champ Clark, Hiram W. Johnson, William Gibbs McAdoo, John Nance Garner, Alfred M. Landon, General Douglas MacArthur, and William Randolph Hearst. Among the men whom he fought while they were in the White House were William McKinley, Theodore Roosevelt, William Howard Taft, Woodrow Wilson, Herbert Hoover, Franklin D. Roosevelt, and Harry S. Truman.

3. What, then, of Hearst as a constructive social force? Certainly he was an advocate of Americanism. But to many his continued espousal of nationalistic policies bordering on jingoism, in a time that demanded American cooperation in international security efforts, was the most distressing feature of his newspapers, And in the 1930s the "Red hunts" his newspapers fostered among the ranks of political leaders, educators, YMCA secretaries, labor leaders, and other citizens were based on the familiar tactics of the demagogue: those who disagreed with Hearst were "Communists." A nationalist-isolationist to the end, Hearst opposed the basic foreign policy adopted by the American people during and after World War II and distrusted the United Nations as thoroughly as he had distrusted the League of Nations.

In domestic affairs, Hearst newspapers continued to give stalwart support to public education and to the idea of public ownership of utilities. But they backslid during the 1920s and 1930s on many of the other progressive features of the Hearst editorial program as written before World War I. Hearst had helped to elect Franklin Roosevelt, and in the spring of 1933 his newspapers applauded vigorously as Roosevelt undertook unemployment relief, suspended exports of gold, and proposed the National Recovery Act—which, a Hearst editorial said, "embodies several basic policies long advocated by the Hearst newspapers."[8] By 1935 the tune had changed. It was the "Raw Deal" and the "National Run Around" in both Hearst news and editorial columns. The unanimous Supreme Court decision outlawing the NRA, which the Hearst papers had once proudly claimed for their own, was greeted with an American flag and the headline: "Thank God for the Supreme Court!"

Other examples in the columns of the Hearst papers of 1935 illustrate the extent to which his earlier beliefs had changed. The publisher who before World War I had been perhaps the most aggressive in supporting the power of labor unions now said "the Wagner Labor Bill . . . is one of the most vicious pieces of class legislation that could be conceived—unAmerican to the core, violative of every constitutional principle and contrary to the whole spirit of American life. Congress in passing it is betraying the country."[9]

The publisher who had fought so long against monopolies and trusts now said "the Wheeler-Rayburn Bill, decreeing death to the holding companies, is PURE VENOM distilled by a PERSONAL and MALIGNANT OBSESSION, without a pretense of economic or legal justification."[10]

The publisher who always believed that he understood the common people, and was understood by them, sparked an extensive front-page coverage of WPA activities in 1936 with headlines like this one: "Taxpayers Feed 20,000 Reds on N.Y. Relief Rolls." And his newspapers warned that the Social Security Act was "A Pay Cut for You! . . . Governor Landon, when elected, will repeal this so-called security act."[11]

Hearst newspapers threw every resource of the editorial and news pages into the campaign to elect Governor Alfred M. Landon of Kansas president in 1936. When President Roosevelt was reelected by the greatest majority in history, carrying all the states but two, Hearst's enemies cried for his scalp. But the triumphant liberals over-reached themselves in launching the Supreme Court reorganization bill of 1937, which was called the "court-packing bill" by those who defeated it. The New Deal reform period came to an abrupt halt. Just as the Hearst papers weathered their economic difficulties in the next few years, they weathered public attacks against them and moved into a different political climate in which they could once more go on the offensive.

COLONEL McCORMICK AND THE *CHICAGO TRIBUNE*

Second only to Hearst in stirring up the wrath of critics was Colonel Robert R. McCormick, publisher of the *Chicago Tribune.* The quarrel with McCormick was not so much that his *Tribune* clung to an outmoded and dangerous nationalist-isolationist point of view in the face of overwhelming public support of efforts to find peace and security through international cooperation. Nor was it so much that his *Tribune* became the principal voice for the ultraconservative right wing in American politics and rejected a President Eisenhower as violently as it had rejected a President Truman. The real quarrel McCormick's critics had with him was that as he tried so hard to prove that the *Tribune* was right and that most everybody else was wrong, editorial columns became bitter personal proclamations whose prejudiced approaches to matters of public interest spilled over into the news columns. McCormick's answer, until death stilled his voice in 1955, was that his *Tribune* was the "World's Greatest Newspaper."

This claim would have had merit if newspaper greatness were measured only in terms of financial success, circulation, and mechanical excellence. In the mid-1950s the *Tribune* carried as much advertising as its three Chicago rivals combined. Its circulation, while down to 900,000 daily from a 1946 high of 1,075,000, was still the largest of any standard-sized American newspaper and was spread through five states in an area McCormick called "Chicago-land." Its 450-person news staff, operating from the 36-story Tribune Tower, provided blanket coverage of local and area events that was the despair of rival city editors. For a venture that rated as the most-often criticized single American newspaper, the *Tribune* was doing all right, and Colonel McCormick frequently reminded his critics of that fact.

Not all of this success was due to McCormick. The *Tribune* has a long history, beginning in 1847. The builder was Joseph Medill, who from 1855 to 1899 devoted his energies to creating a powerful conservative newspaper. Medill left a financial trust that provided for the families of his two daughters—the McCormicks and the Pattersons. The Robert R. McCormick era began in 1914, the year his brother Medill retired from the paper to become a senator. Sharing responsibility for the *Tribune* with the future colonel was his cousin, Joseph Medill Patterson, who founded the *New York Daily News* in 1919. The fourth Medill grandchild, Eleanor Medill Patterson, was to become owner of the *Washington Times-Herald*. The young cousins doubled *Tribune* circulation and advertising during the World War I period. Patterson had a particular brilliance for spotting the best comic strips and other features; McCormick proved to be an able businessperson.

The success of the *New York Daily News,* and the disappearance of Captain Patterson into that venture, further entrenched McCormick's position. The two papers made as much as $13 million a year. The *Tribune-Daily News* feature syndicate, radio station WGN, and Canadian paper and power investments followed. When Captain Patterson died in 1946, McCormick became the head of the *New York Daily News,* although he preferred to exercise influence by remote control. When Eleanor Patterson died in 1948, she willed the *Washington Times-Herald* to seven of her executives, but they sold it to McCormick in 1949 for $4.5 million. The *Tribune* formula did not work in Washington, and in 1954, ill and weary of a paper that was losing $500,000 a year, McCormick sold the *Times-Herald* for $8.5 million to Eugene Meyer's *Washington Post.* But despite this retreat, no one except the Hearst heirs had more readers than McCormick had, with his two big dailies.

The memos signed "R. R. Mc." were law in the *Tribune* empire. The 6-foot 4-inch colonel turned eyes of ice-water blue on all aspects of the business. His private domains were the Tribune Tower and his 1000-acre farm and estate outside Chicago, named Cantigny for the World War I battle in which McCormick participated. McCormick made a deep study of military history, but his opinions about international affairs were based on a belief that foreigners, especially the English, were dangerous. Almost as dangerous, the *Tribune* said, were New York financiers, eastern internationalists, and educators.

Among those who helped to build the *Tribune* as McCormick's aides were Edward Scott Beck, managing editor from 1910 to 1937; J. Loy Maloney, managing editor from 1939 to 1951, when he became executive editor; W. D. Maxwell, city editor who became managing editor in 1951; and sports editor Arch Ward. Heading the Washington bureau were Arthur Sears Henning and his successor, Walter Trohan, who learned to shape their coverage to back up the Colonel's opinions.

McCormick opposed President Franklin Roosevelt and the domestic policies of the New Deal with every resource. As a result, in a 1936 poll of Washington correspondents the *Tribune* was voted as runner-up to the Hearst papers for the title "least fair and reliable." When the World War II crisis began to develop, the *Tribune* bitterly denounced cooperation with Great Britain, the ancient enemy; a typical eight-column banner when the lend-lease bill was under debate read: "HOUSE PASSES DICTATOR BILL." It was this combination of extreme conservatism and nationalism that incited Marshall Field to start the *Chicago Sun* as a rival morning paper (the *Tribune* having inherited the field alone when Hearst retired from it in 1939).

But McCormick's luck held. Three days after the *Sun* appeared, its principal issue of isolationism versus interventionism was exploded by the bombs at Pearl Harbor. McCormick supported the American war effort, although the *Tribune* called American entrance an "FDR war plot." The Washington correspondents again estimated the *Tribune*'s standing in 1947, voting it "the newspaper . . . most flagrant in angling or weighting the news."[12]

HOWARD AND THE SCRIPPS IMAGE

Receiving special attention, too, was Roy W. Howard, the man who by the 1930s had come to dominate the newspapers founded by E. W. Scripps. Howard was held responsible by his critics for a rightward shift in the outlook of the 20 surviving Scripps Howard dailies, which ranked third in circulation behind Hearst and McCormick-Patterson papers. The complaints were not of the same character as those made against Hearst and McCormick; rather they reflected the disappointment and dismay of the liberals that the "people's papers" of Edward Wyllis Scripps had in many respects become conventionally conservative in tone.

Robert Paine Scripps, the founder's youngest son, inherited the controlling interest in the newspapers, the United Press, Acme Newsphotos, Newspaper Enterprise Association, and United Feature Syndicate when his father died in 1926. Robert Scripps had been at the editorial helm as family representative since 1918, while Roy Howard, the architect of the United Press, had taken over business management of the newspaper chain in 1922, the year the Scripps-McRae newspapers were renamed Scripps Howard.

Roy W. Howard, newspaper publisher

(Milton J. Pike)

The son was imbued with the philosophy of the father, although his quiet and sensitive nature kept him from exercising a firm control over policy. When editor Carl Magee in Albuquerque, New Mexico, was persecuted and driven from business in 1922 because of his efforts to expose the political machine headed by Secretary of the Interior Albert B. Fall (later convicted of bribe-taking in the Teapot Dome scandal), Robert Scripps bought Magee's paper, the *Tribune,* and restored him to its editorship. In 1924 the Scripps Howard papers supported Robert M. La Follette, Progressive party candidate for the presidency. The Scripps Howard editors, called into session periodically to decide matters of national policy, backed Herbert Hoover for the presidency in 1928 but swung back to Franklin D. Roosevelt in 1932 and 1936.

Howard's ascendancy in Scripps Howard affairs became apparent in 1937, when the chain's papers broke with Roosevelt over the Supreme Court reorganization bill. Lowell Mellett, editor of the *Washington News,* and other old Scripps men left the organization. Robert Paine Scripps, who had been in virtual retirement, died aboard his yacht in 1938. The Scripps wills provided for Howard, William W. Hawkins of the United Press, and George B. Parker, editor-in-chief of the newspapers, to serve as trustees until the sons of Robert Scripps reached the age of 25. Under this regime the Scripps Howard papers opposed a third term for President Roosevelt in 1940 and supported Republican presidential candidates every four years through 1960. Organized labor no longer found the papers to be stalwart champions. They still reflected variety in outlook and reader appeal, however, and won particular recognition in Memphis and Cleveland. After World War II, Scripps heirs inherited the trustee positions, and Charles E. Scripps became chairman. The eventual leadership in editorial matters fell to Edward W. Scripps II, a Nevadan with traits similar to those of his grandfather.

Howard remained powerful, however, as head of the *New York World-Telegram and Sun* until he died in 1964—just three years before his favorite paper succumbed. His son Jack was high in the councils as president and general editorial manager of the Scripps Howard Newspapers and president of the parent E. W. Scripps Company, in control of far-flung interests in broadcasting, syndicates, and United Press International. In the Far West, the family of James Scripps, eldest son of the founder, who had quarreled with his father in 1920, was successfully rebuilding the once nearly defunct Scripps League by developing small daily newspapers in Utah, Idaho, Montana, and Oregon. Another Scripps grandson, John P. Scripps, had built a chain of small California dailies. The name Scripps seemed certain to remain an important one.

LANDMARK LEGAL DECISIONS: THE FIRST AMENDMENT

Significant episodes involving freedom of the press and the right of the people to know became a part of the record beginning in the 1930s. There were landmark cases in which newspapers appealed to the courts to uphold the historic right, under the First and Fourteenth Amendments, to freedom of expression without prior restraint and without punitive action by government or courts of any level anywhere in the country.

In *Near* v. *Minnesota,* an obscure Minnesota publisher provided a case in which the Supreme Court, in 1931, stated a bedrock doctrine defending the First and Fourteenth Amendment rights of the press that is still basic legal philosophy 65 years later. Citing the incorporation doctrine first articulated in *Gitlow* in 1925, the Supreme Court held for the plaintiff by applying the freedom of press guarantees of the First Amendment against the states through the due-process clause of the Fourteenth Amendment. What was known as the Minnesota "gag law" of 1925, which permitted the suppression of malicious and scandalous publications, had been applied by a court to the *Saturday Press* of Minneapolis in order to stop its smear attacks on public officials. Calling the law a threat to all newspapers, no matter how unworthy the *Saturday Press* might be, chairman Robert R. McCormick of the American Newspaper Publishers Association (ANPA) committee on freedom of the press retained counsel to carry the case to the Supreme Court. There Chief Justice Charles Evans Hughes, speaking for the majority in a 5–4 decision, held the Minnesota law unconstitutional because it permitted prior restraint on publication.[13] Suppression, the Court said, was a greater danger than an irresponsible attack on public officials, who in any event had proper recourse through libel action.

Huey Long, the Louisiana political boss, provided the next major case in 1934. The Long machine obtained passage by the state legislature, of a special 2 percent tax on the gross advertising income of Louisiana papers with a circulation of 20,000 or more. Twelve of the 13 papers affected were opposed to the Long regime. They appealed to the courts, again with the assistance of Colonel McCormick's ANPA committee, and in 1936 the Supreme Court found the punitive tax unconstitutional. Justice George Sutherland wrote a unanimous decision, holding that Long's bill was "a deliberate and calculated device . . . to limit the circulation of information to which the public is entitled by virtue of the constitutional guarantees."[14] Even a discretionary tax that benefits the press may be unconstitutional.

Although the press may not be singled out for discriminatory taxation, it is subject to taxes and other government regulation of general applicability. In the *Associated Press* v. *NLRB,* the Supreme Court said that "the publisher of a newspaper has no special immunity from the application of general laws," thus defining the limits of First Amendment protection the press can expect from the government regulation of business.[15]

Newspapers do have latitude in commenting on judges' activities, but they often have had to appeal to higher courts for relief after being held in contempt by lower courts. A landmark case in this area was decided by the Supreme Court in 1941. This was *Bridges* v. *California,*[16] a companion case to another involving the *Los Angeles Times.* Harry Bridges, the longshoreman labor leader, had been cited for contempt because newspapers had published the text of a telegram he had sent the Labor Department threatening to call a strike if a court decision went against him. The *Times* was cited for publishing editorials deemed threatening by a court. The California Bar Association asked the Supreme Court to declare the two contempt citations unconstitutional. The court did this by applying the sanctions of the First Amendment against the state court under the due-process clause of the Fourteenth Amendment and by utilizing the clear-and-present danger test first applied in the *Schenck* case. In theory newspapers could henceforth comment on a court action not yet closed, without fear of punishment, unless a judge could demonstrate that the press comment created so great and immediate a danger that a defendant's Sixth Amendment rights to a fair trial would be shredded. But state courts continued to resist this trend in thinking, and hard battles have been fought since 1941 to avoid the penalties of contempt charges in other circumstances.[17]

THE RISE OF INTERPRETATIVE REPORTING

The rise of interpretative reporting was the most important development of the 1930s and 1940s. The proper backgrounding of news events and covering of major areas of human activity by specialists were not unknown before that time. But the impact of the political-social-economic revolution of the New Deal years, the rise of modern scientific technology, the increasing interdependence of economic groups at home, and the shrinking of the world into one vast arena for power politics forced a new approach to the handling of news. "Why" became important, along with the traditional "who did what." The coverage of politics, economics and business, foreign affairs, science, labor, agriculture, and social work was improved by reporter-specialists. Editorial pages also became more interpretative. The news magazines and some specialized newspapers and magazines joined in the movement, together with radio commentators. Old-style objectivity, which had been encouraged strongly at the turn of the century by the AP's Melville E. Stone and other leaders, consisted of sticking to a factual account of what had been said or done. This was challenged by a new concept that was based on the belief that an event had to be placed in its proper context if truth was really to be served. Old beliefs that difficult subjects such as science and economics could not be made interesting to general readers were likewise discarded out of sheer necessity. The Washington and foreign correspondents responded with increasing success to the demands thus made on them by the pressure of the news.

The rise of "big labor" to challenge "big business" under the collective-bargaining guarantees of the New Deal brought the labor beat into full prominence. Louis Stark of the *New York Times,* the paper's labor reporter, and, with John Leary of the *New York World,* one of the first reporters in the field, transferred his base of operations to Washington in 1933. There Stark became the acknowledged dean of American labor reporters, as writers covered national labor-management bargaining in the steel and coal industries, the activities of the National Labor Relations Board, and legislative contests that culminated in the replacement of the Wagner Act by the Taft-Hartley Law. Coverage of strikes had always been a part of the nation's news report, but the fuller interpretation of the problems of labor-management relations now became the goal of good reporters. They also sought to increase direct coverage of organized labor's activities and attitudes.[18]

The worlds of science and medicine were better covered, too, by reporters who repaired the damage that had been done by the sensationalized science stories of the days of yellow journalism. Science Service, directed by Watson Davis, did much to improve the science coverage of its subscribers after 1921. The *New York Times* was again early to enter the field. Waldemar Kaempffert, an engineer who had joined the paper as a science specialist in 1927, was in turn joined by William L. Laurence in 1930. Pulitzer Prizes were given in 1937 to a group of pioneer science writers, including Laurence, David Dietz of the Scripps Howard newspapers, Howard W. Blakeslee of the Associated Press, John J. O'Neill of the *New York Herald Tribune,* and Gobind Behari Lal of Hearst's Universal Service. The National Association of Science Writers, formed in 1934, had nearly 1000 members four decades later.[19]

Federal action to stabilize agricultural prices, provide economic security for farmers, and conserve soil resources became major news with the advent of the Agricultural Adjustment Administration. But the agricultural story had been an important one even before the concerted actions of the New Deal. Alfred D. Stedman of the *St. Paul Pioneer Press* and *Dispatch* and Theodore C. Alford of the *Kansas City Star* arrived in Washington in 1929 as the first specialists in agricultural news correspondence.

Several special news and feature services were established for American newspapers after 1900. Newspaper Enterprise Association, founded in 1902 by Robert E. Paine, E. W. Scripps's talented editor-in-chief, offered foreign and Washington correspondence as well as features. The Scripps Howard Newspaper Alliance served only the group's papers. A major reorganization took place in 1930 when a group of metropolitan newspapers founded the North American Newspaper Alliance. It was directed by John N. Wheeler, head of the Bell Syndicate, and absorbed the Associated Newspaper, Consolidated Press, and McClure syndicates.

The extreme in interpretation was reached by the New York tabloid, *PM,* founded in 1940 and financed by Marshall Field. Under the editorship of Ralph Ingersoll, *PM* made it a policy to express its liberal point of view in its news columns, to the point of becoming a daily journal of opinion. The paper had a notable staff and contributed a fighting spirit to New York journalism. But its hopes that it could exist on the basis of its intelligent writing, excellent pictures, and interpretative appeal alone—without solicitation of advertising—had faded by 1946. Even when it accepted advertising, *PM* languished financially. Field sold out in 1948; the paper became the *New York Star* and fought for life under the editorship of Joseph Barnes. It backed President Harry Truman for reelection before suspending publication in 1949.

THE FOREIGN CORRESPONDENTS

No journalists were more crucial as reporters and news interpreters than the foreign correspondents. Only a few American newspapers have maintained significant numbers of staff correspondents abroad to augment the reporting of the press-association staffs. In the 1930s four of the leading groups of foreign correspondents were those of the *Chicago Daily News,* the *New York Times,* the *New York Herald Tribune,* and the *Chicago Tribune.*

The *Chicago Daily News* foreign service grew out of the coverage begun in 1898 by Victor Lawson for the *Daily News* and *Record-Herald.* It won wide attention during World War I through the work of Edward Price Bell in London, Paul Scott Mowrer in Paris, and Raymond Gram Swing in Berlin. But it hit its most remarkable peak of performance in the 1930s and early 1940s under publisher Frank Knox and the foreign news director, Carroll Binder, himself a noted correspondent before he became head of the service in 1937. Pulitzer Prizes were won by Paul Scott Mowrer in 1929 and by Edgar Ansel Mowrer in 1933. This famed foreign service was closed in 1977, a year before the *Daily News* itself suspended publication.

The New York Times News Service was founded in 1917. Three of its staff won Pulitzer Prizes for their European reporting during the 1930s: Walter Duranty, 1932; Anne O'Hare McCormick, 1937; and Otto D. Tolischus, 1940. Duranty won honors for his coverage in the Soviet Union during Stalin's rise to power. McCormick won her spurs with a 1921 story that analyzed an unknown Benito Mussolini and predicted that he would master Italy. In 1937 she was made the *Times'* columnist on international affairs and a member of its editorial board. Tolischus was in Berlin at the outbreak of war in 1939 and in Tokyo on Pearl Harbor day.

The *New York Herald Tribune* foreign service was built on that of the old *Tribune,* which had employed Frank H. Simonds and Richard Harding Davis as World War I writers. Leland Stowe won a 1930 Pulitzer Prize as a *Herald Tribune* correspondent, and Homer Bigart was similarly honored for his World War II work.

The *Chicago Tribune* foreign service had as its World War I stars Floyd Gibbons, Frazier Hunt, John T. McCutcheon, and Sigrid Schultz. Serving the *Tribune* overseas for varying periods were such well known journalists as Vincent Sheean, William L. Shirer, George Seldes, Jay Allen, Henry Wales, and Edmond Taylor. Wilfred C. Barber won the *Tribune* news service's first Pulitzer Prize in 1936.[20]

DURANTY AND THE MOWRER BROTHERS

Of all the foreign correspondents mentioned above special attention must be given to Walter Duranty of the *New York Times* and the Mowrer brothers of the *Chicago Daily News*. Duranty, a British citizen, was a resident correspondent in Russia between 1922 and 1934, and until 1941 he was a special traveling writer, spending an average of five months per year studying the land he loved. Even before he began his initial 13-year stint as the leading foreign reporter in Russia, Duranty had developed a strong philosophy about the rough character of Communist rule. At the outset he hated and feared the Bolsheviks, but as he told H. R. Knickerbocker of the INS in 1935, he learned to appreciate the Russian position. "I don't see that I have been any less accurate about Russia because I failed to stress casualties so hard as some of my colleagues . . . I am a reporter, not a humanitarian."[21]

Duranty was bitterly assailed during the 1930s for his generally noncritical assessment of Stalin's ruthlessness and Soviet goals. Heywood Broun said he wrote "editorials disguised as news dispatches," and others joined the charge that he was too sympathetic. Years later his biographer S. J. Taylor accumulated evidence of Duranty's various journalistic sins. For example, she wrote that he had dismissed the Ukraine famine of 1932–33 during which millions of persons who had been forced onto collective farms died. Duranty—winner of the 1932 Pulitzer for his economic reporting—was merely a shill for Stalin, according to many of his colleagues.[22] It should be noted that he was not the only well-known correspondent to be accused of biased, lopsided coverage of a dictator, but certainly one of the most influential. Hypocrisy enters the story also. A number of writers and editors, including some eager to downgrade Duranty's reputation, were likewise

Walter Duranty, *New York Times*

Edgar Ansel Mowrer, *Chicago Daily News*

slow to criticize the fascists of the twentieth century, from Mussolini and Hitler to the likes of Marcos, Pinocet, and Somoza, particularly those corrupt leaders supported by the American government.

An assessment of Duranty's contributions must include the fact that he had accepted one of the toughest individual reporting assignments: to report the unknown. Stalin consented to talk with Duranty only twice, in the fall of 1930 and at Christmas, 1933. Otherwise Duranty depended on his keen knowledge of Russian history and language to overcome physical handicaps. The politically risky business of collectivization was determining many careers within Russia, like that of Leon Trotsky. Duranty sent long interpretative dispatches to the *New York Times* but rarely did these efforts receive prominent display. America was involved with domestic and European problems. During the crucial winter of 1928–29, when Stalin consolidated power, for example, none of Duranty's nearly 100 stories made page one.[23]

Duranty's intellect and analytical ability made him a valuable member of the growing *Times'* foreign staff, which at that moment included Wythe Williams in Vienna, Paul Miller in Berlin, Arnaldo Cortesi in Rome, and Allen Raymond in London. Duranty was a confident writer, hardened by scenes of death in World War I. He accepted the brutality of Russian life and wrote from that point of view. Stalin moved stealthily, the censor was a barrier, the Soviet press did not report internal arguments in any way, official names were rarely mentioned, and travel was restricted. Yet Duranty was able to give detailed and colorful reports of life in that tormented land.

William Henry Chamberlin lived in Russia from 1922 to 1934, writing for the *Manchester Guardian* and then the *Christian Science Monitor* and *Atlantic*. Louis Fischer authored more than 40 articles, most of them for the *Nation,* between 1925 and 1932. And world traveler Maurice Hindus wrote a dozen articles and a best-selling book, *Red Bread*. Along with Duranty these men gave a few Americans their only look at Russia; the bulk of United States newspapers, including those with prominent foreign staffs, carried only casual mentions of Russian affairs. Duranty filed the only regularly published newspaper accounts in the late 1920s, and his descriptions of Bolshevik behavior helped restore the faith of some in the *Times,* which during the "Red Scare" period had confused readers about Russian Communists and American Socialists. In fact, a special *New Republic* supplement of August 1920, edited by Walter Lippmann and Charles Merz, had charged the usually reliable *Times* with irresponsible coverage. Duranty himself had said his paper's early attitude was caused by a fear of the "Red Bogey," which explains in part why he went to great lengths to provide a different viewpoint.

Paul Scott Mowrer began his long career in 1905, taking a job with the *Chicago Daily News.* Getting the Midwest out of his system proved to be a problem, as he later admitted.[24] While in Chicago he had shunned Stanley Washburn's dispatches from the Russo-Japanese front. He remembered riding in an elevator with Richard Henry Little, who had been captured by the Japanese at Mukden. But Mowrer cared only for Minnesota, Michigan, and the bustling metropolis, which he considered the heart of journalism. In 1910 he arrived in London, joining reporters who worked for other papers: Frederic William Wile, Wythe Williams, and a handful of others who knew Europe before war changed the politics and the boundaries. Writers like Will Irwin occasionally sailed to Europe to write for American magazines, but the years were dull. Earlier, writers had flocked to the Boer War and Boxer Rebellion. The bitter subjugation of the Philippine rebels under Aguinaldo in 1899–1901 had attracted a host of reporters. That United States experiment with colonial power at one point involved 70,000 American troops. The Russo-Japanese War of 1904 to 1905, in which Richard Harding Davis, Jack London, Frederick

Palmer, and another 100 American and British reporters had fought Japanese censorship, gained considerable attention in the United States press. But things were quiet in Europe, as Paul Scott Mowrer discovered when he showed up as a 22-year-old assistant to Edward Price Bell. At the outbreak of war nearly four years later he covered the assassination of French Socialist Jean Jaures and broke in his younger brother, Edgar Ansel Mowrer, who thus began his equally distinguished career. Edgar, who had been contributing to United States and British magazines and studying at the Sorbonne, sneaked through enemy lines for an exclusive story. Then Edgar was allowed to accompany mining engineer Herbert Hoover to Holland, and finally in 1915 he was given the job as Rome correspondent. Paul Scott Mowrer headed for the front and ended up reporting the horrors of Verdun.

Following the war, Paul Scott Mowrer was assigned to direct the *Daily News* bureau at the Versailles conference. Based in Paris, he filed dispatches during the Moroccan campaign of 1924 to 1925 and in 1934 to 1935 became associate editor and chief editorial writer for his paper. The editorship itself was his between 1935 and 1944, until the last year of World War II, when he accepted a position as European editor for the *New York Post*. Edgar Ansel Mowrer was bureau chief of the *Daily News* in Berlin and Paris during the "between-wars" period. Connected with the Office of War Information after having been forced out of Germany at the start of World War II, he was later a columnist and broadcaster and with his brother contributed several books on foreign affairs.

The Mowrer brothers teamed with many famous byliners—including Dorothy Thompson of the *New York Post,* who covered Vienna, Berlin, Moscow, Budapest, and London, and who was expelled from Germany by Hitler in 1934; Webb Miller of the United Press, who reported the rise of Gandhi in India and the Ethiopian war in between European assignments; Louis P. Lochner of the Associated Press, who recorded daily the rise of Hitler from Berlin; Vincent Sheean, talented author and correspondent for the *Chicago Tribune;* Frederick T. Birchall of the *New York Times;* Reginald Wright Kauffman and Harold Scarborough of the *New York Herald Tribune;* and Henry Wales of the *Chicago Tribune*—to cover the League of Nations, the rise of fascism, and the coming of another war. They added color and depth to stories at a time when even familiar European situations were in heavy competition with American domestic concerns for space in newspapers.

(AP-Wide World Photos)

Dorothy Thompson, distinguished political columnist

THE POLITICAL COLUMNISTS

The political column began in the early 1920s with the writings of David Lawrence in his syndicated column and Washington publications, of Mark Sullivan in the *New York Herald Tribune,* and of Frank R. Kent in the *Baltimore Sun.* Walter Lippmann joined this trio as a *Herald Tribune* columnist when his editorship of the *World* ended in 1931. Their columns were concerned with current politics and issues of the day, as contrasted with Arthur Brisbane's philosophical commentary, which began in 1917 and was front-paged by Hearst newspapers for nearly 20 years. But the coming of the New Deal in 1933 and the consequent revolution in Washington coverage brought a new version of the political column to join the syndicated offerings of Lawrence, Sullivan, Kent, and Lippmann.

The four early leaders in political and current-affairs columns, who were called "pundits," wrote in a sober style and with a serious-minded approach. Sullivan and Kent were masters of the practical political scene of the 1920s, but they were not responsive to the social and economic shifts that brought the widespread increase in governmental activity in the New Deal era. Sullivan, who had been an enthusiastic interpreter of Theodore Roosevelt's progressive program and an intimate of President Herbert Hoover, became far better known for his superb journalistic history of 1900–1925, *Our Times,* than for his later columns. Lawrence continued to hold a place as a commentator on national affairs, as did Lippmann in the international field.

A new kind of political column after 1932 was the personalized, or "gossip-type," column. The idea stemmed from the successful book *Washington Merry-Go-Round,* published anonymously in 1931. The authors were soon identified as Drew Pearson of the *Baltimore Sun* and Robert S. Allen of the *Christian Science Monitor.* These two Washington correspondents quickly left their newspapers to coauthor a behind-the-scenes column that Pearson eventually continued alone. Paul Mallon was in the personalized-column competition from the start of the New Deal era; joining in as sympathetic commentators on the New Deal's activities were Ernest K. Lindley, Samuel Grafton, and Joseph and Stewart Alsop, first writing as a team, then separately.

United Features offered a particularly strong and varied group of columnists and commentators in the 1930s. Before his death in a 1944 wartime plane crash, Raymond

(AP/Wide World Photos)
Walter Lippmann, dean of the "pundits"

(Bettmann Archive)
Drew Pearson, gossip columnist

Clapper was recognized as perhaps the best-balanced interpreter of the Washington scene. Clapper's opinions on national and international problems were widely respected, largely because they were based on his reporting ability and on his long experience as a United Press political writer, and as head of the UP Washington bureau and that of the *Washington Post.* Thomas L. Stokes, a hard-working reporter of the Washington scene for the United Press and the Scripps Howard newspapers, developed a large following for his vigorous and crusading columns. Stokes won a Pulitzer Prize for national reporting and a Clapper memorial award for his column before he died in 1958. Carrying on for United Features were Marquis Childs, distinguished Washington correspondent for the *St. Louis Post-Dispatch,* who began his column after Clapper's death, and William S. White of the *New York Times* Washington staff. In 1970 Childs's column won the first Pulitzer Prize given for commentary.

Also in the United Features group of columnists were some commentators of the personal variety. One was Westbrook Pegler, the caustic ex-sports writer and United Press and *Chicago Tribune* writer. Pegler had a distinctive, colorful style and won a 1941 Pulitzer Prize for his exposure-type crusading. Unhappily his work degenerated into monotonous and vicious attacks on three groups—labor unions, New Dealers, and members of the Franklin D. Roosevelt family—and Pegler switched from Scripps Howard to Hearst sponsorship in the mid-1940s, becoming known as "the stuck whistle of journalism." Balancing Pegler was the witty, warm personality of Heywood Broun. Best described as "looking like an unmade bed," Broun was a deceptive writer who could switch from light and easy commentary to a hard-hitting defense of liberal traditions whenever his temper was aroused. His "It Seems to Me" ran first in the *New York Tribune,* then in the *World* during the 1920s, and finally in the Scripps Howard papers. Broun's leading role in the American Newspaper Guild and his liberal line brought a break with Roy Howard, and the column was headed for the *New York Post* when Broun died in 1939. Also writing columns for United Features were Eleanor Roosevelt, who first signed in 1935 in an unprecedented move for a president's wife, and the lovable Ernie Pyle, whose original cross-country tour columns about little people and things were followed by superb personal glimpses of American fighting men in World War II until he was killed on a Pacific island in 1945.

Well to the right of the United Features columnists in political and social outlooks were the King Features group. Best known were Pegler and the conservative George Sokolsky, both of whom died in the 1960s. Later in the field for King were radio commentator Fulton Lewis, Jr., moral philosopher Bruce Barton, and reporter Jim Bishop.

Women journalists won high honors in column writing. One was Dorothy Thompson, a European correspondent for the *Philadelphia Public Ledger* and the *New York Post* during the 1920s and early 1930s. Married to Sinclair Lewis, Thompson returned to the United States and wrote a column on international affairs for the *New York Herald Tribune* until she was dropped for endorsing Franklin Roosevelt for a third term in order to meet the threat of Hitler's regime. Her emotion-charged comments were widely syndicated until her career closed in 1961. In 1954 Doris Fleeson, who came to the columnist field from the *New York Daily News* to write a smooth political commentary until 1970, became the first woman to win the Raymond Clapper award for reporting.

THE EDITORIAL CARTOONISTS

Syndication also affected the profession of editorial cartooning. As in the field of columning, widespread readership offered fame and financial rewards to the talented cartoonist. But despite their proved reader-drawing copy, it was unlikely that a newspaper would "bring up" its own cartoonist or columnist. Local columnists always had great latitude, of course, but serious commentary on national and international affairs by a staff cartoonist became scarcer.

The period after the Civil War saw the development of the political cartoon as an editorial device. Until then, the cartoon was more likely to be seen in magazines because of newspaper production difficulties, but the introduction of stereotyping enabled dailies to use illustrations more readily. Thomas Nast, the cartoonist who so savagely attacked the Tweed political ring, drew for the *New York Times* after 1870, as well as for *Harper's Weekly.* In the magazines of the times, Joseph Keppler's work for *Puck* was outstanding. The presidential-campaign cartoons of Homer Davenport, drawn for Hearst's *New York Journal* in 1896, scored a new high point both in prominence and in bluntness.

The first quarter of the twentieth century was a golden age for political cartoonists. The issues were simple enough for easy pictorial interpretation and elemental enough for clever satire, the two ingredients of the political cartoon. One of the famous cartoonists was John T. McCutcheon, who began drawing for the *Chicago Tribune* in 1903 after serving on the *Chicago Record,* and who won a Pulitzer Prize before he retired in 1946. Clifford K. Berryman, who first appeared in the *Washington Post* as far back as 1889, was closely identified with the *Washington Star* after 1906. He and his son, James T. Berryman, were the only father and son combination to win Pulitzer Prizes for their cartoon work, after the younger Berryman succeeded his father in 1949.

Lesser known to the public but influential among his colleagues, was Arthur Henry Young, who always signed his cartoons "Art Young." He suffered because of his devotion to left-wing causes, especially during World War I, but in his day Young was the cartoonist's cartoonist. He was the first to produce a daily panel, for the Chicago *Inter Ocean,* but the best of his work appeared in *The Masses,* the militantly socialist magazine. Young, unlike earlier cartoonists, strove for simplicity. His technique was to focus attention on a main issue; for example, one of his cartoons showed a ragged child of the slums looking up at the night sky and saying: "Ooh, look at all the stars; they're thick as bedbugs."

(New York World-Telegram)

Rollin Kirby's famous "Two chickens in every garage" barb at Hoover, 1932

(Reprinted with permission of D. R. Fitzpatrick and the St. Louis Post-Dispatch, copyright 1947)

"You gambled but I paid"— Daniel Fitzpatrick in a 1947 crusade

(New York Herald Tribune)

"Halloween, 1936"—Jay ("Ding") Darling jibed at Wallace, Farley, and FDR

Two other great masters of the cartooning art were Rollin Kirby of the *New York World* and Edmund Duffy of the *Baltimore Sun,* both three-time Pulitzer Prize winners. Kirby was a fiercely liberal spirit who began cartooning in 1911 and hit his peak on the old *World* in the 1920s. His "Mr. Dry," a gaunt, black-frocked, blue-nosed caricature of the bigoted prohibitionists, became famous. Duffy exhibited his mastery of satire and caricature for the *Baltimore Sun* for 25 years.

Beginning his work for the *St. Louis Post-Dispatch* in 1913 and continuing until 1958 was Daniel R. ("Fitz") Fitzpatrick, whose devastating cartoon attacks won fame for his paper's editorial page and two Pulitzer Prizes for him. Reminiscent of the old school of flowery technique was Jay N. ("Ding") Darling, who began drawing for the *Des Moines Register* in 1906. Darling then joined the *New York Herald Tribune* and won two Pulitzer Prizes. In this era, too, was Nelson Harding of the *Brooklyn Eagle,* also a two-time Pulitzer award winner.

RADIO NEWS COMES OF AGE

As the 1930s opened, the only daily news broadcast to reach the growing national audience was one sponsored by the sedate *Literary Digest* and read by the flamboyant Floyd Gibbons, the *Chicago Tribune*'s dashing war correspondent who had lost an eye in battle and who wore a white patch as his badge. Positioned in the time slot preceding NBC's *Amos 'n' Andy* show, Gibbons delivered the news with breakneck speed. He had originally been signed by NBC to do a weekly half-hour show called *The Headline Hunter,* on which he would spin yarns about his foreign adventures. He is also credited with the first remote broadcast, which he accomplished because he was carrying a shortwave transmitter when the German dirigible *Graf Zeppelin* landed at Lakehurst, New Jersey, in 1929. Two men with him hoisted an antenna that transmitted Gibbons's voice to NBC's facilities for coast-to-coast listening.

Gibbons presented the news in a folksy, rough manner—the style of the school of Chicago journalism—booming out his "Hello, Everybody," and launching into a series of vivid descriptions. In late 1930, when he was earning $10,000 per week, an enormous salary for those Depression-era days, he alienated his sponsors with his brusque manner. At that moment William S. Paley decided that CBS should try to convince *Literary Digest* publisher R. J. Cuddihy to switch sponsorship to his network, using another announcer. He had in mind Lowell Thomas, a veteran newsperson whose main claim to fame was his exclusive story of the Arabian campaign in World War I, found in his best-selling book, *With Lawrence in Arabia.*

A test broadcast was arranged, during which Thomas read the news on CBS ahead of Gibbons's NBC show. Cuddihy listened to both broadcasts. He decided to let Gibbons go and hired Thomas, who made his first broadcast September 29, 1930. The program became the longest running in broadcast history, lasting until May 14, 1976. The first show included Thomas's comments about Adolf Hitler: "There are now two Mussolinis in the world. . . . Adolf Hitler has written a book (*Mein Kampf*) in which this belligerent gentleman states that a cardinal policy of his powerful German party is the conquest of Russia. That's a tall assignment, Adolf. You just go ask Napoleon."[25] For 6 months both networks carried the nightly show, NBC in the East and CBS in the West. But Cuddihy finally decided to let NBC have exclusive access to Thomas, who inherited the spot before the *Amos 'n' Andy* show. His "Good Evening, Everybody," became a popular phrase in the United States.

Lowell Thomas
(Bettmann Archive)

Radio was building audiences in many ways, and its coverage of the major news events and personalities of the 1930s helped. Hitler and Mussolini used radio to rally their peoples in the name of patriotism. President Roosevelt was one of the world leaders who realized the potential of radio for achieving national unity; during the depths of the Great Depression and World War II he made 28 "fireside chats." People were taken with the president's friendly manner, and it was said that "Washington was no farther away than the radio receiving sets in their living rooms."[26] The presidential nominating conventions and campaigns provided news bulletins, as did such events as the kidnapping of the Lindbergh baby, the Bonus March in Washington, King Edward VIII's abdication speech, the burning of the German airship *Hindenburg,* and the outbreak of hostilities in Manchuria, in China, in Ethiopia, and eventually throughout Europe.

THE NEWSPAPER-RADIO WAR

The AP's furnishing of 1932 presidential-election returns to the radio networks to forestall the sale of election coverage by the United Press precipitated action by the ANPA board of directors in December 1932. The board recommended that press associations should neither sell nor give away news in advance of its publication in the newspapers. The broadcasting of news should be confined to brief bulletins that would encourage newspaper readership, and radio logs should be treated as paid advertising. Many qualified observers felt that radio was too well established as a news medium to be hobbled in this way.[27] But the ANPA recommendations led to a futile two-year effort to eliminate radio news competition. After a spirited fight, the 1933 AP membership meeting voted not to furnish news to the radio networks and to limit the broadcasting of news by AP members to occasional 35-word bulletins. The UP and the INS bowed to their newspaper clients' desires and stopped selling news to radio stations. The answer of the radio industry was to undertake the job of gathering news itself.

The Columbia Broadcasting System set up the leading network news service under the direction of Ed Klauber, a former night city editor of the *New York Times* who was hired by William S. Paley in 1930. Klauber, a strict disciplinarian, quickly rose to second in command of CBS and was instrumental in the network's growth. He served Paley until 1943. Paul White, a former UP reporter, was hired as Klauber's assistant. Together they began staffing bureaus in New York, Washington, Chicago, Los Angeles, and London with other newspaperpeople. CBS built up an extensive system of correspondents and imported the British Exchange Telegraph agency's news report for daily CBS broadcasts. NBC's rival news service was organized by White's counterpart, A. A. Schechter, director of news and special events in the 1930s. Meanwhile, local stations continued to broadcast news regularly by the simple expedient of using the early editions of the newspapers.[28]

The networks found that collecting news was expensive, and the publishers disliked the new competition. So in December 1933, a solution was proposed in the form of the Press-Radio Bureau, which would present two 5-minute, unsponsored news broadcasts daily on the networks using news supplied by the press associations. Bulletin coverage of extraordinary events would also be provided. In return, the networks would stop gathering news.

The Press-Radio Bureau began operating in March 1934, and after a year had 245 subscribers. But it was doomed from the start. Not only was it unrealistic, but it left the door open for the founding of new news-gathering agencies not bound by the agreement. Five news services jumped into the field, led by Herbert Moore's Transradio Press Service, which at its peak in 1937 served 230 radio clients and even signed up several newspapers.

The collapse of the effort to curtail broadcasting came in 1935. The UP and the INS obtained releases from the Press-Radio Bureau agreement so that they could meet Transradio's competition by selling full news reports to stations. The UP began a wire report especially written for broadcasting, which the AP matched after it joined the race for radio clients in 1940. The Press-Radio Bureau suspended operation in 1940; Transradio slumped away and died in 1951.

MUTUAL NETWORK; *THE MARCH OF TIME*

By 1934 CBS had 97 affiliated stations, and the two NBC networks had 127. But with more than 600 commercial stations, there was room for competition in the news field. That year 4 independent stations, headed by WOR, New York, and WGN, Chicago, organized the Mutual Broadcasting System, which primarily served affiliated smaller stations. WLW, Cincinnati, and WXYZ, Detroit, were the other 2 founding stations; CKLW, Windsor, Ontario–Detroit, replaced WXYZ in 1935. The first expansion came in 1936 when 13 New England stations associated with the regional Colonial network and 10 in California belonging to the Don Lee network agreed to be Mutual outlets. Adding 23 Texas stations in 1938, Mutual grew to 160 outlets by 1940. Of these, 25 were also associated with NBC and 5 with CBS, showing the strong interest in Mutual shows like *Lum 'n' Abner* and *The Lone Ranger.*[29] Networks, radio found, could produce more costly and successful programs because they could draw on the support of national advertisers, and their growth made radio a more formidable competitor for the advertising dollar each year.

Also getting attention in the 1930s was *The March of Time,* which brought radio listeners dramatic reenactments of the week's news. Before its final show in 1945, *The March of Time* had been heard on CBS, both NBC networks, and ABC. The idea for such a show began with Fred Smith, who in 1925 had produced *Musical News* for WLW, Cincinnati, a show during which news items were followed by organ music. Listener response was strong, and in 1928 Smith got *Time* magazine to sponsor a weekly news roundup. He joined the *Time* organization later that year, and organized a 60-station syndication of a daily ten-minute news summary. At the time there was no national newscast. This first show, called *NewsCasting,* was carried over WOR, New York, during the dinner hour. Smith claimed that this was the first use of the word *newscast,* which brought together the concepts of news and broadcasting.[30] Smith believed that the daily news should be dramatized, however, and in 1929 he produced weekly five-minute recordings of a show called *NewsActing.* More than 100 stations carried it, and it led to the development of *The March of Time* series. Impersonations of famous personalities, including President Roosevelt, were often the highlights of the show. Later in its history the show used actual news updates and remote broadcasts. Ironically, one of the actors in the series was Orson Welles, whose 1938 Mercury Theatre presentation of "War of the Worlds" caused widespread panic on an East Coast presumably invaded by Martians. *The March of Time* also had film documentary and television versions.

(Bettmann Archive)

Director Orson Welles, when he won attention with his "War of the Worlds" broadcast

COMMENTATORS DEBATE THE NATIONAL ISSUES

As Franklin Roosevelt took hold of the federal machinery and a genuine national debate began over the merits of his New Deal programs, Americans were offered the opinions of a number of highly spirited, controversial broadcasters. The arguments increased in intensity later in the 1930s when the Roosevelt administration took steps to prepare for World War II. The dean of the commentators was Hans Von Kaltenborn, who quit the newspaper business and joined CBS as a full-time commentator in 1930. A foreign correspondent, managing editor, and associate editor of the *Brooklyn Eagle* in his first journalistic assignments, Kaltenborn had started broadcasting news for a local station in 1922. This dignified, civilized man with clipped, high-pitched, precisely accentuated tones made sense of the turmoil in the world, basing his comments on his own extensive travels and on his own decent instincts.

Kaltenborn's internationalistic outlook was similar to that broadcast by Dorothy Thompson, Edward R. Murrow, Raymond Gram Swing, and later Elmer Davis. Lowell Thomas could be included here, except he was loath to give partisan opinions on the air, instead preferring to provide colorful descriptions for the listener. On the conservative side of the ledger were Boake Carter, Upton Close, Fulton Lewis, Jr., and the "Radio Priest," Father Charles Coughlin.

Though not a journalist, Father Coughlin had a tremendous impact on American politics through his Sunday radio show from Royal Oak, Michigan, broadcast nationwide by WJR, Detroit. When he was dropped by CBS in 1931, he set up his own chain of stations. Attacking socialism, communism, and capitalism as evil, Coughlin lashed out angrily at international bankers, Presidents Hoover and Roosevelt, Jewish interests, and even Prohibitionists. He bitterly criticized the breaking up of the Bonus Army encampment in Washington, when Hoover ordered General Douglas MacArthur to use force to rout those seeking pension monies. Yet as the years passed, Father Coughlin's broadcasts took on a pro-Nazi stance. An estimated 30 million listeners followed the man who was considered by progressives to be a dangerous demagogue. Coughlin's organization, the National Union for Social Justice, was due to one thing: radio.

Boake Carter, a close friend of Father Coughlin, earned his reputation as a CBS reporter while covering the Lindbergh baby kidnapping story. Because he had been born in England, Carter's accent gave his broadcasts a unique touch. He was immensely popular; his 1936 to 1938 ratings showed him in a virtual tie with NBC's Lowell Thomas. He presented news and commentary each weekday between January 1933 and August 1938, when he was dropped by CBS—like Coughlin—for reasons not entirely clear. However, he had been extremely harsh in his attacks against President Roosevelt on radio and in his newspaper column, warning repeatedly that the United States was being dragged into coming wars in Europe and Asia. It is suspected that, like Coughlin, Carter was taken off the air because of the increasing "irrationality" of his comments.[31]

Upton Close broadcast news analyses over NBC stations between 1934 and 1944, when he was dropped following concern within NBC over some of his controversial shows. Over the years Close had become less objective and more reactionary, echoing others in their hatred of the British, Jews, and Russians and in their sympathy for right-wing politics. Fulton Lewis, Jr., who began his commentaries over the Mutual stations in 1937, closely followed partisan Republican party ideas. He became an avid supporter of Charles Lindbergh in 1939 during the debate over Britain's ability to stave off the Nazi threat; this earned him the plaudits of conservative listeners.

Dorothy Thompson, Berlin bureau chief for the *Philadelphia Public Ledger* as well as a contributor to other newspapers and magazines while living in Europe between the wars, began delivering commentaries for NBC in 1937. A staunch internationalist, Thompson was widely admired for her interviews with political leaders and for her role in the women's movement.

Raymond Gram Swing worked for several leading dailies before getting involved with broadcasting. In 1932, during the British elections, he and Cesar Saerchinger of CBS conducted the first trans-Atlantic interview. His regular broadcasts began with Mutual in 1936, and within two years he was ranked third to Kaltenborn and Thomas in a poll of radio editors.[32] Like Thompson and Murrow, Swing detested Hitler, was in full sympathy with Britain, and feared for the Jewish people. Also worried about fascism at home, he wrote and lectured on the subject.

Two other leading commentators whose careers began in this era were the snappy Walter Winchell and the predictable Gabriel Heatter. Winchell, mainly involved with Hollywood gossip, underworld tips, and scandals, did enlighten Americans about the German menace and provided Roosevelt with strong support during the 1940 campaign. "Good evening, Mr. and Mrs. North America and all the ships at sea. Let's go to press"—that was the Winchell opening followed by "Predictions of things to come." Despite his many erroneous predictions, Winchell built a huge audience and was number one in the 1946 ratings, with nearly 19 percent of the audience, ahead of Lowell Thomas, at 11 percent, and a host of other famous names. Before his 40-year career ended in 1969, he had been affiliated with several networks. Heatter, fiercely patriotic and emotional, gained fame by broadcasting the trial of Bruno Hauptmann for the Lindbergh baby murder directly from a New Jersey courtroom. A year later he held the Mutual audience for nearly an hour, ad-libbing while waiting for the news of Hauptmann's execution. More than 50,000 letters poured in following the broadcast, and Heatter was given a five-nights-a-week spot for commentary. In his presentations he attempted, for the most part, to comfort the audience rather than take sides in the political battles. His personal views could not be identified as easily as most of the other commentators. At his peak in the postwar years he reached 196 stations and earned $400,000 per year, warming his listeners' hearts with his "There's good news tonight."

THE NETWORKS REACH OVERSEAS

The outbreak of the Spanish Civil War in 1936, followed quickly by Hitler's threats first against Austria and then Czechoslovakia, gave radio newspeople an opportunity they fully accepted. The first of a number of memorable broadcasts made between 1936 and the official start of World War II in 1939 was made by Hans Von Kaltenborn. Wearing his dark business suit and trying to act his usual dignified self, Kaltenborn broadcast from a haystack near the French border with Spain where a battle was raging. After a number of interruptions the American audience heard Kaltenborn's voice for 15 minutes, surrounded by the sounds of gunfire, bringing a bit of understanding about the spreading of fascism. The networks did not have foreign staffs at this time, but instead relied on hastily patched-together transmission systems for occasional broadcasts. Often a news-paper reporter was called upon to provide the short description. This changed in early 1938 when Hitler invaded Austria.

Edward R. Murrow, an unknown CBS program arranger who had been named European news chief, was in London when the crisis developed. He had hired as an assistant William L. Shirer, out of a job since the closing of Hearst's Universal Service. Their pattern was to do cultural programs and human-interest stories for shortwave broadcasts that were rebroadcast by United States stations. On March 12, 1938, Murrow in Vienna

(Bettmann Archive)

H. V. Kaltenborn, pioneer radio commentator

and Shirer in London improvised the first multiple news pickup in history. They quickly asked newspaper reporters Edgar Mowrer, Pierre Huss, and Frank Gervasi to add their impressions from Paris, Berlin, and Rome, respectively. Robert Trout was the anchor. The stage was set for radio coverage of the 20 days of crisis in September, beginning with Hitler's demand that the Czechs give him the German-speaking Sudetenland and ending with the signing of the Munich Pact.

Listeners heard live broadcasts from 14 European cities during the Munich crisis. The voices of Hitler, President Eduard Benés of Czechoslovakia, Chamberlain, Goebbels, Litvinoff, Mussolini, and Pope Pius XI came in firsthand. In his "Studio Nine" in New York City, Kaltenborn spent the three weeks backstopping the CBS European correspondents who conducted the elaborate hookup system known as the *European News Roundup,* giving hours of analysis and commentary. It was Kaltenborn who translated Hitler's fiery oratory for American listeners and who predicted the diplomatic steps that would follow various events. He was heard 85 times during the three weeks; between his stints he cat-napped on a cot. CBS devoted 471 broadcasts—nearly 48 hours of air time—to the crisis; of these 135 were bulletin interruptions, including 98 from European staffers. NBC's two networks logged 443 programs during 59 hours of air time.[33]

NBC's Max Jordan was a worthy competitor for Murrow and Shirer. He had a 46-minute broadcast on the actual text of the Munich Pact, whereby Britain and France backed down in the face of Nazi bullying and allowed the Germans to regain the Sudetenland section of Czechoslovakia. The Czechs had not been allowed to participate in the decision. Broadcasts from Prague were gloomy. While Winston Churchill howled that this was an act of appeasement—it was clear that Hitler was now free to take the rest of Czechoslovakia whenever he wished—many persons heaved sighs of relief. London had prepared for air raids, children had been taken to the country, and American listeners hung on every word, wondering if war could be averted. Thomas E. Dewey was making a major political address in which he was accepting the New York GOP's nomination to run for governor when Jordan's broadcast came through. It was one of the few times a major speech had been canceled.

Jordan had a backup crew of top-flight newspaper and press-association correspondents on whom to draw—for example, Walter Kerr of the *New York Herald Tribune,* Karl Von Wiegand of the International News Service, M. W. Fodor of the *Chicago Daily News* service, and G. Ward Price of the *London Daily Mail,* who conducted an exclusive interview with Hitler at Cologne during which Hitler gave October 1 as his final deadline. Maurice Hindus, a noted author and international observer, assisted CBS. Mutual had John Steele in London and Louis Huot in Paris. Between September 10, when Czech President Benés broadcast his nation's desire to resist Hitler, and the final four-power agreement at Munich on the 29th, Americans responded to the tense, colorful broadcasts with a vast and deep interest. The networks had been assisted, of course, by bulletins from the UP, Transradio, and the Press-Radio Bureau. When World War II came, the networks were ready to cover the far-flung action in Asia and Europe.

At this time more than 91 percent of urban American homes and about 70 percent of rural homes had radios, many because of the Roosevelt administration's programs for rural electrification. In fact, between 1930 and 1938 the number of radio sets had increased more than 100 percent. More homes had radios than telephones.[34] The popular fare, in addition to the many musical programs like *Your Hit Parade,* included *One Man's Family, Gangbusters, Jack Armstrong—The All American Boy, Captain Midnight, The Green Hornet, Baby Snooks,* and *Henry Aldrich.* Jack Benny was the top comedian, Edgar Bergen and his wooden friend Charlie McCarthy had the highest rated show, Kate Smith was the most popular woman singer, and Ted Husing and Clem McCarthy broadcast the biggest sporting events. Other personalities were Bing Crosby, Eddie Cantor, Nelson Eddy, George Burns and Gracie Allen, and Don Ameche. But this lightness and fun was interrupted by the ominous messages from Europe. For those paying attention, World War II was on the horizon, and it was only a matter of time before it would break out. Others, of course, did not believe America would or should get involved and were awakened only on December 7, 1941, when Pearl Harbor was bombed.

TELEVISION: THE COMPETITION OF THE 1930s

The development of television in the 1930s was marked by the competition between Vladimir K. Zworykin, a Russian scientist working for RCA, and Philo T. Farnsworth, a San Francisco inventor who had obtained private backing for his experiments. Their success had been preceded by numerous tests in Europe, where interest in the transmission of images could be traced to proposals for a facsimile device in the 1840s. Between 1890 and 1920 a number of British, French, American, Russian, and German scientists suggested techniques related to the perfection of the television set.

The first public demonstration of a live television picture was conducted by John L. Baird, a Scottish inventor, on January 16, 1926, in London. Onlookers, including a reporter, substantiated that images were transmitted from one room to another, faint and often blurred, but clear enough to be seen on a screen of only a few square inches. Two years later Baird televised a woman's image from London to Hartsdale, New York, using a short-wave band, and also sent images to an oceanliner 1000 miles out at sea. In 1932 more than 4000 persons in a London movie house saw Baird's televised pictures of the English Derby on a large screen.[35] The British Broadcasting Corporation began the world's first regularly scheduled television service on November 2, 1936.

BAIRD, JENKINS, AND IVES: OTHER EXPERIMENTS

Baird and an American competitor, Charles Francis Jenkins, attempted to develop a "mechanical" television system for commercial use that was dependent on a number of moving parts, including scanning drums, to record the minute parts of an image successively and to transmit them in such a way as to give the illusion of motion. Although scanning is the crucial process in the production of television pictures, the "mechanical" system did not offer the clarity—or definition—required for wide-scale acceptance. The pictures were dim, and the screen size was limited to only a few inches. Later the "electronic" method would allow the various elements of the image to be recorded all at once before being translated into the electrical charges that end up as the picture on the screen.

Jenkins used the wireless to send the image of a photograph of President Harding from Washington to Philadelphia in 1923 and transmitted motion pictures (but not live figures) over radio waves in 1925. But after 1930 his company fell into receivership, and his patents ended up with RCA. Baird, who had shown the possibility of color television as early as 1923, continued with his experiments for many years, disappointed that the BBC, which used the "mechanical" system when it introduced general telecasting in 1936, switched over to the more comprehensive "electronic" system.

Another vital cog in the early experimentation was Herbert E. Ives, whose work in the Bell Telephone Laboratories on wire-photo transmission led to the sending of Secretary of Commerce Herbert Hoover's image over wires from Washington to New York in 1927. When Hoover's face appeared on a 2-by-3-inch screen, his voice was also heard; this generated ideas about the possible future use of the Picturephone. Ives was also instrumental in developing a method for relaying television images by coaxial cable and radio, and in inventing a camera that could be used outdoors. AT&T, however, did not attempt to commercialize its inventions.[36]

SARNOFF, ZWORYKIN, AND FARNSWORTH

David Sarnoff was determined to bring television to the public, however, and his vehicle was Zworykin, who had patented the first electronic television camera tube—the iconoscope—in 1923. In 1926 Zworykin invented the kinescope, a cathode ray tube that would be the core of a receiving unit. Impressed with Zworykin's assessments of television's possibilities, Sarnoff arranged for him to join the Westinghouse research unit in 1929. The following year Zworykin joined the large RCA research team in New Jersey when a court ordered Westinghouse and General Electric to separate from RCA. This remarkable group of scientists had already recorded a number of impressive achievements. In 1928 Ernest

F. W. Alexanderson of GE had conducted tests over experimental station W2XAD. The first television drama was telecast, with sound carried by radio station WGY, Schenectady. This was followed by a science-fiction thriller that ended with New York's destruction by a guided missile.

Meanwhile, Farnsworth had also been building a strong reputation. In 1927 he transmitted his first picture, and by the early 1930s he was developing a fully electronic system. San Francisco supporters helped him form Television Laboratories, Inc., which kept him in direct competition with the larger research team at RCA. Both groups were able to produce pictures far superior to anything done before. Zworykin's iconoscope had allowed brighter images and a larger screen size. Farnsworth had devised a way to obtain a picture with 100- to 150-line definition; earlier experiments had been with 30- to 50-line definition. By 1931 RCA was able to transmit a 120-line picture, and the quality thereafter increased steadily.

The resources of RCA proved too much for Farnsworth. In 1932 Sarnoff ordered a television studio to be built in the Empire State Building. RCA's experimental station was 2XBS. Then in 1935, two years after Radio City had become NBC's home, one of its studios was turned into a large television production area. Sarnoff coordinated every detail. Experimental station W2XF became the center for RCA's tests in 1936; a mobile unit was sent out into New York streets in 1937, and its first live telecast in 1938 was of a fire; Sarnoff gave the first large public demonstration of electronic television at the New York World's Fair in 1939, and Franklin Roosevelt became the first president to appear on television. Sarnoff demonstrated a 441-line system, and in 1941 the FCC decided that a 525-line, 30-frames-a-second system—still in effect—would be the standard.[37]

RCA also became deeply involved with the development of FM radio, first supporting it and then fighting the man who had invented the system under RCA auspices, Edwin H. Armstrong. The television and FM signals competed for the same upper frequencies, and when RCA officers were ready to push into television in the mid-1930s, they set aside their enthusiasm for FM. Armstrong, who had conducted a number of tests demonstrating the clarity of FM sound, removed his equipment from the Empire State Building and fought RCA in court until he died a broken man in 1953. In the course of his career he had become a millionaire and had seen FM accepted, but he had not been given full recognition and royalties by Sarnoff.[38]

Meanwhile, Farnsworth and RCA became entangled in a number of disputes over patents, and finally, in 1939, RCA agreed to make a complicated set of royalty payments to Farnsworth in return for the use of patents, the first time RCA had ever agreed to such a procedure instead of purchasing patents outright.

Despite the disagreements, television had arrived. Sets were available in department stores in 1938. Models with screens ranging in size from 3 to 12 inches cost from $125 to $600. By the next year more than a dozen manufacturers were involved, which caused the FCC to step in to standardize equipment.[39]

The FCC gave approval for 18 television stations to begin commercial operation beginning July 1, 1941, and the first 2, ready that day, were the New York stations NBC (WNBT) and CBS (WCBW). Within nine months another 8 stations had joined them, serving viewers of an estimated 10,000 to 20,000 sets. The stations were allowed to offer 15 hours of programming per week. WCBW distinguished itself on December 7, 1941, by offering the latest bulletins on the Pearl Harbor attack and by showing its audience of a few thousand some maps of the war zones. A government freeze in May 1942 halted construction on new stations and most of those in existence drastically cut back on programming. Only 6 stations were still broadcasting at the war's end in 1945, when the freeze was lifted.

THE NEWSREEL AT THE MOVIES

At most movie houses the standard American newsreel ran for ten minutes along with other short subjects between showings of the feature film. Five major production companies released new versions twice weekly, mixing shots of major news events with human interest, sports, and a touch of disaster and crime. The newsreel was in its prime during the 1930s and the war years of the 1940s.

Film historians credit Charles Pathé of France with the first newsreel, the *Pathé Journal* of 1907. In 1911 he also produced the first silent newsreel in the United States, *Pathé's Weekly,* in a New Jersey studio. By 1914 the Pathé Frères company was employing 37 staff camera operators in North America, and had Vitagraph and the Hearst film interests as newsreel competitors.[40]

Fox Movietone News showed the first sound news films in January 1927, then scored a smash hit with a sound film of Charles Lindbergh's takeoff for Paris in May. The first full-length Fox newsreel, shown in October, entranced viewers with the majesty of Niagara Falls, reviewed the "Romance of the Iron Horse," and covered the Army-Yale football game and a rodeo in New York. Hearst Metrotone News (later renamed *News of the Day*) appeared in sound in 1929. The other major producers were Paramount News ("The Eyes and Ears of the World"), Universal News, and Pathé News. In 1937 Castle's *News Parade* began selling 16 mm. and 8 mm. films for home showing of such subjects as the *Hindenburg* disaster, the life of the Duke of Windsor, and the coronation of Edward VIII.

A study of newsreel content from 1938 to 1949 showed that sports used 25 percent of the footage during peacetime. World War II took over 50 percent of the footage during 1943 to 1944, and foreign shots took 30 percent in the postwar years. Government was covered in 5 percent to 10 percent of the films, and disasters and crime never exceeded 4 percent. In a world without television and only recently with picture magazines, the newsreel was eagerly awaited in the movie house, bringing as it did images of the great, the drama of war, and the tragedy of life. But with network television coverage of major news events, the newsreel withered. In November 1949, New York's Embassy Newsreel Theater closed after showing only newsreels to 11 million customers for 20 years. The Trans-Lux newsreel theaters were gone by 1950. Newsreels had one last moment of glory when they could show the 1953 coronation of Queen Elizabeth II as rapidly as did television, which did not yet have trans-Atlantic satellite transmission.

The newsreel companies sought television connections and sold their film libraries. *The March of Time* documentary, a competitor since 1935, transferred to television in 1951. Pathé News closed down in 1956, Paramount in 1957, Fox in 1963, and Hearst and Universal in 1967. The newsreel was no more.

The March of Time, although made in documentary form, was shown with the newsreels in movie houses monthly for 16 years. An estimated 20 million moviegoers saw it in 9000 theaters in the United States and in others around the world. Produced for Time Inc. by Louis de Rochemont, a journalist and filmmaker, it featured nearly 300 episodes exploring social issues, many of them controversial. Westbrook Van Voorhis provided the attention-arresting voice with a crisis-laden, staccato tone. In its reconstructions of events, at times using impersonators, *The March of Time* made attacks on Huey Long, Father

Coughlin, Gerald L. K. Smith, Hitler, and Mussolini, and deplored the Dust Bowl, the plight of migratory workers, and the inequalities of wartime. Through film, radio, and television, Americans heard Van Voorhis intone, "Time Marches On!"

MAGAZINES OF OPINION AND INTERPRETATION: MENCKEN'S *MERCURY*

Some of the country's magazines became important factors in the trend toward interpretation and news specialization. There was a new element injected into the magazine world, however. It was increasingly clear that the small-circulation opinion journals were being hurt by constant boosts in postal rates, high printing costs, and changing newsstand practices, and that the "slicks" were becoming dominant.

In the muckraking era, such general magazines as *Collier's, McClure's, Everybody's,* and the *American* served both as entertainment media and as "people's champions," exposing industrial monopolies and political corruption and crusading for a broadening of political and economic democracy. But that phase had ended by World War I, and the old champions withered. *McClure's* went downhill before 1920 and flickered out in 1933; *Everybody's* died in 1930; and *Collier's* and the *American* in 1956.

Most of the serious magazines that were important as sources of information and as vehicles of opinion before World War I fell by the wayside in the 1920s and 1930s. The *Century* was merged with the *Forum* and then both disappeared into *Current History. World's Work,* one of the best, had to combine with *Review of Reviews,* which in turn was sold to the *Literary Digest.* The *Digest,* founded in 1890 and long a highly popular reporter on American newspaper opinion and current affairs, slumped away before the onslaught of newer-type news magazines and abruptly ended its career by publishing the results of a postcard poll that predicted that Alfred M. Landon would defeat Franklin Roosevelt for the presidency in 1936 (Landon carried two states). Of the distinguished literary magazines, *Scribner's* collapsed in 1939.

Henry Louis Mencken's *American Mercury* was a bright new star of the magazine world in 1924, challenging American complacency, shocking solid citizens, and delighting the young rebels who had already enjoyed the work of Mencken and George Jean Nathan in *Smart Set* since 1914. Mencken was the dominant figure in American criticism in the 1920s, working from his base on the *Baltimore Sun.* He had the air of a disdainful aristocrat, who disliked nearly everything in the country; sometimes he found people or customs distasteful, at other times absurd. His particular targets were Puritanism, Prohibition, and the Anglo-Saxon tradition in literature. His collection of what he called "crack-brained" deeds and words appeared in his column "Americana." The college generation, and young journalists, envied his sophisticated air and writing style, imitating both. But the national mood changed with the Great Depression, and the *American Mercury* declined after Mencken and his associates let it pass into other hands in 1933.

ROSS AND THE *NEW YORKER*

Possibly the most distinctive of American magazines arrived in 1925, when Harold Ross began publication of the *New Yorker.* Ross had been editor of the *Stars and Stripes* in World War I days, and met Franklin P. Adams and Alexander Woollcott on that distinguished staff. In New York in 1925 they helped him get his magazine venture under way, with the fi-

(Fabian Bachrach)

Harold Ross, the *New Yorker* editor

(©1987, The New Yorker, reprinted by permission.)

Eustace Tilley, the *New Yorker*'s trademark

nancial backing of Raoul Fleischmann. The magazine, Ross said, would be a humorous one, reflecting metropolitan life and keeping up with the affairs of the day in a light and satirical vein that would mark it as not being "for the old lady in Dubuque." Ross was a demanding, irascible editor who hired and fired about 100 staff members in the first struggling year-and-a-half before he began to find his stars: E. B. White, conductor of "Talk of the Town"; Rea Irvin, art editor who drew Eustace Tilley, the supercilious dandy who is the *New Yorker*'s trademark; writers James Thurber, Ogden Nash, Wolcott Gibbs, S. J. Perelman, A. J. Liebling, and Frank Sullivan; artists Peter Arno, Helen Hokinson, Otto Soglow, Charles Addams, and a host of others who contributed the famous *New Yorker* cartoons; and editor Katharine White.

But the *New Yorker* was more than cartoons, whimsy, and curiously plotless fiction; it had its penetrating "Profiles," its "Reporter at Large," and other incisive commentaries on public affairs. One of the most famed series was its "Letter from Paris," signed by "Gênet" but written by Janet Flanner. The first of her more than 700 articles from Paris and other European cities was written in 1925, the last in 1975. Flanner described her work as "foreign correspondence with a critical edge." She was the kind of writing stylist Ross so admired. She was also able to bring to her readers both the feel of French society and penetrating comment on the great events of her era.

When Ross died in 1951, his magazine was a solid success, both in circulation and advertising, and under a new editor, William Shawn, it continued its gains. There was some criticism as bylines inevitably changed (*Time* reported in 1960 that Shawn's *New Yorker* had 97 subscribers in Dubuque, including several old ladies). But the magazine won nearly half a million subscribers, who read many pages of sophisticated advertising, the cartoons, and such newer writing talent as Washington correspondent Richard Rovere, writer John Updike, public affairs reporters Calvin Trillin and Jonathan Schell, columnist Elizabeth Drew, and critics Penelope Gilliatt and Michael Arlen.

WALLACE'S *READER'S DIGEST*

Very likely contributing to the demise of the quality magazines was the spectacular success of the *Reader's Digest,* which in 1922 began to print condensed versions of articles of current interest and entertainment value that had appeared in other magazines. The brainchild of DeWitt Wallace and his wife, Lila Acheson Wallace, the *Reader's Digest* slowly won readers during the 1920s and then mushroomed to a 1 million circulation by 1935. The pocket-size style of the magazine, its staff's keen judgment of popular tastes, and the skillful editing for condensation continued to make it a national best seller as circulation reached 3 million in 1938, 5 million in 1942, and 9 million in 1946. Wallace then began to develop his own articles, partly because some magazines began to refuse him reprint rights and partly to support his personal outlook on life. Gradually, during the 1940s, the magazine, which was supposedly an impartial digest of material in other publications, began to acquire a noticeable and conservative point of view of its own. Critics complained that its "inspirational" tone was unrealistic, if not Pollyanna-like, and offered little help in meeting major national and world problems. Nevertheless the *Reader's Digest* grew in size and influence, reaching a nearly 20 million circulation in the United States and an additional 10 or more million for foreign-language editions in 60 countries. Wallace reversed an old ban and accepted advertising, beginning in 1955, which further added to the *Digest*'s profits.

LUCE AND *TIME*

A big new name in magazine journalism was that of Henry R. Luce. He became both an extraordinarily successful and a controversial figure. His weekly news-magazine, *Time,* became dominant in its field, and his picture magazine, *Life,* became a runaway success in circulation and advertising.

(Time Inc.—Halsman)

Magazine founder Henry R. Luce

The story of Time Inc. began in March 1923, when Luce and a fellow Yale graduate, Briton Hadden, brought out the first issue of *Time.* Both had been editors of the *Yale Daily News* and had worked briefly as reporters. The young men looked about them in the era of the 1920s and announced in their prospectus:

> Although daily journalism has been more highly developed in the United States than in any other country in the world—
>
> Although foreigners marvel at the excellence of our periodicals, *World's Work, Century, Literary Digest, Outlook,* and the rest—
>
> People in America are, for the most part, poorly informed.
>
> This is not the fault of the daily newspapers; they print all the news.
>
> It is not the fault of the weekly "reviews"; they adequately develop and comment on the news.
>
> To say with the facile cynic that it is the fault of the people themselves is to beg the question.
>
> People are uninformed because no publication has adapted itself to the time which busy men are able to spend on simply keeping informed.

Time, its editors promised, would organize and departmentalize the news of the week. Its slogan became, "*Time* is written as if by one man for one man." Its coverage of national affairs, foreign news, science, religion, business, education, and other areas was to be written not for people who had expert knowledge of each of the fields but for *Time*'s "busy man." The editors developed the use of the narrative story in telling the news and injected strong elements of human interest. To accumulate myriads of facts that could be woven into each story, *Time* developed an extensive research and library staff as well as a good-sized news-gathering organization of its own to supplement press-association services.

Hadden died in 1929, after seeing *Time* reach a circulation of 200,000, and Luce went on alone. The *March of Time* radio program was begun in 1931 and its motion picture version in 1935. *Fortune,* Luce's lavish magazine for businesspeople, which sold at $1 a copy, was successful even in the depression year of 1930. *Life,* hitting the newsstands in 1936, caught the interest of a photography-conscious people and had customers fighting for copies. *Sports Illustrated,* less of a success, was added in 1954. Time Inc. moved to Rockefeller Center in 1938, opened its own 48-story Time & Life building there in 1960, and counted a record-breaking $270 million annual gross. *Time* claimed three million circulation for its domestic, Canadian, and three overseas editions in 1962. Luce retired as editor-in-chief in 1964 in favor of Hedley W. Donovan and died in 1967.

There were many things about *Time* that aroused criticism. Luce and his editors made no pretense of sticking to the usual concepts of journalistic objectivity, which they considered mythical. Nor did *Time* want to be called impartial, it said; rather, "fairness" was *Time*'s goal. In an historic essay published on its twenty-fifth anniversary, *Time* said: "What's the difference between impartiality and fairness? The responsible journalist is 'partial' to that interpretation of the facts which seems to him to fit things as they are. He is fair in not twisting the facts to support his view, in not suppressing the facts that support a different view."[41]

Some critics felt, however, that sometimes *Time* was not fair to its readers, since it presented opinion and editorial hypothesis intermingled with the straight news. Later *Newsweek* received the same rebukes. The critics disliked the use of narrative and human-interest techniques. Still, *Time* had widespread influence, and it served many readers by summarizing day-by-day news in its weekly digests. Particularly, its specialized departments brought news of science, medicine, religion, business, education, art, radio, the press, and other areas to many who never before had followed happenings in such diverse fields. Its "Essays," begun in the mid-1960s, further enhanced the magazine's appeal for serious readers, and its 1976 special bicentennial editions were outstanding contributions. In that year Time Inc. became the first billion-dollar publishing firm, slightly ahead of the Times Mirror Company of Los Angeles.

NEWSWEEK, U.S. NEWS, AND BUSINESS WEEK

After *Time* bought the remains of the *Literary Digest* in 1938, its only direct competitor was *Newsweek,* founded in 1933. *Newsweek*'s format was almost identical to that of *Time,* but its early editors injected less opinion into its columns. Financed by the wealth of the Astor and Harriman families and directed by Malcolm Muir after 1937, *Newsweek* grew steadily in influence. By 1961 it had a 1.5 million circulation, its own New York headquarters building, two overseas editions, and a network of domestic and foreign news bureaus. That year it was sold to the *Washington Post*'s publisher, Philip L. Graham, for $9 million. Graham then took control of *Newsweek* as chairman of the board but died in 1963 before his plans for the magazine could be fully developed. Katharine Meyer Graham succeeded her husband as head of the *Post* and *Newsweek.*

Devoting itself exclusively to news of national and international importance was *U.S. News & World Report,* a combination of David Lawrence's publishing ventures. Lawrence ran the *United States Daily* in Washington from 1926 to 1933, then changed it to a weekly. In 1946 he launched *World Report,* which he combined with his older journal in 1948. By 1962 the magazine had 1.2 million readers, a large Washington bureau, and several overseas bureaus.

Specializing in news of business and industry was *Business Week,* founded in 1929 by the McGraw-Hill Publishing Company. Along with 30 other McGraw-Hill magazines, it was served by the McGraw-Hill World News Service. *Business Week*'s circulation was substantial, reaching 400,000 in 1962.

PHOTOJOURNALISM: LIFE, LOOK, AND DOCUMENTARIES

Widespread public interest in the newsreel, in newspaper photos transmitted by wire, and in personal photography led Time Inc. to establish the weekly picture magazine *Life* in November 1936. People almost fought in the streets to buy copies, and circulation soared. *Life* was patterned after photographic publications in Germany and Britain, but it introduced a disciplined concept of advance research and planning by the editors that guided the photographers. Even such great photographers as its 1936 stars—Margaret Bourke-White, Alfred Eisenstaedt, Peter Stackpole, and Thomas McAvoy—got suggestions from editor Wilson Hicks about how the key shots were to be made when they arrived on the scene. Hicks came from the Associated Press to be picture editor, then executive editor. He built a staff of 40 within three years and directed it until 1950.

Bourke-White did photographic essays and interpretive picture stories at the close of the Great Depression, captured Gandhi's compelling personality on film in India, and took wartime assignments before illness cut short her career. Robert Capa, W. Eugene Smith, and David Douglas Duncan all recorded the wars, from Capa's great image of a falling

(AP/Wide World Photos)

Margaret Bourke-White captured many *Life* cover shots.

Spanish Civil War soldier to Duncan's chilling sequences in Vietnam. Earlier Duncan had also won acclaim for his Korean War photography. Smith's picture essays, including "Spanish Village," "Country Doctor," and "Nurse Midwife," stand as classics. Other noted photojournalists were Gordon Parks, who interpreted the feelings of black America for *Life*, Gjon Mili, and Carl Mydans. The managing editors were John Shaw Billings, Edward K. Thompson, George Hunt, and Ralph Graves.

Life's circulation success proved its undoing. The broad approach of television siphoned off some advertisers and readers, and other advertisers diverted contracts from the mass-circulation magazines to those with specialized audiences. Circulation dropped from 8.5 million in 1970 to 5.5 million in 1972, and the revenue flow was not enough to sustain publication. With tears and many a fond remembrance, *Life* staffers headed for other jobs in the media world.[42]

Life's suspension in 1972 had followed on the heels of the death of *Look*, its chief competitor in the world of photojournalism. *Look* was begun by Gardner Cowles in 1937. At first it adopted the rotogravure techniques of the Cowles family newspapers in Des Moines and Minneapolis, but gradually it developed major articles on public affairs. A fortnightly, it reached two million circulation in 1945, passed four million in 1955, and had touched eight million when it was suspended in 1971, another victim of inflated costs and deflated advertising revenues. Daniel D. Mich was *Look*'s longtime editor, succeeded by William B. Arthur. Arthur Rothstein came from the Farm Security Administration photojournalism group to be director of photography. Achieving distinction with their cameras were John Vachon, Phillip Harrington, and Paul Fusco. The magazine was a national leader in art direction under art directors Allen Hurlburt and William Hopkins.

Documentary films, recording the lives and social activities of real people, had their beginning in 1922 when a New York fur company commissioned Robert Flaherty to film the life of an Eskimo family. His *Nanook of the North* set a standard for others. John Grierson filmed herring fishermen on the North Sea in 1929 to produce *Drifters,* the first of a series for the British government that he, Paul Rotha, and others continued in the 1930s.

The United States government joined in support of documentary photography through the Farm Security Administration (FSA), which was concerned with soil erosion, dust storms, and their human toll. A team of photo documentarians under the guidance of Roy E. Stryker began touring the Midwest Dust Bowl in 1935, taking pictures that opened the eyes of the nation to the unchronicled devastation of rural poverty. One of the photographers was Dorothea Lange, whose sensitive images stand as examples of still photography at its finest. Others included Carl Mydans, Walker Evans, and Ben Shahn. The FSA project involved 272,000 negatives and 150,000 prints, now stored at the Library of Congress.

The FSA then commissioned documentary films, produced by Pare Lorentz. His *The Plow That Broke the Plains* (1936) was a graphic documentation of the causes of soil erosion and the dust storms that were turning Great Plains farmers into migrant workers. In 1937 Lorenz completed *The River,* addressed to another major national problem, flooding.

During World War II, Hollywood directors such as John Huston, Frank Capra, William Wyler, and John Ford filmed documentaries on and around battlegrounds, including *San Pietro, Memphis Belle,* and *Battle of Midway* during 1944. The British Ministry of Information made three masterful films: *London Can Take It* (1940), *Target for Tonight* (1941), and *Desert Victory* (1942). Most documentary effort was diverted to television in the 1950s, but the cult of *cinéma vérité,* or spontaneous filmmaking, kept the tradition alive.

BOOK PUBLISHING TURNS THE CORNER

Book publishing, a part of American life since colonial days, reached a turning point about 1915, according to the leading historian of the industry, John Tebbel.[43] A rapidly increasing literacy rate and a mushrooming urbanization meant that more people living in city centers, where book stores could prosper, wanted to read books. Tebbel also points out the arrival on the publishing scene of a remarkable number of aggressive builders.

Between 1914 and 1926 the newcomers included Alfred A. Knopf, W. W. Norton, and William Morrow, whose publishing houses, bore their names; Bennett Cerf and Donald Klopfer of Random House; Harold Guinzburg of Viking Press; and four sets of partners who built illustrious houses: Alfred Harcourt and Donald Brace, Richard Simon and Max Schuster, Albert Boni and Horace Liveright, and John Farrar and Stanley Rinehart.[44]

The most exciting publishing house in the 1920s and 1930s was Scribner's. After founder Charles Scribner's death in 1871, the firm became Charles Scribner's Sons, with Charles Scribner II serving as president from 1879 to 1928. Among his authors were Edith Wharton, Henry James, and Richard Harding Davis. His more important action, however, was to bring Maxwell Perkins into the offices in 1910. Perkins served as an editor from 1914 until his death in 1947, and with his associates built a remarkable record for literary successes. It was Perkins who worked with F. Scott Fitzgerald to produce his first novel in 1920, *This Side of Paradise;* it was Perkins who answered a tip from Fitzgerald in 1924 that there was a promising young author in Paris named Ernest Hemingway, whose *The Sun Also Rises* came from Scribner's in 1926; it was Perkins who worked endlessly with a young southern giant named Thomas Wolfe to create in 1929, out of 1100 pages of manuscript, Wolfe's first novel, *Look Homeward, Angel,* and then, out of 3000 pages, his second novel, *Of Time and the River.* Meantime, the Scribner's editorial team was producing the *Dictionary of American Biography.*

Cass Canfield arrived at Harper & Bros. in 1924, and served as chief executive officer from 1931 to 1967. An early coup was Wolfe's move from Scribner's to the editorship of Edward Aswell at Harper's in 1937. D. Appleton & Co. celebrated its one-hundredth birthday in 1925 with such authors as Edith Wharton (*The Age of Innocence* was a 1920 event), Edgar Lee Masters, and Vachel Lindsay. Edward P. Dutton, founder of his firm, died in 1923 after 62 years as president. At Macmillan, George Brett died in 1936, the same year he published *Gone with the Wind.*

Two of the country's leading book clubs, the Book-of-the-Month Club (BOMC) and the Literary Guild, appeared in 1926. The BOMC was begun by Harry Scherman, with Henry Seidel Canby, founder of the *Saturday Review of Literature,* as its first editor-in-chief. The founder of Viking Press, Harold Guinzburg, launched the Literary Guild. Books by mail flourished, partly due to the inadequate organization of the book-selling trade. Book trade associations dated from 1900; the American Book Publishers Council (1946) and the American Textbook Publishers Institute (1942) joined forces in 1970 to become the Association of American Publishers. The stores were organized as the American Booksellers Association.

Paperbacks made their start in this period, notably the Boni & Liveright efforts in 1914, the Little Leather Library, and the Modern Library in 1917. The latter was acquired by Random House in 1925. It was 1939, however, before the promoters of Pocket Books found the right formula and revolutionized the paperback business.

Honolulu Star-Bulletin 1st EXTRA

8 PAGES—HONOLULU, TERRITORY OF HAWAII, U. S. A., SUNDAY, DECEMBER 7, 1941—8 PAGES ★ PRICE FIVE CENTS

WAR!

(Associated Press by Transpacific Telephone)

SAN FRANCISCO, Dec. 7.—President Roosevelt announced this morning that Japanese planes had attacked Manila and Pearl Harbor.

OAHU BOMBED BY JAPANESE PLANES

SIX KNOWN DEAD, 21 INJURED, AT EMERGENCY HOSPITAL

Attack Made On Island's Defense Areas

By UNITED PRESS

WASHINGTON, Dec. 7.—Text of a White House announcement detailing the attack on the Hawaiian islands is:

"The Japanese attacked Pearl Harbor from the air and all naval and military activities on the island of Oahu, principal American base in the Hawaiian islands."

Oahu was attacked at 7:55 this morning by Japanese planes.

The Rising Sun, emblem of Japan, was seen on plane wing tips.

Wave after wave of bombers streamed through the clouded morning sky from the southwest and flung their missiles on a city resting in peaceful Sabbath calm.

According to an unconfirmed report received at the governor's office, the Japanese force that attacked Oahu reached island waters aboard two small airplane carriers.

It was also reported that at the governor's office either an attempt had been made to bomb the USS Lexington, or that it had been bombed.

CITY IN UPROAR

Within 10 minutes the city was in an uproar. As bombs fell in many parts of the city, and in defense areas the defenders of the islands went into quick action.

Army intelligence officers at Ft. Shafter announced officially shortly after 9 a. m. that fact of the bombardment by an enemy but long previous army and navy had taken immediate measures in defense.

"Oahu is under a sporadic air raid," the announcement said.

"Civilians are ordered to stay off the streets until further notice."

CIVILIANS ORDERED OFF STREETS

The army has ordered that all civilians stay off the streets and highways and not use telephones.

Evidence that the Japanese attack has registered some hits was shown by three billowing pillars of smoke in the Pearl Harbor and Hickam field area.

All navy personnel and civilian defense workers, with the exception of women, have been ordered to duty at Pearl Harbor.

The Pearl Harbor highway was immediately a mass of racing cars.

A trickling stream of injured people began pouring into the city emergency hospital a few minutes after the bombardment started.

At The Star-Bulletin office the phone calls deluged the single operator and it was impossible for this newspaper, for sometime, to handle the flood of calls. Here also an emergency operator was called.

HOUR OF ATTACK—7:55 A. M.

An official army report from department headquarters, made public shortly before 11, is that the first attack was at 7:55 a. m.

Witnesses said they saw at least 50 airplanes over Pearl Harbor.

The attack centered in the Pearl Harbor, Army authorities said:

"The rising sun was seen on the wing tips of the airplanes."

Although martial law has not been declared officially, the city of Honolulu was operating under M-Day conditions.

It is reliably reported that enemy objectives under attack were Wheeler field, Hickam field, Kaneohe bay and naval air station and Pearl Harbor.

Some enemy planes were reported shot down.

The body of the pilot was seen in a plane burning at Wahiawa.

Oahu appeared to be taking calmly after the first uproar of queries.

ANTIAIRCRAFT GUNS IN ACTION

First indication of the raid came shortly before 8 this morning when antiaircraft guns around Pearl Harbor began sending up a thunderous barrage.

At the same time a vast cloud of black smoke arose from the naval base and also from Hickam field where flames could be seen.

BOMB NEAR GOVERNOR'S MANSION

Shortly before 9:30 a bomb fell near Washington Place, the residence of the governor. Governor Poindexter and Secretary Charles M. Hite were there.

It was reported that the bomb killed an unidentified Chinese man across the street in front of the Schuman Carriage Co. where windows were broken.

C. E. Daniels, a welder, found a fragment of shell or bomb at South and Queen Sts. which he brought into the City Hall. This fragment weighed about a pound.

At 10:05 a. m. today Governor Poindexter telephoned to The Star-Bulletin announcing he has declared a state of emergency for the entire territory.

He announced that Edouard L. Doty, executive secretary of the major disaster council, has been appointed director under the M-Day law's provisions.

Governor Poindexter urged all residents of Honolulu to remain off the street, and the people of the territory to remain calm.

Mr. Doty reported that all major disaster council wardens and medical units were on duty within a half hour of the time the alarm was given.

Workers employed at Pearl Harbor were ordered at 10:10 a. m. not to report at Pearl Harbor.

The mayor's major disaster council was to meet at the city hall at about 10:30 this morning.

At least two Japanese planes were reported at Hawaiian department headquarters to have been shot down.

One of the planes was shot down at Ft. Kamehameha and the other back of the Wa-

Hundreds See City Bombed

Hundreds of Honolulans who hurried to the top of Punchbowl soon after bombs began to fall, saw spread out a panorama of surprise attack and defense.

Far off over Pearl Harbor the white sky was polka-dotted with antiaircraft smoke.

Names of Dead and Injured

Schools Closed

All schools on Oahu, both public and private, will remain closed until Monday. This does not apply elsewhere in the territory.

Editorial

HAWAII MEETS THE CRISIS

Honolulu and Hawaii will meet the emergency of war today as Honolulu and Hawaii have met emergencies in the past—coolly, calmly and with immediate and complete support of the officials, officers and troops who are in charge.

Governor Poindexter and the army and navy leaders have called upon the public to remain calm, for civilians who have no essential business on the streets to stay off, and for every man and woman to do his duty.

That request, coupled with the measures promptly taken to meet the situation that has suddenly and terribly developed, will be needed.

Hawaii will do its part as a loyal American territory. In this crisis, every difference of race, creed and color will be submerged in the one desire and determination to play the part that Americans always play in crisis.

BULLETIN

Additional Star-Bulletin extras today will cover the latest developments in this war move.

Big type announced Pearl Harbor and the coming of World War II to the United States.

15

A World
at War

**This is a people's war, and to win it the people should know as
much about it as they can.**

—Elmer Davis

The diplomatic bombshell that signaled the opening of World War II was the signing of the German-Russian neutrality pact on August 23, 1939. This sinister deal between the dictators Hitler and Stalin gave the Germans freedom to march against Poland and later their neighbors to the west without fear of Russian intervention. Russia, in return, would annex eastern Poland. The German *blitzkrieg* opened on September 1, and the British and French, who had failed repeatedly to stand up against Hitler and Mussolini, responded with declarations of war on September 3. They did not, however, launch offensives.

President Roosevelt immediately increased his efforts to assist the Allies; the Neutrality Act was revised in November, the first step toward reversal of the isolationist trend. Congress repealed the embargo on arms' sales and authorized a cash-and-carry trade with those resisting aggression. This was met with bitter resentment from the anti-Roosevelt segment of the news media led by the McCormick-Patterson *Chicago Tribune* and *New York Daily News* and radio commentators Fulton Lewis, Jr., Upton Close, and Father Charles Coughlin.

The full nature of Hitler's designs—and its danger to the security of the United States—was revealed in the spring of 1940, when Nazi armies first invaded Denmark and Norway and then launched a gigantic offensive against Holland, Belgium, and France on May 10. The shock of the British evacuation of Dunkerque, the fall of France, and the opening of the Nazi air blitz against Britain in August produced strong pro-Allied sentiment in the United States.

AMERICANS LEARN OF EUROPE'S WAR

Bill Henry of CBS and Arthur Mann of Mutual had been the first front-line radio reporters in 1939, William L. Shirer of CBS and William C. Kerker of NBC had seen Hitler strutting before accepting the French surrender at the railroad car at Compiègne, and night after night in late 1940 Edward R. Murrow told CBS listeners of the Nazi air attacks against London. The greatest impact on American minds was made by his "This Is London" broadcasts, graphically reporting the Battle of Britain. Murrow's quiet but compelling voice brought images of a bomb-torn and burning London that did much to awaken the still-neutral United States to the nature of the war. Later the poet Archibald MacLeish would say of Murrow's broadcasts: "You burned the city of London in our houses and we felt the flames that burned it."[1]

One of the early standouts among newspaper war correspondents was the veteran Leland Stowe of the *Chicago Daily News,* who reported the Russo-Finnish War and the Nazi invasion of Norway, and who in 1941 became the first American to reach the Nazi-Soviet front lines after Hitler's invasion of Russia. Webb Miller of the United Press covered his eleventh war in Finland, then returned to London to be killed in a blackout accident. Frazier Hunt of the INS and M. W. Fodor of the *Chicago Daily News* filed notable accounts of the French retreat in 1940; on the other side, with Hitler's triumphant army, were Louis Lochner of the Associated Press, Pierre J. Huss of the International News Service, and Frederick C. Oechsner of the United Press.

In September 1940, the Selective Service Act was passed, and Roosevelt announced the trade of 50 destroyers to Britain in return for leases on air-sea bases in the western hemisphere. Many American newspapers supported both actions, and Henry Luce's *Time* magazine agreed with them.

ROOSEVELT'S THIRD-TERM CAMPAIGN

Roosevelt was in the middle of his campaign for an unprecedented third term. His opponent, the enthusiastic Wendell Willkie from Indiana, supported aid for Britain, the draft, and the destroyer deal—although he fairly criticized Roosevelt for not including Congress in the decision. Willkie was in turn called a "me-too" candidate by the Republican "old guard." The Republican National Committee went much further than its candidate, issuing radio messages saying, "When your boy is dying on some battlefield in Europe . . . and he's crying out 'Mother! Mother!'—don't blame Franklin D. Roosevelt because he sent your boy to war—blame yourself because you sent Franklin D. Roosevelt to the White House!"[2]

The lines were formed between the isolationists and the interventionists. On one side was the America First Committee, headed by General Robert E. Wood and championed by Colonel Charles A. Lindbergh. Senators Gerald P. Nye and Burton K. Wheeler were also America Firsters. Unfortunately for them, their side drew such assorted rabble rousers as Father Coughlin, Gerald L. K. Smith, William Dudley Pelley of the fascist Silver Shirts, Fritz Kuhn of the German-American Bund, and Communists William Z. Foster and Earl Browder. On the other side was the Committee to Defend America by Aiding the Allies, headed by the distinguished Kansas editor William Allen White. The White group attracted many influential writers and editors and carried out a newspaper-advertisement campaign that resulted in the formation of hundreds of local committees. Among these journalistic leaders were columnist Joseph Alsop, radio commentator Elmer Davis, and playwright Robert E. Sherwood.

The voters decided not to change leadership in the midst of crisis and gave Roosevelt 27 million popular votes to 22 million for Willkie. John L. Lewis of the United Mine Workers urged Roosevelt's defeat, but Roosevelt held the majority of his coalition together. In November 1940, a Gallup poll showed that 50 percent of the Americans favored helping England, even at the risk of intervention in Europe; by December that total would mount to 60 percent.

THE ARSENAL OF DEMOCRACY

In December 1940, President Roosevelt called on the nation to become "the great arsenal of democracy." He told a worldwide radio audience that if Britain were defeated, the Axis powers would "control the continents of Europe, Asia, Africa, Australasia, and the high seas." He continued, "It is no exaggeration to say that all of us in the Americas would be living at the point of a gun—a gun loaded with explosive bullets, economic as well as military."[3] But, he predicted, the Axis nations would not win the war if America would speed up its arms production. Earlier that year Winston Churchill, who had emerged from political exile to become Britain's prime minister, had thrilled the free nations with his "blood and tears, toil and sweat" speech, also heard on radio.

The Lend-Lease Act of 1941, which empowered the president to provide goods and services to those nations whose defense he deemed vital to the defense of the United States, represented a victory for the pro-Allied group. It also served to make the United States a nonbelligerent ally of the British, to the disgust of Senators Robert Taft and Arthur Vandenberg, Joseph P. Kennedy, and John Foster Dulles. Ironically, it was Taft who also noted Roosevelt's unhappiness with Japanese aggression in Southeast Asia. Taft said that no American mother was ready to have a son die "for some place with an unpronounceable name in Indo-china."[4]

In May 1941, Roosevelt proclaimed an unlimited state of national emergency to facilitate the American mobilization program. In August he and Churchill met on the high seas and announced their peace aims in the Atlantic Charter. The isolationists were far from beaten, however; that same month the House of Representatives continued the military draft by the narrow margin of one vote.

WAR BREAKS IN THE PACIFIC

Unity for war was achieved on December 7, 1941, when radio brought the astounding news that Japanese planes had bombed the U.S. Pacific Fleet at their Pearl Harbor base in the Hawaiian Islands. Len Sterling, an announcer for Mutual, broke into the broadcast of a professional football game coming from the Polo Grounds in New York. At 2:22 P.M. the press associations had flashed the White House announcement of the attack—"White House says Japs attack Pearl Harbor"—and were relaying news from correspondents in Honolulu. The United Press provided the first direct account of the attack before military censors cut off communications from Hawaii.

Mrs. Frank Tremaine, wife of the UP's Hawaiian manager, made the call to San Francisco, repeating information from her husband and other staffers. One of those reporters was Francis McCarthy, whose byline appeared over this story:

Honolulu, Dec. 7 (UP)—War broke with lightning suddenness in the Pacific today, when waves of Japanese bombers assailed Hawaii and the United States Fleet struck back with a thunder of big naval rifles.

It was afternoon on the East Coast and a few minutes after the Mutual break-in. John Daly of CBS came on the air at 2:31 P.M. with: "The Japanese have attacked Pearl Harbor, Hawaii, by air, President Roosevelt has just announced. The attack was also made on naval and military activities on the principal island of Oahu."[5] The incredible announcement was repeated by NBC announcers, and during the rest of the day the radio carried bulletins— and some commentary based on rumor as much as fact.

In Honolulu, editor Riley Allen of the *Star-Bulletin* and his staff managed to issue a detail-filled extra headlined, "WAR! OAHU BOMBED BY JAPANESE PLANES," within 90 minutes, which was followed by a wave of extras in mainland cities.[6] The following day a record 79 percent of American homes listened to Roosevelt's speech before Congress, when he asked for a declaration of war by beginning, "Yesterday, December 7, 1941, a date which will live in infamy. . . ."

All of the grim facts of the United States' humiliating losses at Pearl Harbor and the disgraceful lack of preparation were not immediately known. In all, 2403 Americans died, and another 1178 were wounded. The battleship *Arizona* sank at its berth, and 17 other ships were sunk or damaged, along with more than 200 planes that were destroyed or damaged. But on that first day it was clear that this had been a great defeat. That evening Eric Sevareid, who had joined Murrow's staff in Europe in 1939, broadcast from the White House press room: "There is one report that I must give you that is not all confirmed—a report which is rather widely believed here and which has just come in. And that is that the destruction at Hawaii was indeed very heavy, more heavy than we really had anticipated."[7]

Although the Pacific war opened with the "sneak attack," it can be argued that war between the United States and Japan had been inevitable because of the American presence in the Philippines since 1898, Japan's desire to spread its Greater East Asia Co-Prosperity Sphere without Western interference, longstanding grudges against the United States because of discrimination against Japanese immigrants, and finally, American insistence that Japan abandon its attempts to occupy Manchuria and China. A final straw had been the American embargo on scrap iron and steel shipments to Japan in September 1940, which made the Japanese warlords more fearful of United States intentions. In their minds the large U.S. Pacific Fleet was a threat to their nation's Pacific destiny. In fact, the Japanese newspaper *Yomiuri* had stated this position at the time of the embargo: "Britain, the United States, and France must be forced out of the Far East. Asia is the territory of the Asians."[8] The *New York Herald Tribune* understood this too, saying after the attack, "Since the clash now seems to have been inevitable, its occurrence brings with it a sense of relief." While many other papers vented their anger and frustration in bitter denunciations of the "Japs" and vowed that the Japanese homeland would be destroyed, the *Herald Tribune* calmly stated, "The air is clearer. Americans can get down to their task with old controversies forgotten."[9]

Hitler made Roosevelt's task easier on December 11, when, against the advice of many of his military chiefs, he declared war against the United States. Now there could be no argument against fighting on the European front. The president's isolationist foes were shocked into silence.

CENSORSHIP AND PROPAGANDA RENEWED

With organization of the country for war, newspaperpeople recalled that the Espionage Act and Trading-with-the Enemy Act of 1917 were still on the statute books. The more sweeping generalities of the Sedition Act had been repealed in 1921, however. Use of these acts to bar publications from the mails and to suppress free speech was more sharply limited than during World War I, however, and mainly affected pro-Fascist and subversive propaganda sheets. The greatest invasion of civil liberties took place during the early years of the war, when Japanese living in the United States, including many American citizens of Japanese ancestry, were rounded up and kept in isolated camps.

Byron Price, executive news editor of the Associated Press, was named director of the Office of Censorship. Probably no other person could have held the respect and confidence of newspaperpeople everywhere better than Price, who was temperamentally and intellectually equipped to handle the most difficult part of his job—the direction of the voluntary press censorship.[10]

The *Code of Wartime Practices for the American Press,* issued on January 15, 1942, carefully outlined to those who published printed materials what would constitute the improper handling of news having to do with troops, planes, ships, war production, armaments, military installations, and weather. Similar instructions were given to radio stations. The code became a bible for American newspeople, who usually erred in the direction of oversuppression of news possibly harmful to the war effort.

Most of the 14,462 persons in the Office of Censorship were engaged in the mandatory censorship of mail, cables, and radio communications between the United States and other countries. Price's Office of Censorship in World War II thus combined the World War I operations of the Censorship Board and the voluntary press-censorship portion of George Creel's work. Price, however, had nothing to do with originating the news or with the government's propaganda effort. Those aspects of the work of the World War I Committee on Public Information were handled during World War II by a separate agency, the Office of War Information (OWI), which was established by an executive order of the president in June 1942 to supersede four earlier government agencies. Roosevelt made a wise choice in the person of Elmer Davis as director. Davis had served on the *New York Times* staff for ten years, and had been a news analyst and commentator for the Columbia Broadcasting System.[11]

One function of the OWI was to act as a city desk for the nation's war news. Government departments and war agencies continued to handle approximately 40 percent of government publicity stories without reference to the OWI. But those news releases relating significantly to the war effort or dealing with activities affecting more than one government agency had to pass through the OWI News Bureau. The News Bureau operated on a $1 million annual budget with 250 regular employees. Three hundred reporters and correspondents used its facilities, including some 50 reporters working full time in the OWI pressroom. Copy flowed from the general news desk, where policy decisions were made, to the domestic and foreign news desks, the radio news desk, the picture desk, and the feature desk. Cartoons, pictures, features, weekly digests, and fillers became a part of the OWI offering. Background information concerning desired propaganda and informational objectives of the government was given to editorial writers, cartoonists, and columnists. In all of this work the OWI had the cooperation of the War Advertising Council and the nation's publishers. The government paid for recruiting advertising, but all other war-related newspaper, magazine, radio, and billboard advertising space was donated by the media or by national and local advertisers.

The overseas section of the OWI received up to 30,000 words a day of teletyped news from the domestic OWI News Bureau. The overseas offices in New York and San Francisco used also the news reports of the press associations, radio networks, and OWI's own regional offices. At its height of activity in 1943, the overseas news and features bureau, headed by Edward Barrett, cabled 65,000 words daily to all parts of the world, mailed hundreds of thousands of words of feature material, and airmailed or radioed 2500 pictures.[12] OWI also operated the Voice of America on radio.

MILITARY CENSORSHIP

Military censorship during World War II picked up where it had left off at the end of World War I, with the added problem of controlling radio broadcasts. In the early months of the war British censorship was blundering and severe, and it remained tight even after the Ministry of Information became better organized. Nazi Germany was not so badly handicapped by Allied control of cables during World War II, since wireless and radio facilities were available. The Nazis did not censor foreign correspondents before publication, but if they sent stories that Dr. Joseph Goebbels's Ministry of Propaganda did not like, they were subject to expulsion from Germany. Two victims of this policy in the first few months of World War II were Beach Conger of the *New York Herald Tribune* and Otto D. Tolischus of the *New York Times*. Edgar Ansel Mowrer of the *Chicago Daily News* was compelled to leave by threats against his person. Joseph W. Grigg of the UP, the only American reporter to cover the first day and the last day of World War II in Berlin, spent five months in internment after being arrested by the Nazis in 1941.

As the war developed, newspeople found the British Admiralty and the U.S. Navy Department most prone to suppressing news of war actions. The American Navy withheld details of the Pearl Harbor disaster and of the sinking of ships in the Pacific for long periods on the plea that the Japanese should not be given such vital information. Reporters grumbled, however, that evidence of inefficient naval operations also was being kept back.

The *Chicago Tribune* was involved in two major incidents in which vital information was disclosed to the enemy. Several days prior to Pearl Harbor the *Tribune* had published the Roosevelt administration's contingency "war plans." This publication, which showed that American officials felt that only an American expeditionary force could help save the British and Russians, and that the war should be fought in Europe first while the Japanese were held in check in the Pacific, infuriated Roosevelt. But the *Tribune*'s McCormick was robbed of a chance to exploit the matter when the Japanese bombed Pearl Harbor. Later, while announcing victory at the battle of Midway in June 1942, the paper also carried a story indirectly stating that military intelligence had broken the secret Japanese code. The *Tribune* gave full attention to how American commanders knew the position of the oncoming Japanese carriers. In this case the government considered prosecution, but dropped the matter after considerable publicity.[13]

On the other hand, the British censorship in Egypt, conflicting British and American censorship in the India-Burma theater, the Chinese censorship in Chungking, and General Douglas MacArthur's censorship in the Pacific also drew heavy fire from correspondents and editors. Many newspeople said that MacArthur's information officers insisted unduly on personal glorification of the commander.

Techniques used by General Dwight D. Eisenhower in Europe were considered generally satisfactory. However, the coverage of the German surrender in Europe ended with arguments over censorship and the confusing case of Edward Kennedy. Kennedy, the AP chief on the Western front, was one of 16 Allied correspondents taken to the military headquarters in Reims to witness the German surrender. All were pledged not to release their stories until an officially prescribed time. Kennedy, angered by the news that the German radio was announcing the surrender in advance of the time set by American, British, and Russian political leaders, made an unauthorized telephone call to London and dictated part of his story for transmission. The AP thus had the official story of the

German surrender a day in advance of V-E Day. But Kennedy's 54 colleagues in Paris charged him with committing "the most disgraceful, deliberate, and unethical double cross in the history of journalism." Kennedy defended his action as necessary to counteract a needless political censorship and won reinstatement as a war correspondent a year after his suspension. But the AP disassociated itself from its stormy petrel, and he left in 1946.

PRESS AND RADIO COVER THE WAR

Coverage of World War II by the American press and radio was considered by most observers to be the best and fullest the world had ever seen. A great share of the credit for this achievement went to the overseas and war-front correspondents for press associations, newspapers, magazines, and radio. As many as 500 full-time American correspondents were abroad at one time. Altogether the United States armed forces accredited 1646 persons. The biggest staffs were those of the press associations and radio networks; the *Times* and *Herald Tribune* in New York; the *Daily News, Tribune,* and *Sun* in Chicago; the *Christian Science Monitor; Baltimore Sun;* and *Time, Life,* and *Newsweek.* Of the 37 American newspeople who lost their lives during the war, 11 were press-association correspondents, 10 were representatives of individual newspapers, 9 were magazine correspondents, 4 were photographers, 2 were syndicated writers, and 1 was a radio correspondent.[14]

The development of mobile units and the use of tape recordings soon brought greatly increased radio coverage. The reports now came from battlefields, from bombers flying over Berlin and Tokyo, and from other action centers. Some of them were especially memorable: Cecil Brown of CBS describing the fall of Singapore; Edward R. Murrow riding in a plane in the great 1943 air raid on Berlin and living to broadcast about it; George Hicks of ABC winning D-Day honors by broadcasting from a landing barge under German fire. Wright Bryan of the *Atlanta Journal* gave NBC and CBS the first eyewitness account from the cross-channel front by flying over it with a planeload of paratroopers.

Perhaps the best-known reporter of World War II was the columnist friend of the G.I., Ernest Taylor Pyle. Pyle had won attention before the war for his personal notes on life in the United States, as observed in his wanderings across the country. In 1940 he told his readers what the people of Britain felt as they resisted the Nazi air blitz. Then he attached himself to the American army, writing in a hometown style of the intimate daily life of the G.I. in Ireland, North Africa, Sicily, Italy, and France. His column for Scripps Howard and his *Here Is Your War* and *Brave Men* won him a national reputation and a Pulitzer Prize. Pyle left Europe in 1944, but after a rest he flew out to cover the final stages of the Pacific war. When a Japanese sniper killed Ernie Pyle on Ie Shima during the Okinawa campaign of April 1945, the saga of a great American war correspondent came to a close.

There was a soldiers' journalism again in World War II, as there had been in World War I. The *Stars and Stripes* reappeared as the leading G.I. newspaper in 1942 and eventually had European and Pacific editions. *Yank,* a magazine with 22 editions, gained a circulation of 2.5 million. The resentments of the enlisted man were portrayed in *Stars and Stripes* by cartoonist Bill Mauldin, and Sgt. George Baker's "Sad Sack" and Milton Caniff's sexy "Male Call" ran in both publications. Almost every major unit and camp had its own publication. And unlike during World War I, the armed services developed extensive public-relations units, of which the combat correspondents of the Marine Corps were the most effective. Sergeant Jim G. Lucas of the Marines, formerly of the *Tulsa Tribune* staff, wrote one of the outstanding eyewitness stories of the war from a beach on the Pacific island of Tarawa, the location of the most bloody of all American invasions.

GOOD NEWS FROM THE FRONT

The turning points in the battles against the Axis powers came in 1942 in the Pacific, Russia, and North Africa. Previously Americans had been treated to only gloomy news, except for General Jimmy Doolittle's surprise raid on Tokyo in early 1942. In May, American forces defeated a Japanese task force in the battle of the Coral Sea, checking the enemy's southward expansion near New Guinea and northern Australia. This was followed quickly by the major naval victory of the Pacific war—the smashing of the Japanese fleet and air forces at the battle of Midway in June.

Had Admiral Yamamoto's forces won, the Japanese would have been free to cut the lifeline between the United States and Australia, where General Douglas MacArthur's forces would have been isolated, to attack Hawaii, and eventually to launch raids on the American West Coast. But instead the Americans under Admiral Chester Nimitz, having cracked the secret Japanese code, were able to locate the oncoming Japanese carriers and destroy four of them, along with 332 planes. A series of fierce air battles decided the outcome, with Japanese planes caught on the deck refueling at a crucial moment. In August, Americans invaded Guadalcanal as a first step toward reclaiming the Japanese-conquered Philippines.

Despite this success in the Pacific, the news from Russia and Africa remained bad. Newsreels and news magazines showed dramatic pictures of German tanks under General Rommel sweeping toward Egypt. In Russia, Hitler's forces were poised outside of Stalingrad. Then the tide changed. The British, led by General Montgomery, stopped Rommel at El Alamein following massive tank battles in the African desert. The Americans invaded North Africa in November, joining the British and setting the stage for the invasion, the next year, of Sicily and Italy, which surrendered in September 1943.

The Russians held Stalingrad and encircled 300,000 Nazi troops in November 1942, taking the offensive for the rest of the war. By the start of 1944 the Allies held air superiority and were preparing for the invasion of Western Europe from England.

It is important to note that the United States did not really get involved in the fighting in Europe until the tide had shifted in the Allies' favor. The Russians had asked for a second, western front for two years, but the United States declined until 1944. This became a significant source of tension, and historians trace the beginning of the Cold War to this at least as much, if not more so, than to the dropping of the atomic bombs.[15]

THE PRESS ASSOCIATIONS FLASH NEWS
OF VICTORY AND FDR'S DEATH

Wes Gallagher of the Associated Press, who had covered every aspect of the European fighting, was fully prepared for the Allied invasion of France on June 6, 1944. He pounded out a 1700-word story, sweeping the play across the United States. This was his lead:

> **SUPREME HEADQUARTERS, ALLIED EXPEDITIONARY FORCE, June 6—American, British and Canadian troops landed in northern France this morning, launching the greatest overseas military operation in history with word from their supreme commander, Gen. Dwight D. Eisenhower, that "We will accept nothing except full victory" over the German masters of the continent.[16]**

As General Patton's Third Army stormed across the Rhine River on its way toward Berlin, and the Russians moved in from the east, Hitler's days were numbered. Meanwhile, in the Pacific, American forces triumphed in the Solomon Islands and New Guinea, and then moved into the Philippine Islands, where General MacArthur gained immense publicity by dramatically wading ashore. In early 1945 U.S. Marines were ready to assault yet another small Pacific island, Iwo Jima, the tiny strip of land memorialized by AP photographer Joe Rosenthal's photograph of six Marines planting the Stars and Stripes atop Mount Suribachi. The United Press bureau in San Francisco, receiving the communiqué from the Pacific military radio, flashed the news of the landing ahead of the AP. The lead of the first story read:

> **GUAM, Feb. 19 (U.P.)—American Marines, protected by a great sea and air bombardment, have invaded the eight-square-mile island of Iwo Jima. This amphibious assault carried the United States Pacific offensive within 750 miles of bomb-blasted Tokyo.**[17]

Victory was at hand—the only question was when the Germans and Japanese would finally quit.

President Roosevelt was serving his fourth term, after conducting an exhausting campaign against Thomas E. Dewey, which he won by the most narrow of his four margins: 54 percent of the popular vote. He had the editorial support of only 22 percent of those dailies endorsing candidates, compared to as much as 38 percent in 1932. It had been an increasingly bitter campaign, marked by Dewey's charges of Communist influence in America and Roosevelt's derisive speeches about GOP tactics. Seriously ill and preoccupied with postwar contingencies, Roosevelt went to his Warm Springs, Georgia, retreat for a two-week rest. It was there, on April 12, 1945, that he suffered a massive cerebral hemorrhage and died at age 63, having served as president longer than any other American.

In Washington the three press-association offices were not as busy as usual because the president was away. Arthur Hermann of the INS, Joe Myler of the UP, and Gardner Bridge of the AP all lifted their phones when notified by their switchboards of an urgent conference call coming through. The caller was Steve Early, Roosevelt's press secretary, who said, "I have a flash for you. The President died suddenly this afternoon. . . ." Hermann bellowed instinctively to his wire operator, "Flash! FDR Dead!" Thirty seconds later the UP followed with its flash, and the AP was right behind.[18] The news circuits were flooded within minutes and the shock hit around the world, particularly overseas, where American soldiers were told their commander-in-chief was gone.

In Warm Springs the UP's Merriman Smith, who 18 years later would win a Pulitzer Prize for his coverage of President John Kennedy's assassination, hurried to the cottage of the president's secretary, William Hassett. Harold Oliver of the AP and Bob Nixon of the INS were with him. As Hassett told them the sad news, they jumped for available phones and began dictating. This story appeared under Smith's byline:

> **WARM SPRINGS, (GA) April 12 (U.P.)—Franklin D. Roosevelt, president for 12 of the most momentous years in this country's history, died at 3:35 p.m. C.W.T. today in a small room in the "Little White House" here.**[19]

TRUMAN AND THE ATOMIC BOMB: THE COLD WAR BEGINS

Harry S Truman was sworn in as president less than three hours later, setting in motion the final drama of World War II: the decision to use the atomic bomb. The Germans surrendered to the Allies on May 7. Japan was being bombed unmercifully, but there was no sign of its surrender. American officials faced several choices. They could launch a massive invasion of the Japanese mainland or use the secret atomic weapon that had been developed during the war. Less well known is their third alternative: on July 2, 1945, Secretary of War Henry L. Stimson wrote a memo to Truman reporting that Japan might be close to surrender and stating that a carefully worded call to Japan to lay down its arms—including a promise that Emperor Hirohito could remain on his throne—might bring that surrender about. The Potsdam Ultimatum of July 26 followed Stimson's suggestions closely, with one important exception: it made no mention of the Japanese emperor. The democratization of Japan was a goal throughout the war, but there were strong differences of opinion within FDR's and Truman's administrations over how to achieve this, including whether the Emperor should remain.[20] Truman, under extraordinary pressure, made the decision to use the bomb.

On August 6, 1945, three giant Superforts took off from the island base of Tinian, rendezvoused over Iwo Jima, and sped toward Japan. The strike plane, the *Enola Gay,* approached Hiroshima, and at 9:15 A.M. a bomb with power equivalent to 20,000 tons of TNT slipped into the morning air. Sixty seconds later it exploded, opening the Atomic Age. In the city below several square miles disappeared. More than 60,000 people were killed. Correspondents on Tinian, unaware of the bombing, were told the planes were returning. They were overcome with feeling when told in the press hut that an incredible new weapon had been used. In Washington, President Truman was telling the world of the event, while other officials revealed details of the test that had been conducted in New Mexico several weeks earlier, on July 16.

Three days later William L. Laurence of the *New York Times* rode in one of the planes that flew to Nagasaki to drop the second atomic bomb. Within seconds there was a blinding flash brighter than the midday sun, and a massive cloud boiled 45,000 feet into the sky. Laurence, the only reporter to witness the New Mexico test, had been promised a "front-row" seat in return for secrecy about his knowledge of the Manhattan Project, which had developed the bomb. The *New York Times* of September 9 carried his eyewitness description, including these words:

> **. . . the pillar of purple fire had reached the level of our altitude. Only about forty-five seconds had passed. Awe-struck, we watched it shoot upward like a meteor coming in from the earth instead of from outer space, becoming more alive as it climbed skyward through the white clouds. It was no longer smoke, or dust, or even a cloud of fire. It was a living thing, a new species of being, born right before our incredulous eyes.[21]**

Laurence, a science expert who had won a Pulitzer Prize in 1937, won a second one for this article and a series of ten others that followed.

World War II officially ended September 2, 1945, when the Japanese signed surrender documents on the battleship *Missouri* in Tokyo Bay, with General MacArthur presiding. Wirephotos of that solemn ceremony filled front pages nationwide. But the joyous occasion was accompanied by doubts and fears about the intentions of the Russians. One reason for dropping the atomic bomb quickly was to end the war before the Russians had advanced too far into Asia. They already occupied all of Eastern Europe, and there were arguments over the control of Berlin. President Truman decided that Stalin could not be trusted, and an uneasy peace fell across the world.

Not only had the Cold War begun, but questions were soon raised about Roosevelt's agreements with Stalin at the Yalta conference in early 1945, when the future of Eastern Europe was discussed. The use of the atomic bomb frightened many, and the moral question was debated, particularly in intellectual magazines. A 1946 issue of the *New Yorker* carrying John Hersey's *Hiroshima* awakened many consciences. Postwar publication of fuller details of the Holocaust, the killing of six million Jews by the Nazis, raised queries as to how much Allied officials had known—and when—about the extent of the wholesale slaughter. These arguments have not yet been settled. Another rumor—spread by various books—was that Roosevelt knew that the Japanese fleet was headed for Pearl Harbor and that he let the tragedy occur. However, this was a complex issue. The historian John McKechney argues that Roosevelt, while most certainly doing nothing to provoke the Japanese attack or encourage it, did welcome the opportunity it provided for silencing isolationist sentiment. And Roberta A. Wohlstetter emphasizes the limits of intelligence operations at the time; the United States anticipated an attack, perhaps in the Philippines, but not at Pearl Harbor.[22] Thus did the postwar period begin, with the seeds of recrimination that would multiply in the next few years.

POSTWAR ADJUSTMENTS AT HOME AND ABROAD

President Truman moved the nation into the postwar period with a steady hand. Brisk and sober-minded, Truman provided a sharp contrast to the jovial, witty Roosevelt. He had his own brand of humor, directly related to the ordinary citizen. He earned the respect of Democratic party leaders and some of his Republican opponents with his bluntness and honesty; he spoke with rare candor. He also needed all of the support that he could get because he was faced with a series of labor disputes and foreign crises as he finished Roosevelt's term.

On the domestic front, Truman was challenged by the leader of the United Mine Workers, John L. Lewis, who ordered a strike of 400,000 coal miners in 1946, about the same time a railroad strike threatened to paralyze the transportation industry. Truman forced a settlement of the railroad dispute by seizing control of the lines, and he got Lewis to call his miners back to work. Accused of being antilabor in these actions, Truman attempted to take a middle course: he vetoed the Taft-Hartley Act of 1947, a Republican-sponsored law that tightened regulations governing strikes at companies engaged in interstate commerce. One of the most controversial provisions outlawed the closed shop and set up election procedures for union shops. Amidst a great furor, Congress passed the law over Truman's veto. Over time the president was seen as a champion of workers but a foe of anyone whom he suspected of acting against the public interest.

While he battled the Congress and tried to push for his Fair Deal—a series of laws dealing with employment practices, social-security benefits, public housing, price and rent controls, and other social actions stemming from the New Deal days—Truman was forced to cope with increasing pressure from the Russians. In May of 1946 a strong protest from the United States had forced the Soviets to remove troops from Iran, where they attempted to detach one province and threatened to swallow the entire country.

The fear of international Communism, coupled with the disclosure of Soviet spy activity in the United States and the relentless attacks of the House Un-American Activities Committee (HUAC), filled the nation's press and airwaves with charges and countercharges. Fear replaced logic, as it had in the "Red Scare" of 1918 to 1920.

Winston Churchill, who had maintained the traditional British opposition to the Soviet Union throughout the war, traveled to the United States in 1946. Appearing with Truman in Fulton, Missouri, he coined the phrase "Iron Curtain," saying "From Stettin in the Baltic to Trieste in the Adriatic an iron curtain has descended across the Continent." The Cold War rhetoric increased in intensity. In later years historians criticized Truman and other Allied leaders for not presenting a more compromising program to the Soviets but instead triggering their fears that a hostile Anglo-American alliance was being set up to thwart their natural interests, as it had been following World War I.

On the other hand, the Soviet occupation of Eastern Europe, arguments over the reunification of Germany, and a generally belligerent Russian attitude did little to reassure Americans about Stalin's motives. Truman feared Communist expansion into southern Europe, and acted quickly in 1947 to promise economic aid to Greece and Turkey. These acts were part of the Truman Doctrine—the beginning of America's "containment policy." This included the Marshall Plan for the redevelopment of Western Europe in 1947, the air-lifting of supplies to break a Soviet blockade of Berlin in 1948, the Point Four Program for underdeveloped nations in 1949, and the creation of the North Atlantic Treaty Organization (NATO), also in 1949. These constituted a mixture of humanitarian and military programs, meshing together as elements of the Cold War. Another factor was the difficulty of reporting anything that conflicted with the anti-Communist crusade. The first postwar press martyr was George Polk, chief Middle East correspondent for CBS, who was murdered in May 1948 because of his criticism of the Greek government and his refusal to take its side against Communist guerrillas involved in a civil war. The truth about his death was covered up for years by Greek, U.S., and British officials.

Europe was made secure against the perceived Communist threat there, but the president and his advisers could do little about the spread of Communism in Asia. Despite sizable American assistance, the Nationalist forces of warlord Chiang Kai-shek were losing the struggle with the People's Liberation Army under Mao Tse-tung. The Truman administration sent General George C. Marshall on a futile mission to attempt a coalition of the Nationalist and Communist regimes in the wake of a disastrous effort by the nearly senile American ambassador, General Patrick Hurley, to have Chiang and Mao meet. Hurley resigned, and blamed the State Department China experts and embassy staff for losing China, a theme picked up in the McCarthy era by the entire right wing of American thought. China scholars in American universities and American journalists in China were likewise harassed when they objectively forecast the impending victory of Mao's Marxist forces over Chiang's Kuomintang party. The Luce publications, the Scripps Howard newspapers, and others built up Chiang's reputation, despite well-documented evidence of his regime's corruptness and unpopularity with the Chinese people. In the Cold War atmosphere, American public opinion dismissed Mao, Chou En-lai, and other new Chinese statesmen as "Red bandits" who had hoodwinked the correspondents. The leading authority on the press corps in China summed up his findings: "If Americans had a persuading encounter with Chinese Communists, they had a repelling encounter with Chinese Nationalists." He added that Western correspondents in China viewed the Kuomintang as "rotten to the core" and "an old-fashioned dictatorship, feudal, decadent, and probably beyond repair."[23]

THE "CHINA WATCHERS" EMERGE

Edgar Snow, whose 1938 book *Red Star over China* introduced Mao to the outside world, came to China in 1928 as a protégé of Thomas F. Millard, a controversial journalist who turned propagandist during his three pioneering decades in China, 1900 to 1929. Millard, founder of the *China Press* in 1911 and the *China Weekly Review* in 1917, was appointed the first *New York Times* correspondent in China in 1925. A University of Missouri journalism graduate, he welcomed a flow of that school's students to internships and then to regular media posts, where they joined such noted correspondents as Demaree Bess of the

Philadelphia Public Ledger, Hallett Abend of the *New York Times,* and John B. Powell, who edited the *China Weekly Review* in the extraterritorial safety of Shanghai.[24]

Snow worked for Powell's liberal paper, freelanced, and lectured in journalism at Yenching University in Peking (now Beijing University). In 1936 he made a hazardous trip to the isolated Shensi province headquarters of Mao and the Chinese Communist army units who had survived a 6000-mile "Long March," ending in their wartime stronghold of Yenan. Snow spent four months with the Communists, came back famous, and was named chief Far East correspondent for the *London Daily Herald.* He sold 75 photos to *Life,* wrote for the *Saturday Evening Post,* and published *Red Star over China,* in which he interpreted Mao and his political philosophy.

Snow's wife, Helen Foster Snow, eluded the Kuomintang and reached Yenan in 1937 to gather material for her book, *Inside Red China.* There she found another woman journalist in the Mao circle. She was Agnes Smedley, embittered daughter of a Colorado mining family with only a grade-school education. Smedley arrived in China in 1928 as correspondent for the *Frankfurter Zeitung.* As the only Western journalist with Communist party contacts before 1936, Smedley served other correspondents as go-between. She wrote the biography of General Chu Teh of "Long March" fame, lived in one of Yenan's caves, and helped with food and medicine. She became the *Manchester Guardian* correspondent from 1938 to 1940, and wrote *Battle Hymn of China* in 1943.

Anna Louise Strong, in contrast, was a college graduate and a minister's daughter. She traveled in China and the Soviet Union in the 1920s and 1930s as author and journalist. It was to her in Yenan that Mao addressed his words, "All reactionaries are paper tigers." The site of the interview is now a historical monument; reporting the phrase made Strong famous. She lived in China in her later years. Snow, Smedley, and Strong were memorialized in the 1980s in China by the founding of the 3-S Society.

In the wartime press corps at the Kuomintang capital of Chungking was Annalee Jacoby of *Time,* who had escaped in 1942 with her correspondent husband Mel from the Philippines to Australia, where he died in a plane crash. Among others active there were Theodore White of *Time, Life* photographer Carl Mydans, Tillman Durdin of the *New York Times,* A. T. Steele of the *Chicago Daily News,* Vincent Sheean of the *New York Herald Tribune,* Albert Ravenholt of the UP, Jack Belden of the INS, and Snow. Israel Epstein, UP correspondent in the 1930s, represented the *New York Times* when six correspondents made a breakthrough trip to Yenan in 1944.[25]

The harassment of the China correspondents began as the war ended. When Theodore White and Annalee Jacoby published *Thunder out of China* in 1946, reporting Mao's strength and the Chinese desire for change, they found themselves denounced by conservative U.S. newspapers and politicians. They later testified along with John Hersey that their copy was grossly altered by *Time's* anti-Communist foreign news editor, Whittaker Chambers, with Henry Luce's support.[26] Snow fled the U.S. for Switzerland as the McCarthy-era persecution intensified. John W. (Bill) and Sylvia Powell of the *China Weekly Review* were charged in the United States in 1953 with sedition for publishing the names of American prisoners taken by the Chinese in the Korean War; so was writer Julian Schuman, who had covered the 1949 fall of Shanghai for ABC. They won dismissal after seven years of charges and trials. In the 1980s Schuman became sports editor of the English-language *China Daily* in Beijing. Epstein, who had been brought to China from Poland at the age of two, founded what had become by the 1980s, under his editorship, the glossy, multilanguage magazine *China Reconstructs.*

When Mao's army entered the Chinese capital in 1949 and Chiang fled to Formosa (later called Taiwan), American diplomatic and journalistic ties with the new People's

Republic of China ceased. Snow, who left in 1949, returned in 1960 to Beijing, where for a decade he was the only American correspondent. In 1970 he was saluted alongside Mao at Tienanmen Square. He died just before President Richard Nixon arrived in China, an event foreshadowing the rehabilitation of the China diplomats, scholars, and correspondents of the 1940s.

But in 1949 these Chinese supporters suffered the wrath of those who felt the United States's postwar role was to be the world's policeman. The right wing's anger was only increased by the news that the nationalist-Marxist forces of Ho Chi Minh in Indochina were slowly winning their war against the American-supported French army. Truman was ardently anti-Communist—as demonstrated by his tough actions in Europe—and he gave American aid during these Asian civil wars, but he argued strongly against all-out intervention.

NEW YORK DAILIES REACH THEIR PEAK

The flourishing of newspapers in the immediate postwar years is best illustrated in New York, where the nine major dailies boasted a daily circulation of slightly more than 6 million, nearly double the 1987 total for the four major dailies. Every Sunday readers bought 10.1 million copies of the six available newspapers, including 4.7 million copies of the *Daily News*, which reached its all time circulation peak in 1947, selling 2.4 million copies of its daily morning edition.

Hearst's *Journal-American* sold nearly 1.3 million copies on Sunday and about 700,000 every evening, and his *Mirror* topped that, with 2.2 million in Sunday sales and slightly more than 1 million on weekday mornings. The *Times* had reached the 1 million mark in Sunday sales the previous year and had morning sales of about 545,000. The *Herald Tribune* sold 680,000 copies on Sunday and 320,000 each morning. Another 300,000 persons bought the Sunday edition of *PM,* which was nearing the end of its publishing life as a daily journal of opinion and interpretation.

The Hearst and McCormick-Patterson companies greatly outsold their more moderate rivals, the *Times* and the *Herald Tribune,* at the time that President Truman and the Democrats began to look ahead to the 1948 campaign.

TRUMAN'S ELECTION: THE MIRACLE OF 1948

Facing an election in 1948, Truman was not given much of a chance of continuing in office. Southern Democrats, led by Strom Thurmond of South Carolina, bolted from the party and founded the Dixiecrats. The loss of the Democratic party's traditional hold on the "Solid South" was compounded when former Vice President Henry Wallace challenged Truman under the banner of the Progressives and stole some liberal support. Sensing an easy victory, Republicans nominated the popular governor of New York, Thomas E. Dewey, who had lost to Roosevelt in 1944.

Throughout the summer the nation's leading editorial writers and political columnists described Dewey's strength and Truman's inability to forge a winning coalition. Walter Lippmann, Drew Pearson, Joseph and Stewart Alsop, Marquis Childs, and others wrote of the coming disaster to the Democratic party. But that fall the determined president retaliated by taking his case to the people in the most dramatic "whistlestop" campaign of the twentieth century. In town after town Truman pulled no punches, attacking the Republican Congress and relating to problems in that particular locality. Republicans pounded away on the issue of "Communist subversion." But as the campaign drew to a close, Truman's crowds grew in size and enthusiasm. Although this was noted by some of the traveling reporters, others dismissed the change in atmosphere. By November 1 Truman had caught Dewey, but the Gallup Poll, as reported that morning by the *Washington Post,* predicted Dewey's win: "Gallup Gives Dewey 49.5%, Truman 44.5% of Popular Vote."[27] The November 1 *Life* magazine included a photo of Dewey, with the caption: "The next President travels by ferry boat over the broad waters of San Francisco Bay."[28]

An early edition of the *Chicago Tribune* was handed to Truman when the White House-bound presidential train reached St. Louis on November 3, the day after the election. The unforgettable headline blared, "Dewey Defeats Truman," and the *Tribune* never lived it down. During the previous evening NBC commentator Hans Von Kaltenborn had been telling his listeners that the early Truman lead in popular vote could not hold up. But it did, providing an enormous excitement over Truman's achievements. The *Washington Post* of November 4 paid Truman the ultimate tribute, running on page one a copy of a telegram the paper had sent inviting him to a "crow banquet" to which "this newspaper proposes to invite newspaper editorial writers, political reporters and editors, including our own, along with pollsters, radio commentators and columnists for the purpose of providing

Prime evidence of Republican overconfidence—one of the most quoted headlines in history

a repast appropriate to the appetite created by the late elections."[29] Truman not only upset Dewey; he carried a Democratic Congress into office with him, despite having the support of only 15 percent of the dailies endorsing a candidate that year.

Still, the real majority was a coalition of Republicans and Southern Democrats—and the Republican campaign of fear was hardly conquered. In fact, McCarthyism and the Red Scare flourished after Truman's reelection, serving partisan political purposes. Historians point out that "McCarthy served some conservative Republicans as a blunt instrument they used to damage the Democrats." William L. O'Neill even contends that if a Republican had been elected in 1948, the Red Scare would have been blunted considerably.[30]

TRUMAN AND THE PRESS CONFERENCE

The relationship of the president and the news media underwent drastic changes during Truman's nearly eight years in office. The Truman style, the complexity of events after World War II, and the growth of the news-gathering apparatus—particularly broadcasting—during and after the war contributed to the metamorphosis.

Although Truman and the newspeople around him enjoyed a cordial personal relationship—they generally liked each other—professionally, they remained sharp adversaries throughout his 93 months in office. As president, he held 324 news conferences, averaging 3 to 4 a month. This was half of Roosevelt's annual total, but nearly twice as many as any of his successors. The president's abrupt and sometimes unpredictable comments at these sessions often appeared strangely contradictory to a period dominated by the realities of atomic energy and Cold War politics.

If reporters relished the Truman news conferences for the possibility of an unexpected and sensational utterance, they also came to realize that the structure of the conferences was changing to give the administration more control over them. Truman began meeting with press secretary Charles G. Ross and others of his staff for preconference briefings, and greatly increased the use of carefully prepared opening statements to which he would refer a questioning reporter when he chose not to elaborate on a matter.

In the spring of 1950, the location of presidential news conferences was moved from the intimate atmosphere of the Oval Room of the White House to a 230-seat room in the Executive Office Building. Though the change was brought about because of the growth in the number of Washington correspondents, its effect was to formalize the presidential press conference further. The move also ushered in the use of microphones and, by 1951, the need for presidential authorization to broadcast excerpts of recordings on news programs. As news conferences thereby became increasingly public during the Truman years, the president was obliged to exercise greater control over them, to come to them better prepared, and to respond during them with greater care. Truman's tendency to speak his mind, or to "shoot from the hip" as some critics termed it, was not obscured entirely by the new overlay of safeguards. Salty, sometimes embarrassing slips continued despite preparation to prevent them. But the groundwork of control was laid for his successors.

Apart from the news conference, another effort to control information created a furor among publishers and correspondents during the Korean War. Convinced that magazines and newspapers were guilty of leaking most of America's military secrets, Truman ordered all government agencies handling military information to classify it at their discretion and to restrict its use by the media. Despite a wave of criticism, the order stood.

Truman responded to harsh and continuing criticism of himself and his administration by the news media with strong denunciations of the media. After his stunning election in 1948 the president lashed out at "the kept press and the paid radio." He attacked what he called the "confusion of fact with mere speculation by which readers and listeners were undoubtedly misguided and intentionally deceived."

Only when he prepared to leave office in January 1953 did some media opponents relent. Some even saluted him affectionately. It was an unexpected pleasure for the retiring Truman, who later recalled that "some editors ate crow and left the feathers on."[31]

THE WAR IN KOREA, 1950 TO 1953

The news of the Communist North Korean attack on the Republic of South Korea on June 25, 1950, was first flashed to the world by Jack James of the UP. Headed for a Sunday morning picnic, James stumbled onto the invasion story at the U.S. embassy in Seoul and after confirming it got off his bulletin, which beat the ambassador's cable to Washington by 20 minutes.

Korea had been divided at the thirty-eighth parallel for occupation purposes in 1945. Russian troops left North Korea after the establishment of a Communist government there in 1948, and the Americans left South Korea, save for a small advisory force, early in 1949. No one expected an attack in Korea; State Department representative John Foster Dulles had been in Seoul a week before and had left reassured of the area's stability. The bad news that James and others sent by wireless brought a decision by Secretary of State Dean Acheson and President Truman to seek a United Nations armed intervention, which was voted by the Security Council on June 28 after Truman had ordered General Douglas MacArthur to force the North Koreans back.

Walter Simmons of the *Chicago Tribune,* who had traveled to Seoul with Dulles, stayed on and filed the first action story by a newspaper correspondent. The press associations rushed in Peter Kalischer and Rutherford Poats of the UP; O. H. P. King and photographer Charles P. Gorry of the AP; and Ray Richards of the INS. Richards was the first to fly over the battle area; caught with a lost battalion at Chonan, he was killed ten days after his arrival. Eleven American correspondents were killed before the war was over, among a total of 18 from all nations.[32]

Two of the toughest and most outspoken stars of the Korean news brigade flew to Seoul on June 27 from Tokyo under fighter escort. They were Marguerite Higgins of the *New York Herald Tribune* and Keyes Beech of the *Chicago Daily News.*[33] Landing with them at Kimpo airfield were Burton Crane of the *New York Times* and Frank Gibney of *Time.* They were routed from the city during the night as Seoul fell; the men missed death by 25 yards at the River Han, and Higgins flew back to Tokyo to file her story. She returned on June 29 with General MacArthur on his first visit to the front and got an exclusive interview on the return trip. The next day she, Beech, Tom Lambert of the AP, and Gordon Walker of the *Christian Science Monitor* were at the fall of Suwon airfield. With Carl Mydans of *Life* and the bureau chief of Reuters, Ray McCartney, Higgins saw the first U.S. soldier killed in action July 5. David Douglas Duncan of *Life* was taking the first of his great Korean war photographs, and *Life*'s July 10 issue brought the war home to a country not yet linked by television.

The South Koreans and their American reinforcements were being forced back on the beachhead port of Pusan. Its outer defense, Taejon, fell in late July, and General William P. Dean was captured. By now many more reporters were risking their lives in the foxholes, rice paddies, and back roads. The *Herald Tribune* sent Homer Bigart to relieve Higgins, but she refused to leave Korea and engaged in a give-and-take duel with Bigart for front-page play. Edward R. Murrow came to tie CBS coverage together; broadcast coverage was essentially by radio, with film being shot for television and newsreels.[34]

The Korean War opens for U.S. troops; Marguerite Higgins and Homer Bigart
report

Instead of being driven off the Korean beachhead, MacArthur mounted a brilliant
amphibious landing with troops from Japan at Inchon on September 15, and he recaptured
Seoul on September 26, thus cutting off the North Koreans to the south. One of the correspondents present was Jim Lucas, the chronicler of Tarawa, now reporting for Scripps
Howard. Lucas was to win a 1954 Pulitzer Prize for his stories of "Porkchop Hill" during
the long stalemate.

MACARTHUR AND THE PRESS: CENSORSHIP IMPOSED

General MacArthur, as the United Nations commander in Korea, at first left correspondents to
their own devices, refusing to institute the field censorship that had prevailed during both
World Wars I and II. In the confused situation of the first months of the fighting, the traditional-

minded "team member" reporters found themselves on their own in the thick of battle. Ironically, they also found themselves subject to harsh criticism from MacArthur's staff for stories filed without receiving minimum military assistance. Lambert of the AP and Kalischer of the UP temporarily lost their accreditations on charges of giving aid and comfort to the enemy. Relations between Colonel Marion P. Echols, MacArthur's press officer, and the correspondents became even more strained than they had been during the years of the occupation of Japan, when dissenting reporters had found their accreditations endangered.

The September 1950 victories following MacArthur's Inchon landing brought an easing of the correspondents' problems. Their interviews with critical and despondent soldiers, which had aroused MacArthur's ire earlier in the summer, were at an end. Nearly 300 correspondents from 19 countries were reporting the controversial advance of United Nations troops toward the Yalu. Then came the entry of the Chinese Communist army into the war and a disastrous retreat of the UN's units, best pictured by *Life*'s Duncan, with the Marines at Chosin reservoir. Seoul fell to the Chinese in January but was regained two months later as the UN forces stabilized a line near the thirty-eighth parallel. Keyes Beech had reported that at the height of the retreat panic MacArthur had recommended withdrawal from Korea, and other correspondents had criticized MacArthur's tactics in splitting the commands of his forces in northern Korea. The general's answer was the institution of a full and formal censorship, which he claimed had been recommended by the country's top newspaper executives.[35]

The stringent regulations imposed in January 1951 went further, however, than any reporters would have desired.[36] These regulations covered not only censorship of military information but also all statements that would injure the morale of UN forces or that would embarrass the United States, its allies, or neutral countries. Correspondents complained that the censors interpreted the use of the word *retreat* as being embarrassing, and they contended that MacArthur had brought about a political and psychological censorship as well as a military one. The most dangerous provision of the new censorship was one making correspondents subject to trial by court martial for serious violations of the rules.

TRUMAN FIRES MACARTHUR: A PRESIDENTIAL CRISIS

President Truman and his commander in the field were at odds throughout the war. MacArthur had received high marks for his handling of Japan's postwar problems—and in fact he was later called the "father of modern Japan" because of his keen understanding of sensitive issues—but he was also giving the impression that he intended to make American foreign policy. In July 1950, his visit to Formosa was seen at home as a new step in United States–Nationalist China relations, despite State Department and White House misgivings about Chiang Kai-shek. The general also ignored Pentagon and White House instructions on the issue of public statements, particularly after disagreements arose on how to conduct the war.

Of concern in Washington was MacArthur's desire to use Chiang's troops against mainland China. In this plan he was supported by Senator Robert A. Taft of Ohio and other Republican conservatives who had been sniping at Truman for "losing China to the Communists." Civilian control of the military was at stake. Truman and MacArthur met on Wake Island in October 1950 and appeared to reach some sort of understanding, but MacArthur persisted in pushing his ideas through friendly members of Congress. This greatly irritated Truman, who became enraged on April 5, 1951, when Joseph Martin, the House minority leader, released a letter from MacArthur in which the general complained about White House restrictions on his battle plans. One of his ideas was to use Allied planes to bomb across the Yalu River, the dividing line between North Korea and Chinese-held Manchuria. The use of the atomic bomb against the Chinese was fully contemplated and was encouraged by MacArthur's supporters.

The *New York Times* reported MacArthur's plans for a second front and greatly expanded war: "M'Arthur Wants Chiang Army Used on China Mainland."[37] This was followed by a week of intense controversy in American and European newspapers. Senator Joseph McCarthy of Wisconsin called it "high treason" to refuse MacArthur permission to use Chiang's troops. Others protested MacArthur's disdain of Truman and the United Nations, under whose command he was to serve. Then on April 11 Truman acted, removing MacArthur from all responsibility.

"Impeach Truman," cried the *Chicago Tribune* in a page-one editorial. "President Truman must be impeached and convicted. His hasty and vindictive removal of Gen. MacArthur is the culmination of a series of acts which have shown he is unfit, morally and mentally, for the office."[38] Truman defended his decision in a nationwide broadcast in which he said that MacArthur's actions had threatened a general war—in effect, World War III. The *New York Times, St. Louis Post-Dispatch,* and a number of other major newspapers fully supported Truman, while the Gallup Poll showed that nearly 70 percent of the people were caught up in the enthusiasm for MacArthur. Millions watched MacArthur's speech to a joint session of Congress and showered him with affection during ticker-tape parades in major cities, beginning in San Francisco. Paying tribute to a military hero of gigantic proportions, the crowds were giving belated thanks for MacArthur's World War II service as much as certifying his Korean record.

A new offensive in Korea and the passing of time took the edge off the story, however, and the general soon passed into private life. As he had told Congress, ". . . old generals never die, they just fade away." Seen in a different light, years later, Truman's action appeared vindicated because of MacArthur's reckless handling of his forces when Communist China entered the war in October 1950 and his deliberate attempts to disobey orders. In addition to the conventional criticism of MacArthur's attitude and handling of his command, alternative journalists I. F. Stone and James Aronson added their interpretations. In *The Hidden History of the Korean War,* written in 1952, Stone offered evidence that MacArthur had forced the Chinese into combat by probing dangerously close to the Yalu River, thus ignoring a buffer zone, a point that has been supported by more recent scholarship.[39] He also strongly suggested that American fears of a Communist Chinese presence in the United Nations ruined chances for an early armistice, despite Russian attempts to bring the fighting to a halt.[40]

A TRUCE IN KOREA

The removal of MacArthur for insubordination brought an easing of censorship, although his chief intelligence officer, Major General C. A. Willoughby, continued to attack such respected reporters as Hal Boyle, Hanson W. Baldwin, Homer Bigart, and Joseph Alsop as "inaccurate, biased, and petulant." When truce negotiations began in Korea in July 1951, the United Nations Command insisted that reporters be permitted to cover the truce site. Reporting of the war during the prolonged negotiations became a routine affair, punctuated by excitement over the status of prisoners of war. The Defense Department issued new field-censorship instructions in December 1952, which transferred censorship duties from intelligence officers to public-relations officers, and put the Army, Navy, and

Air Force under a uniform plan. Censorship for reasons other than those involving security was forbidden, but as usual the disagreement between newspeople and censors about a definition of "security" continued.

The signing of a truce at Panmunjom in July 1953 brought an end to the fighting phase of the Korean War. The repatriated prisoners, whose fate had been such an issue, reappeared at the "Bridge of No Return." In the 1990s the UN Command, through U.S. troops, still stood guard at Panmunjom. No peace had yet been signed. The war cost 33,629 United States dead, 1263 other UN–allied dead, some 2 million Korean casualties, and several hundred thousand Chinese losses. The principle involved, that the will of the United Nations could not be openly flouted, had been defended. But one view held that it had been defended by the first recapture of Seoul and that MacArthur's advance to the Yalu River boundary of Communist China had changed the character of the war and had polarized Chinese-American relations for two decades.

The Korean fighting soon merged in the minds of Americans with other events, but future generations would learn of the tragedy, irony, and humor of those days through the television show *M*A*S*H,* which used the Korean experience to focus on the United States' war in Vietnam. The partisanship of those in the field who were questioning the purpose of the war and who were commenting about the sides people were taking at home applied to both wars and became a part of television history. And, as William L. O'Neill has noted, the stalemate in Korea badly damaged American morale at home, thus removing the lid from defense spending and invigorating the arms race. For Koreans the legacy of the war was a series of repressive governments—strongly supported by the United States—who used the belligerent North Korean regime as an excuse to unleash brutal force against those seeking basic reforms. About 40,000 U.S. troops remained in Korea nearly 40 years after the signing of the truce.

An RCA television assembly line, 1950

16

Television Takes
Center Stage

> It is much easier to report a battle or a bombing than it is to do an
> honest and intelligible job on the Marshall Plan, the Taft-Hartley
> Law or the Atlantic Pact.
>
> —*Edward R. Murrow*

The decade of the 1950s is best remembered for Lucille Ball, Ed Sullivan, and Edward R. Murrow on television, Dwight Eisenhower, Adlai Stevenson, and Joseph McCarthy in politics, the New York Yankees, Elvis Presley, Madison Avenue, hula hoops, drive-in movies, suburban tract homes, interstate highways, and jet airplanes. Later portrayed in the television show *Happy Days* and the motion picture *American Graffiti* as a tranquil, rather uneventful time, the period was actually filled with moments of grave consequence for Americans, as the nation moved toward the explosions of the 1960s and early 1970s.

In the postwar years the nation entered into the longest period of prosperity in its history. Consumer and business spending, coupled with government spending (including for the GI Bill), fueled a postwar economic boom. Still, America struggled with several problems of postwar adjustment, including labor strife, a sometimes faltering economy that raised fears that the hard times of the 1930s could return, and a housing shortage. (The latter was met with a housing construction boom that led to the suburbanization of America and ultimately a whole other set of challenges).[1]

And all along, seeds were being sown for future confrontations. The "containment policy" of Truman became the "brinkmanship policy" of Eisenhower and his secretary of state, John Foster Dulles. A decision was made to ignore the victory of Communist guerrillas in Indochina and to assume the French role there by aiding a weak government in Saigon. This fear of international Communism and internal subversion turned neighbor against neighbor as Senator McCarthy, Richard Nixon, and others skillfully exploited the situation.

Long-suffering blacks in Montgomery boycotted the local bus company, and a dispute over the integration of a Little Rock high school became a nationwide controversy. Martin Luther King, Jr.'s name appeared in the *New York Times* for the first time. A Supreme Court ruling that the "separate but equal" doctrine for the nation's schools was unconstitutional gave blacks hope that other doors would soon be opened.

Little was said about damage to the environment, abuses by law-enforcement officials, or the need for greater consumer protection, except in alternative publications or in an occasional news story or broadcast documentary. Yet those problems existed while the powerful business and industrial community consolidated its hold on the nation's political, economic, and social life during the 1950s.

Instead, the entertainment media—television, radio, movies, magazines, books— aimed to treat the American viewer and reader in an unprecedented way. "See the USA, in a Chevrolet, America's the greatest land of all," crooned Dinah Shore. Such messages struck a common nerve. Americans were ready for fun and excitement after a number of tough years. They were upset that the Korean War had broken out. The Russians and Chinese ruled a good share of the globe, Communist spies had stolen atomic secrets, and the good life was still around the corner. But this was their chance to strive for the American dream, as presented to them daily through mass-media advertising and certified by public relations.

Newspapers, the press associations, news magazines, and radio and television news departments also began to change, faced with the task of interpreting the meaning of those days, when the simplicity of American life began to get confusingly complex.

TELEVISION SHAPES THE 1952 CAMPAIGN

Television became the dominant force in the American political process during the 1952 presidential campaign between General of the Army Dwight D. Eisenhower, the candidate of a frustrated Republican party, and Illinois governor Adlai E. Stevenson, the choice of Democratic leaders hoping for another four years of power. For the first time the public was exposed to commercials, documentaries, and election-night specials, all planned by political consultants and paid for by campaign boosters. The excitement began with Eisenhower's televised announcement that he would challenge Senator Robert A. Taft for his party's nomination, and grew as the conventions of the summer of 1952 drew near.[2]

The audience not only recognized the familiar faces of political heroes but also saw new heroes created. The manipulations of rival groups were clear to all, particularly during the Republican convention when Eisenhower forces—pleading for "fair play"— broke Taft's hold on the convention by challenging the accreditation of delegates from several states. Another high point came when Everett Dirksen of Illinois, a candidate for a Senate seat, pointed at Thomas E. Dewey and cried, "We followed you before and you took us down the path to defeat."[3]

The mistake of Taft managers in banning television cameras from credentials hearings gave Eisenhower forces more ammunition for their appeal to the delegates for fairness. The home audience was given the impression that Taft was associated with backroom politics, while "Ike" was above such shady dealings. Actually both men had reasonable claims to the disputed delegates. Finally Eisenhower floor managers convinced delegates to defeat a Taft-sponsored amendment dealing with the credentials fight. The momentum switched to Eisenhower, who came within a few votes of victory at the end of the first ballot. Television cameras picked up the waving Minnesota standard and the official switch of that state's votes, which gave Eisenhower the nomination.

Appearing on television screens during the bitterly contested fight had been Senator Joseph McCarthy of Wisconsin, who scornfully referred to Secretary of State Dean Acheson as "the Red Dean" and Democrats in general as "Commie loving." Richard Nixon, selected by Eisenhower to be his running mate, joined in the denunciation of the "whining, whimpering, groveling" Democrats, as did John Foster Dulles. During lulls a young actress named Betty Furness became famous by opening and shutting the doors of Westinghouse refrigerators for the estimated 50 million persons who tuned in for at least one of the sessions.

When the Democrats met to find a replacement for President Truman, who had decided not to run again, they settled on Stevenson and Senator John Sparkman of Alabama, a credible southern leader but one lacking the flair of the 1956 Stevenson running mate, Senator Estes Kefauver of Tennessee, who gained fame from televised crime probes and Davy Crockett coonskin caps. Stevenson began the campaign with a remarkable speech, saying that the nation was "on the eve of great decisions" and reminding Americans that they lived "in an hour of history haunted with those gaunt, grim specters of strife, dissension, and materialism at home, and ruthless, inscrutable, and hostile power abroad."

As the campaign developed, television gave the public a chance to learn about the liberal, idealistic Stevenson, the articulate and witty public servant who built a cadre of devoted followers from the progressive wing of the Democratic party. While listening to his polished speeches, they also saw his flaws, however, and many of them came to agree with the disparaging comment made by columnist Stewart Alsop and popularized by others that Stevenson was an "egghead." Republicans used this in their anti-Communist crusade, implying that the intellectuals had "lost China" and "sold out" Eastern Europe.

While Stevenson was presenting himself as a gentleman and a scholar as well as a man of high integrity, Eisenhower's advertising experts took advantage of his sweeping arm waves to crowds and his infectious hearty grin to portray him as a strong leader, a "man of peace." Whereas Eisenhower's 30-minute television shows contained several minutes of opening and closing scenes, Stevenson often had problems fitting his speeches into the half-hour format, and audiences saw him still speaking as the shows were cut off the air.

The campaign intensified in September when the Republicans used the slogan "Communism, Corruption, and Korea" to refer to the Roosevelt-Truman years. Nixon, who had become famous during his investigation of the discredited State Department official Alger Hiss, used the name of the convicted perjurer to link Stevenson unfairly to the stealing of secret documents by Russian agents. Newspapers, greatly favoring Eisenhower—only 14.5 percent endorsed Stevenson—freely carried this kind of charge, later causing Stevenson to issue a complaint against a "one-party press in a two-party country."

Finally it was Nixon himself in the glare of unfavorable publicity. The *New York Post* broke the story that Nixon's supporters had maintained a "secret slush fund" to help defray campaign expenses. Pressure grew for Nixon to explain the situation in full and for Eisenhower to drop the Californian from the campaign, which had been built on the image of high-level integrity. The Republican National Committee arranged for a nationwide hookup of 64 NBC television stations, 194 CBS radio stations, and the Mutual Radio Network, then 560 stations. Speaking with great emotion from a Los Angeles studio, Nixon won back Eisenhower's confidence and that of many Republican voters by offering precise details of his personal expenses, and by referring to his wife Pat's cloth coat and his daughters' dog Checkers. The speech became known in broadcast history as the "Checkers speech."[4]

Eisenhower's smashing victory in November ended 20 years of Democratic rule. He had made a pledge during the campaign to "go to Korea," and that December he visited the troops there, with television cameras recording his every move.

EISENHOWER AND THE PRESS

President Eisenhower was not comfortable with television, nor was he able to relax much with reporters. Like other presidents, he had his favorites, but overall he was a private man more familiar with the military life than with the public requirements of his new office. Because of this, he depended on the services of a talented press secretary, James C. Hagerty, who held the post for Eisenhower's two terms and who was tauntingly called by some of the newspeople he bested in professional duels "the best Republican president who was never elected." This was unfair to Hagerty, who prided himself on knowing how best to use the press to serve his boss. Eisenhower, in turn, maintained a presidential reserve and dignity in his relations with others, even though they called him Ike.

Eisenhower continued the large, formal news conferences that had begun with Truman, having 250 correspondents at his first session and 309 at his final one, eight years and 190 press conferences later. He permitted direct quotations and taping for later television release, new gains for the press corps. Hagerty, however, had to check the material. Eisenhower made many slips of the tongue, thought faster than he talked, and skipped parts of sentences so that press-conference transcripts had to be reworded to be intelligible. A penetrating personal question might bring a display of the famed Eisenhower controlled anger. But generally he was not too concerned with the press. He told one conference that he went over the important sections of the Sunday papers that re-

(UPI)

President Eisenhower and James Hagerty

viewed world events and studied them carefully—"but the kind of things you talk of, cartoons and unfriendly quips, I just can't be bothered with."[5] The President had a few bad
incidents: Hagerty was mobbed by left-wing demonstrators at the Tokyo airport, forcing
cancellation of a presidential visit, and the U-2 spy-plane controversy in 1960 brought
about a debacle at the Paris summit conference.

It was the U-2 spy-plane incident that triggered the start of what journalists later
called "the credibility gap" between the White House, the press, and the public. When
pilot Gary Powers was shot down over Russia, the American government issued a statement that he had been flying a weather-surveillance plane that had accidentally strayed
off course. But when the Russians produced Powers, a confessed CIA agent, an embarrassed Eisenhower was forced to admit that his administration had lied. The public shock
was reflected in the nation's news media. It was one thing to conduct secret operations; it
certainly was another thing to lie about it. And Eisenhower, of all persons, was held to be
above such conduct. During the next two decades the credibility gap widened considerably, and historians pointed to the U-2 story as one glaring starting point for the unfortunate turn of events.

As the first president to travel extensively by jet plane, Eisenhower produced some
exciting television coverage of overseas trips. Robert J. Donovan of the *New York Herald
Tribune* speculated that the "arrival of the jets . . . changed the presidency more than people realized. There was Eisenhower's great trip to India in 1959—which I covered and
which I think was the great spectacle of my life."[6]

In recent years historians have considerably revised their estimation of Eisenhower,
especially after scrutinizing his papers, which reveal a president of underestimated intelligence who was very engaged in the issues of the day.[7]

EXPANSION OF THE NETWORKS: TV'S GOLDEN AGE

Television had gained a significant place in the American market by 1952. More than 34
percent of the homes—15 million—had television sets. By the end of the decade this figure was 86 percent. NBC and CBS were battling to increase their number of affiliated stations; NBC led, 64 to 31, with the upstart ABC network trailing with 15. DuMont
attempted to form a fourth network but dropped from competition in 1955. Regular network service was under way with shows like Milton Berle's *Texaco Star Theatre* and Ed
Sullivan's *Toast of the Town.*

In all, there were 108 stations on the air, the number allocated by the FCC when it
"froze" the television industry in 1948 to allow for study of a number of issues, particularly for debates over color television and the number of channels needed to meet future
demand.[8] In 1952 the FCC provided for VHF (very-high-frequency) television to include
channels 2 to 13 and UHF (ultra-high-frequency) stations to range to channel 83. Regarding color, in 1950 the FCC approved a CBS system after acrimonious hearings, but RCA
had the support of major manufacturing firms such as DuMont and Philco. CBS was unable to progress, and in 1953 the FCC switched its approval to RCA's compatible color
system, which enabled either color or black-and-white sets to receive a show.

Coast-to-coast broadcasting was made possible with the development of coaxial
cable. The first lines had been laid by 1946 between New York, Philadelphia, and Washington, and by 1947 to Boston. By 1948 the Midwest was included so that network shows
were received simultaneously in the middle and eastern parts of the nation. Finally, in
1951, AT&T completed a microwave relay system to the West Coast, in time for President

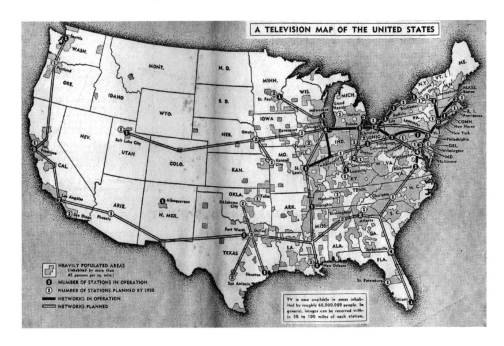

Truman to address the San Francisco peace conference that officially ended the Pacific war in September. That speech was carried by 94 stations. Regular network broadcasting followed, and one of the first shows to be aired was Edward R. Murrow's *See It Now*.

In these formative years the bulk of network programming was arranged in New York by imaginative people like Sylvester L. "Pat" Weaver of NBC, who conceived the *Today* and *Tonight* shows. Beginning in 1952 many Americans awakened to the voice of Dave Garroway, the first host of the *Today* show, which came on the air at 7 A.M. Eastern time. Steve Allen was the host of the first *Tonight* show in 1954, and was followed over the years by Jack Parr and then Johnny Carson.

Television was live in the early days.[9] Milton Berle was called "Mr. Television." Sid Caesar and Imogene Coca starred on *Your Show of Shows,* Ed Sullivan's *Toast of the Town* became the *The Ed Sullivan Show,* Arthur Godfrey and Ted Mack brought their talent-scout shows from radio, and a half-dozen dramatic programs such as *Kraft Television Theatre* and *Studio One* carried the works of leading authors and playwrights into the living room. Comedy shows featured Jimmy Durante, Bob Hope, Jack Benny and Mary Livingston, George Burns and Gracie Allen, Edgar Bergen, and Red Skelton. The learned Bishop Fulton J. Sheen used his chalkboard to lecture on the evils of Communism, glibly telling the audience that his "guardian angel" had erased the board. Bing Crosby, Perry Como, and the singers on *Your Hit Parade* offered light fare. Soap operas also made their way from radio to television.

Youngsters who talked their teachers into letting their classes watch the World Series saw games played at Yankee Stadium, Ebbets Field, and the Polo Grounds, as sporting events became regular features on television. Other radio shows coming to television were Eve Arden's *Our Miss Brooks, The Goldbergs, The Life of Riley, The Adventures of Ozzie and Harriet,* and *Amos 'n' Andy.* Children watched *Howdy Doody* and *Kukla, Fran, and Ollie,* appealing shows with puppets, and *Ding Dong School* with Miss Frances. *Mama,* starring Peggy Wood, was a favorite family show.

The most spectacular audience during television's golden years of the 1950s was recorded in January 1953, when 72 percent of the nation's 21 million television homes tuned in to see the *I Love Lucy* show during which Lucille Ball, pregnant in real life, gave birth to a son.

Program content began to change in the middle 1950s, however, when most production activities moved from New York to the Hollywood studios. A half-dozen Westerns were put on the air, led by the popular *Gunsmoke.* An actor named Ronald Reagan was the host of *Death Valley Days.* By 1959, when *Bonanza,* another long-running show appeared, there were 30 regular Western shows. Among a long line of popular detective shows at that time were *Perry Mason* and *Dragnet.*

Television suffered a setback in the late 1950s when it was learned that some of the quiz shows were rehearsed. The CBS show *$64,000 Question* was television's highest rated show in 1955. But by 1958 it was determined that there had been a wholesale cheating of the public, and 20 quiz shows were taken off the air. A New York grand jury investigation in 1959 brought out all of the details. Television's credibility had been hurt, but only temporarily. The 1994 motion picture *Quiz Show* alerted another generation to the ethics problems.

MURROW AND MCCARTHY: THE DEBATE
OVER "DISLOYALTY AND DISSENT"

At no time in the 1950s was the marriage between the emerging television system and partisan politics so clearly displayed than during the encounters of broadcaster Edward R. Murrow and Senator Joseph R. McCarthy of Wisconsin, men who had built their careers in the public eye and who saw the problems of international Communism and internal security—and journalism—quite differently.

Murrow remains the conscience of responsible broadcast journalists because of his relentless pursuit of the truth, his fondness for the English language, and his deep affection for the best in America's heritage. This, of course, includes the First Amendment guarantees to free and vigorous debate, open assemblies, independent gathering of the news, and critical commentaries about public affairs. This sophisticated man's devotion to hard work and his feeling for the common people's rights were developed by his own tireless Quaker parents who had moved from their native North Carolina to the farms and logging mills of Washington when Murrow was a boy.

The 1948 political conventions brought Murrow to the television audience, but it was on November 18, 1951, that he made a full introduction of his style and personality. That first *See It Now* show featured Murrow sitting before two monitors, one showing the Golden Gate Bridge and the San Francisco skyline, and the other the Brooklyn Bridge set into New York's profile. During those 30 minutes the cameras showed Murrow in New York and Eric Sevareid in Washington talking about the Korean War, and Howard K. Smith in Paris during a prefilmed telephone conversation with Murrow. Murrow and Fred W. Friendly, his coproducer of radio and television documentaries for the next 10 years, were bringing their *Hear It Now* radio show to the new medium.

For the next seven years *See It Now* broke the trail, bringing Americans many moments of hard journalism. Murrow believed that the message was more vital than the medium, and his zeal for fine writing and carefully edited film was contagious. This was the time of live television, and Murrow was able to transmit his sense of honesty and

Edward R. Murrow, the great CBS commentator

(CBS)

accuracy into the nation's living rooms. His familiar deep voice, rich with conviction, added to the impact of the shows, as did his solemn face and dignified manner.

Gradually the *See It Now* show moved from three or four brief looks at various subjects to occasional longer presentations. One milestone was achieved in late 1952 when Murrow took a large reporting and film crew to Korea for *See It Now*'s first full-hour show, the highly acclaimed "Christmas in Korea." It was television's first full-length combat report, and it drove home the fact that this war was stalemated.

Then in October 1953, Murrow moved into the most controversial issue of those years, McCarthyism. The tension at CBS was at a peak as Murrow and Friendly prepared the story of a young Air Force reserve officer, Milo Radulovich, who had been classified as a security risk because his father and sister read "subversive" newspapers. The frequently abrasive nature of Murrow's previous shows had caused problems within CBS, and this time the network refused to advertise *See It Now*. Instead Murrow and Friendly used $1500 of their own funds to buy a *New York Times* advertisement, while CBS felt strong pressure against the show from its own corporate advertisers.

Murrow and his cameras probed into the Dexter, Michigan, community of the Radulovichs and showed that the paper the father read was a Serbian-language one that supported Marshall Tito in Yugoslavia, five years after Tito had broken from Russian control. Murrow's final words included an offer to the Air Force for a reply and then this:

> Whatever happens in this whole area of the relationship between the individual and the state, we will do ourselves; it cannot be blamed upon Malenkov, Mao Tse-tung or even our allies. It seems to us—that is, to Fred Friendly and myself—that this is a subject that should be argued about endlessly.[10]

Lieutenant Radulovich was cleared of being a security risk, and the Murrow-Friendly team moved deeper into the emotion of the day. Within a month they produced "An Argument in Indianapolis," which dealt with the local American Legion using its influence to stop a newly formed American Civil Liberties Union group from hiring a hall. CBS cameras filmed the Legion and the ACLU meetings being held at different locations on the same evening, and the viewer was allowed to judge which speakers were following the dictates of the Constitution.

It also was in 1953 that Murrow began his famed interview show, *Person to Person.* Murrow's distaste for the show-business aspects of television had already caused disagreements between him and CBS executives and had strained his longtime relations with CBS president Frank Stanton. But after a shaky start Murrow grew to like the more informal style in which he was able to sit in the studio and discuss the lighter side of life with America's personalities.[11]

The *Person to Person* show featured 500 guests before it ended on June 26, 1959. It was in the top ten in the ratings and brought many a thoughtful moment as Murrow, cigarette in hand, quietly probed and tried to make his famous guests at ease. But he reserved his loyalty for *See It Now.*

The March 9, 1954, broadcast of *See It Now* was one of the most controversial in broadcast history. Fully disgusted with the tactics employed by Senator McCarthy in charging numerous Americans with subversive activities, Murrow pulled out all the stops. In his broadcast that night, while showing films of McCarthy in action, Murrow said:

> As a nation we have come into our full inheritance at a tender age. We proclaim ourselves—as indeed we are—the defenders of freedom abroad, what's left of it, but we cannot defend freedom abroad by deserting it at home. The actions of the junior Senator from Wisconsin have caused alarm and dismay amongst our allies abroad and given considerable comfort to our enemies, and whose fault is that? Not really his. He didn't create this situation of fear; he merely exploited it, and rather successfully. Cassius was right: "The fault, dear Brutus, is not in our stars but in ourselves". . . Good night, and good luck.[12]

Later that spring the public got another chance to see Senator McCarthy in action during the sensational Army-McCarthy hearings, an investigation of alleged pro-Communist activities within the U.S. Army itself. Bitter arguments and legal maneuvering produced a huge daytime audience. But McCarthy was wearing thin, and in August a Gallup Poll showed that only 36 percent of the public felt "favorable" toward him. Censured by Senate colleagues for his bullying tactics, McCarthy left center stage. He died in 1957.

Murrow had tried to educate the public about the difference between disloyalty and dissent. But the strain of unending work and dissatisfaction with trends in television were taking their toll. Board chairman William S. Paley decided to discontinue *See It Now,* and the last show ran on July 9, 1958.[13] Throughout this period Murrow had continued his nightly radio news show and had often appeared on television twice a week. He also continued his earlier association with *CBS Reports,* as part of which he narrated *Harvest of Shame,* which showed the plight of the migrant worker, in 1960. Then in 1961, greatly disappointed about the commercial nature of television and signs that television news itself would become locked into the ratings scramble, Murrow resigned to take charge of the U.S. Information Agency. Illness forced his retirement in December 1963.

When Murrow died from cancer in April 1965, two days after his fifty-seventh birthday, Eric Sevareid said of his mentor—whose skill and imagination set future standards for news and documentary broadcasting—"He was a shooting star. We shall live in his afterglow a very long time . . . we shall not see his like again."[14] Ironically, while Murrow argued for public understanding of the dangers of McCarthyism, there were many within the broadcasting, film, and advertising industries who bowed to pressure and agreed to the "blacklisting" of certain writers, actors, producers, and directors because of allegations that they were somehow linked to Communism. Indeed, in June 1950, a blacklisting group issued *Red Channels: The Report of Communist Influence in Radio and Television.* The monograph listed more than 150 broadcast employees and suggested that they should not be trusted as loyal Americans. The FBI hounded the New York City Photo League into dissolution. Loyalty oaths were the order of the day, even in universities, as blacklisting became a common practice because of fear and cowardice. It was in this grim atmosphere that Murrow, Friendly, and other courageous journalists worked.

Powerful publications like Henry Luce's *Time* and *Life,* McCormick's *Chicago Tribune,* and the Hearst newspapers, joined by many other newspapers across the land, added to the sensationalizing of the "Red" issue. Sickened by this trend, the alternative journalist I. F. Stone cried out in his July 19, 1954, issue of *I. F. Stone's Weekly:* "The Time to Save America from Fascism Is Now." He told of the House Un-American Activities Committee bill requiring all "subversive" organizations to register their printing facilities, even their mimeograph machines, "so fearful are we becoming of the printed word."[15]

NBC NEWS: HUNTLEY AND BRINKLEY

For 14 long years, from the 1956 political conventions to the unrest of 1970, the unusual team of Chet Huntley—the deep-voiced, rough-hewn Montanan—and David Brinkley—the dry, cynically whimsical reporter from North Carolina—formed an unlikely match that made millions for NBC.

The Huntley-Brinkley team was conceived for the 1956 conventions by Robert Kintner, then president of NBC News, who brought a surge of excitement to the division. The CBS team of Murrow and Walter Cronkite had outclassed NBC in 1952. At one point, to the sheer frustration of NBC and ABC executives, Richard Nixon used the headset of a CBS floor reporter to give Cronkite and Murrow an exclusive statement on his nomination as Eisenhower's running mate.[16] But it was a different story in 1956, with Huntley and Brinkley working perfectly together, playing to each other's words, while Cronkite and Murrow fared poorly.

NBC first paired Huntley and Brinkley on its evening news show, called *The Huntley/Brinkley Report,* on October 29, 1956, and by 1960 they had overtaken CBS in the ratings chase. NBC's rise to the top of the television news business in the 1950s began with John Cameron Swayze's show of 1949 to 1956, *The Camel News Caravan,* a 15-minute show during which Swayze narrated newsreel clips. CBS had initiated the concept the previous year with *Douglas Edwards with the News.*

The team lasted until 1970, when Huntley retired. When he died of cancer in 1974, Brinkley told the television audience of the many times he and his partner had been told by young persons, "I grew up with you guys." Indeed, many Americans did grow to adulthood with Huntley reading the news from New York and Brinkley adding his part from Washington, each time signing off with the somewhat silly and often imitated exchange: "Goodnight, Chet." "Goodnight, David, and goodnight for NBC News." The NBC news division recorded many triumphs, with the *Today* show, well-edited instant specials on days of unusual news significance, and live coverage of historic moments. But it was clear that the hub of the success was the attention gained by Huntley and Brinkley, whose familiar faces and voices dominated political conventions until 1968, when CBS began to gain ground. CBS regained the ratings lead in the 1969 to 1970 season.

Although the industrious *Huntley/Brinkley Report* added much to America's knowledge of itself, the two men were not that close. Huntley was more conservative in outlook, a businessman by nature who retired to his $20 million Big Sky resort complex, defended himself against the protests of conservationists, and did commercials for American Airlines. His many admirers praised his warmth, courage, and strong patriotism. No less patriotic, Brinkley, on the other hand, reflected more of the Washington viewpoint. As early as July 1967, he publicly criticized the American involvement in Vietnam and said that the air war over North Vietnam should be stopped.[17]

Following Huntley's retirement, Brinkley temporarily found himself in an awkward "troika" arrangement with John Chancellor and Frank McGee. He separated from this to do *David Brinkley's Journal,* a nightly commentary. Chancellor emerged as the sole anchorperson, and McGee took over the popular *Today* show. Then in 1976 Brinkley returned to coanchor the evening news when NBC executives decided to intensify the attack against CBS's hold on the ratings. The result was that NBC brought the numbers almost even. Brinkley later joined ABC.

RADIO ADJUSTS TO TELEVISION

Television had written radio's obituary, many observers said. But time proved that there was room for both. Network radio withered, as its established stars moved (with the advertising budgets) to network television. The value of time sales for national radio networks was $40 million in 1935, rose to a high of $133 million in 1948, then dropped back to $35 million in 1960. But the time sales for all of radio increased virtually every year. The "music, news, and sports" pattern proved successful for the spreading number of smaller stations. Incessant newscasts, rather than longer and more meaningful ones, proved annoying, but radio still produced many excellent network and local news and public-affairs broadcasts.

The networks, with the exception of the loosely organized Mutual, moved into television, but they also stayed in radio. The American Broadcasting Company (the NBC Blue network until 1943) merged with Paramount Theatres in 1953 in a mutual defense pact against television. ABC had 1348 radio station affiliates in 1975 in four subnetworks, CBS had 258, and NBC had 232. Mutual, serving 560 stations, went into bankruptcy in 1959 but was successfully reorganized. The number of regional radio networks increased to 81 by 1961.

FM (frequency modulation) radio—given its first public demonstration by Edwin Armstrong in 1935—made a bid against the normal AM (amplitude modulation) radio in the 1940s, as Table 16–1 shows. FM radio was looked on as the means of providing thousands of smaller towns with radio stations, since FM covers a smaller area with better reception. But only a few hundred FM stations survived in the 1950s, primarily as "better-listening" stations, because transistor radio sets produced by mass methods did not tune in FM channels until the mid-1960s. From then on, FM became one of the fastest growing elements in American broadcasting. There were several reasons for this mushrooming of FM broadcasting: (1) a better chance of success for investors than in network-dominated television and the badly overcrowded AM field; (2) an increased interest in cultural affairs and classical music; (3) the arrival of stereo and the high-fidelity industry, coinciding with this interest in better music; (4) various FCC decisions that helped give FM a separate identity from AM, its longtime subsidizer; (5) the driving away of some of the audience by the poor programming of television and AM; (6) the increasing use of FM by advertisers as the quality and quantity of its audience became known; and (7) the growing sales of FM sets, from 2 million a year in 1960 to 21 million in 1968. By the 1970s combined AM-FM sets were commonplace.

Appearing on the scene with FM was facsimile broadcasting, also limited in scope of reception. Facsimile broadcasting, begun on a daily basis by KSD, St. Louis, in 1938,

TABLE 16–1   Numbers of Radio and Television Stations and Sets in Use

YEAR	AM STATIONS (on the air)	FM STATIONS (on the air)	TV STATIONS	RADIO SETS (millions)	TV SETS (millions)
1930	612			13	
1935	605			30	
1940	814			51	
1945	943	53	9	60	(8000)
1950	2086	733	97	80	6
1955	2669	552	439	115	33
1960	3398	688	573	156	55
1965	4009	1270	586	228	61
1970	4269	2476	872	303	84
1975	4463	3571	962	413	120
1980	4575	4350	1020	456	150
1985	4805	5066	1220	489	180
1990	4984	5810	1469	533	210
1994	4948	6595	1516	575[*]	240[*]

Source: Broadcasting Yearbooks. Radios were in 96 percent of all households in the United States in 1950, 98.6 percent in 1970. Television household figures were 13 percent in 1950, 68 percent in 1955, 99 percent in 1994. Of the 533 million radio sets in 1990, 343 million were in homes, and 190 million were out of homes. [*]Estimate.

was viewed as a possible way of delivering printed newspapers into the home. But the innovation failed to reach mass-production use.

THE PRESS ASSOCIATIONS: THE AP'S KENT COOPER

The name of Kent Cooper came to dominate the history of the Associated Press in the 1920s, and his long shadow remained over that news organization through the 1950s. An Indianan, Cooper had started reporting for his local paper at 14. His college education was interrupted by the death of his father, and he left school to join the *Indianapolis Press.* From there he went to the Scripps-McRae news service, and he became head of the Indianapolis bureau of what was to become the AP's major rival. There Cooper got the idea that out-of-the-way papers could be better served by a system of telephoning rather than telegraphing the news report. In 1910 he so impressed General Manager Melville E. Stone of the AP with his knowledge of news-communications methods that he was made AP traffic chief. He became an assistant general manager in 1920 and became general manager in 1925 after Stone's retirement. Cooper demonstrated strong administrative qualities, but he was never a "newspaperman's newspaperman."

Cooper had plans for improving the efficiency and quality of the AP service, and many changes came with his rise to control. The number of bureaus was increased, and staffs were expanded. Human-interest stories, long frowned on by the AP, gained favor. The transition was marked by the AP's first Pulitzer Prize, won by Kirke L. Simpson in 1922 for a series on the burial of the Unknown Soldier in Arlington Cemetery. State services, permitting the exchange of regional news on teletype wires subsidiary to the main AP trunk wires, were expanded. A news photo service was established in 1927, and after a sharp clash between picture-minded publishers and their more conservative colleagues, the AP Wirephoto system was approved in 1935. Automatic news printers, called teletypes, were first used in 1913 and gradually replaced Morse code operators.

The pressures of competition from other news services and of World War II coverage requirements brought further advances. In 1934 the AP management had finally brought an end to their restrictive arrangements with European news agencies that had prevented the sale of AP news abroad, and an AP World Service was begun in 1946. The AP had leased cable and radio-teletype circuits across the North Atlantic, European-leased land circuits, and an overseas radio-photo network. The character of the news report was subjected to increasingly intensive review by members of the Associated Press Managing Editors Association, a group formed in 1931. The managing editors of member papers criticized the AP news coverage and writing style orally until 1947, when the reports of a Continuing Study Committee were printed annually. State members made similar analyses. The AP management hired readability expert Rudolph Flesch to advise its staff, and correspondents like James Marlow of the Washington bureau did excellent work in pointing the way to better writing.

One change came involuntarily. This was in the membership-protest right, by which an AP member could blackball a new applicant in his own city. It took a four-fifths vote of the entire membership to override a blackball, a vote rarely obtained. This restriction was challenged by the *Chicago Sun,* which was founded by Marshall Field in 1941 as a morning competitor to the *Tribune.* Court action was begun in 1942, and in 1945 the U.S. Supreme Court held that the AP bylaws concerning protest rights constituted unfair restriction of competition. The AP thereupon amended its membership rules and elected several newspapers previously denied admission. On another front, and after a bitter battle, the AP began to sell its news report to radio stations in 1940, five years later than the UP and INS. Radio stations were granted associate membership, without voting rights, in 1946. The Associated Press Radio-Television Association was formed in 1954.

New faces appeared in the AP management. Two of the men most respected by their colleagues for their capabilities as journalists were Byron Price and Paul Miller. Both served as chiefs of the Washington bureau. Price became the AP's first executive news editor in 1936, before retiring from the news service to become director of the Office of Censorship during World War II and later Assistant Secretary General of the United Nations. Miller, after being named an assistant general manager, quit the AP to become an executive of the Gannett newspapers. Their departures left veteran Frank J. Starzel as the logical successor to Cooper when he retired in 1948.

Wes Gallagher, the AP's leading World War II war correspondent and postwar foreign-bureau chief, returned to the New York office in 1954 to be groomed as Starzel's 1962 successor. Gallagher, an aggressive AP spokesperson, instituted "task-force" reporting by a ten-person team based in Washington, opened AP reporting ranks to younger men and also to women, and presided over a massive reorganization of the transmission wires. He retired in 1976.[18]

There were flaws in news coverage during this period, AP's generally excellent reputation notwithstanding. In Dallas in 1963 the AP trailed the UPI badly in early reports of the Kennedy assassination, and carried several major false and confusing reports, including that Lyndon Johnson had been shot and that a Secret Service man and policeman had been killed. In other years, the AP erroneously reported that civil rights activist James Meredith had been killed by an assassin and that President Reagan's press secretary, James

Brady, had been killed in an assassination attempt. It also said initially that Reagan had escaped unharmed.[19]

THE UP AND THE INS BECOME THE UPI

The United Press and the International News Service established themselves as competitive news agencies during the 1920s and 1930s. They expanded rapidly in response to the pressures of World War II and the growth of the mass media in the postwar years, and then in 1958 combined their forces as the United Press International—a news organization which competed strongly with the Associated Press for another three decades.

The UP jumped into several fields ahead of the AP, just as it did in developing its foreign news service. Acme Newspictures began operating in 1925, two years earlier than the AP picture service was established. The UP pioneered in supplying news to radio stations and, with the INS, was first into the television news field in 1951. Acme became United Press Newspictures in 1952 and handled UP Telephoto, a rival to AP Wirephoto. In 1954 both services began supplying pictures by facsimile, over the UP Unifax and AP Photofax networks. The teletypesetter, producing a tape that automatically runs a typesetting machine, arrived in 1951, and both UP and AP set up teletypesetter circuits for smaller papers, sports, and financial services.

Roy Howard's successors as president of the United Press all came up through the ranks. Two strong men were Karl A. Bickel and Hugh Baillie. Bickel took over in 1923 and became a leader in furthering the freedom of international news coverage, while advancing the UP's own position in worldwide service.

Baillie, who succeeded Bickel in 1935, loved nothing better than to whip his competitors with an exclusive story, preferably a vivid one. He traveled extensively, impressing his own competitive drive for news on his staff and keeping in touch by personally covering some of the major events.

Two of the UP's outstanding editors over the years were Earl J. Johnson and Roger Tatarian. Johnson became working head of the news operation in 1935 and retired as editor in 1965, widely praised for his energetic leadership. Tatarian was the UP's European news chief in the 1950s and succeeded Johnson as editor. He became known throughout the news world before a heart attack forced his early retirement to a professorship.

The United Press spawned some legendary newspeople. One was Merriman Smith, who spent 30 years covering six presidents and intoning the traditional, "Thank you, Mr. President," as senior White House correspondent. Another was Henry Shapiro, who arrived in Moscow in the 1930s and served as bureau chief until the 1970s, dominating Moscow coverage of the Stalin, Khrushchev, and Brezhnev eras.

Editor-in-chief Barry Faris of the International News Service developed full 24-hour operations for his agency by 1928. Added as talented featured writers were Bob Considine and Inez Robb, joining the team of Floyd Gibbons, James L. Kilgallen, and H. R. Knickerbocker. Kilgallen's daughter Dorothy became a noted byliner. Other glamour names on the INS wire were Quentin Reynolds, Frank Gervasi, Paul Gallico, and Damon Runyon. In a final burst of glory, the 1956 Pulitzer Prize for international reporting was won for the INS and the Hearst newspapers by William Randolph Hearst, Jr., Kingsbury Smith, and Frank Conniff, who conducted interviews with Communist political leaders behind the Iron Curtain.[20]

There were lumps in many throats when the hard-hitting INS staff of 450 saw their agency merged with the UP in May 1958. William Randolph Hearst, Jr., and two of his associates took minority seats on the board of directors of the new United Press International, and some INS staffers joined the UPI. A few of the brightest INS stars went to work for the newly formed Hearst Headline Service. Otherwise the INS was no more.

THE USIA AND THE VOICE OF AMERICA

The creation of an autonomous United States Information Agency (USIA) in 1953 gave stability to a program established in 1945, when tension and uncertainty was felt in the postwar world and American officials decided that the work of the Office of War Information should be continued in peacetime. That first operation was the Office of International Information and Cultural Affairs, established within the State Department.

In 1948, under the Smith-Mundt Act, the functions were split into an Office of International Information and an Office of Cultural Exchange, with a small combined annual budget of $12 million, about one-third that of OWI.

With the Soviet Union consolidating its grip on the satellite states of Eastern Europe and attempting the 1948 Berlin blockade, and with the Korean War beginning in 1950, congressional appropriations rose swiftly. By 1952 the revamped International Information Administration had $87 million, 25 percent of which was for the Voice of America (VOA). After 1953 the annual budget for the USIA was maintained at well over $100 million, adjusted for inflation. By 1970 the Voice of America was being heard in 40 languages over 92 transmitters by an estimated audience of 43 million. The overseas United States Information Service was operating information libraries and reading rooms in 70 countries, and was distributing news services, motion pictures, magazines, and pamphlets. The policy and planning and the research and assessment sections were involved in the country's foreign-policy making, but not enough to satisfy many of the staff.

During the 1950s and 1960s there was a running duel between the professionals who viewed the USIA and the Voice of America as agencies for "tell it like it is" journalism, properly interpreting United States involvement in news events, and officials who wished the agencies to reflect their image of how the world should respond to current U.S. policy and who wished to minimize news of any conflict with such an image. Increasing White House concern with the war in Vietnam polarized the debate after 1965.[21]

In 1977 President Jimmy Carter announced a reorganization plan that would combine the USIA and the State Department's educational and cultural-affairs activities in a new International Communication Agency. The Voice of America and overseas USIS would operate as before, and the broadcasters would be assured of freedom of action. But by 1982 the familiar USIA symbol was again in use. The Reagan administration tinkered with the agency's structure and caused controversy by renewing the 1950s debate over content of programming by the Voice of America. A brief attempt to harden a propaganda line died in the face of staff resistance. Radio Marti, a controversial shortwave broadcast beamed at Cuba, began operating in 1985.

By 1990 the USIA operating budget stood near $700 million, including $172 million for the Voice of America. The VOA played a major role in providing information during the 1989 liberation of Eastern European countries and China's student protest movement.

By 1995 VOA's 24-hour service was broadcasting in 45 languages with an estimated worldwide audience of about 130 million persons, or almost twice as much as the British Broadcasting Corporation (BBC). There were USIS libraries in 125 nations and the USIA's budget was more than $700 million. With the demise of communism, the VOA assumed many technical operations of two warriors of the propaganda battles, Radio Free Europe (1951) and Radio Liberty (1953), whose offices were moved from Munich to Prague as part of the general post-Cold War realignment.

ADVERTISING: MADISON AVENUE, U.S.A.

Martin Mayer's 1958 book about the advertising agencies, *Madison Avenue, U.S.A.*, helped popularize the image of the man in the gray flannel suit who contributed to what E. S. Turner called *The Shocking History of Advertising* in a constructively critical 1953 study. Advertising was in full stride, with the volume of total expenditures doubling in the first decade of network television, and Madison Avenue was the symbol of its success.

During World War II, with consumer products in short supply, advertising made points by being both institutional and patriotic. Lucky Strike cigarettes had been packaged in green, with a red bull's-eye in the center. When the armed forces needed green dye, Luckies switched to a white package with the same red center spot and launched a full-scale campaign, "Lucky Strike green has gone to war." The company donated thousands of cartons to servicepeople overseas and watched its sales curve mount upward (women, it seemed, also preferred the new white packaging). Ford, producing solely for the military, like other auto companies, dinned the slogan, "There's a Ford in your future," so successfully that the company led postwar sales. One of the most famed of the institutional advertisements was the New Haven Railroad's 1942 page, "The Kid in Upper 4," reprinted countless times. A wartime Advertising Council was created by the agencies, the media, and the advertisers to promote sales of war bonds, blood donations, rationing, and the like; after the war the Council continued to sponsor some two dozen public-service campaigns annually.

Television advertising by large companies began for the few thousand set owners of 1944 with commercials for clothing makers and Lifebuoy soap, which joined those of *Reader's Digest* and oil and utility companies. The 30-second television commercials invented for network broadcasts were relentlessly repetitious, but they sold goods. Programs sponsored by Alcoa, Du Pont, General Electric, and other large corporations sold images. By 1957 advertisers were spending more than $1.5 billion for television time, talent, and production costs to reach 37 million set owners.

The criticisms of advertising made in the 1930s were renewed in earnest in the late 1950s and early 1960s, leading to a deeper questioning of the "cult of consumerism" that advertising fosters. Vance Packard's best-selling *The Hidden Persuaders* (1956) attacked advertising for using the techniques of depth psychology to raise "subliminal anxieties" and manipulate desires for alcohol, cigarettes, and other consumer goods. In *The Affluent Society* (1958) John Kenneth Galbraith pointed out that advertising was encouraging wasteful consumption of scarce resources by a small portion of the world's people, to the detriment of both human beings and their environment. In *The One-Dimensional Man* (1964) Herbert Marcuse explained advertising as the means by which technology reached into an individual's consciousness and destroyed his or her freedom. Sloan Wilson's *The Man in the Gray Flannel Suit* (1967) was far more critical than the books of the 1950s.

The techniques of some advertising people aroused criticisms. Ted Bates & Company originated the manipulative technique of the "unique selling proposition" (usp) to increase the sales of mass-produced products that in reality differed little from rival brands ("Cleans your breath while it cleans your teeth," for Colgate, and "Washed with live

A famous 1942 institutional advertisement

steam," for Schlitz to win finicky beer-bottle users). Ernest Dichter's motivational research was used by Chrysler to suggest to men with secret desires to have mistresses that their hardtop convertibles combined feelings of sinning with assurances of safety. There was also considerable discussion of subliminal advertising, by which momentary stimulations were said to trigger responses. One example of such advertising was to project flickering messages that said "Coke" or "popcorn" to stimulate movie-house sales of those products. College students found the research theory's possibilities intriguing.

On another research front, C. E. Hooper made his first television-audience study in 1948, and Dr. Claude Robinson and Dr. George Gallup formed a service to measure the effectiveness of advertising. In 1950 A. C. Nielsen took over the Hooper radio rating service and soon extended it to television.

The first serious attempt at self-regulation of advertising occurred in 1952, when the National Association of Broadcasters (NAB), nudged by the FCC, established extensive sets of guidelines for both programs and advertising. A NAB code authority professional staff began clearing commercials prior to their airing; each network also reviewed the commercials for truth, taste, and fairness.

Two new advertising-agency leaders appeared: Ogilvy & Mather in 1948 and Doyle Dane Bernbach in 1949. David Ogilvy, an Englishman, emphasized brand image in his advertising campaigns, thus creating distinction for the product on the basis of "snob appeal." In his Hathaway shirt ads, which first appeared in 1951, the shirts were modeled by Russian nobles who wore black eyepatches and had the air of upper-class taste and distinction. This image would transfer to the buyer of a Hathaway shirt, the argument ran; during an eight-year campaign Hathaway's sales increased 250 percent. Schweppes, another Ogilvy account, had a bearded English commander for its image. William Bernbach, creative leader of Doyle Dane Bernbach for its first three decades, offered an opposite style: low-key, ironic, and endearing. His slogan for Avis Rent-a-Car swept the country: "We try harder. We're only Number 2." His long advertising campaign for the Volkswagen beetle ran against American buying habits—"Think small"—but it made the Volkswagen the first successful automobile import. Bernbach's New York City billboard campaign, begun in 1963, relaxed ethnic tensions when it showed a smiling young black boy with the slogan, "You don't have to be Jewish to love Levy's real Jewish rye."

When *Printers' Ink* published its seventy-fifth anniversary issue in 1963, it found that it could run pictures of five women vice-presidents of major advertising agencies. Three had come up through the creative side: Jean Brown of Benton & Bowles, Jean Wade Rindlaub of Batten, Barton, Durstine & Osborn (BBDO), and Margot Sherman of McCann-Erickson. Genevieve Hazzard of Campbell-Ewald had been account executive for Chevrolet; Nancy Stephenson of J. Walter Thompson focused on copywriting. A New York advertising leader was Bernice Fitz-Gibbon, who wrote the slogan, "It's smart to be thrifty," for Macy's, then moved to Gimbel's and wrote, "Nobody but nobody undersells Gimbel's," before opening her own agency in 1954.

Stanley Resor spent 40 years as J. Walter Thompson's president, 1916 to 1955. Bruce Barton, Ben Duffy, and Charles H. Brower were BBDO presidents. Also notable were Fairfax M. Cone, partner and creative director for Foote, Cone & Belding and a leading industry spokesperson; George Gribbin, copy chief and then president of Young & Rubicam; and Marion Harper, Jr., who became president of McCann-Erickson at the age of 32, revolutionizing that agency's activities.

In 1962 the largest agencies, by client billings, were J. Walter Thompson, Young & Rubicam, BBDO, McCann-Erickson, Leo Burnett, Ted Bates, N. W. Ayer, Foote, Cone &

The man in the Hathaway shirt

David Ogilvy's best "brand image" ad

Belding, and Benton & Bowles. The leaders had made notable expansions in foreign accounts in the postwar years, particularly J. Walter Thompson and McCann-Erickson. By the early 1960s, 12 of the 20 largest U.S. agencies had overseas subsidiaries.

Advertising volume as a percentage of all consumer expenditures peaked at 4.7 percent in 1922. It plummeted during the Depression years, then reached a plateau of 3.5 percent throughout the 1950s. Total advertising volume was $2 billion in 1940, $6 billion in 1950, $10 billion in 1955, and $12 billion in 1960.

THE EXPANSION OF CORPORATE PUBLIC RELATIONS

The 1950s were marked by a rapid advance in corporate public relations. Individual firms opened new public-relations departments or expanded older ones. Recognition of public relations as a management concept increased, and the number of public-relations counsels retained by businesses and groups grew. *Public Relations News,* the leading journal of the field, defined public relations as "the management function which evaluates public attitudes, identifies the policies and procedures of an individual or an organization with the public interest, and executes a program of action to earn public understanding and acceptance." The development of modern public-opinion and marketing-survey techniques, beginning in the 1930s, by George Gallup, Elmo Roper, Claude Robinson, and others, provided a tool by which public-relations counselors could evaluate public attitudes quantitatively and could therefore obtain more objective measurements than their personal estimates of public opinion.

Sales booms in many manufacturing fields and businesses following the end of World War II benefited the public-relations field. By 1950 there were an estimated 17,000 men and 2000 women employed as experienced practitioners in public relations and publicity. In 1960 the census counted 23,870 men and 7271 women; others estimated a 35,000 total. The largest numbers were in manufacturing, business services, finance and insurance, religious and nonprofit groups, public administration, and communications. J.A.R. Pimlott, a British scholar, wrote in 1951, "Public relations is not a peculiarly American phenomenon, but it has nowhere flourished as in the United States. Nowhere else is it so widely practiced, so lucrative, so pretentious, so respectable and disreputable, so widely suspected and so extravagantly extolled."[22]

Detailed descriptions of the public-relations departments of major companies were given in published proceedings of forums sponsored by the Minnesota chapter of the Public Relations Society of America (PRSA) in the early 1950s.[23] The PRSA had been formed in 1948 from existing organizations and offered the forums at the University of Minnesota as a showcase. General Mills, which had a staff of three in its Department of Public Services in 1945, reported a professional staff of nearly 20 by 1952 and an outside public-relations consultant of national reputation. The milling firm had offices for press relations, internal communications, stockholder communications, consumer services, rural services, special services and contributions, nutrition education, and economic education. It published an employee newspaper monthly and a stockholder report quarterly, and it made a 16-mm color newsreel for employee viewing. Betty Crocker was still the company's most famous symbol, however.

The Aluminum Company of America in 1953 had a vice president serving as director of public relations and advertising, with an assistant public-relations director and an advertising manager. Departments included community relations, employee publications, the news bureau, trade-press relations, product publicity, motion pictures and exhibits, and industrial economics (speech writing and educational relations). The company published the *Alcoa News* for employees and 20 additional plant publications. Its most prestigious effort was its sponsoring of Edward R. Murrow's *See It Now* program.

Standard Oil Company of Indiana in 1955 focused on six defined areas or publics: employees, stockholders, dealers, suppliers, customers, and special publics. Its public-relations director gave a sampling of statistics for 1954 activity: 900 company speakers made 3528 speeches to 435,000 persons; 120,000 stockholders received the annual report and two management letters; 30,000 employees received the company magazine and four management letters; 50,000 persons made plant tours; and the company gave $2 million in philanthropic contributions. In contrast, only 113 general press releases were issued. Thus had public relations advanced from press-agent days.

In the early 1960s the largest public-relations counseling firms were Carl Byoir & Associates, Hill & Knowlton, and Ruder & Finn. Advertising agencies leading in public-relations services were N. W. Ayer, J. Walter Thompson, and Young & Rubicam. Some of the most extensive public-relations departments were found at General Motors, AT&T, United States Steel, and Du Pont.

MAGAZINES OF THE 1950s

The most popular magazines of the 1950s, in addition to the *Reader's Digest,* were *Life, Look, Collier's,* and the *Saturday Evening Post,* all similar to television and the movies in their general appeal. Only *Reader's Digest* survived the fierce competition for the advertising dollar, partly because of a decision in 1955 to accept advertising in the publication's thirty-third year. DeWitt and Lila Wallace stuck to the basic format, condensing articles from leading periodicals that dealt with informative subjects and ideas of value. Often attacked for its conservative, progovernment, and business approach, the *Reader's Digest* outlasted many of its critics.

Henry Luce expanded his Time-Life empire in 1954 by establishing *Sports Illustrated,* a flashy magazine that coincided with the expansion of major-league sports in the late 1950s and early 1960s. Luce continued to use his prime publications—*Time, Life,* and *Fortune*—to further his goal of playing an important role in American life. The friend of presidents and prime ministers, he pushed hard during the anti-Communist crusade, attacking President Truman, Secretary of State Dean Acheson, and Adlai Stevenson. Day by day *Time* maintained its circulation lead over rivals *Newsweek* and *U.S. News and World Report. Life* was in a class by itself, with its glossy stock and letterpress printing, as compared with *Look*'s rotogravure.

The *Saturday Evening Post* was special in that its short stories and articles continued to feature the United States' well-known authors and journalists. Under editor George Horace Lorimer, the *Post* had become the reflection of traditional middle-class Americans, with inspirational biographies and business success articles interspersed with stories by Clarence Buddington Kelland and other homey writers. After Lorimer's retirement in 1937, the *Post* had a shakedown under editor Ben Hibbs, was modernized, and reached 6.5 million in circulation before Hibbs passed the editorship to Robert Fuoss in 1961. Suddenly the *Post*'s profits translated into heavy losses as television competition took its toll, and a succession of editors compounded its difficulties with poor judgments that alienated readers and lost a major libel suit. Seventy-two years after it had been purchased by Cyrus H. K. Curtis, the *Post* ceased publishing in 1969, joining its rival *Collier's,* which had closed down in 1956 after 68 years. It was the last of its kind.[24]

HARPER'S, ATLANTIC, AND *SATURDAY REVIEW*

Harper's, once a leading literary journal, became primarily a public-affairs magazine after the mid-1920s and reached its hundredth anniversary in 1950 under the editorship of contemporary historian Frederick Lewis Allen. John Fischer succeeded Allen as editor in 1953 and furthered *Harper's* position among high-grade magazines. His reading audience, he once said, was 85 percent college graduates; more than half had taken some graduate work and had traveled abroad within the calendar year surveyed. But only 6 percent read the more literary-based *Atlantic.* It was this audience that in 1965 attracted John Cowles, Jr., a Harvard graduate who was president of the Minneapolis Star and Tribune Company, to buy a half-interest from Harper & Row, successor to the House of Harper dating from 1817.

Willie Morris, a liberal young writer who had achieved notice for his muckraking articles for the *Texas Observer,* joined the *Harper's* staff in 1963 and was Cowles's choice, at the age of 32, to succeed Fischer in 1967 as *Harper's* eighth editor in 117 years. Morris built a freewheeling staff of executive editor Midge Decter; managing editor Robert Kotlowitz; and contributing editors David Halberstam, Larry L. King, John Corry, and Marshall Frady. The magazine became an unpredictable, imaginative vehicle for personal journalism of social and political concern. Morris ran huge excerpts of William Styron's *The Confessions of Nat Turner* and Norman Mailer's *The Armies of the Night.* But a storm broke at *Harper's* in March 1971, when Mailer's earthy essay on the women's liberation movement, "The Prisoner of Sex," appeared in an effort to bolster declining circulation. When the uproar was over, Cowles had made Robert Shnayerson the ninth editor of *Harper's;* most of its distinguished new staff had resigned.

Things were quieter at the 120-year-old *Atlantic.* It also had shifted toward public-affairs articles but to a lesser degree, after Edward A. Weeks replaced longtime editor Ellery Sedgwick in 1938. The pages that once carried the contributions of Emerson, Thoreau, and Longfellow continued to present the literary great: Ernest Hemingway, Edwin O'Connor, Saul Bellow, and Lillian Hellman. Public-affairs articles gained ground with the 1964 appointment of Robert Manning as executive editor. Manning was an experienced newspaperperson and had been assistant secretary of state for public affairs. He became the *Atlantic's* tenth editor-in-chief in 1966, with Michael Janeway as managing editor. Elizabeth Drew wrote the Washington commentary.

The *Saturday Review of Literature* had expanded its interests to include music, science, education, communications, and travel. In 1952 it shortened its name to the *Saturday Review.* Founded in 1924 by Henry Seidel Canby, the first editor-in-chief of the Book-of-the-Month Club, the *Saturday Review* began to grow steadily after Norman Cousins assumed the editorship in 1942. With circulation mounting to 265,000, the magazine put its business affairs in the hands of the *McCall's* publishing corporation in 1961. Cousins advocated restraint in seeking circulation, yet the *Saturday Review* had 615,000 readers by 1970. The publication then went into a period of instability under several owners, losing much of its influence.

BUCKLEY'S *NATIONAL REVIEW*

The strongest and most intelligent voice of the far right in American political opinion was that of the *National Review.* Founded in 1955 by William F. Buckley, Jr., it had 32,000 readers and an $860,000 deficit by 1960. Buckley and the leaders of political conservatism persisted, and by 1977 circulation was 110,000. The 1970 election of William's brother James, Conservative party candidate, to a United States Senate seat for New York, stimulated the Buckley family and its publishing enterprise. The editor's sister, Priscilla, was managing editor. Other key staff editors included James Burnham and Russell Kirk. James Jackson Kilpatrick and Ralph de Toledano were contributing editors. Also reaching the American right was the *Alternative,* edited in Bloomington, Indiana, by R. Emmett Tyrrell, Jr., who had started it as a campus paper in 1966 and began nationwide distribution in 1970. William Buckley, Irving Kristol, Sidney Hook, and Senator Daniel Patrick Moynihan were among its impressive list of contributors.

THE LIBERAL LEFT OPINION JOURNALS

Among the struggling opinion magazines operating at the liberal left during the reactionary 1950s were the *Nation* (founded in 1865) and the *New Republic* (founded in 1914). E. L. Godkin's *Nation* was owned by the Villard family from 1881 to 1934 and followed Oswald Garrison Villard's liberal, pacifist course. Freda Kirchwey became editor in 1937 and Carey McWilliams in 1955, as the magazine passed through financial crises and intrastaff dissensions over policy toward the Soviet Union. George Kirstein, publisher from 1955 to 1965, stabilized the budget and gave McWilliams firm support as the magazine reached its centennial year. A vigorous liberalism prevailed, and by the mid-1960s the *Nation* made perhaps the most passionate attacks on the intensified war in Vietnam. McWilliams and Washington correspondent Robert Sherrill wrote incisive, fact-supported editorials that accompanied the magazine's articles and sections on books and the arts. Advertising was meager, and circulation was scant, perhaps 25,000. McWilliams retired in 1976, and Blair Clark became editor.

The *New Republic,* founded with money from the Willard D. Straight family in 1914, exerted influence during the Wilsonian era with the writings of editor Herbert Croly and Walter Lippmann. It again had force in the 1930s under editor Bruce Bliven. When Michael Straight took over its direction in 1946 he appointed Henry A. Wallace editor. Circulation touched 100,000, but Wallace's involvement in the ultraliberal Progressive party as its 1948 presidential candidate brought his resignation. Sales slumped but were restored after 1956 by editor Gilbert A. Harrison. One bright feature was a column of hard-hitting comment from Washington, begun in 1943 and signed merely "TRB," which was eventually identified as the moonlighting activity of Richard L. Strout, mild-mannered *Christian Science Monitor* staff writer. Strout continued until 1983. *New Republic* later swung to the right politically.

Not as fortunate was the *Reporter,* launched in 1949 by Max Ascoli as a fortnightly. It won widespread praise from its liberal and academic audience for its high-grade research articles and sharply pointed opinion pieces, but audience enthusiasm waned when Ascoli supported the escalated war in Vietnam. Despite 200,000 circulation, the disappointed Ascoli sold out in 1968 to *Harper's,* which discontinued it. Douglass Cater had been its star Washington correspondent.

Other opinion magazines with smaller circulations were also being published. The *Progressive,* founded in 1909 by the La Follette family in Wisconsin, continued its excellent work under the editorship of Morris H. Rubin. The *New Leader,* Socialist but strongly anti-Communist in its origins, appeared in 1924 as a tabloid and adopted magazine format in 1950. Samuel M. (Sol) Levitas made it a stronghold of intellectual thought from 1930 until his death in 1961.

THE RELIGIOUS PRESS

Joining the liberal left opinion magazines were some religiously oriented publications, led by the widely respected *Catholic Worker.* It was founded in 1933 by Dorothy Day, who edited it until 1980 with a tenaciously held editorial philosophy of personalist Christianity, active pacifism, and nonviolent social justice (see pages 419–420).

Other journals espousing social justice themes were the Protestant *Christianity in Crisis,* which grew out of the religious ferment of the 1960s; *Salt,* edited since 1980 for "fair-shake Catholics" by the Claretian fathers and brothers; and *Sojourners,* Protestant-edited with a radical evangelical slant. On the liberal Catholic side were the *National Catholic Reporter, Jubilee,* and *Critic,* a unique arts magazine that flourished during the 1960s.

There were 1700 religious magazines by 1970, including 1100 Protestant, 400 Catholic, and 200 Jewish. Numbers had been growing the past two decades, but circulation declines ranging from 25 to 50 percent hit many religious journals in the early 1970s. This was particularly true of the denominational publications. Gaining attention were the ecumenical magazines, small in circulation but widely quoted and influential in American society. Best known were *Christian Century* and *Commonweal.*

A nondenominational Protestant organ dating from 1884, *Christian Century* was given a stature by editor-owner Charles Clayton Morrison between 1908 and 1947 that was retained by his successors, Dr. Paul Hutchison, Harold E. Fey, and James M. Wall. They edited a vigorous independent journal of intellectual depth and liberal outlook, trying to apply Christian principles to contemporary concerns. *Commonweal,* formed in 1924 by a group of Catholics, won wide respect under the editorship of Edward Skillin. Its opposition to Franco in the Spanish Civil War cost *Commonweal* one-fourth its readers and editor George Schuster. It was then edited by John Deedy, James O'Gara, and Peter Steinfels as a widely quoted journal of social awareness.

At the right among ecumenical magazines was *Commentary,* founded in 1945 by the American Jewish Committee of New York as a journal of significant thought and opinion on Jewish affairs and contemporary issues. Begun as a liberal publication, it began shifting to the right when Norman Podhoretz was named editor in 1960. Known for its distinguished contributors and provocative articles, *Commentary* had a mostly male, upper-class readership. Two other ecumenical journals of opinion were *America,* begun in 1909 by the Jesuits, and the *Friends Journal,* interpreting Quaker pacifism and social concerns. By far the biggest success was the *Catholic Digest,* founded in 1936 and published at the College of St. Thomas in Minnesota. A family magazine modeled after the *Reader's Digest,* its circulation reached 600,000.

Among denominational publications, the longtime leaders were Presbyterian and Methodist. *Presbyterian Life,* which had 1.1 million circulation in the 1960s, had half that many readers when it merged with a United Church of Christ publication in 1972, under the name *A.D.* The Methodists' *Christian Advocate* (1826) and *Together* (1956) became *United Methodists Today* in 1974. Both it and *A.D.* retained circulations near 200,000. Others included *The Lutheran, The Episcopalian,* the Catholic *Extension,* and *American Judaism,* official magazine since 1873 of Hebrew congregations.

Evangelical in nature were the *Moody Monthly,* published since 1900 by the Moody Bible Institute with a strong Baptist flavor, and *Christianity Today. The Wanderer* of St. Paul was aggressively right wing in Catholic advocacy. *The Watchtower* was circulated in 70 countries to 5 million readers by the Jehovah's Witnesses.

But typical of most of the religious press was the venerable *Christian Herald,* begun in 1888 as a family inspirational magazine and still circulating several hundred thousand copies.

PHOTOJOURNALISM: *EBONY, NATIONAL GEOGRAPHIC,* AND *SMITHSONIAN*

John H. Johnson started *Ebony*, imitating the format of *Life,* in 1945 with a press run of 50,000. A friend of Henry Luce, Johnson previously had published *Negro Digest. Ebony* became "a pictorial Who's Who in Black America," a high-quality magazine aiming at middle-class readership but dealing with all aspects of poverty and success.[25] In the late 1960s it became more activist. Johnson later published *Jet, Tan Confessions,*

Magazine owner John H. Johnson

(Ebony)

Ebony Jr. for children, and *Black Stars.* With the other big picture magazines, *Life* and *Look,* gone by the early 1970s, *Ebony* was left alone in this category of magazine and was eminently successful.

The demise of *Life* and *Look* left a void for outstanding photographers, a number of whom joined the venerable *National Geographic,* a one-time travelogue journal begun in 1888. By the 1950s it was an old favorite, but it shot upward in circulation and moved into the general-interest level as other magazines closed their doors. It became a center of photojournalism progress as well, with Robert E. Gilka as director of photography. Gilbert Grosvenor was editor when the *National Geographic* reached 9 million circulation by 1977.

Among the refugees from *Life* was Edward K. Thompson, who turned *Smithsonian* into a superb example of photojournalism. Founded in 1970 by that Society in Washington, *Smithsonian* filled its pages with color photography, became fat with advertising, and ran its circulation to 1.5 million monthly by the late 1970s.

BOOK PUBLISHING: THE OLD HOUSES LEAD A POSTWAR BOOM

It became obvious in the first few years after World War II that the major publishing houses and the new paperback producers would give the reading public a greater choice than ever. The old firms led the way, developing new authors and expanding into uncharted areas. The largest firm was Doubleday & Co., developed by Frank Nelson Doubleday and his son

Nelson Doubleday, heralded as two of the greatest booksellers of the twentieth century.[26] Doubleday opened the 1950s with *The Caine Mutiny* by Herman Wouk, who later authored *The Winds of War.* Following in the tradition of *Crusade in Europe*—Doubleday's 1948 publication of Dwight Eisenhower's wartime memoirs—the firm released Harry Truman's *Years of Decision* in 1955. The former president sat in a Kansas City hotel and autographed nearly 4000 books in one day, setting some sort of record. Doubleday survived as the last of the major independent publishing houses.

The energy at Random House came from Bennett Cerf, known better, perhaps, for a number of humor books, but known in the trade as a strong leader who brought into his line the works of Truman Capote, Irwin Shaw, John O'Hara, and Moss Hart. *Witness,* the story of Whittaker Chambers, the man who had accused Alger Hiss of treason, became a best seller, as did Don Whitehead's *The FBI Story.* Macmillan also used the 1950s to move ahead; its president George P. Brett, Jr., introduced Arthur Koestler, Mary Ellen Chase, and poet Marianne Moore. Walter Lippmann was a Macmillan author.

Alfred A. Knopf, who loved history, fashioned a distinguished list of authors for his business. *The Prophet*, by the mystical Lebanese poet Kahlil Gibran, had been an enormous success, and Knopf was attracted to international literature. That firm was purchased by Random House in 1960, and later—an example of the spread of conglomerate power— both were bought by RCA.

Cass Canfield dominated Harper & Bros.; as his first contribution he brought in Robert Sherwood's *Roosevelt and Hopkins.* Deeply interested in politics, he used his connections to obtain John Kennedy's *Profiles in Courage.* The firm became Harper & Row in 1962 after it acquired Row, Peterson & Co. In 1966 Canfield was the center of a bitter controversy over William Manchester's *Death of a President,* parts of which were offensive to the Kennedy family.

Gore Vidal, Anaïs Nin, Mickey Spillane, and Françoise Sagan became best sellers with E. P. Dutton & Co. When Elliott Macrae assumed his father's position there, he added a number of exciting works, such as *Annapurna,* Maurice Herzog's story of the conquest of Mount Everest.

The Henry Holt house boasted an impressive list of authors during World War II years, including Ernie Pyle's books and Bill Mauldin's collection of cartoons, but it was in need of stronger leadership by the 1950s, even though books of the stature of Norman Mailer's *The Naked and the Dead* had been listed. Texas oil millionaire Clinton Murchison became involved, purchasing 40 percent of Holt stock; his friend Edgar Rigg became president. The firm added *Field and Stream* to its successful magazine list and dramatically built its textbook sales so that by the end of the 1950s it was outsold only by McGraw-Hill and Prentice Hall. Then in 1959 Rigg acquired Rinehart & Co. and the John C. Winston Co., giving the company a new name, Holt, Rinehart & Winston. CBS took control in 1967, with executives William S. Paley and Frank Stanton taking seats as directors. This followed the pattern of many conglomerate takeovers in which, in the words of historian John Tebbel, publishing houses would be "run by executives who were not bookpeople and who assumed that these houses could be run like any other business."[27]

William Jovanovich was elected president of Harcourt, Brace & Co, in 1955. He soon added his name to the title, as he quickly aimed his firm in the direction of highly diversified activities. Among other things, he was the first modern publisher to arrange for "copublishing," a technique whereby outstanding editors published with him under a joint agreement.

Other major houses were Viking, which in 1975 added Penguin Publishing Ltd. to form Viking Penguin; Simon & Schuster, part of Marshall Field's enterprises for 13 years until it broke loose in 1957; G. P. Putnam's Sons, which took on Mailer's *The Deer Park* and then caused a sensation by publishing Vladimir Nabokov's *Lolita;* Houghton Mifflin, a traditional Boston firm that gave the public Rachel Carson's warnings about the environment, *Silent Spring;* and Little, Brown, another Boston house that became part of the Luce empire in 1968 and later published such notable authors as Frances FitzGerald (*Fire in the Lake,* a distinguished book on Vietnam) and William Manchester (*American Caesar,* the life of Douglas MacArthur).

A major development in 1957 was the establishment of the Atheneum house by the three publishing leaders. Simon Michael Bessie, a senior editor at Harper & Bros., was joined by Hiram Haydn, editor-in-chief at Random House, and Alfred Knopf, Jr., vice president of his father's house. The firm got off to a good start with Jan de Hartog's *The Inspector,* and in 1961 jumped to success by publishing Theodore H. White's *The Making of the President,* which won the Pulitzer Prize for nonfiction. Frederick A. Praeger founded his firm in 1950, starting from scratch and working into the field with books like Hugh Seton-Watson's *From Lenin to Malenkov.* The company became the leading publisher of books about the Cold War; in 1957 it released ex-Communist Howard Fast's repudiation of Communism, *The Naked God,* and Milovan Djilas's *The New Class,* a book written by a Yugoslavian who had split with Marshall Tito.

THE PAPERBACK EXPLOSION

In the paperback field, the Pocket Books company introduced low-cost books to the public in 1939,[28] following the ideas of Robert de Graff and Leon Shimkin. De Graff had been involved with selling inexpensive reprints for years, and Shimkin was a partner with Richard Simon and Max Schuster. De Graff was backed by Pocket Books and given 51 percent control. Within three years 23 million of the 25-cent Pocket Books had been sold, and by the 1950s the company was printing 180 million books annually.

Bantam Books entered the pocket book field in 1945. It later became a leader by publishing topical books soon after major events, rushing into print with Bantam Extras. Fawcett Publications, with *True Confessions, Woman's Day, Mechanix Illustrated,* and other magazines, had been developed by the family of Wilford H. Fawcett. It joined the paperback competition in 1950 with Gold Medal books. This led to the development of Crest Books, which issued the first paperback to break the $1 price, William L. Shirer's *The Rise and Fall of the Third Reich,* which sold for $1.65. Shirer was paid $400,000 for rights to the book, a then unheard of amount.

Dell began issuing its small-sized books in 1942 as an outgrowth of George T. Delacorte's massive publishing business, which turned out 160 million magazines and comic books per year, including *Walt Disney's Comics* and *Looney Tunes.* It was estimated that in 50 years Dell had published between 600 and 700 magazines and that Delacorte himself had owned, at one time or another, more than 200 of them. A number had press runs of more that one million copies. Much of the success was due to the shrewd marketing techniques of Helen Meyer, who finally became president of the firm after working with Delacorte from the opening of the business in 1921.

A quality line of paperbacks was published by New American Library (NAL), founded in 1948 by Kurt Enoch and Victor Weybright, who developed the Signet and Mentor lines for their company. Introducing the "king-size" paperback and better printing, New American Library offered Theodore Dreiser's *An American Tragedy,* Erskine Caldwell's

God's Little Acre, and similar works. NAL set the standard for the future distribution of literature in paperback form. After spectacular success, it was purchased by the Times Mirror Co. in 1966.

Following the rush of paperback publishing in the 1940s and 1950s, publishing leaders began to develop marketing strategies that would allow the systematic distribution of first the hardcover and then the softcover editions of popular books. Later lucrative tie-ins to motion pictures and television productions were engineered, adding yet another dimension to the growing publishing field.

THE MOVIES FACE TV'S CHALLENGE

In the late 1940s the movies were still prosperous. Television was not yet a dangerous rival. Hollywood had a huge worldwide market for more than 400 films yearly. The studios turned out major dramatic films, using the actors they had under contract, and they also made a steady run of low-budget B films. Five of the eight big studios owned chains of theaters that had first pick of the new releases, although they, and the independent theaters, had to take movies sight-unseen under the block-booking system. There were still nearly 20,000 movie houses, and attendance was good, although down one-third in 1950 from an estimated 90 million weekly high.

But Hollywood was soon staggering under three blows. The first was the unexpectedly rapid growth of television, whose nationwide transmission networks were completed by 1951. Mass sales of sets for entertainment at home cut into the number of trips to the neighborhood movie houses for millions of families. The second blow came from a series of consent decrees ordered by the federal courts to break up the practice of block-booking and to force the major producing companies to sell their strings of movie houses. Coming between 1946 and 1948, these decrees hastened the end of the low-budget films, brought a sharp decline in the contract player system, and reduced the number of movies made annually by nearly half. Within another decade the number of movie houses would be reduced one-fourth. The third blow, more psychological than economic, resulted from a series of investigations of the film-making industry by the House Un-American Activities Committee (HUAC). Beginning in 1947 the HUAC subjected hundreds of "suspect" liberal writers and directors to cross-examinations, jailed 10 as unfriendly witnesses, and condemned many others to an informal "blacklisting" ordered by the frightened industry leaders. Jack Warner renounced his wartime film, *Mission to Moscow,* even though it had merely recounted that wartime alliance, and the studios ground out movies extolling the FBI and the anti-Communist crusade.

One response by Hollywood to television was the introduction of the wide screen. Since the pictures on early television sets were very small, the massive scope of the wide screen could hopefully be used to lure audiences back into the movie houses. The standard screen shape since the Kinetoscope had been a rectangle 20 feet wide and 15 feet high, representing a ratio of 1.33 to 1. The new screens were almost twice as wide as they were high; the most successful, Cinemascope, had a proportion of 2.55 to 1. Twentieth Century-Fox released the first wide-screen film, *The Robe,* in 1953.

The new screen permitted further experimentation in visual composition and other movie-making techniques. There had been significant advances during the 1940s, notably by director-actor Orson Welles. His 1941 film, *Citizen Kane,* reflected exciting experimentation, particularly in the technique of narration. The story of an immensely wealthy and domineering businessman, it was clearly identified as a psychological study of publisher William Randolph Hearst. As the decades passed, students of the film ranked it among the top pictures ever made. Director John Ford's production of John Steinbeck's *The Grapes of Wrath* in 1939 had set another standard for the examination of significant social issues. The best of the Hollywood wartime films, produced in 1942, was *Casablanca,* directed by Michael Curtiz and starring Humphrey Bogart and Ingrid Bergman. Katharine Hepburn offered sophisticated comedy, in 1940 with Cary Grant in *The Philadelphia Story* and in 1942 with Spencer Tracy in *Woman of the Year*—the first of eight films for that pair. Bette Davis specialized in melodramas, notably *Jezebel* (1938) and *Little Foxes* (1942); Joan Crawford did the same in *Mildred Pierce* (1945). William Wyler's *Best Years of Our Lives* was a 1946 postwar hit—but was soon condemned by the HUAC as unpatriotic.

Aside from Orson Welles's work, the most significant 1940s films came from abroad. Roberto Rossellini's *Open City* ushered in neorealism in 1945. It was followed by fellow Italian Vittorio de Sica's *The Bicycle Thief* (1947). These war-related films gave way to another theme in Federico Fellini's *La Dolce Vita* (1960). The French "new wave" of 1958 to 1964 took the camera into the streets for imaginative, unstructured story telling best done by François Truffaut and Jean-Luc Godard. British contributions to realism included Tony Richardson's *Room at the Top* (1958), an examination of social mobility, and *A Taste of Honey* (1961). The feelings of a young Russian couple under wartime stress offered reality to viewers of *The Cranes Are Flying* (1957).

Some of these films were breaking down the strictures of the industry production code. In 1956, revisions in the code permitted the depiction of drug addiction, kidnapping, prostitution, and abortion. The 1953 movie *The Moon Is Blue* had depicted adultery. Otto Preminger's *The Man with the Golden Arm* opened up the subject of drugs in 1956. Prostitution was the subject of two 1960 films, *Butterfield 8* and *Girl of the Night.* All were released bearing the Motion Picture Seal of Approval.

There were more conventional films that won critical attention: George Stevens's *Shane,* a 1953 Western; Marlon Brando in *On the Waterfront* (1954); Elizabeth Taylor in *Suddenly Last Summer* (1959), directed by Joseph Mankiewicz. Alfred Hitchcock came to the United States in 1940 after making *The 39 Steps* (1935) in England, in which he used new sound-montage techniques like merging a woman's scream into a train whistle. Hitchcock communicated obsessive or compulsive behavior with maximum intensity in his thrillers *Rear Window* (1954), *Vertigo* (1958), and *Psycho* (1960). David Lean produced notable epics: *Bridge on the River Kwai* (1957), *Lawrence of Arabia* (1962), and *Dr. Zhivago* (1965). The older era of Hollywood filmmaking and "going to the movies" ended on the high note of a new all-time box-office champion in 1965—*Sound of Music* with Julie Andrews, which depicted a joyful outwitting of the Nazis.

Weekly movie attendance had dropped to 40 million by 1960. Movie houses with no more than 500 seats were built at shopping centers, and drive-ins dotted the landscape. The big studios began selling their old films to television beginning in 1955, soon peddling a total of 9000 pre-1948 movies. CBS paid MGM $25 million for the rights to *Gone With the Wind.* The cooperative venture of televising the annual Academy Awards shows helped the movies maintain their image. Still, by 1965 more than 6000 movie houses had shut down. RKO, Republic, and Monogram were gone, and the remaining studios were issuing scarcely 200 films a year.

A SERIES OF ALARMS

As the decade of the 1950s ended it appeared that the United States' problems tended to multiply rather than be solved. President Eisenhower had been reelected in 1956 by an overwhelming margin, over Adlai Stevenson, by stressing his attempts to keep peace in the world. There had been a brief thaw in the United States–Soviet relations, high-lighted by Nikita Khrushchev's "secret" anti-Stalin speech in February 1956. But this came to an end just before the presidential election, when Russian tanks crushed a revolt in Hungary that had won the sympathy of the world but not its active support. The Sovi-ets also were active in the Middle East, where the establishment of Israel in 1948 after a bitter war for independence had triggered a series of crises. Soviet leaders gained new stature in the area through their support of Egypt's Gamal Nasser, who had seized the Suez Canal, the lifeline to the Persian Gulf oil fields. Israel, Britain, and France attempted to regain the canal, but were forced to withdraw after a strong American protest. Following this attempt to act as peacemaker, the Eisenhower administration fashioned the "Eisen-hower Doctrine": a pledge that the United States would assume responsibility to defend the territory and resources of the Middle East, including Turkey, Iran, Iraq, and Pakistan. Israel, however, was not promised direct assistance because of a fear that this would further alienate the Arab states.

In Asia there was continued controversy over Quemoy and Matsu, two small islands in the Formosa Straits close to the Chinese mainland. The Communist shelling of the islands, which were held by Chiang Kai-shek's Nationalists, had caused angry outbursts in Congress about the need to punish "Red China." Communist control of Indochina's northern area was considered a threat to the American-backed Saigon government, and the general American response to Asian Communism had been the formation of the Southeast Asian Treaty Organization (SEATO), the counterpart to Europe's NATO (where tension also increased in 1958 and 1959 during another crisis over Berlin's status). In fact, between 1947 and 1961 the United States had entered into mutual defense agreements with every major friendly nation in the world.

(AP/Wide World Photos)

Vice President Richard Nixon and Soviet Premier Nikita Khrushchev engaged in a spontaneous debate while visiting the kitchen area of a United States exhibit in Moscow. The July 1959 "kitchen debate" height-ened Nixon's reputation. On Nixon's right is Leonid Brezhnev, who later assumed power.

There was trouble on the horizon in Africa, where the force of nationalism would sweep nearly every nation in the 1960s; in Cuba, where Fidel Castro was soon to win and become a declared enemy of the United States; and in Central America, where in Guatemala the CIA engineered the overthrow of the democratically elected government in 1954, and where in Nicaragua the U.S.-backed dictator Anastasio Somoza ruthlessly used his National Guard to crush his opposition. In India, Prime Minister Jawaharlal Nehru was irritating American policy makers by attempting to be neutral in world affairs and by dealing with China.

Domestically, there was increased racial tension in the South. The wide-scale civil-rights movement was close at hand. The Russian success with Sputnik had activated American scientists, and the "space race" was under way. And another presidential campaign was in the making, with Vice President Richard M. Nixon the apparent choice of Republicans.

In December 1959, Americans indicated that newspapers were slightly more believable than television news reports, 32 percent to 29 percent, followed by other media. Within two years this would switch to television's favor, 39 percent to 24 percent. But when asked which medium of communication they would retain if allowed to keep only one, 42 percent said television, 32 percent newspapers, and 19 percent radio.[29] Television's impact—as an entertainment medium as well as a distributor of vital news—would be felt even more strongly in the 1960s.

Walter Cronkite of CBS excelled in reporting the first manned space flights. Below, the NBC team of Chet Huntley and David Brinkley led in election-night coverage during the 1960s.

(CBS)

17

Challenges
and Dissent

**The United States might leave Vietnam, but the Vietnam War
would now never leave the United States.**

—Frances FitzGerald in Fire in the Lake

If in later years some Americans harked back to the 1950s, trying to regain a lost sense of
security and discipline, others recalled with mixed feelings the traumas and satisfactions
of the 1960s when the nation was swept along the gamut of emotions. Shocking news
bulletins telling of assassinations, race riots, and escalations of the Vietnam War produced
reactions of anger, fear, sadness, and sheer bewilderment. But contentment was felt by
those supporting the enforcement of new civil-rights laws and the expansion of political
participation. And there was a swelling of pride throughout the land in July 1969, when
Americans stood on the moon.

The images of the decade, captured by print and broadcast journalists, are unforgettable. A panorama of scenes would show President Kennedy fending off tough questions
with wit and charm at one of his televised news conferences, Attorney General Robert
Kennedy on the phone planning strategy during a civil-rights confrontation in the South,
Mrs. Kennedy taking a television crew on a White House tour, and the same Mrs. Kennedy
stepping off Air Force One with her husband's coffin in view behind her. There would be
Martin Luther King, Jr., giving his "I Have a Dream" speech in Washington, Lyndon Johnson and his advisers pondering the next step during the war, antiwar demonstrators being
clubbed by Chicago police, Richard Nixon on the campaign trail again, women parading
for equality, and national guardsmen riding through city streets brandishing machine guns.
It all began in the spring of 1960, when John Fitzgerald Kennedy entered the presidential
primaries, declaring that it was time for a new generation to hold power.

NIXON VERSUS KENNEDY: "THE GREAT DEBATES"

In late June 1960, Congress suspended Section 315 of the Communications Act of 1934, the so-called equal-time rule requiring broadcasters to offer equal time to candidates for every party seeking a political office. This allowed the campaign managers for Nixon and Kennedy to begin negotiations leading to four televised debates in September and October. Kennedy had won the Democratic nomination with primary-election victories over Hubert H. Humphrey in Wisconsin and West Virginia and through a demonstration of power at the Los Angeles convention after delegates and supporters of Adlai E. Stevenson erupted into a frenzied, memorable demonstration that momentarily threatened to halt the Kennedy surge. Vice President Nixon had bested New York governor Nelson Rockefeller to win the Republican nomination during a Chicago convention at which many of the charges of the 1950s about China, Korea, and internal security were repeated.

More than 85 million Americans tuned in to at least one of the Kennedy-Nixon debates. But the first debate, moderated by CBS news correspondent Howard K. Smith and carried on the three major networks, provided the crucial moment of the campaign. It was that evening in Chicago, September 26, that the less well known Kennedy showed that he was an even match for the vice president.[1]

As the two men traded comments about the United States' economic health and their own qualifications, Kennedy looked poised and fit, while Nixon seemed weary and somewhat gray. Occasionally the camera showed a worried Nixon listening to Kennedy, while a few minutes later a confident Kennedy was shown listening to one of Nixon's counter-charges. From this point on Kennedy would be free of being called immature.

Kennedy's November victory by the margin of only 118,550 votes was attributed to his favorable television image. At age 43 he was the youngest man, and the first Roman Catholic, to be elected president.

KENNEDY AND THE PRESS: LIVE NEWS CONFERENCES

Kennedy introduced the live televising and broadcasting of presidential press conferences, an innovation with mixed blessings. The White House correspondents found that their home offices heard and saw the presidential responses long before the news stories clattered into their news desks. The mystique of the White House press conference in the Oval Room was gone. A skilled president could use the correspondents as foils or actors, and a few correspondents became actors by choice. On the positive side, millions of Americans could see the press conferences for themselves, live at the moment or digested in the evening news. Most of Kennedy's press conferences were in the afternoons, in time for Walter Cronkite and Huntley-Brinkley to feature their highlights. Kennedy handled the star role far better than any of the presidents of his period; he was young, charming, stylish, and as disarmingly humorous or severely grave as circumstances dictated. In short, he put on a good show.

Behind this Kennedy the public knew was a president who was anxious for his administration's image, who gave frequent individual interviews and had correspondents among his friends, who read a half-dozen leading papers daily and resented their criticisms so much that he once banned the *Herald Tribune* temporarily. His press secretary, Pierre Salinger, took a hard line with the correspondents, as did Pentagon spokesperson Arthur Sylvester, who uttered the ill-fated comment about "the government's inherent right to lie" in cases in which government officials claim that the national security is at stake.

Threat to UN Eases; Peking Casts Shadow

By the Associated Press
New York

President Eisenhower and British Prime Minister Harold Macmillan agreed Sept. 27 to give "full support" to United Nations Secretary-General Dag Hammarskjold in his tasks. Mr. Hammarskjold has been a target of Soviet Premier Nikita S. Khrushchev.

By Joseph C. Harsch
Special correspondent of
The Christian Science Monitor
United Nations, N.Y.

The delicate compromise of Indian Prime Minister Jawaharlal Nehru and the phlegmatic urbanity of British Prime Minister Harold Macmillan flowed over the United Nations scene as the General Assembly went into the second week of its extraordinary session here in New York.

The effect was steadying on all—with, of course, the exception of Premier Fidel Castro of Cuba, who embarrassed his apparent friends and bored the rest of his audience with his inability to distinguish interminable rhetoric from logic.

The importance of Soviet

Premier Nikita S. Khrushchev's role has visibly diminished as the awareness spreads that he has neither wrecked the UN nor possesses the capacity to do so. Dag Hammarskjold is still Secretary-General and will continue to be so.

A count of hands shows that Mr. Khrushchev could barely get 15 votes for his proposals which sounded so ominous a few days before, and the conviction grew that he had launched his assault on the UN—and for an instant expecting to get anywhere with it, but primarily as a talking point for his cunning argument with the Chinese Communists, with some incidental possible bargaining value here.

It is conceivable that he might at some point withdraw his threats against the UN in return for some benefit in future negotiations with the West, but his main purpose, it was agreed among Western diplomats, had been to forge a weapon he could use in the mighty waters of Communist-bloc politics.

Mr. Nehru and Mr. Macmillan arrived on the scene not overawed by the superficial dis-

cussions on disarmament which rejected the theoretical purpose of this gathering; and not unduly disturbed by the flurry over the UN which struck both of the new arrivals as equally unrealistic. Mr. Khrushchev had produced massive sound and fury which on examination proved to be nothing but froth.

Nehru's Concern

What concerned Mr. Nehru the most was not Dr. Castro's display of vulgar histrionics, but the flexing muscles of the Chinese giant across his northern frontier. And what was reportedly uppermost in Mr. Macmillan's thinking was the long-term implication of the Soviet-managed operation of recent weeks in the Congo.

The real dangers, as these men see them, and as their Washington colleagues agreed, are not immediate nor here in the UN, but in the fact that Moscow was able to deploy hundreds of "technicians" in the Congo on the first visible sign of an opportunity to make a new conquest for communism there, and of the even more disturbing implication that this abrupt action reflected a trend of willingness in Moscow to take and dangerous risks with the peace under the steady glare of Peking excitement to violence which is the brand of Communist bloc behavior the year.

Key Question Cited

The visitors from London have been sobered by the Congo operation and while Mr. Macmillan himself can still see much theoretical merit in reviving the personal relations with Mr. Khrushchev, he and his associates have forced the fact that Moscow proved in the Congo both its possession of a highly trained apparatus for suddenly exploiting an opportunity that conquest far beyond its frontiers and the cynical willingness to use it.

The visitors from India have been sobered by their own experience under the shadow of Chinese expansionism and the many current indications that the dragon is still hungry and is still pushing with increasing truculence against the world around it.

The real question which the Western statesmen talked about off the UN stage in the hotel rooms was the long-term problem of how to persuade, some would say help, Mr. Khrushchev to resist the arguments would have for months been heating upon him from Peking to revert to ever greater violence and revolution in a major Communist attack.

Soviet Task?

The most significant event at this session may well prove to be the meeting between Mr. Nehru and Mr. Khrushchev, although it will certainly be years, if ever, before the real essence of this encounter will be spread on the public record.

It is perfectly obvious that Mr. Nehru called on Mr. Khrushchev to discover in best he could whether Mr. Khrushchev either willingly or under pressure which he thinks he can no longer resist is committed to the Chinese deflated course. Mr. Nehru is far too responsible a statesman to disclose what, if anything, he learned.

The dominant fact overshadowing this meeting is that Mr. Khrushchev, while clinging to his theories of the inevitability of communist conflict "peaceful co-existence," has done in the Congo precisely the sort of thing which Peking has been urging. In he committed permanently down this line, or is he treading it to build strength within the Communist bloc for a showdown with Peking which some Western experts increasingly regard may be the greatest struggle looming on the world's horizon today?

Meeting Unlikely

Communist labor leadership is hidden to assemble in Moscow in early November. Every Communist move here is quite probably shaped to that gathering of the clan where the issues outstanding between Moscow and Peking must be thrashed out by another whether China is represented or stays away.

Under these circumstances it may now be assumed that the idea of any major effort to bring agreement with Communist China, then there is no possibility of any news here of a surprise meeting between the two new leaders of Peking and Moscow either in Paris last May.

The most alarming possibility is that the failure of the Congo venture and the impending possibility here to stampede the new African countries into the Communist field can good Mr. Khrushchev not toward moderation but toward even more dangerous ventures.

In the meantime, though, the excitement is diminishing here and the British intend to express their views on all this to much help both their Prime Minister and their Foreign Minister back in London come next weekend.

John F. Kennedy
Resolved ...

Debate Winner? Voters of Nation

By Godfrey Sperling, Jr.
Chief of the Central News Bureau of The Christian Science Monitor
Chicago

The focal point of some 130,000,000 eyes, the presidential candidates squared off in the first of four unprecedented joint appearances before a vast TV audience.

The winner? The American public was the winner.

The silent Chicago streets, the cavernous ball park, the almost empty theaters. All this attested to the public's intense interest in the two candidates and a clash that centered on the farm, the aged, the schools, the economic growth rate, the lowering of the national debt, the relative maturity and experience of the two men. But that impact naturally spilled over into America's posture in the world today, and who was best qualified to provide leadership for the next four or eight years.

For reporters who have been following the candidates around the United States, there was little that was new in what the two men said. Senator John F. Kennedy, again, was saying that America's prestige, vis-à-vis the Soviet Union, was not good enough. Vice-President Richard M. Nixon was saying it had, indeed, been good enough. And both were agreeing that there must be a step up for the future—militarily, scientifically, educationally, economically.

In the main, the verbal exchanges here showed that the objectives of the two candidates are quite similar. The difference lies in the means—and the cost of the means.

Mr. Nixon said, as he has said before, that he has tabulated the Democratic program and thinks it will cost $13,200,-000,000 to perhaps $18,000,-000,000 while, he said, his own program would cost some $4,000,000,000 to $4,900,900,-900.

Richard M. Nixon
Resolved ...

Not One Slip On Banana Peel!

By Richard L. Strout
Staff Correspondent of The Christian Science Monitor
Washington

The first reception of the unprecedented Nixon-Kennedy debate in millions of homes was a gasp of surprise. For till that had been written about it in advance, most viewers were not prepared for the bare, bleak, brutal stage, utterly devoid of any titivating background of decoration, this two men sent flying in space for 65 million to watch.

As the ordeal continued, many viewers must have had a sense of sympathy for either candidate, whichever first could stub a toe, either in physical affiliation, at the terrible stress to which they were subjected. Any slip might have swelled run for either candidate and his party's hopes. The bare stage was actually strewn with invisible banana peels, and it was hard for the viewer not to feel a sense of admiration for the sure-footed young men, each of whom, in the opinion of many, displayed a quite astonishing grasp of detail and fluidity for quick calculation or ideas.

Rise to Challenge

The cameras showed closeups of the listening candidate's face while the other talked. Senator John F. Kennedy, his chin raised in a Roosevelt tilt with clean profile and lips slightly moving; Vice-President Richard M. Nixon, in turn, pointing to many more—and-possibly with chin perspiring with the hot TV lights, the tropical glare. No other candidates in American presidential history went through such an ordeal, watch seemed as almost unreal in its revealing details.

The candidates rose to the challenge, however, and after a preliminary period of rigidity seemed to relax in the home-long interrogation and reply which is the first of four such performances.

By the loss of a coin Mr. Kennedy not merely spoke first but had the last word, an advantage which Mr. Nixon will have in inter meetings. Some observers felt that Senator Kennedy was energized in his opening statement, which was composed of fragments of campaign speeches which he had by heart. In turn, Mr. Nixon seemed to gather strength as the proceedings continued as he drew constantly increasing objections in the guts of Mr. Kennedy's prevailing composure.

To some Senator Kennedy seemed to have a second problem—a very advantage in that he was making the attack on the Eisenhower-Republican policies, while Mr. Nixon, so first, was in the position of a defender. As interior...

State of the Nations

Who Pays for Reform?

By William H. Stringer
Chief, Washington News Bureau, The Christian Science Monitor
Washington

The first Nixon-Kennedy televised debate points up a behavior in the business community.

♦ ♦ ♦

Quite evidently, Senator John F. Kennedy would proceed more vigorously—or drastically—using more costly programs than would Vice-President Richard M. Nixon, and in his efforts to handle the problems of aid to education, minimum wage, federal power, medical care for the elderly, perhaps defense. The question then is not merely that raised by Mr. Nixon, which is whether Congress would approve the 90 days of vigorous legislation which a President Kennedy in the White House would favor.

The question is also whether the business and industrial community of the United States would take this added burden, which almost certainly would mean an additional tax burden, in the proper...

Text of Statements
In TV Debate: Page 16

a display of outstanding mental capacity or was this, at least in part, the expression of countless little ceremonial speeches? The limitations of TV could not assure this with a certainty, although the viewers—and particularly those who had already chosen up sides—probably resolved this question to their own satisfaction.

Actually, the question—from panel format is not one that brings about a clear clash of the "debaters." There was really little opportunity for either of the candidates to probe the other's mind—or to pressure the other with new questions.

Production Figures

It was Mr. Nixon, the man of experience under fire, the man of the kitchen debates with Soviet Premier Nikita S. Khrushchev, who looked strained in the early minutes of the discussion. He calling well, but Kennedy had probably made a point. His contained poise no doubt helped to put the immaturity charge to rest—for the evening, and perhaps the entire campaign.

In the exchange of figures on economic growth, Mr. Nixon flatly said that the Soviet production rate was 44 per cent that of the United States—the same that it was 20 years ago.

Senator Kennedy seemed to accept this figure but said it was important that the Soviets' production did not rise to 60 or 70 per cent in the next few years. Earlier, Mr. Nixon had said that the Soviet's economic growth rate had been good in late years only because it was measured against a very low base.

Had Mr. Nixon asked Senator Kennedy on the acceptance of a production figure, an acceptance that current productions were not as bad as he had pictured? Perhaps so, but then, again, maybe only in the midst of Mr. Nixon's partisan ...

Public the Critic

Actually, this was a strange occasion, where the press was not reporting anything that the public was not, itself, seeing—and analyzing for itself. And even a supercritical critique seems inconsequential. For the viewers are the critics.

Was Senator Kennedy or Mr. Nixon more persuasive than the other? How many votes were changed or won? The real critiques will be coming in on Nov. 8, in terms of votes for the next President of the United States.

Inside Reading

Facts and fireworks over school center managers.
Page 2

Lynn residents take strike threat in stride.
Page 2

Congo: Ghana keeps up pressure.
Page 19

Glitter gone from golden Prague.
Page 12

Research by NASA discloses goals for moon probing.
Page 9

Southern Democrats take stand on foreign policy.
Page 14

MDC Probe Hears Political Echoes

By Albert D. Hughes
Staff Writer of The Christian Science Monitor

Political overtones today were injected into the special Massachusetts Senate committee investigation of the Metropolitan District Commission.

Senator John R. Powers (D) of Boston implied that the administration of Gov. Christian A. Herter and MDC commissioner Charles W. Greenough rolled off the Pleasure Bay project in his testimony. The project was an enclosed area along a Boston harbor which would be free of tides and available throughout most of the day as a bathing beach.

Associate Commissioner Greenough, who was on the witness stand, suggested that the project was large and had been politically controversial. He furthermore asserted "I was not ordered to roll it off."

Start Recalled

The associate commissioner testified that the Pleasure Bay project originated in a telephone call between himself and Senator Powers while he was on a vacation in Maine. Upon his return the then Commissioner said he sat down with Senator Powers and talked over the project.

Mr. Greenough further asserted that the Herter administration had concerned itself as strongly opposed to the project. Earlier in his testimony Senator Powers interrupted Mr. Greenough to ask him what steps he had taken to reorganize the MDC after he became Commissioner.

Mr. Greenough displayed copies of bills which he had placed in the Legislature to put the executive and administrative of the MDC under the Commissioner rather than the Board of Commissioners.

Bill Quoted

Senator Powers took a copy of the bill and stated that nowhere in it was there any indication that an MDC official was interested in the legislation, even though it concerned the MDC.

Resentment of key career employees over politics and events in the operations of the Metropolitan District Commission was illustrated in testimony of Benjamin W. Fink, of Newton, chief engineer in the MDC Parks Division, before the special Senate committee investigating the MDC.

A career employee with the MDC for 30 years and for 12 years head of the Parks Division, Mr. Fink charged that the MDC is wasting half of the mil-

lions it spends on consultants' fees.

The special inquiry is expected to conclude today with testimony from MDC Commissioner John E. Maloney and Associate Commissioners Charles W. Greenough and John Hill.

Already, disclosures of the hearings have promoted new reform and other changes are in stores for the MDC. At its regular meeting last week no Tuesday voted to review all new under-$1,000 contracts.

On the subject of these contracts, which it is charged were split to evade requirements for public bidding, Mr. Fink said political assertions were responsible for "poor supervision" of such contracts.

Mr. Fink testified he was forced to rely on subordinates for checking the under-$1,000 contracts and stated that it was a "plastic impossibility" for him to oversee this work personally, though it carried his approving signature.

The MDC engineer who testified that members of his staff split bids or order to evade the under-$1,000 bid provisions over the under-$1,000 "political controls" to the bearing.

The Newton engineer also said that he too imposed all payment of under-$1,000 contracts, but since the investigations began, expert for emergency work.

Mr. Fink also testified he too has overruled the specters he suggested as an instance of the kind of the idea of any major effort to bring agreement with Communist China, then there is no possibility of any news here of a surprise meeting between the two new leaders of Peking and Moscow either in Paris last May.

Resignations Sought

Mr. Fink also testified he too posting that qualified steel inspectors be engaged when the Longfellow Bridge contract was begun and of being turned down by the commission. He said the MDC had five inspectors on the Longfellow Bridge job but none of them were qualified steel inspectors.

The disclosures brought from George A. McLaughlin, chief counsel a statement that "we are going to ask, in our final report, that the Legislature abolish to build all steel roads, bridges, buildings, both for the state and the MDC, and that it be properly staffed with a central engineering division, and that it pay these engineers the going rates."

Senator Francis X. McCann (D), of Cambridge, committee member, also remarked "I think something was wrong here, dangerous ventures."

The Cambridge legislator made this statement after hearing testimony of William A. Meagher, of Wakefield, administrative assistant to Commissioner Moloney.

Pictures: Page 2

U.S. and U.A.R. Presidents Meet

President Eisenhower (left) and United Arab Republic President Nasser had a show of hands as they met at President Eisenhower's hotel suite in New York Sept. 26. Mr. Eisenhower arrived from Washington earlier and held talks with various foreign dignitaries in New York for the 15th UN General Assembly. President Nasser is reported to have invited Mr. Eisenhower to pay a visit to the U.A.R. as Mr. Nasser's guest of honor. Eisenhower's hurried New York day: Page 3

Goldfine Case To Open in Boston

The World's Day

New England: Tax-Evasion Trial Set for Oct. 3

The $400,000 tax-evasion case of industrialist Bernard Goldfine will open Monday, Oct. 3, in United States District Court, Boston. Mr. Goldfine, currently in the Federal Correctional Institution in Danbury, Conn., on a contempt-of-court sentence ending Monday, will be brought to Charles Street Jail this weekend. United States Attorney Elliot L. Richardson will prosecute the case.

National: Candidates Back on Campaign Trail

Following the "great debate" Vice-President Richard M. Nixon headed south for campaign activities in Tennessee and Arkansas. Senator John F. Kennedy flew to Ohio for a one-day political swing.

The father of 15-year-old Caryl Ann Powers, who failed in attempts to see Soviet Premier Nikita S. Khrushchev on behalf of his son, appealed to the Kremlin leader through the Dave Garroway "Today" show on NBC television.

Asia: South Korea Plans to Grant Pardons

Premier John M. Chang's South Korean Government decided to grant pardons or reduction of sentences to nearly 1,000 prisoners Oct. 1 in celebration of the founding of the Second Republic. Dr. Meanwhile, the government prosecution demanded capital punishment for four top-ranking police officials charged with rigging national elections last March.

Weather: Cloudy Tonight and Wednesday [Page 2]

Arts, Music, Theater: Page 7. Radio, TV, FM: Page 6

Just Before the Opening Gavel

Presidential candidates Nixon and Kennedy trade grins

The crucial first "Great Debate" on television decided the 1960 presidential race.

The press was upset in April 1961 when it was given clouded information about the Bay of Pigs, the futile attempt by the Kennedy administration to support a CIA-planned invasion of Castro's Cuba by a small army of exiles. The expedition, planned by the Eisenhower administration and agreed to by Kennedy upon advice from CIA officials, was a disaster. Kennedy accepted full responsibility and angrily dismissed CIA head Allen W. Dulles.

The Kennedy administration unified its news sources, sought to manage the contacts between officials and the press, and was accused of seeking to manage the news itself. During the Cuban Missile Crisis of 1962, when Kennedy grimly told the nation that Russian missiles in Cuba were a threat to the United States and could lead to nuclear war, the administration insisted that the crisis was so severe as to require press self-control and privately suggested possible censorship of the press in the event of actual hostilities. Publication of the "Pentagon Papers" in 1971 proved a far deeper American involvement in Vietnam affairs by 1963 than the Kennedy administration had ever acknowledged, including a share of responsibility for the assassination of President Diem, and showed that the Saigon press corps had been essentially correct in vainly protesting the deepening entanglement in a "quagmire." While public opinion supported the president, there was enough doubt to indicate that a credibility gap existed.

Following the tradition of previous Democratic presidents, Kennedy had received marginal support from newspapers during the campaign, getting only 16 percent of the endorsements. The *New York Times,* however, had swung behind him after supporting Eisenhower twice, and his friend Philip L. Graham headed the *Washington Post.* But after receiving careful treatment from old family friend Henry Luce during the campaign—until the end, when Nixon received the coveted endorsement—Kennedy fell into disfavor with *Time* and *Life* and continued to irritate conservative publishers.[2]

Kennedy was hardly "soft on Communism," however, as some publishers and columnists suggested. The Soviets repeatedly put him to test, first in August 1961, when they built the Berlin Wall. During the Cuban Missile Crisis in October, 1962, Nikita Khrushchev played brinkmanship to the hilt, forcing Kennedy to declare a blockade of Cuba and to threaten the use of arms if the Soviets persisted in setting up missile bases. On October 22 Kennedy made a historic 17-minute address, informing frightened Americans of his ultimatum. Khrushchev backed down in return for a pledge that the United States would not attack Cuba in the future. Later Kennedy visited Berlin, and home viewers saw him honored by millions of West Germans as he said in German, "I am a Berliner." Meanwhile, on the domestic front, the Kennedy brothers used the federal government to protect the civil rights of southern blacks. Robert Kennedy put Teamsters President James Hoffa in prison, and the president made headlines by attacking the steel industry when leaders attempted to obtain a price hike. During his "1000 days" in office Kennedy was an exciting personality. The Washington press corps responded with uncounted stories about the Kennedy "clan" as well as those on traditional topics. Because of this general fondness for Kennedy he was spared hard looks into his personal life that might have revealed sensual interests capable of destroying his presidency. He was especially appreciated by television news executives, who liked his manner and the drama surrounding him.

THE KENNEDY ASSASSINATION: THE END OF THE "1000 DAYS"

There were many reasons in November 1963 why a group of conspirators—or a lone deranged killer—would have wished John Fitzgerald Kennedy dead. First there was the "Cuban problem." The island remained in Castro's hands, despite a CIA vendetta against him that was disclosed later. Organized crime leaders were furious over the loss of hundreds of millions of dollars in gambling and prostitution revenues due to federal crackdowns. Ex-CIA officials and veterans of the Bay of Pigs failure were embittered over JFK's decision not to use American forces in 1961 and during the crisis of 1962. Mob leaders worried how far Robert Kennedy might go in his racket-busting campaign, already having obtained a conviction of Teamsters boss James Hoffa. Kennedy had signed a nuclear test-ban treaty with the Soviet Union in June 1963, and finally, in August, he issued a strong statement of support after Martin Luther King, Jr., and other black leaders led the largest civil-rights rally in the nation's history, 200,000 strong, at the Lincoln Memorial.

Looking ahead to the 1964 campaign, Kennedy agreed to travel to Texas in November. Vice President Lyndon Johnson wanted Kennedy to help mend some political fences. It was a bright, sunny day, November 22, when the president's motorcade headed through downtown Dallas on its way to the Trade Mart, where Kennedy was to address a luncheon audience. Merriman Smith of the United Press International was in the front seat of a "pool" car—next to a telephone—and three other reporters were in the back seat. Then, as the Kennedy car slowly turned a corner at the end of the parade route, shots were fired. It was 12:30 P.M.

The president's limousine and its police and Secret Service escorts roared off at high speed. Smith wrote later: "Our car stood still for probably only a few seconds, but it seemed

(Edwin Emery personal collection)

President Kennedy and Merriman Smith

like a lifetime. One sees history explode before one's eyes and for even the most trained observer, there is a limit to what one can comprehend."[3] As the pool car careened along the freeway, Smith dialed the Dallas UPI number and reached William Payette, the southwestern division manager. At 12:34 P.M. the UPI "A" wire carried these words:

DALLAS, NOV. 22 (UPI) THREE SHOTS WERE FIRED AT PRESIDENT KENNEDY'S MOTORCADE TODAY IN DOWNTOWN DALLAS, JT1234PCS

The New York UPI office broke in with, "Dallas it's yours," meaning that all other bureaus should refrain from transmitting. The wire was kept open. In the pool car Smith held onto the phone, while Jack Bell of the AP pounded him on the back, yelling, "Smitty, give me the phone." When the car reached Parkland Hospital Smith threw Bell the phone and rushed to the Kennedy car. He saw both the president and Texas Governor John B. Connolly cradled in their wives' arms. Smith asked about the president and heard Secret Service agent Clint Hill say, "He's dead." With that Smith ran into the hospital amidst the hysteria. He managed to reach the Dallas bureau and began to dictate what would become a Pulitzer Prize–winning story. Smith's "flash" and story were jammed onto the wire. The unusually long "flash" was jumbled. Official style was lost for a few seconds.

> FLASH
> FLASH
> KENNEDY SERIOUSLY WOUNDED. PERHAPS SERIOUSLY
> PERHAPS FATALLY BY ASSASSIN'S BULLETS
> UP19N BULLETIN 1ST LEAD SHOOTING
> PRESIDENT KENNEDY AND GOV. JOHN B. CONNOLLY OF
> TEXAS WERE CUT DOWN BY ASSASSIN'S BULLETS AS THEY
> TOURED DOWNTOWN DALLAS IN AN OPEN AUTOMOBILE TO-
> DAY
> More JT1241PCS

Jack Fallon took charge of the writing within the bureau and was later credited with the smooth flow of the copy. The story was rushed onto the UPI broadcast wire, and within minutes AP wires were confirming the horrifying news. Then at 1:32 P.M. the AP flashed, "TWO PRIESTS SAY KENNEDY DEAD." By this time, television sets around the nation had been switched on. In New York City the audience jumped from 30 percent to 70 percent. At CBS Cronkite had rushed into the newsroom to begin broadcasting the first details. Now he and his counterparts at the other networks had the AP flash. CBS radio, through the reporting of Dan Rather in Texas, had already announced the president's death. Then came the confirmation of the AP reports. At 1:35 P.M. UPI said, "FLASH. PRESIDENT DEAD." Tears welled in Cronkite's eyes, and in those of millions of others.

There was no other news that day. The press associations used every available wire to pump the Dallas news and reaction stories to their media outlets. Regular television programming was canceled. Radio stations played somber music. Then came the news that Lee Harvey Oswald, a member of the left-wing Fair Play for Cuba Committee, had been arrested and charged with the assassination.

Later it was said the days November 22 to 25 were the finest in television history. Calm, comprehensive coverage of the news from Dallas and Washington—the transition from Kennedy to Lyndon Johnson—gave the nation a sense of security. On the evening of November 22, Air Force One returned to Washington. The public saw Jacqueline Kennedy,

The great *New York Herald Tribune* records history with superb journalistic skill.

still wearing her blood-stained pink suit, accompanying her husband's body and being comforted by Robert Kennedy and other family members. Lyndon Johnson made a brief statement at the airport. Smith and Charles Roberts of *Newsweek* were the pool reporters on that historic flight. Meanwhile, major news organizations sent additional reporters, photographers, and television crews to Dallas to assist the exhausted members of the White House press corps.

Several young reporters established their reputations on the day of Kennedy's assassination. Rather distinguished himself and afterwards was named White House correspondent. CBS felt that Rather, a Texan, might gain some advantage with Johnson. Tom Wicker of the *New York Times* also produced an amazingly comprehensive story by running from one location to another throughout the day.

On Sunday, November 24, television cameras were focused on the scene in the Capitol rotunda, where President Kennedy's body had rested overnight. Leaders of the free world were headed to Washington for Monday's funeral. Sunday was a day of eulogies and pleas for an end to violence and hatred. Shortly after 12:30 P.M. Oswald was being transferred from the Dallas police station to the county jail. The scene was picked up on monitors in the three network control rooms in New York. NBC made the decision to switch to Dallas immediately, while CBS and ABC stayed with the pictures from the Capitol, where Mrs. Kennedy and her children stood near the coffin.

Tom Pettit of NBC was only a few feet from Oswald when the suspect was led through the basement door and into an underground parking garage in Dallas. As Pettit began to describe the scene a burly man shoved his way through the edge of the crowd of police, reporters, and photographers. Jack Ruby, handgun extended, fired one shot into Oswald's body. The shot was plainly heard. It was television's first live murder. CBS and ABC videotaped the scene, and the three networks showed it repeatedly throughout the rest of the day and evening.[4]

Oswald died one hour later, ten feet from where Kennedy had died. Americans sat stunned in their living rooms, speculating about the bizarre turn of the events. The next day they watched the funeral. Television cameras were stationed at every major Washington intersection, and correspondents sometimes failed to hold back their emotions as the casket passed and the bands played sad hymns. The nation fell silent as the final words were said at Arlington National Cemetery and military planes roared over, with one plane missing from the formation as a symbol of loss.

President Johnson ordered a complete investigation of Kennedy's killing, and a commission was established under the leadership of Chief Justice Earl Warren. In 1964 the Warren Commission issued its findings: that Oswald had acted alone and that he had fired three shots, killing Kennedy with the third shot, which hit the president in the head. There was instant rebuttal of these findings and critics like Mark Lane, author of *Rush to Judgment,* used a homemade movie taken by Abraham Zapruder of Dallas to make their case. A frame-by-frame analysis showed that Oswald had 4.6 seconds to fire the second and third shots. The Warren Commission thesis rested on the statement that there were *three* shots. If so, one shot had to have hit both Kennedy and Connolly, because one bullet hit the street and another shot clearly hit the president in the head.

Among news organizations, *Life* offered the best examination of the evidence, partially because the magazine had purchased Zapruder's film. In October 1964, *Life* said of the Warren report, "The major significance . . . is that it lays to rest the lurid rumors and wild speculations."[5] But in November 1966, *Life,* relying on Connolly's testimony that he had not been hit by the same bullet as Kennedy, demanded that the case be reopened. A year later *Life* offered unpublished photos by onlookers that suggested the possibility of a conspiracy but fell short of proving it. In December 1967, the *Saturday Evening Post* claimed that Kennedy was killed by three assassins who fired from different angles.

Major papers shied from the conspiracy story, out of disbelief and also because such an investigation would require an enormous amount of time and money. In 1966 the *New York Times* finally decided to go ahead with an investigation, with Harrison Salisbury as the reporter, but he was granted his visa to visit Hanoi at that time and the project was dropped. CBS News, with Rather the reporter, produced a documentary and decided that there was little, if any, evidence of a conspiracy. Prior to his death in 1972, however, former President Johnson told Cronkite that he had never believed the Warren Commission report. The comment was part of a taped interview, but Johnson refused to permit its broadcast, despite Cronkite's pleadings. In 1978 the House Select Committee on Assassinations held hearings on the deaths of President Kennedy and Martin Luther King, Jr. While the committee issued the startling report that both leaders likely were victims of conspiracies, no hard evidence that might have led to further investigations was revealed. Throughout the years a plethora of books, videos, and motion pictures have attempted to prove a number of conspiracy theories. On the thirtieth anniversary of the Kennedy killing, numerous television news reports and documentaries refueled the old arguments, but not with the uproar caused by Oliver Stone's film *J.F.K.*, with its wide-ranging accusations and dramatic use of the Zapruder film.

THE PROTEST MOVEMENTS FIGHT RACISM, SEXISM, AND IMPERIALISM

The powerful antiestablishment movements of the 1960s were the culmination of many previous efforts to change laws discriminating against minorities and women and to halt imperialistic adventures that depleted the nation's treasure. Much of the activity can be traced to the student movements of the late 1950s at Berkeley, Chicago, Columbia, Michigan, and Oberlin. When young blacks staged a sit-in at a F. W. Woolworth store in Greensboro, North Carolina, in February 1960, they triggered a nationwide reaction. College students in other states began picketing Woolworth stores, which eventually led to the desegregation of public facilities. Also in 1960, a number of Berkeley students protesting a House Un-American Activities Committee session in San Francisco were beaten by police and arrested.

The first Freedom Riders made their way into the South in May 1961, continuing the sit-ins and demanding an end to restrictions in voting laws. Television news teams soon spread images of angry whites and defiant southern authorities. Ku Klux Klansmen organized opposition to the Freedom Riders, and on several occasions buses were burned and the riders severely beaten. During the early 1960s several civil-rights workers were murdered. Paving the way for other protesters were members of the Congress of Racial Equality (CORE), led by James Farmer, and the Student Nonviolent Coordinating Committee (SNCC).

Attorney General Robert Kennedy petitioned the Interstate Commerce Commission to desegregate all airport terminals and railroad depots. The "white" and "colored" signs were taken down by the end of 1961. That year the Kennedys also used federal power to force the University of Mississippi to register James Meredith, an Air Force veteran. Dozens of federal marshals were injured, some of them by snipers' bullets, and two people were killed when a large mob attacked those protecting Meredith. Regular U.S. Army troops were used to quell the bloody rioting.

The Bay of Pigs disaster of 1961 and the terrible fear of nuclear war brought more campus protests. The Students for a Democratic Society (SDS) issued their Port Huron Statement in 1962, denouncing domestic racism and overseas imperialism. Until its dissolution into warring factions in 1969, SDS was the organizational soul of the New Left, as described by Todd Gitlin in his media analysis *The Whole World Is Watching.*

Then, in 1963, the civil-rights movement hit full stride, as did its media coverage. Martin Luther King, Jr., declared war on Birmingham, Alabama, which he considered the citadel of racism. The police chief there, T. Eugene "Bull" Connor, became a symbol of southern resistance. While King led a series of sit-ins and marches, the Kennedys were determined to integrate the University of Alabama in a showdown with the rebellious governor George C. Wallace.

Wallace did stand in the doorway of a university building, reading for the television cameras a proclamation forbidding the intrusion of the federal government. But the black students Vivian J. Malone and Jimmy A. Hood were registered at the university, one more step in ending segregation in universities. Meanwhile, Birmingham blacks had taken to the streets in protest of the vicious use of police dogs against demonstrators. Pictures of police using dogs and fire hoses against defenseless blacks circulated the world, creating an embarrassing image for the United States.

The first of the "long hot summers" began in 1964 in Harlem, where blacks went on a rampage after a police officer shot a 14-year-old boy. Waves of hostility long kept under control burst loose. The next summer riots broke out in the Watts section of Los Angeles. More than 20,000 National Guardsmen and local authorities were called into a 50-square-mile riot area. After six days of burning and fighting, 34 people were dead and another 1000 injured. A split occurred in the black leadership in 1966 when Stokely Carmichael took over SNCC and Floyd McKissick replaced Farmer at CORE. Carmichael and McKissick urged strong action, but King, the National Association for the Advancement of Colored People (NAACP), and the Urban League stuck to the nonviolent course. "Black power" inevitably became the byword for thousands of angry young blacks, some of them devoted to the dissident Muslim leader Malcolm X. In 1966, for a great variety of reasons, there were several dozen racial outbreaks in the United States. In 1967 there was major fighting in Newark, Detroit, and Cambridge, Maryland; in Detroit alone 41 persons were killed. Following the April 4, 1968, assassination of Martin Luther King in Memphis, while he was urging restraint during a sanitation workers' strike, rioting broke out again in many cities, with much violence in Washington and Chicago. Television brought nightly scenes of anger in the streets.

Running parallel to the civil-rights strife were the "free-speech," antiwar, and women's movements. The so-called free-speech movement began on the University of California's Berkeley campus in 1964, when Mario Savio and other students protested an administration decision banning on-campus rallies in support of off-campus demonstrations. Police arrested hundreds of students in the first of the student-administration battles that spread to many other campuses during the decade. By 1965 there were anti-Vietnam rallies at Berkeley and the University of Michigan. Radical students were sometimes opposed by Young Americans for Freedom, a conservative organization built by followers of Senator Barry Goldwater of Arizona.

Leading the drive for sexual equality was the National Organization for Women (NOW), founded at the University of Wisconsin in 1966. Other pioneers were the Women's Equity Action League (WEAL) and Federally Employed Women (FEW). Much of the legal planning and leadership was provided by the American Civil Liberties Union's Women's Rights Project. The first female picket line organized by NOW was set up in 1967 to protest the Equal Employment Opportunities Commission's wording of want ads. NOW members

The killing of Martin Luther King added to the nation's shame.

had gained experience in the civil-rights movement and union activities, and their leaders urged parades and picketing to protest discrimination in employment and sexist portrayals of women in the mass media. Because some of the leaders were skilled at public relations, the movement gained much public attention.

But a younger branch of the movement gradually turned to small-scale activities as more effective ways of raising the consciousness of America. By the 1970s there was a cohesive women's movement, based on the concept that consciousness raising (studying the gamut of women's lives) would keep women from becoming involved in single-issue campaigns and would eventually gain the movement more popular support.[6] Among the encouraged consciousness-raising activities were the establishment of women's centers, abortion counseling, film and tape production, research, and the publication of feminist newspapers and magazines.

But before that happened the women's liberation movement took hold with street demonstrations. In the late 1960s thousands of women marched in Chicago, New York, Boston, and other cities. Gloria Steinem, Betty Friedan, and others addressed rallies and conventions. The movement tackled the problems faced by the growing women's labor force and later affected the whole of male-female relationships, including family life and the educational process. One major goal was not realized, however: passage of the Equal Rights Amendment (ERA), the proposed Twenty-seventh Amendment to the Constitution.

Gays and lesbians were forging their own liberation movement in the late 1950s and 1960s, generally ignored by establishment media. A defining moment came in 1969, when New York police and gays battled outside a bar in what became known as the Stonewall riots. The open resistance to harassment was hailed by gays and lesbians nationwide as they struggled for acceptance in a society where homosexuality was ridiculed.

Of all the demonstrations of the 1960s, the most spectacular in size and media impact were King's march on Washington in 1963, the battles between antiwar demonstrators and police at the 1968 Chicago Democratic National Convention, and the antiwar marches in Washington in the fall of 1969.

TELEVISION NEWS: CRONKITE AND CBS

Walter Cronkite, an amiable native of St. Joseph, Missouri, with the stamina of a workhorse, became the leading CBS News personality in the 1960s. By the mid-1970s he was hailed as one of the most admired people in America, after having anchored dozens of CBS specials on presidential elections, the Vietnam agony, racial conflicts, assassinations, Watergate, and the many space flights.

Unlike others within CBS News, Cronkite was not one of Edward R. Murrow's protégés, although Murrow had tried to hire him away from the UP during World War II and eventually did hire him in 1950. Instead of reporting from Korea as planned, Cronkite ended up earning a reputation at CBS's Washington station, WTOP-TV. He did not present CBS executives with the outwardly intellectual image of Eric Sevareid or Charles Collingwood but was noted for his devotion to the hard news story. Coming out of the press-association tradition, Cronkite went for the bulletin lead or the exclusive interview. But over the years he also became the star of many CBS documentary shows, including *Eyewitness to History, Twentieth Century,* and *CBS Reports,* and was heard regularly on a CBS radio show.

Cronkite's straight delivery of the news, with a heavy note of seriousness, earned him the evening newscaster spot in 1962. He replaced Douglas Edwards, who had been hired in 1948 to begin a news show. It had been Edwards's fate to be pitted against the popular John Cameron Swayze's *Camel News Caravan* on NBC and later the Huntley-Brinkley team. Cronkite's job was to push CBS up in the ratings.

On Labor Day, 1963, Cronkite and the CBS crew, which included the reliable Sevareid in Washington, inaugurated the first 30-minute network news show. That morning, Cronkite interviewed President Kennedy at Hyannisport and asked JFK about the growing war in Vietnam, where 47 Americans had been killed. A young field reporter, Dan Rather, bluntly described a confrontation between police and blacks in the South, and the veteran Peter Kalischer was in Tokyo. During the next few years, with Cronkite serving as managing editor of the evening news show, CBS's reputation as a no-nonsense news organization grew steadily.

Cronkite suffered a personal setback before the 1964 Democratic National Convention when CBS executives replaced him with veteran Bob Trout and a young reporter named Roger Mudd. Cronkite had been the regular convention anchor since 1952, and he was the backbone of the CBS team originally put together by news chief Sig Mickelson and later Richard Salant. But the Huntley-Brinkley team had run away with the ratings. Trout and Mudd did not fare better, however, and Cronkite was given priority from then on.

During the American involvement in Vietnam, Cronkite, like most journalists, did not seriously question the nature of the United States commitment until the late 1960s. In 1965 he rode in a Canberra jet that dive-bombed in the jungle near Danang, just as he had flown in a bomber over Germany in 1943. But in 1968, after visiting Vietnam for a special on the Tet offensive, Cronkite was sufficiently convinced of the futility of the war to end his broadcast with "to say we are mired in stalemate seems the only realistic, yet unsatisfactory conclusion . . . the only rational way out . . . will be to negotiate [and] not as victors."[7] That was the turning point, and in following years the CBS coverage contained more criticism of American tactics.

The CBS team suffered the wrath of Mayor Richard Daley of Chicago during the riotous 1968 Democratic National Convention, when Cronkite, watching Rather being slugged by a so-called security guard, called the guards "thugs." With typical fairness, however, he granted Daley a long interview the next day and passed up the chance to criticize Chicago's boss for the tactics used by police on journalists and innocent bystanders. Cronkite in turn was criticized for such politeness, but he continually stressed the need for news credibility and insisted that the cameras spoke for themselves.

Although Lyndon Johnson constantly complained to Cronkite following evening news broadcasts, he had respect for Cronkite's sense of fairness. But the White House of Richard Nixon thought of CBS as a prime enemy. And although television journalists in general did a poor job of analyzing the Watergate-related events in 1972 and 1973—before the open revelations of scandal—Cronkite was credited with the best performance. One study showed that between September 14, 1972, and election day, CBS devoted twice as much air time to the Watergate story as either NBC or ABC.[8]

The tough CBS approach to news and Sevareid's voice of reason earned the network the top spot in the ratings by 1969–70. Another reason for the upsurge was Cronkite's ability as a space reporter. Throughout the 1960s he had covered the Mercury and Apollo programs with an interest dating to his World War II UP stories about the German rocket attacks on London. Finally, on July 20, 1969 the normally reserved Cronkite shared his feelings about the United States' incredible achievement. As the *Eagle* descended to the moon, Cronkite murmured, "Boy, what a day." Then, as former astronaut Walter Shirra, sitting with Cronkite, exclaimed, "We're home," Cronkite said, "Man on the moon . . . Oh, Boy! . . . Whew! Boy! . . . Boy! There they sit on the moon! . . . on

Newspapers reproduced television's historic news beats on their front pages.

green with the flight plan, all the way down. Man finally is standing on the surface of the moon. My golly!"[9]

When President Carter held an unprecedented radio talk show with the public in 1977, it was Walter Cronkite who sat in the Oval Office as moderator—the same "Uncle Walter" who babysat Americans through the killing and funeral for John Kennedy, the dangerous reentry periods of the space missions, and the anxiety of the Watergate crisis. He was counted on to hold the fort, and he did until one evening when he intoned: "And that's the way it is, Friday, March 6, 1981. I'll be away on assignment, and Dan Rather will be sitting in here for the next few years. Goodnight." Cronkite became a special correspondent, making occasional appearances.

Sevareid, the acknowledged dean of the television news analysts who had logged 38 years with CBS, including 15 political conventions, had announced his retirement in 1977. Beginning his CBS career as part of Murrow's *World News Roundup* team, he covered various aspects of World War II from Paris, London, Washington, the China-Burma theater, and finally Europe again. He spent almost all of the postwar years in the Washington bureau—with the exception of 1959 to 1961, when he was a roving correspondent in Europe—where he delivered regular evening commentaries once CBS moved to a 30-minute format.

The CBS team was a formidable unit. Mudd had become well established as a political reporter, Fred P. Graham offered excellent reports on legal affairs, Charles Kuralt was a favorite for his "On the Road" segments, Bernard and Marvin Kalb covered the State Department with thoroughness, and Lesley Stahl was a leading correspondent on her way to a White House assignment.[10] The documentary show *60 Minutes* became television's top-ranked program, the first time a news show had made the top 10 in the ratings. Rather, Mike Wallace, and Morley Safer brought the program into the limelight, and later Ed Bradley and Harry Reasoner appeared. (Reasoner began his career with CBS and then transferred to ABC for a number of years.) Mayra McLaughlin was CBS's first woman reporter in 1965; longtime correspondent Daniel Schorr was forced from his job in 1976 after he gave a controversial report on the CIA to the *Village Voice* and was threatened with contempt of Congress in a much-debated episode.

NBC: CHANCELLOR AND MCGEE

John Chancellor, one of the most thoughtful and conscientious broadcasters to address the public, assumed the NBC anchor spot in 1970 and temporarily found himself in an awkward "troika" arrangement with Brinkley and Frank McGee. Brinkley left to do a nightly commentary, *David Brinkley's Journal,* and McGee went on to the *Today* show. This left Chancellor to guide his viewers through the maze of the last stages of the Vietnam War, Watergate, and the Ford, Carter, and Reagan years, although Brinkley did return to coanchor in 1976 in an effort to close the gap with CBS.

That year, with the nature of television news being discussed in dozens of periodicals, Chancellor offered this simple explanation of his confident performance:

> What you do is say, "I got up at 10 o'clock this morning, and I worked all day, and read all the wires, and called up a lot of people. Now over there is the news. Let's look at it together. I'll be your guide."[11]

Chancellor, who began his NBC career in 1950, was a floor reporter at a number of political conventions along with Sander Vanocur, Edwin Newman, and McGee, and had headed several NBC foreign bureaus. He took one brief break in service to run the Voice of America for Lyndon Johnson.

NBC had always fielded a strong lineup of reporters. McGee was one of the most perceptive people in the business. As early as December 20, 1965, in an NBC special on the war, he concluded that if the United States government could not make a compelling argument why an independent South Vietnam was so vital to American national interests that "it transcends doubts about the legality and morality of the war," then the United States should withdraw.[12] Later he narrated the sensitive "Same Mud, Same Blood," documentary about black and white soldiers surviving or dying together. McGee also covered the South for NBC during the civil-rights battles, anchored many broadcasts of space flights, and anchored the desk for 12 hours on the day of John Kennedy's assassination. He died of cancer in April 1974, at the age of 52.

In addition to excellent field reporting, NBC compiled an impressive list of documentaries, headed by the NBC *White Paper* and the two-hour *First Tuesday.* Chemical and biological warfare, Army intelligence units spying on civilians, migrant labor problems, and the nation's pension plans were among the controversial topics covered. In early 1976 NBC canceled an entire evening of prime time—something that would have made Edward R. Murrow happy—and offered a three-hour analysis of foreign-policy problems. Later a magazine-type show was instituted, *NBC Magazine,* to compete with *60 Minutes,* but despite some successes, the ratings did not show much public support.

Among women working for NBC were Pauline Frederick, who in 1948 was the first woman to cover a political convention for a network and who stayed until 1974 as UN correspondent; Barbara Walters of *Today* show fame, an expert interviewer for NBC before she left for ABC; Marilyn Berger, who was appointed White House correspondent to replace Tom Brokaw; and Catherine Mackin, a high-ranking political correspondent and commentator.[13] Jessica Savitch and Connie Chung emerged as leading NBC anchorpersons.

ABC NEWS: WALTERS AND REYNOLDS

The television news world awoke one morning in 1976 to discover that Barbara Jill Walters, the star of NBC's *Today* show, would be joining ABC with a five-year contract calling for $5 million. But the biggest news was that the highest-paid news personality would be coanchoring the evening news with veteran Harry Reasoner, who immediately began to pout. Cronkite at CBS and Chancellor at NBC were shocked, and critics immediately castigated ABC for its show-business approach to the news. ABC executives came to the defense, though, and pointed out Walters's long record as a writer and interviewer of leading personalities.

It was not the first time that ABC had been criticized for its news tactics. The network had been playing catch-up in the ratings race since 1953, when John Daly was the first in a long line of anchors. Daly lasted until 1960, when John Cameron Swayze had a brief stint. He was followed by Ron Cochran (1963 to 1965), Peter Jennings (1965 to 1968), Bob Young (1968), and Howard K. Smith and Frank Reynolds (1968 to 1970). Smith and Reasoner had begun a partnership in 1970, but Smith eventually fell into a commentator's slot, leaving Reasoner alone, or so he thought.

Besides hiring Walters in an effort to put life into the ratings, ABC began experimenting with the heavy use of feature material. The ABC system's encouragement of the so-called happy talk format for its local stations in the early 1970s brought strong criticism from traditionalists, who found the joking and exchanges of light comments out of line.

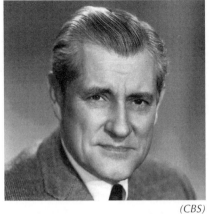

In their prime: Eric Sevareid, CBS commentator, and Lesley Stahl, CBS correspondent

John Chancellor, NBC anchor, and Connie Chung, ABC news correspondent

Frank Reynolds, ABC anchor, and Barbara Walters, ABC interviewer

ABC heavily promoted the "marriage" of Walters and Reasoner, but from the beginning there was doubt whether, as one critic put it, "the mix of Manhattan moxie and Iowa wry will chemically click."[14] In addition to the evening news, Walters was scheduled to host a number of special interview shows. Her producer was Lucy Jarvis, who, as the first American to receive an invitation from the People's Republic of China to film a news documentary, produced "The Forbidden City" for NBC in January 1973.

The Walters-Reasoner experiment failed, and Walters left the anchor post to devote herself exclusively to interviews. She recorded a number of notable exchanges with President Anwar Sadat of Egypt and other international figures, as well as with political and show-business personalities. Her yearly salary was more than $1.3 million, topped only by Rather's $1.6 million.[15] Reasoner left ABC in time to rejoin CBS for the 1978–79 season, taking a spot with the top-ranked *60 Minutes* show.

Roone Arledge brought ABC Sports into first place with *Wide World of Sports, Monday Night Football,* and spectacular Olympic coverage—particularly of the 1972 games in Munich, when Howard Cosell and other sportscasters helped describe the massacre of Israeli athletes by terrorists. Becoming head of ABC News in 1977, a controversial switch debated in the industry, Arledge instituted the "roving-anchor" concept the following year, with Walters in New York, Frank Reynolds in Washington, Peter Jennings in London, and Max Robinson in Chicago. Later, with Walters out of the daily picture, Reynolds assumed a more prominent role on ABC's *World News Tonight.*

Nancy Dickerson and Lisa Howard were among the first women reporters. A number of other women were involved, including Ann Compton, the first woman assigned by a network to cover the White House. Marlene Sanders, a Vietnam correspondent who became a vice president and director of documentaries, was one of the leaders in that field. In fact, Sanders had anchored the network evening news as a substitute during a strike in 1964; she later anchored the weekend news for several months in 1971. In 1977 her main project was the prestigious *ABC Closeups* series, with Smith as the main narrator. Reasoner had also been involved with a number of those shows as well as *ABC News Reports,* the network's principal documentary efforts outside of special reports. One of Sanders's major productions was "Women's Health: A Question of Survival" in 1976. She was a strong advocate of young women broadcasters and gave much time to that cause. ABC, like the other networks, also had talented women at key network stations.[16]

THE QUAGMIRE IN VIETNAM

Robert Capa, the Hungarian-born photographer who was world renowned for his graphic pictures of the Spanish Civil War and the Normandy invasion beaches, was the first American journalist to die in Vietnam. He stepped on a land mine while photographing for Magnum in 1954, the year the French extricated themselves from the Indochina quagmire by surrendering at Dienbienphu. The French watched as the Americans then took their places in the quagmire that swallowed up one president and was linked to the resignation of another.[17]

The American phase of the 30-year struggle in Indochina—in Vietnam, in Cambodia, and in Laos—became perhaps the most thoroughly covered war in history. Certainly it caused more moral searching than ever, and by the time the United States withdrew in 1975, it seemed that it represented a revulsion against the Cold War mentality and an ebbing of the spirit of "Manifest Destiny." Much credit should accrue to the print and broadcast correspondents and photographers covering the war, including the more than 50 who died, as well as those few who clarified the issues through their dissent at home.

Vietnam's national hero, Ho Chi Minh, proclaimed a Democratic Republic of Vietnam at Hanoi in 1945, in the wake of the Japanese surrender. But by 1946 the French, who had returned to Saigon, were engaged in hostilities with Ho's Viet Minh forces. Ex-emperor Bao Dai was installed in 1948 as chief of state in Saigon by the French, who then obtained financial aid from the United States in 1950 at the time of the Korean crisis. The United States carried up to 80 percent of the cost, but the French were humiliated at Dienbienphu. The Geneva agreements of 1954 ending hostilities provided for the partitioning of Vietnam at the seventeenth parallel and reunification through national elections in 1956. The Bao Dai government did not sign or honor the agreement; the United States created the SEATO alliance and included South Vietnam in the protected areas. Premier Ngo Dinh Diem ousted Bao Dai, refused to allow the elections, and obtained the help of the U.S. Military Assistance Advisory Group to train his army beginning in 1955. Diem's opposition in South Vietnam formed the National Liberation Front and its guerrilla force, called the Viet Cong by South Vietnamese and Americans.

By 1960 there were 686 United States military advisers, a figure raised to 3200 at the close of President Kennedy's first year in office (1961) as insurgency grew. Diem, his sister-in-law Mme. Nhu, and the ruling Catholic party became increasingly oppressive. The Buddhist uprisings of 1963 in Saigon and Hue, together with countryside insurgency, brought a November coup and the death of Diem. The American supporters, now transformed into a U.S. Military Assistance Command with 16,300 men, took over military affairs as ten Saigon governments came and went in the next 18 months. A new president was also entering the White House three weeks after the Saigon coup.

THE SAIGON PRESS CORPS FORMS

The Saigon press corps had already distinguished itself by the time of Diem's downfall. Its dean was Homer Bigart, now of the *New York Times,* whose critical analyses scorched desks in Washington. Three who became the leaders in pointing out the quagmire's dangers were Malcolm Browne, who went to Vietnam in November 1961 for the Associated Press; Neil Sheehan, who went in April 1962 for the United Press International; and David Halberstam, who joined them in May, for the *New York Times,* replacing Bigart. François Sully, the French reporter who had covered Dienbienphu and who stayed on to interpret the war for *Newsweek* and others until he died in Laos in 1971, was expelled by Diem in 1962 and could not return until Diem's overthrow. Among others who appeared in 1962 were Horst Faas, photographer, and Peter Arnett, correspondent, for the AP; Peter Kalischer, now with CBS; Charles Mohr for *Time;* and Beverly Deepe for *Newsweek,* a freelancer who took Sully's place and who later joined the *Christian Science Monitor.* Another female correspondent, freelancer Dickey Chapelle, made her first trip in 1961.

These and other correspondents had bad news to report about the progress of the war, about the weaknesses of the Diem government, and about the very ability of anyone to achieve what the U.S. government had set out to do in Vietnam. But the spirit of the military command and of the civilians in the embassy and aid missions was most often one of "we have a policy and it has to work if we just try hard enough." Anyone reporting facts that pointed in a contradictory direction was labeled noncooperative. When Sheehan and Halberstam viewed a military debacle at Ap Bac in January 1963 that proved that the U.S. military advisers had a long way to go to infuse a winning spirit in their allies, they reported on the failure of South Vietnamese arms. But the U.S. command described this as a victory, and the undermining of the journalistic reputations of the Saigon press corps had begun.[18]

(AP/Wide World Photos)

(Left to right): David Halberstam (*New York Times*), Malcolm Browne (*AP*), and Neil Shee-han (*UPI*) chat between lifts during operation in the Mekong Delta.

THE SAIGON PRESS CORPS UNDER ATTACK

As Buddhists set themselves afire and the pressures against the Diem dictatorship increased, the Saigon press corps also found conflict within its own ranks. Going to Saigon for varying amounts of time were Joseph Alsop, the columnist; Marguerite Higgins of the *New York Herald Tribune* and Keyes Beech of the *Chicago Daily News,* veterans of World War II and Korean press corps; and Jim Lucas of Scripps Howard, who was to win the 1964 Ernie Pyle award for his coverage in Vietnam. These correspondents were typified by Lucas: hard-nosed, ready to fight any attempt at censorship but more or less willing to accept war as a necessary fact of life, and not activist in probing into the humaneness of the military tactics. Indeed, correspondent Higgins was an avowed "hawk" who advocated the use of the atomic bomb if needed to repel the Communists wherever they were; tragically, Higgins fell victim to an Asiatic infection on a 1965 trip and died a lingering death in 1966. The criticism by Alsop, Higgins, Beech, and Lucas of the reporting and interpretation given by Browne, Sheehan, Halberstam, and Kalischer left the established Saigon press corps vulnerable to attack by outsiders.

These attacks mounted in 1963. The correspondents had fought off a State Department "press guidance" issued in 1962 by Carl T. Rowan saying that "newsmen should be advised that trifling or thoughtless criticism of the Diem government would make it difficult to maintain proper cooperation between the United States and Diem," only to find in 1963 that Diem's police would beat them over the head and smash their cameras.[19] The pot boiled over in September 1963, when *Time* attacked the Saigon press corps as propagandists plotting to overthrow the Diem government and, through distorted reporting, "helping to compound the very confusion that it should be untangling for its readers at home."[20] *Time* correspondents Charles Mohr and Mert Perry resigned in outraged protest; Mohr joined the *New York Times* and Perry *Newsweek* to stay in Saigon. Mme Nhu castigated the AP, UPI, *New York Times, Washington Post,* and *Newsweek* as enemies of Diem. *Time,* unrepentant, continued to doubt the analysis of the Saigon correspondents until long after their definition of a quagmire had been accepted by all disinterested observers of the Vietnam War.

The attacks on the integrity of the press led Halberstam, Sheehan, Browne, and later others to undertake activist roles in writing books and lecturing at home about the nature of the Vietnamese conflict and the danger to the U.S. national interest of a "win-at-any-cost" policy there. Halberstam and Browne shared the 1964 Pulitzer Prize for international reporting. Sheehan joined the *New York Times* staff in 1964 and in 1971 was instrumental in the *Times'* publishing of the Pentagon Papers, taken from a secret analysis by Pentagon researchers and validating the 1961 to 1965 reporting of the Saigon press corps. The furor over this, and the problem of the "credibility gap," which came to affect the mass media as well as Presidents Johnson and Nixon, was a polarizing issue affecting all aspects of American life.

In Vietnam the central problem was not only that the military deliberately falsified information, but also that it more often withheld information detrimental to continued belief in the eventual success of U.S. policies and established elaborate statistical counts to justify the policies of the White House and the Pentagon. General William Westmoreland became the American commander in Saigon in 1964 and remained until Paris peace talks were begun in 1968; it was through him that the twin "search and destroy" and "bomb the North" policies were instituted. The first employed the famed "body-count" statistics used by Defense Secretary Robert McNamara to prove that the enemy was being exhausted. The second utilized minute reports of "precision bombing" of enemy convoys, roads, factories, and troop concentrations at an unprecedented saturation level. At the daily briefing in Saigon, dubbed "The Five O'Clock Follies" by the correspondents, communiqués on the previous day's action were read; it was folly to attend, the press corps said, because the briefing officer only knew what was in his communiqué. Critics of the press contended that the correspondents nevertheless filed stories filled with the body-count reports they doubted as major news events and thus created an illusion of conventional battle warfare when none really existed, except in calculated situations.

JOHNSON AND THE PRESS: THE WAR ESCALATES

No president worked harder in trying to make himself available to the White House "regulars" than Lyndon Johnson. He did not care to undertake immediately the televised conferences so expertly run by Kennedy, so he called the two dozen or so regular correspondents into his office, plied them with food, and answered their questions. He took them with him to the LBJ Texas ranch and held barbecues; he argued with them on walks in the White House garden; he swam with them in the pool; he even subjected himself to 135 regular press conferences, a slightly better average than Eisenhower or Kennedy. In 1964 Johnson was elected president in his own right with a record popular majority and the support of all but a dozen of the country's major newspapers. The next year his "Great Society" legislation consolidated the gains the country wanted to make in civil rights, aid to education, medical benefits, and other social issues. Yet, for all this, the credibility gap grew as the war in Vietnam grew.

The decision to make the war in Indochina a major U.S. war came in August 1964, when the administration asserted that two American destroyers on patrol in the Gulf of Tonkin had been attacked by North Vietnamese PT boats. It developed later that the official version so readily accepted by news media was false. Nevertheless, President Johnson requested, and Congress quickly approved, a resolution giving him power to repel attacks and to prevent further aggression. It was the contention of Secretary of State Dean Rusk that an aggression from the North was in progress; others contended that the war in Vietnam was a civil war, particularly the actions involving the Viet Cong, the guerrilla arm of the South Vietnamese National Liberation Front. The incident of the Gulf of Tonkin seemed to foreclose the issue. Bombings of North Vietnam, secretly planned since the previous August, began in earnest in February 1965, and U.S. advisers went into combat in June, 23,000 strong. By the end of 1965 there were 160,000 more Americans in Vietnam. Intensified bombing of the Hanoi-Haiphong area was carried out during 1966. U.S. troops launched search-and-destroy missions and supported the pacification program aimed at regaining control of the villages.

At the same time President Johnson's 1965 decision to send U.S. Marines to intervene in a Dominican Republic dispute caused 160 journalists to flock to the scene. First to arrive was an old Latin American hand, Jules Dubois of the *Chicago Tribune.* Offering heavy interpretation of the U.S. were Bernard Collier of the *New York Herald Tribune,* Dan Kurzman of the *Washington Post,* Ted Szulc of the *New York Times,* and Ruben Salazar of the *Los Angeles Times.* CBS's Bert Quint drove to the rebels' section and later reported first-hand observations. But this crisis ended quickly, and Vietnam was back in the headlines.

Two major controversies developed in this period, not between the correspondents and the military, but between the correspondents and the public. In August 1965, Morley Safer of CBS News and two Vietnamese photographers shot "The Burning of the Village of Cam Ne." U.S. Marines had been fired on in the village area and in retaliation (after the Viet Cong had slipped away) leveled the 150-home village. "This is what the war in Viet Nam is all about," Safer narrated as he stood in front of the burning huts. "The Viet Cong were long gone . . . the action wounded three women, killed one baby, wounded one Marine and netted four old men as prisoners."[21] Walter Cronkite used the film; a storm broke. The film was too realistic, its critics contended; American soldiers should not be criticized; the presentation was one-sided and negative. Safer, who had thought to show the inhumanity of war, nearly lost his job.

But a greater sensation came in December 1966, when the respected Harrison Salisbury, a senior editor-correspondent of the *New York Times,* was granted a visa and began filing stories from Hanoi. Salisbury's series of stories, filled with detailed observations and accompanied by photographs, directly contradicted much of the claimed success of the U.S. bombing program. The bombing had not been pinpointed on military targets; many smaller towns had been reduced to ghostly ruins; bombs had been dumped indiscriminately by fliers who needed to lose their payloads; and, worst of all, the unprecedented bombing attack had scarcely made a dent in the transportation and war-supplies capability of the North Vietnamese. Angry attacks were made on Salisbury and the *Times;* a judging committee denied him a Pulitzer Prize for what most newspeople conceded was the outstanding news beat of 1966.

The administration claimed that it was grinding out a victory and that Secretary McNamara could see "a light at the end of the tunnel," a phrase that became a bitter joke for cartoonists. President Johnson, visiting Camranh Bay in late 1966, had urged his soldiers to "come home with that coonskin on the wall"[22] and his commanders were trying to

A confident President Johnson exhorted, "Come home with that coonskin on the wall."

oblige. Some journalists, including columnists Joseph Alsop and Hanson W. Baldwin, were assessing the North Vietnamese as badly hurt and incapable of winning. But more were foreboding. Peter Arnett of the AP, whose tireless reporting had won him the 1966 Pulitzer Prize, said that Westmoreland was "in a critical position." Ward Just, *Washington Post* correspondent, said that all the statistics reported by the government gave a false picture of conditions; the country was not pacified when you could not travel on the roads. R. W. Apple, Jr., of the *New York Times* said: "Victory is not close at hand. It may be beyond reach." Robert Shaplen, the *New Yorker* magazine's talented correspondent, and Denis Warner of the *Reporter* magazine added their realistic estimates of a stalled effort in Vietnam.[23]

Those who read and believed these leading members of the Saigon press corps were not as badly surprised as most of the public, the U.S. Command in Saigon, and official Washington by the fury of the Tet offensive of late January 1968. The National Liberation Front forces assaulted Saigon and put the U.S. Embassy under siege, held Hue for 25 days, and wiped out most of the pacification program in the countryside. General Westmoreland asked President Johnson for another 206,000 troops. The answer was a topping off at a total of 538,900, and a reassessment of the Vietnam War policy.

By that time Senator Eugene McCarthy's antiwar movement was sweeping Johnson out of the presidential race. On March 31—facing a defeat in the Wisconsin primary—the president stunned a vast television audience by withdrawing. He sharply limited the bombing of North Vietnam and initiated plans for preliminary peace talks in Paris that got under way in May. But a combination of public disbelief, disillusionment, and distaste for violence led to a stalemate in public opinion. The assassination of Senator Robert Kennedy in June, minutes after he had defeated McCarthy in the California primary, tore the heart out of the Democratic political campaign and opened the way for a fatal compromise in the welter of Chicago's street demonstrations and riots.

The administration's candidate was Vice President Hubert H. Humphrey, who, despite his liberal domestic achievements, had inherited Johnson's war mantle. He was challenged by his old Minnesota colleague McCarthy and Senator George McGovern of South Dakota, who had picked up some of Robert Kennedy's support. An emotional attempt to recruit Senator Edward Kennedy failed. Faced with the prospect of a continuation of Johnson's war policies—and ignoring the possibility that Richard M. Nixon might be worse for their long-range goals—thousands of demonstrators expressed their disappointment and anger.

CHICAGO, 1968, AND THE WALKER REPORT

Late in 1968, after the Humphrey presidential hopes had been wrecked by the image created during the turbulent Democratic convention in Chicago, a study of that convention, known as the Walker Report, was issued. Chicago attorney Daniel Walker made the report for the National Commission on the Causes and Prevention of Violence. His staff took statements from 1410 eyewitnesses and participants, and had access to over 2000 interviews conducted by the FBI. The Walker Report, calling the event "a police riot," said that conditions were worse than the media had described them.[24] The final report, made in December 1969, said that Chicago police had used excessive force not only against the provocateurs but also against peaceful demonstrators, passive bystanders, and news reporters and photographers.

If these were the documented conclusions of a distinguished national commission appointed by President Johnson—the man against whom much of the bitterness at Chicago in 1968 was directed—how did the media come out with tarnished public images?

Here best operated William Small's warning: the public, rather than accept reality, will prefer "to kill a messenger." The messenger was primarily television. CBS anchor Walter Cronkite found himself exploding with wrath when he saw (as did the audience) a floor guard slug CBS correspondent Dan Rather senselessly, but Cronkite later found himself meekly interviewing Chicago's political boss, Mayor Richard J. Daley, on whom rested primary responsibility for using "law and order" to create disorder. NBC correspondent Sander Vanocur never recovered professionally from the public disfavor he incurred while covering the convention and retired from NBC in 1971. The flow of antimedia letters was so intense that the Federal Communications Commission felt compelled to conduct an investigation of the news coverage of the affair by the networks. The networks agreed to cooperate, reluctantly; in September 1969, the FCC reported that the networks had been fair.

Most Americans saw a 17-minute television sequence reporting the police-crowd confrontation on Wednesday night of convention week in front of the Conrad Hilton Hotel. There, and on the side streets, police brutality reached its peak, the Walker Report said.

What most viewers would scarcely believe is the fact that those 17 minutes comprised half of the time CBS used to cover the demonstrations—32 minutes out of 38 hours of network time devoted to covering the week's activities. NBC devoted 36 minutes to violence on the floor out of 35 hours of coverage, 28 minutes to demonstrations outside the hall. ABC devoted 14 minutes to the disorders. Thus only a little more than 1 percent of network time was devoted to violence during the turbulent week, 99 percent to events on the floor, discussions, and the boredom of political-convention coverage.[25]

The public, however, criticized the media for paying too much attention to the demonstrators and for reporting too much violence. A study reported by *Broadcasting* magazine put the Wednesday night audience at 90 million, of whom 21.3 percent thought the police used excessive force and 56.8 percent thought they did not. Only 13 percent thought the tight security measures on the convention floor were unjustified—even though one critic commented that Humphrey was nominated "in a stockade." Altogether the news media, equally divided between the electronic and print media, suffered some 70 injuries at the hands of the police. But scant attention was paid to them. Eric Sevareid summed up the dilemma:

> The explanation seems obvious. Over the years the pressure of public resentment against screaming militants, foul mouthed demonstrators, arsonists, and looters had built up in the national boiler. With Chicago it exploded. The feelings that millions of people released were formed long before Chicago. Enough was enough: the police *must* be right. Therefore, the reporting *must* be wrong.[26]

It was a sobering experience for the media. It was a disastrous week for the Democratic party and Hubert Humphrey, whose campaign fell apart fatally in Chicago. The image of violence and radicalism projected from Chicago alienated one group of voters; Humphrey's defense of the Vietnamese war turned off the liberal left that once had supported him. Republican Richard Nixon adroitly used telecasts, and won, by a hairline decision despite Humphrey's valiant closing rush, the White House that had eluded him in 1960. The public, already recoiling from rioting and racial violence in the cities, rejected violence on its campuses and in its politics. It also rejected the free-speech movement with its four-letter words. Nixon and Spiro T. Agnew were a calm refuge for just enough voters to give them victory.

THE UNDERGROUND PRESS

The roots of the "underground press" movement that swelled to prominence in the mid-1960s can be found in the words of all the radicals of American journalism, starting with James Franklin and including more recently the radical *Guardian,* founded in New York City in 1948, and *I. F. Stone's Weekly.* The inspiration for the movement came from men like Allan Ginsberg, Bob Dylan, Jack Kerouac, Lenny Bruce, and Norman Mailer. The immediate stimuli were the four-letter word movement, the sex revolution, the generation and credibility gaps that created the antiestablishment era, and, above all, the bitter antiwar protest typified by the march on the Pentagon.

Underground papers, printed cheaply by offset, were free-swinging in style and content, uninhibited in graphic design, unrestricted in viewpoint, and in many cases unprofitable. They reflected a rebellion not only against the national establishment but also against its conventional mass media. The best of the underground papers did a capable job of criticizing both and of breathing new life into the dead-center American social and political scene of the 1960s. By the mid-1970s much of the spark had left the movement.

One historian of the underground papers, Robert Glessing, listed 457 titles of papers in his 1970 book,[27] and commented that they were coming and going almost too rapidly to list. Included in his total were 55 military papers and campus, black, and Chicano publications. He estimated that there were 3000 underground high-school papers.

First of the underground papers was the *Village Voice,* a sensational weekly when it was founded in Greenwich Village in 1955. Its creators were Daniel Wolf, a freelance writer who became editor; Edward Fancher, a psychologist who became publisher; and novelist Norman Mailer. Its political line was antiestablishment Democrat, it exhibited the Village interest in books and the arts, and its great coup was to break the four-letter word barrier. It started cartoonist Jules Feiffer on his way, helped Jack Newfield upward, and ran contributions from most of the writers who also appeared in the new-journalism columns of *Esquire, New York,* and *Harper's.* It became a fat 48 pages, with top "underground" circulation of 150,000 in the 1970s.

Most successful of the really radical underground publishers of the 1960s was former machinist Art Kunkin, who used $15 to start his *Los Angeles Free Press* in 1964. By 1970 his estimated circulation was 95,000, and Kunkin had not missed a week with his antipolice cartoons, his swinging classified ads, and his put-downs of politicians and society leaders. His paper gained additional attention through serious comment on both national and local issues, however startling the language. A four-year battle between Kunkin and the Los Angeles police over his right to a press pass ended in March 1971, when the Supreme Court refused to hear the *Free Press*'s appeal of an appellate-court decision holding that the weekly paper did not automatically qualify for a press pass under the First Amendment. In New York a media council granted press passes to underground papers, but Los Angeles police were adamant about Kunkin, who had published a list of names of narcotics undercover agents in one defiant episode. He lost financial control of the paper late in 1971, and became a freelance writer and journalism professor.

Best known and most successful of campus-related papers was the *Berkeley Barb,* born in the summer of 1965 out of the students' passionate dislike for the University of California administration and the excitement of the Berkeley free-speech movement. Its founder, Max Scherr, was in his fifties but was still in touch with the alienated people of the streets. The *Barb* produced major Bay-area exposés, led the disruptive student protests that split the campus apart, advanced to the sex revolution's frontiers, and grew fat on profits from suggestive classified ads and circulation. In 1969 Scherr and some of his staff split, and the dissidents produced the *Tribe.* The resulting controversies diminished the influence of the *Barb.*

There were other important underground papers of the mid-1960s: Detroit's *Fifth Estate* of 1965, the *Washington Free Press* of 1966, and three products of the climactic year of 1967: *Seed* in Chicago, *Kaleidoscope* in Milwaukee, and *Distant Drummer* in Philadelphia. Praised for their graphic effects were Boston's *Avatar* of 1967 and the *San Francisco Oracle,* a 1966 sensation for its psychedelic effect. Closely connected to rock music were John Bryan's *Open City* of 1967 to 1969 in Los Angeles and San Francisco's later *Rolling Stone.* Breaking down the barriers the *Village Voice* had not tested in New York City were Paul Krassner's *Realist,* founded in 1958, and the *East Village Other,* a 1965 protest journal with innovative art forms that grew in influence. New York's radical political paper, the *Guardian,* became underground in outlook by 1970. The dismal wind-down of the Vietnam War proved I. F. Stone and his *Weekly* to have been right as well as cantankerous.

ALTERNATIVE JOURNALISTS

The incomparable I. F. Stone—working only with his wife and an occasional research assistant—began publishing his *I. F. Stone's Weekly* in 1953, biting at the proponents of McCarthyism. He continued the newsletter until 1971, writing of controversies caused by the Korean War, the problems of the blacks, the early days of Vietnam, and the steady encroachment on private rights in the anti–Vietnam War demonstration days.[28] Stone's documented exposés, often taken from the printed records of the government, fed many other writers and activists with ammunition. Stone emerged as one of America's most distinguished and consistent journalists, along with Carey McWilliams of the *Nation* and Dorothy Day of the *Catholic Worker.* All had to be content with small circulations, but had the satisfaction of knowing that their dedicated readers included some activists and policy makers who eventually made inroads against the status quo in the 1970s. Stone retired from active combat to become a contributing editor for the *New York Review of Books,* where he continued his critical writing until his death in 1989.

Carey McWilliams came to the editor's chair of the *Nation* in 1955, succeeding Freda Kirchwey, who had steered the magazine through money shortages and staff crises involving the policy line toward the Soviet Union. McWilliams maintained a vigorous liberalism and by the *Nation*'s 100th anniversary in 1965 it was making the most incisive, fact-supported editorial attacks on the Vietnam War found in American publications. McWilliams continued his investigative journalism during the Watergate period, again putting the *Nation* in the forefront of aggressive attack.

Like Stone, Dorothy Day exhibited a compelling, tenacious, and consistent journalistic purpose. Her influence reached far beyond the circulation of her *Catholic Worker,* a monthly paper that cost but a single penny, and that was graced by the illustrations of Fritz Eichenberg and Adé Bethune, and the writings of Jacques Maritain, J. F. Powers, Michael Harrington, Thomas Merton, poets Brother Antoninus and Claude McKay, and others. The Catholic Worker movement the paper nurtured acted as a leaven on American social

(AP/Wide World Photos)   (Marquette University Archives)

I. F. Stone and Dorothy Day, alternative journalists

consciences, and its soup kitchens and residences for the poor spread across a recession-hit America in the 1980s, just as they had in the Depression. The *Catholic Worker* publication has surpassed all others by maintaining a consistent editorial line for more than half a century: an advocacy of personal activism ("personalism") to achieve nonviolent social justice, a thoroughgoing devotion to pacifism, and a philosophy of communitarian Christianity, concludes professor Nancy Roberts.[29] Until her death in 1980, Dorothy Day was clearly the spiritual and temporal leader of the movement and its paper.

Born into a newspaper family, Day left college at 18 to become an activist reporter for the *Socialist Call* and the *Liberator,* hobnobbing in Greenwich Village with young writers like Eugene O'Neill and Hart Crane, writing for the *Masses,* and picketing the White House for women's suffrage. Converted to Catholicism in 1927, she started the *Catholic Worker* in 1933 with a French Catholic sidewalk philosopher, Peter Maurin, and saw its circulation reach 190,000 by 1938. Steadfastly pacifist, Day ran counter to majority American Catholic support of Franco in the Spanish Civil War and for American military action in World War II, when circulation fell as low as 50,000. Day aimed to reform the Catholic Church, never to break with it. She urged it to resist bourgeois culture and to return to its radical, pristine beginnings. The left attacked her for her opposition to the revolutionary class struggle as determinedly as the right shunned her for her pacifism and concern for the poor. The *Catholic Worker* opposed the 1940 draft, Father Coughlin's anti-Semitism, Japanese internment in California, the atomic bomb, the 1948 peacetime draft, the Korean War, and the Rosenberg executions. Keeping alive the peace movement in the 1950s meant Day went to jail four times for opposing mandatory civil-defense drills as militarist devices.

Catholic Worker circulation, which rebounded as pacifism became popular again in the Vietnam era, eventually reached 100,000, where it stood throughout the 1990s. The *Catholic Worker* supported draft-card burning but not sabotaging the draft-board offices, which Day believed could spark violence. Day's antiwar stand coincided with that of Pope John XXIII; she was in the company of Thomas Merton, Father Robert Drinan, Philip and Daniel Berrigan, *Commonweal, Jubilee, Critic,* and the *National Catholic Reporter,* of the liberal church press. At 75, Day was arrested while picketing with Cesar Chavez in California. Before she died, Notre Dame University honored her with its Laetare Medal for her influence upon both her country and her church. A campaign has begun to petition for Day's canonization in the Catholic Church.

Joining in the alternative-journalism category as journals of tough-minded criticism in the 1960s were the *Village Voice, Bay Guardian, Cervi's Rocky Mountain Journal,* and *Texas Observer.* Each attacked the established press in its area, as well as the political and social establishments, in the best tradition of crusading journalism. The *Bay Guardian*'s editor, Bruce Brugmann, ended up suing the San Francisco dailies for abridging freedom of the press through their joint publishing agreement and won awards for his paper's reporting. Two decades later he and his associate editor, his wife Jean Dibble, were still in business, pounding away at San Francisco's business establishment, the local newspapers, and anyone threatening press freedom, They featured a series of investigative stories exposing illegal Reagan administration actions supporting the Contras in Nicaragua. Meanwhile the *Voice* emerged as a prosperous leader of the alternatives by using investigative journalism and commentaries to excoriate conservatives, defend civil and sexual rights, and challenge its heavily Jewish audience by examining sacred cows like the State of Israel. The atmosphere at the *Voice* changed in 1994, when publisher David Schneiderman instituted tough cost-cutting measures, fired some veteran editors and reporters, moved away from its strong foreign coverage, and in general followed conventional establishment lines by softening the product. In a rush for more advertising dollars, Schneiderman purchased the *Los Angeles Weekly,* itself in a transition period.

Behind the underground-press revolution were its press associations. One, the Liberation News Service, was founded in 1967 during the march on Washington by two graduate students who had been editors of their college papers, Ray Mungo and Marshall Bloom. The Underground Press Syndicate, organized in 1966 and developed by Tom Forcade, became a trade-association clearing house and advertising representative for the papers. Forcade later argued for and won the right to cover Congress.

While a number of underground and alternative publications either died or slipped in influence in the 1970s, one early leader became a huge financial success: *Rolling Stone.* Jann Wenner was 21 when his first issue rolled off the presses in 1967, and ten years later he headed a $10-million-a-year enterprise with circulation approaching 500,000. *Rolling Stone* contributors ranged from the sophisticated Tom Wolfe to the eccentric Hunter Thompson, the proponent of "Gonzo" journalism. By moving his headquarters from San Francisco to New York, Wenner confirmed *Rolling Stone*'s place in the establishment world. The main focus remained music, although tough stands had been taken during the Vietnam War, and political and social commentary continued to be part of the attractive package.

Of the many women's magazines—traditional and feminist—that were born in the 1960s and 1970s the most influential was *Ms.,* edited by Gloria Steinem. Letty Pogrebin, Patricia Carbine, and a dozen other active writers assisted with the editing chores in this unusually democratic group effort. *Ms.* not only attacked the white male establishment but also offered a wide range of views on financial, sexual, psychological, and family matters. *Ms.* had reached a circulation of 500,000 by 1983 with Carbine as publisher, but then faltered in advertising revenues, and passed through two ownerships before being redesigned by Dale Lang, publisher of several women's magazines. In July 1990 he put *Ms.* back on the newsstands as an adless, sophisticated monthly; by 1994 its circulation had reached 166,000, with Robin Morgan as editor.

Remaining active in staunch liberal journalism were the *Jewish Daily Forward* (1898), the last Yiddish-language daily in North America, and the *Partisan Review* (1937). Under editor Abraham Cahan, the *Forward* carried analyses and reviews with a Socialist orientation, but mellowed with its readership in later years. Writer Isaac Bashevis Singer joined the staff in 1935 and editor Simon Weber in 1940; they became survivors of economic hardship that saw circulation drop from a peak of 220,000 in 1924 to 35,000 in 1982. The *Forward* then became a weekly. Weber retired in 1987, and new editors launched a weekly English-language edition in 1990. Singer, a Nobel prize winner in literature, died in 1991.

One of *Partisan Review*'s founding editors, William Phillips, remained at his desk, editing the anti-Soviet prose and poetry. His cofounder, Philip Rahv, died in 1974. While its heyday was in the 1940s and 1950s, the *Partisan Review* remained true to its original Socialist goal, publishing pieces praising the Polish Solidarity campaign of the 1980s.

The Communist party's *Daily Worker,* founded in 1924, had a 100,000 circulation in the late 1930s, but only 5600 when it dropped to weekly status in 1958. In 1968 it resumed morning publication as the *People's Daily World,* claiming a 62,000 circulation in 1989. But in 1990 it became the *People's Weekly World,* citing rising costs.

INVESTIGATIVE REPORTING

Digging into the activities of the Pentagon, Central Intelligence Agency, Federal Bureau of Investigation, Teamsters' Union, organized crime syndicates, and corrupt politicians were the so-called investigative journalists of the 1960s and 1970s. Investigative reporting meant developing sufficient sources and documents over a long period to offer the public a strong interpretation of an event. The term *investigative* became extremely popular after Seymour Hersh uncovered the story of the My Lai massacre in Vietnam and joined the *New York Times* staff in time to look into the CIA. Jack Nelson of the *Los Angeles Times* helped demythologize FBI Director J. Edgar Hoover, and Bob Woodward and Carl Bernstein of the *Washington Post* became national heroes during Watergate. But by its very nature, true investigative reporting could be conducted by only the most wealthy and influential media outlets, who rarely accepted the challenge.

Investigative journalism did not begin with the 1960s, however. It was a continuation of the muckraking tradition, which had never really died. From the 1920s to the present day, small circulation magazines like the *Nation* and the *New Republic* have kept reform ideas alive. Heywood Broun, McAlister Coleman, Lewis Gannett, and Louis Adamic wrote for their pages in earlier days. Matthew Josephson attacked large-scale arms spending in the *Nation* in 1956, the same year Fred J. Cook wrote "The Shame of New York." Editor Carey McWilliams developed special issues on the FBI in 1958 and the CIA in 1962. Ralph Nader's first series, including "The Safe Car You Can't Buy," appeared in the *Nation* in 1959, and as early as 1953 McWilliams was linking cigarettes and lung cancer.

Major contributions to investigative reporting also came from books. Carey McWilliams' *Factories in the Field* and John Steinbeck's *The Grapes of Wrath* brought the plight of the migrant worker to Americans' attention in the 1930s. Later, writers like Michael Harrington, Dwight MacDonald, and Herman Miller helped discover the forgotten poor. In the Vietnam and Watergate eras a spate of books uncovered governmental deception, white collar and organized crime, and a general neglect of the quality of life. In the broadcasting field CBS led the way, first with Edward R. Murrow's documentaries, and then with "Hunger in America" and "The Selling of the Pentagon." All three networks and public television looked at the problems of drugs, crime, excessive wealth, and corruption, but for the most part, investigative journalism remained television news' biggest weakness.

Others who made strong efforts in investigative reporting included syndicated columnist Jack Anderson, Bob Greene, George Reasons, Denny Walsh, Robert Sherrill, Sanford Watzman, Nick Kotz, Tom Whiteside, Les Whitten, Joseph Goulden, and Robert Scheer. The controversial Anderson won the 1972 Pulitzer Prize for his exposure of the Nixon administration's deception during the India-Pakistan war; Greene headed a special investigative team at *Newsday* that turned out several important stories, including one on Nixon's Florida connections; and Reasons led the *Los Angeles Times* group that won a Pulitzer Prize for finding corruption in that city's harbor commission. Walsh won a Pulitzer Prize for his *Life* magazine exposé on organized crime. *Life* and *Look* made a number of attempts to investigate problems in America before they fell victim to economic and management problems. Scheer edited *Ramparts,* a leftist magazine in the 1960s, which among other things exposed the CIA's infiltration of the international student movement. After writing one of the first critical books of the war, *How the U.S. Got into Vietnam,* he became a freelance writer and later reported for the *Los Angeles Times.* Don Bolles of the *Arizona Republic* was killed by a car bomb in 1976 while investigating mob activities. His work was continued by fellow investigative reporters whose *Arizona Project,* a 33-part series, led to the formalization of Investigative Reporters and Editors, Inc. (IRE), which by 1991 claimed 3200 members and held national conventions. Despite these investigative efforts, the record showed that a number of stories that did not receive adequate investigation included the role of major oil companies during energy crises, white-collar crime in general, the backgrounds of persons appointed to public office or regulatory commissions on all levels, bribery involving arms sales, and other subjects involving power and money.

In 1992 Manuel de Dios Unanue, editor of the Spanish-language daily *El Diario/La Prensa* was shot to death in a New York restaurant. De Dios was targeted by a Colombian cocaine mob because of his relentless antidrug crusades.

THE NEW JOURNALISTS

It was in the early 1960s that the term "new journalism" again came into use. Used during the days of Pulitzer and Hearst, it referred to a fresh approach to newsgathering.[30] Then in the age of disillusionment, writers like Tom Wolfe, Joan Didion, Jimmy Breslin, Gay Talese, Truman Capote, and Norman Mailer began to experiment with what was later called "new nonfiction reportage," or literary journalism. This took different forms, but generally it meant using perception and interviewing techniques to obtain an inside view of an event, instead of relying on the standard information-gathering, stock-question approach common to conventional journalism. It also meant focusing on writing style and on the quality of description, using literary techniques.

The bulk of the so-called new journalists were newspaper reporters who spent much of their spare time and a good deal of company time trying to sell articles to magazines like *Esquire, New York,* and the *New Yorker.* Wolfe had worked for the *Washington Post* before joining the *New York Herald Tribune* staff where Breslin was already a newsroom curiosity. Talese wrote for the *New York Times.* It was natural that these writers would approach *Esquire* with their off-beat portraits of people and life styles. For years Arnold Gingrich, who founded *Esquire* in 1933, had been running the top bylines in American writing, while at the same time dropping away from his habit of filling pages with sexy material. Hemingway, Faulkner, and Steinbeck had preceded the new journalists. Harold T. P. Hayes and Don Erickson were top editors in the 1960s, and Garry Wills and Robert Sherrill were among the contributing editors.

The most spectacular magazine success in the 1960s was that of *New York.* More than a typical city magazine such as those that appeared in other metropolitan centers, *New York* was a continuation of the magazine supplement of the *Herald Tribune.* Editor Clay Felker had developed a style there, printing such new journalism writers as Wolfe, Breslin, and Peter Maas. In 1967 Felker obtained the right to the name and recruited enough support to launch the magazine in April 1968. He aimed it at the young city dwellers and was rewarded with some 150,000 readers within a year, including a 25,000 newsstand sale that exceeded that of the proud *New Yorker.* Felker's business associate was publisher George Hirsch. Wolfe, Breslin, and Maas continued as contributing editors, along with Judith Crist and George J. W. Goodman ("Adam Smith"). The star writer was Gloria Steinem, whose articles had appeared in other magazines. *New York* did some muckraking, but more often carried articles, departments, and tips to better living that served its city audience. It also interested out-of-towners, who upped circulation to 375,000.

Felker moved on to assume editorial control of the *Village Voice* and then created the splashy *New West,* copying the cover and internal design of *New York.* His empire collapsed in early 1977, however, when Australian press lord Rupert Murdoch outbid Katharine Graham of the *Washington Post* and gained control of three publications by paying $9 million to Felker's fellow stockholders.

Among the other city magazines—some of which resembled Chamber of Commerce sheets—*Philadelphia* magazine was twice honored with National Magazine Awards for its tough reporting. In 1970 the magazine exposed a scandal in the Pearl S. Buck Foundation, and in 1972 it examined the management of the Delaware Port Authority, a case not covered by other media. *Los Angeles* magazine gained attention for its life-style coverage and tremendous advertising volume.

Using sights, sounds, and inner thoughts, the new journalists tackled a wide variety of subjects with their individual styles. In the June 1966 *Atlantic,* writer Dan Wakefield credited Wolfe's *The Kandy-Kolored Tangerine-Flake Streamline Baby* and Capote's *In Cold Blood* with causing the literary world to consider new journalism as a serious art form. Dozens of articles and several books appeared on the subject, but no single definition was agreed upon.[31] But whether new journalism was merely a concentrated use of old feature-writing techniques or a genuine breakthrough in gaining "the truth," these writers made a mark. As early as 1952 Lillian Ross of the *New Yorker* contributed *The Picture,* a factual report of a movie company done in novel form. Even earlier, in the late nineteenth century, journalists such as Mark Twain, Stephen Crane, George Ade, and Lafcadio Hearn had written journalism with the scope and power traditionally associated with works of literary fiction. Later Breslin's looks at the "little people" were found in *The World of Jimmy Breslin* (1968), Mailer poured out his experiences on a march against the Pentagon in his *Armies of the Night* (1968), Wolfe described the age of drugs in his *Electric Kool-Aid Acid Test* (1969), and Talese tattled on his former bosses at the *Times* with marvelous detail in his *The Kingdom and the Power* (1969).

Although examples of the new nonfiction reportage appeared in various magazines and books, the writing movement did not spread to newspapers. Of the major writers, only Breslin continued to turn out newspaper columns while doing other forms of writing. Most editors frowned on new journalism techniques and mistakenly linked them with "advocacy" or "activist" reporting. In addition to this confusion, another group claimed that it had the answer to reporting problems: those advocating the use of social-science survey techniques in reporting. Called "precision journalists," they learned from the example of Philip Meyer, who covered Washington for the Knight newspapers and in 1991 authored the book *Precision Journalism.* Of note was his study, *Return to 12th Street,* in which a reporting team examined the Detroit riot of 1967 through interviews with hundreds of black residents. Haynes Johnson and a *Washington Post* team used similar tactics in covering national politics. The object was to gather news data that could be used to interpret trends or describe conditions under which people were living.

URBAN AND ENVIRONMENT WRITERS

An Urban Writers' Society was formed in 1968, reflecting the concern of Americans about urban society and the environment. Outstanding among the urban specialists were Ada Louise Huxtable, architecture critic of the *New York Times* since 1963 and winner of the 1970 Pulitzer Prize for criticism; Wolf Von Eckardt, urban and architecture specialist for the *Washington Post* since 1964; George McCue, art and urban-design critic for the *St. Louis Post-Dispatch;* and Allan Temko, urban columnist for the *San Francisco Chronicle.* When in 1970 *Editor & Publisher* asked the nation's dailies to send in the names of their writers specializing in environmental news coverage on the ecology beat, 100 responded.[32]

Environmental concerns became paramount in the late 1970s, and reporters struggled to explain such things as environmental impact reports, nuclear power plants, liquified natural gas, water projects, zoning regulations, and, of course, the economic implications of all this to the tax-paying public. Among the environment and ecology specialists were Gladwin Hill of the *New York Times,* Margaret Freivogel of the *St. Louis Post-*

Dispatch, Steve Wynkoop of the *Denver Post,* David Ross Stevens of the *Louisville Courier-Journal,* and Paul Hayes of the *Milwaukee Journal.*

The need for alternative energy sources and water conservation became acute in 1976–77, when a terrible drought struck the western half of the nation while the eastern half was hit by an unusually severe winter that nearly exhausted fuel supplies. Changing weather patterns were also examined by reporters, who interpreted the divergent viewpoints of leading scientists. This interest continued, and, in 1990, the Society of Environmental Journalists was formed with Jim Detjen of the *Philadelphia Inquirer* serving as the first president.

THE BLACK PRESS SURVIVES

At the close of World War II the "big three" of the black newspapers—the *Chicago Defender* (1905), the *Pittsburgh Courier* (1910), and the *Afro-American* of Baltimore (1892)—could be purchased as easily in Mississippi or in Florida as in their hometowns. Gunnar Myrdal's classic study of 1945, *An American Dilemma,* reported that "the Negro press . . . is rightly characterized as the single greatest power in the Negro race."[33] The *Defender* boasted a circulation of 257,000; the *Courier,* 202,000; and the *Afro-American,* 137,000. The impact of two world wars and heavy black migration to northern industrial cities had created this peak of circulation influence. But within a few years a general decline began, and nationally circulating papers lost ground to community-based ones, leaving small stable papers as the survivors during the civil-rights battles of the 1960s.

For the most part the older, somewhat conservative black papers were left behind by the rush of events and black militancy in the 1960s. In many cities small organizational newspapers were published to offer a point of view not found in the established white or black press. In Chicago, for example, *Black Truth, Black Liberator,* and *Black Women's Committee News* were among a number of newspapers challenging the *Defender.* The black press concentrated on the routine coverage of the community and was ambivalent to the cries of young blacks for direct action. Fear of losing newly gained white advertising accounts kept some black papers from joining more vigorously in the black revolution. It was not until the Black Panthers party was ruthlessly treated by law-enforcement agencies that some black papers questioned the role of whites in dealing with the militant group, particularly after the killing of Panther leader Fred Hampton in a 1969 raid on his Chicago apartment.

Nevertheless, the black press survived the economic hardships and the community political pressures. By 1970 the circulation of the *Defender* had dropped to 33,000 and that of the *Pittsburgh Courier* to 20,000. The circulation leader was the nationally distributed *Muhammad Speaks,* the voice of the Black Muslim movement founded by Malcolm X in 1961, with an estimated 700,000. Copies were sold on street corners, proclaiming the programs of Elijah Muhammad and condemning the Vietnam War. Also prominent was the *Black Panther,* founded in 1966 by San Francisco blacks who led the fight against alleged police abuse of minorities. Circulation ran around 100,000 during the late 1960s, and the paper was available in major cities. *The Voice* in Jamaica, New York, boasted a circulation of 90,000, and the *Sentinel-Bulletin* of Tampa had 75,000.

Although the bulk of the papers resisted pressure to take up the slogans of black militants, editors did keep an eye on problems with local law-enforcement officials. Another theme was news of federal-government programs, and there was considerable criticism of Washington during the Nixon years. This was repeated later during the Reagan administration's attempts to trim community-assistance programs and health benefits.

BLACK PRESS LEADERS

John H. Sengstacke, editor and publisher of the *Chicago Daily Defender* and head of the Sengstacke Newspapers group, was elected to the board of directors of the American Society of Newspaper Editors in 1970. He was the first black editor to be so honored. The personal recognition reflected the status of the Sengstacke group. In 1998 the *Chicago Daily Defender*, with a circulation of about 23,500, remained a leader among the 185 black newspapers listed by *Editor and Publisher*. It had achieved daily status in 1956. The other African-American daily was Brooklyn's *New York Daily Challenge/Afro Times*, with a circulation of 78,000, founded as a daily in 1972. In 1970 Atlanta's *Daily World* (1928) dropped from the daily status it had enjoyed since 1932 to a four-day publishing schedule. It had a circulation of about 18,000.

Leaders in audited circulation included Philadelphia's triweekly *Philadelphia Tribune* (1884), 26,400; and these weeklies: *San Francisco Metro Reporter*, 100,210; *Washington* (D.C.) *Informer*, 30,000; New York's *Amsterdam News* (1909), 29,000; the *Los Angeles Sentinel* (1934), 19,000. Also in the Sengstacke group were Detroit's *Michigan Chronicle* (1936), 31,000, and the *New Pittsburgh Courier*, 30,000, purchased by Sengstacke in 1966 with the Courier group. The trend among black newspapers indicated declining circulation and increasing problems in gaining advertising and maintaining staffs.

Yet there were exceptions, such as the *Afro-American* group, published by John J. Oliver, Jr., in Baltimore and Richmond, with an edition published in Washington, D.C., by Francis L. Murphy II. After near-bankruptcy in the 1980s, the chain survived to celebrate its one-hundredth anniversary in 1992. From a high of 200,000 during the 1950s, its circulation had declined to 20,000 in 1989. But by the mid-1990s circulation had grown to about 24,000.[34] Elizabeth Murphy Moss, vice president of the group, was a leading reporter and war correspondent. So was Ethyl Payne, Washington correspondent for the Sengstacke papers and the only black newspaperwoman to cover the Vietnam War.

The *Amsterdam News*, the largest circulating of the standard black community papers, was purchased by Dr. C. B. Powell in 1936 and was controlled by him until 1971, when ownership passed to Clarence B. Jones. Wilbert A. Tatum later became publisher. This paper concentrated on local items and sensationalized crime and sex news to combat its competition in Harlem from Congressman Adam Clayton Powell's *People's Voice* and the old *New York Age*. Like the *Afro-American* and *Defender* papers, it became moderate in tone, heavily local in news coverage, strong in sports and women's news, and occasionally crusading.

The New York *Daily Challenge* was under the direction of longtime editor Dawad Philip. The Atlanta *Daily World* was founded by William A. Scott, who was assassinated in 1934; his successor, Cornelius A. Scott, edited a consistently conservative paper in news content, typographical appearance, and editorial direction. Its world news coverage was good. It supported the Republican party politically and opposed such militant black action as economic boycotts of white merchants who discriminated in hiring blacks.

The *Los Angeles Sentinel*, brought to prominence by Ruth Washington, continued as the most important black publication in Los Angeles, where it displayed a mildly sensational front page and a liberal-moderate editorial page. Other noteworthy black papers were the *Atlanta Inquirer* (1960), Norfolk's *Journal and Guide* (1909), the semiweekly *Tampa Sentinel-Bulletin* (1945), the *Kansas City Call* (1919), and the *Louisiana Weekly* (1926). There were large free-circulation shopping papers like the Wave Publications in Los Angeles, with a distribution of 379,000.

(Chicago Defender)

John H. Sengstacke, head of the *Defender* newspaper group

Thieves slay blind man
(see page 3)

Chicago Defender
SENGSTACKE Newspaper

CHICAGO'S DAILY PICTURE NEWSPAPER

WEATHER
Today will be partly sunny, high in upper 70s.

VOL. LXXI - NO. 111   WEDNESDAY, OCTOBER 8, 1975   15¢ 20¢ Outside Of Chicago

Islamic groups unite in fete
(see page 4)

HEW tells board end teacher bias
(see page 3)

At showdown...
Dr. James G. Haughton (left photo), director of Cook County Hospital, warned the hospital's 548 doctors and interns yesterday that if their dispute is not settled soon, they could face "maximum discipline," including being fired. Some of the dissatisfied doctors and interns (right) appear bored as they listen to Haughton's recommendations. Members of house staff have said they are prepared to lose their jobs if it will improve patient care and overall working conditions. Dr. Haughton says that many of the criticisms about the care of patients are unfounded. (Defender photos by Phyllis Doering).

She wants cash for 'lemon'
(see page 3)

A front page of a leading black paper

427

Like the regular weeklies, the black weeklies usually appeared on Thursdays. Advertising occupied about one-third of the total space, with two-thirds or more of that local in origin. Most of the national black papers and largest weeklies subscribed to the United Press International for their state, regional, national, and international news. The best known of the specialized press services was the Associated Negro Press (ANP), founded in 1919 by Claude A. Barnett. It peaked in 1945 with 112 American subscribers. Barnett made many trips to Africa after World War II, adding 100 subscribers there as well as developing African news. But by 1966 the ANP had so much competition in the coverage of black news that it went out of business.[35] The National Negro Press Association, with Louis Lautier as Washington correspondent, operated between 1947 and 1960 with the support of the larger black papers, and it began service again in 1974 with John W. Lewis, Jr., as correspondent.

The number of black papers dropped from 213 to 165 between 1974 and 1979, according to Henry G. LaBrie III, noted for his research in the area. In earlier studies LaBrie had discovered that fewer than 40 black papers had their own printing facilities and that only a small number had circulations verified by ABC audit.[36] The only paper distributed nationally was the *Bilalian News,* the Orthodox Muslim publication that was formerly *Muhammad Speaks* (now known as the *Muslim Journal*).

THE BLACK MAGAZINES

John H. Johnson's *Ebony* reached a circulation of 1.9 million in the late 1980s, appealing mainly to urban, middle-class blacks. After founding *Ebony* in 1945, Johnson quickly discovered that sensationalism did not pay, but that quality photographs and a serious presentation of black life did. Era Bell Thompson was a leading editor at the magazine for more than a quarter-century. During the turmoil of the 1960s *Ebony* became more concerned with black problems and ran extensive articles on these subjects in addition to pictures and cartoons. Johnson's other main publication, *Jet,* had a circulation of 923,400 in 1999. It was started as a pocket-sized news weekly to carry material that would not fit into *Ebony.* In 1986, Johnson added *EM* to his empire, a men's fashion magazine. In addition to the enormously profitable Johnson Publishing Co., he was president of three radio stations and involved with other enterprises. In 1987 he named his daughter, Linda Johnson-Rice, president of the Johnson Publishing Company, sharing power with her.

The leading publication for black women was *Essence,* begun in 1970. By the mid-1990s, its circulation had climbed to more than one million. For its first 10 years *Essence* was edited by Marcia Ann Gillespie, who kept the magazine tied to its roots in the black-power movement of the 1960s. The goal was to relate to the lives of black women and to create awareness among advertisers of the potential of this audience. In 1998, some 310,000 African American businessmen and women read *Black Enterprise* (1970); civil-rights and race-relations advocates were devoted to *Crisis* (1910); college students could buy the *Black Collegian* (1970); and intellectuals read *Reconstruction* (1990). Among other noteworthy black magazines were *Black Enterprise* (1970), for professionals and entrepreneurs, with a circulation of 310,000; *EMERGE, Black America's Newsmagazine* (1989), with a circulation of 200,000; *Black Family Today;* and *American Visions* (1986). Many magazines were available in online versions as well. Of special note was *Legacy,* a joint venture started in 1995 by *American Heritage* (the history magazine owned by Forbes Inc.) and RJR Communication, Inc. (headed by Rodney J. Reynolds) to cover African American history. By 1998 it boasted a circulation of 508,000.

THE LATINO MEDIA

The rising consciousness of Latinos in the 1960s, sparked by the leadership of Cesar Chavez, led to the founding of several dozen newspapers dedicated to the organization of Latinos as sensitive, progressive communities. As Chavez led his United Farm Workers union against the powerful California grape growers in the San Joaquin Valley, *El Malcriado,* published from a shack in Delano, became the official union voice in 1964. The movement spread from the fields to the cities, and in 1967 *La Raza* appeared in Los Angeles, speaking loudly for improvement in educational opportunities, better housing, and an end to what young Latinos called police harassment. The protests followed in the tradition of earlier Mexican newspapers.

The United Farm Workers succeeded in improving the working conditions of migrant workers in California, and Chavez attempted to bring pressure on growers in Texas and Florida, where discrimination was rampant. California had a long history of racist attacks against those who did the necessary inexpensive labor. Native Americans, Chinese, and Japanese took their turn picking the crops and doing other hard labor, while being ruthlessly victimized by violence and discriminatory laws. The Native Americans were driven to the mountain areas, the Chinese and Japanese were excluded by immigration laws, and from the 1920s on the fields were worked by Mexicans and, to a lesser but significant degree, Filipinos. Carey McWilliams summed up the long-standing grievances of the farm workers in his *Factories in the Field.* There were many strikes along the West Coast in the twentieth century, but little support from organized labor until the 1960s. Gompers of the AFL had laid down the rules in the early 1900s—no Mexican or Asian could share a union with whites—but later auto workers, longshoremen, and AFL-CIO workers around the nation supported Chavez.

Other events in the 1960s caused a number of Latino papers to appear. *El Rebozo,* published by women in San Antonio, was among five Texas papers; other papers were *El Gallo* in Denver, *La Guardia* in Milwaukee, *Adelante* in Kansas City, and *Lado* in Chicago.

Latinos are the fastest-growing minority group in the United States. By 2000 they are expected to be 15 percent of the population. Latinos are dispersed across the nation, mainly in urban areas. Nearly 80 percent listed themselves as bilingual in Spanish and English. However, as a group, Latinos experience a continuation of past educational, health, and employment problems, some of them due to unequal political representation.

The national media's discovery of the previously invisible Latinos in the 1960s was attributed by researcher Félix Gutiérrez to their "virtually nonexistent" coverage in the first 70 years of the twentieth century. Studies of both national and local coverage show a pattern similar to that experienced by blacks: "When Mexican labor or immigration impacted national policy or when Latinos were involved in civil strife"—such as the Pauhuco race riots in Los Angeles in the early 1940s or the attempts to seal off the Mexican border to stop immigration—the headlines appeared.[37]

Several newspapers, appreciating the advertising potentiality, began to address their Latino populations. The *Miami Herald* introduced a Spanish-language section in 1976, and was followed in this effort in 1981 by the *Chicago Sun-Times* and *Arizona Republic.* The *Los Angeles Times* began a monthly section called *Nuestro Tiempo.* The Gannett Corporation bought New York's Spanish-language daily, *El Diario/La Prensa,* in 1981, after completing an extensive study of Latino media habits and attitudes. Gannett later sold the daily in 1989. Several NBC television stations in New York, Chicago, and Los Angeles began simulcasts of evening news broadcasts on local Spanish-language radio stations, and many television stations began to follow this practice. There were other positive responses.

The *New York Times* won a Pulitzer Prize for John Crewdon's examination of immigration, and the *Los Angeles Herald-Examiner* was widely praised for Merle Wolin's series on the Los Angeles garment district, for which the reporter posed as an undocumented worker, in the spirit of Annie Laurie of Hearst's day. A *Los Angeles Times* series by Chicano reporters captured a Pulitzer Prize.

Latinos found it difficult to enter the mainstream reporting and editing ranks, however, just as blacks and other minorities did. The situation was slightly better in broadcasting, because of federal regulations and the pressure of a 1977 federal study, "Window Dressing on the Set," that pointed out gross inequities in the hiring and promoting of minorities. By 1998 *Editor and Publisher Yearbook* listed 117 Latino newspapers, including these circulation leaders: *El Vocero,* San Juan, Puerto Rico, 259,000; *Novedades,* in Los Angeles, 113,000; *La Opinion,* 102,800; *El Nuevo Herald,* 100,000; *Diario de las Americas* in Miami, 68,000; *El Diario/La Prensa* in New York, 49,700; *Noticias del Mundo* in New York, 25,000.

In the magazine field, *Vista,* an English-language magazine for Latinos distributed within newspapers, claimed a circulation of 1,075,000. Among other general English-language magazines was *HISPANIC,* published in Austin, Texas. Among the specialty magazines in English was the nationally distributed *Hispanic Business,* published in Santa Barbara, California (200,000). In addition, *Cosmopolitan, Good Housekeeping, Parents,* and other major magazines printed Spanish editions.

It was obvious that major media corporations recognized the advertising potential of the Latino audience—the fastest growing in the U.S. market. The biggest excitement came in the broadcasting, where Univision had 22 full-power stations (six in California, five in

Front page of *Wassaja* (left); New York's leading Latino daily, a *El Diario/La Prensa*

Texas, two each in New Mexico and Arizona, and one each in Florida, Maryland, New York, Massachusetts, and Illinois) and an additional 27 affiliates. It commanded a prime-time audience of about $1\frac{2}{3}$ million adults through its broadcast and cable affiliates nationwide. The other U.S.-based network, Telemundo, had seven full-power stations (San Jose–San Francisco, New York, Miami, Los Angeles, Houston, San Antonio, and Chicago), fourteen low-power stations spread across the United States, and 32 broadcasting affiliates, plus 118 direct-affiliate cable systems. Various cable systems spread the programming nationwide, along with that of Televisa, the Mexican network.

NATIVE AMERICAN NEWSPAPERS

The Native American press of the 1990s was almost entirely printed in English, although some newspapers were used to teach tribal languages. There were 220 newspapers listed by the Native American Journalists Association (formerly Native American Press Association), scattered across 32 states and Canada.[38]

The driving force behind the formation of the association in 1984 was Tim A. Giago, Jr., whose name in the Oglala Sioux tribe meant "He Stands Up for Them." Giago founded *The Lakota Times* in 1981 (now called *Indian Country Today*) and turned it into the largest weekly in South Dakota. With more than 17,000 circulation, it is the largest independent Native American owned paper in the United States. Giago's column, "Notes from Indian Country," was syndicated in 14 establishment papers and won the *Baltimore Sun*'s H. L. Mencken Writing Award.[39]

Fewer than a quarter of the Indian newspapers were weeklies; most were published monthly or less often. There was one daily from 1984 to 1987, *The Navajo Times Today,* of Window Rock, Arizona. Some of the papers were truly independent, but many were owned by tribes. The approach was to be editorially autonomous, but that wasn't always possible.

Two national newspapers were the 10,000 circulation *Akwesasne Notes,* a 48-page tabloid published six times annually as the official publication of the Mohawk nation, and *Wassaja,* a bimonthly of 24 to 32 pages sponsored by the American Indian Historical Society and devoted to Native American self-determination and education.

The *Cherokee Phoenix,* the first Native American paper, appeared in Georgia from 1828 to 1832. It continues as the *Cherokee Advocate.* Other early papers were the Sioux-language *Shawnee Sun* (*Siwinowe Kesibwi*), and the *Cherokee Rose Bud,* founded in 1848 by Native American women seminary students in present-day Oklahoma.

Native American papers suffered from limited funding, editorial inexperience, and tribal conflicts such as those experienced within the Mohawk community. But they were cause-oriented, promoted the welfare and self-pride of Native Americans, preserved and restored the Indian heritage, and functioned as mirrors of their communities and their readerships by presenting their points of view.

THE GAY AND LESBIAN PRESS

At the turn of the twenty-first century, the gay and lesbian press continued to thrive, emerging as a lucrative niche for advertisers. Led by a vocal new generation of gay men and lesbians, around the country some 850 gay weeklies, biweeklies, monthlies, and quarterlies covered local events and news for an audience of at least two million, while others, such as *Genre,* a life-style magazine for gay men published in Los Angeles, reached a national audience of 100,000 and commanded advertising from national companies such as Absolut vodka and the Columbia House record club.[40] Three circulation leaders were the *San Francisco Bay Times,* the *Seattle Gay News,* and the *Washington Blade.* Some publications were traditional bar giveaways heavily dependent upon sexually oriented advertising, but increasingly, many more sought a more mainstream image. One was New York's *Out,* which described itself as "a gay and lesbian *Mirabella* or *Esquire* with a little bit of gay and lesbian *Cosmo* thrown in."[41] By 1998 its paid circulation exceeded 136,000.

The National Lesbian and Gay Journalists Association, founded in 1990, encouraged gay and lesbian journalists working in mainstream media to come out in order to demystify homosexuality and foster better coverage of issues related to it.[42] At the group's first conference in San Francisco, *New York Times* publisher Arthur O. Sulzberger, Jr., pledged that his paper would eventually give health insurance and other benefits to the partners of gay employees. Meanwhile, the *New Republic* became the first mainstream national magazine with an openly gay editor, Andrew Sullivan.[43] Andrew Kopkind, one of the most influential gay journalists, died in 1994 at age 59 after a long career that included positions with the *Washington Post, Time, Village Voice, The New Republic,* and the *Nation.* He was a leader in the reporting of the civil rights and antiwar movements. His friend Alexander Cockburn, himself a radical syndicated columnist, called Kopkind "the best radical reporter and writer of this time, the most graceful stylist, and spiritually the least amenable to conformity I've ever met."[44]

18

A Crisis
of Credibility

The press was to serve the governed, not the governors.

—Justice Hugo L. Black

The credibility gap as an institution became painfully apparent in American life by 1970. There were gaps between president and people, president and press, press and people. To these were added gaps between old and young, black and white, intellectuals and silent majority.

One reason for the difficulties of the presidents was the growth of a cult of disbelief. At his height, Senator Joseph McCarthy had half of the American people believing in him, which meant they believed their government was a combination of Communism and corruption—even the army harbored treason, McCarthy said. The senator was unable to bring down war hero Eisenhower, who was less affected than were his successors by the credibility gap. John F. Kennedy inherited a Cuban crisis; news was managed, and many disbelieved their government's explanations. The Warren Commission hearings failed to keep Americans from doubting accounts of President Kennedy's assassination; that doubt increased over the years. Senator Barry Goldwater could offer rueful testimony about the depth of disbelief he encountered in his disastrous 1964 presidential campaign. Senator Eugene McCarthy found in the winter of 1967–68 that President Johnson's public support was a hollow shell; his "children's crusade" and the reality of the Tet attacks in Vietnam shattered belief in the war effort. The credibility gap that had been attributed to the Lyndon Johnson personality persisted for Richard Nixon as his problems multiplied, partially for the same reason but also partly because it was part of the American way of life.

Another reason for the difficulties of both presidents and press was the steady diet of bad news that characterized the 1950s and 1960s, despite many years of prosperity

The Weather

The Washington Post

Index

97th Year — No. 247   FRIDAY, AUGUST 9, 1974   Phone (202) 223-6000   15¢

Nixon Resigns

By Carroll Kilpatrick

Ford Assumes Presidency Today

By Jules Witcover

Era of Good Feeling
Congress Expects Harmony

By Spencer Rich and Richard L. Lyons

A Solemn Change
Power Is Passed Quietly

By Richard Harwood and Haynes Johnson

President Nixon and daughter Julie embracing Wednesday after the President's decision to resign.

THE NIXON YEARS

A 24-page special section on the Nixon presidency—inside today.

The climax of two years of persistent investigative reporting

and notable accomplishments. Americans did not want to hear that they had to settle for a stalemate in Korea—"Communism, Corruption, and Korea" was a 1952 election slogan to explain the bad news, not the hard facts of a capable Chinese army opponent. A recession in the late 1950s; antagonistic receptions abroad of Vice President Nixon and even President Eisenhower; and a challenge to American prestige by Charles de Gaulle were all unwanted subjects. They piled up in the 1960s and early 1970s: the Bay of Pigs, the Berlin Wall, the assassination of a president, the Vietnam War, racial riots in big cities, college-campus riots, the assassinations of Senator Robert Kennedy and Martin Luther King, the collapse of the promise of victory in Vietnam, long hair, sex and four-letter words in the open, drug addiction, Kent State, My Lai, a near depression, and Watergate. Traditionally a president pays politically for adverse news, particularly of an economic nature. But as William Small of CBS put it in a book title, the public, like the kings of old seemed willing "to kill a messenger"—in this case, CBS and the other networks, the *Washington Post* and other liberal newspapers, and even the objectivity-seeking press associations that brought them the bad news.

The situation was ripe for demagogues. There was much bad news people did not want to believe, much reality they did not want to have exist. One group did not believe the president; another did not believe the press. And both president and press encouraged people not to believe the other. It was easy to argue, as it is now, that reporting bad news was unpatriotic; to say that those who made bad news—as at Kent State or in the streets of Chicago—were un-American and deserving of their fates. The only solace defenders of freedom had was that such credibility gaps had existed before and that with determination this one also could be overcome. However, during the Iran-Contra scandal of 1986–87 the credibility of the Reagan administration hit new lows. And, of course, the media took their share of the blame in the Clinton-Lewinsky scandal that broke in January 1998.

In seeking to understand the development of the credibility gap, one continues with the record of the relationships between the presidents and the press, examines the overt attacks on the press, estimates the extent of the gap between the press and the people, and also records the frictions between government and press that resulted in legislation and court decisions involving freedom of the press.

In the 1990s, the credibility gap continued. A 1997 study by the Newseum found that although 80 percent of Americans see the role of the media as crucial to a free society, 64 percent say the news is too sensational. People view journalists as insensitive and biased, while less than a third trust newspaper reporters. And journalists are perceived to be ethically equivalent to individuals with agendas, such as politicians, lawyers, and corporate managers. Perhaps most frightening of all, the study found that if the press freedoms guaranteed in the Constitution were put to a popular vote today, it is unlikely that they would survive.

NIXON AND AGNEW

Richard Nixon had spent years studying his mistakes in the 1960 presidential race, with its "great debates" on television, and in his 1962 failure in California, which ended with his ill-tempered attack on the press. But in 1968 he used television skillfully, appearing before controlled audiences with filtered questions rather than giving set speeches. He held standard press conferences only rarely, at one-third the rate of recent presidents. Instead he relied on a technique Johnson had developed when he had dramatic war news to announce: request prime-time network television for a brief appearance. He did this 37 times while in office, at a higher frequency than any other president. Nixon averaged 11 regular press conferences a year during his first two years in the White House, but then trailed off and ended with a total of 38. A committee of the Associated Press Managing Editors, made up of executives of three conservative papers that had supported Nixon (the *Christian Science Monitor, Washington Star,* and *Philadelphia Bulletin*), criticized him for using press conferences to "raise questions about the credibility of the press."

Vice President Spiro Agnew aroused a stormy debate late in 1969, when he declared that the networks and newspapers with multiple media holdings (his favorite targets were the *Washington Post, Newsweek,* and Katharine Graham's TV stations) exercised such powerful influence over public opinion that they should vigorously endeavor to be impartial and fair in reporting and commenting on national affairs. Specifically, Agnew criticized network management for using commentators with an "Eastern Establishment bias" and for failing to provide a "wall of separation" between news and comment.

A research study comparing random samples of newscast items reporting administration activities for one-week periods in 1969 and 1970 bore out the contention that the Agnew-generated criticism had affected the newscasts in the direction of "safe" handling.[1]

The vice president went into eclipse after the Republican setbacks in the 1970 congressional elections, but CBS gave him another opening when it screened "The Selling of the Pentagon" early in 1971. A congressional committee attempted to subpoena all records and unused film CBS had filed in making the Pentagon film; Representative Harley O. Staggers, West Virginia Democrat, obtained the support of the Commerce Committee in requesting the House of Representatives to try CBS and CBS President Frank Stanton on charges of contempt of Congress. This the House refused to do, voting 226 to 181 in July 1971 to return the request to the committee. The refusal, while encouraging to free-press advocates, was more politically shocking (such turndowns by the House have been rare) than legally reassuring.

Nixon's major accomplishment during this period was helping to part the "Bamboo Curtain." In 1971 an American ping-pong team was invited to play in Peking. China-watcher correspondents routinely asked to accompany them and were astounded to be admitted in some cases. John Roderick of the AP revisited China after an absence of 23 years. So did veterans John Rich of NBC and Tillman Durdin of the *New York Times.* A large contingent traveled with Nixon on his trip to China in 1972, and the networks broadcast many of the proceedings live, using satellite transmissions. The age-old American love affair with China was resumed but suspicions remained on both sides because of the Taiwan problem, which occasionally flared into the headlines.

PRIOR RESTRAINT: THE PENTAGON PAPERS CASE

In June 1971, the United States government attempted to impose prior restraint on American newspapers, and for 15 days it successfully stopped one of the country's most influential dailies from publishing a vital news story. For those 15 days the clock was turned back to the time of Henry VIII, who in 1534 had imposed prior restraint on the English press. Prior restraint ended in England in 1694 and in the colonies in 1721, to be temporarily revived exactly 250 years later.

That the Supreme Court came to the rescue of press freedom and the First Amendment guarantee on June 30, 1971, by vacating its own temporary stay order of June 25 and earlier lower-court orders, afforded some reassurance. But the fact that President Nixon had ever instructed Attorney General John Mitchell to go to court to seek the imposition of a prior restraint on publication did great damage to the concept of liberty of the press that had so painstakingly developed through historical evolution and legal decisions since 1694. In the history of the republic, no other president had so acted.

In the judgment of legal scholars, the Pentagon Papers case left little legal residue and will be remembered far longer for its political implications than for its legal stature.[2] In that respect it perhaps paralleled the Zenger case of 1735; there was no guarantee after Zenger's acquittal that another editor would not be charged in another government effort to muzzle the press, but it never seemed politically feasible for colonial administrators to try in the same manner. Possibly the next president faced with circumstances similar to those involved in the Pentagon Papers case will seek a postpublication criminal prosecution, if one seems warranted, rather than attempt again to impose prior restraint on publication. In that sense, the case is worth detailed examination.

Sometime in March 1971, the *New York Times* came into possession of a 47-volume study entitled "History of the U.S. Decision-Making Process on Vietnam Policy," compiled for the Pentagon at the order of former Defense Secretary Robert McNamara. Its contents were historical and nonmilitary in character but highly explosive in terms of political and diplomatic interest. All such documents were classified "top secret" under a 1953 executive order. *Times* correspondent Neil Sheehan, who had represented the UPI in the original Saigon press corps and who in 1971 covered the Pentagon, was a key figure in the development of the Pentagon Papers series for the paper. Managing editor Abe Rosenthal assigned several leading *Times* staffers to weeks of painstaking work in a hotel room hideaway. On June 13 the *Times* printed the first installment.

Attorney General Mitchell asked the *Times* to stop the series; it refused. The government then went to a federal district judge just appointed by President Nixon and serving the first day on his new bench with its unprecedented prior restraint order request. Judge Murray Gurfein issued a temporary restraining order on June 15, forcing the *Times* to stop after the third installment. On June 19 Judge Gurfein refused to grant a permanent restraining order, saying that the government had failed to prove its case other than to plead a "general framework of embarrassment." But he let the temporary order stand. On June 23, the U.S. Court of Appeals in New York reversed Gurfein's decision. In the meantime, the *Washington Post* had started a series of its own and had won a clear-cut victory when Judge Gerhard A. Gesell ruled that the government could not "impose a prior restraint on essentially historical data." The U.S. Court of Appeals for the District of Columbia upheld Gesell, and the two cases reached the U.S. Supreme Court on June 25. There, with Justices Black, Douglas, Brennan, and Marshall dissenting, the court voted 5–4 to hear testimony and continue the temporary order of prior restraint.

At this point the case collapsed as a legal landmark. The newspaper attorneys, shaken by the adverse 5–4 vote of the Supreme Court continuing a temporary prior restraint, refused to gamble on a plea that the First Amendment prohibited prior restraint under any and all circumstances. Instead, they preferred to win the immediate case on the grounds that the government could not prove that national security was involved. This they did, on a 6–3 *per curiam* decision.[3] It was based on *Near* v. *Minnesota* and two more recent press-freedom decisions. There were then nine individual decisions, with Justices Black and Douglas arguing that freedom of the press is absolute; Justices Brennan and Stewart declaring that the government had not proved its case; Justice Marshall rejecting the contention that the president had inherent power to declare a document nonpublishable in the national interest; Justice White joining the majority but inviting a criminal prosecution of newspapers in the future; Chief Justice Burger and Justice Blackmun, in dissent, objecting to the haste shown in the case and requesting an exhaustive review of the documents; and Justice Harlan, in dissent, indicating that he believed the president

(© 1971, New York Times)

The *New York Times* reports its victory; inset, Frank Stanton and CBS avoid censure.

should have the power to foreclose publication of any document whose disclosure would, in the president's judgment, be harmful to national security.

The anonymous writer of the *per curiam* decision did cite *Near* v. *Minnesota,* the landmark 1931 case defending liberty of the press and extending the protection of the First amendment against acts of Congress to include a ban on state action. The government cited *Near* also. Also cited were two quotations, one from an earlier case, the second from a concurrent case. The rule of the earlier case became the rule of the Pentagon Papers case in particular and of prior restraint in general:

> Any system of prior restraints of expression comes to this court bearing a heavy presumption against its constitutional validity.[4]
>
> The Government thus carries a heavy burden of showing justification for the enforcement of such a restraint.[5]

Prior restraint for purposes of national security was imposed again in 1979, when the government obtained a restraining order that temporarily stopped *Progressive* magazine from publishing an article telling how hydrogen bombs are built, even though the author had obtained his information from public sources. The magazine had voluntarily submitted the detailed story to the government for examination. The *Progressive* appealed a lower-court ban to the 7th Circuit Court of Appeals, but the government withdrew its charges when the *Madison Press Connection* went ahead and published nearly identical information. The likely outcome of such cases would be more self-censorship, it was feared, in the face of government harassment.

THE WATERGATE STORY

The most widespread political corruption in the nation's history, involving more than a dozen major events conveniently listed under the headline word *Watergate,* forced the resignation of Richard Nixon and deepened the cynicism of a public already battered by the endless Vietnam fighting, partisan politics, and economic chaos. The scope and magnitude of the illegal activities and deceptions revealed during Nixon's desperate fight to save his presidency between 1972 and 1974 shocked Republicans and Democrats alike, most of whom were loath to believe that men who had entered the White House on a strict "law and order" platform had misused their power, money, and public trust.

Watergate was not an aberration. As discussed, its roots lay deep in the misdeeds of other administrations. But these specific events were unprecedented because of the scope and magnitude of the totalitarian methods used by Nixon and his closest advisers to discredit their foes and maintain their long-sought control over America's destiny.[6]

Crucial to the events that followed was Nixon's decision to begin a secret bombing campaign against neutral Cambodia in March 1969. Enmity and distrust between the White House and Congress grew when the Senate twice rejected Nixon's nominations to the Supreme Court. Then came massive public demonstrations against an open invasion of Cambodia and the killing of four Kent State University students. The White House atmosphere became one of tenseness, and a number of news leaks added to the pressure.

In June 1970, Nixon agreed to a plan advanced by White House aide Tom Huston that called for a domestic security group to be formed from representatives of the White House, FBI, CIA, and other government agencies. It was to be authorized to wiretap, commit burglary, and violate other laws, if necessary, in the interest of providing intelligence information on persons disloyal to the administration. FBI Director J. Edgar Hoover, jealously protecting his hold over domestic intelligence gathering, refused to cooperate. Nixon then recalled his memos to the other organizations. The White House learned a lesson here. In the future, if sensitive missions needed to be carried out, they would have to be conducted by persons not connected to any official agency.[7]

In the absence of any such secret group, however, Nixon authorized FBI wiretaps on 4 newsmen and 13 government officials between May 1969 and February 1971. Secretary of State Henry Kissinger, fearful of possible leaks from members of his staff, encouraged some of the wiretaps. A turning point came in June 1971 with the publication of the Pentagon Papers. Worried that his own secret foreign maneuverings, including the Cambodian bombing,[8] might be revealed, Nixon authorized the establishment of a White House surveillance team—later to be called the "Plumbers." Their chief assignment was to plug leaks of classified information. On September 3, 1971, several of the unit's members broke into the office of Daniel Ellsberg's psychiatrist in an effort to find personal information that might discredit the man who brought the Pentagon Papers to the *New York Times.*

That same week White House aide Charles Colson, one of Nixon's closest personal confidants, gave John Dean, the president's counsel, a "priority list" of 20 "political enemies." The list, later expanded, contained the names of journalists, politicians, movie stars, and other prominent Americans. From this time until June 1972, operatives hired by persons with White House contacts attempted to disrupt the campaigns of Democratic candidates, especially the acknowledged front runner, Senator Edmund Muskie. Their object was to destroy Muskie's candidacy in the hopes that a more vulnerable candidate, Senator George McGovern, might emerge as Nixon's opponent in the 1972 elections. Nixon's White House chief of staff, H. R. ("Bob") Haldeman, was kept advised of these activities, known later as the "dirty tricks" campaign.

It was the White House "Plumbers" who, on June 17, 1972, entered the Washington headquarters of the Democratic National Committee, located in the Watergate apartment complex. Washington police caught five men redhanded, planting listening devices in the office of Lawrence F. O'Brien, chairperson of the Democratic party. It was later determined that this break-in was part of a large-scale plan to spy on Democratic leaders that was financed by contributions (some of them illegal) to the Committee to Re-Elect the President, called CREEP.[9]

The *Washington Post* ran as its second lead on June 18 an 83-inch story that linked Watergate burglar James McCord to the CIA. The *New York Times* ran a 13-inch story on an inside page, as did most newspapers. Since this broke as a local story, the *Post* assigned several metropolitan reporters to it, including Bob Woodward and Carl Bernstein. It was Woodward who traced the name of E. Howard Hunt, found in one burglar's address book, to a White House office.

The pattern of media coverage quickly developed. As the *Post* pushed onward with its stories by Woodward and Bernstein, assisted by the mysterious contact "Deep Throat," White House spokespeople branded them as being false or misleading. These official rebuttals received more attention than the original stories.

The *Post*'s major breakthrough came in October, when Woodward and Bernstein wrote that Watergate had been only part of a White House plan for massive spying and political espionage. However, studies of press performance during the fall of 1972 revealed that Watergate got little attention from the bulk of the news media. One critic calculated that of 433 Washington-based reporters who could have been assigned to the story, only 15 were. Television networks also treated the story in such a routine way that only 52 percent of Americans polled by the Gallup organization recognized the word Watergate.[10]

Bob Woodward and Carl Bernstein

It was in this atmosphere that Nixon was reelected. While the *Washington Post, New York Times, Louisville Courier-Journal, St. Louis Post-Dispatch,* and *Minneapolis Tribune* clamored against his policies, the bulk of the press gave him its blessing, including the *Los Angeles Times,* which lived to regret its decision.

Watergate became the biggest story in 1973 but not merely because of investigative reporting. The trial of the burglars began in Judge John T. Sirica's courtroom in January, and in February the Senate Select Committee on Presidential Campaign Activities, headed by Senator Sam J. Ervin, Jr., of North Carolina, began hearing testimony. The American public began hundreds of hours of television viewing. But behind all of this was a growing revolt against Nixon by people in the FBI and Department of Justice, and finally by Republican congressmen and papers that had endorsed him.

The lid could not be kept on the cover-up. Media pressure intensified, and a number of stories contained allegations of serious misconduct. Seymour Hersh of the *New York Times,* Jack Nelson of the *Los Angeles Times,* and writers for *Time* and *Newsweek* joined in. Dan Rather of CBS and Nixon engaged in combat at several news conferences. But the most startling discovery came on July 16, when presidential aide Alexander Butterfield told the Senate committee that since 1970 Nixon had been secretly taping all of his conversations.

The "battle over the tapes" raged until July 24, 1974, when the Supreme Court voted 8–0 that Nixon had to turn over his recordings to Judge Sirica. On October 10, during the middle of this crisis, Vice President Agnew resigned after pleading no contest on charges of income tax evasion. Nixon picked Gerald Ford to replace him and isolated himself from the calls for impeachment that would not be quieted.

In early 1974 the dam broke when it was discovered that a strange 18½-minute gap in a tape recording of a Nixon–Haldeman talk on June 20, 1972, was caused by manual erasure. The House voted 410–4 to begin impeachment hearings, an action that culminated in late July, when the bipartisan House Judiciary Committee voted three articles of impeachment: obstruction of justice, abuse of power, and contempt of Congress for refusing to turn over the tapes.

Several hold-out Republicans on the Judiciary Committee dropped their staunch support on August 5, when Nixon, complying with the Supreme Court order, released the transcript of his June 23, 1972, talk with Haldeman. It was the "smoking gun" that proved that for two years Nixon had been lying to the public, his supporters, and even his lawyers about his lack of knowledge of the break-in.

The end came on the evening of August 8, when Nixon, defending his overall record as he had on so many other occasions during the 26-month ordeal, told a stunned nation he would resign effective the following noon. The next morning he gathered his cabinet and staff for an emotional farewell, which was also televised. A few minutes later Gerald Ford took the oath of office and attempted to reassure the country by saying, "Our long national nightmare is over. Our Constitution works."

Nixon's life and the entire Watergate affair were revisited on a grand scale after his death in 1994 and the gathering of former presidents at his funeral. While there was a generous forgiving of Nixon's transgressions by former political and media foes, some, like David Halberstam, bluntly reminded audiences that Nixon's Vietnam policies were an opportunistic sham and that his funeral—with eulogies for a wise elder statesman—was designed to erase memories of the angry, vindictive man from California.

NIXON AND THE WAR

President Nixon announced a "Vietnamization" policy in November 1969, under which the defense of South Vietnam would be turned over to South Vietnamese troops. As U.S. troops were gradually withdrawn, the command ceased placing troops in exposed positions, as had occurred at Con Thien in 1967 and at Khesanh in 1968, in order to draw the enemy out.

One of the biggest stories of the war in Vietnam escaped the Saigon press corps at about the same time: the massacre of civilians by U.S. troops at My Lai, for which Lieutenant William Calley was convicted of murder in 1971. Even though military pictures were taken at the massacre scene and floating stories existed of the "Pinkville" affair, the story did not break until November 1969, after a freelance writer in Washington was tipped to Calley's interrogation. The writer, former AP Pentagon reporter Seymour M. Hersh, won the 1970 Pulitzer Prize for international reporting for a story he had to market through the unknown Dispatch News Service. It was only then that major media outlets began to develop the story. The turning point was on November 24, when former soldier Paul Meadlo appeared on Walter Cronkite's *CBS Evening News* and described how he had executed dozens of Vietnamese civilians. On December 5 *Life* published former Army photographer Ron Haeberle's shocking pictures. My Lai was a story Americans did not want to read, just as they had not wanted to see and hear Morley Safer's anguished broadcast from Vietnam in 1965.

Early in 1969 Nixon began planning his secret bombing campaign against neutral Cambodia. For 14 months, beginning in March 1969, American B-52s pulverized the Cambodian countryside with more than 3600 sorties and 100,000 tons of bombs. Records of the raids were falsified with the knowledge of the president and high military officers. When the story emerged in July 1973, through the congressional testimony of an Air Force officer—not from the news media—there was cynical speculation that Nixon's 1968 campaign pledge to use a "secret peace plan" to end the war actually masked a scheme to bomb the opposition into submission. There also were secret bombings in Laos prior to a 1971 U.S.–South Vietnamese invasion that was a complete failure.

Thus the nation was unaware of the full scope of the Asian war when the president appeared on nationwide television on April 30, 1970, to announce the ground invasion of Cambodia. Nixon claimed that American policy since the Geneva Agreement of 1954 had been to "scrupulously respect the neutrality of the Cambodian people," but that North Vietnamese troops were using Cambodian sanctuaries to attack South Vietnam. News reports of the war's expansion triggered shock and anger throughout the nation. Protests, some violent, broke out on college campuses, and there were clashes between students and local police. Peaceful marches were held in many communities. But at Kent State University in Ohio, tired and edgy National Guardsmen fired on a crowd of demonstrating students, killing four persons in the area, including one walking to class. Anguish and more anger were the result; some newspapers and broadcast stations supported Nixon's criticism of "these bums . . . blowing up the campuses."[11]

Journalist J. Anthony Lukas later wrote that the Cambodian and Kent State experiences, coupled with Senate setbacks, marked a turn as Nixon moved toward a policy of "positive polarization." This meant punishing his enemies and trying to capture the votes of the so-called silent majority.[12]

In July 1973, Murrey Marder, diplomatic correspondent for the *Washington Post,* added another dimension with his analysis that the Nixon group had fought the 1971 disclosure of the Pentagon Papers—and created the "Plumbers" unit as part of a system of illegal wiretapping and break-ins—because of the risk of exposure of its Cambodian bombing campaign and other sensitive plans of the president and Secretary of State Henry Kissinger. "Facts now available not only overturn the official version of how the United States entered the Cambodian war," Marder wrote, "they illuminate the kind of thinking that led to Watergate."[13]

THE PRESS CORPS: PRIZES AND CASUALTIES

The large number of correspondents who covered the Vietnam story makes it impossible to describe the accomplishments of more than a few. Heading any list, if for no other reason than seniority, would be reporters like Keyes Beech and Peter Arnett. The majority of the journalists, even some of the most well known, had relatively short stints.[14] Malcolm Browne shifted to ABC News in 1965 and later joined the *New York Times* staff. Sheehan also joined the *New York Times.* David Halberstam served briefly as a contributing editor for *Harper's* and then devoted his time to books and articles.

Among the photographers who won Pulitzer Prizes for their work in Vietnam was the German-born Horst Faas, a 1965 winner, who sparked the AP coverage from the beginning, was wounded in 1967, and met the Tet crisis while still convalescing. Kyoichi Sawada of the UPI was the 1966 Pulitzer winner for a picture of a Vietnamese family swimming together in a river current, children's heads bobbing. Sawada won many other prizes, then was killed in 1970 in Cambodia. Toshio Sakai reported for the UPI in 1968. Edward T. Adams of the AP swept all 1969 competition with his photo of the Saigon police chief executing a Viet Cong during the Tet offensive. David Douglas Duncan of *Life* won the 1967 Robert Capa Award, and Catherine Leroy, a freelancer for the AP, won an Overseas Press Club award.

Death struck heavily in the ranks of photographers. Besides Sawada, two other prize winners died: Larry Burrows of *Life,* in Vietnam since 1962 and twice a Capa award winner, and Henri Huet, who had worked for both the UPI and AP and had won a Capa

IN CAMBODIA—American soldiers try to spot enemy through rubber trees in the Fishhook region.

IN KENT, OHIO—National guardsmen advance during clash in which four students were killed.

Los Angeles Times

LARGEST CIRCULATION IN THE WEST. WEEKDAYS DAILY, 1,217,229 SUNDAY.

VOL. LXXXIX   SEVEN PARTS—PART ONE   CC , F   TUESDAY MORNING, MAY 5, 1970   110 PAGES   DAILY 10c

DEATH ON THE CAMPUS—A girl screams over the body of a student shot at Kent State University.

Troops Kill Four Students in Antiwar Riot at Ohio College

Large S. Viet-U.S. Force Opens Third Cambodia Offensive

WAR SITUATION AT A GLANCE

Guards' Gunfire Wounds 11 at Kent University

KENT, Ohio (UPI)—Four students were shot to death on the Kent State University campus Monday when national guardsmen, believing a sniper had attacked them, fired into a crowd of rioting antiwar protesters.

At least 11 persons were wounded, three critically, before order was restored. The university was shut down for at least a week.

The town of 18,000 was sealed off and a judge ordered the university's

California student protesters disrupt campuses. See Page 3, Part 1.

ALABAMA ELECTION

Wallace's Drive for Presidency at Stake Today

BY KENNETH REICH
Times Staff Writer

Hopes Rise for Teacher Strike Settlement by End of the Week

BY HARRY BERNSTEIN
Times Labor Writer

New U.S. Air Raids Halted Over North, but Option Remains

BY TED SELL
Times Staff Writer

My Lai Disclosure Wins Pulitzer Prize

BY RICHARD DOUGHERTY
Times Staff Writer

Index to The Times

THE WEATHER

U.S. Weather Bureau forecast: Night and morning low clouds with local drizzle but hazy afternoon sunshine today and Wednesday. High today, 70. High Monday, 80; low, 55.

Smog report and complete weather information in Part 2, Page 4.

award. They died together covering the 1971 Laos invasion. The UPI lost three other staff men: Hiromichi Mine, Kent Potter, and Charles Eggleston. Bernard J. Kolenberg of the AP and Dickey Chapelle of the *National Observer* died in 1965. Robert J. Ellison of Empire/Black Star was killed at Khesanh. Paul Schutzer of *Life* won a 1965 Capa award in Vietnam, then died in the 1967 Israeli war.

Bernard Fall, the distinguished historian of the Indochina war, was a 1967 casualty. *Look* editor Sam Castan was killed in 1966. Among the dead and missing in the Cambodian invasion were Frank Frosch of the UPI, George Syvertsen and Gerald Miller of CBS, and Welles Hangen of NBC.

MILITARY CENSORSHIP IN VIETNAM

To the credit of the U.S. military command in Saigon, only a minimum of censorship was imposed on the Saigon press corps, whose principal troubles were with the South Vietnamese government and critics at home. When bombings of North Vietnam were stepped up in 1965 and troop ships flooded in, some correspondents among the 150 Americans and 400 or more other newspeople ran afoul of military police. As casualties mounted, exact numbers were discontinued in daily briefings in favor of weekly totals, another minor complaint. After Tet and the limiting of United States military actions, a simple field censorship was imposed that correspondents readily accepted. Major complaints were heard during news blackouts preceding the Cambodian and Laos invasions of 1970 and 1971. In the latter, restrictions on the use of helicopters by photographers cost the lives of four in the crash of a Vietnamese substitute craft. Among correspondents, François Sully had been an early victim of expulsion by the Vietnamese; Homer Bigart narrowly missed the same fate, as did Everett Martin of *Newsweek*. Jack Foisie, *Los Angeles Times;* George Esper, AP; and John Carroll, *Baltimore Sun,* had their credentials temporarily suspended by the U.S. command for reporting military actions prematurely.

Major censorship in Vietnam affected the newspaper of the GIs, the *Stars and Stripes,* and the Armed Forces Vietnam Network, supplying radio programs and news to the troops. The Armed Forces Network particularly fell under the heavy hand of the U.S. command's Office of Information, which endeavored to eliminate stories that would embarrass the South Vietnamese government or adversely affect morale. The result was a rebellion of staff people amid charges that the Saigon command was violating Defense Department regulations and policy. The controversy simmered down, with the censors still in control. *Stars and Stripes* weathered charges that it was undermining morale by reporting life in Vietnam "like it is." The most sharply censored press in Vietnam was, of course, the local one in Saigon, whose ranks were thinned periodically of political dissenters by charges of aid to the enemy.

DEFEAT AND SURRENDER

The end to 30 years of war occurred quickly when it finally came. On April 30, 1975, a handful of reporters stood on the roof of the famed Caravelle Hotel in downtown Saigon and watched helicopters carry away the last evacuees from the roof of the American Embassy. They reported that the "Stars and Stripes" no longer flew over the embattled city and that Saigon had surrendered. The final stage of the long battle for national unification was over, and the vast American military machine had fallen victim to the persistence of Ho Chi Minh's followers, as had the French 21 years earlier. A demoralized South Vietnamese army, denied further U.S. aid, in turn fell victim to its own corruption, inefficiency, and poor training. The Communists unleashed full-scale attacks in January, and when Danang fell on March 29, a horrified American television audience saw South Vietnamese troops fighting civilians to board transports leaving the city.

The "peace with honor" that President Nixon and Secretary of State Kissinger had proclaimed in January 1973 was forgotten. So were the formal agreements signed in Paris by the United States, North and South Vietnam, and the Viet Cong. Pressures for negotiations had mounted after the United States mined Haiphong harbor in May 1972 and unloaded the heaviest bombing of the entire war at Christmastime of that year. The last American combat troops had departed in August, along with a good number of journalists who moved on to other breaking stories. In March 1973, the nation watched with mixed emotions as American prisoners of war returned, but the issue of men missing in action added to the debate over how the war should be ended and whether the United States should pay to reconstruct the land it had helped destroy.

The gleaming black granite wall of the Vietnam Veterans Memorial dedicated in Washington on Veteran's Day 1982 is inscribed with the names of 58,132 Americans who died in Vietnam. Several hundred thousand others suffered wounds. There was no estimate of how many millions of Vietnamese, Cambodians, and Laotians were killed or wounded between 1961 and 1975. There seemed to be a consensus that for the most part American journalists had brought the Vietnam dilemma home to the public, but there was continued concern over the failures of the Saigon and Washington press corps to press quickly on stories that would have given some of the fragments greater meaning, such as the Tonkin Gulf incident, My Lai, Cambodian and Laotian bombings and raids, and the bombing of North Vietnam.

It has been noted that most American journalists—except those writers and editors for alternative and underground publications—were very slow to truly understand the futility of the Vietnam experience. So were most citizens, and Congress lagged even further behind. The most severe criticism of the news media, however, might be its failure to put the war into a historical perspective. With the exception of an occasional "blockbuster" interpretative article or a television documentary, American journalists reported everything about the war except the essence of why it was being fought. David Halberstam had strong feelings about this and undoubtedly spoke for the handful of journalists who had tried to explain it in the 1950s and early 1960s:

> The problem was trying to cover something every day as news when in fact the real key was that it was all derivative of the French Indo-China war, which is history. So you really should have had a third paragraph in each story which would have said, ". . . none of this means anything because we are in the same footsteps as the French and we are prisoners of their experience," but given the rules of newspaper reporting you can't really do that. That is not usually such a problem for a reporter, but to an incredible degree in Vietnam I think we were haunted and indeed imprisoned by the past.[15]

VIETNAM RECONSIDERED: LESSONS OF THE WAR

Eight years after Saigon's surrender an unlikely mix of former Vietnam correspondents, antiwar activists, spies, generals, government press spokespeople, veterans, and Vietnamese—all participants in the United States' Asian nightmare—met in Los Angeles to discuss the lessons of Vietnam. There were disagreements over the causes and strategies of the war, but it was clear that deep wounds had not healed and that Vietnam had indeed become a myth destined to influence the actions of future generations.[16]

Harrison Salisbury warned against accepting a "revisionist" view that the war had been lost because of "liberal" reporting and not because of blind, imperialistic motives. Salisbury described Vietnam as an "anomaly" and said that Americans should not take it for granted that their government would allow open criticism of its actions in a future conflict. He said the "Vietnam model" was there for all to see, including those who do not respect press freedoms.

Joining in the defense of critical coverage were David Halberstam, Morley Safer, John Laurence, Peter Arnett, and Garrick Utley. Adding their poignant memories were Gloria Emerson, Frances FitzGerald, and Jack Langguth, who had written a bitter denunciation of United States policy for the *New York Times Magazine* after returning home in 1965 following a tour as Saigon bureau chief.

Halberstam said that in retrospect he wished that the press corps had been much more critical during the war's opening days, from 1962 to 1964. Salisbury agreed, noting how the correspondents had been caught in the middle, pleasing neither side at home. The purge of progressives from the State Department in the late 1940s and 1950s, Halberstam said, denied Saigon reporters the kind of open-minded sources within the embassy staff that could have produced more analytical, truthful stories. On the other hand, he said, reporters did find such sources within the United States adviser groups, but generally not within higher commands. Similarities were noted in dealing with State Department officials in Central America, where in the early 1980s, some of the same military and diplomatic planners were involved, repeating tactics that had failed in Vietnam.

Peter Braestrup's thesis, found in *Big Story*, that Saigon reporters had misrepresented the 1968 Tet offensive and had helped cause the downfall of the United States mission, was angrily refuted by Laurence and Arnett.[17] Michael Arlen, who coined the phrase "living room war" with his book, warned against continued parochialism in American reporting, characterized by only defining events in terms of U.S. interests, as in Vietnam. Filmmaker Peter Davis noted that after a long, articulate report viewers often knew more about the star television reporter than about the Vietnamese family being filmed, a criticism that held true later. The oldest Asian veteran, Keyes Beech, lamented the loss of Vietnam to the Communists and said that in general the coverage had been "lopsided" against United States efforts to stabilize the area.

It became clear that the intramural press war of the early 1960s had not ended and that the victims of the war—the Vietnamese and the veterans—had been ignored by the nation as a whole. While Vietnamese refugees became part of the United States' urban poor, thousands of angry veterans demanded recognition in the form of better hospital treatment and benefits. Lyndon Johnson's press secretary, George Reedy, and playwright Arthur Miller argued that Americans shared a collective guilt for Vietnam and that images of the War will continue to pose problems until political leaders and educators come to grips with this reality. President Reagan's claim that Vietnam had been a "noble cause" was ridiculed. Instead, Seymour Hersh angrily said that the war had been "racist," and in this he was joined by others.

In the fall of 1983 Americans intently watched a 13-part documentary, "Vietnam: A Television History," on Public Broadcasting Service stations. It was the most ambitious PBS project ever undertaken, requiring nearly $5 million and six years to complete. Critics hailed it as a stunning achievement and the best film chronology of a war ever assembled. Richard Ellison was executive producer, and longtime Vietnam War correspondent Stanley Karnow was chief correspondent. Earlier viewers had seen a Canadian-produced series, "Vietnam: The 10,000 Days War," also an excellent effort.

In April 1985, more than 150 U.S. journalists broadcast and wrote from Ho Chi Minh City (Saigon) on the tenth anniversary of the end of the fighting. Ironically, live satellite reports featuring interviews with Vietnamese officials were part of the painful reliving of those years. A new Vietnam scholarship was in evidence at major universities by the mid-1980s: comprehensive study of the causes and effects of the nation's unresolved experience that had left so much divisiveness. Included was the viewing of some of the 10,000 pieces of film shown on evening news shows between 1965 and 1975. When shown along with David Douglas Duncan's haunting black-and-white photographs, images of Vietnam intensified with a hold hard to shake.

With each passing year, film and dramatic television interpretations of the Vietnam War multiplied, spurring some new insights and resolutions.[18] Nevertheless, at the turn of the twenty-first century, the most persistent Vietnam myth held that news media all but lost the war for the United States by their unabashedly critical reporting of the government's conduct of the war. Richard Nixon passionately expressed this perspective in his memoirs:

> In each night's TV news and each morning's paper the war was reported battle by battle, but little or no sense of the underlying purpose of the fighting was conveyed. . . . More than ever before, television showed the terrible human suffering and sacrifice of war [and] the result was a serious demoralization of the home front, raising the question whether America would ever again be able to fight an enemy abroad with unity and strength of purpose at home.[19]

In the view of Nixon and many others, television is a "transparent window to reality." But as Clarence R. Wyatt pointed out in a 1993 monograph, "research over the past few years has indicated that such a belief is misplaced. Content analyses of newspaper and television coverage show that, more often than not, the press reported official information, statements, and views with relatively little dissent."[20] A classic study by Daniel C. Hallin, *The "Uncensored War": The Media and Vietnam* demonstrates this, at least for CBS and *New York Times* coverage of the war.[21]

Still, conventional wisdom maintains that during the Vietnam War, dovish U.S. journalists lionized antiwar protesters, speeding the war's end. Such was not the case, as Todd Gitlin shows in his landmark study, *The Whole World Is Watching: Mass Media in the Making & Unmaking of the New Left.*[22] And, recent scholarship by Melvin Small decisively debunks this myth. He found, for example, that mass media frequently communicated an expectation of violence associated with antiwar demonstrations. Also, the presence or absence of "bizarre or countercultural behavior" was often cause for comment in news accounts, whereas most journalists completely missed the political intricacies of the antiwar demonstrators' rationales.[23]

It is helpful here to consider Brigitte Lebens Nacos's argument that in "acute crisis" periods "when the chips are down, when the nation is faced with an emergency, the press—regardless of its previous editorial positions—tends to react like the political elite in that it either rallies behind the chief executive or mutes its criticism."[24]

Ironically, then, even though during war and other crisis periods national security needs may act to restrict journalists' freedom, they may voluntarily (and often inadvertently) give up some of that freedom in order to get on the side of national policy. Such seems to have been the case in the Vietnam War.

CHINA AND THE PACIFIC RIM

Much of the United States' attention was focused after 1950 on its wars in Korea and Vietnam, but there was also increasing realization of the importance of what became known as the "Pacific Rim." Japan and the Philippines had been particularly associated with American interests, and Tokyo and Manila served as news centers for United States media, along with Hong Kong and Singapore. But in the 1970s the People's Republic of China became the media story.

Mao Tse-tung's victory in 1949 over Chiang Kai-shek's Kuomintang and China's intervention in the Korean war put China behind a bamboo curtain for Americans. Mao and Chou En-lai broke with the Soviet Union in the 1960s, but the onset of the chaotic Cultural Revolution, lasting for a decade, delayed reconciliation. China's admission to the UN in 1971 was followed by President Nixon's week-long visit to China in 1972 and a gradual thaw. President Jimmy Carter's diplomatic recognition of China at the close of 1978 then opened the door to American news bureaus in Beijing and to exchanges of students and faculty.

When John Roderick of the AP and Robert Crabbe of the UPI arrived in Beijing in March 1979 they found about 50 foreign correspondents. Toronto's *Globe and Mail* had opened the third Western news office in 1959; Edgar Snow lived in Beijing during the 1960s. By August 1980 there were 10 United States correspondents, including Fox Butterfield of the *New York Times,* Linda Matthews of the *Los Angeles Times,* her husband Jay Matthews of the *Washington Post,* and Frank Ching of the *Wall Street Journal.* Aline Mosby of the UPI and Victoria Graham of the AP had taken over those offices. The *Baltimore Sun, Newsday, Chicago Tribune,* and Knight-Ridder were other early arrivals, along with the networks and news magazines. Meanwhile, Peng Li opened a Xinhua news agency bureau in Washington with Yu Enguang as White House correspondent. Yu became a resource person at one press conference.

In the 1970s the Hong Kong China-watchers were important media interpreters. Among them were Robert S. Elegant of the *Los Angeles Times,* Keyes Beech of the *Chicago Daily News,* Peter Kann of the *Wall Street Journal,* Joseph Lelyveld of the *New York Times,* and Robert Shaplen of the *New Yorker.* A careful count of correspondents for all United States media around the Pacific Rim in 1975 totaled 136, with 48 in Tokyo and 40 in Hong Kong. In 1986 American newspapers had 29 of their own correspondents in five cities: Tokyo, 13; Beijing, 8; Manila, 3; Hong Kong, 2; and Bangkok, 3.

There were 29 Americans among 115 foreign correspondents in Beijing in 1986. The All-China Journalists Association sponsored an informal press center and encouraged Chinese ministries to hold Western-style news conferences. Among effective correspondents were Daniel Southerland of the *Washington Post,* Julian Baum of the *Christian Science Monitor,* and James Mann of the *Los Angeles Times.* Fox Butterfield's book about China made his hosts unhappy; his successor for the *New York Times,* John F. Burns, was jailed and expelled for breaking travel regulations. Mark Hopkins was a resourceful Voice of America bureau chief whose broadcasts had impact in China.

This era of liberalized Chinese press policies ended in January 1987 with the ousting of Hu Yaobang as Communist party leader. Hu's death in April 1989 sparked widespread demonstrations against the right-wing government. Students occupied Tiananmen Square, seeking democratic reforms. They won the support of the majority of Chinese journalists and extensive press coverage. Troops brought to Beijing attacked the students and their worker supporters, clearing Tiananmen Square in a bloody June 3 night encounter.

Nicholas D. Kristof and Sheryl WuDunn, a *New York Times* husband-and-wife team, won a Pulitzer Prize for their months-long interpretation of the protest and their Tiananmen Square reporting. Television anchors and staffers, on hand for a visit by Premier Gorbachev, filled U.S. screens with the drama and horror of the protest climax. Dan Rather of CBS and Bernard Shaw of CNN won special recognition for live reporting in the midst of Beijing's political turmoil.

Premier Li Peng ousted moderate party leader Zhao Ziyang and hard-nosed conservatives took control of the government and Chinese media. John E. Pomfret of the AP and Mark Hopkins and Alan Pessin of the Voice of America were expelled for violating tight censorship. Still, in 1990 there were 170 foreign correspondents in Beijing, including 34 Americans.

This general pattern continued, with Tokyo clearly the headquarters for Western journalists. Despite China's enormous importance, the number of U.S. reporters stationed there dropped. The television networks pulled out their crews, citing budgetary problems. The press associations' skeleton forces in Beijing provided basic government news, while a handful of reporters for the top dailies occasionally traveled into the provinces for badly needed information about China's economic and social life.

Another dramatic story from the Pacific Rim was the 1986 revolution in the Philippines, led by Corazon Aquino, that overthrew dictator Ferdinand Marcos in a classic demonstration of "people power." American networks carried the dramatic story live, sending their anchors to Manila, and along with reporting by the news services and major newspapers, raised American interest to an enthusiastic high. A wave of public support for "Cory" overcame President Reagan's longtime preference for Marcos and brought about his last-moment recognition of Aquino's new government.

FORD ATTEMPTS TO RESTORE CREDIBILITY

President Gerald Ford served as both vice president and president without being elected to either office by the people. A friendly, down-to-earth man, Ford quickly earned the praise of a press corps tired of the daily battles with the Nixon administration. He had inherited the disengagement from Vietnam, a high inflation rate, and a higher degree of public cynicism about politicians. But Ford's honeymoon ended only a month after it began, at the moment he appeared on television on September 8, 1974, to announce that he was giving Richard Nixon a full presidential pardon for any offenses he may have committed, before all investigations had been completed. J. F. terHorst, Ford's press secretary, resigned in protest, and the president was subjected to criticism from all quarters. Former NBC newsman Ron Nessen was named press secretary and served with mixed success, frequently butting heads with a press corps whose skepticism had been quickly revived. It was during Ford's tenure that the nation's institutions, including the news media, would undergo a wholesale reappraisal of basic values. In this post-Watergate era, Ford was credited with bringing to the White House a humility it had lacked for some time.

Ford held 39 regular press conferences during his busy two and one-half years in office: 5 in the balance of 1974, 19 in 1975, and 15 more in 1976. A stubborn man, he spoke bluntly and plainly, maintaining his conservative credentials. The Nixon pardon hurt his credibility, as did his link to the Nixon years in general. His selection of Nelson A. Rockefeller as vice president was one move toward unity in his party and the nation, and Ford gave the country some reassurance in that respect.

The 1976 campaign began in August with President Ford 13 points behind in his bid for his own term. It ended with Georgia's former governor Jimmy Carter winning the presidency by 2 poll points and 297 electoral votes, a squeak-through majority. Carter was hurt by media overexposure and repeated charges that he was "fuzzy" on the main issues, despite his issuance of dozens of position papers by his staff. He was also attacked for granting a candid interview with *Playboy* magazine. Ford was belittled for a generally dull performance, and the "trivialization of the news" included accounts of his hitting his head on plane doors and slipping several times. Also hurtful was his association with Earl Butz, the secretary of agriculture, whose antiblack comment was reported by former Nixon aide John Dean in *Rolling Stone* and explained more fully by *New Times*. Media critics said events like this distracted from major foreign-policy and domestic issues that needed further amplification.[25]

Three nationally televised debates between Carter and Ford, and one between vice presidential candidates Walter Mondale and Robert Dole, gave millions of Americans the chance to judge the candidates for themselves. Sponsored by the League of Women Voters, the debates (called news conferences by critics who wanted point-by-point challenges by the men) allowed Carter the opportunity to demonstrate his knowledge of foreign-policy issues and his capacity to handle himself under pressure against the more experienced Ford. After a shaky start in the first debate, Carter came on strong in the final two and headed into election day with a slight advantage in poll points, which he held.

"THE BOYS ON THE BUS": PRESIDENTIAL CAMPAIGNS

The long, grueling presidential contests of the 1970s were marred by the lavish spending of advertising monies designed to package the candidates for television and the preoccupation of many press-corps members with the contender's personal styles rather than the substance of ideas. At times the storytellers became the story, as hordes of tired journalists chased the equally exhausted politicians from dawn to midnight, through state after state. If anything, the situation was worse by the mid-1990s.

The tendency of the journalists to report basically the same things gave rise to the terms "pack" and "herd" journalism, while the soft content of much of the reporting led to comments about "news trivia" and "junk news." Coverage devoted to the latest public-opinion poll was called "horse-race" reporting. Feeding the American public a steady diet of news were the well-known national political reporters and columnists who joined the circuit for the pivotal moments; the regular reporters for prestige newspapers and magazines and a few smaller papers; the network television and radio correspondents; and the handful of press-association reporters.

It was clear that the whistle-stop technique was still a basic part of political campaigning even if candidate appearances were arranged to entice coverage by the ever-present network television cameras. Although research indicated that most voters cast their ballots along traditional lines and did not make up or change their minds during actual campaigns, the number of close elections (1948, 1960, 1968, 1976) showed media influences to be crucially important.

The newspaper reporter with the most personal influence on the coverage by the traveling press corps in the 1970s was R. W. ("Johnny") Apple, Jr., of the *New York Times,* who had been with the paper since 1963. Because the *Times* was the only paper regularly available on many stops, Apple's stories provided continuity for the group. An industrious, aggressive man, Apple worked around the clock to provide the *Times* with updated information and fresh insights. Key press association correspondents were Walter Mears of the AP and Arnold Sawislak of the UPI. Some of the most astute commentaries were by the *New Yorker*'s Elizabeth Drew, who turned her diaries into a book.

"The boys on the bus," as they were called by Timothy Crouse in his classic description of the 1972 campaign,[26] received a great amount of criticism as did their successors. They were accused of following the lead of a Johnny Apple or a Walter Mears and of not developing their own story angles, partly because of laziness and partly because their editors also followed what the *New York Times,* AP, or UPI said. Some writers were said to be partial to a particular candidate; some were said to be rude, arrogant, and too ambitious; others were said to be easily manipulated by candidates or their campaign aides. Suggestions were made for more pool reporting and less emphasis on routine speeches.

As the years passed veteran print reporters spent much less time on the campaign trail and television reporters began to switch off, instead of sticking with one candidate.

The preoccupation with television meant that syndicated columnists and political writers had to resort to specially arranged interviews. At times these "exclusives" given to selected writers served the same purpose as full news conferences. They also were part of the candidate's control of the news flow.

White House speechwriter Peggy Noonan, who created some of the famous Reagan "soundbites," and critic Mark Hertsgaard wrote popular books describing media manipulation.[27] Particularly distressing was the admission of a number of top journalists that collectively the press corps had stopped asking candidate George Bush tough Iran-Contra questions in 1988 because of their perception that people were tired of the issue. The traveling journalists became victims of their own technology, political pollsters, and the timidity of their editors and producers. In 1992 candidate Bill Clinton knew that one quick quip on CNN in Omaha or an appearance on MTV was worth a dozen well-prepared talks to farm organizations. Women reporters, numbering about 20 percent, brought added sensitivity to the coverage of domestic issues such as homelessness, abortion, education, and health care.

The 1996 campaign season was, according to many commentators and political pundits, lackluster and dull. President Bill Clinton enjoyed widespread popularity, and many believed that Republican contender Robert Dole would not be a serious threat. A 1997 study by the Freedom Forum revealed that press coverage of the 1996 campaign had diminished: there were fewer front-page stories about the candidates or campaigns, and network TV newscasts reduced their coverage by 43 percent. Also troubling was the indifferent voting public—the percentage of eligible voters who turned out for the 1996 election was less than 50 percent of the total electorate, and lower than in any presidential election in more than 70 years.[28] Of course, it is not up to the media to make or break a candidate. However, the 1996 election raised more interesting questions about the media's role in shaping a candidate's possibilities of being elected.

THE CARTER YEARS: THE IRANIAN CRISIS

Jimmy Carter's close victory in 1976 brought a new style to the White House. Publicly dedicating himself to total honesty with the public, the religious-minded Carter lost no time in trying to continue where Ford left off in encouraging faith in the nation's cherished institutions. He began holding regular news conferences every two weeks trying to avoid the frequent charges of the campaign days that he was less than precise in his answers. As a further step in communicating with the public, in March of 1977 he conducted a two-hour "phone-in" from the Oval Office. Persons lucky enough to have their calls get through the jammed circuits found themselves talking first to Walter Cronkite and then to the president.

Carter's years in office were marked by his patient attempts to convince the American people to believe in themselves and in his programs. With longtime aide Jody Powell serving as press secretary, Carter made an attempt to be open to the press. He held up well despite the growing inquisitorial nature of the televised news conferences. His major accomplishments came in foreign affairs. In 1978 he successfully negotiated the gradual return of the Panama Canal to Panama, earning the respect of the peoples of Central and Latin America. Full diplomatic relations were opened with the People's Republic of China that year. And it was Carter's persistence that allowed President Anwar Sadat of Egypt and Prime Minister Menachem Begin of Israel to finally agree on peace terms during talks at Camp David in 1979. But the president's first national address on the energy crisis failed when his emotional claim that his program was "the moral equivalent of war" fell on deaf ears. Carter's image also sagged whenever the antics of his troublesome brother Billy became news. Later Billy Carter's financial dealings were categorized by the news media as "Billygate."

Public confidence in Carter dropped further in November 1979, when the American Embassy in Tehran was seized by supporters of the Ayatollah Khomeini and its American occupants were held captive. The humiliating event found the United States powerless to act. The president had bungled his way into the disaster, failing either to defend the Embassy or remove its occupants after pondering the likelihood of a takeover. In April 1980, an attempt at a dramatic helicopter rescue ended in disaster in the Iranian desert, when the mechanical failure of three of the eight helicopters forced Carter to abort the mission. Eight Americans died when two helicopters collided in the confusion of fleeing the area. Carter was also severely criticized for not attempting to support the Shah of Iran prior to Khomeini's seizure of power. That criticism came from Nixon, Kissinger, and others who had formed close friendships with the Shah and tolerated his secret police tactics at a time when the United States had few friends in that part of the world and supposed the Shah was a military bulwark. At this early point few journalists realized the historical significance of the fundamentalists' revolution that Khomeini represented.

Edward Kennedy challenged Carter for the Democratic nomination in 1980, causing great anger in the White House. During this time of enormous pressure, with Carter monitoring the Iranian situation daily, he was obliged to combat the Kennedy threat. Exhibiting a toughness that some characterized as "mean," Carter triumphed over Kennedy, who could not shed the image of Chappaquiddick.

Facing Ronald Reagan in the fall campaign, Carter attempted to portray him as a dangerous man who would lead the nation to the brink of war and divide it along religious and racial lines. But the strategy backfired, as Reagan came across on television as pleasant and open. Finally, on October 28, Reagan and Carter met in a debate from which independent candidate John Anderson had been excluded. While Carter tried to draw a clear distinction between himself and the former California governor on such issues as nuclear proliferation and social security, Reagan was able to reduce the entire campaign to a final series of questions: "Are you better off than you were four years ago? . . . Is America as respected throughout the world as it was? Do you feel that our security is safe, and that we're as strong as we were four years ago?" (It was later revealed that the Reagan camp had had access to Carter's briefing papers and to top secret documents prior to the debate.)

The voters, asked in television advertisements to choose on this basis, decided that Ronald Reagan would be the next president. In a final dramatic action, the Iranians punished Carter by not releasing the 52 hostages until the moment that Reagan was being sworn into office on January 20, 1981. Carter had urged patience despite nightly television scenes of anti-American hatred, and he had suffered through 444 days of waiting. For weeks there had been rumors of an imminent release of the hostages. Only 33 minutes after Reagan took the oath of office, the flight to freedom began, with excited reporters breaking into the inauguration coverage to give the latest details. The next morning many of the nation's newspapers carried huge two-line headlines and two photos, balancing the competing stories. The *New York Times* summed it up: "Reagan Takes Oath as 40th President; Promises an 'Era of National Renewal'; Minutes Later, 52 Hostages in Iran Fly to Freedom after 444-Day Ordeal."[29]

Carter enjoyed a revival of press interest as elder statesman in 1994. He made national headlines when he brokered a peace agreement between the war-torn factions in Bosnia. Earlier that year, he had done the same in North Korea and in Haiti through patience and creative diplomatic tactics.

REAGAN AND THE MEDIA: THE STRUGGLE FOR ACCESS

Ronald Reagan was granted a long and fairly happy honeymoon by the Washington press corps. The president's easy manner and ready smile made him a likable figure, and the excitement of a change in administrations was a welcome relief from the tenseness of the final Carter years. The honeymoon was extended by the attempt on Reagan's life on March 30, 1981, when the president was shot outside of a Washington hotel. His recovery period, marked by his concern for the seriously injured press secretary James Brady, was relatively free of criticism. White House regulars even agreed to raise their hands instead of jumping up to ask questions at news conferences. But by October, after eight months in office, it had become apparent that Reagan was the most inaccessible of the modern presidents, with the exception of Nixon during the Watergate period. At that point he had held only 3 news conferences, while Carter had held 14 and Ford 12. Reagan was to average about 3 per year.

One reason for Reagan's unfavorable news-conference record was his knowledge that he often fared poorly at them. Unlike Carter, who showed up with facts and figures, Reagan tried to handle questions that he seemed unprepared to answer. On several occasions he made historical errors. He once said, for example, that President Kennedy had sent combat troops to Vietnam, when he meant President Johnson. Reagan's aides tried to protect him from meeting with reporters at airports or prior to public appearances because his off-the-cuff comments often made embarrassing headlines. In turn, Reagan complained about the coverage of his administration, particularly by television. He once asked, "Is it news that some fellow out in South Succotash has just been laid off . . . ?" The comment was in reference to frequent television interviews with unemployed workers and charts showing rising unemployment figures. The *Los Angeles Times* replied: "The answer is, it is news. It is news in Los Angeles, Detroit, New York and, yes, South Succotash. Unemployment is news." The editorial was headlined, "Let Them Eat Succotash," and an adjoining cartoon by Paul Conrad, captioned "Reagan Country," showed a sign reading, "Welcome to South Succotash, Population: 9,000,000 Unemployed."[30]

Such editorial barbs increased from 1981 on as Reagan seemed to lose control of events. The recession worsened, before leveling off into a period of uncertainty. Numerous leaks from within the Reagan administration—many of them from the White House itself—brought consternation.

The president's disregard for the press and the public's right to learn about its government was shown in a number of directives that raised serious questions about Reagan's basic attitudes. One new order protecting classified materials said that government employees suspected of leaking classified materials could be required to take lie-detector tests. Those refusing could be demoted or fired. The order also gave federal agencies the power to review and approve articles, books, and speeches by employees or former employees. Thousands of federal employees were required to sign such secrecy agreements.

Earlier Reagan had launched attacks against the Freedom of Information Act (FOIA), increasing the authority of federal agencies to exclude materials from the FOIA's provisions and encouraging agencies to charge fees for information sought. In its 1982 Freedom of Information report card, the Society of Professional Journalists, Sigma Delta Chi, gave the president an "F." The nation's largest journalistic society noted that the Reagan administration gained passage of a bill providing harsh penalties for anyone reporting the name of a past or present CIA agent, regardless of whether the information was already in the public domain or had little value.

    As the number of Reagan's formal meetings with the White House correspondents dropped, they met instead with Larry Speakes, the deputy press secretary (Brady kept his title but was not able to work because of his severe head injuries), who tried to explain the president's reactions to events. This was a thankless job, with ABC's Sam Donaldson, UPI's Helen Thomas, and others complaining about the lack of presidential exposure. It was noted, however, that the press did a poor job of explaining the president's remoteness to the public.[31]

    Reagan won the presidency by pledging to end the New Deal legacy of his former hero, Franklin D. Roosevelt, and to replace it with his brand of economic theology. However, as historian Henry Steele Commager noted, Reagan's ideas were rooted in Herbert Spencer's nineteenth-century concepts of Social Darwinism: "the application of the theory

President and Mrs. Reagan

(UPI Photo)

of the survival of the fittest to society and the economy. In the realm of economics, this principle requires that government keep 'hands off' and give free rein to the competitive instinct nourished by individualism."[32] The result was a strong public feeling that Reagan favored the rich at the expense of the poor, despite his stated concerns for the less fortunate.

Reagan struggled not to deeply offend the right-wing of the Republican party, led by North Carolina Senator Jesse Helms. He made pleas for decency in movies, prayer in public schools, an end to most abortions, and vigorous opposition to guerrilla activity in Central America that threatened American financial interests. But his rigidity—particularly in the area of arms control—alienated many moderate Republicans. Reagan officials said that they believed that the Soviet Union was developing a "first-strike capability," that it was building its defenses so Russia could attack the United States without fear of being completely destroyed in the inevitable counterattack. Reagan strategists indicated that they believed that the United States could survive such an attack and that there could be a "winner" in a nuclear exchange. Thus, the United States could begin planning for a "first-strike capability," something foreign to the thinking of past defense planners, who had advocated "détente" instead of nuclear brinkmanship. *Los Angeles Times* reporter Robert Scheer produced notes and tapes from numerous interviews with Reagan, Vice President George Bush, and others proving that the nation's top leaders were thinking "the unthinkable."[33]

For the first six years of his presidency Reagan enjoyed an amazingly high popularity rating. Despite a number of controversial decisions that caused anger and controversy, the president's affability allowed him to escape personal responsibility for such disasters as the slaughter of U.S. Marines in Beirut, more than a dozen scandals involving administration officials, the building of a trillion-dollar budget, a massive foreign trade imbalance, a cemetery tribute in Germany to Nazi soldiers, and support for South Africa. His confusion following the historic October 1986 meeting with Mikhail Gorbachev in Iceland brought dismay but also some sympathy. But as the question of the president's effectiveness and credibility became an open concern, it was apparent that Reagan, his closest advisers, and influential campaign supporters had a "persistent distaste for the raucous, untidy, rambunctious aspects of democracy,"[34] including the American news media that reported disturbing and unwelcome news.

The public seemed to accept the fact that this president had a loose grasp on public affairs and sometimes gave erroneous accounts of events, but had a keen sense of how to use his office to produce the dramatic moment, especially on nationwide television.[35] A sad footnote was the revelation, several years after Reagan left office, that he suffered from Alzheimer's disease. This led to speculation about whether the condition, while still undiagnosed, might have affected his cognitive abilities as president.

Reagan had built his reputation early in his presidency by tough talk when firing striking air controllers, when insisting on no income tax increases, and especially when addressing the leaders of the "Evil Empire," as he called the Soviet Union. This nononsense approach had appeal. When Korean Air's flight 007 was shot down by a Soviet fighter plane, resulting in the death of 269 persons, the president's angry aggressive style was hard to fault. He often identified himself with the world's "freedom fighters," once saying the Nicaraguan Contras were the "moral equivalent of our Founding Fathers." Later he said, "I am a Contra." Reagan gave every appearance of enjoying his reputation of being the "Rambo" of the world. "They can run but they can't hide," he said after the bombing of Libya, an action that was applauded by many Americans.

The president had other problems. Twice his nominations for a vacant Supreme Court seat failed, trade deficits reached record levels, and the Persian Gulf crisis intensified after the U.S.S. *Stark* was hit by a bomb and 37 sailors died. But such problems paled in the wake of the panic-driven, 500-point "Black Monday" stock market crash of October 19, 1987. Investor losses were nearly double those of the historic Black Monday in 1929. I. F. Stone, writing in the *Nation,* said: "The whole country is in hock. One of the delusions of supply-side economics was that massive tax cuts would lead to a sharp rise in the volume of savings." But the savings rate as a percentage of disposable income after taxes had dropped from 7.1 percent in 1980 to less than 3 percent in 1987. Private debt had doubled in the spending spree, and the public debt had more than doubled. There was widespread agreement that the economic policies called "Reaganomics" were bankrupt. Nearly so was the president's credibility. But he still grinned and waved his arm as he left with the First Lady for Camp David.

THE IRAN-CONTRA SCANDAL

This high credibility was badly damaged in late 1986, however, when the roof fell in on the Reagan administration. On October 5 a C-123 cargo plane carrying arms to Contra forces was shot down by a Sandinista soldier. Two American pilots were killed, but Eugene Hasenfus, a mercenary from Wisconsin, was captured. Documents found in the plane and Hasenfus's testimony at his trial in Managua produced headlines worldwide telling of the secret supply network that had been set up to circumvent Congress during the period when supplying military aid to the Contras was against U.S. law. Major news organizations, led by the *Los Angeles Times, Washington Post, New York Times,* and *Miami Herald,* produced a number of authoritative investigative stories documenting the administration's illegal plans.[36] The White House denied connection to the plane.

On October 31, 1986, the Beirut magazine *Al Shiraa* published a story telling how the Reagan administration had been secretly selling arms to Iran in exchange for hostages, in direct contradiction of an American policy that the administration had been promoting to its allies. U.S. reporters in the Middle East picked up the story a few days later, and by early November the country was in an uproar, with politicians, the public, and news organizations demanding a full-scale investigation. The White House maintained that the shipments were made to begin a dialogue with elements within Iran who might eventually assume leadership after the death of the Ayatollah Khomeini. Nevertheless, the spectacle of the United States selling arms to Iran caused outrage across the United States and made a shambles of its foreign policy apparatus. The anger intensified when it was revealed that the Israelis had been involved in the arms transfers and had been selling arms to Iran for several years.

Months later it became known that Reagan presided over a November 10 White House conference, telling the others "don't talk specifics" about the Iranian arms shipments and to continue saying "no bargaining with terrorists." Notes taken by a participant gave details of what the *Washington Post* called a cover-up. Reagan contended he had still hoped to free more hostages than the three his arms shipments netted (soon four new American hostages replaced them). Another White House group, including the Attorney General Edwin Meese, coached CIA director William J. Casey on how to give cover-up testimony to the House intelligence committee. Casey, who died of brain cancer in early 1987, misled the committee about the Israeli connection, which Reagan had doggedly denied.

Reagan and his spokespeople attempted to repair the damage in a number of statements, but to no avail. The episode led to many cynical late night television jokes about "Iranamuck," "Gippergate," and after more details emerged, "Contragate." Polls showed the vast number of Americans felt the president was not telling the truth. On November 19

Reagan defended his decision at a nationally televised news conference, where he was subjected to what was undoubtedly the most pitiless cross-examination ever of a president by the White House press. Led by the UPI's Helen Thomas and ABC's Sam Donaldson, the reporters accused him of duplicity, challenged his credibility, and shattered his composure. Correspondents for the conservative *Wall Street Journal* and Hearst newspapers were as bitterly critical.

Thomas bluntly asked Reagan to "assess the credibility of your own administration in light of the prolonged deception of Congress and the public in terms of your secret dealings with Iran, the disinformation [about Libya], the trading of Sacharoff for Daniloff."[37] Reagan denied there had been any loss, but Donaldson, after asking how Reagan could "justify this duplicity," persisted:

> Sir, if I may, the polls show that a lot of Americans just simply don't believe you. That the one thing that you've had going for you more than anything else—your credibility—has been severely damaged. Can you repair it? What does this mean for the rest of your presidency?[38]

The president's quiet response, "Well, I imagine I'm the only one around here who wants to repair it and I didn't have anything to do with damaging it."

Six days later Attorney General Meese held a news conference to announce that profits from the arms sales had been diverted to the Contras. This astounding news brought the resignation of Admiral John Poindexter, the president's national security adviser, and the firing of Lieutenant Colonel Oliver L. North, the go-for-broke Marine who had played a key role in the private supply network. Cartoonists and columnists had a field day describing the analogies between the breaking news stories and those of Watergate from 1971 to 1974.

Then in December leading journalists began to fret that the media were being too aggressive. Alleged Watergate "excesses" were condemned by some editors and broadcasters. Instead of being too aggressive, however, some reporters had neglected to investigate North's activities for at least three years because they enjoyed his availability as an off-the-record source. Both the House and Senate appointed select investigative committees, and a special prosecutor was given broad powers to look into the entire scandal. The 100th Congress began its sessions in early 1987.

Media language, even from ordinarily restrained sources, was blunt. The *New York Times* editorialized:

> The whole affair, from Israeli arms shipments through Swiss bank accounts to subsidizing the contras, smacks of a pattern of lawlessness. . . . The most chilling disclosure at the White House yesterday was not any single fact but the evidence of collapse of judgment and values. . . . Poor policies and reckless aides can be replaced. Trust cannot, and now the powder trail runs right to the Oval Office.[39]

Lewis Lapham, speaking from his "easy chair" at *Harper's,* described Reagan as "an aging matinee idol, as well informed about history and geography as any matinee idol"; CIA director William Casey as "a venal autocrat"; and chief of staff Donald Regan as "a bully, noted for his arrogance and stupidity." Lapham added: "Ever since its arrival in Washington in the winter of 1981, the Reagan Administration has made no secret of its contempt for anything as chicken-hearted and un-American as the due process of law."[40]

Senate and House select investigative committees began joint hearings on May 25 and North's appearance was the climax. He was the man who could say that the president had known (but he didn't say). His week of testimony became a major television event. In

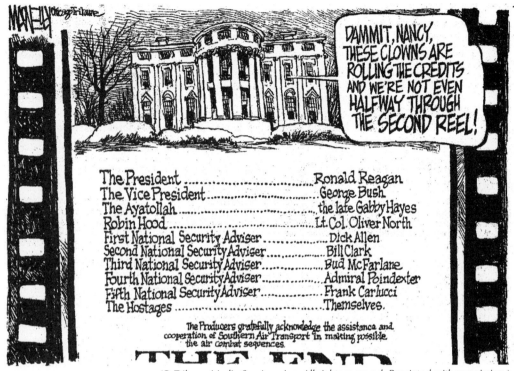

DAMMIT, NANCY, THESE CLOWNS ARE ROLLING THE CREDITS AND WE'RE NOT EVEN HALFWAY THROUGH THE SECOND REEL!

The President .... Ronald Reagan
The Vice President .... George Bush
The Ayatollah .... the late Gabby Hayes
Robin Hood .... Lt. Col. Oliver North
First National Security Adviser .... Dick Allen
Second National Security Adviser .... Bill Clark
Third National Security Adviser .... Bud McFarlane
Fourth National Security Adviser .... Admiral Poindexter
Fifth National Security Adviser .... Frank Carlucci
The Hostages .... Themselves.

The Producers gratefully acknowledge the assistance and cooperation of Southern Air Transport in making possible the air combat sequences.

THE END

The last joke about old movies was on the "Great Communicator" himself.

full uniform with rows of medals, he looked every inch a patriot. *New York Times* correspondent R. W. Apple, Jr., said, "There was a lot of Gary Cooper in him, the lonesome cowboy, a lot of Jimmy Stewart too, the honest man facing down the politicians, and quite a bit of Huck Finn."

After two days of grilling by the committee counsels, North found more receptive questioners and quickly dominated the televised proceedings. He said an Iranian munitions dealer had suggested the idea of diverting arms sales profits to the Contras, and he grinned, "A neat idea, turning the Ayatollah's money over to the Contras." He boasted about shredding stacks of documents that would have been evidence. He winked, and called himself "Ollie."

When it was over, a majority of Americans still said President Reagan was lying about his knowledge of the Contra arms diversion (53 percent). The response was 47 to 33 percent that former National Security Adviser John Poindexter was lying about not telling Reagan. But 70 percent said North was testifying truthfully (although 61 percent said he was not a national hero). The final committee report said the document shredding and Casey's death left the record about Reagan's role in the Contra diversion incomplete. But, it said, "If the President did not know what his national security advisers were doing, he should have." And, the committee declared, it was Reagan's own policy to sell arms secretly to Iran and to support the Contras; the others had followed his lead. It castigated his false statements.

The most tantalizing rumor, persisting into the Bush years, was that on October 18–19, 1980, a deal had been finalized in Paris whereby the American hostages would not be released prior to the November election. The goal was to prevent Carter from obtaining their release and winning re-election. If true, the participants would have been guilty of treason. This story appeared in several alternative publications and in the European press, but was not taken seriously by mainstream U.S. media.

While print journalists, mainly those working for alternative publications, continued to probe the Reagan-Bush ties to Iran-Contra, it was Bill Moyers who gave the widest exposure to misdeeds with his November 1990 PBS show *High Crimes and Misdemeanors*. It was Moyers's judgment that both Reagan and Bush lied about their involvement.[41]

INTERVENTIONS IN CENTRAL AMERICA AND THE CARIBBEAN

North American interventions in the Central American and Caribbean areas in support of U.S. corporate investments and trade profits, often under the guise of fighting international communism, have occurred steadily throughout the twentieth century. In the post-World War II period the Eisenhower administration sent CIA personnel to Guatemala in 1954 to overthrow a democratically elected liberal president. President Kennedy's ill-fated Bay of Pigs invasion of Cuba in 1961 failed to upset Fidel Castro and produced a backlash throughout the Latin world. A massive subversive effort involving sabotage raids and disinformation continued for years. President Johnson sent troops to the Dominican Republic in 1965 to bolster a right-wing dictatorship.

President Nixon, one of the architects of such interventionist policies in the 1950s, involved the CIA in the overthrow of the democratically elected leftist government of Chile in 1973 and continued the support of dictatorships in Nicaragua, El Salvador, and Honduras, all to be in the headlines in the 1980s; in one of the brighter moments, President Carter negotiated Senate approval of a treaty restoring sovereignty over the Panama Canal to Panama, winning widespread approval in later years.

President Reagan ordered the invasion of the tiny Caribbean island of Grenada in 1983—claiming Cubans were setting up an air base that could tip the balance of power in the region—and allowed military commanders to deny access to U.S. reporters trying to cover the initial operations, the first such censorship in the nation's history. Partisans claimed that the "victory" of thousands of North Americans over a handful of Cuban and Grenadian soldiers and several hundred Cuban construction workers showed the United States had recovered from its Vietnam defeat. However, after the televised homecomings had their political effect, the Pentagon's after-action reports showed that the entire operation had been poorly coordinated.[42] News of this led to demands for wholesale changes in U.S. planning and cast doubt upon the administration's glowing reports of success.

Following the pattern of international reporting in general, the bulk of the news media coverage of these interventions failed to provide the reader or viewer with the background information and interpretation necessary for making judgments about the particular situation. In the absence of solid information, including the historical antecedents, the news consumer became the victim of dubious government statements.[43] However, there was considerable improvement in the middle 1980s, when the revolutions in Nicaragua and El Salvador became worldwide news because of U.S. determination to control the destiny of the region.

The North American effort to dominate the life of Nicaraguans was a classic example of economic imperialism. Nicaraguan schoolchildren of the 1980s knew of William Walker, the Nashville adventurer who had competed with Cornelius Vanderbilt for control of their nation in the 1850s. While Vanderbilt was gaining concessions to build a canal across Nicaragua to form an interoceanic passenger route, Walter proclaimed himself president of Nicaragua in 1855. He finally was executed by the British in 1860, after leaving a legacy for other North Americans. An oligarchy tied to U.S. investors ruled for years, with the help of U.S. armed forces who occupied Nicaragua from 1912 to 1933.

Nationalists under the command of the legendary Augusto Cesar Sandino began a guerrilla war in 1926 and outlasted their foes, who resorted to using air power against the Nicaraguans in July 1927, the first time in history it was aimed at a civilian population. The Nicaraguans said 300 persons died in the raids near Ocotal.[44] By 1930 the North Americans had repeated many of the brutal tactics that had been employed in the Philippines at the turn of the century. A few reporters, like the Mexican-based U.S. journalist Carleton Beals, attempted to report favorably about Sandino's cause. His nine-part series was published in the *Nation* in 1928 but such anti-imperialistic articles were rare, as the U.S. press followed the traditional line that highlighted official government statements and denigrated the Nicaraguans.[45] Unable to enforce their will upon the determined Nicaraguans, the U.S. Marines finally withdrew. But the United States left the National Guard in command of Anastasio Somoza, who ordered the assassination—and unwittingly the martyrdom—of Sandino on February 21, 1934.

The Somoza family controlled the country until the heirs of Sandino, who formed the Sandinista National Liberation Front (FSLN) in 1961, toppled the U.S.-backed National Guard on July 19, 1979. More than 50,000 Nicaraguans died in the final years of the revolution against the last Somoza, who ordered Nicaraguan cities bombed in the final days. The deliberate murder of ABC correspondent Bill Stewart by Somoza's soldiers furnished an on-camera killing for U.S. television audiences, who generally had been unaware of the long Sandinista struggle. At the end a broad-based civilian coalition took part, led by the fighting arm, the Sandinistas, and a flock of print and broadcast reporters were in Managua for the victory processions.

As U.S. reporters made their way to Nicaragua and neighboring El Salvador, where a similar revolution had turned into a civil war in 1979, the stage was being set for a propaganda battle that would last into the 1990s. While initial news reports from the field generally showed the Sandinistas and their supporters in a favorable light, partially because of the ugly excesses of Somoza and his thugs, the news from Washington had a different tone. The Sandinista leaders, with their Marxist orientation toward the distribution of economic power, offered a model that frightened U.S. leaders, particularly because guerrillas in El Salvador were inspired by the downfall of Somoza. If allowed to stand, the Nicaraguan revolution would be the first leftist movement in Central America to succeed.

While the Carter administration took cautious steps to deal with the new Nicaraguan government, the CIA began negotiating with members of Somoza's National Guard in the first stages of what became an all-out U.S. effort to resume control over Nicaragua. Ronald Reagan's 1980 presidential campaign included bitter attacks against Nicaraguan leaders and claims that Democrats had allowed the creation of a "second Cuba." Upon taking power in 1981 Reagan devoted enormous energy to funding an anti-Sandinista force led primarily by former Nicaraguan National Guard officers, known in later headlines as the "Contras."

As it became clear the Sandinista leadership was in firm control, with strong Cuban and Soviet support, the Reagan administration took more drastic measures. In effect war was declared, without informing the public or asking for congressional approval. Claiming that its goal was not a military overthrow but rather the application of political pressure on the Sandinistas, the Reagan administration gained congressional funds beginning in 1981 to assist the Contras.

But in September 1983 and February 1984 the CIA organized the bombing of the Managua airport, the destruction of fuel tanks and pipelines in Nicaragua's ports, and the mining of those harbors.[46] News media disclosures of these illegal actions forced Congress to cut off military aid to the Contras in October 1984. The White House retaliated immediately by allowing the National Security Council and the CIA to work with nongovernment intermediaries for the continuation of the Contra supply network, which involved airfields in Honduras, El Salvador, and Costa Rica. In addition, the U.S. government imposed an economic embargo on trade with Nicaragua, a stranglehold that had devastating effects on the Nicaraguan economy.

The United States made a determined effort to build a southern front along the Costa Rican border against the Sandinistas.[47] Former Sandinista hero Eden Pastora, then head of a Contra guerrilla unit operating out of Costa Rica, refused to merge with the CIA-backed main force in Honduras, however, causing a problem for Washington. A May 30, 1984, assassination attempt against Pastora killed three journalists, including U.S. citizen Linda Frazier, and five Contra guerrillas at a press conference Pastora had called to criticize the CIA. That bomb blast seriously injured U.S. journalist Tony Avirgan. He and his wife, Martha Honey, began a two-year investigation of the bombing, and despite great personal risk, discovered evidence of other illegal activities. In late 1986 they filed a civil suit in a Miami district court against 29 people, including Contras, Cuban-Americans, and former U.S. military and CIA officers who allegedly took part in this assassination attempt and other murder plots, gun-running, drug-smuggling, and other racketeering activities. A public service legal group, the Christic Institute, joined in the suit. One alleged goal of these dealings was to cause an incident—such as the killing of Pastora and journalists—that would justify future U.S. actions against Nicaragua. The case ultimately was rejected in the courts, but the arguments continued.[48]

In June 1986 the International Court of Justice at The Hague (known as the World Court) responded to a suit by Nicaragua and found the United States in gross violation of international law because of its unqualified support of the Contras and their murderous activities.[49] That same month Congress, ignoring the World Court, international opinion, and editorials in leading U.S. newspapers, voted to give the Contras $100 million in military aid. Reagan's lobbying of moderate House members afraid of accusations of being "soft on communism" carried the day.

Steeped in this traditional fear of communism and believing official statements that the Sandinistas were a threat to the United States and their neighbors, the public acquiesced with the understanding that American troops would not be sent into combat. Ignored were statements from Latin leaders critical of the Contra aid program, who instead favored continuation of the Contadora peace talks, which had been stymied by a U.S.-Nicaraguan dispute over the future role of the Contras in Nicaraguan politics.[50] The stalemate at the peace table allowed the U.S. to accelerate the fighting in 1987, as thousands of Contras infiltrated into Nicaragua to disrupt the coffee harvest, destroy schools and health facilities, and mine roads. But a change came in late 1987, when President Oscar Arias Sánchez of Costa Rica won Central American support for a peace plan that won him the Nobel Peace Prize.

Three years later the U.S.-backed candidate for president, Violeta Chamorro, defeated Daniel Ortega in a shocking upset. War-weary Nicaraguans, harassed by the embargo and looking for relief, found solace in Chamorro's pleas for national unity. She was the widow of Pedro Joaquin Chamorro, the famed newspaper publisher murdered by Somoza's thugs in 1978, an incident that had helped spark the Sandinista revolution. The Sandinistas remained the strongest political force, in Ortega's words "governing from below," while former Contras, defeated in the field, turned in their arms and returned home to join the political battles of the future. There were fears that the grandmotherly Chamorro would not be able to control events as inflation soared and partisan feelings intensified. Ironically, U.S. news reports of the Sandinista defeat generally concentrated on their poor economic performance while barely mentioning the effects of the U.S.-sponsored war and trade embargo on the population.

Stephen Kinzer of the *New York Times* was the most prominent of the U.S. journalists covering the Nicaraguan revolution and the Contra war. A history major at Boston University, Kinzer was only 25 when he showed up in Managua as a freelance journalist in 1976. After authoring a 1977 piece on Nicaragua for the *New Republic* he was hired by the *Boston Globe,* for whom he covered the Sandinista triumph. On January 1, 1983, he opened the Managua Bureau of the *New York Times* as its bureau chief, and until late 1986 remained the only full-time U.S. newspaper journalist permanently stationed in Managua.

Teaming with Kinzer to give the *Times* extensive coverage throughout Central America was James LeMoyne, who in addition to producing major stories from Nicaragua also spent considerable time in El Salvador and Honduras. Kinzer's byline also appeared frequently from Honduras. A prolific writer, he also was known for his book *Bitter Fruit,* the story of the 1954 U.S. coup in Guatemala. As the Contra war progressed Kinzer was roundly criticized by some of his colleagues and U.S. peace activists for not offering more interpretation in his stories to show the brutality of the U.S.-sponsored war and the better points about the revolution: health care, increased literacy, effective land reform, few human rights abuses. Instead, his critics contended, he, and his editors, concentrated too much on the faults of the Sandinista government that had closed the opposition newspaper *La Prensa* and exiled several priests who clashed with authorities. His supporters, however, pointed at the great variety of political and military stories produced with what they called an even-handedness. Like his *New York Times* predecessors in Vietnam and other flash points, he was on the spot and was resigned to that reality.[51] A number of other U.S. journalists in Nicaragua and El Salvador were criticized for either following the line of the American Embassy or for showing too much sympathy for the other side. LeMoyne was one who fell under unusually harsh criticism from progressives for some of his El Salvador work, despite his stories about the guerrillas that brought fire from conservatives.

Marjorie Miller of the *Los Angeles Times,* based in El Salvador, earned a solid reputation for her reporting. William Long of the *Times* traveled many Central American roads, to be followed later by Richard Boudreaux, who established the paper's first permanent Managua bureau in late 1986. The *Miami Herald,* famed for its Latin American coverage, had Sam Dillon, Don Bohning, and Tim Golden roaming the region. Edward Cody and Julia Preston shared major stories for the *Washington Post.* The text and photos produced by *Newsweek*'s Rod Nordland and Bill Gentile offered some of the war's best "inside" looks at both the Contras and the Sandinistas.[52]

An active group of freelancers, many from Europe, Canada, and Australia, were important in the coverage of Central America, providing reports from Managua, San Salvador, Tegucigalpa, and San Jose. While some worked for major newspapers, the bulk filed radio reports overseas or to the United States. The National Public Radio (NPR) system was praised for its interpretative and timely military and political stories. NPR and Pacifica radio reporters often were ahead with details on Contra-related activities. The U.S. television networks maintained stringer camera crews in the various capitals but flew in on-air reporters from the United States for the major reports.

The administration's focus on Nicaragua and the heightened tension there distracted from the coverage of El Salvador, which in the early 1980s had been the region's number one hot spot. More than 450 U.S. journalists covered the national elections in 1982. There an inept government, a merciless military force, and a lawless right-wing "death squad" operation had brought death to thousands of civilians, including democratic-minded intellectuals, journalists, rebellious farmworkers, and Catholic priests, including Archbishop Oscar Romero. The murder of four North American women, including three nuns, in 1980, two U.S. agricultural aid workers in 1981, and six Jesuit priests in 1989 aroused strong opposition to U.S. military involvement, particularly in Roman Catholic church circles, where the problems of poverty and oppression were recognized as the primary ones by those priests and nuns practicing the new "liberation theology."

Out of these events emerged a familiar pattern of U.S. thinking: the dissenting intellectuals, church leaders, and workers were perceived as a "left" tainted by Marxist thought and association with the neighboring Sandinistas, who briefly supplied arms to the El Salvador guerrillas. Instead, the Reagan and Bush administrations supported the dominant "right" composed of wealthy landowners, the military, and the managers of hundreds of American-owned corporate enterprises. El Salvador and Honduras joined Israel, Egypt, Turkey, and Pakistan among the nations receiving the most U.S. aid.[53]

The United States also provided the Salvadoran government with dozens of helicopter gunships and planes that were used to bombard the rural areas dominated by the Farabundo Marti National Liberation Front and the Democratic Revolutionary Front (FMLN/FDR). Critics of U.S. policy contended that the mainstream media failed to report the severity of these bombings. Proponents said the tactics were part of a winning strategy, and the arguments over the quality of coverage remained unresolved.[54] But in 1991 the government was hopelessly adrift, threatened by guerrillas who controlled about one-third of the country and opposed politically by a large coalition of farm cooperatives and labor unions. The fighting that had taken more than 50,000 lives continued in the wake of a 1986 earthquake that killed 1000 and left 200,000 homeless.

Women played an important role in covering El Salvador's war. Providing some of the most graphic descriptions of the bloody killing of civilians were Joanne Omang of the *Washington Post;* Beth Nissen of *Newsweek*; Laurie Becklund of the *Los Angeles Times;* and Lynda Schuster of the *Wall Street Journal.* Shirley Christian won the 1981 Pulitzer Prize for the *Miami Herald* and later joined the *New York Times,* where she fell under criticism from liberals for her ideological stance, a pro-Contra viewpoint demonstrated in her book *Nicaragua: Revolution in the Family.*

In a classic case of injustice, Raymond Bonner of the *New York Times* was removed from his El Salvador position after he aggressively reported the massacre of civilians that Salvadoran and U.S. officials said never happened. Bonner quit the paper and later was completely exonerated. Joining the lecture circuit to denounce U.S. policies were the former U.S. ambassador to El Salvador Robert E. White, former Contra leader Edgar Chamorro, former CIA agent David McMichael, and Dr. Charles Clements, who wrote the anguishing behind-the-lines account of the guerrilla war *Witness to War.*[55] At least 20 foreign journalists, including a Dutch television crew of four ambushed by government troops, died in El Salvador. Killed on the Honduran-Nicaraguan border in June 1983 were Dial Torgerson, longtime and trusted *Los Angeles Times* Latin American correspondent, and freelance photographer Richard Cross.

The 1989 invasion of Panama by U.S. forces seeking to overthrow Manuel Noriega led to a further deterioration of the U.S. reputation in Central America. There was less opposition to a 1994 intervention in Haiti, but the move reminded observers of the many previous interventions and was perceived as another attempt to enhance U.S. power in the region.

BUSH AND THE "NEW WORLD ORDER"

When George Bush emerged from the 1988 campaign a winner over Governor Michael S. Dukakis of Massachusetts, his first task was to escape the image of a mud-slinging, whining, nasty man who had used negative advertising to downgrade his opponent. Once accomplished, his next transformation would be from the invisible man on the Reagan team, the man who had escaped severe scrutiny in the Iran-Contra investigations, to the leader of a rapidly changing world. He couldn't have dreamed of how much the world would change in his first year in office.

The Soviet Union's Eastern European block crumbled, from Poland to Romania, and the fabled Berlin Wall fell along with it as Soviet leader Mikhail Gorbachev's policy of *glasnost* swept across previously closed borders. Checkpoint Charlie, the main crossing point between East and West Berlin, was removed by a crane in June 1989 as Secretary of State James Baker and Soviet Foreign Minister Eduard Shevardnadze watched.

For the first time in their history, the Soviets allowed contested elections. But strikes in the Soviet Union and outbursts of nationalism, particularly in the annexed Baltic States and Moslem areas, portended problems. There were early signs that Gorbachev's *perestroika,* the restructuring of the Soviet economy, might falter. If so, it was feared that conservative forces would demand an end to political and media openness.

The *New York Times* declared "The Cold War Is Over" on April 2, 1989, citing the end to "poisonous Soviet-American feelings . . . [and] domestic political hysteria."[56] Another relief came when Soviet troops began to withdraw from Afghanistan after ten years of fighting. At the same time Vietnam promised to withdraw from Cambodia unconditionally after years of occupation, the Soviets disassociated themselves from Cuba, and there were rumblings of great changes within China.

Those hopes were dashed in Beijing's Tiananmen Square on the night of June 3, 1989, when Chinese soldiers massacred hundreds and perhaps thousands of students and workers who demanded their version of democracy. Emotional television coverage notified the world that China's old guard was firmly in control. The White House responded to China's crackdown with displeasure but did not cut economic ties. There was muffled joy in Washington over the breakup of Eastern Europe, and some inappropriate boasting that Western-style democracy was sweeping the world. There were some old scores to settle, however, and one of them was in Panama.

The year ended on a sour note when Bush ordered U.S. troops into Panama in an effort to seize Manuel Noriega, the Panamanian leader who for years had been involved with international drug smuggling and espionage. Bush claimed other reasons were to protect the lives of U.S. residents, guarantee operation of the Panama Canal, and install a democratic government. The code name for the invasion, which led to the destruction of a civilian area of the city, was "Operation Just Cause." Following the censorship pattern set during the 1983 invasion of Grenada, the U.S. media pool was denied access to the action; the press pool of 16 reporters and photographers did not produce one eyewitness account. Arguments continued about the actual number of civilians killed, with the U.S. claiming 200 and human rights investigators listing as many as 4000. There also were charges that the U.S. had installed a new government that could be manipulated from Washington.[57]

Noriega sought sanctuary at the Vatican Embassy and finally surrendered. He was taken to Florida and jailed on drug trafficking charges. His history included years of working with the CIA and Israel's Mossad in a number of treacherous operations. Bush had a long relationship with Noriega dating to 1976, when he headed the CIA. Noriega's excesses had been excused as long as he was willing to be a broker for information, particularly about

Cuba and Nicaragua. But he became a liability because of his drug activities and because of his support for a Central American peace plan to end the Nicaraguan fighting. Tom Wicker of the *New York Times* concluded, "The more one looks into President Bush's invasion of Panama, the more one should—and the more one wonders why those of us in the press have been so uncritical about both the 'justification' and the consequences of this egregious misuse of U.S. military power."[58]

Perhaps one reason was that the Washington press corps found Bush to be friendly and accessible. He endured a great amount of criticism when he announced that he would raise taxes (his famous "read my lips" campaign promise was shown repeatedly) and for being part of the Reagan team that had spawned the huge federal deficit. He also was successful in dodging questions about the mushrooming savings and loan scandals that involved the loss of hundreds of millions of taxpayers' dollars. There was embarrassment when it was learned one of the president's sons was under fire for his savings and loan dealings. The scandals had evolved over several years, but the press was slow to dig into the reasons for this national disaster, including the campaign contributions to many senators and representatives who overlooked signs of wrongdoing.

Bush earned high marks in 1990 when Gorbachev visited Washington to sign major military and trade agreements. Photos of the smiling Barbara Bush and Raisa Gorbachev reassured Americans about true progress in Soviet relations. He had earned the respect of the American people and the press corps for establishing his own personality in the wake of Reagan's popular style, and he had completely erased his "wimp" image from his vice-presidential days. His frequent news conferences and his general availability were in marked contrast to Reagan's policy of ignoring reporters. His critics noted, however, that Bush had no clear agenda for domestic policy and that his foreign policy models were those who encouraged covert action and manipulation to achieve U.S. military and economic goals abroad.

Bush's promise to provide a "kinder and gentler America" was held up to scrutiny in 1990, when he decided to send U.S. troops to Saudi Arabia in Operation Desert Shield as the first step to drive invading Iraqi troops from neighboring Kuwait.

Instead of enjoying the fruits of a world finally free of East-West tensions, and positive news from South Africa and Chile, Americans found themselves in the midst of a major crisis. While the majority supported Bush's action, many were confused about the goals of U.S. policy. Bush took the high road, proclaiming that it was time for a "New World Order," with the U.S. taking the lead role in maintaining political and economic stability.

A GROWING U.S. ROLE IN THE MIDDLE EAST

The seemingly insoluble differences between Arabs and Jews—particularly over control of the Holy Land called Palestine by the Arabs and Israel by the Jews—have been the subject of news items and editorials around the world throughout the twentieth century. From all of the claims of sovereignty, charges of injustice, appeals to the United Nations, and propaganda barrages, only two facts emerged clearly. The Jewish people had a national homeland and state; the Palestinian people did not. And in the early 1990s that remained the crux of an excruciating dilemma that threatened the peace of the world.

Writers and journalists have played a part on both sides of this struggle from the beginning. Theodore Herzl, considered the father of the Zionist movement, issued his pamphlet *Der Judenstaat* in 1896, wherein he called for a political solution to the "Jewish Question"—the establishment of a Jewish state. Negib Azouri, a Christian Arab who edited an independent Arab newspaper in Paris, called for the secession of Arab lands from the Ottoman Empire in 1905. The seeds of Arab revolt can be traced to the decision of Turkish reformers to no longer rule in the name of Islamic brotherhood but rather in the nonreligious British and French colonial style, thus eliminating any reason for Arab submission.

The drive by Jews and Arabs to revive their historic pasts was fueled by the excitement at the end of World War I. Arabs sought to take advantage of the Allies' defeat of the Turks and the disintegration of the Ottoman Empire. But Arab desires were sidetracked by one agreement made secretly during the war by the British and French (Sykes-Picot, 1915–16) that set up their postwar division of the Middle East's Fertile Crescent. One of the provisions of the complicated agreement eventually gave Great Britain control of Palestine.

The Balfour Declaration of 1917, which demonstrated the growing British commitment to the creation of a Jewish home within Palestine, was put into operation in 1923. Accepting this mandate under the League of Nations, the British carefully controlled an immigration policy from this time to the end of World War II, insisting that Palestine should never fall under the control of either Arabs or Jews. Arabs were disbelieving, however, and rebelled against the British during 1936–39.

The German policy of genocide against the Jews led to heavy immigration into Palestine from Europe and increased demands for a political solution. Jewish terrorist groups attacked British troops and installations to intensify the pressure. Finally, one of several partition plans was adopted by the United Nations General Assembly's Resolution 33-13 (the U.S. and U.S.S.R. voted for it) in November 1947.

The Arab Higher Executive Council was opposed to this compromise, partially because the plan gave the small Jewish population a disproportionately high percentage of land; the Jewish Agency, which also had objections, agreed to the settlement. As arguments raged and the issue became a worldwide story, the Israeli Proclamation of Independence was issued in Tel Aviv on May 14, 1948; the British Mandate ended the next day; and about 20,000 soldiers from neighboring Arab nations came to the assistance of the Palestinian Arabs who opposed the formation of the new state on the basis of the partitioning plan. The regular Jewish forces totaled about 40,000; the first of the Israeli-Arab wars was under way, with its accompanying myths and propaganda.

When the fighting ended with a truce, the Israelis occupied considerably more territory, including half of Jerusalem, than they would have under the partition plan. An estimated 800,000 Palestinians lost their homes, fleeing across the borders. Hatreds flared that remain to this day. Jewish leaders said the Arabs had never wanted them to have even a modest share of Palestine; Arabs claimed the Jewish forces were brutal in forcing them to leave. Historians and journalists later documented the murder of innocent persons by both sides, including the infamous massacre of about 250 unarmed Arabs at Deir Yassin, a village on the western outskirts of Jerusalem.[59]

The pattern for future wars and a growing refugee problem was set. Americans saw newsreel pictures of Palestinians in the dreadful Gaza Strip or read an occasional newspaper story, but lacked the background knowledge for understanding the complexities of the story. During these years of remarkable achievements and admirable courage, the Israeli government—strongly supported by U.S. politicians and numerous organizations—created a favorable media image, while the Arab world, despite all of its own accomplishments, retained its image of being the land of camels and sword-carrying sheiks. A number of studies have demonstrated the imbalance in coverage of the Arab-Israeli conflicts and the stereotyping of Arabs in general, not dissimilar from that suffered by Jews over previous centuries.[60]

The almost daily conflict soon involved the great powers and the world press. In 1956 the British and French conspired with the Israelis to allow them to seize the Suez Canal. The Israelis had complained for years of Egyptian interference with free trade. In this instance the Eisenhower administration forced the Israelis to halt their advance in favor of a U.N. peacekeeping arrangement. Then in June 1967 the Israelis smashed their Egyptian, Syrian, and Jordanian enemies in the fighting that became glorified as the Six-Day War. Throughout these conflicts the strategic interests of the United States and the Soviet Union formed the backdrop for the news stories of tank battles and air attacks.

In the 1967 battles the Israelis gained East Jerusalem and the West Bank from Jordan, the Golan Heights from Syria, and the Gaza Strip near the Sinai Peninsula from Egypt. In seizing this territory they took on the responsibility for approximately one million more Arab inhabitants, adding to their enormous refugee problem. Ted Yates, an NBC producer, and Paul Schutzer, *Life* photographer, were casualties during this period as they and dozens of U.S. journalists tried to capture the confusing story.

This was the highpoint for the Israelis. The Arab world seemed cowed, and Israeli troops appeared invincible. In November 1967 the U.N. Security Council passed Resolution 242, which called for peace based on Israeli withdrawal from the Golan Heights, Gaza, and the West Bank in return for being recognized as an independent state—with all states having the right to live within secure and defined borders. Arguments over interpretations of Resolution 242—including the future status of Jerusalem—and the possibility of its implementation have not ceased.

The 1970 civil war in Jordan provided another benchmark in this long struggle. Jordan had become the base for Palestinian attacks against Israel after the 1967 Israeli occupation of the West Bank. The Palestine Liberation Organization (PLO) under the chairmanship of Yasir Arafat assumed too much power—it became a state within a state— and Jordan's King Hussein used his armed forces to drive out the Syrian-supported PLO. There was extensive media coverage. The PLO fled to southern Lebanon, where they eventually became involved in the disastrous fighting there. The result of the Jordanian fighting was the continued fragmenting of the Palestinian effort to gain a homeland, with the press, including the *New York Times,* assisting by its failure to accept the PLO as the legitimate representative of the Palestinian people.[61]

The most shocking story broadcast was from Munich during the 1972 Olympic Games, when Arab terrorists murdered Israeli athletes in the Olympic village. That plus other raids by various Palestinian guerrilla groups and numerous Israeli retaliation attacks in neighboring countries kept the Middle East in a state of high tension.

Israel suffered a setback in 1973, when Egypt and Syria attacked on the Yom Kippur holy day and surprised the Israeli forces. Only massive American airlifts helped the Israelis to push their foes back and avoid the threat of a major war. But after another ceasefire agreement, Egyptian president Anwar Sadat became interested in a more permanent arrangement. This eventually led to the Camp David accords signed by President Carter, Israeli Prime Minister Menachem Begin, and Sadat, to the dismay of Arabs who were left out of the process.

Israel's international reputation hit an all-time low in 1982 following its decision to invade southern Lebanon to oust PLO forces. Syria had occupied northern Lebanon, and the PLO had set up a governmental headquarters in Beirut. Instead of halting about 25 miles past the border, according to an announced plan, the Israeli government mounted an all-out assault, laid siege to Beirut, and temporarily drove out the PLO guerrillas. But television reports of the bombings of Lebanese villages and air attacks in the Beirut area brought Israeli tactics into question.

In previous years there had been little anger expressed through the U.S. establishment media over Israel's supplying of arms to repressive regimes in South Africa, Chile, El Salvador, Honduras, Iran, and other nations, including Nicaragua when the dictator Somoza was in charge. Those acts clearly were in line with U.S. foreign policy goals and received scant attention. But a debate began over Israel's conduct in Lebanon, particularly after the sickening massacre in September 1982 of more than 700 refugee Palestinians in two Beirut camps by Lebanese Christian Phalangists allied with Israel. Loren Jenkins of the *Washington Post* and Thomas Friedman of the *New York Times* shared the 1983 Pulitzer international reporting award for their stories of the fighting. Friedman later detailed this in his autobiography *From Beirut to Jerusalem.* AP photographer Bill Foley won the 1983 Pulitzer prize and AP Managing Editors Award for his pictures of the massacre camp. Walter Wisniewski and Jack Redden of UPI received the Overseas Press Club award for their massacre coverage.

American policy became further fragmented when the administration sent U.S. Marines to Lebanon as part of an international peacekeeping force. In October 1983 a truck-bomb attack in Beirut killed 241 of the Marines. The horrifying television footage of the attack, blamed on a pro-Iranian group, added to the sense of futility still felt by Americans in the aftermath of the hostage crisis. The indiscriminate shelling of Lebanese villages by the battleship *New Jersey* only added to the anti-U.S. passions in the Arab world, as did President Reagan's April 1986 decision to bomb Libya in an attempt to kill Libyan President Muammar Qaddafi.

The Reagan administration suffered another severe loss of credibility in late 1986, when it was discovered that the president—the man who had admonished U.S. allies on how to deal with terrorists—had secretly authorized the sale of arms to Iran in hopes of exchanging them for several hostages, including AP bureau chief Terry Anderson,[62] and that some of the funds had been diverted to support the administration's pet project, the overthrow of the Nicaraguan government. The scandalous news shocked not only Americans angry over the Iranian hostage debacle, but also the entire Arab world, mostly hostile to Iran and supportive of Iraq in the long Iran-Iraq War. That Arab shock turned to anger when it was learned how Israel had played a key role in the arms transfer.

A series of plane hijackings and the bloody seizure of the Italian cruise ship *Achille Lauro* by members of fringe groups damaged the Palestinians' long struggle for their homeland, submerging it under the emotional issue of international terrorism. But on December 9, 1987, Palestinian nationalists in Gaza began an all-out revolt against Israeli occupation, known as the Intifada, and were joined the next day by residents of the West Bank and East Jerusalem. Within days it was clear that the stone-throwing young people, fully supported by their parents and grandparents, could not be controlled, and frustrated Israeli soldiers resorted to widespread beatings, tear gassings, and shootings.[63]

On November 15, 1988, Yasir Arafat, chairman of the Palestine Liberation Organization, read the Palestinian Declaration of Independence in Algiers. In December he publicly recognized Israel's right to exist. As world sympathy grew for the Palestinian cause, long ignored by the Western media, the Israelis—encouraged by former Secretary of State Henry Kissinger—instituted strict censorship, frequently denying correspondents access to the refugee camps and villages where violent clashes took place.

By 1991 more than 1000 Palestinians had been killed, many by live ammunition, and thousands more had suffered from brutal beatings, all documented by various human rights organizations. Several thousand dissenters were jailed for months without charge; homes were demolished as part of the Israelis' well-known "collective punishment" policy; and many Palestinian leaders, including moderates who called for peace talks, were expelled.

In October 1990 Israeli border police killed 17 Palestinians in Jerusalem during a disturbance triggered by a Jewish extremist group.[64] Worldwide coverage added to a growing debate over whether the Palestinian question should be linked to efforts to force Iraqi President Saddam Hussein to withdraw from occupied Kuwait. President Bush strongly rejected that notion, and when war broke out on January 17, 1991, the Israelis put the 1.7 million Palestinians under curfew.

Following the Persian Gulf War positive steps were taken that led to Arab-Israeli negotiations beginning in 1991. A major breakthrough occurred on September 13, 1993, when Arafat and Israeli Prime Minister Yitzhak Rabin shook hands at the White House, offering mutual recognition. Israel agreed to transfer governing authority to Palestinians in Gaza and the historic West Bank town of Jericho as the first step in a multiyear withdrawal plan. Arafat agreed to accept limited autonomy during the transition period, deeply disappointing many of his most devoted supporters in the Occupied Territories, who felt the basic Palestinian right to self-determination had been compromised. By mid-1994 Arafat had appointed the majority of positions in a Palestinian National Authority. The PLO chairman returned "home" for the first time in 27 years on July 1. The television audience saw this smiling symbol of Palestinian independence greeted by a tumultuous crowd in Gaza. But the euphoria quickly disappeared in the wake of bloody attacks by Palestinian and Israeli extremists. While many obstacles remained to a legitimate peace—particularly the final status of illegal Israeli settlements and occupied East Jerusalem—Israelis and the Palestine Liberation Organization were openly dealing with each other after nearly five decades of hostility.

THE GULF WAR

During the confusing aftermath of the United States' Gulf War victory over Iraq, those journalists and members of the public concerned about the meaning of President Bush's "New World Order" began to assess the consequences of the electronically controlled *blitzkrieg* that had set Iraq back into the preindustrial age. Despite the maze of contradictions between Washington's officially stated policies and the results in Kuwait and Iraq, several things were clear.

First, the United States and Great Britain were free to physically control events in the oil-rich Gulf for the foreseeable future; the Palestinian question was back at the top of the Middle East agenda; as the world's remaining superpower, the United States was willing to use massive force against any nation interfering with its long-range economic goals; a precedent had been created for continued wide-ranging censorship of U.S. correspondents covering overseas conflicts; and the U.S. government was satisfied with its use of CIA and psychological operations disinformation that had proved so effective in disarming both press and public between the time of Saddam Hussein's invasion of Kuwait on August 2, 1990, and February 27, 1991, when President Bush halted the slaughter of fleeing Iraqi soldiers and the bombing elsewhere in Iraq.

Most Americans assumed Iraq's President Saddam Hussein was a U.S. ally when his forces seized neighboring Kuwait after a long dispute over war reparations, control of two islands blocking Iraqi access to the Arabian Gulf, and Iraqi charges that Kuwait had been stealing oil from a field on a disputed boundary. After all, it had been a public U.S. policy all summer to continue to support Iraq economically, assisting the nation that had borne the brunt of the eight-year war against a U.S. enemy, Iran.

But evidence emerged later that the United States and Britain had begun to "tilt" against Iraq as early as August of 1988, when the Iran-Iraq war ended with Iraq as the strongest military power in the region. It has been consistent U.S. and British Middle East policy to keep heavily populated Iraq and Iran as weak and separate as possible to protect the Western oil interests in the lightly populated, more vulnerable Gulf states.[65]

The president's public reaction to Iraq's invasion was a mixture of anger and caution. While denouncing the aggression and invoking the image of Adolph Hitler, Bush and his advisers worked skillfully to build broad-based support for the military action that they had decided upon during these early stages. Using UN resolutions as a base, he sent U.S. forces to Saudi Arabia on August 7, claiming that Iraqi tanks threatened to sweep into the oil kingdom. Then on September 11 he addressed the American people, telling them that U.S. goals were (1) Iraqi withdrawal from Kuwait; (2) the return of the Kuwaiti Emir to power; (3) assurance of stability in the Gulf region; and (4) the protection of U.S. citizens in the area. Later that evening Peter Jennings offered an ABC special, *A Line in the Sand,* praised by critics as one of the best programs broadcast during the build-up period.

In May 1991 the *Washington Post's* Bob Woodward joined those questioning the origins and outcomes of the war by publishing another best-selling book, *The Commanders,* where he described how the strong desire of President Bush, Secretary of Defense Richard Cheney, and others for armed conflict essentially eliminated the chance for an Arab world solution to the crisis or a long-term application of economic sanctions by the UN coalition. Woodward reported that one person advocating a softer approach in the beginning was General Colin Powell, chairman of the Joint Chiefs of Staff, who could not find any allies within the top circle of advisers.

From these opening moments the bulk of the U.S. media faithfully reported White House, State Department, and Pentagon interpretations of the growing crisis—and a constant demonizing of Saddam Hussein not unlike the personalizing of the Panamanian conflict with General Manuel Noriega—while the efforts of those citizens participating in a small but significant antiwar movement were trivialized by the news media.[66] As the first of what would become a force of more than 430,000 Americans arrived in Saudi Arabia, the Pentagon announced a complicated press pool plan designed to curtail the media's activities and control the flow of news back home.

While there were numerous skirmishes between reporters and press officers, and between reporters competing for valuable spots in a pool, there was little protest by the owners and managers of the news media systems. If anything there was a resignation that the Pentagon had all of the power and that a prowar public would accept even more censorship if the government imposed it. Arguments over the arbitrariness of the press pool rules —including one that reporters had to be escorted at all times—continued long after the fighting ceased. But the goal of putting the loss in Vietnam out of the public mind one of the government's objectives in going to war) had been achieved, and there was little chance of returning to a more open style of giving reporters access to U.S. personnel in the field.[67]

One journalist who attempted to circumvent the pool coverage was CBS's Bob Simon, who was captured along with his crew and spent the war in an Iraqi prison. The only journalist killed during the war and the period immediately afterward was freelance photographer Gad Schuster Gross, a native of Romania and a Harvard graduate who was killed March 29 by Iraqi soldiers while working for *Newsweek* in northern Iraq. Two of his freelance colleagues, Frank Smyth of the *Village Voice* and CBS and Alain Buu of Gamma-Liaison, were captured by Iraqis and released three weeks later. Caryle Murphy of the

Washington Post, who hid in Kuwait for 26 days after the invasion and phoned out information, won the Pulitzer Prize.

The public soon became familiar with the faces and bylines of the U.S. press corps in Saudi Arabia, Jordan, and Israel, and later in Kuwait, Iraq, and Turkey. On November 8, two days after the midterm elections, Bush announced he was doubling U.S. forces, bringing them to Vietnam-era strength. The standoff between Bush and Saddam Hussein continued, accompanied by continuous speculation by a horde of Middle East experts who dominated television programming. Dan Rather, Tom Brokaw, and Ted Koppel reported from the Middle East, with Rather securing an exclusive interview with Saddam Hussein. At one point NBC's *Today* show originated from Saudi Arabia, with Bryant Gumbel sitting in a chair on a red carpet. Bush had given Saddam Hussein until January 15 to retreat from Kuwait. It was television's crisis as the tension built in early January, and it was television's war when the bombs fell on Baghdad. Operation Desert Shield had become the Operation Desert Storm of the U.S. commander, general H. Norman Schwarzkopf.

Gary Shepard of ABC reported the flashes of light first, from his room in Baghdad's Al-Rashid Hotel during a live conversation with anchor Peter Jennings. It was 6:35 P.M. (eastern standard time), January 16, 1991: "It's like fireworks on the Fourth of July, multiplied by 100!" A few minutes later ABC and other organizations lost their telephone connections, but CNN had made advance arrangements at $16,000 per month for a special telephone line to Amman, Jordan, that connected with a satellite relay. This foresight guaranteed CNN a place in broadcast news history.

CNN reporters Peter Arnett and John Holliman were in their room with anchor Bernard Shaw in Baghdad, awaiting an interview with Saddam Hussein, when Cruise missiles and squadrons of F-15E fighter-bombers took over. They reported the flashes of light for 15 or 20 minutes, and at 7 P.M. Holliman said, "The war has begun in Baghdad." Across the United States people eating dinner or driving home heard the initial reports, and within an hour most of them were listening to the voices of Arnett, Holliman, and Shaw describe, in the World War II style if not the prose of Edward R. Murrow, a sky filled with anti-aircraft fire. Thunderous explosions were heard in the background, sometimes accompanied by an "oooh" from one of the reporters, as bombs hit near the center of the city. Chuckles and nervous laughter were part of the uninhibited report. That evening Bush spoke to the biggest audience for a single news event in television history, an estimated 61 million households.

ABC broadcast the first pictures of the attack, taken by a World Television News (WTN) cameraman and carried out by Shepard. The next day Holliman and Shaw left with more than 40 other journalists, leaving Arnett and two technicians behind. He remained in contact with the Atlanta desk throughout the entire war, eventually being supplied with a satellite dish so he and his crew could transmit live pictures. Arnett became the object of extreme hostility from some quarters because of his reporting of bomb damage. He also was praised by the majority of his colleagues for his courage and his calm assessment of the situation. He told his audience he was accompanied by censors, but at times even his own CNN anchors seemed embarrassed by his reporting. If anything, Arnett occasionally contradicted Pentagon claims that the destruction of nonmilitary targets was only "collateral" or accidental damage, as explained away by military briefers at the U.S. Central Command center in Riyadh, Saudi Arabia.

The antiseptic nature of the air war was difficult to erase, even when two bombs from a U.S. Stealth fighter-bomber incinerated more than 300 Iraqi civilians in a Baghdad bomb shelter in mid-February. While Arnett and other journalists reported the carnage, U.S. military spokesmen insisted the shelter was a military command post. But Iraqi Scud missile alerts in Israel and Saudi Arabia were televised live, and casualties and damage in Israel evoked considerable empathy in the United States. Scenes of Israelis and television reporters with gas masks brought home the horrors of war, while the absence of cameras in Iraq meant that thousands of Arab deaths were invisible to the world audience.

For the bulk of the war there was scant regard or even wonderment in the U.S. media about Iraqi casualties. Later a United Nations report of March 1991 detailed the destruction of Iraq's infrastructure, calling it "near-apocalyptic." News media reports then began quoting Air Force statistics showing that most bombs dropped were not precision-guided and that 70 percent missed their targets, along with 10 percent of the "smart bombs" equipped with cameras that had held viewers in awe.[68]

Watching the war on television became such a ritual that when the war ended some persons had great difficulty adjusting to the lack of excitement. They missed CNN reporters Wolf Blitzer at the Pentagon, Charles Jaco in Saudi Arabia, Christine Amanpour in Amman—and the dry Richard Blystone in Tel Aviv. NBC's Arthur Kent became a "heart-throb" of female viewers. ABC's Dean Reynolds, NBC's Martin Fletcher, and CBS's Tom Fenton became familiar during Scud attacks in Israel.[69]

Accompanying the sheer novelty of seeing live press briefings or live pictures of Patriot missiles hitting incoming Scuds was a growing jingoism within the U.S. population, fed in part by lopsided local television and newspaper coverage. KABC-TV in Los Angeles banned coverage of local antiwar protests, ignoring a City Hall protest that was the biggest there since the Vietnam War. Newspapers ran double-spreads featuring yellow ribbons and decorated their city rooms with prowar symbols. Disc jockeys promoted new prowar songs, while talk shows for the most part were dominated by hosts and callers who gloried in the "precision bombings" and "high-tech efficiency of American war technology," while reserving criticism for Peter Arnett and other journalists who were skeptical about U.S. claims.

There was a collective sigh of relief at the beginning of the air war when it was learned U.S. casualties were minimal. The government had prepared the public for thousands of deaths in the event of all-out war. A sense of quiet satisfaction was evident also when military briefers displayed videotapes of missiles squarely hitting their targets, a demonstration of U.S. industrial capabilities. A public used to hearing negative news understandably relished the almost completely positive news flowing from the Gulf.

Once the air war was under way, and more than 100,000 sorties had been flown against Iraqi targets, the final phase of the war became obvious, the ground war. President Bush again gave a deadline, this time February 23. As the final minutes ticked off, combat pool reporters prepared to head into occupied Kuwait with the lead elements. CBS's Bob McKeown scored a dramatic coup with joyous live coverage of Kuwait being liberated, momentarily lifting spirits within a network that had been battered by CNN and ABC for the bulk of the war. NBC had not fared much better.

There were about 1000 journalists and technicians from dozens of nations, mainly the United States, awaiting pool assignments in Saudi Arabia. Veterans like the *New York Times*'s Malcolm Browne and R. W. ("Johnny") Apple, Jr., were surrounded by hundreds of young reporters covering their first war, armed with enthusiasm but with little knowledge of the roots of the conflict. For the most part they acquitted themselves well, providing comprehensive reports about every aspect made available. Many of them outfoxed the censorship rules when the ground war broke out, and chaos reigned along the roads to Kuwait. The *Los Angeles Times* had the biggest Middle East contingent, and one of the best, assigning nine reporters to the region. Another contingent winning professional approval for its work was that of the *Wall Street Journal*. The news weeklies geared up with about a dozen staffers each. The Associated Press battled Reuters for wire service beats, while the understaffed UPI steadfastly held on.

The ground war officially lasted only 100 hours as Coalition forces—U.S., British and Arabs—easily sliced through Iraqi defenses and captured about 100,000 Iraqis. Another 100,000 Iraqis were killed, the majority by continuous bombing raids prior to the attack. An estimated 15,000 Iraqi civilians were killed by bombings, a statistic contested by both peace activists and military supporters. When the fighting ended in late February U.S. forces were in southern Iraq, but U.S. involvement in the Middle East then took a different course. Some of the most graphic pictures of misery seen in years came from the coverage of Kurdish refugees fleeing into Turkey ahead of Iraqi troops. The anguish in the United States was so great that Bush belatedly was forced to send U.S. troops into northern Iraq to support the Kurds. UN forces were to assume control, but the length of the U.S. commitment in Iraq and in Kuwait, the scene of great disorder and environmental damage caused by burning oil wells, was undetermined.

The war, conducted at a high level by the White House and the Pentagon, ended on a sour note. There was not increased stability in the Middle East, and Saddam Hussein was still in power, along with hundreds of thousands of his troops who had escaped defeat. Kuwait's undemocratic rulers returned and set up trials for hundreds of Palestinians and others accused of being subversives. Israelis, expecting special treatment for not retaliating against Iraq during the war, vowed to settle Russian Jews in the Occupied Territories, throwing up an obstacle to U.S.-encouraged peace talks with the Arab states and Palestinians.

In retrospect, the war consisted of a massive propaganda blitz, replete with welcome-home parades festooned with yellow ribbons. But, as the *Wall Street Journal* summed up:

> One year after Saddam Hussein invaded Kuwait, the lingering air of defeat and destruction—of lives, livelihoods, and pride—shrouded Arab thinking about the crisis . . . From the U.S. standpoint, the humbling of Iraq may have been a victory, yet for Arabs it has come at a horrific price.

During the troop build-up in October 1990 public opinion polls gave Bush as high as a 78 percent approval rating (ABC-*Washington Post*), and on the eve of the air war this remained remarkably high at 69 percent. But once the war ended, with U.S. troops in northern Iraq and massive debts riddling the domestic economy, his ratings began to erode. As for the news media, a series of polls taken in early 1991 showed that 89 percent used television as the main source of war news, 67 percent said follow-ups in newspapers gave them the same basic information, and the vast majority (91 percent for television and 85 percent for newspapers) responded very favorably to the news media's war performance.

On the negative side, 39 percent said Saddam Hussein was given too much opportunity to make his case, 44 percent said the news media are often inaccurate, and 64 percent said the news media made it difficult for U.S. officials to conduct the war. Only 51 percent read a newspaper daily, a fact that reinforces the importance of television news coverage.

One of former President Reagan's advisers, public relations expert Michael Deaver, summed up the establishment's attitude about the war and its coverage. He noted how top officials had become sophisticated in their approach to controlling the news media, especially television: "The coverage on television has been a combination of Lawrence of Arabia and Star Wars, and since television is where 80 percent of the people get their news, it couldn't be better."[70]

CLINTON'S STRUGGLE FOR APPROVAL

Bill Clinton became the third president to conquer the mysteries and fears of television, joining Kennedy and Reagan, both of whom knew how to use the medium. Beginning with his erratic drive for the 1992 Democratic nomination—one marred by public allegations of sexual misconduct during his 12 years as governor of Arkansas and confusion over his draft status during the Vietnam War—Clinton demonstrated an affinity for the camera, smiling broadly and talking in an engaging "aw shucks" manner.

He was surrounded by a horde of staff members attracted by his centrist, populist outlook. One was Dee Dee Myers, who later served for two years as the first woman presidential press secretary. Clinton evoked comparisons with Kennedy, his boyhood idol, whom he had met at the White House as a teenager, and his wife, Hillary Rodham Clinton, was likened to Eleanor Roosevelt.

From the outset of the primary campaign, however, many reporters maintained an emotional distance from Clinton, complaining that they did not feel comfortable with his various explanations for his position changes and for his personal problems. The media highlight of the primary season came when the Clintons appeared on *60 Minutes* to answer questions about his marital fidelity and their marriage, an image that later became haunting in the wake of continued allegations of Clinton's sexual improprieties.

Called "Slick Willie" by his Republican enemies in Arkansas, Clinton was disappointed when the moniker was applied to him during his campaign against the incumbent Bush. Some critics wondered why a press corps that had backed off from challenging Reagan and Bush with embarrassing questions would seem to delight in tackling Clinton day after day. One answer was that this friendly, idealistic, and accessible candidate provided an easy target for the cynical Washington journalists. George McGovern and Jimmy Carter had similarly suffered.

The campaign became a three-ring circus, with Texas billionaire Ross Perot mounting a full-fledged independent campaign. His main target was Bush, for whom Perot harbored longtime grudges. Meanwhile Clinton—this child of television—broke with tradition by appearing on MTV and every possible radio and television talk show, and even playing the saxophone on the Arsenio Hall program. Vague and inexperienced in the foreign policy arena, Clinton argued eloquently for cuts in the trillion-dollar deficit, reform within the burgeoning federal government, and implementation of a middle-class tax cut.

In his "campaign of hope," Clinton urged Americans to break from a malaise that affected confidence in government and general productivity, reminding voters that the deficit had grown drastically in the Reagan-Bush years. Inexplicably, Bush ran a lackluster campaign and squandered the overwhelming support he had enjoyed following the Gulf War. The president never recovered from a decision to allow the conservative right to dominate the GOP convention, which at times turned into an antiwomen, antihomosexual statement.

Perot self-destructed as well, emerging on the *Larry King Live* and other talk shows as a stubborn man filled with homilies but with no specific suggestions or answers. Despite this, a disillusioned and fragmented electorate gave Perot 19 percent of the vote, the strongest third party showing since Theodore Roosevelt had gained 27 percent with his 1912 Progressive party campaign. The traditional two-party system so easily taken for granted seemed ready to be shattered by the right person.

Clinton defeated Bush handily, 43 to 38 percent, but he was decidedly a minority president. At age 46 he was the first president to be born after that great dividing line, World War II—one of the "baby boomers." His inauguration symbolized his dreams for a diverse and just society, with the reading by Maya Angelou forcing comparisons with Robert Frost's poetry at Kennedy's inauguration.

Clinton then received the shortest honeymoon accorded a modern president as White House staff and reporters began sniping at one another almost immediately. Clinton's support for gays in the military—a campaign pledge he tried to keep—elicited a torrent of abuse from conservatives and many in the news media said Clinton equivocated when settling for a "don't ask, don't tell," compromise with the Pentagon.

During his first two years Clinton successfully managed several narrow but significant legislative victories including a deficit-cutting budget; a ban against assault weapons (opposed by the National Rifle Association, the nation's strongest lobby); and various educational programs. The most ambitious program, directed primarily by the articulate and energetic First Lady, was designed to overhaul the nation's health care system. Two years of effort crumbled, however, when Democratic congressional leaders signaled their surrender to a myriad of hostile forces.

The Clintons were bitterly criticized by friends for trying to accomplish too much at once in the health area, and by foes for challenging the insurance companies and private health groups opposed to change. Media coverage was open to criticism, too. One major study supported the First Lady's contention that many stories did not relate to the average reader. Over a four-month period only 12 percent of newspaper stories of the proposed health care changes focused on their potential impact on individuals and their families, while 41 percent dealt with their possible impact on the system as a whole and 23 percent on their political ramifications.[71] Despite his setbacks, Clinton maintained a public cheery attitude with reporters while jogging and at impromptu sessions. He and the First Lady dazzled everyone with their long, detailed answers to complicated questions. Vice President Al Gore and his wife provided solid support for the Clintons, with Gore emerging as a creditable spokesman in his own right.

The president was at his best at news conferences, where he usually was able to field tough questions from UPI's ageless Helen Thomas, ABC's aggressive Brit Hume, or

President Clinton

(Photo by Michael Emery)

CNN's imperturbable Wolf Blitzer. But at times he showed his frustration. On one occasion, the nomination of Supreme Court Justice Ruth Bader Ginsburg, Clinton rebuked Hume for a rude, out-of-place question and stalked off. In private he was known to fume over news reports, and he indicated more than once, usually on a radio interview show, that he felt unappreciated by the news media—that he had taken on tough tasks and accomplished far more than the public realized, because, he said, "the media didn't tell them." Among major newspapers the president received his strongest criticisms on the editorial pages of the *Wall Street Journal.*

In 1993 Clinton temporarily eased his media problems by appointing Republican image-maker David Gergen his director of communications, but the hassles with the media soon returned, and Gergen moved backstage. One of the president's self-made problems from the outset was that despite his ability to handle a full-fledged news conference, he held them infrequently (only three in his first 20 months) and preferred to by-pass the White House corps by answering questions during televised meetings with average citizens or appearing on talk shows. Jack Nelson, Washington bureau chief of the *Los Angeles Times* said:

> He has turned out to be one of the most activist, ambitious, controversial, undisciplined, procrastinating presidents. . . . He's into everything. He's late for almost everything, even for making the State of the Union address. . . . one of his aides said he's inventing a new form of chaos that works for him. . . . But despite his eccentricities and many ups and downs . . . I think his harshest critics would agree that he's delivered on one or two of his major promises. Whether you like him or whether you don't like him, he has delivered on diversity and he has delivered on change.[72]

While no one suggested that Clinton had committed any wrong-doing while in the White House, he was continually held up to scrutiny by conservatives and their talk show advocate Rush Limbaugh, who viciously attacked the president from every level, passing on rumors with abandon, including some about the suicide of Clinton's deputy White House counsel and close friend Vincent Foster. An Arkansas scandal dubbed "Whitewater" dominated headlines for months and at times threatened to engulf Clinton's presidency. Major news organizations, led by the *New York Times,* and tabloid journalists combed Arkansas for anything new about Hillary Clinton's former law firm, Foster's death, the couple's association with developers and investors, and a savings and loan failure. *New York Times* columnist Anthony Lewis wrote: "The press has its own version of Gresham's Law: the tendency, in the competition for readers [or viewers], to let the scandalous and sensational drive out serious news."[73] Media critic Todd Gitlin of the University of California at Berkeley agreed. Noting the tendency of the news media to "lean so hard on Democrats," he said:

> As for reporters, they are often Democrats themselves and bend over backward to prove they are "objective". . . Most of all, the press has no built-in sense of proportion. Maniacal competition fuels the search for the smoking misdeed. . . . Thus do the guardians of public information put the Clintons in their place—in the gutter, with the rest of the country.[74]

While some of the Clintons' associates were linked to wrongdoings, the president and his wife were not. Then came another sex scandal—a young woman went on national television to charge the president with making unsolicited advances toward her when he was governor. Clinton was granted some relief when a court ruled this lawsuit could be delayed until after his presidency.

Seeking to override these distractions, in 1994 Clinton pointed to a drop in unemployment and a pleasing rise in the national economy. His foreign policy record was generally positive. He set a record for presidential travel in a calendar year in 1994 with six overseas trips, including one grueling, six-nation tour of the Middle East, as his administration struggled for a consistent policy in a post–Cold War world where situational ethics were more practical. With the Soviets out of the picture, there were no measuring sticks to determine whether to intervene in a foreign matter. Clinton earned respect in Europe and Asia after public appearances; he supported the hotly debated North American Fair Trade Agreement (NAFTA); and he was a leader in the creation of the World Trade Organization, a new international body created to direct commerce.

Clinton avoided, temporarily at least, potential disasters in Haiti and North Korea, both times allowing former President Jimmy Carter to handle the negotiations. An invasion of Haiti was avoided at the last minute when former President Jean-Bertrand Aristide was restored to office. Clinton demonstrated firmness against Iraq's Saddam Hussein on several occasions, ordering bombing once, and he continued the United States' closed-fist policy against Fidel Castro's Cuba. He disagreed with his European allies on the Bosnian question, pushing unsuccessfully for the bombing of Serbian Bosnian positions and an end to an arms embargo against beleaguered Bosnian Muslims.

Overall, however, Clinton's liberal critics too often found him supporting programs that they said promoted the rich and powerful in direct contrast to his stated personal philosophy. For example, NAFTA may cut tariffs and open trade, but offered no protection for the exploited Mexican workers living in squalor just south of the U.S. border. The Clinton administration was no different from its predecessors in selectively signaling displeasure with human rights violations. China and Indonesia, for example, escaped sanctions because of lucrative trade agreements; the administration looked the other way when Israel violated international law by continuing to build settlements and confiscate land in the West Bank and Gaza; and the United States did nothing when Russian President Boris Yeltsin unleashed his armed forces against the runaway Republic of Chechnya, as Western journalists reported horrors similar to those committed by Serbs at Sarajevo.

Clinton's supporters argued that he had inherited his problems: the budget deficit that multiplied following the criminal savings and loan scandals that everyone seemed to forget; the Bosnian war ignored by Bush; the shrinking resources in Europe and Japan; a declining U.S. educational system; massive illegal immigration; growing voter dissatisfaction with government in general; and an Islamic fundamentalism that no one understood.

The voters delivered Clinton a resounding blow at the 1994 midterm elections by returning the Republicans to power in both houses of Congress for the first time since 1954. Senate Majority Leader Robert Dole and Speaker of the House Newt Gingrich pledged to challenge the president in almost every area. Gingrich, once an obscure Georgia college history professor, developed an unusual ability to raise a political war chest. He became a hero to conservatives disgusted by "big government" and "liberal causes." Calling the Clintons "counterculture McGovniks," Gingrich and his fellow Republicans set out to fulfill their "Contract with America," a specific campaign pledge signed on the Capitol steps.

Washington's biggest question in 1995 was: would Clinton recover from his political wounds and run for a second term? The answer was yes. Clinton beat Republican challenger Bob Dole by eight percentage points in a campaign that vacillated between down-and-dirty attack ads and apparent political lethargy. Both candidates vied for the centrist position, seemingly favored by most Americans. The Democratic ticket of Clinton and Al Gore, according to postdebate polls, won all three debates. However, Clinton was faced in his second term by a Republican-controlled Congress. Some commentators attributed this division of political power between the parties to voters' desires to avoid ideological extremes and to favor a centrist government.

Tragically, midway through his second term the most salient aspect of Clinton's presidency became his affair with a 21-year-old White House intern named Monica Lewinsky. The scandal became the focus of a special investigation headed by prosecutor Kenneth Starr, whom many perceived as a neo-Puritan engaged in a moral vendetta. In his grand-jury testimony (which was telecast nationally, a precedent), Clinton did not give straight-forward answers about his relationship with Lewinsky, leading to allegations that he lied under oath and resulting in a historic vote by Congress, largely along party lines, to impeach him. In early 1999 amid simultaneous calls for Clinton's resignation and expressions of dismay that a sitting president could be potentially removed from office in this manner, the Senate struggled to agree on procedural rules for the conduct of the impeachment trial. Ultimately there were insufficient votes to remove him from office. Clinton remained resolute in his determination to finish out his term, claiming that his behavior, while objectionable, did not merit impeachment and possible removal from office, and the public strongly approved of his job performance.

THE PUBLIC PERCEPTION OF MEDIA CREDIBILITY

The understanding of news media credibility was enhanced in the 1980s and 1990s by major studies that added to the knowledge accumulated since 1959 by polls taken by the Roper Organization. The Roper polls showed that television had ousted newspapers as the prime news source in 1963. Other polls showed that the news media ranked ahead of other institutions—schools, local government, police, business, organized religion—in public esteem, despite a disenchantment with it.

The most extensive of the new studies were commissioned by the Times Mirror Corporation and conducted by the Gallup Organization. Called "The People & the Press," a prime 1986 study offered several conclusions that challenged the conventional wisdom concerning public opinion and the nation's news media. There was no credibility crisis for the media, the study maintained, if credibility was being defined as believability. Secondly, the data did not confirm journalists' concern that the public perceived them as being arrogant and inaccurate.

The overall measures showed a wide range of public support, but not a deep reservoir. The public indicated its appreciation of the press's watchdog role against the government, which outweighed the dissatisfactions with news media performance. The public gave the news media good but not excellent marks for believability. In another bit of caution, the researchers pointed out that media critics are more critical than supporters are supportive, indicating some softness in the overall support. The Times Mirror survey concluded that the public is ready to side with the press in matters of governmental wrongdoing:

> The public says "no" to formal censorship and says "no" to prior restraint. The public says "no" to government requiring fairness in news coverage. The public says "no" to the government requiring equal advertising time on television or space in newspapers for political candidates. And the public says "yes" emphatically, to publishing a story such as the Pentagon Papers.[75]

The Minneapolis-based MORI Research, Inc. conducted a study of adults for the American Society of Newspaper Editors (ASNE) entitled "Newspaper Credibility: Building Reader Trust." This study, which gave more emphasis to public dissatisfactions, found that three-fourths of adults had some problem with media credibility and that one-sixth expressed frustration with the news media.

However, the two studies demonstrated similar credibility rates for newspapers and television. The Times Mirror survey showed 70 percent of people in positive categories and 30 percent among the negative. The ASNE study said 75 percent gave a high or medium rating to newspapers and 73 percent such ratings to television news. Interestingly, the Times Mirror study showed that some readers with the highest regard for the press as an institution were among its more severe critics of performance. Forty-five percent said newspapers were politically biased, and 34 percent said they often were inaccurate. For these reasons newspapers trailed television slightly in the "highly believable" category (see Table 18–1). White House correspondents ranked lower than anchorpeople, and President Reagan's total believability rating was 68, well below that of media personalities and institutions, which recorded ratings above 80 percent. (See Table 18–2.)

A third study, conducted by MORI for the Associated Press Managing Editors Association, examined the opinions of 1,333 journalists from 51 newspapers selected randomly. The goal was to analyze the credibility gap that many journalists perceived as existing between them and readers. It was called "Journalists and Readers: Bridging the Credibility Gap." The study uncovered strong feelings of worry about the media and the public trust, particularly among senior editors. While the journalists thought their newspapers were more credible and accurate than readers had indicated in the ASNE study, they agreed almost unanimously that credibility was a serious problem. A major concern of journalists was the lack of public knowledge and interest about issues vital to the survival of the press system. Results from the other surveys substantiated this concern. Only 45 percent of respondents to the Times Mirror survey could identify the First Amendment or the Bill of Rights as providing for freedom of the press.

The fourth major effort was made by the Gannett Center for Media Studies at Columbia University, which published "The Media and the People," a review of polling and research findings about media credibility over a 50-year period.

TABLE 18–1   Believability Rankings (Times Mirror)

NEWS INSTITUTION	HIGHLY BELIEV- ABLE	TOTAL FOR BELIEV- ABILITY	NEWS PERSONALITY	HIGHLY BELIEV- ABLE	TOTAL FOR BELIEV- ABILITY
Wall Street Journal	45	87	Walter Cronkite (CBS)	57	92
Readers' Digest	40	81	Dan Rather (CBS)	44	89
Cable News Network	38	84	McNeil-Lehrer (PBS)	43	83
Local TV news	36	85	Ted Koppel (ABC)	41	88
Time	35	85	Peter Jennings (ABC)	40	90
National TV news	34	87	John Chancellor (NBC)	39	89
Newsweek	31	86	David Brinkley (ABC)	38	90
Radio news	30	84	Tom Brokaw (NBC)	37	88
Local daily newspaper	29	84	Mike Wallace (CBS)	35	83
National newspapers	25	78	Barbara Walters (ABC)	30	78

TABLE 18–2   Public Attitudes toward Newspapers (Times Mirror)

ATTITUDES TOWARD NEWSPAPERPEOPLE	*ATTITUDES TOWARD NEWSPAPERS*
Percent Favorable	*Percent Unfavorable*
79 Care about quality of work	73 Invade people's privacy
78 Fair to President Reagan	60 Too much bad news
72 Highly professional	55 Try to cover up mistakes
55 Get the facts straight	53 Favor one side (biased)
52 Stand up for America	53 Often influenced by powerful

Times Mirror and the Gallup organization reported a follow-up study in November 1989 that showed some decline in press believability since 1985, averaging 5 or 6 percentage points for news organizations. But the overall favorability of the press still stood at 82 percent for network TV news, 80 percent for local TV news, and 77 percent for newspapers. Cable News Network showed a 5 percent gain in "most highly believable" to rank second to the *Wall Street Journal.* The survey also showed rising support for press freedom and the watchdog function of the press. But only 45 percent could identify the Bill of Rights and First Amendment, and 63 percent criticized the press for overzealous coverage of ethics scandals as opposed to straight news reporting.

Later studies supported the relatively strong confidence level that accompanied the public's bluntly stated unhappiness with certain aspects of news media performance. A 1993 Times Mirror poll reported that 42 percent of respondents said they had "quite a bit" or "a great deal" of confidence in newspapers. That was the highest confidence rating since a 51 percent score in a 1979 Gallup poll. Overall, 88 percent said the news media do a "very good or fairly good" job. Nevertheless, there was growing disenchantment with sensationalism, bias, and inaccuracy. Significantly, persons in the 45-to-64 age category said they had less confidence than when they first began reading newspapers and watching television news.[76] In a 1992 postelection survey, Times Mirror reported that voters felt campaign coverage had vastly improved in comparison with the 1988 campaign, with 77 percent stating they had had enough information to make an informed judgment—a strong sign of confidence.[77]

In the 1990s, the credibility problem continued. A 1995 Freedom Forum report entitled "Nothing Sacred: Journalism, Politics and Public Trust in a Tell-All Age," found that people think that journalists are too interested in power relationships as a news topic. A whopping 71 percent agreed that the country is governed by a few powerful politicians, journalists, and businesses, and that nothing the public does matters. A 1997 Newseum study entitled "News Junkies, News Critics" found that 63 percent believed that the press is "too manipulated by special interests." Some also thought that big business (49 percent) and elected officials (39 percent) exercise undue influence on news judgment. A significant 63 percent thought that "the profit motive" improperly influences reporting, and 54 percent believed that corporate media owners and advertisers have too much power.

On a more positive note, a 1997 study conducted by the Newspaper Association of America and ASNE found that people rely heavily on local newspapers for news about their local communities, local government, and political views, and information to help the community deal with problems. But the Pew Research Center found that favorability ratings are declining for media across the board: For example, in 1985, local newspapers received an 81 percent favorability rating, compared to 78 percent in 1992 and 74 percent in 1997.

CRITICISM OF TELEVISION NEWS

The emotions of the 1960s brought the first strong criticisms of television news. Southerners charged that network film crews had distorted the racial picture during the Freedom Rides; blacks and whites alike were angered by coverage of the urban riots; doves and hawks both thought the Vietnam news to be slanted; some veteran broadcasters, like Fred W. Friendly, thought their bosses sought ratings at the expense of public service; and conservatives led by former Vice President Agnew thundered against the perceived "liberal bias" of the commentators and reporters covering the Nixon administration. The criticism of general programming, given impetus by FCC Chairman Newton Minow's "vast wasteland" speech in 1961, soon spread to every area of the system.

But beginning in the 1970s and continuing into the 1990s, the criticisms focused on the very essence of television news, the variables that make it what it is. Edith Efron had written *The News Twisters* in 1971 as an attempt to discredit the major networks, but in 1973 media critic Edward J. Epstein published his scholarly *News from Nowhere,* which simply showed how economic and logistical factors as much as subjective judgments severely hampered the scope and quality of television news.[78] Then followed a rash of criticism in popular publications of the so-called happy-talk format devised by ABC for its stations; the hiring of nonjournalistic consultants to advise on the hiring of anchorpeople; the designing of fancy sets; and the length of story and film segments (the "top-40" concept); the overuse of "pretty faces"; the team approach in which several persons sit around a table; and the extensive use of feature material in a magazine format.

Leading newscasters like Walter Cronkite and David Brinkley readily admitted the weaknesses of the existing system; Cronkite severely criticized the "pretty faces" on local television shows and pushed for a one-hour evening news show in an effort to avoid some of the superficiality. That extra half-hour would have come from local station time, however, and plans for one-hour news shows were shelved by all three networks. To the consternation of traditionalists, the major gains in ratings were made by those local stations that pushed ahead with the lighter approach to news through "mini-documentaries" dealing with sensational subjects and specialists who lined up to report on health tips and consumer news. Increasingly large local stations sent their own correspondents to the scene of world and national events, or received the news from satellite syndicates such as CONUS Communications or Cable News Network. This made affiliates less dependent on the networks. In fact, network affiliation dropped slightly (ABC/Capital Cities, 230; CBS and NBC, about 200), thus opening the door for Rupert Murdoch to launch a news division within his Fox Network that was built around seven Fox-owned stations and had the potential of 140 affiliates, some of whom had been lured away from CBS. The former president of CBS News, Van Gordon Sauter, was hired to grab a share of the quickly fragmenting audience. Adding to the uncertainty of the news divisions, all three networks were open for sale, with Time-Warner, the Walt Disney Company, Viacom, and the Turner Broadcasting Company among the interested parties. Time-Warner and Viacom began small networks in 1995 (Warner Brothers Network and United Paramount Network), trying to follow in Fox's footsteps by leading with entertainment shows.

The networks' vulnerability to the advances of cable television and the independents was troublesome. Their share of the viewing audience dropped to 57 percent in the 1994–95 season and was eroding about 4 percent per year. In 1995 ABC led in overall ratings, while CBS plunged to alarming low audience figures. Nevertheless, the three original networks demonstrated their worth during times of historical moment. Anchors Peter Jennings, Tom Brokaw, and Dan Rather and a slew of supporting reporters could be counted on to provide the appropriate background and drama. The news divisions also maintained their ability to stitch together late-evening "news specials." But much of this was minimized by broadcast veterans, who harked back to the 1960s and 1970s, when it was possible to air a long documentary dealing with an important subject, and network newsrooms were filled with people who felt they had a higher calling in life.

Rather looked back on broadcast news history in 1993, telling broadcast executives that a collective lack of courage—the type of bravery once demonstrated by his hero Edward R. Murrow—was the cause of the demise of broadcast news. The reason, in Rather's view, that the line between news and entertainment vanished was that

> we've gone Hollywood—we've all succumbed to the Hollywoodization of the news—because we were afraid not to. We trivialize important subjects. We put videotape through a Cuisinart trying to come up with high speed, MTV-style cross-cuts. And just to cover our asses, we give the best slots to gossip and prurience.[79]

Times had changed so drastically that major news organizations, both print and broadcast, felt free to quote the *National Enquirer* and the *Star* while reporting allegations of sexual misconduct by Bill Clinton prior to his election, the Tonya Harding–Nancy Kerrigan ice skating rivalry that led to an attack on Kerrigan, and other bizarre stories involving sex and scandal. The main question for television news executives was: if the tabloid television shows like *Hard Copy* and *Inside Edition* are running with a rumor-filled story, should they ignore it or run with it? Too often they included the rumors in their account.

O. J. Simpson's arrest after a Los Angeles freeway chase in 1994 televised worldwide by CNN led to virtual nonstop coverage for weeks with a flurry of stories that obliterated news from Washington, Bosnia, and North Korea. In what became the most publicized trial in U.S. history—more television time was devoted to Simpson than to the Gulf War—the world was fascinated by the speculation that the handsome former football great and Hollywood celebrity may have murdered his beautiful ex-wife and a young man and left behind telltale clues. The media mob outside of the Los Angeles courthouse turned the area into a circus whenever Simpson's lawyers walked through or whenever a new rumor surfaced. While the reporting of the courtroom proceedings was generally well handled, reporters passed on a number of rumors harmful to Simpson that proved to be false.

Brokaw, like Rather and Jennings, was willing to take his share of responsibility for some of the sensationalized stories that appeared on his evening news show. But he worried that too many in journalism were content to "live by O. J. alone":

> We are becoming a tribal America. . . . Every ethnic, financial, cultural, political, and religious group looks to its own interests, each trying to exploit the weakness of the other. . . . That's a story that will continue well beyond the end of the O. J. Simpson trial—and it will have a far greater effect on this country.[80]

The tragic and untimely death of Diana, Princess of Wales, in August 1997 in a Paris car accident, resulted in a deluge of media coverage. In the weeks following the accident, the most photographed individual in the world became the center of the world's attention.

ABC, NBC, and CBS devoted 197 minutes to the story during that week, at that time second only to the 1991 coverage of the coup against Mikhail Gorbachev (225 minutes of coverage).

People tuned in and read voraciously about the princess's final days. CNN reported that on August 31, 1997, the night of Diana's death, viewership peaked at 4.6 million households. It continued its network-wide coverage with an hour-long primetime special edition of "Impact" on the life and legacy of Diana. *Time* magazine's first issue about Diana's death had newsstand sales of 850,000 (up 650,000 from usual). *USA TODAY*'s circulation rose several hundred thousand during the week after the accident. More than 50 million people watched the August 31 "60 Minutes" report on Diana.

Coupled with the public's insatiable consumption of news about the princess was a vitriol directed against the media, and against paparazzi in particular, who were alleged to have played a part in the accident. Laws protecting personal privacy against intrusion were introduced in legislatures all over the world. As the public ate up news and information about Diana, they grumbled about media overkill as many stations carried live or taped broadcasts of the entire funeral procession. And many complained about the relatively small amount of coverage given to the death of Mother Teresa of Calcutta, who died the day before Diana's funeral.

The coverage of Diana's death was eclipsed just over a year later, when the Center for Media and Public Affairs reported that ABC, NBC, and CBS aired more coverage of the Clinton-Lewinsky allegations in the first seven days than they did in the first week of coverage about Diana's accident and death. The three networks devoted 67 percent of their total coverage to the emerging scandal.

In July 1999 when John Fitzgerald Kennedy, Jr.'s small plane crashed in the Atlantic Ocean near Martha's Vinyard, killing him and his wife and sister-in-law, the familiar criticism of media excess was again raised. For a week, front-page news stories and continuous live television coverage eclipsed all other news, including compelling revelations of Serb atrocities and mass graves in the aftermath of the recent NATO bombing campaign. Reporters staked out the Kennedy compound in Hyannisport and published accounts that were often little more than inconsequential gleanings, as the Navy and Coast Guard searched for and retrieved the wreckage and bodies. "The media, in making so much of this particular bad news, imposed their own love for the newsworthy Kennedys upon the public," wrote John Updike in the *New Yorker.* "The news frenzy's object might have smiled one of his light, practiced smiles of forbearance at seeing his privacy definitively invaded in one wrapup after another, and such a tide of eulogy whipped up for a man whose life . . . could be described as a glamorous preamble."[81]

Most criticism of television news centered on the local product. "If it bleeds, it leads, if it votes, it don't," was the cynical headline over a FAIR-sponsored survey of local news in Los Angeles, where stations devoted from 30 to 54 percent of air time to crime news and virtually ignored preelection coverage of the 1994 California gubernatorial primary. Included on that ballot was Proposition 187, which gained national attention by calling for the end to health and education support for undocumented immigrant workers and their families. During 35 hours of air time, only two of seven stations mentioned the primaries and then for only a total of eight minutes.[82] Sadly, a Times Mirror survey of "The People, the Press & Politics" showed that a majority of people under age 35 depended on television for campaign news.[83]

Meanwhile the chase for high-paid local anchors continued in the age of agents and media consultants. In major cities it was not uncommon for some anchors to receive from $1 to $2 million per year at the same time that executives blamed declining revenues for newsroom cutbacks. By the early 1990s the poor morale in most television newsrooms had become the major topic of conversation. Of course there were exceptions: some major market stations, like WFAA in Dallas–Fort Worth, maintained high professionalism, while a number of others in middle and smaller markets exhibited admirable performance levels.[84]

But for the most part, when people discussed local television news they talked of helicopter coverage of freeway chases, bodies in the street following another drive-by shooting, and the crushed hulls of automobiles. Missing on all levels—from the networks to small-town stations—were clearly told stories about the effects of global economic pressures, the decline of public education, and the reasons for community violence.

TELEVISION'S BIGGEST AUDIENCES

The growth of broadcasting, with its accompanying economic power, was startling (see Table 18–3), as was its coverage of public events. More than 61 million households—about 150 million people—were tuned to President Bush's speech on the first day of the Gulf War in 1991, the largest audience for a single news event in U.S. television history. Audiences from 100 to 130 million were recorded for such events as the 1969 moon landing, President Nixon's 1972 China visit, the Munich Olympic tragedy of that year, Nixon's resignation in 1974, the 1976 Bicentennial celebrations, the attempt on President Reagan's life in 1981, and festivities at the Statue of Liberty in 1986, plus Super Bowls, World Series, and other special events. The O. J. Simpson freeway chase of 1994 was seen by an estimated 95 million people. The largest worldwide audiences were for World Cup matches, where satellites had the potential to bring images to an estimated 1 billion people.

The dependency on television was demonstrated on January 28, 1986, when the space shuttle Challenger blew up seconds after lift-off, killing the crew. Within 30 minutes 69 percent of American adults had heard of the tragedy, from word of mouth (37 percent), television (36 percent), or radio (22 percent). But 82 percent said they eventually got most of their news from television.[85] When news of President Kennedy's assassination in 1963 became known, the New York City television audience jumped from 30 percent to 70 percent and rose to 93 percent during the funeral service, when for a few moments the nation fell silent.

In the non-news field, 110 million people watched *Gone with the Wind* in 1976; the following year *Roots,* a series tracing black history, set a number of records for that period. During the eight consecutive nights that it was aired, it was seen by an estimated 130 million people. ABC repeated its success in 1983 with a week-long showing of *The*

TABLE 18–3   The Growth of Broadcasting

	1961	*1985*	*1997*
On-air AM stations	3,539	4,805	4,863
On-air FM stations	815	4,888	7,271
On-air TV Stations	583	1,194	1,554
Households with radio	49,500,000	86,700,000	98,800,000
Households with TV	47,200,000	85,900,000	97,000,000
Households with cable	725,000	34,740,000	64,020,000

Source: *Broadcasting & Cable Yearbook, 1997*

Winds of War. The highest-rated single program in television history was the 2½-hour final episode of CBS's 11-year series *M*A*S*H,* shown on February 28, 1983, to 77 percent of all U.S. homes watching television. Technically the all-time record for a single program belonged to a January 1953 segment of the *I Love Lucy* show during which Lucille Ball, pregnant in real life, gave birth to a son. However, there were only 21.2 million television sets at the time.[86]

CBS NEWS

Dan Rather inherited Walter Cronkite's anchor chair at the *CBS Evening News* in 1981 after signing an $8 million 5-year contract, and he immediately felt the tremendous pressure of trying to maintain the CBS lead in the ratings. After getting off to a slow start as the audience became used to Rather's intensity and rapid delivery, CBS ran off a string of 213 consecutive weeks in first place before slipping in June 1986. Rather had clearly become comfortable with his audience. His trademarks were his sincerity, his ready smile, and his pullover sweaters.

The ratings war became a three-way battle in 1986, when NBC's *Nightly News* topped CBS in the fourth quarter, the first time NBC had won a quarter since 1967.[87] Deep concern set in at "Black Rock," the CBS headquarters that only months before had survived a questionable "junk bonds" takeover bid by the flamboyant Ted Turner. A series of management shifts saw 84-year-old William S. Paley come out of retirement to resume his old board chairman's position, Laurence Tisch of the Loews corporate empire become the chief operating officer, and veteran producer Howard Stringer assume the presidency of CBS News. By late 1987 the *CBS Evening News* again had a narrow lead.

During the 1988 campaign Rather became the center of controversy when he aggressively challenged candidate George Bush about his Iran-Contra connections, only to have the vice president counter with a tongue-lashing for raising the issue. During one heated exchange Bush chided Rather for an earlier episode when Rather, angry over a mix up, left his CBS anchor chair—and the network—empty for several embarrassing minutes while his producers tried to find him. However, many journalists praised Rather for his courage in asking about Bush's mysterious involvement, and later it was learned Bush was in fact considerably involved with various Iran-Contra aspects.

CBS dropped its *CBS Morning News* show in late 1986 after more than three decades. A number of experiments with anchors had failed to boost ratings. The unveiling of a new magazine format show, the jazzy *West 57th St.,* featuring four young and relatively unknown reporters, brought mixed reviews, but the short-lived (1985–88) show scored with news beats on involvement of Contra arms suppliers with drug smuggling. The Sunday news-interview show *Face the Nation,* dating to November 7, 1954, ended its run in 1983.

However, the *60 Minutes* magazine show continued as the most profitable and, in terms of ratings, the most popular news program in television history. Executive Producer Don Hewitt's CBS career dated to the days of Douglas Edwards and Edward R. Murrow. His sense of storytelling and dramatic investigation made *60 Minutes* the provocative, oft-quoted show that brought its viewers the unexpected. His ratings success easily allowed him to weather criticism that the show exploited its reporters' fame and was too sensational.[88]

When CBS emerged from its internal battling it was clear that the network would no longer be able to dominate its rivals. Times had changed. In effect, the three evening news shows were similar in content, quality, and personalities. So were their 1986–87 ratings of 12 each for CBS and NBC, and 10.6 for ABC. CBS's days as ratings leader were numbered however with ABC poised to take over. By 1990 the news organization faced huge cuts in operating expenses. At the start of the Gulf War the network had only 30 staffers in the area, half that of NBC and ABC, while CNN had 130. All of this combined to plunge CBS to third place in the ratings after which more foreign and domestic bureaus were closed.

CBS made a highly publicized move to regain lost ratings in 1994, when Connie Chung joined Rather as co-anchor and shared major assignments. The experiment failed and an unhappy Chung left CBS in 1995. Rather, in his fourth decade with CBS, continued with his *48 Hours* magazine show. The sensitive, poetic Charles Kuralt retired that year after 37 years with CBS, leaving a distinguished record as anchor of the *Sunday Morning* show. Rita Braver was dependable on the White House beat.

In this wild rush for survival the networks did not hesitate to raid each other, breaking up some old reporting teams. Familiar faces from one network would suddenly appear on another, reflecting the million dollar salaries being offered.

One of those wooed to CBS twice was Bill Moyers, a former press secretary for Lyndon Johnson who became alienated by the Vietnam War and accepted the publisher's chair at *Newsday.* From there Moyers went to public television, where his sharp intellect produced some moving looks at world events. He briefly became involved with *CBS Reports* before returning to public television to produce *Bill Moyers' Journal,* a long-running series dealing with current events and the human condition. Later his 17-part *Creativity* series traced the achievements of productive people. Finally he was back with CBS, this time giving nightly news commentaries, in Eric Sevareid's old spot, planning documentaries, and hosting the short-lived *Our Times.* His frank approach to life, keen perception, and Texas populism combined to make him one of the most respected of television's observers. In his warm, soft style, he likened television to a "national campfire" around which the nation sits listening. But the minister's son could be severe with those who pushed for a war in Central America or who threatened the health of the nation's poor.

(© CBS News 1996)   *(©1999, ABC, Inc.)*

Dan Rather, CBS anchor   Diane Sawyer, ABC News

On those occasions he spoke in the tradition of Murrow and Sevareid, informing the people of their history and their responsibility. Shoved into the background by a new format that allotted more time for news features, Moyers left CBS in 1986 to form his own production company. He would be back in the public television business. The infrequent CBS commentaries gave "time only to make your point but not to build your case," he said.

Diane Sawyer, one of several CBS reporters targeted for success, became well known on the morning show and as a regular on *60 Minutes*. Hailed for her sharp intellect, interviewing skill, and easy manner, Sawyer brought a distinctive charm to CBS programming before she left to join ABC. A veteran of Washington politics, she had worked in the Nixon White House. This originally alarmed some of her new colleagues, but she earned their respect through her fair-minded reporting. Lesley Stahl and Steve Kroft later filled prized *60 Minutes* spots, while Andy Rooney continued his humorous commentaries.

The training of new reporters in CBS traditions had been part of Paley's style before he retired in September 1982 after 54 years of running the company that he had founded. Throughout the years Paley had kept his keen eyes on the news department, working first with Ed Klauber and Paul White and later with Frank Stanton to develop top-rated news teams. He was not without faults; he argued with Ed Murrow and Fred Friendly about their shows, and during the Vietnam-Watergate years he was regarded as being too friendly to the Johnson-Nixon point of view. But, overall, Paley was a strong leader who helped his CBS News employees develop standards for others to follow.

NBC NEWS

Tom Brokaw, a former White House correspondent who had dueled with Rather for scoops before becoming host of the *Today* show in the early 1970s, was named sole anchor of the *NBC Nightly News* in July 1983, after briefly sharing the anchor responsibilities with former CBS reporter Roger Mudd.

Although he did not achieve the top spot in the ratings chase, the urbane Brokaw maintained NBC's high credibility and generally escaped criticism, although during the Reagan years there were complaints that he was too critical of the administration.[89] On one occasion Reagan singled out both Rather and Brokaw as examples of powerful broadcasters who were giving the public a poor impression of his programs. By 1990 NBC had moved ahead of CBS but trailed front-running ABC by a wide margin, as an increasingly conservative audience felt more comfortable with ABC's approach.

Judy Woodruff led NBC White House coverage before leaving for public television. Chris Wallace, the son of CBS's Mike Wallace, became a fixture at the White House. Connie Chung was anchor of the early morning news show in 1983 and graduated to key evening and anchor spots before joining CBS.

John Chancellor left his anchor position with hopes that network news would expand to an hour format. He expressed regrets over what he termed a lack of sophistication in television's ability to select stories and to deliver enough important facts to help the viewer understand the stories. "We could have a three-hour program every day and not be able to cover adequately some of the elements of the news which I regard as important. However big the vessel is, it just is not designed to provide a full service."[90]

NBC's success in the evening news ratings was matched by its morning *Today* show, which had fallen behind ABC's *Good Morning America* in 1980. In early 1986 the combination of Bryant Gumbel and Jane Pauley passed rival David Hartman in the audience count. The happiness was short-lived, however. The ratings slipped, and Pauley's position became a revolving door beginning in 1990, when she was replaced after an embarrassing

Tom Brokaw, NBC anchor

*(© National Broadcasting Company, Inc.
1999. All Rights Reserved.)*

internal squabble. She emerged with her own news-magazine show and frequent fill-ins for Brokaw, while *Today* began to battle back with Katie Couric as Gumbel's sidekick.

There was other controversy. In late 1985 General Electric bought RCA, NBC's parent company, in the biggest media merger in U.S. history, a $6.28 billion deal. GE Chairman John F. Welch, Jr., had the reputation of being a tough cost-cutter, and NBC news executives eventually felt the effects. In 1990 the network was accused of broadcasting reenactments of news stories, and in 1993 there was severe criticism of a *Dateline NBC* report that showed a General Motors pickup truck catching fire upon impact. NBC admitted that the truck was rigged to break into flames. Battling GE's incessant cuts and—like its two old network rivals—cable television and Fox Broadcasting, the news division responded with an expanded schedule for *Dateline NBC,* airing the show on three evenings with Pauley and Stone Phillips as principal anchors and Brokaw, Gumbel, Couric, and Maria Shriver anchoring and reporting.

The talent was there. Brian Williams was a highly touted White House correspondent, replacing the indefatigable Andrea Mitchell, who became chief foreign affairs correspondent. In one year Mitchell reported 184 times, 40 more than her nearest competitor. Her colleague on Capitol Hill, Lisa Myers, was close behind, while Tim Russert emerged as a leading political commentator. He served as host of *Meet the Press,* television's longest-running program, which dated to November 6, 1947. Bill Moyers, always thoughtful and sometimes refreshingly provocative, assumed the role as commentator for the evening news show in 1995, filling a void left by Chancellor's retirement. While NBC maintained that tradition, David Sarnoff and his son, Robert, builders of the vast empire, were gone.[91] And gone too was NBC Radio, founded in 1926 as the first national network. It was sold in 1987 to Westwood One, Inc., a youth-oriented California company in which GE would hold an investment interest. NBC kept its radio stations.

ABC NEWS

Peter Jennings, a Canadian national with 15 years of foreign reporting experience, was named anchor of ABC's *World News Tonight* show in September, 1983 following the death of anchor Frank Reynolds. Reynolds, who had anchored breaking events like the assassination attempt on President Reagan's life with a quiet professionalism, had earned a reputation for his direct questions and dogged persistence. Despite Reynolds' high energy level, the recruitment of good talent, and ABC's innovative use of flashy graphics, Jennings inherited a show that lagged behind number one ranked CBS.

Jennings had held the anchor post once before. He took over at age 26 in 1964 and lasted until 1968 when all parties admitted the experiment had been a mistake. He then reported extensively from abroad, particularly the key London post, from where he joined Reynolds and Max Robinson in the 1978 three-anchor format which also failed to generate success. In the age of satellite delivery the home audience got used to seeing the polished Jennings anchor *World News Tonight* from Tokyo, Moscow, and other scenes of historic events, battling with Brokaw and Rather for nightly ratings.

Generating audience support through his calm treatment of the news, with his Canadian accent showing occasionally when he came to "a-bout," Jennings brought ABC into the lead in 1989. Surveys showed audience confidence in Jennings' knowledge of world affairs and his ability to bring troubling news in a non-threatening manner. He was cited for his insight and sensitivity in the coverage of the many Middle East crises, particularly the Gulf War where he and his fellow anchors found themselves reporting from the war zone. The *World News Tonight* program also featured the aggressive White House reporting of Sam Donald-

(© 1999, ABC, Inc.)

Peter Jennings, ABC anchor

son and later Brit Hume, and the work of specialty reporters like Peggy Wehmeyer, the first network correspondent assigned to cover religious and spiritual news on a full-time basis.

Roone Arledge, the colorful president of ABC's news division, assembled an impressive lineup of reporters, writers, producers and anchors. In addition to Jennings on the evening news show and Ted Koppel on *Nightline,* Diane Sawyer gave luster to *Prime Time Live* and Barbara Walters and Hugh Downs held their own with *20-20.*

Koppel was the most exciting ABC personality, an English-born journalist who in 1963, at age 23, became the youngest network correspondent in television history. After covering Vietnam and the State Department during the Nixon and Ford years, Koppel emerged as the no-nonsense host of *Nightline,* a show that ran from 11:30 to midnight, Eastern time, in competition with NBC's Johnny Carson show. Beginning as a 15-minute update of the Iranian crisis in March 1980, the show evolved into nightly looks at one of the events or personalities currently in the news, often related to that day's leading news story. Live interviews were the main feature, with Koppel asking questions back and forth to guests of opposing views.

In following years the audience became used to Koppel telling the affiliates that the show would be running over. Viewers knew that on the evening of any big news day Koppel and his crew would be ready to add to the news, not just repeat it. A series of broadcasts from South Africa that brought leaders from opposing sides together earned praise in 1986, as did a historic program from Jerusalem in 1988, when Jews and Palestinian Arabs came together. In addition to assisting with many special events, he also presided over ABC's *Viewpoint,* a novel show on which correspondents, news subjects, and members of a studio audience discussed the responsibilities and tastes of the broadcasters.

Like its opponents in the television wars, ABC suffered its share of setbacks. With less money it had kept pace over the years by offering as news commentators Howard K. Smith, known for his blunt, crisp phrases, Quincy Howe of World War II fame, and Reynolds, also one of ABC's top political reporters. Then, when the network was hitting its stride in the 1980s, it was hurt by the same cutbacks that slowed CBS and NBC. Capital Cities Communications bought the American Broadcasting Company in early 1985 and assumed control in January 1986, paying $3.5 billion. A stringent cost-cutting program followed.

Roone Arledge retained his position as president of ABC News when Capital Cities took over, but gave up his other longtime job as president of ABC Sports. The network's *Wide World of Sports, Monday Night Football,* and Olympic coverage had been sensationally successful. Among the innovations of the Arledge years were the slow-motion cameras and instant replays that were so common later. Commentator Howard Cosell was ABC's most prominent sports personality. Arledge came under criticism during the 1984 Olympic Games in Los Angeles, however, when critics said the coverage was jingoistic, with producers opting for extra shots of U.S. athletes and ignoring some of the outstanding foreign achievements. Cynics said ABC was "America's network." There was an outpouring of protest from a newly established group, Fairness and Accuracy in Reporting (FAIR), and many other media critics in 1987 when ABC broadcast a 14½-hour miniseries *Amerika* that portrayed a United States conquered by the Soviets and run by United Nations occupation troops with the help of American appeasers.

While the *Close-Up* documentary staff was affected by budget cuts, efforts were made to maintain the *20-20* magazine show hosted by Hugh Downs, who had logged more hours on national commercial television than anyone in broadcasting history. The show had been designed to compete with CBS's *60 Minutes.* Walters joined him later, and the show remained popular. ABC launched *Good Morning America* in 1975, and it battled NBC's *Today* show for ratings. The ABC *Issues and Answers* news-interview show, a fixture since

Ted Koppel

Bernard Shaw

1961, was replaced in 1981 by *This Week with David Brinkley.* That show, also featuring Donaldson, Cokie Roberts of National Public Radio, and conservative syndicated columnist George Will, became the leading Sunday morning attraction, topping *Meet the Press* and out-classing *The McLaughlin Group.*[92]

ABC, like its competitors, suffered cutbacks under the ownership of Capital Cities/ABC, whose executive officers complained about Arledge's free spending as he moved the news division into first place. However, there was enough in 1994 for the network to outbid NBC and resign Sawyer to a contract calling for an annual salary estimated to be about $6 million. In addition to *Prime Time Live,* she was tabbed to join Walters and Forrest Sawyer on other magazine shows. Catherine Crier, a Texas judge who became a popular CNN news anchor and talk show host, was added to the *20-20* line-up and given major anchoring assignments. ABC dealt NBC another blow by forming a partnership with the British Broadcasting Corporation (BBC) to share worldwide television and radio news coverage. Besides exchanging footage and audio tapes, the organizations agreed to plan coverage together and share correspondents and production teams in a giant cost-saving effort. NBC and CBS would continue a limited exchange of video news footage with the BBC. The contract also was aimed at trimming Cable News Network's lead in world coverage, for the BBC actively planned to compete with CNN.

CABLE NEWS NETWORK

Ted Turner, the creator of "superstation" WTBS in Atlanta, launched his Cable News Network in June 1980 after first using a satellite to offer cable stations sports and reruns of movies. Turner began the satellite service in 1976, a year after Home Box Office's successful satellite-cable experiments.

Making a direct challenge to the three established networks, CNN's 24-hour service included hourly news summaries, heavy treatment of sports and business, news specials, and lengthy interviews on various subjects throughout the day. The initial experiment met with mixed reviews: critics complained about poor visual quality and inexperienced reporters. However, the quick access to news and a direct, no-nonsense approach pleased many viewers who were impressed with the overall coverage.

By the late 1980s there was full professional recognition of CNN's reporting of world and national events. The CNN achievements during the Gulf War came as no surprise to those who had noted a steady string of successes. The first came in 1981, when CNN was the first to report that President Reagan had not escaped injury during the assassination attempt. Because of its ability to stay on the air long after the other networks had returned to regular programming, CNN began to build a loyal audience.[93]

Another scoop came when CNN's films of the El Salvador fighting showed an American military "adviser" carrying a weapon contrary to regulations. This caused a nation-wide furor. Demanding to share White House pool responsibilities, Turner won a court battle to have his network represented. Former CBS correspondent Daniel Schorr was an early CNN commentator, bringing with him an audience following.

CNN reports were beamed by satellite to many stations outside of the cable network and during such events as the congressional inquiry into the Iran-Contra scandal, viewers automatically turned to CNN for gavel-to-gavel coverage. Despite its popularity, critics contended that CNN was merely a "common carrier" of information, like a press association, running live press conferences and updating breaking news without offering much background interpretation. Defenders cited shows like *Larry King Live* and *World Report,* among the best on television, and a wide range of general information, business, and sports programming. Added prestige came in 1990, when Tom Johnson left his post as publisher of the *Los Angeles Times* to become president and chief executive of CNN.

There was a bizarre quality to CNN's popularity. It became common for a person in one country to call someone at the scene of a world crisis in another country and learn that the other person was getting prime information from CNN. This happened during the 1989 invasion of Panama, when residents of Panama City saw CNN's coverage of shooting scenes occurring only a few blocks away from their apartments. During the Gulf War diplomats and generals throughout the Middle East as well as in the Pentagon kept tuned for the latest CNN update. The highest praise came from NBC's Tom Brokaw, who on the first night of the Gulf War introduced his viewers to CNN's team in Baghdad. After showing CNN footage and talking with CNN's Bernard Shaw, Brokaw said, "CNN used to be called the little network that could. It is no longer a little network."

Indeed it wasn't, with its sprawling Atlanta broadcast center, large Washington staff, 10 U.S. bureaus, and 24 more overseas. In 1999 CNN and its separate Headline News channel had access to 76 and 71 million U.S. homes, respectively, through more than 11,000 cable clients. CNN International (CNNI), the world's only 24-hour global news network, was transmitted to more than 200 nations and territories over a dozen satellites to an estimated audience of 150 million persons, including thousands of hotels, government offices and businesses. Much of CNNI's programming originated in London; Asian production facilities were in Hong Kong. Believing that the U.S. audience wanted more foreign news, the company made CNNI available to its domestic clients in 1995. Four international feeds from Atlanta served viewers in North America, Latin America, Europe, and Asia. At the turn of the 21st century, CNN's Spanish-language channel was available in 7.9 million households, in Latin America and some regions of the United States.

Overall, CNN boasted more than 800 broadcast affiliates worldwide, more than any other news group, including more than 400 U.S. stations affiliated with CBS, NBC, ABC,

Christiane Amanpour, CNN commentator

Judy Woodruff, CNN anchor

or Fox, and about 200 independent stations. Its U.S. staff of more than 3500 was about twice as large as those of its competitors. However, salary schedules were lower, leading to the loss of some talented journalists. In one case, however, loyalty won out over money. CNN's star foreign correspondent, Christiane Amanpour, ended a bidding war with other networks by saying she enjoyed the freedom found at CNN.

At the heart of the operation was the low-keyed, straightfaced Shaw, the principal anchor who became part of the original 1980 anchoring team after successful years with CBS. Well known to worldwide viewers were anchor Judy Woodruff, legal analyst Greta Van Susteren, John King at the White House, Andrea Koppel at the State Department, Jamie McIntyre at the Pentagon, and television's leading talk show personality, Larry King. Expecting instantaneous coverage, many viewers instinctively tuned to CNN whenever a major story was breaking.

FOX BROADCASTING

Rupert Murdoch and Barry Diller founded Fox Broadcasting in 1987, and its first prime-time offering was the sitcom *Married . . . with Children,* an "aggressively tacky" show with "bite," in the words of one commentator. At the time of Fox's debut, most observers scoffed at the concept of a fourth network. But Fox's willingness to take risks while the older networks rested on their laurels allowed it to gain a respectable chunk of network viewership. In fact, although it remained fourth in primetime ratings for the 1998 season, it averaged 12 million viewers per hour of prime time, compared to 15.4 million for NBC, 13.9 million for CBS, and 13.7 million for ABC, according to Nielsen Media Research.

Fox's willingness to take on challenges usually ducked by the other networks manifested itself in such durable shows as the offbeat cartoon *The Simpsons* and the stylistically

Greta Van Susteren, CNN legal analyst

(Fox News)

Brit Hume, Fox News

dramatic and dark *X-Files*. Fox also designated portions of its schedule specifically for African Americans; one of its most notable offerings in this area was *In Living Color,* which included sketches mostly spoofing African Americans. Fox also catered to the younger crowd with shows like *Ally McBeal, Party of Five, Beverly Hills, 90210,* and *Melrose Place*. In fact, Fox did so well with the younger demographic that it tied with ABC for second place among 18- to 49-year-olds, trailing NBC. Fox also managed to grab the NFL games from CBS.

As Fox celebrated its tenth anniversary, it had proved the naysayers wrong about the potential for a fourth network. It had an impact on the medium and on society. As one commentator put it, "It was the first broadcast network for the MTV generation. It played an influential role in the spread of hip-hop and grunge as youthful sounds and styles of the 1990s."[94] Fox also laid the groundwork for new network startups UPN and the WB.

UPN AND THE WB

Both UPN and WB (Warner Brothers network) started in January 1995, but with very different philosophies. While WB targeted specific demographic groups, UPN's programming was intended for a very broad audience. Early on, UPN's strategy seemed to be the more promising, as it consistently edged out WB in ratings and had twice the affiliates. But toward the end of 1998, WB struck back and began to top UPN's ratings. UPN readjusted its programming toward more specific targets in response but still maintained the need for a "shared experience" in network programming.

Both networks devote a sizable portion of their schedules to African American programming and to the younger crowd. WB offerings included *Dawson's Creek, Buffy the Vampire Slayer,* and *Felicity*—all with young stars and youthful musings and plots. UPN had as one of its crown jewels *Star Trek: Voyager,* the fourth in the *Star Trek* series. It remains to be seen whether one or both fledgling networks can survive.

PUBLIC BROADCASTING: MACNEIL-LEHRER

A long effort to establish public broadcasting in the United States at the level at which it exists in other countries was given stability in 1967, when Congress chartered the Corporation for Public Broadcasting (CPB) to dispense funds for a unified system of national and local programming. Much of the original programming was done by the well-established National Educational Television (NET). After 1970, the country's noncommercial and educational television stations were connected through the Public Broadcasting Service (PBS), which hopefully called itself "the fourth network." In radio, many of these stations were linked by the National Public Radio (NPR) network.

The future of public financing remained in question, largely because of a threat by Newt Gingrich, speaker of the House of Representatives, who vowed to end federal funding for public radio and television, selling the Corporation for Public Broadcasting to private business. The conservative politicians said that public broadcasting was politically slanted to the left, while liberal critics of public broadcasting said this was nonsense, that the annual threats of budget cuts had led to an increase in conservative programming.

In addition to the threats of political intervention, the budget cuts and internal financial disputes threatened the viability of public broadcasting. There was enormous pressure on PBS and NPR stations to raise private funds to supplement their meager budgets. Only about 15 percent of PBS's budget came from the government. There also was considerable discussion whether public stations should accept advertising. Proponents pointed at the longtime underwriting of major shows by corporate grants; opponents said that the purity of public broadcasting should not be violated, and the question of advertising remained.

Public television's best-known success was *Sesame Street,* which first captured the imaginations of the country's moppets in 1969. Kermit the Frog and his fellow Muppets were the spontaneous creations of Jim Henson (who gave Kermit his voice). As the Muppets became world-famous, Henson also entertained adults with *The Muppet Show.* His mid-career death in 1990 brought dismay, but *Sesame Street*'s veteran production company kept Kermit and his friends on PBS. Another educational program, *The Electric Company,* aimed at third to fifth graders. Kenneth Clark's series called *Civilisation* was another high-level success; so were *The Forsythe Saga, The First Churchills, The Great American Dream Machine, Washington Week in Review,* and *Wall Street Week.* There were such innovative programs as the production of an actual courtroom trial and *The Global Village.* Two educational stations pioneering in such efforts were WGBH, Boston, and KQED, San Francisco. NET had other staple programs, such as another delightful children's hour, *Mister Rogers's Neighborhood, NET Playhouse, Nova,* and *NET Festival.* Other major producers were KCET, Los Angeles; WNET, New York; WETA, Washington; and WTTV, Chicago.

The programming, supplemented by the best in British television, continued to improve. Critically acclaimed were series like *The Story of English, Wonderworks, Great Performances, Heritage: Civilization and the Jews,* and *The American Experience.* Earlier hit shows had included *Upstairs, Downstairs, Shoulder to Shoulder, Monty Python, The Adams Chronicles,* and *The Incredible Machine.* Public television provided gavel-to-gavel coverage of the Watergate hearings, and a number of candid documentaries appeared, including *Vietnam: A Television History, Baseball,* and *The Civil War.* In 1994 a huge worldwide audience watched "the three tenors" (José Carreras, Placido Domingo, and Luciano Pavarotti) perform in a spectacular Los Angeles setting.

Alistair Cooke retired in 1992 at age 83 after 21 years of public television appearances. As host of *Masterpiece Theatre,* the former British newspaper reporter probed into the manners and mores of different periods, inserting astute observations about the behavior of the principal characters. News buffs relied on NPR's *All Things Considered* for interpretations of the day's events, as well as the *MacNeil-Lehrer NewsHour.*

Robert MacNeil and Jim Lehrer brought their print journalism experience to public television in 1975 with a 30-minute show focusing on one major topic. In 1983 the report was expanded to a one-hour format. Underwritten by CPB, AT&T, and the member stations of PBS, the show was a pacesetter in television news and won numerous awards. MacNeil, who began his career with Reuters in 1955, retired in 1995. That same year a controversy developed when MacNeil-Lehrer Productions, the show's producer, sold two thirds of its holdings to Liberty Media, a subsidiary of TCI, the nation's largest cable system company, known for its ruthless business tactics. While PBS welcomed the infusion of capital into the *NewsHour* show, critics worried about the possibility that political pressure could be applied, especially when they learned that MCI planned to give increased access to National Empowerment Television shows hosted by Gingrich and conservative groups like Accuracy in Media (AIM).

Chief correspondents were Charlayne Hunter-Gault and Judy Woodruff. Hunter-Gault was known for in-depth national and international reports, while Woodruff, a former NBC Washington reporter, reported for the evening news show and anchored the *Frontline* investigative show, hailed for its hard-hitting reports. She joined CNN in 1993, replaced on the evening show by *Newsweek*'s Margaret Warner.

One study showed that about 60 percent of public television's evening programming was devoted to national nonpublic-affairs shows, while 33 percent was in the category of national public affairs. Only about 7 percent was devoted to local programming, a major flaw in the national system caused mainly by the underfunding of local stations.[95]

(PBS/Don Perdue)

Jim Lehrer, executive editor and anchor of
The News Hour with Jim Lehrer

(PBS/Christopher Little)

Charlayne Hunter-Gault

THE HIRING OF MINORITIES

Part of the angry public reaction to violence on television screens undoubtedly stemmed from reporting on news and public-affairs shows of turbulence in cities and on campuses, of disorders and riots in black communities, and of the tragedies of assassination. Following the scenes of destruction in Newark and Detroit, President Johnson appointed the National Advisory Commission on Civil Disorders, with Governor Otto Kerner of Illinois as chairperson. Chapter 15 of its March 1968 report dealt with the mass media and the president's question, "What effect do the mass media have on the riots?"[96] The answers offered lessons for the future.

The Kerner Commission said that on the whole the media had tried hard to give a balanced, factual account of the 1967 disorders. There had been some evidence of sensationalism, distortion, and inaccuracy; most of the shooting had been done by the National Guards and police officers, not by blacks; there was no organized conspiracy spurring the rioting, but mainly hostile young ghetto blacks; and property damage was exaggerated, by as much as ten times by one AP dispatch from Detroit. In many cases of error, the media had relied on police authorities for their information. This observation by the commission was graphically reinforced in 1971, when false official statements said that the prison guards who died at Attica in New York State had had their throats slashed, while in reality they had been shot by their would-be rescuers. A courageous coroner and determined media reporters forced a prompt retraction of the false statements in fairness to the black convicts.

Television fared well in its riot coverage. When the commission staff looked at 955 sequences of news, it classified 494 as "calm" treatment and 262 as "emotional." Moderate black leaders were shown three times as often as militants. Because most of the soldiers and police were white, television scenes of actual rioting tended to make viewers think they were witnessing a black-white confrontation, when actually the riots were in black slum areas. Overall, both network and local television coverage was cautious and restrained, the Kerner report said.

But the commission made a ringing indictment of the mass media, which was also an indictment of American society because the performance of the media largely reflected the public attitude of the times. The communications media, the commission said,

> . . . have not communicated to the majority of their audience—which is white—a sense of the degradation, misery, and hopelessness of living in the ghetto. They have not communicated to whites a feeling for the difficulties and frustrations of being a Negro in the United States. They have not shown understanding or appreciation of—and thus have not communicated—a sense of Negro culture, thought, or history. . . . When the white press does refer to Negroes and Negro problems it frequently does so as if Negroes were not part of the audience . . . such attitudes, in an area as sensitive and inflammatory as this, feed Negro alienation and intensify white prejudices.[97]

There has been no serious reporting of the black community, the commission said; there are few black reporters and fewer race experts. "Tokenism—the hiring of one Negro reporter, or even two or three—is no longer enough. Negro reporters are essential, but so are Negro editors, writers, and commentators," the report declared.

The commission also recognized the problem conscientious journalists face when it commented:

> Events of these past few years—the Watts riot, other disorders, and the growing momentum of the civil rights movement—conditioned the responses of readers and viewers and heightened

their reactions. What the public saw and read last summer thus produced emotional reactions and left vivid impressions not wholly attributable to the material itself.[98]

A CBS News survey in 1968 pointed up this public fear; 70 percent of whites responding thought the police should have been tougher in putting down riots. In the case of Watts, the white community later denied that the area badly needed hospital facilities, even though the *Los Angeles Times* had won a Pulitzer Prize for its analysis of the Watts problem—after the riot was over.

Other studies bore out the Kerner Commission's statements about lack of black participation in the mass media. A 1969 study covering 32 of 48 major newspapers in 16 of the 20 largest cities showed that of 4095 news executives, deskpersons, reporters, and photographers, 108, or 2.6 percent, were black, including only 1 news executive and 6 on desks.[99] A 1970 survey by *Time* listed the *Washington Post* as the most integrated newspaper, with 19 black editorial staffers, or 8.5 percent. In 1977 the *Post* reported 34 black professionals, or 10 percent. A 1977 ASNE survey obtained responses from 28 percent of the dailies with at least 16,000 employees; they reported 563 black newsroom employees, or 3.5 percent. Among them were Carl T. Rowan, syndicated columnist; William Raspberry, *Washington Post* columnist; Charlayne Hunter (later Hunter-Gault), *New York Times*; L. F. Palmer, Jr., *Chicago Daily News* columnist; and William A. Hilliard, city editor of the *Oregonian* in Portland. Hilliard later became editor and was slated to become the first black ASNE president in 1994.

In 1994, the ASNE reported one of the biggest gains in the history of the surveys. About 10.9 percent of the more than 60,000 persons working in the nation's newsrooms were minorities, with about 5 percent African Americans, followed by Hispanics, Asian Americans, and Native Americans. About 6 percent of newsroom supervisors were non-white, and the number of newspapers with no minority journalists was about 50 percent. Most smaller papers remained homogeneous. Statistics indicated that minorities held about 14 percent of the jobs in television news and 10 percent in radio news, but that these figures included many low-level jobs that didn't lead to advancement.[100]

The most prominent black print journalist was Robert C. Maynard, who became editor, publisher, and owner of the *Oakland Tribune,* across the bay from San Francisco, in 1983. Maynard was the first black to direct a general circulation metropolitan daily. Self-educated, he got a job on the *York Gazette* in Pennsylvania, won a 1965 Nieman Fellowship to Harvard, reported for the *Washington Post,* and directed media minorities programs at Columbia and Berkeley before becoming editor in heavily black-populated Oakland in 1979 for the Gannett group, which then sold the paper to Maynard and others.

Battling against an increasing debt, Maynard sold the paper in 1992 to the Alameda Newspaper Group, part of the Singleton chain. Named as editor was Pearl Stewart, the first black woman to head a major metropolitan daily. Maynard died in 1993. In 1981 Gannett named Pamela McAllister Johnson as the first black woman publisher of a general circulation daily, the *Ithaca Journal* in New York State. Gannett has more cultural diversity in its newsrooms than any other organization, with about 19 percent minority and 44 percent female representation. Meanwhile, Bob Herbert, a seasoned black New York City journalist, became a *New York Times* op-ed columnist in 1993. Also that year, Jill Nelson, a black former staff writer for the *Washington Post,* lobbed furious criticism at that paper's treatment of minority reporters in a book called *Volunteer Slavery.*

Minorities were more conspicuous on network television, with first ABC's Max Robinson and later NBC's Bryant Gumbel and CNN's Bernard Shaw holding anchor spots. Many local stations had at least one minority person at an anchor position. A continuing problem for minorities in radio and television was in the writing and producing area, where

Robert C. Maynard

(Oakland Tribune)

it was difficult for them to obtain decision-making jobs. One criticism was that minorities were being "used" on camera but were not allowed to shape the coverage. A National Association of Black Journalists (NABJ) was formed in 1975; by 1999 it had 3000 members, with 74 affiliated professional and 51 student chapters.

Meanwhile, a 1993 survey by the 2400-member NABJ indicated that members felt they faced "barriers to advancement, lack of mentors and role models."[101] The 1997 ASNE report "Journalists in the 1990s" claimed that minorities' representation continues to lag behind their proportions in the national population, making up only 11 percent (compared to 26 percent representation in the national population). However, the survey suggests that this is an increase since 1988.

CONCERNS ABOUT TELEVISION PROGRAMMING

Violence has been a central theme of countless plays, novels, movies, comic books, and television scripts, from the times of the Greek dramatists to those of *NYPD Blue.* Television, which in the 1960s had a full quota of real violence to report from battlefields and urban riots, also loaded its programming with fantasy violence. The assassinations of John and Robert Kennedy and Martin Luther King, coupled with urban rioting and campus disorders, gave the opponents of programmed violence an opportunity.

Dr. George Gerbner, dean emeritus at the Annenberg School for Communication at the University of Pennsylvania, studied television violence for more than 20 years. In 1994 he estimated that the average 16-year-old had witnessed 200,000 violent acts, including 33,000 murders, on television. Over two decades, he said, the networks averaged about five acts of violence per hour in prime time. On Saturday mornings, when small children are active watchers, there were about 25 acts of violence per hour—about half of what was broadcast in the early 1970s. The Fox network logged slightly more violent acts than the other networks, but cable programming had the highest rates.[102]

Congressional hearings on television violence held in 1993 led to another nationwide scrutiny of its possible effects on children. Most researchers said that there was a statistically significant connection between watching violence and participating in it, but there was disagreement about what percent of violence could be attributed to television. Some said that violence in adulthood could be traced to heavy childhood viewing. Gerbner maintained that while television's contribution might be only 5 percent, heavy watchers of violence suffer from a "mean world syndrome" whereby they overestimate the level of actual crime, buy guns for protection, and develop an insecurity that leads to a "self-reinforcing cycle." The villains here were local news programs as well as entertainment shows.[103]

One incident that triggered outrage against television was the burning to death of a two-year-old Ohio girl by her five-year-old brother. The boy had seen two characters on an MTV cartoon show, *Beavis and Butt-head,* playing with fire and giggling about how much fun it was to burn things. MTV responded to criticism by eliminating a 7 P.M. airing of the show, leaving one at 10:30 P.M. Fox, ABC, NBC, and CBS attempted to offset criticism by airing parental advisories and sponsoring a three-year study of their programming, while cable television stations signed up for a similar three-year project. Cynics said such studies were unnecessary—that the causal links were obvious—and that the FCC should limit the amount of televised violence between 6 A.M. and 10 P.M. Others argued for the installation of an electronic blocking device so parents could control the television set, but unsupervised watching was a main source of the problem.

While the networks were prime targets for criticism, the worse offenders were cable operators and independent syndicators. They seemed to ignore how a significant part of the audience was becoming increasingly uncomfortable with the violence, sex, nudity, vulgarity, smoking, and drinking heard and seen on television. Nothing seemed to change over the years. In 1975 the FCC encouraged the networks and National Association of Broadcasters to adopt a "family viewing time," known later as the "family hour." The idea was to keep shows with high amounts of sex and violence, like *Kojak, Hawaii Five-O,* and *Charlie's Angels,* off the air until young children were in bed.

Coupled with the high degree of violence was the increasing abandonment of entertainment taboos, as demonstrated by the hit of 1975 to 1976, *Mary Hartman, Mary Hartman.* Public awareness of the problem was heightened by the movie *Network,* the Academy Award winner of 1977 that bitterly satirized the ratings system. In 1978 *Dallas* led off an era of primetime soap operas laced with sex, violence, and deception; the show lasted until 1991. But certain shows earned the praise of the most stubborn critics. One was *M*A*S*H,* the story of the Korean War exploits of the 4077th Mobile Army Surgical Hospital team, starring Alan Alda. It brought home with unusual perception and candor the tragedy, humor, and above all, the poignance of wartime experiences. During these years breakthrough comedies created by Norman Lear, particularly *All in the Family, Maude,* and *Good Times,* dealt with subjects that television comedies previously had avoided—race, religion, abortion, rape. Progressives were pleased, but traditionalists were appalled. This also was the era when *Mary Tyler Moore* began a long tradition of shows where the workplace was the center of the action, and co-workers replaced family members as confidants.

Former FCC commissioner Nicholas Johnson's group encouraged a boycott of the advertisers of the highest-rated violent shows, claiming that the real power was in the hands of the consumer audience. Other changes were effected by Action for Children's Television (ACT), formed by a Newton, Massachusetts, housewife, Peggy Charren, who was perturbed about programming and advertisements shown to children.

Then, in 1976, the American Medical Association, the American Psychiatric Association, and the national Parent-Teacher Association pushed national campaigns against televised violence. The J. Walter Thompson and other advertising companies started to disassociate themselves from violent programming, but the battle was far from over.

Coming to the defense of the American television system, while citing its fine achievements and acknowledging its faults, was CBS News commentator Eric Sevareid. Noting the adversarial relationship between print and electronic journalism, Sevareid challenged print journalists who criticize television to look at their own products:

> Don't publish lofty editorials and critiques berating the culturally low common denominator of TV entertainment programming and then feature on the cover of your weekly TV supplements, most weeks of the year, the latest TV rock star or gang-buster character. Or be honest enough to admit that you do this, that you play to mass tastes for the same reason the networks do—because it is profitable. Don't lecture the networks for the excess of violence—and it is excessive—on the screen and then publish huge ads for the most violent motion pictures in town, ads for the most pornographic films and plays, as broadcasting does not.[104]

Nevertheless, in the mid-1980s, strong objections continued to be raised about televised violence. Adding his voice was the Reverend Jerry Falwell, leader of the Moral Majority organization. Leading researchers, including George Comstock and George Gerbner, agreed that television is a main agent for socialization, because it brings into the often-unsupervised home "information and portrayals not duplicated or readily testable in their real-life environment . . . viewing of violence increases the likelihood of aggressive behavior on the part of the young."[105] But it was also stressed that the influence of parents, teachers, and religious persons modified the effects of television.

By the late 1980s there had been changes in both content and technology. *Miami Vice,* which debuted in 1984, pioneered a new trend in television. The fast-moving crime show employed video techniques copied from MTV. These floating images and unusual camera angles, accompanied by music, also had influenced many television commercials. The show sometimes deviated to take on political issues, including the Miami community's connection with the Contra war in Nicaragua. Another show credited with helping to change the look of television was the critically acclaimed police drama *Hill Street Blues.* This series began in 1981 and had a hard reality to it. A technical success was the use of hand-held cameras for action scenes. Another police drama, *Cagney and Lacey,* focused on women and their problem-solving ability and *L.A. Law* became a favorite.

In addition to the portrayal of violence and women, critics paid attention to shows featuring minorities. NBC's *The Cosby Show* became one of the nation's favorites. It was a gentle comedy about an upper-class black family, and unlike earlier shows, such as *The Jeffersons* and *Good Times,* its scripts did not dwell on racial issues. Some thought *Cosby* was unrealistic, however, and argued that *A Different World,* a spinoff from *Cosby* and produced by the comedian himself, more properly put blacks in a black context. ABC's *Family Matters* also was hailed, while the Fox Entertainment Network's syndicated comedy and variety show *In Living Color* gained mixed reviews for its blunt satire.

Women were featured prominently in a number of shows, including *Murder She Wrote* and *The Golden Girls.* Game shows became immensely popular, as they had been in the late 1950s, with *Wheel of Fortune* leading the pack. Dominating the cable networks were a half-dozen powerful preachers who gave messages designed to offset any sex and violence on other channels, and to raise millions of dollars for their causes.

In 1990 Congress passed the Children's Television Act, which had little if any effect. Ironically, many of the best children's shows were on public television, but the federal government regularly cut its share of funding. In 1995 Newt Gingrich, the new Republican Speaker of the House, pledged to eliminate funding for public television at a time when the afternoon and primetime soap operas were more explicit than ever, daytime talk shows exhibited the lowest level of human behavior, late night talk shows spared no one in providing a parade of degrading jokes, comedians on cable television ridiculed persons of every ethnic and cultural persuasion, and regular shows like *Married . . . with Children, Melrose Place, Baywatch,* and *Real Stories of the Highway Patrol* appealed to every base instinct. In addition the proliferation of cable channels brought the television productions and movies of the previous thirty years into the home, for better or worse.

Congress passed the Telecommunications Act in 1996, which included a provision for a technological device called the V-chip. This device was to enable parents to block television content carrying ratings that they deemed unacceptable for their children. All new televisions over 13 inches were to have the chip by January 2000. There was already a ratings system in place, developed by the networks and approved by the FCC. While some hailed this as a way to put control of what children see back into the hands of their parents, critics claimed that to mandate a ratings system was a form of governmental control and thus unacceptable. Content providers might fear that getting a high rating for violence or sexual content could result in their programming being blocked and thus might self-censor.

THE FCC AND THE BROADCASTERS: LICENSING

Radio and television were still under public regulation, by means of the Federal Communications Commission, but the government eased up on the reins in the 1980s during the Reagan and Bush years. Individuals could own up to 18 AM, 18 FM, and 12 television stations. The television stations could not reach more than 25 percent of the national viewing potential. Broadcast groups that invested in stations more than half-owned by minorities could own up to 21 AM, 21 FM and 14 television stations, and could reach up to 30 percent of the potential television audience.

There were a number of restrictions regarding multimedia ownership. Newspaper owners could not purchase a broadcast station in the same market area. Nor could a radio station owner purchase a television station, nor a television owner acquire a radio station. A television station owner could not own a local cable franchise; the major networks were forbidden from owning any cable systems.

On the other hand, the policy of deregulation presided over by FCC Chairman Mark Fowler was generous toward broadcasters, allowing them to devote a minimum of time to news and "public service" programs. Included here might be children's programming, religious shows, and public-affairs presentations. Instead the FCC expanded the time that can be devoted to commercials. Fowler, who once said, "Television is just another appliance; it is a toaster with pictures,"[106] urged the commission to go further. The license period was extended from three years to five for television and to seven for radio, and owners were protected from challenges by the elimination of regulations calling for them to keep program logs that could be evaluated.

Television found itself subjected to other regulations. For health reasons, Congress passed legislation banning cigarette advertising from the screens beginning in 1971 (magazine cigarette advertising promptly doubled and that in newspapers also increased). The immediate loss to the broadcast industry was $225 million in advertising revenues, unless the time was sold to other advertisers. And the FCC voted to limit network-television affiliate stations in the top 50 markets to three hours of network programming in prime time (this prime-time access rule forced the stations to scramble around for 30 minutes of fill-in each evening between 7:30 to 8 P.M., E.S.T.).

Following the general philosophy set by the Reagan administration in 1981, the FCC approved the licensing of 125 new AM radio stations, increasing competition in that area, and then set the deregulation of television in motion. As an initial action it approved the construction of low-power television stations to provide access to segments of society not well served. In the mid-1990s the majority were in Alaska. The FCC gave its blessing to teletext operations and, importantly, to direct broadcasting from satellite to home.

The major concern with deregulation, articulated by noted television critic Les Brown and others, was that the networks and individual stations could exploit the situation and not adhere to the concept of fairness. Concern was heightened when Fowler advocated "no renewal filings, no ascertainment exercises, no content regulation, no ownership restrictions beyond those that apply to media generally, free resale of properties, no petitions to deny, no brownie points for doing this right, no finger-wagging for doing that wrong." Brown replied, "Television without referees is a commercial free-for-all, a sport for scoundrels."[107]

In 1996, Congress passed the 1996 Telecommunications Act, the first truly comprehensive rewrite of the Communications Act of 1934. By and large, cross-market entry barriers were eliminated and merger rules relaxed. The act was hailed as a boon to the consumer because it was intended to foster additional competition and give consumers choices about who provides their telecommunications services.

The act relaxed ownership restrictions on radio and television stations even more. A single entity could now own any number of television stations nationally as long as the total audience did not exceed 35 percent. On the local level, the FCC eliminated the one-per-owner rule and considered other options for regulation. Nationally, a single entity could own any number of radio stations, while locally the restrictions were relaxed according to market size (e.g., in a market with 45 or more stations, one owner could own up to eight, with no more than five AM or five FM stations). The FCC could also waive these radio restrictions to increase the number of stations in an area. Restrictions were also relaxed on cross-media ownership (television/cable, newspaper/broadcast), with the possibility of waivers permitting additional voices to be heard in the community.

In the early 1990s it was predicted that the FCC's greatest challenges would be in the technology area, dealing with conflicts over the use of fiber optics, the expansion of spectrum space, and other factors related to High Density Television (HDTV) signals from satellites and Digital Audio Broadcasting (DAB), a technology that broadcasters said could replace the AM and FM systems. Congress, the FCC, and the courts were still struggling with these issues in the late 1990s. However, opinions differed about the effectiveness of the Telecommunications Act. Critics suggested that, despite Congressional intentions to encourage competition as a benefit to the end-user, the act facilitated the purchase of radio stations by large corporations all over the country (to such a degree, in fact, that the FCC was still trying to decide how to handle television station ownership deregulation so as to avoid the same scenario). Some commentators said that it was too early to say whether the other provisions of the act, such as the ones covering telephony, would have an impact on the face of American telecommunications.

THE FCC FAIRNESS DOCTRINE

The problems of editorializing on the air and showing fairness in presenting all sides of public issues were others involving the stations and the FCC over many decades. In a 1941 ruling, called the "Mayflower decision" because it involved the renewal of a Boston station license held by the Mayflower Broadcasting Corporation, the FCC said, "The broadcaster cannot be an advocate." Radio supporters presented arguments against this policy, and in 1949 the FCC decided broadcasters could—and should—"editorialize with fairness." Station owners were cautious in taking up the invitation, but by 1967 a survey showed that 57 percent of radio and television stations were presenting editorial opinion, one-third of them either daily or weekly, the rest occasionally. This figure steadily increased. Some problems of covering politics were removed in 1959, when bona fide newscasts and news programs were exempted from the FCC's "equal-time" rule, but the basic problem of obtaining "fairness" in access to the air and in presenting all sides of controversial issues remained.

The requirement to be "fair" was based on two arguments: the airwaves are public property, by act of Congress, and the FCC was given power to license broadcasters in the "public interest, convenience, and necessity." The public interest is served, the FCC held, if the airwaves are made accessible to many viewpoints.

Broadcasters said that it was hard to define the "public interest" legally. They also said such extreme efforts to balance editorial comment and interpretive documentaries mitigated against broadcasters covering important social issues. If, as the FCC implied, a station had to go out and look for at least one other side to any issue it discussed in order to be fair, it would not go out at all (as in the case of CBS looking for the other side to the migrant labor problem or of military propaganda, for example). And if the "other side" came in with program demands by any number of offended or interested groups (as in the case of the Vietnam War and activist resistance to war), the station's time would be filled with programming of little interest to the majority of viewers (any newspaper editor knows that a large percentage of citizens is not interested in a given social or political issue, a fact confirmed by opinion polls). In a 1969 decision the Supreme Court did not agree to all this.[108]

In another decision affecting access to the airwaves and public discussion, the FCC reversed a policy that had encouraged antismoking, environmentalist, and other groups to seek access. The FCC narrowed previous rulings that held that all broadcast advertising was subject to the "fairness doctrine" and had to be balanced with "counter-advertising" whenever controversies were involved. The new ruling was that ads designed merely to sell products did not have to be balanced with opposing viewpoints, but that advertisements dealing with issues were still subject to the provisions calling for balance. However, the FCC and Supreme Court ruled that broadcasters could not be required to sell advertising space to anyone who had the money and were only expected to make a "good faith effort" to ensure balance in their overall programming, as opposed to any one program. The inquiry was intended to settle questions that had arisen during license disputes and was considered to be different from "right-of-reply" and "equal-time" problems.

In an extension of regulations governing advertising, in 1978 the Supreme Court ruled that the Federal Trade Commission (FTC) had the authority to enforce corrective advertising. Advertisers found guilty of using false advertising were required to devote a certain percentage of future advertising to acknowledging previous falsehoods. The FTC had decided that advertising for Listerine, which for 100 years had claimed that the product helped cure colds and sore throats, needed correcting. The Supreme Court agreed to this concept of fairness in advertising.

By the mid-1980s there was a rising cry against the fairness doctrine, however. As could be expected, broadcast executives were opposed to its continuation. They argued that the networks should be free to cover controversial issues without the fear of government intervention. Cynics suspected that some executives also wanted to be free of pressure from minorities, women, senior citizens, and others demanding balanced coverage. But leading journalists, including many sympathetic to those often denied access, joined in the arguments for the abolition of the fairness doctrine. Both Walter Cronkite and Eric Sevareid said that there were so many ways for the average citizen to hear different viewpoints that there was no reason to assume that the television networks held as much power as in the days when broadcasting frequencies were limited.

Finally the FCC itself assailed the fairness doctrine. In August 1985 the commission said the regulation no longer served the public interest because it violated the First Amendment guarantees of freedom of speech, but would continue to be enforced. This in turn brought protests from more than 100 groups. But the following year a dozen media organizations, led by CBS, asked a federal appeals court to stop the FCC from enforcing the fairness rules. The case remained unresolved. Congress voted in 1987 to give the FCC fairness rules the force of law, but President Reagan killed the bill with a veto. The FCC thereupon abolished the fairness doctrine.

Occasionally there are calls for a return to the fairness doctrine. In 1993 a bill was again introduced to write the doctrine into law, amid speculation that President Clinton might be willing to sign it. Coalitions of concerned individuals also petitioned the courts to reinstate the doctrine. However, none of these efforts were successful. Critics of the doctrine claim that broadcasters who do not want to cover all sides of controversial issues might steer away from these kinds of issues altogether. And, some say that the fairness doctrine was just one more governmental regulation on freedom of the press, and the fact that it was abolished should be celebrated.

PRIVACY CONCERNS

In the 1990s, with the ever-increasing availability of online databases, some raised concerns about protecting personal data. Parents were also concerned about their children visiting a website that asks for personal information about them or their families in exchange for a free trinket.

In 1998 the Federal Trade Commission published a report entitled *Privacy Online: A Report to Congress.* In this report, the FTC noted that it had been following the concerns of citizens about online privacy of data, and that it had surveyed over 1400 websites and recorded their data privacy policies. It found that 85 percent of all websites gather personal information about visitors, while only 14 percent of those sites offered notice that they were doing so. Most children's sites (89 percent) also gathered information from children surfing by, and most of those sites did not ask children to get their parents' permission before providing the information, notify parents of the information gathered, or provide parental control over the data collected from their children.

The report concluded that children's privacy was not adequately protected, nor was that of adult consumers. The Congressional response was the 1998 Children's Online Privacy Protection Act, which required the FTC to require commercial websites to "follow fair information practices in connection with the collection and use of personal information from children under age 16, including by obtaining verifiable parental consent for the collection, use or disclosure of personal information from children under the age of 13." The FTC will doubtless encourage the passage of other laws to protect privacy for adults surfing the Internet.

19

Efforts to Improve
the Media

There can be no such thing as a free press and no such thing as the integrity of the news if the men and women who write the news live in fear of the security of their jobs.

—Heywood Broun

The picture on the following page is symbolic of the element of change in media history. Taken at the 1986 convention of the American Newspaper Publishers Association (ANPA), it shows *Washington Post* board chairperson, Katharine Graham, greeting luncheon speaker Richard M. Nixon, whom her newspaper had helped force from the office of president in 1974. "I want this shot," Nixon smiled. "Bygones are bygones," commented *Post* publisher Donald Graham (whose mother was the first woman to serve as ANPA president, another evidence of change).

Through all the years of media criticism, which gathered force in the 1930s and escalated steadily beginning in the 1960s, one continuing problem was the involvement of the press in partisan politics, making it difficult to maintain media credibility in the public mind. The Graham gesture in the conservative atmosphere of spring 1986 addressed this concern.

But if those within the profession were responding to external pressures upon the print and broadcast media, they also were creating some pressures of their own. Their responses took the forms of improving professional working conditions, establishing effective media associations, writing voluntary codes of conduct, developing professional organizations devoted to the high purposes of journalism, encouraging education for journalism, supporting studies of the press, sponsoring press councils and journalism reviews, exploring new theories of community journalism, improving the status of minorities and women in the profession, and defending the press against legal and governmental pressures. This chapter elaborates on the degrees of success of these efforts to improve the media.

The *Washington Post*'s Katharine Graham greets Richard Nixon at the 1986 ANPA convention.

(presstime/photo)

THE PRESS IN PRESIDENTIAL ELECTIONS

Criticism of newspapers since the 1930s have centered on, more than anything else, their editorial positions in political campaigns. Historically, a small but definite majority of the daily newspapers giving editorial-page support to a presidential candidate was to be found on the side of the Republican party. As Franklin Roosevelt entered the first of his four presidential campaigns in 1932, he had the support of 38 percent of the nation's dailies, compared to 55 percent for President Hoover. In 1936, Roosevelt was backed by 34 percent of the dailies, Republican Alfred M. Landon by 60 percent. These figures are approximations gathered by *Editor & Publisher* when it launched, in 1940, a comprehensive preelection poll of dailies concerning editorial-page support. Approximately three-fourths of all dailies, with 90 percent of total daily newspaper circulation, responded to the polls until the 1970s, when the character of the contests caused the response to dwindle. The number of dailies supporting Roosevelt declined to 22 percent for both his 1940 and 1944 races with Wendell Willkie and Thomas E. Dewey, respectively.

Press critics chortled in 1948 when Harry S. Truman upset Dewey and the public opinion pollsters to win reelection. Dewey had enjoyed the support of 65 percent of the papers responding to the *Editor & Publisher* poll with 78 percent of the circulation; Truman garnered only 15 percent with a record circulation low of 10 percent. It was the fifth consecutive time the leader in editorial endorsements had lost the election.

But in 1952 the highly popular Dwight D. Eisenhower swept both the newspaper editorial support and the election over the darling of the intellectuals, Adlai E. Stevenson. Eisenhower had an all-time high of 80 percent of the circulation of reporting dailies, Stevenson 10.8 percent. The 1956 outcome was the same.

John F. Kennedy edged out Richard M. Nixon in 1960, despite the handicap of having endorsements from just 15.8 percent of the reporting circulation against Nixon's 70.9. But Kennedy had endorsements by more large papers countrywide than any Democrat since 1944.[1]

Then came political upheaval stemming from the assassination of President Kennedy. His successor, Lyndon Johnson of Texas, became the first southerner to win the Democratic nomination in modern times. His opponent, Senator Barry M. Goldwater, represented the frustrated right wing of the Republican party. Given such a choice, newspaper publishers and editors chose to endorse President Johnson for reelection. The scales were essentially turned. Among dailies over 100,000 in circulation, Nixon had enjoyed the support of 87 to 22 for Kennedy in 1960. Johnson won 82 to his side four years later, and Goldwater only 12.[2] Johnson's figure of 61.5 percent of the reporting circulation was an all-time Democratic high, and Goldwater's 21.5 a historic Republican low.

Four years later came more upheaval—the assassination of Senator Robert Kennedy, the forced withdrawal of President Johnson from the Democratic race by the Eugene McCarthy crusade, and the nominations in vacuums of Hubert Humphrey and Richard M. Nixon. The scales tilted back, and the big dailies divided 78 for Nixon and 28 for Humphrey. Humphrey's percentage of the reporting circulation was only 19.3 to Nixon's 70, but he barely lost the presidency.[3]

In 1972 it was the Democrats' turn to nominate a candidate from an extreme wing of their party, Senator George McGovern, who won only one state. Dailies representing only two-thirds of the total circulation responded to the poll, and the big dailies split 66 for President Nixon and 9 for McGovern, who had an all-time low of 7.7 percent of the circulation.[4]

Then came the Watergate scandal. The forced resignations of President Nixon and Vice President Spiro Agnew led many embarrassed Republican newspapers to avoid a 1976 presidential endorsement. Among 114 dailies with more than 100,000 circulation, 50 backed President Gerald Ford, 21 Democratic candidate Jimmy Carter of Georgia, and 43 blanked out.[5] Carter was elected, although he had only 22.8 percent of reporting circulation to Ford's 62.2.

In the 1980s, presidential elections were dominated by television and interest in newspaper endorsements was low. Only half the dailies responded to *Editor & Publisher*'s poll. Dailies not making endorsements rose from 40 percent in 1980 to 55 percent in 1988. Ronald Reagan defeated Carter handily in 1980, although he had only 48.6 percent of circulation of reporting papers.[6] Democrat Walter Mondale won but a single state from Reagan in 1984 despite a prestigious list of newspaper supporters.[7] In 1988, the dailies responding to the *Editor & Publisher* poll split 428 for no endorsement, 241 for Vice President George Bush, and 103 for Democratic governor Michael Dukakis of Massachusetts. Dukakis lost badly even though he was supported by 9 of the 15 leading newspapers, Bush by only 2.

Four years later President Bush's public and newspaper editorial support both collapsed along with the recession-wracked economy. The 1992 *Editor & Publisher* poll showed 45 percent of responding newspapers opting for no endorsement, 35 percent for Democrat Bill Clinton, and 19.6 percent for Bush—2 points lower than Goldwater's previous Republican low. Among the 15 leading dailies, Clinton won 11, Bush only the *Chicago Tribune* (the *Los Angeles Times, Miami Herald,* and *Wall Street Journal* did not endorse). Only half the dailies took part in the poll.[8]

In 1996, *Editor & Publisher* reported that Republican challenger Robert Dole had won a solid majority of daily newspaper endorsements—111 to Clinton's 65. Libertarian party candidate Harry Browne also received an endorsement, the only one outside the major parties. An additional 166 papers planned not to endorse anyone, and 249 papers had not chosen a candidate to endorse. Nevertheless, Clinton went on to win his second term.

After the 1994 midterm election, in which Minnesota voter turnout hit an all-time low despite several hotly contested races, Tom Hamburger, Washington bureau chief of the Minneapolis *Star Tribune,* proposed the Minnesota Compact. This voluntary "experiment" asks all participants in elections, from candidates to the media to voters, to pledge in advance to reach for higher standards during election seasons. The compact suggests that candidates cease attack advertising on television; the media commit to providing substantive coverage of campaigns and refrain from "horserace" reporting; candidates participate in debates and community discussion; and citizens get involved in thinking about and discussing issues and candidates. A coalition of citizen groups, business associations, journalists, and educators formed in 1996 to implement the values of the compact. Although the compact has not gained widespread recognition, E. J. Dionne, Jr., of the *Washington Post* wrote an op-ed piece applauding the concept and wondering how it could be applied to presidential elections.

THE NEWSPAPER GUILD

In the crisis year of 1933, gaining adequate income and job security for newspaper men and women was their first prerequisite. While other workers in newspaper plants had long since unionized, the editorial employees remained unorganized and relatively underpaid. Section 7-a of the National Industrial Recovery Act (NRA) of 1933 offered them their chance, since it guaranteed the right of collective bargaining. The NRA also contained licensing provisions that alienated conservative leaders of the American Newspaper Publishers Association. This made the writing of a daily newspaper code under the "Blue Eagle" provisions a grueling duel. The final version provided a 40-hour work week in bigger cities, minimum salaries, and an open-shop provision. But its $11 to $15 weekly salary minimum did nothing to further the professional status of journalism or the economic security of its workers. New York reporters considered $40 a week equitable at the time.

Reporters and desk workers around the country began talking about forming collective bargaining units in the summer of 1933, when the trend of the code negotiations became apparent. Heywood Broun, the liberal and combative columnist for the *New York World-Telegram,* sounded a call for action in his syndicated column for August 7, 1933, which sparked the translation of talk into deeds. Broun deftly chastised his fellow newspaper workers for not having formed a union like those of the better-paid printers and gently chided those who feared "the romance of the game" would be lost if they organized. Then in typical Broun style he concluded:

> But the fact that newspaper editors and owners are genial folk should hardly stand in the way of the organization of a newspaper writers' union. There should be one. Beginning at nine o'clock in the morning of October 1, I am going to do the best I can in helping get one up. I think I could die happy on the opening day of the general strike if I had the privilege of watching Walter Lippmann heave a brick through a *Tribune* window at a nonunion operative who had been called in to write the current "Today and Tomorrow" column on the gold standard.[9]

The cautious Lippmann ignored Broun's call to arms, but the newspaper people across the country who read his column did not, nor did they wait until October 1. Cleveland's reporters were the first to respond, forming what became the first local of the Newspaper Guild on August 20. The Twin Cities, Minneapolis and St. Paul, and New York were next in line.[10]

Heywood Broun

New York newspeople, headed by Broun, issued the first number of the *Guild Reporter* on November 23, and called for a national convention to be held in Washington, D.C., on December 15. Delegates from 30 cities responded. Broun was elected president, a post he held until his death in 1939, and Jonathan Eddy became the first executive secretary. The newspapermen and -women were seeking, they said, "to preserve the vocational interests of the members and to improve the conditions under which they work by collective bargaining, and to raise the standards of journalism."

By the time the first annual convention met in St. Paul in June 1934, the Guild had 8000 members. But only one of its local units had a contract with a publisher. The 1934 Guild convention called for more contracts covering minimum wages and maximum hours, paid holidays and vacations, overtime pay, sick leave, severance pay, and other usual trade-union contract provisions—goals that still remained to be gained by the average newspaper staff. Publishers who disliked seeing the Guild take on the form of a trade-union organization were further antagonized when the convention approved a code of ethics that listed what the Guild regarded to be harmful practices of newspapers. The Guild thereafter stuck closely to problems of salaries and working conditions when dealing with employers.

Head-on clashes became unavoidable. The Guild did not shrink from using the strike and picket line, and was involved in 20 strikes during its first five years. Bitterest was a 508-day strike against Hearst newspapers in Chicago; the longest in Guild history was the strike called in 1967 against Hearst's *Los Angeles Herald-Examiner* that eventually led 15 years later to non-Guild agreements. But in the main the Guild negotiated peacefully. It developed Guild shop provisions to ensure 80 percent membership, joined the CIO in 1937, and broadened the membership base to office employees. All this aroused controversy, but by 1938 the Guild had 75 newspaper contracts.[11]

But the biggest early Guild victory was gained in a court case involving a single Associated Press staff member, Morris Watson. Watson, who had been discharged by the AP in 1935, asserted that he had been dismissed for Guild activities. He appealed to the National Labor Relations Board (NLRB) for an order compelling his reinstatement under the provisions of the Wagner Labor Relations Act of 1935. When the NLRB ruled in favor of Watson in 1936, the AP carried the case to the Supreme Court, contending that the Wagner Act was unconstitutional and that in any event it did not apply to newspapers or press associations.

The Supreme Court, which had ruled adversely on much New Deal legislation in 1935 and 1936, announced a series of decisions in April 1937 upholding the constitutionality of the Wagner Act. Among the cases decided was that of Morris Watson. Justices Hughes and Roberts swung to the liberal side to join Justices Brandeis, Stone, and Cardozo in ordering the AP to reinstate Watson in his job. The five justices ruled that Watson had been illegally discharged for union activity, and it was on that point that the case turned.[12] But the majority also observed that "the publisher of a newspaper has no special immunity from the application of general laws."

The upholding of the Wagner Act was a great Guild victory. It assured the Guild a permanent place in newspaper life. Gradually contracts were won in larger cities, including one with the *New York Times,* whose staff had long been skeptical of the Guild. But the road was still a rocky one. The recession years of 1937 to 1939 brought widespread newspaper closings and staff prunings that left thousands of newspapermen and -women unemployed and made contract negotiation difficult.

The Guild became engaged in a bitter fight between conservative, or "pro-Guild," members and left-wing elements who were strongest in the New York City locals. Forcing an election of officers by nationwide referendum, however, brought victory to the "pro-

Guild" group managed by Wilbur Bade, early editor of the *Guild Reporter.* Under the leadership of presidents Milton M. Murray and Harry Martin, and executive presidents Sam Eubanks and Ralph B. Novak, the Guild remained vigorously liberal.[13]

World War II brought a general "freezing" of labor-relations activities. As the war ended, the Guild's goal was a top minimum of $65 a week for all contracts. Then in 1946 the goal was set at a seemingly impossible $100 level. When it was reached with ease by 1954, new goals were set. Founders would have been amazed by the breaking of the $500 a week level at the *Washington Post* in 1977 and top minimums exceeding $1000 weekly. The average top minimum reporting salary in 1994 was $715 weekly ($37,180 annually). The average starting salary for reporters in Guild shops was $457 ($23,764), with 20 percent of contracts at $500 weekly or more, and the *New York Times* at $1,238. Of course salaries for other newsroom employees were higher; for example, total average compensation for managing editors was about $60,000. It should be noted that despite the advances made for its members, the Guild's influence had declined considerably. Guild leaders since 1950 have included Joseph F. Collis, Arthur Rosenstock, William J. Farson, Charles A. Perlik, Jr., and Charles Dale.

Although its original hopes for influencing journalistic standards had been shelved, the Guild revived such interests in the 1960s. It established the Mellett Fund for a Free and Responsible Press to finance press councils in local communities. It encouraged establishment of critical media reviews, and Guild members cautiously sought more voice in advising newspaper management on institutional policy. In 1970 the Guild changed its name to the Newspaper Guild to acknowledge its Canadian members. Race discrimination, reporters' privilege, restrictions on the press, and physical harassment of reporters were other issues occupying Guild attention. Remembering their founder, in 1940 the Guild established an annual award for newspaper work "in the spirit of Heywood Broun."

In 1995 the Guild endorsed a merger with the Communication Workers of America and elected its first woman president, Linda Foley. The merger, which took place in 1997, was an acknowledgment of the increasingly important role of communications technology to the newspaper industry.

THE AMERICAN NEWSPAPER PUBLISHERS ASSOCIATION/NEWSPAPER ASSOCIATION OF AMERICA

The American Newspaper Publishers Association (ANPA), founded in 1887 as the trade association of the dailies, had grown to 850 members by the 1930s. In contrast to its position on the Guild, the ANPA had sponsored an imaginative policy of voluntary arbitration with the printing unions after 1900. Its Bureau of Advertising was involved in the *Continuing Study of Newspaper Reading.* It had sponsored research in printing processes and had defended newspaper owners' interests in newsprint tariffs and postage rates.

But in the 1930s its leadership proved unresponsive to changing social and economic conditions. Its manager, Lincoln B. Palmer, and counsel, Elisha Hanson, put the ANPA in full opposition to the major legislation of the New Deal. Exemptions for the newspaper business were asked when reform legislation was before the Congress. After Cranston Williams became general manager in 1939, the uncompromising conservative stance was altered. By the time Stanford Smith took charge in 1960, the ANPA was a typical trade association with a progressive flair. Membership rose to 1200 dailies.

The publishers had long supported a mechanical department devoted to the study of improvements in the printing processes. After World War II they felt the growing pressures of a "cold-type revolution" brought about by the introduction of the photographic process into printing. In 1947 a research director was named and funds were voted to establish a research center in Easton, Pennsylvania, which formally opened in 1951. It was incorporated as the ANPA Research Institute in 1954, and moved to Reston, Virginia, after ANPA established its Newspaper Center there in 1972. Working in ultramodern research laboratories with printing industry support, an ANPA staff headed by William D. Rinehart made printing technology breakthroughs in rapid etch, photocomposition, offset printing, plastic printing plates, digital computers, color inks, and the flexographic press. Its annual Mechanical Conference drew more than 10,000 visitors in the mid-1980s.

The ANPA Foundation was chartered in 1961 to develop funding for outreach programs. By 1987 it had an endowment exceeding $6 million. Under director Judith D. Hines it sponsored research projects, worked with journalism educators, held professional advancement workshops, helped to develop opportunities for minorities in newspapering, and directed activities in the strengthening of freedom of speech and press.

The ANPA's biggest legislative victory was the passage of the Newspaper Preservation Act, after three years of debate in the Congress. The act exempted from antitrust suits the joint-printing operations of 44 newspapers in 22 cities and overturned a Supreme Court decision dissolving a pooled business operation in Tucson. Opponents said the new law, signed by President Nixon in 1970, would perpetuate the status quo.

Jerry W. Friedheim succeeded Smith as chief executive officer in 1975. He reorganized the staff-operated departments, creating those in human resources and personnel, telecommunications, and legal and government affairs. Among highlights of his regime were the founding in 1979 of *presstime* as the association's expertly edited monthly trade journal, major confrontations with the telephone companies and the U.S. Postal Service over encroachments upon sources of newspaper financial stability, and negotiations with the White House and the Joint Chiefs of Staff not to repeat their ban on reportorial coverage of the 1983 invasion of Grenada. As the ANPA celebrated its centennial year in 1987, its member papers totaled 1400 and its annual budget was more than $10 million. But in 1991 concerns over the roles of print media organizations brought Friedheim's retirement as chief executive officer in favor of Cathleen Black, the publisher of *USA Today* since 1984.

The ANPA disappeared on June 1, 1992 when it merged with the NewspaperAdvertising Bureau and five other associations under the name Newspaper Association of America (NAA). The nonprofit organization served 1050 newspapers in the United States and Canada. In 1998 NAA members accounted for nearly 90 percent of United States daily circulation newspapers as well as a wide range of nondailies and many Canadian and international papers. Its current efforts are to retain and build newspapers' advertising share and sales, support the First Amendment, encourage diversity in the newspaper workforce, research new opportunities for growth and development, and provide technical guidance for newspapers to serve their readership. Leadership in 1999 included chairman Richard Gottlieb and president/CEO John Sturm.

ASNE, NAB, AND CODES OF CONDUCT

The American Society of Newspaper Editors (ASNE) was organized in 1922, under the leadership of Casper S. Yost of the *St. Louis Globe-Democrat,* to fill a long-felt need. As the group's constitution pointed out, "Although the art of journalism has flourished in America for more than two hundred years, the editors of the greater American newspapers have not hitherto banded themselves together in association for the consideration of their common problems and the promotion of their professional ideals." State and regional newspaper associations had considered news and editorial problems, but the ANPA had virtually excluded all but business topics from its agendas.

Membership in the ASNE was limited to editors-in-chief, editorial-page editors, and managing editors of dailies published in cities of more than 100,000 population, a figure soon reduced to 50,000. Limited numbers of editors of smaller dailies were admitted in later years.

Early meetings of the society were enlivened by a bitter dispute over the power of the group to expel a member, Fred G. Bonfils of the *Denver Post,* who stood accused of blackmailing oil millionaire Harry Sinclair in connection with the Teapot Dome scandal. At one point a vote of expulsion was taken, but the action was rescinded, and the Denver editor was permitted to resign. Later the ASNE clarified its power to expel a member for due cause, but the Bonfils incident made it clear that the group did not propose to serve as a policing organization. Willis J. Abbot of the *Christian Science Monitor* and Tom Wallace of the *Louisville Times* were leaders in the fight for a stern policy, but Yost and others held to a middle course.

A code of ethics, called the "Canons of Journalism," was presented to the first annual meeting in 1923. Chief author was H. J. Wright, founder of the *New York Globe.* Some of the key paragraphs read as follows:

> The right of a newspaper to attract and hold readers is restricted by nothing but considerations of public welfare. The use a newspaper makes of the share of public attention it gains serves to determine its sense of responsibility, which it shares with every member of its staff. A journalist who uses his power for any selfish or otherwise unworthy purpose is faithless to a high trust.
>
> Freedom of the press is to be guarded as a vital right of mankind. It is the unquestionable right to discuss whatever is not explicitly forbidden by a law, including the wisdom of any restrictive statute.
>
> Freedom from all obligations except that of fidelity to the public interest is vital.
>
> Partisanship, in editorial comment which knowingly departs from the truth, does violence to the best spirit of American journalism; in the news columns it is subversive of a fundamental principle in the profession.[14]

Annual meetings of the ASNE are held each April, often in Washington. Proceedings are reported in a series of books, dating from 1923, titled *Problems of Journalism,* which offer significant discussions of professional matters.[15] Lively debate is found in the monthly *ASNE Bulletin.*

The first version of the Society of Professional Journalists' Code of Ethics was borrowed from the ASNE canon in 1926. In 1973 SPJ wrote its own code and continued to revise it in 1984 and 1987. The version of the SPJ Code of Ethics in use in 1999 was adopted in September 1996 and provided journalists with four major ethical principles by which to abide: Seek truth and report it; minimize harm; act independently; and be accountable. Each principle is followed by a list of ways to practice it. This brief code hangs above many reporters' and editors' desks and is often adopted in its entirety by news organizations.

ASNE's most ambitious undertaking was the Journalism Credibility Project, started in 1997 and continuing. This study attempted to help newspaper editors better understand the public's increasing loss of trust in journalism. Initial findings of the project included the public's concern with inaccuracies, overcoverage of certain stories, and journalistic biases perceived to influence news coverage.

Codes of conduct for the broadcasting industry were developed by its trade association, the National Association of Broadcasters (NAB). The NAB was founded in 1923 during a skirmish between the radio station owners and ASCAP over fees the latter insisted be paid for broadcasting music of ASCAP members. Paul Klugh was the first NAB managing director. The role of the trade association expanded to include its relationships with advertising and then, increasingly, with the Federal Communications Commission.

The NAB Code of Ethics and the NAB Standards of Commercial Practice were adopted in March 1929, as the first voluntarily imposed regulations on broadcasters. More detailed documents, the NAB Radio Code and the NAB Television Code, were added. About half of all commercial radio and television stations subscribed to the codes. There were other major codes and statements, particularly those of the Radio-Television News Directors Association and the programming standards of the networks and many individual stations.

Headquarters of the NAB are in Washington, with a large staff for administration, legal problems, station services, broadcast management, government affairs, public relations, and research. The NAB Code Authority staff hears complaints concerning violations by those subscribing to the codes. There are also review boards for the Television Code and Radio Code.

In 1997 a coalition of NAB, the Motion Picture Association of America (MPAA), and the National Cable Television Association (NCTA) worked together to create and implement a set of television ratings for all programming. The TV Parental Guidelines were developed in accordance with the Telecommunications Act of 1996, which also includes a provision that by January 2000 televisions 13 inches or larger be equipped with a device known as a V-chip. This chip, which was anticipated to be on the market sometime in 1999, was designed to allow parents to program their TVs to block content with ratings they find objectionable. The guidelines, approved by the FCC in 1998, include ratings that describe categories of content such as violence, strong language, and sexual situations. Networks have already incorporated the ratings into much of their programming.

NCEW, APME, AND RTNDA

Editorial-page editors and editorial writers who wanted a smaller and more vigorous "working" organization than the 450-member ASNE formed the National Conference of Editorial Writers (NCEW) in 1947. The idea came from a group attending an American Press Institute session at Columbia University[16] and was promoted by Leslie Moore of the *Worcester Telegram* and *Gazette.* Beginning in 1947 annual sessions were held that featured small-group critique panels in which members appraised the editorial-page efforts of their colleagues. A quarterly magazine, the *Masthead,* and convention proceedings were published. A code of principles was adopted in 1949 and revised in 1975 "to stimulate the conscience and the quality of the American editorial page."[17] This document was revised and renamed "Statement of Principles" in 1975. Six articles outline legal and ethical considerations such as: responsibility to the public; freedom of the press; and journalistic independence, impartiality, and dedication to truth and accuracy. The statement concludes with a declaration that "these principles are intended to preserve, protect and strengthen the bond of trust and respect between American journalists and the American people, a bond that is essential to sustain the grant of freedom entrusted to both by the nation's founders."

Another important national group, the Associated Press Managing Editors Association (APME), was formed in 1931 by news executives who found the annual meetings of the ANPA and the AP too little concerned with improving the news columns' content. The AP news report was analyzed and criticized orally in annual meetings until 1947, when a printed report was prepared by a Continuing Study Committee. Although the studies of the different portions of the AP news report were penetrating enough to arouse replies from the AP management, they were made public as the *APME Red Book* beginning in 1948.[18] Setting the pattern for the Continuing Study reports were the first chair people, William P. Steven of the *Minneapolis Tribune* and Lee Hills of the *Miami Herald*. The group published *APME News*.

The equivalent organization in broadcasting is the Radio-Television News Directors Association (RTNDA), which was founded in 1946 as the National Association of Radio News Directors. Among early leaders were Sig Mickelson, WCCO, Minneapolis, and Jack Shelley, WHO, Des Moines. Its publication was the *RTNDA Communicator*. The group set broadcast news standards and worked closely with journalism schools.

OTHER PROFESSIONAL GROUPS

Other professional groups were concerned with varying aspects of journalistic problems: the National Newspaper Association, representing weeklies and some smaller dailies; the Magazine Publishers Association; the National Association of Educational Broadcasters; the National Radio Broadcasters Association; the National Press Photographers Association; the Society of Newspaper Design; and many regional organizations. Some schools of journalism joined with newspeople in sponsoring various professional conferences dealing with journalistic problems. Awards for outstanding achievement were inaugurated by Sigma Delta Chi, the professional journalism society begun in 1909 at DePauw University and expanded to include professional chapters and both men and women, under the name of Society of Professional Journalists. Its journal is the *Quill*. Research on journalism was encouraged by annual awards by both Sigma Delta Chi and Kappa Tau Alpha, a journalism scholastic society founded in 1910 at the University of Missouri. Theta Sigma Phi, a women's journalism society founded in 1909 at the University of Washington, stimulated interest through its annual Matrix table gatherings; it became Women in Communications, Inc., and published *The Professional Communicator*.

A UNITY Convention was held in Atlanta in 1994 for four associations of minority journalists: the National Association of Black Journalists, the Asian American Journalists Association, the National Association of Hispanic Journalists, and the Native American Journalists Association. A second UNITY convention was held in 1999 in Seattle. The mission of the UNITY coalition, which is made up of these four associations, is "to advance the growth and leadership of people of color in the global news industry." The convention is intended to raise public awareness of the challenges faced by journalists of color and to educate mainstream media on the importance of newsroom diversity.

EDUCATION FOR JOURNALISM BEGINS

The ties between campus and city room were strengthened greatly in the second quarter of the twentieth century. The famous cartoon showing a city editor asking a young hopeful, "And what, may I ask, is a school of journalism?" no longer held true. It was now likely that the city editor was a journalism school graduate also—or at least a college graduate with an appreciation of the necessity for sound educational training for newspeople.

The first definitely organized curriculum in journalism was offered at the University of Pennsylvania from 1893 to 1901 by Joseph French Johnson, a former financial editor of the *Chicago Tribune.* The University of Illinois organized the first four-year curriculum in journalism in 1904 under the direction of Frank W. Scott. The first separate school of journalism, with newspaperman Walter Williams as dean, opened in 1908 at the University of Missouri.[19]

In this first period of journalism education, emphasis was placed on establishing technical courses. But journalism teachers, often getting their starts in English departments, had to win academic recognition as well as the confidence of the newspaper profession. Their most successful early leader in this regard was Willard G. Bleyer, who began teaching journalism at the University of Wisconsin in 1904. Bleyer advocated integrating journalism education with the social sciences, and through his development of this concept and his own journalism history research, he established Wisconsin as a center for graduate study by future journalism teachers. Other early leaders were Eric W. Allen of the University of Oregon, Leon N. Flint of the University of Kansas, Merle H. Thorpe of the University of Washington, and Talcott Williams and John W. Cunliffe of Columbia University, the first two men to head the Pulitzer School of Journalism, opened in 1912 with a $2 million endowment from the *New York World* publisher.

JOURNALISM AS A SOCIAL INSTITUTION

During the second phase of journalism education emphasis was placed on the study of journalism history and of the press as a social institution, and instruction was widened to areas other than that of the daily and weekly newspapers. Pioneer textbooks had been written by Bleyer, Harry F. Harrington of Northwestern, Grant M. Hyde of Wisconsin, and M. Lyle Spencer of Syracuse. In the early 1920s the books by Bleyer on journalism history and by Flint and Nelson Antrim Crawford of Kansas State on newspaper ethics pointed the way toward integration of technical training with analysis of the social responsibilities of the journalists. Coming into importance were the American Association of Teachers of Journalism, founded in 1912, and the American Association of Schools and Departments of Journalism, established in 1917.

Other publishers than Pulitzer aided in the establishment of journalism schools. Second in size to the Pulitzer gift to Columbia University was the endowment fund provided in 1918 by William J. Murphy, publisher of the *Minneapolis Tribune,* for journalism education at the University of Minnesota, augmented in 1977 by publisher John Cowles. The owners of the *Chicago Tribune* established the Medill School of Journalism at Northwestern University in 1921. State press associations helped establish other schools and departments.

The 1920s saw the founding of the *Journalism Quarterly* (now *Journalism and Mass Communication Quarterly),* devoted to research studies in the field of mass communications. It began as the *Journalism Bulletin* in 1924, taking the title *Quarterly* in 1930. Frank Luther Mott of Iowa (later Missouri) and Ralph D. Casey and Raymond B. Nixon of Minnesota set its tone as initial editors. The educators successively founded *Journalism Educator* (now *Journalism and Mass Communication Educator), Journalism Monographs* (now *Journalism and Mass Communication Monographs),* and *Journalism Abstracts* (now *Journalism and Mass Communication Abstracts).* Among other research journals were *Journalism History, American Journalism, Journal of Broadcasting* (now *Journal of Broadcasting and Electronic Media), Journal of Communication, Public Opinion Quarterly, Journal of Popular Culture, Critical Studies in Mass Communication,* and *Journal of Mass Media Ethics.*

JOURNALISM AS A SOCIAL SCIENCE

A third phase of journalism education was developing by the 1930s. The fuller integration of journalism education with the social sciences was the goal, and the leading schools and departments understood research and teaching in the field of communications as a whole. Journalism students, it was recognized, should receive broad liberal-arts educations, sound journalistic technical training, and understanding of the social implications of their chosen profession. Northwestern University developed a five-year plan for professional training in 1938; the Pulitzer School at Columbia in 1935 had restricted its one-year course to holders of bachelor's degrees. Graduate-level instruction along with research in mass communications was expanded at other institutions. Among early leaders in mass-communications research based on the social and behavioral sciences were Chilton R. Bush of Stanford University, Ralph O. Nafziger of Minnesota (later Wisconsin), Wilbur Schramm of Iowa (later Illinois and Stanford), and Paul F. Lazarsfeld of Columbia.

MEDIA SUPPORT FOR EDUCATION

Closer ties between newspaperpeople and schools were established during the 1930s. The idea of a joint committee that would include representatives of the principal newspaper associations and the schools and departments of journalism was suggested by Fred Fuller Shedd, the editor of the *Philadelphia Bulletin* who had been instrumental in the founding of the department at Pennsylvania State. Journalism educators, led by Bleyer of Wisconsin, Allen of Oregon, and Frank L. Martin of Missouri, joined in the plan in 1931. The project lapsed during the Great Depression years but was brought into full operation in 1939 through the efforts of Kenneth E. Olson of Northwestern University. The American Council on Education for Journalism (ACEJ) was formed by journalism educators and 5 major newspaper organizations; more than 50 professional associations in broadcasting, magazine publishing, advertising, business communications, and public relations later joined in the council's work. The ACEJ established an accrediting program and approved studies in one or more areas of journalism at 40 schools and departments in the late 1940s. The number of accredited institutions increased to more than 90 by 1990.

In 1949 the American Association of Teachers of Journalism reorganized as the Association for Education in Journalism (AEJ). Accepting coordinate roles within the AEJ structure were the American Association of Schools and Departments of Journalism (now composed of the accredited schools) and the American Society of Journalism School Administrators, founded in 1944. They merged in 1984 as the Association of Schools of Journalism and Mass Communication (ASJMC). The AEJ similarly became the AEJMC.

Journalism schools in the 1990s were thus well established in the fields of teaching, research, and service. They had close ties with the profession, and their scope of interests included daily and weekly newspapers, magazines, radio, television, photojournalism, advertising, the graphic arts, industrial editing, and public relations. A doctorate in mass communications was offered at more than a score of universities in the fields of communication theory, mass-communications history, law and social institutions, and international communication.

A million-dollar endowment left to Harvard University in 1936 by the widow of Lucius W. Nieman, founder of the *Milwaukee Journal,* was used for a different type of educational opportunity. The Nieman Foundation, beginning in 1937, annually selected a dozen highly qualified working newspaperpeople for a year of study at Harvard as Nieman

Fellows, on leave from their newspapers or press associations. Louis M. Lyons, first curator of the foundation, established a thoughtful quarterly magazine, *Nieman Reports,* in 1947.

EFFORTS TO IMPROVE: STUDIES OF THE PRESS

Other attempts to study the responsibilities and the character of the American press were made in the years after World War II. Magazine publisher Henry R. Luce financed an important private study by the Commission on Freedom of the Press. The commission was headed by Chancellor Robert M. Hutchins of the University of Chicago and was composed chiefly of social-science professors outside the field of journalism. No journalists were invited to sit on the commission. Its summary report, *A Free and Responsible Press* (1947), covered newspapers, radio, motion pictures, magazines, and books, and consisted of a general statement of principles. The commission itself conducted only a limited research program in the making of its report, but it sponsored the publication of important books, including Zechariah Chafee, Jr.'s *Government and Mass Communications,* William E. Hocking's *Freedom of the Press,* and Llewellyn White's *The American Radio.* It has heard over 120 cases, and its determinations are not legally enforceable. Participants also waive their rights to litigate the matter after the determination. The parties appear before the council to present their sides, and the council discusses the issues and votes on them the same day. Decisions are publicized through local media.

A major contribution to the elevation and advancement of the mass media was made in 1984 by the Trustees of the Gannett Foundation, founded in 1935 by Frank Gannett, when they established a center for media studies at Columbia University. The foundation was renamed the Freedom Forum in 1991, with Allen H. Neuharth serving as chairman of the board of trustees. Charles L. Overby was named president.

In addition to the Media Studies Center in New York, the Freedom Forum operated the First Amendment Center at Vanderbilt University, the Pacific Coast center in Oakland, and The Newseum, a major tourist attraction at its World Center in Arlington, Virginia. The nation's only comprehensive memorial to journalists killed while reporting news was built in Freedom Park adjoining the Newseum.

The Freedom Forum commissioned numerous studies of media relationships with the public, government, and business, and frequently held seminars at its World Center. It was recognized for its devotion to the improvement of education and professional opportunities for minorities. In 1995 Neuharth announced a $1 million study of Congress and the news media. The Media Studies Center sponsored annually a variety of conferences, seminars, and briefings; conducted a technology studies program; developed a research library; and became a major producer of books, pamphlets, and a noteworthy scholarly quarterly, *Media Studies Journal.* The foundation made other substantial contributions to professional and scholarly media events and publications.

EFFORTS TO IMPROVE: PRESS COUNCILS

The example of the successful British Press Council, established in 1953 to hear complaints against newspapers under rules carefully drawn to protect the rights of both editors and citizens, led to movements to create press councils in the United States. The first to appear were the local press councils organized in the late 1960s under the auspices of the Newspaper Guild's Mellett Fund.

One effort was made on the West Coast under the direction of William L. Rivers and his associates from Stanford University; another in Sparta and Cairo, Illinois, by Kenneth

Starck and others from Southern Illinois University. A media-black council, to develop a better understanding between media executives and the black community, was directed by Lawrence Schneider of the University of Washington in Seattle for 19 months. In 1971, the first statewide press council was established in Minnesota through the efforts of the Minnesota Newspaper Association, the Newspaper Guild, the Society of Professional Journalists, other media leaders, and public officials. The council membership was evenly divided between representatives of the media and the public, with a state supreme court justice serving as chair. Hawaii's council was formed the same year, but it survived only as a Honolulu press council. A regional council combines parts of Washington and Oregon. Minnesota's remained the only state council.[20]

Efforts to establish a national press council bore fruit in 1973 with the establishment of the National News Council. A task force supported by the Twentieth Century Fund set as its goals "to examine and report on complaints concerning the accuracy and fairness of news reporting in the United States, as well as to initiate studies and report on issues involving the freedom of the press." At first shunned by major media leaders, the National News Council gained support through its handling of issues presented to it for consideration by ten public members and eight professional members. William B. Arthur was executive director, and Norman E. Isaacs was chairman, followed by Richard Salant. Beginning in 1977 its reports were printed first in the *Columbia Journalism Review* and later in *Quill.* But support waned, and the council closed its doors in 1983.[21] But recently there have been calls to revisit the national news council concept, most notably from Mike Wallace, who appeared at the twenty-fifth anniversary of the Minnesota News Council in 1996 to encourage the media to consider a new national news council to bolster its sagging credibility.

EFFORTS TO IMPROVE: OMBUDSMEN

The employment of an ombudsman to monitor a newspaper's performance and review public complaints began at the *Louisville Courier-Journal* in 1967. But by 1998 only 32 other dailies were employing an ombudsman and publishing his or her comments.

The Organization of News Ombudsmen, formed in 1980, has an international membership. Its goals include education about the position of news ombudsmen and aid in establishing ombudsmen in newspapers and elsewhere in the media. An annual meeting is held in a member's country to discuss ethical issues and trade ideas.

EFFORTS TO IMPROVE: JOURNALISM REVIEWS

Another phenomenon was the journalism review. Prior to 1968 only three existed: the *Montana Journalism Review* (1958), *Columbia Journalism Review* (1961), and *Seminar,* a review of sorts published by Copley Newspapers (1966). The *Chicago Journalism Review* (1968 to 1975) inspired a number of local and journalism department reviews, but of the approximately 40 established between 1968 and 1976, fewer than a dozen survived in 1977, including the Columbia and Montana reviews; *MORE,* a national review published in New York; *Accuracy in Media (AIM),* a conservative newsletter; *Media Report to Women; feed/back,* published in San Francisco; the *St. Louis Journalism Review;* the *Twin Cities Journalism Review; Pretentious Idea* in Tucson; and *Lexington Media Review* (Kentucky).[22] *The Washington Journalism Review* (*WJR*) began publishing in 1977. A magazine bluntly titled *Lies of Our Times* appeared between 1990 and 1994. The 1991 survivors were the *American Journalism Review* (formerly *WJR*), *CJR, Extra* (by Fairness and Accuracy in

Reporting), *St. Louis Journalism Review, Media Report to Women,* and *AIM.* Edward S. Herman of the University of Pennsylvania was senior editor and Ellen Ray was executive editor of this publication aimed principally at the *New York Times.* Contributors included Noam Chomsky of the Massachusetts Institute of Technology, who teamed with Herman in numerous books and articles to castigate news organizations for their failures in the coverage of U.S. foreign policy, human rights and illegalities in government and business.

The *Chicago Journalism Review* appeared in the wake of the riots at the 1968 Democratic convention. Edited by Ron Dorfman, the monthly afforded an aggressive criticism of the city's press and a forum for issues of press criticism and self-improvement among young new reporters. It inspired not only local imitators but also the development of informal "reporter-power" groups in city rooms, where young staff members met to seek improvements in their professional contributions. In some cities regular meetings of journalists and management resulted.

In 1998 *Brill's Content* came out, with its mission to be a general audience publication covering media ethics and accountability. The magazine, subtitled "The Independent Voice of the Information Age," elicited mixed reactions. Its first cover story, on the Clinton–Lewinsky scandal, drew a terse and lengthy rebuttal letter from independent council Kenneth Starr. Articles in the first few issues included a look at Matt Drudge, a controversial reporter who admits that he does not check his stories but often rushes them into print, but whose online *Drudge Report* broke the Lewinsky story before the mainstream media did. *Brill's Content* employs an ombudsman.

EFFORTS TO IMPROVE: PUBLIC/CIVIC JOURNALISM

A new form of journalism called public or civic journalism has become popular in the last few decades. Two of its creators and top defenders are Jay Rosen, the Director of the Project on Public Life and the Press at New York University and Davis "Buzz" Merritt, editor of the *Wichita Eagle.* According to Rosen, public journalism's primary claim is that the media can and should improve civic discussion and engage in community problem solving. From this perspective, the media have become detached from the public they serve, and public journalism is a way to reconnect the two. Public journalism projects have gathered people at events such as community roundtables to address issues such as crime or education, or have sponsored voter registration drives.

Many newspapers have either undertaken public journalism projects or reorganized their newsrooms to reflect some of the concerns public journalism identifies. For example, in "The People's Voice," the *Boston Globe* and several local television and radio stations teamed up to give their citizens a voice in the 1994 elections. In Madison, Wisconsin, people participated in "We The People" town hall meetings and debates, which were organized by the *Wisconsin State Journal* and a coalition of other Madison media organizations; television and radio stations rebroadcast the events to thousands more.

Proponents of public journalism claim that journalism and public life have been historically intertwined and should be connected this way. Journalists have always been involved in public life, they say, and this is no different. Opponents assert that public journalism removes objectivity. No longer observers and reporters, journalists help to set agendas for public discussion and action rather than reporting on them. Traditional journalists cover a parade while public journalists march in it. Despite the division among American journalists, the practice of public journalism has not yet reached its peak, and it is likely that more newspapers will give the concept a try in an attempt to better relate to the public whose readership they are rapidly losing.

WOMEN IN THE MEDIA

The pressure of the feminist movement increased the representation of women in the media, but there was concern in the 1990s that more needed to be done despite evidence of progress in a number of areas. In the newspaper field, fewer than 20 percent of news, advertising, and circulation managers were women. While Cathleen Black was publisher of *USA Today,* fewer than 60 other women (7 percent) ran U.S. dailies. Women managers or editors were in the majority only in the classified advertising area, the business office, and the feature and life-style sections. Roughly 30 to 40 percent of newsroom staffs were female.

Pacesetters were Katherine Fanning, editor of the *Christian Science Monitor,* and Mary Anne Dolan, editor of the *Los Angeles Herald-Examiner.* Knight-Ridder named Janet Chusmir executive editor of the *Miami Herald.* Later Marty Claus, managing editor for features and business at the *Detroit Free Press,* was named vice president for news for Knight-Ridder. Margaret Downing became the first woman managing editor at the *Houston Post.* Kathryn Christensen, former senior editor at the *Wall Street Journal* and senior producer at ABC's *World News Tonight,* was named managing editor of the *Baltimore Sun.* At the *New York Times,* Linda Matthews, formerly with the *Los Angeles Times* and *World News Tonight,* became national editor—the first outsider (not trained within the paper) to head a news division at the *Times* in 30 years. By 1995 women held important editing positions at most major papers.

Cathleen Black took over as president of Hearst Magazines in late 1995, where she oversaw financial performance and development of magazines such as *Cosmopolitan, Esquire, Good Housekeeping, Harper's Bazaar,* and *Redbook.* She was included in the 25 top-ranked most powerful women in American business by *Fortune* magazine that year. In 1998, Tina Brown made national headlines when she left the editorship of *The New Yorker* for a position as executive editor of a new monthly magazine at Miramax. Ruth Whitney, editor-in-chief at Conde Nast's *Glamour* magazine, retired in 1998 after 31 years at the helm; she was succeeded by Bonnie Fuller, editor-in-chief of *Cosmopolitan,* and that position was taken by Kate White, formerly of *Redbook.*

More women were active in national associations. For example, the editor of the *Miami Herald*'s Broward edition, Sue Reisinger, was the first woman president of the Associated Press Managing Editors; Cathleen Black moved from head of the American Newspaper Publishers Association to president of the Newspaper Association of America; Jane Healey, managing editor of the Orlando (Fla.) *Sentinel* and a Pulitzer Prize–winning editorial writer, was a longtime board member of the American Society of Newspaper Editors. Women also held the presidencies of the Society of Professional Journalists, the Association for Education in Journalism and Mass Communication, and other organizations.

The gender gap was narrowing, according to a study sponsored by the Freedom Forum's Media Studies Center, *The American Journalist in the 1990s,* conducted in 1992 by David Weaver and G. Cleveland Wilhoit. Women journalists numbered 34 percent, a figure unchanged in a decade. But their pay averaged 81 percent of that of male colleagues, an increase of 10 percent. A growing number of women were reported to hold some sort of supervisory position. In the newspaper world, women had their highest employment percentage on papers with circulations of 25,000 to 100,000, but even so few made it into top leadership roles. On the positive side an increased number of women were active in political journalism and in the foreign correspondence field.

A 1997 report showed very little change for women in the newsroom. ASNE's study, "Journalists in the 1990s," revealed that 36 percent of newsroom staffers were women— very little change from 1992. Of those women, more than one-quarter were age 30 or younger, compared to 15 percent of men. In the over-50 age group, only 22 percent were women.

Interestingly, ASNE's 1997 study showed little difference between the sexes in areas such as job satisfaction, reasons for leaving the newspaper business, and evaluations of their managers and the needs of the newsroom. But women were more likely than men to desire more one-on-one communication, and they tended to aspire to positions within the newsroom rather than to the top publisher spot.

In broadcasting there were steady improvements in the numbers of women hired on all levels. Studies of visibility on the networks' nightly news programs showed the number of reports by women reporters increased 87 percent from 1990 to 1993. Overall, women reported about one-fourth of evening news stories and made up about a quarter of the national evening news corps. Veteran Washington journalist Mary Tillotson hosted *CNN & Co.,* a popular all-woman news-talk show. In radio it became common to hear a woman delivering the news, and an increasing number became news directors. In television women were seen as reporters and anchors in almost every community, and began to make inroads in producing, but men still dominated the executive offices.

In the primetime entertainment field the number of women producers, directors, and writers remained low. In the major industry segments, women had the most success in public relations and advertising, where they often were the top executive or the owner. The magazine area also was more open, as was the book publishing business. Nancy Evans, editor-in-chief of the Book of the Month Club, became publisher of Doubleday. In the film industry, also a longtime bastion of iron-willed men, it was difficult for women seeking a top-level position. Overall, networking was paying off for women, but true equality in decision making and compensation was far from being achieved, with sexual harassment cases a continual reminder of the challenge. The long-range forecast was for improvement, however, because more than 60 percent of the nation's journalism students were women. Assisting women working in the media or teaching journalism were *Media Report to Women,* the nation's oldest such newsletter, founded by Donna Allen; and *Women's Words,* published by the Commission on the Status of Women of the Association for Education in Journalism and Mass Communication.

LANDMARK LEGAL CASES: LIBEL

The historic law providing citizens recourse against defamation of character in the press always provided occasion for fair comment on, and criticism of, those who were in the public eye when they became involved in the news. But in the 1960s the Supreme Court so clarified and extended the media's protections against libel that a new theory emerged, called the "public law of libel." The Court also constitutionalized libel by making it a matter of the First Amendment. Under this theory public officials and public figures cannot recover for libel unless they can prove deliberate lying or extreme recklessness in publishing without an attempt to ascertain the truth.[23] This requirement is called "actual malice," which must be proven by the person bringing the lawsuit.

The landmark case was *New York Times Co.* v. *Sullivan,* decided in 1964. In 1960 the Times had published an advertisement protesting police actions in Montgomery, Alabama, against followers of the Reverend Martin Luther King, Jr. Sullivan, a police commissioner, sued for libel and was awarded $500,000 damages in a state court. Reversing the judgment, the Supreme Court held that errors contained in the advertisement were not malicious and that the First Amendment protects "uninhibited robust and wide-open" debate of public issues without any test of truth, which became known as the *"New York Times* doctrine."[24]

In 1967 the Supreme Court extended this theory to cover "public figures" as well as "public officials" but drew a line concerning recklessness in not following professional precautions in checking for truth when time permits. The Court reversed a $500,000 judgment a right-wing spokesperson, General Edwin A. Walker, had obtained against the Associated Press, ruling that Walker was a public figure subject to criticism. But it upheld a $460,000 judgment given to University of Georgia football coach Wallace Butts for a story in the *Saturday Evening Post* accusing him of throwing games. The court said handling of the story "involved highly unreasonable conduct constituting an extreme departure from the standards of investigation and reporting ordinarily adhered to by responsible publishers."[25]

In 1971, the Supreme Court, which had "buried the common law crime of seditious libel" in *Sullivan,* extended its "actual malice" requirement from public officials and public persons to include even private individuals who had been projected into the public-interest area. The case, *Rosenbloom* v. *Metromedia,* involved a broadcaster's references to a book dealer's "obscene" literature.

By a 5–4 majority in 1974, however, the Court held in *Gertz* v. *Robert Welch, Inc.,* that private citizens, even if involved in events of public interest, were entitled to recover damages without having to prove the *New York Times* malice test, but only if they could prove actual damages. The *Times* malice rule still applied to a plaintiff who sought punitive damages. In 1976 the Court, in *Time Inc.* v. *Firestone* narrowed its definition of "public figures" to only those who have roles to play in the resolution of public issues, while giving a prominent socialite libel damages against *Time.*[26]

Three 1986 Supreme Court decisions gave new support to the *Sullivan* doctrine. In *Anderson* v. *Liberty Lobby* the Court ruled 6–3 that a public-figure libel plaintiff must demonstrate "actual malice" by "clear and convincing evidence" to overcome a defendant's motion that a summary judgment dismissing the suit be granted by a trial judge. The political action organization had sued columnist Jack Anderson.

In *Hepps* v. *Philadelphia Newspapers Inc.* the Court ruled 5–4 that states may not place the burden on media libel defendants to prove truth in suits brought by private figures if they involve coverage of issues of public concern. Justice Sandra Day O'Connor said this reversal of common law tradition was necessary to protect the constitutional interest in open debate of issues of public concern. The *Inquirer* had linked a beverage-store owner with members of organized crime. Showing proof or falsity would remain the plaintiff's responsibility.

A third 1986 Court action bulwarked the "actual malice" standard by letting stand a U.S. court of appeals ruling affirming a summary judgment for CBS that dismissed a libel claim by Lieutenant Colonel Anthony Herbert, a Vietnam War hero who had charged that Mike Wallace had in effect called him a liar during a 1973 *60 Minutes* broadcast. In 1979 the Supreme Court had ruled that Herbert was entitled to probe the thoughts of Wallace in order to help prove his case. Herbert spent more than $3 million on the lengthy case, and CBS $4 million. In 1985 CBS also successfully repelled a $120 million libel claim made by General William Westmoreland in the wake of another Mike Wallace news documentary about Vietnam.

A sweeping reaffirmation of the *Sullivan* decision protecting criticism of public figures came in the Court's 1988 unanimous decision in the *Hustler Magazine* v. *Falwell* case. The Court overturned a $200,000 award to the Reverend Jerry Falwell for "emotional distress" caused by a *Hustler* parody portraying him as an incestuous drunk. The case was important because it could have opened the floodgates to suits by people claiming emotional distress in order to avoid the legal burden of proving libel.

In 1990 the Supreme Court ruled 7–2 in *Milkovich* v. *Lorain Journal Co.* that opinion is not protected when based on false facts. Chief Justice William Rehnquist said the statement in *Gertz* v. *Welch* that "under the First Amendment there is no such thing as a false idea" was not intended "to create a wholesale defamation exemption for anything that might be labeled 'opinion.'" Media leaders found the decision "unsettling," but the other side of the coin was that the Court had extended the protections of *Sullivan* to opinion as it had to satire in the *Falwell* case. Subsequent cases have upheld the general rule that opinion based on false facts may not be protected. But at least the context of an opinion will be considered.[27]

But libel remains an uncertain area for the media. Libel awards against media organizations—particularly punitive damages, those meant to punish the offender—continue to grow. In 1997 a Texas jury awarded $22.7 million in actual damages and a staggering $200 million in punitive damages, the largest such award, against the *Wall Street Journal* for a story about a troubled Houston bond-trader. Plaintiff MMAR Group alleged that the *Journal* probably knew the information in the story was false and published it anyway, and the information was damaging enough to cause several clients to withdraw their business. MMAR Group went out of business a few weeks later. The damage award was subsequently reduced and the verdict appealed, but the message to the media was clear: Libel, when it can be demonstrated, will be harshly punished.[28]

In another interesting media law development, a plaintiff skirted traditional First Amendment issues (which usually involve high burdens of proof for plaintiffs) and sued on the basis of employment law and trespass. In 1992 two employees of the ABC news magazine *PrimeTime Live* posed as deli workers with falsified resumes and got jobs at a Food Lion grocery store to follow up on a story about unsafe food handling practices in the chain. *PrimeTime Live* filmed hours of hidden-camera tape trying to dig up misdeeds by Food Lion and showed excerpts from these tapes. Food Lion, alleging that the tapes were severely edited and framed to show what *PrimeTime Live* wanted to show, bypassed traditional claims of libel and instead went for claims of fraud, trespass, and breach of loyalty, claiming that the *PrimeTime Live* employees got their jobs by lying. In 1997 a North Carolina jury awarded Food Lion only $1402 in actual damages but over $5.5 million in punitive damages, which was also subsequently reduced. However, should this trend continue, many find it disturbing to see the creative ways in which plaintiffs bypass the difficult First Amendment route to attack the media on other grounds.[29]

Until recently, online libel was a difficult and unsettled area. Lower courts had disagreed on whether an operator of an online service can be held liable for defamatory statements posted by users. In 1991 a district court in New York held that CompuServe, an online service, could not be held liable for information loaded onto its bulletin boards as part of an "electronic library" that it had not had the opportunity to review. CompuServe was determined to be a distributor, not a publisher, of this information, and thus not liable for the content it had distributed.[30] But in 1995 another court in New York held that Prodigy, a service similar to CompuServe, was found to be responsible for its content by exercising editorial review and control procedures and advertising these procedures as benefits to its potential market. Thus Prodigy was a publisher of the defamatory material, not just a distributor. The judge, while agreeing with the CompuServe court, distinguished the Prodigy case by the level of control or review of the material prior to its loading into the computer banks. This unpublished opinion did not have the force of law.[31] However, a trio of cases involving the online service provider America Online seemed to settle the matter once and for all. After the 1995 case against Prodigy, Congress enacted "Good Samaritan" provisions (Section 230) to the Communications Decency Act (a part not held to be unconstitutional by the Court in *Reno versus ACLU*). This section established that online service providers are neither publishers nor speakers of content passing through their systems and could not be expected to monitor that vast amount of content. Courts have interpreted Section 230 to create an absolute immunity for online service providers with respect to third-party content.[32]

OBSCENITY AND PORNOGRAPHY

Courts have long struggled with the regulation and definition of sexual materials. The words *pornography* and *obscenity* are often used interchangeably; however, they are not legally the same. While both words connote sexual content, material that a court deems to be obscene because it meets the criteria outlined in the three-part *Miller* test (described below) is not afforded any protection by the First Amendment and can be censored. Pornography is protected by the First Amendment because despite its sexual nature, it has not met the *Miller* test.

It was not an easy task to determine what was obscene, however, and society's standards on that subject, as they affected newspapers, magazines, and films, changed dramatically in the 1960s and 1970s, This was particularly true in the areas of four-letter words and nudity. But the Supreme Court was slow to find clear-cut guides. A landmark case came in 1957 with *Roth* v. *United States*. Roth, who sold distasteful material, had been convicted under the federal obscenity statute. The court upheld his conviction but set a new standard for testing obscenity: "Whether to the average person, applying contemporary community standards, the dominant theme of the material taken as a whole appeals to prurient interest."[33] To this the Court in later decisions added a test of "redeeming social importance"; if this were present, the law need not apply. Under this interpretation, *Fanny Hill* was cleared, but Ralph Ginzburg, publisher of *Eros,* was not. The Court ruled that he had flouted this test and had commercially exploited erotic materials solely on prurient appeal.[34] How to define these terms remained a puzzle.

A 5–4 majority of the Supreme Court revised the *Roth* standard in *Miller* v. *California,* a 1973 case.[35] The Court held that to be judged obscene the work must specifically lack "serious literary, artistic, political or scientific value," and added that the contemporary community standards against which the jury is to measure prurient appeal and patent offensiveness are to be the standards of the state or local community. This ruling, which left standards of taste to individual communities, posed serious problems for products distributed nationwide for audiences of diverse sophistication, and the courts were left grappling with the problem of how to define these terms. There was no significant change in the *Miller* ruling during the next decade, although in a 1978 decision the Court added that "community standards did not necessarily mean a majority view," and that an "average" person would have to be a "reasonable" person.[36] The *Miller* test still remains the governing law in determining whether material of a sexual nature receives First Amendment protection and thus cannot be censored. The *Miller* test has been also been used to determine whether sound recordings are obscene and can be censored.[37]

Both legislatures and courts are grappling with the question of sexual material available online. Because children have easy access to computers and the Internet, many parents want the ability to control very carefully what their children see online. The first Congressional attempt to regulate online sexual material was part of the Telecommunications Act of 1996. Titled the Communications Decency Act, or CDA, it criminalized the knowing transmission of sexual material to anyone under 18 years of age, and outlined broad definitions of what constituted prohibited sexual material. A district court overturned the CDA as overbroad and vague, and in 1997 the Supreme Court agreed.

In *Reno* v. *American Civil Liberties Union,* the Supreme Court, in its first decision to address the Internet as a mass medium, said that the CDA was "a content-based blanket restriction on speech" that could not withstand First Amendment scrutiny. Because the definitions were so vague and broad, any communication of a sexual nature could be covered—including, for example, e-mail communication between parents and children involving sexual themes. Justice John Paul Stevens, writing for the majority, noted, "Under the CDA, a parent allowing her 17-year-old to use the family computer to obtain information on the Internet that she, in her parental judgment, deems appropriate could face a lengthy prison term." The Court refused to reduce Internet content to what is only appropriate for children. Stevens wrote, "In order to deny minors access to potentially harmful speech, the CDA effectively suppresses a large amount of speech that adults have a constitutional right to receive and to address to one another." This case was also important because the Court refused to apply the strong regulations traditionally applied to the broadcast medium to the Internet. However, the Court did not specifically outline a standard by which the Internet is to be judged.[38]

Not long after the CDA was overturned, Congress began work on other versions of a bill intended to protect children from online sexual materials. Dubbed "Sons of CDA" or "CDA IIs" in the press, these bills were new attempts to define limits for online sexual content deemed inappropriate for minors. Late in 1998, Congress passed the Child Online Protection Act (COPA), in which commercial websites that provided access to pornographic material would be required to employ some form of age verification or be subject to sanctions. The definition provided for material considered to be "harmful to minors" closely resembled the three-part obscenity test the Supreme Court created in *Miller* in 1973. The ACLU immediately petitioned for a temporary restraining order against the act's enforcement, which was granted until early 1999, when hearings were scheduled. Some commentators suggested that this act stood a better chance than did the CDA did of passing constitutional muster because the obscenity definition in this act mimicked the Court's own language in the *Miller* case, and the act was targeted only at commercial websites. Critics, however, alleged that this act suffered from the same defects as the CDA did—it would have the effect of discouraging the circulation of otherwise constitutionally protected sexual material.

In early February 1999, COPA was struck down as constitutionally flawed. The district court judge replaced the earlier restraining order with a preliminary injunction to block its enforcement, claiming that "we do the minors of this country harm if First Amendment protections, which they will with age inherit fully, are chipped away in the name of their protection." The government plans to appeal the ruling to the Third Circuit.

CENSORSHIP

The Post Office Department, with its power to exclude publications from the mails under certain conditions, has at times been a threat to freedom of the press. Over the years, court decisions and administrative actions—and during World War I, the sweeping use of the postmaster's power to throw socialist publications out of the mails—built up a spirit of censorship in the Post Office. In 1943, however, when the Postmaster General proposed to withdraw use of the second-class mailing rate from *Esquire* magazine, the Supreme Court stepped in on the side of the magazine. Justice William Douglas pointed out that to allow this action would be to open the floodgates for additional censorious actions on the basis of a single official's opinion.[39]

The Court considered censorship of publications in 1988. In *Hazelwood School District* v. *Kuhlmeier,* the Court ruled that a Missouri school administration could censor some student "speech that is inconsistent with the school's basic educational mission." Some students and media representatives attacked the decision as a restriction on student journalists' exploration of such issues as drug and alcohol abuse, AIDS, teen pregnancy, and effects of divorce on children. A few states have laws specifically protecting student press rights to combat the *Hazelwood* decision, but most do not.

Internet censorship remained one of the hottest legal topics at the turn of the twenty-first century. Not only material of a sexual nature is targeted by laws like the CDA, but websites that contain hate messages have also been threatened. Not everyone agrees on the worth of websites that promote anti-Semitic or other racist views. Filtering software is one option that some argue can help screen out not only sexual material but also hate speech. These programs contain lists of search terms and web addresses that are blocked when a user tries to access them, and some can be customized. In theory, this software helps parents control what sites their children can access. However, many proprietary filtering companies do not release their lists of blocked sites or search terms, and it has been suggested that some blocking is politically motivated. Mandates for public libraries to install filtering software on computers available for patron Internet use were among the bills circulating in Congress in the late 1990s.

COMMERCIAL SPEECH

In another First Amendment area deserving attention, there was concern that government had extended its regulatory control in the fields of advertising and other promotional activities. The Supreme Court's involvement dated to 1942 when in *Valentine* v. *Chrestensen* it ruled the Constitution placed no restraints upon government regulation of commercial speech. By the 1970s a number of decisions had given regulators fairly broad control over such things as door-to-door solicitation and in some cases advertising leaflets. There was a brief reversal in the 1975–79 period when the Court protected the advertising of prescription drug prices and the circulation of information about abortions. But in the 1980 case of *Central Hudson Gas & Electric Corp.* v. *Public Service Commission* the Court approved a four-part test for future commercial speech cases and in doing so removed some of the protection bestowed in the previous five-year period.[40]

The 1990s saw both gains and losses for commercial speech interests. In a 1996 case, the Supreme Court overturned a Rhode Island law banning the advertisement of retail liquor prices except at the place of sale. Justice John Paul Stevens, using the test outlined in the 1980 *Central Hudson* case, concluded that the ban on advertisements that provide the public with accurate information about retail liquor prices is an unconstitutional abridgment of freedom of speech. Blanket bans such as Rhode Island's, Stevens said, must be viewed with special care, and a heavy burden is placed on the state to justify such laws. Rhode Island did not meet this burden. The Court also emphasized the importance of advertising and other commercial speech in modern society, and thus its need for First Amendment protection.[41] But a year later in 1997, the Court said that a requirement that fruit growers help subsidize generic advertising for peaches, nectarines, and plums—

advertising that not only promoted them but also their competitors—did not violate the First Amendment. This seems to be a step back from the Court's expansion of First Amendment protection for commercial speech.[42]

PUBLIC ACCESS TO THE MEDIA

The concept of "fairness" involving the right of access to the broadcast media by people or ideas, has already been discussed in Chapter 18. The theory of a public right of access to the print media was advanced by law professor Jerome A. Barron in a 1967 *Harvard Law Review* article that envisioned a two-dimensional First Amendment that not only forbade the inhibiting of expression by the government, but also, in some circumstances, mandated government affirmative action to provide for public access to the media.[43]

Barron's concept was unanimously rejected by the Supreme Court in a constitutional test of a 1913 Florida law granting a political candidate the right of reply to criticism and attacks on his record by a newspaper. Chief Justice Warren Burger ruled for the Court in the 1974 *Tornillo* case that mandatory access was unconstitutional: "a responsible press is an undoubtedly desirable goal, but press responsibility is not mandated by the Constitution and like many other virtues it cannot be legislated."[44]

Although media spokespeople agree that efforts should be made to open more time and space to individuals, minority groups, unpopular ideas, and simply nonconsensus thinking, they also quail at the idea of compulsory acceptance of everything offered by a station, newspaper, or magazine. There are movements to make the media more accessible. As noted earlier in this chapter, mechanisms such as press councils, ethics codes, and news ombudsmen are traditional ways to increase the public's access to the media. and public journalism is a relatively new movement designed to connect the media more closely to the public they serve.

FREE PRESS, FAIR TRIAL

The weighing of the rights of a free press and its readers against the rights of an accused to a fair trial continued in the 1980s and 1990s as a major problem, with the O. J. Simpson criminal trial bringing the issue to much of the public's attention. In this area, the courts clearly had their way, and in the end the press generally agreed that the placing of restrictions on reporters, photographers, and broadcasters was warranted—provided that they stemmed from cooperative agreements and not from judicial fiat.

Early action centered about the presence of photographers in the courtroom. The American Society of Newspaper Editors, the National Press Photographers Association, and the National Association of Broadcasters waged a battle through the 1950s to gain access to courtrooms for newspaper and television photographers. Their argument that the photographers need not be interrupting the trials had merit, for pictures could be made without noise or light. But lawyers said the publicity stemming from photographs served to frighten witnesses and accused persons, affected juries, and offended the judicial feeling. In 1959 the American Bar Association did agree to review its Canon 35 regulating such activity in the courtroom. But no action resulted, and the admission of cameras remained a local decision of a judge or a state decision.

Meanwhile other events vastly broadened the "free press, fair trial," debate. The assassination of President Kennedy and the haphazard conditions surrounding the killing of the accused by Jack Ruby in a press-filled area brought a plea for reform from the Warren Commission. After a Texas judge had permitted television cameras into the trial of financier Billy Sol Estes, the Supreme Court reversed his conviction.[45] That 1965 decision was followed by one in 1966 ruling that Dr. Sam Sheppard had been deprived of a fair trial in Cleveland on a charge of murdering his wife because the trial judge had failed to protect him from massive prejudicial "trial by newspaper" before and during his prosecution.[46]

The Reardon Report of the American Bar Association came out of the debate. Issued in October 1966 by a 10-member committee of lawyers and judges headed by Justice Paul C. Reardon of Massachusetts, the report favored putting the responsibility on judges to curtail pretrial publicity generated either by the prosecution or the defense. The commission recommended withholding such information as the prior criminal record of the accused, existence of a confession, names of prospective witnesses, speculation on a possible plea, and interviews or photographs obtained without the consent of the accused. The American Bar Association adopted the Reardon Report in 1968, leaving the spelling out of specific provisions to negotiations with media representatives. By the fall of 1969 the press-bar committees of the bar and the ASNE had found common ground for the imposition of the "fair-trial" provisions that did not endanger the "free press." The media, in major trials of the later 1960s and 1970s, resorted to using artists to make sketches of courtroom scenes for both print and television use, thus reverting to the late nineteenth-century practice of using artists' skills to catch the drama of an event.

A breakthrough came in 1981 when the Supreme Court ruled unanimously in *Chandler* v. *Florida* that states have the right to allow television, radio, and photographic coverage of criminal trials, even if the defendant objects. The decision bolstered media efforts to permit still and television cameras in trial and appellate courts. By 1995 courts in 48 states were permitting television and still-photo coverage of trials under varying conditions. Cameras were still prohibited in federal courtrooms. The Senate and House of Representatives also voted to permit radio and television coverage under controlled conditions. In 1995 C-Span cameras were allowed in committee meetings. However, the Supreme Court still does not permit television coverage of its proceedings.

Reporters were placed in the position of having either to face contempt charges or obey a judicial ruling, even if unconstitutional, after a 1972 Louisiana case, *United States* v. *Dickinson.*[47] A judge ordered the press not to report a hearing held in open court, and two reporters who wrote stories despite the warning were then convicted of contempt. The appeals court said the order was unconstitutional but upheld the conviction, saying the reporters should have obeyed the order and appealed it. The Supreme Court declined to review the case, letting the decision stand.

In another 1972 case, *Branzburg* v. *Hayes,* the Supreme Court ruled that reporters had the same obligations as other citizens to respond to legitimate grand jury subpoenas and answer questions relevant to an investigation of a crime. Three reporters had refused to testify about information they had received in confidence. The decision ran counter to the concept of shield laws, passed in many states, allowing reporters to protect the confidentiality of news sources.[48] Many of these laws apply the three-part test of relevance, compelling public need, and the lack of alternative sources cited in a *Branzburg* dissent. There is no federal shield law, but many federal jurisdictions as well as some of the 19 states without shield laws recognize the three-part test. State laws vary greatly in what kind of information is protected and under what circumstances.

A Nebraska murder trial in 1976 brought another press-bar confrontation when the trial judge entered an order that, as modified by the state supreme court, restrained the news media from reporting (1) the existence of any confession or admissions made by the defendant to law-enforcement officers or third parties, except members of the press; (2) the substance of these confessions or statements; and (3) other facts "strongly implicative" of the defendant. The order, designed to follow *Sheppard* guidelines concerning pretrial publicity, expired when the jury was impaneled.

Chief Justice Burger, speaking for the Supreme Court, struck down this order, commenting that the media can report evidence presented at an open preliminary hearing and also that the prohibition on "implicative" information was "too vague and too broad" to survive scrutiny given restraints on First Amendment rights. The press victory was somewhat diluted, however, in that the Supreme Court denied a motion to expedite the appeal, which was not heard until it was moot. Also, the wording of the opinion did not preclude future "gag" orders. "We need not rule out the possibility of showing the kind of threat to fair trial rights that would possess the requisite degree of certainty to justify restraint," Burger wrote, but "the barriers to prior restraint remain high and the presumption against its use remains intact."[49]

The 1979 decision of the Supreme Court in *Gannett* v. *DePasquale* muddied the press-bar situation momentarily. In it, the Court ruled that members of the public have no constitutional right under the Sixth and Fourteenth Amendments to attend criminal trials.[50] Judges across the country began closing courtrooms—in one year 126 pretrial proceedings and 34 trials.

Then came Chief Justice Burger's 7–1 decision in 1980 in *Richmond Newspapers* v. *Commonwealth of Virginia.* Burger declared the public has a constitutional right to attend criminal trials even when defendants want to exclude them, citing the First Amendment.[51] The decision left pretrial hearings still subject to closing. That gap was eliminated in 1986, when Burger ruled in *Press Enterprise Company* v. *Superior Court of California* that the public has the same right to attend pretrial sessions. In a 1984 case the Riverside paper had won the opening of the jury selection process to the public and press.

Public defense of press rights was further demonstrated after police raided the office of the student-run *Stanford Daily,* seeking photographs of a campus sit-in. The Supreme Court decided in *Zurcher* v. *Stanford Daily* that the First Amendment provides the press no special protection from police searches.[52] The result was passage by Congress in 1980, virtually without opposition, of legislation that banned similar police raids on newsrooms.

THE RIGHT TO KNOW

The battles for freedom to print and freedom to criticize, carried on in the courtrooms, were important ones. But just as important were the fights waged for the right to have access to the news—since the right to publish news is worthless if the sources of information have dried up.

Freedom of information and open records campaigns were carried on beginning in the late 1940s by the ASNE, the Associated Press Managing Editors Association, the Radio-Television News Directors Association, and the Society of Professional Journalists. Through their efforts, and those of others, by 1970 all but five states had some sort of laws requiring open public records and open meetings for conduct of public business. Leaders of the fight included James S. Pope, *Louisville Courier-Journal;* J. R. Wiggins, *Washington Post;* V. M. Newton, Jr., *Tampa Tribune;* and Harold L. Cross, ASNE legal counsel.

The creation of the House Subcommittee on Government Information in 1955, headed by Representative John E. Moss of California, brought a campaign against secrecy to the federal level. In 1958, aided by the news media groups, the Moss committee won revision of the 1789 "housekeeping statute" to stop its use in denying access to records. It also won some ground in opposing the claim of executive privilege by the president and his subordinates, and reported success in 95 of 173 cases exposing undue federal censorship of information during 1958 to 1960. Controversy between the Kennedy administration and the press flared up during the Cuban crisis and gave impetus to an effort to adopt the Freedom of Information Act, which was passed and signed by President Johnson on July 4, 1966. It provided that after one year a citizen could go to court if a federal official arbitrarily withheld information of a public transaction other than in the areas specifically exempted under the law. There were nine such areas, including the all-important "national defense or foreign policy." Nevertheless, Representative Moss and others said a victory had been scored. The effect was as much to aid businesspeople and average citizens seeking information from federal offices as to aid reporters.

In an effort to speed up the search process, the Freedom of Information Act (FOIA) was amended in 1974, requiring each federal agency to promulgate detailed regulations implementing the substance of the amendments and outlining information-request procedures, appeal procedures, and search and duplicating costs. The amendments sought to eliminate agency stalling by shortening the allowable response time by agencies, providing for judicial review of denial decisions, and authorizing fines for officials who arbitrarily refused to release information. The Reagan administration sought to exclude more agencies from the inquiry procedure and institute fees for searches, but legislation was stalled until 1986 when mild amendments were approved, including a preferential level of fee charges for media requests.

But despite the FOIA's emphasis on timely response, government agencies continued to have long backlogs of requests, sometimes measured in years, due to short FOIA staffing and increasing numbers of requests. In 1996, Congress passed the Electronic Freedom of Information Act Amendments. These amendments to the FOIA were intended to provide for public access to information in an electronic format, in hopes of speeding up the lengthy and often unwieldy FOIA process. Congress acknowledged that most agency records were now kept on computer disks and CD-ROMs rather than on paper. The EFOIA, as it was known, mandated that records subject to the FOIA would be made available under the FOIA when those records are maintained in electronic format. Inquirers may request records in any form in which the agency maintains the records. Agencies must also make a reasonable effort to comply with requests to furnish records in other formats.

Another encouraging sign in the battle for the right to know was the enactment by Congress of a Government in Sunshine Law that took effect early in 1977. This law requires open meetings of more than 50 federal boards and agencies with two or more members. The Sunshine Law allows meetings to be closed for certain specified reasons, but requires that those reasons be certified by the chief legal officer or general counsel of the agency. In 1995, all 50 states had both open records and open meetings laws, although again there is wide variation in their wording from state to state.

The Goldstone Deep Space Communications Complex, located in the Mojave Desert in California, is one of three complexes that make up NASA's Deep Space Network (DSN). The DSN provides radio communications for all of NASA's interplanetary spacecraft and is also utilized for radio astronomy and radar observations of the solar system and the universe.

20

Media Technology: The Challenge of the Twenty-First Century

> Each of these planetary corporations plans to gather under its control every step in the information process, from creation of "the product" to all the various means of which modern technology delivers media messages to the public.
>
> —*Ben Bagdikian*

As the twentieth century entered its last moments, journalists and marketing specialists gave increased attention to gaining access to the fragments of American society. The future was limited only by the ability of the consumers within these specialized audiences to purchase what manufacturers and advertisers agreed was the next item in an endless list of electronic communication tools. Cellular telephones, facsimile machines, home-earth receivers, decoders, personal computers, low-power television, optic fibers, direct satellite broadcasting, pagination, digital darkrooms, memory clips, high-definition television, CD-ROM, microbooks, teletext, Internet, and World Wide Web were only some of the media terms added to the language.

The world's largest corporations took the lead in developing the new technology, investing uncounted billions in research and development and racing for patents just as the inventors of radio and television had competed fiercely in the early twentieth century and the penny-press leaders raced for news in the previous century. The invention of the semiconductor chip by Jack Kilby and Robert Noyce in 1958–59 was an astounding technological and commercial breakthrough, ranking with the contributions of Bell, Edison, and Ford. The integration of all parts of the electronic circuit—resistors, transistors, capacitors, and diodes—in one tiny piece of material turned the media world upside down.

The age of electronic marvels was also an age of contradiction. While millions could obtain instant world news by satellite and use two-way data-processing systems to produce information on their color television screens, there was deep concern that the gap between classes would widen—that the new information machines would not benefit those in the lower segment of society who badly needed help in surviving the severity of everyday life. There was equal concern that the news component would diminish, become corrupted, or at the least would not be driven by an intensity and professional pride required to keep pace with the money-brokers and manipulators seeking political and social power. The moral and legal problems of the computer age were as perplexing as the possibilities for expansion into untapped areas of money making.

THE UNITED STATES IN THE 1990s

The nation moved past the two-hundredth anniversary of the Bill of Rights in a state of uncertainty. The confusion over values was evident in all phases of government and private life, inconsistencies that needed to be addressed. The richest nation in the history of the world officially joined the debtor class because of a massive trade imbalance and an inability to compete with foreign competitors. The collapse of the savings and loan banking structure in a series of unprecedented scandals forced a negligent federal government to pass on to future taxpayers an additional debt of hundreds of billions of dollars.

The Gulf War cost taxpayers up to $1 billion per day, while federal, state, and local health and education programs were cut. The influx of needy immigrants from Third World nations grew, 85 percent coming from Asia and Latin America, while U.S. arms merchants sold high-technology weapons to those same nations and cigarette companies poured millions into foreign advertising, aiming the messages for their cancer-causing product at children. Millions of Americans mobilized to save the environment, but the U.S. government consistently refused to join in worldwide plans to save the oceans and the atmosphere. James A. Michener's description of the 1980s as "The Ugly Decade" applied to the 1990s as well; critical problems were avoided by a "general know nothingness."[1]

Optimism has been a hallmark of American life, but there was deep concern about the health of the nation and its future. Jonathan Kozol's *Illiterate America* described a people exiled from the written word, where 60 million adults among the nation's 250 million citizens could not read and understand the Bill of Rights. The United States fell far below the world's developed nations in literacy. The collective annual loss, in terms of welfare costs, accidents, and lost financial opportunities, was estimated at $120 billion.[2] A government study said that between 17 and 21 million adults could not pass a simple test. Of these people, only 41 percent lived in metropolitan areas; 41 percent were English-speaking whites; 40 percent were between the ages of 20 to 39, productive years.[3] There were many cries for reform of the educational system and the establishment of special literacy programs because the existence of an uneducated underclass posed a threat to democracy. It also hampered any efforts for the widespread technological changes needed to keep up with the Europeans and Asians.

The makeup and location of this population had changed dramatically over a 20-year span. More than 60 million people lived in the three major Sunbelt states of Florida, Texas, and California. Los Angeles passed Chicago to become the second largest city, after New York, and was home to the most diverse population. California, with 30 million residents, was the most populous state, taking in a large share of the Asians and Latins who made up the bulk of the nation's new immigrants.

This diversity was both a strength and a weakness. The strength was in the richness of the different cultures—old and new—and in the determination of all groups to work for their goals with spirit. The weakness was that all of this made communication more difficult. When it came to elections, for example, politicians increasingly resorted to slick television packages to reach the fragmented audiences. On all levels voters had less allegiance to parties and more devotion to their own special interests.

Despite the long Reagan-Bush era and the emergence of a Republican congressional majority in 1994, it remained unclear whether there had been a long-term realignment by the majority of the electorate into a predictable pattern of right or center-right politics. Voter turnouts were embarrassingly low. Lobbying groups were everywhere, from the city council to the White House, while hundreds of organizations aimed a bewildering blitz of information at a generally confused public. Obviously the role of the news media in translating all of this was more important than ever. This in turn led to numerous discussions about media bias in the handling of this information.

The technological age also saw a decline in the strength of the organized labor movement. Deregulation was the order of the day, and corporate mergers were commonplace. When creative innovations were demanded to help the long-suffering farmers of middle America and the workers in the aging eastern cities of the Rustbelt, the average American was becoming increasingly isolationist in the face of challenges from abroad: protectionism, terrorism, anti-Americanism. Instead of joining in the spirit of turning up the heat of competition, Americans accommodated themselves to the status quo.

One of the goals of the Reagan and Bush administrations was to create a resurgence of national pride, nurtured by hard-nosed diplomacy and military action against Grenada, Libya, Panama, and Iraq. In addition, Americans savored their country's accomplishments in space with moon landings, space probes to Mars, and shuttle flights with payloads. The image on television screens in January 1986 of the shuttle Challenger dissolving into plumes of smoke remained etched on the minds of a nation. The crew of seven died, along with faith in American technological invulnerability and space superiority. This was revived in 1990 when the Voyager spacecraft completed a 12-year, 4.4 billion mile journey to Neptune, sending back scores of close-up color photographs.

Racism and discrimination were evident in American life, and minorities complained of a slowdown in educational and employment opportunities. After the 1986 celebration of the Statue of Liberty, Rosa Parks, the black woman whose 1955 arrest touched off the historic Montgomery bus boycott, said, "We still have a long way to go." The National Urban League claimed that the percentage of blacks living below the poverty line was increasing. While this debate raged it was obvious that women in general had made advancements. They were more than half of the professional ("white collar") workers. In the nation's universities, women were one-third of the medical students, 40 percent of the business and law students, more than one-third of the computer science students, and almost one-fifth of those in engineering. And 60 percent of journalism–mass communication students were women.[4]

Other changes reflected strong movements in religion, most noticeably in the Christian evangelical arena, where television played a major role. This fundamentalist approach to life challenged the values of those who sought liberalization in such areas as abortion, birth control, sex education, homosexuality, and divorce. Emotions in the pro-choice, anti-abortion battle escalated along with violence at health clinics where intimidation and even murder frequently became news and fodder for talk shows. Religious organizations led the debate about the distribution of X-rated, sexually explicit, and excessively violent films over some cable systems seemingly immune from responsibility. Such materials were available through store sales of cassettes for use on home video units. These advocates were challenged by groups who feared that efforts to regulate such materials would lead to abuses in First Amendment rights and move censorship into the political arena.

The 1990s also saw the rise of "political correctness" as an attempt to combat stereotypes in language. Many were concerned with terminology that they perceived to keep women, gays and lesbians, ethnic and racial minorities, and those with disabilities in a repressed position in society. This resulted in continued shifts in language toward gender-neutral terms such as *flight attendant, chairperson,* and *workers' compensation* (in place of *chairman, stewardess,* and *workman's compensation*) and the use of modifiers such as *African American, Asian American,* and *Native American* to reflect full rights of citizenship in these groups. *Black* and *queer* came to have somewhat radical overtones, while African Americans reclaimed the use of *nigger* among themselves as a political and cultural statement. But political correctness also came under attack as an advanced form of censorship when campuses such as the University of Wisconsin and Stanford implemented restrictive speech codes, later scaled back or overturned in lawsuits.[5] And some are hypersensitive about language to the point of error. In January 1999 a Washington, D.C., mayor's office administrator was fired for his use of the term *niggardly* (meaning "stingy or miserly") in describing a budget to two African American aides. He resigned amid a flood of controversy, but the NAACP and others came to his defense, encouraging D.C. Mayor Anthony Williams to reinstate him.[6]

Overall, Americans retained their ties to religion, despite irregular attendance patterns. New technologies helped create amazing changes in the worlds of science and health. These brought hopes for the cure of cancer and the deadly AIDS epidemic, which killed tens of thousands as it spiraled out of control.

The space shuttle Challenger remained the symbol of both high hopes and disillusionments. It stood for everything marvelous and yet it contained fatal uncorrected flaws. While many things needed correcting in U.S. society and in the fast-changing media world, the reassurance of journalist James Reston deserved attention. At the time of the Statue of Liberty celebration he recalled the words of Alexis de Tocqueville in his *Democracy in America,* as he described the United States of the 1830s:

> No sooner do you set foot on American ground than you are stunned by a kind of tumult; a confused clamor is heard on every side, and a thousand simultaneous voices demand satisfaction of their social wants. Everything is in motion around you.[7]

DISTURBING TRENDS IN JOURNALISM

It seemed appropriate that *Lies of Our Times,* an obscure but potent critic of the *New York Times* and other media, would die from financial strangulation. In its final 1994 issue senior editor Edward S. Herman and his staff said, "The evil that *LOOT* was designed to confront, institutional bias in the major media, has not abated in the past five years; it remains as powerful as ever, and will become so as the media become increasingly concentrated in conglomerates of global scope."[8]

To keep such concerns in context, it is wise to recall that these gloomy predictions echo E. L. Godkin's railing against the yellow journalism excess of his day, Upton Sinclair's bitter writings, and George Seldes's attacks on the newspaper barons of his times. The disturbing difference, however, was the change from the era of personal journalism—when, for better or worse, powerful individuals and their families could more easily control their product—to one of corporate decision making, where in the middle 1990s about 25 conglomerates with interconnecting alliances controlled most of the nation's newspaper, magazine, book, broadcast, film, and electronic information service businesses in the United States, with many having major foreign holdings as well.

Previous discussions have detailed the outstanding news efforts in journalism history, at times suggesting directly or implicitly that the public service heralded by Pulitzer Prizes and other awards was dictated by personal or corporate motives as much as by simply a high calling to tell the truth. One premise here is that despite their high-profile coverage of major events—wars, elections, riots, economic downfalls—news organizations have found it difficult or inconvenient to understand and report on a regular basis the patterns of government and corporate culture that inevitably have led to misguided or immoral U.S. government policies overseas, and to continued discrimination and economic exploitation at home. It was clear to the best professional journalists that "objectivity" was a myth, something for offenders to hide behind, while the only acceptable goal was to seek accuracy, comprehensiveness, and above all fairness to both source and audience.

One commonly heard rationalization about the serious faults in the U.S. media system was that it was the inevitable by-product of capitalism and that its benefits outweighed its sins. Opponents, like Herman and his partner in media analysis, MIT's Noam Chomsky, argued that change could occur only with public awareness that the media's lies "are more than literal falsehoods; they encompass subjects that have been ignored, hypocrisies, misleading emphases, and hidden premises—the biases which systematically shape reporting."[9] This book underscores the stories of those men and women who have sought the truth at the most discouraging moments in U.S. history, either from inside a news organization or as an outside commentator. Those stories will continue, but in the meantime it is instructive to look at the news media performance from a critical standpoint.

Some of the criticism is in the philosophical realm. Michael Massing maintained that a flurry of compassionate newspaper articles, books, and films about black society actually contributed to the collective negative attitude about the inner city because black adults rarely came off well in these otherwise good-hearted descriptions, leaving the impression that their children's fate is essentially their fault—and that the situation is hopeless.[10] Such criticism, which appeared to put journalists in a no-win situation, raised awareness.

In that same league was the stream of articles and reviews of Richard Herrnstein and Charles Murray's widely publicized book *The Bell Curve,* suggesting blacks are genetically inferior. Publicity given to these eugenicists and their colleagues unleashed a furor of criticism, raising many questions. How do you discuss a repugnant belief without offending victims and their protectors? When is it the news media's social obligation to squash a potentially harmful notion before it takes root? A number of publications refused to accept advertising that challenged the reality of the Jewish Holocaust, saying that the media had no responsibility to publicize lies. There was general support for such actions, but some First Amendment supporters said they were a bad precedent.

There was legitimate concern that the concept of "political correctness" would be extended unreasonably in the news and commentary columns to reflect more than sensitivity toward women, minorities, gays and lesbians, and the physically disadvantaged. The pushing of this further by various self-interest groups, liberal or conservative, would add to the list of dilemmas. One existing problem was the reporting of rape victims' names, as in the William Kennedy Smith case, where the Associated Press, the *New York Times,* and NBC bowed to self-induced competitive pressures and revealed the victim's identity.

The O. J. Simpson trial in Los Angeles exposed again the problem with revealing details about the private lives of people in the public eye, famous or not, and passing on unsubstantiated rumors, true or not, before a jury could be chosen and justice served. As discussed, the coverage of the Clinton presidency proved that no future occupant of the White House would be spared extreme scrutiny—the privacy line for all public officials had been eliminated. On the other hand, Oliver North could come within an eyelash of winning a U.S. Senate seat by benefiting from the immense news coverage that mentioned his lies to Congress but touched only briefly on his role in illegally perpetuating the Contra war in which many innocent Nicaraguans were murdered by U.S.-supported agents.

Many concerns were raised in the coverage of foreign news. For a variety of reasons, most revolving around problems of time and space, stories about U.S. policies and actions rarely were placed in a historical context and in a format in which cynical government motives were revealed. Few Americans realized their nation was the world's largest supplier of arms, gaining enormous wealth and political leverage from these transactions with some of the earth's worst human rights violators; few also knew that despite constant news coverage given to opponents of foreign aid, the wealthiest nation in the world's history stood above only Ireland at the bottom of the list in terms of its percentage of gross national product (GNP) given to other nations.

The bulk of the responsibility for the flaws in foreign news coverage belonged to home-based editors and producers, not the men and women in the field who often worked under censorship and difficult personal situations. By the mid-1990s the average foreign correspondent was a well-educated, multilingual observer ready to take personal risks in the interests of the story. Despite this some correspondents too easily fell into the trap of believing the local U.S. embassy's version of an event or sticking too closely to U.S. business interests in the region.

The major blame for news distortions could be traced to a native provincialism found on too many home desks, where people without much knowledge of world history and recent foreign events edited copy and tapes from overseas. For example, when Soviet President Boris Yeltsin, a celebrated friend of the United States, decided to postpone elections, there was no serious comment in the U.S. media; it was almost not a story. Only his brutal armed attack against the runaway republic of Chechnya elicited personal criticism. It was also acceptable in U.S. media circles for Israel to interfere in elections planned for Palestinians, thus causing a delay. But if the Nicaraguan Sandinistas had considered a postponement of their 1990 elections, the splash of headlines and nightly news lead-offs would have been spectacular.

Too often the common assumption, stereotype, or in some cases pure racial or political prejudice overcame any instinct to push for "the other side." Such an outlook, often clouded by years of U.S. government complicity, made it difficult for the downtrodden peoples of such places as East Timor, Armenia and Karabakh, Gaza, Kashmir, Tibet, and Honduras to get adequate attention, even if they engaged in war and revolt against their oppressors. It was odd that despite a historic reputation for being a supporter of the underdog—another myth destroyed—the U.S. and its media system most often sided with the most powerful and wealthy power broker on the scene.

It was the responsibility of the home editors to provide the necessary background sidebar stories and to edit context into foreign stories. It was the job of broadcast producers to argue for late-night news specials that did more than rehashes of tapes already seen on the evening news. Editorial writers, columnists, and cartoonists needed to seize the moment and drive home any omissions or misconceptions raining in by satellite. With the exception of the Gulf War, which was a momentary distraction, the nation had withdrawn from foreign involvement since the end of the Vietnam War. The Central American involvement was largely a covert action that became public, and there was little interest in it, despite the many news stories and the resulting scandal.

The most telling moments that demonstrated the disengagement of the United States from the world came during the criminal shelling of Sarajevo, the city that had captivated the globe during a previous Winter Olympics. Despite stark reports from the *New York Times*'s John Burns, CNN's Christiane Amanpour, *Nightline,* and U.S. and European colleagues—coverage that cried for intervention in the name of humanity—there was no measurable response from the public or politicians. The Lorena Bobbitt trial got equal time. In the spring of 1999, the United States was a major participant in the three-month NATO air strike campaign in the former Yugoslavia. The bombing had been delayed since the previous fall to allow diplomatic solutions to be fully tried. Through much of 1998 and well into 1999, as the Balkan crisis escalated, this important international news story was largely eclipsed by repetitive accounts of the Clinton sex scandal and eventual impeachment proceedings. Furthermore, there were scarcely any U.S. casualties in the Balkans—supporting the truism that, regarding television coverage of foreign events, the medium's influence on policy increases if U.S. lives were in jeopardy. In keeping with their new range of investments, major media corporations devoted an increased amount of overseas attention to business news but trimmed their regular coverage of foreign events. In fact, in a November 1998 article in *American Journalism Review,* CNN correspondent Peter Arnett noted that foreign news is disappearing from many American newspapers and suggested that "a foreign story that doesn't involve bombs, natural disasters or financial calamity has little chance of entering the American consciousness."[11] Most dailies contain very little world coverage, and most of that gained from AP or other wire services. Arnett also observed that after the Vietnam War, public desire for more local and service-oriented features supplanted the already-dwindling international news slot.

There was a contradiction here, however, because despite the growing importance of understanding the financial world and a rising interest among readers, journalists as a group were underprepared for the task. The exceptions were well known, and cable television provided a number of new business-related programs. But there was evidence that major organizations were not that serious about reporting the basics of national economic policy. Among the larger newspaper groups in 1995, Knight-Ridder, Newhouse, Gannett, Scripps Howard, Copley, and Cox had no full-time reporters covering the Federal Reserve and related agencies. Neither did the *Boston Globe, Chicago Tribune,* and *Baltimore Sun.* The top four papers—*New York Times, Los Angeles Times, Wall Street Journal,* and *Washington Post*—and the *Dallas Morning News* filled the gap. The *Morning News* gave frequent page-one play to reporter Robert Dodge's reports. Otherwise the major papers' syndicated services and the press associations carried the main economic news. Brief nightly news television reports alerted people to major developments, but were not credited with increasing any understanding of economic complexities.

This admittedly was a difficult task. Eileen Shanahan, a 30-year veteran of Washington economic reporting, pointed out that the enormous increase in international trade and competition, along with effects of widespread layoffs in the manufacturing sector and other changes in work and investment habits deserved attention.[12] This lack of experience and interest contributed to the news media's failure to force the savings and loan industry scandal into the national consciousness, despite the efforts of the *Houston Post*'s Pete Brewton, who broke the original story and then met with increased opposition as he suggested there were culprits in the White House and CIA.[13]

Along those lines, major newspapers serving Orange County, California—the *Register* and the *Los Angeles Times*—failed to understand and interpret substantial evidence presented to them that the county treasurer's unusually high investment risks could bring the county to ruin. In one of the worst such disasters in U.S. history, the county declared bankruptcy in 1995. On the positive side, the *Cleveland Plain Dealer* staff saved taxpayers a considerable loss by exposing a similar high risk investment plan. On all levels of economic/business reporting there was a need to adhere to the standards set by Leonard Silk, a pioneer in simplifying these complex issues while writing editorials and columns for *Business Week* and the *New York Times* from the 1960s to the early 1990s. The holder of a Ph.D. in economics, his reputation was based on his ability to clearly explain issues and to interpret their meaning.

Journalism history is filled with examples of excess in coverage of crime and violence. But it is much harder to get a handle on stories like the spread of the AIDS epidemic into the nation's mainstream. Randy Shilts, a gay reporter for the *San Francisco Chronicle* and the author of three best-selling books, led the way. Shilts tracked AIDS across the world, trying to bring the gravity of the situation to the attention of skeptical journalists and an ignorant Reagan administration. He was internationally known for his 1987 book *And the Band Played On,* which became a movie. Despite his pioneering work the mainstream media took years to get AIDS-related stories onto their agendas. Suddenly it was the leading cause of death among Americans between the ages of 25 and 44. Shilts died of complications of the disease in 1994 at age 42, truly one of those journalists who was faithful to his calling.[14]

Leo Bogart, internationally known in the public opinion and advertising fields, argued persuasively that "in one form or another, and sooner or later, the content and control of mass media is likely to become an issue of political debate." He called for looking at communications policy as a whole, as the nation did with environmental policy, and then protecting it. Noting the steady expansion of the advertising base for all media as part of the race for audience and dollars, he said, "The largest of our mass media, the daily press, traditionally the forum for contention and irreverence, has undergone a steady attrition of competition and a general retreat to the safety of middle ground. Left to their own devices, the public persistently drifts toward amusement rather than enlightenment, avoiding confrontation with the pressing, perhaps overwhelming problems that confront the nation and the world."[15]

Consumers looking for investigative journalism got a sample in the bushel of television magazine news shows that appeared. While *60 Minutes, 20-20, Frontline,* and others occasionally provided shocking new information about a major topic, the segments often were tied to disturbing stories already in the news—child beating, inner-city crime, discrimination on the job—or had a soft, entertaining angle. Certainly there was room for light fare, but one bothersome trend in modern journalism was that few organizations were hustling in their communities, Washington, or overseas to break stories with major political, social, or economic consequence—stories about wrongdoing, hypocrisy, and thievery on a big scale. *Time* and *Newsweek,* caught up with their own competition for cover stories (and cover matching), often were disappointingly shallow, offering rewrites with little interpretation of what the reader already had seen on television or in the daily press.

So it should come as no surprise that few Americans knew that 40 percent of corporations doing business in the U.S. with assets of $250 million or more either paid no income taxes or paid taxes of less than $100,000. The *Nation* told them, however, and other watchdogs, such as the *Progressive, Z Magazine, Extra!,* and some high-quality newsletters and small publishing companies, keep their ears up. On the conservative side, *Accuracy in Media (AIM)* continued its drumfire, now aided by radio and television talk-show stars such as Rush Limbaugh and shockjock Howard Stern.

Magazines devoted to media criticism included *American Journalism Review* and *Columbia Journalism Review,* both targeted toward the industry, with circulations of around 30,000 each. The splashy new *Brill's Content,* targeted toward a general audience, made its debut in August 1998 to a flurry of controversy. The first cover story, "Pressgate," alleged that Independent Counsel Kenneth Starr had inappropriately leaked information to some reporters in violation of the law in his investigation of the Clinton-Lewinsky scandal. Starr denied the impropriety and illegality of the leaks in a lengthy letter that the magazine ran in its second issue. But some commentators noted that Steven Brill (former owner of Court TV and *The American Lawyer* magazine), editor and publisher of *Brill's Content* as well as author of "Pressgate," had fallen into some of the same ethical traps as he was claiming to reveal in other media; for example, conflicts of interest and questionable reportorial tactics.

Overall, the "news business," as it was called, was caught up in the cultural changes sweeping the nation, as movie stars, athletes, and television personalities commanded the most attention, and as the pressure to survive or excel economically overshadowed the basic needs of citizenship: the education necessary to understand rights and responsibilities, the ability to gather information for proper decision making at election time, and the opportunity to petition effectively for changes vital to mental and physical health and safety.

In the age of "peeping Tom" tabloid journalism and a preoccupation with bottom-line financing, it was clear at the turn of the twenty-first century that the nation's news organizations were falling short of the mark in living up to their obligations. In fact, the issue of "ambush journalism" became so problematic that in the aftermath of the 1997 death of Diana, Princess of Wales, the "Personal Privacy Protection Act" (dubbed the "anti-paparazzi bill" in the press) was introduced in Congress. The act established criminal penalties for pursuing individuals to record or photograph them for commercial purposes "in a manner which causes them to have reasonable fear of bodily injury."

In many ways—writing, photography, videotape editing, graphics—journalists excelled. They were hailed as being better educated and more sensitive than their predecessors. That was encouraging. All they needed was a commitment from management that basic news and strong interpretation still counted, plus some of that valuable space and time required for a comprehensive presentation.

PRINT TECHNOLOGY

The revolution in the newspaper, magazine, and book-publishing industries caused by the introduction of the video display terminal (VDT) was accelerated by experiments with pagination—the direct transmission of complete pages from computer memory to printing plates. The entire process of producing the daily newspaper, the weekly news magazine, and the paperback book was computerized. The work on pagination that had begun with research at Brown University in 1973–75 under the leadership of Dr. Hans Anderseen led to pioneering experiments in 1981 at the Westchester Rockland Newspapers in Harrison, New York.[16] Equipment manufacturers were eager to become involved, as they were in the 1970s and early 1980s, when video display terminals replaced typewriters.

Publishers watched carefully, too, because of the heavy expenses involved with pagination, but the conversion was inevitable. The ultimate step was to install photo and graphics subsystems so that an entire page could be fed automatically without any delay. Facilitating rapid changes in the newsroom was the continued development of the personal computer, introduced by Apple in 1977. By the 1990s many newspapers used the Macintosh and a laser jet printer to produce color information graphics. Smaller publications used such a combination, perhaps involving an IBM model, to produce an entire newspaper, magazine, or brochure in what was called "desktop publishing."

Leading programs for desktop publishing included QuarkXPress and Adobe PageMaker. The wide availability of these applications, coupled with graphics packages such as Adobe Photoshop, Adobe Illustrator, and Macromedia Freehand, as well as CorelDraw and others, enabled even small newspapers to produce excellent results.

Other major developments, spurred by research sponsored by the American Newspaper Publishers Association and continued by the Newspaper Association of America,

Desktop publishing software makes it much easier for small newspapers to get good results. Many newspapers have moved from traditional layout techniques to desktop publishing to produce their pages.

(Nancy Roberts)

were the introduction of flexographic newspaper presses and anilox inking systems—both designed to give cleaner, brighter images.

Before these breakthroughs, the major change in print technology came with the introduction of the "cold-type" process, which introduced photography into printing. Such machines of the 1950s as the Fotosetter, Linofilm, and Photon produced words on film and transferred them directly to a printing plate. Widely used in advertisement composition, they proceeded to make steady inroads on "hot-metal" typesetting.

Offset printing, based on the age-old lithography process, avoids both typesetting and photoengraving by the use of pasteups photographed onto flexible printing plates. The *Opelousas Daily World* in Louisiana, begun in 1939, was the first successful daily to print by offset. The Phoenix *Arizona Journal,* founded in 1962 as a rival to the jointly owned *Arizona Republic* and *Gazette,* was the first attempt at producing an offset daily in a metropolitan competitive situation. It died in 1964, but the *Oklahoma Journal* founded that year was still printing by offset against two established rivals in 1980, when economic recession killed it.

The conversion from hot type to photocomposition of type was completed. Figures showed that 99 percent of dailies used photocomposition, even though a quarter of all dailies still used letterpress technology for printing. In fact, those using letterpress accounted for more than half of the daily circulation.[17] The slow process of purchasing new presses and the introduction of flexography would change this figure in the future.

Keeping pace with the developments were the Associated Press and United Press International. Instead of sending stories at the old speed of 60 words per minute on an old-fashioned teletype machine, the press associations used high-speed computers to process stories and send data at speeds of up to 9000 words per minute. Dish-type antennas were installed at newspapers to receive satellite transmissions. Pictures flashed to newspaper offices from around the world, with the press associations using satellites and cables, lasers, and electronic darkrooms to bring high-quality photos to editors within minutes. Lightweight portable transmitters, some weighing only 15 pounds, allowed photographers to beam photos to relay points from near the scenes of action, saving precious time. AT&T closed its last teletype line in 1991.

Reporters equipped with laptop computers could go anywhere in the world where there was telephone service and send stories to home-based computers. Within minutes stories could be edited and sent into production through the pagination process. Such laptops were commonly used at major sporting events and political conventions. The reporter typed the story into the laptop, edited it if there was time, and then used a modem to send it to the main office. Later developments in satellite technology allowed a reporter covering a major breaking story to beam a signal to a satellite, using satellite time purchased or owned by the newspaper, magazine, or press association.

In addition to *USA Today,* the national satellite newspaper, the *Wall Street Journal, Christian Science Monitor,* and *New York Times* used satellites for domestic delivery. Publishers, too, began the distribution of national advertising by satellite through a facsimile advertising project.

Miniature cassette recorders used by reporters were called electronic notebooks. Less than one-inch thick and weighing only a few ounces, they became tools of the trade. Larger models allowed speeches and interviews to be played back at high speeds without changes in the pitch of the sound; this allowed the reporters to find important quotations quickly.

From the first thoughts of Gutenberg to the computerized newsroom, the implications of printing technology had enormous impact. By the 1990s those involved with the distribution of printed information had quickly integrated themselves with the emerging broadcast technology, trying to avoid being swallowed up by the avalanche of new television systems. As they had done with the first radio and television stations, newspaper publishers moved into ownership positions. However, there were many questions to resolve regarding the future of the newspaper, magazine, and book industries. Table 20–1 lists the top 10 newspapers.

TABLE 20–1   Top Ten Newspapers—1997 Daily and Sunday

DAILY	*CIRCULATION*	*SUNDAY*	*CIRCULATION*
1. *Wall Street Journal*	1,774,880	1. *New York Times*	1,658,718
2. *USA Today*	1,629,665	2. *Los Angeles Times*	1,361,748
3. *New York Times*	1,074,741	3. *Washington Post*	1,102,329
4. *Los Angeles Times*	1,050,176	4. *Chicago Tribune*	1,023,736
5. *Washington Post*	775,894	5. *Philadelphia Inquirer*	878,660
6. *New York Daily News*	721,256	6. *Detroit News & Free Press*	829,178
7. *Chicago Tribune*	653,554	7. *New York Daily News*	807,788
8. *Newsday*	568,914	8. *Dallas Morning News*	789,004
9. *Houston Chronicle*	549,101	9. *Boston Globe*	758,843
10. *Chicago Sun-Times*	484,379	10. *Houston Chronicle*	748,036

(average daily circulation for six months ending September 30, 1997)

Source: Standard and Poor's Industry Surveys—Publishing (April 23, 1998).

THE TELECOMMUNICATIONS ACT OF 1996

One of the most interesting technological developments of the 1990s had to do with the concept of technological convergence. Convergence is the idea that although consumers now get their telecommunications signals through a variety of resources, many of those resources are multipurpose. Where once most households had separate resources for their television signals and telephones, one line could conceivably carry them both, as well as additional services such as fax and cable TV. Professor Thomas Krattenmaker of William and Mary School of Law has described convergence like this:

> Today, most Americans receive their television programming over a wire, the medium we call "cable television." Millions of telephone calls every day in the United States are broadcast from cellular (mobile) telephones. It would probably be impossible, and certainly difficult, to define today the difference between a telephone and a computer. Tomorrow it will be equally challenging to distinguish a television set with a VCR and a cable connection from a computer with a monitor, CD-ROM, and a good modem. . . .
>
> In short, telecommunications law is converging. More precisely . . . we are witnessing a convergence of devices accompanied by a plethora of transmission paths. The telecommunications receiver is a radio, computer, television, telephone, VCR, and fax machine all rolled into one. We can get information to such devices by broadcast, microwave, satellite, tape or disk, copper wire, or optic fiber.[18]

In February 1996 President Clinton signed into law the Telecommunications Act of 1996, the first truly comprehensive revision of the Communications Act of 1934. The act was passed by a bipartisan Congress and it opened up nearly every area of telecommunications, including long-distance and local telephony and cable, to competition. By and large, cross-market entry barriers have been eliminated and merger rules relaxed. The act was hailed as a boon to the consumer because it was intended to foster additional competition and give consumers choices about who provides their telecommunications services. The act also deregulated ownership limitations, modified spectrum allocation, and created the Communications Decency Act.

Most notably for this discussion, the act acknowledged the idea of convergence and began to make regulations based upon the idea of "one-stop shopping": the possibility of a single delivery platform to provide multiple services (for example, cable modem service that provides high-speed Internet service via broadband). The goals of the Telecom Act are threefold: (1) to promote competition and reduce regulation to secure lower prices and higher quality services; (2) to encourage new telecommunications technologies; and (3) to prevent harm to consumers from the implementation of competition.

Telephony   In 1983, because of antitrust concerns, AT&T was split into seven "Regional Bell Operating Companies" (RBOCs). These seven companies were further divided into 20 Bell Operating Companies (BOCs). The 1983 consent decree breaking up AT&T placed severe restrictions on what the BOCs could do. At the time of the split, BOCs could not fully enter the long-distance market; they were limited to offering long-distance only within their own regions. The Telecom Act removed this restriction, as well as the restriction that BOCs could not offer telecommunications services between regions. Now BOCs may fully enter the long-distance market. To do so, they must meet FCC requirements set out to enable competition to flourish with minimal impact on consumers. Essentially the 1983 consent decree has no more legal effect.

Much of the act is devoted to opening up competition in telephony. Existing local telephone service companies are required to allow competitors to interconnect seamlessly with their systems to minimize negative impact on consumers. These existing companies must also negotiate for these connections in good faith, and they must permit reselling of their services by their competitors at a competitive rate. Once competitors develop their own networks, they must permit others in under the same rules as the existing service companies do. The act also provides for mediation of disputes between companies by state commissions. Companies may appeal these rulings in federal court, and many have already done so.

Another major section of the act says that states or municipalities cannot "prohibit or have the effect of prohibiting the ability of any entity to provide any interstate or intrastate telecommunications services." This opens up the telecommunications market to anyone who wishes to get in: electric utility companies, natural gas providers, cable companies, and even cities and municipalities themselves. While it may seem odd that such companies may want to enter the telecom market, they have access to their own fiber optic and other kinds of cable that could be converted to telecom service. States do have the ability to regulate these new forays, however.

The act also mandates as a social policy that all Americans have access to telephone service at an affordable rate—the so-called "universal service" policy. Although most Americans do have telephone service, minority families are less likely than Caucasian families to have service. Telephone companies have been rate-shifting to accommodate the new policy, although some consumers may see a rate increase as subsidies to their bills are shifted toward other groups. Toward the goal of providing all American children access to the Internet, schools and libraries are to receive discount-rate services based on their economic status (that is, economically disadvantaged schools and libraries receive deeper discounts).

Ownership Issues   Ownership restrictions on radio stations have been relaxed. Prior to the act, a single owner was limited in the actual number of stations owned. But the act now provides that nationally, a single entity can own any number of radio stations, while locally the restrictions have been relaxed according to market size (for example, in a market with 45 or more stations, one owner can own up to eight, with no more than five AM or five FM stations). The FCC may also waive these radio restrictions to increase the number of stations in an area. Critics suggest that, despite Congressional intentions to encourage competition as a benefit to the end-user, the act has facilitated the purchase of radio stations by large corporations all over the country (to such a degree, in fact, that the FCC is still trying to decide how to handle television station ownership deregulation so as to avoid the same scenario).

The act also relaxes ownership restrictions on television stations. A single entity can now own any number of television stations nationally as long as the total audience does not exceed 35 percent. On the local level, the FCC has eliminated the one-per-owner rule and is considering other options for regulation.

However, some cross-ownership controls are still in force. In a local market, one company cannot own two TV stations (duopoly), a newspaper and a TV station or radio station, or both a radio and a television station (one-to-a-market). However, the FCC does grant waivers even to these controls and is considering whether to relax them. It is now acceptable to own both a television network and a cable system, and the FCC is considering whether to permit ownership of both a television station and a cable system serving the same community.

Television Technology   The Telecom Act requires that the FCC provide the option to existing television stations to acquire an additional channel to provide "advanced" digital television services (DTV). The quality of the DTV image is significantly improved over the standard analog signal. Thus, broadcast licensees have the ability to offer two channels: one "standard" analog channel, and one carrying DTV broadcasts, provided free from the FCC. At the end of 1998, about 50 DTV stations were in operation. Of course, consumers must have a television capable of receiving the DTV signal (currently $5000–$10,000, though prices will fall), and there must be compatible cable boxes available to provide cable access to these channels. By the end of 1999, about 50 percent of U.S. households were expected to have access to DTV.

One issue that remains unresolved is whether cable systems will be required to carry DTV signals. Currently, cable systems are required to carry local over-the-air broadcast signals, a provision of the 1992 Cable Act that was upheld by the Supreme Court in 1994. Opponents of the must-carry provisions (often cable system operators) claim that in order to carry the new digital signals, they would have to drop other channels and anger subscribers. Proponents (broadcasters) argue that for the new format to survive and flourish, mandatory carriage is essential. The FCC is currently mulling over the issue.

Cable Television   Nonbasic cable rates (that includes most nonbroadcast and satellite programming offered by cable systems) were deregulated, quickly for small cable systems, and more gradually for larger ones. The "open video" system designation was created; this is a system that offers most of its channels to outside programming but can still retain up to a third for its own programming. They are subject to many of the same rules as the telephone industry, with the intent to open competition and make transitions between companies as seamless as possible.

Is Convergence a Good Thing?   While the idea of convergence is exciting, some have concerns about the desirability of "one-stop shopping" for telecommunications service. One company providing a number of services can be convenient for the consumer (one bill to pay, one company to call for service questions or requests), but critics suggest that convergence really means a reduction in the number of options consumers have in selecting telecommunications services from a broad range of providers. If the choice is between one full-service provider and another, without the ability to pick and choose among individual services, the end result might be an overall decrease in the number of points of view available to anyone.

DOMESTIC BROADCAST TECHNOLOGY

It was inevitable that the emerging broadcast technologies would end up competing for the same advertising dollars. The development of domestic satellites led to the quick expansion of the cable television system, with entrepreneurs like Ted Turner of Atlanta starting their own news, sports, and religious networks and competing with the three major networks. But before the nation's cable pattern was established, in 1982 the Federal Communications Commission approved roles for direct broadcast satellites (DBS) and rival companies began planning for home delivery of high definition images (HDTV) in competition with cable operators and regular broadcasters.

By the mid-1990s predictions of future media possibilities came at a dizzying pace. The key was digital electronics, defined as the conversion of information, sound, video, text, and images into a single code that can be decoded at the other end. Rushing into this future were the huge communication, computer, electronics and entertainment conglomerates. One important prediction was that high definition television, interactive services, and image processing would be brought to home and office over fiber optic telephone lines, and not necessarily via cable television. The telephone companies known as the Baby Bells received court approval to provide news, sports, movies, shopping, and other information over their phone lines and that was only the beginning. In 1995 the Walt Disney Co. and three Baby Bells announced a $500 million venture to provide such programming over phone lines to a potential audience of 50 million persons in 19 Southern and Midwestern states. There also was a flurry of activity whereby phone and cable firms negotiated mergers; cable customers would be offered cheaper phone service and lower cable costs if facilities could be shared.

Regardless of how information eventually reached private homes, consumers were asked to pay for a dizzying number of services. In the previous decade, advertisers became interested in teletext, the printing of messages on television screens, sometimes accompanied by elaborate color graphics. The first American broadcast of commercial teletext was in September 1981, when Chicago viewers read "pages" of information on their screens. The teletext operation allowed information to stay on the screen for about 20 seconds before the next appeared. Over a number of years there had been previous experiments in Britain, France, and Japan.[19]

There were also experiments in the United States, Europe, and Japan with two-way interactive systems. Causing attention was Warner Cable's QUBE system in Columbus, Ohio, whereby viewers participated in public-opinion polls by punching buttons in their homes.[20] The common name for the interactive systems was videotex. However, some referred to them as viewdata systems, saying that videotex was a generic term covering all such techniques, including teletext. The sending of information to a selective audience was dubbed narrowcasting. Audiotext involved the use of the telephone to transmit a message onto a screen.

The future of teletext and videotex was highly problematical, for it depended on the general economy, the whims of investors, and the desires of advertisers. Neither service posed an immediate threat to newspapers or broadcast news. By the 1990s, several expensive electronic-publishing ventures had folded. Warner ended the six-year QUBE experiment in 1984.

Meanwhile, the number of homes wired for cable television (64 million in 1998) rapidly reached the point at which advertisers considered the medium a major marketing possibility. Nearly 60 percent of television homes had cable programming. Industry experts said the turning point was January 1, 1987, when cable fees charged by 9900 operators were deregulated, and operators began to earn big profits by raising the price for their basic channels.[21] The domestic satellite system was the heart of this transformation. Pay cable operators, led by Time Inc.'s Home Box Office and Viacom's Showtime/The Movie Channel, were forced to compete by cutting rates as subscriber interest in these optional services waned. Lagging far behind was the pay-per-view (PPV) system, where subscribers received unscrambled signals for movies, sports, and music.

In 1997, there were 11,800 operating cable systems in the United States, serving 34,000 communities. The largest single system, Time Warner Cable in New York, had more than a million subscribers. The largest multiple system operator was Tele-Communications Inc. (TCI) with 14 million subscribers, followed by Time Warner with 12 million, Media-One with 5 million, and Comcast with 4.4 million.[22]

In general there was much freedom for broadcasters. In 1982 the FCC ruled in favor of increasing the general television service to any given area. Earlier, the Copyright Reform

Act of 1976 had made it legal for cable firms to sell a "secondary transmission" of a signal. The development of domestic satellites and the growth of the home satellite dish market created a market for small firms able to pass on the signal of a larger company. In addition, in 1972 the FCC had opened up the nation's skies to all financially responsible firms interested in providing satellite transmission of television, telephone, news, and data services.

The first private domestic satellite was Western Union's Westar, launched in April 1974. Seven others were launched by RCA, Communications Satellite Corporation (called Comsat), and Western Union in the next three years, as satellite transmission became less costly than land transmission for sending one message to multiple sites. By the 1990s, fiber optic cables emerged as a competitor to satellites for point-to-point communications and several large firms made plans to switch telephone traffic from satellites to fiber optic lines. Even so, there were two dozen domestic satellites servicing the nation's television system.

Time Inc. inaugurated the concept of linking satellite programming to cable systems on September 30, 1975, with its showing of the Ali-Frazier prize fight from Manila. Its Home Box Office (HBO) dated to 1972, but it was not until 1975 that the satellite was utilized. The financial success of HBO was staggering. In 1980 Time Inc.'s Video Group, headed by HBO and Time's cable company, American Television & Communications, earned more money than the entire NBC network.[23]

Time Inc. also became Hollywood's largest financier of movies. HBO needed 200 new films per year for its broadcasting schedule and threatened to become the dominant economic force in the movie business. The six major studios—Columbia, MGM/UA, 20th Century Fox, Paramount, Universal, and Warner Bros.—failed to recognize the growing consumer demand for televised films, and their slowness cost them dearly. When a movie was shown in a theater, the studio that distributed it earned about 45 cents per box-office dollar. When HBO distributed the film by satellite to the home, the studio ended up with only 20 cents, with HBO earning the lion's share of the profits.

Independent producers, heavily dependent on the studios in the past, began to look to HBO, while the major studios and HBO's pay-cable competitor, The Movie Channel/ Showtime, made efforts to form alliances in order to stop HBO from controlling the industry. While HBO planned to remain primarily a financier of movies, with investments of more than $1 billion in future films, it did join with Columbia and CBS to form Tri-Star Pictures. The goal was to become Hollywood's seventh major studio. In addition, HBO money financed two other production companies that in return gave HBO exclusive cable rights to their films. The trend was clear: Americans were spending more money than ever before on home movies, rivaling the amount spent at conventional theaters. Noting their declining income, movie studios fought against anything that would reduce their share of VCR and pay-per-view revenues. This included opposition to a plan whereby HBO and other pay networks would offer feature films over the pay channels at the same time they were opening in movie theaters.

THE INTERNET

In 1966, four computers were linked together via telephone lines. Two basic concepts shaped the ancestor of the Internet, the ARPAnet: it was a "distributed" system, so that if one computer went down, communication among the remaining units was not lost; and it connected computers together regardless of their makes or models. From this modest beginning arose the newest mass medium, the powerhouse of 1990s communication, the Internet. Anyone with a computer, modem, and telephone line could dial in to a vast amount of information on any topic imaginable. Libraries, government offices, and public and private companies put up their sites, filled with history, information, and resources of all kinds. Individuals could also enter this new mass medium with an unprecedented ease of access—and they did, in droves. Millions of individual web pages, containing personal information, photographs, and more, appeared on local servers all over the world.

The Internet is made of a number of different systems, among them e-mail, chatrooms (wherein participants may type comments to one or more other individuals that can be read in real time), newsgroups (where users can post messages for later comment by others), and the World Wide Web, containing millions of individual web pages formatted in HTML (Hyper-Text Markup Language), the standard for displaying text and images online.

Among the big Internet service providers (ISPs—companies that provide gateways for users to get online) were American Online (AOL), Compuserve, Netcom, and AT&T. Local ISPs could also get in on the act; in fact, 38 percent of all business Internet connections were provided by local companies, followed by AOL at 26 percent and others such as Compuserve in the single digits.[24] AOL recently passed the 10 million subscriber mark, making it the largest overall service in the nation. Electronic commerce began to be a serious contender in sales, estimated to hit $30 billion by the year 2000.

Many desktop publishing packages and word processors could also create web pages in HTML, thus making it easy for individuals to move into the online environment. Standalone web design software like Microsoft FrontPage and Adobe PageMill made web publishing accessible to nearly everyone with a computer and a modem. Some entrepreneurial online companies also made server space available for free to individuals who wanted to publish their own pages on nearly any topic they chose. Geocities, Tripod, Angelfire, Virtual Avenue, and Xoom were among the many options. In fact, with more than 2 million members in June 1998, Geocities was so popular that it received 26.8 per cent of all Internet hits in 1998.[25]

THE TURNER BROADCASTING SYSTEM

The spectacular worldwide success of Cable News Network allowed the swashbuckling Ted Turner to move headlong into other ventures, as his stock soared in value and cash poured in. The Turner Broadcasting System added a new entertainment channel called Turner Network Television (TNT), and there was talk of adding a Spanish-language entertainment channel. Another experiment was the Checkout Channel, where CNN was seen in supermarkets.

The ambitious Georgian rebounded from a 1986 setback when, after an aborted attempt to gain control of CBS, he purchased majority shares of MGM/UA for $1.78 billion. That same year he launched his Goodwill Games in Moscow, an expensive but creative experiment that allowed his network and independent subscribers to receive nearly 200 hours of exclusive programming. A year later, badly in debt, he sold 37 percent of the firm to Time Inc. and Tele-Communications, the nation's largest operator of cable stations. But he retained use of MGM/UA's giant film library as a nucleus for entertainment broadcasting.

Then came the upswing, with CNN expanding its list of foreign bureaus and using its satellites to simultaneously reach viewers throughout the world. The payoff came when the network outdistanced the established networks in covering the Gulf War. This was followed by expansion of the overseas cable operations, the development of more original domestic cable programming, and adding other communications companies to the list of Turner Broadcasting System properties. Noncombative when speaking in public, Turner

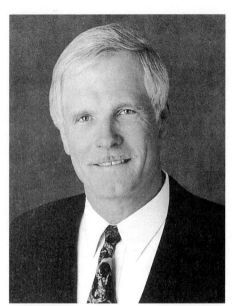

Ted Turner

*(1999, Photograph provided courtesy of CNN.
A Time Warner Company. All Rights Reserved.)*

continually stressed his belief that television could be used for peaceful purposes and for saving the environment—for bringing people together. He was a throwback to an earlier age, an unusual character loose in the cutthroat corporate world.

Other entrepreneurs also sensed the vulnerability of the established networks and used developments in satellite communications to their advantage. Satellite news gathering (SNG) cooperatives competed for the attention of network affiliate and independent stations by offering a video version of the press associations. Leaders were Hubbard Broadcasting's CONUS system and Group W's Newsfeed. The *Chicago Tribune*'s Independent Network News service, established in 1981, eagerly served more than 60 U.S. clients and in 1987 began transmitting a daily feed to a small number of European clients. But it was Stanley S. Hubbard, the son of broadcasting pioneer Stanley E. Hubbard, who caused a commotion in 1984 by establishing CONUS, a consortium of local stations. Hubbard sold these stations, mobile units, a fleet of vans equipped with cameras, editing equipment, and uplinks to satellites. Within minutes of a major event a three-person crew could send a live report to any of ten channels available on two satellites using the newly developed Ku-band system (Ku-band frequencies can be transmitted and received by smaller satellite dishes than the traditional C-band and in general allow for better reception). The reports were received in the CONUS headquarters in St. Paul and distributed by satellite to subscribing stations. CONUS grew to more than 110 U.S. clients and expanded to Australia, Asia, and Europe. For particular stories a crew working for a station in one city could communicate directly with the newsroom of a station in another city. CONUS also joined with the AP to form TV Direct, a company that distributed television news of Washington events along with AP news photos. Soon the four major networks joined in, offering deals to affiliates for the sharing of newsgathering costs and the coordination of satellite transmissions originating from mobile units.

Mobile units had been used for years to transmit signals back to a main studio, but the SNG innovation allowed local broadcasters to share their work with colleagues around

CNN, Atlanta

the nation who did not wish to be dependent on the network feed for a particular story. Network affiliates joined the list of those stations subscribing to one of the cooperatives, but the main target was the growing group of independent stations, about 250 strong and commanding roughly 20 percent of the viewing audience. It was Hubbard's dream to eventually move into the entertainment field and to again challenge network programming.

The networks' first reaction to the emerging cable business was to compete head-on.[26] They started overnight news programs for the millions of night owls who watch television when most persons are sleeping. All three invested in cable cultural, sports, or movie programming.

The networks also competed heavily to retain their contracts with professional sports leagues, paying billions of dollars for multiyear contracts. Despite all of this activity, the network share of viewing time continued to drop. Profits began to drop accordingly, as cable operators and programming syndicators moved into the picture. The percentage of advertising profit for local stations remained constant; it was the networks who suffered from the changes.

CONGLOMERATES: MEDIA WEALTH AND INFLUENCE

Corporate mergers, hostile takeovers, and leveraged buyouts financed with junk bonds permeated the U.S. business world of the later 1980s. The collapse of the Drexel Burnham Lambert brokerage house, Wall Street's "junk bond" leader, ended such money orgies as the bitter $25 billion takeover battle for the RJR Nabisco conglomerate.

More happy was the outcome of the second largest financial deal—the $14 billion merger of Time Inc. and Warner Communications in 1989. The spectacle of this merger was breathtaking: its major components were the largest U.S. print media company, the famed Warner Bros. film studio, Lorimar Telepictures (making TV series like *Dallas*), and Home Box Office.

The deal arranged by Steve Ross of Warner and Nick Nicholas of Time Inc. left Time Warner with a $10.8 billion merger debt. Revenues in 1991 remained more than ample to service interest but not to retire the debt without paring away some assets. Time Warner had many: 21 magazines, 5 book companies, 6 recording companies, the Comedy Channel, 3 major cable companies, a 42 percent interest in 7 television stations, and 17 percent of Turner Broadcasting System.

The merger was defensive on the part of Time Inc., regarded by Wall Street as vulnerable to a takeover due to its stock price levels. Indeed, Paramount Communications vainly mounted a hostile bid. When the new management took form, the major operating units were the Cable-TV group and the Time Warner Publishing Co., composed of Time Trade Books and the Time Inc. Magazine Co. Thus, Time Inc. editor-in-chief Jason McManus had protected both the name and his flock—including *Time, People,* and *Sports Illustrated,* the top three U.S. magazines in advertising revenue and among the top five in circulation revenue. He celebrated by buying the influential western magazine, *Sunset,* in 1990.

Staggering amounts of money were involved in these 1985–90 properties transactions. General Electric Company took over the RCA Corporation and its National Broadcasting Company for $6.3 billion, at that moment the biggest merger in media history. Capital Cities Communications, Inc., a print media giant, bought the American Broadcasting Company for $3.5 billion. Ted Turner got into the movie business by paying $1.78 billion for control of MGM/UA, before selling off the UA part for $470 million. The Tribune Company paid $510 million for Los Angeles television station KTLA. The Gannett Company, owner of 130 newspapers, paid $635 million for four major metropolitan dailies. Hachette of France bought magazines, paid $712 million for Diamandis Communications, and spent $450 million for Grolier books. The Doubleday book firm went to Bertelsmann of Germany for $475 million. Sony of Japan bought CBS Records for $2 billion and Columbia Pictures for $3.4 billion, while Matsushita paid $6.9 billion for MCA. Table 20–2 lists the top 15 media companies.

The whirling tranactions continued into the 1990s. These headlines show the scope of the business deals: "Sony Takes a $2.7-Billion Hit on Studios," "Time, TCI Mull Plan for Turner Takeover," "QVC Wins a Round in Court In Its Bid to Buy Paramount, "Paramount to Acquire Macmillan," "Media Giants Said to be Negotiating for TV Networks." Around and around they went, with Disney interested in CBS and Time Warner looking at both CNN and NBC. Book companies were bought and sold with abandon, as were valuable broadcast properties. Unlike the days of Pulitzer and Hearst, the media deals came so fast that they became indistinguishable; it was hard to tell who owned whom without an annual report.

In 1998, the merger wars were still being waged. Three important mergers stood out: a $56 billion arrangement between Ameritech and SBC Communications (which would reduce the number of regional Bell Operating Companies to four); Bell Atlantic's $52 billion purchase of GTE, and the $32 billion deal for AT&T to buy TCI (still held up in the FCC). Internet companies were also watching the mergers closely. AOL wanted the FCC to regulate high-speed cable Internet services; its competitor, the cable Internet service @Home, is part of the AT&T/TCI merger. Cable Internet service was still relatively uncommon (only about 250,000 subscribers) but was expected to take off in the next few years.

Some personalities stood out for both their successes and their love of adventure. One was Microsoft Chairman Bill Gates, number one on *Forbes* list of the 400 richest persons with a net worth of $90 billion as of mid-1999. The king of computer software had his eyes on the movie industry and was seeking investments. However, Gates ran into trouble with the Department of Justice over his plans to integrate his Internet browser,

TABLE 20–2   Top 15 Companies by Media Revenue, in Millions of Dollars (1996)

COMPANY	HQ	TOTAL MEDIA REVENUE	NEWS-PAPER	MAGA-ZINES	TV & RADIO	CABLE	OTHER MEDIA
1. Time Warner	New York	11,851.1	—	2,764.1	87.0	9,000.0	—
2. Walt Disney Co.	Burbank, CA	6,555.9	119.0	321.9	4,425.0	1,690.0	—
3. Tele-Communications Inc.	Denver	5,954.0	—	—	—	5,954.0	—
4. NBC TV (GE Co.)	Fairfield, CT	5,230.0	—	—	4,940.0	290.0	—
5. CBS Corp.	New York	4,333.5	—	—	4,323.5	10.0	—
6. Gannett Co.	Arlington, VA	4,214.4	3,335.2	—	685.0	194.2	—
7. News Corp.	Sydney	4,005.0	115.0	660.0	2,500.0	20.0	710.0
8. Advance Publications	Newark, NJ	3,385.0	2,209.0	1,176.0	—	—	—
9. Cox Enterprises	Atlanta	3,075.3	1,033.0	—	582.0	1,460.3	—
10. Knight-Ridder	Miami	2,851.9	2,851.9	—	—	—	—
11. New York Times Co.	New York	2,615.0	2,335.3	161.1	118.6	—	—
12. Hearst Corp.	New York	2,568.4	865.0	1,303.0	400.4	—	—
13. Viacom	New York	2,404.0	—	—	390.3	2,013.7	—
14. Times Mirror Co.	Los Angeles	2,321.0	2,080.2	240.8	—	—	—
15. Tribune Co.	Chicago	2,106.0	1,336.0	24.8	745.2	—	—

Source: Advertising Age, August 18, 1997.

Microsoft Explorer, into the hugely popular Windows operating system for PCs. In the so-called browser wars, Justice officials wanted to demonstrate that Microsoft, in its quest to take over the Internet market, engaged in practices that violated antitrust laws. E-mails containing messages from financial incentives to outright threats to incorporate Microsoft's browser and not its competitor, Netscape Navigator, were entered into evidence against Microsoft, which claimed that it was just practicing aggressive business tactics. After 76 days, testimony ended in late June 1999, and a verdict could come as late as early 2000. Meanwhile, Ted Turner's estimated net worth was $5 billion in 1999. Some relative unknowns got into the act as well. John Malone, holder of a Ph.D. in industrial engineering, forged his Tele-Communications, Inc. (TCI) to the top of the cable world. Billions of dollars rolled in and out as he expanded his cable systems and prepared for an acceleration in the digital, fiber optic age. Earlier, Sumner M. Redstone of Boston, owner of a chain of theaters, led the $3.4 billion takeover of Viacom International's properties, including Showtime/The Movie Channel and MTV. And George Gillette of Denver owned the largest group of affiliate television stations, with 13 percent of the national audience. Table 20–3 lists the top 10 television station owners.

Rupert Murdoch was the most conspicuous of the high rollers in the media acquisition business. In rapid order he bought the 20th Century Fox studios for $575 million, seven major television stations for $1.55 billion, Harper & Row book publishers for $300 million, and Triangle Publications, including *TV Guide,* for $3 billion. He deftly used the Fox properties and the television stations to form the Fox Broadcasting Company as a fourth television network and to make a major dent in the television series production business.

Murdoch had more than 150 media properties in his News Corp. Its News America subsidiary retained the *Boston Herald* and *San Antonio Express-News* in the 1990s. Murdoch's Scottish book firm, William Collins, was merged with the Harper & Row and Scott,

TABLE 20–3   TV's Top Ten Station Owners

COMPANY	NUMBER OF STATIONS	PERCENT OF U.S. TV HOUSEHOLDS COVERED
1. Fox Television Studios	23	34.9
2. Paxson Communication	55	30.9
3. CBS	14	30.8
4. NBC	12	26.9
5. Tribune Broadcasting	19	26.5
6. ABC	10	23.9
7. Chris Craft/United Television	10	18.7
8. Gannett Broadcasting	19	16.5
9. USA Broadcasting	13	15.5
10. A. H. Belo Corp.	17	14.2

Source: Standard & Poor's Industry Surveys—Broadcasting & Cable (July 2, 1998), from Broadcasting & Cable.

Foresman textbook publishers to form a powerful HarperCollins house. In Britain, he had 5 national newspapers including *The Times* of London and more than 50 other papers, totaling a third of British circulation, plus 8 magazines. In his native Australia, Murdoch owned 9 magazines and more than 100 newspapers, accounting for nearly 60 percent of press circulation.

But there was a price to pay. News Corp. had accumulated an $8.2 billion debt by early 1991. Part of it, more than $600 million, came from the launching of Sky Television in early 1989, an ambitious effort to bring programming to British homes by satellites. Murdoch reluctantly joined forces with rival British Satellite Broadcasting to help stem losses, and like other high-rollers looked for renegotiated bank loans. Murdoch's most spectacular success was in the 1993 purchase and expansion of Star TV, a small Hong Kong satellite company with enormous potential. Plunking down $525 million in another huge risk, Murdoch created two networks, one for China and the Pacific Basin and the other for India and the Middle East. He planned to expand offerings to 32 channels, dumping old movies, talk shows and other examples of Western culture into these regions in return for the hope of creating an advertising base. Star also carried the BBC's world news service. Although its future was uncertain, Star came close to being a world network. Movies produced by 20th Century Fox could be shown over Star and by Sky TV in Europe, which expanded into a system known as B Sky B. Sports was another commodity and in Murdoch paid $1.6 billion for Fox's right to broadcast National Football League games which had been within CBS' province for 38 years. He also bought Genie, one of the top five "online" computer information companies.

Never satisfied, and feeling hampered by U.S. laws prohibiting ownership of broadcast properties by foreign companies, Murdoch gained the support of Speaker of the House Newt Gingrich and other conservatives who welcomed Murdoch's business style. Gingrich, however, ran into heavy criticism when he accepted a multimillion book deal from HarperCollins, one of Murdoch's companies, for a novel about Washington political life. Gingrich backed off from the agreement. Murdoch a U.S. citizen, ran into more problems when a Federal Communications Commission official charged that his purchase of six television stations in 1985—later the base of his Fox Network—were illegal because 99 percent of the equity was owned by his Australian company. The full extent of Murdoch's power in the U.S. remained an open question.

INTERMEDIA ADVERTISING COMPETITION

The story of the competition for advertising among the media since the rise of television can be simply told. Total expenditures for advertising in the United States in 1990 were an estimated $129 billion. Of that sum, approximately 60 percent was allocated to the mass media, according to McCann-Erickson, Inc., estimates. Newspapers received 26.4 percent of that allocation, television 22.2, radio 6.8, and magazines 5.3. In 1950, newspapers had received 36.5 percent, radio 10.7, magazines 9, and fledgling television only 3 percent.

But another analysis of the figures shows the sharp impact television made in winning national advertising revenues, reducing the percentage received by newspapers by two-thirds in those 40 years and that of radio by three-fourths.

Table 20–4 shows the division among the major mass media of the national and local advertising revenues spent on them alone. In other words, the four major media together were allotted varying amounts of advertising expenditures each year by national and local advertisers. How were these total sums split among the contestants? Table 20–4 shows that television became dominant in this division of national advertising, cutting most sharply into radio's and newspapers' shares. Table 20–5 continues the trend from 1990.

Table 20–5 demonstrates that only small increases were expected in the percentages of advertising dollars in the decade of the 1990s. Because no one can accurately forecast

TABLE 20–4   Percentage of Advertising Expenditures Allotted Only to the Mass Media

YEAR	NATIONAL ADVERTISING IN				LOCAL ADVERTISING IN		
	News-papers	Magazines	Radio	Television	News-papers	Radio	Television
1950	33.6	32.4	24.8	9.2	82.4	14.6	3.0
1960	25.0	28.0	7.9	39.1	80.2	12.0	7.8
1970	18.1	23.0	7.2	51.7	75.6	13.6	10.8
1980	15.7	21.7	6.3	56.3	69.9	14.5	15.6
1990	11.8	20.6	6.4	61.2	65.6	15.3	19.1

Source: McCann-Erickson, Inc., estimates

TABLE 20–5   Advertising Media: Shares of the Market (in percent)

MEDIA	1990	1991	1992	1993	1994	1995	1996	1997	F1998
Newspapers	25.1	24.2	23.4	23.2	22.9	22.6	22.0	22.1	22.0
Magazines	5.3	5.2	5.3	5.3	5.3	5.3	5.2	5.3	5.3
Television	22.1	21.6	22.4	21.1	22.8	22.0	23.3	22.7	22.9
Radio	6.8	6.7	6.6	6.8	7.0	7.0	7.0	7.1	7.1
Other	40.8	42.3	42.3	42.5	42.0	43.1	42.5	42.8	42.7
Total	100.0	100.0	100.0	100.0	100.0	100.0	100.0	100.0	100.0
National	56.6	57.5	57.9	57.9	58.2	58.6	58.8	58.9	58.9
Local	43.4	42.5	42.1	42.1	41.8	41.4	41.2	41.1	41.1
Total	100.0	100.0	100.0	100.0	100.0	100.0	100.0	100.0	100.0

F = forecast

Source: Standard & Poor's Industry Surveys—Publishing (April 23, 1998), from McCann-Erickson.

the potential impact of the Internet on the advertising area, the "other" section, which presumably includes formats like billboards and online ads, might be higher than the table anticipates toward the close of the century.

The percentage of total newspaper advertising revenue coming from local advertisers increased from 70 percent to 91 percent between 1950 and 1990; the percentage of total radio advertising revenue coming from local sources jumped from 41 percent to 76 percent. Television stayed even with one-fourth local advertising. Radio thus joined newspapers as primarily a local advertising medium. Magazines have no advertising categorized as local, although they offer split-runs so that advertisers can buy space in copies being distributed in restricted areas; perhaps 15 percent of advertising revenue is regional in origin.

Table 20–6 indicates advertising expenditures as allotted among various electronic media. It is anticipated that cable will more than triple its market share.

Table 20–7 includes a breakdown among other kinds of media than the electronic media. According to these data, newspapers are still getting the lion's share of advertising revenue, but because the various types of electronic media are broken out in this table rather than combined as in Table 20–6, the impression of newspapers' wide margin might be misstated. Note also the difference in some of the estimates between sources.

TABLE 20–6   Cable, Radio, and Television Advertising Expenditures (in billions of dollars)

	1990	1995	1996	1997	E1998
Broadcast TV	22.62	27.91	31.27	32.46	34.10
Cable TV	2.88	5.11	6.44	7.95	9.30
Radio	8.75	11.47	12.41	13.49	14.70
Total	34.25	44.49	50.12	53.90	58.10

E = estimated

Source: Standard & Poor's Industry Surveys—Broadcasting & Cable (July 2,1998), from Television Bureau of Advertising; Radio Advertising Bureau.

TABLE 20–7   Advertising Expenditures by Media Channel (projected 1998—in millions of dollars)

Newspapers	40,140
Network TV	14,876
Magazines	14,504
Radio	11,524
Spot TV (local)	11,251
Spot TV (national)	9,825
Cable TV	6,231
Outdoor	1,933
Syndication	1,641

Source: Adweek, September 8, 1997, p. 6, from Zenith Media Worldwide.

AM/FM RADIO

By the 1990s, there were more than 530 million radio sets in the United States; 99 percent of the homes had at least one radio. More than 12,000 radio stations were on the air in 1997.

While news and talk shows were popular in major market areas, the leading formats were adult contemporary music and the Top 40 shows, followed by country music. The enormous recording industry, with annual revenues of more than $4 billion, gave radio its many options for music. There were more than 2000 country and western stations on the air, challenging for audiences. Radio had something for everyone, with music, news, and sports the backbone of the system. Actually the total amount of radio news declined, particularly at smaller stations, following the loosening of FCC standards.

Audiences for FM stations continued to grow while AM stations held even, as radio proved to be a stable medium and satellites helped bring a new life. One headache for AM owners was the large-scale conversion to stereo transmission, which had been slowed by technical problems following its inauguration in 1982 at KDKA in Pittsburgh. Another possibility for the improvement of radio was the use of cable, which would mean higher fidelity sound. Overall, radio was popular, with 95 percent of the audience above 12 years old listening at least once a week. In the era of deregulation the FCC created the opportunity for another 1000 stations by 1990.

In addition 161 nations aired shortwave radio programs, led by the British Broadcasting Corporation (BBC), which claimed that 100 million adults listened weekly. The Soviet Union produced the most programming.[27]

In 1995 six giant firms, led by Time Warner's WEA, dominated the record business tied so closely to radio. The old record label names, Capitol, RCA, Columbia, Motown, and others were subsumed under corporate names: UNI, CEMA, Polygram, BMG, and Sony. Independent distributors accounted more only about 15 percent of the business.

Early in 1999, the FCC issued a study that indicated that radio stations serving minorities do not get a fair share of advertising revenue—a claim minority-owned stations had been making for years. The report said that 91 percent of minority-owned stations had encountered advertiser dictates not to buy time there. The FCC encouraged advertisers to eliminate bans against buying ads on minority-owned or targeted stations.[28]

MOTION PICTURES HOLD THEIR PLACE

Buffeted by the competition of television and by the changing entertainment preferences of Americans, the movies sank to an all-time low of 17.7 million weekly attendance in 1970. But by 1975 the figure had rebounded to approximately 20 million and stayed above that figure during the 1980s. Box-office receipts, which had dipped below $1 billion in 1963, hit a new high of $4 billion in 1984—due in good part, of course, to inflation and rising ticket prices—and topped $5 billion in 1989 and 1990. In the early 1990s, theater grosses were just below $5 billion, reaching approximately $5.42 billion in 1994. Videotapes and cable television receipts accounted for 57 percent of studio revenues, compared to 30 percent for movie houses. But by 1994 there were more than 25,000 movie outlets, many of them clusters of small auditoriums sharing the same popcorn stand. Most of the studios had changed hands. MGM auctioned off its props, including Clark Gable's trenchcoat, Ben Hur's chariot, and Judy Garland's red shoes, before the lion stopped roaring in 1973. But at Academy Award time each spring, there was proof that "going to the movies" was still an American habit.

A "new American cinema" appeared in the late 1960s, an extension of the French "new wave." Its guiding light was the magazine *Film Culture,* produced by the Mekas brothers. Jonas Mekas made *The Brig* in 1964, and Kenneth Anger made *Scorpio Rising* in 1966. The high point was reached with Dennis Hopper's *Easy Rider,* a 1969 low-budget film ($370,000) that won widespread audience support. Hopper, Peter Fonda, Jack Nicholson, and Karen Black topped the cast, making a rebellious statement to their youthful audiences. This marked the emergence in the United States of the "*auteur* theory" of cinema, which views the director as the primary creative force.

Warren Beatty and Faye Dunaway exhibited a taste for "violence for violence's sake" in Arthur Penn's 1967 *Bonnie and Clyde.* Two films depicting the generation gap were Mike Nichols's *The Graduate* (1967), introducing Dustin Hoffman, and *Goodbye Columbus* (1969). Robert Altman's 1970 movie *M*A*S*H* ushered in a Korean War legacy for television. Francis Ford Coppola directed Marlon Brando in *The Godfather* (1972), the story of the Mafia. In comedy, Paul Newman and Robert Redford won acclaim for *The Sting* (1973) and Woody Allen and Diane Keaton for *Annie Hall* in 1977.

In 1981 Warren Beatty, epitomizing the *auteur,* wrote, directed, and acted in *Reds,* the story of John Reed and the American radical movement that was confounded by the 1917 Russian Revolution. The epic *Gandhi,* a 1982 effort at portraying an historical event starring Ben Kingsley as the Mahatma, was directed by Richard Attenborough. Another off-beat Oscar winner, in 1984, was Milos Forman's *Amadeus,* a fictional account of the last years of Mozart.

Two pictures shared 11 nominations each for the 1985 Oscar awards, but only one received honors. Sydney Pollack's *Out of Africa,* starring Meryl Streep as the ill-fated Isak Dinesen, swept seven awards. Steven Spielberg's *The Color Purple,* in which Whoopi Goldberg rose to stardom as a black woman subjugated by her husband, received none. Spielberg, director of four of the top ten all-time box-office successes, including *The Extra Terrestrial,* went unnominated that year but won in 1993 for *Schindler's List,* which also won six other Oscars. The war in Southeast Asia spawned two graphic, violent films: Oliver Stone's autobiographical *Platoon* about Vietnam and *The Killing Fields,* depicting the Cambodian morass; *Platoon* won the 1986 Oscar. Veteran Jessica Tandy and *Driving Miss Daisy* won in 1989, and Kevin Costner's *Dances with Wolves,* an epic of Native American life, swept seven awards in 1990.

Sexuality, horror, and rock music characterized many films, made for audiences more than half of whom were under 25. Sylvester Stallone's violent, chauvinistic *Rocky,* followed by sequels *II, III,* and *IV,* illustrated Hollywood's "make-a-buck" trends. Stallone's *Rambo* became a household name. 1994's *Pulp Fiction* raised, once again, the issue of Hollywood's seemingly gratuitous violence.

On the basis of box-office draw, three science-fiction or fantasy features led the all-time list of American movies. Number one, with more than $300 million in U.S. and Canadian receipts, was a human-interest triumph—*E.T.* (1982)—about a little visitor from outer space and his young friends on earth. Runner-up was *Jurassic Park* (1992), Steven Spielberg's dinosaur thriller. Close behind was *Star Wars,* the first of George Lucas's dramatic action films about Luke Skywalker, R2-D2, and the worlds beyond. Pressing close was *The Lion King* (1994), the animated Disney children's tale, along with *Forrest Gump* (1994), the story of a childlike innocent who survives the cataclysms of the 1960s and beyond. But still in the box-office top 20 were *Jaws* (1975) and George Lucas's *Star Wars* sequel, *Return of the Jedi* (1983).

In early 1995 the announcement of a new firm company called Dream Works, led by Steven Spielberg, threatened to shake up the studio lineup. At the same time the Seagram

TABLE 20–8   Top Grossing Films of All Time (in millions of dollars, as of July 27, 1999)

	TOTAL DOMESTIC GROSS	*YEAR RELEASED*
Titanic	601	1997
Star Wars	461	1977
Star Wars: The Phantom Menace	403	1999 (still in release)
E. T.	400	1982
Jurassic Park	357	1993
Forrest Gump	330	1994
The Lion King	313	1994
Return of the Jedi	307	1983
Independence Day	306	1996
The Empire Strikes Back	290	1980
Home Alone	285	1990
Jaws	260	1975

Source: USA TODAY, March 16, 1998, p. D1, from Exhibitor Relations Co. Inc., and Exhibitor Relations Co., Inc., statistics [http://movieweb.com/movie/alltime.html].

Co. acquired MCA, Inc. and ended up with majority ownership of Universal Pictures. The other players were: Warner Brothers, Sony, Paramount, Disney, Fox, and MGM/UA, all susceptible to reorganizations and ownership changes. The 1998 movie season saw the blockbuster *Titanic,* directed by James Cameron and starring Kate Winslet and Leonardo di Caprio, break many long-held records. The movie won most of the major Oscars and took first place in the top-grossing films of all time (see Table 20–8). 1997 saw the re-release of the *Star Wars* trilogy, with additional scenes that further developed the characters and plots as well as newly remastered imagery that amazed audiences. The *Star Wars* series remained a surefire draw with the 1999 release of *Star Wars: Episode I—The Phantom Menace,* which grossed more than $403,000,000 in its first ten weeks.

MAGAZINES FOR THE 21ST CENTURY

One of the most influential and successful media groups in the United States remained Time Warner's Time Inc. Magazine Co. Henry Anatole Grunwald was succeeded by Jason McManus as editor-in-chief in 1987. He gave managing editor Henry Muller freedom to change traditional ways; for example, by 1991 a third of *Time*'s articles were being written and signed by correspondents, not homogenized in New York. In 1992 McManus supervised a bold, clean new design and organization for *Time.* He retired in 1995, and Norman Pearlstine became the fifth editor-in-chief, dating back to Henry Luce.

In 1997 domestic circulation for *Time* exceeded 4.1 million copies weekly; worldwide circulation, adding five non-U.S. regional editions, was above 5.5 million. Satellite transmissions carried images of *Time* pages to printing plants in the United States, Europe, and Asia. By the early 1990s, *Time* had at least 29 correspondents in 19 bureaus abroad, 40 in 10 bureaus at home, and 450 staffers in New York. Time Warner was the largest U.S. print media company, with $2.5 billion in annual revenue. Its fluffy *People Weekly* at 3.6 million copies and *Sports Illustrated* at 3.2 million copies were also good sellers. A revived monthly edition of *Life,* without its famed photojournalism impact, sold 1.8 million copies, and *Fortune* circulated 732,000 biweekly.

Time Inc. experimented with several new magazines in the late 1970s and the 1980s. Only one, *Money,* was successful, with 2.1 million circulation by 1994. Costly failures were *TV-Cable Week* and *Picture Week;* disappointing were *Entertainment Weekly, Leisure,* and *Discover,* a news magazine of science. Time Inc. bought *Asiaweek, Progressive Farmer,* and three women's magazines, headed by *Southern Living,* as well as part-interests in *Working Woman, Working Mother,* and *Parenting.* Elizabeth Valk Long became Time Inc.'s first woman publisher, at *Life,* in 1986; she became publisher of *Time* in 1991 and then president. Patricia Ryan, managing editor of *People* since 1982, took the same job at *Life* in 1987.

Newsweek remained *Time*'s major rival at 3.2 million copies weekly, with Richard M. Smith as editor-in-chief and multiple domestic and foreign bureaus. *U.S. News and World Report,* purchased by media investor Mortimer B. Zuckerman in 1984, rose to 2.2 million copies as a conservative-leaning news magazine. *Business Week,* at 886,000 copies, was a solid competitor. The owners of the conservative *Washington Times* founded the weekly news magazine *Insight* in 1985 with Arnaud de Borchgrave as editor-in-chief; the lavishly printed journal had a circulation of 440,000 in 1994. *Ebony,* the black-owned picture magazine, sold 886,000 monthly.

Among the quality and opinion magazines, the *New Yorker* remained a jewel of American journalism. William Shawn, successor to founder Harold Ross as editor in 1951, retired involuntarily in 1987. Samuel I. Newhouse, Jr., who had bought the *New Yorker* for $142 million in 1985, named as its third editor Robert A. Gottlieb, 55-year-old editor-in-chief of Alfred A. Knopf publishing house, another Newhouse property. Circulation was 620,000. Newhouse also owned *Vogue,* with 1.3 million circulation, and in 1983 resuscitated *Vanity Fair,* published for the reading rich from 1914 to 1936. In 1994 it had reached 1.2 million copies, with the Englishwoman Tina Brown, and then Graydon Carter, as editors. After the *New Yorker* lost $10 million in 1991 under Gottlieb's editorship, Newhouse quickly replaced him with Tina Brown, stunning the publishing industry. Brown left the *New Yorker* in 1998.

Esquire also made news. Its quality declined after founder Arnold Gingrich sold out in 1976, but it was restored by Philip Moffitt and Christopher Whittle. Moffitt escalated a $20 million investment into an estimated $80 million payoff when he sold *Esquire* to the Hearst Corp. magazine group at the close of 1986. By 1994 it had its first woman publisher, Nancy Nadler LeWinter, and 713,000 readers. *New York,* purchased by Rupert Murdoch in 1977, lost much of its sophisticated appeal but retained 427,000 readers. It was bought in 1991 by K-III Holdings partnership.

Smithsonian, strong in photographic skills and travel appeal, sold 2.2 million copies with Don Moser as editor. The venerable *Atlantic,* sold to Mortimer Zuckerman in 1980, ran startling public-affairs articles and by 1994 had built a 461,000 circulation with William Whitsworth as editor and James Fallows as Washington editor. *Harper's,* rescued from a closing in 1981 by new publisher John R. MacArthur, gained a respite during the 18-month editorship of Michael Kinsley. When Kinsley took over the TRB column in the *New Republic* in late 1983, former editor Lewis Lapham again filled the "Easy Chair" for *Harper's,* now circulating 207,000. *Saturday Review* closed down in 1982 but was temporarily revived in 1983, first by Jeffrey and Debra Gluck and then by David L. Simpson II and Paul Dietrich, who made it a bimonthly.

Texas Monthly, founded in 1973, won 310,000 circulation for its iconoclastic, investigative style. *In These Times,* founded by James Weinstein in 1976, offered a strong voice on the left. The news weekly had a circulation of about 32,000 in 1994. Another new entry among the activist opinion journals was *Mother Jones,* a cooperative staff effort that appeared in San Francisco in 1976. Headed by Deidre English and Michael Moore, its circulation reached 115,000 by the mid-1990s. Starting in 1969 editor-in-chief Charles Peters put out the sprightly *Washington Monthly* as a keen commentary on the capital. By 1994 editor Victor Navasky had 96,000 readers for the *Nation,* compared to 100,000 for the less radical *New Republic,* edited by Andrew Sullivan, and 168,000 for William Buckley's conservative *National Review.* Erwin Knoll kept the *Progressive* contributing to liberal thought and criticism in Wisconsin. He died in 1994, but the magazine continued.

Science magazines, buoyant in the 1970s, lost support in the mid-1980s. *Scientific American,* founded in 1846 and read by a highly professional 663,000 subscribers, suffered sharp advertising declines. *Science Digest* suspended in 1986; *Science '86* sold its 635,000 subscription list to Time Inc.'s *Discover,* which needed it to become profitable at a 1 million copy level. *Discover* reached that level after it was sold to the Family Media Group in 1987. *Omni,* the Playboy International entry publishing science fiction and fantasy, had the most advertising and 703,000 readers in 1994.

Reader's Digest had the largest circulation of U.S. magazines, with 16.3 million copies sold at home and 12 million more in 40 international editions published in 16 languages. *TV Guide* sold 14.9 million copies in regional editions. The *National Geographic,* a family favorite, had difficulty producing enough copies as circulation reached 9.7 million.

In all, there were nearly 16,000 periodicals of all types in 1994. About 3000 were consumer magazines considered of general interest. The biggest subfields included business and trade publications, 8,649; religious magazines, 802; and agricultural journals, 628. Each year some 600 hopefuls launch new magazines. Table 20–9 shows the magazines with the highest circulations.

TABLE 20–9   Top Magazines—1997

	CIRCULATION
Modern Maturity	20,390,755
Reader's Digest	15,038,708
TV Guide	13,103,187
National Geographic	9,012,074
Better Homes & Gardens	7,605,187
Family Circle	5,107,477
Good Housekeeping	4,739,592
Ladies' Home Journal	4,590,155
The Cable Guide	4,544,778
Woman's Day	4,461,023
McCall's	4,216,145
Time	4,155,806
People	3,608,111
Prevention	3,310,278
Sports Illustrated	3,223,810

Source: Advertising Age, February 23, 1998, p. 28.

BOOK PUBLISHING

The U.S. book publishing industry enjoyed gross sales of over $23 billion in 1998. Trade books, fiction, and nonfiction sold to the reading public doubled in sales, reaching $4 billion in 1990, nearly $5 billion in 1994, and $6.15 billion in 1998. Public school and college textbooks topped $4 billion, while paperbounds reached $1.5 billion. The largest increases were in children's books.

More than 22,000 publishing houses issued 49,000 new titles or editions each year, and produced a total of nearly 2 billion copies. There were 27,809 book outlets of all kinds, of which half handled new trade books. More than half of trade and paperback sales were made by two nationwide chains, Waldenbooks and B. Dalton/Barnes & Noble, which employed computerized inventory control and ordering systems. B. Dalton's 800 stores were bought in 1986 by the New York booksellers, Barnes & Noble. Online bookseller Amazon.com, started in 1995, reported sales in the first quarter of 1999 of $293.6 million. Besides books the company also sells music, videos, and gifts online and has recently added an auction site.

Simon & Schuster, led by Richard E. Snyder as chief executive since 1975, emerged as the world's largest publishing house with sales of $1.4 billion under some 40 names by 110 operating units. Its principal subsidiary was Prentice Hall, a leading publisher of educational and business information books, purchased in 1984 for $710 million; in 1992 Prentice Hall was eliminated as a separate imprint to cut costs. Both were part of the Paramount Communications conglomerate until 1994, when Viacom Inc. acquired Paramount. In the second quarter of 1994, Viacom's total revenues were $1.7 billion, with more than $469 million from publishing alone. In November 1998, Pearson PLC acquired Simon & Schuster's textbook division for $4.6 billion, which made it the world's largest educational publisher with one-third of the U.S. market.

Random House, owned by the Newhouse family's Advance Publications, was the largest trade publisher after its 1988 acquisition of the Crown Publishing Group. Random House also owned Alfred A. Knopf, Pantheon, Times Books, Villard, Ballantine Books, and Fawcett. Bantam Doubleday Dell was second largest, followed by Simon & Schuster (which purchased Macmillan), HarperCollins, Penguin USA, and Putnam Berkley.

A mass resignation of frustrated editors at Pantheon resulted in the naming of a black executive editor, Errol McDonald, in 1990, to stem the dissent and Pantheon's losses. Newhouse counted on Italian-born Alberto Vitale to smooth away turbulence as the new chief executive of Random House. At prestigious Alfred A. Knopf, Newhouse named Ajai Singh Mehta as editor-in-chief, succeeding Robert A. Gottlieb when he became *New Yorker* editor. Mehta, a citizen of India and Cambridge graduate, had directed the largest paperback house in Britain.

Rupert Murdoch's News Corp. created HarperCollins out of a three-way merger in 1990. The new firm mounted an aggressive challenge in trade book publishing and was the fifth largest publisher of college texts. Harper & Row's employees had sold their stock to Murdoch in 1987. In 1989 he completed his purchase of a major British house, William Collins & Sons, and bought textbook publishing house Scott, Foresman from Time Warner. Scotsman George Craig was chief executive of HarperCollins and Susan Moldow was editor-in-chief of its adult trade division.

Sales of American book firms to European houses marked the mid-1980s. The Holtzbrinck Group of Germany bought Holt, Rinehart & Winston (renamed Henry Holt) from CBS. Penguin Publishing Company of London included New American Library and its hard-cover affiliate, E. P. Dutton, in its worldwide operations. Bertelsmann A.G.

TABLE 20–10   Leading Book Publishers—1997

HARDCOVERS	SHARE IN PERCENTAGE	PAPERBACKS	SHARE IN PERCENTAGE
Random House Inc.	22.8	Random House Inc.	23.2
Time Warner	15.3	Penguin Putnam Inc.	18.8
Penguin Putnam Inc.	13.7	Bantam Doubleday Dell	17.7
Simon & Schuster	11.1	Simon & Schuster	14.0
Bantam Doubleday Dell	11.0	Health Communications	7.0
HarperCollins	10.7	Time Warner	6.5
Hearst	3.0	Hearst	4.3
Hyperion	2.9	HarperCollins	2.9
Von Holtzbrink	2.4	Hyperion	2.7
Grove/Atlantic Monthly	1.7	Andrews McMeel	1.1
Norton	1.7	Other	1.8
Longstreet	1.6		
Other	2.1		

Shares are shown based on 1530 hardcover and 1530 paperback bestseller positions during 1997.

Source: Publishers' Weekly, January 5, 1998, p. 40.

of Germany paid $475 million for Doubleday & Company; it had acquired Bantam Books in 1980 for its worldwide group of 30 publishing houses.

The rise of the "superstores" such as Barnes & Noble, as well as the online book-selling giant, Amazon.com, has heightened competition. Many independent bookstores had to close their doors as the number of superstores was estimated to top 950 in number at the end of 1997. Table 20–10 outlines some of the heavy hitters in the book publishing industry. It is interesting to note the variations between hardcover and paperback publishers.

PUBLIC RELATIONS AS A PROFESSION

An estimated 150,000 practitioners worked in public relations and its affiliated functions in the United States. Most of them were specialists in some form of communications activity; some were generalists at the executive or managerial level. There were some 1500 public-relations counseling firms, and about one-third of large American companies retained an outside consultant, according to a comprehensive survey by *O'Dwyer's Directory of Corporate Communications*. Eighty percent of 2675 large companies and trade associations reported an identifiable public-relations activity under such organizational titles as public relations, corporate relations, public information, corporate communications, or external relations.

The largest public relations counseling service, with a lion's share of billings, was Young & Rubicam, followed by Ketchum Communications, I.M.S. International and BDO Health and Medical. Rounding out the top 10 were: Mickelberry, Carlson Marketing Group, Chiat/Day/Mojo Advertising, Hill & Knowlton, Entergy Services, and Croswell, Munsell, Fultz & Zirbel. A third of the top 50 public-relations firms were advertising agency subsidiaries. The public-relations arms of such groups as the American Medical Association, the AFL/CIO, the National Association of Manufacturers, and the National Rifle

Association, were both large and controversial. Those of leading corporations were involved in both public-relations management decisions and operating functions using communications techniques.

The Public Relations Society of America (PRSA), founded in 1948, had 15,000 members, half of whom were female. About 3000 had won professional accreditation since the group began a stiffly operated accrediting program in 1965. PRSA membership tended to be concentrated among the generalist professionals, while the International Association of Business Communicators flourished with 11,000 members among publications editors and information specialists. The International Public Relations Association, founded in 1955, had 700 members in 50 countries. There were perhaps two dozen specialized public-relations associations in such fields as finance, agriculture, education, and social work. Whatever the level of operation, those involved tended to strive for acceptable performance standards.

PRSA's mission includes the goal of uniting members of the profession, encouraging continuing education in the field, and maintaining high standards of conduct and public service. At the turn of the twenty-first century, PRSA had 109 chapters throughout the United States grouped into 10 geographical areas and offered membership in diverse professional-interest sections to further enhance connections among public-relations practitioners.

WORLDWIDE ADVERTISING

The world's largest advertising company was the WPP Group of London, which expanded in the late 1980s with the purchases of several top U.S. firms, including J. Walter Thompson and Ogilvy & Mather. WPP's gross income of more than $2.8 billion far surpassed the number two company, Interpublic Group New York, with $1.99 billion. Interpublic's holdings included the well-known McCann-Erickson Worldwide.

Others high in the billings were Omnicom Group, New York; Saatchi & Saatchi, London, world leader through most of the 1980s; Dentsu of Tokyo; and Young & Rubicam, New York.

Total annual advertising volume in the United States reached $130 billion, more than doubling since 1980. Some 400,000 people worked in primary advertising jobs, another million in related ones. There were about 5000 advertising agencies; the 700 members of the American Association of Advertising Agencies (AAS) controlled three-fourths of the business.

One trend in the field was comparative advertising, particularly on television. The Federal Trade Commission encouraged comparative ads on the theory that consumers would be enlightened. The public was witness to battles between pizza makers, Jeno's and Totino's; fast-food chains, McDonald's and Burger King; soft drinks, Pepsi and Coke; and video game makers, Atari and Intellivision. Sometimes these battles ended up in court. The rule was that you could disparage your competitor so long as you did not lie or mislead. Another trend was corporate advertising. GTE and TRW aimed to make the public as conscious of their names as of IBM.

In the 1980s the effort to position the product in the public mind took the form of target advertising—how does the product fit into different life-styles? Intensive research into psychographics—the grouping of people by values and life-styles as well as by age, sex, and income—formed the basis of the campaigns. The Stanford Research Institute created VALS—Values and Life Styles—as a way to divide the total public into clumps, rather than by age groups or occupations.

Enormous increases in the cost of television commercials brought advertiser resistance. There were experiments with 15-second commercials (two related products sharing a 30-second spot) and 90-second "blockbusters." Buying 30 seconds of time on a primetime network cost up to $250,000; if you wanted 30 seconds with the 1995 Super Bowl, it was $1 million. Since the one-time showing of the famous Apple commercial during the 1984 Super Bowl, many people tune into the Super Bowl just to see the commercials, and advertisers like that just fine. Although the 1999 Super Bowl garnered a rating of only 40.2 percent (compared with 44.5 percent for the 1998 Super Bowl), most participants note that they can reach more customers with a 60-second spot on the Super Bowl than they can with a year's worth of advertising in most other media.

Rankings within the industry tabulated by *Advertising Age* consistently named J. Walter Thompson and Ogilvy & Mather as the two best advertising agencies. Chiat/Day/Mojo ranked high for creativity, along with Fallon McElligott of Minneapolis. Other regional agencies winning attention were Hill, Holliday, Conners, Cosmopulos of Boston; Ketchum Advertising and Goodby, Berlin & Silverstein of San Francisco; Martin Agency in Richmond, Virginia; Livingston & Company of Seattle; Wieden & Kennedy in Portland, Oregon; and the Richards Group of Dallas.

Women began to break through to highest ranks. Charlotte Beers of Tatham-Laird became the first woman president of the 4As. Louise R. McNamee became the first woman with her name in an advertising agency's name when Della Femina McNamee WCRS was formed in 1988. She was agency president. The Interpublic Group reported that two of its subsidiaries had 50 percent women in professional jobs.

INTERNATIONAL SATELLITE TECHNOLOGY

The global satellite network, the core of private, commercial and governmental communications systems, was changing as fast as the other technological areas. One example: the heads of the nation's largest cellular telephone company and the largest computer software company planned to build a $9 billion system using 840 satellites, a plan that dwarfed any others. William Gates of Microsoft and Craig McCaw, who built McCaw Cellular Communications, formed Teledesic Corporation.

The idea was to place smaller than normal satellites in low earth orbit, about 435 miles high. These satellites, about 12 feet by three, would be equipped with a new video transmission system which would compete with high-capacity copper and fiber optic systems. However, in order to cover the earth's expanse the many satellites would be required to orbit along at least 20 different routes. Before the full system could go into operation, the permissions of international regulatory organizations and perhaps individual nations would be required. The Motorola Corporation planned a 66-satellite telephone system.

The intense competition of the 1990s was fueled by a 1986 Reagan Administration decision to turn over the business of launching private satellites to private U.S. rocket makers. The turning point was the January 1986 destruction of the space shuttle Challenger. The government, of course, continued to launch its own space shuttles carrying both military and scientific payloads.

The main U.S. firms involved in international and domestic traffic were AT&T, General Electric, GTE Corp., Hughes Aircraft, Western Union, and Satellite Business Systems. Among many other services, AT&T's Telstar satellites carried ABC and CBS; General Electric served NBC and used RCA's Satcom satellites to become a major carrier of cable networks, along with Hughes Aircraft; Western Union carried PBS and NPR; SBS specialized in teleconferencing, computer, and other business communications. However, the plans by U.S. firms to launch privately owned satellites for international communications were opposed by developing nations who were members of the International Telecommunications Union (ITU), an agency of the United Nations responsible for satellite regulation.

The United States became involved with international satellite communication when the successful launching of AT&T's Telstar on July 10, 1962, permitted the first live transmission of pictures between the United States and Europe. These were staged shows lasting for the few minutes that the signal could be bounced off the moving satellite. RCA's Relay carried pictures to 23 nations at the time of President Kennedy's assassination. The effort to develop continuous service by launching a satellite that would achieve a fully synchronous orbit (an orbit and speed that keep the craft directly over one spot on earth) met success when Howard Hughes launched Syncom III in 1964. Four such satellites, equally spaced around the world, could provide television coverage to all inhabited portions of the planet.

The Communications Satellite Corporation, formed by Congress in 1962 to unify the U.S. effort and to provide international leadership, carried out technical progress under the leadership of Joseph V. Charyk, its president for the first 22 years.

Comsat's achievements included the launching in 1965 of Earlybird, the world's first commercial communications satellite, assisting with the planning of many of the nation's domestic satellite systems, and the successful coordination with Intelsat, the International Telecommunications Satellite Consortium. Comsat held a 25 percent share of Intelsat. In May 1971, a 79-nation Intelsat conference revised its rules, but it was not until after 1975 that there was much enthusiasm for international satellites. This was in the wake of the Home Box Office success.

By 1977 the Intelsat IV satellites were carrying more than 4000 voice circuits, and that figure jumped to more than 35,000 for the Intelsat VI series in 1986. The 1988 and 1989 Intelsats had ten times that capacity and the numbers rapidly increased. Intelsat had 16 satellites serving 170 nations, including 110 who were full-fledged members of the organization. These satellites carried about two-thirds of the international telephone traffic and nearly all of the television programming. One threat to Intelsat's dominance was the switch by some phone companies to fiber optics and the setting up of new systems.

The commercial communications satellites orbited the earth at an altitude of 22,300 miles.

The uses of international satellites were virtually unlimited. The BBC considered being co-producer of a weekly global television news program, called Planet 3, where a comparison would be offered of how news events were covered in different parts of the world. The first news pictures of the 1986 nuclear plant disaster at Chernobyl in the Soviet Union were passed on by American and French satellites. But there were some concerns, also. The American and French satellites easily could pick up military installations, nuclear test sites, and evidence of military maneuvers. There was a proposal for a media satellite owned by the networks and other organizations that could provide images more detailed than possible through Landsat and SPOT. The Pentagon reacted with alarm, arguing for enforcement of a 1978 executive order signed by President Carter that limited satellites to a higher resolution than desired by news executives. The "spy-in-the-sky" debate involving national security protections and First Amendment rights would continue. Libertarians were worried also by reports of systemized government monitoring of international communications.

Table 20–11 demonstrates the worldwide nature of satellite activity. Russia has outranked the United States in satellites since 1966. The "Payload" column indicates the number of satellites each country or company has in orbit.

TABLE 20–11   Space Objects Box Score for December 31, 1998

SOURCE/ ORGANIZATION	OBJECTS IN ORBIT			DECAYED OBJECTS		
	Payload	Debris	Total	Payload	Debris	Total
AB = Arab Sat. Comm. Org.	6	0	6	0	0	0
AC = ASIASAT Corp.	2	0	2	0	0	0
ARGN = Argentina	6	0	6	0	0	0
AUS = Australia	8	1	9	2	0	2
BRAZ = Brazil	8	0	8	0	0	0
CA = Canada	15	1	16	1	1	2
CHLE = Chile	1	0	1	0	0	0
CIS = Russia/USSR	1367	2604	3971	1698	10070	11768
CZCH = Czechoslovokia	4	0	4	1	0	1
EGYP = Egypt	1	0	1	0	0	0
ESA = European Space Agency	31	209	240	4	493	497
ESRO = Euro. Space Res. Org.	0	0	0	7	3	10
EUTE = Euro. Telec. Sat. Org	14	0	14	0	0	0
FGER = France/Fed. Rep. Ger.	3	0	3	0	0	0
FR = France	30	16	46	7	59	66
GER = Germany	17	1	18	7	1	8
GLOB = Global	8	0	8	0	1	1
IM = Int. Marit. Sat. Org.	9	0	9	0	0	0
IND = India	17	4	21	7	8	15
INDO = Indonesia	8	0	8	1	0	1
IRID = Iridium	86	0	86	0	12	12
ISRA = Israel	3	0	3	2	3	5
ISS = International Space Station	1	0	1	0	1	1
IT = Italy	8	2	10	6	0	6
ITSO = Int. Telec. Sat. Org.	56	0	56	1	0	1
JPN = Japan	68	51	119	12	94	106
KOR = Korea	4	0	4	0	0	0
LUXE = Luxembourg	8	0	8	0	0	0
MALA = Malaysia	2	0	2	0	0	0
MEX = Mexico	6	0	6	0	0	0
NATO = North At. Treaty Org.	8	0	8	0	0	0
NETH = Netherlands	0	0	0	1	0	1
NOR = Norway	3	0	3	0	0	0
ORB = Orbital Telecommucation	28	0	28	0	0	0
PAKI = Pakistan	0	0	0	1	0	1
POR = Portugal	1	0	1	0	0	0
PRC = Peoples Rep. of China	27	98	125	31	118	149
RP =	2	0	2	0	0	0
SPN = Spain	5	0	5	0	0	0
STCT = Singapore/Taiwan	1	0	1	0	0	0
SWED = Sweden	8	0	8	0	0	0
THAI = Thailand	4	0	4	0	0	0
TURK = Turkey	2	0	2	0	0	0
UK = United Kingdom	16	1	17	8	4	12
US = United States	765	3178	3943	684	3421	4105
Column Totals	2667	6166	8833	2481	14289	16770
Sum Totals						25603

THE INTERNATIONAL FLOW OF THE NEWS

In the years after World War II it became clear that there was an international flow of the news, made increasingly immediate, if not instantaneous, by the miracles of media technology. It was also clear that there was a need for better collection, writing, and distribution of news and information so that they served people more evenly on a worldwide basis, recognizing both their interests and their needs.

There were barriers to such communication improvements. One was the long Cold War between the United States and its Western allies and the USSR and its Eastern bloc. Outside stood what became known as the Non-Aligned Countries, which evolved a New World Information Order envisioning the full participation of the Third World in exchange of news and information. With the support of UNESCO, the large Non-Aligned group brought about a full debate of the issue, and increased activity on the part of the West to improve its news and information systems.

A literature also developed that examined the role of the American media in the cultural and political development of the rest of the world. Some viewed the United States media as an arm of American economic and military imperialism, distorting, on one hand, the images the American public received about events abroad and policies of foreign powers, and attempting to "sell," on the other hand, the advantages of American social and political beliefs to those living abroad. Wherever the balance of truth was to be found, it was clear that the American news media—particularly its press associations, news magazines, and broadcast programs—had major influence in all parts of the world. So, increasingly, were the media of other nations coming to the attention of media personnel, political and educational leaders, and informed audiences in the United States.

Of course, the Internet has broadened the scope of news to the international forum. Anyone anywhere in the world can access the Internet, and this, coupled with the success of CNN in Gulf War coverage, has shortened the news cycle considerably. Where once there was sufficient lag time to fully develop news stories before publishing them in any format, now there is pressure for a 24/7/365 news cycle. Some critics claim that this cycle creates time pressure problems on journalists to keep up and results in less fact-checking taking place before the news hits press and thus more errors and ethical problems. However, the trend is unlikely to change, so journalists will have to develop systems to cope with the increasing pressure.

U.S. NEWS AGENCIES: AP AND UPI

The AP and UPI intensified their competition in the wake of the merger of the United Press and International News Service. By the late 1970s, both had 400,000 miles of leased telephone wires in the United States for the transmission of news and pictures. Both used satellite channels, radio teleprinters, and underwater cables to carry their news reports to more than 100 countries. Both had teletype circuits covering more than 20,000 miles in Europe, where their news reports were translated and fed into national wires, and both transmitted pictures worldwide. Both had automated their transmission facilities, using video display terminals and computers to perfect information storage and retrieval systems. The domestic news wire could deliver copy to news offices at 1200 words a minute, 10 times earlier speeds. A news report could be flashed around the world, using the automatic editing system, within a single minute.

The systems still worked, as the 1980s began, but the UPI found great difficulties in coping with sharp inflation of costs and the effects of a worldwide recession which intensified at home. Its parent E. W. Scripps Company reported losses running into the millions after 1980. They sought to sell shares in the UPI to media using its services, negotiated with the British news agency Reuters about a possible merger, and finally negotiated a sale in June 1982 to Media News Corporation, a group of American newspaper, cable, and television station owners. UPI President Robert W. Beaton retired and was succeeded by William J. Small, a former executive of both CBS News and NBC News. Maxwell McCrohon, *Chicago Tribune* news executive, became editor-in-chief. Key news operations were shifted from New York to Washington.

Continuing losses and court battles over control cut the UPI to the bone, and in 1985 the agency filed for protection from its creditors. The bankruptcy proceedings ended in June 1986, when Mario Vázquez Raña, the owner of more than 60 Mexican newspapers, was approved as the new owner and became chairman. The price was only $41 million. A running debate began in media circles about the appropriateness of the sale of a U.S. firm to a foreign owner with political friends, but it was pointed out that many U.S. publishers have been close to major political figures.

As 1987 began, the AP officially counted up 6145 users of its services worldwide. These included 1365 member papers and 3954 radio and television stations in the United States. It had 2950 employees, including 1520 news staff members, in 222 bureaus serving 108 countries. Best estimates for the UPI were 5000 users of its services worldwide, including 700 papers and 3330 stations in the United States. The UPI had 1200 employees working in 230 bureaus located in more than 100 countries. Both delivered news by satellite to virtually all U.S. users. But the UPI continued to flounder.

Vázquez turned over control in early 1988 to an investor group, Infotechnology, Inc., which also controlled Financial News Network. All three firms were plagued by insufficient cash flow. Pieter VanBennekom succeeded H. L. Stevenson as the UPI's vice president for editorial operations. In late 1990 he announced more layoffs and plans to concentrate news coverage in 15 states, offering specialized segments of the news report. The UPI was down to fewer than 400 newspaper clients, and its staff agreed to a 35 percent paycut while management sought a buyer. In February 1991, the UPI was gamely offering its Gulf War Frontline news package to any takers.

The agency was rescued from the bankruptcy court in June 1992 by Middle East Broadcasting Center, Ltd., a television news and entertainment company based in London but owned by Walid Al-Ibrahim, brother-in-law of Saudi Arabia's King Fahd, and Rafik al-Hariri, Saudi radio station owner. The purchase price was $3.95 million. At that moment UPI found itself reduced to about 450 fulltime employees and 2,000 part-time correspondents working in 33 domestic bureaus (in 22 states) and 73 foreign countries. While the number of overseas clients was not known, it was estimated that UPI's contracts with U.S. dailies had dropped to about 100 and that another 100 weeklies were being served. The new owners pledged to maintain the integrity of the news operation—not to politicize it—and to invest about $50 million in order to expand coverage and gain more clients. Veteran international journalist Raphael Calis was executive editor and vice president.

Perhaps the UPI's greatest asset was its White House correspondent, Helen Thomas, who succeeded the legendary Merriman Smith upon his death in 1970. Thomas was the first woman to head the White House Correspondents Association and was showered with many honors as she became a legend herself. At a 1991 Gulf War press conference, President Bush as usual opened by calling out "Helen," but this time questions were also put by women representing the *New York Times,* the *Wall Street Journal,* and the AP. Thomas,

(UPI)

(Silha Center, University of Minnesota)

Helen Thomas, UPI's White House
correspondent

Louis D. Boccardi, AP president

still covering the White House in 1999, received the third annual Edward W. Estlow Anvil of Freedom award from the University of Denver in October 1998 recognizing professional excellence in the service of the First Amendment.

Within the AP structure, Keith Fuller replaced Wes Gallagher as president and general manager. In 1984 he was replaced by Louis D. Boccardi, who spearheaded the AP's drive for technological breakthroughs. Walter Mears was the star of political reporting. Stanley Swinton, head of the AP World News Service since its inception, died in 1982 and was replaced by Larry Heinzerling. William E. Abeam became executive editor in 1990.

Boccardi sought to improve AP news coverage and writing, but he emphasized financial, weather, and election news coverage. The AP enhanced its international laserphoto and was the first news agency to own satellite transponders. It added an electronic darkroom, an all-digital photo system, and APTV, a global news video service. In 1991 the AP had more than 1540 U.S. newspaper members, as it moved toward news service dominance.

But in the wake of UPI's demise as a competitive force there were concerns expressed, summed up by press critic David Shaw of the *Los Angeles Times:*

> Critics say that too much AP writing is bland and unimaginative, too few AP stories take real risks, either journalistically, politically, or stylistically, and too many AP bureaus in this country and abroad spend too much time rewriting stories from the local papers and not enough time doing their own reporting. . . .
>
> . . . Many past and present AP staffers say that AP's performance on the Watergate, My Lai and Cambodian stories is symptomatic of a fundamental problem that continues today. . . . There are still some kinds of stories that AP is not comfortable doing. Stories that challenge the White House and make America look bad in the eyes of the world are, they say, among them.[29]

U.S. NEWS SERVICES ABROAD

It was ironic that as U.S. news organizations approached the end of the century, their managers assigned only about 1000 U.S. nationals to cover the world population of more than 6 billion. Half of the overseas Americans worked for one of the press associations. While there was retrenchment within the news operations, there was no slowdown in the selling of news and features to overseas clients.

One leader of the newspaper syndicates was the New York Times News Service. Founded in 1917, it was claiming more than 600 users in 54 countries. Newest on the scene was the Los Angeles Times–Washington Post News Service, begun in 1962 by publishers Otis Chandler and Philip L. Graham. It claimed more than 650 clients in 56 countries.

More than 200 foreign clients of Knight-Ridder/Tribune Information Services had access to the news filed by foreign correspondents and domestic news bureaus of the participating newspapers, the Knight-Ridder papers and the *Chicago Tribune.*

Other important supplementary news services used by American media were the Dow Jones News Service, specializing in economic news; the Copley News Service, focusing on Latin America; and the Scripps Howard News Service. The Religious News Service and the Catholic News Service operated widely.

Winning a place in U.S. newspapers was Reuters from Great Britain, founded in 1851 and the oldest of the world's current news services. In the 1980s Reuters built up a North American organization as a supplement to its worldwide service and later purchased the UPI photo division. Reuters Monitor was a specialized financial report competing with Dow Jones, Knight-Ridder Financial News, AFX (a joint venture of Agence France–Presse and Extel Financial, Ltd, London) and other emerging high-technology financial news firms. Reuters joined the AP and UPI with guaranteed seats on Air Force One.

THE NEW WORLD INFORMATION ORDER

The flow of news between nations became an increasingly sensitive international issue in the 1970s as Third World leaders spoke out loudly and clearly about the urgent need to reorder the traditional international communication system in order to achieve a better balance of information. By the mid-1980s the Western countries had a better grasp of Third World concerns, if not a willingness to adopt what was being called the New World Information Order.

Among the world's many press associations or news agencies, the four Western transnationals—the Associated Press, United Press International, Reuters, and Agence France–Presse—along with TASS of the Soviet Union, provided more than 90 percent of the daily international news fare. Western powers also were the most advanced in the use of telecommunications channels, including satellites; in 1982 developing nations representing 70 percent of the world's population had only 5 percent of the television transmitters and 12 percent of television receivers. The nonaligned and some other nations viewed this dominance of communication channels as a vestige of colonialism that inhibited them culturally, politically, and economically. Their goal of a New International Economic Order, proclaimed in 1973, could not be achieved without a new information or communication order, they said.

There were efforts to address the problem as early as the 1953 flow-of-news study by the International Press Institute, whose data showed the one-way flow. The IPI was dedicated to the Western-style free press system, but also worked to develop the press in Asia and Africa. So did the Thomson Foundation in Britain, which since 1963 has provided practical training for Third World journalists. UNESCO in 1960 undertook a worldwide survey of press, radio, film, and television, providing data illuminating the problem. It also encouraged the development of national and regional news agencies in Asia, Africa, and Latin America. By 1972 UNESCO had developed a declaration of guiding principles on the use of satellite broadcasting for the free flow of information.

But all this did not satisfy the Third World. The 1970 UNESCO General Assembly asked its Director General to examine communication policies, and began a discussion of the phrase "right to communicate." The issue exploded in 1973 at the fourth conference of Heads of State of Non-Aligned Countries, held in Algeria. They called for "reorganization of existing communication channels which are the legacy of the colonial past" and which hampered intercommunication among developing countries, for cheaper press cable rates, and for collective ownership of communications satellites. They also began planning the Non-Aligned News Pool, which began operating in 1975 under the guidance of the Yugoslav agency, Tanjug.

The issues were sharpened in an escalating series of meetings in Paris, Tunis, New Delhi, New York, and San José, Costa Rica. The last named meeting, in July 1976, introduced the phrase "free and balanced flow" of the news. The Tunisian foreign minister, Mustapha Masmoudi, earlier had contributed a detailed document of complaints, and the Soviet Union put even more drastic proposals to the 1976 General Assembly of UNESCO at Nairobi in October 1976. A breakdown between the Western bloc and the Soviet-supported Non-Aligned group was avoided when the Assembly agreed to a two-year delay and the appointment of a 16-person International Commission for the Study of Communication Problems, under the chairmanship of Sean MacBride of Ireland, recipient of both the Lenin and Nobel Peace prizes.

At its 1978 General Assembly, UNESCO dropped the "free and balanced flow" concept, using the phrase "a free flow and a wider and better balanced dissemination of information." In return for this concession, the Western group admitted that it was "necessary to correct the inequalities in the flow of information to and from developing countries, and between those countries." The 1980 final report of the MacBride Commission rejected proposals for licensing of journalists or affording them "special protections" beyond those of all citizens; condemned censorship; and argued for right of access to private as well as public sources of information. It failed to put private ownership of news media and communications facilities on the same plane as public control, and in the view of Western press leaders left the transnational agencies open to pressure to transmit stories promoting government-set economic and political goals, regardless of newsworthiness or propaganda content.

The 1980 General Assembly in Belgrade did not vote on the MacBride report, but did adopt a resolution containing many of its principles. UNESCO began a lengthy series of regional meetings on the issues of the New World Information Order and the concept of the "right to communicate." Western press leaders, particularly the American-sponsored World Press Freedom Committee, raised more than a million dollars for training programs and equipment shipments to three continents. Third World journalists were invited to internship experiences, and the U.S. government provided free transponder time on Intelsat to the developing world.

But the Third World's basic political objections were not yet met. UNESCO's 1984–85 discussion program still talked of state-run news agencies, codes of conduct for journalists, and the removal of obstacles to the flow of news from the developing countries to the developed areas of the world—with the Third World definition of what is important news. Like the New International Economic Order, the New World Information Order was beset with difficulties stemming from basic North-South economic and East-West political confrontations. The withdrawal by the United States from UNESCO in 1985 left matters at an impasse, which had not yet been broken in 1995 despite a complete retreat by Third World UNESCO members.

In September 1998 UNESCO counseled the World Association of Press Councils (WAPC) against developing a set of global guidelines for media ethics and creating a world press council to hear transnational complaints on media conduct. *The Times* of London strongly recommended distancing Britain's Press Complaints Commission from the WAPC's agenda, fearful that this could constitute a repeat of the New World Information Order fiasco.[30]

LESSONS FOR THE AGE OF TECHNOLOGY

In this age of power and influence it was incumbent upon the men and women who worked in the rush of technological change not to forget that the freedom to speak and write the truth is never secure, never certain, always capable of being lost. Louis D. Boccardi, president and general manager of the Associated Press, reminded journalists of both their rights and responsibilities. Preserving rights, he said, is linked to media credibility. Freedom of gathering and disseminating information depends on the level of tolerance in a society. He told media managers that while their business pressures were multiplying, their main challenge was to maintain public support.

Journalists need occasional reminders of their faults. The overreliance on anonymous sources hurts credibility. So does any reliance on "tabloid sources." A rush of libel suits may indicate overzealousness as much as tough journalism. There are two rational sides to the debate over national security versus a free press. Keeping events in perspective is difficult, and Boccardi urged journalists not to risk frightening their audience with a torrent of information that lacks meaningful background and interpretation.

"The parking lots at convention centers have become electrified forests of satellite dishes," he said, marvelling at the age of technology. But he also warned that if media credibility drops, then courts, legislatures, and even a constitutional convention could dictate new laws, with the ultimate result that the public upon whom freedoms ultimately rest could turn aside.[31] Such warnings about the danger to media freedoms should be taken seriously, but not just because of the abundance of poor practices. Journalism history shows that a generally responsible and vigilant media is the first target of oppressive leaders.

In 1971 the United States government tried to deny its people the right to read a report prepared by their own government about a war in which they had fought and died. At the same time the president and his staff used illegal means to try to intimidate members of the news media and others who opposed his policies. Later other presidents adversely affected U.S. media coverage by denying U.S. correspondents access to war zones. These crises passed, but others were sure to occur.

Yet there is room for optimism. Using the sophisticated electronic equipment available to them, today's print and broadcast news managers brought the celebrations of the two-hundredth anniversary of the Constitution to the entire nation and transmitted the Olympic Games to the entire world. Their continual challenge was to help people better understand the pressing economic, military, and social issues of the times.

The rights of citizens are only as strong as their will to defend them. This includes their willingness to defend those who bring them news and opinion with no self-interest. From James Franklin the printer to Edward R. Murrow the broadcaster, men and woman have so tried.

Notes

CHAPTER 1: THE HERITAGE OF THE AMERICAN PRESS

1. Elizabeth Eisenstein, *The Printing Press as an Agent of Change* (Cambridge, England: Cambridge University Press, 1980), product of a 15-year exploration of early European printing history.

2. Robert W. Desmond, *The Information Process: World News Reporting to the Twentieth Century* (Iowa City: University of Iowa Press, 1978), vol. 1, p. 14. This first volume of a four-volume series offers a most detailed explanation of ancient communication methods that led to the development of printing. Important also is Mitchell Stephens, *History of News from the Drum to the Satellite* (New York: Viking, 1988). A brief account appears in John Hohenberg's *Free Press/Free People: The Best Cause* (New York: Columbia University Press, 1971). As could be expected, there are some discrepancies in these and other accounts of the "firsts" in printing and newspaper history. See also Karlen Mooradian, "The Dawn of Printing," *Journalism Monographs,* XXIII (May 1972).

3. Paul Lunde, "A History of the World," *Aramco World Magazine,* XXXII (January–February 1981), 3. This article is accompanied by full-page photographs of the manuscript.

4. There is no agreement on when the first press was introduced in America, but the 1536 date is accepted by most modern Mexican scholars. See Victoria Goff's paper "*Hojas Volantes:* The Beginning of Print Journalism in the Americas," American Journalism Historians Association (AJHA) convention, 1990. The heyday of the *hojas* was the seventeenth century. An extensive collection is housed in the Benson Latin American Collection at the University of Texas at Austin. Also see Goff's "Print Journalism in Mexico: From Printing Press to Revolutionary Press," AJHA convention, 1994. For a comprehensive treatment of Spanish contributions to journalism in America, see the "Spanish Language Media Issue" of *Journalism History,* IV (Summer 1977), edited by Félix Gutiérrez; and *Journalism History,* VI (Autumn 1979), including "Newspapers and Newspaper Prototypes in Spanish America, 1541–1750," by Al Hester, and "The 1541 Earthquake: Dawn of Latin American Journalism," by Félix Gutiérrez and Ernesto Ballesteros. The cover of the eight-page pamphlet is reproduced and a full translation of the 1541 news report is included. The Spanish contribution was discussed by Isaiah Thomas in the opening pages of his 1810 *History of Printing in America,* but that section was excised from the 1874 edition. In his *American Journalism,* Frank Luther Mott made footnote reference (p. 6, 1941 edition) to the 1541 news sheet and to *relaciones* in the Spanish colonies, but he also said that "no regularly published newspaper on the continent antedated the earliest Boston papers." There is some question whether the first news account was printed in 1541 or 1542, but the majority of Latino historians favor the 1541 date. So does Desmond, *The Information Process,* p. 37.

5. See Félix Gutiérrez's tracing of the roots of news recording and book publishing in *Journalism History,* IV (Autumn 1979), 79, and Al Hester's description of the *relaciones,* including the 1594 Lima publication, ibid., 76.

6. Hester, "Newspapers and Newspaper Prototypes," p. 77. For example, the printing firm founded by Bernardo Calderon in Mexico City in 1631 lasted for 132 years. His widow, Paula de Benavides, assumed control upon his death in 1641 and published *hojas* until 1684. But in their publications she and other women printers were listed as a*viuda* (widow) of the particular printer. See Victoria Goff, *"Hojas Volantes."*

7. Desmond, *The Information Process,* p. 32.

8. No evidence exists that any of these copies were preserved, so there is some doubt about these news accounts. Hohenberg, *Free Press/Free People,* p. 13, claims that the first news sheet was printed in Augsburg in 1505.

9. Folke Dahl, ed. *The Birth of the European Press* (Stockholm: The Royal Library, 1960), summarizes much of this research. Dahl found local news emphasized in a Viennese paper of 1629—an unusual development. The oldest known Swedish paper was printed at Strängnäs in 1624.

10. Desmond, *The Information Process,* p. 33, offers no date for this newspaper. Mott, *American Journalism,* p. 116 (1941 edition), says that the *Leipzig Zeitung* (under an earlier title) was a daily for several years beginning in 1660, but that the first successful German daily was the Augsburg *Ordinari-Zeitung,* begun in 1718.

11. Relatively speaking, that is. The wars continued after his death in 1483, when his heir was pushed aside by Richard of Gloucester. Gloucester was ultimately defeated by young Henry Tudor at Bosworth Field. There was a period under Edward IV when England was peaceful, however, and it is to this time that the text refers.

12. It has not been absolutely established where Caxton set up his press, but the consensus is that it was in the abbey. In 1660, Richard Atkyns, a Stuart supporter, tried to prove that the first press was established by royal grant in 1468. Atkyns

was trying to show precedent for royal control of printing. Caxton apparently began printing on his own initiative and without sanction. Most authorities on the subject now agree that there is no validity to the Atkyns claims. See Fredrick Seaton Siebert, *Freedom of the Press in England, 1476–1776* (Urbana: University of Illinois Press, 1952), pp. 22–24.

13. Ibid., Chapter 1, describes the situation admirably.

14. Ibid., Chapter 3, contains a detailed discussion of the Stationers Company. Siebert has found that some of these dates have been incorrectly reported.

15. Carter's was the only execution of this type under the Tudors, however.

16. As Siebert points out, the first real English reporters were the "intelligencers" John Chamberlain, John Pory, William Locke, and the Reverends Larkin and Mead.

17. These six *corantos,* bearing only the initials "N.B." as publisher, have perplexed English historians. They were probably issued by Nicholas Bourne (discussed next), but they could have been a continuation of Nathaniel Butter's summer series. The account here of the first London *corantos* is based upon Siebert, who found evidence in records and correspondence going beyond that offered by the surviving *corantos.* See also Matthias A. Shaaber, *Some Forerunners of the Newspaper in England, 1476–1622* (Philadelphia: University of Pennsylvania Press, 1929), pp. 314–18. The accounts of Desmond, *The Information Process,* p. 33, and Hohenberg, *Free Press/Free People,* p. 21, offer different names for the first titled *coranto,* but the Siebert account was based on an observation of the preserved copies.

18. Milton's ideas and even some of his phrases had already been expressed by Peter Wentworth, who made a speech in Parliament in 1571 on freedom of discussion. Milton's Parliament speech, later published as *Areopagitica,* rose out of his difficulties with the Stationers Company after Milton published a series of licensed and unlicensed pamphlets on divorce.

19. Quoted from Rufus Wilmot Griswold, ed., *The Prose Works of John Milton,* vol. 1 (Philadelphia: J. W. Moore, 1856), p. 189. Milton's glory is dimmed somewhat by the fact that he himself was serving as licenser and censor only seven years later.

20. The Separatists, one of many dissenting sects, were strong believers in the separation of church and state. The Lilburne thesis was that the English had a birthright in speaking out fearlessly on all measures and that restrictions were a usurpation of power.

21. Siebert, *Freedom of the Press in England,* p. 262, from T. B. Macaulay, *History of England* (London: J. M. Dent and Sons, Ltd., 1906), vol. 3, p. 328.

22. An excellent description of the paper is given by Marvin Rosenberg, "The Rise of England's First Daily Newspaper," *Journalism Quarterly,* XXX (Winter 1953), 3–14.

23. Ibid., p. 4.

24. The first series appeared in the *Independent Whig* between January 20, 1720, and January 4, 1721. Much of the text in the 53 essays was concerned with religious liberty. After the financial crash known as the "South Sea Bubble,"

the authors wrote 144 more letters on the responsibilities of government in protecting citizens. These appeared in the *London Journal* and the succeeding *British Journal* between November 12, 1720, and December 7, 1723.

25. Siebert, *Freedom of the Press in England,* p. 10. For a scholarly proof of Siebert's proposition ("The area of freedom contracts and the enforcement of restraints increases as the stresses on the stability of the government and of the structure of society increase"), see Donald L. Shaw and Stephen W. Brauer, "Press Freedom and War Constraints: Case Testing Siebert's Proposition II," *Journalism Quarterly,* XLVI (Summer 1969), 243, an analysis of the threats against a North Carolina Civil War editor.

CHAPTER 2: THE COLONIAL YEARS

1. John M. Murrin, "Beneficiaries of Catastrophe: The English Colonies in America," in Eric Foner, ed. *The New American History,* rev. and exp. ed. (Philadelphia: Temple University Press, 1997), p. 3.

2. Murrin, ibid., pp. 7, 5, 8; also see James H. Merrell, *The Indians' New World: Catawbas and Their Neighbors from European Contact through the Era of Removal* (Chapel Hill: University of North Carolina Press, 1989); Daniel H. Usner, Jr., *Indians, Settlers, and Slaves in a Frontier Exchange Economy: The Lower Mississippi Valley before 1783* (Chapel Hill: University of North Carolina Press, 1992); Richard White, *The Middle Ground: Indians, Empires and Republics in the Great Lakes Region, 1650–1815* (Cambridge and New York: Cambridge University Press, 1991).

3. Stephen Daye, a London printer, was brought to operate the press. He began printing in January 1639, issuing the *Freeman's Oath* and "an almanack," according to printing historian Isaiah Thomas. His first book, 300 pages of Psalms printed in 1640, was titled *The Psalms in Metre, Faithfully Translated for the Use, Edification, and Comfort of the Saints in Public and Private, Especially in New England.* Later editions added hymns and spiritual songs. Thomas, *The History of Printing in America* (New York: Weathervane Books, 1970), pp. 50–54.

4. Sara Evans, *Born for Liberty,* 2nd ed. (New York: Free Press, 1997), p. 28.

5. Mary Beth Norton, "The Evolution of White Women's Experience in Early America," *American Historical Review,* 89:3 (June 1984), pp. 593–619.

6. For a fuller picture of colonial New England life, consult Jack P. Green, *Pursuits of Happiness: The Social Development of Early Modern British Colonies and the Formation of American Culture* (Chapel Hill: University of North Carolina Press, 1988) and Bernard Bailyn, *The Peopling of British North America: An Introduction* (New York: Knopf, 1986).

7. True, the farm colonist might have settled in other areas, but New England had its share, along with its middle-class émigrés.

8. James M. McPherson, *Ordeal By Fire, Volume I: The Coming of War,* 2nd ed. (New York: McGraw-Hill, 1993), p. 17.

9. A good source on the development of slavery in the colonial period is Ira Berlin, "Time, Space, and the Evolution of Afro-American Society in British Mainland North America," *American Historical Review,* 85 (1980), pp. 44–78.

10. Professor Robert L. Baker of Pennsylvania State University made this evaluation of Smith's contribution in a paper, "The Genesis of Journalism in America: Captain John Smith and the 1608 Publication of *Newes from Virginia,*" presented at the 1987 Midwest Journalism History Conference, Urbana, Illinois.

11. He was never tried. Indeed, he was soon returned to favor and came back to America as governor of Virginia.

12. Even on this count it would fail to qualify technically as a newspaper because Harris intended to issue the paper only once a month, unless an "unusual glut of occurrences" made greater frequency of publication practicable.

13. From a facsimile filed in the London Public Office 1845), as reprinted in Willard G. Bleyer, *Main Currents in the History of American Journalism* (Boston: Houghton Mifflin, 1927) p. 45.

14. From a facsimile in the Library of the State Historical Society of Wisconsin.

15. David Paul Nord, "Teleology and News: The Religious Roots of American Journalism, 1630–1730," *The Journal of American History,* LXXVII (June 1990), 9.

16. The Mathers were insufferable in the sense that their righteousness made them too sure of themselves, but this does not detract from their important place in colonial history. Increase was licenser of the press after 1674, in addition to being the leading minister of the dominant Puritans. He was president of Harvard and was a respected agent of Massachusetts in London. Cotton opposed the arrogant Sir Edward Andros, ousted from New England after the Revolution of 1688. The Mathers were prolific writers of considerable merit. They were also outstanding historians. In later life they became more tolerant.

17. Professor C. Edward Wilson of the University of Western Ontario offered some differing interpretations of this episode in "The Boston Inoculation Controversy: A Revisionist Interpretation," *Journalism History,* VII (Spring 1980), 16. It was not until 1796 that Dr. Edward Jenner developed the safer smallpox vaccination using the milder cowpox virus.

18. As quoted in Frank Luther Mott, *American Journalism* (New York: Macmillan, 1950), p. 20. Colonial writing style called for use of many hyphens, such as in "New-England," which are not used here.

19. James's widow, two daughters, and a son carried on the printing business in Newport. In 1758, James, Jr., with the help of his rich uncle Benjamin, established the *Newport Mercury,* which survived until 1934. Its name was then retained in a small weekly edition of the *Newport News.*

20. As quoted in Carl Van Doren, *Benjamin Franklin* (New York: Viking, 1938), p. 100.

21. The three colonies with earlier newspapers were Massachusetts, Pennsylvania, and New York. Other firsts in their respective colonies were the *Rhode Island Gazette* and *South Carolina Gazette,* 1732; *North Carolina Gazette,* 1751; *Connecticut Gazette,* 1755; *New Hampshire Gazette,* 1756; *Georgia Gazette,* 1763; *New Jersey Gazette,* 1777; *Vermont*

Gazette, 1780; and *Delaware Gazette,* 1785. James Parker, one of Ben Franklin's protégés, founded the Connecticut paper. Another of Franklin's "boys" established the South Carolina paper, although there is some doubt as to which one of two has the more valid claim.

22. There were two great Bradford printing families. William Bradford was founder of the Pennsylvania line and was a pioneer printer in Philadelphia and New York. His son, Andrew, established the first newspaper in Philadelphia. William Bradford III was the famous soldier-editor of the Revolution and publisher of the *Pennsylvania Journal* in Philadelphia. His son, Thomas, succeeded him as editor. John Bradford, no relative of the Pennsylvania clan, was a surveyor who founded the first paper in Kentucky, at Lexington. His brother Fielding was also active in journalism. James, another member of this branch, founded the first newspaper in Louisiana and may have been the first American war correspondent, according to Mott, *American Journalism,* p. 196. The Greens were prominent in New England. Bartholomew and Samuel were pioneers in the Boston-Cambridge area, the former as printer of the first successful newspaper in America. From Samuel Green of Cambridge descended a long line of printer-journalists. Timothy, Jr., founded the New London, Connecticut, *Summary* in 1758. His son Timothy III changed the name to the *Gazette* after Timothy, Jr.'s death. Samuel and Thomas founded the first paper in New Haven in 1767. Thomas, the brother of Timothy III, founded the *Connecticut* (now *Hartford*) *Courant* in 1764. Timothy IV was cofounder of the first Vermont paper. The fourth printing family were the Sowers, Germans who settled near Philadelphia. First in the printing dynasty was Christopher, who, with the encouragement of Benjamin Franklin, established one of the earliest foreign-language newspapers, the Germantown *Zeitung.* A mechanical genius, Christopher constructed his own press and made his own ink and paper. His sons carried on the business, but Christopher III was a Tory during the Revolution, and his journalistic career was ruined by the American victory. The Franklin influence in Massachusetts, Rhode Island, and Pennsylvania has been described.

23. Clarence S. Brigham, *History and Bibliography of American Newspapers, 1690–1820* (Worcester, MA: American Antiquarian Society, 1947), p. xii.

24. These aspects of development are admirably presented in Sidney Kobre, "The Revolutionary Colonial Press—A Social Interpretation," *Journalism Quarterly,* XX (September 1943), 193–97.

25. Frank Presbrey, *The History and Development of Advertising* (Garden City, NY: Doubleday, 1929), p. 56.

26. Ibid., p. 70.

27. Warren C. Price, "Reflections on the Trial of John Peter Zenger," *Journalism Quarterly,* XXXII (Spring 1955), 161, provides many new data on the Zenger case and points to the land-grabbing episode as one reason why public opinion swung to the Zenger-Morris side so heavily. Cosby Manor at Utica, 20 miles by 10 miles in extent, was an example of the governor's greed.

28. See also Isaiah Thomas, *The History of Printing in America,* edited by Marcus A. McCorison from Thomas' second edition (New York: Weathervane Books, 1970), pp. 487–491; *Howell's State Trials* (1783).

29. Jeffery A. Smith, *Printers and Press Freedom: The Ideology of Early American Journalism* (New York: Oxford University Press, 1988).

30. The others are: (1) the right to publish without official license, established in America by James Franklin; and (2) the right to report matters of public interest, which was not widely recognized until well into the nineteenth century and is still contested.

31. Harold L. Nelson, "Seditious Libel in Colonial America," *American Journal of Legal History,* III (April 1959), pp. 160–72. See also Jeffery A. Smith, "A Reappraisal of Legislative Privilege and American Colonial Journalism," *Journalism Quarterly,* LXI (Spring 1984), 97.

CHAPTER 3: THE PRESS AND THE REVOLUTION

1. Bernard Bailyn, *The Ideological Origins of the American Revolution* (Cambridge, MA: Harvard University Press, 1967), updated in *Faces of Revolution* (New York: Alfred A. Knopf, 1990).

2. Linda Kerber, "The Revolutionary Generation: Ideology, Politics, and Culture in the Early Republic," in Eric Foner, ed. *The New American History,* rev. and exp. ed. (Philadelphia: Temple University Press, 1997), p. 35. Also see Joyce Appleby, "Republicanism in Old and New Contexts," *William and Mary Quarterly,* 43 (1986).

3. Jesse Lemisch, "The American Revolution Seen from the Bottom Up," in Barton Bernstein, ed. *Towards a New Past: Dissenting Essays in American History* (New York: Pantheon, 1968), pp. 3–45; Kerber, "The Revolutionary Generation," pp. 31–59; Edward Countryman, *Americans, A Collision of Histories* (New York: Hill and Wang, 1996); Don Higginbotham, *War and Society in Revolutionary America: The Wider Dimensions of Conflict* (Columbia: University of South Carolina Press, 1988).

4. "Resolutions of the House of Representatives of Massachusetts, October 29, 1765," in Harry R. Warfel, Ralph H. Gabriel, and Stanley Williams, eds. *The American Mind* (New York: American Book, 1937), p. 138.

5. Curtis P. Nettels, "The Money Supply of the American Colonies before 1720," *University of Wisconsin Studies,* No. 20 (1934), pp. 279–83.

6. See Arthur M. Schlesinger, *Prelude to Independence: The Newspaper War on Britain, 1764–1776* (New York: Knopf, 1958), for the story of the use of the press by the Radical propagandists.

7. Kerber, "Revolutionary Generation," p. 36.

8. William V. Wells, *The Life and Public Services of Samuel Adams,* vol. 1 (Boston: Little, Brown, 1865), p. 48.

9. Philip Davidson, *Propaganda and the American Revolution 1763–1783* (Chapel Hill: University of North Carolina Press, 1941), quoted from the Norton Library edition (New York, 1973), p. 237.

10. Rider Paul Revere was an influential member of the Patriot group and made engravings for their publications. A major mission of the riders was to warn Samuel Adams and John Hancock that General Gage had ordered their arrests.

11. *Massachusetts Spy*, May 3, 1775. This appeared on the inside (page 3) of the paper under a Worcester dateline. After moving to Worcester, Thomas described his paper in a page-one skyline as "THE MASSACHUSETTS SPY, or American ORACLE of Liberty."

12. Paine is usually identified as a writer or political philosopher. In this book the journalist is defined as one who acts as the transmission belt carrying ideas, information, and inspiration to the general public, which is dependent on such resources for rational opinion. This was Paine's prime function during the American Revolution. His work for Aitken on the *Pennsylvania Magazine,* often ignored in sketches about him, also qualifies him for consideration as a journalist, in the broad sense.

13. *Pennsylvania Evening Post,* July 2, 1776.

14. Dunlap was also the first to print the Constitution and Washington's Farewell Address. Journalism historian Frederic Farrar examined many of these early newspapers and displayed them around the United States.

15. Frank Luther Mott, *American Journalism*, rev. ed. (New York: Macmillan, 1962), p. 100.

16. From *America Goes to Press,* by Laurence Greene, copyright 1936, used by special permission of the publishers, Bobbs-Merrill.

17. Robert E. Dreschel, *Newsmaking in the Trial Courts* (New York: Longman, 1982), pp. 35 ff.

18. Al Hester, Susan Parker Hume, and Christopher Bickers, "Foreign News in Colonial North American Newspapers, 1764–1775," *Journalism Quarterly,* LVII (Spring 1980), 18. Newspapers sampled were the *Boston Gazette, Maryland Gazette,* and *Pennsylvania Gazette.*

19. Marion Marzolf, "The Woman Journalist: Colonial Printer to City Desk," *Journalism History,* I (Winter 1974), 100. See also bibliographies for Chapter 2 and this chapter.

20. Letter from Sarah Goddard to William Goddard, early 1768, quoted by Susan Henry in "Sarah Goddard, Gentlewoman Printer," *Journalism Quarterly,* LVII (Spring 1980), 28.

21. Ibid.

22. The other early women printers were: Anna Catherine Zenger (widow of John Peter), *New York Journal,* 1746–48; Cornelia Bradford (widow of Andrew), *American Weekly Mercury,* Philadelphia, 1742–52; Anne Green, *Maryland Gazette,* 1767–75; Clementina Rind, *Virginia Gazette,* 1773–74; Mary Crouch, *Charleston Gazette,* 1778–80, and *Salem Gazette,* 1781; Elizabeth Boden, *South Carolina Weekly Advertiser,* 1783; Ann Timothy (widow of Peter), *Gazette of the State of South-Carolina,* 1782–92; and Elizabeth Holt (widow of John), *New York Journal,* 1784–85.

CHAPTER 4: FOUNDING THE NEW NATION

1. Useful sources on this period include Forrest McDonald, *E Pluribus Unum: The Formation of the American Republic, 1776–1790* (Boston: Houghton Mifflin, 1965) and Gordon Wood, *The Creation of the American Republic, 1776–1790* (Chapel Hill: University of North Carolina Press, 1969). Also consult Richard Beeman, Stephen Botein,

and Edward C. Carter II, eds., *Beyond Confederation: Origins of the Constitution and American National Identity* (Chapel Hill: University of North Carolina Press, 1987); Patrick T. Conley and John P. Kaminski, eds., *The Bill of Rights and the States: The Colonial and Revolutionary Origins of American Liberties* (Madison, WI: Madison House, 1992); Jack N. Rakove, *Original Meanings: Politics and Ideas in the Making of the Constitution* (New York: A. A. Knopf, 1990); and Staughton Lynd, *Class, Conflict, Slavery, and the United States Constitution* (Indianapolis: Bobbs-Merrill, 1967).

2. Linda Kerber, "The Revolutionary Generation," p. 51.

3. Henry Steele Commager, ed., *Documents of American History* (New York: Appleton-Century-Crofts, 1934), p. 104, Article XII, and p. 109, Article XVI.

4. Historians differ on the ultimate influence wielded by *The Federalist* articles, but in any case they were a brilliant analysis of the failures of the Articles of Confederation and of the complex nature of federalism.

5. Claude G. Bowers, *Jefferson and Hamilton* (Boston: Houghton Mifflin, 1925), p. 31.

6. Ibid., p. 26. Bowers, it should be pointed out, is a respecter, but no admirer, of Hamilton.

7. As quoted in Wilfred E. Binkley, *American Political Parties: Their Natural History* (New York: Knopf, 1943), p. 32.

8. Quoted from Vernon L. Parrington, *Main Currents in American Thought,* vol. 1 (New York: Harcourt Brace Jovanovich, 1927), p. 321.

9. *National Gazette,* December 19, 1791.

10. Ibid., February 9, 1792.

11. *Porcupine's Gazette*, November 16, 1797.

12. See, for example, B. E. Martin, "Transition Period of the American Press," *Magazine of American History,* XVII (April 1887), 273–94.

13. It is remarkable that all during these critical years all roads to safety eventually led right back to Washington. He was not a political genius, but he appeared to know instinctively the policies that would offer the greatest security to the nation he had saved in war.

14. *U.S. Statutes at Large,* "The Sedition Act," I, Sec. 2, p. 596.

15. Larry D. Eldridge's *A Distant Heritage: The Growth of Free Speech in Early America* (New York: New York University Press, 1994) is a useful account of the evolution of ideas about free speech.

16. The key votes in the House of Representatives on the Sedition Act were almost entirely on party lines. There were 47 Federalists, 39 Anti-Federalists. The bill passed, 44–41, with 43 Federalist votes. Six Federalists joined in the modifications involving truth as a defense. The jury provision, however, was backed by all 39 Anti-Federalists and 28 Federalists. See John D. Stevens, "Constitutional History of the 1798 Sedition Law," *Journalism Quarterly,* XLIII (Summer 1966), 247.

17. James M. Smith, *Freedom's Fetters: The Alien and Sedition Laws and American Civil Liberties* (Ithaca, NY: Cornell University Press, 1956), verifies 14 indictments under the Sedition Act. Other totals are from Frank Luther Mott, *American Journalism* (New York: Macmillan, 1950), p. 149.

18. Stevens, "Constitutional History," p. 254.

19. David Sloan, "The Early Party Press," *Journalism History,* IX, no. 1 (Spring 1982), 19.

20. Arthur M. Schlesinger, Jr., *The Age of Jackson* (Boston: Little, Brown and Company, 1946), p. 282.

21. Thomas Adams was the first important editor to be indicted under the Sedition Act. Before he could be tried, he was indicted under the common law for criticizing the Massachusetts legislature. He was too sick to stand trial, but his brother, Abijah, was convicted and jailed for a month, although he too was ailing. The defiant Thomas, faced with both federal and state sedition trials, sold the *Chronicle* in May 1799, two weeks before he died.

CHAPTER 5: WESTWARD EXPANSION

1. Coleman was a great admirer of Burr and remained loyal to him even after Burr killed Hamilton in a duel in 1804. By that time the editor of the *Post* was expressing himself independently.

2. In 1804 President Jefferson helped Thomas Ritchie found the *Richmond Enquirer*, soon the most influential paper in Virginia. Ritchie was political boss of his state; his views were therefore of significance throughout the South, where they were widely reprinted.

3. From the *Letters,* quoted from Saul K. Padover, *Thomas Jefferson on Democracy* (New York: Penguin, 1939), pp. 92–93. Copyright 1939, D. Appleton-Century Company, Inc.

4. To Volney, 1802. New York Public Library, Manuscript II, 199, in ibid., p. 95.

5. Most of the newspaper figures and comments in this section are based on Clarence S. Brigham, *History and Bibliography of American Newspapers, 1690–1820,* 2 volumes (Worcester, MA: American Antiquarian Society, 1947).

6. Regulations such as this and the law requiring publication at state cost of lists of letters uncalled for at the post office were also a means of rewarding proadministration editors. As administrations changed, political rivals found ready-made organs of expression.

7. Sharon M. Murphy and James E. Murphy, *Let My People Know: American Indian Journalism* (Norman: University of Oklahoma Press, 1981), pp. 20–31.

8. The Turner theory, first suggested by the Wisconsin historian in 1893 and elaborated by him and an entire school of historians, is explained in Turner, *The Significance of Sections in American History* (New York: Holt, Rinehart & Winston, 1933); in Walter Prescott Webb, *The Great Plains* (Boston: Ginn, 1931); and with a modified updating in Ray A. Billington, *America's Frontier Heritage* (New York: Holt, Rinehart & Winston, 1967). It is opposed by Henry Nash Smith in *The Virgin Land* (Cambridge, MA: Harvard University Press, 1950); by Fred A. Shannon in "Critiques of Research in the Social Sciences," *Social Science Research*

Council Bulletin, no. 46 (New York: The Council, 1940); and by Louis M. Hacker in "Sections or Classes," *Nation,* CXXXVII (July 26, 1933), 108. For a well-balanced discussion of Turner's influence on American historiography, see Richard White, "Western History," in Eric Foner, ed. *The New American History,* rev. and exp. ed. (Philadelphia: Temple University Press, 1997), pp. 203–30.

9. See Richard White, "Western History," ibid. as well as Patricia Nelson Limerick, *The Legacy of Conquest: The Unbroken Past of the American West* (New York: Norton, 1987); Richard White, *"It's Your Misfortune and None of My Own": A New History of the American West* (Norman: University of Oklahoma Press, 1991); and William Cronon, *Nature's Metropolis: Chicago and the Great West* (New York: Norton, 1991), an ecological history.

10. This was a useless victory, because the armies to be supplied by the Great Lakes route, such as Hull's command, were ineffective by the time Commodore Perry had cleared the enemy from the lake.

11. The treaty was signed December 24, 1814. Jackson won his remarkable victory on January 8, 1815. News of the battle reached Washington on January 28; news of the treaty reached New York by ship on February 11. As a result, many Americans believed that Jackson's victory had much to do with the successful negotiations.

12. Roger H. Brown, *The Republic in Peril: 1812* (New York: Columbia University Press, 1964).

13. Helpful sources are: Burton Spivak, *Jefferson's English Crisis: Commerce, Embargo, and the Republican Revolution* (Charlottesville: University Press of Virginia, 1979), the best work on the embargo and how it affected American party politics; J. C. A. Stagg, *Mr. Madison's War: Politics, Diplomacy and Warfare in the Early American Republic, 1783–1830* (Princeton, NJ: Princeton University Press, 1983), which analyzes the War of 1812; and Reginald Horsman, *The Diplomacy of the Early Republic, 1776–1985* (Arlington Heights, IL: Harlan Davidson, 1985), which discusses America's foreign policy goals in this period.

14. See Elizabeth Gregory McPherson, "Reporting the Debates of Congress," *Quarterly Journal of Speech,* XXVIII (April 1942), 141–48.

15. William E. Ames, "Federal Patronage and the Washington, D.C., Press," *Journalism Quarterly,* XLIX (Spring 1972), 22.

16. This is just one of many colorful phrases of Major Benjamin Russell of the *Columbian Centinel* in Boston, which were widely quoted. Another had its birth in 1812, when a man named Gerry was governor. The Republican legislature of Massachusetts had divided a political district into a weird shape in order to gain voting power. According to one account, Gilbert Stuart called Russell's attention to the new district's resemblance to a salamander. "Better say a Gerrymander!" replied the Federalist editor, although in truth the governor had had no part in the original "gerrymandering."

17. Merle Curti, *The Growth of American Thought* (New York: Harper & Row, 1943), p. 215.

18. See Godfrey T. Vique, "Six Months in America"; Thomas Hamilton, "Men and Manners in America"; Harriet Martineau, "Society in America"; reprinted in Allan Nevins, ed., *American Social History* (New York: Holt, Rinehart & Winston, 1923).

19. Translation by Arpad Kadarkay, *Los Angeles Times,* May 31, 1976, Part 2, p. 7. The original was not published in English.

20. Sean Wilentz, "Society, Politics, and the Market Revolution, 1815–1868," in Eric Foner, ed. *The New American History,* rev. and exp. ed. (Philadelphia: Temple University Press, 1997), p. 61.

21. Richard Hofstadter, *The American Political Tradition* (New York: Vintage Books, 1948), p. 55.

22. Arthur M. Schlesinger, Jr., *The Age of Jackson* (Boston: Little, Brown, 1945), p. 306.

23. All quotes in this paragraph from ibid., p. 14.

24. See, for example, Charles Sellers, *The Market Revolution: Jacksonian America, 1815–1846* (New York: Oxford University Press, 1991), a comprehensive look at the rise of market capitalism.

25. Anthony Wallace, *The Long, Bitter Trail: Andrew Jackson and the Indians* (New York: Hill and Wang, 1993); Sean Wilentz, "Society Politics, and the Market Revolution, 1815–1868," pp. 61–84.

26. *New York Evening Post,* June 13, 1836.

27. The *electric* telegraph had not been invented at that time. The name probably derived from the semaphore signal.

28. Schlesinger, *The Age of Jackson,* p. 73.

CHAPTER 6: A PRESS FOR THE MASSES

1. The paper had strong religious undertones, but it was aggressive in its news policies and business coverage. We refer to it again in a later discussion on the development of cooperative news gathering.

2. By 1837 the *Sun* was printing 30,000 copies a day, which was more than the total of all New York daily newspapers combined when it had first appeared.

3. *New York Sun,* January 3, 1835.

4. Michael Schudson, *Discovering the News* (New York: Basic Books, 1978), pp. 12–60.

5. It would be ridiculous to maintain that the penny press avoided partisanship. Papers like the *Herald* took up issues every day, and often fought for them as violently as in the old partisan-press days. But that was not the purpose of these papers, as it had been when papers reflected factions and parties. The newspaper was a little more impersonal than the viewspaper but the development of objectivity had barely started, and the goal had not been reached more than 150 years later. All such progress must be measured relatively.

6. *New York Herald,* June 4, 1836 (*Morning* was dropped from the name plate in 1835).

7. John R. Commons, "Horace Greeley and the Working Class Origins of the Republican Party," *Political Science Quarterly,* XXIV (September 1909), 472.

8. Harrison's running mate, John Tyler of Virginia, proved as president to be more Southern than Whig and vetoed Clay's pet bills. In the 1844 presidential year the Whigs ditched Tyler for Clay, but Democrat James K. Polk won.

9. H. L. Stoddard, *Horace Greeley* (New York: G. P. Putnam's Sons, 1946), p. 322.

10. Willard G. Bleyer, *Main Currents in the History of American Journalism* (Boston: Houghton Mifflin, 1927), p. 240.

11. Gerald W. Johnson, et al., *The Sunpapers of Baltimore* (New York: Knopf, 1937), p. 50.

12. Ibid., p. 51.

13. The North Carolina–based study, directed by Donald Lewis Shaw with the assistance of Mary E. Junck and David Pace, was reported by Professor Shaw in an unpublished paper presented at the 1981 Association for Education in Journalism (AEJ) convention, and was condensed in "At the Crossroads: Change and Continuity in American Press News, 1820–1860," *Journalism History,* VIII (Summer 1981), 38. The extensive sampling study covered sources of news items, topics of stories, locations of news events, and time lag in publishing. Papers presented to the AEJ in 1976 by David H. Weaver, "U.S. Newspaper Content from 1820 to 1860: A Mirror of the Times?" and by Gerald J. Baldasty, "The South Carolina Press and National News, 1807–47," reflect similar interest. In a random sample study of North Carolina–collected data, Weaver found that papers in all sections of the country emphasized general community, general political, and intellectual and cultural news; paid attention to economic news and science and technology, but little to education; and gave little emphasis to the conflict issues of slavery, abolition, expansionism, and sectional differences, except in the Lower South. The sample, of course, could not measure news play at exact moments of major sectional conflict events. Baldasty found that the South Carolina press depended heavily on the Washington press, particularly the *National Intelligencer,* through the 1830s, then reflected more diversity as technological change occurred. Baldasty's paper was later published (see the Bibliography for this chapter).

14. Richard B. Kielbowicz, *News in the Mail: The Press, Post Office, and Public Information, 1700–1860s* (Westport, CT: Greenwood Press, 1989), is the authoritative study.

15. Frederick B. Marbut, *News from the Capital: The Story of Washington Reporting* (Carbondale: Southern Illinois University Press, 1971), pp. 29–37.

16. Maurine Beasley, *The First Women Washington Correspondents* (Washington, DC: GW Washington Studies, no. 4, 1976), pp. 3–9.

17. The *Courier and Enquirer* had found the cost of maintaining a pony route too great. But the *Journal of Commerce* continued its private express and even extended it to Washington to gain a day over rival New York papers depending on the government's Philadelphia–New York express. Other papers were showing similar news enterprise, particularly those in Boston, the *Providence Journal,* and the *Charleston Courier.*

18. Richard A. Schwarzlose, "The Nation's First Wire Service: Evidence Supporting a Footnote," *Journalism Quarterly,* LVII (Winter 1980), 555.

19. Frederic Hudson, *Journalism in the United States* (New York: Harper & Row, 1873), pp. 366–67. Oliver Gramling in *AP: The Story of News* (New York: Farrar, Straus & Giroux, 1940), presents a dramatic account of the beginnings of the Associated Press, but the historical basis for the details he relates had never been established.

20. Richard A. Schwarzlose, "Early Telegraphic News Dispatches: Forerunner of the AP," *Journalism Quarterly,* LI (Winter 1974), 595. The *Courier and Enquirer,* also studied, ran the identical story on July 7.

21. Richard A. Schwarzlose, *The Nation's Newsbrokers,* 2 vols. (Evanston, IL: Northwestern University Press, 1989–90), vol. 1, pp. 96–105.

22. Victor Rosewater, *History of Cooperative News-Gathering in the United States* (New York: Appleton-Century-Crofts, 1930), pp. 64–66.

23. Richard A. Schwarzlose, "Harbor News Association: The Formal Origin of the AP," *Journalism Quarterly,* XLV (Summer 1968), 253.

24. Reprinted in Rosewater, *History of Cooperative News-Gathering,* pp. 381–88.

25. Schwarzlose, *The Nation's Newsbrokers,* vol. 1, p. 106, and vol. 2, pp. 35–37.

26. *Baltimore Sun,* April 12, 1847.

27. *New York Herald,* May 15, 1846.

28. *New York Tribune,* May 12, 1846.

29. *New York Herald,* May 12, 1846.

30. *New York Herald,* February 26, 1846.

31. The best known of these New Orleans papers were the *Picayune, Delta, Crescent, Tropic, Commercial Times,* and *Bee.*

32. Tom Reilly, "A Spanish-Language Voice of Dissent in Antebellum New Orleans," *Louisiana History,* XXIII (Fall 1982), 327. The paper, founded in 1845, appeared under three names before it was destroyed by a mob on August 21, 1851, after criticizing the Cuban filibustering expedition. As *La Patria,* it was a daily from the fall of 1847 to early 1848. Invading U.S. troops founded the first English-language newspaper in Mexico in 1846, *The American Star,* a semi-weekly that lasted until troops withdrew in July 1848 after the signing of the Treaty of Guadelupe Hidalgo. See Victoria Goff's unpublished paper, "Mexico's Press during the Early National Period (1821–1867)."

33. The other seven were Francis A. Lumsden, Daniel Scully, Charles Callahan, and John E. Durivage of the *Picayune;* George Tobin, the *Delta;* William C. Tobey ("John of York"), *Philadelphia North American;* and John Warland, *Boston Atlas.*

34. *New York Sun,* January 20 and April 15, 19, 1847. For a detailed study see Thomas W. Reilly, "American Reporters and the Mexican War, 1846–1848" (Ph.D. thesis, University of Minnesota, 1975).

35. For a full description of these early Spanish-language papers, see the special issue of *Journalism History,* IV (Summer 1977), edited by Félix Gutiérrez.

CHAPTER 7: THE IRREPRESSIBLE CONFLICT

1. Arthur Charles Cole, *The Irrepressible Conflict* (New York: Macmillan, 1934). See also Avery Craven, *The Repressible Conflict* (Baton Rouge: Louisiana State University Press, 1939).

2. See, for example: Eric Foner, "Slavery, the Civil War, and Reconstruction," in Eric Foner, ed. *The New American History,* rev. and expanded ed. (Philadelphia: Temple University Press, 1997), pp. 85–106; James M. McPherson, *Ordeal by Fire: The Civil War and Reconstruction* (New York: Alfred A. Knopf, 1982), p. 1; William J. Cooper, *The South and the Politics of Slavery, 1828–1856* (Baton Rouge: Louisiana State University Press, 1978); Eric Foner, *Free Soil, Free Labor, Free Men: The Ideology of the Republican Party before the Civil War* (New York: Oxford University Press, 1970); William Freehling, *The Road to Disunion, 1776–1854* (New York: Oxford University Press, 1990); David Potter, *The Impending Crisis, 1848–1861* (New York: Harper & Row, 1976).

3. Both quotations are reprinted in Louis L. Snyder and Richard B. Morris, eds., *A Treasury of Great Reporting* (New York: Simon & Schuster, 1949), pp. 124–25.

4. Wendell Phillips Garrison and Francis Jackson Garrison, *William Lloyd Garrison: The Story of His Life Told by His Children,* vol. 1 (New York: Appleton-Century-Crofts, 1885), p. 200.

5. Vernon L. Parrington, *Main Currents in American Thought,* vol. 2 (New York: Harcourt Brace Jovanovich, 1927), p. 356. Parrington's fascinating analysis of the abolitionist leader quotes many such statements by Garrison.

6. Kendall justified his action by holding that each issue of the *Liberator* reaching a southern state was a criminal libel, that is, a threat to public peace. He tried to explain the situation in his annual report for 1835, when he asked Congress for an official banning of "obnoxious" literature in southern states. This would have taken the responsibility out of the hands of the postmaster general and indicates that Kendall knew that his actions had been arbitrary. It is interesting to see the South's great leader, John C. Calhoun, challenge the constitutionality of Kendall's request. Calhoun's alternative was a recommendation for states with appropriate laws to ban such literature at the source.

7. Carter R. Bryan, "Negro Journalism in America before Emancipation," *Journalism Monographs,* no. 12 (September 1969), 1, 30–33.

8. I. Garland Penn, *The Afro-American Press and Its Editors* (Springfield, MA: Wiley, 1891), p. 28. Stewart is one of 11 African American women journalists discussed in Rodger Streitmatter's *Raising Her Voice: African-American Women Journalists Who Changed History* (Lexington: University Press of Kentucky, 1994). Others included Mary Ann Shadd Cary, Ida B. Wells-Barnett, Ethyl Payne, and Charlayne Hunter-Gault.

9. Armistead S. Pride, *A Register and History of Negro Newspapers in the United States* (Ph.D. thesis, Northwestern University, 1950), p. 4.

10. Bryan, "Negro Journalism," pp. 11–14.

11. Ibid., p. 17.

12. Roland E. Wolseley, *The Black Press, U.S.A.* (Ames: Iowa State University Press, 1971), pp. 24–25.

13. As quoted in Bryan, "Negro Journalism," p. 19, from the *Ram's Horn,* November 5, 1847, p. 4.

14. Wolseley, *The Black Press,* pp. 22–23.

15. Tom Reilly, "Early Coverage of a President-Elect: Lincoln at Springfield, 1860," *Journalism Quarterly,* XLIX (Autumn 1972), 469–79. Also see "Lincoln-Douglas Debates of 1858 Forced New Role on the Press," *Journalism Quarterly,* LVI (Winter 1979), 734.

16. For a discussion of the relations between Lincoln and the press, see James E. Pollard, *The Presidents and the Press* (New York: Macmillan, 1947), pp. 312–97.

17. Ibid., p. 360.

18. The *New York Times* climbed from 45,000 to about 75,000 in the same period. The daily *New York Tribune* trailed behind, but the weekly edition, largely responsible for Greeley's national reputation, reached more than 200,000. This was the largest circulation of any single American paper. The *New York Ledger* had almost twice that many subscribers, but it was not a newspaper, rather a weekly story periodical.

19. Lincoln had only 40 percent of the popular vote in 1860, and he won by only 400,000 votes in 1864, when none of the southern Democrats had any voice in the elections. This was a serious consideration for Republican leaders contemplating the postwar political problem.

20. An outstanding study of this problem is Quintus Wilson, "A Study and Evaluation of the Military Censorship in the Civil War" (Master's thesis, University of Minnesota, 1945).

21. Ibid., p. 50.

22. Louis L. Snyder and Richard B. Morris, eds., *A Treasury of Great Reporting* (New York: Simon & Schuster, 1949), p. 130.

23. Ibid., p. 146.

24. Ibid., p. 149.

25. This subject is presented in detail by Quintus C. Wilson, "The Confederate Press Association: A Pioneer News Agency," *Journalism Quarterly,* XXVI (June 1949), 160–66.

26. Ibid., p. 162.

27. J. Cutler Andrews, *The South Reports the Civil War* (Princeton: Princeton University Press, 1970), pp. 26–33.

28. Ibid., p. 50.

29. *Charleston Daily Courier,* September 29, 1862.

30. Andrews, *The South Reports the Civil War,* pp. 316–17.

31. It was not impossible to print spread headlines and large maps on the earlier type-revolving presses, but it was

hazardous and inconvenient, because the column rules had to be locked tight to keep the metal type from flying out as the presses revolved. It was accomplished now and then, however. Big maps were printed by the newspapers in the Mexican War period.

32. As must happen to all news photographers, Brady missed some great picture opportunities. He had his camera trained on President Lincoln at the time the immortal Gettysburg Address was delivered. Edward Everett, famous orator and the main speaker at the memorial, talked so long that Brady had to keep changing his plates, which had to be exposed while still wet with sensitizing solution. He was in the midst of removing a dried-out plate when the president arose to speak. The inspiring message was so short that Brady's assistant could not fetch a fresh plate from the portable dark room in time to photograph Lincoln before he bowed and retired. One of the great "news shots" of American history was thereby lost to posterity.

33. The word "instantaneous" had a much broader meaning then than now. It could mean anything up to several minutes.

34. This period is well described in Robert Taft, *Photography and the American Scene: A Social History, 1839–1889* (New York: Macmillan, 1938).

35. Beaumont Newhall, *The History of Photography,* 4th ed. (New York: Museum of Modern Art, 1978), pp. 67–72.

CHAPTER 8: A REVOLUTION IN NATIONAL LIFE

1. Henry Steele Commager, *The American Mind* (New Haven: Yale University Press, 1950), p. 41.

2. Eric Foner, "Slavery, the Civil War, and Reconstruction," also see Eric Foner, *Reconstruction: America's Unfinished Revolution, 1863–1877* (New York: Harper & Row, 1988), the definitive comprehensive work.

3. James Cobb, *The Most Southern Place on Earth: The Mississippi Delta and the Roots of Regional Identity* (New York: Oxford University Press, 1992) is a well-researched account of how blacks fared during and after Reconstruction.

4. This is a brief summary of the farmers' problems, which are fully analyzed in such studies as John D. Hicks, *The Populist Revolt* (Minneapolis: University of Minnesota Press, 1931), and Solon J. Buck, *The Granger Movement* (Cambridge, MA: Harvard University Press, 1913).

5. Fuller details are given in Gustavus Myers, *The History of Tammany Hall* (New York: Boni and Liveright, 1917).

6. Frank M. O'Brien, *The Story of the Sun* (New York: George H. Doran Company, 1918), p. 231; new edition (New York: Appleton-Century-Crofts, 1928), p. 151.

7. As quoted in Allan Nevins, *American Press Opinion* (New York: Heath, 1928), p. 299.

8. Godkin's full statement of purpose is found in Rollo Ogden, *Life and Letters of Edwin Lawrence Godkin,* vol. 1 (New York: Macmillan, 1907), pp. 237–38.

9. As noted, the *New York Tribune*'s founder, Horace Greeley, had been the first president of New York City's Typographical Union No. 6, founded in 1850.

10. The younger Villard sold the *Evening Post* in 1918 but remained at the helm of the *Nation* until 1933.

11. Arthur Krock, ed., *The Editorials of Henry Watterson* (New York: Doran, 1923), p. 15.

12. Tom Wallace, "There Were Giants in Those Days," *Saturday Evening Post,* August 6, 1938 (reprinted in John E. Drewry, ed., *Post Biographies of Famous Journalists* Athens: University of Georgia Press, 1942).

13. The Scott and Pittock family heirs retained control of the *Oregonian* until 1950, when the 100-year-old paper was sold to Samuel I. Newhouse. See the *Oregonian,* December 11, 1950.

14. Documented in Allan Nevins, *The Emergence of Modern America, 1865–1898* (New York: Macmillan, 1927), and Ida M. Tarbell, *The Nationalizing of Business, 1878–1898* (New York: Macmillan, 1936). David M. Potter, in *People of Plenty* (Chicago: University of Chicago Press, 1954), argued that economic abundance, not activists, provided the touchstone for unified progress.

15. The following figures show what was happening to the United States. Total manufacturing production increased sevenfold between the end of the Civil War and 1900: using a base figure of 100 for the years 1909 to 1913, the index figure for 1865 was 8.5; in 1880 it was 27, and by 1900 it was 61. There were 140,000 industries of all types in 1860. By 1880 there were 250,000, and by 1900 the number was over 500,000. The number of persons employed in those industries doubled each 20 years. Statistical information is from the U.S. Department of Commerce, *Historical Statistics of the United States, 1789–1945* (Washington, D.C.: U.S. Government Printing Office, 1949).

16. An excellent New Left economic analysis of U.S. expansionism is Walter LaFeber, *The New Empire: An Interpretation of American Expansionism, 1860–1898* (Ithaca, NY: Cornell University Press, 1963), while a strong analysis of business and diplomatic interests in overseas expansion is Robert L. Beisner, *From the Old Diplomacy to the New, 1865–1900,* 2nd ed. (Arlington Heights, IL: Harlan Davidson, 1986).

17. Schlesinger's *The Rise of the City, 1878–1898* (New York: Macmillan, 1932) is a classic study of the transformation of American life stemming from the economic revolution. See also Blake McKelvey, *The Urbanization of America, 1860–1915* (New Brunswick, NJ: Rutgers University Press, 1969), and its companion volume, *The Emergence of Metropolitan America, 1915–1966* (1968).

18. The census figures for totals of all types of dailies were 574 in 1870 and 2226 in 1900. The figures used in the text are more comparable to twentieth-century statistics.

19. This topic is well discussed in Commager, *The American Mind.*

20. The predominant Social Darwinism theory is attacked, but its influence acknowledged, in Richard Hofstadter, *So-*

cial Darwinism in American Thought, 1860–1915 (Philadelphia: University of Pennsylvania Press, 1955).

21. Jack Nelson, *"The Golden Era:* The Most Important Magazine on the Pacific Coast," paper presented to Western Journalism Historians Conference, University of California-Berkeley, 24–25 February 1995.

22. Leon Fink, *Workingmen's Democracy: The Knights of Labor and American Politics* (Urbana: University of Illinois Press, 1983); also, for a discussion of the Knights of Labor and women workers, see Susan Levine, *Labor's True Woman: Carpet Weavers, Industrialization, and Labor Reform in the Gilded Age* (Philadelphia: Temple University Press, 1984).

23. In Philadelphia, two newcomers in the 1870s were the *Record* and the *Times.* The *Record,* begun in 1870, was taken over in 1877 by William M. Singerly, a millionaire railroad builder who cut the paper's price to one cent, brightened its makeup and writing, and engaged in popular crusades against local abuses. By the early 1880s the *Record* was outselling its famous competitor in the morning field, the *Public Ledger,* which had been purchased from the Swain family in 1864 by the able George W. Childs. The *Times* (1875), published by reform-conscious Alexander K. McClure, also pushed into the top circulation bracket, along with the *Evening Item* (1847), which hit its stride in the 1880s as a crusading penny paper, and the *Press* (1857). The *Evening Bulletin* (1847) and the *Inquirer* (1829), ultimately the two survivors in the Philadelphia field, trailed the *Public Ledger* in prestige and the other papers in circulation. The trend was similar in other eastern cities. Baltimore's new entry was the *Evening News* (1872), which in the 1890s, under fighting editor Charles H. Grasty, rose to challenge the famous *Sun.* The *Evening Penny Press* of Pittsburgh appeared in 1884 as the forerunner of the *Pittsburgh Press* and promptly undertook civic improvement campaigns. The Butler family's *Buffalo News* dates from 1880, and it immediately asserted leadership in the newspaper field as an aggressively run evening paper. Another influential leader in the 1880s was the evening *Brooklyn Eagle,* begun in 1841. In Providence, the *Journal* (1829) saw the trend early and established the *Evening Bulletin* in 1863. The Noyes and Kauffmann families gave Washington a local evening paper in 1852, and by 1890 their *Evening Star* had as its only competitor the morning *Post* (1877). Crosby S. Noyes and Samuel H. Kauffmann were leading men in the early years of the *Star;* Noyes's sons, Frank and Theodore, became active before 1890 and guided the *Star* until the 1940s.

24. Raymond B. Nixon, "Henry W. Grady, Reporter: A Reinterpretation" *Journalism Quarterly,* XII (December 1935), 343.

25. In the South, Henry Watterson's well-established *Louisville Courier-Journal* started the *Times* as an evening edition in 1884 and soon saw it outsell the parent morning paper. New Orleans's morning leader, the *Picayune* (1837), found new competition from two evening papers, the *Item* (1877) and the *States* (1879). Two other New Orleans morning papers, the *Times* (1863) and the *Democrat* (1875), found the going more difficult and merged in 1881. A famous editor

appeared in Raleigh, North Carolina, in 1885, when Josephus Daniels took over the *State Chronicle,* which he soon merged into the *News and Observer,* thereby establishing what became a great Daniels family newspaper.

26. The *Commercial Gazette* resulted from an 1883 merger of the *Gazette* (1815) and the *Commercial* (1843), which Halstead had edited since 1865. After Halstead left Cincinnati in 1890 to go to Brooklyn, the *Commercial Gazette* became the *Commercial Tribune* in 1896. It disappeared into the *Enquirer* in 1930.

27. Rivaling the *Daily News* in Chicago as an exponent of the new order in journalism was the *Herald,* founded by James W. Scott in 1881 as a low-priced, liberal-independent morning paper. Scott had difficulties providing sufficient capitalization for his expanding paper, but it quickly won the runner-up position to the *Daily News* in circulation. The ambitious Scott followed William M. Singerly of the *Philadelphia Record* as the second president of the newly formed American Newspaper Publishers Association, serving from 1889 to 1895. With his business associates he founded the *Evening Post* in 1890, and in 1895 he consolidated the older *Times* (1854) with the *Herald* as the *Times-Herald.* At this moment of glory, Scott died, and his papers passed into less talented hands. The *Times,* under editor Wilbur F. Storey, had become known for its shocking sensationalism. Its most famous headline, over an 1875 story of the hanging of four repentant murderers, read "Jerked to Jesus."

28. Melville E. Stone, *Fifty Years a Journalist* (Garden City, NY: Doubleday, 1921), p. 44.

29. William Allen White, "The Man Who Made the *Star,"* *Collier's,* LV (June 26, 1915), 12.

30. Two of the challengers were Scripps with his *Kansas City World* (1897) and the Denver team of Bonfils and Tammen, who operated the *Kansas City Post* from 1909 to 1922. Neither paper survived.

CHAPTER 9: THE NEW JOURNALISM

1. In a poll of American editors conducted by *Editor & Publisher* in 1934.

2. Cockerill's biographer contends that his experience in exploiting local news as managing editor of the *Cincinnati Enquirer* and his subsequent exposures to national and international news in Washington and Baltimore and as a war correspondent made Cockerill a definitely superior newsman to Pulitzer. Much of the imaginative handling of the news and the sensational approach in Pulitzer's papers is credited to Cockerill. See Homer W. King, *Pulitzer's Prize Editor: A Biography of John A. Cockerill, 1845–1896* (Durham, NC: Duke University Press, 1965).

3. As quoted in Don C. Seitz, *Joseph Pulitzer: His Life and Letters* (New York: Simon & Schuster, 1924), p. 101. The name of the paper was soon changed to the *Post-Dispatch.*

4. As quoted in *The Story of the St. Louis Post-Dispatch* (St. Louis: Pulitzer Publishing Company, 1949), p. 3.

5. Documented in the chapter, "A Sensational Newspaper," in Julian Rammelkamp, *Pulitzer's Post-Dispatch, 1878–1883* (Princeton, NJ: Princeton University Press, 1967), pp. 163–206. On the whole Rammelkamp endorses Pulitzer's record.

6. Rammelkamp points out that Pulitzer "mobilized the middle class elements of St. Louis into a dynamic movement of reform" that finally bore fruit early in the twentieth century (ibid., p. 303).

7. As quoted in Willard G. Bleyer, *Main Currents in the History of American Journalism* (Boston: Houghton Mifflin, 1927), p. 325.

8. *New York World,* May 11, 1883.

9. As quoted in Bleyer, *Main Currents in the History of American Journalism,* p. 328.

10. *Journalist,* August 22, 1885.

11. James Creelman, "Joseph Pulitzer—Master Journalist," *Pearson's,* XXI (March 1909), p. 246.

12. As quoted in Seitz, *Joseph Pulitzer,* p. 286.

13. Indicative of that frailty that led to conspicuous failings was Pulitzer's admiration of three publishers in particular whose newspapers utilized sensational techniques but did not measure up to the *World* in high-quality performance. They were William M. Singerly, *Philadelphia Record;* Charles H. Taylor, *Boston Globe;* and the British newspaper popularizer, Alfred Harmsworth, who later became Lord Northcliffe.

14. Three New York newspapers repeated the stunt in 1936. H. R. Ekins of the *World-Telegram* won with a time of 18½ days, defeating Dorothy ("Nellie Bly") Kilgallen of the *Journal* and Leo Kiernan of the *Times.*

15. Ted Curtis Smythe, "The Reporter, 1880–1900," *Journalism History,* VII (Spring 1980), describes in detail the primitive working conditions and their effect on the news products. In his "The Cooperative Impulse in American Journalism: Rivals as Partners" (West Coast Journalism Historians Conference, 1990), he urges study of his theory that cooperation among various news agencies and syndicates shaped U.S. journalism as much as competition.

16. Marion Marzolf, *Civilizing Voices: American Press Criticism 1880–1950* (New York: Longman, 1991), and Hazel Dicken-Garcia, *Journalistic Standards in Nineteenth-Century America* (Madison: University of Wisconsin Press, 1989).

17. For a full discussion of these women and dozens more, see Marion Marzolf, *Up from the Footnote: A History of Women Journalists* (New York: Hastings House, 1977).

18. Robert W. Desmond's books on international communications, particularly pp. 165–68 of *The Information Process* and pp. 384–92 of *Crisis and Conflict,* offer excellent descriptions of the Ring Combination's financial and political dealings.

19. The definitive account of this subject is Richard A. Schwarzlose, *The Nation's Newsbrokers,* 2 vols. (Evanston, IL: Northwestern University Press, 1989–90).

20. Alfred M. Lee, *The Daily Newspaper in America* (New York: Macmillan, 1937), p. 511.

21. For details see Harlan S. Stensaas, "The Rise of Objectivity in U.S. Daily Newspapers, 1865–1934" (Ph.D. dissertation, University of Southern Mississippi, 1986).

22. The detailed story is told in Frank Presbrey, *The History and Development of Advertising* (New York: Doubleday, 1929).

23. William Marz, "Patent Medicine Advertising: Mass Persuasion Techniques and Reform, 1905–1976" (M.A. thesis, California State University at Northridge, 1977).

24. The International Typographical Union (ITU) was reorganized in 1852. The International Printing Pressmen and Assistants' Union split off from the ITU in 1886, the International Photo-Engravers' Union in 1900, and the International Stereotypers' and Electrotypers' Union in 1901.

25. Lee, *The Daily Newspaper in America,* pp. 743–45.

26. *Cosmopolitan,* XI (August 1891).

27. Beaumont Newhall, *The History of Photography,* 4th ed. (New York: Museum of Modern Art, 1978), pp. 138–42.

28. Paula Pierce, "Frances Benjamin Johnston, Mother of American Photojournalism," *Media History Digest,* V (Winter 1985), 54.

29. Will Irwin, "The Fourth Current," *Collier's,* XLVI (February 18, 1911), 14.

30. Ibid. Estimate by Will Irwin in 1911, for the period up to then.

31. Ferdinand Lundberg, *Imperial Hearst: A Social Biography* (New York: Equinox Cooperative Press, 1936), p. 50. Lundberg presents much information about Hearst's finances but paints the publisher in the blackest possible fashion. For the best balanced accounts see John Tebbel, *The Life and Good Times of William Randolph Hearst* (New York: Dutton, 1952), and W. A. Swanberg, *Citizen Hearst* (New York: Scribner's, 1961).

32. *New York World,* May 1, 1898, p. 7 (supplement).

33. Willard G. Bleyer, *Main Currents in the History of American Journalism* (Boston: Houghton Mifflin, 1927), pp. 357–64. This book documents the case against the *Journal's* rampant yellow journalism.

34. William Rockhill Nelson, editor of the *Kansas City Star,* had also used his own funds to fight court battles on behalf of the public interest, but not so sensationally.

35. Marcus M. Wilkerson, *Public Opinion and the Spanish-American War* (Baton Rouge: Louisiana State University Press, 1932), and Joseph E. Wisan, *The Cuban Crisis as Reflected in the New York Press* (New York: Columbia University Press, 1934).

36. Richard Dean Burns, ed., *Guide to American Foreign Relations since 1700,* edited for the Society for Historians of American Foreign Relations (Santa Barbara, CA and Oxford, England: ABC-Clio, 1983), pp. 349–350. Also see Robert L. Beisner, *From the Old Diplomacy to the New, 1865–1900,* 2nd ed. (Arlington Heights, IL: Harlan Davidson, Inc., 1986); Emily S. Rosenberg, *Spreading the American Dream: American Economic and Cultural Expansion, 1890–1945* (New York: Hill and Wang, 1982). An earlier interpretation advanced by the New Left historians of the 1960s and early 1970s argued that economic reasons—

search for markets for surplus products and opportunities for capital investments, and so on—spurred U.S. intervention in the Spanish-Cuban conflict; see William Appelman Williams, *The Tragedy of American Diplomacy,* rev. ed. (New York: Dell, 1972) and *The Roots of the Modern American Empire: A Study of the Growth and Shaping of Social Consciousness in a Marketplace Society* (New York: Random House, 1969). However, recent scholarship challenges this interpretation by pointing to important ideological factors underlying the decision to intervene.

37. John D. Hicks, *A Short History of American Democracy* (Boston: Houghton Mifflin, 1943) p. 605.

38. Wisan, *The Cuban Crisis,* p. 460.

39. Wilkerson, *Public Opinion and the Spanish-American War,* p. 40.

40. There was competition between the Associated Press and the old United Press until 1897. After that time, all the major New York papers except the *New York Sun* were AP members.

41. James Creelman, *On the Great Highway* (Boston: Lothrop Publishing, 1901), p. 178.

42. Wisan, *The Cuban Crisis,* p. 331.

43. Arthur Brisbane, "The Modern Newspaper in War Time," *Cosmopolitan,* XXV (September, 1898), 541.

44. Don C. Seitz, *Joseph Pulitzer* (New York: Simon & Schuster, 1924), p. 312.

45. Wisan, *The Cuban Crisis,* p. 417.

46. Their story is told by Charles H. Brown in *The Correspondents' War* (New York: Scribner's, 1967). Also, Joyce Milton's *The Yellow Kids: Foreign Correspondents in the Heyday of Yellow Journalism* (New York: Harper & Row, 1990) offers rich details about the reporters and The Kid.

47. Richard O'Connor, *Pacific Destiny* (Boston: Little, Brown, 1969), p. 256.

48. Stanley Karnow, *In Our Image: America's Empire in the Philippines.* (New York: Random House, 1989).

49. Carl Schurz, "Manifest Destiny," *Harper's* (October 1893), 737–46, cited in William Appleman Williams, *The Roots of the Modern American Empire* (New York: Random House, 1969), p. 365, as part of Williams's contention that the agricultural majority played the prime role in forcing the war against Spain in order to open more markets. Also see his *The Contours of American History* (Cleveland: World Publishing, 1961, reissued 1973) for an analysis of the effects of Frederick Jackson Turner's frontier theory on U.S. expansion, and the relationship between expansionism and the reform movement.

50. As cited by Leon Wolff in his *Little Brown Brother* (New York: Doubleday, 1961), p. 270.

CHAPTER 10: THE PEOPLE'S CHAMPIONS

1. One documented study of the period is Harold U. Faulkner, *The Quest for Social Justice, 1898–1914* (New York: Macmillan, 1931). A full and fascinating account by a journalistic historian is found in the first three volumes of Mark Sullivan, *Our Times* (New York: Scribner's, 1926–1935). For a revisionist study with a New Left emphasis, see Gabriel Kolko, *The Triumph of Conservatism: A Reinterpretation of American History 1900–1916* (Chicago: Quadrangle Books, 1967).

2. Richard L. McCormick, "Public Life in Industrial America, 1877–1917," in Eric Foner, ed. *The New American History,* rev. and exp. ed. (Philadelphia: Temple University Press, 1997), pp. 107–132; Willard Gaylin, Ira Glasser, Steven Marcus, and David Rothman, *Doing Good: The Limits of Benevolence* (New York: Pantheon Books, 1978).

3. Sara Evans, *Born for Liberty,* 2nd ed. (New York: Free Press, 1997); Kathryn Kish Sklar, "Hull House in the 1890s: A Community of Women Reformers," *Signs,* 10:41 (1985), 658–677; Allan Davis, *Spearheads for Reform: The Social Settlements and the Progressive Movement, 1890–1914* (New York: Oxford University Press, 1967).

4. Louis Hartz in *The Liberal Tradition in America* (New York: Harcourt Brace Jovanovich, 1955), p. 6, offers this explanation: "It is not accidental that America which has uniquely lacked a feudal tradition has uniquely lacked also a socialist tradition. The hidden origin of socialist thought everywhere in the West is to be found in the feudal ethos."

5. Sources on women's reform work include: Evans, *Born for Liberty;* Anne Firor Scott, *Natural Allies: Women's Associations in American History* (Urbana: University of Illinois Press, 1992); Paula Baker, "The Domestication of Politics: Women and American Political Society, 1780–1920," *American Historical Review,* 89 (June 1984), 620–647; Robyn Muncy, *Creating a Female Dominion in American Reform, 1890–1935* (New York: Oxford University Press, 1991); Harriet Hyman Alonso, *Peace as a Women's Issue: A History of the U.S. Movement for World Peace and Women's Rights* (Syracuse, NY: Syracuse University Press, 1993).

6. Marion Marzolf, *Up From the Footnote: A History of Women Journalists* (New York: Hastings House, 1977), pp. 219 ff.

7. Rosalyn Terborg-Penn, *African American Women in the Struggle for the Vote, 1850–1920* (Bloomington: Indiana University Press, 1998); Evans, *Born for Liberty.*

8. David Paul Nord, "The *Appeal to Reason* and American Socialism, 1901–1920," *Kansas History,* I (Summer 1978), 75.

9. For a sketch of Cobb and a collection of his important editorials, see John L. Heaton, *Cobb of "The World"* (New York: Dutton, 1924).

10. W. A. Swanberg, in *Citizen Hearst* (New York: Scribner's, 1961), contends that the Hearst of 1904 presidential ambitions was not a demagogue but sincerely believed he was the best-fitted Democrat to run. For his estimates of Hearst, see pages 208–219 for this period, and the summation, pages 523–527, in which he concludes that Hearst was two men, "a Prospero and a Caliban."

11. *Los Angeles Examiner,* December 12, 1903, p. 4.

12. As quoted in Oliver H. Knight, ed., *I Protest: The Selected Disquisitions of E. W. Scripps* (Madison: University of Wisconsin Press, 1966), p. 270. Knight edited from the

Scripps papers a variety of Scripps' personal views that establish the publisher as a thinking observer of American affairs.

13. The editorial is reprinted in *The Autobiography of William Allen White* (New York: Macmillan, 1946), pp. 280–83. It also appears in Allan Nevins, *American Press Opinion* (Boston: Heath, 1928), pp. 419–22.

14. One account, not confined to this period, is Silas Bent, *Newspaper Crusaders* (New York: Whittlesey House, 1939). Another is Jonathan Daniels, *They Will Be Heard: America's Crusading Newspaper Editors* (New York: McGraw-Hill, 1965).

15. The full story was first told in C. C. Regier, *The Era of the Muckrakers* (Chapel Hill: University of North Carolina Press, 1932). However, Regier ignored the contributions of the newspapers in crusading.

16. One of the Chinese leaders was *Wah Kee* (1875–79). There were seven by 1914, all but two dailies. The first two papers in Japanese appeared in 1890–1900. For a comprehensive treatment of the early ethnic press see Clint Wilson II and Félix Gutiérrez, *Minorities and the Media: The End of Mass Communication* (Beverly Hills: Sage Publications, 1985).

17. Barbara Straus Reed, "The Antebellum Jewish Press: Origins, Problems, Functions," *Journalism Monographs* 139 (June 1993). See also her article on Robert Lyon in *American Journalism*, VII (Spring 1990), 77.

18. See Victoria Goff's paper "Spanish-Language Newspapers in California during the Nineteenth Century" (American Journalism Historians Association convention, 1994). Also, see her paper "Spanish-Language Newspapers in California during the 1860s" (Association for Education in Journalism and Mass Communication convention, 1994). Important statistics are found in Carlos E. Cortés, "The Mexican-American Press," in *The Ethnic Press in the United States: A Historical Analysis and Handbook,* ed. Sally M. Miller (New York: Greenwood Press, 1987). For the description of activism see Félix Gutiérrez, "Latinos and the Media," in *Readings in Mass Communication,* ed. Michael Emery and Ted Curtis Smythe (Dubuque, IA: William C. Brown, 1989), and in annual customized collections.

19. Armistead Scott Pride, "Negro Newspapers: Yesterday, Today and Tomorrow," *Journalism Quarterly,* XX–VIII (Spring 1951), 179.

20. Substantial accounts of leading black papers can be found in Roland E. Wolseley, *The Black Press, U.S.A.* (Ames, IA: Iowa State University Press, 1971).

Many tributes to Van Anda from leaders in his profession are found in a short biography: Barnett Fine, *A Giant of the Press* (New York: Editor & Publisher Library, 1933). Berger carries the story of Van Anda's achievements through several chapters.

3. For the full story of the *Titanic* coverage see Berger, *The Story of the New York Times,* pp. 193–201. A contemporary account by Alexander McD. Stoddart appeared in the *Independent,* LXII (May 2, 1912), 945.

4. *New York Times,* October 18, 1907, p. 1.

5. See, for example, *Herald* pages in Michael C. Emery et al., *America's Front Page News, 1690–1970* (New York: Doubleday, 1970), pp. 83, 104, 109, 124.

6. Don C. Seitz, *The James Gordon Bennetts* (Indianapolis: Bobbs-Merrill, 1928), p. 377.

7. In *Outing,* LIII (March 1909), 690.

8. Some of the color of the *Sun* is found in Frank M. O'Brien, *The Story of the Sun* (New York: George H. Doran Company, 1918). Church's "Is There a Santa Claus?" is reprinted on pp. 409–10.

9. The story of the *Inter Ocean* is told in Walter E. Ewert, "The History of the Chicago *Inter Ocean,* 1872–1914" (Master's thesis, Northwestern University, 1940).

10. See Jack R. Hart, *The Information Empire* (Washington, DC: University Press of America, 1981).

11. Victor Rosewater, *History of Cooperative News-Gathering in the United States* (New York: Appleton-Century-Crofts, 1930), pp. 182–89.

12. For a description of Stone's activities see *"M.E.S."—His Book* (New York: Harper & Row, 1918).

13. As quoted in Rosewater, *History of Cooperative News-Gathering,* p. 354.

14. As quoted in Charles R. McCabe, ed., *Damned Old Crank* (New York: Harper & Row, 1951), p. 219.

15. Howard gave his explanation in Webb Miller, *I Found No Peace* (New York: Simon & Schuster, 1936), p. 96. The Associated Press blunder on the Hauptmann verdict stemmed from the setting up of a signal system to get the news out of the courtroom. An overeager AP man got the wrong signal and flashed news of a life sentence when the verdict was death. The premature 1944 D-Day flash by the AP was sent by a woman teletype operator who was "practicing," the AP said. The UP was similarly victimized by an employee who flashed the end of the Japanese war prematurely in 1945.

16. McCabe, *Damned Old Crank,* p. 204.

CHAPTER 11: BASTIONS OF NEWS ENTERPRISE

1. *New York Times,* August 19, 1896, p. 1.

2. See Elmer Davis, *History of the New York Times, 1851–1921* (New York: The New York Times, 1921), p. 274, and Meyer Berger, *The Story of the New York Times, 1851–1951* (New York: Simon & Schuster, 1951), p. 160 for two estimates of Van Anda's role in building the *Times.*

CHAPTER 12: WAR COMES TO THE UNITED STATES

1. As quoted in Mark Sullivan, *Our Times,* vol. 5 (New York: Scribner's, 1933), p. 32. Sullivan's six-volume journalistic coverage of the years 1900 to 1925 reflects both the life and history of the United States in an engrossing manner.

2. Edwin Costrell, "Newspaper Attitudes toward War in Maine, 1914–17," *Journalism Quarterly,* XVI (December

1939), 334. This measurement of an immediate anti-German reaction, before the introduction of concerted propaganda by the belligerents and before the cutting of cable communications with Germany, is significant.

3. Among the more responsible books of the era of disillusionment were Walter Millis's *Road to War* (Boston: Houghton Mifflin, 1935), H. C. Peterson's *Propaganda for War: The Campaign Against American Neutrality, 1914–1717* (Norman, Oklahoma: University of Oklahoma Press, 1939), and Harold D. Lasswell, *Propoganda Technique in the World War* (New York: Peter Smith, 1927).

4. Lloyd E. Ambrosius, *Wilsonian Statecraft: Theory and Practice of Liberal Internationalism during World War I* (Wilmington, DE: Scholarly Resources, 1991) discusses Wilson's liberal capitalist ideology and how he tried to transform the world to conform to it. For a New Left interpretation of Wilson's foreign policy, see Lloyd C. Gardner, *Safe for Democracy: The Anglo-American Response to Revolution, 1913–1923* (New York: Oxford University Press, 1987).

5. British journalist Phillip Knightley, in his *The First Casualty* (New York: Harcourt Brace Jovanovich, 1975), contended that between 1914 and 1918 "more deliberate lies were told than in any other period of history, and the whole apparatus of the state went into action to suppress the truth" (p. 80). His book is a harsh appraisal of war correspondence and government manipulation from the Crimean War to Vietnam.

6. The best-balanced picture of American press difficulties in covering the war is found in Ralph O. Nafziger, *The American Press and Public Opinion during the World War, 1914 to April, 1917* (Ph.D. thesis, University of Wisconsin, 1936). Nafziger ranks overt propaganda efforts as having less effect on American news presentation than (1) rigid war censorships and (2) limited and controlled communications facilities.

7. Charles DeBenedetti, *The Peace Reform in American History* (Bloomington and London: Indiana University Press, 1980), p. 79; Nancy L. Roberts, *American Peace Writers, Editors, and Periodicals: A Dictionary* (Westport, CT: Greenwood Press, 1991), pp. 329–330; also see Harriet Hyman Alonso, *Peace as a Women's Issue: A History of the U.S. Movement for World Peace and Women's Rights* (Syracuse, NY: Syracuse University Press, 1993); Charles Chatfield, *For Peace and Justice: Pacifism in America, 1914–1941* (Boston: Beacon Press, 1971).

8. Frank Luther Mott, *American Journalism* (New York: Macmillan, 1950), p. 616.

9. George Creel, *How We Advertised America* (New York: Harper & Row, 1920), p. 4.

10. See Harold D. Lasswell, *Propaganda Technique in the World War* (New York: Peter Smith, 1927), p. 20.

11. Walton E. Bean, "The Accuracy of Creel Committee News, 1917–1919: An Examination of Cases," *Journalism Quarterly,* XVIII (September 1941), 272. The major study of the CPI is James R. Mock and Cedric Larson, *Words That Won the War* (Princeton: Princeton University Press, 1939).

12. Paxson eventually wrote a three-volume series titled *American Democracy and the World War.* The war itself is covered in detail in the second volume, *America at War, 1917–1918* (Boston: Houghton Mifflin, 1939).

13. James West Davidson, Mark H. Lytle, Christine Leigh Heyrman, William E. Gienapp, and Michael B. Stoff, *Nation of Nations: A Narrative History of the American Republic, Volume Two: Since 1865,* 3rd ed. (Boston: McGraw-Hill, 1998), pp. 816–817. Also see: Chapter 6, "Homogenizing a Pluralistic Culture: Propaganda during World War I," in William Bruce Wheeler and Susan D. Becker, *Discovering the American Past: A Look at the Evidence, Volume II: Since 1865,* 3rd ed. (Boston: Houghton Mifflin, 1994), pp. 165–193; Stephen Vaughn, *Holding Fast the Inner Lines: Democracy, Nationalism, and the Committee on Public Information* (Chapel Hill: University of North Carolina Press, 1979).

14. The AP committed a familiar journalistic blunder by adding a "no" to a La Follette statement concerning the American declaration of war, making it read "we had no grievance." An unsuccessful move to oust La Follette from the Senate resulted.

15. Enlarged and brought up to date in Chafee, *Free Speech in the United States* (Cambridge, MA: Harvard University Press, 1941).

16. James R. Mock, *Censorship 1917* (Princeton: Princeton University Press, 1941), pp. 81, 93.

17. Mark Sullivan, *Our Times,* vol. 5 (New York: Scribner's, 1933). This is a contemporary account by a noted newspaper columnist. See Chapter 27 for a discussion of Wilson's treaty effort.

18. Harvey Wish, *Society and Thought in Modern America* (New York: David McKay, 1962), p. 420.

19. Fred J. Cook, *The FBI Nobody Knows* (New York: Macmillan, 1964), pp. 89–95.

20. *Schenck* v. *United States, 249 U.S. 47 (1919).*

21. *Abrams* v. *United States*, 250 U.S. 616 (1919).

22. *Gitlow* v. *People of the State of New York, 268 U.S. 652 (1925).*

23. *Whitney* v. *California, 274 U.S. 357 (1927).*

24. *Dennis* v. *United States, 341 U.S. 494 (1951).* A subsequent decision of 1957 in the Yates case narrowed the grounds for Smith Act convictions and freed five defendants.

25. David Nord, "The *Appeal to Reason* and American Socialism, 1901–1920," *Kansas History,* vol. 1, no. 2, Summer 1978.

26. Alfred McClung Lee, *The Daily Newspaper in America* (New York: Macmillan, 1937), pp. 191–92.

CHAPTER 13: THE TWENTIES: RADIO, MOVIES, AND JAZZ JOURNALISM

1. Alan Brinkley, "Prosperity, Depression, and War, 1920–1945," in Eric Foner, ed. *The New American History,* rev. and exp. ed. (Philadelphia: Temple University Press, 1997), p. 142; also see Robert F. Himmelberg, *The Origins of the National Recovery Administration: Business, Government, and the Trade Association Issue, 1921–1933* (New

York: Fordham University Press, 1976); Louis Galambos, *The Rise of the Corporate Commonwealth: United States Business and Public Policy in the Twentieth Century* (New York: Basic Books, 1988); Ellis W. Hawley, *The Great War and the Search for a Modern Order: A History of the American People and Their Institutions, 1917–1933* (New York: St. Martin's Press, 1979).

2. Studies of the Klan include Kathleen M. Blee, *Women of the Klan: Racism and Gender in the 1920s* (Berkeley: University of California Press, 1991); Shawn Lay, ed., *The Invisible Empire in the West: Toward a New Historical Appraisal of the Ku Klux Klan of the 1920s* (Urbana: University of Illinois Press, 1992); Nancy MacLean, *Behind the Mask of Chivalry: The Making of the Second Ku Klux Klan* (New York: Oxford University Press, 1994). On fundamentalism, consult George M. Marsden, *Fundamentalism and American Culture: The Shaping of Twentieth-Century Evangelicalism, 1870–1925* (New York: Oxford University Press, 1980). Discussions of Americanization campaigns can be found in Gary Gerstle, *Working-Class Americanism* (New York: Cambridge University Press, 1989) and Gary Gerstle, "The Protean Character of American Liberalism," *American Historical Review,* 99:4 (October 1994), 1043–1073.

3. Elliot N. Sivowitch, "A Technological Survey of Broadcasting's Prehistory, 1876–1920," *Journal of Broadcasting,* XV (Winter 1970–71), 1–20. This article was reprinted along with a number of other important research articles in Lawrence W. Lichty and Malachi C. Topping, *American Broadcasting: A Source Book on the History of Radio and Television* (New York: Hastings House, 1975).

4. Thomas W. Hoffer, "Nathan B. Stubblefield and His Wireless Telephone," *Journal of Broadcasting,* XV (Summer 1971), 317–29. For details of these early experiments see also Erik Barnouw, *A Tower in Babel* (New York: Oxford University Press, 1966); Christopher H. Sterling and John M. Kittross, *Stay Tuned: A Concise History of American Broadcasting* (Belmont, CA: Wadsworth, 1978); and Sydney W. Head and Christopher Sterling, *Broadcasting in America* (Boston: Houghton Mifflin, 1982).

5. *New York Times,* October 18, 1907.

6. Sterling and Kittross call this the "first publicly announced broadcast of radio telephony," *Stay Tuned,* p. 28. Sivowitch, "Technological Survey," offers the most detailed description; see also Barnouw, *A Tower in Babel,* p. 20.

7. This is supported by evidence gathered by Gordon Greb, "The Golden Anniversary of Broadcasting," *Journal of Broadcasting,* III (Winter 1958–59), 3–13, and confirmed by Sterling and Kittross in a lengthy discussion, *Stay Tuned,* p. 40.

8. Susan L. Douglas, *Inventing American Broadcasting, 1899–1902* (Baltimore: Johns Hopkins University Press, 1987), places radio development in a social and cultural context. Also see Susan Smulyan, *Selling Radio: The Commercialization of American Broadcasting, 1920–1934* (Washington, D.C.: Smithsonian, 1994).

9. Sydney W. Head, *Broadcasting in America* (Boston: Houghton Mifflin, 1976), p. 113, cites Department of Commerce records.

10. The full story of RCA's rise and of other concentration of radio control is told in Lewellyn White, *The American Radio* (Chicago: University of Chicago Press, 1947).

11. In 1921 the *Kansas City Star* offered a combination radio-newspaper rate for advertising users of the *Star* and its station WDAF, but there were few immediate takers.

12. From testimony by Ralph D. Casey, director of the University of Minnesota School of Journalism, before the FCC. The testimony was reprinted in part by the Newspaper-Radio Committee in *Freedom of the Press* (booklet, 1942), pp. 5–21.

13. Wayne M. Towers, "World Series Coverage in New York City in the 1920s," *Journalism Monographs,* LXXIII (August 1981), 5–6.

14. Lichty and Topping, *American Broadcasting,* p. 158, cite an article by Bruce Barton in the *American Magazine,* August 1927, describing his participation at this extravaganza.

15. John Wallace, "What We Thought of the First Columbia Broadcasting Program," *Radio Broadcast* (December 1927), 140–41.

16. White, *The American Radio,* pp. 144–47.

17. The story of the newspaper-radio struggle and ANPA's part in it is told in Edwin Emery, *History of the American Newspaper Publishers Association* (Minneapolis: University of Minnesota Press, 1950), Chap. 13.

18. Mitchell V. Charnley, *News by Radio* (New York: Macmillan, 1948), p. 9.

19. George A. Lundberg, "The Content of Radio Programs," *Social Forces,* VII (1928), pp. 58–60, cited by Lichty and Topping, *American Broadcasting,* p. 323.

20. Barnouw, *A Tower in Babel,* p. 229.

21. The name comes from the title of a history of the tabloids: Simon M. Bessie, *Jazz Journalism* (New York: Dutton, 1938).

22. As quoted in ibid., p. 82.

23. William H. Taft, "Bernarr Mcfadden: One of a Kind," *Journalism Quarterly,* XLV (Winter 1968), 631.

24. Gauvreau used this phrase as the title for a thinly fictionalized account of his editorship of the *Graphic:* Emile Gauvreau, *Hot News* (New York: Macaulay Company, 1931).

25. As quoted in Helen M. Hughes, *News and the Human Interest Story* (Chicago: University of Chicago Press, 1940), p. 235.

26. See Walter E. Schneider, "Fabulous Rise of *N.Y. Daily News,*" *Editor & Publisher,* LXXII (June 24, 1939), 5, for an extensive account of 20 years of the paper's history. Patterson's obituaries appeared in *Editor & Publisher,* LXXIX (June 1, 1946), 9, and in *Time,* LXVII (June 3, 1946), 87.

27. Royal H. Ray, *Concentration of Ownership and Control in the American Daily Newspaper Industry* (New York: Columbia University Microfilms, 1951), pp. 401–8. A summary of this Ph.D. dissertation was published in *Journalism Quarterly,* XXIX (Winter 1952), 31.

28. Census population figures and newspaper-circulation totals are conveniently tabulated in the appendices of A. M.

Lee, *The Daily Newspaper in America* (New York: Macmillan, 1937). Advertising revenue totals are from figures of the ANPA Bureau of Advertising.

29. Data for 1880 tabulated by Edwin Emery from S.N.D. North, *History and Present Condition of the Newspaper and Periodical Press of the United States* (Washington, DC: Government Printing Office, 1884). For 1900 to 1920, W. Carl Masche, "Factors Involved in the Consolidation and Suspension of Daily and Sunday Newspapers in the United States Since 1900: A Statistical Study in Social Change" (Master's thesis, University of Minnesota, 1932), and Morris Ernst, *The First Freedom* (New York: Macmillan, 1946), p. 284. For 1930, Alfred McClung Lee, "The Basic Newspaper Pattern," *The Annals of the American Academy of Political and Social Science,* CCXIX (January 1942), 46, except figures for one-daily cities of specified population, from Masche.

Numbers of English-language general circulation dailies for 1880 tabulated from North; for 1900, from Masche; for 1910, from Royal H. Ray (*see n. 25 above*); for 1920 to 1930, *Editor & Publisher International YearBook* figures. The census counts of daily publications, which included foreign-language, religious, trade, and technical dailies, were 971 dailies in 1800, 2226 in 1900, 2600 in 1910, and 2441 in 1920. But those figures do not compare with the *Editor & Publisher YearBook* figures available after 1920. Masche, Ernst, and Ray tabulated their data from Ayer directories; Lee used *Editor & Publisher International YearBook* data.

30. Willard G. Bleyer, "Freedom of the Press and the New Deal," *Journalism Quarterly,* XI (March 1934), 29. Early in this period such morning papers as the *Atlanta Constitution, Indianapolis Star, Minneapolis Tribune,* and *St. Paul Pioneer Press* were alone in their fields. They were joined in 1915 by the *Detroit Free Press,* with the death of the old *Tribune.* In 1917 Cleveland saw the *Leader* disappear into the *Plain Dealer,* leaving the latter as the only morning paper. Elimination of the *Free Press* in Milwaukee in 1919 left the *Sentinel* without morning competition. The same year the *St. Louis Globe-Democrat* bought its morning rival, the *Republic.* In Buffalo in 1926 the merger of the *Courier* (1831) and the *Express* (1846) ended that city's long morning rivalry. Pittsburgh's morning dailies were reduced to one in 1927, and Kansas City joined the trend in 1928. The *Cincinnati Enquirer* closed out its competition in 1930 by buying the *Commercial Tribune,* successor to Murat Halstead's old *Commercial Gazette.* Other cities with just one morning daily but with two or more evening papers were Baltimore, Providence, Rochester, Syracuse, Dayton, Columbus (Ohio), Louisville, Richmond, Memphis, Houston, Dallas, Fort Worth, Oklahoma City, Portland (Oregon), and Seattle. Those cities with just one morning and one evening paper were Hartford, New Haven, Tampa, Chattanooga, Knoxville, Grand Rapids, Tulsa, and Denver. One company owned all the dailies published in six cities: New Bedford and Springfield, Massachusetts, Duluth, Des Moines, Wilmington, Delaware, and Charleston, South Carolina. Springfield, however, had two morning and two evening dailies operating under a single ownership headed by Sherman H. Bowles of the historic *Republican* family.

31. Morning paper mergers were the most spectacular in the first decades after 1900, but overall consolidation of metropolitan newspapers, and concentration of ownership, continued from coast to coast. Entry of the Hearst papers into Detroit through purchase of the *Times* in 1921 prompted the *News* (founded by James E. Scripps) to buy out the *Journal* in 1922. Thus Detroit, with more than a million in population, was left with but three newspapers, the morning *Free Press* and the evening *News* and *Times.* In New Orleans, the *Times-Democrat* and the *Picayune* were merged in 1914, leaving the new *Times-Picayune* alone in the morning field for ten years. The *Times-Picayune,* owned by L. K. Nicholson, bought Colonel Robert Ewing's *States* in 1933 for an evening edition. The other evening paper, the *Item,* published a morning edition, the *Tribune,* from 1924 to 1941. St. Louis afternoon journalism was dominated by Pulitzer's *Post-Dispatch.* The *Chronicle,* the Scripps-McRae entry of 1880, merged with the *Star* (1884), in 1905. The *Times* (1907) joined forces with the *Star* in 1932 as the *Star-Times,* leaving St. Louis with three ownerships. Kansas City rivals of Nelson's *Star* found the going equally difficult. Nelson bought the morning *Times* in 1901. The Scripps-McRae *World,* founded in 1897, faded from the picture. The evening *Post,* started in 1906 and bought by Bonfils and Tammen of *Denver Post* fame in 1909, was sold in 1922 to the owners of the morning *Journal* (1868), and the two papers became the *Journal-Post* in 1928. Kansas City thus dropped to two ownerships.

32. In Boston, where the Hearst-owned evening *American* was founded in 1904, the publisher bought the century-old *Daily Advertiser* in 1917 and the *Record* in 1920. The two papers were juggled in an effort to bring tabloid publication to Boston, with the name *Record* surviving for the morning Hearst paper. Meanwhile the *Boston Herald* was buying the *Traveler* in 1912 for an evening edition and was absorbing the Munsey-owned *Journal* in 1917. Thus Boston, which in 1900 had 11 major newspapers operated by seven ownerships, by 1930 had eight newspapers and five ownerships. The others were Edwin A. Grozier's highly successful morning *Post,* the Taylor family's morning and evening *Globes,* and the limping but traditional *Transcript.*

Baltimore was less fortunate. The *Sun,* the original penny paper of 1837, took over the *Evening World* in 1910 and made it the *Evening Sun.* The *Herald,* a morning penny paper, died in 1906. The *Evening News,* Grasty's crusading paper that fell into Munsey's control, was consolidated with the *Star* in 1921, and the paper was sold to Hearst in 1922. The *American,* dating from 1799, also passed from Munsey to Hearst and after 1928 was published only as a Sunday paper. A 1922 Scripps Howard entry, the *Post,* was sold to Hearst in 1934. The Hearst *News-Post* thus opposed the *Sun* papers.

Pittsburgh's newspapers were also shuffled by the Hearst and Scripps Howard organizations. The Scripps Howard group bought the well-established *Press* in 1923 for $6 million, under an agreement with the city's other newspaper owners that the *Dispatch* and *Leader* would be bought out and killed. Four years later Hearst and Paul Block, a Hearst associate and newspaper broker, bought the remaining four

Pittsburgh dailies. The morning *Sun* and *Chronicle Tele-graph* were transformed into the Hearst-owned *Sun-Tele-graph;* the evening *Post* and *Gazette Times,* into the Block-owned *Post-Gazette.*

Arthur Brisbane and Hearst teamed up in Milwaukee at the end of World War I, with the result that the *Evening Wis-consin,* the *News,* and the *Telegram* were rolled into the *Wis-consin News,* Hearst-owned after 1919. The morning *Sentinel* joined the Hearst group in 1924 to give the chain two footholds against the steadily increasing pressure of the *Milwaukee Journal.* Also in the Midwest, the *Omaha News* and *Bee* were bought by Hearst in 1928 and merged as the *News-Bee,* a morning, evening, and Sunday publication. Among Hearst's other purchases were the *Atlanta Georgian,* 1912; *Detroit Times,* 1921; *Seattle Post-Intelligencer,* *Rochester Journal,* and *Syracuse Telegram,* 1922; *Albany Times-Union* and *San Antonio Light,* 1924; and *Syracuse Journal* (combined with the *Telegram*), 1925.

Strengthening of the Scripps Howard properties by elimi-nating the competitors took place in several cities. Knoxville saw the *News-Sentinel* created by the merger of the *News,* started in 1921, and the *Sentinel,* bought in 1926. The *El Paso Post,* founded in 1922, became the *Herald-Post* with the acquisition of the *Herald* in 1931. The *Akron Press,* begun in 1899 by E. W. Scripps, received a badly needed transfusion in 1925 with the purchase of the *Times,* to form the *Times-Press.* The *Memphis Press,* founded in 1906, be-came the *Press-Scimitar* by absorbing the *News-Scimitar* in 1926; ten years later Scripps Howard added the morning *Memphis Commercial Appeal* to the chain. The *New York Telegram* bought in 1927, became the *World-Telegram* in 1931, when Howard negotiated the purchase of the famous Pulitzer paper. The *Pittsburgh Press* was acquired in 1923 in a deal that eliminated the *Dispatch* and *Leader.* On the loss side, Scripps Howard sold the *Des Moines News, Sacra-mento Star,* and *Terre Haute Post* to competitors during the 1920s, and the *Baltimore Post* to Hearst in 1934. The *Wash-ington Daily News, Fort Worth Press,* and *Birmingham Post* were founded in 1921. Scripps Howard purchased the *Indi-anapolis Times* and *Youngstown Telegram* in 1922, the *New Mexico State Tribune* in Albuquerque in 1923, and the *Buf-falo Times* in 1929. The *Rocky Mountain News* and *Times* were bought in 1926; the chain consolidated its *Denver Ex-press* and *Times,* then killed the paper in 1928.

33. Roland Marchand, *Advertising the American Dream* (Berkeley: University of California Press, 1985), pp. 32–36.

34. Cutlip traces the history of public relations in his *Effec-tive Public Relations,* which he coauthored with Allen H. Center (Englewood Cliffs, NJ: Prentice-Hall, 1986).

35. Eric F. Goldman, *Two-Way Street* (Boston: Bellman Publishing, 1948), tells the story.

CHAPTER 14: DEPRESSION AND REFORM

1. James West Davidson et al., *Nation of Nations,* 2nd ed. (Boston: McGraw-Hill, 1999). For a brief overview of the causes of the Depression, see Gerald Nash, *The Crucial Era:* *The Great Depression and World War II, 1929–1945,* 2nd ed. (New York: St. Martin's Press, 1992).

2. *Out of Our Past* (New York: Harper, 1959).

3. *Franklin D. Roosevelt and the New Deal, 1932–1940* (New York: Harper & Row, 1963).

4. See, for example, Barton J. Bernstein, "The New Deal: The Conservative Achievements of New Deal Reform," in Barton J. Bernstein, ed., *Towards a New Past: Dissenting Es-says in American History* (New York: Pantheon, 1968).

5. See, for example, Julia Kirk Blackwelder, *Women of the Depression: Caste and Culture in San Antonio, 1929–1939* (College Station: Texas A & M University Press, 1984); Jill S. Quadagno, *The Transformation of Old Age Security: Class and Politics in the American Welfare State* (Chicago: University of Chicago Press, 1988).

6. Betty Houchin Winfield, "Roosevelt and the Press: How Franklin D. Roosevelt Influenced News-gathering, 1933–1941" (Ph.D. thesis, University of Washington, 1978), pp. 46, 200–204.

7. Betty Houchin Winfield, "Franklin D. Roosevelt's Ef-forts to Influence the News during His First Term Press Con-ferences," *Presidential Studies Quarterly* (Spring 1981), 192, 196.

8. *San Francisco Examiner,* May 6, 1933.

9. Ibid., May 29, 1935.

10. Ibid., June 21, 1935.

11. Ibid., October 30, 1936.

12. *Time,* XLIX (June 9, 1947), 68. The 1936 survey of Washington correspondents, cited here, was taken by Leo C. Rosten for his book, *The Washington Correspondents* (New York: Harcourt Brace Jovanovich, 1937). Cited most often as "least fair and reliable" by 93 correspondents were, in order, the Hearst newspapers, the *Chicago Tribune,* the *Los Angeles Times,* and the Scripps Howard newspapers. Cited most often as "most fair and reliable" by 99 correspondents were, in order, the *New York Times, Baltimore Sun, Christ-ian Science Monitor,* the Scripps Howard papers, and the *St. Louis Post-Dispatch.*

13. *Near* v. *Minnesota ex rel. Olson,* 283 U.S. 697 (1931).

14. *Grosjean* v. *American Press Co.,* 297 U.S. 233 (1936). In a 1983 case brought by the *Minneapolis Star* and *Tribune,* the court voided a Minnesota law imposing a 6 percent tax on newsprint and ink used by larger newspapers, thus ex-tending its doctrine on discriminatory taxation.

15. *Associated Press* v. *NLRB,* 301 U.S. 103 (1937); regard-ing discretionary taxes, see *Minneapolis Star and Tribune Co.* v. *Minnesota Commission of Revenue,* 460 U.S. 575 (1983).

16. *Bridges* v. *California,* 314 U.S. 252 (1941).

17. *United States* v. *Noriega* (*In re* Cable News Network, Inc.), 917 F.2d 1543 (11th Cir.), *cert. denied,* 498 U.S. 976 (1990).

18. Others noted over the years included such reporters as Edwin A. Lahey of the *Chicago Daily News,* Fred Carr of the *Christian Science Monitor,* John Turcott of the *New York Daily News,* John F. Burns of the *Providence Journal,* A. H.

Raskin of the *New York Times,* and a score or more of equally competent associates.

19. Other top science writers included Arthur J. Snider of the *Chicago Daily News,* Victor Cohn of the *Washington Post,* David Perlman of the *San Francisco Chronicle,* Josephine Robertson of the *Cleveland Plain Dealer,* Harry Nelson of the *Los Angeles Times,* Walter Sullivan of the *New York Times,* Christine Russell of the *Washington Star,* John Durham of the *Houston Chronicle,* Earl Ubell of NBC, Delos Smith of UPI, and Alton Blakeslee, Frank J. Carey, and John Barbour of the AP. One of their major concerns was space science.

20. Ranking with the Mowrer brothers as among the best of American foreign correspondents were John Gunther in London, William Stoneman in Moscow and London, Wallace Deuel in Rome and Berlin, Helen Kirkpatrick in Paris, and David Nichol in Berlin and Moscow. Other leading *Chicago Daily News* foreign correspondents were Leland Stowe, Robert J. Casey, William McGaffin, Paul Ghali, Ernie Hill, Nat A. Barrows, A. T. Steele, Georgie Anne Geyer, and George Weller, a Pulitzer Prize winner for distinguished reporting. Keyes Beech and Fred Sparks won Pulitzer awards for Korean War coverage. Paul Leach, Edwin A. Lahey, and Peter Lisagor were Washington bureau chiefs.

Herbert L. Matthews covered the Ethiopian war for the *New York Times* and then Germany; active in Europe were Cyrus L. Sulzberger, chief foreign correspondent, Drew Middleton, and Flora Lewis. Other leading *Herald Tribune* correspondents of the war period were Walter Kerr, Joseph Barnes, Major George Fielding Eliot, Russell Hill, Joseph Driscoll, and John O'Reilly. While he was Washington bureau chief, Bert Andrews won the 1948 Pulitzer Prize for national reporting. Jack Steele was a leading Washington staff member in the early 1950s before becoming Scripps Howard's chief political writer. Homer Bigart and Marguerite Higgins won Pulitzer Prizes as Korean War correspondents. In 1962 columnist Walter Lippmann won the paper's final Pulitzer Prize before its death in 1966. Correspondents of other foreign and Washington services outshone the *Chicago Tribune*'s writers until 1975, when William Mullen, a white reporter, and Ovie Carter, a black photographer, won the Pulitzer Prize for international reporting with a series on famine in Africa and India.

21. Walter Duranty, *I Write as I Please* (New York: Halcyon House, 1935), pp. 166–67.

22. See S. J. Taylor, *Stalin's Apologist* (London: Oxford University Press, 1990). Also see Whitman Bassow's *The Moscow Correspondents* (New York: William Morrow, 1988).

23. See Michael Emery, *On the Front Lines* (Washington, DC: American University Press, 1995), Chapter 2.

24. Paul Scott Mowrer, *The House of Europe* (Boston: Houghton Mifflin, 1945), p. 70. For his brother's personal account, see Edgar Ansel Mowrer, *Triumph and Tragedy* (New York: Weybright and Talley, 1968).

25. Lowell Thomas, *Good Evening, Everybody* (New York: William Morrow, 1976), p. 311.

26. Lawrence W. Lichty and Malachi C. Topping, *American Broadcasting: A Source Book on the History of Radio and Television* (New York: Hastings House, 1975), p. 302.

27. Including *Editor & Publisher,* which expressed skepticism in its issue of December 10, 1932, p. 5.

28. The AP won suits against KSOO, Sioux Falls, South Dakota, and KVOS, Bellingham, Washington, to stop this practice. Eventually the period of time during which there is a protectible property right in news came to be recognized as a minimum of four to six hours after publication.

29. *Report on Chain Broadcasting* (Federal Communications Commission Order No. 37, May 1941), pp. 26–28.

30. Lawrence W. Lichty and Thomas W. Bohn, "Radio's March of Time: Dramatized News," *Journalism Quarterly,* LI (Autumn 1973), 458–62.

31. For the best treatment of radio commentators in the 1930s and 1940s see Irving Fang, *Those Radio Commentators!* (Ames: Iowa State University Press, 1977). Other prominent commentators included Frederick William Wile and David Lawrence, who were listed in newspaper columns along with Kaltenborn as commentators prior to 1930; Edwin C. Hill; and John W. Vandercook.

32. Fang, *Those Radio Commentators!,* p. 161.

33. Michael Emery, "The Munich Crisis Broadcasts: Radio News Comes of Age," *Journalism Quarterly,* XLII (Autumn 1965), 576.

34. Christopher H. Sterling and John M. Kittross, *Stay Tuned: A Concise History of American Broadcasting* (Belmont, CA: Wadsworth, 1978), pp. 182–83.

35. Ibid., pp. 100–101.

36. For a survey of television experiments dating to 1875, see David T. MacFarland, "Television: The Whirling Beginning" in Lichty and Topping, *American Broadcasting: A Source Book,* pp. 46–52.

37. The story of RCA's dominance of early television is found in Erik Barnouw, *Tube of Plenty: The Evolution of American Television* (New York: Oxford University Press, 1975), and his more detailed studies, *A Tower in Babel,* (New York: Oxford University Press, 1966) and *The Golden Web* (New York: Oxford University Press, 1968); and in Sydney W. Head, *Broadcasting in America* (Boston: Houghton Mifflin, 1976); F. Leslie Smith, *Perspectives in Radio and Television* (New York: Harper & Row, 1984). Lichty and Topping, *American Broadcasting;* and Sterling and Kittross, *Stay Tuned.*

38. Barnouw, *Tube of Plenty,* pp. 78–83, 143–45.

39. Although RCA dominated the early years, a number of other companies had been active, including CBS, the DuMont Laboratories, Philco Radio and Television Corp., and AT&T. By 1937 there were 17 experimental stations on the air.

40. See Raymond Fielding, *The American Newsreel, 1911–1967* (Norman: University of Oklahoma Press, 1972), for a definitive history and bibliography. Fielding is also the author of *The March of Time, 1935–1951* (New York: Oxford University Press, 1978), the story of that film documentary.

41. *Time,* LI (March 8, 1948), 66.

42. Chris Welles, "Lessons from *Life,*" *World* (February 13, 1973). *Life* later reappeared, but with a much different format.

43. John Tebbel, *History of Book Publishing in the United States,* is a four-volume effort (see bibliography for Chapter 2).

44. There were also older family names whose publishing companies had already survived for a century: John Wiley, 1807; Harper & Bros., 1817; Appleton, 1825; G. P. Putnam, 1836; Dodd of Dodd, Mead, 1839; Scribner's, 1842; A. S. Barnes, 1845; E. P. Dutton, 1852. After the Civil War came a Macmillan branch from England in 1869; Henry Holt & Co., 1871; Funk & Wagnalls and Thomas Y. Crowell, 1876; David McKay, 1882; Frank N. Doubleday's first firm, 1897; the McGraw and Hill firms in 1899 and 1902; and Prentice-Hall, 1913. In Boston, Little, Brown and Houghton Mifflin, dating from 1837 and 1848, respectively, rivaled the dominant New York firms and those in Philadelphia, led by J. B. Lippincott, 1836.

CHAPTER 15: A WORLD AT WAR

1. Erik Barnouw, *The Golden Web* (New York: Oxford University Press, 1968), p. 151.

2. William Manchester, *The Glory and the Dream* (Boston: Little, Brown, 1973), p. 273.

3. *Atlanta Constitution,* December 30, 1940, p. 1.

4. Manchester, *The Glory and the Dream,* p. 267.

5. Christopher H. Sterling and John M. Kittross, *Stay Tuned: A Concise History of American Broadcasting* (Belmont, CA: Wadsworth, 1978), p. 203.

6. Alf Pratte, "The *Honolulu Star-Bulletin* and the 'Day of Infamy,' " *American Journalism,* V (1988), 5.

7. Ernest D. Rose, "How the U.S. Heard about Pearl Harbor," *Journal of Broadcasting,* V (Fall 1961), 285–98.

8. Gordon W. Prague, *At Dawn We Slept* (New York: McGraw-Hill, 1981), p. 5.

9. Ibid., p. 583.

10. The activities of the Office of Censorship and the work of other individuals are described by Theodore F. Koop, an AP man and assistant to Price, in *Weapon of Silence* (Chicago: University of Chicago Press, 1946). John H. Sorrells, Nat. R. Howard, managing editor Jack Lockhart of the *Memphis Commercial Appeal,* and Koop were successive heads of the voluntary press-censorship division. J. Howard Ryan directed the radio division.

11. Elmer Davis, "OWI Has a Job," *Public Opinion Quarterly,* VII (Spring 1943), 8. For Davis's account of his stewardship, see "Report to the President," *Journalism Monographs,* No. 7 (August 1968), edited by Ronald T. Farrar. See also Robert L. Bishop and LaMar S. Mackay, "Government Information in World War II," *Journalism Monographs,* No. 19 (May 1971).

12. The OWI operated everywhere abroad except in Latin America, where Nelson Rockefeller's Office of the Coordinator of Inter-American Affairs held jurisdiction.

13. Jerome E. Edwards, *The Foreign Policy of Col. McCormick's Tribune, 1929–1941* (Reno: University of Nevada Press, 1971), pp. 176–179, 209.

14. There were many distinguished examples of war correspondence and many personal stories of performance in the face of danger by reporters. Pulitzer Prizes went to Larry Allen of the AP for his exploits with the British Mediterranean fleet; to Hal Boyle and Daniel De Luce of the AP European staff; to military analyst Hanson W. Baldwin of the *New York Times;* to Ira Wolfert of the North American Newspaper Alliance; to Mark S. Watson of the *Baltimore Sun;* to Homer Bigart of the *New York Herald Tribune;* to AP war photographers Frank Noel, Frank Filan, and Joe Rosenthal; and to Ernie Pyle of the Scripps Howard Newspaper Alliance. Clark Lee of the AP and Melville Jacoby of *Time* were among the newspeople who shared the dangers of the Bataan evacuation; Jacoby died later in a plane crash, but Lee survived to become an INS byline writer. Among other leading war reporters were Vern Haugland and Wes Gallagher of the AP, Quentin Reynolds of *Collier's,* Edward W. Beattie and Henry T. Gorrell of the UP, James Kilgallen and Richard Tregaskis of the INS, Drew Middleton of the *New York Times,* and Russell Hill of the *Herald Tribune.*

World War II also had women correspondents. The INS sent its featured writer, Inez Robb, to North Africa and Europe. Three other INS women war correspondents were Lee Carson with the U.S. First Army, Dixie Tighe with the British, and Rita Hume in Italy. Among the UP women correspondents were Eleanor Packard and Dudley Anne Harmon; the AP correspondents were Ruth Cowan and Bonnie Wiley in the field. Other correspondents were Helen Kirkpatrick, *Chicago Daily News;* Peggy Hull (Mrs. Harvey Deuel) of the *Cleveland Plain Dealer,* who had also served in World War I; Margaret Bourke-White, photographer for *Time* and *Life;* Iris Carpenter, *Boston Globe;* Marguerite Higgins, *New York Herald Tribune,* who became Berlin bureau chief, and Leah Burdette of *PM,* who lost her life in Iran.

15. Mark A. Stoler, *The Politics of the Second Front: American Military Planning and Diplomacy in Coalition Warfare, 1941–1943* (Westport, CT: Greenwood, 1977).

16. *St. Joseph's Gazette,* June 6, 1944, p. 1, a typical front page that day.

17. *San Francisco Chronicle,* February 19, 1945, p. 1.

18. For the full story, see Bernard Asbell, *When F.D.R. Died* (New York: Holt, Rinehart & Winston, 1961).

19. *New York Herald Tribune,* April 13, 1945, p. 1.

20. Martin J. Sherwin, *A World Destroyed: The Atomic Bomb and the Grand Alliance* (New York: Alfred A. Knopf, 1975); Martin J. Sherwin, *A World Destroyed: Hiroshima and the Origins of the Arms Race* (New York: Vintage, 1975).

21. *New York Times,* September 9, 1945, p. 1.

22. John McKechney, "The Pearl Harbor Controversy: A Debate Among Historians," *Monumenta Nipponica,* 18:1 (1963), pp. 45–88; Roberta A. Wohlstetter, *Pearl Harbor: Warning and Decision* (Stanford, CA: Stanford University Press, 1962).

23. Kenneth E. Shewmaker, *Americans and Chinese Communists, 1927–1945: A Persuading Encounter* (Ithaca, NY: Cornell University Press, 1971), pp. 320–21.

24. Other U.S. correspondents in China of the 1920s included Randall Gould, UP (later *Christian Science Monitor*); Edna Lee Booker and John Goette, INS; Charles Dailey, *Chicago Tribune;* Grover Clark, the *Monitor* and *Peking Leader;* and George Sokolsky. Other activist Shanghai papers included the *China Forum,* founded by Harold Isaacs in 1932, and the *Voice of China,* run by Max Granich.

25. Also in Chungking were Peggy Durdin and Shelley Mydans, both with *Time;* Leland Stowe, *Chicago Daily News;* Betty Graham, NEA; Walter Rundle and John Hlavacek, UP; Clyde Farnsworth, J. R. O'Sullivan, and Spencer Moosa, AP; Sonia Tamara, *New York Herald Tribune;* and Royal Arch Gunnison, *Collier's.* Harrison Forman of the *Times of London* and the *New York Herald Tribune* and Gunther Stein of the AP and the *London News Chronicle* led the 1944 trip to Yenan. In the theater were Darrel Berrigan and Hugh Crumpler of the UP; Frank L. Martin, Jr., of the AP; China-Burma-India, Eric Sevareid of CBS, and James R. Shepley of *Time.*

26. See Theodore White, *In Search of History* (New York: Harper & Row, 1978), pp. 254–58, and James C. Thomson, Jr., and Walter Sullivan, "China Reporting Revisited . . . The Crucial 1940s," *Nieman Reports,* XXXVII (Spring 1983), 30–34, a report on a 1982 reunion of surviving U.S. correspondents. Epstein also gave access to his papers from that conference. Other postwar correspondents included Walter Sullivan and Henry Lieberman, *New York Times,* Phillip Potter, *Baltimore Sun;* Pegge Parker Hlavacek, *New York Daily News;* and Hugh Deane, *Christian Science Monitor.*

27. *Washington Post,* November 1, 1948, p. 1.

28. *Life,* November 1, 1948, closing page.

29. *Washington Post,* November 4, 1948, p. 1.

30. James West Davidson et al., *Nation of Nations,* 2nd ed. (Boston: McGraw-Hill, 1999), pp. 101–103; William L. O'Neill, *American High: The Years of Confidence, 1945–1960* (New York: Free Press, 1986).

31. See Randall L. Murray, "Harry S. Truman and Press Opinion, 1945–53" (Ph.D. thesis, University of Minnesota, 1973).

32. Four of the dead were from the INS: Ray Richards and Frank Emery, correspondents, and Charles D. Rosecrans, Jr., and Ken Inouye, photographers. Nine of the total 18 died in front-line fighting, 9 in air crashes. Among them were Wilson Fielder, *Time-Life;* Charles O. Supple, *Chicago Sun-Times;* Albert Hinton, *Norfolk Journal and Guide,* the first black correspondent to lose his life covering a U.S. war; and Ernie Peeler, *Pacific Stars and Stripes.*

33. For an evaluation and account of the early weeks of the war coverage, see Michael Emery, *On the Front Lines* (Washington, DC: American University Press, 1995), Chapter 4.

34. The AP sent Relman Morin, Don Whitehead, and Hal Boyle, all veteran war reporters. Fred Sparks came to work with Keyes Beech for the *Chicago Daily News.* When the Pulitzer Prize committee met the following April they honored the *Herald Tribune,* the *Daily News,* and the AP by giving six awards to Bigart and Higgins, Beech and Sparks, Morin and Whitehead. (At that point in time, no one from the UP or the INS had ever won a Pulitzer Prize.) Later another Pulitzer award went to Max Desfor, AP photographer. Behind the correspondents at the front were the bureau chiefs in Tokyo: Earnest Hoberecht of the UP, Russell Brines of the AP, Howard Handleman of the INS, and William H. Lawrence coordinating for the *New York Times.*

35. In a letter to *Editor & Publisher,* LXXXIV (January 20, 1951), 7.

36. The text of the censorship code was carried in *Editor & Publisher,* LXXXIV (January 13, 1951), 8.

37. *New York Times,* April 6, 1951, p. 1.

38. *Chicago Tribune,* April 12, 1951, p. 1.

39. William L. O'Neill, "War in Korea." *American High.*

40. I. F. Stone, *The Hidden History of the Korean War* (New York: Monthly Review Press, 1952). See Chapter 18, "First Warnings," and Chapter 38, "Every Time Stalin Smiles."

CHAPTER 16: TELEVISION TAKES CENTER STAGE

1. William H. Chafe, "America Since 1945," in Eric Foner, ed. *The New American History,* rev. and exp. ed. (Philadelphia: Temple University Press, 1997), pp. 159–177.

2. Sig Mickelson, *The Electric Mirror: Politics in an Age of Television* (New York: Dodd, Mead 1972), offers an analysis of television's changing role in the campaigns of the 1950s and 1960s. As president of CBS News, Mickelson was involved with many of the decisions.

3. William Manchester, *The Glory and the Dream* (Boston: Little, Brown, 1973), gives a colorful description of the 1952 conventions and campaign in Chapter 19, "Right Turn." Television's first widescale convention coverage is also discussed in a number of broadcasting histories.

4. Erik Barnouw, *The Tube of Plenty: The Evolution of American Television* (New York: Oxford, 1975), pp. 137–39, includes quotations from the speech.

5. *New York Herald Tribune,* May 12, 1960, as quoted in James E. Pollard, *The Presidents and the Press: Truman to Johnson* (Washington, DC: Public Affairs Press, 1964).

6. See Godfrey Sperling, Jr.'s interview with Donovan, *Christian Science Monitor,* September 15, 1982 and Donovan's second volume on the Truman presidency, *Tumultuous Years* (New York: Norton, 1982). Donovan covered Washington for more than 20 years.

7. Two important revisionist works on Eisenhower are Stephen E. Ambrose, *Eisenhower,* 2 vols. (New York: Simon and Schuster, 1984) and Robert A. Divine, *Eisenhower and the Cold War* (New York: Oxford University Press, 1981).

8. For a complete description of the historic "freeze" and the FCC's comprehensive report, see Sydney W. Head, *Broadcasting in America* (Boston: Houghton Mifflin, 1976), pp. 162–69.

9. The best descriptions of the golden age of programming are found in Christopher H. Sterling and John M. Kittross, *Stay Tuned: A Concise History of American Broadcasting* (Belmont, CA: Wadsworth, 1978); Erik Barnouw, *The Tube of Plenty, The Golden Web* (New York: Oxford, 1968), and *The Image Empire* (New York: Oxford, 1970); and Lawrence W. Lichty and Malachi C. Topping, *American Broadcasting: A Source Book an the History of Radio and Television* (New York: Hastings House, 1975).

10. "The Case against Milo Radulovich, A0589839," *See It Now,* CBS News, October 20, 1953.

11. Alexander Kendrick, who for 20 years worked with Murrow, provides the full story of Murrow's life, including his many battles with CBS, in *Prime Time* (Boston: Little, Brown, 1969).

12. "Senator Joseph R. McCarthy," *See It Now,* CBS News, March 9, 1954.

13. John Crosby, television critic for the *New York Herald Tribune,* wrote, "*See It Now . . .* is by every criterion television's most brilliant, most decorated, most imaginative, most courageous and most important program. The fact that CBS cannot afford it but can afford *Beat the Clock* is shocking." Cited by Erik Barnouw, *The Image Empire* (New York: Oxford University Press, 1970), p. 116. For a critical look at the world of William S. Paley, Frank Stanton, and CBS News from the Murrow years through Cronkite, see David Halberstam, *The Powers That Be* (New York: Knopf, 1979).

14. For a poignant remembrance of Murrow, see Edward Bliss, Jr., "Remembering Edward R. Murrow," *Saturday Review* (May 31, 1975), 17.

15. *I. F. Stone's Weekly,* July 19, 1954, p. 1.

16. David Halberstam, *The Powers That Be* (New York: Knopf, 1979), p. 422. In addition to the Kintner story, of interest is the role played at CBS by producer Don Hewitt, who was instrumental at the conventions, with the *See It Now* series and later with *60 Minutes.*

17. *TV Guide,* July 1, 1967, as cited by Erik Barnouw, *The Image Empire,* p. 301.

18. Alan J. Gould, sports editor since 1932, served as executive editor from 1941 to 1963. Lloyd Stratton directed the AP service abroad until Stanley Swinton was named director of the World Service in 1960, to serve until 1982. Also, the names of the AP staff should not be ignored. Serving in Washington were such newspeople as David Lawrence, who left the AP to become a columnist and news magazine publisher, and Stephen T. Early, who became President Franklin D. Roosevelt's press secretary. Pulitzer Prize winners of the 1930s were Francis A. Jamieson, who covered the Lindbergh baby kidnapping story; Howard W. Blakeslee, AP science editor; and Louis P. Lochner, Berlin bureau chief. Among other noted byliners were Edward J. Neil, killed during the Spanish Civil War; Hal Boyle, whose featurized stories were religiously run as columns by small, rank-and-file dailies; the tenaciously hard-working Marvin Arrowsmith, whose fate was to duel with the UP's flamboyant Merriman Smith on the White House beat during the 1950s before becoming Washington bureau chief; longtime European correspondent Eddy Gilmore; and special correspondent Saul Pett. Other major AP figures through the 1950s included general news editors Paul Mickelson and Samuel G. Blackman, foreign editor Ben Bassett, political writer Jack Bell, and news analyst John Hightower.

Other major AP figures have included general news editor Rene Cappon, foreign editor Nate Polowetsky, Washington bureau chief William L. Beale, Jr., White House correspondents Ernest B. Vaccaro and Frank Cormier, political writers Douglas Cornell and Relman Morin, news analysts J. M. Roberts, Jr., and William L. Ryan, special correspondent George Cornell, and court trial specialist Linda Deutsch. Some noted byliners were Brian Bell, Larry Allen, Daniel De Luce, Lloyd Lehrbas, Don Whitehead, Edward Kennedy, C. Yates McDaniel, Malcolm Browne, and Peter Arnett. Overseas correspondents have been W. F. Caldwell, Richard O'Regan, Henry Bradsher, Richard K. O'Malley, and David Mason in Europe; Lynn Heinzerling and son Larry Heinzerling in Africa, Nick Lundington in the Middle East, Myron Belkind in India, and George Esper in Asia.

19. David Shaw, "The AP: It's Everywhere and Powerful," *Los Angeles Times,* April 3, 1988, pp. 1, 22.

20. Winning wide respect for their work for the UP were Lyle Wilson, Washington bureau chief, Harrison Salisbury, wartime foreign-news editor who won fame with the *New York Times;* Walter Cronkite, who was a wartime London correspondent before he joined CBS; diplomatic reporters Stewart Hensley in Washington and K. C. Thaler in London; Supreme Court reporter Charlotte Moulton; European news chiefs Virgil Pinkley and Daniel Gilmore; George Marder, whose "Under the Capitol Dome" was a broadcast feature from 1945 to the late 1970s; and foreign editors Joe Alex Morris and Phil Newsome. Russell Jones won a 1957 Pulitzer Prize for covering the Budapest uprising. Reynolds and Eleanor Packard were a colorful overseas reporting team.

Other major UP figures were Frank Tremaine, war correspondent and longtime executive; Washington bureau chiefs Julius Fransden and Grant Dillman; political writers Raymond Lahr and Richard Growald; women's editor Gay Pauley; and European news chiefs Harry Ferguson and Julius B. Humi. Reporting abroad in the 1940s were Frederick C. Oechsner, Ralph Heinzen, Phillip H. Ault, Edward W. Beattie, M. S. Handler, William F. Tyree, William B. Dickinson, and H. D. Quigg. Byliners abroad in the 1950s and 1960s included Joseph W. Grigg, Norman Montellier, Frederick Kuh, A. L. Bradford, W. R. Higginbotham, Joseph W. Morgan, H. R. Ekins, Henry Gorrell, Robert Musel, and Jack Fox. Also prominent for the INS were Arthur "Bugs" Baer, Louella Parsons, and Edwin C. Hill. The Hearst organization killed its morning-paper news agency, Universal News Service, in 1937, and gave business control of the INS first to Joseph V. Connolly and, after 1945, to Seymour Berkson.

The INS foreign service developed stature by the 1930s. Among its leaders were J. C. Oestreicher, foreign editor; Pierre J. Huss, Berlin bureau chief; and J. Kingsbury Smith, who became European general manager. Top World War II correspondents were Howard Handleman, Kenneth Downs, Merrill Mueller, George Lait, Graham Hovey, Frank Conniff, Richard Tregaskis, Lee Van Atta, and Clarke Lee. In

Washington were George R. Holmes, William K. Hutchinson, George E. Durno, and Robert G. Nixon. Among the INS women correspondents, Rose McKee achieved prominence for political reporting.

21. For an account of the USIA from 1948 to 1960, see Wilson P. Dizard, *The Strategy of Truth* (Washington, DC: Public Affairs Press, 1960). Analysis of the ups and downs is given by Ronald I. Rubin, *The Objectives of the U.S. Information Agency: Controversies and Analysis* (New York: Praeger, 1968).

22. J. A. R. Pimlott, *Public Relations and American Democracy* (Princeton, NJ: Princeton University Press, 1951), p. 3.

23. *Proceedings of Minnesota Public Relations Forum* (Minneapolis: Public Relations Society and participating company, 1952–55).

24. A revival of the *Post* as a quarterly, using its old-time flavor and material, appeared on newsstands in 1971; this was succeeded by a monthly version in 1977.

25. William H. Taft, *American Magazines in the 1980s* (New York: Hastings House, 1982), p. 242. This work deals with more than 650 magazines, offering historical background on all leading magazines as well as advertising trends.

26. John Tebbel, *A History of Book Publishing in the United States,* vol. 4 (New York: R. R. Bowker Company, 1981), p. 109. This volume, which covers 1940 to 1980, is part of two decades of research leading to this monumental set of books.

27. Ibid., p. 165.

28. The first softcover books appeared in 1842. From 1870 to 1890 there was great interest in dime novels and other paperbacks. The third wave of interest came with Pocket Books.

29. *A Ten-Year View of Public Attitudes Toward Television and Other Mass Media,* 1959–68, a report by Roper Research Associates, pp. 4–5.

CHAPTER 17: CHALLENGES AND DISSENT

1. The most descriptive account of the Kennedy-Nixon encounters is found in Theodore H. White, *The Making of the President 1960* (New York: Atheneum, 1961). See also Sig Mickelson, *The Electric Mirror: Politics in an Age of Television* (New York: Dodd, Mead, 1972), for an explanation of Nixon's poor performance and of various camera and lighting techniques agreed to by the two sides.

2. W. A. Swanberg, *Luce and His Empire* (New York: Scribner's, 1972), pp. 412–16. The influence of Joseph Kennedy, Sr., is clearly demonstrated.

3. Merriman Smith, United Press International, November 23, 1963.

4. The videotape recorder, produced by Ampex in 1956, was first used that year by Huntley and Brinkley, who played back President Eisenhower's inauguration speech. CBS developed the sports "instant replay" in 1963.

5. *Life,* October 2, 1964, p. 41. See also *Life,* November 25, 1966, p. 53, and November 24, 1967, pp. 87–95, and *Saturday Evening Post,* December 2, 1967, p. 27.

6. For a complete analysis of the social movements of the 1960s, see Mayer N. Zald and John D. McCarthy, *The Dynamics of Social Movements* (Cambridge: Winthrop, 1979). The role of NOW is discussed on pp. 176–82.

7. See Leonard Zeidenberg, "Lessons of a Living Room War," *Broadcasting* (May 19, 1975), for an analysis of reporting achievements.

8. This study was conducted by Edwin Diamond, then codirector of the Network News Study Group at the Massachusetts Institute of Technology, and his students in 1973.

9. CBS News, July 20, 1969.

10. Other CBS reporters included Bob Schieffer, Bill Henry, Robert Pierpoint, Martin Agronsky, Winston Burdett, Morton Dean, Phil Jones, Michelle Clark, Sylvia Chase, Ed Rabel, Richard Threlkeld, Joe Benti, Susan Peterson, Sharon Lovejoy, Heywood Hale Broun, Susan Spencer, Renee Poussaint, and Connie Chung.

11. For a long interview with Chancellor, see Philip Noble, "The Cool and Confident Anchorman," *MORE* (May 1976), 7. Also see Barbara Matusow, "Intrigue at NBC," *Washington Journalism Review* (July–August, 1983), pp. 50–62.

12. NBC News, December 20, 1965, McGee, along with CBS's Morley Safer, was one of the first broadcasters to openly question the United States role. Jerry Jacobs produced the Vietnam segments and wrote much of the script. The program was aired after discussion within NBC News about the conclusion.

13. Other NBC radio and television reporters and commentators were Edwin Newman, the veteran who anchored many NBC specials; Joseph C. Harsch, Irving R. Levine, Elie Abel, Hugh Downs, Ray Scherer, Herbert Kaplow, Tom Pettit, Robert Goralski, Peter Hackes, Clifton Utley, Morgan Beatty, Merrill Mueller, and Garrick Utley. Also prominent were Richard Valeriani, Bob Jamieson, Ford Rowan, John Hart, David Burrington, Floyd Kalber, Don Oliver, Jack Reynolds, John Dancy, Douglas Kiker, Richard Hunt, and Frank Blair.

14. "The New Look of TV News," *Newsweek* October 11, 1976, p. 76.

15. *Forbes,* December 7, 1981, p. 133.

16. Other leading correspondents on the team originally built by James C. Hagerty and later Elmer Lower and William Sheehan included Edward P. Morgan, William H. Lawrence, John Scali, Robert Clark, White House reporter Tom Jarriel, Peter Jennings, Peter Clapper, Aline Saarinen and Esther Tufty (both on the air early), Judy Woodruff, Linda Ellerbee, Carole Simpson, and Betty Rollins.

17. *The Making of a Quagmire,* by David Halberstam (New York: Random House, 1965), sets this tone. Halberstam, the Pulitzer Prize–winning correspondent of the *New York Times* in Vietnam, forecast the tragedy.

18. Dale Minor, *The Information War* (New York: Hawthorn Books and Tower Publications, 1970), pp. 29–34. Minor, who finds both heroes and villains in the Saigon press corps,

dismisses the war correspondents of earlier wars as "team players" who accepted the official "line" and the necessity of the war itself. His analysis of the conflict between press and government in Vietnam, and between moral philosophies and concerns for humanity, is perceptive.

19. *Newsweek,* October 7, 1963, pp. 98–99; Malcolm W. Browne, "Viet Nam Reporting: Three Years of Crisis," *Columbia Journalism Review,* III (Fall 1964), 4.

20. *Time,* September 20, 1963, p. 62, and October 11, 1963, p. 55.

21. *Time,* October 14, 1966, p. 58.

22. As reported in the *Chicago Daily News,* October 26, 1966, p. 1. For a series of front pages depicting the Indochina war, see Michael C. Emery, et al., *America's Front Page News, 1690–1970* (New York: Doubleday, 1970).

23. Minor, *The Information War,* pp. 95–100: *Newsweek,* November 13, 1967, pp. 68–69.

24. As quoted in William Small, *To Kill a Messenger* (New York: Hastings House, 1970), p. 211.

25. Ibid., p. 214.

26. Ibid., p. 216.

27. Robert Glessing, *The Underground Press in America* (Bloomington: Indiana University Press, 1970).

28. In addition to numerous articles and books by Stone and Carey McWilliams, see Leonard Downie, *The New Muckrakers* (Washington, DC: New Republic, 1977), which examines their work and that of other leading investigative reporters.

29. Nancy L. Roberts, *Dorothy Day and the "Catholic Worker"* (State University of New York Press, 1984).

30. An early use of the term was in Matthew Arnold's attack against a plan for Irish home rule and the British journalists who supported it, found in his "Up to Easter," *Nineteenth Century* (May 1887), 638–39.

31. See Tom Wolfe, "The Birth of 'The New Journalism': Eyewitness Report by Tom Wolfe," *New York* (February 14, 1972). For useful overview of history, terms, and definitions, consult Thomas B. Connery, "Discovering a Literary Form" (introductory essay) in Connery, ed., *A Sourcebook of American Literary Journalism: Representative Writers in an Emerging Genre* (Westport, CN: Greenwood Press, 1992), pp. 3–28. For a breakdown of different types of new journalism writing and a discussion of leading proponents, see also Everette Dennis and William Rivers, *Other Voices: The New Journalism in America* (San Francisco: Canfield, 1974).

32. *Editor & Publisher,* August 8, 1970, p. 45.

33. As quoted by L. F. Palmer, Jr., "The Black Press in Transition," in Michael Emery and Ted C. Smythe, *Readings in Mass Communication* (Dubuque: William C. Brown, 1972), p. 226.

34. *Editor & Publisher,* September 7, 1991, p. 37. The annual edition of the *Editor & Publisher International Year-Book* carries a list of all black newspapers, The regular compiler was Henry G. LaBrie III.

35. Richard L. Beard and Cyril E. Zoerner II, "Associated Negro Press: Its Founding, Ascendency and Demise," *Jour-*

nalism Quarterly, XLVI (Spring 1969), 47. Also see C. S. K. Jameson and C. E. Zoerner, Jr., "History Overlooked: The Associated Negro Press," *The Journalist* (October, 1986), 18.

36. See Henry G. LaBrie III, "A Survey of Black Newspapers in America," *presstime* October 1980, p. 54. See also *Perspectives on the Black Press 1974* (Kennnebunkport, ME: Mercer House Press, 1974), and *The Black Press: A Guide* (Iowa City: University of Iowa Press, 1970).

37. Félix Gutiérrez, "Latinos and the Media," in Emery and Smythe, *Readings in Mass Communication.* This article is a complete description of the history and current status of Latino media, based on the author's extensive research.

38. Native American Journalists Association *Media List,* 1999. See the various publications of the Native American community, including *The Native American Press Association Newsletter, The American Native Press Archives, Native Press Research Journal* (affiliated with the American Native Press Research Association), and *American Indian and Alaska Native Newspapers and Periodicals, 1826–1985* (Westport, CN: Greenwood, 1985). In addition there was a flourishing literary press with a history dating to 1826. See *American Native Press Archives* (Spring 1986). Important is James E. and Sharon Murphy, *Let My People Know: American Indian Journalism 1828–1978* (Norman: University of Oklahoma Press, 1981), which was the first comprehensive synthesis.

39. *Editor & Publisher,* November 23, 1985, p. 38.

40. Rodger Streitmatter, *Unspeakable: The Rise of the Gay and Lesbian Press in America* (Boston: Faber and Faber, 1995), p. 339.

41. See Rodger Streitmatter, "The *Advocate:* Setting the Standard for the Gay Liberation Press," *Journalism History* (Vol. 19, No. 3, Autumn 1993); Deirdre Carmody, "New Gay Press is Emerging, Claiming Place in Mainstream," *New York Times,* March 2, 1992.

42. Jennifer Juarez Robles, "Out of the Newsroom: How Gay and Lesbian Journalists Are Changing Mainstream Media," *Extra!* (June 1993), p. 19.

43. Stuart Elliott, " 'Hot Editor' Phenomenon Benefits the *New Republic,*" *New York Times,* March 26, 1992.

44. *Village Voice,* December 6, 1994, p. 17.

CHAPTER 18: A CRISIS OF CREDIBILITY

1. Dennis T. Lowry, "Agnew and the Network TV News: A Before/After Content Analysis," *Journalism Quarterly,* XLVIII (Summer 1971), 205.

2. See Don R. Pember, "The 'Pentagon Papers' Decision: More Questions Than Answers," *Journalism Quarterly,* XLVIII (Autumn 1971), 403, whose conclusions were endorsed by other mass-communications law scholars.

3. *The New York Times Company* v. *United States* and *United States* v. *The Washington Post Company,* 403 U.S. 713 (1971). The government soon admitted its error by selling 43 volumes of the Pentagon Papers from its Printing Office to all comers.

4. *Bantam Books Inc.* v. *Sullivan,* 372 U.S. 58 (1963).

5. *Organization for a Better Austin* v. *Keefe,* 402 U.S. 215 (1971).

6. The public record is found in *Watergate: The Chronology of a Crisis* (Washington, DC: Congressional Quarterly, 1975), a documentary review of the impartial and authoritative research organization.

7. For background on the Nixon years, see the Bibliography for this chapter. In particular, see David Wise, *The Politics of Lying,* for a detailed examination of wide-scale government deceit over two decades.

8. The recipient of one news leak was William Beecher of the *New York Times,* who reported on May 9, 1969, that secret B-52 raids were being conducted in Cambodia. The full story did not emerge until 1973. See the journalism review *MORE* (October 1973, p. 17). Other reporters claimed that they knew of the Cambodian bombings but did not consider them major news. After the one story in the *New York Times,* only *Newsweek,* once in its news-brief section, mentioned the bombing during the 14-month period.

9. O'Brien was a likely target because of his friendship with Edward Kennedy, his demands for investigation of the ITT case, and his possible knowledge of a $100,000 contribution given to Nixon's friend Charles ("Bebe") Rebozo by billionaire Howard Hughes that was not passed on to CREEP. A 1971 memo from Nixon to Haldeman, released in 1987, suggested the need for more information about O'Brien's public relations contract with Hughes; this was for possible use in the 1972 campaign.

10. Edwin Diamond's 1973 study was part of an effort by the Network News Study Group at MIT, of which he was codirector. See also Edward J. Epstein, "How the Press Handled the Watergate Scandal," *Los Angeles Times,* September 14, 1973.

11. Dan Rather and Gary Paul Gates, *The Palace Guard* (New York: Harper & Row, 1974), pp. 182–83. Rather, the former CBS White House correspondent, takes a critical look at the inner working of Nixon's operations.

12. J. Anthony Lukas, *Nightmare: The Underside of the Nixon Years* (New York: Viking Press, 1976), p. 3. Lukas, whose remarkable Watergate account filled an entire *New York Times Magazine* issue in July 1973, comprehensively documents all of the Watergate-related incidents and the administration's fear that radicals might disclose some "really damaging secrets" or pass them to the Soviets (p. 71).

13. Opinion Section, *Los Angeles Times,* July 29, 1973, p. 1. The story originally appeared in the *Washington Post* and was distributed to United States and foreign clients by the *Los Angeles Times–Washington Post* News Service.

14. The UPI team included Bryce Miller, Alvin Webb, and Dan Southerland. William Tuohy won a Pulitzer Prize for his reporting for the *Los Angeles Times.* Sydney Schanberg of the *New York Times* won the Pulitzer Prize for his coverage of the surrender in Cambodia. Peter Braestrup divided four years between the *New York Times* and *Washington Post.* Charles Mohr of the *New York Times* won high praise. Richard Critchfield won distinction for the *Washington Star.* CBS reporters producing field reports and documentaries included Peter Kalischer, Morley Safer, John Laurence, Don Webster, Dan Rather, and Murray Fromson. Among others reporting for NBC were Frank McGee, Ron Nessen, Kenley Jones, and Howard Truckner; for ABC, Dan North and Roger Peterson. In Cambodia were Laurence Stern, *Washington Post;* Henry Kamm, *New York Times;* Raymond Coffey, *Chicago Daily News;* the indefatigable Arnett of the AP; and two who were captured and released, Richard Dudman, *St. Louis Post-Dispatch,* and Elizabeth Pond, *Christian Science Monitor.* There were other women correspondents, including the *New York Times's* Gloria Emerson; Elaine Shepard of Mutual; columnist Georgie Anne Geyer; freelancer Helen Musgrove; magazine journalist Frances FitzGerald; ABC's Marlene Sanders; and Maggie Kilgore, Betty Halstead, and Kate Webb of the UPI. Webb and Michele Ray, a French freelancer, were captured and released. Philippa Schuyler of the *Manchester Union-Leader* died in a 1967 helicopter crash.

15. As quoted by Phillip Knightley in *The First Casualty* (New York: Harcourt Brace Jovanovich, 1975), p. 423.

16. The conference, the only such gathering held in the post-Vietnam era, was held at the University of Southern California. The proceedings were videotaped for later release. Many of the 85 participants were journalists. See Fox Butterfield, "The New Vietnam Scholarship," *New York Times Magazine,* February 13, 1983.

17. Peter Braestrup, *Big Story* (New Haven: Yale University Press, 1977). Braestrup claimed that shocked Saigon reporters overreacted to the Communist attack and that some confused Saigon and Washington officials added to a distortion of reality. See also Braestrup's letter to the editor, *ASNE Bulletin,* April 1978, p. 20, defending his work.

18. See Michael Anderegg, ed., *Inventing Vietnam: The War in Film and Television* (Philadelphia: Temple University press, 1991).

19. Richard Nixon, *The Memoirs* (New York: Grosset and Dunlap, 1978), p. 350.

20. Bruce Cumings, *War and Television* (New York: Verso, 1992) p. 84; Clarence R. Wyatt, *Paper Soldiers: The American Press and the Vietnam War* (New York: W. W. Norton, 1993) p. 7.

21. New York: Oxford University Press, 1986.

22. Berkeley: University of California Press, 1980.

23. Melvin Small, *Covering Dissent: The Media and the Anti-Vietnam War Movement* (New Brunswick, NJ: Rutgers University Press, 1994).

24. Brigitte Lebens Nacos, *The Press, Presidents, and Crises* (New York: Oxford University Press, 1990), p. 187.

25. Roger Morris, "Foreign Policy Reporting: Quarantined for the Campaign," *Columbia Journalism Review* (November–December 1976), 19.

26. Timothy Crouse, *The Boys on the Bus* (New York: Random House, 1973). Other regulars included Jules Witcover, who left the *Los Angeles Times* to join the *Washington Post,* a veteran of more than 25 years; Haynes Johnson of the *Washington Post,* a leader in reporting voter preferences; Jack Germond, another 25-year veteran who headed Gannett's coverage before becoming chief political writer for the

Washington Star; the old reliable of the *Baltimore Sun,* Phil Potter; James McCartney of the Knight newspapers; Curtis Wilkie, who made his mark in 1972 with Wilmington's *News Journal* and later became the *Boston Globe*'s White House correspondent; Kenneth Reich of the *Los Angeles Times,* who gained attention during the 1976 campaign; and Jim Perry of the *National Observer.* Eleanor Randolph of the *Chicago Tribune* and Roger Simon of the *Chicago Sun-Times* were cited for their 1976 stories.

Dozens of correspondents reported for the press associations and television networks. Walter Mears, Saul Pett, and Karl Leubsdorf of the AP, and Arnold Sawislak, Clay Richards and Steve Gerstel of the United Press International had leading bylines. On television in 1976, CBS's Ed Bradley, ABC's Sam Donaldson, and NBC's Judy Woodruff and Don Oliver led in covering Carter. Tom Jarriel, ABC, Phil Jones, CBS, and Bob Jamieson, NBC, followed Ford. Cassie Mackin, NBC, Ann Compton, ABC, and Sharon Lovejoy, CBS, were active on camera.

27. Peggy Noonan, *What I Saw at the Revolution* (New York: Random House, 1990); Mark Hertsgaard, *On Bended Knee: The Press and the Reagan Presidency* (New York: Farrar, Straus & Giroux, 1989).

28. John W. Mashek, with Lawrence T. McGill and Adam Clayton Powell III, *Lethargy '96: How the Media Covered a Listless Campaign* (Arlington, VA: The Freedom Forum, 1997).

29. *New York Times,* January 21, 1981, p. 1.

30. *Los Angeles Times.* March 19, 1982, p. 10.

31. *Editor & Publisher,* October 9, 1982, reported that the *New York Times* had not been granted a one-on-one interview even though such success had been given to the *Washington Times,* the paper owned by the "Moonies." Ranking reporters were quoted on the access problem. See also *Editor & Publisher,* April 9, 1983.

32. *Los Angeles Times,* January 24, 1982, Opinion Section, p. 2.

33. Robert Scheer, *With Enough Shovels: Reagan, Bush, & Nuclear War* (New York: Random House, 1982).

34. Phil Kerby, "When Reagan Chides the Press, There's a Difference," *Los Angeles Times,* April 14, 1983, Part II, p. 1.

35. The development of Reagan's "performer's magic" from boyhood to the presidency is traced by Garry Wills in *Reagan's America* (New York: Doubleday & Company, 1987). Also see Leon Wieseltier, "What Went Wrong: An Appraisal of Reagan's Foreign Policy," *The New York Times Magazine,* December 7, 1986, p. 43.

36. The Washington bureau of the *Los Angeles Times,* led by the reporting of Doyle McManus, distinguished itself during these days with several exclusive stories. Also see the *Chicago Tribune* of November 16, 1986, which featured major investigative efforts on both the illegal covert operations and Israel's campaign to steal U.S. secrets.

37. Transcript of presidential news conference, November 19, 1986.

38. Ibid.

39. *New York Times,* November 26, 1986, p. 26.

40. *Harper's,* February 1986, p. 8.

41. See Seymour M. Hersh, "Did They Protect Reagan?" *The New York Times Sunday Magazine,* April 29, 1990, p. 47. For the emerging of the "guns for no hostages deal" information, see Gary Sick's "The Election Story of the Decade," *New York Times,* April 15, 1991, p. A15; Robert Parry's investigation on PBS's *Frontline,* April 16, 1991; a series of articles by Joel Bleifuss in *In These Times* beginning with "Did Reagan Steal the 1980 Election," June 24, 1987, and including "Truth: The Last Hostage," April 17, 1991; various columns by Christopher Hitchens in *The Nation;* and Barbara Honegger's book *October Surprise.*

42. The Pentagon later confirmed that the U.S. came dangerously close to having its assault aircraft shot down in the opening minutes of the invasion. Aboard were more than 300 U.S. Rangers. This was only two days after the 241 U.S. Marines were killed in Beirut. See Michael Emery, "The Grenada Story That No One Wanted," in Michael Emery and Ted Curtis Smythe, eds., *Readings in Mass Communication* (Dubuque, IA: William C. Brown Co., 1992).

43. See William A. Dorman, "Peripheral Vision: U.S. Journalism and the Third World," *World Policy Journal,* III (Summer 1986). Cited on the issue of Latin American coverage is Joseph P. Lyford's critical assessment, "The Times and Latin America" (Freedom of Information Center, Publication No. 93, School of Journalism, University of Missouri). Also see Tad Szulc, "Government Deception, Disinformation, Delusion," *Los Angeles Times* Opinion Section, November 2, 1986, p. 3. Szulc is a former *New York Times* reporter.

44. See "Sandinista Foreign Policy: Strategies for Survival," *NACLA Report on the Americas,* XIX (May–June 1985), 18, which includes a historical introduction and a thorough discussion of the role of *Sandinismo* in Nicaraguan society.

45. See John Britton, "Carleton Beals and Central America after Sandino: Struggle to Publish," *Journalism Quarterly,* LX (Summer 1983), 240. In a similar case William Krehm of *Time,* a reporter in Central America and the Caribbean, published a controversial book in Spanish about the region in 1948, containing some information turned down by timid *Time* editors because it might offend the government and large corporations. The book finally appeared in English in 1984 as *Democracies and Tyrannies of the Caribbean.*

46. See Marlene Dixon and Susanne Jones, eds., *Nicaragua under Siege* (San Francisco: Synthesis Publications, 1984); and Marlene Dixon, ed., *On Trial: Reagan's War against Nicaragua* (San Francisco: Synthesis Publications, 1985). Also see Noam Chomsky, *Turning the Tide: U.S. Intervention in Central America and the Struggle for Peace* (Boston: South End Press, 1985), which cites many media sources.

47. See Michael Emery, "Contragate: The Costa Rican Connection," *San Francisco Bay Guardian,* December 3, 1986, p. 1, which details the investigation of journalists Martha Honey and Tony Avirgan into the Contras and their lawsuit in Miami against Contra leaders and U.S. accom-

plices accused of murder and drug-running. Also see *San Francisco Bay Guardian* articles by Michael Emery, February 4 and May 27, 1987; by Michael Emery, Martha Honey, and Tony Avirgan, April 1, 1987; and by Martha Honey, May 27, 1987. The *Bay Guardian's* four-part examination of this wide-ranging conspiracy was unmatched for detail.

48. Martha Honey and Tony Avirgan, "The Carlos File," *Nation* (October 5, 1985); Martha Honey and Tony Avirgan, *La Penca: Pastora, the Press and the CIA* (published in Spanish in Lima, Peru, 1985); Joel Millman, "Whodunit: The Pastora Bombing," *Columbia Journalism Review* (March–April 1986); Jacqueline Sharkey, "Disturbing the Peace," *Common Cause* (September–October 1985); Robert Parry, Brian Barger, and Murray Waas, "The Secret Contra War," *New Republic* (November 24, 1986); and the script for the June 25, 1986, segment of *West 57th St.* containing interviews with participants in the Contra supply operation. In 1993 journalists agreed that the La Penca bomber was working with the Sandinista organization; a CIA tie was not clear. See the *Miami Herald*, August 8, 1993, p. 1; *San Francisco Chronicle*, August 9, 1993, Foreign News Section. For the La Penca story see Martha Honey's *Hostile Acts: U.S. Policy in Costa Rica in the 1980s* (Gainesville: University Press of Florida, 1994).

49. *Nicaragua* v. *U.S.A.* (International Court of Justice: The Hague, The Netherlands, June 27, 1986).

50. See editorial, *Los Angeles Times*, December 26, 1986.

51. Joe Klein, "Our Man in Managua," *Esquire* (November 1986), p. 103; and Michael Emery, interview with Kinzer in Managua, July 1986.

52. Chris Hedges of the *Dallas Morning News*, Joanne Omang of the *Washington Post* and the *Post's* stringer John Lantigua, Dennis Volman of the *Christian Science Monitor*, Andrew Maykuth of the *Philadelphia Inquirer*, William Gasperini of *In These Times*, freelancers Nancy Nusser and June Erlick, and Mary Jo McConahay of Pacific News Service made valuable contributions. So did Anne-Marie O'Connor of Reuters, based in Honduras, and Marc Cooper, Frank Smyth, and Chris Norton in El Salvador. Among other newspapers the *Boston Globe* had strong coverage and op-ed page analysis, with Pamela Constable contributing to both. The AP had veteran Reid Miller, based in San Jose, as its roving correspondent., The AP had a two-person bureau in Managua. Tracy Wilkinson set up the UPI's two-person Managua bureau in 1985 and later joined the *Los Angeles Times*. Both services relied heavily on nationals, full-time and stringers. Only a few of the Central American press association reporters were U.S. citizens. Of the television reporters, Peter Collins of ABC had logged five years of Central American work by 1986; Leigh Green of CNN was known for his even-handed treatment; Jamie Gangel made several trips for NBC; and Mike O'Connor was in action for CBS.

Among other El Salvador correspondents winning attention were Loren Jenkins, *Washington Post*; Raymond Bonner, *New York Times*; Anne Nelson, freelancer and *Nation* writer; Geri Smith and Cindy Karp, UPI; Hilary Brown, ABC News; Zoe Trujillo, CNN; Susan Meiselas, once-wounded Magnum photographer; and James Dickson, *Dallas Times Herald*, who won the 1983 Pulitzer Prize for feature photography.

53. A statistical breakdown of the expanding U.S. aid to the region is found in Barry and Deb Preusch, *The Central America Fact Book* (New York: Grove Press, 1986), Chapter 3.

54. One episode is found in Alexander Cockburn's "Beat the Devil" column in *Nation* (June 1, 1985), p. 662, in which he compares coverage about the bombings. Also see "Behind the Death Squads," *Progressive* (May, 1984), for an extensive examination of the U.S. role that began in the early 1960s.

55. Charles Clements, *Witness to War* (New York: Bantam, 1984). The Epilogue contains quotations from dozens of stories written about El Salvador. In 1992 a U.N.-supported truth commission said the January 1982 stories about a massacre at El Mozote filed by Bonner and the *Washington Post's* Alma Guillermoprieto were accurate. See the *New York Times*, October 22, 1992, p. 4. In its December 6, 1993, issue the *New Yorker* filled almost the entire magazine with Mark Danner's "The Truth of El Mozote," complete with Susan Meiselas's original photographs. Tim McCoy of California State University, Hayward authored a scathing criticism, "The *New York Times'* Coverage of El Salvador," in *Newspaper Research Journal* (Summer 1992).

56. *New York Times*, April 2, 1989, p. 30.

57. See Mark Cooper, "The Press and the Panama Invasion," *The Nation*, June 18, 1990, p. 850.

58. *New York Times*, April 19, 1990, p. 19.

59. David K. Shipler, *Arab and Jew: Wounded Spirits in a Promised Land* (New York: Times Books, 1986) p. 39. This is a monumental reporting effort by a neutral party, non-Arab and non-Jew, the *Times* correspondent in Jerusalem; it is excellent on recent history. Also see the writings of Edward W. Said, including *After the Last Sky: Palestinian Lives* (New York: Pantheon Books, 1986) and *The Israel-Arab Reader*, eds. Walter Laqueur and Barry Rubin (New York: Penguin Books, 1985). Also, Michael Emery, interview with Israeli military historian and journalist Uri Milstein, Jerusalem, July 30, 1987.

60. See the studies of Janice Terry and Michael Suleiman in various publications, including *Arabs in America: Myths and Realities* (The Medina University Press International, 1975); for other books also see Noam Chomsky, *The Fateful Triangle* (Boston: South End Press, 1983); Jack Shaheen, *The TV Arab* (Bowling Green, Ohio: Bowling Green University, Popular Press, 1984); Issam S. Mousa, *The Arab Image in the U.S. Press* (New York: Peter Lang Publishers, Inc., 1984); Russ Braley, *Bad News: The Foreign Policy of the New York Times* (Chicago: Regnary Gateway, 1984); and Howard Davis and Paul Walton, ed., *Language, Image, Media* (New York: St. Martin's Press, 1983).

Terry conducted three content analyses of Arab-Israeli coverage from 1948 to 1974. See Abdeen Jabara and Janice Terry, eds., *The Arab World from Nationalism to Revolution* (The Medina University Press International, 1971), pp. 94–113, and "1973 U.S. Press Coverage of the Middle East," *Journal of Palestine Studies* (Autumn 1974), 120. In four studies Suleiman focused on the Arab image in news magazines during the 1956, 1967, and 1973 crises. See "An Evaluation of Middle East Coverage in Seven American News-Magazines," *Middle East Forum* (Autumn 1965), 9; "American Mass Media and the Time Conflict," in Ibrahim Abu-Lughod, ed., *The Arab Perspective* (Chicago: Northwestern University Press, 1970), pp. 138–154; "National Stereotypes as Weapons in the Arab-Israeli Conflict," *Journal of Palestinian Studies* (Spring 1974), 109.

Also see Janice Monti Belkaoui, "Images of Arabs and Israelis in the Prestige Press, 1966–1974," *Journalism Quarterly,* LVI (Winter 1979), 732; Robert H. Trice, "The American Elite Press and the Arab-Israeli Conflict," *The Middle East Journal* (Summer 1979), 304; David Daugherty and Michael Warden, "Prestige Press Editorial Treatment of the Mid-East during 11 Crisis Years," *Journalism Quarterly,* LVI (Winter 1979), 776; V. M. Mishra, "News from the Middle East in Five U.S. Media," *Journalism Quarterly,* LVI (Summer 1979), 374; Daniel Sneebny "American Correspondents in the Middle East, Perceptions and Problems," *Journalism Quarterly,* LVI (Summer, 1979), 386; and Beverly S. Marcus, *The Changing Image of the Palestinians in Three U.S. Publications, 1948–1974* (M.A. Thesis, University of Wisconsin, 1975).

61. The most thorough treatment of this September 1970 crisis is found in Salwa Shtieh Rifai's *The Palestinian Guerrillas' Image in the New York Times during the Jordan Crisis, 1970* (M.A. thesis, California State University, Northridge, 1986).

62. Anderson was captured in 1985, and in 1991 remained a hostage. Jeremy Levin of CNN was seized in 1984 and held for 11 months before he escaped

63. For various views of the Palestinian Intifada, see Ze'ev Schiff and Ehud Ya'ari, *Intifada: The Palestinians and the Uprising–Israel's Third Front* (New York: Simon and Schuster, 1990); Geoffrey Aronson, *Israel, Palestinians and the Intifada* (London: Kegan Paul International, 1990); Alan Hart, *Arafat: a Political Biography* (Bloomington: Indiana University Press, 1988); and Thomas L. Friedman, *From Beirut to Jerusalem* (New York: Farrar Straus Giroux, 1989). Also see the numerous articles by Robert I. Friedman in New York's *Village Voice* and analyses in other alternative publications such as Chicago's *In These Times.*

64. Michael Emery, "New Videotapes Reveal Israeli Coverup," *Village Voice* (November 13, 1990).

65. See Bob Woodward, *The Commanders* (New York: Simon & Schuster, 1991), and Pierre Salinger and Eric Laurent, *Secret Dossier* (New York: Penguin, 1991). Also see the numerous *Village Voice* investigations between August and April, including Michael Emery, "The War That Didn't Have to Happen," *Village Voice* (March 5, 1991), featuring an exclusive interview with King Hussein; the *Los Angeles Times* (March 3, 1991), Opinion Section version of that interview; Christopher Hitchens, "Why We Are Stuck in the Sand," *Harper's Magazine* (January 1991); and various *New Yorker* Notes and Comments sections during the crisis.

66. See Vincent Carroll, "The Scarcity of Anti-War Editorial Voices," *Washington Journalism Review* (January–February

1991). Carroll reported that as of mid-November 1990, of the top 25 largest newspapers, only the *Rocky Mountain News* argued consistently against military action as a last resort. Also see the publications of FAIR (Fairness and Accuracy in Reporting), which reported on January 16 that of a total of 2855 minutes of network television coverage devoted to the August–January build-up, only 29 minutes, or 1 percent, was given to "popular opposition."

67. *New York Times,* two-part series, May 5–6, 1991. See also Lewis H. Lapham's savage attack on the news media's weak performance, "Trained Seals and Sitting Ducks," *Harper's Magazine* (May 1991); and David Lamb, "Pentagon Hardball," *Washington Journalism Review* (April 1991).

68. See "The Report to the Secretary-General on Humanitarian Needs in Iraq . . . " (March 20, 1991); and "The Damage Was Not Collateral," *New York Times,* March 24, 1991, editorial.

69. The reporters were too numerous to include (see *Broadcasting, Editor & Publisher,* and other journals for various updates); among women television correspondents were ABC's Linda Patillo and CBS's Martha Teichner; Kim Murphy was in the front lines for the *Los Angeles Times* and Molly Moore for the *Washington Post;* and Geraldine Brooks of the *Wall Street Journal* shared an Overseas Press Club award with colleague Tony Horowitz.

70. *New York Times,* February 15, 1991, p. 9.

71. "Newspaper Coverage of Health Care Reform," a joint project of the Kaiser Family Foundation, Times Mirror Center for The People & The Press, and *Columbia Journalism Review* (issued as supplement to the *Review's* issue of November–December 1993).

72. Remarks to the Los Angeles World Affairs Council, February 2, 1994.

73. *New York Times,* December 24, 1993, p. 13.

74. *Los Angeles Times,* April 3, 1994, p. M5.

75. "The People & the Press," Times Mirror Corporation study on media credibility, 1986, p. 57.

76 *Los Angeles Times,* March 31, 1993, p. 1.

77. *Editor & Publisher,* November 21, 1992, p. 13.

78. Edith Efron, *The News Twisters* (Los Angeles: Nash, 1971); and Edward J. Epstein, *News from Nowhere* (New York: Random House, 1973).

79. Remarks by Rather to Radio and Television News Directors Association Convention, Miami, September 29, 1993.

80. *Los Angeles Daily News,* December 11, 1994, L.A. Life Section, p. 4.

81. John Updike, "The Talk of the Town: Comment," *New Yorker,* August 2,1999, p. 24.

82. Barbara Bliss Osborn, *Extra!* (September–October 1994), p. 15. This is the publication of FAIR, based in New York.

83. *Editor & Publisher,* July 18, 1992, p. 4.

84. Joe Holley, "Bright Spot in the Lone Star State," *Columbia Journalism Review* (January–February 1994), p. 21.

85. Television Information Office, bulletin of May 1986.

86. *The Winds of War* attracted the second largest miniseries audience ever recorded: 54 percent of television sets turned on, compared to 66 percent for *Roots.* But because there were 83.3 million television households in 1983—about 140 million—compared with 71.2 million in 1977, more persons saw at least part of one segment of *The Winds of War.*

The previous record for a single program was held by the 1981 segment of the *Dallas* series during which the villain, J. R., was shot by an unknown person. As for the last episode of *M*A*S*H,* there was a long advertising build-up for the show, which received a 76 share. However, the "rating" for *M*A*S*H* (the measurement of all television sets as compared with the "share" of those sets turned on during the broadcast) was 60.3 and for *Dallas,* 53.3. Ranking behind *Dallas* were the last episode of *Roots* and the first two parts of *The Winds of War.* The *M*A*S*H* show also set advertising records for that period; a 30-second commercial cost $450,000. The rating for the *I Love Lucy* show was 71.8, and the share was 92 percent.

87. Each rating point represents a certain number of homes with television. In 1990 the figure used was 1 percent of homes, or 930,000. For example, in early June 1986 CBS had a 10.3 rating and 22 share, NBC had 9.7 and 22, and ABC had 9.4 and 21. Also see Alex S. Jones, "The Anchors," *The New York Times Magazine* (July 27, 1986), p. 13; and Peter J. Boyer, "CBS News in Search of Itself," *The New York Times Magazine* (December 28, 1986), p. 15.

88. William A. Henry III, "Don Hewitt: Man of the Hour," *Washington Journalism Review* (May 1986), 25 and Judy Flander, "Hewitt's Humongous Hour," *Washington Journalism Review,* (April 1991), p. 26.

89. Lynn Darling, "Country Boy Makes Good," *Esquire* (March 1986), p. 90, offers a profile of Brokaw, from Yankton, South Dakota, and how he ended up in New York and Washington.

90. *Christian Science Monitor,* November 18, 1982, magazine section. For a detailed examination of news values, see Herbert J. Gans, *Deciding the News: A Study of CBS Evening News, NBC Nightly News, Newsweek, and Time* (New York: Vintage, 1979).

91. See Kenneth Bilby, *The General: David Sarnoff and the Rise of the Communications Industry* (New York: Harper & Row, 1987). The author traces the post-Sarnoff malaise within RCA and the takeover by General Electric.

92. Barbara Matusow, "Sunday Best," *Washington Journalism Review* (June, 1985), 23. Good summary of the three Sunday morning shows.

93. See "The Network That Couldn't, Did," *Insight,* June 25, 1990, p. 56.

94. John Carman, "Fox Grows Older, Not Up," *San Francisco Chronicle,* April 3, 1997, p. E1.

95. "The Broken Promise of Public Television," *Extra!* (September–October 1993), p. 8.

96. *Report of the National Advisory Commission on Civil Disorders* (New York: Bantam Books, 1968).

97. Ibid., p. 383.

98. Ibid., p. 365.

99. Edward J. Trayes, "The Negro in Journalism," *Journalism Quarterly,* XLVI (Spring 1969), 5.

100. See Clint Wilson II and Félix Gutiérrez, *Minorities and Media* (Beverly Hills, CA: Sage Publications, 1985), p. 161. Also see *Minorities in the Newspaper Business,* the reports of the American Newspaper Publishers Association.

101. Pat Guy, "Black Journalists Cite Frustrations," *USA Today,* July 22, 1993, p. 4B.

102. *New York Times,* December 14, 1994, p. 13.

103. Dr. Gerbner's video, "The Killing Screens: Media and the Culture of Violence," summarizes the statistics.

104. Eric Sevareid, "What's Right with Sight-and-Sound Journalism," *Saturday Review* (October 10, 1976), 19.

105. George Comstock, "The Impact of Television on American Institutions," in Michael C. Emery and Ted C. Smythe, eds., *Readings in Mass Communication* (Dubuque, IA: Wm. C. Brown, 1983), p. 232. See also, in that volume, George Gerbner and Kathleen Connolly, "Television as New Religion," an examination of violence on television.

106. Bernard D. Nossiter, "The FCC's Big Giveaway Show," *Nation* (October 26, 1985), 402.

107. *Channels* (March–April 1983), 27. See *Broadcasting,* March 2, 1981, for discussion of the Reagan administration's plans, radio deregulation, and low-power television stations.

108. *Red Lion Broadcasting Co., Inc.,* v. *Federal Communications Commission,* 394 U.S. (1969).

CHAPTER 19: EFFORTS TO IMPROVE THE MEDIA

1. Among major dailies outside the South supporting Kennedy in 1960 were the *New York Times, St. Louis Post-Dispatch, Milwaukee Journal, Louisville Courier-Journal, New York Post, Newsday, Long Island Press, Pittsburgh Post-Gazette, Toledo Blade, Hartford Times, Denver Post,* and *Sacramento Bee.* The *Washington Post* did not endorse, but favored, Kennedy.

2. The 12 major dailies supporting Goldwater in 1964 were the *Chicago Tribune* and *American, Los Angeles Times, Oakland Tribune, Cincinnati Enquirer, Columbus Dispatch, Milwaukee Sentinel, Richmond Times-Dispatch, Richmond News Leader, Nashville Banner, Tulsa World,* and *Birmingham News.*

3. Nine major dailies that had supported Nixon in 1960 swung to Humphrey in 1968: Hearst's *San Francisco Examiner* and *Boston Record-American,* the Cowles' *Minneapolis Star* and *Tribune* and *Des Moines Register* and *Tribune,* the Ridder's *St. Paul Dispatch* and *Pioneer Press,* and Newhouse's *Newark Star-Ledger.* Four that had backed Kennedy in 1960 now endorsed Nixon: *Newsday,* the *Toledo Blade,* Gannett's *Hartford Times,* and the Ridders' *Long Beach Press-Telegram.*

4. The nine major dailies supporting McGovern in 1972 were the *New York Times, New York Post, Louisville Courier-Journal, Minneapolis Tribune, St. Louis Post-Dispatch,* Portland's *Oregon Journal, Arkansas Gazette, Bergen County* (NJ) *Record,* and *St. Petersburg Independent.*

5. Switching to the Democrats with Carter in 1976 were the *Chicago Sun-Times* and *Daily News* and the *Detroit Free Press.* Although he carried virtually the entire South, Carter had the backing of only six major southern dailies: *Atlanta Journal* and *Constitution, Charlotte Observer, St. Petersburg Independent, Nashville Tennessean,* and Little Rock's *Arkansas Gazette.* Other Carter supporters, in addition to McGovern's 1972 list, included the *Des Moines Register, Denver Post, Dayton News, Long Island Press, Milwaukee Journal,* and *Minneapolis Star.*

6. In 1980 Carter retained all of the papers of McGovern's 1972 list except the *New York Post* (which had been sold). His other major endorsements were from the *Philadelphia Inquirer, Detroit Free Press, Chicago Sun-Times, Milwaukee Journal, Kansas City Star, Baltimore Sun* and *News-American, Dayton News, Atlanta Constitution, St. Petersburg Times, Raleigh News and Observer,* and *Sacramento Bee.*

7. In 1984 Mondale had a prestigious list of supporters: the *New York Times, Washington Post, Boston Globe, Philadelphia Inquirer, Milwaukee Journal, St. Louis Post-Dispatch, Louisville Courier-Journal and Times, Detroit Free Press, Minneapolis Star* and *Tribune, St. Paul Pioneer Press and Dispatch, Atlanta Constitution, St. Petersburg Times, Orlando Sentinel, Miami News, Nashville Tennessean, Oakland Tribune, Des Moines Register,* and *Philadelphia Daily News.* Nearly all also supported Dukakis in 1988 (the *Washington Post* did not endorse).

8. For Clinton data see *Editor & Publisher,* October 24 and November 7, 1992.

9. Broun's column is reprinted in the *Guild Reporter,* XVI (December 9, 1949), which contains several pages reviewing early Guild history and Broun's career. The early years of the Guild are examined in Daniel J. Leab, *A Union of Individuals: The Formation of the American Newspaper Guild 1933–1936* (New York: Columbia University Press, 1970).

10. Earlier AFL efforts are summarized in National Labor Relations Board, *Collective Bargaining in the Newspaper Industry* (Washington, DC: Government Printing Office, 1939), and in Alfred McClung Lee, *The Daily Newspaper in America* (New York: Macmillan, 1937). The most successful locals were in Scranton, Milwaukee, Boston, New York, Philadelphia, and Columbus, Ohio.

11. The details can be followed in the *Guild Reporter* and *Editor & Publisher,* and are summarized in the NLRB's *Collective Bargaining in the Newspaper Industry* and in a special issue of the *Guild Reporter,* XVI (December 9, 1949).

12. *Associated Press* v. *NLRB,* 301 U.S. 103 (1937).

13. This subject is explored in detail in Sam Kuczun, "History of the American Newspaper Guild" (Ph.D. thesis, University of Minnesota, 1970). Some other data in this account are taken from Kuczun's research in Guild archives and other documentary sources.

14. Found in *Problems of Journalism,* published annually by the ASNE.

15. The proceedings of the twenty-fifth annual ASNE meeting, in 1947, contain on pages 39–53 historical reminiscences of three early members, Grove Patterson of the *Toledo Blade,* Marvin H. Creager of the *Milwaukee Journal,* and Donald J. Sterling of the *Oregon Journal.*

16. The American Press Institute was founded in 1946 through the efforts of Sevellon Brown of the *Providence Journal* and *Bulletin.*

17. The NCEW code of principles appears in *Editor & Publisher,* LXXXII (October 29, 1949), 7.

18. The *APME Red Book* for 1948 opens with a history of the organization and its Continuing Study activities to that time.

19. See Albert A. Sutton, *Education for Journalism in the United States* (Evanston: Northwestern University Press, 1945), and Edwin Emery and Joseph P. McKerns, *AEJMC: 75 Years in the Making,* Journalism Monographs, no. 104 (1987).

20. See *Communication Law and Policy* issues devoted to the fiftieth anniversary of the Hutchins Comission Report, vol. 3, no. 2 (Spring 1998), pp. 133–365 and vol. 3, no. 3 (Summer 1998), pp. 367-447.

21. For an overview of the National News Council, see Patrick Brogan, *Spiked: The Short Life and Death of the National News Council* (New York: Priority Press, 1985).

22. This was the unpublished report of Claude-Jean Bertrand, University of Paris–Nanterre, studying American media from 1976 to 1977.

23. See Donald M. Gillmor and Jerome A. Barron, *Mass Communication Law: Cases and Comment* (St. Paul: West Publishing, 1969), pp. 250 ff.

24. *New York Times Co.* v. *Sullivan,* 376 U.S. 245 (1964).

25. *Curtis Publishing Co.* v. *Butts and Associated Press* v. *Walker,* 388 U.S. 130 (1967).

26. *Gertz* v. *Robert Welch, Inc.,* 418 U.S. 323 (1974); *Time Inc.* v. *Firestone,* 96 S. Ct. 958 (1976). Gertz won $100,000 actual damages and $300,000 punitive damages from Welch and a John Birch Society publication in a retrial and appeals court confirmation. Mrs. Firestone waived her $100,000 award rather than go through a second trial to determine *Time*'s degree of negligence in erroneously reporting a charge of adultery.

27. *Moldea* v. *New York Times Co., Inc.,* 22 Med. L. Rptr. 1681 (D.C. Cir. 1994).

28. *MMAR Group, Inc.* v. *Dow Jones & Co., Inc.,* 987 F. Supp. 535 (S.D. Tex. 1997).

29. *Food Lion, Inc.* v. *Capital Cities/ABC, Inc.,* 984 F. Supp. 923 (M.D.N.C. 1997).

30. *Cubby, Inc.* v. *CompuServe, Inc.,* 776 F. Supp. 135 (S.D.N.Y. 1991).

31. *Stratton Oakmont, Inc.* v. *Prodigy Services Co.* (unpublished opinion), 1995 WL 323710 (N.Y. Sup. 1995).

32. *Zeran* v. *America Online,* 129 F.3d 327 (4th Cir. 1997); *Blumenthal* v. *Drudge,* 992 F. Supp. 44 (D.D.C. 1998); *Doe*

v. *America Online,* No. CL 97-631AE (Fla. Cir., 15 Jud. Cir., Palm Beach County, June 26, 1997).

33. *Roth* v. *United States,* 354 U.S. 476 (1957).

34. *Ginsburg* v. *United States,* 383 U.S. 463 (1966).

35. *Miller* v. *California,* 413 U.S. 15 (1973).

36. *Pinkus* v. *United States,* 436 U.S. 293 (1978).

37. *Luke Records Inc.* v. *Navarro,* 20 Med. L. Rptr. 1114 (1992).

38. *Reno* v. *American Civil Liberties Union,* 117 S. Ct. 2329 (1997).

39. *Hannegan* v. *Esquire,* 327 U.S. 146 (1946).

40. For a full discussion see Karl A. Boedecker, Fred W. Morgan, and Linda Berns Wright, "The Evolution of First Amendment Protection for Commercial Speech," *Journal of Marketing* (January 1995), pp. 38–47.

41. *44 Liquormart* v. *Rhode Island,* 517 U.S. 484 (1996).

42. *Glickman* v. *Wileman Brothers & Elliott, Inc.,* 117 S. Ct. 2130 (1997).

43. Jerome A. Barron, "Access to the Press–A New First Amendment Right," 80 *Harvard Law Review* 1641 (1967). See also Jerome A. Barron, *Freedom of the Press for Whom? The Right of Access to Mass Media* (Bloomington: Indiana University Press, 1973).

44. *Miami Herald Publishing Co.* v. *Tornillo,* 418 U.S. 241 (1974).

45. *Estes* v. *State of Texas,* 381 U.S. 532 (1965).

46. *Sheppard* v. *Maxwell,* 384 U.S. 333 (1966).

47. *United States* v. *Dickinson,* 46496 (5th Cir. 1972).

48. The *Branzburg* ruling also included *In re Pappas* and *U.S.* v. *Caldwell.* Paul Branzburg of the *Louisville Courier-Journal* refused to tell a grand jury about drug violations he had observed. Earl Caldwell of the *New York Times* and Paul Pappas, a Massachusetts television reporter, refused to give grand juries information about Black Panther members they had interviewed.

49. *Nebraska Press Association* v. *Stuart,* 427 U.S. 539 (1976).

50. *Gannett* v. *DePasquale,* 99 S. Ct. 2898 (1979).

51. *Richmond Newspapers* v. *Commonwealth of Virginia,* 448 U.S. 555 (1980).

52. *Zurcher* v. *Stanford Daily,* 436 U.S. 547 (1978).

CHAPTER 20: MEDIA TECHNOLOGY: THE CHALLENGE OF THE TWENTY-FIRST CENTURY

1. James A. Michener, "You Can Call the 1980s 'The Ugly Decade,' " *New York Times,* January 1, 1987, p. 19.

2. Jonathan Kozol, speech to American Newspaper Publishers Association, San Francisco, April 21, 1986. See also Kozol's *Illiterate America* (New York: New American Library, 1985).

3. "Losing the War of Letters," *Time,* May 5, 1986, p. 68.

4. *presstime,* October, 1986, p. 32.

5. "Court Overturns Stanford University Code Barring Bigoted Speech," *New York Times* , March. 1, 1995, p. B8.

6. Sam Fulwood III, "D.C. Mayor under Fire in War of Words over Word Use," *Los Angeles Times,* January 29, 1999, p. A15.

7. James Reston, *New York Times,* July 2, 1986, p. 27.

8. *Lies of Our Times* (September–December 1992), p. 3; also see Donna Allen, *Media Without Democracy* (Washington, DC: Women's Institute for Freedom of the Press, 1991), which is no. 3 in a booklet series dealing with restructuring the communications media.

9. *Lies of Our Times* (September–December 1992), p. 2; also see Charles M. Young's interview with Noam Chomsky in "American Radical," *Rolling Stone,* May 28, 1992, p. 42.

10. Michael Massing, "Ghetto Blasting," *New Yorker,* January 16, 1995, p. 32.

11. Peter Arnett, "Goodbye, World," *American Journalism Review,* Nov. 1998, p. 50.

12. Eileen Shanahan, "How to Fathom the Fed," *Columbia Journalism Review* (January–February 1995), p. 38; also, for a comprehensive and critical look at reporting practices, see John Quirt, *The Press and the World of Money* (Los Angeles: Anton/Courier, 1993).

13. Dennis Bernstein, "Interviewing Pete Brewton," *Z Magazine* (November 1992), p. 42.

14. See Steven Konick, "A Comparison of Verbal and Visual Themes in Network News Coverage of AIDS," paper presented at the Association for Education in Journalism and Mass Communication convention, August 1994.

15. Leo Bogart, *The American Media System and Its Commercial Culture* (March 1991), p. 14. This booklet was issued by the Freedom Forum Media Studies Center at Columbia University as part of a series.

16. See the April 1981 issue of *presstime* for a description of the pioneering work with pagination.

17. The September 11, 1980, report of the American Newspaper Publishers Association, no. 80–6, said that 24.7 percent of dailies in the United States accounted for 57.8 percent of the daily circulation, or 36.9 million. There were 439 letterpress operations among the dailies.

18. Thomas G. Krattenmaker, "The Telecommunications Act of 1996," 29 *Connecticut Law Review* 123 (Fall 1996), p. 127.

19. See Kenneth Edwards, "Delivering Information to the Home Electronically," in Michael Emery and Ted C. Smythe, *Readings in Mass Communication* (Dubuque: Wm. C. Brown, 1983). Edwards has written extensively on the subject.

20. Ralph Lee Smith, "The Birth of a Wired Nation," *Channels* (April–May 1982).

21. "Wall Street's Affairs with the Wire," *Channels Field Guide,* 1987 edition, p. 87.

22. *Standard & Poor's Industry Surveys—Broadcasting & Cable* (July 2, 1998), from *Broadcasting & Cable,* p. 15.

23. *Channels* (December 1981–January 1982), p. 36. See also Robert Lindsey, "Home Box Office Moves in on Hollywood," *New York Times Magazine,* June 12, 1983, p. 31.

24. *PC Magazine,* March 10, 1998, p. 10.

25. Saul Hansell, "Geocities' Cyberworld Is Vibrant, But Can It Make Money?" *New York Times,* July 13, 1998.

26. For a thorough analysis of new patterns in television news, see Jerry Jacobs's *Changing Channels* (Mountain View, CA: Mayfield, 1990), which offers a worldwide analysis of the rush for ratings. Also see Dennis Hart, "The 11 O'Clock News—Can You Hear Clicking," *Communicator* (February 1991).

27. "Catching the Shortwave," *Christian Science Monitor,* March 11, 1987, p. 16.

28. David Hinckley, "FCC Sees Bias in Ad Revenues," *New York Daily News,* January 14, 1999, p. 108.

29. David Shaw, "The AP: It's Everywhere and Powerful," *Los Angeles Times,* April 3, 1988, pp. 1, 22–24.

30. "Bad Order," *The Times,* September 26, 1998.

31. Louis D. Boccardi, president and general manager of the Associated Press, comments at the AP's annual meeting, New York, May 4, 1987.

Annotated Bibliography*

CHAPTER 1: THE HERITAGE OF THE AMERICAN PRESS

Books

BACKSCHEIDER, PAULA R. *Daniel Defoe: His Life*. Baltimore: Johns Hopkins University Press, 1989. Focuses on Defoe as a journalist and propagandist; best of Defoe biographies.

BLACK, JEREMY. *The English Press in the Eighteenth Century*. Philadelphia: University of Pennsylvania Press, 1987. Relates press growth to social, political history; extensive use of quotes.

BLAGDEN, CYPRIAN. *The Stationers Company*. London: Allen & Unwin, 1960. A scholarly account of licensing and control of printing.

BLEYER, WILLARD GROSVENOR. *Main Currents in the History of American Journalism*. Boston: Houghton Mifflin, 1927. Chapter 1 is a good description of early English journalism, to about 1750.

BOND, DONOVAN H., AND W. REYNOLDS MCLEOD, eds. *Newsletters to Newspapers: Eighteenth-Century Journalism*. Morgantown, WV: West Virginia University, 1977. Symposium papers covering England and the colonies.

BOND, RICHMOND P. *The Tatler: The Making of a Literary Journal*. Cambridge, MA: Harvard University Press, 1971. Addison and Steele's paper.

CAREY, JOHN, ed. *Eyewitness to History*. Cambridge, MA: Harvard University Press, 1988. Firsthand accounts of great events since 43 B.C.

CARTER, THOMAS F. *The Invention of Printing in China and Its Spread Westward*, rev. by L. Carrington Goodrich. New York: Ronald Press, 1955. The standard source.

CRANFIELD, G. A. *The Press and Society: From Caxton to Northcliffe*. London: Longman, 1978. A British overview. See also Cranfield, *The Development of the Provincial Newspaper, 1700–1760* (London: Oxford University Press, 1962), research-based.

DESMOND, ROBERT W. *The Information Process: World News Reporting to the Twentieth Century*. Iowa City: University of Iowa Press, 1978. A scholarly, comprehensive survey integrating worldwide data from the invention of alphabets to 1900. It is the first of a four-volume series, also including *Windows on the World: World News Reporting 1900–1920* (1980); *Crisis and Conflict: World News Reporting between Two Wars 1920–1940* (1982); and *Tides of War: World News Reporting 1931–1945* (1984). The series won three national research prizes.

EISENSTEIN, ELIZABETH. *The Printing Press as an Agent of Change*. Cambridge, England: Cambridge University Press, 1980. A depth analysis of communications and cultural change to 1600. A more readable, one-volume edition is titled *The Printing Revolution in Early Modern Europe* (1984).

FORD, EDWIN H., AND EDWIN EMERY, eds. *Highlights in the History of the American Press: A Book of Readings*. Minneapolis: University of Minnesota Press, 1954. Selected articles; four on England.

FRANK, JOSEPH. *The Beginnings of the English Newspaper*, Cambridge, MA: Harvard University Press, 1961. Carries the story through the Restoration of 1660. See also Frank, *Cromwell's Press Agent: A Critical Biography of Marchamont Nedham, 1620–1678* (Washington, DC: University Press of America, 1980); readable, scholarly.

GHIGLIONE, LOREN. *The American Journalist*. Washington, DC: Library of Congress, 1990. An oversized, illustrated companion to the Library's journalism history exhibit.

HART, JIM ALLEE. *Views on the News: The Developing Editorial Syndrome, 1500–1800*. Carbondale: Southern Illinois University Press, 1970. An overview of the opinion-giving function.

HOGBEN, LANCELOT. *From Cave Painting to Comic Strip: A Kaleidoscope of Human Communication*. New York:

*The Introductory Bibliography preceding Chapter 1 contains references to other bibliographies, encyclopedias, studies of historiography, and guides to reference materials and major library collections for the mass media.

Chanticleer Press, 1949. Illustrated chronology of communication systems and technology.

HUTT, ALLEN. *The Changing Newspaper: Typographic Trends in Britain and America, 1622–1972.* London: Gordon Fraser, 1973. A standard work.

KOSS, STEPHEN. *The Rise and Fall of the Political Press in Britain.* Vol. 1, *The Nineteenth Century.* Vol. 2, *The Twentieth Century.* Chapel Hill: University of North Carolina Press, 1981, 1984. By a noted historian.

KUNZLE, DAVID. *The Early Comic Strip: Narrative Strips and Picture Stories in the European Broadsheet from c. 1450 to 1825.* Berkeley: University of California Press, 1973. A 471-page artistic analysis.

LEE, ALAN J. *The Origins of the Popular Press in England.* Totowa, NJ: Rowan and Littlefield, 1976. Highly interpretive, broadly Marxian approach to the press of second half of the nineteenth century.

McDONALD, IVERACH. *The History of "The Times."* Vol. V, *Struggles in War and Peace, 1939–1966.* London: Times Books, 1984. The first four volumes, beginning with 1785, were published during 1935–48.

McMURTRIE, DOUGLAS C. *The Book: The Story of Printing and Bookmaking.* New York: Oxford University Press, 1943. Tells the Gutenberg story, and traces the spread of printing to the New World.

MORAN, JAMES. *Printing Presses: History and Development from the Fifteenth Century to Modern Times.* Berkeley: University of California Press, 1973. Detailed and illustrated.

MORGAN, EDMUND S. *Inventing the People: The Rise of Popular Sovereignty in England and America.* New York: Norton, 1988. Colonials substituted people power for Parliamentary power.

OZMENT, STEVEN. *Protestants: The Birth of a Revolution.* New York: Doubleday, 1992. The scholar's examination of the impact of the Protestant Reformation and its pamphleteers.

O'BRIEN, CONOR CRUISE. *The Great Melody: A Thematic Biography and Commented Biography of Edmund Burke.* Chicago: University of Chicago Press, 1992. Best of many efforts.

PAINTER, GEORGE D. *William Caxton.* New York: George Putnam, 1977. England's first printer and the times in which he lived. See also Edmund Childs, *William Caxton: A Portrait in a Background.* New York: St. Martin's Press, 1976.

SCHRAMM, WILBUR. *The Story of Human Communication: Cave Printing to Microchip.* New York: Harper & Row, 1988. The noted communications scholar focuses on ancient writing and printing developments in this highly readable volume.

SHAABER, MATTHIAS A. *Some Forerunners of the Newspaper in England, 1476–1622.* Philadelphia: University of Pennsylvania Press, 1929. Authoritative.

SIEBERT, FREDRICK SEATON. *Freedom of the Press in England, 1476–1776.* Urbana: University of Illinois Press,

1952. The outstanding study of the subject. Corrects inaccuracies of older histories.

SMITH, ANTHONY. *The Newspaper: An International History.* London: Thames and Hudson, 1979. Races over 400 years, drawing the story together in 192 pages and with 111 illustrations. See also Smith, *The British Press Since the War* (Totowa, NJ: Rowan and Littlefield, 1974), beginning in 1945.

STEINBERG, S. H. *Five Hundred Years of Printing.* New ed. rev. by John Trevitt. New Castle, DE: Oak Knoll Press, 1996. Well-illustrated classic account, updated to trace the interrelation of printing and culture from 1450 into the contemporary era of massive technological changes.

STEPHENS, MITCHELL. *History of News from the Drum to the Satellite.* New York: Viking, 1988. Focus is on content of the news, including sensationalism.

TUNSTALL, JEREMY. *The Media in Britain.* New York: Columbia University Press, 1983. Industry trends and policies, since 1945. Annotated bibliography.

VON KLARWILL, VICTOR, ed. *The Fugger News Letters,* first series. New York: G. P. Putnam's Sons, 1924. Second series, 1926. An interesting study of the content of news before the days of newspapers.

WEBER, HAROLD M. *Paper Bullets: Print and Kingship under Charles II.* Lexington: University Press of Kentucky, 1995. Press control is essential to political power.

WERKMEISTER, LUCYLE. *The London Daily Press, 1772–1792.* Lincoln: University of Nebraska Press, 1963. Only detailed history of the period.

WIENER, JOEL H. ed. *Papers for the Millions: The New Journalism in Britain, 1850s to 1914.* Westport, CT: Greenwood Press, 1988. Symposium.

WILLIAMS, FRANCIS. *Dangerous Estate: The Anatomy of Newspapers.* New York: Macmillan, 1958. The British press as a social institution since 1702.

Periodicals and Monographs

ALLEN, ERIC W. "International Origins of the Newspapers: The Establishment of Periodicity in Print," *Journalism Quarterly,* VII (December 1930), 307. Discusses qualifications of the true newspaper.

BAKER, HARRY T. "Early English Journalism," *Sewanee Review,* XXV (October 1917), 396. A detailed account that highlights Nathaniel Butter and Sir Roger L'Estrange.

BLEYER, WILLARD G. "The Beginnings of English Journalism," *Journalism Quarterly,* VIII (September 1931), 317. A study of foreign news in *corantos.*

FACKLER, MARK, AND CLIFFORD G. CHRISTIANS. "John Milton's Place in Journalism History: Champion or Turncoat?" *Journalism Quarterly,* LVII (Winter 1980), 563. Milton is judged a champion for his *Areopagitica.*

GIFFARD, C. A. "Ancient Rome's Daily Gazette," *Journalism History,* II (Winter 1975), 106. A study of the *Acta Diurna,* begun in 59 B.C. by Julius Caesar.

———. "The Anglo-Saxon Chronicle: Precursor of the Press," *Journalism History,* IX (Spring 1982), 11.

GUTIÉRREZ, FÉLIX, AND ERNESTO BALLESTEROS. "The 1541 Earthquake: Dawn of Latin American Journalism, *Journalism History,* VI (Autumn 1979), 78.

HARRIS, MICHAEL, AND TOM O'MALLEY. *Studies in Newspaper and Periodical History 1995 Annual.* Westport, CT: Greenwood Press, 1995. Essays with an international perspective on serial publication from 1700 through the 1970s.

HESTER, AL. "Newspapers and Newspaper Prototypes in Spanish America, 1541–1750," *Journalism History,* VI (Autumn 1979), 73. Best sources.

LOWENTHAL, LEO, AND MARJORIE FISKE. "Reaction to Mass Media Growth in 18th-Century England," *Journalism Quarterly,* XXXIII (Fall 1956), 442. Discusses how literary tastes were lowered.

MOORADIAN, KARLEN. "The Dawn of Printing," *Journalism Monographs,* 23 (May 1972). First steps of printing—stamp and cylinder seals—found in Mesopotamia and Crete; movable type in Crete dates 3000 years before its use in China.

ROSENBERG, MARVIN. "The Rise of England's First Daily Newspaper," *Journalism Quarterly,* XXX (Winter 1953), 3. An excellent study of the *Courant.*

STEPHENS, MITCHELL. "Sensationalism and Moralizing in 16th and 17th Century Newsbooks and News Ballads," *Journalism History,* XII (Autumn–Winter 1985), 92.

WILSON, C. EDWARD. "The First Daily Newspaper in English," *Journalism Quarterly,* LVIII (Summer 1981), 286. Oliver Williams published *A Perfect Diurnal or the Dayly Proceedings in Parliament* for four weeks in 1660.

CHAPTER 2: THE COLONIAL YEARS

Books: Bibliographical Essay

For the general reader the most useful books from among histories of American journalism earlier than this volume are those by Mott, Bleyer, A. M. Lee, and Payne, listed in the following bibliography. The earliest attempt at a general account was that by Isaiah Thomas in 1810 (see following). Next were those by Frederic Hudson in 1873 and by S.N.D. North in 1884 (see bibliographies for Chapters 6 and 8, respectively). These three books remain of special use to journalism historians. Other general histories have been those by James Melvin Lee, *History of American Journalism* (Boston: Houghton Mifflin, 1917), the first by a journalism educator; Robert W. Jones, *Journalism in the United States* (New York: Dutton, 1947); Edith M. Bartow, *News and These United States* (New York: Funk & Wagnalls, 1952); John W. Tebbel, *The Compact History of the American Newspaper* (New York: Hawthorn, 1963), a readable but quick survey of high points; Sidney Kobre, *Development of American Journalism* (Dubuque, IA: Wm. C. Brown, 1969), a revision of his sociologically oriented earlier works that adds details about many regional papers; Robert A. Rutland, *The Newsmongers* (New York: Dial Press, 1973), a readable popular supplement to basic journalism history books; John W. Tebbel, *The Media*

in America (New York: Thomas Y. Crowell, 1974), a popular account emphasizing the nineteenth century; George N. Gordon, *The Communications Revolution* (New York: Hastings House, 1977), an uneven account lacking a framework of interpretation; Jean Folkerts and Dwight L. Teeter, Jr., *Voices of a Nation: A History of the Media in the United States*, 3rd ed. (Boston: Allyn and Bacon, 1998), designed as a core textbook; and W. David Sloan, James G. Stovall, and James D. Startt, eds., *The Media in America: A History,* 3rd ed. (Northport, AL: Vision Press, 1996), 24 chapters contributed by 24 authors, of uneven quality. For analysis of the subject, see Chapter 1 of Stevens and Dicken-Garcia, *Communication History*; the annotations in Price, *The Literature of Journalism,* pp. 3–7; and Allan Nevins, "American Journalism and Its Historical Treatment," *Journalism Quarterly,* XXXVI (Fall 1959), 411. An invaluable general reference work is Margaret Blanchard, ed., *History of the Mass Media in the United States: An Encyclopedia* (Chicago, London: Fitzroy Dearborn, 1998), whose entries provide excellent overviews and bibliographies.

For historical accounts of the roles of women in United States journalism, see the following citations for Marion Marzolf, Susan Henry, and Madelon Schilpp and Sharon Murphy, and others in bibliographies for succeeding chapters, especially 3, 6, 9, 10, 11, 18, and 19. Extensive unannotated bibliographies were published in *Journalism History I* (Winter 1974), 117, and III (Winter 1976), 116.

Especially recommended for background reading in American history are histories by: William Chafe, *The Unfinished Journey: America since World War II* (New York: Oxford University Press, 1991), Mary Beth Norton, et al., *A People and a Nation,* 5th ed. (Boston: Houghton Mifflin, 1998), and William Appleman Williams, *The Contours of American History* (cited below). The best broad treatment of women's history is Sara Evans, *Born for Liberty,* 2nd ed. (New York: Free Press, 1997). Also recommended is Ronald Takaki, *A Different Mirror: A History of Multicultural America* (Boston: Little, Brown, 1993).

Other useful, regularly updated general texts include: James L. Roark, et al., *The American Promise* (Boston: Bedford Books, 1998) and James West Davidson, et al., *Nation of Nations,* 2nd ed. (Boston: McGraw-Hill, 1999). Also, the American History Series of short, highly readable books on a range of specific topics in U.S. history published by Harlan Davidson (Arlington Heights, IL) is recommended for supplementary reading.

Good sources on U.S. historiography are: Eric Foner, ed., *The New American History,* rev. and exp. ed. (Philadelphia: Temple University Press, 1997) and Gerald N. Grob and George A. Bilias, *Interpretations of American History: Patterns and Perspectives,* Vol. 1, *To 1877,* 6th ed. (New York: Free Press, 1992), and Vol. 2, *Since 1877,* 6th ed. (New York: Free Press, 1992).

Books: Background History

FISCHER, DAVID H. *Albion's Seed.* New York: Oxford University Press, 1989. Diverse values of settlers from various sections of England created distinctive U.S. regional cultures.

KAMMEN, MICHAEL. *People of Paradox: An Inquiry Concerning the Origins of American Civilization.* New York: Oxford University Press, 1972. Won a 1973 Pulitzer Prize.

KULIKOFF, ALLAN. *Tobacco and Slaves: The Development of Southern Cultures in the Chesapeake, 1680–1800.* Chapel Hill: University of North Carolina Press, 1986. One of the most significant recent studies of Chesapeake society.

MCCUSKER, JOHN J., AND RUSSELL R. MENARD. *The Economy of British America, 1607–1789.* Chapel Hill: University of North Carolina Press, 1985. A comprehensive assessment of research on the pre-Revolutionary economy that considers the colonies from Canada to the Caribbean.

MILLER, PERRY. *The New England Mind: The Seventeenth Century.* New York: Macmillan, 1939; and *The New England Mind: From Colony to Province.* Cambridge, MA: Harvard University Press, 1953. The first volume, covering to 1660, is a readable interpretation of the Puritan character. The second volume discusses society and thought to 1730.

SILVERMAN, KENNETH. *The Life and Times of Cotton Mather.* New York: Harper & Row, 1984 First comprehensive biography of James Franklin's protagonist. See also Michael G. Hall, *The Life of Increase Mather 1639–1723* (Middletown, CT: Wesleyan University Press, 1988), Cotton's father.

WILLIAMS, WILLIAM APPLEMAN. *The Contours of American History.* Cleveland: World Publishing, 1961. A groundbreaking reinterpretation of moral, social, and economic development since colonial times; a New Left outlook by a major spokesperson.

WOOD, GORDON S. *The Radicalism of the American Revolution.* New York: Alfred A. Knopf, 1992. How a revolution transformed a monarchical society into a democratic one unlike any that had ever existed.

Books: Journalism History

BEASLEY, MAURINE, H., AND SHEILA GIBBONS. *Taking Their Place: A Documentary History of Women in Journalism.* Lanham, MD: American University Press, 1993. Revised and expanded version of the 1977 classic, covering the period from Mary Katherine Goddard to *Ms.* magazine.

BLEYER, WILLARD GROSVENOR. *Main Currents in the History of American Journalism.* Boston: Houghton Mifflin, 1927. One of the standard histories of journalism—reliable and detailed. Emphasizes leading editors after the 1830s.

BOWEN, CATHERINE D. *The Most Dangerous Man in America: Scenes from the Life of Benjamin Franklin.* Boston: Little, Brown, 1974. See also Ronald W. Clark, *Benjamin Franklin* (New York: Random House, 1983); and Esmond Wright, *Franklin of Philadelphia* (Cambridge, MA: Harvard University Press, 1986). Best recent biographies.

BRIGHAM, CLARENCE S. *History and Bibliography of American Newspapers, 1690–1820.* 2 vols. Worcester, MA: American Antiquarian Society, 1947. Gives brief descriptions of all newspapers up to 1820. Indispensable for the colonial historian.

————. *Journals and Journeymen.* Philadelphia: University of Pennsylvania Press, 1950. Fifteen essays on the colonial press; particularly interesting one on advertising.

BROWN, RICHARD D. *Knowledge Is Power: The Diffusion of Information in Early America, 1700–1865.* New York: Oxford University Press, 1989. Overview of the informal spreading of news.

Cambridge History of American Literature. Vol. 1. New York: G. P. Putnam's Sons, 1917–21. Vol. 1 of this four-volume work discusses Franklin (pp. 90–110) and newspapers and magazines (pp. 111–23).

CHIASSON, LLOYD, ed. *The Press in Times of Crisis.* Westport, CT: Praeger, 1995. Ten authors critique press performance in about a dozen different periods.

CLARK, CHARLES E., DAVID PAUL NORD, GERALD BALDASTY, MICHAEL SCHUDSON, AND LOREN GHIGLIONE. *Three Hundred Years of the American Newspaper.* Worcester, MA: American Antiquarian Society, 1991. A slim but useful collection of essays published to celebrate the 300th anniversary of *Publick Occurrences.*

COOK, ELIZABETH C. *Literary Influences in Colonial Newspapers, 1704–1750.* New York: Columbia University Press, 1912. Describes the role of the press in satisfying the craving for popular literature.

COPELAND, DAVID A. *Colonial American Newspapers: Character and Content.* Newark, NJ: University of Delaware Press, 1997. Detailed, insightful analysis of 79 different English-language newspapers printed during the colonial period.

DE ARMOND, ANNA JANNEY. *Andrew Bradford: Colonial Journalist.* Newark, DE: University of Delaware Press, 1949. Well documented.

EMERY, MICHAEL C., R. SMITH SCHUNEMAN, AND EDWIN EMERY, eds. *America's Front Page News 1690–1970.* New York: Doubleday, 1971. Some 300 newspaper pages reproduced to trace main themes of United States political history, wars, popular movements, triumphs, and tragedies. See also Edwin Emery, *The Story of America as Reported by Its Newspapers 1690–1965* (New York: Simon & Schuster, 1965).

FRANKLIN, BENJAMIN. *The Autobiography of Benjamin Franklin,* ed. Leonard W. Labaree. New Haven: Yale University Press, 1964.

HUDSON, ROBERT V. *Mass Media: A Chronological Encyclopedia of Television, Radio, Motion Pictures, Magazines, Newspapers, and Books in the United States.* New York: Garland, 1987. A remarkably useful 435-page work with a vital 75-page index; its detailed entries are in 16 sections, 1638–1965.

KOBRE, SIDNEY. *The Development of the Colonial Newspaper.* Pittsburgh: The Colonial Press, 1944. A short but classic study of the integration of political, social, and economic forces in the development of the American press.

LEE, ALFRED McCLUNG. *The Daily Newspaper in America.* New York: Macmillan, 1937. A topical history with a sociological approach, especially useful for its discussions of economic factors.

MARZOLF, MARION. *Up from the Footnote: A History of Women Journalists.* New York: Hastings House, 1977. A study from colonial days to the present. See also Marzolf, "The Woman Journalist: Colonial Printer to City Desk," *Journalism History,* I–II (Winter 1974–Spring 1975).

McCHESNEY, ROBERT, AND WILLIAM SOLOMON. *Ruthless Criticism: New Perspectives in U.S. Communication History.* Minneapolis: University of Minnesota Press, 1993. Useful anthology covering both print and broadcasting industries and cultures.

MOTT, FRANK LUTHER. *American Journalism.* New York: Macmillan, 1941, rev. eds. 1950, 1962. A detailed general reference book by an outstanding scholar of American journalism. The revisions add sections for the 1940s and 1950s.

PANETH, DONALD, ed. *The Encyclopedia of American Journalism.* New York; Facts on File, 1983. Has 1000 entries covering print and electronic media and film, plus bibliographies.

PAYNE, GEORGE H. *History of Journalism in the United States.* New York: Appleton-Century-Crofts, 1920. An old history, but accurate and detailed, particularly useful for the period up to 1800.

PICKETT, CALDER M. *Voices of the Past: Key Documents in the History of American Journalism.* Columbus, OH: Grid Publishing, 1977. A storehouse of firsthand materials.

POPE, DANIEL. *The Making of Modern Advertising.* New York: Basic Books, 1983. A careful historical study using theoretical perspectives grounded in economics. Concentrates on the nineteenth century.

PRESBREY, FRANK. *The History and Development of Advertising.* Garden City: Doubleday, 1929. Longtime standard account, especially useful for its details and numerous illustrations.

REMER, ROSALIND. *Printers and Men of Capital: Philadelphia Book Publishers in the New Republic.* Philadelphia: University of Pennsylvania Press, 1994. Useful summary of early book publishing's business side.

SCHILPP, MADELON GOLDEN, AND SHARON M. MURPHY. *Great Women of the Press.* Carbondale: Southern Illinois Press, 1983. Eighteen working journalists from colonial era to present are portrayed. Barbara Belford deals with 24 in her biographical anthology, *Brilliant Bylines* (New York: Columbia University Press, 1986).

SLOAN, W. DAVID, AND JULIE HEDGEPETH WILLIAMS. *The Early American Press, 1690–1783.* Westport, CT: Greenwood Press, 1994. Well-researched account that reveals the press was quite sophisticated.

STREITMATTER, RODGER. *Mightier than the Sword: How the News Media Shaped American History.* Boulder, Co: Westview Press, 1997. Fourteen significant episodes in which mass media played an important role, including the Revolution, abolition movement, Vietnam, civil rights struggle, and Watergate.

TEBBEL, JOHN W. *A History of Book Publishing in the United States.* Vols. 1–4. New York: Bowker, 1972, 1975, 1978, 1981. Vol. 1 covers 1630–1865, Vol. 2, 1865–1919; Vol. 3, 1920–1940; Vol. 4, 1940–1980. The standard authority. A single-volume summary, *Between Covers,* appeared in 1986.

The Papers of Benjamin Franklin. Vol. 1. New Haven: Yale University Press, 1959. Covers the period to 1734, including "Silence Do-Good" and "Busy-Body" letters. Extensive introduction by editor Leonard W. Labaree.

THOMAS, ISAIAH. *History of Printing in America.* 2 vols. Worcester, MA.: Isaiah Thomas, Jr. (first printing), 1810; Albany, NY: Joel Munsell, 1874. The standard authority on colonial journalism; contains biographies of printers and accounts of newspapers in all colonies and in some new states.

WROTH, LAWRENCE C. *The Colonial Printer.* Portland, ME: Southworth-Anthoensen Press, 1938. An excellent study of the printing craft.

Books: Press Freedom

ALEXANDER, JAMES. *A Brief Narrative of the Case and Trial of John Peter Zenger, Printer of the New York "Weekly Journal,"* ed. Stanley N. Katz. Cambridge, MA: Harvard University Press, 1963. Scholarly reprint with annotations by Zenger's lawyer.

BURANELLI, VINCENT, ed. *The Trial of Peter Zenger.* New York: New York University Press, 1957. Reprint of the text of the trial, with biographical information and an analysis of its meaning.

DUNIWAY, CLYDE A. *The Development of Freedom of the Press in Massachusetts.* New York: Longmans, Green & Company, 1906. A detailed and invaluable contribution.

INGELHART, LOUIS EDWARD. *Press and Speech Freedoms in America, 1619–1995: A Chronology.* Westport, CT: Greenwood Press, 1997. A descriptive overview of press and speech freedoms in the United States from 1619 through 1995.

LEVY, LEONARD W., ed. *Freedom of the Press from Zenger to Jefferson.* Durham, NC: Carolina Academic Press, 1997. A reprint of the classic 1966 edition, a collection of documents tracing theories of freedom of the press and the rise of libertarianism.

———. *Emergence of a Free Press.* New York: Oxford University Press, 1985. Revised and enlarged edition of Levy's *Legacy of Suppression* (1960); he now finds newspapers had more freedom in the pre-1800 era than previously described.

———. *The Establishment Clause: Religion and the First Amendment.* New York: Macmillan, 1986. Historical analysis supporting the argument for absolute disestablishment of religion.

MacCRACKEN, HENRY NOBLE. *Prologue to Independence: The Trials of James Alexander, 1715–1756.* New York: Heineman, 1964. The lawyer who edited Zenger's paper.

OSGOOD, HERBERT L. *The American Colonies in the Eighteenth Century.* Vol. 2. New York: Columbia University Press, 1924. Pages 443–82 give the political background for the Zenger trial.

Powe, Lucas A., Jr. *The Fourth Estate and the Constitution: Freedom of the Press in America.* Berkeley: University of California Press, 1991. Overview for print media by law professor who is the author of *American Broadcasting and the First Amendment.*

Rabban, David M. *Free Speech in Its Forgotten Years, 1870–1920.* New York: Cambridge University Press, 1997. Uncovers free speech history between the Civil War and World War I.

Sheridan, Eugene R. *Lewis Morris 1671–1746: A Study in Early American Politics.* Syracuse, NY: Syracuse University Press, 1981. Morris defended the interests of landed aristocracies in New Jersey and New York.

Smith, Jeffery A. *Printers and Press Freedom: The Ideology of Early American Journalism.* New York: Oxford University Press, 1988. Persuasively argued, scholarly review of the press freedom concept as developed in the colonies.

Periodicals and Monographs

Covert, Cathy. " 'Passion Is Ye Prevailing Motive': The Feud Behind the Zenger Case," *Journalism Quarterly,* L (Spring 1973), 3. Zenger was the printer of James Alexander's ideas.

Ford, Edwin H. "Colonial Pamphleteers," *Journalism Quarterly,* XIII (March 1936), 24. A scholarly discussion including Increase and Cotton Mather and Samuel Sewall. Reprinted in Ford and Emery, *Highlights in the History of the American Press.* Minneapolis: University of Minnesota Press, 1954.

Frasca, Ralph. "Benjamin Franklin's Printing Network," *American Journalism,* V (1988), 145. The emphasis is upon economics.

Hudson, Robert V. "The English Roots of Benjamin Franklin's Journalism," *Journalism History,* III (Autumn 1976), 76. Influence of essayists.

King, Marion Reynolds. "One Link in the First Newspaper Chain, the *South Carolina Gazette,*" *Journalism Quarterly,* IX (September 1932), 257. Describes the arrangement by which Franklin financed his apprentices.

Kobre, Sidney. "The First American Newspaper: A Product of Environment," *Journalism Quarterly,* XVII (December 1940), 335. Social and economic factors leading to the founding of the press.

———. "The Revolutionary Colonial Press—A Social Interpretation," *Journalism Quarterly,* XX (September 1943), 193. A digest of a more detailed study, useful for its background information.

Lipper, Mark. "Comic Caricatures in Early American Newspapers as Representations of the National Character," Ph.D. thesis, Southern Illinois University, 1973. Concludes they were primarily vehicles for satire.

Mott, Frank Luther. "What Is the Oldest U.S. Newspaper?" *Journalism Quarterly,* XL (Winter 1963), 95. The title goes to the *Hartford Courant,* founded as the weekly *Connecticut Courant* in 1764, daily since 1837.

Nelson, Harold L. "Seditious Libel in Colonial America," *American Journal of Legal History,* III (April 1959), 160. Establishes the thesis that after the Zenger trial, printers were disciplined by legislatures or governors' councils rather than by trial courts. Exhaustive study by a legal scholar.

Nord, David Paul. "The Authority of Truth: Religion and the John Peter Zenger Case," *Journalism Quarterly,* LXII (Summer 1985), 227. Argues that freedom of expression had important religious roots.

———. "Teleology and News: The Religious Roots of American Journalism, 1630–1730," *Journal of American History,* LXXI (June 1990). p. 9.

Parkes, H. B. "New England in the Seventeenth-Thirties," *New England Quarterly,* III (July 1930), 397. A valuable appraisal of the Puritan traditions; also discusses the effect of British essay papers.

Price, Warren C. "Reflections on the Trial of John Peter Zenger," *Journalism Quarterly,* XXXII (Spring 1955), 161. Scholarly commentary.

Shaaber, Matthias A. "Forerunners of the Newspaper in America," *Journalism Quarterly,* XI (December 1934), 339. Describes predecessors of *Publick Occurrences.* Reprinted in Ford and Emery, *Highlights in the History of the American Press.*

Steffens, Pete. "Franklin's Early Attack on Racism," *Journalism History,* V (Spring 1978), 8. Ben wrote a 1764 essay against a massacre of Indians.

Thorn, William J. "Hudson's History of Journalism Criticized by His Contemporaries," *Journalism Quarterly,* LVII (Spring 1980), 99. *Herald*'s managing editor was suspect.

Wilson, C. Edward. "The Boston Inoculation Controversy: A Revisionist Interpretation," *Journalism History,* VII (Spring 1980), 16. Detailed research in newspaper files and documents.

CHAPTER 3: THE PRESS AND THE REVOLUTION

Books

Aldridge, Alfred O. *Man of Reason: The Life of Thomas Paine.* Philadelphia: Lippincott, 1959. The best study of Paine since Moncure D. Conway's two-volume *Life of Thomas Paine* (London: Putnam's, 1892). See also Mary A. Best, *Thomas Paine* (New York: Harcourt Brace Jovanovich, 1927).

Bailyn, Bernard. *The Ordeal of Thomas Hutchinson.* Cambridge, MA: Harvard University Press, 1974. Sam Adams's conservative victim.

———. *The Ideological Origins of the American Revolution.* Cambridge, MA: Harvard University Press, 1967. A structured study, utilizing the Harvard Library pamphlet collection, that exhibits feeling for the radical nature of the Revolution. See also Bailyn, *Origins of American Politics* (Cambridge, MA: Harvard University Press, 1968).

————. *Faces of Revolution.* New York: Knopf, 1990. An updating of his ground-breaking *Ideological Origins.*

BEER, GEORGE L. *British Colonial Policy.* New York: Macmillan, 1907. Presents the British point of view in a way that may not be familiar to the reader.

BOWEN, CATHERINE D. *John Adams and the American Revolution.* New York: Little, Brown, 1950. Follows the school of historical writing that allows the author to describe the feelings of her subjects.

BULLION, JOHN L. *A Great and Necessary Measure: George Grenville and the Genesis of the Stamp Act.* Columbia, MO: University of Missouri Press, 1982.

CALHOON, ROBERT M. *The Loyalists in Revolutionary America, 1760–1781.* New York: Harcourt Brace Jovanovich, 1973. Traces the Loyalists' enunciation of principles, search for accommodation, and final appeal to doctrine.

COMMAGER, HENRY STEELE, ed. *Documents of American History.* New York: Appleton-Century-Crofts, 1934; Hawthorn Books, 1969. Contains writings of Dickinson, the Adamses, Madison, and Jefferson.

DAVIDSON, PHILIP. *Propaganda and the American Revolution.* Chapel Hill: University of North Carolina Press, 1941. Reveals the tremendous impact of pamphlets, broadsides, newspapers, and books in conditioning the public to rebellion.

DEMETER, RICHARD L. *Primer, Presses, and Composing Sticks: Women Printers of the Colonial Period.* Hicksville, NY: Exposition Press, 1979. Incomplete 155-page study of nine women printers.

DRECHSEL, ROBERT E. *Newsmaking in the Trial Courts.* New York: Longman, 1982. Includes a historical review chapter on court reporting in the eighteenth and nineteenth centuries, based on literature review and substantial content analysis of leading U.S. papers. Based on Ph.D. thesis, University of Minnesota, 1980.

FLOWER, MILTON E. *John Dickinson, Conservative Revolutionary.* Charlottesville: University Press of Virginia, 1983. Examines the pattern of his political and private life.

FONER, ERIC. *Tom Paine and Revolutionary America.* New York: Oxford University Press, 1976. Places Paine in the American setting as a radical contributing to a new society.

GREENE, LAURENCE. *America Goes to Press.* Indianapolis: Bobbs-Merrill, 1936. Goes to source materials to describe how the news of important events reached the people through the press.

GROSS, ROBERT. *The Minutemen and Their World.* New York: Hill and Wang, 1976. How society was changing at the time of the Revolution and the impact of those changes on American policy.

HIXSON, RICHARD F. *Isaac Collins: A Quaker Printer in 18th-Century America.* New Brunswick, NJ: Rutgers University Press, 1968. The scholarly biography of a Patriot printer-editor.

HUDAK, LEONA M. *Early American Women Printers and Publishers, 1639–1820.* Metuchen, NJ: Scarecrow Press, 1978. Brief biographies and library collection listings on twenty-five women printers.

JONES, MICHAEL WYNN. *Cartoon History of the American Revolution.* New York: G. P. Putnam's Sons, 1975. Both an illustrated history of the period and a collection of drawings.

KERBER, LINDA K. *Women of the Republic: Intellect and Ideology in Revolutionary America.* Chapel Hill: University of North Carolina Press, 1980. A key overview of women in the Revolutionary period.

LORENZ, ALFRED L. *Hugh Gaine: A Colonial Printer-Editor's Odyssey to Loyalism.* Carbondale: Southern Illinois University Press, 1972. Business conservatism led to Gaine's moderate politics. His "turncoat" *New York Gazette and Mercury* did not survive.

MARBLE, ANNIE R. *From 'Prentice to Patron—The Life Story of Isaiah Thomas.* New York: Appleton-Century-Crofts, 1935. The standard biography.

MIDDLEKAUFF, ROBERT. *The Glorious Cause: The American Revolution, 1763–1789.* New York: Oxford University Press, 1982. The first volume of the *Oxford History of the United States.*

MILLER, JOHN C. *Sam Adams: Pioneer in Propaganda.* Boston: Little, Brown, 1936. A "debunking" treatment of Adams; sometimes vague, but useful.

MINER, WARD L. *William Goddard, Newspaperman.* Durham, NC: Duke University Press, 1962. Detailed study; also covers his mother and sister.

MONTROSS, LYNN. *Rag, Tag and Bobtail.* New York: Harper & Row, 1952. Demonstrates that the people's army and government operated remarkably effectively.

NASH, GARY. *The Urban Crucible: Social Change, Political Consciousness, and the Origins of the American Revolution.* Cambridge, MA: Harvard University Press, 1979. Economic and demographic changes in urban America that helped precipitate the Revolution.

NORTON, MARY BETH. *Liberty's Daughters: The Revolutionary Experience of American Women, 1750–1800.* Boston: Little, Brown, 1980, 1996 (with a new preface). A major study of women in the Revolutionary period.

PAINE, THOMAS. *The Life and Major Writings of Thomas Paine,* ed. Philip S. Foner. New York: Citadel Press, 1961. Annotated texts of Paine's major works.

SCHLESINGER, ARTHUR M. *Prelude to Independence: The Newspaper War on Britain, 1764–1776.* New York: Knopf, 1958. An excellent detailed study of the role of the newspaper in promoting revolution, and a history of the press for the period.

SMITH, PAGE. *A New Age Now Begins: A People's History of the American Revolution.* New York: McGraw-Hill, 1976. A two-volume narrative of the Revolutionary era. Newspapers were used extensively to provide precise details for its 1900 pages.

SNYDER, LOUIS L., AND RICHARD B. MORRIS. eds. *A Treasury of Great Reporting.* New York: Simon & Schuster, 1962.

This book contains excerpts from outstanding journalistic writings between colonial times and post–World War II.

WALETT, FRANCIS G. *Patriots, Loyalists, and Printers.* Worcester, MA: American Antiquarian Society, 1976. Bicentennial booklet containing many reprints. See also Walett, *Massachusetts Newspapers and the Revolutionary Crisis, 1763–1776* (Boston: Massachusetts Bicentennial Commission, 1974).

WOOD, GORDON S. *The Creation of the American Revolution, 1776–1787.* Chapel Hill: University of North Carolina Press, 1969. An analysis of political and social thought and the institutions shaping it.

YOUNG, ALFRED. *The American Revolution: Explorations in the History of American Radicalism.* DeKalb: Northern Illinois University Press, 1976.

———. *Beyond the American Revolution: Explorations in the History of American Radicalism.* DeKalb: Northern Illinois University Press, 1993. New Left, "history-from-the-bottom-up" interpretations of the American Revolution.

Periodicals and Monographs

BRADLEY, PATRICIA. "Slavery in Colonial Newspapers: The Somerset Case," *Journalism History,* XII (Spring 1985), 2. Content analysis.

CULLEN, MAURICE R., JR. "Benjamin Edes: Scourge of Tories," *Journalism Quarterly,* LI (Summer 1974), 213. Traces Edes's life and role in the Sons of Liberty.

———. "The Boston Gazette: A Community Newspaper," *Journalism Quarterly,* XXXVI (Spring 1959), 204. Tells how the *Gazette* reflected Boston life in the 1760s and 1770s.

DICKEN-GARCIA, HAZEL. "Of Punctilios among the Fair Sex: Colonial American Magazines, 1741–1776," *Journalism History,* III (Summer 1976), 48. The bulk of material printed about or for women came from men.

FARRAR, FREDERIC. "Constitution Era Newspapers: Fourteen Survive," *Media History Digest,* VII (Spring–Summer 1987), 43.

HENRY, SUSAN. "Colonial Woman Printer as Prototype: Toward a Model for the Study of Minorities," *Journalism History,* III (Summer 1976), 20. Argues for the use of social, biological, economic, and local history sources.

———. "Notes toward the Liberation of Journalism History: A Study of Five Women Printers in Colonial America," Ph.D. thesis, Syracuse University, 1976. The five are Ann Franklin, Sarah Goddard, Margaret Draper, Hannah Watson, and Mary Crouch. See also Henry, "Sarah Goddard, Gentlewoman Printer," *Journalism Quarterly,* LVII (Spring 1980), 23; and "Exception to the Female Model: Colonial Printer Mary Crouch," *Journalism Quarterly,* LXII (Winter 1985), 725.

HESTER, AL, SUSAN PARKER HUME, AND CHRISTOPHER BICKERS. "Foreign News in Colonial North American Newspapers, 1764–1775," *Journalism Quarterly,* LVII (Spring 1980), 18. Content analysis of three leading papers.

HIXSON, RICHARD F. "Literature for Trying Times: Some Pamphlet Writers and the Revolution," *Journalism History,* III (Spring 1976), 7. A survey.

HOOPER, LEONARD J. "Women Printers in Colonial Times," *Journalism Educator,* XXIX (April 1974), 24. A factual survey. See also Susan Henry, "Margaret Draper: Colonial Printer Who Challenged the Patriots," *Journalism History,* I (Winter 1974), 141; and Norma Schneider, "Clementina Rind: 'Editor, Mother, Wife,' " *Journalism History,* I (Winter 1974), 137, for sketches of Massachusetts and Virginia women printers.

JENSEN, MERRILL. "The American People and the American Revolution," *Journal of American History,* LVI (June 1970), 5. Excellent example of newspaper, pamphlet, and broadside use.

MOTT, FRANK LUTHER. "The Newspaper Coverage of Lexington and Concord," *New England Quarterly,* XVII (December 1944), 489. A day-by-day analysis of how the news was spread. Reprinted in Ford and Emery, *Highlights in the History of the American Press.*

PARKER, PETER J. "The Philadelphia Printer: A Study of an 18th-Century Businessman," *Business History Review,* XL (Spring 1966), 24. The colonial artisan becomes a fledgling capitalist.

STEIRER, WILLIAM F., JR. "A Study in Prudence: Philadelphia's 'Revolutionary' Journalists," *Journalism History,* III (Spring 1976), 16. The journalists shied away from social and political issues. Uses stand on slavery as basis for judgment.

TEETER, DWIGHT L. " 'King' Sears, the Mob, and Freedom of the Press in New York, 1765–76," *Journalism Quarterly,* XLI (Autumn 1964), 539. The mob, disrespectful of the freedom of ideas, drove James Rivington out of business.

———. "Press Freedom and the Public Printing: Pennsylvania, 1775–1783," *Journalism Quarterly,* XLV (Autumn 1968), 445.

"Tom Paine's First Appearance in America," *Atlantic Monthly,* IV (November 1859), 565. Describes Paine's propaganda activities and journalistic contributions. Reprinted in Ford and Emery, *Highlights in the History of the American Press.*

YODELIS, MARY ANN. "The Press in Wartime: Portable and Penurious," *Journalism History,* III (Spring 1976), 2. Apparently subscriptions and advertising paid for newspaper printing costs, with profits coming from other printing. General and religious customers, rather than government and political patrons, were major sources of that income.

———. "Who Paid the Piper? Publishing Economics in Boston, 1763–1775," *Journalism Monographs,* XXXVIII (February 1975). Based on a Ph.D. thesis, University of Wisconsin, 1971. See also Yodelis, "Courts, Counting House and Streets: Attempts at Press Control, 1763–1775," *Journalism History,* I (Spring 1974), 11; and "Advertising in the Boston Press," *Journalism History,* III (Summer 1976), 40. In-depth studies by colonial journalism scholar.

CHAPTER 4: FOUNDING THE NEW NATION

Books

ALEXANDER, JOHN K. *The Selling of the Constitutional Convention: A History of News Coverage.* Madison House, 1990. Explores the media's role in the Constitution's adoption.

APPLEBY, JOYCE O. *Capitalism and a New Social Order: The Republican Vision of the 1790s.* New York: New York University Press, 1984. Hamilton's vision of the future of the republic.

AUSTIN, ALEINE. *Matthew Lyon: "New Man" of the Democratic Revolution, 1749–1822.* University Park, PA: Pennsylvania State University Press, 1981. Definitive.

AXELRAD, JACOB. *Philip Freneau: Champion of Democracy.* Austin: University of Texas Press, 1967. Carefully researched biography.

BAILEY, THOMAS A. *A Diplomatic History of the American People.* Englewood Cliffs, NJ: Prentice Hall, 1980. Tenth edition of a leading work on foreign policy.

BOORSTIN, DANIEL. *The Americans: The National Experience.* New York: Random House, 1965. Consensus history; traces social history to the Civil War, minimizing political conflicts and clashes of ideas.

BOWERS, CLAUDE G. *Jefferson and Hamilton.* Boston: Houghton Mifflin, 1925. This book is particularly interesting to the student of journalism because the author draws heavily on newspaper sources. Strongly Anti-Federalist.

COBBETT, WILLIAM. *Selections.* Oxford: Clarendon Press, 1923. These excerpts from the journalist's detailed *Works* demonstrate style and content.

HENDRICKSON, ROBERT A. *The Rise and Fall of Alexander Hamilton.* New York: Van Nostrand Reinhold, 1981. Definitive biography.

HUMPHREY, CAROL SUE. *The Press of the Young Republic, 1783–1833.* Westport, CT: Greenwood Press, 1996. Asserts the important political role of the press in the early national period as partisanship grew.

LEARY, LEWIS. *That Rascal Freneau.* New Brunswick, NJ: Rutgers University Press, 1941. The standard "life" of the Anti-Federalist editor.

LEVY, LEONARD W. ed. *Freedom of the Press from Zenger to Jefferson.* Durham, NC: Carolina Academic Press, 1997. See entry in bibliography for Chapter 2.

MCCOY, DREW. *The Elusive Republic: Political Economy in Jeffersonian America.* Chapel Hill: University of North Carolina Press, 1980. Jefferson's views on expansion and American capitalism.

MCMASTER, JOHN BACH. *A History of the People of the United States from the Revolution to the Civil War.* 8 vols. New York: Appleton-Century-Crofts, 1883–1913. McMaster is chosen from among some of the best historians who wrote of this period, because he depended on newspaper sources to bring out the flavor and temper of the times.

MILLER, JOHN C. *Crisis in Freedom: The Alien and Sedition Acts.* Boston: Little, Brown, 1951. A relatively brief account of passage of the laws and details of the trials. See also Miller, *Alexander Hamilton: Portrait in Paradox* (New York: Harper & Row, 1959); and *The Federalist Era* (Harper & Row, 1960).

NEVINS, ALLAN. *American Press Opinion, Washington to Coolidge.* Boston: Heath, 1928. An excellent selection of the partisan editorials of the period.

OSBORNE, JOHN W. *William Cobbett: His Thought and His Times.* New Brunswick, NJ: Rutgers University Press, 1966. Biography of the Federalist editor of *Porcupine's Gazette.*

POLLARD, JAMES E. *The Presidents and the Press.* New York: Macmillan, 1947. The attitude of the Chief Executive regarding the press is an indicator of journalistic prestige and power, decade by decade.

RUTLAND, ROBERT ALLEN. *The Birth of the Bill of Rights, 1776–1791.* Chapel Hill: University of North Carolina Press, 1955. A documented study. See also Rutland, *The Ordeal of the Constitution* (Norman: University of Oklahoma Press, 1966).

SISSON, DANIEL. *The American Revolution of 1800.* New York: Knopf, 1974. Scholarly.

SMITH, JAMES M. *Freedom's Fetters: The Alien and Sedition Laws and American Civil Liberties.* Ithaca, NY: Cornell University Press, 1956. Detailed and documented analysis of the laws and court cases.

SMITH, JEFFERY A. *Printers and Press Freedom: The Ideology of Early American Journalism.* New York: Oxford, 1987. The ideology of the eighteenth-century press emphasized that press freedom existed so the press could expose governmental misconduct.

———. *Franklin and Bache: Envisioning the Enlightened Republic.* New York: Oxford, 1990. Ben and his grandson.

STEWART, DONALD H. *The Opposition Press of the Federalist Period.* Albany: State University of New York Press, 1969. A scholarly study of the partisan press with much new detail.

TEBBEL, JOHN, AND SARAH MILES WATTS. *The Press and the Presidency from George Washington to Ronald Reagan.* New York: Oxford University Press, 1985. Strongest in nineteenth century; conventional criticism of recent presidents.

TUGG, JAMES. *Benjamin Franklin Bache and the "Philadelphia Aurora."* Philadelphia: University of Pennsylvania Press, 1991. First modern biography of Bache.

Periodicals and Monographs

BALDASTY, GERALD J. "Toward an Understanding of the First Amendment: Boston Newspapers, 1782–1791," *Journalism History,* III (Spring 1976), 25. Revises Levy by focusing on the common law of defamation rather than on seditious libel.

BOSTON, RAY. "The Impact of 'Foreign Liars' on the American Press (1790–1800)," *Journalism Quarterly,* L (Winter 1973), 722. Political refugees from Britain spearheaded press attack on Federalists.

"Cobbett," *Fraser's Magazine,* XII (August 1835), 207. A personality sketch that brings out the journalist's wit and pugnacity.

COLL, GARY. "Noah Webster: Journalist, 1783–1803," Ph.D. thesis, Southern Illinois University, 1971. Assesses his contributions to both form and content of the newspaper and magazine.

———. "Noah Webster, Magazine Editor and Publisher," *Journalism History,* XI (Spring–Summer 1984), 26.

DOWLING, RUTH N. "William Cobbett, His Trials and Tribulations as an Alien Journalist, 1794–1800," Ph.D. thesis, Southern Illinois University, 1972. Seven libel charges, some unfairly made, prompted Cobbett to leave for England.

GOLDSMITH, ADOLPH O. "The Roaring Lyon of Vermont," *Journalism Quarterly,* XXXIX (Spring 1962), 179. The stormy career of Congressman Lyon, who was reelected while in jail for sedition.

GROTTA, GERALD L. "Phillip Freneau's Crusade for Open Sessions of the U.S. Senate," *Journalism Quarterly,* XLVIII (Winter 1971), 667. The editor wins out.

HUMPHREY, CAROL SUE. " 'Little Ado about Something,' Philadelphia Newspapers and the Constitutional Convention," *American Journalism,* V (1988), 63. In-depth data study.

KNUDSON, JERRY W. "Political Journalism in the Age of Jefferson," *Journalism History,* I (Spring 1974), 20. Summarizes Knudson's Ph.D. thesis, University of Virginia, 1974. Jefferson faced criticism of a predominantly Federalist press.

LIST, KAREN K. "Realities and Possibilities: The Lives of Women in Periodicals of the New Republic," *American Journalism,* 11:1 (Winter 1994), 20–38. Award-winning research.

———. "The Role of William Cobbett in Philadelphia's Party Press, 1794–1799," *Journalism Monographs* 82 (1983), 1–41. Well-researched study.

———. "Two Party Papers' Coverage of Women in the New Republic," *Critical Studies in Mass Communication,* 2:2 (June 1985), 52. Cobbett and Bache aided the cause of women in politics.

PRINCE, CARL E. "The Federalist Party and Creation of a Court Press, 1789–1801," *Journalism Quarterly,* LIII (Summer 1976), 238. Political rivalries and favors transform the press system.

REITZEL, WILLIAM. "William Cobbett and Philadelphia Journalism," *Pennsylvania Magazine,* LIX (July 1935), 223. An excellent interpretation of the journalist. Reprinted in Ford and Emery, *Highlights in the History of the American Press.*

SLOAN, WILLIAM DAVID. "The Party Press: The Newspaper Role in National Politics, 1789–1816," Ph.D. thesis, University of Texas, 1981. Finds party press played a constructive role in U.S. political development. See *Journalism History,* IX (Spring 1982), 18, for his article.

———. " 'Purse and Pen': Party-Press Relationships, 1789–1816," *American Journalism,* VI (1989), 103. See also Sloan, "Scurrility and the Party Press, 1789–1816," *American Journalism,* V (1988), 97. By an authority.

SMITH, JEFFERY A. "Public Opinion and the Press Clause," *Journalism History,* XIV (Spring 1987). Bill of Rights press guarantee had public backing. See also Carol Sue Humphrey, "The Bulwark of Our Liberties," p. 34.

STEVENS, JOHN D. "Congressional History of the 1798 Sedition Law," *Journalism Quarterly,* XLIII (Summer 1966), 247. A detailed report of the partisan battle in the House, with analysis of votes.

CHAPTER 5: WESTWARD EXPANSION

Books

ADAMS, HENRY. *History of the United States of America During the Administration of Thomas Jefferson.* New York: A. & C. Boni, 1930. The first two volumes of Adams's brilliant history; the next two cover Madison. Adams's first six chapters magnificently portray the United States of 1800. The nine-volume work first appeared in 1889–91.

AMBROSE, STEPHEN E. *Undaunted Courage: Meriwether Lewis, Thomas Jefferson, and the Opening of the American West.* New York: Simon and Schuster, 1996. The Lewis and Clark expedition and Jefferson's relationship with Lewis.

AMES, WILLIAM E. *A History of the "National Intelligencer."* Chapel Hill: University of North Carolina Press, 1972. Intensive use of files and other documentary materials; covers Smith, Gales, Seaton and other editors of the outstanding paper. See also Ames, "Samuel Harrison Smith Founds the *National Intelligencer,*" *Journalism Quarterly,* XLII (Summer 1965), 389; and "Federal Patronage and the Washington, D.C. Press," *Journalism Quarterly,* XLIX (Spring 1972), 22.

BARTLETT, RICHARD A. *The New Country: A Social History of the American Frontier, 1776–1890.* New York: Oxford Press, 1974. Updating of interpretations.

BENNION, SHERILYN COX. *Equal to the Occasion: Women Editors of the Nineteenth-Century West.* Reno: University of Nevada Press, 1990. Covers the lives, work, and historical contexts of at least 35 women editors from 1854 to the turn of the century.

BROOKS, VAN WYCK. *The World of Washington Irving.* New York: Dutton, 1944. An interpretation of the period through the literary contributions of American writers.

BROWN, CHARLES H. *William Cullen Bryant.* New York: Scribners', 1971. A comprehensive study of the editor of the *New York Evening Post.*

Cambridge History of American Literature. Vol. 2. New York: G. P. Putnam's Sons, 1917–21. Pages 160–75 describe magazines during 1783–1850; pages 176–95 describe the general newspaper picture from 1775 to 1860. Book publishing is surveyed in Volume 4 (pp. 533–53).

CLOUD, BARBARA. *The Business of Newspapers on the Western Frontier.* Reno: University of Nevada Press, 1992. Illuminates little-studied economic aspects of the frontier press.

DOOLEY, PATRICIA L. *Taking Their Political Place: Journalists and the Making of an Occupation.* Westport, CT: Greenwood Press, 1997. Thoroughly researched study that illuminates how journalists established occupational boundaries separating their work from that of politicians.

ECKHARDT, CELIA MORRIS. *Fanny Wright: Rebel in America.* Cambridge, MA: Harvard University Press, 1984. Passionately written biography of the radical freethinker.

FARAGHER, JOHN MACK. *Sugar Creek: Life on the Illinois Prairie.* New Haven: Yale University Press, 1986. A social and political history of westward expansion in one central Illinois community.

FORD, WORTHINGTON C. *Jefferson and the Newspaper, 1785–1830.* New York: Columbia University Press, 1936. Gives examples of how Jefferson regarded journalists.

FORSYTH, DAVID P. *The Business Press in America, 1760–1865.* Philadelphia: Chilton, 1964. A prize-winning history of business journalism.

LUXON, NORVAL NEIL. *Niles' Weekly Register.* Baton Rouge: Louisiana State University Press, 1947. This doctoral dissertation contains the best information on this influential paper.

LYON, WILLIAM H. *Those Old Yellow Dog Days: Frontier Journalism in Arizona.* Tucson, AZ: Historical Society, 1994. By a respected historian of the West.

MALONE, DUMAS. *Jefferson and His Time.* 5 vols. Boston: Little, Brown, 1962–75. Volume 3, *Jefferson and the Ordeal of Liberty,* is followed by two on his presidential terms.

MOTT, FRANK LUTHER. *History of American Magazines, 1741–1850.* New York: Macmillan, 1930. Volume one of a series by the outstanding authority on the subject. The author won a Pulitzer award for his study.

———. *Jefferson and the Press.* Baton Rouge: Louisiana State University Press, 1943. An excellent monograph.

NELSON, HAROLD L. *Freedom of the Press from Hamilton to the Warren Court.* Indianapolis: Bobbs-Merrill, 1967. A collection of documents, cases, and essays, with a lucid introduction by the editor summarizing press freedom trends since 1800.

PERDUE, THEDA, ed. *Cherokee Editor: The Writings of Elias Boudinot,* Knoxville: University of Tennessee Press, 1983. First Native American editor.

PETERSON, MERRILL D. *Thomas Jefferson and the New Nation.* New York: Oxford University Press, 1970. Biography by a leading Jeffersonian scholar covering his entire life.

PRESTON, DICKSON J. *Newspapers of Maryland's Eastern Shore.* Centreville, MD: Cornell Maritime Press, 1986. Handsomely printed and illustrated account of newspapers from colonial times to the present.

REMINI, ROBERT V. *Andrew Jackson and the Course of American Democracy.* New York: Harper & Row, 1984. Winner of the 1984 nonfiction American Book Award.

———. *Henry Clay: Statesman for the Union.* New York: W. W. Norton, 1991. Excellent biography that covers perhaps the most important statesman of the 1812–50 period.

RILEY, SAM G. *Magazines of the American South.* Westport, CT: Greenwood Press, 1986. Essays cover 89 magazines since 1764.

SCHLESINGER, ARTHUR M., JR. *The Age of Jackson.* Boston: Little, Brown, 1945. A penetrating study of the political backgrounds by a Pulitzer Prize winner. Includes a chapter on the press. A classic study, but it seriously overstates the democracy of Jacksonian politics. See also Glyndon G. Van Deusen, *The Jacksonian Era* (New York: Harper & Row, 1959); and Edward Pessen, *Jacksonian America* (New York: Dorsey, 1969), whose revisionist study counters Schlesinger.

SMITH, CULVER H. *The Press, Politics and Patronage.* Athens, GA: University of Georgia Press, 1977. A detailed account for 1789 to 1875.

TOCQUEVILLE, ALEXIS DE. *Democracy in America.* New York: Doubleday, 1969. Editions have been appearing since 1835 of this famous French observer's study of American democracy and its effect on the social system. For a 1980s version, see Richard Reeves, *American Journey: Traveling with Tocqueville in Search of "Democracy in America"* (New York: Simon & Schuster, 1982).

WALTER, RONALD G. *American Reformers, 1815–1860.* New York: Hill and Wang, 1978. Places pre–Civil War reform movements in their broader cultural contexts.

WHITE, RICHARD. *A New History of the American West.* Norman: University of Oklahoma Press, 1991. Massive compilation of anecdotal material on a rootless social world.

WILENTZ, SEAN. *Chants Democratic: New York City and the Rise of the American Working Class, 1788–1850.* New York: Oxford University Press, 1984. A well-written scholarly interpretation.

William Winston Seaton. Boston: James R. Osgood and Company, 1871. The biography of the great Washington editor of the *National Intelligencer,* with notes of family and friends.

WOOD, JAMES PLAYSTED. *Magazines in the United States.* New York: Ronald Press, 1956. A study of the influence of magazines on American society.

Periodicals and Monographs

AVERY, DONALD R. "The Newspaper on the Eve of the War of 1812: Changes in Content Patterns, 1808–1812," Ph.D. thesis, Northern Illinois University, 1982. Content analysis of a 10 percent sample of 1810 newspapers showed foreign news declining, domestic news increasing, and one-half of the space devoted to advertising. See also "The Emerging American Newspaper: Discovering the Home Front," *American Journalism* I:2 (1954), 51.

BALDASTY, GERALD J. "The Press and Politics in the Age of Jackson," *Journalism Monographs,* LXXXIX (August 1984). See also Baldasty, "The Boston Press and Politics in Jacksonian America," *Journalism History,* VII (Autumn–Winter 1980), 104; and "The Washington, D.C.,

Political Press in the Age of Jackson," *Journalism History,* X (Autumn–Winter 1983), 50.

CLARK, CARLISLE. "The Old Corner Printing House," *Granite Monthly,* XXX (August 1901), describes the *Farmer's Weekly Museum,* started by Isaiah Thomas.

DICKEN-GARCIA, HAZEL. "Communication in the Migration to Kentucky, 1789–1792," Ph.D. thesis, University of Wisconsin, 1977. An examination of all aspects.

FINNEGAN, JOHN R., JR. "Politics, Defamation, and the Social Process of Law in New York State, 1776–1860," Ph.D. thesis, University of Minnesota, 1985.

FRANCKE, WARREN. "Sensationalism and the Development of 19th-Century Reporting," *Journalism History,* XII (Autumn–Winter 1985), 80.

GARRISON, BRUCE L. "Robert Walsh's *American Review:* America's First Quarterly," *Journalism History,* VIII (Spring 1981), 14. Published 1811–12.

GLICKSBERG, CHARLES. "Bryant and the United States Review," *New England Quarterly,* VII (December 1934), 687. Describes early nineteenth-century periodicals.

HAGE, GEORGE S. "Anti-Intellectualism in Press Comment: 1828 and 1952," *Journalism Quarterly,* XXXVI (Fall 1959), 439. Comparison of newspaper content in two presidential elections.

JONES, CHARLOTTE D. "The Penny Press and the Origins of Journalistic Objectivity," Ph.D. thesis, University of Iowa, 1985.

KIELBOWICZ, RICHARD B. "Party Press Cohesiveness: Jackson Newspapers, 1832," *Journalism Quarterly,* LX (Autumn 1983), 518. Considerable local discretion.

LEE, ALFRED MCCLUNG. "Dunlap and Claypoole: Printers and News-Merchants of the Revolution," *Journalism Quarterly,* XI (June 1934), 160. The story of the first successful American daily.

LUEBKE, BARBARA F. "Elias Boudinot, Cherokee Editor: The Father of American Indian Journalism," Ph.D. thesis, University of Missouri, 1981.

LYLE, CORNELIUS R., II "New Hampshire's *Sentinel:* The Editorial Life of John Prentiss, 1799–1846," Ph.D. thesis, Northwestern University, 1972. A weekly editor, first a Federalist, then a Whig.

MARTIN, BENJAMIN ELLIS. "Transition Period of the American Press—Leading Editors in This Century," *Magazine of American History,* XVII (April 1887), 273. Describes battles between Federalist and Republican journalists. Facsimile examples.

MELTON, BAXTER F., JR. "Amos Kendall in Kentucky, 1814–1829," Ph.D. thesis, Southern Illinois University, 1977. Pre-Washington years.

MILLER, ALAN R. "America's First Political Satirist: Seba Smith of Maine," *Journalism Quarterly,* XLVII (Autumn 1970), 488. The creator of Major Jack Downing at the *Portland Courier.*

NORD, DAVID PAUL. "The Evangelical Origins of Mass Media in America, 1815–1835," *Journalism Monographs,* LXXXVIII (May 1984). Evangelical impulse brought the mass printing of religious tracts.

PLASTERER, NICHOLAS N. "The Croswell Case: Paradox of History," *Journalism Quarterly,* XLIV (Spring 1967), 125. Argues that Croswell deserves more attention than Zenger.

REED, BARBARA STRAUS. "A History and Content Analysis of the Pioneer English-Language American Jewish Periodical Press, 1823–1858," Ph.D, thesis, Ohio University, 1987. The Jewish press began with magazines (*The Jew,* 1823) rather than later Yiddish newspapers.

RILEY, SAM G. "*The Cherokee Phoenix:* The Short Unhappy Life of the First American Indian Newspaper," *Journalism Quarterly,* LIII (Winter 1976), 666. The 1834 *Phoenix* succumbed to tribal problems and white harassment.

———, AND GARY SELNOW. "Southern Magazine Publishing, 1764–1964," *Journalism Quarterly,* LXV (Winter 1988), 898. Analysis of data for twelve states.

SINGLETARY, MICHAEL W. "The New Editorial Voice for Andrew Jackson: Happenstance or Plan?" *Journalism Quarterly,* LIII (Winter 1976), 672. Discussion of Blair.

STEWART, ROBERT K. "The Exchange System and the Development of American Politics in the 1820s," *American Journalism,* IV (1987), 30. Much data.

———. "Jacksonians Discipline a Party Editor," *Journalism Quarterly,* LXVI (Autumn 1989), 591. Philadelphia editor Stephen Simpson feels the wrath.

TEETER, DWIGHT L., JR. "John Dunlap: The Political Economy of a Printer's Success," *Journalism Quarterly.* LII (Spring 1975), 3. Making of a fortune by the publisher of the *Pennsylvania Packet.*

ZIMMER, ROXANNE M. "The Urban Daily Press: Baltimore, 1797–1816," Ph.D. thesis, University of Iowa, 1982. News emphasis was on shipping and trade; little local news, much advertising.

CHAPTER 6: A PRESS FOR THE MASSES

Books

BALDASTY, GERALD J. *The Commercialization of News in the Nineteenth Century.* Madison: University of Wisconsin Press, 1992. Well-researched history of partisan giving way to commercial newspapers.

BARNES, THURLOW WEED, AND HARRIET WEED. eds. *Life of Thurlow Weed.* 2 vols. Boston: Houghton Mifflin, 1883. The Albany editor.

BLANCHARD, PAULA. *Margaret Fuller: From Transcendentalism to Revolution.* New York: Delacorte, 1978. Readable biography.

BROWN, FRANCIS. *Raymond of the "Times."* New York: Norton, 1951. A first-rate biography.

CAPPER, CHARLES. *Margaret Fuller: An American Romantic Life.* Vol. 1, *The Private Years.* New York: Oxford University Press, 1993.

CARLSON, OLIVER. *The Man Who Made News.* New York: Duell, Sloan & Pearce, 1942. The best biography of James Gordon Bennett, Sr.

CHEVIGNY, BELL GALE. *The Woman and the Myth: Margaret Fuller's Life and Writings.* Old Westbury, NY: Feminist Press, 1976. Biography of this famed intellectual leader of the 1840s.

COPELAND, FAYETTE. *Kendall of the "Picayune."* Norman: University of Oklahoma Press, 1943. An interesting account of the life and times of a New Orleans editor and Mexican War correspondent.

CROUTHAMEL, JAMES L. *James Watson Webb, A Biography.* Middletown, CT: Wesleyan University Press, 1969. Carefully documented study of a leader in news gathering.

————. *Bennett's "New York Herald" and the Rise of the Popular Press.* Syracuse, NY: Syracuse University Press, 1989. Scholarly, detailed.

DABNEY, THOMAS E. *One Hundred Great Years.* Baton Rouge: Louisiana State University Press, 1944. The centennial of the *New Orleans Times-Picayune.*

DAVIS, ELMER. *History of the "New York Times," 1851–1921.* New York: The New York Times Company, 1921. Valuable for the early years.

DICKEN-GARCIA, HAZEL. *Journalistic Standards in Nineteenth-Century America.* Madison: University of Wisconsin Press, 1989. Award-winning study of journalistic standards and press criticism.

EISENHOWER, JOHN S. D. *So Far from God: The U.S. War with Mexico, 1846–1848.* New York: Random House, 1989. Primarily a military history. See also K. Jack Bauer, *The Mexican War* (New York: Macmillan, 1974), also a military study.

EMERSON, EVERETT. *A Literary Biography of Samuel L. Clemens.* Philadelphia: University of Pennsylvania Press, 1984. Based on unpublished archives.

GLEASON, TIMOTHY W. *The Watchdog Concept: The Press and the Courts in 19th-Century America.* Ames: Iowa State University Press, 1990. The publishers staked their claim to role.

GRAMLING, OLIVER. *AP: The Story of News.* New York: Farrar, Straus & Giroux, 1940. A colorful account of the rise of the AP, not always accurate.

GREELEY, HORACE. *Overland Journey from New York to San Francisco in the Summer of 1859,* edited with notes by Charles T. Duncan. New York: Knopf, 1963. Valuable biographical material as well as Greeley's view of the West.

————. *Recollections of a Busy Life.* New York: J. B. Ford and Company, 1868. The editor's own version of his career.

HAGE, GEORGE S. *Newspapers on the Minnesota Frontier, 1849–1860.* St. Paul: Minnesota Historical Society, 1967. What frontier journalism was like. Carefully researched and well written.

HARLOW, ALVIN F. *Old Wires and New Waves: The History of the Telegraph, Telephone, and Wireless.* New York: Appleton-Century-Crofts, 1936. First half of the book covers the pre–Civil War period.

HOE, ROBERT. *Short History of the Printing Press.* New York: R. Hoe & Company, 1902. Obviously a promotional venture, but valuable in describing presses.

HUDSON, FREDERIC. *Journalism in the United States, 1690–1872.* New York: Harper & Row, 1873. One of the oldest journalism histories, but especially useful in the description of the mid-nineteenth century because the author knew many of the persons he discusses.

HUNTZICKER, WILLIAM. *The Popular Press, 1833–1865.* Westport, CT: Greenwood, 1999. An excellent study that covers a wide range, including specialized and alternative newspapers as well as the New York press and western newspapers.

HUTTON, FRANKIE, AND BARBARA STRAUS REED, eds. *Outsiders in 19th Century Press History: Multicultural Perspectives.* Bowling Green, OH: Bowling Green State University Popular Press, 1995. Essays on 11 alternative presses, including those of Native Americans, African Americans, Jews, and peace advocates.

JOHN, RICHARD R. *Spreading the News: The American Postal System from Franklin to Morse.* Cambridge, MA: Harvard University Press, 1995. Indispensable study about the development of the postal system as a communication technology; a major contribution.

JOHNSON, GERALD, et al. *The Sunpapers of Baltimore.* New York: Knopf, 1937. An excellent case history of the penny press outside New York.

KIELBOWICZ, RICHARD B. *News in the Mail: The Press, Post Office, and Public Information, 1700–1860s.* Westport, CT: Greenwood Press, 1989. The definitive study of the relationship between newspapers and the post office. Based on exhaustive documentary research.

LENNON, NIGEY. *The Sagebrush Bohemian: Mark Twain in California.* New York: Paragon House, 1991. Sam Clemens as an 1860s newsman.

LEONARD, THOMAS C. *The Power of the Press: The Birth of American Political Reporting.* New York: Oxford University Press, 1986. Focuses on nineteenth-century episodes.

MARBUT, FREDERICK B. *News from the Capital: The Story of Washington Reporting.* Carbondale: Southern Illinois University Press, 1971. History of reporting, both print and broadcast, by a longtime student of the Washington press corps.

MAVERICK, AUGUSTUS. *Henry J. Raymond and the New York Press.* Hartford: A. S. Hale and Company, 1870. An outstanding authority, this book contains many valuable documents.

McLAWS, MONTE BURR. *Spokesman for the Kingdom: Early Mormon Journalism and the Deseret News, 1830–1898.* Provo, UT: Brigham Young University Press, 1977. Scholarly study.

McMURTRIE, DOUGLAS C., AND ALBERT H. ALLEN. *Early Printing in Colorado.* Denver: Hirschfeld Press, 1935. McMurtrie also wrote about the journalism of other western states.

MERRIAM, GEORGE S. *Life and Times of Samuel Bowles.* New York; Appleton-Century-Crofts, 1885. Full of interesting letters and documents.

MITCHELL, CATHERINE C., ed. *Margaret Fuller's New York Journalism: A Biographical Essay and Key Writings.*

Knoxville: University of Tennessee Press, 1995. Includes a substantial biographical essay.

O'BRIEN, FRANK M. *The Story of "The Sun."* New York: George H. Doran Company, 1918. Revised ed. New York: Appleton-Century-Crofts, 1928. The standard history of the first penny newspaper.

PARTON, JAMES. *Life of Horace Greeley.* New York; Mason Brothers, 1855. The standard reference, written by a contemporary.

RHODES, JANE. *Mary Ann Shadd Cary: The Black Press and Protest in the Nineteenth Century.* Bloomington: Indiana University Press, 1998. Journalist and activist who used the press to fight slavery and advance human rights.

RITCHIE, GEORGE A. *Press Gallery: Congress and the Washington Correspondents.* Cambridge, MA: Harvard University Press, 1991. Brief survey emphasizing emblematic correspondents.

ROSEWATER, VICTOR. *History of Cooperative News-Gathering in the United States.* New York: Appleton-Century-Crofts, 1930. Superseded by Schwarzlose.

RUSSO, ANN, AND CHERIS KRAMARAE. *The Radical Women's Press of the 1850s.* London and New York: Routledge, Chapman and Hall, 1991.

SCHILLER, DAN. *Objectivity and the News: The Public and the Rise of Commercial Journalism.* Philadelphia: University of Pennsylvania Press, 1981. Links rise of objectivity with 1830s penny press; content analysis of the *National Police Gazette* (1845).

SCHUDSON, MICHAEL. *Discovering the News: A Social History of American Newspapers.* New York: Basic Books, 1978. Five essays dealing with the penny press, reportorial trends, and objectivity.

SCHWARZLOSE, RICHARD A. *The Nation's Newsbrokers.* Vol. 1, *The Formative Years, from Pretelegraph to 1865.* Vol. 2, *The Rush to Institution, from 1865 to 1920.* Evanston, IL: Northwestern University Press, 1989–90. Absolutely definitive, based on a 25-year study of primary sources.

SIBLEY, MARILYN M. *Lone Stars and States Gazettes: Texas Newspapers before the Civil War.* College Station: Texas A&M University Press, 1983.

SPENCER, DONALD M. *Louis Kossuth and Young America.* Columbia: University of Missouri Press, 1977. How the Hungarian patriot interacted with U.S. audiences in 1851.

STEELE, JANET E. *The Sun Shines for All: Journalism and Ideology in the Life of Charles A. Dana.* Syracuse: Syracuse University Press, 1993. Argues Dana was a great innovator and influence on newspaper development.

STILGOE, JOHN R. *Origins of the American Suburb, 1820–1939.* New Haven, CT: Yale University Press, 1989. A well-written social document.

SWISSHELM, JANE GREY. *Half a Century.* Chicago: Jansen, McClurg and Co., 1880. Autobiography of the first woman Washington correspondent.

VAN DEUSEN, GLYNDON GARLOCK. *Horace Greeley: Nineteenth-Century Crusader.* Philadelphia: University of Pennsylvania Press, 1953. This is the best, and most detailed, of the Greeley biographies.

WARREN, JOYCE W. *Fanny Fern: An Independent Woman.* New Brunswick, NJ: Rutgers University Press, 1992. First biography of the widely read newspaperwoman.

Periodicals and Monographs

BALDASTY, GERALD J. "The Charleston, South Carolina, Press and National News, 1808–47," *Journalism Quarterly,* LV (Autumn 1978), 519. The *National Intelligencer* was a major source.

BEASLEY, MAURINE. *The First Women Washington Correspondents.* Washington, DC: GW Washington Studies, no. 4, 1976. Report on seven nineteenth-century newswomen. See also Beasley, "Pens and Petticoats: Early Women Washington Correspondents," *Journalism History,* I (Winter 1974), 112; and "The Curious Case of Anne Royall," *Journalism History,* III (Winter 1976), 98.

BJORK, ULF JONAS. "The Commercial Roots of Foreign Correspondence: The *New York Herald* and Foreign News, 1835–1839." *American Journalism,* XI:2 (1994). Added details about Bennett's pivotal role.

BORDEN, MORTON. "Some Notes on Horace Greeley, Charles Dana and Karl Marx," *Journalism Quarterly,* XXXIV (Fall 1957), 457. It was Dana who kept Marx on the *Tribune*'s payroll. See also the Summer 1959 issue for texts of five letters from Dana to Marx (p. 314).

BOVÉE, WARREN G. "Horace Greeley and Social Responsibility," *Journalism Quarterly,* LXIII (Summer 1986), 251. He "anticipated" the Commission on Freedom of the Press.

BRADFORD, GAMALIEL. "Samuel Bowles," *Atlantic Monthly,* CXVI (October 1915), 487. An excellent character study. Reprinted in Ford and Emery, *Highlights in the History of the American Press.*

BROWN, JUNIUS HENRI. "Horace Greeley," *Harper's New Monthly Magazine,* XLVI (April 1873), 734. Describes Greeley's idiosyncrasies.

BUDDENBAUM, JUDITH M. "The Religion Journalism of James Gordon Bennett," *Journalism History,* XIV (Summer–Autumn 1987), 54. Detailed analysis of Bennett's extensive coverage.

CARTER, JOHN D. "*The San Francisco Bulletin, 1855–1865,*" Ph.D. thesis, University of California, 1941. A study of the beginnings of Pacific coast journalism.

CLOUD, BARBARA L. "Start the Presses: The Birth of Journalism in Washington Territory," Ph.D. thesis, University of Washington, 1979. Covers 1852 to 1882; young printers seeking profits were founders rather than editors with political motives.

COLEMAN, ALBERT E. "New and Authentic History of the Herald of the Bennetts," *Editor & Publisher,* LVI–LVIII, March 29, 1924–June 13, 1925.

COMMONS, JOHN R. "Horace Greeley and the Working Class Origins of the Republican Party," *Political Science Quar-*

terly, XXIV (September 1909), 468. A significant article by a great authority on labor.

DYER, CAROLYN S. "The Business History of the Antebellum Wisconsin Newspaper, 1833–1860," Ph.D. thesis, University of Wisconsin, 1978. Study of the concentration of ownership and diversity of views.

EBERHARD, WALLACE B. "Mr. Bennett Covers a Murder Trial," *Journalism Quarterly,* XLVII (Autumn 1970), 457. The 1830 trial of a sea captain.

ENDRES, FREDERIC F. "Frontier Obituaries as Cultural Reflectors," *Journalism History,* XI (Autumn–Winter 1984), 54. Ohio frontier papers.

ENDRES, KATHLEEN. "Jane Grey Swisshelm; 19th-Century Journalist and Feminist," *Journalism History,* II (Winter 1975), 128. Early Washington correspondent.

FIREBAUGH, DOROTHY GILE. "*The Sacramento Union:* Voice of California 1851–75," *Journalism Quarterly,* XXX (Summer 1953), 321.

"Frontier Press Issue," *Journalism History,* VII (Summer 1980), ed. Thomas H. Heuterman and Jerilyn S. McIntyre. Contains articles by Carolyn S. Dyer, Hazel Dicken-Garcia, Barbara L. Cloud, Roy A. Atwood, and Fred F. Endres.

GREGG, LEIGH F. "The First Amendment in the 19th Century: Journalists' Privilege and Congressional Investigations," Ph.D. thesis, University of Wisconsin, 1984. Case of James W. Simonton of the *New York Times.*

HALL, MARK W. "1831–49: The Pioneer Period for Newspapers in California," *Journalism Quarterly,* XLIX (Winter 1972), 648.

HERBERT, WILLIAM. "Jackson, the Bank, and the Press," Ph.D. thesis, University of Missouri, 1975. Newspapers overlooked changing economics in the debate on the Second Bank of the United States.

HOLLAND, DONALD R. "Volney B. Palmer (1799–1864): The Nation's First Advertising Agency Man," *Journalism Monographs,* XLIV (May 1976). Palmer began work in 1842 and had an agency by 1849.

"Journalism of the West," *Journal of the West,* XIX (April 1980). Articles by William H. Lyons and Thomas H. Heuterman.

KIELBOWICZ, RICHARD B. "Newsgathering by Printers' Exchange before the Telegraph," *Journalism History,* IX (Summer, 1982), 42. An important device.

———. "Speeding the News by Postal Express, 1825–1861; The Public Policy of Privileges for the Press," *Social Science Journal,* XXII (January 1985).

LORENZ, ALFRED L. " 'Out of Sorts and Out of Cash': Problems of Publishing in Wisconsin Territory, 1833–1848," *Journalism History,* III (Summer 1976), 34. See also Lorenz, "Hamilton Reed: An Editor's Trials on the Wisconsin Frontier," *Journalism Quarterly,* LIII (Autumn 1976), 417.

MARBUT, FREDERICK B. "Early Washington Correspondents: Some Neglected Pioneers," *Journalism Quarterly,* XXV (December 1948), 369. See also Marbut, "The United States Senate and the Press, 1838–4l," *Journalism Quarterly,* XXVIII (Summer 1951), 342.

MCINTYRE, JERILYN. "Communication on a Western Frontier—Some Questions about Context," *Journalism History,* III (Summer 1976), 33. News-use patterns.

MELLOW, JAMES R. "Brook Farm: An American Utopia," *Dialogue,* XIII:4 (1980), 44. Examines that literary-oriented communal experiment.

MITCHELL, CATHERINE C. "Horace Greeley's Star: Margaret Fuller's *New York Tribune* Journalism, 1844–1846," Ph.D. thesis, University of North Carolina–Asheville, 1987. Fuller was one of four editing the literary section.

NELSON, JACK A. "The Pioneer Press of the Great Basin, Ph.D. thesis, University of Missouri, 1971. Nevada and Utah editors lacked news ethics.

NILSSON, NILS G. "The Origin of the Interview," *Journalism Quarterly,* XLVIII (Winter 1971), 707. Police and court reporting of 1830s were the progenitors of the interview.

PEEBLES, PAUL. "James Gordon Bennett's Scintillations," *Galaxy,* XIV (August 1872), 258. A revealing and rewarding study of the editor. Reprinted in Ford and Emery, *Highlights in the History of the American Press.*

PICKETT, CALDER M. "Technology and the New York Press in the 19th Century," *Journalism Quarterly,* XXXVII (Summer 1960), 398.

REILLY, THOMAS W. "American Reporters and the Mexican War, 1846–1848," Ph.D. thesis, University of Minnesota, 1975. Coverage of the war was extensive and reinforced the American belief in Manifest Destiny.

———. "Newspaper Suppression during the Mexican War," *Journalism Quarterly,* LIV (Summer 1977), 262.

———. "A Spanish-Language Voice of Dissent in Antebellum New Orleans," *Louisiana History,* XXIII (Fall 1982), 325.

RUSSO, ANN, AND CHERIS KRAMARAE. *The Radical Women's Press of the 1850s.* London and New York: Routledge, Chapman and Hall, 1991.

SCHWARZLOSE, RICHARD A. "Early Telegraphic News Dispatches: Forerunner of the AP," *Journalism Quarterly,* LI (Winter 1974), 595. Pinpoints the AP's birth.

———. "Harbor News Association: Formal Origin of the AP," *Journalism Quarterly,* XLV (Summer 1968), 253.

———. "The Nation's First Wire Service: Evidence Supporting a Footnote," *Journalism Quarterly,* LVII (Winter 1980), 555. The New York State Associated Press is nominated.

———. "The Foreign Connection: Transatlantic Newspapers in the 1840s," *Journalism History,* X (Autumn–Winter 1983), 44.

SHAW, DONALD LEWIS. "At the Crossroads: Change and Continuity in American Press News, 1820–1860," *Journalism History,* VIII (Summer 1981), 38–53. Detailed report on major flow of the news research project.

———, AND JOHN W. SLATER. "Sensationalism in American Press News, 1820–1860," *Journalism History,* XII (Autumn–Winter 1985), 86.

SLOAN, W. DAVID. "George W. Wisner, Michigan Editor and Politician," *Journalism History,* VI (Winter 1979–80), 113. See also James Stanford Bradshaw, "George W. Wisner and the *New York Sun,*" ibid., p. 112. Two studies of the *Sun*'s police reporter.

TAYLOR, SALLY. "Marx and Greeley on Slavery and Labor," *Journalism History,* VI (Winter 1979–80), 103. Marx was a *Tribune* correspondent.

"The Herald—Onward," Democratic Review, XXXI (November 1852), 409. A favorable appraisal of a maligned newspaper.

TURNBULL, GEORGE. "Some Notes on the History of the Interview," *Journalism Quarterly,* XIII (September 1936), 272. Holds that Greeley was the founder of the modern interview.

WEIGLE, CLIFFORD F. "San Francisco Journalism, 1847–1851," *Journalism Quarterly,* XIV (June 1937), 151. The beginnings of a colorful journalism.

WHITBY, GARY L. "The New York Penny Press and the American Romantic Movement," Ph.D. thesis, University of Iowa, 1984. Influence of the Romantic movement on the content, style, and mission of the 1830s press is examined.

CHAPTER 7: THE IRREPRESSIBLE CONFLICT

ANDREWS, J. CUTLER. *The North Reports the Civil War.* Pittsburgh: University of Pittsburgh Press, 1955. Most extensive (813 pages) of the histories of Civil War reporting, and thoroughly documented. Lists several hundred northern reporters.

———. *The South Reports the Civil War.* Princeton: Princeton University Press, 1970. Like Andrews's *The North Reports the Civil War,* a prize-winning job of research and writing.

BLASSINGAME, JOHN W. *The Slave Community: Plantation Life in the Antebellum South.* New York: Oxford University Press, 1972; rev. ed., 1976. Superb look at slave culture, including music, family, food, and religion.

BUCKLAND, GAIL. *Fox Talbot and the Invention of Photography.* Boston: David R. Godine, 1980. Pioneer English photographer of 1830s–40s; one-third illustrations.

CROZIER, EMMET. *Yankee Reporters, 1861–65.* New York: Oxford University Press, 1956. A readable account of correspondents' work.

DANN, MARTIN E., ed. *The Black Press: 1827–1890.* New York: G. P. Putnam's Sons, 1971. A collection of articles from black newspapers with the theme of the quest for national identity.

DETWEILER, FREDERICK G. *The Negro Press in the United States.* Chicago: University of Chicago Press, 1922. Quotes extensively from the papers.

DICKERSON, DONNA LEE. *The Course of Tolerance: Freedom of Press in Nineteenth-Century America.* Westport, CT: Greenwood Press, 1990. A good overview.

DILLON, MERTON L. *The Abolitionists: The Growth of a Dissenting Minority.* DeKalb, IL: Northern Illinois University Press, 1974. Unravels abolitionist ideologies and strategies, and places them in context.

———. *Elijah P. Lovejoy, Abolitionist Editor.* Urbana: University of Illinois Press, 1961. Used primary sources.

DONALD, DAVID HERBERT. *Lincoln.* New York: Simon & Schuster, 1995. Winner of the Pulitzer Prize. Recent and best biography of Lincoln.

DOUGLASS, FREDERICK. *My Bondage and My Freedom.* Chicago: Johnson Publishing Company, 1970. Second of three autobiographical chronicles, originally published in 1855. Others: *Narrative of the Life of Frederick Douglass* (1845); *Life and Times of Frederick Douglass* (1878).

FAHRNEY, RALPH RAY. *Horace Greeley and the "Tribune" in the Civil War.* Chicago: University of Chicago Press, 1929. Documented.

FAUST, DREW GILPIN. *James Henry Hammond and the Old South.* Baton Rouge: Louisiana State University Press, 1982. The best look at a planter family and the slave economy.

FONER, PHILIP S. *Frederick Douglass.* New York: Citadel Press, 1963. By the author of the outstanding four-volume *Life and Writings of Frederick Douglass.*

GARRISON, WENDELL PHILLIPS, AND FRANCIS J. *William Lloyd Garrison.* 4 vols. New York: Appleton-Century-Crofts, 1885–89. The life story of the famous abolitionist, told by his children.

GENOVESE, EUGENE D. *The Political Economy of Slavery.* New York: Pantheon, 1965. A New Left historian uses the comparative approach. See also *Roll, Jordan, Roll* (New York: Pantheon, 1975), his story of the world slaves made.

GILL, JOHN. *Tide without Turning: Elijah P. Lovejoy and Freedom of the Press.* Boston: Beacon Press, 1958. A well-documented biography.

GOBRIGHT, LAWRENCE A. *Recollections of Men and Things at Washington during a Third of a Century.* Philadelphia: Claxton, Remsen, and Haffelfinger, 1869. By the AP correspondent.

HARPER, ROBERT S. *Lincoln and the Press.* New York: McGraw-Hill, 1951. Readable and detailed account of Lincoln's press relations after 1858; written from newspaper sources.

HORAN, JAMES D. *Mathew Brady: Historian with a Camera.* New York: Crown, 1955. A good biography, with 453 pictures.

ISELY, JETER ALLEN. *Horace Greeley and the Republican Party, 1853–1861.* Princeton: Princeton University Press, 1947. Analysis of Greeley's writings about slavery in the *New York Tribune.*

JOYNER, CHARLES. *Down by the Riverside: A South Carolina Slave Community.* Urbana: University of Illinois Press, 1984. Recreates with vivid detail the daily life of slaves.

KLEMENT, FRANK L. *The Copperheads in the Middle West.* Chicago: University of Chicago Press, 1960. Wilbur Storey, C. L. Vallandigham, and Samuel Medary are among those covered.

LEVINE, LAWRENCE. *Black Culture and Black Consciousness: Afro-American Folk Thought from Slavery to Freedom.* New York: Oxford University Press, 1977.

MATHEWS, JOSEPH J. *Reporting the Wars.* Minneapolis: University of Minnesota Press, 1957. History of war news reporting since the mid-eighteenth century. See also F. L. Bullard, *Famous War Correspondents* (Boston; Little, Brown, 1914).

MCFEELY, WILLIAM S. *Frederick Douglass.* New York: Norton, 1991. A Pulitzer Prize–winning historian provides a penetrating analysis of both the man and his mission.

MCPHERSON, JAMES M. *Battle Cry of Freedom: The Civil War Era.* New York: Oxford University Press, 1989. Readable scholarly account of 1846 to 1865.

MEREDITH, ROY. *Mr. Lincoln's Camera Man, Mathew S. Brady.* New York: Scribner's, 1946. A colorful account of the pioneer war photographer, with some of his best pictures.

NEVINS, ALLAN. *"The Evening Post": A Century of Journalism.* New York: Boni and Liveright, 1922. See especially Chapters 4–7.

OKKER, PATRICIA. *Our Sister Editors: Sarah J. Hale and the Tradition of Nineteenth-Century American Women Editors.* Athens: University of Georgia Press, 1995. A rigorous scholarly examination that places the editor of *Godey's Lady's Book* in the larger context of women editors.

PALUDAN, PHILLIP S. *A People's Contest: The Union and the Civil War, 1861–1865.* New York: Harper & Row, 1988. Explores how northern society and culture changed during the war.

PANZER, MARY. *Mathew Brady and the Image of History.* Washington, D.C.: Smithsonian, 1997. Brady's photography portrayed a stable republic even as the national identity was shattering.

PENN, I. GARLAND. *The Afro-American Press and Its Editors.* Springfield, MA: Wiley Company, 1891. The source book for the nineteenth-century black press.

Photographic History of the Civil War. New York: Review of Reviews Company, 1911. 10 vols. A very complete collection of Brady's pictures, with explanatory material.

POTTER, DAVID M. *The Impending Crisis, 1848–1861.* New York: Harper & Row, 1976. Political study; winner of the 1977 Pulitzer Prize for history.

REYNOLDS, DONALD E. *Editors Make War: Southern Newspapers in the Secession Crisis.* Nashville, TN: Vanderbilt University Press, 1970. Research in the files proved that most southern editors were in the forefront of the secession movement.

STAMPP, KENNETH M. *America in 1857: A Nation on the Brink.* New York: Oxford University Press, 1990. Dred Scott, financial panic, and "Bloody Kansas."

STARR, LOUIS M. *Bohemian Brigade: Civil War Newsmen in Action.* New York: Knopf, 1954. One of the best studies of reporting, editing, censorship.

STREITMATTER, RODGER. *Raising Her Voice: African-American Journalists Who Changed History.* Lexington: University Press of Kentucky, 1994. Biographical sketches of 11 journalists, from the early nineteenth century to the present.

THOMAS, JOHN L. *The Liberator: William Lloyd Garrison, a Biography.* Boston: Little, Brown, 1963. Excellent biography, but focuses on politics.

TRIPP, BERNELL. *Origins of the Black Press: New York 1827–1847.* Vision Press, 1992. Good source on the early black press.

WHITE, DEBORAH GRAY. *Ar'n't I a Woman? Female Slaves in the Plantation South.* New York: W. W. Norton, 1985. A groundbreaking book that explores slave women's roles within the family and community and shows how they contrasted sharply with traditional female roles in the larger American society.

WHITE, LAURA A. *Robert Barnwell Rhett.* New York: Appleton-Century-Crofts, 1931. Describes the southern "fire-eater" and his role.

WOLSELEY, ROLAND E. *The Black Press, U.S.A.* Ames: Iowa State University Press, 1990. Chapter 2 deals with nineteenth-century black papers.

Periodicals and Monographs

BLACKMON, ROBERT E. "Noah Brooks: Reporter in the White House," *Journalism Quarterly,* XXXII (Summer 1955), 301. Brooks was the Washington correspondent of the *Sacramento Union* in wartime.

BRYAN, CARTER R. "Negro Journalism in America before Emancipation," *Journalism Monographs,* XII (September 1969). Careful study of the early black press.

CHIASSON, LLOYD. "A Newspaper Analysis of the John Brown Raid," *American Journalism,* II:1 (1985), 22. The *New Orleans Daily Picayune* and *New York Tribune* compared.

CHU, JAMES C. Y. "Horace White: His Association with Abraham Lincoln, 1854–60," *Journalism Quarterly,* XLIX (Spring 1972), 51. White was a reporter and adviser.

CULLEN, MAURICE R., JR. "William Gilmore Simms, Southern Journalist," *Journalism Quarterly,* XXXVIII (Summer 1961), 298. A South Carolina editor first opposes secession, then defies the invading army.

EATON, CLEMENT. "The Freedom of the Press in the Upper South," *Mississippi Valley Historical Review,* XVIII (March 1932), 479. A study of the muzzling of press freedom prior to the Civil War.

GOLDSMITH, ADOLPH O. "Reporting the Civil War: Union Army Press Relations," *Journalism Quarterly,* XXXIII (Fall 1956), 478. A good summary.

GUBACK, THOMAS H. "General Sherman's War on the Press," *Journalism Quarterly,* XXXVI (Spring 1959), 171. A well-done account, featuring Sherman's famous clash with the *New York Herald*'s Knox.

JENSEN, OLIVER. "War Correspondent: 1864," *American Heritage,* 31 (August–September 1980), 48. Discusses James E. Taylor of *Frank Leslie's Illustrated*

Newspaper, who left a manuscript memoir of his illustrator assignment.

KENNEDY, FRONDE. "Russell's Magazine," *South Atlantic Quarterly*, XVIII (April 1919), 125. Analysis of the periodical published at Charleston, which argued the proslavery viewpoint.

MARTIN, ASA EARL. "Pioneer Anti-Slavery Press," *Mississippi Valley Historical Review*, II (March 1916), 509. Describes the *Philanthropist*.

PETERSON, DONALD CHRISTIAN. "Two Pioneer American Picture Magazines," Master's thesis, University of Wisconsin, 1953. A detailed study of *Harper's Weekly* and *Frank Leslie's Illustrated Newspaper*.

PRIDE, ARMISTEAD S. "A Register and History of Negro Newspapers in the United States," Ph.D. thesis, Northwestern University, 1950. Most scholarly effort to identify black newspapers.

REILLY, THOMAS W. "Early Coverage of a President-Elect: Lincoln at Springfield, 1860," *Journalism Quarterly*, XLIX (Autumn 1972), 469. Henry Villard reports for the *New York Herald*. Taken from "Henry Villard: Civil War Journalist," Master's thesis, University of Oregon, 1970. A discerning, carefully researched study of early news reporting.

————. "Lincoln-Douglas Debates of 1858 Forced New Role on the Press," *Journalism Quarterly*, LVI (Winter 1979), 734. Detailed analysis of the on-spot coverage.

SHAW, DONALD LEWIS. "News about Slavery from 1820–1860 in Newspapers of South, North, and West," *Journalism Quarterly*, LXI (Autumn 1984), 483. All papers increased slavery news; southern editors were the most alarmed.

STEWART, JAMES B. "Young Turks and Old Turkeys: Abolitionists, Historians, and Aging Processes," *Reviews in American History* (June 1983), 226. Discussion of recent book-length studies of abolitionism.

WEEKS, JAMES. "The Civil War's Greatest Scoop," *American Heritage* (July–August 1989), p. 100. How George W. Smalley got his exclusive, graphic story from Antietam for the *Tribune*.

WILSON, QUINTUS C. "A Study and Evaluation of the Military Censorship in the Civil War," Master's thesis, University of Minnesota, 1945. A well-documented study of the subject.

CHAPTER 8: A REVOLUTION IN NATIONAL LIFE

Books

AARON, DANIEL. *Men of Good Hope: A Story of American Progressives*. New York: Oxford University Press, 1951. Studies, among others, Henry George, Edward Bellamy, Henry Demarest Lloyd. Thorstein Veblen, William Dean Howells, and Theodore Roosevelt.

AYERS, EDWARD. *The Promise of the New South: Life after Reconstruction*. New York: Oxford University Press,

1992. How the New South dealt with the changes brought about by the war and reconstruction.

BAEHR, HARRY W., JR. *The "New York Tribune" Since the Civil War*. New York: Dodd, Mead, 1936. One of the better histories of newspapers.

BROWN, DEE. *Bury My Heart at Wounded Knee*. New York: Holt, Rinehart & Winston, 1971. The history of the West as finally written by the losers, the Native Americans.

BYRNES, GARRETT D., AND CHARLES H. SPILMAN. *The "Providence Journal": 150 Years*. Providence, RI: Journal Company, 1983. Oldest U.S. paper in continuous circulation as a daily.

Casual Essays of "The Sun." New York: R. G. Cooke, 1905. A collection of *Sun* editorials including "Dear Virginia."

CLAYTON, CHARLES G. *Little Mack: Joseph B. McCullagh of the "St. Louis Globe-Democrat."* Carbondale: Southern Illinois Press, 1969. Helps to illuminate a great newspaper figure.

CURL, DONALD W. *Murat Halstead and the "Cincinnati Commercial."* Gainsville: University Presses of Florida, 1980 Brief conventional biography.

DUNCAN, BINGHAM. *Whitelaw Reid: Journalist, Politician, Diplomat*. Athens, GA: University of Georgia Press, 1975. A leading conservative voice at the *New York Tribune*.

FONER, ERIC. *Reconstruction: America's Unfinished Revolution, 1861–1877*. New York: Harper & Row, 1988. Prize-winning nine-year feat of synthesis.

GRAYBAR, LLOYD J. *Albert Shaw of the "Review of Reviews": An Intellectual Biography*. Lexington: University Press of Kentucky, 1974.

HART, JIM ALLEE. *A History of the "St. Louis Globe-Democrat."* Columbia: University of Missouri Press, 1961. The story of founder J. B. McCullagh within a social framework.

HEUTERMAN, THOMAS H. *Movable Type: Biography of Legh R. Freeman*. Ames: Iowa State University Press, 1979. Skillfully presents the attention-winning editor of the "Press on Wheels" in the post–Civil War West.

JACKSON, KENNETH T. *Crabgrass Frontier: The Suburbanization of the United States*. New York: Oxford University Press, 1986. Documented history of the growth of the suburbs.

KAROLEVITZ, ROBERT F. *Newspapering in the Old West*. Seattle: Superior Publishing, 1965. Pictorial history of "how it was" on the frontier.

KELLER, MORTON. *The Art and Politics of Thomas Nast*. New York: Oxford University Press, 1968. A beautifully printed, illustrated, and researched story of the great cartoonist.

KROCK, ARTHUR E. *The Editorials of Henry Watterson*. New York: George H. Doran Company, 1923. Excellent preface.

LOGSDON, JOSEPH. *Horace White, Nineteenth-Century Liberal*. Westport, CT: Greenwood Publishing, 1971. Discusses an editor of the *Chicago Tribune* and owner of the *New York Evening Post*.

McJimsey, George T. *Genteel Partisan: Manton Marble, 1834–1917.* Ames: Iowa State Press, 1971. Discusses the editor of *New York World* in the 1860s, and his Spencerian social philosophy.

McKelvey, Blake. *The Urbanization of America, 1860–1915.* New Brunswick, NJ: Rutgers University Press, 1969.

———. *The Emergence of Metropolitan America, 1915–1966.* New Brunswick, NJ: Rutgers University Press, 1968. Two detailed studies of the trend.

Mindich, David T. Z. *Just the Facts: How "Objectivity" Came to Define American Journalism.* New York and London: New York University Press, 1998. A thoughtful and well-written analysis of the development of five concepts related to journalistic objectivity during the nineteenth century: detachment, nonpartisanship, inverted pyramid, facticity, and balance.

Mott, Frank Luther. *A History of American Magazines.* Vol. 2, *1850–1865;* Vol. 3, *1865–1885;* Vol. 4, *1885–1905.* Cambridge, MA: Harvard University Press, 1938–57. Volume 5, *1905–1930* (1968), of Mott's authoritative study has a cumulative index.

Myers, John Myers. *Print in a Wild Land.* Garden City, NY: Doubleday, 1967. Racy account of newspaperin' in the Old West.

Nixon, Raymond B. *Henry W. Grady: Spokesman of the New South.* New York: Knopf, 1943. The definitive biography of a leading southern editor.

North, Simeon N. D. *History and Present Condition of the Newspaper and Periodical Press of the United States.* Washington, DC: U.S. Government Printing Office, 1884. Published as a part of the 1880 census.

O'Brien, Frank M. *The Story of the "Sun."* New York: George H. Doran Company, 1918. Revised ed., New York: Appleton-Century-Crofts, 1928. One of the most readable histories.

Ogden, Rollo. *Life and Letters of Edwin Lawrence Godkin.* New York: Macmillan, 1907. The standard biography.

Paine, Albert Bigelow. *Th. Nast, His Period and His Pictures.* New York: Macmillan, 1904. Well illustrated with Nast's famous cartoons.

Painter, Nell Irwin. *Standing at Armageddon: The United States, 1877–1919.* New York: Norton, 1987. Overview that includes considerable social and cultural history.

Robertson, Michael. *Stephen Crane, Journalism, and the Making of Modern American Literature.* New York: Columbia University Press, 1997. A major study.

Schlereth, Thomas J. *Victorian America: Transformations in Everyday Life, 1878–1915.* New York: HarperCollins, 1991. The things people bought, mass produced, and advertised; illustrated.

Schlesinger, Arthur M. *The Rise of the City, 1878–1898.* Vol. 10 of *A History of American Life.* New York: Macmillan, 1932. A social history of a crucial period. See also Ida M. Tarbell, *The Nationalizing of Business, 1878–1898.* Vol. 9 of *A History of American Life* (1936).

Stone, Candace. *Dana and the "Sun."* New York: Dodd, Mead, 1938. The top-ranking biography of Dana, critical in tone.

Stone, Melville E. *Fifty Years a Journalist.* Garden City, NY: Doubleday, 1921. The first portion deals with Stone's Chicago career, the latter with the AP.

Summers, Mark W. *The Press, Gang, Newspapers & Politics, 1865–1878.* Chapel Hill, NC, and London: University of North Carolina Press, 1994. How reporters gathered the news and slanted it.

Trefousse, Hans L. *Carl Schurz, A Biography.* Knoxville: University of Tennessee Press, 1982. Fresh biographical study; Schurz viewed as ethnic mediator.

Walsh, Justin E. *To Print the News and Raise Hell.* Chapel Hill: University of North Carolina Press, 1968. Biography of Wilbur F. Storey, controversial editor of the *Chicago Times.*

Wall, Joseph F. *Henry Watterson: Reconstructed Rebel.* New York: Oxford University Press, 1956. A well-documented study.

Watterson, Henry. *"Marse Henry"; An Autobiography.* New York: George H. Doran Company, 1919. The Louisville editor's own pungent story.

Wiebe, Robert. *The Search for Order, 1877–1920.* New York: Hill and Wang, 1968. Examines how the United States developed from a nation composed primarily of rural, isolated communities to an urbanized, industrial society. See also Robert G. McCloskey, *American Conservatism in the Age of Enterprise, 1865–1910* (New York: Harper & Row, 1971).

Wish, Harvey. *Society and Thought in Modern America.* New York; Longmans, Green, 1962. The second volume in Wish's social and intellectual history, beginning with 1865.

Woodward, C. Vann. *Origins of the New South, 1877–1913.* Baton Rouge: Louisiana State University Press, 1951. Prize-winning study of the South's emergence from the Civil War.

Young, John P. *Journalism in California.* San Francisco: Chronicle Publishing, 1913. Principally a history of the *San Francisco Chronicle.*

Periodicals and Monographs

Baldasty, Gerald J. "The Economics of Working-Class Journalism: The E. W. Scripps Newsletter Chain, 1878–1908," *Journalism History,* 25:1 (Spring 1999), 3–12. Thoughtful interpretation of Scripps's strategies.

Belman, Lary S. "Robert Ezra Park: An Intellectual Portrait of a Journalist and Communication Scholar," *Journalism History,* II (Winter 1975), 116.

Brakeman, Mark. "Thomas Nast: Pen with Power," *Media History Digest,* V (Fall 1985), 23.

Caudill, Edward. "E. L. Godkin and the Science of Society," *Journalism Quarterly,* LXVI (Spring 1989), 57. The *Nation's* editor helps shape a new "social" science by providing ideas and a forum.

Child, Theodore. "The American Newspaper Press," *Fortnightly Review,* XLIV (December 1, 1885) 827. A meaningful evaluation.

Cloud, Barbara. "Establishing the Frontier Newspaper: A Study of Eight Western Territories," *Journalism Quarterly,* LXI (Winter 1984), 805. Uses the census of 1880.

DAVIS, HAROLD E. " 'A Brave and Beautiful City': Henry Grady's New South," *American Journalism,* V (1988), 131. By Grady's biographer.

DOWNEY, MATTHEW T. "Horace Greeley and the Politicians," *Journal of American History,* LIII (March 1967), 727. Liberal Republican convention of 1872.

FEDLER, FRED. "Mrs. O'Leary's Cow and Other Newspaper Tales about the Chicago Fire of 1871," *American Journalism,* III:1 (1986), 24. Study of reporting inaccuracies and their causes.

"Fifty Years of Harper's Magazine," *Harper's,* C (May 1900), 947.

FOLKERTS, JEAN. "Functions of the Reform Press," *Journalism History,* XII (Spring 1985), 22. Focuses on Farmers' Alliance papers of the 1880s.

HALL, MARK W. "The *San Francisco Chronicle:* Its Fight for the 1879 Constitution," *Journalism Quarterly,* XLVI (Autumn 1969), 505. From Hall's Master's thesis, University of Missouri, 1967.

HUNTZICKER, WILLIAM E. "Historians and the American Frontier Press," *American Journalism,* V (1988), 28. Historiographical essay in depth.

IRWIN, WILL. "The Power of the Press," *Collier's,* XLVI (January 21, 1911), 15. The first article in Irwin's "The American Newspaper" series, discussing the birth of modern journalism and such publishers as William Rockhill Nelson of the *Kansas City Star* and Harrison Gray Otis of the *Los Angeles Times.*

KIELBOWICZ, RICHARD B. "Origins of the Second-Class Mail Category and the Business of Policymaking, 1863–1879," *Journalism Monographs,* XCVI (April 1986). See also his "The Growing Interaction of the Federal Bureaucracy and the Press: The Case of a Postal Rule, 1879–1917," *American Journalism,* IV:1 (1987), 5. By a leading authority on postal affairs.

LEITER, KELLY. "U.S. Grant and the *Chicago Tribune,*" *Journalism Quarterly,* XLVII (Spring 1970), 71.

MANN, RUSSELL A. "Investigative Reporting in the Gilded Age: A Study of the Detective Journalism of Melville E. Stone and the *Chicago Morning News,* 1881–1888," Ph.D. thesis, Southern Illinois University, 1977.

McCORKLE, WILLIAM L. "Nelson's *Star* and Kansas City, 1880–1898," Ph.D. thesis, University of Texas, 1968. Scholarly study with fresh interpretations.

MITCHELL, EDWARD P. "The Newspaperman's Newspaper," *Scribner's,* LXXVI (August 1924), 149. A vivid portrait of Dana and his *Sun* by a longtime *Sun* editor.

MOTT, FRANK LUTHER. "Fifty Years of *Life:* The Story of a Satirical Weekly," *Journalism Quarterly,* XXV (September 1948), 224.

MURRAY, RANDALL L. "Edwin Lawrence Godkin: Unbending Editor in Times of Change," *Journalism History,* I (Autumn 1974), 77. Godkin laments late 1880s social change.

NEVINS, ALLAN. "E. L. Godkin: Victorian Liberal," *Nation,* CLXXI (July 22, 1950), 76. An interpretative essay, followed by a study written by Lewis Gannett, of Oswald Garrison Villard's editorship.

NIXON, RAYMOND B. "Henry W. Grady, Reporter: A Reinterpretation," *Journalism Quarterly,* XII (December 1935), 341. Reprinted in Ford and Emery, *Highlights in the History of the American Press.*

NORD, DAVID PAUL. "Working-Class Readers: Family, Community, and Reading in Late Nineteenth-Century America," *Communications Research,* XIII (April 1986), 156. Analysis of data on working-class families to determine newspaper and book readership patterns.

PLUMMER, L. NIEL. "Henry Watterson's Editorial Style: An Interpretative Analysis," *Journalism Quarterly,* XXIII (March 1946), 58.

PRINGLE, HENRY F. "Godkin of *The Post,*" *Scribner's,* XCVI (December 1934), 327; and "Kentucky Bourbon—Marse Henry Watterson," *Scribner's,* XCVII (January 1935), 10. Reprinted in Ford and Emery, *Highlights in the History of the American Press.*

Quarterly of the Oregon Historical Society, XIV:2 (June 1913). An issue devoted to Harvey W. Scott, editor of the *Oregonian.*

REED, V. DELBERT. "A Last Hurrah for the Frontier Press," *American Journalism,* VI (1989), 65. The Coeur d'Alene frontier of Idaho in the 1880s.

ROGERS, CHARLES E. "William Rockhill Nelson and His Editors of the *Star,*" *Journalism Quarterly,* XXVI (March 1949), 15. Based on the author's *William Rockhill Nelson: Independent Editor and Crusading Liberal* (Ph.D. thesis, University of Minnesota, 1948).

RUTENBECK, JEFFREY B. "The Rise of Independent Newspapers in the 1870s: A Transformation in American Journalism," Ph.D. thesis, University of Washington, 1990. Focus on newspapers in New York, California, Ohio, and Illinois.

STEWART, WALTER H. "The Editorial Paragraph: A Century and More of Development," Ph.D. thesis, Southern Illinois University, 1970. Investigates 14 newspaper editorialists.

THORP, ROBERT K. " 'Marse Henry' and the Negro: A New Perspective," *Journalism Quarterly,* XLVI (Autumn 1969), 467. It was not as Marse Henry remembered it; he was scarcely their champion.

TURNBULL, GEORGE. "The Schoolmaster of the Oregon Press," *Journalism Quarterly,* XV (December 1938), 359. A study of the influence of Harvey W. Scott by the author of the *History of Oregon Newspapers* (1939).

WHITE, WILLIAM ALLEN. "The Man Who Made the *Star,*" *Collier's,* LV (June 26, 1915), 12. A portrait of William Rockhill Nelson by the editor of the *Emporia Gazette.* Reprinted in Ford and Emery, *Highlights in the History of the American Press.*

WHITE, Z. L. "Western Journalism," *Harper's,* LXXVII (October 1888), 678. A contemporary picture of Ohio journalism, including the Scripps enterprises, and from farther West.

WILEY, BONNIE. "History of the Portland *Oregonian,*" Ph. D. thesis, Southern Illinois University, 1965. From Harvey Scott to Samuel Newhouse.

CHAPTER 9: THE NEW JOURNALISM

Books

The *Union List of Newspapers,* beginning where Brigham's bibliography leaves off in 1820, is supplemented by directories: *Geo. P. Rowell & Co.'s American Newspaper Directory* (1869), and *N. W. Ayer & Son's American Newspaper Annual* (1880), later called the *Directory of Newspapers & Periodicals.* The *Editor & Publisher International YearBook* dates from 1921.

ABRAMSON, PHYLLIS LESLIE. *Sob Sister Journalism.* Westport, CT: Greenwood Press, 1990. The Harry Thaw trial as covered by Annie Laurie, Dorothy Dix, Nixola Greeley-Smith, and Ada Patterson.

BARRETT, JAMES W. *Joseph Pulitzer and His World.* New York: Vanguard, 1941. A colorful, rambling story of the *New York World* by its last city editor.

BEISNER, ROBERT L. *Twelve Against Empire: The Anti-Imperialists, 1898–1900.* New York: McGraw-Hill, 1968. Two of the 12 were Godkin and Schurz.

BENNION, SHERILYN COX. *Equal to the Occasion: Women Editors of the Nineteenth-Century West.* Reno: University of Nevada Press, 1990. Covers 35 editors in 13 states.

BLEYER, WILLARD G. *Main Currents in the History of American Journalism.* Boston: Houghton Mifflin, 1927. The chapter on Hearst admirably documents charges of sensationalism.

BROWN, CHARLES H. *The Correspondents' War.* New York: Scribner's, 1967. All the details of the press corps for the Spanish-American War.

CARLSON, OLIVER. *Brisbane: A Candid Biography.* New York: Stackpole Sons, 1937. A good critical analysis of the famous Hearst editor.

———, AND ERNEST SUTHERLAND BATES. *Hearst, Lord of San Simeon.* New York: Viking, 1936. Better than other early biographies by John K. Winkler and Mrs. Fremont Older. Still useful for the early Hearst period, but supplanted by Tebbel and Swanberg (see later reference).

CARNES, CECIL. *Jimmy Hare, News Photographer.* New York: Macmillan, 1940. The biography of one of the early leading press photographers.

DAVIS, RICHARD HARDING. *Notes of a War Correspondent,* New York: Scribner's, 1910. An American war correspondent in Cuba, Greece, South Africa, and Manchuria, covering four wars.

ELLIS, L. ETHAN. *Newsprint: Producers, Publishers, Political Pressures.* New Brunswick, NJ: Rutgers University Press, 1960. The economics of print paper (includes Ellis's 1948 study, *Print Paper Pendulum*).

EMERY, EDWIN. *History of the American Newspaper Publishers Association.* Minneapolis: University of Minnesota Press, 1950. Covers the activities of the organized daily newspaper publishers in the fields of labor relations, newsprint, advertising, mailing privileges, mechanical research, and legislative lobbying, from 1887 to 1950. Updated in "ANPA's First 100 Years," *presstime* (May 1987), 28.

GERSHEIM, HELMUT. *A Concise History of Photography.* London: Thames and Hudson, 1965. Well illustrated; begins with the 1830s.

GOBLE, GEORGE CORBAN. *The Obituary of a Machine: The Rise and Fall of Ottmar Mergenthaler's Linotype at U.S. Newspapers.* Ann Arbor, MI: University Microfilms International, 1986 (from Goble's Ph.D. thesis, Indiana University, 1984). Excellent in-depth study.

GOLDSTEIN, TOM, ed. *Killing the Messenger: 100 Years of Media Criticism.* New York: Columbia University Press, 1989. Selection of 15 classic articles and essays.

GRAHAM, THOMAS. *Charles H. Jones, Journalist and Politician of the Gilded Age.* Tallahassee, FL: A&M University Press, 1990. A Pulitzer editor.

HARDT, HANNO, AND BONNIE BRENNEN. *Newsworkers: Toward a History of the Rank and File.* Minneapolis: University of Minnesota Press, 1995. Cultural studies perspectives on reporters, editors, and newsboys, concentrating on the years 1890–1940.

HOWER, RALPH M. *The History of an Advertising Agency: N. W. Ayer & Son at Work, 1869–1949.* Cambridge, MA: Harvard University Press, 1949.

IRWIN, WILL. *The American Newspaper,* ed. Clifford F. Weigle and David G. Clark. Ames, IA: State University Press, 1969. Reproductions of the original series in *Collier's* of 1911.

———. *The Making of a Reporter.* New York: G. P. Putnam's Sons, 1942. Autobiography of a discerning newspaperperson who ranked with the best.

JAKES, JOHN. *Great Women Reporters.* New York: G. P. Putnam's Sons, 1969. The stories of dozens who competed with men for news.

JONES, EDGAR R. *Those Were the Good Old Days: A Happy Look at American Advertising, 1880–1930.* New York: Simon & Schuster, 1959. Illustrations.

JUERGENS, GEORGE. *Joseph Pulitzer and the "New York World."* Princeton, NJ: Princeton University Press, 1966. A detailed, enthusiastic account of Pulitzer's first four years at the *World,* 1883 to 1887.

KARNOW, STANLEY. *In Our Image: America's Empire in the Philippines.* New York: Random House, 1989. A sweeping narrative from 1521 to Cory Aquino.

KING, HOMER W. *Pulitzer's Prize Editor: A Biography of John A. Cockerill, 1845–1896.* Durham, NC: Duke University Press, 1965. Only detailed study.

KNIGHT, OLIVER A. *Following the Indian Wars: The Story of the Newspaper Correspondents among the Indian Campaigners, 1886–1891.* Norman: University of Oklahoma Press, 1960. Well documented.

KROEGER, BROOKE. *Nellie Bly: Daredevil, Reporter, Feminist.* New York: Times, 1994. Well-researched, definitive biography.

LANCASTER, PAUL. *Gentlemen of the Press: The Life and Times of an Early Reporter, Julian Ralph of the "Sun."* Syracuse: Syracuse University Press, 1992. Vivid biography that illuminates the professionalization of journalism in the late nineteenth century.

LAWSON, LINDA. *Truth in Publishing: Federal Regulation of the Press's Business Practices, 1880–1920.* Carbondale: Southern Illinois University Press, 1993. First in-depth study of the press's business practices and the Newspaper Publicity Act of 1912, during the Progressive Era.

LOFT, JACOB. *The Printing Trades.* New York: Holt, Rinehart & Winston, 1944. An inclusive account. See also Elizabeth F. Baker, *Printers and Technology: A History of the International Printing Pressmen and Assistants' Union* (New York: Columbia University Press, 1957).

LUBOW, ARTHUR. *The Reporter Who Would Be King: A Biography of Richard Harding Davis.* New York: Scribner's, 1992. Well-written biography of the glamour boy of early modern journalism.

LUNDBERG, FERDINAND. *Imperial Hearst: A Social Biography.* New York: Equinox Cooperative Press, 1936. A bitter attack on the chain publisher; valuable particularly for financial data.

MARZOLF, MARION. *Up from the Footnote: A History of Women Journalists.* New York: Hastings House, 1977. From colonial days to present, by the bibliographer of the subject. Also see Marzolf, "The Woman Journalist: Colonial Printer to City Desk," *Journalism History,* I–II (Winter 1974–Spring 1975).

————. *Civilizing Voices: American Press Criticism 1880–1950.* New York: Longman, 1991. Reports in depth the debate over newspaper performance.

MATHEWS, JOSEPH F. *George Washburn Smalley: Forty Years a Foreign Correspondent.* Chapel Hill: University of North Carolina Press, 1973. Covers the years 1867–1906.

MILTON, JOYCE. *The Yellow Kids: Foreign Correspondents in the Heyday of American Journalism.* New York: Harper & Row, 1989. Time frame is 1895 to 1898.

NEWHALL, BEAUMONT. *The History of Photography from 1839 to Present.* New York: Museum of Modem Art, 1982. The standard reference.

NORD, DAVID PAUL. *Newspapers and New Politics: Midwestern Municipal Reform 1890–1900.* Ann Arbor: UMI Research Press, 1981. Based on his 1979 Ph.D. thesis, University of Wisconsin. Reform succeeds in Chicago, fails in St. Louis. See also Nord, "The Politics of Agenda Setting in Late Nineteenth-Century Cities," *Journalism Quarterly,* LVIII (Winter 1981), 563.

O'CONNOR, RICHARD. *Pacific Destiny: An Informal History of the U.S. in the Far East.* Boston: Little, Brown, 1969. Thesis is that the U.S. moved from an Atlantic to a Pacific role through deep desires and motives of political, military, and religious leaders at pivotal moments, from Commodore Perry's time to Vietnam. Detailed treatment of the Philippine Insurrection.

POORE, BEN: PERLEY. *Perley's Reminiscences of Sixty Years in the National Metropolis.* 2 vols. Philadelphia: Hubbard, 1886. Political, social, and journalistic life in Washington, 1820s to 1880s. Poore was the *Boston Journal*'s correspondent.

POPE, DANIEL. *The Making of Modern Advertising.* New York: Basic Books, 1983. Theoretical approach based on economics and business. Mainly focused on the nineteenth century.

PRESBREY, FRANK. *The History and Development of Advertising.* New York: Doubleday, 1929. Long the standard history in its field.

RALPH, JULIAN. *The Making of a Journalist.* New York: Harper & Row, 1903. The autobiography of another top-ranking reporter of the period.

RAMMELKAMP, JULIAN S. *Pulitzer's "Post-Dispatch," 1878–1883.* Princeton: Princeton University Press, 1966. Documented study of the evolving journalistic style of Pulitzer, Cockerill, and others; restrained approval of Pulitzer's soial contributions, criticism of his sensationalized news.

ROSS, ISHBEL. *Ladies of the Press.* New York: Harper & Row, 1936. Valuable for stories of early women journalists, by one of the most famous.

SEITZ, DON C. *Joseph Pulitzer: His Life and Letters.* New York: Simon & Schuster, 1924. The first Pulitzer study; others draw upon it. Written by Pulitzer's business manager.

SWANBERG, W. A. *Pulitzer.* New York: Scribner's, 1967. Best of the studies of the tempestuous editor-publisher.

————. *Citizen Hearst.* New York: Scribner's, 1961. A highly readable study, covering available printed sources in meticulous detail.

TEBBEL, JOHN. *The Life and Good Times of William Randolph Hearst.* New York: Dutton, 1952. A well-balanced biography and the best-documented study of the Hearst newspaper empire.

TURNER, E. S. *The Shocking History of Advertising.* Harmondsworth, England: Penguin Books, 1965. An updated revision of a good history.

WARE, LOUISE. *Jacob A. Riis.* New York: Appleton-Century-Crofts, 1938. Biography of a socially conscious reporter.

WATKINS, JULIAN L. *The 100 Greatest Advertisements,* 2nd ed. New York: Moore Publishing, 1959. Discusses who wrote them and what they did.

WILKERSON, MARCUS M. *Public Opinion and the Spanish-American War.* Baton Rouge: Louisiana State University Press, 1932. A scholarly study of war propaganda and press influence.

WISAN, JOSEPH E. *The Cuban Crisis as Reflected in the New York Press.* New York: Columbia University Press, 1934. A good specialized study.

WOOD, JAMES PLAYSTED. *The Story of Advertising.* New York: Ronald Press, 1958. Fairly detailed from the 1860s on.

Periodicals and Monographs

The trade journals became available in this period. The leaders were the *Journalist* (1884–1907), the *Fourth Estate* (1894–1927), and *Editor & Publisher* (1901) in the daily newspaper field; the *Publishers' Auxiliary* (1865) in the weekly newspaper field; and *Printers' Ink* (1888) in advertising. The fiftieth anniversary numbers of *Editor & Publisher* (July 21, 1934), and of *Printers' Ink* (July 28, 1938) are particularly valuable sources.

BALDASTY, GERALD J., AND JEFFREY RUTENBECK. "Money, Politics and Newspapers," *Journalism History,* XV (Summer–Autumn 1988), 60. Press partisanship declined as business relationships of papers grew.

BANKS, ELIZABETH. "American Yellow Journalism," *Nineteenth Century,* XLIV (August 1898), 328.

BEASLEY, MAURINE. *The First Women Washington Correspondents.* Washington, DC: GW Washington Studies, No. 4, 1976. Covers six post–Civil War women.

BENNION, SHERILYN COX. "A Working List of Women Editors on the 19th-Century Frontier," *Journalism History,* VII (Summer 1980), 60.

———. "Fremont Older: Advocate for Women," *Journalism History,* III (Winter 1976–77), 124. San Francisco *Bulletin*'s women reporters and editors.

———. "Women Editors of California: 1854–1900," *Pacific Historian,* XXVIII (Fall 1984).

BERG, MEREDITH AND DAVID. "The Rhetoric of War Preparation: The New York Press in 1898," *Journalism Quarterly,* XLV (Winter 1968), 653. Analysis of New York dailies after the sinking of the *Maine.*

BRIDGES, LAMAR W. "Eliza Jane Nicholson of the *Picayune,*" *Journalism History,* II (Winter 1975), 110. Owner, 1876 to 1896.

BRISBANE, ARTHUR. "Joseph Pulitzer," *Cosmopolitan,* XXXIII (May 1902), 51. An intimate contemporary portrait by his editor.

———. "The Modern Newspaper in War Time," *Cosmopolitan,* XXV (September 1898), 541. The Journal editor confesses his sins. See also Brisbane, "Yellow Journalism," *Bookman,* XIX (June 1904), 400; and XXIV (June 1909), 403.

BROMLEY, JOHN C. "Richard Harding Davis and the Boer War," *American Journalism,* VII (1990), 12.

BROWN, CHARLES H. "Press Censorship in the Spanish-American War," *Journalism Quarterly,* XLII (Autumn 1965), 581. It was more extensive and effective than believed.

COMMANDER, LYDIA K. "The Significance of Yellow Journalism," *Arena,* XXXIV (August 1905), 150. A contemporary analysis.

CONNERY, THOMAS B. "Fusing Fictional Technique and Journalistic Fact: Literary Journalism in the 1890s Newspaper," Ph.D. thesis, Brown University, 1984.

———. Julian Ralph: Forgotten Master of Descriptive Detail," *American Journalism,* II:2 (1985), 165. A *New York Sun* great.

DANIELS, ELIZABETH A. "Jessie White Mario: 19th-Century Correspondent," *Journalism History,* II (Summer 1975), 54. Correspondent in Italy for the *Nation,* 1866 to 1904.

DICKERSON, DONNA. "William Cowper Brann: Nineteenth Century Press Critic," *Journalism History,* V (Summer 1978), 42. Brann published *The Iconoclast* in Waco, Texas, 1895 to 1898, and wrote 18 essays on the "yellow press."

DONALD, ROBERT. "Sunday Newspapers in the United States," *Universal Review,* VIII (September 1890), 79. A look at a then-new medium.

EK, RICHARD A. "Victoria Woodhull and the Pharisees," *Journalism Quarterly,* XLIX (Autumn 1972), 453. Exposure of minister's adultery brings reprisals against editor.

FRANCKE, WARREN. "An Argument in Defense of Sensationalism," *Journalism History,* V (Autumn 1978), 70. Analyzes differing perceptions of the word *sensationalism* in journalism history.

GABLER, WILLIAM G. "The Evolution of American Advertising in the Nineteenth Century," *Journal of Popular Culture,* II (Spring 1978), 763.

GREEN, NORMA, STEPHEN LACY, AND JEAN FOLKERTS. "Chicago Journalists at the Turn of the Century: Bohemians All?" *Journalism Quarterly,* LXVI (Winter 1989), 813. Detailed data for 1300 newspeople.

HART, JACK R. "Horatio Alger in the Newsroom: Social Origins of American Editors," *Journalism Quarterly,* LIII (Spring 1976), 14–20. Shows that editors of 1875 and 1900 are comparable to executives in other major industries.

HENRY, SUSAN. "Reporting 'Deeply at First Hand': Helen Campbell in the 19th-Century Slums," *Journalism History,* II (Spring–Summer 1984), 18. Reporter for *New York Tribune* and muckraker.

HUDSON, ROBERT V. "Journeyman Journalist: An Analytical Biography of Will Irwin," Ph.D. thesis, University of Minnesota, 1970. Reportorial career researched in depth.

INGLIS, WILLIAM. "An Intimate View of Joseph Pulitzer," *Harper's Weekly,* LV (November 11, 1911), 7. An obituary with considerable insight.

IRWIN, WILL. "The American Newspaper," *Collier's,* XLVI–XLVII (January 21–July 29, 1911). A series of 15 articles that constitutes a history of journalism after the Civil War. The sins of yellow journalism are described in February 18 and March 4 issues.

JONES, DOUGLAS C. "Remington Reports from the Badlands: The Artist as War Correspondent," *Journalism Quarterly,* XLVII (Winter 1970), 702. His drawings were in *Harper's Weekly.*

———. "Teresa Dean: Lady Correspondent among the Sioux Indians," *Journalism Quarterly,* XLIX (Winter 1972), 656.

KAHAN, ROBERT S. "The Antecedents of American Photojournalism," Ph.D. thesis, University of Wisconsin, 1969. The artist versus the camera.

KNIGHT, OLIVER A. "Reporting a Gold Rush," *Journalism Quarterly,* XXXVIII (Winter 1961), 43. The story of two young reporters from the *Inter Ocean* and the *New York Herald* in the Black Hills of 1875.

KNIGHTS, PETER R. "The Press Association War of 1866–1867," *Journalism Monographs,* VI (December 1967).

MCKERNS, JOSEPH P. "Ben:Perley Poore's Reminiscences: A Reliable Source for Research?" *Journalism History,* II (Winter 1975), 125.

———. "Benjamin:Perley Poore of the *Boston Journal:* His Life and Times as a Washington Correspondent, 1850–1887," Ph.D. thesis, University of Minnesota, 1979.

A well-written, exhaustively researched biography placed in context.

MANDER, MARY S. "Pen and Sword: Problems of Reporting the Spanish-American War," *Journalism History,* IX (Spring 1982), 2.

MARZOLF, MARION T. "American 'New Journalism' Takes Root in Europe at End of 19th Century," *Journalism Quarterly,* LXI (Autumn 1984), 529. Depth of U.S. influence documented.

MOTT, FRANK L. "The First Sunday Paper: A Footnote to History," *Journalism Quarterly,* XXXV (Fall 1958), 443. The *Boston Globe.*

NORD, DAVID PAUL. "The Public Community: The Urbanization of Journalism in Chicago," *Journal of Urban History,* II (August 1985).

———. "The Business Values of American Newspapers: The 19th Century Watershed in Chicago," *Journalism Quarterly,* LXI (Summer 1984), 265. Newspapers have uniqueness as a business that helps shape editorial values.

Outlook. XCIX (November 11, 1911), 603 and 608, contains two estimates of Pulitzer and *The World.*

PETERS, GLEN W. "The *American Weekly,*" *Journalism Quarterly,* XLVIII (Autumn 1971), 466. A review of the Sunday supplements, especially Hearst's.

PIERCE, PAULA M. "Frances Benjamin Johnston: Mother of American Photojournalism," *Media History Digest,* V (Winter 1985), 54. Unconventional career highlighted by McKinley assassination photos.

PIERCE, ROBERT N. "Lord Northcliffe: Trans-Atlantic Influences," *Journalism Monographs,* XL (August 1975).

SAALBERG, HARVEY. "The *Westliche Post* of St. Louis: A Daily Newspaper for German-Americans, 1857–1938," Ph.D. thesis, University of Missouri, 1967. Pulitzer, Schurz, and Preetorius figure in the story. See also Saalberg, "The *Westliche Post* of St. Louis: German Language Daily, 1857–1938," *Journalism Quarterly,* XLV (Autumn 1968), 452.

SCHUNEMAN, R. SMITH. "The Photograph in Print: An Examination of New York Daily Newspapers, 1890–1937," Ph.D. thesis, University of Minnesota, 1966. The rise of photojournalism is developed by extensive research.

———. "Art or Photography: A Question for Newspaper Editors of the 1890s," *Journalism Quarterly,* XLII (Winter 1965), 43. Why the halftone waited until 1897 in big dailies.

SEITZ, DON C. "The Portrait of an Editor," *Atlantic Monthly,* CXXXIV (September 1924), 289. Reprinted in Ford and Emery, *Highlights in the History of the American Press.* Joseph Pulitzer portrayed.

SMYTHE, TED CURTIS. "The Reporter, 1880–1900: Working Conditions and Their Influence on the News," *Journalism History,* VII (Spring 1980), 1.

———. "The Advertisers' War to Verify Newspaper Circulation; 1870–1914," *American Journalism,* III:3 (1986), 167. Founding of Audit Bureau of Circulations.

STEFFENS, LINCOLN. "Hearst, the Man of Mystery," *American Magazine,* LXIII (November 1906), 3. Penetrating study based on interviews of Hearst.

STENSAAS, HARLAN S. "The Objective News Report: A Content Analysis of Selected U.S. Daily Newspapers for 1865 to 1954," Ph.D. thesis, University of Southern Mississippi, 1986. Percentage of stories rated objective rose from one-third in 1865–74 to two-thirds in 1905–14, then to 80 percent by 1925–35. Connects rise in objectivity with inverted pyramid format and use of authoritative sources.

VANDERBURG, RAY. "The Paradox That Was Arthur Brisbane," *Journalism Quarterly,* XLVII (Summer 1970), 281. Study of the great Hearst editor.

WARD, HILEY. "A Popular History of the National Newspaper Association," *Publishers' Auxiliary,* CX (July 10, 1975), 14. First of a series extending to 1977, substantially researched. Based on Ward's Ph.D. thesis, University of Minnesota, 1977.

ZOBRIST, BENEDICT KARL. "How Victor Lawson's Newspapers Covered the Cuban War of 1898," *Journalism Quarterly,* XXXVIII (Summer 1961), 323. The nonsensational *Chicago Record* and *Daily News.*

CHAPTER 10: THE PEOPLE'S CHAMPIONS

For references to the literature about Hearst and Pulitzer see the Bibliography for Chapter 9. Volume 4 of Mott's *History of American Magazines* covers this period (see Chapter 8).

Books: Background History

COOPER, JOHN M., JR. *The Warrior and the Priest: Woodrow Wilson and Theodore Roosevelt.* Cambridge, MA: Harvard University Press, 1985. Deemed principal architects of modern American politics.

CORNWELL, ELMER E., JR. *Presidential Leadership of Public Opinion.* Bloomington: Indiana University Press, 1965. The press conference from Theodore Roosevelt to John Kennedy.

DALLEK, ROBERT. *The American Style of Foreign Policy.* New York: Knopf, 1983. A provocative synthesis.

ELLIS, ELMER. *Mr. Dooley's America.* New York: Knopf, 1941. The life and times of Finley Peter Dunne, humorist and reformer.

EVANS, SARA M., AND HARRY C. BOYTE. *Free Spaces: The Sources of Democratic Change in America.* New York: Harper & Row, 1986. Examples are women's voluntary associations, black churches, Knights of Labor, and Farmers' Alliance.

FLEXNER, ELEANOR. *Century of Struggle.* Cambridge, MA: Belknap Press, 1959. Leading history of the women's equality movement. See also Susan Ware, *Holding Their Own: American Women in the 1930s* (Boston: Twayne, 1982), a widely used study.

HOFSTADTER, RICHARD. *The Age of Reform.* New York: Knopf, 1955. From Bryan to FDR, the Populists, Progressives, and liberals wend their way.

HOWE, IRVING. *Socialism and America.* San Diego: Harcourt Brace Jovanovich, 1986. Analytical review of U.S. socialist movement by the editor of *Dissent* and admirer of Eugene Debs.

HUNTER, JANE. *The Gospel of Gentility: American Women Missionaries in Turn-of-the-Century China.* New Haven: Yale University Press, 1984. Well-researched study.

JOHNSON, WALTER. *William Allen White's America.* New York: Holt, Rinehart & Winston, 1947. Important as an interpretation of the swiftly changing half-century in which White was a national figure.

KOLKO, GABRIEL. *The Triumph of Conservatism: A Reinterpretation of American History, 1900–1916.* Chicago: Quadrangle, 1967. A revisionist study by a leading New Left historian.

LINK, ARTHUR S. *Woodrow Wilson and the Progressive Era, 1910–1917.* New York: Harper & Row, 1954. A volume in the New American Nation series by Wilson's biographer.

MAY, HENRY F. *The End of American Innocence.* New York: Knopf, 1969. Intellectual history of the period from 1912 to 1917.

MORRIS, EDMUND. *The Rise of Theodore Roosevelt.* New York: Coward, McCann and Geoghegan, 1979. A highly readable biography.

MOWRY, GEORGE E. *Theodore Roosevelt and the Progressive Movement.* Madison: University of Wisconsin Press, 1946. Traces the relationship of Roosevelt to radicalism.

PAINTER, NELL IRWIN. *Standing at Armageddon: The United States, 1877–1918.* New York: Norton, 1987. An overview of a period of "radicalism in flower."

PRINGLE, HENRY F. *Theodore Roosevelt.* New York: Harcourt Brace Jovanovich, 1931. A Pulitzer Prize–winning biography of the key figure of the muckraking era by a former newspaperperson.

REGIER, C. C. *The Era of the Muckrakers.* Chapel Hill: University of North Carolina Press, 1932. An exhaustive study of the crusading magazines and their writers.

SHAPIRO, ROBERT. *A Turning Wheel.* New York: Random House, 1979. Thirty years of Asian revolution, by a *New Yorker* correspondent.

SKLAR, MARTIN J. *The United States as a Developing Country.* New York: Cambridge University Press, 1992. Seven essays by noted scholars of the early twentieth-century Progressive and Wilsonian eras.

SULLIVAN, MARK. *Our Times.* 6 vols. New York: Scribner's, 1926 ff. Newspaperman Sullivan's six volumes are crowded with the color and the drama of the years 1900 to 1929.

THOMSON, JAMES C., JR., PETER W. STANLEY, AND JOHN CURTIS PERRY. *Sentimental Imperialists: The American Experience in East Asia.* New York: Harper & Row, 1981. Dovish view of East Asian mistakes, 1784 to Vietnam, by three East Asian scholars.

WELCH, RICHARD E., JR. *Response to Imperialism: The United States and the Philippine-American War, 1899–1902.* Chapel Hill: University of North Carolina Press, 1979. A public-opinion study; the first comprehensive treatment of that war's press coverage.

WILIAMS, WILLIAM APPLEMAN. *The Roots of the Modern American Empire.* New York: Random House, 1969, A leader of New Left historians dissents from United States foreign policy since the 1890s. See also Williams, *The Contours of American History* (Cleveland: World Publishing, 1961; reissued 1973).

———. *Empire as a Way of Life.* New York: Oxford University Press, 1980. An essay tracing imperialism in the United States from colonial times.

WINTERS, DONALD E., JR. *The Soul of the Wobblies: The I.W.W., Religion, and American Culture in the Progressive Era, 1905–1917.* Westport, CT: Greenwood Press, 1985. The I.W.W.'s religious orientation.

Books: Newspapers

BALDASTY, GERALD. *E. W. Scripps and the Business of Newspapers.* Urbana: University of Illinois Press, 1999. An excellent business history that is based on substantial archival research.

BOSWELL, SHARON A., AND LORRAINE MCCONAGHY. *Raise Hell and Sell Newspapers: Alden J. Blethen and the Seattle Times.* Pullman, WA: Washington State University Press, 1996. Well-researched and written biography grounded in U.S. social and intellectual history.

BRITT, ALBERT. *Ellen Browning Scripps: Journalist and Idealist.* London: Oxford University Press, 1961. Adds to the early Scripps story, when Ellen worked with and advised E. W.

COCHRAN, NEGLEY D. *E. W. Scripps.* New York: Harcourt Brace Jovanovich, 1933. A more factual biography than Gilson Gardner's *Lusty Scripps* (New York: Vanguard, 1932).

DANIELS, JOSEPHUS. *Tar Heel Editor.* Chapel Hill: University of North Carolina Press, 1939. This first volume of the Daniels autobiography deals with his early newspaper career.

Editorials from the Hearst Newspapers. New York: Albertson Publishing, 1906. Selected reprints of the Hearst editorial-page offerings.

ELLIS, ELMER, ed. *Mr. Dooley at His Best.* New York: Scribner's, 1938. Writings of Finley Peter Dunne, the famed Chicago columnist.

GRIFFITH, SALLY FOREMAN. *Home Town News: William Allen White and the "Emporia Gazette."* New York: Oxford University Press, 1989. Cultural history; less a biography than a reconstruction of small-town American life seen through the life of White.

HEATON, JOHN L. *Cobb of "The World."* New York: Dutton, 1924. Includes a sketch of Frank I. Cobb and a collection of his *New York World* editorials.

HILDERBRAND, ROBERT C., ed. *The Papers of Woodrow Wilson: The Complete Press Conferences, 1913–1919.*

Vol. 50. Princeton, NJ: Princeton University Press, 1985. Pioneering presidential effort.

HOWE, E. W. *Plain People.* New York: Dodd, Mead, 1929. The story of an unusual Kansas editor in the usual small town, and of the *Atchison Globe.*

JUERGENS, GEORGE. *News from the White House.* Chicago: University of Chicago Press, 1981. Presidential-press relationships for Roosevelt and Wilson.

KNIGHT, OLIVER H., ed. *I Protest: Selected Disquisitions of E. W. Scripps.* Madison: University of Wisconsin Press, 1966. An admirable, condensed biography is followed by Scripps's private writings as a "thinker." Best book on Scripps.

LINN, JAMES W. *James Keeley, Newspaperman.* Indianapolis: Bobbs-Merrill, 1937. The biography of the *Chicago Tribune*'s crusading managing editor.

LITTLEFIELD, ROY EVERETT, III. *William Randolph Hearst: His Role in American Progressivism.* Lanham, MD: University Press of America, 1980. Hearst of 1895 to 1920 played a progressive role as reformist and social activist. See Carlisle listing in the Chapter 14 Bibliography.

MCRAE, MILTON A. *Forty Years in Newspaperdom.* New York: Brentano's, 1924. Autobiography of E. W. Scripps's partner and business manager.

MAHIN, HELEN O., ed. *The Editor and His People.* New York: Macmillan, 1924. An excellent collection of William Allen White's editorials.

MARZOLF, MARION. *Up From the Footnote: A History of Women Journalists.* New York: Hastings House, 1977. Includes one chapter on the women's movement.

MORRISON, JOSEPH L. *Josephus Daniels Says.* Chapel Hill: University of North Carolina Press, 1962. Detailed biography of the editor of the *Raleigh News-Observer* from 1894 to 1913; his crusading battles, his white supremacy.

NIVEN, PENELOPE. *Carl Sandburg: A Biography.* New York: Scribner's, 1991. In-depth research by a Sandburg specialist.

OLDER, FREMONT. *My Own Story.* New York: Macmillan, 1926. The fighting San Francisco editor tells his piece.

PICKETT, CALDER M. *Ed Howe: Country Town Philosopher.* Lawrence: University Press of Kansas, 1969. Prize-winning biography of the editor of the *Atchison Globe.*

TRIMBLE, VANCE H. *The Astonishing Mr. Scripps.* Ames: Iowa State University Press, 1992. New biographical material by a former Pulitzer Prize–winning reporter.

Books: Magazines, Muckraking

BAKER, RAY STANNARD. *An American Chronicle.* New York: Scribner's, 1945. The autobiography of one of *McClure's* writers.

BANNISTER, ROBERT C. *Ray Stannard Baker: The Mind and Thought of a Progressive.* New Haven: Yale University Press, 1966. One of the reporters for *McClure's.*

BOK, EDWARD W. *The Americanization of Edward Bok.* New York: Scribner's, 1920. The famous autobiography of the editor of the *Ladies' Home Journal.*

BRADY, KATHLEEN. *Ida Tarbell: Portrait of a Muckraker.* New York: Seaview/Putnam, 1984. Well-balanced biography of pioneering journalist. See also Mary E. Tomkins, *Ida M. Tarbell* (New York: Twayne, 1974).

BRASCH, WALTER M. *Forerunners of Revolution: Muckrakers and the American Social Conscience.* Lanham, MD: University Press of America, 1990. How reporters exposed exploitation of the people.

CHALMERS, DAVID M. *The Social and Political Ideas of the Muckrakers.* New York: The Citadel Press, 1964. A brief analysis of 13 muckrakers.

DIGBY-JUNGER, RICHARD. *The Journalist as Reformer: Henry Demarest Lloyd and Wealth Against Commonwealth.* Westport, CT: Greenwood Press, 1996. Biography of the well-known muckraker.

FILLER, LOUIS. *Crusaders for American Liberalism.* New York: Harcourt Brace Jovanovich, 1939. A study of the 1902 to 1914 muckrakers based on *The Muckrakers* (University Park: Pennsylvania State University Press, 1976).

FORCEY, CHARLES. *The Crossroads of Liberalism.* New York: Oxford University Press, 1961. A case study of Herbert Croly, Walter Weyl, Walter Lippmann, and the 1914 *New Republic.*

HAPGOOD, NORMAN. *The Changing Years.* New York: Holt, Rinehart & Winston, 1930. The reflections of the editor of *Collier's.*

KAPLAN, JUSTIN. *Lincoln Steffens: A Biography.* New York: Simon & Schuster, 1974. Points to discrepancy between Steffens's autobiography and real life.

KOCHERSBERGER, ROBERT C. *More Than a Muckraker: Ida Tarbell's Lifetime in Journalism.* Knoxville: University of Tennessee Press, 1994. Demonstrates Tarbell's literary side; she wrote books and articles into her 80s.

LEVY, DAVID W. *Herbert Croly of the New Republic: The Life and Thought of an American Progressive.* Princeton, NJ: Princeton University Press, 1985. New study of the founder.

LINGEMAN, RICHARD. *Theodore Dreiser: At the Gates of the City, 1871–1907.* New York: Putnam's, 1986. First volume of a biography by a cultural historian ends with the success of *Sister Carrie.*

LYON, PETER. *Success Story: The Life and Times of S. S. McClure.* New York: Scribner's, 1963. His muckraking magazine provides the climax of this prize-winning biography.

MARCOSSON, ISAAC F. *David Graham Phillips and His Times.* New York: Dodd, Mead, 1932. The biography of a muckraker.

MAREK, JAYNE E. *Women Editing Modernism: "Little" Magazines & Literary History.* Lexington, KY: University Press of Kentucky, 1995. Seven women who edited *The Dial,* the *Little Review, Poetry,* and others during the 1910s and 1920s.

MCCLURE, S. S. *My Autobiography.* New York: Frederick A. Stokes & Company, 1914. The story of the magazine publisher.

OHMANN, RICHARD. *Selling Culture: Magazines, Markets, and Class at the Turn of the Century.* London, New York:

Verso, 1996. The connection of mass-circulated magazines and advertising to mass culture.

O'CONNOR, RICHARD. *Jack London.* Boston: Little, Brown, 1964. A popular biography.

PHILLIPS, DAVID GRAHAM. *The Treason of the Senate,* ed. George E. Mowry and Judson A. Grenier. Chicago: Quadrangle, 1964. Excellent discussion by the editors precedes the texts of Phillips's famed articles in *Cosmopolitan.*

RILEY, SAM G., ed. *American Magazine Journalists, 1741–1850; 1850–1900; 1900–1960, First Series; 1900–1960, Second Series.* Detroit: Gale Research, 1988; 1989; 1990; 1994. Four invaluable volumes in the Dictionary of Literary Biography series cover the key figures with biographies and bibliographies.

SCANLON, JENNIFER. *Inarticulate Longings:* The Ladies' Home Journal, *Gender and the Promises of Consumer Culture.* New York: Routledge, 1995. The *Journal* both reflected and shaped emerging consumer culture, 1910–30.

SCHNEIROV, MATTHEW. *The Dream of a New Social Order: Popular Magazines in America, 1893–1914.* New York: Columbia University Press, 1994. How magazines became the first national mass medium and expressed a uniquely American vision of a better future.

SEDGWICK, ELLERY. *The Happy Profession.* Boston: Little, Brown, 1946. Includes a description of the hurly-burly times at *Leslie's,* the *American,* and *McClure's* before Sedgwick became owner and editor of the *Atlantic* in 1909.

SMITH, STEVEN E., et al., eds. *American Book and Magazine Illustrators to 1920.* Detroit: Gale Research, 1998. Dictionary of Literary Biography volume includes biographies and bibliographies.

STEFFENS, LINCOLN. *The Autobiography of Lincoln Steffens.* New York: Harcourt Brace Jovanovich, 1931. One of the great journalistic autobiographies.

TARBELL, IDA M. *All in the Day's Work.* New York: Macmillan, 1939. The chief woman muckraker reviews her career.

VILLARD, OSWALD GARRISON. *Fighting Years.* New York: Harcourt Brace Jovanovich, 1939. The autobiography of the publisher of the *Nation* and *New York Post.*

WEINBERG, ARTHUR AND LILA, eds. *The Muckrakers.* New York: Simon & Schuster, 1961. A compilation of some of the best magazine articles by the muckrakers.

WILSON, HAROLD S. *"McClure's" Magazine and the Muckrakers.* Princeton, NJ: Princeton University Press, 1970. Solid contribution to the subject.

Books: Alternative Press, Minorities, Foreign-Language Press

APTHEKER, HERBERT, ed. *Against Racism.* Amherst: University of Massachusetts Press, 1985. Unpublished essays, paper, and addresses of W.E.B. Du Bois, 1887–1961.

BACKLUND, JONAS O. *A Century of the Swedish-American Press.* Chicago: Swedish-American Newspaper Co., 1952. Nearly all were rural weeklies.

BULLOCK, PENELOPE L. *The Afro-American Periodical Press, 1839–1909.* Baton Rouge: Louisiana State University Press, 1981. Precedes in time Abby and Roland Johnson, *Propaganda and Aesthetics: The Literary Politics of Afro-American Magazines in the Twentieth Century* (Amherst: University of Massachusetts, 1979).

BUNI, ANDREW. *Robert L. Vann of the "Pittsburgh Courier": Politics and Black Journalism.* Pittsburgh: University of Pittsburgh Press, 1974.

CAHAN, ABRAHAM. *The Education of Abraham Cahan,* trans. Leon Stein. New York: Jewish Publication Society, 1969. Founder of the *Jewish Daily Forward.*

CLARKE, JOHN H., et al. *Black Titan W.E.B. Du Bois: An Anthology by the Editors of "Freedomways."* Boston: Beacon Press, 1970. Writings about Du Bois, first editor of *The Crisis* and legendary black leader.

CONLIN, JOSEPH R., ed. *The American Radical Press, 1880–1960.* Westport, CT: Greenwood Press, 1974. Collection of articles; includes *Appeal to Reason.*

DETWEILER, FREDERICK G. *The Negro Press in the United States.* Chicago: University of Chicago Press, 1922. Basic historical study together with Vishnu V. Oak, *The Negro Press* (Yellow Springs, OH: Antioch Press, 1948).

DU BOIS, W. E. B. *The Autobiography of W. E. Burghardt Du Bois,* New York: International Publishers, 1968. Written at age 90 by the editor of *The Crisis* as volume 3 of his autobiography.

FOX, STEPHEN R. *"The Guardian" of Boston: William Monroe Trotter.* New York: Atheneum, 1971. Trotter's *Guardian* was a leader of 1900 to 1920.

HARMON, STEVEN, W. *The "St. Josephs–Blatt", 1896–1919.* Peter Lang, 1989. Concentrates on the World War I period, a difficult time for the German-American press.

HUTTON, FRANKIE. *The Early Black Press in America, 1827–1860.* Westport, CT: Greenwood, 1993. Demonstrates that early black press editors were interested in many concerns besides antislavery.

LEWIS, DAVID LEVERING. *W.E.B. DuBois: Biography of a Race, 1868–1919.* New York: Holt, 1993. First in two-volume study; acclaimed as the best biography of Du Bois.

MARZOLF, MARION T. *The Danish-Language Press in America.* New York: Arno Press, 1979. Based on a Ph.D. thesis, University of Michigan, 1972. The small ethnic press grew from 1872 to 1914.

MILLER, SALLY M., ed. *The Ethnic Press in the United States: A Historical Analysis and Handbook.* Westport, CT: Greenwood Press, 1987. Scholarly essays on the pre-1914 era's 1300 foreign-language papers of 27 immigrant groups.

PARK, ROBERT E. *The Immigrant Press and Its Control.* New York: Harper, 1922. Descriptive and analytical. Finds the high point of 1323 papers in the United States in 1917.

PRIDE, ARMISTEAD. *The Black Press: A Bibliography.* Jefferson City, MO: Lincoln University Department of Journalism, 1968. Major scholarly effort.

RISCHIN, MOSES, ed. *Grandma Never Lived in America: The New Journalism of Abraham Cahan.* Bloomington:

Indiana University Press, 1986. Writings of the editor of the *Jewish Daily Forward.*

RUSSO, PIETRO. *Italian American Periodical Press, 1836–1980: A Comprehensive Bibliography.* Staten Island, NY: Center for Migration Studies, 1983.

SHORE, ELLIOT. *Talkin' Socialism, J. A. Wayland and the Role of the Press in American Radicalism, 1890–1912.* Lawrence: University of Kansas Press, 1988. The story of his *Appeal to Reason.*

STREITMATTER, RODGER. *Raising Her Voice: African-American Women Journalists Who Changed History.* Lexington: University Press of Kentucky, 1994. Biographical sketches of 11 journalists, from Maria W. Stewart to Charlayne Hunter-Gault.

SUGGS, HENRY LEWIS, ed. *The Black Press in the South, 1865–1979.* Westport, CT: Greenwood Press, 1983. A comprehensive study of 12 states.

THORNBROUGH, EMMA L. *T. Thomas Fortune: Militant Journalist.* Chicago: University of Chicago Press, 1972. Black editor of the *People's Advocate.*

WELLS-BARNETT, IDA B. *Crusade for Justice.* Chicago: University of Chicago Press, 1970. Writings of a black journalist and reformer, 1887–1931, edited by John Hope Franklin.

WILSON, CLINT, AND FÉLIX GUTIÉRREZ. *Minorities and the Media: The End of Mass Communication.* Beverly Hills: Sage Publications, 1985.

WITTKE, CARL F. *The German-Language Press in America.* Lexington: University of Kentucky Press, 1957. A history from 1732 to 1956.

WOLSELEY, ROLAND E. *The Black Press: U.S.A.* Ames: Iowa State University Press, 1990. A comprehensive survey, with substantial historical material for black newspapers, magazines, and broadcasting.

Periodicals and Monographs

AJAMI, JOSEPH G. "The Arabic Press in the United States Since 1842: Socio-Historical Study," Ph.D. thesis, Ohio University, 1987.

ATWOOD, ROY A. "Telephony and Its Cultural Meanings in Southeastern Iowa, 1900–1917," Ph.D. thesis, University of Iowa, 1984. Grassroots development of small co-ops. See also Atwood's article in *Journalism History,* X (Spring–Summer 1983), 16.

BEASLEY, MAURINE. "The Muckrakers and Lynching: A Case Study in Racism," *Journalism History,* IX (Autumn–Winter 1982), 86.

BENNION, SHERILYN COX. "Woman Suffrage Papers of the West, 1869–1914," *American Journalism,* III:3 (1986), 125.

BJORK, ULF JONAS. "The Swedish-American Press: Three Newspapers and Their Communities," Ph.D. thesis, University of Washington, 1987. Time frame for content study, 1908–10 and 1921–23.

BRADSHAW, JAMES S. "The Journalist as Pariah: Three Muckraking Novels by Samuel Hopkins Adams," *Journalism History,* X (Spring–Summer 1983), 10.

BURT, ELIZABETH V. "Dissent and Control in a Woman Suffrage Periodical: 30 Years of the *Wisconsin Citizen,*" *American Journalism,* 16:2 (Spring 1999), 39–61. The *Wisconsin Citizen* "often suppressed debate among its constituents in the interest of maintaining an appearance of unity within the movement and the dominance of movement leaders."

COBB-REILEY, LINDA. "Aliens and Alien Ideas: The Suppression of Anarchists and the Anarchist Press in America 1901–1914," *Journalism Quarterly,* LXV (Summer 1988), 50. Identification of anarchists as immigrants compounded their problems.

COOPER, ANNE M. "Suffrage as News: Ten Dailies' Coverage of the Nineteenth Amendment," *American Journalism,* I (Summer 1983), 73. Content analysis and evaluation.

CRAMER, JANET M., "Cross Purposes: Gender, Race, and Nation in the U.S. Women's Missionary Press, 1880–1905," Ph.D. thesis, University of Minnesota, 1999. How mass media function to perpetuate social structures and to form community.

———. "Woman as Citizen: Race, Class, and the Discourse of Women's Citizenship, 1894–1909," *Journalism and Mass Communication Monographs,* 165 (1998), 1–39.

DOMKE, DAVID S., "Journalists, Framing, and Discourse about Race Relations," *Journalism and Mass Communication Monographs,* 164 (1997), 1–55. Based on his award-winning Ph.D. thesis, "The Press, Social Change and Race Relations in the Late Nineteenth Century," University of Minnesota, 1996.

DORWART, JEFFERY M. "James Creelman, the New York *World* and the Port Arthur Massacre," *Journalism Quarterly,* L (Winter 1973), 697. Eyewitness report.

ERICKSON, JOHN E. "Newspapers and Social Values: Chicago Journalism, 1890–1910," Ph.D. thesis, University of Illinois, 1973. The press reported and embodied values marking entry into the twentieth century.

EVENSEN, BRUCE J. "The Evangelical Origins of the Muckrakers," *American Journalism,* VI (1989), 5. Analysis of the *McClure's* group.

FOLKERTS, JEAN LANGE. "William Allen White's Anti-Populist Rhetoric as an Agenda-Setting Technique," *Journalism Quarterly,* LX (Spring 1983), 28. Based on her Ph.D. thesis, University of Kansas, 1981 (author, Lange).

———. "William Allen White: Editor and Businessman During the Reform Years, 1895–1916," *Kansas History,* VII (Summer 1984).

FRANCKE, WARREN T. "Investigative Exposure in the Nineteenth Century: The Journalistic Heritage of the Muckrakers," Ph.D. thesis, University of Minnesota, 1974. Muckraking proves to be part of an earlier reporting tradition.

GATEWOOD, WILLARD B., JR. "A Negro Editor on Imperialism: John Mitchell, 1898–1901," *Journalism Quarterly,* XLIX (Spring 1972), 43. Mitchell saw the claims of liberating peoples from Spain as a mask for American imperialism.

GRENIER, JUDSON A. "Muckraking and the Muckrakers: An Historical Definition," *Journalism Quarterly,* XXXVII (Autumn 1960), 552. A study of the years 1902 to 1914.

GROSE, CHARLES W. "A Century of Black Newspapers in Texas, 1868–1969," Ph.D. thesis, University of Texas, 1972. Depression broke the GOP's hold on the papers.

HARRISON, JOHN M. "Finley Peter Dunne and the Progressive Movement," *Journalism Quarterly,* XLIV (Autumn 1967), 475. Mr. Dooley's creator was a philosophical anarchist.

HOWE, GENE. "My Father Was the Most Wretchedly Unhappy Man I Ever Knew," *Saturday Evening Post,* October 25, 1941. A dramatic story about E. W. Howe, reprinted in John E. Drewry, *Post Biographies of Famous Journalists* (1942).

KESSLER, LAUREN J. "A Siege of the Citadels: Access of Women Suffrage to the Oregon Press, 1884–1912," Ph.D. thesis, University of Washington, 1980.

KIELBOWICZ, RICHARD B. "The Limits of the Press as an Agent of Reform: Minneapolis 1900–1905," *Journalism Quarterly,* LIX (Spring 1982), 21. Minimizes influences.

KIMBROUGH, MARVIN G. "W.E.B. Du Bois as Editor of the *Crisis,*" Ph.D. thesis, University of Texas, 1974. Study of the NAACP's paper from 1910 to 1934.

KLASSEN, TERESA C., AND OWEN V. JOHNSON. "Sharpening of the *Blade:* Black Consciousness in Kansas, 1892–97," *Journalism Quarterly,* LXIII (Summer 1986), 298. An activist, small-town, black-owned newspaper.

KNIGHT, OLIVER. "Scripps and His Adless Newspaper, *The Day Book,*" *Journalism Quarterly,* XLI (Winter 1964), 51. Full story of the effort to create an adless daily.

KREILING, ALBERT L. "The Making of Radical Identities in the Black Press: A Cultural Analysis of Race Journalism in Chicago, 1878–1929," Ph.D. thesis, University of Illinois, 1973. Differing cultural groups find expression.

LAWSON, LINDA. "Truth in Publishing: The Newspaper Publicity Act as Government Regulation of the Press," Ph.D. thesis, University of Washington, 1988. It fell short of expectations.

MASEL-WALTERS, LYNNE. " 'Their Rights and Nothing More': A History of *The Revolution,* 1868–70," *Journalism Quarterly,* LIII (Summer 1976), 242–51. Details the beginning of women's political journalism and a short-lived national publication.

———. "A Burning Cloud by Day: The History and Content of the *Woman's Journal,*" *Journalism History,* III (Winter 1976–77), 103. Organ of the feminist movement from 1869 to 1931.

———. "Margaret Sanger and *The Woman Rebel,*" *Journalism History,* XI (Spring–Summer 1984), 3. Censorship of her paper under Anthony Comstock's laws, 1914.

MATHER, ANNE. "A History of Feminist Periodicals," *Journalism History,* I–II (Autumn 1974–Spring 1975). Three-part article.

McGLASHAN, ZENA BETH. "Club 'Ladies' and Working 'Girls': Rheta Childe Dorr and the *New York Evening Post,*" *Journalism History,* VIII (Spring 1981), 7. Turn of the century.

MIRALDI, ROBERT. "The Journalism of David Graham Phillips," Ph.D. thesis, New York University, 1985. See also his article in *Journalism Quarterly,* LXIII (Spring 1983), 83.

NORD, DAVID PAUL. "The *Appeal to Reason* and American Socialism, 1901–1920," *Kansas History,* I (Summer 1978), 75. Sixty-issue sampling of leading Socialist weekly.

PARMENTER, WILLIAM. "*The Jungle* and Its Effects," *Journalism History,* X (Spring–Summer 1983), 14.

PONDER, STEPHEN E. "News Management in the Progressive Era, 1898–1909," Ph.D. thesis, University of Washington, 1985. The conservation crusade.

PRIDE, ARMISTEAD SCOTT, comp. "The Black Press to 1968: A Bibliography," *Journalism History,* IV (Winter 1977–78), 148. Books by subject areas.

PRINGLE, HENRY F. "The Newspaper Man as an Artist," *Scribner's,* XCVII (February 1935), 101. The artist was Frank I. Cobb, editor of the *World.*

REAVES, SHIELA. "How Radical Were the Muckrakers?: Socialist Press Views, 1902–1906," *Journalism Quarterly,* LXI (Winter 1984), 763. Enthusiasm of five socialist papers for muckrakers waned.

REED, BARBARA STRAUS. "The Antebellum Jewish Press: Origins, Problems, Functions," *Journalism Monographs* 139 (June 1993). Includes treatment of Jewish immigration.

———. "Unity, not Absorption: Robert Lyon and the *Asmonean,*" *American Journalism,* VII (1990), 77. First U.S. English-language Jewish weekly.

ROBERTS, NANCY L. " 'Ten Thousand Tongues' Speaking for Peace: Purposes and Strategies of the Nineteenth-Century Peace Advocacy Press," *Journalism History* XXI:1 (Spring 1995), 16–28. Eight peace society periodicals and two Quaker publications.

SARASOHN, DAVID. "Power without Glory: Hearst in the Progressive Era," *Journalism Quarterly,* LII (Autumn 1976), 474. Examines Hearst's power and his squandering of political capital.

STEFFENS, PETE. "The Identity Struggle of Lincoln Steffens—Writer or Reporter?" *Journalism History,* II (Spring 1975), 16. By his son. Lincoln Steffens hesitated to make reporting a career.

STEIN, HARRY H. "American Muckrakers and Muckraking: The 50-Year Scholarship," *Journalism Quarterly,* LVI (Spring 1979), 9. Evaluation of the literature.

STEINER, LINDA. "The Women's Suffrage Press, 1850–1900; A Cultural Analysis," Ph.D. thesis, University of Illinois, 1979. See also Steiner, "Finding Community in Nineteenth-Century Suffrage Periodicals," *American Journalism,* I (1983), 1.

STEVENS, GEORGE E. "A History of the *Cincinnati Post,*" Ph.D. thesis, University of Minnesota, 1968. Emphasizes local issues and political coverage of a mainstay Scripps daily. See Stevens, "Scripps' *Cincinnati Post:* Liberalism at Home," *Journalism Quarterly,* XLVIII (Summer 1971), 231.

STREITMATTER, RODGER. "William W. Price: First White House Correspondent," *Journalism History,* XVI (Spring 1989), 32. Stood outside the door in 1895.

THEUS, KATHRYN T. "From Orthodoxy to Reform: Assimilation and the Jewish-English Press of Mid-Nineteenth-Century America," *American Journalism,* I:2 (1984), 15.

THORNBROUGH, EMMA LOU. "American Negro Newspapers, 1880–1914," *Business History Review,* XL (Winter 1966), 467. Of hundreds of papers, only a few subsidized ones survived any length of time.

WEIGLE, CLIFFORD F. "The Young Scripps Editor: Keystone of E. W.'s 'System,' " *Journalism Quarterly,* XLI (Summer 1964), 360. A case study of the founding of the *Houston Press.*

WEISSBERGER, S. J. "The Rise and Decline of the Yiddish-American Press," Ph.D. thesis, Syracuse University, 1972. Yiddish papers since 1870.

WHITE, W. L. "The Sage of Emporia," *Nieman Reports,* XXIII (March 1969), 23. Human-interest piece by William Allen White's son.

CHAPTER 11: BASTIONS OF NEWS ENTERPRISE

Books

BERGER, MEYER. *The Story of the "New York Times," 1851–1951.* New York: Simon & Schuster, 1951. Mainly the story of the *Times* after Ochs bought it; other books are better for the pre-Ochs period. But reporter Berger gets many reporters into his story, too rare an event in newspaper history telling, and thus has a lively book. The *Times* also issued *One Hundred Years of Famous Pages from the "New York Times"* in 1951 and many later reprint volumes.

BOND, F. FRASER. *Mr. Miller of "The Times."* New York: Scribner's 1931. The biography of *New York Times's* editor Charles R. Miller.

DAVIS, ELMER. *History of the "New York Times," 1851–1921.* New York: The New York Times, 1921. Still good for its period.

DESMOND, ROBERT W. *The Information Process: World News Reporting to the Twentieth Century.* Iowa City: University of Iowa Press, 1978. Most exhaustive scholarly study of news agencies and leading publications.

DORNFELD, A. A. *Behind the Front Page: The Story of the City News Bureau of Chicago.* Chicago: Academy, 1983. Famed training ground.

GORDON, GREGORY, AND RONALD E. COHEN. *Down to the Wire: UPI's Fight for Survival.* New York: McGraw-Hill, 1989. Award-winning recounting of UP and UPI history by two UPI editors.

HARRISON, JOHN M. *The Man Who Made Nasby, David Ross Locke.* Chapel Hill: University of North Carolina Press, 1969. An excellent biography of the editor of the *Toledo Blade,* who was the creator of Petroleum V. Nasby.

HUDSON, ROBERT V. *The Writing Game: A Biography of Will Irwin.* Ames: Iowa State University Press, 1982. Definitive study of Irwin's professional work and life.

JOHNSON, GERALD W. *An Honorable Titan.* New York: Harper & Row, 1946. A good, but comparatively uncritical, biographical study of Adolph S. Ochs.

McCABE, CHARLES R., ed. *Damned Old Crank.* New York: Harper & Row, 1951. Contains a chapter in which E. W. Scripps explains why he started the United Press, and gives some financial details.

"M.E.S." His Book. New York: Harper & Row, 1918. A book commemorating Melville E. Stone's first 25 years as the AP's general manager. Much of Stone's own writing and his major speeches are included along with other historical materials. See also Stone's autobiography, *Fifty Years a Journalist* (1921).

MITCHELL, EDWARD P. *Memoirs of an Editor.* New York: Scribner's, 1924. By the distinguished editor of the *New York Sun.*

MORRIS, JOE ALEX. *Deadline Every Minute: The Story of the United Press.* New York: Doubleday, 1957. By a UP staff member, observing the press association's fiftieth anniversary. Highly readable; covers both UP executives and newspeople.

SCHWARZLOSE, RICHARD A. *The Nation's Newsbrokers.* 2 vols. Evanston, IL: Northwestern University Press, 1989–90. Definitive news services account from pre-telegraph to 1920.

SEITZ, DON C. *The James Gordon Bennetts.* Indianapolis: Bobbs-Merrill, 1928. The younger Bennett brings the *New York Herald* to its downfall.

WATSON, ELMO SCOTT. *A History of Newspaper Syndicates in the United States, 1865–1935.* Chicago: Publishers' Auxiliary, 1936. Source for the story of the Western Newspaper Union.

Periodicals and Monographs

ABBOT, WILLIS J. "Melville E. Stone's Own Story," *Collier's,* LXV (February 7, 1920), 51. A well-written portrait of the AP general manager.

EWERT, WALTER E. "The History of the Chicago *Inter Ocean,* 1872–1914," Master's thesis, Northwestern University, 1940. An excellent account of a famous paper.

FINE, BARNETT. "When 'Boss' Lord Ruled *The Sun,*" *Editor & Publisher,* LXVI (April 22–July 15, 1933). A series of articles about Chester S. Lord, managing editor of the *New York Sun* for 33 years.

HUDSON, ROBERT V. "Will Irwin's Pioneering Criticism of the Press," *Journalism Quarterly,* XLVII (Summer 1970). 263. Authoritative biographical writing.

IRWIN, WILL. "The New York Sun," *American Magazine,* LXVII (January 1909), 301. The story of the *Sun's* school of journalism by one of its pupils.

———. "United Press," *Harper's Weekly,* LVIII (April 25, 1914), 6. An estimate of early UP progress by a topflight newsman.

MAGYAR, LINDA FEINFELD. "The Evolution of Presidential Press Secretaries," *Media History Digest,* V (Spring 1985), 2. A résumé of McKinley and Theodore Roosevelt years.

NATHAN, GEORGE JEAN. "James Gordon Bennett, the Monte Cristo of Modern Journalism," *Outing,* LIII

(March 1909), 690. The dramatic critic criticizes an erratic publisher.

SIMS, NORMAN H. "The Chicago Style of Journalism," Ph.D.
thesis, University of Illinois, 1979. Features Opie Read,
George Ade, Ben Hecht, and Whitechapel Club.

STOLBERG, BENJAMIN. "The Man Behind *The Times*," *Atlantic Monthly*, CXXXVIII (December 1926), 721. A
discerning study of Adolph S. Ochs. Reprinted in Ford
and Emery, *Highlights in the History of the American
Press.*

WIETEN, JAN. "Howard and Northcliffe: Two Press Lords on
the Warpath," *Roy W. Howard Monographs* (Bloomington: Indiana University School of Journalism, 1990).

CHAPTER 12: WAR COMES TO THE UNITED STATES

Books

CHAFEE, ZECHARIAH, JR. *Free Speech in the United States.*
Cambridge, MA: Harvard University Press, 1941. The
major study of the problem, by a Harvard law professor.

CHRISLOCK, CARL H. *Watchdog of Loyalty: The Minnesota
Commission of Public Safety during World War I.* St.
Paul: Minnesota Historical Society, 1991. Part of the
story of the hysteria that swept the Midwest during these
years.

CORNEBISE, ALFRED E. *Ranks and Columns: Armed Forces
Newspapers in American Wars.* Westport, CT: Greenwood, 1993. From 1776 through the Persian Gulf War.

———. *"The Stars and Stripes": Doughboy Journalism in
World War I.* Westport, CT: Greenwood Press, 1984.

CREEL, GEORGE. *How We Advertised America.* New York:
Harper & Row, 1920. The chairman of the World War I
Committee on Public Information makes his report to the
public. See also Creel's autobiography, *Rebel at Large*
(New York: G. P. Putnam's Sons, 1947).

CROZIER, EMMET. *American Reporters on the Western Front,
1914–1918.* New York: Oxford University Press, 1959.
Much detail about both star reporters and "specials."

EARLY, FRANCES H. *A World Without War: How U.S. Feminists and Pacifists Resisted World War I.* Syracuse, NY:
Syracuse University Press, 1997. Analysis of women's
political activism by an award-winning historian.

FERRELL, ROBERT. *Woodrow Wilson and World War I.* (New
York: Harper & Row, 1985). A balanced and straightfor-
ward account.

FISHBEIN, LESLIE. *Rebels in Bohemia: The Radicals of The
Masses, 1911–1917.* Chapel Hill: University of North
Carolina Press, 1982. Discusses Max Eastman, editor of
The Masses, John Reed, Emma Goldman, Floyd Dell,
Upton Sinclair, and others.

FLACKS, RICHARD. *Making History: The American Left and
the American Mind.* New York: Columbia University
Press, 1989. A synthesis of American left-wing politics by
a SDS founder, now a professor.

GILBERT, MARTIN. *The First World War: A Complete History.*
New York: Henry Holt & Company, 1994. A humaniza-
tion of the fighting in all sectors; detailed chronology.

KENNEDY, DAVID M. *Over Here: The First World War and
American Society.* New York: Oxford University Press,
1980. Best book about changes in U.S. society brought on
by the war. Especially good on the rise of centralized
government.

KNIGHTLEY, PHILLIP. *The First Casualty.* New York: Harcourt
Brace Jovanovich, 1975. A critical study of war correspondence from the Crimean War to Vietnam. Says most
war coverage has been poor.

KNOCK, THOMAS J. *To End All Wars: Woodrow Wilson and
the Quest for a New World Order.* New York: Oxford University Press, 1992. Well-researched, balanced account.

LANDE, NATHANIEL. *Dispatches from the Front: A History of
the American War Correspondent.* New York: Oxford
University Press, 1995. Excellent anthology of war correspondence from the Revolution to the Persian Gulf War,
with brief interpretive essays.

LASSWELL, HAROLD D. *Propaganda Technique in the World
War.* New York: Peter Smith, 1927. A standard source for
World War I propaganda efforts in the major belligerent
countries.

MOCK, JAMES R. *Censorship 1917.* Princeton: Princeton
University Press, 1941. The major work on World War I
censorship.

MOCK, JAMES R., AND CEDRIC LARSON. *Words That Won the
War.* Princeton: Princeton University Press, 1939. Best account of the work of the Committee on Public Information during World War I.

MURPHY, PAUL L. *World War I and the Origins of Civil Liberties.* New York: W. W. Norton, 1979. The classic, critical account.

PALMER, FREDERICK. *With My Own Eyes.* Indianapolis:
Bobbs-Merrill, 1933. Biographical account by a leading
World War I correspondent who became military field
censor.

POLENBERG, RICHARD. *Fighting Faiths: The Abrams Case,
the Supreme Court, and Free Speech.* New York: Viking
Penguin, 1988. The stories of those involved, from Justice
Holmes to J. Edgar Hoover.

ROTH, MITCHEL P. *Historical Dictionary of War Journalism.*
Westport, CT: Greenwood Press, 1997. Entries cover reporters, photographers, and artists who represented various news sources, from 1846 to the Persian Gulf War and
Yugoslavian conflict.

SALVATORE, NICK. *Eugene V. Debs: Citizen and Socialist.* Urbana: University of Illinois Press, 1983. Debs's Socialist
party failed but paved way for 1930s unions.

SCHREINER, GEORGE A. *Cables and Wireless.* Boston: Strat-
ford, 1924. Analyzes the effect of World War I on
communications.

SMITH, JEFFEREY A. *War and Press Freedom: The Problem
of Prerogative Power.* New York: Oxford University
Press, 1999. From the ratification of the Bill of Rights in
1791 through the Gulf War of 1991, this compelling study

discusses the evolution of wartime restrictions on the news media.

THOMPSON, JOHN A. *American Progressive Publicists and the First World War.* New York: Cambridge University Press, 1986. Analysis of confrontation of reform tradition with World War I.

WILLIAMS, WYTHE. *Passed by the Censor.* New York: Dutton, 1916. A World War I correspondent's story. Twenty years later his *Dusk of Empire* pictured the decline of Europe into another war.

WISH, HARVEY. *Society and Thought in Modern America.* New York: David McKay, 1962. Includes a lively discussion of the "Red Scare."

WITTKE, CARL F. *The German-Language Press in America.* Lexington: University of Kentucky Press, 1957. A history from 1732 to 1956; three chapters devoted to World War I.

ZURIER, REBECCA. *Art for the Masses: A Radical Magazine and Its Graphics, 1911–1917.* Philadelphia: Temple University Press, 1988. 150 illustrations.

Periodicals and Monographs

BEAN, WALTON E. "The Accuracy of Creel Committee News, 1917–1919; An Examination of Cases," *Journalism Quarterly,* XVIII (September 1941), 263.

BECK, ELMER A. "Autopsy of a Labor Daily: The *Milwaukee Leader,*" *Journalism Monographs,* XVI (August 1970).

BRITTON, JOHN A. "In Defense of Revolution: American Journalists in Mexico, 1920–1929," *Journalism History,* V (Winter 1978–79), 124. Carleton Beals, Ernest Gruening, and Frank Tannenbaum oppose U.S. State Department's concern for property rights and opposition to revolution, in pages of the *Nation* and the *New Republic.*

COBB-REILEY, LINDA. "The Meaning of Freedom of Speech and the Progressive Era: Historical Roots of Modern First Amendment Theory," Ph.D. thesis, University of Utah, 1986.

COHEN, JEREMY. "*Schenck* v. *United States:* A Clear and Present Danger to the First Amendment," Ph.D. thesis, University of Washington, 1983. Revisionist study. See also his article in *American Journalism,* II:1 (1985), 49.

CRAIG, ROBERT L. "The Journalism of Josephine Herbst," *American Journalism* XI:2 (1994). An advocacy writer is blackballed during the "Red Scare."

FOUGHT, JOHN P. "News and Editorial Treatment of Alleged Reds and Radicals by Selected Newspapers and Periodicals during 1918–1921," Ph.D. thesis, Southern Illinois University, 1970. The *New York Times* and *New York Tribune* had heavy bias.

LARSON, CEDRIC. "Censorship of Army News during the World War, 1917–1918," *Journalism Quarterly,* XVII (December 1940), 313.

LINK, ARTHUR S. "That Cobb Interview," *Journal of American History,* LXXII:1 (June 1985), 7. An exercise in historiography revising the account of the Wilson-Cobb interview.

MANDER, MARY SUE. "Pen and Sword: A Cultural History of the American War Correspondent, 1895–1945," Ph.D.

thesis, University of Illinois, 1979. Flamboyant correspondents disappeared with the cavalry by 1917.

———. "The Journalist as a Cynic," *Antioch Review* (Winter 1980), 92. Reporting of World War I examined.

McGLASHAN, ZENA BETH. "Women Witness the Russian Revolution: Analyzing Ways of Seeing," *Journalism History,* XII (Summer 1985), 54. Correspondents Bessie Beatty and Rheta Childe Dorr.

PICKETT, CALDER M. "A Paper for the Doughboys: *Stars and Stripes* in World War I," *Journalism Quarterly,* XLII (Winter 1965), 60. The flavor of the soldiers' paper is captured.

STEVENS, JOHN D. "Press and Community Toleration: Wisconsin in World War I," *Journalism Quarterly,* XLVI (Summer 1969), 255. Based on his Ph.D. thesis, University of Wisconsin, 1967.

CHAPTER 13: THE TWENTIES: RADIO, MOVIES, AND JAZZ JOURNALISM

Books: Background History

ALLEN, FREDERICK LEWIS. *The Big Change.* New York: Harper & Row, 1952. See also Lloyd Morris, *Postscript to Yesterday* (New York: Random House, 1947); Dixon Wecter, *The Age of the Great Depression, 1929–1941.* Vol. 13 of *A History of American Life* (New York: Macmillan, 1948); Harvey Wish, *Contemporary America: The National Scene Since 1900* (New York: Harper & Row, 1966). Excellent social histories.

COVERT, CATHERINE L., AND JOHN D. STEVENS, eds. *Mass Media between the Wars: Perceptions of Cultural Tensions, 1918–1941.* Syracuse, NY: Syracuse University Press, 1984. Twelve substantive studies, bibliographical essay.

FASS, PAULA S. *The Damned and the Beautiful: American Youth in the 1920s.* New York: Oxford University Press, 1977. A well-researched and well-written social history.

LEUCHTENBURG, WILLIAM E. *The Perils of Prosperity, 1914–1932.* 2nd ed. Chicago: University of Chicago Press, 1993. Update of the classic 1958 overview that traces the political, economic, social, and cultural phenomena that transformed the United States in this period.

LEWIS, DAVID L. *When Harlem Was in Vogue.* New York: Knopf, 1981. A major study of the flowering of black culture in Harlem.

LIEBOVICH, LOUIS. *Bylines in Despair: Herbert Hoover, the Great Depression, and the U.S. News Media.* A presidential administration that failed to communicate.

MURRAY, ROBERT K. *The Harding Era.* Minneapolis: University of Minnesota Press, 1969. A detailed study of the ill-fated Harding administration.

PERRETT, GEOFFREY. *America in the 20's: A History.* New York: Simon & Schuster, 1982. Detailed study.

TEAFORD, JON C. *The Twentieth-Century American City.* Baltimore: Johns Hopkins, 1986. Urban realities have stymied social progress.

Books: Newspapers

BARRETT, JAMES W. *"The World," the Flesh, and Messrs. Pulitzer.* New York: Vanguard, 1931. The best story of the sale of the *World,* by the last city editor.

BESSIE, SIMON M. *Jazz Journalism.* New York: Dutton, 1938. The best story of the tabloids, prefaced with an account of the rise of sensationalism.

BOYLAN, JAMES, ed. *"The World" and the Twenties: The Golden Years of New York's Legendary Newspaper.* New York: Dial Press, 1973. Captures the flavor and writing skill.

BRITT, GEORGE. *Forty Years—Forty Millions: The Career of Frank A. Munsey.* New York: Holt, Rinehart & Winston, 1935. A critical biography.

CHAPMAN, JOHN. *Tell It to Sweeney: The Informal History of the "New York Daily News."* New York: Doubleday, 1961. Light-touch account.

DENNIS, CHARLES H. *Victor Lawson: His Time and His Work.* Chicago: University of Chicago Press, 1935. The authorized story of Lawson and the *Chicago Daily News.*

DORNFELD, A. A. *Hello Sweetheart, Get Me Rewrite!* Chicago: Academy Chicago Publications, 1988. Originally published as *Behind the Front Page.*

EVENSEN, BRUCE. *When Dempsey Fought Tunney: Heroes, Hokum, and Storytelling in the Jazz Age.* Knoxville: University of Tennessee Press, 1996. Mass media's role in the cultivation of celebrity, and the emergence of the sportswriter.

FOWLER, GENE. *Timber Line.* New York: Covici-Friede, 1933. The colorful story at the Bonfils and Tammen era at the *Denver Post.* No tale was too tall for Denver news writers.

HOSOKAWA, BILL. *Thunder in the Rockies: The Incredible "Denver Post."* New York: Morrow, 1976. An update by the executive news editor.

HUGHES, HELEN M. *News and the Human Interest Story.* Chicago: University of Chicago Press, 1940. A sociological study of the feature story and sensationalism, with some discussion of the tabloid era.

HUTCHENS, JOHN K., AND GEORGE OPPENHEIMER, eds. *The Best in the "World."* New York; Viking Press, 1973. Selections from 1921 to 1928.

PERKIN, ROBERT L. *The First Hundred Years: An Informal History of Denver and the "Rocky Mountain News."* New York: Doubleday, 1959. By a staff member of Colorado's first paper.

STEVENS, JOHN D. *Sensationalism and the New York Press.* New York: Columbia University Press, 1991. Concentrates on the penny press, yellow journalism, and the 1920s.

VILLARD, OSWALD GARRISON. *The Disappearing Daily.* New York: Knopf, 1944. Criticism of the trend toward consolidation and bigness.

———. *Some Newspapers and Newspaper-Men.* New York: Knopf, 1923. Like *The Disappearing Daily,* this book discusses newspapers in major cities as well as major publishers.

Books: Comics

BLACKBEARD, BILL, AND MARTIN WILLIAMS. *The Smithsonian Collection of Newspaper Comics.* Washington, DC: Smithsonian Institution Press, 1977. A hundred strips, 94 color pages, annotated index.

COUPERIE, PIERRE, AND MAURICE C. HORN. *A History of the Comic Strip.* New York: Crown, 1968. Covers worldwide with emphasis upon American.

GIFFORD, DENIS, *American Comic Strip Collections, 1884–1939: The Evolutionary Era.* Boston: G. K. Hall, 1990. The first authoritative listing of early comic collections, comprehensive bibliography.

KUNZLE, DAVID. *The History of the Comic Strip: The Nineteenth Century.* Berkeley: University of California Press, 1990. Covers European and U.S. artists, 1827 to the Yellow Kid, in 390 pages.

MARSCHALL, RICHARD. *America's Great Comic Strip Artists.* New York: Abbeville Press, 1989. Three hundred color and black-and-white illustrations.

ROBINSON, JERRY. *The Comics: An Illustrated History of Comic Strip Art.* New York: Putnam's, 1974. Perhaps the best one-volume overview.

WAUGH, COULTON. *The Comics.* New York: Macmillan, 1947. A first-rate history of the comic pages; detailed but well written and well illustrated.

WEBSTER, H. T. *The Best of H. T. Webster.* New York: Simon & Schuster, 1953. One of the best collections of humorous newspaper drawings.

Books: Broadcasting

AITKEN, HUGH G. J. *The Continuous Wave: Technology and American Radio, 1900–1932.* Princeton, NJ: Princeton University Press, 1985. Continues the author's *Syntony and Spark* (1976), covering the 1880s to 1900. Best-written history of technical development.

BARFIELD, RAY. *Listening to Radio, 1920–1950.* Westport, CT: Praeger, 1996. Oral histories of early listeners explore radio's impact.

BARNOUW, ERIK. *A History of Broadcasting in the United States.* Vol. 1, *A Tower in Babel* (to 1933); vol. 2, *The Golden Web* (1933–53); vol. 3, *The Image Empire* (from 1953). New York: The Oxford Press, 1966, 1968, 1970. Best account of radio and television; third volume necessarily becomes less historical in tone.

———. *Media Marathon: A Twentieth-Century Memoir.* Durham, NC: Duke University Press, 1996. Reflections on a life in broadcasting and teaching.

———. *Tube of Plenty.* New York: Oxford Press, 1990. Condensed, updated version of television history.

BILBY, KENNETH. *The General: David Sarnoff and the Rise of the Communications Industry.* New York: Harper & Row, 1986. Best biography of RCA's leader.

Broadcasting, 50th anniversary issue, October 12, 1981. A 314-page issue including a 57-page chronology of broadcast history.

CLOUD, STANLEY, AND LYNNE OLSON. *The Murrow Boys.* Boston, MA: Houghton Mifflin, 1996. Early radio's inner circle of reporters, including Eric Sevareid, Richard Hottelet, Cecil Brown, and Mary Marvin Breckinridge.

DE FOREST, LEE. *Father of Radio: The Autobiography of Lee De Forest.* Chicago: Wilcox & Follett, 1950. The early years.

DOUGLAS, SUSAN J. *Inventing American Broadcasting, 1899–1922.* Baltimore: Johns Hopkins, 1987. Best history of early radio and the forces at work in society and business.

DUNNING, JOHN. *Tune in Yesterday: The Ultimate Encyclopedia of Old-Time Radio, 1925–1976.* Englewood Cliffs, NJ: Prentice Hall, 1976. Narrative and data listings.

ELY, MELVIN P. *The Adventures of Amos 'n' Andy: A Social History of an American Phenomenon.* New York: Free Press, 1991. Radio's top show.

EMERY, WALTER B. *Broadcasting and Government.* Rev. ed. East Lansing: Michigan State University Press, 1971. An encyclopedic survey of all aspects of government interest in and regulation of U.S. broadcasting.

GODFREY, DONALD G. comp. *A Directory of Broadcast Archives.* Washington, DC: Broadcast Education Association, 1983.

HEAD, SYDNEY W., CHRISTOPHER STERLING, AND LEMUEL SCHOFIELD. *Broadcasting in America.* 7th ed. Boston: Houghton Mifflin, 1995. Sterling joins Head as coauthor of this classic.

HILMES, MICHELLE. *Radio Voices: American Broadcasting, 1922–1952.* Minneapolis: University of Minnesota Press, 1997. Programs' social and popular culture contexts.

HINDS, LYNN BOYD. *Broadcasting the Local News, the Early Years of Pittsburgh's KDKA-TV.* University Park, PA: Pennsylvania State University Press, 1995. The evolution of local news on KDKA.

JACKAWAY, GWENYTH L. *Media at War: Radio's Challenge to the Newspapers, 1924–1939.* Westport, CT: Greenwood Press, 1995. How newspapers sought to preserve their institutional power in the face of a new media technology.

KAHN, FRANK J. ed. *Documents of American Broadcasting.* 4th ed. Englewood Cliffs, NJ: Prentice Hall, 1984. The pertinent documents and cases.

KEMPLER, CANDYCE, ed. *The First Fifty Years of Broadcasting.* Washington, DC: Broadcasting Publications, 1982. Edited reprint of weekly articles in *Broadcasting* magazine.

LICHTY, LAWRENCE W., AND MALACHI C. TOPPING. *American Broadcasting: A Sourcebook on the History of Radio and Television.* New York: Hastings House, 1975. Eight-year editing project yields more than 700 pages of data, chronologies, and findings.

MACDONALD, J. FRED. *Don't Touch That Dial!: Radio Programming in American Life from 1920 to 1960.* Chicago: Nelson-Hall, 1979. Radio's varied contributions to U.S. culture.

MCCHESNEY, ROBERT W. *Telecommunications: Mass Media and Democracy: The Battle for the Control of U.S. Broadcasting, 1928–1935.* New York: Oxford University Press, 1994. Revisionist scholar uncovers the losing battle waged by reformers that failed to stop commercial interests from 1934 FCC victory and complete entrenchment.

SARNOFF, DAVID. *Looking Ahead: The Papers of David Sarnoff.* New York: McGraw-Hill, 1968. Papers of the broadcasting pioneer.

SMITH, F. LESLIE. *Perspectives on Radio and Television: An Introduction to Broadcasting in the United States.* New York: HarperCollins, 1990. A good history of broadcasting.

SMULYAN, SUSAN. *Selling Radio: The Commercialization of American Broadcasting, 1920–1934.* Washington, DC: Smithsonian, 1994. Excellent history of advertising's role in early radio.

STERLING, CHRISTOPHER H., AND JOHN M. KITTROSS. *A Concise History of American Broadcasting.* Belmont, CA: Wadsworth, 1990. Leading synthesis; highly usable.

TEBBEL, JOHN W. *David Sarnoff: Putting Electrons to Work.* Chicago: Encyclopedia Britannica, 1964. A biography of the RCA chairman.

WHITE, LLEWELLYN. *The American Radio.* Chicago: University of Chicago Press, 1947. A publication of the Commission on Freedom of the Press. Best analysis of radio's growth.

Books: Film, Motion Pictures

BERG, A. SCOTT. *Goldwyn: A Biography.* New York: Knopf, 1989, A top-flight biographer selects a good subject for both substance and color.

BOGLE, DONALD. *Toms, Coons, Mulattoes, Mammies, & Blacks: An Interpretive History of Blacks in American Films.* 3rd ed. New York: Continuum, 1996. Useful catalogue of popular film interpretations of African Americans.

BORDWELL, DAVID, JANET STAIGER, AND KRISTIN THOMPSON. *The Classical Hollywood Cinema.* New York: Columbia University Press, 1985. A first-rate new version of film history, 1895–1960.

COOK, DAVID A. *A History of Narrative Film.* 3rd ed. New York: Norton, 1996. One of the widely used survey texts, along with Gerald Mast and Bruce F. Kawin, *A Short History of the Movies,* 6th ed. (Boston: Allyn and Bacon, 1996); and Jack C. Ellis, *A History of Film,* 3rd ed. (Englewood Cliffs, NJ: Prentice Hall, 1990).

GIANNETTI, LOUIS. *Masters of the American Cinema.* Englewood Cliffs, NJ: Prentice Hall, 1981. Chapters on 18 great directors and artists.

GOMERY, DOUGLAS. *Movie History: A Survey.* Belmont, CA: Wadsworth, 1990. By a film scholar.

HARPOLE, CHARLES, ed. *A History of the American Cinema.* 10 vols. New York: Charles Scribner's Sons, 1990 ff. Volumes 1–3 cover to 1928.

JOWETT, GARTH. *Film: The Democratic Art.* Boston: Little, Brown, 1976. Social impact of the movies and economic, political, and cultural adjustments.

KNIGHT, ARTHUR. *The Liveliest Art.* New York: Hastings House, 1978. Particularly good for the period from 1895 to 1930. See also D. J. Wenden, *The Birth of the Movies* (New York: Dutton, 1975).

MOSLEY, LEONARD. *Disney's World.* New York: Stein and Day, 1985. Biography of Walt Disney, creative genius of the film.

ROBINSON, DAVID. *Chaplin: His Life and Art.* London: Collins, 1985. Uses Chaplin archives; complements autobiography.

SCHICKEL, RICHARD. *D. W. Griffith: An American Life.* New York: Simon & Schuster, 1984. Authoritative and readable.

SOLOMON, CHARLES. *Enchanted Drawings: The History of Animation.* New York: Knopf, 1989. More than 400 illustrations adorn this volume.

Books: Advertising, Public Relations

BERNAYS, EDWARD L. *Biography of an Idea.* New York: Simon & Schuster, 1965. Memoirs of a pioneer public-relations counselor.

CUTLIP, SCOTT M. *Public Relations History: From the 17th to the 20th Century.* Hillsdale, NJ: Lawrence Erlbaum Associates, 1995. Argues that press agentry, lobbying, publicity, and other public relations functions were essential in the early U.S. republic, as well as later.

————. *The Unseen Power: Public Relations, A History.* Hillsdale, NJ: Lawrence Erlbaum Associates, 1994. Well researched, comprehensive history of key early public-relations agencies and their contribution to the field's development.

————, ALLEN H. CENTER, AND GLEN M. BROOM. *Effective Public Relations.* Englewood Cliffs, NJ: Prentice Hall, 1985. Long-used survey text with extensive historical account.

GUNTHER, JOHN. *Taken at the Flood: The Story of Albert D. Lasker.* New York: Harper & Row, 1960. The career of a famed advertising-agency executive.

HIEBERT, RAY E. *Courtier to the Crowd: The Life Story of Ivy Lee.* Ames: Iowa State University Press, 1966. Pioneer publicist and public-relations practitioner.

HOLME, BRYAN, ed. *Advertising Reflections of a Century.* New York: Viking, 1982. More than 500 ads, mostly in color, with commentary.

LEARS, JACKSON. *Fables of Abundance: A Cultural History of Advertising in America.* New York: Basic Books, 1994. A significant, sweeping analysis that reinterprets the cultural role of advertising.

MARCHAND, ROLAND. *Advertising the American Dream.* Berkeley: University of California Press, 1985. A major contribution; uses a cultural approach to the formative period of advertising, 1920–40, describing it as both promoting technological modernity and offering relief from self-image anxiety. See also Stephen Fox, *The Mirror Makers: A History of American Advertising and Its Creators* (New York: Wm. Morrow, 1984), for the story through the 1970s, concentrating on the impact of creative people.

NEWSOME, DOUG, ALAN SCOTT, AND JUDY VAN SLYKE TURK. *This Is PR: The Realities of Public Relations.* Belmont, CA: Wadsworth, 1989. Widely used survey text.

NORRIS, JAMES D. *Advertising and the Transformation of American Society, 1865–1920.* Westport, CT: Greenwood Press, 1990. Advertising's role in developing a national market for consumer goods.

POPE, DANIEL. *The Making of Modern Advertising.* New York: Basic Books, 1983. A thoughtful, analytic history of advertising to 1920.

Printers' Ink, 75th anniversary issue, "Advertising: Today, Yesterday, Tomorrow," June 14, 1963. A 474-page historical review, compiled by 100 staff members and advertising-industry authorities. Both facts and color.

RAUCHER, ALAN R. *Public Relations and Business, 1900–1929.* Baltimore: Johns Hopkins University Press, 1968. An excellent monograph.

TURNER, E. S. *The Shocking History of Advertising.* Harmondsworth, England: Penguin Books, 1965. An updated reprinting of a good history.

TYE, LARRY. *The Father of Spin: Edward L. Bernays and the Birth of Public Relations.* New York: Crown Publishers, Inc., 1998. A thorough account, distinguished by the author's access to Bernays's extensive papers.

WATKINS, JULIAN L. *The 100 Greatest Advertisements.* 2nd ed. New York: Moore Publishing, 1959. Histories of all the ads, prepared by a veteran copywriter.

WILCOX, DENNIS L., PHILLIP H. AULT, AND WARREN K. AGEE. *Public Relations: Strategies and Tactics.* New York: HarperCollins, 1991. Newest survey, combining breadth and depth, in a historical unit.

WRIGHT, JOHN W., ed. *The Commercial Connection: Advertising and the American Mass Media.* New York: Dell, 1979. Anthology dealing with audiences and content.

Periodicals and Monographs

ALEXANDER, JACK. "Vox Populi," *New Yorker,* XIV (August 6–20, 1938). A profile of Captain Patterson.

BARCUS, FRANCIS E. "A Content Analysis of Trends in Sunday Comics, 1900–1959," *Journalism Quarterly,* XXXVIII (Spring 1961), 171. The first report from a major study of comics at Boston.

BEASLEY, MAURINE. "A 'Front Page Girl' Covers the Lindbergh Kidnapping: An Ethical Dilemma," *American Journalism,* I:1 (Summer 1983), 63. Reporter was Lorena A. Hickok of the AP, later Eleanor Roosevelt's friend.

BENJAMIN, LOUISE M. "Radio Regulations in the 1920s," Ph.D thesis, University of Iowa, 1985. Free speech issues and the 1927 Radio Act.

BENNION, SHERILYN COX. "Reform Agitation in the American Periodical Press, 1920–29," *Journalism Quarterly,* XLVIII (Winter 1971), 652. General circulation periodicals largely ignored the reform impulse, reflecting public opinion.

BERNAYS, EDWARD L. "Emergence of the Public Relations Counsel: Principles and Reflections," *Business History Review,* XLV (Autumn 1971), 296. Memoir of a pioneer.

BLEYER, WILLARD G. "Freedom of the Press and the New Deal," *Journalism Quarterly,* XI (March 1934), 22. Report on the trend toward newspaper combinations.

BROD, DONALD F. "Church, State, and Press: Twentieth-Century Episodes in the United States," Ph.D. thesis, University of Minnesota, 1968. Examines newspaper coverage of the Scopes trial, Vatican relations, and the 1928 and 1960 elections.

DENNIS, EVERETTE, AND CHRISTOPHER ALLEN. "*Puck,* the Comic Weekly," *Journalism History,* VI (Spring 1979), 14. Hearst's great comics.

DUFFUS, ROBERT L. "Mr. Munsey," *American Mercury,* II (July 1924), 297. A gently critical rejection of Munsey as a newspaper owner. Reprinted in Ford and Emery, *Highlights in the History of the American Press.*

EVANS, JAMES P. "Clover Leaf: The Good Luck Chain, 1899–1933," *Journalism Quarterly,* XLVI (Autumn 1969), 482. The chain had a *Daily News* in Omaha, St. Paul, and Des Moines, and a *Kansas City World.*

FURLONG, WILLIAM B. "The Midwest's Nice Monopolists, John and Mike Cowles," *Harper's,* CCXXVI (June 1963), 64. A sketch of responsible monopoly publishers.

GARVEY, DANIEL E. "Secretary Hoover and the Quest for Broadcast Regulation," *Journalism History,* III (Autumn 1976), 66. Hoover sought stronger regulation than Congress granted.

GODFREY, DONALD G. "The 1927 Radio Act: People and Politics," *Journalism History,* IV (Autumn 1977), 74. Led to FCC.

HENRY, SUSAN. "Anonymous in Her Own Name: Public Relations Pioneer Doris E. Fleischman," *Journalism History,* 23:2 (Summer 1997), 50–62. Detailed, well-documented account.

———. " 'There is Nothing in This Profession . . . That a Woman Cannot Do': Doris E. Fleischman and the Beginnings of Public Relations," *American Journalism,* 16:2 (Spring 1999), 85–111. Her early career as publicist, fundraiser, and newspaper reporter, based on substantial research, including oral histories.

HYNES, TERRY. "Media Manipulations and Political Campaigns: Bruce Barton and the Presidential Elections of the Jazz Age," *Journalism History,* IV (Autumn 1977), 93. BBDO enters politics.

MADDOX, LYNDA M., AND ERIC J. ZANOT. "The Image of the Advertising Practitioner as Presented in the Mass Media, 1900–1972," *American Journalism,* II:2 (1985), 117.

MANDER, MARY S. "The Public Debate about Broadcasting in the Twenties: An Interpretive History," *Journal of Broadcasting,* XXVIII:2 (Spring 1984), 167. Analysis of ways in which people dealt with problem of a new medium.

MARTINSON, DAVID L. "New Images of Presidential Candidates, 1920–24: A Survey of Three Major Newspapers," Ph.D. thesis, University of Minnesota, 1974. Surveys the *Chicago Tribune, St. Louis Post-Dispatch,* and *New York Times.*

MCCHESNEY, ROBERT W. "The Battle for the U.S. Airwaves, 1928–1935," *Journal of Communication* (Autumn 1990), 29. Broadcasters fend off public and congressional impact on policy.

MCKERNS, JOSEPH P. "Industry Skeptics and the Radio Act of 1927," *Journalism History,* III (Winter 1976–77), 128.

MERRICK, BEVERLY. "Ishbel Ross, on Assignment with History: The Formative Years, 1895–1923," Ph.D. thesis, Ohio University, 1989. Ross was the top woman reporter in New York in the 1920s.

NELSON, HAROLD L. "The Political Reform Press: A Case Study," *Journalism Quarterly,* XXIX (Summer 1952), 294. An analysis of an almost-successful farmer-labor newspaper, the *Minnesota Daily Star* (1920 to 1924).

NIXON, RAYMOND B. "Trends in U.S. Newspaper Ownership: Concentration with Competition," *Gazette,* XIV:3 (1968), 181. A review with comprehensive data. See also Raymond B. Nixon and Jean Ward, "Trends in Newspaper Ownership and Inter-Media Competition," *Journalism Quarterly,* XXXVIII (Winter 1961), 3.

OLASKY, MARVIN. "Edward Bernays and the Salvation of Society Through Public Relations," *Journalism History,* XII (Spring 1985), 17. Pioneer in public opinion.

———. "Retrospective: Bernays' Doctrine of Public Opinion," *Public Relations Review,* X (Fall 1984), 3. Closes gap in Bernays literature.

———. "The Development of Corporate Public Relations," *Journalism Monographs,* CII (April 1987). Treats press agentry for railroads and utilities.

SAALBERG, HARVEY. "Don Mellett, Editor of the *Canton News,* Was Slain While Exposing Underworld," *Journalism Quarterly,* LIII (Spring 1976), 88.

SEITZ, DON C. "The American Press," *Outlook,* January 6–February 3, 1926. A six-part series by the manager of the *New York World.*

SMYTHE, TED C. "A History of the *Minneapolis Journal,* 1878–1939," Ph.D. thesis, University of Minnesota, 1967. Leading Minneapolis afternoon daily.

TAFT, WILLIAM H. "Bernarr Macfadden: One of a Kind," *Journalism Quarterly,* XLV (Winter 1968), 627. Based on extensive research about the publisher.

"The Twenties," articles by Cathy Covert, Garth S. Jowett, James W. Wesolowski, George E. Stevens, Robert V. Hudson, June Adamson, and W. Richard Whitaker, in *Journalism History,* II (Autumn 1975).

VAUGHN, STEPHEN. "Morality and Entertainment: The Origins of the Motion Picture Production Code," *Journal of American History,* LXXI (June 1990), 39.

WASSMUTH, BIRGIT L. "Art Movements and American Print Advertising: A Study of Advertising Graphics 1915–1935," Ph.D. thesis, University of Minnesota, 1983. Traces uses of art forms and the rise of art directors.

WEINFELD, WILLIAM. "The Growth of Daily Newspaper Chains in the United States: 1923, 1926–1935," *Journalism Quarterly,* XIII (December 1936), 357. The first important study of the problem.

WHITAKER, W. RICHARD. "The Night Harding Died," *Journalism History,* I (Spring 1974), 16. Based on his "Warren G. Harding and the Press," Ph.D. thesis, Ohio University, 1972.

WILLIAMSON, MARY E. "Judith Cary Waller: Chicago Broadcasting Pioneer," *Journalism History,* III (Winter 1976–77), 111. First station manager of the *Daily News*'s WMAQ, 1922; 50-year career.

CHAPTER 14: DEPRESSION AND REFORM

Books: New Deal, Press Freedom

BARONE, MICHAEL. *Our Country: The Shaping of America from Roosevelt to Reagan.* New York: Free Press, 1990. Highly praised for its remarkably complete summary of factual research.

BAUMAN, JOHN F., AND THOMAS H. COODE. *In the Eye of the Great Depression.* DeKalb, IL: Northern Illinois University Press, 1992. Stories of 16 journalists sent by the Emergency Relief Administration to report on the extent of poverty; covers two years of reports.

BEASLEY, MAURINE, ed. *White House Press Conferences of Eleanor Roosevelt.* New York: Garland Publishing, 1983. Transcripts of 100 women-only press conferences, 1933 to 1945.

BRINKLEY, ALAN. *Voices of Protest: Huey Long, Father Coughlin, and the Great Depression.* New York: Knopf, 1982. Pictures them as Populists, reaching masses by radio, rivaling FDR.

———. *The End of Reform: New Deal Liberalism in Recession and War.* New York: Knopf, 1995. A major reinterpretation of the New Deal that argues that the liberalism of the early reform years gave way to a contemporary liberalism that is less hostile to corporate capitalism and more solicitous of individual rights.

CONKIN, PAUL. *The New Deal.* 3rd ed. Wheeling, IL: Harlan Davidson, 1992. Analyzes the New Deal as a social and political movement.

CONRAD, DAVID E. *The Forgotten Farmers: The Story of Sharecroppers in the New Deal.* Urbana: University of Illinois Press, 1965. An economic history of changes occurring in the South during the Depression years.

CULLEN, MAURICE R., JR. *Mass Media & the First Amendment.* Dubuque, IA: Wm. C. Brown, 1981. Introduces media through the First Amendment door.

FREIDEL, FRANK. *Franklin D. Roosevelt: A Rendezvous With Destiny.* Boston: Little, Brown, 1990. A one-volume summation of a lifelong study of FDR.

FRIENDLY, FRED W. *Minnesota Rag.* New York: Random House, 1981. The story of *Near* v. *Minnesota,* the 1931 case that became the First Amendment bedrock.

GALBRAITH, JOHN KENNETH. *The Great Crash, 1929.* 3rd ed. Boston: Houghton Mifflin, 1972. A classic, comprehensive exploration of the causes of the 1929 crash by an eminent economist.

GARRATY, JOHN A. *The Great Depression: An Inquiry into the Causes, Course, and Consequences of the Worldwide Depression of the Nineteen Thirties, as Seen by Contemporaries and in the Light of History.* New York: Harcourt Brace Jovanovich, 1986.

GERALD, J. EDWARD. *The Press and the Constitution.* Minneapolis: University of Minnesota Press, 1948. Freedom-of-the-press cases from 1931 to 1947.

HACHTEN, WILLIAM A., ed. *The Supreme Court on Freedom of the Press: Decisions and Dissents.* Ames: Iowa State University Press, 1968. The main historical story, with commentaries.

PHILLIPS, CABELL. *From the Crash to the Blitz, 1929–1939.* New York: Macmillan, 1969. Newspaper based.

SCHLESINGER, ARTHUR, JR. *The Age of Roosevelt.* 3 vols. Boston: Houghton Mifflin, 1957–60. Vol. 1, *The Crisis of the Old Order* (1957), covers 1919 to 1933; vol. 2, *The Coming of the New Deal* (1958), covers 1933 to 1934; vol. 3, *The Politics of Upheaval* (1960), covers 1935 to 1936.

TERKEL, STUDS. *Hard Times.* New York: Pantheon, 1970. An oral history of the Great Depression.

WHITE, GRAHAM J. *FDR and the Press.* Chicago: University of Chicago Press, 1979. Examines FDR's good relations with reporters and his dislike of publishers. Finds better support for FDR in press than the president pictured.

WILLIAMS, T. HARRY. *Huey Long.* New York: Knopf, 1969. Best study of Long and the South during the period.

WINFIELD, BETTY HOUCHIN. *FDR and the News Media.* New York: Columbia University Press, 1994 (first published 1990). Meticulously researched scholarly account of FDR's techniques in news management and dueling with White House press.

Books: Newspapers, Correspondents

BASSOW, WHITMAN. *The Moscow Correspondents: Reporting on Russia from the Revolution to Glasnost.* New York: Morrow, 1988. A former one surveys more than 300 American correspondents.

BRENDON, PIERS. *The Life and Death of the Press Barons.* New York: Atheneum, 1983. The Bennetts, Pulitzer, Hearst, McCormick, Patterson, and in Britain, W. T. Stead, Northcliffe, Beaverbrook, and Murdoch made newspapers a rich variety.

CARLISLE, RODNEY P. *Hearst and the New Deal: The Progressive as Reactionary.* New York: Garland Publishing, 1979. Opposite view to Littlefield (see Chapter 10 Bibliography).

CHISHOLM, ANNE, AND MICHAEL DAVIE. *Lord Beaverbrook.* New York: Alfred A. Knopf, 1993. A meticulous study of William Maxwell Aitken, who became Britain's most powerful press lord.

CROWL, JAMES W. *Angels in Stalin's Paradise: Western Reporters in Soviet Russia, 1917 to 1939. A Case Study of Louis Fischer and Walter Duranty.* Washington, DC: University Press of America, 1982. How Soviets sought to manipulate key reporters.

DREWRY, JOHN E., ed. *Post Biographies of Famous Journalists.* Athens: University of Georgia Press, 1942. Contains articles about Hearst, Roy Howard, and McCormick.

FORD, EDWIN H., AND EDWIN EMERY, eds. *Highlights in the History of the American Press.* Minneapolis: University of Minnesota Press, 1954. Contains articles about Hearst, Scripps Howard, and McCormick.

HEALD, MORRILL. *Transatlantic Vistas: American Journalists in Europe 1900–1940.* Kent, OH: Kent State University Press, 1989. A survey.

HOHENBERG, JOHN. *Foreign Correspondence: The Great Reporters and Their Times.* New York: Columbia University Press, 1964. Foreign correspondence since the French Revolution; best survey of the reporters and the trends.

HOOPES, ROY. *Ralph Ingersoll.* New York; Atheneum, 1985. Biography of the editor of the adless newspaper *PM.*

KROCK, ARTHUR. *Memoirs: Sixty Years on the Firing Line.* New York: Funk & Wagnalls, 1968. By the longtime Washington Chief of the *New York Times.*

MILLER, WEBB. *I Found No Peace.* New York: Simon & Schuster, 1936. One of the best of the foreign correspondents' books, by a longtime United Press correspondent.

MOWRER, EDGAR ANSEL. *Triumph and Turmoil: A Personal History of Our Times.* New York: Weybright and Talley, 1968. Autobiography of one of the greatest foreign correspondents.

SELDES, GEORGE. *Witness to a Century.* New York: Ballantine Books, 1987. Sparkling anecdotes from a caustic critic and skilled correspondent.

SMITH, RICHARD N. *The Colonel: The Life and Legend of Robert R. McCormick, 1880–1955.* Boston: Houghton Mifflin, 1997. First biography based on McCormick's papers.

STARTT, JAMES D. *Journalism's Unofficial Ambassador: A Biography of Edward Price Bell, 1869–1943.* Athens: Ohio University Press, 1979. *Chicago Daily News* correspondent.

SULZBERGER, C. L. *A Long Row of Candles.* New York: Macmillan, 1969. Memoirs and diaries of the chief *New York Times* foreign correspondent, 1934–54. His *The Last of the Giants* (1970) carried the story through 1963.

SWANBERG, W. A. *Citizen Hearst.* New York: Scribner's, 1961. Highly readable, detailed.

TAYLOR, S. J. *Stalin's Apologist: Walter Duranty, The "New York Times'" Man in Moscow.* New York: Oxford University Press, 1990. Indifferently written but well-researched revisionist account.

TEBBEL, JOHN. *An American Dynasty.* New York: Doubleday, 1947. An analysis of the McCormick-Patterson publishing empire.

———. *The Life and Good Times of William Randolph Hearst.* New York: Dutton, 1952. Best single book about both Hearst and his publishing empire.

WALDROP, FRANK C. *McCormick of Chicago.* Englewood Cliffs, NJ: Prentice Hall, 1966. Best biography of the *Chicago Tribune* publisher. See also Jerome E. Edwards, *The Foreign Policy of Col. McCormick's Tribune,*

1929–1941 (Reno: University of Nevada Press, 1971), a carefully researched analysis.

Books: Radio, Correspondents

BANNERMAN, R. LEROY. *Norman Corwin and the Golden Years of Radio.* New York: Lyle Stuart, 1990. CBS writer, director, and producer.

BULMAN, DAVID, ed. *Molders of Opinion.* Milwaukee: Bruce Publishing Company, 1945. Includes chapters on H. V. Kaltenborn, Gabriel Heatter, Fulton Lewis, Jr., and Raymond Gram Swing.

BURLINGAME, ROGER. *Don't Let Them Scare You: The Life and Times of Elmer Davis.* Philadelphia; Lippincott, 1961. A good biography of a top-flight news analyst.

CULBERT, DAVID HOLBROOK. *News for Everyman.* Westport, CT: Greenwood Press, 1976. Account of how American radio affected foreign affairs during the 1930s.

FANG, IRVING E. *Those Radio Commentators!* Ames; Iowa State University Press, 1977. Study of major commentators of the 1930s and 1940s.

HOSLEY, DAVID H. *As Good As Any: Foreign Correspondence on American Radio, 1930–1940.* Westport, CT: Greenwood Press, 1984. Superb reporting of an exciting decade.

KALTENBORN, H. V. *Fifty Fabulous Years, 1900–1950: A Personal Review.* New York: G. P. Putnam's Sons, 1950. Autobiography of a commentator who began on the air in 1922.

SCHECHTER, A. A. WITH EDWARD ANTHONY. *I Live on Air.* New York: Frederick Stokes, 1941. NBC's first director of news and special events.

SHIRER, WILLIAM L. *20th-Century Journey.* New York: Simon & Schuster, 1976. The 1920s in Paris. *The Nightmare Years, 1930–1940* (Boston: Little, Brown, 1984), continues the CBS radio correspondent's story, recorded in part in *Berlin Diary: A Native's Return, 1945–1988* (Little, Brown, 1990), which completes the trilogy.

THOMAS, LOWELL. *Good Evening Everybody.* New York: Morrow, 1976. Autobiography of the pioneer CBS radio newscaster, 1930–76.

Books: Columnists

ANDERSON, JACK, WITH JAMES BOYD. *Confessions of a Muckraker.* New York: Random House, 1979. Covers the Pearson-Anderson team years, 1947–69.

BRADEN, MARIA. *She Said What? Interviews with Women Newspaper Columnists.* Lexington: University Press of Kentucky, 1993. Profiles 13, including Mary McGrory, Erma Bombeck, Georgie Anne Geyer, Ellen Goodman, Anna Quindlen, and Molly Ivins.

CHILDS, MARQUIS. *Witness to Power.* New York: McGraw-Hill, 1975. Autobiography.

DAM, HARI N. *The Intellectual Odyssey of Walter Lippmann.* New York: Gordon Press, 1973. The columnist's public philosophy, 1910–60, is analyzed in scholarly, readable style.

See also John Luskin, *Lippmann, Liberty and the Press* (University, AL: University of Alabama Press, 1972).

FARR, FINIS. *Fair Enough: The Life of Westbrook Pegler.* New Rochelle, NY: Arlington House, 1975. Favorable biography of the sportswriter and political columnist.

FISHER, CHARLES. *The Columnists.* New York: Howell, Soskin, Publishers, 1944. A lively study, outdated but still valuable for its period.

KURTH, PETER. *American Cassandra: The Life of Dorothy Thompson.* Boston: Little, Brown, 1990. Readable and informative.

MEYER, KARL E. *Pundits, Poets, and Wits: An Omnibus of American Newspaper Columnists.* New York; Oxford University Press, 1990. Samples 72 writers from Ben Franklin to Molly Ivins.

O'CONNOR, RICHARD. *Heywood Broun: A Biography.* New York: G. P. Putnam's Sons, 1975. Newest study; well done. See also Dale Kramer, *Heywood Broun* (New York: A. A. Wyn, 1949).

PILAT, OLIVER. *Drew Pearson: An Unauthorized Biography.* New York: Harper's Magazine Press, 1973. Pearson had questionable news-gathering ethics, but many readers.

PYLE, ERNEST. *Ernie's America.* New York: Random House, 1989. Best of his 1930s travel columns.

RILEY, SAM G. *Biographical Dictionary of American Newspaper Columnists.* Westport, CT: Greenwood Press, 1995. Well-researched entries on 600 diverse newspaper columnists, from the Civil War to the present.

SANDERS, MARION K. *Dorothy Thompson: A Legend in Her Time.* Boston: Houghton Mifflin, 1973. Prize-winning biography of an outstanding foreign correspondent and columnist.

STEEL, RONALD. *Walter Lippmann and the American Century.* Boston: Atlantic-Little, Brown, 1980. A major effort to place the columnist in perspective.

STOKES, THOMAS L. *Chip Off My Shoulder.* Princeton: Princeton University Press, 1940. Autobiography of a distinguished reporter-columnist.

SULLIVAN, MARK. *The Education of an American.* New York: Doubleday, 1938. The autobiography of one of the first political columnists.

Books: Editorial Cartoonists

HESS, STEPHEN, AND MILTON KAPLAN. *The Ungentlemanly Art: A History of American Political Cartoons.* New York: Macmillan, 1968. A well-done survey from Franklin to Herblock.

JOHNSON, GERALD W. *The Lines Are Drawn.* Philadelphia: Lippincott, 1958. A study of Pulitzer Prize–winning cartoons.

LENDT, DAVID L. *Ding: The Life of Jay Norwood Darling.* Ames: Iowa State University Press, 1979. Cartoonist for *Des Moines Register* and *New York Herald Tribune.* See also John M. Henry, ed. *Ding's Half Century* (New York: Duell, Sloan and Pearce, 1962).

MURRELL, WILLIAM. *A History of American Graphic Humor, 1865–1938.* New York: Macmillan, 1938. The second volume of a work that reproduces many cartoons.

NEVINS, ALLAN, AND GEORGE WEITENKAMPF. *A Century of Political Cartoons.* New York: Scribner's, 1944. The cartoons are presented in a historical setting.

PRESS, CHARLES. *The Political Cartoon.* East Brunswick, NJ: Associated University Presses, 1981. History and analysis, including 250 examples since the seventeenth century.

SPENCER, DICK, III. *Pulitzer Prize Cartoons.* Ames: Iowa State College Press, 1953. A history of the winning cartoons since 1922.

WEST, RICHARD S. *Satire on Stone: The Political Cartoons of Joseph Keppler* (Urbana: University of Illinois Press, 1988). The great *Puck* cartoonist.

Books: Magazines, Book Publishing

BAINBRIDGE, JOHN. *Little Wonder.* New York: Reynal & Hitchcock, 1946. A critical study of the *Reader's Digest,* which originally appeared as a *New Yorker* profile.

BAKER, CARLOS. *Ernest Hemingway: A Life Story.* New York: Scribner's, 1969. By far the best biography of Hemingway. See also Scott Donaldson, *By Force of Will* (New York: Viking Press, 1977); and Jeffrey Meyers, *Hemingway* (New York: Harper & Row, 1985).

BAUGHMAN, JAMES L. *Henry R. Luce and the Rise of the American News Media.* Boston: Twayne, 1987. *Time's* founder and his empire well analyzed.

BERG, A. SCOTT. *Maxwell Perkins, Editor of Genius.* New York: Dutton, 1978. *Scribner's* great editor who worked with Tom Wolfe, Scott Fitzgerald, and Ernest Hemingway.

BOK, EDWARD W. *A Man from Maine.* New York: Scribner's, 1923. A life of Cyrus H. K. Curtis by his editor.

BUSCH, NOEL F. *Briton Hadden.* New York: Farrar, Straus & Giroux, 1949. The biography of the co-founder of *Time.*

DAVIS, LINDA H. *Katharine S. White: Onward and Upward.* New York: Harper & Row, 1987. The great *New Yorker* editor and wife of E. B. White.

DESSAUER, JOHN. *Book Publishing: What It Is, What It Does.* New York: Bowker, 1981. A readable survey.

DONOVAN, HEDLEY. *Right Times, Right Places: Forty Years of Journalism, Not Counting My Paper Route.* New York: Holt, 1989. An editor-in-chief of *Time.*

DOUGLAS, GEORGE, H. *The Smart Magazines: 50 Years of Literary Revelry and High Jinks at "Vanity Fair," "The New Yorker," "Life," "Esquire," and "The Smart Set."* Hamden, CT: Archon, 1991.

ELSON, ROBERT T. *Time Inc.: The Intimate History of a Publishing Enterprise, 1923–1941.* New York: Atheneum, 1968. Successfully done under company auspices. See also Elson, *The World of Time Inc. (1941–1960)* (Atheneum, 1973); and Curtis Prendergast with Geoffrey Colvin, *The World of Time Inc.: The Intimate History of a Changing Enterprise, 1960–1980* (Atheneum, 1986).

FLANNER, JANET. *Janet Flanner's World.* New York: Harcourt Brace Jovanovich, 1979. See also Flanner, *Paris Was*

Yesterday (New York: Viking, 1972). Her *New Yorker* columns, signed Gênet, 1925 to 1939.

FORD, JAMES L. C. *Magazines for Millions.* Carbondale: Southern Illinois University Press, 1969. An account of specialized publications.

HACKETT, ALICE P., AND JAMES H. BURKE. *80 Years of Best Sellers, 1895–1975.* New York: Bowker, 1977. Frank Luther Mott's *Golden Multitudes* (1950) is more scholarly.

HEMINGWAY, ERNEST. *By-Line: Ernest Hemingway,* ed. William White. New York: Scribner's 1967. His stories in papers and magazines over four decades.

JONES, MARGARET C. *Heretics & Hellraisers: Women Contributors to "The Masses," 1911–1917.* Austin: University of Texas Press, 1993. Covers Louise Bryant, Dorothy Day, Mabel Dodge, Mary Heaton Vorse, and others.

KRAMER, DALE. *Ross and the New Yorker.* Garden City, NY: Doubleday, 1951. See also Brendan Gill, *Here at the New Yorker* (New York: Random House, 1975); and James Thurber, *The Years with Ross* (Boston: Little, Brown, 1957).

Magazine Profiles. Evanston, IL: Medill School of Journalism, 1974. Studies by 12 graduate students of nearly 50 then-current magazines.

MANCHESTER, WILLIAM. *Disturber of the Peace.* New York: Harper & Row, 1950. Best of the biographies of H. L. Mencken, whose autobiography is titled *The Days of H. L. Mencken* (New York: Knopf, 1947). See also Carl Bode, *Mencken* (Carbondale: Southern Illinois University Press, 1969); and George H. Douglas, *H. L. Mencken, Critic of American Life* (Hamden, CT: Archon Books, 1978).

MARTIN, RALPH G. *Henry and Clare: An Intimate Portrait of the Luces.* New York: Putnam's, 1991. Human-interest history of Time Inc.

MITCHELL, JOSEPH. *Up in the Old Hotel and Other Stories.* New York: Pantheon, 1992. Strong anthology of classic *New Yorker* pieces.

MOTT, FRANK LUTHER. *A History of American Magazines.* Vol. 5, *Sketches of 21 Magazines, 1905–1930.* Cambridge, MA: Harvard University Press, 1968. Contains index for all five volumes.

PETERSON, THEODORE. *Magazines in the Twentieth Century.* Urbana: University of Illinois Press, 1964. A gold mine of interpretation and factual detail about the magazine industry.

ROBERTS, NANCY L., AND ARTHUR W. ROBERTS, eds. *'As Ever, Gene': The Letters of Eugene O'Neill to George Jean Nathan.* Cranbury, NJ: Fairleigh Dickinson University Press, 1987. Shows the influence of a major drama critic and magazine editor on America's foremost dramatist.

ROVERE, RICHARD. *Final Reports.* New York: Doubleday, 1984. Posthumous collection of reflections on politics and the times.

SCHREINER, SAMUEL A., JR. *The Condensed World of the Reader's Digest.* New York: Stein and Day, 1977. Highly recommended in reviews.

SCRIBNER, CHARLES, JR. *In the Company of Writers.* New York: Scribner's, 1990. History of the great book firm.

SOKOLOV, RAYMOND. *Wayward Reporter: The Life of A. J. Liebling.* New York: Harper & Row, 1980. First full-scale biography.

SWANBERG, W. A. *Luce and His Empire.* New York: Scribner's, 1972. Critical study of Luce and his influence on American life.

TEBBEL, JOHN. *A History of Book Publishing in the United States* (see Chapter 2 bibliography).

———, AND MARY ELLEN ZUCKERMAN. *The Magazine in America: 1741–1990.* New York: Oxford University Press, 1991. A comprehensive history.

WINEAPPLE, JANET. *Gênet: A Biography of Janet Flanner.* New York: Ticknor & Fields, 1990. Many details but inadequate evaluation.

WOOD, JAMES PLAYSTED. *Magazines in the United States.* New York: Ronald Press, 1956. Social background is provided.

ZUCKERMAN, MARY ELLEN. *History of Popular Women's Magazines in the United States, 1792–1995.* Westport, CT: Greenwood Press, 1998. A detailed, readable study grounded in economic and cultural history.

Books: Photojournalism, Documentaries

BARNOUW, ERIK. *Documentary: A History of the Non-Fiction Film.* New York: Oxford University Press, 1974. A leading study, well-integrated analysis.

BOURKE-WHITE, MARGARET. *Portrait of Myself.* New York: Simon & Schuster, 1963. Illustrated autobiography of *Life's* great photojournalist.

CARLEBACH, MICHAEL L. *American Photojournalism Comes of Age.* Washington, D.C.: Smithsonian, 1997. In-depth study of the formative years, late nineteenth and early twentieth centuries.

———. *The Origins of Photojournalism in America.* Washington, D.C.: Smithsonian, 1992. Covers 1839–80, from the daguerreotype to the halftone process.

DUNCAN, DAVID DOUGLAS. *Yankee Nomad.* New York: Holt, Rinehart & Winston, 1966. A photographic autobiography by a great photojournalist who won his spurs with *Life.* See also *I Protest!,* Duncan's 1968 collection from Vietnam, and *War Without Heroes* (1970).

EISENSTAEDT, ALFRED. *Witness to Our Times.* New York: Viking, 1966. Photographs over 40 years of one of *Life's* best.

EVANS, HAROLD, AND HUGH B. KING. *Front Page History: Events of Our Century That Shook the World.* Salem, NH: Salem House, 1984. Pictures, 1900–1984.

FABER, JOHN. *Great Moments in News Photography.* New York: Nelson, 1960. Covers from Mathew Brady to Robert Capa in 57 photographs. See also Associated Press, *The Instant It Happened* (New York: Associated Press, 1974).

FIELDING, RAYMOND. *The March of Time, 1935–1951.* New York: Oxford University Press, 1978. The complete story of the film documentary made for the movie houses.

GIDAL, TIM N. *Modern Photojournalism Origin and Evolution, 1910–1933.* New York: Macmillan, 1973. Account of photographers and editors who developed the first picture magazines in Germany between 1928 and 1931.

GOLDBERG, VICKI. *Margaret Bourke-White, A Biography.* New York: Harper & Row, 1986. Carefully researched story of a *Life* star.

HAMBLIN, DORA JANE. *That Was the Life.* New York: Norton, 1977. *Life* magazine photographers were gods, their chronicler says. Amusing anecdotes.

JACOBS, LEWIS, ed. *The Documentary Tradition.* New York: Norton, 1979. Updates 1971 book.

JOHNSON, WILLIAM S., ed. *W. Eugene Smith: Master of the Photographic Essay.* Millerton, NY: Aperture, 1982. More than 1800 photographs, all small.

KOZOL, WENDY. *"Life"'s America.* Philadelphia: Temple University Press, 1994. Shows how *Life* legitimized the affluent, middle-class, nuclear family.

"Life," The First Fifty Years, 1936–1986. Boston: Little, Brown, 1986. More than 4000 photographs. See also *Life*'s 50th anniversary edition, November 1986; and Doris O'Neil, ed. *"Life": The Second Decade, 1946–1955* (Boston: Little, Brown, 1984).

LORENTZ, PARE. *F.D.R.'s Moviemaker: Memoirs and Scripts.* Reno: University of Nevada Press, 1992. The glory years of social documentary filmmaking.

MACDONALD, GUS. *Victorian Eyewitness.* New York: Viking Press, 1979. Classic images from 1826 to 1913.

MYDANS, CARL. *Carl Mydans, Photojournalist.* New York: Abrams, 1985. The *Life* photographer's pictures tell his story.

NEWHALL, BEAUMONT. *The History of Photography from 1839 to the Present Day.* 5th ed. New York: Museum of Modern Art, 1982. The standard account.

NORBACK, CRAIG T., AND MELVIN GRAY, eds. *The World's Great News Photos, 1840–1980.* New York: Crown, 1980. Some 250 photos, many from Bettmann Archive.

OHRN, KARIN BECKER. *Dorothea Lange and the Documentary Tradition.* Baton Rouge, Louisiana State University Press, 1980. Lavishly illustrated, well integrated; based on her Ph.D. thesis, Indiana University, 1977. See *Journalism History,* IV (Spring 1977), for a Lange photographic essay on a 1942 Japanese-American internment camp.

PARKS, GORDON. *Voices in the Mirror.* New York: Doubleday, 1991. Autobiography of black *Life* photographer and film director.

PHILLIPS, JOHN. *It Happened in Our "Lifetime."* Boston: Little, Brown, 1985. A memoir with 500 photographs by a *Life* photographer.

POLLACK, PETER. *A Picture History of Photography.* New York: Abrams, 1969. Some classics.

ROTHA, PAUL, SINCLAIR ROAD, AND RICHARD GRIFFITH. *The Documentary Film.* London: Faber and Faber, 1966. The standard work.

TRACHTENBERG, ALAN. *Reading American Photographs: Images as History, from Mathew Brady to Walker Evans.* New York: Hill and Wang, 1989.

WHELAN, RICHARD. *Capa.* New York: Knopf, 1985. A biography. See also *Robert Capa Photographs,* ed. Cornell Capa and Richard Whelan (New York: Knopf, 1985).

Periodicals and Monographs

ALSOP, JOSEPH AND STEWART. "Our Own Inside Story," *Saturday Evening Post,* CCXXXI (November 8–15, 1958). How they operated from 1946 to 1958.

ANDERSON, DOUGLAS A. "The Muckraking Books of Pearson, Allen and Anderson," *American Journalism,* II:1 (1985), 5.

BARTNESS, GAROLD L. "Hearst in Milwaukee," Ph.D. thesis, University of Minnesota, 1968. Study of the *Wisconsin News,* "a real Hearst newspaper," from 1918 to 1939.

BEASLEY, MAURINE. "Eleanor Roosevelt's Press Conferences: Symbolic Importance of a Pseudo-Event," *Journalism Quarterly,* LXI (Summer 1984), 274. Opened the path for women journalists.

———. "Lorena A. Hickok, Woman Journalist," *Journalism History,* VII (1980), 92. On the AP staff.

BLANCHARD, MARGARET A. "Press Criticism and National Reform Movements: The Progressive Era and the New Deal," *Journalism History,* V (Summer 1978), 33. Well documented.

———. "Freedom of the Press and the Newspaper Code: June 1933–February 1934," *Journalism Quarterly,* LIV (Spring 1977), 40. Detailed analysis of the NRA code.

BROWN, PAMELA A. "George Seldes and the Winter Soldier Brigade: The Press Criticism of *In Fact,* 1940–1950," *American Journalism,* VI (1989), 86.

BURD, GENE. "The Newspaper Critic and His Critics: George Seldes and Press Criticism," *Southwestern Mass Communication Journal,* I:2 (1985), 43. Seldes advocated ombudsmen and journalism reviews in 1930s.

CARLISLE, RODNEY P. "William Randolph Hearst: A Fascist Reputation Reconsidered," *Journalism Quarterly,* L (Spring 1973), 125. Hearst supported the early New Deal.

CASWELL, LUCY SHELTON. "Edwina Dumm, Pioneer Woman Editorial Cartoonist, 1915–1917," *Journalism History,* XV (Spring 1988), 2.

CHENEY, LYNNE. "Cissy Patterson," *Washington Journalism Review* (December 1985), 33. In-depth portrait of legendary *Washington Times-Herald* owner.

"The Chicago Tribune," *Fortune,* IX (May 1934), 101. Detailed study.

CLARK, DAVID G. "The Dean of Commentators: A Biography of H. V. Kaltenborn," Ph.D. thesis, University of Wisconsin, 1965. Written from the Kaltenborn papers.

———. "H. V. Kaltenborn's First Year on the Air," *Journalism Quarterly,* XLII (Summer 1965), 373. The *Brooklyn*

Eagle editor takes to the air in 1923 on WEAF for a stormy year.

CRANSTON, PAT. "Political Convention Broadcasts: Their History and Influence," *Journalism Quarterly,* XXXVII (Spring 1960), 186. A survey from 1924 to 1956.

DENNIS, EVERETTE E., AND CLAUDE-JEAN BERTRAND. "Seldes at 90: They Don't Give Pulitzers for That Kind of Criticism," *Journalism History,* VII (Autumn–Winter 1980), 81. Interview recalling Seldes's *Tell the Truth and Run* (1953).

EMERY, MICHAEL C. "The American Mass Media and the Coverage of Five Major Foreign Events, 1900–1950: The Russo-Japanese War, Outbreak of World War I, Rise of Stalin, Munich Crisis, Invasion of South Korea," Ph.D. thesis, University of Minnesota, 1968. The press corps and how the media used their coverage.

———. "The Munich Crisis Broadcasts: Radio News Comes of Age," *Journalism Quarterly,* XLII (Autumn 1965), 576. Kaltenborn, Murrow, and Shirer penetrate American minds. Detailed analysis of CBS, NBC, and Mutual broadcasts.

GALLAGHER, ROBERT. "Good Evening Everybody," *American Heritage* (August–September 1980), 32. Well-illustrated interview with Lowell Thomas.

GIBBS, WOLCOTT. "*Time-Fortune-Life*-Luce," *New Yorker,* XII (November 28, 1936), 20. A dissection of the Luce empire.

HIMEBAUGH, GLENN A. "Donald Ring Mellett, Journalist: The Shaping of a Martyr," Ph.D. thesis, Southern Illinois University, 1978. Career of a crusading editor.

JOHNSON, CARL E. "A Twentieth-Century Seeker: A Biography of James Vincent Sheean," Ph.D. thesis, University of Wisconsin, 1974. Sheean spent 50 years abroad.

KRAFT, SCOTT. "The Chronicles of Calvin Trillin," *Washington Journalism Review* (December 1985), 43. Writer for *New Yorker* and the *Nation.*

KROMPACK, FRANK J. "Socio-Economic Influences Affecting Texas Press in the Great Depression," Ph.D. thesis, University of Texas, 1975. Most papers survived declining revenues and circulation by economizing.

———. "A Wider Niche for Westbrook Pegler," *American Journalism,* I (Summer 1983), 31. Emphasis is on Pegler's humor.

LASCH, ROBERT. "*PM* Post-Mortem," *Atlantic Monthly,* CLXXXII (July 1948), 44. An excellent analysis of the *PM* experiment and the reasons for its failure.

LICHTY, LAWRENCE W., AND THOMAS W. BOHN. "Radio's *March of Time:* Dramatized News," *Journalism Quarterly,* LI (Autumn 1974), 458. The beginning of this technique.

LIEBLING, A. J. "Publisher," *New Yorker,* XVII (August 2–23, 1941). Critical profile of Roy W. Howard.

LIEBOVICH, LOUIS. "Press Reaction to the Bonus March of 1932," *Journalism Monographs,* CXXII (August 1990).

MARBUT, FREDERICK B. "Congress and the Standing Committee of Correspondents," *Journalism Quarterly,* XXXVIII (Winter 1961), 52. The history of the press gallery rules is traced from 1879.

MCCHESNEY, ROBERT W. "Franklin Roosevelt, His Administration, and the Communications Act of 1934," *American Journalism,* V (1988), 204.

MILLER, MERLE. "Washington, the World, and Joseph Alsop," *Harper's,* CCXXXVI (June 1968), 43. The imperious columnist examined.

MONED, DAVID H. "Historical Trends in the Criticism of the Newsreel and Television News," *Journal of Popular Film and Television,* XII (Fall 1984).

OGLES, ROBERT M., AND HERBERT H. HOWARD. "Father Coughlin in the Periodical Press, 1931–1942," *Journalism Quarterly,* LXI (Summer 1984), 280. Seven major magazines compared.

PARMENTER, WILLIAM. "The News Control Explanation of News Making: The Case of William Randolph Hearst, 1920–1940," Ph.D. thesis, University of Washington, 1979. Finds overwhelming evidence of control in the Hearst newspapers.

PEARSON, DREW. "Confessions of 'an S.O.B.'," *Saturday Evening Post,* CCXXIX (November 3–24, 1956). Story of an "inside" columnist.

PFAFF, DANIEL W. "The Press and the Scottsboro Rape Cases, 1931–32," *Journalism History,* I (Autumn 1974), 72. News and editorial coverage.

RANTANEN, TERHI. "Howard Interviews Stalin: How the AP, UP, and TASS Smashed the International News Cartel," *Roy W. Howard Monographs,* III (May 1994). Howard's 1936 interview was released to other agencies, but not to Hearst's INS. See also Rantanen, "Mr. Howard Goes to South America," *Roy W. Howard Monographs,* II (May 1992).

SENTMAN, MARY ALICE. "Black and White: Disparity in *Life* Magazine from 1937 to 1972," *Journalism Quarterly,* LX (Autumn 1983), 501.

SMITH, C. ZOE. "Emigré Photography in America: Contributions of German Photojournalism from Black Star Picture Agency to *Life* Magazine, 1933–1938," Ph.D. thesis, University of Iowa, 1983. See also her article in *Journalism History,* XIII (Spring 1986), 19.

———. "Great Women in Photojournalism," *News Photographer,* January–April 1985.

———. "An Alternative View of the '30s: Hine's and Bourke-White's Industrial Photos," *Journalism Quarterly,* LX (Summer 1983), 305.

STREITMATTER, RODGER. "Theodore Roosevelt: Public Relations Pioneer," *American Journalism,* VII (1990), 96. How he controlled White House news.

STROUT, RICHARD L. "Tom Stokes: What He Was Like," *Nieman Reports,* XIII (July 1959), 9. A portrait of a great Washington reporter.

TAYLOR, FRANK J. "The Incredible House That Hearst Built," *Saturday Evening Post,* CCXXXII (May 9, 1959), 38. Hearst's San Simeon estate becomes a California Historical Monument.

TAYLOR, SALLY. "The Life, Work, and Times of Walter Duranty, Moscow Correspondent for the *New York Times,*

1921–1941," Ph.D. thesis, Southern Illinois University, 1979. Says his influence waned with inadequate reporting of the Ukrainian famine.

"The Story of an Experiment," *Time,* LI (March 8, 1948), 55. *Time* evaluates itself after 25 years.

WINFIELD, BETTY HOUCHIN. "FDR's Pictorial Image: Rules and Boundaries," *Journalism History,* V (Winter 1978–79), 110. A seldom-discussed problem.

———. "Mrs. Roosevelt's Press Conference Association," *Journalism History,* VIII (Summer 1981), 54. Eleanor shines a light on herself.

———. "The New Deal Publicity Operation," *Journalism Quarterly,* LXI (Spring 1984), 40.

CHAPTER 15: A WORLD AT WAR

Books

BLUM, JOHN. *V Was For Victory: Politics and American Culture during World War II.* New York: Harcourt Brace Jovanovich, 1976. Scholarly history, including material on propaganda.

BRAVERMAN, JORDAN. *To Hasten the Homecoming: How Americans Fought World War II through the Media.* Lanham, MD: Madison Books, 1996. How mass media bolstered morale at home.

CHAFE, WILLIAM H. *The Unfinished Journey: America Since World War II.* New York: Oxford University Press, 1990. A sprightly, clear style.

COLE, WAYNE S. *America First: The Battle against Intervention, 1940–1941.* Madison: University of Wisconsin Press, 1953. Still the classic study of America First, and of isolationism generally.

DAWIDOWICZ, LUCY S. *The War against the Jews, 1933–1945.* New York: Holt, Rinehart and Winston, 1975. An examination of U.S. inaction relative to the Holocaust.

DIGGINS, JOHN PATRICK. *The Proud Decades.* New York: Norton, 1988. America in war and peace, 1941–60.

DONOVAN, ROBERT J. *Conflict and Crisis: The Presidency of Harry S. Truman, 1945–48.* New York: Norton, 1977. See also Donovan, *Tumultuous Years, 1949–53* (1982). Well-balanced accounts.

DOWER, JOHN W. *War without Mercy: Race and Power in the Pacific War.* New York; Pantheon, 1986. Extreme racial propaganda in U.S. and Japan led to ferocious combat.

FARRAR, RONALD T. *The Reluctant Servant: The Story of Charles G. Ross.* Columbia: University of Missouri Press, 1969. Ross was a longtime *St. Louis Post-Dispatch* star before serving as President Truman's press secretary.

GERVASI, FRANK. *The Violent Decade.* New York: Norton, 1989. Memoir of the foreign correspondent, 1935–45, at the fall of France and in Mediterranean.

GOLDMAN, ERIC F. *The Crucial Decade: America, 1945–1955.* New York: Knopf, 1956. A sequel to *Rendezvous*

with Destiny. See also Peter Joseph, *Good Times: An Oral History of America in the Nineteen Sixties* (New York: Charterhouse, 1973).

HARSCH, JOSEPH C. *At the Hinge of History: A Reporter's Story.* Athens, GA: University of Georgia Press, 1993. The veteran broadcast and print reporter offers his interpretation of world events beginning with World War II.

HASTINGS, MAX. *The Korean War.* New York: Simon & Schuster, 1987. Carefully researched, balanced.

HAMILTON, JOHN MAXWELL. *Edgar Snow: A Biography.* Bloomington: Indiana University Press, 1989. Vividly written. See also Hamilton's article in *Media History Digest,* VII (1987), 55.

IRONS, PETER. *Justice at War: The Story of the Japanese American Internment Cases.* New York: Oxford University Press, 1983. Liberals failed to defend civil rights principles.

KEEGAN, JOHN. *The Second World War.* New York: Viking, 1990. Rated as the best account.

KETCHUM, RICHARD M. *The Borrowed Years, 1938–1941: America on the Way to War.* New York: Knopf, 1990. Americans didn't believe Europe's war against Hitler was theirs.

KOOP, THEODORE F. *Weapon of Silence.* Chicago: University of Chicago Press, 1946. The story of the World War II Office of Censorship by one of its principal executives.

LIEBOVICH, LOUIS. *The Press and the Origins of the Cold War, 1944–1947.* New York: Praeger, 1988. News coverage reinforced popular images of the USSR; focus is on *New York Herald Tribune, Chicago Tribune, San Francisco Chronicle,* and *Time.*

LIPSTADT, DEBORAH E. *Beyond Belief: The American Press and the Coming of the Holocaust, 1933–1945.* New York: The Free Press, 1985. A sorry record for the U.S. news media. See also David S. Wyman, *The Abandonment of the Jews* (New York: Pantheon, 1985).

MACDONALD, CALLUM A. *Korea: The War before Vietnam.* New York: Free Press, 1987. Emphasis is on domestic and international politics, not battles.

MACKINNON, JANICE AND STEPHEN. *Agnes Smedley: The Life and Times of an American Radical.* Berkeley: University of California Press, 1988. Authors obtained the FBI's Smedley dossier and other new data.

MACKINNON, STEPHEN, AND ORIS FRIESEN. *China Reporting.* Berkeley: University of California Press, 1987. Report of reunion of wartime China hands.

MAY, ANTOINETTE. *Witness to War: A Biography of Marguerite Higgins.* New York: Penguin, 1985. A great correspondent with personal problems.

MCCULLOUGH, DAVID. *Truman.* New York: Simon & Schuster, 1992. Appreciation for the "common-man" president and for the role individuals play in shaping history.

MEYER, ROBERT, JR. *The "Stars and Stripes" Story of World War II.* New York: McKay, 1960. Anthology of stories, with background.

MIDDLETON, DREW. *Where Has Last July Gone? Memoirs.* New York: Quadrangle, 1973. Details his career as a *New York Times* correspondent, with focus on World War II.

MILLER, LEE G. *The Story of Ernie Pyle.* New York: Viking, 1950. Biography of the famed World War II columnist.

MILLER, MERLE. *Plain Speaking.* New York: G. P. Putnam's Sons, 1973. An oral biography of Harry S Truman that gives, among many other opinions, the ex-president's views on the press.

MILLER, WEBB. *I Found No Peace.* New York: Simon & Schuster, 1936. One of the best of the foreign correspondents' books by a longtime UP star.

POLLARD, JAMES E. *The Presidents and the Press: Truman to Johnson.* Washington, DC: Public Affairs Press, 1964. Continues his earlier study.

PRANGE, GORDON W. *At Dawn We Slept: The Untold Story of Pearl Harbor.* New York: McGraw-Hill, 1981. Definitive account from Japanese and U.S. sources. See also his *Pearl Harbor: The Verdict of History, Dec. 7, 1941* (New York: McGraw-Hill, 1986); and *Miracle at Midway* (with Donald M. Goldstein and Katherine V. Dillon) (New York: McGraw-Hill, 1982).

PYLE, ERNEST TAYLOR. *Here Is Your War.* New York: Holt, Rinehart & Winston, 1943. A compilation of Pyle's columns. See also *Ernie's War,* ed. David Nichols (New York: Random House, 1986).

SALISBURY, HARRISON E. *The Long March.* New York: Harper & Row, 1985. Step-by-step recreation of Mao's retreat to Yenan, base of Chinese Communist power.

SHERWOOD, ROBERT E. *Roosevelt and Hopkins.* New York: Harper & Row, 1948. An intimate history of the wartime partnership by the writer-confidant of FDR.

SHEWMAKER, KENNETH E. *Americans and Chinese Communists, 1927–1945: A Persuading Encounter.* Ithaca, NY: Cornell University Press, 1971. Basic source for the history of the press corps in China. Leaders and their major books included Edgar Snow, *Red Star over China* (1938); Agnes Smedley, *China's Red Army Marches* (1934); Anna Louise Strong, *China's Millions* (1935); and Theodore White and Annalee Jacoby, *Thunder Out of China* (1946).

SNOW, HELEN FOSTER. *My China Years.* New York: Wm. Morrow, 1984. Autobiography of Edgar Snow's first wife, who as Nym Wales wrote *Inside Red China* (New York: Doubleday, Doren, 1939) after her trip to Yenan.

SNOW, LOIS WHEELER. *Edgar Snow's China.* New York: Random House, 1981. His second wife covers Snow's reporting career, from 1928 to 1949, using his writing and photos. Snow foresaw Mao's victory.

SNYDER, LOUIS J., ed. *Masterpieces of War Reporting.* New York: Julian Messner, 1962. Great moments of World War II.

SORENSEN, THOMAS C. *The World War: The Story of American Propaganda.* New York: Harper & Row, 1968. Focuses on the USIA in postwar crises.

STEIN, M. L. *Under Fire: The Story of American War Correspondents.* New York: Julian Messner, 1968. Good, popularly written history.

STRONG, TRACY B., AND HELENE KEYSSAR. *Right in Her Soul: A Biography of Anna Louise Strong.* New York: Random House, 1983. Correspondent with Mao in Yenan.

TERKEL, STUDS. *"The Good War": An Oral History of World War II.* New York: Pantheon, 1984. A Pulitzer Prize winner.

THOMSON, CHARLES A. H. *Overseas Information Service of the United States Government.* Washington: Brookings Institution, 1948. Authoritative account.

TOLAND, JOHN. *The Rising Sun: The Decline and Fall of the Japanese Empire 1936–1945.* 2 vols. New York: Random House, 1970. A comprehensive account of the war in the Pacific.

TUCKER, ROBERT C. *Stalin in Power: The Revolution from Above, 1928–1941.* New York: W. W. Norton Co., 1990. See also Tucker, *Stalin as Revolutionary, 1879–1929* (New York: W. W. Norton Co., 1973). Scholarly examinations of Stalin's life and rise to power.

VOSS, FREDERICK S. *Reporting the War: The Journalistic Coverage of World War II.* Washington, DC: Smithsonian Institution Press for the National Portrait Gallery, 1994. Oversized, illustrated documentation of all media people who covered the war.

WADE, BETSY, ed. *Forward Positions: The War Correspondence of Homer Bigart,* ed. Betsy Wade. Little Rock: University of Arkansas Press, 1993. 51 battlefront dispatches from World War II and Korea from *The New York Herald Tribune* and the *New York Times,* by the Pulitzer Prize winner.

WAGNER, LILYA. *Women War Correspondents in World War II.* Westport, CT: Greenwood Press, 1989. Interviews with 18; lists accredited women reporters with newspapers and wire services.

WASHBURN, PATRICK S. *A Question of Sedition: The Federal Government's Investigation of the Black Press During World War II.* New York: Oxford University Press, 1986. J. Edgar Hoover's FBI tries to repeat the harassment practiced during World War I.

WEINBERG, GERHARD L. *World at Arms: A Global History of World War II.* Cambridge, England and New York: Cambridge University Press, 1994. A comprehensive view of World War II from a truly global perspective.

WHITE, WILLIAM ALLEN. *The Autobiography of William Allen White,* ed. Sally Foreman Griffith. Lawrence: University Press of Kansas, 1990. No one should miss this autobiography, and few do.

WILLIAMS, HERBERT LEE. *The Newspaperman's President: Harry S. Truman.* New York: Nelson-Hall, 1984. A labor of love.

WINKLER, ALLAN M. *The Politics of Propaganda: The Office of War Information, 1942—1945.* New Haven: Yale University Press, 1978. Favorable, detailed account.

ZELIZER, BARBIE. *Remembering to Forget: Holocaust Memory through the Camera's Eye.* Chicago: University of Chicago Press, 1998. A well-researched and thoughtful account of how photojournalists represented the Allied liberation of German concentration camps in 1945.

Periodicals and Monographs

The files of the *Journalism Quarterly* and *Public Opinion Quarterly* contain many important articles about World War II censorship and propaganda activities. See particularly the Spring 1943 issue of *Public Opinion Quarterly,* and *Journalism Quarterly* from 1942 to 1944. Other important articles include the following:

BISHOP, ROBERT L., AND LAMAR S. MACKAY. "Mysterious Silence, Lyrical Scream: Government Information in World War II," *Journalism Monographs,* XIX (May 1971). The OWI.

BROWNE, DONALD R. "The Voice of America: Policies and Problems," *Journalism Monographs,* XLIII (February 1976). A comprehensive account.

BLANCHARD, MARGARET A. "Americans First, Newspapermen Second? The Conflict Between Patriotism and Freedom of the Press During the Cold War, 1946–1952," Ph.D. thesis, University of North Carolina at Chapel Hill, 1981.

BRAESTRUP, PETER. "Battle Lines," *Nieman Reports,* XXXIX:3 (Autumn 1985), 43. The military-press relationship: an uneasy alliance.

CARDOZO, ARLENE ROSSEN. "American Magazine Coverage of the Nazi Death-Camp Era," *Journalism Quarterly,* LX (Winter 1983), 217. Content analysis and evaluation.

DAVIS, ELMER. "Report to the President," ed. Ronald T. Farrar, *Journalism Monographs,* VII (August 1968). On his OWI stewardship.

FARRAR, RONALD. "Harry Truman and the Press: A View from Inside," *Journalism History,* VIII (Summer 1981), 56. Based on research in the Truman Library.

HAMILTON, MARY A. "J. W. Gitts: The Cold War's Voice in the Wilderness," *Journalism Monographs,* XCI (February 1985). Only daily publisher to support Henry Wallace in 1948.

KESSLER, LAUREN. "Fettered Freedoms: The Journalism of World War II Japanese Internment Camps," *Journalism History,* XV (Summer 1988), 70. See also John Hersey, "Behind Barbed Wire," *New York Times Magazine,* September 11, 1988, 57.

LIEBOVICH, LOUIS. "H. V. Kaltenborn and the Origins of the Cold War," *Journalism History,* XIV (Summer 1987), 46. Warmth for Soviet Union in 1943 turned cool by 1946.

MANDER, MARY S. "American Correspondents During World War II," *American Journalism,* I:1 (Summer 1983), 17. Interpretive study.

MILLER, ROBERT C. "Censorship in Korea," *Nieman Reports,* VI (July 1952), 3.

MURRAY, RANDALL L. "Harry S. Truman and Press Opinion: 1945–1953," Ph.D. thesis, University of Minnesota, 1973. Documented analysis of the influence of press opinion on the president; also excellent for details of Truman's press relations.

PFAFF, DANIEL W. "Joseph Pulitzer II and the European War, 1938–1945," *American Journalism,* VI (1989), 143. Ups and downs of *St. Louis Post-Dispatch* policy analyzed by biographer of Pulitzer II.

PRATTE, ALF. "The *Honolulu Star-Bulletin* and the 'Day of Infamy,' " *American Journalism,* V (1988), 5. Riley Allen and his staff issued three extras.

STEELE, RICHARD W. "News of the 'Good War': World War II News Management," *Journalism Quarterly,* LXII (Winter 1985), 707. FDR's news management gained public support.

STEVENS, JOHN D. "From the Back of the Foxhole: Black Correspondents in World War II," *Journalism Monographs,* XXVII (February 1973).

WASHBURN, PATRICK S. "The Federal Governments' Investigation of the Black Press During World War II," Ph.D. thesis, Indiana University, 1984. Francis Biddle stood off censors. See also Washburn's article in *Journalism History,* XIII (Spring 1986), 26.

———. "FDR Versus His Own Attorney General: The Struggle over Sedition, 1941–42," *Journalism Quarterly,* LXII (Winter 1985), 717. Francis Biddle cooled off FDR's complaints against the press.

———. "The *Pittsburgh Courier*'s Double V Campaign in 1942," *American Journalism,* III:2 (1986), 73. Victory in war and victory over racism.

CHAPTER 16: TELEVISION TAKES CENTER STAGE

Books: Background, Newspapers

BAUGHMAN, JAMES L. *The Republic of Mass Culture: Journalism, Filmmaking, and Broadcasting in America Since 1941.* 2nd ed. Baltimore: Johns Hopkins University Press, 1997.

BAYLEY, EDWIN R. *Joe McCarthy and the Press.* Madison: University of Wisconsin Press, 1981. Won a national research award. See also an excellent biography, Thomas C. Reeves, *The Life and Times of Joe McCarthy* (New York: Stein & Day, 1982).

BLUMBERG, NATHAN B. *One Party Press?* Lincoln: University of Nebraska Press, 1954. How 35 large dailies covered the 1952 campaign; news essentially fair.

BRANCH, TAYLOR. *Parting the Waters: America in the King Years, 1954–63.* New York: Simon & Schuster, 1988. A broad overview of the civil rights movement.

FRIED, RICHARD M. *Nightmare in Red: The McCarthy Era in Perspective.* New York: Oxford University Press, 1990. McCarthy analyzed in the context of twentieth-century anti-Communist politics.

GELB, NORMAN. *The Berlin Wall.* New York: Times Books, 1987. Kennedy vs. Khrushchev; by Mutual network's correspondent on the scene.

HALBERSTAM, DAVID. *The Powers That Be.* New York: Knopf, 1979. Examines in detail the influence of the *Washington Post, Los Angeles Times,* Time Inc., CBS, and their owners.

———. *The Fifties.* New York: Villard Books, 1993. A searching look at the events of the decade of nostalgia that spawned the upheavals of the 1960s.

ISAACSON, WALTER, AND EVAN THOMAS. *The Wise Men: Six Friends and the World They Made: Acheson, Bohlen, Harriman, Kennan, Lovett, McCloy.* New York: Simon & Schuster, 1986. America's postwar diplomats and newsmakers.

KLUGER, RICHARD. *Simple Justice: The History of Brown v. Board of Education and Black America's Struggle for Equality.* New York: Knopf, 1976. In-depth study.

KUTLER, STANLEY J. *The American Inquisition: Justice and Injustice in the Cold War.* New York: Farrar, Straus & Giroux, 1983. Scholarly analysis of specific cases.

MAY, ELAINE TYLER. *Homeward Bound: American Families in the Cold War Era.* New York: Basic Books, 1988. Pathbreaking study that connects U.S. containment policy to domestic affairs, arguing that containment also describes the homefront during these years.

MCCORMICK, THOMAS J. *America's Half-Century: United States Foreign Policy in the Cold War and After.* 2nd ed. Baltimore: Johns Hopkins University Press, 1995. A New Left examination of the United States's role in the world.

MORRIS, ALDON D. *The Origins of the Civil Rights Movement: Black Communities Organizing for Change.* New York: Free Press, 1984.

NEVILLE, JOHN F. *The Press, the Rosenbergs, and the Cold War.* New York: Praeger, 1995. Describes the biased press coverage of the atomic spy case.

OSHINSKY, DAVID M. *A Conspiracy So Immense: The World of Joe McCarthy.* New York: Free Press, 1983. A compelling, well-researched analysis.

PATTERSON, JAMES T. *Grand Expectations: The United States, 1945–1974.* New York Oxford University Press, 1996. Winner of the 1997 Bancroft Prize in History. The most readable and balanced overview of this period.

ROBINSON, JO ANN GIBSON. *The Montgomery Bus Boycott and the Women Who Started It: The Memoir of Jo Ann Gibson Robinson.* Edited by David J. Garrow. Knoxville: University of Tennessee Press, 1987. An in-depth account of the boycott; correctly points out the importance of the African American Women's Political Council.

ROWSE, ARTHUR E. *Slanted News.* Boston: Beacon Press, 1957. Analysis of how 31 large dailies reported the "Nixon fund" episode in 1952.

SCHRECKER, ELLEN W. *Many Are the Crimes: McCarthyism in America.* Boston: Little, Brown, 1998.

WHITFIELD, STEPHEN J. *The Culture of the Cold War.* 2nd ed. Baltimore: Johns Hopkins University Press, 1996. How the Cold War affected American culture—including television, movies, and religion.

Books: Broadcasting

ALLEN, CRAIG. *Eisenhower and the Mass Media: Peace, Prosperity, and Prime Time TV.* Chapel Hill: University of North Carolina Press, 1993. Some insights into television and politics.

BARNOUW, ERIK. *Tube of Plenty: The Evolution of American Television.* New York: Oxford, 1990. Update by broadcast history author (see Chapter 13 Bibliography).

BERGREEN, LAURENCE. *Look Now, Pay Later: The Rise of Network Broadcasting.* Garden City, NY: Doubleday, 1980. Best to date.

BLISS, EDWARD J. *Now the News.* New York: Columbia University Press, 1991. A comprehensive, anecdotal history of broadcast news by a former CBS writer-producer.

BLUEM, A. WILLIAM. *The Documentary in American Television.* New York: Hastings House, 1965. Includes historical development and 100 pages of photographs.

BOYLE, DIEDRE. *Subject to Change: Guerrilla Television Revisited.* New York: Oxford University Press, 1997. Well-written, analytical history of alternative television in the late 1960s and early 1970s, with useful bibliography and other research resources.

Broadcasting: The First 50 Years of Broadcasting. Washington, DC: 1981. A year-by-year informal history.

COMSTOCK, GEORGE. *Television in America.* Beverly Hills: Sage, 1980. Synthesis of published research on the impact of television on society.

CRONKITE, WALTER. *A Reporter's Life.* New York: Knopf, 1996. Autobiography by the dean of broadcast reporters.

DAY, JAMES. *The Vanishing Vision: The Inside Story of Public Television.* Berkeley, CA: University of California Press, 1995. A well-documented, insider history.

ENGELMAN, RALPH. *Public Radio and Television in America: A Political History.* Thousand Oaks, CA: Sage Publications, 1996. A critical analysis of the origins and development of the major institutions, including National Public Radio, Radio Pacifica, and the Public Broadcasting Service.

FEDERAL COMMUNICATIONS COMMISSION. *Annual Report for Fiscal Year 1964.* Washington, DC: Government Printing Office, 1964. Summarizes, as a 30th anniversary issue, communication developments since 1934.

FRIENDLY, FRED W. *Due to Circumstances Beyond Our Control. . . .* New York: Random House, 1967. The story of life with Edward R. Murrow, of their controversial CBS documentaries, and of Friendly's break with CBS.

GABLER, NEAL. *Winchell: Gossip, Power, and the Culture of Celebrity.* New York: Alfred A. Knopf, 1994. A skillful synthesis of biographical highlights with cultural and social history.

KENDRICK, ALEXANDER. *Prime Time: The Life of Edward R. Murrow.* Boston: Little, Brown, 1969. Biography of the great commentator; thorough but misses catching drama of great events.

METZ, ROBERT. *CBS: Reflections in a Bloodshot Eye.* Chicago: Playboy Press, 1975. CBS viewed this critical study with silence.

MURRAY, MICHAEL D., ed. *Encyclopedia of Television News.* Phoenix, AZ: Oryx, 1998. Reference covers TV journalism from its beginnings.

———— AND DONALD G. GODFREY, eds. *Television in America: Local Station History from across the Nation.* Ames, IA: Iowa State University Press, 1997. The first broad study of local television history, placed in a national context.

MURROW, EDWARD R. *In Search of Light: The Broadcasts of Edward R. Murrow, 1938–1961.* New York: Knopf, 1967. Broadcast history through memorable scripts.

NELSON, MICHAEL. *War of the Black Heavens: The Battles of Western Broadcasting in the Cold War.* Syracuse, NY: Syracuse University Press, 1997. Western radio—including the Voice of America—was a strong force in the fight against communism.

NEWCOMB, HORACE, ed. *Museum of Broadcast Communications Encyclopedia of Television,* 3 vols. Chicago and London: Fitzroy Dearborn, 1997. A superb historical analysis of television in the United States, Britain, Canada and Australia, presented in about 1000 entries.

PALEY, WILLIAM S. *As It Happened.* Garden City, NY: Doubleday, 1979. Story of CBS by its founder.

PERSICO, JOSEPH E. *Edward R. Murrow: An American Original.* New York: McGraw-Hill, 1989. Combines comprehensive detail with well-told anecdotes.

QUINLAN, STERLING. *Inside ABC: American Broadcasting Company's Rise to Power.* New York: Hastings House, 1979. By an ABC executive.

ROMAN, JAMES. *Love, Light, and a Dream: Television's Past, Present, and Future.* Westport, CT: Praever, 1996. Informative history and survey of television as both business and cultural institution.

SCHROTH, RAYMOND A. *The American Journey of Eric Sevareid.* South Royalton, VT: Steerforth Press, 1995. Well-researched biography.

SHIERS, GEORGE, ed. *Technical Development of Television.* New York: Arno Press, 1977. Thirty articles surveying progress from the 1870s to 1975.

SMITH, ANTHONY, ed. *Television: An International History.* New York: Oxford University Press, 1995. Seventeen experts contribute essays documenting television's global evolution.

SMITH, SALLY BEDELL. *In All His Glory: The Life of William S. Paley: The Legendary Tycoon and His Brilliant Circle.* New York: Simon & Schuster, 1990. A best seller; her five-year study presents Paley, warts and all.

SPERBER, ANN M. *Murrow: His Life and Times.* New York: Freundlich, 1986. A lengthy but absorbing biography of the CBS broadcaster. See also Betty Houchin Winfield and Lois B. DeFleur, *The Edward R. Murrow Heritage* (Ames: Iowa State University Press, 1986), based on a major 1983 symposium honoring Murrow.

STEMPEL, TOM. *Storytellers to the Nation: A History of American Television Writing.* Syracuse, NY: Syracuse University Press, 1996. Oral-history interviews with 42 writers.

STEPHENS, MITCHELL. *The Rise of the Image, the Fall of the Word.* New York: Oxford University Press, 1998. Analyzes previous communications revolutions to argue that the contemporary dominance of the moving image over print may lead to cultural renaissance.

WATSON, MARY ANN. *Defining Visions: Television and the American Experience since 1945.* New York: Harcourt Brace, 1997. Explores television's connection to U.S. culture as well as its social history.

Books: Press Associations

BAILLIE, HUGH. *High Tension.* New York: Harper & Row, 1959. Readable autobiography of the former UP president. See also Joe Alex Morris, *Deadline Every Minute: The Story of the United Press* (Garden City, NY: Doubleday, 1957).

CONSIDINE, BOB. *It's All News to Me.* New York: Meredith, 1967. Autobiography of a great reporter for the INS and Hearst.

COOPER, KENT. *Kent Cooper and the Associated Press.* New York: Random House, 1959. Autobiography of the former general manager. For the story of the AP's restrictive news-exchange agreements, see his *Barriers Down* (New York: Holt, Rinehart & Winston, 1942).

ISRAEL, LEE. *Kilgallen.* New York: Delacorte, 1979. Story of Dorothy of the INS.

SMITH, MERRIMAN. *A White House Memoir.* New York: Norton, 1972. How the UPI's great White House correspondent covered from FDR to Nixon.

Books: Magazines, Book Publishing

ALPERN, SARA. *Freda Kirchwey: A Woman of the Nation.* Cambridge: Harvard University Press, 1987. Kirchwey guided the *Nation* through crisis years.

COHN, JAN. *Creating America: George Horace Lorimer and the "Saturday Evening Post".* Pittsburgh: University of Pittsburgh Press, 1989. Well written.

COUSINS, NORMAN. *Present Tense: An American Editor's Odyssey.* New York: McGraw-Hill, 1967. The history of the *Saturday Review* at age 25 by its editor.

DAVIS, KENNETH C. *Two-Bit Culture: The Paperbacking of America.* Boston: Houghton Mifflin, 1984. Best account, well researched.

DESAULNIERS, LOUISE, ed. *119 Years of the "Atlantic."* Boston: Little, Brown, 1979. Selections.

FRIEDRICH, OTTO. *Decline and Fall.* New York: Harper & Row, 1970. About the death of the *Saturday Evening Post.* See also Joseph C. Goulden, *The Curtis Caper* (New York: G. P. Putnam's Sons, 1965).

JUDIS, JOHN B. *William F. Buckley, Jr.: Patron Saint of the Conservatives.* New York; Simon & Schuster, 1989. A solid evaluation.

MARTY, MARTIN E., JOHN G. DEEDY, JR., AND DAVID W. SILBERMAN. *The Religious Press in America.* New York: Holt, Rinehart & Winston, 1963. Protestant, Catholic, and Jewish editors combine to analyze their subject.

PAYNE, DARWIN. *The Man of Only Yesterday: Frederick Lewis Allen.* New York: Harper & Row, 1975. Excellent biography of editor of *Harper's* and author of *Only Yesterday.*

PETERSON, THEODORE. *Magazines in the Twentieth Century.* Rev. ed. Urbana: University of Illinois Press, 1964. The most comprehensive discussion of magazine economics.

SCHWED, PETER. *Turning the Pages: An Insider's Story of Simon & Schuster, 1924–1984.* New York: Macmillan, 1984. By a longtime friend.

TEBBEL, JOHN W. *George Horace Lorimer and the "Saturday Evening Post."* Garden City, NY: Doubleday, 1948. Lorimer edited the *Post* from 1899 to 1937.

WAGNER, PHYLLIS CERF, AND ALBERT ERSKINE. *At Random: The Reminiscences of Bennett Cerf.* New York: Random House, 1977. Based on 21 tape-recorded interviews.

WALTERS, RAY. *Paperback Talk.* Chicago: Academy, 1985. Selections from the author's *New York Times* Sunday columns of the preceding decade.

Books: Film

BEHLMER RUDY, ed. *Inside Warner Bros. (1935–1951).* New York: Viking, 1985. Annotated selection from the studio's files.

BRADY, FRANK. *Citizen Welles.* New York: Scribner's, 1989. Serious, well-written biography of Orson Welles. See also Robert L. Carringer, *The Making of "Citizen Kane"* (Berkeley: University of California Press, 1985).

GIANNETTI, LOUIS, AND SCOTT EYMAN. *Flashback.* Englewood Cliffs, NJ: Prentice Hall, 1986. World cinema since the 1920s.

KOBAL, JOHN. *People Will Talk.* New York: Knopf, 1986. Life in Hollywood's golden age.

Books: Advertising, Public Relations

BARTOS, RENA, AND ARTHUR S. PEARSON. *The Founding Fathers of Advertising Research.* New York: Advertising Research Foundation, 1977. Brief paper account of Ernest Dichter (motivation), George Gallup (polling), Alfred Polits (sampling), Henry Brenner (entrepreneur), Hans Ziesel (sociologist), Frank Stanton (audience), and Archibald Crossley and A. C. Nielson, Sr. (ratings).

BERNAYS, EDWARD L. *Public Relations.* Norman: University of Oklahoma Press, 1979. A case-history type of discussion of the field by one of its founders.

CONE, FAIRFAX M. *With All Its Faults: A Candid Account of Forty Years in Advertising.* Boston: Little, Brown, 1969. By the head of famed Foote, Cone & Belding agency.

GOODRUM, CHARLES, and HELEN DALRYMPLE. *Advertising in America: The First 200 Years.* New York: Abrams, 1990. Overview history and 250 illustrated pages with 566 ads.

GOLDEN, L.L.L. *Only by Public Consent.* New York: 1968. Story of Paul W. Garrett and General Motor's public-relations program.

HILL, JOHN W. *The Making of a Public Relations Man.* New York: McKay, 1963. Counsel.

MAAS, JANE. *Adventures of an Advertising Woman.* New York: St. Martin's Press, 1986. Worked in top agencies, headed one.

MAYER, MARTIN. *Madison Avenue, U.S.A.* New York: Harper, 1958. A picture of advertising in the 1950s. See also Sloan Wilson, *The Man in the Gray Flannel Suit* (New York: Pocket Books, 1967).

OGILVY, DAVID. *Confessions of an Advertising Man.* New York: Atheneum, 1964. Fascinating account of advertising work by a founder of a leading agency.

ROSS, IRWIN, *The Image Merchants.* Garden City, NY: Doubleday, 1959. New York public-relations practitioners of the era described.

TEDLOW, RICHARD S. *New and Improved: The Story of Mass Marketing in America.* New York: Basic Books, 1990. Mass culture advertising.

Periodicals and Monographs

ALSDURF, PHYLLIS E. "Telling the Untold Story: An Examination of the History of the Religious Press in America," paper presented to Association for Education in Journalism and Mass Communication annual convention, Washington, D.C., 1995. Detailed review of the scholarship with prescription for a cultural studies approach.

ATWATER, TONY, "Editorial Policy of *Ebony* before and after Civil Rights Act of 1964," *Journalism Quarterly,* LIX (Spring 1982), 87. Photo-editorial coverage increased.

BAUGHMAN, JAMES L. "Television in the 'Golden Age': An Entrepreneurial Experiment," *Historian,* XLVII (February 1985).

BEASLEY, MAURINE AND PAUL BELGRADE. "Media Coverage of a Silent Partner: Mamie Eisenhower as First Lady," *American Journalism,* III:1 (1986), 39.

BENÉT, STEPHEN VINCENT. "The United Press," *Fortune,* VII (May 1933), 67. A compact treatment of UP history and its 1933 status.

BETHUNE, BEVERLY M. "A Case of Overkill: The FBI and the N.Y. City Photo League," *Journalism History,* VII (Autumn–Winter 1980), 87.

BOGART, LEO. "Magazines Since the Rise of Television," *Journalism Quarterly,* XXXIII (Spring 1956). 153. Magazine readership and economics from 1946 to 1955.

"Broadcasting at 50," *Broadcasting,* LXXIX (November 2, 1970). A special issue, including a year-by-year review of major events from 1931 to 1970.

"CBS: The First Five Decades," *Broadcasting,* XCIII (September 19, 1977), 45–116. Extensive survey.

GOEBBEL, ALFRED R. "*The Christian Century:* Its Editorial Policy and Positions, 1908–1966," Ph.D. thesis, University of Illinois, 1967. Descriptive study.

GOMERY, DOUGLAS. "Rethinking TV History," *Journalism Quarterly* 74:3 (Autumn 1997), 501–14.

GOODSON, MARK. "If I'd Stood up Earlier," *New York Times Magazine,* January 13, 1991, p. 22. A TV producer recounts the dark terror of blacklists.

GOULD, LEWIS. "First Ladies and the Press: Bess Truman to Lady Bird Johnson," *American Journalism,* I:1 (Summer 1983), 47.

HARRISON, RICHARD EDES. "AP," *Fortune,* XV (February 1937), 89. The rise of the AP and a contemporary picture of its operations.

KARNICK, KRISTINE. "NBC and the Innovation of Television News," *Journalism History,* XV (1988), 26. Economic and organizational emphasis.

LEAB, DANIEL J. " 'The Iron Curtain' (1948): Hollywood's First Cold War Movie," *Historical Journal of Film, Radio and Television,* VIII (1988), 153. Hollywood's first effort for the anti-Red movement.

LEAMING, DERYL RAY. "A Biography of Ben Hibbs," Ph.D. thesis, Syracuse University, 1969. Discusses the editor of the *Saturday Evening Post.*

MANAGO, B. R. "The *Saturday Evening Post* under Ben Hibbs, 1942–1961," Ph.D. thesis, Northwestern University, 1968. Decline began in the 1950s.

MARSH, HARRY D. "Hodding Carter's Newspaper on School Desegregation, 1954–55," *Journalism Monographs,* XCII (May 1985). Mississippi's champion of racial equality.

MCKERNS, JOSEPH P. "Television Docudrama: The Image as History," *Journalism History,* VII (Spring 1980), 24. A study of documentaries.

MURRAY, MICHAEL D. "Television's Desperate Moment: A Conversation with Fred W. Friendly," *Journalism History,* I (Autumn 1974), 68. Interview about Senator Joseph McCarthy and the media.

PFAFF, DANIEL W. "Joseph Pulitzer II and Advertising Censorship, 1929–1939," *Journalism Monographs,* LXXVII (July 1982). Reform at the *Post-Dispatch.*

RENAUD, JEAN-LUC. "U.S. Government Assistance to AP's Worldwide Expansion," *Journalism Quarterly,* LXII (Spring 1985), 10. Kent Cooper got governmental favors.

SCHWARZLOSE, RICHARD A. "The American Wire Services: A Study of Their Development as a Social Institution," Ph.D. thesis, University of Illinois, 1965. By a leading student of the press associations.

———. "Trends in U.S. Newspapers' Wire Service Resources, 1934–66," *Journalism Quarterly,* XLIII (Winter 1966), 627. A lessening of competitive service appears in these detailed figures.

SHAPLEN, ROBERT. "A Farewell to Personal History," *Saturday Review,* XLIII (December 1, 1960), 46. Network coverage abroad in the 1950s.

SWINDLER, WILLIAM F. "The AP Antitrust Case in Historical Perspective," *Journalism Quarterly,* XXIII (March 1946), 40. Scholarly analysis.

CHAPTER 17: CHALLENGES AND DISSENT

Books: Background History, Vietnam

ASSOCIATED PRESS. *Triumph and Tragedy: The Story of the Kennedys.* New York: William Morrow, 1968. Discusses the assassinations of JFK and RFK. See also United Press International, *Assassination: Robert F. Kennedy* (New York: Cowles, 1968).

BLIGHT, JAMES G., AND DAVID A. WELCH. *On the Brink: Americans and Soviets Reexamine the Cuban Missile Crisis.* New York: Hill & Wang, 1989. Participants in the 1962 crisis reexamine the events and perceptions.

BRAESTRUP, PETER. *Big Story: How the American Press and Television Reported and Interpreted the Crisis of Tet 1968 in Vietnam and Washington.* 2 vols. Boulder, CO: Western

Press, 1977. A 1500-page analysis by the Saigon bureau chief of the *Washington Post.*

DONOVAN, ROBERT J. *Nemesis: Truman and Johnson in the Coils of War in Asia.* New York: St. Martin's Press, 1985. Skillful comparison of the two men and events, rich in anecdotes.

ELWOOD-AYERS, VIRGINIA. *Women War Correspondents in the Vietnam War, 1961–1975.* MeFuchen, NJ: Scarecrow Press, 1988. Covers 74 correspondents.

EMERSON, GLORIA. *Winners and Losers.* New York: Random House, 1977. A former *New York Times* reporter wrote this so Americans would not forget Vietnam.

FALL, BERNARD B. *The Two Viet-Nams: A Political and Military Analysis.* 2nd rev. ed. New York: Praeger, 1967. The most important study of the historical background and changing nature of the war.

FITZGERALD, FRANCES. *Fire in the Lake.* Boston: Little, Brown, 1972. The story of the people of Vietnam by an acclaimed journalist. Hailed as one of the best books on the consequences of the war.

GITLIN, TODD. *The Whole World Is Watching.* Berkeley: University of California Press, 1980. This study by a one-time SDS president shows that the demonstrations of the 1960s were played out in the media spotlight, treating the anti-war movement as an oddity or crime, and making celebrities of New Left leaders.

———. *The Sixties: Years of Hope, Days of Rage.* New York: Bantam, 1987. Strong on politics and culture.

HALBERSTAM, DAVID. *The Making of a Quagmire.* New York: Random House, 1965. By the *New York Times*'s Pulitzer Prize winner in Vietnam. See also his *The Best and the Brightest* (New York: Random House, 1972). A thoroughly researched analysis of the Ivy Leaguers and Cold Warriors who created the Vietnam War.

HALLIN, DANIEL C. *The "Uncensored War": The Media and Vietnam.* New York: Oxford University Press, 1986. Refutes charge that network news opposed and lost the Vietnam War.

HAMMOND, WILLIAM M. *Reporting Vietnam: Media and Military at War.* Lawrence: University Press of Kansas, 1998. By the author of several books on Vietnam War coverage and media–military relations. Based on both classified and recently declassified government documents.

KAISER, CHARLES. *1968 in America.* New York: Weidenfeld & Nicolson, 1988. Music, politics, chaos, counterculture, and the shaping of a generation.

KALVEN, HARRY, JR. *A Worthy Tradition: Freedom of Speech in America.* New York: Harper & Row, 1988. Thorough coverage of domestic communism-related cases of the 1940s to 1960s.

KARNOW, STANLEY. *Vietnam: A History.* New York; Viking, 1983. Companion to the PBS television series. Authoritative source, acclaimed for balance and documentation.

KEARNS, DORIS. *Lyndon Johnson and the American Dream.* New York: Harper & Row, 1976. The best study of LBJ, by a scholar and confidante; portrays his strengths and weaknesses.

KERN, MONTAGUE, PATRICIA W. LEVERING, AND RALPH B. LEVERING. *The Kennedy Crises.* Chapel Hill: University of North Carolina Press, 1984. Laos, the Berlin Wall, Cuba, Vietnam.

KOLKO, GABRIEL. *Confronting the Third World: United States Foreign Policy, 1945–1980.* New York: Pantheon, 1988. A punishing attack by a leading revisionist historian.

LEVY, DAVID. *The Debate over Vietnam.* Baltimore: Johns Hopkins University Press, 1991. Examines the bitter national discussion over the necessity and morality of the war.

MILLER, JAMES. *Democracy Is in the Streets.* New York: Simon & Schuster, 1987. Story of the SDS from its idealistic Port Huron statement of 1962 to the 1968 siege of Chicago, featuring Tom Hayden, Todd Gitlin, and others.

MINOR, DALE. *The Information War.* New York: Hawthorn, 1970. Perceptive analysis of press-government conflict in Vietnam.

O'CONNOR, RICHARD. *Pacific Destiny: An Informal History of the U.S. in the Far East.* Boston: Little, Brown, 1969. An excellent account.

PIKE, DOUGLAS. *People's Army of Vietnam.* San Francisco: Presido, 1986. Major reason for U.S. loss in Vietnam, a leading scholar says.

PROCHNAU, WILLIAM. *Once upon a Distant War: Young War Correspondents and the Early Vietnam Battles.* New York: Times Books, 1995. Detailed, well-written insider history.

Report of the National Advisory Commission on Civil Disorders. New York: Bantam Books, 1968. Chapter 15 discusses the mass media.

Reporting Vietnam: American Journalism 1959–1975. Part One: American Journalism, 1959–1969, 858 pp.; *Part Two: American Journalism, 1969–1975,* 857 pp. New York, NY: Library of America, 1998. An excellent anthology of more than 80 writers, including Peter Arnett, Homer Bigart, Phil Caputo, David Halberstam, Seymour Hersh, Sydney Schanberg, and Neil Sheehan. Includes all of Michael Herr's *Dispatches.*

SALISBURY, HARRISON. *Behind the Lines.* New York: Harper & Row, 1967. The *New York Times* editor's trip to Hanoi opened many eyes to the conduct of the war; almost won him a Pulitzer Prize.

———. *Vietnam Reconsidered: Lessons from a War.* New York: Harper & Row, 1984. Proceedings of major conference of Vietnam participants and newsmen.

SHEEHAN, NEIL. *A Bright, Shining Lie: John Paul Vann and America in Vietnam.* New York: Random House, 1988. Sheehan interprets the war through the flawed personality of an Army friend and wins a Pulitzer Prize.

———, et al. *The Pentagon Papers.* New York: Quadrangle Books, 1971. The documents showing early U.S. involvement in Vietnamese affairs and plans for expansion of this role.

———. *After the War Was Over.* New York: Random House, 1992. Poignant reflections of a former Vietnam correspondent after 1989 visit.

SMALL, WILLIAM. *To Kill a Messenger.* New York: Hastings House, 1970. A prize-winning study of "television news and the real world" by the CBS Washington news manager.

SORENSEN, THEODORE C. *Kennedy.* New York: Harper & Row, 1965. One of the best of the studies of President Kennedy and his administration.

TURNER, KATHLEEN J. *Lyndon Johnson's Dual War: Vietnam and the Press.* Chicago: University of Chicago Press, 1985. Excellent analysis of Johnson's inability to communicate.

UNITED PRESS INTERNATIONAL. *Four Days: The Historical Record of the Death of President Kennedy.* New York: Simon & Schuster, 1964. An *American Heritage* volume, includes journalistic coverage. See also The Associated Press, *The Torch Is Passed* (New York: The Associated Press, 1964).

WATSON, MARY ANN. *The Expanding Vista: American Television in the Kennedy Years.* New York: Oxford University Press, 1990. Incisive account of TV's transition.

WELCH, RICHARD E., JR. *Response to Revolution: The United States and the Cuban Revolution, 1959–1961.* Chapel Hill: University of North Carolina Press, 1985. U.S. actions facilitated Castro's leftward turn.

WHITE, THEODORE H. *The Making of the President—1960.—1964.—1968.—1972.* New York: Atheneum, 1961, 1965, 1969, 1973. The campaigns and their journalistic developments. For a revised version of 1972, see his *Breach of Faith: The Fall of Richard Nixon* (New York: Atheneum, 1975).

WYATT, C. R. *Paper Soldiers: The American Press and the Vietnam War.* Chicago: University of Chicago Press, 1995. Well-documented refutation of the myth that the U.S. press caused the war's failure.

YOUNG, MARILYN B. *The Vietnam Wars, 1945–1990.* New York: Harper & Row, 1991. A global history of the entire conflict from beginning to end.

ZAROULIS, NANCY, AND GERALD SULLIVAN. *Who Spoke Up?: American Protest Against the War in Vietnam, 1963–1975.* New York: Doubleday, 1985. Nonstudent protests are also well covered.

ZIEGER, ROBERT H. *American Workers, American Unions, 1920–1985.* Baltimore: Johns Hopkins University Press, 1986. Unions grew from the 1930s, declined after 1968 election.

Books: Civil Rights Movement

ALBERT, PETER J., AND RONALD HOFFMAN, eds. *We Shall Overcome: Martin Luther King, Jr. and the Black Freedom Struggle.* New York: Pantheon Books, 1990. Essays by major authorities, including David J. Garrow and John Hope Franklin.

CARSON, CLAYBORNE. *In Struggle: SNCC and the Black Awakening of the 1960s.* Cambridge, MA: Harvard University Press, 1981. Based on extensive oral history and archival research.

GARROW, DAVID J. *Bearing the Cross: Martin Luther King, Jr., and the Southern Christian Leadership Conference.* New York: Morrow, 1986. The definitive study.

LAWSON, STEVEN F. *Running for Freedom: Civil Rights and Black Politics in America since 1941.* Philadelphia: Temple University Press, 1991. An interpretive synthesis that connects local and national civil rights efforts.

MCADAM, DOUG. *Freedom Summer.* New York: Oxford University Press, 1988. History of the 1964 Mississippi Freedom Summer campaign.

MEIER, AUGUST, AND ELLIOTT M. RUDWICK. *CORE: A Study in the Civil Rights Movement, 1942–1968.* Urbana: University of Illinois Press, 1973. The growth and the decline of one of the leading civil rights organizations.

OATES, STEPHEN B. *Let the Trumpet Sound: The Life of Martin Luther King, Jr.* New York: Harper & Row, 1982. Major biography.

PAYNE, CHARLES. *I've Got the Light of Freedom: The Organizing Tradition and the Mississippi Freedom Struggle.* Berkeley: University of California Press, 1995.

PERRY, BRUCE. *Malcolm: The Life of a Man Who Changed Black America.* Barrytown, NY and Station Hill, NY: Talman Co., 1991. Well-researched, readable biography.

VAN DEBURG, WILLIAM L. *New Day in Babylon: The Black Power Movement and American Culture, 1965–1975.* Chicago: University of Chicago Press, 1993. A key work.

Books: Gay and Lesbian History

D'EMILIO, JOHN. *Sexual Politics, Sexual Communities: The Making of a Homosexual Minority in the United States, 1940–1970.* Chicago: University of Chicago Press, 1983. A solid overview.

DUBERMAN, MARTIN, MARTHA VICINUS, AND GEORGE CHAUNCEY, JR., eds. *Hidden from History: Reclaiming the Gay and Lesbian Past.* New York: NAL Books, 1989.

DUBERMAN, MARTIN. *Stonewall.* New York: Dutton, 1993.

FADERMAN, LILLIAN. *Odd Girls and Twilight Lovers: A History of Lesbian Life in Twentieth-Century America.* New York: Penguin Books, 1991.

Books: Investigative Reporting, New Journalism, Radical and Underground Press

AARON, DANIEL. *Writers on the Left: Episodes in American Literary Communism.* New York: Harcourt Brace Jovanovich, 1961. Left-wing writers from 1912 to 1940s in *The Masses, Liberator, New Masses, Daily Worker,* and *Partisan Review.*

ARMSTRONG, DAVID. *A Trumpet to Arms: Alternative Media in America.* Los Angeles: J. P. Tarcher, 1981. Covers alternative and "underground" media.

BELFRAGE, CEDRIC, AND JAMES ARONSON. *Something to Guard: The Stormy Life of the "National Guardian," 1948–1967.* New York: Columbia University Press, 1978. By the editors of the non-Communist, radical paper.

BRESLIN, JIMMY. *The World According to Jimmy Breslin.* New York: Ticknor and Fields, 1984. Best of his *New York Daily News* columns.

CHRISTMAN, HENRY W. ed. *One Hundred Years of the "Nation."* New York: Macmillan, 1965.

CONLIN, JOSEPH R. ed. *The American Radical Press 1880–1960.* 2 vols. Westport, CT: Greenwood Press, 1974. Fifty-eight authors detail left-wing writing.

CONNERY, THOMAS B., ed. *A Sourcebook of American Literary Journalism.* Westport, CT: Greenwood, 1992. Thoughtful essays analyzing writers from Mark Twain to Truman Capote.

COOK, FRED J. *Maverick: Fifty Years of Investigative Reporting.* New York: Putnam's, 1984. Compelling writing.

COOPER, MARC. *Roll Over Che Guevara: Travels of a Radical Reporter.* London and New York: Verso, 1994. A wide-ranging collection of articles written mainly for the *Village Voice.*

COTTRELL, ROBERT C. *Izzy: A Biography of I. F. Stone.* New Brunswick, NJ: Rutgers University Press, 1992. A good introduction to the fabled journalist's life and work.

DENNIS, EVERETTE E., AND WILLIAM L. RIVERS. *Other Voices: The New Journalism in America.* San Francisco: Canfield, 1974. Identifies types of New Journalism and leading personalities.

DOWNIE, LEONARD. *The New Muckrakers.* Washington, DC: New Republic, 1977. Profiles of Stone, Woodward, Bernstein, Anderson, Hersh, McWilliams and others.

ETTEMA, JAMES S., AND THEODORE L. GLASSER. *Custodians of Conscience: Investigative Journalism and Public Virtue.* New York: Columbia University Press, 1998. Fruits of a decade's research.

GARRISON, DEE. *Mary Heaton Vorse: The Life of an American Insurgent.* Philadelphia: Temple University Press, 1989. Labor and war reporter for 35 years. Greenwich Village leader.

HARRINGTON, MICHAEL. *Socialism: Past and Future.* New York: Arcade Publishing, 1990. Harrington wrote *The Other America* in 1962, sparking JFK's war on poverty, and was a socialist intellectual.

KAUL, ARTHUR J., ed. *American Literary Journalists, 1945–1995.* Detroit: Gale Research, 1997. Biographies and bibliographies of the key figures.

KEITH, MICHAEL C. *Voices in the Purple Haze: Underground Radio and the Sixties.* Westport, CT: Praeger, 1997. Engaging oral history of some 30 of the most prominent figures in underground radio.

KERRANE, KEVIN, AND BEN YAGODA, eds. *The Art of Fact: A Historical Anthology of Literary Journalism.* New York: Scribner, 1997. Selections from 56 authors, mostly American with a few British, from Daniel Defoe to Joan Didion.

KESSLER, LAUREN. *The Dissident Press.* Beverly Hills: Sage, 1984. Examines the journalistic tradition of "other voices" over two centuries, including those of war resisters, radicals, feminists, utopians, immigrants, and blacks.

KLEJMENT, ANNE, AND ALICE KLEJMENT. *Dorothy Day and the "Catholic Worker": A Bibliography and Index.* New York: Garland, 1986.

KOPKIND, ANDREW. *The Thirty Years' War: Dispatches and Diversions of a Radical Journalist 1965–1994.* London and New York: Verso, 1995. The writings of one of the most perceptive and nonconforming American journalists.

LEAMER, LAURENCE. *The Paper Revolutionaries: The Rise of the Underground Press.* New York: Simon & Schuster, 1972. History of the 1960s with many reproductions. See also Robert J. Glessing, *The Underground Press in America* (Bloomington: Indiana University Press, 1970).

MAIK, THOMAS A. The Masses *Magazine: Odyssey of an Era.* New York: Garland, 1994. In-depth portrait of the famous radical magazine.

MCAULIFFE, KEVIN MICHAEL. *The Great American Newspaper: The Rise and Fall of the "Village Voice."* New York: Scribner's, 1978. One of first underground papers goes above ground.

MILLER, WILLIAM D. *Dorothy Day: A Biography.* New York: Harper & Row, 1982. The famous radical editor. See also Mel Piehl, *Breaking Bread: The Catholic Worker and the Origin of Catholic Radicalism in America* (Philadelphia: Temple University Press, 1983).

The Nation, special issue on the editorship of Carey McWilliams, December 2, 1978.

NEKOLA, CHARLOTTE, AND PAUL A. RABINOWITZ, eds. *Writing Red: An Anthology of American Women Writers, 1930–1940.* New York: Feminist Press, 1987. Biographical sketches and writings of 50 authors.

PECK, ABE. *Uncovering the Sixties: The Life and Times of the Underground Press.* New York: Pantheon, 1985. Entertaining account by a *Chicago Seed* editor turned professor.

ROBERTS, NANCY L. *Dorothy Day and the "Catholic Worker."* Albany: State University of New York Press, 1984. Best study of Day's journalistic influence.

———. *American Peace Writers, Editors, and Periodicals: A Dictionary.* Westport, CT: Greenwood Press, 1991. Profiles of more than 400 peace advocates and publications since colonial times; extensive bibliography.

SEEGER, ARTHUR. *The Berkeley Barb.* New York: Irvington, 1983. By its managing editor.

SIMS, NORMAN, ed. *Literary Journalism in the Twentieth Century.* New York: Oxford University Press, 1990. Covers the Hemingway era, the *New Yorker,* and New Journalism.

———. *The Literary Journalists.* New York: Ballantine, 1984. Well-conceptualized anthology of twentieth-century writers, including John McPhee, Tom Wolfe, and Joan Didion, with an excellent introductory essay.

SIMS, NORMAN, AND MARK KRAMER, eds. *Literary Journalism: A New Collection of the Best American Nonfiction.* New York: Ballantine, 1995. Excellent anthology that includes Joseph Mitchell, Jane Kramer, and many contemporary writers.

STEINEM, GLORIA. *Outrageous Acts and Everyday Rebellions.* New York: Holt, Rinehart & Winston, 1983. Autobiography of *Ms.* founder.

STONE, I. F. *Polemics and Prophecies 1967–1970.* New York: Random House, 1970.

———. *In a Time of Torment.* New York: Vintage, 1964. Collections of the writings of the distinguished independent journalist.

WACHSBERGER, KEN, ed. *Voices from the Underground.* Vol. 1, *Insider Histories of the Vietnam Era Underground Press.* Vol. 2, *A Directory of Sources and Resources on the Vietnam Era Underground Press.* (Tempe, AZ: Mica's Press, 1993). Detailed, scholarly participant case histories.

WITTNER, LAWRENCE S. *Rebels Against War: The American Peace Movement 1933–1983.* Philadelphia: Temple University Press, 1994.

WOLFE, TOM. *The New Journalism.* New York: Harper & Row, 1973. Defends the genre, traces the history, and reprints examples.

Books: Magazines

ABRAHAMSON, DAVID. *Magazine-Made America: The Cultural Transformation of the Postwar Periodical.* Cresskill, NJ: Hampton Press, 1996. Sociocultural context of the transformation of U.S. consumer magazines during the 1960s.

ALWOOD, EDWARD. *Straight News: Gays, Lesbians, and the News Media.* New York: Columbia University Press, 1996. The evolution of the relationship between gay men, lesbians, and the U.S. news media since World War II.

DOUDNA, MARTIN K. *Concerned about the Planet: The "Reporter" Magazine and American Liberalism, 1949–1968.* Westport, CT: Greenwood Press, 1977. Relates the magazine to the environment.

DRAPER, ROBERT. *"Rolling Stone" Magazine: The Uncensored History.* New York: Doubleday, 1990. Vivid portrait of Jann Wenner and his magazine.

GINGRICH, ARNOLD. *Nothing but People: The Early Days at Esquire.* New York: Crown Publishers, 1971. The founder's account of *Esquire*'s pioneering graphics and literary strengths.

HULSETHER, MARK. *Building a Protestant Left:* Christianity and Crisis *Magazine, 1941–1993.* Knoxville: University of Tennessee Press, 1999. Insightful study of religion, mass media, and the American political and social landscape.

LUTZ, CATHERINE A., AND JANE L. COLLINS. *Reading "National Geographic".* Chicago: University of Chicago Press, 1993. Shows how past and present editors have used photographs to reinforce popular U.S. views of life abroad.

MCWILLIAMS, CAREY. *The Education of Carey McWilliams.* New York: Simon & Schuster, 1978. By a great editor of *The Nation.*

OSMER, HAROLD H. *U.S. Religious Journalism and the Korean War.* Washington, DC: University Press of America, 1980. Follows Martin Marty's *The Religious Press in America* (1963).

ROSS, ROBERT W. *So It Was True: The American Protestant Press and the Persecution of the Jews.* Minneapolis: University of Minnesota Press, 1980. A scholarly study.

THOM, MARY. *Inside Ms.: 25 Years of the Magazine and the Feminist Movement.* New York: Henry Holt & Co., 1997. A critical, engaging account.

Books: Minorities and Ethnic Media

COWARD, JOHN M. *The Newspaper Indian: Native American Identity in the Press, 1820–90.* Urbana: University of Illinois Press, 1999. The nineteenth-century press's role in creating and publicizing Native American stereotypes such as the barbarian and the noble savage.

DANIEL, WALTER C., ed. *Black Journals of the United States.* Westport, CT: Greenwood Press, 1982. Contains narrative histories and a bibliography.

DATES, JANNETTE L., AND WILLIAM BARLOW, eds. *Split Image: African Americans in the Mass Media.* Washington, DC: Howard University Press, 1990. A study of the dual reflections of African Americans in the mass media: the self-image of blacks and the image created by whites.

DAWKINS, WAYNE. *Black Journalists: The NABJ Story.* Sicklerville, NJ: August Press, 1993. Covers the National Association of Black Journalists' founding years, 1975–83.

FARRAR, HAYWARD. *The "Baltimore Afro-American," 1892–1950.* Westport, CT: Greenwood, 1998. Based on his doctoral dissertation at the University of Chicago.

FINKLE, LEE. *Forum for Protest: The Black Press During World War II.* Cranbury, NJ: Fairleigh Dickinson University Press, 1975. Study of editorial policies and campaigns of major black newspapers.

HAYS, ROBERT G. *A Race at Bay:* New York Times *Editorials on the "Indian Problem," 1860–1900.* Carbondale: Southern Illinois University Press, 1997. A detailed sample of the nearly 1000 editorials, and analysis.

HENRITZE, BARBARA K. *Bibliographic Checklist of African American Newspapers.* Baltimore: Genealogical Publishing, 1990. Useful identifier of 5539 newspapers that may be available in various historical societies and state archives.

HOGAN, LAWRENCE D. *A Black National News Service: The Associated Negro Press and Claude Barnett, 1919–1945.* Cranbury, NJ: Fairleigh Dickinson University Press, 1984.

HUNTER-GAULT, CHARLAYNE. *In My Place.* New York: Farrar, Straus, & Giroux, 1992. Memoir of the first black woman student at the University of Georgia turned PBS news staffer.

KEEVER, BEVERLY ANN DEEPE, CAROLYN MARTINDALE, AND MARY ANN WESTON, eds. *U.S. News Coverage of Racial Minorities: A Sourcebook, 1934–1996.* Westport, CT: Greenwood Press, 1997. How the U.S. mainstream press historically has covered communities of color.

KERN-FOXWORTH, MARILYN. *Aunt Jemima, Uncle Ben, and Rastus: Blacks in Advertising, Yesterday, Today, and Tomorrow.* Westport, CT: Greenwood Press, 1994. Stereo-

typing throughout U.S. history, from slavery ads to network television.

LA BRIE, HENRY G., III. *A Survey of Black Newspapers in America.* Kennebunkport, ME: Mercer House Press, 1979. A 72 page listing, updating La Brie, *The Black Press in America: A Guide* (1970). Shows declines in the numbers of papers and circulations.

————, ed. *Perspectives of the Black Press: 1974.* Kennebunkport, ME: Mercer House Press, 1974. Thoughts of black editors.

MAYNARD, ROBERT C., WITH DORI J. MAYNARD. *Letters to My Children.* Kansas City, MO: Andrews and McMeel, 1995. Collection of Maynard's columns, 1980–1993.

MILLER, SALLY M., ed. *The Ethnic Press in the United States: A Historical Analysis and Handbook.* Westport, CT: Greenwood Press, 1987. Covers the foreign-language press of 27 ethnic areas.

MURPHY, JAMES E., AND SHARON M. MURPHY. *Let My People Know: American Indian Journalism 1828–1978.* Norman: University of Oklahoma Press, 1981. First comprehensive synthesis.

MURPHY, SHARON. *Other Voices: Black, Chicano, and American Indian Press.* Dayton, OH: Pflaum/Standard, 1974. A monograph using survey findings.

NELSON, JACK A., ed. *The Disabled, the Media, and the Information Age.* Westport, CT: Greenwood Press, 1994. Essays on stereotyping in print, film, and broadcasting.

PRIDE, ARMISTEAD S., AND CLINT C. WILSON II. *A History of the Black Press.* Washington, D.C.: Howard University Press, 1997. Covers the black press from its start in 1827 to the present, with attention to the development of New York City papers.

ROWAN, CARL. *Breaking Barriers: A Memoir.* Boston: Little, Brown, 1991. Reporter, columnist, diplomat, and black.

STREITMATTER, RODGER. *Unspeakable: The Rise of the Gay and Lesbian Press in America.* Boston, London: Faber & Faber, 1995. Well-researched social history.

SUGGS, HENRY LEWIS, ed. *The Black Press in the Middle West, 1865–1985.* Westport, CT: Greenwood Press, 1996. A companion to his *The Black Press in the South, 1865–1983* (Westport, Ct: Greenwood Press, 1983), with a third volume planned to cover the West.

————. *P. B. Young, Newspaperman.* Charlottesville: University Press of Virginia, 1988. Race, politics, and journalism in the New South, 1910–62. Young owned Norfolk's *Journal and Guide.*

TRAHANT, MARK N. *Pictures of Our Nobler Selves: A History of Native American Contributions to News Media.* Nashville, TN: Freedom Forum First Amendment Center, 1995. Brief, readable survey.

VECIANA-SUAREZ, ANA. *Hispanic Media, USA.* Washington, DC: Media Institute, 1987. National guide and directory of print and electronic areas.

WESTON, MARY ANN. *Native Americans in the News: Images of Indians in the Twentieth Century Press.* Westport, CT:

Greenwood Press, 1996. Analyzes how Native Americans have been depicted in the press, especially in the twentieth century.

WILLIAMS, GILBERT A. *Legendary Pioneers of Black Radio.* Westport, CT: Praeger, 1998. One-on-one interviews with Jack Gibson, "Joltin' Joe" Howard, and other male African American disk jockeys.

WILSON, CLINT C., II, AND FÉLIX GUTIÉRREZ. *Minorities and Media: Diversity and the End of Mass Communication.* Beverly Hills, CA: Sage Publications, Inc., 1985. Authors contend the media are no longer mass, but segmented, in relationships with minorities.

Books: Newspapers

ANGELO, FRANK. *On Guard: A History of the "Detroit Free Press."* Detroit: The Free Press, 1981. A 150-year review by a *Free Press* editor.

ASHLEY, PERRY J., ed. *American Newspaper Publishers, 1950–1990.* Detroit: Gale Research, 1993. Biographies and bibliographies of key figures.

BARLETT, DONALD L., AND JAMES B. STEELE. *America: What Went Wrong?* Kansas City, MO: Andrews & McMeel, 1992. *Philadelphia Inquirer* Pulitzer Prize–winners look at economic woes in a nine-part series reprinted as a book.

BECKER, STEPHEN. *Marshall Field III: A Biography.* New York: Simon & Schuster, 1964. Good portrait of the founder of *PM* and the *Chicago Sun.*

BERGER, MEYER. *The Story of the "New York Times," 1851–1951.* New York; Simon & Schuster, 1951. The best history of the *Times.*

BERGES, MARSHALL. *The Life and Times of Los Angeles.* New York: Atheneum, 1984. A friendly account of the *Los Angeles Times,* concentrating on the 1980s.

BOGART, LEO. *Press and Public.* Hillsdale, NJ: Eribaum. 1990. Analysis of readership studies.

BRADDON, RUSSELL. *Roy Thomson of Fleet Street.* London: Collins, 1965. A detailed and favorable portrait of a world press lord.

BRALEY, RUSS. *Bad News: The Foreign Policy of the "New York Times."* Chicago: Regnery Gateway, 1984. A longtime *New York Daily News* European correspondent takes aim at *Times* reportage he claims follows the paper's liberal editorial line.

BRAY, HOWARD. *The Pillars of the "Post."* New York: W. W. Norton, 1980. Emphasis is on personalities and office problems at the *Washington Post.*

BRENNER, MARIE. *House of Dreams: The Bingham Family of Louisville.* New York: Random House, 1988. Won the Mott-Kappa Tau Alpha research award.

BRODER, DAVID S. *Behind the Front Page.* New York: Simon & Schuster, 1987. Reminiscences of the *Washington Post* veteran correspondent and columnist.

CANHAM, ERWIN D. *Commitment to Freedom: The Story of the "Christian Science Monitor."* Boston: Houghton Mifflin, 1958. By the editor of the *Monitor.*

CATLEDGE, TURNER. *My Life and the "Times."* New York: Harper & Row, 1971. A readable autobiography of a capable newspaperman, reaching a climax with the struggle for "the kingdom and the power." Candid evidence given.

CHANEY, LINDSAY, AND MICHAEL CIEPLY. *The Hearsts: Family and Empire—The Later Years.* New York: Simon & Schuster, 1981. Hearst empire since his 1951 death.

CLAIBORNE, JACK. *The "Charlotte Observer": Its Time and Place, 1869–1986.* Chapel Hill: University of North Carolina Press, 1986. By the associate editor.

CONRAD, WILL C., KATHLEEN F. WILSON, AND DALE WILSON. *The "Milwaukee Journal": The First Eighty Years.* Madison: University of Wisconsin Press, 1964. A good newspaper history of a great daily.

COONEY, JOHN. *The Annenbergs: The Salvation of a Tainted Dynasty.* New York: Simon & Schuster, 1982. Moses and his son Walter (*TV Guide, Seventeen*).

"Christian Science Monitor," The First 80 Years. Boston: The *Monitor,* 1988. Contains the entire first issue and nearly 200 front pages.

COSE, ELLIS. *The Press.* New York: Morrow, 1988. Gossipy, episodic account of *New York Times, Los Angeles Times, Washington Post,* Gannett and Knight-Ridder.

DAVIS, DEBORAH. *Katharine the Great: Katharine Graham and the "Washington Post."* New York: Harcourt Brace Jovanovich, 1979. Treats both the woman and the publisher.

DRYFOOS, SUSAN W. *Iphigene: Memoirs of Iphigene Ochs Sulzberger of the "New York Times" Family.* New York: Dodd, Mead, 1981. Frank comments by the daughter, widow, and mother of three *Times* publishers, edited by a granddaughter.

EAGLES, CHARLES W. *Jonathan Daniels and Race Relations.* Knoxville: University of Tennessee Press, 1983. Evolution of a southern liberal at Raleigh.

Editor & Publisher, March 31, 1984. 100th anniversary edition; reprints from a century of issues.

EMERY, MICHAEL. *America's Leading Daily Newspapers: A Media Research Institute Survey.* Indianapolis: R. J. Berg & Co., 1983. In-depth report of a major poll and profiles of 15 top-ranking papers.

FELSENTHAL, CAROL. *Power, Privilege, and the "Post": The Katharine Graham Story.* New York: Putnam, 1993. An unhappy personal story in contrast to corporate success.

The Front Page, 1887–1980. New York: Arno Press, 1981. Reproduces 129 front pages of the old *Paris Herald* and the *International Herald Tribune.*

GHIGLIONE, LOREN, ed. *Gentlemen of the Press.* Indianapolis: News & Features Press, 1983. Editors' profiles drawn from pages of the *ASNE Bulletin.*

———, ed. *The Buying and Selling of America's Newspapers.* Indianapolis: R. J. Berg, 1984. Ten stories of sales.

GOTTLIEB, ROBERT, AND IRENE WOLT. *Thinking Big: The Story of the "Los Angeles Times," Its Publishers, and Their Influence on Southern California.* New York: Putnam's, 1977. Unauthorized work; relates development of the paper and city; critical.

GOULDEN, JOSEPH C. *Fit to Print: A. M. Rosenthal and His "Times."* Secaucus, NJ: Lyle Stuart, 1988. Triumphs and shortcomings of Abe.

GRAHAM, KATHARINE. *Personal History.* New York: Knopf, 1997. Engaging, insightful autobiography by the president of the Washington Post Company.

GRIFFIN, DICK, AND ROB WARDEN, eds. *Done in a Day: 100 Years of Great Writing from the "Chicago Daily News."* Chicago: Swallow Press, 1977.

HARRISON, JOHN M. *The "Blade" of Toledo: The First 150 Years.* Toledo, OH: The Blade, 1985. A readable history of a regional leader.

HART, JACK R. *The Information Empire: The Rise of the "Los Angeles Times" and the Times Mirror Corporation.* Washington, DC: University Press of America, 1981. A first-rate account, based on Hart's Ph.D. thesis, University of Wisconsin, 1975.

HART, JIM ALLEE. *A History of the "St. Louis Globe-Democrat."* Columbia: University of Missouri Press, 1961. Tells the story of St. Louis's "other paper" in a social and political framework.

HEARST, WILLIAM RANDOLPH, JR., WITH JACK CASSERLY. *The Hearsts, Father and Son.* Niwot, CO: Robert Rinehart, 1991. Defense of father; 100 rare photos.

HOHENBERG, JOHN. *The Pulitzer Prizes.* New York: Columbia University Press, 1974. A meticulous accounting of the first 714 awards. See also his *The Pulitzer Prize Story, II* (1980), a supplement covering 1959 to 1980.

HYNDS, ERNEST C. *American Newspapers in the 1980s.* New York: Hastings House, 1980. Detailed study.

JOHNSON, GERALD W., et al. *The Sunpapers of Baltimore.* New York: Knopf, 1937. An outstanding newspaper history over a 100-year span.

KEELER, ROBERT F. *"Newsday": A Candid History of the Respectable Tabloid.* New York: Morrow, 1990. Anecdotal account of first 50 years.

KERBY, WILLIAM F. *A Proud Profession.* Homewood, IL: Dow Jones-Irwin, 1981. By a leading editor of the *Wall Street Journal.*

KLUGER, RICHARD. *The Paper: The Life and Death of the "New York Herald Tribune."* New York: Knopf, 1986. A fascinating, yet detailed, account of *"The Trib"* by its last book editor; probably the best yet written about an American newspaper.

KOBRE, SIDNEY. *Development of American Journalism.* Dubuque: Wm. C. Brown, 1969. Traces in detail the twentieth-century histories of many leading newspapers.

KURTZ, HOWARD. *Media Circus: The Trouble with America's Newspapers.* New York: Times Books, 1993. Nationally known media critic for the *Washington Post* skims across a myriad of problems and controversies.

LEAPMAN, MICHAEL. *Arrogant Aussie: The Rupert Murdoch Story.* New York: Lyle Stuart, 1985. Brief account by a British newsman.

LYONS, LOUIS M. *Newspaper Story: One Hundred Years of the "Boston Globe."* Cambridge: MA: Harvard University Press, 1971. Much internal detail.

MARKHAM, JAMES W. *Bovard of the "Post-Dispatch."* Baton Rouge: Louisiana State University Press, 1954. A discerning biography.

MARTIN, RALPH G. *Cissy: The Extraordinary Life of Eleanor Medill Patterson.* New York: Simon & Schuster, 1979. Falls short in analyzing her journalistic role.

MARTIN, SHANNON E., AND KATHLEEN A HANSEN. *Newspapers of Record in a Digital Age: From Hot Type to Hot Link.* Westport, CT: Praeger, 1998. Superb, up-to-date analysis of the "newspaper of record" concept in the digital media environment, with excellent historical grounding.

McNULTY, JOHN B. *Older Than the Nation.* Stonington, CT: Pequot Press, 1964. A well presented, scholarly history of the *Hartford Courant* on its 200th birthday.

MEEKER, RICHARD H. *Newspaperman: S. I. Newhouse and the Business of News.* New York: Ticknor & Fields, 1983. Newspaper and magazine owner.

MILLER, ALAN ROBERT. *The History of Current Maine Newspapers.* Lisbon Falls, ME: Eastland Press, 1978. Excellent state history.

NEUHARTH, AL. *Confessions of an SOB.* New York: Doubleday, 1989. By Gannett's chairman.

POUND, REGINALD, AND GEOFFREY HARMSWORTH. *Northcliffe.* London: Cassell, 1959. Based on family papers, best of 15 biographies.

PRICE, WARREN C. *The "Eugene Register-Guard."* Portland, OR: Binford & Mort, 1976. A leading journalism scholar tells the story of a distinguished smaller daily as a citizen of its community and state.

PRICHARD, PETER. *The Making of McPaper: The Inside Story of "USA Today."* Kansas City, MO: Andrews, McMeel & Parker, 1987. An editor recounts tumultuous events and Neuharth's role.

PULLIAM, RUSSELL. *Gene Pulliam, Last of the Newspaper Titans.* Ottawa, IL: Jameson Books, 1984. An in-house biography.

PUSEY, MERLO J. *Eugene Meyer.* New York: Knopf, 1974. A prize-winning biography of the *Washington Post* publisher, father of Katharine Graham.

QUIRT, JOHN. *The Press and the World of Money.* Byron, CA: Anton/California Courier, 1993. The best look at the inner workings of America's business press and its top reporters.

RIVERS, WILLIAM L., AND DAVID M. RUBIN. *A Region's Press: Anatomy of Newspapers in the San Francisco Bay Area.* Berkeley: Institute of Governmental Studies, University of California, 1971. Contemporary study with some historical material.

ROBERTS, CHALMERS M. *In the Shadow of Power: The Story of the "Washington Post."* Washington, DC: Seven Locks Press, 1989. Updates 1977 edition.

ROBERTSON, CHARLES L. *"The International Herald Tribune": The First Hundred Years.* New York: Columbia University Press, 1987. See also his *"Everybody's*

Favorite Newspaper Turns 100," *Washington Journalism Review* (April 1987), 36.

ROSENBERG, JERRY MARTIN. *Inside the "Wall Street Journal."* New York: Macmillan, 1982. History of the *Journal* and assessment of its influence; some criticism.

RUCKER, BRYCE W., ed. *Twentieth-Century Reporting at Its Best.* Ames: Iowa State University Press, 1964. Good collection.

SAGE, JOSEPH. *Three to Zero: The Story of the Birth and Death of the "World Journal Tribune."* New York: American Newspaper Publishers Association, 1967. A brief analysis placing most blame for the fiasco on labor unions.

SALISBURY, HARRISON E. *Without Fear or Favor.* New York: Times Books, 1980. A personalized account of recent *Times* history, by one of its leading foreign correspondents.

————. *A Journey for Our Times* (New York: Harper & Row, 1983); and *A Time of Change* (Harper & Row, 1988), two volumes of memoirs.

SIM, JOHN CAMERON. *The Grass Roots Press: America's Community Newspapers.* Ames: Iowa State University Press, 1969. The most penetrating study of weeklies, rural and suburban, and their community roles.

SINGER, BRUCE., ed. *100 Years of the Paris "Trib."* New York: Harry Abrams, 1987. Brief text; 171 front pages reporting great events.

SLOAN, WM. DAVID, ed. *Pulitzer Prize Editorials: America's Best Editorial Writing, 1917–1979.* Ames: Iowa State University Press, 1980. Reprints and comments on winners.

SLOAN, WM. DAVID, VALARIE MCCRARY, AND JOHANNA CLEARY, eds. *The Best of Pulitzer Prize News Writing.* Columbus, OH: Publishing Horizons, Inc., 1986. Anthology of 71 winners.

SNYDER, LOUIS L., AND RICHARD B. MORRIS. *Treasury of Great Reporting.* New York: Simon & Schuster, 1962. Excellent historical work.

SQUIRES, JAMES D. *Read All About It: The Corporate Takeover of America's Newspapers.* New York: Times Books, 1993. Former *Chicago Tribune* editor condemns intrusion into editorial practices and fears the demise of newspapers.

STEWART, KENNETH, AND JOHN TEBBEL. *Makers of Modern Journalism.* Englewood Cliffs, NJ: Prentice Hall, 1952. Contains extensive comment on many of the newspapers and people covered in this chapter; see index.

TALESE, GAY. *The Kingdom and the Power.* New York: New American Library, 1969. Penetrating, informative recent history of the *New York Times.*

TIFFT, SUSAN E., AND ALEX S. JONES. *The Patriarch: The Rise and Fall of the Bingham Dynasty.* New York: Summit Books, 1991. Psychodrama of a feuding family.

WENDT, LLOYD. *The "Wall Street Journal": The Story of Dow Jones & the Nation's Business Newspaper.* Chicago: Rand McNally, 1982. Authorized history of the *Journal,* but written independently by a *Chicago Tribune* staff member and author.

————. *"Chicago Tribune": The Rise of a Great American Newspaper.* Chicago: Rand McNally, 1979. An 861-page

balanced, comprehensive look at the *Tribune* by a staff member who wrote independently.

WHITED, CHARLES. *Knight: A Publisher in the Tumultuous Century.* New York: E. P. Dutton, 1988. A readable biography of John S. Knight.

WILLIAMS, HAROLD A. *The "Baltimore Sun," 1837–1987.* Baltimore: Johns Hopkins University Press, 1987.

WILDS, JOHN. *Afternoon Story: The History of the "New Orleans States-Item."* Baton Rouge: Louisiana State University Press, 1976. A popular account of city's journalism.

Books: Columnists, Cartoonists

ALSOP, JOSEPH AND STEWART. *The Reporter's Trade.* New York: Reynal & Company, 1958. A discussion of Washington reporting and a compilation of the Alsop brothers' columns from 1946 to 1958.

BLOCK, HERBERT L. *The Herblock Gallery.* New York: Simon & Schuster, 1968. One of several collections of the great cartoonist's work; for his anti-Nixon best, see *Herblock Special Report* (New York: W. W. Norton, 1974).

CATER, DOUGLASS. *The Fourth Branch of Government.* Boston: Houghton Mifflin, 1959. Surveys the Washington press corps.

GRAUER, NEIL A. *Wits & Sages.* Baltimore, MD: Johns Hopkins University Press, 1984. Twelve popular 1980s columnists.

KRAMER, DALE. *Heywood Broun.* New York: A. A. Wyn, 1949. Biography of the Guild's founder, a famous columnist.

RIVERS, WILLIAM L. *The Opinionmakers.* Boston: Beacon Press, 1965. A top-flight study of Washington journalists. See also his *The Adversaries* (1970).

Books: Politics, Presidents, and Policies

BERNSTEIN, IRVING. *Promises Kept: John F. Kennedy's New Frontier.* New York: Oxford University Press, 1991. Emphasis on JFK's domestic problems and policies.

VAUGHN, DAVIS BORNET. *The Presidency of Lyndon B. Johnson.* Lawrence: University Press of Kansas, 1983. Detailed, readable volume in the American Presidency series.

CONKIN, PAUL K. *Big Daddy from the Pedernales: Lyndon Baines Johnson.* Boston: Twayne, 1986. Insightful biography.

KEARNS, DORIS. *Lyndon Johnson and the American Dream.* New York: Harper & Row, 1976. Engaging, well-researched account of Johnson's career.

REEVES, RICHARD. *President Kennedy: Profile of Power.* New York: Simon and Schuster, 1993. Readable, well-researched interpretation of Kennedy's three years in office.

Books: Protest Movements—General

ANDERSON, TERRY H. *The Movement and the Sixties.* New York: Oxford University Press, 1995. A balanced study with a national perspective.

BURNS, STEWART. *Social Movements of the 1960s: Searching for Democracy.* Boston: Twayne, 1990. A history of the four key social movements of the 1960s and early 1970s: black freedom and Black Power; New Left; anti-Vietnam War; feminist.

ISSERMAN, MAURICE. *If I Had a Hammer . . . : The Death of the Old Left and the Birth of the New Left.* New York: Basic Books, 1987. A reappraisal of twentieth-century American radicalism that sheds new light on the 1950s.

MILLER, JAMES. *"Democracy is in the Streets": From Port Huron to the Siege of Chicago.* Reprint ed. Cambridge, MA and London: Harvard University Press, 1994. A new introduction relates the 1960s to the 1990s.

SALE, KIRKPATRICK. *SDS.* New York: Vintage Books, 1983.

The Women's Movement

ECHOLS, ALICE. *Daring to Be Bad: Radical Feminism in America, 1967–1975* . Minneapolis: University of Minnesota Press, 1989. A vivid, well-researched account.

EVANS, SARA. *Personal Politics: The Roots of Women's Liberation in the Civil Rights Movement and the New Left.* New York: Vintage Books, 1978. An eyewitness account that has become a classic.

FREEMAN, JO. *The Politics of Women's Liberation: A Case Study of an Emerging Social Movement and Its Relation to the Policy Process.* New York: Longman, 1975. Social movements, public policy, and feminism.

GIDDINGS, PAULA. *When and Where I Enter: The Impact of Black Women on Race and Sex in America.* New York: Bantam Books, 1984. A narrative survey from the seventeenth century to the present.

HARRISON, CYNTHIA. *On Account of Sex: The Politics of Women's Issues, 1945–1968.* Berkeley: University of California Press, 1988. A study of policy made to serve women's rights.

Periodicals and Monographs

ARONSON, JAMES. "A Radical Journalist in the 1950's," *Nieman Reports,* XXIX (Spring and Summer 1975), 34, 16. Two-part recollection of his 19 years with the radical *National Guardian.*

BAILEY, GEORGE A., AND LAWRENCE W. LICHTY. "Rough Justice on a Saigon Street: A Gatekeeper Study of NBC's Tet Execution Film," *Journalism Quarterly,* XLIX (Summer 1972), p. 221. Step-by-step on the decision to use the execution episode.

BAIN, DAVID H. "Letter from Manila," *Columbia Journalism Review* (May–June 1986), 27. Scholarly account of how the press helped topple Marcos.

BECKER, ROBERT, et al. "The Charge of the Right Brigade," *Washington Journalism Review* (November 1981), 21. Graduate students survey the New Right press.

BERNER, R. THOMAS. "Literary Newswriting," *Journalism Monographs,* XCIX (October 1986). A succinct analysis of its history and style.

BROWNE, MALCOLM W. "Viet Nam Reporting: Three Years of Crisis," *Columbia Journalism Review,* III (Fall 1964), 4. By the AP senior correspondent in Saigon.

BURD, GENE. "Urban Magazine Journalism Thrives During City Crises," *Journalism Quarterly,* L (Spring 1973), 77. Muckraking spirit reborn in 1960s urban magazines. See also Ben L. Moon, "City Magazines, Past and Present," *Journalism Quarterly,* XLVII (Winter 1970).

CORNWELL, ELMER E., JR. "The Johnson Press Relations Style," *Journalism Quarterly,* XLIII (Spring 1966), 3. The press got much attention from LBJ.

DANIELSON, WAYNE A., AND JOHN B. ADAMS. "Completeness of Press Coverage of the 1960 Campaign," *Journalism Quarterly,* XXXVIII (Autumn 1961), 441. Sample of 90 dailies.

FERRETTI, FRED. "The White Captivity of Black Radio," *Columbian Journalism Review,* IX (Summer 1970), 35. Of 310 radio stations serving blacks at least in part, only 16 were owned by blacks.

FLANERY, JAMES A. "Chicago Newspapers' Coverage of the City's Major Civil Disorders of 1968," Ph.D. thesis, Northwestern University, 1971. Violence by police minimized in stories.

GRABER, DORIS A. "Press Coverage and Voter Reaction in the 1968 Presidential Election," *Political Science Quarterly,* LXXXIX (March 1974), 68. Study of 16 dailies found personalities emphasized.

GREENBERG, BRADLEY S., et al. "Local Newspaper Coverage of Mexican Americans," *Journalism Quarterly,* LX (Winter 1983), 671.

GUTIÉRREZ, FÉLIX F. "Spanish-Language Radio and Chicano Internal Colonialism," Ph.D. thesis, Stanford University, 1976. Non-Chicanos largely in charge.

———, ed. "Spanish-Language Media Issue," *Journalism History,* IV (Summer 1977).

———. "Marketing the News in Third World America," *Gannett Center Journal,* I:1 (Spring 1987), 88. Rise of market segmentation spurs Hispanic and black news coverage.

HALL, NORA D. "On Being an African-American Woman: Gender and Race in the Writings of Six Black Women Journalists, 1849–1936," Ph.D. thesis, University of Minnesota, 1998. Detailed, critical, award-winning analysis of six important figures, including Ida B. Wells Barnett and Mary Ann Shadd Cary.

HAUSMAN, LINDA WEINER. "Criticism of the Press in U.S. Periodicals, 1900–1939: An Annotated Bibliography," *Journalism Monographs,* IV (August 1967). What the magazines said about newspapers.

HENRY, WILLIAM A., III. "Don Hewitt: Man of the Hour," *Washington Journalism Review* (May 1986), 25. The producer of *60 Minutes.*

HIRSCH, PAUL M. "An Analysis of *Ebony:* The Magazine and Its Readers," *Journalism Quarterly,* XLV (Summer 1968), 261. Covers 1945 to 1966.

HOLDER, DENNIS. "The Little Journal That Did," *Washington Journalism Review* (April 1984), 51. The *Texas Observer.*

HUTCHISON, EARL R. "Kennedy and the Press: The First Six Months," *Journalism Quarterly,* XXXVIII (Autumn 1961), 453.

———. "John H. Johnson of *Ebony,*" *Nation's Business,* LXII (April 1974), 45.

KESSLER, LAUREN. "Against the American Grain: The Lonely Voice of *Politics* Magazine, 1944–1949," *Journalism History,* IX (Summer 1982), 49.

———. "Up the Creek Without a Paddle," *Quill* (November 1984), 40. Alternative journalism.

KOPKIND, ANDREW, "The Importance of Being Izzy," *Ramparts,* XII (May 1974), 39. I. F. Stone's *Weekly* (from 1953 to 1971) celebrated.

LA BRIE, HENRY G., III. "A Profile of the Black Newspaper Old Guard," Ph.D. thesis, University of Iowa, 1972. Based on 93 interviews.

———, AND WILLIAM J. ZIMA. "Directional Quandaries of the Black Press in the United States," *Journalism Quarterly,* XLVIII (Winter 1971), 640. Black editors reexamine the function of their press in an in-depth survey.

MARTINDALE, CAROLYN, et al., "Diversity in the Media: An Annotated Bibliography," *The Diversity Factor,* 53 (Spring 1997), 46–49.

MATHEWS, JAY. "Edgar Snow Told You So," *Washington Monthly,* July–August 1989. The Tiananmen Square crackdown should have come as no surprise.

McNULTY, THOMAS M. "Network Television Documentary Treatment of the Vietnam War, 1965 to 1969," Ph.D. thesis, Indiana University, 1974. Reaction to spot news, not preconceived notions, determined content.

McWILLIAMS, CAREY. "One Hundred Years of *The Nation,*" *Journalism Quarterly,* XLII (Spring 1965), 189. By the then-current editor.

MURPHY, JAMES E. "The New Journalism: A Critical Perspective," *Journalism Monographs,* XXXIV (May 1974). A careful attempt to define this approach to journalistic writing.

PALMER, L. F., JR. "The Black Press in Transition," *Columbia Journalism Review,* IX (Spring 1970), 31. A survey from 1945 to 1970.

PASADEOS, YORGO. "The Greek-American Press: A 90-Year Compendium," *Journalism Quarterly,* LXII (Spring 1985), 140. First newspaper begun in 1892.

PAYNE, DARWIN. "The Press Corps and the Kennedy Assassination," *Journalism Monographs,* XV (February 1970). Newspaper and broadcast performance at Dallas.

PROCHNAN, WILLIAM. "Vietnam: Halberstam's War," *Gannett Center Journal,* III (Fall 1989), 16. Excerpt from book on early Saigon reporters.

REICHLEY, A. JAMES. "How John Johnson Made It," *Fortune,* LXXVIII (January 1968), 152. Profile of the black publisher.

REILLY, TOM, ed. "American Indians and the Media," *Journalism History,* VI (Summer 1979). A special issue. See also "The Roots of Black Journalism," *Journalism History,* IV (Winter 1977–78), another special issue.

"Remembering Bobby," *Newsweek,* May 9, 1988. A special report on Robert Kennedy's legacy.

RILEY, SAM G. "*Indian Journal,* Voice of Creek Tribe, Now Oklahoma's Oldest Newspaper," *Journalism Quarterly,* LIX (Spring 1982), 46.

———. "Alex Posey: Creek Indian Editor/Humorist, Poet," *American Journalism,* I:2 (1984), 67. Editor of *Indian Journal,* 1902–08.

ROBERTS, NANCY L. "Journalism for Justice: Dorothy Day and the *Catholic Worker,*" *Journalism History,* X (Spring–Summer 1983), 2. The noted pacifist editor.

SAUNDERS, SUSAN. "Berkeley's Free Speech Movement: A Study of Press Reaction to First Amendment Issues," Ph.D. thesis, University of Washington, 1989. Press did not defend students' rights.

SCHOENFELD, A. CLAY. "The Environmental Movement as Reflected in American Magazines," *Journalism Quarterly,* LX (Autumn 1983), 470. Historical review of specialized environmental magazines and study of the 1960s–70s.

SEVAREID, ERIC. "The Power and the Press," *Nieman Reports,* XXXVIII:3 (Autumn 1984), 4. Reflections on his 50-year career.

SINGERMAN, ROBERT. "The American Jewish Press, 1823–1983: A Bibliographic Survey of Research and Studies," *American Jewish History,* LXXIII (June 1984).

"The Spanish-Language Media," special report in the *Washington Journalism Review* (November 1980), 21. Three articles on television and newspapers.

SPAULDING, NORMAN W. "History of Black-Oriented Radio in Chicago 1929–1963," Ph.D. thesis, University of Illinois, 1981. Black radio is a cultural common denominator.

STEMPEL, GUIDO H., III. "The Prestige Press in Two Presidential Elections," *Journalism Quarterly,* XLII (Winter 1965), 15. Study of 15 leading papers' news coverage in 1960 and 1964.

———. "The Prestige Press Meets the Third-Party Challenge," *Journalism Quarterly,* XLVI (Winter 1969), 685. Coverage of 1968 campaign by 15 major dailies.

"A Surging New Spirit," *Time,* July 11, 1988. The Hispanic influence is exploding into the American cultural mainstream.

TEEL, LEONARD RAY. "W. A. Scott and the *Atlanta World,*" *American Journalism,* VI (1989), 158. The first successful black daily.

"Tracing the Roots of the New Journalism," a symposium by Warren T. Francke, Jay Jensen, Joseph M. Webb, and Frederick D. Buchstein, in *Journalism History,* I (Summer 1974).

WHITEFIELD, STEPHEN J. "The Jewish Contribution to American Journalism," *American Journalism,* III:2 (1986), 99. An overview documenting its impact.

WILSON, NOEL AVON. "The *Kansas City Call:* An Inside View of the Negro Market," Ph.D. thesis, University of Illinois, 1968. History and influence.

CHAPTER 18: A CRISIS OF CREDIBILITY

Books: Politics and Press, Watergate

BARRETT, MARVIN, ed. *The Politics of Broadcasting.* New York: Thomas Y. Crowell, 1973. This fourth duPont-Columbia University survey finds that Nixon intimidated the press.

———, ed. *Moments of Truth.* New York: Thomas Y. Crowell, 1975. Fifth duPont-Columbia survey of broadcast journalism compresses the story of the 1973–75 confrontation.

BERNSTEIN, CARL, AND BOB WOODWARD. *All the President's Men.* New York: Simon & Schuster, 1974. The *Washington Post* reporters tell how they laid the groundwork for toppling Nixon; transformed into a top-ranking motion picture. See also Bob Woodward and Carl Bernstein, *The Final Days* (New York; Simon & Schuster, 1976).

BRESLIN, JIMMY. *How the Good Guys Finally Won.* New York: Viking, 1975. A great reporter produces one of the best step-by-step accounts of the Nixon impeachment.

CALIFANO, JOSEPH A., JR. *The Triumph and Tragedy of Lyndon Johnson: The White House Years.* New York: Simon & Schuster, 1991. By LBJ's close political adviser; balanced.

CANNON, LOU. *President Reagan: The Role of a Lifetime.* New York: Simon & Schuster, 1991. "Simply an actor on loan from Hollywood," says a correspondent for the *Washington Post* in a detailed biography.

CARTER, JIMMY. *Keeping Faith.* New York: Bantam Books, 1982. Presidential memoirs. See also Hamilton Jordan, *Crisis: The Last Year of the Carter Presidency* (New York: Putnam's 1982). The Iran hostage negotiations from the inside.

HERMAN, EDWARD S., AND NOAM CHOMSKY. *Manufacturing Consent: The Political Economy of the Mass Media.* New York: Pantheon, 1988. Authors maintain media are propagandists for right-wing elements, covering up errors and deceptions in U.S. foreign policy.

HERTSGAARD, MARK. *On Bended Knee: The Press and the Reagan Presidency.* New York: Farrar, Straus & Giroux, 1989. The press presented Reagan in favorable situations, shied away from exposures.

JENSEN, CARL. *Censored: The News That Didn't Make the News—and Why.* New York: Four Walls, Eight Windows, 1994. The annual yearbook of Project Censored.

KUTLER, STANLEY I. *The Wars of Watergate.* New York: Knopf, 1990. A distinguished historian "wraps it up," with a synthesis in perspective.

LANG, GLADYS ENGEL, AND KURT LANG. *The Battle for Public Opinion: The President, the Press, and the Polls during Watergate.* New York: Columbia University Press, 1983. An excellent survey of the role of the media and public reaction.

LEE, MARTIN A., AND NORMAN SOLOMON. *Unreliable Sources: A Guide to Detecting Bias in the News Media.* Secaucus, NJ: Lyle Stuart, 1990. Charges from a liberal perspective that the media are messenger services for government and businesses placating conservatives.

MAYER, JANE, AND DOYLE MCMANUS. *Landslide: The Unmaking of the President, 1984–1988.* Boston: Houghton Mifflin, 1988. The unraveling of the Reagan presidency, depicted by correspondents.

OUDES, BRUCE, ed. *From: The President: Richard Nixon's Secret Files.* New York: Harper & Row, 1989. Excerpts reprinted in *Columbia Journalism Review,* May–June 1989, covering networks.

The Pentagon Papers. New York: Bantam, 1971. Publication in paperback of the decisions and documents, edited by the *New York Times.*

PORTER, WILLIAM E. *Assault on the Media: The Nixon Years.* Ann Arbor: University of Michigan Press, 1976. Penetrating analysis of the 1969–72 Nixon-Agnew assault on the media.

ROZELL, MARK J. *The Press and the Bush Presidency.* Westport, CT: Praeger, 1996. Between 1988 and 1992, print news media did not treat Bush sympathetically.

RUDENSTINE, DAVID. *The Day the Presses Stopped: A History of the Pentagon Papers Case.* Berkeley, CA: University of California, 1996. A balanced, definitive analysis.

SCHLESINGER, ARTHUR M., JR. *The Cycles of American History.* Boston: Houghton Mifflin, 1986. Discerning essays on past and future U.S. policies.

SHILTS, RANDY. *And the Band Played On: Politics, People, and the AIDS Epidemic.* New York: St. Martin's Press, 1987. Political and social aspects of the disease, which public policy makers at first did not take seriously.

STOLER, PETER. *The War Against the Press: Politics, Pressure and Intimidation in the 1980s.* New York: Dodd, Mead, 1987. Press urged to fight back more aggressively.

TAYLOR, PAUL. *See How They Run: Electing the President in an Age of Mediacracy.* New York: Knopf, 1990. The 1988 election. See also Sidney Blumenthal, *Pledging Allegiance: The Last Campaign of the Cold War* (New York: HarperCollins, 1990). Both authors are *Washington Post* reporters.

Watergate: Chronology of a Crisis. Washington: Congressional Quarterly, 1975. A thousand-page documentary study on a week-by-week basis.

WILLS, GARY. *Reagan's America: Innocents at Home.* New York: Doubleday, 1987. Comprehensive, interpretive biography showing effects of movie career on presidency.

WISE, DAVID. *The Politics of Lying.* New York: Vintage Books, 1973. A veteran journalist traces the credibility gap, from the U-2 to Watergate.

WOODWARD, BOB. *VEIL: The Secret Wars of the CIA, 1981–1987.* New York: Simon & Schuster, 1987. A prime source is Director William Casey.

Books: Foreign Affairs

ARNETT, PETER. *Live from the Battlefield.* New York: Simon & Schuster, 1994. The personal story of this premier correspondent, from Vietnam to Baghdad.

ATKINSON, RICK. *Crusade: The Untold Story of the Persian Gulf War.* New York: Houghton Mifflin, 1993. Highly detailed description of U.S. senior commanders and their war machine.

BILL, JAMES A. *The Eagle and the Lion: The Tragedy of American-Iranian Relations.* New Haven: Yale University Press, 1988. Scholarly overview.

BESCHLOSS, MICHAEL R., AND STROBE TALBOTT. *At the Highest Levels.* Boston: Little, Brown, 1993. By CNN commentator and *Time* columnist; inside details of U.S.-Soviet affairs during Bush-Gorbachev years.

BLACK, ERIC. *Parallel Realities: A Jewish/Arab History of Israel/Palestine.* Minneapolis: Paradigm Press, 1992. Excellent background; balanced to show both sides.

BONNER, RAYMOND. *Waltzing with a Dictator: The Marcoses and the Making of American Foreign Policy.* New York: Times Books, 1987. U.S. policy makers play on the public's fear of Communism to support dictators against militant nationalists who threaten to deprive American business interests of their special privileges.

———. *Weakness and Deceit: U.S. Policy and El Salvador.* New York: Times Books, 1984. By a former *New York Times* reporter who covered the region.

BRANDON, HENRY. *Special Relationships: A Foreign Correspondents's Memoirs from Roosevelt to Reagan.* New York: Atheneum, 1989. Washington correspondent for the *Sunday Times* of London, 1945–83.

BRITTON, JOHN A. *Carleton Beals: A Radical Journalist in Latin America.* Albuquerque: University of New Mexico Press, 1987. A prophet without honor in his own country.

BROWNE, MALCOLM. *Muddy Boots and Red Socks.* New York: Times Books, 1993. The memoirs of the famed AP and *New York Times* correspondent.

BUCKLEY, KEVIN. *Panama: The Whole Story.* New York: Simon & Schuster, 1991. *Newsweek* correspondent traces Noriega involvement and the invasion debacle.

BURTON, SANDRA. *Impossible Dream: The Marcoses, the Aquinos, and the Unfinished Revolution.* New York: Warner Books, 1989. By a *Time* staffer.

CHOMSKY, NOAM. *Turning the Tide: U.S. Intervention in Central America and the Struggle for Peace.* Boston: South End Press, 1985. Strong attack against governmental deceits and media failures.

———. *The Fateful Triangle: The United States, Israel and the Palestinians.* Boston: South End Press, 1983. History and media analysis of the 1982 invasion of Lebanon.

———. *World Orders Old and New.* New York: Columbia University Press, 1994. Cites falsehoods and the cheerleading of establishment media; updated through Haiti.

CLARK, RAMSEY. *The Fire This Time.* New York: Thunder's Mouth Press, 1992. International lawyer bitterly criticizes Gulf War policy and media coverage.

COHEN, WILLIAM S., AND GEORGE J. MITCHELL. *Men of Zeal.* New York: Viking, 1988. A candid inside story of the Iran-Contra hearings.

DENNIS, EVERETTE E., et al. *The Media at War: The Press and the Persian Gulf Conflict.* New York: The Freedom Forum Studies Center, 1991. The most detailed study of attitudes of correspondents and editors about pool systems and barriers to full coverage; lists correspondents and news organizations.

DICKEY, CHRISTOPHER. *With the Contras: A Reporter in the Wilds of Nicaragua.* New York: Simon & Schuster, 1986. By a *Washington Post* correspondent, 1980–83.

DIEDERICH, BERNARD. *Somoza and the Legacy of U.S. Involvement in Central America.* Maplewood, NJ: Waterfront Press, 1989. Personal account of the Managua press corps veteran gives the background for the U.S.-supported Contra war.

DRAPER, THEODORE. *A Very Thin Line: The Iran-Contra Affairs.* New York: Hill & Wang, 1991. Detailed exposure of Reagan era illegalities.

ECHIKSON, WILLIAM. *Lighting the Night: Revolution in Eastern Europe.* New York: Morrow, 1990. By the *Christian Science Monitor* correspondent. See also his *The Collapse of Communism* (*New York Times* Books, 1990).

EMERY, MICHAEL. *On the Front Lines: Following America's Foreign Correspondents Across the Twentieth Century.* Washington, DC: American University Press, 1995. Traces barriers to news flow during seven periods; argues against cuts in foreign news; focuses on reporting achievements, government and self-censorship, propaganda.

FIALKA, JOHN. *Hotel Warriors: Covering the Gulf War.* Washington, DC: The Woodrow Wilson Center Press, 1992. A lively rundown of high and low points in press coverage.

FREEDMAN, LAWRENCE, AND EFRAIM KARSH. *The Gulf Conflict 1990–1991: Diplomacy and War in the New World Order.* Princeton: Princeton University Press, 1993. Focuses on the five months of gamesmanship that preceded the war against Iraq.

FRIEDMAN, ROBERT I. *Zealots for Zion: Israel's West Bank Settler Movement.* New York: Random House, 1992. Veteran journalist writes from personal experiences.

FRIEDMAN, THOMAS L. *From Beirut to Jerusalem.* New York: Farrar, Straus & Giroux, 1989. An account of his ten years of interpretive reporting for the *New York Times* that won him two Pulitzer Prizes.

GJELTEN, TOM. *Sarajevo Daily: A City and Its Newspaper Under Siege.* New York: HarperCollins, 1995. The miracle of publishing under cannon fire.

GLENNY, MISHA. *The Fall of Yugoslavia: The Third Balkan War.* New York: Penguin Books, 1992. The BBC's Central European reporter traces the breakup of Yugoslavia, 1990–92.

GREENBERG, BRADLEY, AND WALTER GANTZ, eds. *Desert Storm and the Mass Media.* Cresskill, NJ: Hampton Press, 1993. Collection of articles on different aspects.

HONEY, MARTHA. *Hostile Acts: U.S. Policy in Costa Rica in the 1980s.* Gainesville: University Press of Florida, 1994. Definitive work on this period.

HOURANI, ALBERT. *A History of the Arab Peoples.* Cambridge, MA: Harvard University Press, 1991. Best contribution to Arab studies in two decades, said the History Book Club. Gulf War made it a best seller.

KARNOW, STANLEY. *In Our Image: America's Empire in the Philippines.* New York: Random House, 1989. Panoramic overview from 1521 to Cory Aquino.

KELLNER, DOUGLAS. *The Persian Gulf TV War.* Boulder, CO: Westin Press, 1992. A leading critic of the war's media coverage documents the one-sided presentations.

KINZER, STEPHEN. *Blood of Brothers: Life and War in Nicaragua.* New York: Putnam's, 1991. Fascinating contemporary history of Sandinista decade (1979–89) by a witness, the *New York Times*'s Managua bureau chief.

LAMB, DAVID. *The Arabs: Journeys Beyond the Mirage.* New York: Random House, 1987. The author of this well-crafted, thoughtful study of the Arab peoples—a veteran *Los Angeles Times* correspondent—believes that many Middle East problems can be attributed to ignorance in the West of Arab culture, history, and legitimate rights.

LEDERMAN, JIM. *Battle Lines: The American Media and the Intifada.* New York: Henry Holt and Company, 1992. Analysis of the coverage of the Palestinian revolt against Israeli rule; covers December 1987–June 1988.

MACARTHUR, JOHN. *Second Front: Censorship and Propaganda in the Gulf War.* New York: Hill and Wang, 1992. *Harper's* publisher bitterly criticizes news managers and reporters.

MOORE, MOLLY. *A Woman at War.* New York: Charles Scribner's Sons, 1993. *Washington Post* reporter, the only woman on the front lines in Saudi Arabia, offers a fascinating interpretation of the build-up to war.

MOWLANA, HAMID, GEORGE GERBNER, AND HERBERT I. SCHILLER. *Triumph of the Image: The Media's War in the Persian Gulf—A Global Perspective.* Boulder: Westview Press, 1992. Twenty full-length articles and shorter pieces by academics and journalists from 18 nations.

PARRY, ROBERT. *Fooling Around: How Washington Insiders Twist the Truth and Manufacture Conventional Wisdom.* New York: William Morrow and Company, 1992. Startling evidence of media bias during Iran-Contra and other events.

PEDELTY, MARK. *War Stories: The Culture of Foreign Correspondents.* New York: Routledge, 1995. The lives and work of reporters in El Salvador by an anthropologist who accompanied them into the field and observed them in the office.

RIEFF, DAVID. *Slaughterhouse: Bosnia and the Failure of the West.* New York: Simon & Schuster, 1995. A shocking tale of complacency that allowed murder and dislocation.

SAID, EDWARD S. *Covering Islam.* New York: Pantheon, 1981. Critical analysis and cultural explanations; includes the Iran story.

SALISBURY, HARRISON E. *Heroes of My Time.* New York: Walker & Company, 1993. The 29th and last book in a 65-year career; recollections of famous people met along the way.

———. *The New Emperor: China in the Era of Mao and Deng.* Boston: Little, Brown, 1992. Insider interviews produce top-flight vivid history.

SCHIFF, ZA'EV, AND EHUD YA'ARI. *Intifada: The Palestinian Uprising—Israel's Third Front.* New York: Simon & Schuster, 1990. Two Israeli journalists cover events since 1967, showing an understanding of the Palestinian dilemma.

SCHLESINGER, STEPHEN, AND STEPHEN KINZER. *Bitter Fruit.* Garden City, NY: Anchor Books, 1982. Highly praised investigative account of the 1954 CIA coup in Guatemala.

SICK, GARY. *All Fall Down: America's Tragic Encounter with Iran.* New York: Random House, 1985. Details of 1978–81 events.

SMITH, HEDRICK. *The New Russians.* New York: Random House, 1990. By longtime correspondent.

ULAM, ADAM B. *The Communists: The Story of Power and Lost Illusions, 1948–1991.* New York: Scribner's, 1992. Summation of the Harvard scholar's studies of Communism, featuring Stalin, Tito, Mao, and Gorbachev.

WOODWARD, BOB. *The Commanders.* New York: Simon & Schuster, 1991. Detailed report of how Bush planned for war in the Gulf.

WIENER, ROBERT. *Live from Baghdad: Gathering News at Ground Zero.* New York: Doubleday, 1992. By the CNN producer in Baghdad; covers August 1990–January 1991.

YERGIN, DANIEL. *The Prize: The Epic Quest for Oil, Money, and Power.* New York: Simon & Schuster, 1990. The historical trail ends in Saudi Arabia.

Books: Washington Reporting, Media Performance

CROUSE, TIMOTHY. *The Boys on the Bus: Riding with the Campaign Press Corps.* New York; Random House, 1973. The reporters' wolf pack and their presidential quarries.

DEAKIN, JAMES. *Straight Stuff: The Reporters, the White House, and the Truth.* New York: Wm. Morrow, 1984. *St. Louis Post-Dispatch* White House correspondent of 1965–80 offers an anecdotal account.

DONALDSON, SAM. *Hold On, Mr. President!* New York: Random House, 1987. ABC's White House correspondent tells how it was.

GANS, HERBERT J. *Deciding What's News: A Study of CBS Evening News, NBC Nightly News, Newsweek, & Time.* New York: Pantheon, 1979. Content analysis.

GRIDER, WILLIAM. *Who Will Tell the People: The Betrayal of American Democracy.* New York: Simon & Schuster, 1992. A scathing review of recent media coverage.

HALBERSTAM, DAVID. *The Powers That Be.* New York: Knopf, 1979. Lengthy accounts of CBS News and William Paley, *Time* and Henry Luce, the *Washington Post* and the Grahams, the *Los Angeles Times* and the Chandlers.

HESS, STEPHEN. *The Washington Reporters.* Washington, DC: Brookings Institution, 1981. A critical, factually detailed analysis. See also Michael B. Grossman and Martha J. Kumar, *Portraying the President: The White House and the News Media* (Baltimore: Johns Hopkins University Press, 1981). Institutional analysis.

McClendon, Sarah. *My Eight Presidents.* New York: Wyden Books, 1978. View from the woman with the embarrassing questions at press conferences.

Powell, Jody. *The Other Side of the Story.* New York: William Morrow, 1984. Carter's press secretary dissects White House coverage in lively style.

Reston, James. *Deadline: A Memoir.* New York: Random House, 1991. Fifty years of *New York Times* leadership; forceful comments about failures of the Vietnam era.

Rivers, William L. *The Other Government: Power and the Washington Media.* New York: Universe, 1982. Updating of his studies of the capital press corps.

Robinson, Michael J., and Margaret A. Sheehan. *Over the Wire and on TV: CBS and UPI in Campaign '80.* Beverly Hills, CA: Sage, 1983. Lively comparison,

Rosen, Jay, and Paul Taylor. *The New News vs. the Old News: The Press and Politics in the 1990s.* New York: Twentieth Century Fund, 1992. Essays analyzing campaigns to mid-1992.

Spear, Joseph. *Presidents and the Press: The Nixon Legacy.* Cambridge, MA: MIT press, 1984. Nixon led the way in press manipulation.

Thomas, Helen. *Dateline: White House.* New York: Macmillan, 1975. UPI's top correspondent.

Willis, Jim. *The Shadow World: Life between the News Media and Reality.* New York: Praeger, 1991. A detailed look at agenda-setting and self-censorship, including foreign news.

Books: Broadcasting

Auletta, Ken. *Three Blind Mice: How the TV Networks Lost Their Way.* New York: Random House, 1991. Consequences of 1986 takeovers; ABC fared best.

Barrett, Marvin, et al., eds. *Broadcast Journalism, 1979–1981: The Eighth Alfred I. duPont/Columbia University Survey.* New York: Everest House, 1982. The first survey was published in 1968; issued every two years.

Baughman, James L. *Television's Guardians: The FCC and the Politics of Programming, 1958–1967.* Knoxville: University of Tennessee Press, 1984. The FCC fell captive to the industry it was to regulate.

Block, Alex Ben. *Outfoxed: Marvin Davis, Barry Diller, Rupert Murdoch, Joan Rivers, and the Inside Story of America's Fourth Television Network.* New York: St. Martin's Press, 1990. A lively account of Fox.

Campbell, Richard. *60 Minutes and the News: A Mythology for Middle America.* Champaign: University of Illinois Press, 1991. Reporters please viewers by performing as detectives, analysts, tourists, or arbiters. Overall, a favorable account.

Diamond, Edwin, and Stephen Bates. *The Spot: The Rise of Political Advertising on Television.* Cambridge, MA: MIT Press, 1988.

Donahue, Hugh Carter. *The Battle to Control Broadcast News.* Cambridge, MA: MIT Press, 1989. First Amendment problems chronicled.

Epstein, Edward J. *News from Nowhere: Television and the News.* New York: Random House, 1973. The organization and economics of television news.

Friendly, Fred W. *The Good Guys, the Bad Guys, and the First Amendment.* New York: Random House, 1975, 1976. Attack on the "fairness doctrine."

Gelfman, Judith S. *Women in Television News.* New York: Columbia University Press, 1976. Interviews with 30 newswomen, including Barbara Walters, Pauline Frederick and Lesley Stahl.

Gerbner, George, et al. *Violence Profile No. 7: Trends in Network Drama and Viewer Conceptions of Social Reality, 1967–1975.* Philadelphia: Annenberg School of Communication, 1976. Violence diminished little, "family hour" proved ineffective.

Gitlin, Todd. *Inside Prime Time.* New York: Pantheon, 1985. Discerning criticism of television's past decade; very readable.

Gunther, Marc. *The House That Roone Built.* Boston: Little, Brown, 1994. Detailed look at Arledge's maneuvers that built ABC into a media power.

Hammond, Charles M., Jr. *The Image Decade: Television Documentary, 1965–1975.* New York: Hastings House, 1981. Updates earlier studies.

Hewitt, Don. *Minute by Minute.* New York: Random House, 1985. By the producer of CBS's *60 Minutes.*

Jacobs, Jerry. *Changing Channels.* Mountain View, CA; Mayfield, 1990. Issues and realities in television news.

Kuralt, Charles. *On the Road with Charles Kuralt.* New York: Putnam's, 1985. Human interest for CBS.

Looker, Thomas. *The Sound and the Story: NPR and the Art of Radio.* Boston: Houghton Mifflin, 1994. What it takes to get some of radio's best shows on the air.

MacNeil, Robert. *The Right Place at the Right Time.* Boston: Little, Brown, 1982. By PBS co-anchor.

Matusow, Barbara. *The Evening Stars.* Boston: Houghton Mifflin, 1983. Lively portraits of anchor persons.

Montgomery, Kathryn C. *Target Prime Time: Advocacy Groups and the Struggle over Entertainment Television.* New York; Oxford University Press, 1989. Survey begins in the 1970s.

Rather, Dan, with Mickey Herskowitz. *The Camera Never Blinks.* New York: Moffow, 1977. The candid autobiography of the CBS anchor. See also their *The Camera Never Blinks Twice* (New York: William Morrow, 1994). Covers the later period.

Schoenbrun, David. *On and Off the Air: An Informal History of CBS News.* New York: E. P. Dutton, 1989. Views and anecdotes since 1940.

Schorr, Daniel. *Clearing the Air.* Boston: Houghton Mifflin, 1982. CBS stormy petrel tells his side of controversies and reviews his career.

Whittemore, Hank. *CNN: The Inside Story.* Boston: Little, Brown, 1990. An up-and-down account, primarily of early years.

Periodicals and Monographs

ALEXANDER, S. L. " 'May the Good News Be Yours,' Ralph Renick and Florida's First TV News." *Mass Comm Review,* 1992. He delivered 50,000 editorials in his 35 years on the air.

ALLMAN, T. D. "PBS's Vietnam: How TV Caught the Unprintable Truth," *Channels of Communication* (November–December 1983), 10.

ARMSTRONG, SCOTT. "Iran-Contra: Was the Press Any Match for All the President's Men?" *Columbia Journalism Review* (May–June 1990), 27. Critical.

AULETTA, KEN. "Why ABC Survived Best," *New York Times Magazine,* July 28, 1991, p. 20. Events at ABC News, 1986–91, in the wake of 1986 network takeovers.

BATTIATA, MARY. "Lesley Stahl," *Washington Journalism Review* (October 1982), 43. White House correspondent for CBS; now with *60 Minutes.*

BLONSKY, MARSHALL. "Ted Koppel's Edge," *New York Times Magazine,* August 14, 1988. His aggressive interviewing causes listeners to examine their consciences.

BOOT, WILLIAM. "Campaign '88: TV Overdoses on the Inside Dope," *Columbia Journalism Review* (January 1989), 23. Dukakis-bashing.

———. "Iranscam: When the Cheering Stopped," *Columbia Journalism Review* (March–April 1987), 25. Collapse of the Reagan "great leader" legend. See also Martha Honey, "Contra Coverage—Paid for by the CIA," ibid., 31.

BOYLAN, JAMES. "Declaration of Independence," *Columbia Journalism Review* (November–December 1986), 29. Perceptive review of reporters' efforts, 1961–86, in the 25th anniversary issue of *CJR.*

BRITTON, JOHN. "Carleton Beals and Central America After Sandino: Struggle to Publish," *Journalism Quarterly,* LX (Summer 1983), 240. Very few cared for the truth.

"The Broadcast Media and the Political Process: 1976," *Broadcasting,* XCII (January 3, 1977), 33–76. A special issue on all aspects of the Ford-Carter campaign.

BROWNE, MALCOLM W. "The Military vs. the Press," *New York Times Magazine,* March 3, 1991, p. 27. By veteran *Times* war correspondent. See also William Prochnau, "If There's a War, He's There," ibid., 30. An account of Peter Arnett.

CAPO, JAMES A. "Network Watergate Coverage Patterns in Late 1972 and 1973," *Journalism Quarterly,* LX (Winter 1983), 595.

Columbia Journalism Review (March–April 1991); *Washington Journalism Review* (March 1991); and *Washington Monthly* (April 1991); devoted their entire issues to coverage of the Gulf War.

ELLIOTT, OSBORN. "And That's the Way It Is," *Columbia Journalism Review* (May–June 1980), 50. An interview with the retiring Walter Cronkite.

EMERY, MICHAEL. "The War That Didn't Have to Happen," *Village Voice,* March 5, 1991, p. 22. Based on an in-depth interview with King Hussein of Jordan. See also *Los Angeles Times,* March 3, 1991, p. 3, Opinion Section.

———, AND SUZANNE STEINER EMERY. "Reporting Proposition 13: Business as Usual," *Columbia Journalism Review* (November–December 1978), 31. California papers were not much help to voters in pointing out the pitfalls.

ENGELMAN, RALPH. "The Origins of Public Access Television, 1966–1972," *Journalism Monographs,* CXXIII (October 1990).

ERLICK, JUNE CAROLYN. "Women as the New War Correspondents," *Washington Journalism Review* (June 1982), 42. Detailed report by an El Salvador correspondent on women there. See also Joanne Omang, "How the Fourth Estate Invaded the Third World," ibid., 45. By a correspondent.

EVARTS, DRU, AND GUIDO H. STEMPEL, III. "Coverage of the 1972 Campaign by TV, News Magazines and Major Newspapers," *Journalism Quarterly,* LI (Winter 1974), 645. The study indicates that the media generally showed no news bias.

"The First Amendment on Trial," a special issue containing 13 articles on the Pentagon Papers case, *Columbia Journalism Review* (September–October 1971).

FLANDER, JUDY. "Women in Network News," *Washington Journalism Review* (March 1985), 39. Ten reporters and anchors.

———. "Hewitt's Humongous Hour," *Washington Journalism Review* (April 1991), 26. Update of *60 Minutes.*

FURLONG, WILLIAM B. "Dan ('Killer') Schorr, The Great Abrasive," *New York,* VIII (June 16, 1975), 41. How the controversial CBS correspondent faced his critics.

GAZIANO, CECILIE. "How Creditable Is the Credibility Crisis?" *Journalism Quarterly,* LXV (Summer 1988), 267. Four 1985 surveys, taken together, do not indicate a crisis in public confidence in the media.

GRANATO, LEONARD A. "Prior Restraint: Resurgent Enemy of Freedom of Expression," Ph.D. thesis, Southern Illinois University, 1973. From fourteenth-century England to now.

GREENFIELD, JEFF. "Making TV News Pay," *Gannett Center Journal,* I:1 (Spring 1987), 21. ABC News analyst reviews TV news economics. See also Gary Cummings, "The Watershed in Local TV News," ibid., 40.

HALBERSTAM, DAVID. "Press and Prejudice," *Esquire,* LXXXI (April 1974), 109. Subtitle: "How Our Last Three Presidents Got the Newsmen They Deserved," by one of them.

HANNON, ELIZABETH. "Censorship During the Grenada Invasion: The Pentagon, the Press, and the Public," *International Communication Bulletin,* XXIII (Fall 1988), 15. Reagan's news blackout was politically motivated.

HERSH, SEYMOUR M. "The Iran-Contra Committee: Did They Protect Reagan?" *New York Times Magazine,* April 29, 1990. The answer is yes.

HOPKINS, MARK. "Watching China Change," *Columbia Journalism Review* (September 1989), 35. By the Voice of America bureau chief in Beijing until expelled. See also John Schidlovsky, "Tiananmen Square: A Correspondent's Story," ibid., 19.

"International News and Foreign Policy," *Gannett Center Journal*, III (Fall 1989), contains a special section on China and Tiananmen crisis.

KARP, WALTER. "All the Congressmen's Men: How Capitol Hill Controls the Press," *Harper's* (July 1989). A critical essay that discusses a dozen 1980s books on the media and politics.

KLEIN, JOE. "Our Man in Managua," *Esquire* (November 1986), 103. Stephen Kinzer of the *New York Times* portrayed excellently.

KNIGHTLEY, PHILLIP. "The Falkands: How Britannica Ruled the News," *Columbia Journalism Review* (September–October 1982), 51. A classic case of news management.

LAMB, DAVID. "Pentagon Hardball," *Washington Journalism Review* (April 1991), 33. The problem of Gulf War reporter pools.

LENTZ, RICHARD. "Sixty-five Days in Memphis," *Journalism Monographs*, XCVIII (August 1986). A garbage strike leads to the death of Martin Luther King, Jr.

LOWRY, DENNIS T. "Agnew and the Network TV News: A Before/After Content Analysis," *Journalism Quarterly*, XLVIII (Summer 1971), 205. Networks played it somewhat safer post-Agnew.

———. "Measures of Network News Bias in the 1972 Presidential Campaign," *Journal of Broadcasting*, XVIII (Fall 1975), 387. Content analysis shows anti-GOP.

MARDER, MURREY. "Operation Washington Shield," *Nieman Reports* (Summer 1991), 1. Lead article in issue devoted to Gulf War news manipulation.

MARRO, ANTHONY. "When the Government Tells Lies," *Columbia Journalism Review* (March–April 1985), 29. An excellent survey of the previous three decades by veteran journalists.

MARTINSON, DAVID L. "Coverage of La Follette Offers Insights for 1972 Campaign," *Journalism Quarterly*, LII (Autumn 1975), 539. How the press stereotypes in campaigns.

MASLOW, JONATHAN EVAN, AND AVA ARANS. "Operation San Salvador," *Columbia Journalism Review* (May–June 1981), 52. U.S. press falls in line with Reagan policy.

"Media and Election '88," *Gannett Center Journal*, II (Fall 1988) contains five articles about the campaign's problems and campaign diaries by Sam Donaldson, ABC, covering Dukakis, and by David Hoffman, *Washington Post*, analyzing Bush.

NELSON, ANNE. "Remembering the Dutchmen: One Way to Kill the Story," *Nation* (July 24–31, 1982). 75. El Salvador correspondent reports on slain TV newsmen.

NOBILE, PHILIP. "What Makes the Apple Machine Run?" *More*, VI (July–August 1976), 23. Interview with R. W. Apple of the *New York Times*, rated the ablest of the 1976 boys-on-the-bus.

"NBC: 50th Anniversary; Spearhead of Broadcast Industry Marks Beginning." *Television/Radio Age*, XXIV (June 21, 1976), special issue. See also *Broadcasting*, XCI (June 21, 1976).

PATTERSON, OSCAR, III. "The Vietnam Veteran and the Media: A Comparative Content Analysis of Media Coverage of the War and Vietnam, 1968–1973," Ph.D. thesis, University of Tennessee, 1982. Studied network TV, *Time*, *Newsweek*, and *Life*.

———. "Television's Living Room War in Print: Vietnam in the News Magazines," *Journalism Quarterly*, LXI (Spring 1984), 35. Coverage took 6.4 percent of space; few bloody pictures.

RANLY, DONALD P. "The Challengers: Social Pressures on the Press, 1965–75," Ph.D. thesis, University of Missouri, 1975. Exhaustive history of nongovernmental pressures brought by individuals, groups, and various forms of media review.

"Regulating the Media," *Gannett Center Journal*, II (Winter 1988). Contains 12 articles about deregulation, fairness, and the First Amendment.

"Reporting the 1976 Campaign," *Columbia Journalism Review* (January–February 1977). Articles by participants and observers.

SAID, EDWARD W. "Iran and the Press," *Columbia Journalism Review* (March–April 1980), 23. American press went to war with Islam and Iran, scholar says. See also "Iran and the Press in Retrospect," a special report on media coverage of the hostage crisis in *Washington Journalism Review* (May 1981).

SEEGER, MURRAY. "A Keyhole View: The Press and the Campaign," *Nieman Reports*, XXXVIII:4 (Winter 1984), 5. The 1984 campaign analyzed.

SPEAKES, LARRY. "The Press Gets Its Report Card," *Editor & Publisher*, Feb. 7, 1987, p. 9. Reagan's press chief interviews himself. See also Eleanor Clift, "The Legacy of Larry Speakes," *Washington Journalism Review* (March 1987), 40.

STEINER, LINDA, AND SUZANNE GRAY. "Genevieve Forbes Herrick: A Front-Page Reporter," *Journalism History*, XI (Spring 1985), 8. Noted *Chicago Tribune* reporter and Washington correspondent in 1920–30s.

STEMPEL, GUIDO H., III, AND JOHN W. WINDHAUSER. "The Prestige Press Revisited: Coverage of the 1980 Presidential Campaign," *Journalism Quarterly*, LXI (Spring 1984), 49. Press gets good marks.

———. "Coverage by the Prestige Press of the 1988 Presidential Campaign," *Journalism Quarterly*, LXVI (Winter 1989), 894. Even-handed; quality improved.

STONE, VERNON A. "Trends in the Status of Minorities and Women in Broadcast News," *Journalism Quarterly*, LXV (Summer 1988), 288. RTNDA data show women gained but blacks did not, 1978–86.

STOVALL, JAMES G. "Coverage of the 1984 Presidential Campaign," *Journalism Quarterly*, LXV (Summer 1988), 443. Republicans had fewer events but more press coverage.

STREITMATTER, RODGER. "Front Page from the White House: A Quantitative Study of Personal News Coverage from Teddy Roosevelt to Ronald Reagan," Ph.D. thesis, American University, 1988. Percentage of personal news in total coverage declined steadily, as types of White House news shifted.

SWAIN, BRUCE M. "The *Progressive,* the Bomb and the Papers," *Journalism Monographs,* LXXVI (May 1982). A U.S. government effort at prior restraint fails.

SWERDLOW, JOEL. "The Decline of the Boys on the Bus," *Washington Journalism Review* (January–February 1981), 15. Print reporters shoved to back of bus by TV correspondents.

WEINBERG, STEVE. "CNN Goes for the Gold," *Columbia Journalism Review* (September 1990), 21. CNN hires an investigative team.

"When CNN Hits Its Target." *Newsweek,* January 28, 1991, p. 41. An evaluation of impact on other networks of CNN's historic Baghdad broadcast of Gulf War's opening. See also *Time,* January 28.

CHAPTER 19: EFFORTS TO IMPROVE THE MEDIA

Discussions involving media problems are to be found in the American Society of Newspaper Editors' *Problems of Journalism* series, in the Associated Press Managing Editors' *APME Red Book* series, and in the periodicals *Journalism Quarterly, Journal of Broadcasting, Columbia Journalism Review, American Journalism Review, Nieman Reports, Masthead, Quill, Grassroots Editor, Editor & Publisher, Broadcasting, Advertising Age, Publishers' Auxiliary, Public Relations Journal, Publishers' Weekly, ASNE Bulletin, RTNDA Bulletin,* and ANPA's *presstime.*

Books: Role of the Press, Media Organizations

AGEE, WARREN K., ed. *The Press and the Public Interest.* Washington, DC: Public Affairs Press, 1968. Collection of 18 William Allen White lectures at the University of Kansas by leading journalists.

BOSTROM, BERT N. *Talent, Truth and Energy: Society of Professional Journalists, Sigma Delta Chi.* Chicago: SPJ, SDX, 1984. Celebrates its 75th anniversary, copious data.

BROGAN, PATRICK. *Spiked: The Short Life and Death of the National News Council.* New York: Priority Press, 1986. A hasty, critical account. See the council's three volumes of cases, 1973–83.

CASEY, RALPH D., ed. *The Press in Perspective.* Baton Rouge: Louisiana State University Press, 1963. Seventeen addresses in critical vein by leading journalists and writers, in Guild Lecture series at University of Minnesota.

CENTO, W. F., ed. *Fifty and Feisty—APME: 1933 to 1983.* St. Paul, MN: North Central, 1983. Associated Press Managing Editors.

COMMISSION ON FREEDOM OF THE PRESS. *A Free and Responsible Press.* Chicago: University of Chicago Press, 1947. A penetrating summary.

DENNIS, EVERETTE E., AND ELLEN WARTELLA, eds. *American Communication Research: The Remembered History.* Mahwah, NJ: Lawrence Erlbaum, 1996. The field, its founders, and perspectives.

ELLIS, L. ETHAN. *Newsprint: Producers, Publishers and Political Pressures.* New Brunswick: Rutgers University Press, 1960. Study of costs from 1940 to 1960.

EMERY, EDWIN. *History of the American Newspaper Publishers Association.* Minneapolis: University of Minnesota Press, 1949. Updated in 1962 in 75th anniversary booklet (New York: ANPA), and in 1987 in "ANPA's First 100 Years," *presstime* (May 1987), 28.

HOCKING, WILLIAM E. *Freedom of the Press: A Framework of Principle.* Chicago: University of Chicago Press, 1947. Discusses philosophical problems, written for the Commission on Freedom of the Press.

KAROLEVITZ, ROBERT F. *From Quill to Computer: The Story of America's Newspapers.* Washington, DC: National Newspaper Association, 1985. Commemorating NNA's centennial.

LEAB, DANIEL J. *A Union of Individuals: The Formation of the American Newspaper Guild 1933–1936.* New York: Columbia University Press, 1970. Scholarly detail.

LEVY, H. PHILLIP. *The Press Council: History, Procedure and Cases.* London: Macmillan, 1967. The British Press Council examined in detail, 1953 to 1967. For U.S. examples, see Kenneth Starck, "What Community Press Councils Talk About," *Journalism Quarterly,* XLVII (Spring 1970), 20; William B. Blankenburg, "Local Press Councils," *Columbia Journalism Review,* VIII (Spring 1969), 14; Lawrence Schneider, "A Media-Black Council: Seattle's 19-Month Experiment," *Journalism Quarterly,* XLVII (Autumn 1970), 439; and Rivers, Bertrand, and Rampal references listed below.

LINDSTROM, CARL E. *The Fading American Newspaper.* New York: Doubleday, 1960. A strong critique of trends and methods by a 40-year newspaperman (*Hartford Times*).

MACDOUGALL, A. KENT, ed. *The Press: A Critical Look from the Inside.* Princeton, NJ: Dow Jones Books, 1972. Reflections on the press from the columns of the *Wall Street Journal.*

MARTIN, L. JOHN, ed. *Role of the Mass Media in American Politics.* Annals of the American Academy of Political and Social Science, No. 427, September 1976. A special issue with 13 articles on media coverage, effects, image building, and perspectives.

MOTT, FRANK LUTHER. *The News in America.* Cambridge, MA: Harvard University Press, 1952. An excellent discussion of news gathering and distribution and of sociopolitical responsibilities.

MOTT, FRANK LUTHER, AND RALPH D. CASEY, eds. *Interpretations of Journalism.* New York: Appleton-Century-Crofts, 1937. The most important historical collection of statements on press problems.

NATIONAL LABOR RELATIONS BOARD. *Collective Bargaining in the Newspaper Industry.* Washington, DC: Government

Printing Office, 1938. Studies both the Guild and printing union movements.

NERONE, JOHN C. *Last Rights: Revisiting Four Theories of the Press.* Champaign: University of Illinois Press, 1995. New perspectives on a classic study.

PRATTE, PAUL ALFRED. *Gods within the Machine: A History of the American Society of Newspaper Editors.* Westport, CT: Greenwood Press, 1995. The first critical history of the ASNE shows its uneven record of dealing with ethics, press freedom and other issues. See also an informal account published in 1974, *Read All About It—Fifty Years of ASNE,* by Alice Fox Pitts.

RESTON, JAMES B. *The Artillery of the Press.* New York: Harper & Row, 1967. Essays discussing press influence on foreign policy.

RIVERS, WILLIAM L., AND WILBUR SCHRAMM. *Responsibility in Mass Communication.* New York: Harper & Row, 1969. An examination of the social problem, also done by J. Edward Gerald in *The Social Responsibility of the Press* (Minneapolis: University of Minnesota Press, 1963), and by John Hohenberg in *The News Media* (New York: Holt, Rinehart & Winston, 1968).

RIVERS, WILLIAM L., WILLIAM B. BLANKENBURG, KENNETH STARCK, AND EARL REEVES. *Backtalk: Press Councils in America.* San Francisco: Canfield Press, 1971. By men who operated several local press councils.

RUCKER, BRYCE W. *The First Freedom.* Carbondale: Southern Illinois University Press, 1968. Prize-winning analysis of the position of mass media, designed as an updating of Morris Ernst's *The First Freedom* (1946).

SCHRAMM, WILBUR. *The Beginnings of Communication Study in America: A Personal Memoir.* Ed. by Steven H. Chaffee and Everett M. Rogers. Thousand Oaks, CA: Sage, 1997. An eyewitness account by a key founding figure in the field of communication studies.

SLOAN, W. DAVID, ed. *Makers of the Media Mind: Journalism Educators and Their Ideas.* Hillsdale, NJ: Erlbaum, 1990. Thirty-eight leaders.

WEAVER, DAVID H., AND G. CLEVELAND WILHOIT. *The American Journalist in the 1990s: U.S. News People at the End of an Era.* Mahwah, NJ: Erlbaum, 1996. The standard reference, giving a comprehensive portrait of the demographic backgrounds, professional and ethical values, and working conditions of 1410 representative U.S. print and broadcast journalists working in the 1990s. Updates John W. C. Johnstone et al., *The News People: A Sociological Portrait of American Journalists and Their Work.* Urbana: University of Illinois Press, 1976. Both based on scientific surveys.

Books: Women in Journalism

BELFORD, BARBARA. *Brilliant Bylines.* New York: Columbia University Press, 1986. Twenty-four total.

CLABES, JUDITH G., ed. *New Guardians of the Press.* Indianapolis: News & Feature Press, 1983. Profiles of women editors.

CREEDON, PAMELA J., ed. *Women in Mass Communication: Challenging Gender Values.* 2nd ed. Newbury Park, CA: Sage, 1993. Sixteen papers with feminine views.

DOUGLAS, SUSAN. *Where the Girls Are: Growing Up Female with the Mass Media.* New York: Times Books, 1994. Images of 40 years that both fostered and hurt feminism.

DOW, BONNIE. *Prime-Time Feminism: Television, Media Culture, and the Women's Movement since 1970.* Philadelphia: University of Pennsylvania Press, 1996. The rise of "media-friendly feminism" has mixed implications for women.

EDWARDS, JULIA. *Women of the World: The Great Foreign Correspondents.* Boston: Houghton Mifflin, 1988. Spans 140 years.

ENDRES, KATHLEEN L., AND THERESE L. LUECK, eds. *Women's Periodicals in the United States: Social and Political Issues.* Westport, CT: Greenwood Press, 1996. Essays on 70 individual nineteenth- and twentieth-century periodicals created by women to address social, political, and economic issues.

EVANS, SARA M. *Born for Liberty: A History of Women in America.* 2nd ed. New York: Free Press, 1997. By a leading women's history scholar. See also William H. Chafe, *The Paradox of Change: American Women in the 20th Century* (New York: Oxford, 1991).

GELFMAN, JUDITH S. *Women in Television News.* New York: Columbia University Press, 1976. Survey.

HALSELL, GRACE. *In Their Shoes.* Fort Worth: Texas Christian University Press, 1996. Compelling autobiography by reporter who covered war, civil rights, and adventures abroad for major newspapers.

HOSLEY, DAVID H., AND GAYLE K. YAMADA. *Hard News: Women in Broadcast Journalism.* Westport, CT: Greenwood Press, 1987. Historical overview.

MILLS, KAY. *A Place in the News: From the Women's Pages to the Front Pages.* New York: Columbia University Press, 1990. Reprint of the 1988 book—with a new preface.

ROBERTSON, NAN. *The Girls in the Balcony: Women, Men and "The New York Times".* New York: Random House, 1992. Covers gender issues from the 1850s to the present.

SANDERS, MARLENE, AND MARCIA ROCK. *Waiting for Prime Time: The Women of Television News.* Urbana: University of Illinois Press, 1989. Sanders's autobiography and interviews with six women.

SCHLIPP, MADELON GOLDEN, AND SHARON M. MURPHY. *Great Women of the Press.* Carbondale: Southern Illinois University Press, 1983. Eighteen biographies.

SIGNORIELLI, NANCY, ed. *Women in Communication: A Biographical Sourcebook.* Westport, CT: Greenwood Press, 1996. Biographical profiles of 48 outstanding women in communication including journalists and scholars in the field of communication, from Anne Newport Royall to Connie Chung.

Books: Media Law, Freedom of Information

ADLER, RENATA. *Reckless Disregard: Westmoreland v. CBS et al.; Sharon v. Time.* New York: Knopf, 1986. Two tumultuous libel cases. See also Bob Brewin and Sydney Shaw. *Vietnam on Trial: Westmoreland vs. CBS* (New York: Atheneum, 1987).

BITTNER, JOHN R. *Broadcast Law and Regulation.* Englewood Cliffs, NJ: Prentice-Hall, 1982. Leading book in its field.

BRUCKER, HERBERT. *Freedom of Information.* New York: Macmillan, 1949. Able defense of press by *Hartford Courant* editor.

CHAFEE, ZECHARIAH, JR. *Government and Mass Communication.* Chicago: University of Chicago Press, 1947. Commission on Freedom of the Press study.

CROSS, HAROLD L. *The People's Right to Know.* New York: Columbia University Press, 1953. Scholarly, detailed study of the problems of access to news.

DEVOL, KENNETH S., ed. *Mass Media and the Supreme Court: The Legacy of the Warren Years.* Mamaroneck, NY: Hastings House, 1990. Commentaries, notes.

GILLMOR, DONALD M. *Free Press and Fair Trial.* Washington, DC: Public Affairs Press, 1966. Scholarly survey and analysis of critical cases, best of the literature. See also John Lofton, *Justice and the Press* (Boston: Beacon Press, 1966).

———, *Power, Publicity, and the Abuse of Libel Law.* New York: Oxford Press, 1992. Argues that public figures should not be allowed to sue for libel and that they only have the right of reply.

———, JEROME A. BARRON, TODD SIMON, AND HERBERT TERRY. *Mass Communication Law: Cases and Comments.* St. Paul, MN: West, 1990. Comprehensive casebook, comments.

HOLSINGER, RALPH. *Media Law.* New York: Random House, 1986. Combines casebook and narrative.

NELSON, HAROLD L. *Libel in News of Congressional Investigating Committees.* Minneapolis: University of Minnesota Press, 1961. Scholarly study of problems faced in reporting attacks on individuals.

NERONE, JOHN. *Violence against the Press: Policing the Public Sphere in U.S. History.* New York: Oxford University Press, 1994. Excellent documentation of attacks and antipress attitudes, with a focus on the pre–World War II era.

PEMBER, DON R. *Mass Media Law.* Madison, WI: Brown & Benchmark, 1993. Leading textbook synthesis of media law.

ROBINS, NATALIE. *Alien Ink: The FBI's War on Freedom of Expression.* New York: William Morrow, 1992. Superb documentation beginning with harassment of World War I writers; focus on criticism of J. Edgar Hoover.

SMOLA, RODNEY A. *Free Speech in an Open Society.* New York: Knopf, 1992. Commentary on recent court decisions by College of William and Mary scholar.

TEETER, DWIGHT L., JR., AND DON R. LEDUC. *Law of Mass Communications: Freedom and Control of Print and Broadcast Media.* Westbury, NY: Foundation Press, 1995. Casebook exploring trends in communications law.

WIGGINS, JAMES RUSSELL. *Freedom or Secrecy.* New York: Oxford University Press, 1964. A summation of access-to-news problems by an ASNE leader.

Periodicals and Monographs

American Journalism, VII (1990), 33–35. Contains a bibliography on women in journalism, compiled by Catherine C. Mitchell.

ANDERSON, DAVID H. "Media Success in the Supreme Court," a working paper (New York: Gannett Center for Media Studies, 1987).

BEASLEY, MAURINE. "The Women's National Press Club," *Journalism History,* XV (Winter 1988), 112. Seventy years of history.

BOGART, LEO. "Newspapers in Transition," *Wilson Quarterly,* 1982. Special issue devoted to the news media.

BROUN, HEYWOOD. "An Army with Banners," *Nation,* CXL (February 13, 1935), 154. The Guild president's own account.

BLANCHARD, ROBERT O. "Present at the Creation: The Media and the Moss Committee," *Journalism Quarterly,* XLIX (Summer 1972), 271. Story of the information crusade.

BOTTOROFF, DANA. "Mary Anne Dolan: Woman Editor of the Year," *feed/back* (Spring 1982), 12. First nonowner woman editor of a major daily, the *Los Angeles Herald Examiner.* See also Dennis Holder, "Mary Anne Dolan," *Washington Journalism Review* (June 1982), 19.

CONN, EARL L. "The American Council on Education for Journalism: An Accrediting History," Ed.D. thesis, Indiana University, 1970. Traces the growth of accrediting standards.

DENNIS, EVERETTE E. "Purloined Information as Property: A New First Amendment Challenge," *Journalism Quarterly,* L (Autumn 1973), 456. Based on his Ph.D. thesis, University of Minnesota, 1974, which covers episodes in 1795, 1848, and 1970s.

EMERY, EDWIN, AND JOSEPH P. MCKERNS. "AEJMC: 75 Years in the Making," *Journalism Monographs,* CIV (July 1987). History of journalism educator organizations.

ENDRES, KATHLEEN L. "Capitol Hill Newswomen: A Descriptive Study," *Journalism Quarterly,* LIII (Spring 1976), 132. Background material and current research.

FLANDER, JUDY. "Women War Correspondents: On the Fields of Macho," *Washington Journalism Review* (January 1990), 38. Survey of current leaders.

GILLMOR, DONALD M. "The Puzzle of Pornography," *Journalism Quarterly,* XLII (Summer 1965), 363. Traces court decisions in the area of obscenity including *Roth.* For *Ginzburg* case and aftermath, see Kenneth S. Devol, "The Ginzburg Decision: Reactions in California," *Journalism Quarterly,* XLV (Summer 1968), 271.

GORDON, A. DAVID. "Protection of News Sources: The History and Legal Status of the Newsman's Privilege," Ph.D. thesis, University of Wisconsin, 1971. Cases from 1848.

GLEASON, TIMOTHY W. "Historians and Freedom of the Press Since 1800," *American Journalism,* V (1988), 230. A comprehensive essay.

GUIMARY, DONALD L. "Ethnic Minorities in Newsrooms of Major Market Media in California," *Journalism Quarterly,* LXI (Winter 1984), 827. Improvement since 1979.

KEATING, ISABELLE. "Reporters Become of Age," *Harper's,* CLXX (April 1935), 601. One of the best early articles about the Guild.

KUCZUN, SAM. "History of the American Newspaper Guild," Ph.D. thesis, University of Minnesota, 1970. Comprehensive overview based on access to Guild archives.

MAHONEY, KATHLEEN P. "The Formation of the National Radio Broadcasters Association," Ph.D. thesis, Indiana University, 1983. Growth of rival to NAB, 1959–80.

MCCHESNEY, ROBERT W. *Corporate Media and the Threat to Democracy,* Open Media Pamphlet Series. New York: Seven Stories Press, 1997. Media mergers threaten the future of American democracy.

MCGLASHAN, ZENA BETH. "The Evolving Status of Newspaperwomen," Ph.D. thesis, University of Iowa, 1978. Historical base and case studies of five women managers.

MCINTYRE, JERILYN S. "Repositioning a Landmark: The Hutchins Commission and Freedom of the Press," *Critical Studies in Mass Communication,* IV (October 1987), 6.

MINER, MICHAEL. "Maynard of Oakland," *The Quill* (May 1982), 9. Editor of *Oakland Tribune* and highest-ranking black journalist.

"National Security and the First Amendment," special issue of the *William & Mary Law Review,* XXVI:5 (1984–85).

PETRICK, MICHAEL J. "Inspection of Public Records in the States: The Law and the News Media," Ph.D. thesis, University of Wisconsin, 1970. Covers 1824 to 1969.

PFAFF, DANIEL W. "The First Amendment and Symbolic Speech: Toward a Rationale of the Public Forum," Ph.D. thesis, University of Minnesota, 1972. Sit-ins, flag burnings.

————. "Race, Libel, and the Supreme Court," *Columbia Journalism Review,* VIII (Summer 1969), 23. Surveys Supreme Court libel decisions of 1960s that involved press freedom; points out connection to racial decisions.

PLAMONDON, ANN L. "Recent Developments in Law of Access," *Journalism Quarterly,* LXIII (Spring 1986), 61. A trilogy of 1984 cases.

Quill (February 1990). Special edition with 15 articles about women in the news business.

RASKIN, A. H. "The Once and Future Newspaper Guild," *Columbia Journalism Review* (September–October 1982), 26. Veteran labor writer evaluates 50-year-old Guild.

"The 'Red Lion' Decision," *Journal of Broadcasting,* XIII (Fall 1969), 145. Text of Supreme Court decision on application of the fairness doctrine.

ROBINSON, JOHN P. "The Press as King-Maker: What Surveys from Last Five Campaigns Show," *Journalism Quarterly,* LI (Winter 1974), 587. Excellent summary from Michigan Survey Center.

ROGERS, EVERETT M., AND STEVEN H. CHAFFEE. "Communication and Journalism from 'Daddy' Bleyer to Wilbur Schramm: A Palimpsest," *Journalism Monographs,* CXLVIII (December 1994). The evolution of journalism and communication scholarship and education.

SAALBERG, HARVEY. "The Canons of Journalism: A 50-Year Perspective," *Journalism Quarterly,* L (Winter 1973), 731. History of ASNE's code of ethics.

SCHAFER, ROBERT. "The Minnesota News Council: Developing Standards for Press Ethics," *Journalism Quarterly,* LVIII (Autumn 1981), 355. Leading state council at 10 years.

SCHER, JACOB. "Access to Information: Recent Legal Problems," *Journalism Quarterly,* XXXVII (Winter 1960), 41. An authoritative summary for the 1950s by a Northwestern journalism professor who was special counsel for the Moss committee.

SINICHAK, STEVEN. "The Chicago Journalism Review," *Grassroots Editor,* XI (July–August 1970), 10. Story of the journal's first two years.

STONECIPHER, HARRY, AND ROBERT TRAGER. "The Impact of *Gertz* on the Law of Libel," *Journalism Quarterly,* LIII (Winter 1976), 609. Case of *Gertz* v. *Robert Welch, Inc.*

WARD, HILEY H. "Ninety Years of the National Newspaper Association," Ph.D. thesis, University of Minnesota, 1977. The history of the weekly newspaper group.

WILDER, ROHIN G. "The Mind of Heywood Broun," Ph.D. thesis, University of Wisconsin, 1984.

WILSON, JEAN GADDY. "Women in the Newspaper Business," *presstime* (October 1986), 30. Promoters and salaries lagging, an in-depth study shows. See complete data for 1977–86 in *ASNE Bulletin,* (November 1986), 4; 1991 update in *ASNE Bulletin* (April 1991), 17.

CHAPTER 20: MEDIA TECHNOLOGY: THE CHALLENGE OF THE TWENTY-FIRST CENTURY

Books: Media Surveys, Evaluations

AGEE, WARREN K., PHILLIP H. AULT, AND EDWIN EMERY. *Introduction to Mass Communications.* 10th ed. New York: HarperCollins, 1991. Current status of mass media, research.

BAGDIKIAN, BEN H. *Media Monopoly.* Boston; Beacon Press, 1990. Study of corporate influence on publishing and adverse effects of conglomerates.

BOWER, TOM. *Maxwell: The Outsider.* New York: Viking, 1992. British account of the decade of greed; most comprehensive study of his empire's growth and collapse.

BRUCK, CONNIE. *Master of the Game: Steve Ross and the Creation of Time Warner.* New York: Simon & Schuster,

1994. The magnetic man who forged the $14 billion merger.

CLURMAN, RICHARD M. *To the End of Time.* New York: Simon & Schuster, 1992. Describes "the seduction and conquest of a media empire" by Warner's Steve Ross.

CZITROM, DANIEL J. *Media and the American Mind: From Morse to McLuhan.* Chapel Hill: University of North Carolina Press, 1982. Describes impacts of the telegraph, motion pictures, and radio, and analyzes theories of audience responses.

EMERY, MICHAEL, AND TED CURTIS SMYTHE, eds. *Readings in Mass Communication: Concepts and Issues in the Mass Media.* 11th ed. Dubuque, IA: William C. Brown, 1995. Articles examining principal issues and changing media images.

Forbes Media Guide 500: A Critical Review of the Media. New York: Forbes, Inc., 1994. Annual review of the 500 most important journalists and other data. Edited by Jude Wanniski.

FORNATELE, PETER, AND JOSHUA MILLS. *Radio in the Television Age.* Woodstock, NY: Overlook Press, 1980. Descriptive account of how radio fared.

FULLER, JACK. *News Values: Ideas for an Information Age.* Chicago: University of Chicago Press, 1996. Prescriptions to ensure the survival of the daily newspaper business.

HALBERSTAM, DAVID. *The Next Century.* New York: Avon Books, 1992. An assessment of changes in the media and concerns about growing U.S. isolationism.

ISAACS, NORMAN E. *Untended Gates: The Mismanaged Press.* New York: Columbia University Press, 1986. Sharp criticism of news management. See also Tom Goldstein. *The News at Any Cost: How Journalists Compromise Their Ethics to Shape the News* (New York: Simon & Schuster, 1985).

KOZOL, JONATHAN. *Illiterate America.* New York: Doubleday, 1985. One-third of Americans are functionally illiterate.

LICHTER, S. ROBERT, LINDA RICHTER, AND STANLEY ROTHMAN. *Prime Time: How TV Portrays American Culture* (Washington, DC: Regnery, 1994).

MAIER, THOMAS. *Newhouse.* New York: St. Martin's Press, 1994. Portrays the secretive press baron as an unworthy steward of the public trust.

MAYER, MARTIN. *Whatever Happened to Madison Avenue?* Boston: Little, Brown, 1991. Pessimistic outlook on future of advertising agencies.

MILLMAN, NANCY. *Emperors of Adland: Inside the Advertising Revolution.* New York: Warner Books, 1988. Covers the Saatchi brothers, Omnicom Group, WPP Group, and J. Walter Thompson.

NESS, RICHARD R. *From Headline Hunter to Superman: A Journalism Filmography.* Lanham, MD: Scarecrow Press, 1997. Detailed, well-researched summary of film images of the reporter across the decades.

NOURIE, ALAN AND BARBARA, eds. *American Mass-Market Magazines.* Westport, CT: Greenwood Press, 1990.

PHILLIPS, KEVIN. *The Politics of the Rich and Poor.* New York: Random House, 1990. A noted writer predicts revulsion from the excesses of the 1980s. See also Robert Kuttner, *The End of Laissez-Faire* (New York: Knopf, 1991).

ROTZELL, KIM B., JAMES E. HAEFNER, AND CHARLES H. SANDAGE. *Advertising in Contemporary Society.* Columbus, OH: Grid, 1976. Excellent structural explanation of how consumer movements waxed and waned. See also John S. Wright and John E. Mertes, *Advertising's Role in Society* (St. Paul: Webb, 1976).

SCHILLER, HERBERT I. *Culture, Inc.: The Corporate Takeover of Public Expression.* New York: Oxford University Press, 1989. Analyzes a wide range of news and entertainment media.

SCHUDSON, MICHAEL. *Advertising: The Uneasy Profession.* New York: Basic Books, 1984. A historical, critical approach.

————. *The Power of News.* Cambridge, MA: Harvard University Press, 1995. A collection of the author's essays, some historical and others on changes in the press, 1960–90.

SHAWCROSS, WILLIAM. *Murdoch.* New York: Simon & Schuster, 1993. Excellent storytelling of the ups and downs of Murdoch's empire-building; portrayed as ruthless but not a monster.

STERLING, CHRISTOPHER H., AND TIMOTHY R. HAIGHT, comps. *The Mass Media: Aspen Institute Guide to Communication Industry Trends.* New York: Praeger, 1978. Contemporary picture. See also William L. Rivers et al., *The Aspen Handbook on the Media, 1977–79 ed.* (New York: Praeger, 1977). Selective guide to research, organizations, and publications in communications.

TEBBEL, JOHN, AND MARY ELLEN ZUCKERMAN. *The Magazine in America, 1741–1990.* New York: Oxford Press, 1991. A fact-packed 433-page overview.

UNDERWOOD, DOUG. *When MBAs Rule the Newsroom.* New York: Columbia University Press, 1993. Reflects the disillusionment felt by many in this age of marketing the smartly packaged news.

Books: Media Technology

BAGDIKIAN, BEN H. *The Information Machines.* New York: Harper & Row, 1971. A provocative book based on a RAND Corporation study dealing with the news-communication methods for the next three decades.

BALDWIN, THOMAS F., AND D. STEVENS McVOY. *Cable Communication.* Englewood Cliffs, NJ: Prentice Hall, 1988. Broad introduction and survey of cable technology, services, public policy, organization, and operations.

BROOKS, JOHN. *Telephone: The First Hundred Years.* New York: Harper & Row, 1976. A popular history of AT&T.

GROSS, LYNNE S. *Telecommunications: An Introduction to Radio, Television, and the Developing Media.* Dubuque, IA: Brown, 1990. Overviews of the new technologies.

SMITH, ANTHONY. *Goodbye Gutenberg: The Newspaper Revolution of the 1980s.* New York: Oxford University Press, 1980. A British media critic evaluates the effects of technological change on the appearance and role of the newspaper.

STERLING, CHRISTOPHER H., ed. *Electronic Media: A Guide to Trends in Broadcasting and Newer Technologies, 1920–1983.* New York: Praeger, 1984. Basic reference work.

TUNSTALL, JEREMY. *Communications Deregulation: The Unleashing of America's Communications Industry.* Oxford, England: Blackwell, 1986. A lively, informative analysis.

WHITEHOUSE, GEORGE E. *Understanding the New Technologies of the Mass Media.* Englewood Cliffs, NJ: Prentice Hall, 1986. Inclusive survey.

WILLIAMS, CHRISTIAN. *Lead, Follow, or Get Out of the Way: The Story of Ted Turner.* New York: Times Books, 1982. Atlanta's cable king.

Books: Film

BURGOYNE, ROBERT. *Film Nation: Hollywood Looks at U.S. History.* Minneapolis: University of Minnesota, 1997. Analyzes how five films (including *Forrest Gump* and *Born on the Fourth of July*) challenge traditional myths about national identity and the nature of U.S. history.

GOMERY, DOUGLAS. *Movie History: A Survey.* Belmont, CA: Wadsworth, 1991. Covers 1895–1975.

JOWETT, GARTH. *Film: The Democratic Art.* Boston: Little, Brown, 1976. Film's social impact, economic and political adjustments.

KAEL, PAULINE. *State of the Art.* New York: Dutton, 1985. By the noted film critic.

LEES, DAVID, AND STAN BERKOWITZ. *The Movie Business.* New York: Vintage, 1981. Contemporary picture. See also Michael F. Mayer, *The Film Industry* (New York: Hastings House, 1978).

MCCREADIE, MARSHA. *Women in Film: The Critical Eye.* New York: Praeger, 1983. A discussion of the work of 12 major women film critics.

MONACO, JAMES. *American Film Now.* New York: Oxford University Press, 1980. Films of the 1970s.

Books: World News Agencies, Press Associations

BOYD-BARRETT, OLIVER. *The International News Agencies.* Beverly Hills: Sage, 1980. Includes the AP, UPI, Reuters, AFP, TASS, Non-Aligned News Pool, Inter Press.

DESMOND, ROBERT W. *Windows on the World: World News Reporting 1900–1920.* Iowa City: University of Iowa Press, 1980. *Crisis and Conflict: World News Reporting between Two Wars 1920–1940* (1982). *Tides of War, World News Reporting 1940–1945* (1984). Volumes 2, 3, and 4 of a prize-winning study (see Chapter 1 Bibliography).

FENBY, JONATHAN. *The International News Services.* New York: Schocken Books, 1986. By a former Reuters editor; description and analysis of AP, UPI, AFP, and Reuters, with emphasis on Third World concerns.

FRIEDLAND, LEWIS A. *Covering the World: International Television News Services.* New York: Twentieth Century Fund, 1992. Detailed essay examining 1980s to 1992.

GORDON, GREGORY, AND RONALD E. COHEN. *Down to the Wire: UPI's Fight for Survival.* New York: McGraw-Hill, 1989. Two UPI editors write an award-winning account of UP and UPI history.

KIM, SOON JIN. *EFE: Spain's World News Agency.* Westport, CT: Greenwood Press, 1989.

OSLIN, GEORGE P. *The Story of Telecommunications.* Macon, GA: Mercer University Press, 1992. History of telecommunications from the telegraph through the break-up of AT&T in the early 1990s.

READ, DONALD. *The Power of News: The History of Reuters.* New York: Oxford University Press, 1992. From the days of colorful scoops to the emphasis on business.

STOREY, GRAHAM. *Reuters.* New York: Crown, 1951. Standard account to that time.

UNESCO. *News Agencies: Their Structure and Operations.* New York: Columbia University Press, 1953. Includes discussions of the AP, UP, and INS.

Books: International News Flow, World Press

ANDERSON, MICHAEL H. *Madison Avenue in Asia: Politics and Transnational Advertising.* Rutherford, NJ: Fairleigh Dickinson University Press, 1984. Uses case studies from China, Singapore, Malaysia, and Indochina.

BLANCHARD, MARGARET A. *Exporting the First Amendment: The Press-Government Crusade of 1945–1952.* New York: Longman, 1986. U.S. diplomats and journalism leaders joined in an effort to write the American free press concept into postwar agreements, planting seeds for UNESCO programs.

CHANG, WON HO. *Mass Media in China.* Ames: Iowa State University Press, 1989. By Missouri journalism scholar; describes media changes from 1979 to 1989.

DUNNETT, PETER J. S. *The World Newspaper Industry.* New York: Routledge, 1988. Economic analysis.

FISCHER, HEINZ-DIETRICH, ed. *Outstanding International Press Reporting.* Berlin: Walter de Gruyter, 1984.

HACHTEN, WILLIAM A. *The World News Prism: Changing Media, Clashing Ideologies.* 3rd ed. Ames: Iowa State University Press, 1992. A superb, 133-page introduction to the New World Information Order controversy of the 1970s.

———. *Muffled Drums: The News Media in Africa.* Ames: Iowa Sate University Press, 1971. Descriptive account by a leading U.S. scholar on the subject.

———, WITH HARVA HACHTEN. *The Growth of Media in the Third World.* Ames: Iowa State University Press, 1993. Analysis of African failures, Asian successes.

HALBERSTAM, DAVID. *The Next Century.* New York: Morrow, 1991. Shortest and best book scouring the past for hints of the future, based on the author's 30 years covering Asia and Eastern Europe.

HEAD, SYDNEY W. *World Broadcasting Systems: A Comparative Analysis.* Belmont, CA: Wadsworth, 1985. First worldwide comparison.

HOHENBERG, JOHN. *Free Press/Free People—The Best Cause.* New York: Columbia University Press, 1971. A sweeping review of the coverage of major world events with a concentration on the twentieth century.

HOPKINS, MARK W. *Mass Media in the Soviet Union.* New York: Pegasus, 1970. See also International Organization of Journalists, *Mass Media in CMEA Countries* (Prague: International Organization of Journalists, 1976), covering Eastern Europe and the USSR.

KATZ, ELIHU, AND GEORGE WEDELL. *Broadcasting in the Third World: Promise and Performance.* Cambridge, MA: Harvard University Press, 1978. Data on 91 developing countries, including 11 in-depth case studies.

KESTERTON, WILFRED H. *A History of Journalism in Canada.* Toronto: McClelland and Stewart, 1967. The standard account.

KURIAN, GEORGE, ed. *World Press Encyclopedia.* 2 vols. New York: Facts on File, 1982. Profiles of the press for most countries. Updates earlier surveys by UNESCO and by John C. Merrill et al., *The Foreign Press: A Survey of the World's Journalism* (Baton Rouge: Louisiana State University Press, 1970).

LEE, CHIN-CHUAN. *Media Imperialism Reconsidered.* Beverly Hills: Sage, 1980. Focuses on television, using examples of China, Taiwan, and Canada.

LENT, JOHN A., ed. *The Asian Newspapers' Reluctant Revolution.* Ames: Iowa State University Press, 1971. Essays on history and current status, by country.

———. *Mass Communications in the Caribbean.* Ames: Iowa State University Press, 1990. Handbook of historical and current information.

MACBRIDE, SEAN, et al. *Many Voices: One World.* New York: Unipub, 1980. The MacBride Commission report on the proposal for a New World Information Order and increased Third World participation in news flow. See ten articles on the subject in *Journal of Communication,* XXXI (Autumn 1981), 102–87.

MARTIN, L. JOHN, AND ANJU GROVER CHAUDHARY, eds. *Comparative Mass Media Systems.* New York: Longman, 1983. Chapters by 18 scholars addressing six major aspects of the mass media, from Western, Communist, and Third World viewpoints in each case.

MERRILL, JOHN C., et al. *Global Journalism.* New York: Longman, 1995. Six coauthors survey the world's mass media. Also see Merrill, John C., and Harold A. Fisher. *The World's Great Dailies: Profiles of 50 Newspapers.* New York: Hastings House, 1980.

MOWLANA, HAMID. *Global Information and World Communication.* New York: Longman, 1986. New frontiers in international relations.

NORDENSTRANG, KAARLE, AND HERBERT I. SCHILLER, eds. *Beyond National Sovereignty: International Communica-*

tion in the 1990s. Norwood, NJ: Ablex, 1993. Examination of the flow of ideas and images in a shrinking world by world-renowned scholars.

OLSON, KENNETH E. *The History Makers.* Baton Rouge: Louisiana State University Press, 1966. A survey of European press history.

READ, WILLIAM H. *America's Mass Media Merchants.* Baltimore: Johns Hopkins University Press, 1977. Examines overseas impact of 10 specific media, including the AP, UPI, *Time, Newsweek, Reader's Digest,* and major news syndicates.

RICE, MICHAEL, AND JAMES A. CRONEY, eds. *Reporting U.S.-European Relations.* New York: Pergamon Press, 1982. Aspen Institute comparative study of the *New York Times, Times* of London, *Le Monde,* and *Frankfurter Allgemeine Zeitung.*

RICHSTAD, JIM, AND MICHAEL H. ANDERSON, eds. *Crisis in International News: Policies and Prospects.* New York: Columbia University Press, 1981. Balanced compilation of major scholarly articles dealing with New World Information Order movement.

RIGHTER, ROSEMARY. *Whose News? Politics, the Press, and the Third World.* London: Times Books, 1978. IPI-sponsored, essentially Western press viewpoint.

SCHILLER, HERBERT I. *Mass Communications and American Empire.* 2nd ed. Boston: Beacon Press, 1992.

SCHRAMM, WILBUR, AND L. ERWIN ATWOOD. *Circulation of News in the Third World—A Study of Asia.* Hong Kong: Chinese University Press, 1981. Analyzes flow of agency news to 19 Asian dailies.

SLIDE, ANTHONY, ed. *International Film, Radio, and Television Journals.* Westport, CT: Greenwood Press, 1985. Evaluations of more than 200 periodicals.

STEVENSON, ROBERT L., AND DONALD LEWIS SHAW, eds. *Foreign News and the New World Information Order.* Ames: Iowa State University Press, 1984. Content analysis of major transnational news agencies and media of 17 Third World countries.

TUNSTALL, JEREMY. *The Media Are American.* New York: Columbia University Press, 1977. An examination of the influence of Anglo-American media in the world.

UNESCO. *World Communication Report.* Paris: UNESCO, 1989. A global survey of communication developments with 550 pages of data.

Periodicals and Monographs

ARMSTRONG, DAVID. "A Thinking Approach to News," *Columbia Journalism Review* (September–October 1978), 61. Pacific News Service operates from California base.

AULETTA, KEN. "John Malone: Flying Solo," *New Yorker,* February 7, 1994, p. 52.

BLAIR, GWENDA. "Citizen Peretz," *Esquire* (July 1985), 86. *New Republic* owner profiled moving Left to Right.

BLANCHARD, MARGARET A. "The Crusade for Worldwide Freedom of Information: American Attempts to Shape

World War II Peace Treaties," *Journalism Quarterly,* LX (Winter 1983), 583. Similar goals as Third World movement now.

BOZMAN, SUSANLEE MARDER. "Asking the Hard Questions at the White House: A Biography of UPI Reporter Helen Thomas," Master's thesis, California State University, Northridge, 1990. A thorough examination of Thomas's career, including family and professional influences.

CLIFT, ELEANOR. "Helen Thomas, Dauntless Dean of the White House Press," *Washington Journalism Review,* (November 1986).

DEARMAN, MARION, AND JOHN HOWELLS. "Computer Technology and the Return of the Printer-Journalist," *Journalism History,* II (Winter 1975), 133. New technology's outcome.

"Do You Believe in Magic?" *Time,* April 25, 1988. Starring in its own Cinderella story, Disney transforms itself.

EMERY, MICHAEL. "An Endangered Species: The International News Hole," *Gannett Center Journal,* III (Fall 1989), 151. A content analysis with charts and graphs reaches disturbing conclusions about the ten best American dailies.

GIFFARD, C. ANTHONY. "The InterPress Service: New Information for a New Order," *Journalism Quarterly,* LXII (Spring 1985), 17. News agency covers 60 countries.

GUIDRY, VERNON A., JR. "Minding the Wire: Lou Boccardi and the Associated Press," *Washington Journalism Review* (May 1984), 21. AP's president.

HALL, PETER. "Making Quirkiness Work," *Columbia Journalism Review* (March–April 1982), 51. *The Economist* reaches 70,000 U.S. circulation. See also reminiscence of retiring editor Alastair Bumet in "After 10 Years," *The Economist,* October 12–26, 1974, p. 15.

HAMILL, PETE. "Mario Vazquez Raña: The Mexican Press Lord and His Plans for UPI," *Washington Journalism Review* (April 1986), 16.

HERNDON, KEITH. "CNN Turns a Corner," *Washington Journalism Review* (December 1985), 28. Ted Turner builds a fourth network news team.

HOWARD, HERBERT H. "Broadcast Station Group Ownership: A 20th-Century Phenomenon," *Journalism History,* II (Autumn 1975), 68. Study of the top 100 markets.

———. "An Update on Cable TV Ownership: 1985," *Journalism Quarterly,* LXIII (Winter 1986), 706.

———. "Group and Cross-Media Ownership of TV Stations: A 1989 Update," *Journalism Quarterly,* LXVI (Winter 1989), 785. FCC relaxation of ownership rules brings growth of group ownership.

HOYT, MICHAEL, AND MARY ELLEN SCHOONMAKER. "Onward—and Upward?—With the Newhouse Boys," *Columbia Journalism Review* (July–August 1985), 37. Sizing up the *New Yorker*'s new owners.

KLIESCH, RALPH E. "History and Operations of the McGraw-Hill World News Service," Ph.D. thesis, University of Minnesota, 1968. Describes McGraw-Hill news gathering since the 1880s and the World News Service from 1945 to 1968.

———. "The U.S. Press Corps Rebounds," *Newspaper Research Journal,* XII:1 (Winter 1991), 24. Increase of 150 percent since 1975 study author made.

KOEHLER, MARY A. "Facsimile Newspapers: Foolishness or Foresight?" *Journalism Quarterly,* XLVI (Spring 1969), 29. History of a disappointment.

LACY, STEPHEN, TONY ATWATER, AND ANGELA POWERS. "Use of Satellite Technology in Local Television News," *Journalism Quarterly,* LXV (Winter 1988), 925. Three-fourths of stations use SNG feeds.

LEE, SANG-CHUL. "The Japanese Image Projected in Four U.S. Dailies (1905–1972)," Ph.D. thesis, University of Minnesota, 1979.

LITTLEWOOD, THOMAS B., AND RAYMOND DE LONG. "Supplemental News Services," *Newspaper Research Journal,* II:4 (July 1981), 9. Review as of 1981.

MALL, ELYSE. "Dale Lang's City of Women," *Manhattan Inc.* (March 1990). Portrait of owner of *Working Woman, Working Mother, Sassy,* and *Ms.*

McCHESNEY, ROBERT W. "Off Limits: An Inquiry into the Lack of Debate over the Ownership, Structure, and Control of Mass Media in U.S. Political Life," *Communication,* XIII (1992).

McNICHOL, TOM, AND MARGARET CARLSON. "A Developer Remodels *U.S. News,*" *Columbia Journalism Review* (July–August 1985), 31. Profile of Mortimer B. Zuckerman.

MERRY, ROBERT W. "The Ferment at the *New Republic,*" *Washington Journalism Review* (July 1985), 22. Martin Peretz, Fred Barnes, and Michael Kinsley in action.

O'CONNOR, ANNE-MARIE. "Dateline: Honduras/Subject: The Contras," *Columbia Journalism Review* (May–June 1987). News Service correspondent details coverage difficulties. See also Rod Nordland, "The New Contras?" *Newsweek,* June 1, 1987, p. 32. Nordland and photographer Bill Gentile provide one of the war's best accounts.

ODENDAHL, ERIC M. "The Story and Stories of the Copley News Service," Ph.D. thesis, University of Missouri, 1966. History of the service and analysis of its content.

QUIGG, H. D. "UPI . . . As It Was and It Is," *Editor & Publisher* (September 25, 1982), 16. One of several articles in the issue observing the UPI's 75th anniversary and 1982 sale. See also Quigg's "Goodbye Mr. Scripps," *feed-back* (Summer 1982).

"Rush Limbaugh's Reign of Terror," *Extra!* (July–August 1994), 10–18. Includes factual corrections of the conservative talk show host's most outlandish statements.

RUTH, MARCIA. "Covering Foreign News," *presstime* (April 1986), 28. Special report on foreign reporting by individual U.S. papers.

SHANOR, DONALD, AND DONALD R. JOHNSTON. "Third World News in America Media," *Columbia Journalism Monographs,* IV (1983).

SHAW, DONALD L. "The Rise and Fall of American Mass Media: Roles of Technology and Leadership," Roy W.

Howard Public Lectures, Indiana University School of Journalism, No. 2, April 4, 1991. A historical analysis.

SINGLETARY, MICHAEL W. "Newspaper Use of Supplemental Services: 1960–73," *Journalism Quarterly,* LII (Winter 1975), 748.

SMITH, EDWARD J., AND GILBERT L. FOWLER, JR. "The Status of Magazine Group Ownership," *Journalism Quarterly,* LVI (Autumn 1979), 572.

STERLING, CHRISTOPHER H. "Newspaper Ownership of Broadcast Stations, 1920–68," *Journalism Quarterly,* XLVI (Summer 1969), 227. Data and discussion of issues.

———. "Decade of Development: FM Radio in the 1960s," *Journalism Quarterly,* XLVIII (Summer 1971), 222. Analysis of reasons for rapid growth.

———. "Trends in Daily Newspaper and Broadcast Ownership, 1922–70," *Journalism Quarterly,* LII (Summer 1975), 247. More concentration.

THOMPSON, TOBY. "Prince Donny," *Esquire* (April 1985), 79. Profile of *Washington Post* publisher Donald Graham.

WHITESIDE, THOMAS. "Onward and Upward with the Arts: The Blockbuster Complex," *New Yorker,* September 29, October 6 and 13, 1980. Three-part series on the book-publishing business.

"World Media," *Gannett Center Journal,* IV (Fall 1990). A special issue on problems and updates.

Index

Abbott, Lyman, 224
Abbott, Robert, 228–230
Abbot, Willis, 515
Abell, Arunah S., 104, 113, 115
Abolitionist press, 123–128
Accuracy in Media, 497
Action for Children's Television, 501
Adams, Brooks, 204
Adams, Edward T., 443
Adams, Franklin P., 215, 249, 330
Adams, Henry, 159
Adams, Isaac, 94
Adams, Samuel, 48–50, 52
Adams, Samuel Hopkins, 224, 241
Adams, Thomas, 75
Addams, Charles, 331
Addams, Jane, 205
Adding machine, 156
Addison, Joseph, 14, 25, 29
Ade, George, 166
Adler, Julius Ochs, 240
Advertising
    in 1880–1920, 183–188
    in 1920–1940, 292–296
    in 1940–1960, 376–379
    in 1960–1999, 451, 557–559,
        566–567
    Advertising Council, 343, 377
    agencies, 183–185, 292–296,
        376–379, 381, 566–567
    brand names and, 185–187, 191,
        292–296, 376–379, 566–567
    Bureau of Advertising, 188
    in colonial period, 20, 29–30,
        34–35, 56–57
    criticism of, 187, 296, 376
    examples of copy, 30, 87, 185, 191,
        294, 295, 377, 379
    fraudulent, 187, 226, 296
    intermedia competition and,
        557–558
    market research and, 292–293,
        376, 378
    in penny press period, 100–101, 131
    regulations on, 224, 226, 378

revenues, 295, 296, 379, 555–556
slogans, 292–296, 376–379
subliminal, 376, 378
tax on, 15
African American media
    advertising, 428
    alternative publications, 417
    circulation, 426, 428
    civil rights movement and,
        401–404
    during Civil War, 126–130
    leaders of, 426–427
    magazines, 384–385, 428
    minorities, media employment of,
        499
    in muckraking era, 231–235
    news organizations, 428
    in post–World War II period, 425–428
    television, 495–496
    women writers in, 181, 425–426
Agnew, Spiro T., 435–436, 441
Aguinaldo, Emilio, 204–205
Aitken, Robert, 55, 85
Albany Evening Journal, 106
Albuquerque Tribune, 309
Alexander, Peter W., 139–140
Alexanderson, Ernest F. W., 327–328
Alford, Theodore C., 311
Alien and Sedition Acts, 71–74, 580
Alienated American, The, 128
Allen, Frederick Lewis, 381
Allen, Jay, 312
Allen Riley, 342
Allen, Robert S., 316
Allen, William V., 204
Al Shiraa, 457
Alsop, Joseph, 316, 340, 352, 358,
        412, 415
Alsop, Stewart, 316, 352, 363
Alternative journalism
    Communist Party press, 421
    gay and lesbian press, 431–432
    investigative reporting in, 421–423
    journalists in, 419–421
    New Journalism of 1960s, 423–425

protest press, 419–421
Socialist press, 212–213, 256–257,
        263–264, 318, 383, 421
underground press publications,
        417–418
Amanpour, Christiane, 473, 494, 540
America-China Development Com-
        pany, 204
American Association of Advertising
        Agencies, 296
American Association of Schools and
        Departments of Journalism,
        518
American Broadcasting Company
        (ABC)
    correspondents of, 345, 408–410,
        455, 458, 461, 476
    criticism of, 490–492, 500–503
    documentaries of, 471, 492
    foreign news reporting by, 473
    founding of, 274
    minority hiring by, 499
    networks, 490–492
    news, 322, 370–371, 400, 405,
        408–410, 417, 443, 472
    news magazine programming of,
        490–492
    ratings of, 490–492
    sports programming of, 410, 491
    stations, 365, 371
American Civil Liberties Union
        (ACLU), 367
American Council on Education for
        Journalism, 519
American Federation of Labor, 188,
        210, 214
American Magazine, 226, 330
American Mercury, 330
American Museum, 85
American Newspaper Directory, 184
American Newspaper Guild, 317
American Newspaper Publishers As-
        sociation, 184, 188–189, 276,
        310, 320–321, 507, 510–511,
        513, 543